The Life of the Venerable
Servant of God
Vincent de Paul

Si tu veux dans vn seul visage
Voir le Portrait de deux grands Saints:
Icy Paul et Vincent sont peints;
Mais pour l'Esprit, lis cet ouurage

The Life of the Venerable Servant of God
Vincent de Paul

Founder and First Superior General
of the
Congregation of the Mission

(Divided Into Three Books)

by
Louis Abelly, Bishop of Rodez

BOOK ONE

New City Press

edited by
John E. Rybolt, C.M.

translated by
William Quinn, F.S.C.

notes by
Edward R. Udovic, C.M. and John E. Rybolt, C.M.

introduction by
Stafford Poole, C.M.

index
translated and edited
from the Pémartin edition of 1891,
with additional annotations, by
Edward R. Udovic, C.M

Published in the United States by New City Press
86 Mayflower Avenue, New Rochelle, New York 10801
©1993 Vincentian Studies Institute

Library of Congress Cataloging-in-Publication Data:

Abelly, Louis, 1604-1691.
   [Vie du vénérable serviteur de Dieu, Vincent de Paul. English]
   The life of the venerable servant of God Vincent de Paul : founder
and first superior general of the Congregation of the Mission :
(divided into three books) / by Louis Abelly ; [edited by John E.
Rybolt ; translated by William Quinn ; introduction by Stafford
Poole].
   Includes bibliographical references and index.
   ISBN 1-56548-052-X : $49.00
   1. Vincent de Paul, Saint, 1581-1660. 2. Christian saints—
France—Biography—Early works to 1800. I. Rybolt, John E.
II. Title.
BX4700.V6A48   1993
271'.7702—dc20
[B]   93-9446

The original edition of Abelly contained as a frontispiece an engraving by René
Lochon, based on the portrait by Simon François de Tours of Vincent de Paul in
choir dress. Below the portrait is a quatrain, the translation of which is:
   If you wish to see in a single face
   the portrait of two great saints
   Paul and Vincent are depicted here;
   but for his spirit, read this work.

CONTENTS

Louis Abelly, His Life and Works 9
Editorial Introduction 17
Acknowledgements 21
Dedication to the Queen Mother of the King 22
Foreword 24
Approbations 26
Extract from the Royal Privilege 28

BOOK ONE. The Life of Vincent de Paul 29

CHAPTER ONE. The Church in France at the Time of the Birth of
 Vincent de Paul 31

CHAPTER TWO. The Birth and Education of Vincent de Paul 35

CHAPTER THREE. Studies and Promotion to the Clerical State 38

CHAPTER FOUR. Vincent de Paul is Captured by Pirates and Taken to
 Barbary 42

CHAPTER FIVE. Monsieur Vincent's Return to France; His First Stay in
 Paris 48

CHAPTER SIX. Monsieur Vincent Appointed Pastor of Clichy Where he
 Serves as a Good Shepherd 52

CHAPTER SEVEN. His Associations with the de Gondi House 55

CHAPTER EIGHT. A General Confession Made by a Peasant Occasions
 Monsieur Vincent's First Mission, and This in Turn Leads to Others . 59

CHAPTER NINE. Vincent Secretly Withdraws from the de Gondi House
 but Later Returns There 63

CHAPTER TEN. The Beginnings of the Confraternity of Charity for the
 Sick Poor 72

CHAPTER ELEVEN. The Conversion of Several Heretics whom
 Monsieur Vincent Brought Back to the Catholic Church 74

CHAPTER TWELVE. The Marvelous Change Brought About in the Life of a Noble Person under Monsieur Vincent's Spiritual Direction . . . 77

CHAPTER THIRTEEN. Different Works of Piety that Monsieur Vincent Was Involved with After His Return to the de Gondi Household . . . 80

CHAPTER FOURTEEN. After Appointment as Royal Chaplain of the Galleys, Monsieur Vincent Visits Provence and Guienne to Provide Physical and Spiritual Help to the Convicts 84

CHAPTER FIFTEEN. He Provides for the Physical and Spiritual Necessities of the Poor of Macon, with Excellent Results 87

CHAPTER SIXTEEN. He is Chosen by the Blessed Francis de Sales, Bishop of Geneva, and by Mother de Chantal as the First Spiritual Father and Superior of the Religious of the Visitation of Saint Mary in Paris 90

CHAPTER SEVENTEEN. He is Appointed Head of the College des Bons Enfants, and Later Makes the First Foundation of the Congregation of the Mission 93

CHAPTER EIGHTEEN. Madame de Gondi Passes from This Life to a Better One. Monsieur Vincent Goes to the College des Bons Enfants 97

CHAPTER NINETEEN. Monsieur Vincent's Dispositions of Body and Soul and his Manner of Acting 100

CHAPTER TWENTY. The Birth and Establishment of the Congregation of the Mission 109

CHAPTER TWENTY-ONE. Some Remarkable Statements of Monsieur Vincent Regarding the Spirit of Humility and the Other Virtuous Dispositions He Wished to See as the Foundation of His New Congregation 113

CHAPTER TWENTY-TWO. The Establishment of the Priests of the Congregation of the Mission at Saint Lazare 119

CHAPTER TWENTY-THREE. Account of the Great Good Accomplished in the Church by the Founding of the Congregation of the Mission, of which Monsieur Vincent Was the Prime Mover; First, the Establishment of the Confraternity of Charity for the Corporal and Spiritual Help of the Sick Poor 127

CHAPTER TWENTY-FOUR. The Establishment of the Daughters of Charity, Servants of the Sick Poor 133

CHAPTER TWENTY-FIVE. The Ordination Retreats for the Benefit of Those Wishing to Receive Holy Orders 138

CHAPTER TWENTY-SIX. Spiritual Retreats for Various Groups of People 141

CHAPTER TWENTY-SEVEN. Spiritual Conferences for Clergy 144

CHAPTER TWENTY-EIGHT. The Establishment of the Hospitals in Paris and Marseilles for the Galley Slaves 148

CHAPTER TWENTY-NINE. The Founding of a Group of Women to Serve in the Hotel Dieu Hospital of Paris and for Other Works of Charity in Paris and Elsewhere 152

CHAPTER THIRTY. The Establishment of a Foundling Hospital 160

CHAPTER THIRTY-ONE. The Founding of Several Seminaries for Clergy 164

CHAPTER THIRTY-ONE (BIS). Monsieur Vincent's Collaboration with Father Olier in Various Pious Works 167

CHAPTER THIRTY-TWO. Some Help Given by Monsieur Vincent to the late Commander de Sillery and to the Order of Saint John of Jerusalem, commonly called the Knights of Malta 170

CHAPTER THIRTY-THREE. Missions Given in the Army in 1636, and the Rules Given by Monsieur Vincent to the Missionaries for this Service 174

CHAPTER THIRTY-FOUR. The Establishment of the First Internal Seminary, at Saint Lazare, for the Congregation of the Mission . . 179

CHAPTER THIRTY-FIVE. Monsieur Vincent Devotes Himself to the Poor of Lorraine during the War and Takes Particular Care of Some Gentlemen and Ladies, Refugees in Paris 185

CHAPTER THIRTY-SIX. Services Provided by Monsieur Vincent to the Late King, Louis XIII of Glorious Memory, in His Last Illness, for the Spiritual Good of his Soul 190

CHAPTER THIRTY-SEVEN. Monsieur Vincent is Appointed to the Council for Ecclesiastical Affairs of the Kingdom During the Regency of the Queen Mother 192

CHAPTER THIRTY-EIGHT. Monsieur Vincent's Help in Establishing the Congregation of the Daughters of the Cross and for the Spiritual Good of its Members 195

CHAPTER THIRTY-NINE. Monsieur Vincent's Experiences During the Troubled Times of 1649. What Occurred During Several Trips He Made at that Time 198

CHAPTER FORTY. Monsieur Vincent Works for the Relief of the Poor of the Frontier Regions Devastated by the War, Especially Champagne and Picardy 204

CHAPTER FORTY-ONE. The Death of the Prior of Saint Lazare. Monsieur Vincent's Appreciation of Him 206

CHAPTER FORTY-TWO. The Help Given by Monsieur Vincent to the
   Poor of Paris and Several Other Places During the Troubled Times
   of 1652 and Later 208

CHAPTER FORTY-THREE. Monsieur Vincent in Service to the King and
   Kingdom during the Troubled Times Beginning in 1652 213

CHAPTER FORTY-FOUR. Monsieur Vincent's Opposition to the Errors
   of Jansenism 221

CHAPTER FORTY-FIVE. The Home for the Aged Poor Begun at Paris by
   Monsieur Vincent; The General Hospital for the Poor Begun by
   Him in that Same City 224

CHAPTER FORTY-SIX. A Census of the Houses of the Congregation of
   the Mission Founded During the Lifetime of Monsieur Vincent . . 230

CHAPTER FORTY-SEVEN. Monsieur Vincent Gives the Rules to his
   Congregation. What He Said on this Occasion 237

CHAPTER FORTY-EIGHT. Other Works of Piety in Which Monsieur
   Vincent was Involved Besides His Usual Duties 242

CHAPTER FORTY-NINE. A Reflection on the Pains and Afflictions
   Endured by Monsieur Vincent 245

CHAPTER FIFTY. Monsieur Vincent's Illnesses and the Saintly Use He
   Made of Them 250

CHAPTER FIFTY-ONE. His Preparation for Death 256

CHAPTER FIFTY-TWO. Events Surrounding the Death of Monsieur
   Vincent 259

LOUIS ABELLY, HIS LIFE AND WORKS

In the canon of writings about Saint Vincent de Paul, the biography by Louis Abelly, bishop of Rodez, holds pride of place. Published four years after the saint's death, it is the foundational work on which all subsequent studies have depended. It is, then, surprising that it has never been translated into English, unlike works by lesser authorities, such as Pierre Collet. That deficiency has now been remedied, and after more than three centuries Abelly's landmark work is now available to an anglophone readership.

Data on the life of Louis Abelly are scarce and sometimes contradictory. He was born at Paris in 1604.[1] His father was the treasurer and receiver-general of the financial district of Limoges. He studied at the Sorbonne and though he was called a doctor of the Sorbonne, there is no contemporary record of his having received that degree and he never assumed the title himself. At the age of twenty-six he published his first devotional work, *Considérations sur l'éternité* (Paris: 1626). In all probability he was ordained to the priesthood some time in 1628-1629, and there is evidence that at that time he was in the service of Jean Francois de Gondi, the archbishop of Paris.

It is not certain when he came under the influence of Vincent de Paul. Dodin associates him with Saint Vincent as early as 1625-1626 but cites no documentary proof.[2] Saint Vincent's first recorded mention of him is apparently in a letter to Jean Bécu, May 20 or 21, 1638, "M. Abeline [sic] is a very good man, very prudent and discreet, and M. Le Breton very fervent.... One of them is soon to be the vicar general of Bayonne."[3] The saint's first

---

1. Information on Abelly's life can be found in Pierre Coste, C.M., *The Life and Works of Saint Vincent de Paul*, trans. Joseph Leonard, C.M., 3 vols. (Westminster, Maryland: 1952, reprinted New York: 1987), 1:476-86; Pierre Collet, C.M., *La vie de St. Vincent de Paul, Instituteur de la Congrégation de la Mission, et des Filles de la Charité*, 2 vols. (Nancy: 1748), I:v-xiv; P. Broutin, *La Reforme Pastorale en France au XVIIe siècle*, 2 vols. (Tournai: 1956), 2:331-45; I. Cechetti, "Abelly, Louis," in *Enciclopedia Cattolica*, 12 vols. (Vatican City: 1949-1954), 1:68-69; A. Vogt, *Dictionnaire d'histoire et de géographie ecclésiastique* (Paris: 1912-), 1:97-103; A. Rastoul, "Abelly, Louis," *Dictionnaire de Biographie Française*. eds. J. Balteau, M. Barroux, M. Prevost et al., 17 vols. (Paris: 1933-1989), 1:130-40; André Dodin, C.M., *La Légende et l'histoire: de Monsieur Depaul à Saint Vincent de Paul* (Paris: 1985), 11-79. Coste gives the date of Abelly's birth as 1606, though 1604 is now generally accepted. There is also a possibility that he was born a year earlier.
2. Dodin, *La Légende*, 12.
3. *Saint Vincent de Paul: Conferences, entretiens, documents*, ed. Pierre Coste, C.M., 14 vols. (Paris: 1920-1926), I:277. (Hereinafter cited as CED); *Saint Vincent de Paul: Correspondence, Conferences, Documents. I. Correspondence*, vol. 1 (1607-1639), newly translated, edited, and

known letter to him is dated January 14, 1640.[4] Abelly joined the saint's Tuesday Conferences, a select association of ecclesiastics devoted to personal sanctification and the advancement of Church reform.[5] Like other members of the Conference he participated in the missions sponsored by Saint Vincent, one of which is the subject of the letter to Bécu. In 1639 Saint Vincent secured for him an appointment as vicar general to Francois de Fouquet, who had just been appointed bishop of Bayonne.[6] Fouquet had also been a member of the Tuesday Conferences, and his mother belonged to Vincent's Ladies of Charity. On his journey to Bayonne Abelly stopped in Dax and made the acquaintance of many of Vincent's relatives. By a remarkable coincidence Bertrand Ducournau served as Fouquet's steward for a brief period during Abelly's stay in Bayonne. Ducournau later joined the Congregation of the Mission, became Vincent de Paul's secretary, and helped Abelly with the writing of the saint's biography.

Administration of the see of Bayonne proved difficult. In 1644, when Fouquet exchanged sees with the bishop of Agde (a native of Bayonne whose name was also Fouquet), Abelly returned to Paris, where he was briefly pastor in a small rural parish. He was soon appointed pastor of Saint Josse (1644-1652), which he determined to make into a model city parish. During this time he became involved in the Jansenist controversies, especially concerning the bull *Unigenitus*. The publication of his theological work, *Medulla Theologica* (Paris: 1650) placed him squarely in the anti-Jansenist camp. In the following year he refused to publish in his parish the archbishop of Paris's censure of an anti-Jansenist polemic.

In 1650 Saint Vincent arranged for Abelly to become spiritual director to the Daughters of the Cross, an order whose amalgamation to the Visitandines the saint had opposed. In 1657 he was made spiritual director of the Hôpital Générale. The Hôpital was a global name for five hospitals consolidated by Louis XIV for enclosing the poor of Paris. Abelly received the position in part because Vincent de Paul refused to allow any of his community to assume administration of what was little better than a prison. It proved a

---

annotated from the 1920 edition of Pierre Coste, C.M., ed. Jacqueline Kilar, D.C., trans. Helen Marie Law, D.C., John Marie Poole, D.C., James R. King, C.M., Francis Germovnik, C.M., annotated John W. Carven, C.M., (Brooklyn: 1985); vol. 2 (January 1640-July 1646), eds. Jacqueline Kilar, D.C., Marie Poole, D.C., trans. Marie Poole, D.C., Esther Cavanagh, D.C., James R. King, C.M., Francis Germovnik, C.M., annotated John W. Carven, C.M. (Brooklyn: 1989), 1:467. Hereinafter cited as SVP.

4. *CED* II:2-6; SVP, 2:3-7.

5. Dodin dates his entry into the Tuesday Conferences in 1633, but without citing any evidence (*La Légende*, 14).

6. It is not clear how Vincent secured the appointment. He was not at that time a member of the Council of Conscience. Fouquet was the brother of the notorious Nicolas Fouquet, superintendent of finances under Louis XIII, who had accumulated great wealth and power in the years just before Louis XIV's assumption of personal rule in 1661.

difficult task and Abelly resigned some time around 1659/1660. Briefly, at some unknown period, he was confessor to Cardinal Mazarin. Anne of Austria, queen mother after Louis XIV's assumption of personal rule in 1661, recommended him for the diocese of Rodez, to which he was appointed in April 1662. Because of a rupture in relations between the king and pope, however, he was not ordained a bishop until September 1664. In his new see he strenuously combated Jansenism and introduced Vincent de Paul's retreats for ordinands. An unfavorable climate and the difficulties of administration proved detrimental to his health, and in 1665 he suffered a stroke that left him partially paralyzed. He retired to Saint Lazare until his death on October 4, 1691, and was buried in one of the chapels of the church there.

Abelly was the author of forty books.[7] Many of them were controversial and anti Jansenist, something that made him enemies in the Jansenist camp. Boileau, a friend of the Abbé de Saint Cyran, wrote, "let each one take in hand the soft Abelly."[8] Many of Abelly's works enjoyed great popularity, not only during his lifetime but also down to the nineteenth century. The *Medulla Theologica* had thirteen editions and *La Couronne de l'Année Chrétienne* (Paris: 1657) went through forty-five. His most famous work, and the one that has best endured the test of the centuries, is *La vie du Venerable Serviteur de Dieu Vincent de Paul Instituteur et Premier Superieur de la Congregation de la Mission* (Paris: 1664), undertaken at the request of René Alméras, Vincent's successor as superior general.[9]

To what extent was Abelly truly the author of this work? That is a question that may never be answered with certainty. Abelly himself claimed to be the author, though he freely acknowledged the help that he received from the members of Vincent's community.

> Some years after the death of M. Vincent, the Gentlemen of the Mission, moved by the affection they cherish for such a worthy founder, and importuned by very many persons of quality who particularly honoured his memory, resolved to present to the public a history of his life; . . . They themselves might have laboured worthily at this task, for their Company is not wanting in persons most capable of bringing it to a successful issue, but the humility bequeathed to them by M. Vincent as their portion led them to

---

7. A survey of these can be found in Dodin, *La Légende*, 50-61.
8. "Que chacun prenne en main le moëlleux Abelly," *Lutrin,* chapter 4, verse 188. "Moëlleux" ("soft, downy," comes from the noun *moëlle*, "marrow") is apparently a play on the title of Abelly's book, *Medulla Theologica*, ["theological marrow."]
9. An Italian translation, by Domenico Acami, was published in 1677; many other editions followed. The Acami edition was translated into German, 1710; several times into Spanish, beginning 1701; the Spanish text, in turn, was translated into Portuguese, 1738. Translations appeared also in Polish, 1688, and Dutch, 1864.

choose a pen from persons outside their Congregation. They cast their eyes on me, perchance because I have had the happiness of knowing M. Vincent and of frequenting his society for many years. However that may be, they submitted this project to me, and when I had accepted it, they sent me all the memoranda collected by themselves or obtained by them from persons who could be trusted.[10]

Abelly went on to cite a testimonial given him by René Alméras, Vincent's successor as superior general, which stated that the bishop's account of the composition of the book was true.[11]

Abelly's authorship was first challenged in the eighteenth century by a Vincentian priest, Claude Joseph Lacour. In a manuscript work, "Histoire générale de la Congrégation de la Mission" completed in 1720, he wrote "The Missionaries worked at this biography by sending him all the memoranda that might prove useful. His Lordship of Rodez . . . was requested to adopt the book, and to put his name to it, out of conformity with the practice left by M. Vincent to all his children not to publish books. This prelate did so to please M. Alméras, who had asked him, and he scarcely made any other contribution to the book. . . . It was M. [François] Fournier principally who worked on it."[12] Because Lacour's work was not published until the twentieth century, and then only in an incomplete version, his statement at first had little impact. Collet, writing twenty years after Lacour, was unaware of it. Lacour's claim was accepted by the Abbé Maynard in the nineteenth century and through him became rather widespread.[13] Pierre Coste, on the other hand, went to great pains to discount Fournier's authorship and restore the credit to the bishop of Rodez.[14]

There is no doubt that in writing his biography Abelly had abundant help from all who had known Saint Vincent, especially from his two secretaries, Bertrand Ducournau and Louis Robineau. The latter wrote a manuscript life of the saint that has only recently been published.[15] Hence it can safely be said that Abelly was substantially the author of the work, although many other hands were involved to an extent now unknown.

Abelly had two great advantages over all subsequent biographers of

---

10. Louis Abelly, *La vrai défense des sentiments du Vénérable Serviteur de Dieu Vincent de Paul* (Paris: 1668), 10, quoted in Coste, *Life and Works*, 3:477-78.
11. Ibid., 478-79.
12. Quoted ibid., 479-80. An edited version of Lacour's manuscript was published in the *Annales de la Congrégation de la Mission* in yearly installments from 62 (1897) to 67 (1902). This quotation is taken from 62:310.
13. Michel Ulysse Maynard, *Saint Vincent de Paul* (Paris: 1860), 1:vii.
14. Coste, *Life and Works*, 3:479-83.
15. André Dodin, C.M., *Monsieur Vincent Raconté par son secrétaire [Louis Robineau]. Remarques sur les actes et paroles de feu Monsieur Vincent de Paul, notre Très Honoré Père et Fondateur* (Paris: 1992).

Vincent de Paul. The first was that of having known the saint personally for more than twenty years. The second was that he had at hand testimonies of indisputable authenticity, many of which have since been lost because of the destruction caused by the French Revolution and the passage of time. These included letters, conferences, juridical documents, and the recollections of the saint's contemporaries. The question that confronts the modern historian or biographer concerns the way in which Abelly used these sources. Abelly's work has serious shortcomings, some of them important enough to give a misleading view of Saint Vincent's life. These have been noted in this translation.

The first of these is to be found in the motivation for writing the biography. One reason, of course, was the desire to commit to writing all known facts of the saint's life before they were lost. More importantly, the book was written with a clear eye toward eventual canonization. The result was a tendency to glorify Vincent even in his earliest days, and to see him as a saint from his very youth, retrojecting the holiness of an old man into his youth. As Dodin has written, "Abelly, after having composed the portrait of M. Vincent in his last years, has projected that picture into all the stages of his existence."[16] This led Abelly, or his helpers, to use a heavy editorial hand, at times making Vincent's statements sound more pious than they originally were, at other times suppressing anything that could be detrimental to the process of canonization. The most serious of these suppressions, or outright fabrications, concerned the dates of Vincent's birth, his ordination to the various major and minor orders, the date of his resignation of the parish of Clichy, his holding of multiple benefices, and the slowness with which he divested himself of some of them.

Abelly gave 1576 as the year of the saint's birth.[17] The commonest explanation for this has been that when the dimissorial letter for Vincent's ordination was discovered after his death, it stated that he was of legitimate age for ordination, that is, twenty-four. A simple calculation yielded the year 1576 and would have made him eighty-four at the time of his death. This age was entered into the funeral registry at Saint Lazare, the various obituaries published after his death, and finally, by order of his successor as superior general, René Alméras, was carved on his tombstone. Saint Vincent, however, had never made any secret of his age, either in his correspondence or his conferences to the Priests of the Mission. There can be no doubt that his true age was widely known. He never, however, mentioned the date of his ordination. The age question did not prove a difficulty until the

---

16. Dodin, *La Légende*, 182.
17. On this question, see Pierre Coste, C.M., "La vraie date de la naissance de Saint Vincent de Paul," Bulletin de la Société de Borda (1922):18-19; Douglas Slawson, C.M., "The Phantom Five Years," *Vincentian Heritage* 2 (1981):81-93.

discovery of the dimissorial letter, which made it clear that Vincent de Paul was ordained to the priesthood at the age of nineteen. It also seems abundantly clear that the alteration of the date was deliberate, because it also required inserting changes in some of the saint's letters and conferences.[18] These have also been noted in this translation Abelly's life of Saint Vincent is written in typical seventeenth century hagiographical form. This means that not only are all possible negative aspects of the life ignored or suppressed, but the picture presented is idealized. It was not a critical age. It was also the golden age of devotional works. Edification was more important than critical analysis. In this regard Abelly's work is no different from almost all the lives of saints to come from that period.

Abelly's hagiographic approach caused him to accept uncritically stories that later authors would find false or based on unreliable testimony. These included the accounts of the false accusation of theft by the judge of Sore, the temptation against faith, and the substitution for the galley slave.[19] He deliberately altered texts so as to make them appear more pious than they originally were or to improve the Saint Vincent's sometimes rough-hewn style. Among the examples given by Coste is that of a letter to Saint Louise de Marillac, in which the saint wrote, "Oh! what a tree in God's sight have you not seemed to-day, since you have produced such good fruit! May you be for ever a beautiful tree of life, bringing forth fruits of love." Abelly gave a different version, "Oh! how you have appeared to-day in the sight of God as a beautiful tree, since, by His grace, you have produced such a fruit! I beseech Him that, in His infinite bounty, you may be ever a veritable tree of life bringing forth fruits of true charity!"[20] Abelly did the same with Saint Vincent's famed letter on his Tunisian captivity, in which the biographer's editorial hand is especially heavy.

Those aspects of the saint's early life that were less than edifying were simply ignored. Abelly mentions nothing about Vincent's desperate search for benefices or the fact that he held multiple benefices, such as the parish of Gamaches (1614) where he was an absentee pastor, or his position on the chapter of Écouis (1615), whose canons complained about his absenteeism. Abelly is equally silent about the fact that Vincent was an absentee pastor at Clichy from 1613 until 1626, during which time he ruled through an administrator while still receiving an income from it.

The arrangement of the book into three divisions of life, work, and virtues

---

18. For examples of these, see Slawson, "The Phantom Five Years," 87-90.
19. On the temptation against faith, see Stafford Poole, C.M., and Douglas Slawson, C.M., "A New Look at an Old Temptation," *Vincentian Heritage* 11 (1990):125-42; on the story of his substitution of himself for a galley slave, see Coste, *Life and Works*, 1:124-31.
20. Coste, *Life and Works*, 3:485. The footnote in Leonard's translation gives the source of the letter as *CED*, I:62, a misprint for I:51-52.

causes confusion and overlapping. It is difficult to know where to look for particular incidents in the saint's life. Some things, like the famous story of Vincent's temptation against faith, which logically belongs in his life, is told only in the section on virtues. Even contemporaries found the book too long and too detailed. The result was that Abelly published an abridged edition in 1668.

Like other hagiographers of the time, Abelly is fond of citing unnamed witnesses, often for extremely important events: "a very virtuous person, who died before he did, declared...,"[21] "another priest of his Congregation has told...,"[22] "a very virtuous priest who knew him well and observed him during many years,"[23] "a woman of great virtue,"[24] "a very trustworthy person,"[25] (the latter testifying to the story of Vincent's temptation against faith).

Abelly read his own strong anti-Jansenism into Vincent's life. The reality of Vincent's opposition to the Jansenist movement is far more complex than Abelly presents. This was especially true with regard to Vincent's relationship with the Abbé de Saint Cyran, which was generally close and amicable until 1644.[26] After Saint Cyran's arrest, Vincent refused to testify against him or gave testimony so confusing that it was useless. Vincent's opposition to Jansenism after 1644 seems to have arisen from the question of frequent communion and especially the impact that Jansenist teaching on this subject had on the parish missions.

In general it can be said that Abelly is more trustworthy when he describes the later years of Saint Vincent than when he describes his youth. The saint was notably reticent about discussing his early years except in stereotypical terms of having been a swineherd or having been ashamed of his father's poverty. For information on Vincent's youth Abelly depended on the Canon de Saint Martin, an old friend of the saint's. As Coste has said, however, the canon "was not the man needed for such a work, for he had neither the taste for research, nor the knowledge of local history, nor the critical flair which every historian needs if he is to distinguish between truth and error in the evidence placed before him. The good old canon's word is not authoritative; facts which he alleges and which have no other foundation rest on a very shaky basis, and it would therefore be wrong to regard them as indubitable."[27] Román, on the other hand, does not accept this sweeping generaliza-

---

21. Abelly, *Vie*, book 3, ch. 2:7.
22. Ibid., ch. 2:6.
23. Ibid., ch. 6:49.
24. Ibid., ch. 7:56.
25. Ibid., ch. 11, sect. 1:117.
26. Dodin, *La Légende*, 166-68.
27. Coste, *Life and Works*, 3:483.

tion, saying that he considered it exaggerated and that "this judgment has been repeated without critical examination."[28] It is clear, however, that Abelly's account of Vincent's younger years contains numerous errors and omissions, such as any reference to the letters on the Tunisian captivity, the devotion to Our Lady of Buglose, the dates of Vincent's ordination to various orders, and the years when the diocese of Dax was vacant. The further back in time Abelly goes, the greater the caution the historian must exercise.

More than three centuries after its publication, Abelly's life of Saint Vincent is now available in English. It is the single most important source of the saint's life; it is unique and indispensable. It is, however, a source that cannot be used uncritically. In the centuries since 1664 there have been major advances in research and historical writing. Biographers today are less concerned about hagiography and edification than they are about reaching more objective conclusions. France of the seventeenth century and of the Catholic Reformation has been intensively studied. Our knowledge of the French social and religious milieu far exceeds that of Vincent de Paul and his contemporaries who lived in it. Jansenism in particular has received a careful reconsideration. Many letters, documents, and historical references dealing with Saint Vincent have come to light, and many more await the patient researcher. This change of approach has not diminished the saint's stature. Rather, it gives us a picture that is simultaneously more realistic and more appealing. Unfortunately, this fresh research and the insights it has engendered have not yet been incorporated into any modern biography. What an English speaking readership still needs is a new, comprehensive, accurate biography based on original documents and the most current research.

---

28. José María Román, *San Vicente de Paúl. I. Biografía* (Madrid: 1981), 33, n. 9.

EDITORIAL INTRODUCTION

This translation owes its existence to the work of the late Christian Brother, William Quinn. He came to know Saint Vincent through his research on Saint John Baptist de la Salle, founder of the Christian Brothers, and sought to contribute to the growing body of materials on Vincent de Paul in English. Because of his familiarity with translating seventeenth century religious writings, he was qualified to undertake the enormous task of rendering Abelly into English. His accustomed method of translation was to prepare a readable and accurate text. Consequently, he simplified the text at points to enhance its readability, while attempting to conserve the flavor of the original. Beginning in 1988, the members of the Vincentian Studies Institute cooperated with Brother Quinn in reviewing and correcting his work at several stages.

Abelly's life of Saint Vincent has undergone many editions and revisions since its publication. The text translated here, however, has been made from the original text of 1664.[1] Research by André Dodin for his doctoral dissertation on Louis Abelly uncovered some small adjustments between two printings of the 1664 version. The one used here is the second printing (also dated 1664.) The slightly emended text in the first printing has been noted where appropriate. The printing errors given in the list of Errata, identical in both printings, have been corrected in this translation. Dodin's careful work has uncovered still more errors, and a few others have also been noted and corrected in this edition.

Following the example of the excellent 1891 French edition of Abelly, prepared by J.B. Pémartin, C.M., the editor has attempted to give references to all quotations. Only direct quotations from the Bible have been cited. Indirect quotations, allusions, or passing references, however, are left as they are without citations. Quotations from the Psalms are given according to modern numbering, but the text remains that of the old psalter as quoted by Abelly. Biblical translations are generally made directly from the *New American Bible*, rather than from the text used by Abelly. The only exceptions are those occasioned by significantly different texts. Patristic citations have been made, wherever possible, to the old edition of Migne, and abbreviated PL (*Patrologia Latina*) and PG (*Patrologia Graeca*).

All other quotations from Saint Vincent and his correspondents have been

---

1. Louis Abelly, *La vie du venerable serviteur de Dieu Vincent de Paul, instituteur et premier superieur general de la Congregation de la Mission. Divisée en trois livres.* Paris: Florentin Lambert, 1664. 3 vols. in 1. Reprinted, Piacenza: 1986.

cross referenced to the edition of Coste. Those not attributed to some source (a speaker or writer) or not otherwise identified are presumed to appear only in Abelly. More research needs to be done on the sources used by Abelly.

Certain French institutions and public officials have names which have different meanings in English. The following list gives the most important of these.

> Chamber of Accounts: a royal council with responsibilities to oversee royal property and finances
> Chevalier: knight, an honorary title
> College: a boarding high school
> Grand'Chambre: a court in a Parlement, which had jurisdiction over the highest ranks in society
> Hotel: a large private mansion in a town
> Hotel Dieu: a traditional name for a hospital
> Lieutenant: (*lieutenant criminel*), an official with powers to pursue and arrest criminals
> Official: an ecclesiastical judge
> Parlement: a judicial body, not a legislature
> President: a presiding judge in a Parlement
> Presidial court: a local court of appeal

Weights and measures, however, have been left in French to preserve the flavor of the original, and to avoid, particularly dealing with money, having to change currency rates. Since values for weights and measures were not uniform throughout France, the descriptions in the following list are often valid only for the Paris region.

> *Chopine*: liquid measure, containing about one pint
> *Denier*: money, a half-*sou*
> *Ecu*: money, also translated as "crown"; 60 *sous* or 3 *livres*
> *Gros:* money, 12 *deniers*
> *League*: distance, about 2 1/2 miles, 4 kilometers
> *Livre*: money, an old name for a *franc*; 20 *sous*
> *Muid*: liquid measure, containing about 59 gallons
> *Piastre*: money, a coin of Italian or Spanish origin, widely used internationally; in the middle east and north Africa, 100 *piastres* were worth 1 *livre*
> *Pistole*: money, 10 *livres*
> *Setier*: liquid measure containing 2 gallons; in Paris, a *demi-setier* contained a half-pint
> *Sou*: also spelled *sol*; money, 1/20 of a *livre*

In addition, other words or longer quotations in Latin have been left in the text, but are translated in square brackets.

Certain other issues of translation should also be explained. The terms "Mission" and "Missionaries" often, but not always, refer to members of the Congregation of the Mission. When the reference is clear, the terms are capitalized. Often, however, the reference is not clear.

The title *Monsieur* was used regularly for secular clergy in France, and was always used by Saint Vincent, who referred to himself as Monsieur Vincent, and never as Monsieur Depaul. The term Monsieur has been retained here to give some flavor of the original text.

Personal names in French or other languages have generally been retained in their original form, unless the English version of the name is normally in use as such in English. For bibliographical references in footnotes, the original forms have been maintained. However, the use of accents in French names has been retained only for references to book titles. All other accents have been eliminated. Hyphens in French given names, such as Jean-Claude, have also been eliminated.

Noble and ecclesiastical titles have been put into English. The only exception is Marquis/Marquise, instead of the less recognizable English Marquess and Marchioness. These titles are capitalized only when they precede the person's name. French *Monseigneur* for bishops has been translated as "Your Excellency," or "Bishop," rather than "My Lord," a more British than American usage. Other ecclesiastical forms of address have been similarly simplified to reflect modern usage.

Moslem has been used instead of Turk, since in the French of the period, the two were identified. The reason was that, particularly in North Africa, there were many ethnic Turks at work in the imperial Ottoman government. At present, the religious term Moslem for a follower of Islam is more accurate than the ethnic term Turk.

Place names have been given in modern French equivalents in those cases where they have been changed from the seventeenth century, such as modern Noyon for Noyons. In addition, the customary English spellings of certain places have been retained instead of the modern French spelling: English Marseilles for French Marseille. Hyphens used in composite names have been eliminated, such as Saint-Germain-en-Laye.

In addition to the references mentioned above in the historical introduction, the following have been cited in the footnotes:

André Dodin, *Monsieur Vincent Raconté par son Secrétaire*. Paris, 1991. (Hereinafter cited as Robineau.)

André Dodin, *Saint Vincent de Paul, Correspondence, Entretiens, Documents. XV. Supplément*. Paris, 1970. (Hereinafter cited as Supplement.)

André Dodin, *Saint Vincent de Paul. Entretiens spirituels aux missionnaires*. Paris, 1960. (Hereinafter cited as Entretiens.)

Annales de la Congrégation de la Mission, hereinafter cited as Annales CM.

Beatificationis et Canonizationis Vener. Servi Dei Vincentij a Paulo . . . Summarium. Rome, 1703. Part II: Ex processu ne pereant probationes auctoritate apostolica fabricato. (Hereinafter cited as Summarium.)

Lettres de S. Vincent de Paul. Edited by Jean-Baptiste Pémartin. 4 vols. Paris, 1880.

ACKNOWLEDGEMENTS

The editor wishes to acknowledge with thanks the contributions of the following to this work. First to the late Brother William Quinn, F.S.C., whose persistence, even in ill health, brought the tedious work of translation to a conclusion. Next, to the members of the Vincentian Studies Institute and to its sponsors, the Vincentian provincial superiors in the United States. The members' quiet work of reviewing and correcting has lightened the editorial work, and the encouragement and financial support of the provincials has smoothed the way. Special thanks are also due to several Vincentian confreres in Paris: To Fathers André Dodin, Georges Baldacchino, Raymond Chalumeau, and especially Paul Henzmann, all of whom researched small details and generously offered their expert opinions. Many others contributed to clarification of obscure points of theology, history, and geography. Father Daniel Schulte, C.M., contributed greatly to the accuracy of the work through his computer analysis of the text. Thanks, too, to the helpful and faith-filled staff of New City Press.

DEDICATION TO THE QUEEN MOTHER OF THE KING

Madame,

THE FAVORABLE reception Your Majesty[1] always gave to Monsieur Vincent during his lifetime and the kindness with which you have honored his memory since his death gives me hope that you would accept this work which is but a sketch of the life and virtues of this great servant of God.[2] I have attempted to trace his career with as much fidelity as humanly possible. There is little in his life to make it striking enough to be suitable for presentation to such a great princess as yourself. But I believe that to the degree that it is simple and straightforward the more it will truly reflect its subject, and even more favorably will it be accepted by Your Majesty. You will more surely recognize Monsieur Vincent in its pages if he is presented in his everyday clothes, that is to say, in his humility, his simplicity and his usual direct speech and action. Even though Monsieur Vincent during his life had taken every care to hide the marvelous graces he had received from God, I have succeeded in allowing him to speak after his death by citing several letters I have been able to gather, reflecting those occasions when his charity overcame his natural reticence about himself.

Should Your Majesty deign to give me audience I shall have the honor of recalling several matters which will without doubt confirm his reputation. They will console you greatly, for you will recognize the great things he accomplished for God and for the building up of the kingdom of Jesus Christ during the regency. These took place not only by your permission and support but even more so by your zeal, your concern and your generosity. What should be a source of joy for you is that all the great enterprises started by Monsieur Vincent still function, better than ever, under the wise guidance of our incomparable monarch who shines like the sun, vivifying all parts of his kingdom, who is very mindful to use all his strength of mind and inexhaustible zeal to preserve true religion and solid piety in all parts of the kingdom.

---

1. Queen Anne of Austria, mother of Louis XIV.
2. After the death of Louis XIII in 1643, his wife, Anne of Austria, became regent and instituted the Council of Conscience to advise her on ecclesiastical affairs. She appointed Monsieur Vincent to this body. Later, Louis XIV, in his letter to Pope Clement XI supporting Vincent's beatification, testified that his mother had recognized Vincent's virtues and that she had shown this by great marks of confidence. According to Louis, at Vincent's death, his mother had exclaimed, "What a loss for the Church and for the poor!"

The innocence and sanctity of him whose life we write, Madame, assure us that he is in heaven with his God. We believe that he is imploring unceasingly God's goodness to shower his blessings upon our great prince, Your Majesty, and all the royal household. What particularly obliges him to this intercession is his recognition of the favors he received from your hands, and continues to receive in the person of the priests of his Congregation.

While he lived on earth, even during most perilous and difficult times, he was ever faithful to the king and devoted to his service. Since the virtues of the saints never die and especially their charity lives on, we can confidently assert that in heaven Monsieur Vincent retains this same affection and zeal to obtain from God all sorts of blessings upon the king, Your Majesty, and all that you hold dear. It surely is no small consolation to know that you have a faithful servant. To put it more fittingly, you have an assured intercessor and protector, like another Jeremiah[3] continually prostrate before the adorable majesty to pray for what he sees in the light of glory to be truly salutary for Your Majesty and helpful to the achievement of your just desires.

For myself, Madame, having been showered with favors from the king without ever having merited them, and having experienced the effects of your own good will, I recognize myself unable to thank Your Majesty enough. I beg you that I may borrow from him whose life I write, to help fulfill this duty of gratitude, and following his example and with the favor his faithful services have earned, I declare myself, with the greatest possible respect,

Your Majesty'

Your very humble, obedient, faithful servant, and subject,

Louis, bishop of Rodez.

---

3. An allusion to the vision of Judas Maccabeus (2 Mac 15:13-16) who had seen Jeremiah in heaven praying for the people and for the holy city.

FOREWORD

Dear reader, I would like to call three things to your attention before you begin to read this book.

First, since truth is the soul of history without which it does not merit the name "history," but rather of "novel" or "romance," you can be assured that it has been faithfully and exactly observed in this work. What you read has been in the public record or gathered from reliable witnesses. Some things I assert that I have seen with my own eyes, or heard with my ears, having had the good fortune of knowing and associating with Monsieur Vincent for many years. I have visited the place of his birth and spoken with his close relatives during a trip I made to Guienne nearly twenty-five years ago.

I have cited several of his letters and conferences to supplement what I learned from others. These extracts are taken from documents collected by members of his Congregation, especially during the later years of his life.[1] I do so because there is no way we can be more certain of his attitudes or his interior disposition of soul than by quoting what he actually said. On occasion charity overcame his personal humility, despite his reluctance to talk about himself. What gives even greater credence to his words is that all who knew him were well aware that there was no trace of vanity or boasting in his makeup. On the contrary, he often sought out occasions for self-deprecation, saying and doing in the sight of others what might draw down disrespect upon himself.

Since this holy man often spoke on the spur of the moment, his conferences were more like talks of a father to his children than the studied

---

1. On August 15, 1657, only three years before the death of the saint, Brother Bertrand Ducournau, his secretary, sent a long memorandum to the assistants of the house of Saint Lazare to persuade them "how important it is for the future of the company that an exact record of the Monsieur Vincent's discourses be preserved." (*Notices sur les prêtres et frères de la Congrégation de la Mission*, 1, 416.) His proposal was accepted and he himself did most of the work of preserving these precious accounts. The same care was taken by the Daughters of Charity, who had earlier begun to preserve the account of the words of their holy founder. Mathurine Guerin, one of the first Daughters of Charity, wrote that "one of the most valuable possessions of our company is the record that Mademoiselle le Gras had made of the instructions of our last most honored father. She so loved these writings that she did not wish to be the one to write them down for fear that she might change the sense of what our blessed father had said, greatly loving his simple and naive style, without trying to polish it in any way. She often said that one day the sisters would be consoled to have the writings of the persons whom we have been privileged to hear and see. Therefore, you must have them all." (Mathurine Guerin to Marguerite Chetif, elected superioress general at the death of Louise de Marillac. *Louise de Marillac, sa Vie, ses Vertues*, 1887, 1, 250.)

discourses of the learned. Despite this we have decided to report them simply. The reader will thereby be the more able to recognize the depth of his soul and the virtue of this great servant of God, for his words flowed from the abundance of his heart.

The second point I call to your attention is the criticism that this work is too long. Some suggest that it would be enough to speak in general terms, and not enter into many topics better passed over in silence. It is not possible to form a correct judgment of things if they are known only superficially or in part. To see the utility and grandeur of the works of Monsieur Vincent which he did with the help of God, I have thought it necessary to speak about them at length, rather than in summary or in general.

Moreover, let the reader remember, please, that you do not have here an elocution piece or a panegyric. You have a simple recital of the life and activities of a servant of God, who had a particular concern to remain ever in the background. It would be contrary to his disposition were this life to be written with flowery language or with worldly eloquence. Style ought to imitate nature; how better to describe the virtues of a saint than to speak of them in the same spirit with which they were practiced.

Lastly, my dear reader, the third thing I would call to your attention is that I declare that I submit completely to the prudent rules established by the Apostolic See in writing about saintly persons. I base my writing solely on human testimony, and not on the authority of the church. I use the word "saint" in some places in the sense that Saint Paul uses it in referring to all the faithful. My meaning in using this word or others like it is no more than to say that this great servant of God was endowed with eminent virtue, and that he surpassed greatly the ordinary Christian man or woman in his life of holiness.[2]

---

2. The author wrote this in 1664. Later, the cause of the servant of God was introduced at Rome. Vincent de Paul was beatified by Benedict XIII on August 13, 1729, and was canonized by Clement XII (see his bull *Superna Jerusalem* of June 16, 1737 in *Acta Apostolica. Bulla, Braevia, et Rescripta in Gratiam Congregationis Missionis*. Paris, 1876, 118-33).

APPROBATIONS[1]

Approbation of the Archbishop of Auch

We, Henri de la Mothe, doctor of the University of Paris and archbishop of Auch, declare that we have read the book entitled *Life of the Venerable Servant of God Vincent de Paul*, written by Monsieur Louis Abelly, bishop of Rodez. In it we have found nothing but what is edifying and which may not serve as an example for all classes of persons to imitate. Its subject and his life's work is described with such force, such sincerity and in such vivid colors that it is not necessary to have known him intimately or to have spoken with him familiarly. He can be found in this book even better than in life, for he kept himself hidden from the eyes of men, to reveal himself to God alone. We judge that this book should be published and read by everyone.

Done at Paris, this thirtieth day of August, 1664.

Henri de la Mothe [Houdancourt], archbishop of Auch.

Approbation of the Bishop of Evreux

The Church has long endured the cruelty of tyrants, but also the shame of the reproaches made by the prophets against the leaders of the people. Ezekiel complained that the flock of the Lord was dispersed for want of a shepherd. Zechariah called the negligent shepherd an idol since he was useless for guarding his flock which he abandoned in times of stress. The Fathers of the Church lamented the same deplorable evil. Saint Gregory of Nazianzus, among others, while expressing his astonishment at seeing how the good shepherd patiently endured all the rigors of the seasons to assure the safety of the sheep whose guardian he was, could only grieve at the sight of the sheepfold of the Savior of the world exposed to the attack of wolves for want of true shepherds. Souls, whom he calls simply thinking sheep, instead of having true pastors are at the whim of mercenaries who abandon the sheep at the first sign of difficulty.

The Sovereign Pastor who watches over his Church has raised up for us in the person of Monsieur Vincent a faithful servant, filled with zeal for his glory and burning with love for the salvation of souls. We have only to read

---

1. These approbations are reproduced above all because they are from two prelates who were friends of Saint Vincent. The bishop of Evreux was Henri Cauchon de Maupas du Tour, 1600-1680, chaplain to Anne of Austria, and later bishop of Le Puy. In 1661 he was named bishop of Evreux. On November 23, 1660, nearly two months after the saint's death, he pronounced the funeral oration at the official memorial service sponsored at Saint Germain l'Auxerrois in Paris by the members of the Tuesday conferences.

this story of his life, written by the bishop of Rodez, to be convinced of this. I attest that I have read and even reread the books so filled with doctrine and piety the bishop has given the public in the past. I have studied them even in a spirit of admiration. I urge the faithful to read and meditate upon his latest work which cannot help being very useful in impressing on their hearts a true and solid devotion.

Given at Evreux on the feast of Saint Bernard, April 20, 1664.

Henri, bishop of Evreux.

EXTRACT FROM THE ROYAL PRIVILEGE

By the grace and privilege of the king, it has been permitted to Florentin Lambert, a bookseller in Paris, to print or to have printed, to sell and to distribute throughout the kingdom, a book entitled *The Life of the Venerable Servant of God Vincent de Paul, Founder and First Superior General of the Congregation of the Mission*, by Monsieur Louis Abelly, Bishop of Rodez; and to do this in the size, character and as many times as he judges it proper, for the period of twenty consecutive years. It is forbidden to all printers, booksellers and others to print, to have printed, to sell, or to distribute this book in whatever way and manner, and under whatever possible pretext, without the agreement of Lambert, or of those so entitled, under pain of confiscation of copies, arbitrary fine, expenses, damages and interest, according as it has been further specified in this privilege, granted at Paris May 19, 1664. And the twenty-second year of our reign. Signed: BARDON

Registered in the volume of the guild of printers and booksellers of this city, August 19, 1664.

E. Martin, Syndic

Printing completed for the first time, September 10, 1664.

Copies have been furnished.

BOOK ONE

The Life of Vincent de Paul

CHAPTER ONE

The Church in France at the Time of the Birth of Vincent de Paul

G OD'S WISDOM and power in guiding his Church are never so admirable as when he uses the very sufferings she endures to exercise his mercy. These turn her losses into gains, her humiliations to his glory and her sterility into his abundance. This reflects what a prophet had said earlier, that when it seems God has abandoned us, it is only to have us experience more forcefully his mercy and love.[1] When he seems to have turned away his face and forgotten us, it is to prepare us for new blessings and to favor us with his special graces.

The writings of Saint Hilary about the Arians express this thought. In their day they held truth captive in injustice: "The Church of Jesus Christ triumphs when she is struck down. She becomes best known when she is the more disfigured by calumnies. She receives the greatest help from God at the very moment she seems bereft of his protection."[2]

This may be verified by a study of Church history. It speaks of this mystic vessel the Church, seemingly about to founder afloat on the stormy sea of this world, threatened by a thousand perils. She is often within a hair's breadth of disaster. Always, however, the hand of God is with her, often using the very storms or adverse winds to bring her safely to port. Not to be overwhelmed by such a vast area of consideration, it would be enough to reflect on the deplorable state of the Church in France toward the middle of the last century. This would show the Lord's paternal care, not only to preserve the Church but also to see to its growth and development. It appeared at times as though he had abandoned her. In the same way we must study the Providence of God in guiding his faithful servant, Vincent de Paul, the great things he wrought in him and by him for the benefit of his holy Church, for his service and for his greater honor and glory. The servant of God was born toward the end of the sixteenth century, when France was caught in several mighty storms. These were the heresies of Luther and Calvin, which had separated a part of the kingdom from the union all Catholics owe to the head of the Church. Soon afterwards an open rebellion took place against the authority of the king. As a holy apostle remarks, heretics reject all submission, even the respect they owe their lawful sovereign.[3]

The terrible scourge of the two evils, heresy and civil war, cannot be

---
1. Isa 54:7.
2. PL 10:202.
3. Jude 8.

described. These lasted many years. They left the once prosperous French nation, until recently among the most flourishing monarchies of the world, almost like a theater of the absurd, where violence and impiety played tragic roles. Churches everywhere were destroyed, altars abused, sacred objects profaned, priests slain, and above all these ills was an almost total rejection of all ecclesiastical order and discipline. In the greater part of the kingdom people were like scattered sheep, without spiritual pasturage, sacraments, instruction, or almost any other external help toward their own salvation.

When the invincible courage and wise direction of Henry the Great[4] of glorious memory had restored peace to France, the bishops received the opportunity to put an end to confusion and restore religion to its true place in the nation. They called various provincial councils, and the bishops applied their wise and salutary laws in their local synods. It proved no easy task to overcome the contagion of heresy and the license of the armies. In fact, the remedies proved inadequate to root out the evils of the times.

Although the authorities in the Church worked strenuously to fulfill their duties, cases of gross scandals continued among the clergy. As a result, the priesthood fell into disrepute. In some places this was so marked that members of the nobility would be ordained simply to have a considerable benefice attached to certain positions. It became a sort of insult to say of an upper-class cleric that he had become a priest.

Another evil developed from the lack of concern and discipline among the clergy, especially in the countryside. The poor people were not instructed in their spiritual duties, and catechizing was almost unknown. For the most part the village pastors, like the shepherds mentioned by the prophet, were content to take the wool and milk from the sheep but did little to provide decent pasturage.[5] Everywhere Christians passed their entire lives in profound ignorance of what was required for eternal salvation. They were unaware of God's existence, the mysteries of the Holy Trinity, or the incarnation of the Son of God: things which should be known explicitly by all Christians. In what concerned the sacraments it was even worse: which ones should they receive, what dispositions they should bring to their reception, and so on. God alone knows the state of their conscience, living in such complete ignorance of what leads to salvation or what they should know about their faith. Almost no one was available to help them in learning what they were obliged to believe.

Those living in the cities had the advantage of preaching given in the parishes and other churches. Assuredly there was greater knowledge and light there, but unfortunately the knowledge remained sterile and the light

---

4. Henry IV.
5. Ezek 34:3.

was often without warmth. Charity, which is known by its works, was practically unheard of. The spiritual works of mercy in favor of one's neighbor were little known among the laity. Alms were usually but a pittance. Even wealthy people believed they did enough in giving a small coin to a beggar. On some special occasion they considered a larger alms a major act of charity.

Such was the state of the Church in France when God, rich in mercy and mindful of the great needs of the Church in one of the main regions of the world, raised up his faithful servant Vincent de Paul, among several other great and saintly persons. Filled with his Spirit and strengthened by his grace, he began with untiring zeal to repair the damages and apply the proper remedies.

He first set himself to make sure that the Church was served by good priests who would work diligently and faithfully in the Lord's vineyard. He developed special activities for ordinands, seminaries, retreats for the clergy, spiritual conferences, and other similar enterprises to further this goal. He either founded these projects or at least promoted them with extraordinary success, as we shall see later in this book.

He combined this zeal for the reformation of the clergy with an ardent charity which moved him to provide instruction and spiritual help to souls in need. He was devoted to the poor country people more than to others, for he judged them to be the most abandoned, and he had a special tenderness for them. It is impossible to describe how hard he labored to deliver them from sin and ignorance by catechizing and helping them to make a general confession. He was not satisfied with the heroic efforts he made for their relief but elicited the support of others to help in the cause as well. His love for the poor was not satisfied until he had founded a new congregation of virtuous missionary priests. They carried on his work not only in France but in many other areas, such as Ireland, Scotland, the Hebrides, Poland, Italy, Barbary, and even in the tropics, on the island of Madagascar. Several of these Gospel messengers even gave their lives there in the service of charity.

Neither was Vincent de Paul satisfied to work simply for the spiritual welfare of the poor. He thought of their bodily needs as well. Having made himself poor for the love of Jesus Christ and having left all to follow him, he had no more worldly goods to give. His heart was so much on fire with that heavenly flame which the divine Savior had come to enkindle upon the earth that he was most successful in awakening this same spirit in some well-disposed persons he encountered.

We shall see in his life some marvelous examples which will show the graces which God had poured forth on this faithful servant. Even amid the corruption of this present age he was able to arouse in many souls the spirit and charity of the first Christians. This happened although it has never been more true, as the apostle says, that everyone looks out for his own interests and not those of Jesus Christ.[6] The example and words of Vincent de Paul sufficed to remove this root of all evil from the hearts of a great number of virtuous persons. The result was that their greatest joy and satisfaction became, and remains even today, not only to give a notable share of their worldly goods to help the poor, but more remarkably to give themselves, their health, and even their lives in the most demanding tasks of Christian charity.

Paris was not the only place to benefit from his efforts in favor of an innumerable multitude of needy men and women of all classes, and ages. Because of the extreme misery accompanying wars and other public calamities, their charity extended to the remote provinces, even to the French frontier, which felt the effects of the war most severely. His practical help reached to Lorraine, the Hebrides, Barbary, and several other remote regions, as we shall see later in this book.

---

6. Phil 2:21.

CHAPTER TWO

The Birth and Education of Vincent de Paul

ON EASTER Tuesday 1576, Vincent de Paul came into the world in the small town of Pouy[1] near Dax,[2] an episcopal city in the Landes of Bordeaux near the Pyrenees.[3] Within the bounds of this parish is a chapel dedicated to the Most Blessed Virgin under the title Our Lady of Buglose.[4] It ordinarily attracted a large gathering of the faithful who would offer their homage and prayers to the Mother of God. This undoubtedly was one of the reasons which led Vincent de Paul from his tenderest years to conceive and nurture a special devotion to the Queen of Heaven. He had been born in a place dedicated to her and under her special protection.

His parents were poor in worldly goods and lived from their work. His father was Jean de Paul, his mother Bertrande de Moras.[5] Both lived beyond reproach, in innocence and rectitude. They owned a house and some small pieces of property they had inherited, which they developed with the help of their six children.[6] These were four boys and two girls. Vincent was the third oldest and, like the others, began his working career as a guardian of the family animals.

It seems as though God wished to raise upon this humble origin the building which was to become so remarkable, that is, the virtuous soul of his faithful servant. As Saint Augustine says so well, "whoever would be great before God should begin by a profound repudiation of his own self.

---

1. This village is now known as Saint Vincent de Paul. A royal ordinance of December 3, 1828, authorized the change of name.
2. The ancient diocese of Dax was suppressed by the Concordat of 1801 and attached to that of Aire.
3. If one accepts the date of 1580 as the correct year for the saint's birth, his birthday was April 5, the feast of Saint Vincent Ferrer; if 1581, it was March 28. By Abelly's reckoning, it was April 24.
4. The Blessed Virgin has been honored at this place of pilgrimage since ancient times. There was, however, no chapel at Buglose in the saint's childhood. According to legend, at the time of the Wars of Religion, the chapel was burned and the local Catholics are said to have protected the statue by hiding it in a nearby bog. Then, in 1620 a farmer came upon one of his cattle licking the mud from the statue. The pilgrimage probably dates from this year. The chapel was confided to the Congregation in 1706, where the priests established a missionary center to evangelize the surrounding districts. It did so until the French Revolution.
5. Collet mistakenly referred to Vincent's father as Guillaume. *Vie*, I:5; this is the original edition, cited in this work.
6. This house, named Ranquine, was preserved and became a place of pilgrimage. Transferred a short distance from its original site, it has been reconstructed several times using such original materials as existed to restore it to its original appearance. In the nineteenth century, the Berceau ("cradle") was established as a pilgrimage site and a center for Vincentian works of charity.

The more he plans to raise an edifice of virtue the deeper must be the foundation of his humility."[7] So it happened that in his later positions of some consequence or amid the tributes to his virtue and accomplishments, Vincent de Paul usually responded that he was merely a poor peasant's son, who had watched over swine, etc.[8] What a sign of real virtue to recall his humble beginnings amid recognition and praise! Saint Bernard had good reason to say that it is a rare treat to find a humble man exalted.[9] Few attain the degree of perfection that they seek out humiliation at the very moment honors rain down on them.

Pearls develop in an unlikely and often soiled surroundings, but even so they do not lose their brightness by being in the mire. This serves only to heighten their luster and emphasize their true worth. The vivacity of spirit with which God had endowed the young Vincent began to appear and was the more noticeable in such surroundings. His father soon realized that this child was destined for other things than pasturing animals. He planned therefore to send him to school, encouraged by his acquaintance with a prior in the neighborhood. This man was from a humble family like himself, but it was known that he supported members of his family from the revenues of a benefice he enjoyed. In his simplicity the father imagined that with a little schooling Vincent too might receive a benefice, and while serving the Church might help to support his family. The thoughts of men are not always the same as those of God, as one of the prophets reminds us, and his designs are above all our imaginings.[10] The father of the young Vincent thought only of the petty advantages his son might win for the family, while in God's design Vincent was to do great good for the entire Church. The parents were to be left in their lowliness and poverty, while Vincent worked solely to advance the building up the kingdom of his Son, Jesus Christ.

Apropos of this subject, Vincent years later once received a visit in Paris from a priest of his native region. He pointed out the poor circumstances of the de Paul family and asked if Vincent could not do something for them. Vincent inquired if they lived by their own labor and in keeping with their social status. After receiving the reply, yes, they did, he thanked his visitor for his concern but recalled the case of the prior spoken of earlier. This clergyman had spent a good part of the revenues of his benefice to support his parents, but they largely dissipated this help both during the lifetime of their son and after his death. They fell into a worse state than before, for, as

---

7. PL 38:441, 2.
8. See also Book Three, ch. 13, sect. 1; also *CED* II:3, 171; IV:215; V:394; VIII:138; IX:81, 673; X:342; XII:432.
9. In Cant. *Magna prorsus et rara virtus, humilitas honorata.* Homily on Missus est, or in laudibus Virginis Mariae; references from Brepols ed.: 4-55-6-9-Miss-4; homily 4, parag. 9.
10. Isa 55:8-9.

Vincent recalled: "In vain do they labor who build the house, if the Lord does not build it."[11] He cited this example to prove what he had often observed, that families are often ruined by the help received from their clerical relatives who gave them money at the expense of the Church. These priests did more harm than good. The money they gave was in reality the dowry of the poor, which sooner or later God would take back from them.

His refusal on this occasion to help his family did not suggest a hard heart or a lack of filial affection. It revealed only his uprightness and pure intention, the soul of all his actions. He ever walked on the straight path that leads to God, without turning aside for any consideration whatsoever. Moreover he had a tender heart for the sufferings of his neighbor and was quick to help them as much as he could. He could say with the ancient patriarch that "mercy had been born with him."[12] He had a particular inclination toward this virtue even from his earliest years. It was noticed that he gave what he could to the poor. Whenever his father sent him to the mill to collect the flour, and he met a poor person along the way and had nothing else to give, he would open the sack and give the poor man handfuls of flour. We are told that his father, a good man, would not object to this. Another time, when about twelve or thirteen years old, he had saved some thirty *sous* from different jobs. At the time, and in the country district where money was scarce, this was regarded as no small sum. However, upon meeting a poor destitute person along the road, he felt moved with compassion and gave away every bit of his small treasure. If we pay close attention to what attracts young people, we can form a judgment about their future dispositions. In Vincent's case we can predict a great and perfect detachment from the things of this world and, by the grace of God, an eminent degree of charity.

---

11. Ps 127:1.
12. Job 31:18.

CHAPTER THREE

Studies and Promotion to the Clerical State

THE FAVORABLE disposition of soul of the young Vincent and his obvious inclination to the good moved his father to send him for schooling to the extent his meager resources would allow. In keeping with this resolution he sent him to the Franciscan fathers of Dax, at a yearly fee of sixty *livres*, according to the custom of the time. Around 1588 he began to study the elements of Latin. He progressed so well that four years later[1] Monsieur de Comet the elder, lawyer of the city of Dax and judge of Pouy, took him under his patronage on the recommendation of the Father Guardian. He developed an appreciation for him and invited him into his own home as tutor for his children. As teacher and guardian of the children, Vincent could earn enough to continue his studies without being a further charge upon his father. He spent nine years at his studies in Dax. At the end of this, his patron Monsieur de Comet, a man of merit and piety, was satisfied with the service the young Vincent had rendered to his children. He had also edified the entire family by his wise and virtuous deportment, so far beyond his years. For this reason, Monsieur de Comet thought it was time for a change.[2]

The light must no longer be kept under a bushel basket but must be placed upon a candlestick to light up the entire Church. He persuaded Vincent de Paul, who respected him deeply and looked upon him as a second father, to give himself totally to God as a cleric. Therefore he received the tonsure and the four minor orders, on September 19, 1596, at the age of twenty.[3]

---

1. Coste reckons that he could not have spent more than two years in Dax. *Life* I:15. Vincent said that he remained in the fields until about age fifteen (*CED* IX:81), consequently he must have begun his studies between 1592 and 1595, depending on his birth date.
2. Monsieur de Comet (or Commet) the elder, an attorney at the Presidial Court of Dax and a judge of Pouy, together with his brother, deserves the credit for discerning the capabilities of the young Vincent. Up to the day of his departure for the University of Toulouse, Vincent allowed himself to be guided by the Comets who, to increase his slim resources, entrusted to him a tutorship in their own family. It must not be said, however, as did the Jansenist Martin de Barcos, that Saint Vincent de Paul received Holy Orders without a vocation so as not to upset his two benefactors. See Martin de Barcos, *Défense de feu Monsieur Vincent de Paul.... contre les faux discours du livre de sa vie publiée par M. Abelly, ancien évêque de Rodez, et contre les impostures de quelques autres écrits sur ce sujet*, 1666, 87.
3. The correct date is December 20, 1596. This ceremony was conducted by Salvat Diharse, bishop of Tarbes, in the collegiate church at Bidache in the diocese of Dax. At that time, the see of Dax was vacant. By modern chronology, Vincent was only fifteen or sixteen years old. The same bishop conferred subdiaconate and diaconate upon Vincent since Dax was still vacant at the time of the subdiaconate, and the bishop, Jean Jacques Dusault, although appointed, had not reached

Now that he was a cleric he took God as his only portion. He left his native area never to return. With his father's blessing and with a small gift from him (the result of a sale of a pair of oxen,) he set off for Toulouse. There he would remain for seven years to study theology. He also spent some time in Spain to complete his studies at Saragossa.[4]

On February 22 and December 29, 1598, he received the orders of subdeacon and deacon, and finally, on September 23, 1600, he was ordained to the priesthood.[5] Since he lived until September 27, 1660, he was a priest of the Church of Jesus Christ for more than sixty years. God alone knows his dispositions on the occasion of his ordination when he received the sacred character of the priesthood. We can judge the tree by its fruit and the cause by its effects. Thus, in view of the perfection and sanctity with which this worthy priest did his duties, we can rightly conclude that at the moment he was consecrated, our Savior Jesus Christ the Eternal Priest and Prince of Priests poured out upon him the fullness of his own priestly spirit. He was so filled with this spirit that he always spoke of the sacred character of the priesthood with great reverence, as something which could never be appreciated enough. He was moved to astonishment when he spoke of God's marvelous power. It imprinted an indelible mark upon the soul of the priest, bestowed the power to forgive sins, and with four or five words empowered him to change bread and wine into the body and blood of Jesus Christ. The priest offered this body and blood in sacrifice to the Father and gave the body of Jesus Christ as the bread of life to nourish the faithful. He was convinced of the great excellence of the priestly character and the obligation of those who received it to lead a pure, holy, and angelic life. This was such that he was often heard later to say that, had he not already been ordained a priest, he would not deem himself worthy to become one.[6] The more deserving he became, the less worthy he judged himself. None deserves advancement to the first places in the nuptial feast of the Lamb so much as the one who puts himself in the lowest.

When or where he celebrated his first mass is unknown. He later was heard to say that his respect for the majesty of this holy action was so great that he trembled before celebrating. He did not have the courage to offer his first mass publicly. He preferred to offer it in a remote private chapel, attended only by another priest and a server.[7]

---

his diocese at the time of the saint's ordination as a deacon. *CED* XIII:1-2.
4. The time spent in Spain must have been brief. Román, *Biografía* 50, n. 25.
5. The correct dates are September 19 and December 19. *CED* XIII:4-7. He was ordained to the priesthood by Francois de Bourdeilles, bishop of Perigueux, at Chateau l'Eveque, one month before his death, October 24.
6. See *CED* V:568, VII:463.
7. Although we do not know the date of his first mass, there is little doubt that he celebrated at least one of his first masses in the pilgrimage chapel of Our Lady of Grace near the village of Buzet

At the instigation of Monsieur de Comet who had such a great appreciation of his reputation, the vicars general of Dax, since the see was vacant, no sooner learned of his ordination than they invited him to accept the pastorate of the place called Tilh.[8] Another candidate contested the appointment and appealed to the court of Rome. Monsieur Vincent preferred not to enter into a lawsuit over this matter. God permitted this to come about to allow him to continue his studies, which he was anxious to do.[9]

By now, his father had been dead for two years, but his will provided for Vincent's education. After seeing to the welfare of the other children, the will stipulated that Vincent should be helped by the remainder of the estate. This could have given him a legitimate claim on his family, but he did not wish to burden them. He saw that he could not support himself in Toulouse, so he decided to accept a tutoring position in the village of Buzet, four leagues from the town.[10] Some gentlemen of the region had Vincent take care of their children. Some students even came from Toulouse to be under his care and instruction, as we learn from a letter he wrote his mother.[11] Because of the great care he gave to the instruction and good education of the children, he was able to return to Toulouse a short time later. With the consent of the parents, he brought the group of students back to the city, enabling him to continue his studies in theology at the university.

A public record attests that he completed his study after seven years. A document shows that in October [12] of 1604 he received the Bachelor of Theology degree from the university. This record is signed by the Augustinian priest, Esprit Larran, Doctor Regent in Theology, by his secretary Assolens, and sealed. Another document of the same month, signed by Andre Gallus, Doctor Regent and rector of the university, by the secretary Assolens, and sealed, attests to the same degree.

By this degree Vincent received authorization to explain and teach the second Book of the Sentences within the university.[12] Still another document of the same year, signed and sealed by the chancellor of the university, Monsieur Coelmez, and by de Soffores, treasurer, mention the same facts. Members of his Congregation found all three of these documents among Vincent's papers after his death. The priests had been completely unaware

---

sur Tarn. Another candidate is Our Lady of Remoulle, now destroyed, but whose altar was removed to Our Lady of Grace.

8. 1600. The see was not vacant, since the bishop had been appointed in 1598.

9. It appears that Saint Vincent made a journey to Rome at this time, in 1600 or 1601. *CED* I:114-15.

10. Buzet sur Tarn was at the time a town of some importance with a gothic church and a fortified castle. It is located some twenty kilometers northeast of Toulouse.

11. This letter is no longer extant.

12. The standard theology textbook, composed by Peter Lombard, later bishop of Paris, where he died in 1160. The "sentences" or opinions of the Fathers were applied to individual theological questions. The second book deals with creation and what relates to it.

of their existence during his lifetime. If we count up the time since he left his native place, he spent more than sixteen years in studies, first at the town of Dax and later at the University of Toulouse.[13]

He was not one of those puffed up by the little they know. On the contrary, he strove to hide what he had acquired. Out of an extraordinary sense of humility, he tried to persuade others that he had little education. He called himself a poor scholar of the fourth class to convey a poor impression of his education.[14] Saying this he did not offend against the truth, for indeed he had passed through the fourth class, but it was an artifice of the virtue of humility. He maintained silence about his later studies.[15] On those occasions when in the interest of truth or of charity he was forced to speak up and reveal that he was not ignorant of the matter at hand, he still was happiest when others judged that he had no training in formal education. He acted in this way to destroy pride, which leads most men to pass themselves off as knowing as much as anyone else or even more, regardless of how uninformed they are.

Despite his academic background, Vincent de Paul took as his motto the words of the holy apostle: "I count all things as loss except the knowledge of Jesus Christ and Jesus Christ crucified."[16] Here was his book of true learning and highest wisdom. This was the one book always open before the eyes of his soul. He drew from it knowledge and light surpassing what he might have gained from the other good and holy sources he had encountered in his years of study.

---

13. More careful reckoning shows that the time spent in studies was less, between nine and twelve years, depending on one's starting point.
14. See *CED* XII:135, 293. By this expression, he implied that he had not finished his secondary education.
15. After the saint's death, his confreres found the papers for his bachelor of theology, received at the University of Toulouse, and those for the licentiate in canon law, conferred by the University of Paris. He had received this degree at least by 1624. *CED* XIII:60, n.1.
16. 1 Cor 2:2.

CHAPTER FOUR

Vincent de Paul is Captured by Pirates and Taken to Barbary

DURING ALL the years Vincent de Paul devoted to his studies, either in Dax or at the University of Toulouse, he acted with such modesty and wisdom that he spread the good odor of his virtues everywhere. He was esteemed and loved by all who came in contact with him. He was particularly devoted to the young students he supervised, not only teaching them well but likewise giving them a strong taste for Christian piety. His reputation in Toulouse was so well founded that his boarding school became popular. We have testimony from a long-time and dear friend, Monsieur de Saint Martin, canon of Dax, who survived him, that at that time there was some hope that he might be made a bishop. The initiative for this came from the duke of Epernon, who had two close relatives among his students.[1] At the beginning of 1605 Vincent traveled to Bordeaux for reasons we do not know, but we have some right to think might have been about the bishopric. In one of the letters he wrote at this time we read, "I have undertaken a costly matter which I can hardly mention without trembling."[2]

Upon returning to Toulouse he learned that a friend who admired his virtuous life had died, leaving him the beneficiary of a will. This entailed spending some time to acquire the legacy. After looking into the matter he discovered that a man who had borrowed four or five hundred *ecus* from the dead person had fled to Marseilles to avoid paying the debt. Vincent went to Marseilles to pursue the man. He succeeded in working out a settlement of three hundred *ecus*. Since it was now July 1605, he proposed to return to Toulouse by land. A gentleman from Languedoc he had met in an inn suggested, however, that he join him in traveling by ship to Narbonne. Vincent was easily persuaded, for the weather was good and the sea voyage would greatly cut down on his travel.

According to the ordinary standards of the world, we might say this was a foolhardy decision. If we look at things with the clear light of faith, we must say, on the contrary, that it was a happy event in the accomplishment of God's designs upon him.

---

1. They were the two grandnephews of the Duke of Epernon, Jean Louis de Nogaret de la Vallette, 1554-1642, the heroic grand master of the order of Saint John of Jerusalem. The duke became powerful at court in the last years of Henry IV, and especially during the regency of Marie de Medici. He became governor of Guienne only in 1622, but often lived in his chateau at Cadillac near Bordeaux.
2. *CED* I:3.

CHAPTER FOUR

Let us listen to Vincent himself as he describes what happened. He did so in a letter written from Avignon after his escape from captivity, dated July 24, 1607, to Monsieur de Comet, the younger. His father had died of the plague some time before.[3]

I set out by ship for Narbonne, to save time and money, but, to say it better, never to be there and to lose everything I had. The wind was favorable, and we should have reached Narbonne that same day (since it is but fifty leagues away) if God had not allowed three Turkish brigantines[4] patrolling the Gulf of Lyons in search of small ships coming from the fair at Beaucaire,[5] one of the best in Christendom, to attack us. They pressed their attack so vigorously that two or three of our party were killed, and everyone else injured. I myself was struck by an arrow, which will ever be my timepiece for the rest of my life. We were obliged to yield to the pirates. They immediately in their rage hacked our captain into a thousand pieces for having killed one of the leaders, besides four or five of their convicts. They chained us afterwards and, after having crudely dressed our wounds, continued their sweep of the gulf. They captured countless others, but after robbing them set them free if they had surrendered without a fight. Finally loaded with stolen goods, after seven or eight days they returned to Barbary, lair of the disreputable robbers unacknowledged by the Grand Turk.[6] Upon arrival we were put up for sale, with a written report of our capture saying that we had been taken from a Spanish ship. This lie sought to prevent our being freed by the king's consul, who looked after French commercial interests there.[7]

As to our sale, we were first stripped, then given a pair of shorts, a linen jacket, and a cap, and then paraded through the streets of Tunis, there to be sold. After we had been taken in chains five or six times around the city, they brought us back to the boat so that buyers could come and inspect us. They looked to see if we could

---

3. This entire account of the captivity has been much debated as to its historical reliability. Abelly's account differs in numerous details from the original text. *CED* I:13.
4. These ships were at that time small, decked craft, rigged with only one sail, and having eight to sixteen benches, each for a single oarsman. The oars were wide and flat. *CED* I:3.
5. Beaucaire was the central market for goods coming from the East. The fair opened each year on July 22 and brought to that city countless boats from Marseilles, Sete, Aigues Mortes and elsewhere. At the time of their departure, the boats that were headed for the open sea formed their own escort or had themselves accompanied by galleys for protection in case of attack. The pirates from the east and from Barbary lay in wait for them, posted on watch all along the coast, not far from the mouths of the Rhone.
6. The sultan or emperor of the Ottoman state, who resided in Turkey and ruled the far flung areas of the empire through beys and other officials.
7. Treaties of 1534, 1569, 1581, and 1604 stipulated that the Barbary pirates would respect the freedom of French trade.

eat or if we had recovered from our wounds. Next they brought us to the city square, where the buyers came just as they do for buying horses or cattle. They made us open our mouths to show our teeth, rapped our sides, checked our wounds, made us walk, trot, and run, lift boxes, and wrestle to judge each one's strength, and a thousand other indignities.

I was sold to a fisherman, but he was soon obliged to get rid of me because I found nothing so repugnant as the sea. He in turn sold me to an old doctor of alchemy, a student of quintessences. He was a kindly and reasonable man, who told me that he had been searching for the philosopher's stone for fifty years.[8] He liked me very much and taught me some of the secrets of alchemy and then his religious beliefs. He used all his efforts to convert me, promising to enrich me and to teach me all he knew. God inspired in me a sure hope that I would be freed because of my earnest prayers and the care of the Virgin Mary, by whose intercession I firmly believe I was restored to liberty. The hope and even firm belief that I had of seeing you again, Monsieur, made me pay close attention to my owner's instruction about how to cure the plague, for every day I saw the marvelous cures he wrought. He taught me all this and even had me prepare and administer the medications. How many times I wished that I had been captured and enslaved before the death of your brother! In that case I feel that I would have learned the secrets of this disease, and he would have escaped death at its cruel hands.

I was with this aged man from September 1605 to the middle of August 1606, when he was captured and taken for the service of the sultan. This did not happen, however, since he died on the way. I was left to his nephew, a man who attributed human form to God. He resold me soon after his uncle's death. He had heard that the ambassador to the Turks, Monsieur de Breves, was on his way with letters from the Great Sultan[9] to free the Christian slaves.[10]

A renegade from Nice in Savoy bought me.[11] He took me to his

---

8. Abelly here omits several details about Saint Vincent's knowledge of alchemy. The "doctor of quintessences," literally a Spagyrite, explained the organic changes of the human body in health and in sickness as the chemists of their day explained those of the inorganic realms. Paracelsus invented the term Spagyrite, and founded this school of thought in the sixteenth century.
9. Ahmed I, died 1617.
10. Francois Savary, Marquis of Breves, was one of the most able negotiators in the reigns of Henry IV and Louis XIII. His arrival was the result of a treaty advantageous to France, signed with the sultan, May 20, 1604. He left with only seventy-two slaves, but before the time narrated here.
11. Renegades were numerous, recruited from among slaves or from foreigners who had come to Barbary to escape their creditors. Those who embraced Islam were freed of all debts. Converted slaves had more freedom than others and were treated less harshly. The most fearsome captains were almost all renegades. Once they had made their fortunes, they enjoyed them in sumptuous

farm which he held as a tenant farmer to the great lord, for there no one owns anything. Everything belongs to the Sultan. His farm was in the mountains, in an extremely hot and dry country. One of his three wives was a Greek Christian, but orthodox. A second was a Moslem. She turned out to be the instrument of God's immense mercy to recall her husband from apostasy and return him to the bosom of the Church and to rescue me from my slavery.

She was curious to know how we Christians lived. She came every day to the fields where I was digging to speak with me. Once she asked me to sing one of our hymns in praise of our God. The memory of *Quomodo cantabimus in terra aliena* ["How will we sing in a foreign land?"] of the children of Israel captive in Babylon brought tears to my eyes, so I began to sing the Psalm *Super flumina Babylonis* ["at the rivers of Babylon"],[12] and then the *Salve Regina* ["Hail Holy Queen"] and several other songs. She was so pleased, it was astonishing. She spoke in the evening to her husband. She told him that he was wrong to leave such a religion as I had explained in telling her of our God and in singing several hymns for her. She said that she had felt such pleasure in my account that she believed that the paradise of her fathers could not be as glorious or accompanied with such joy as she had experienced when she heard me praise the Lord. She thought there was something marvelous in all this.

This woman, like another Caiaphas or Balaam's ass, was so persuasive in her speech that the next day her husband told me that he was awaiting an opportunity to sail to France with some merchandise.[13] He said also that in a few days a remedy to my situation would make me praise God. These few days lasted ten months, during which he sustained my hopes until finally we sailed in a small skiff, landing on June 28 at Aigues Mortes and later at Avignon. Here the vice-legate[14] publicly received the recantation of the renegade. With tears in his eyes and a sob in his voice, he was reconciled to God in the Church of Saint Peter, to the honor of God and the edification of all present. The vice-legate kept us both with him for some time. Then he directed us to Rome, where he promised to come as soon as his own successor[15] arrived in Avi-

---

palaces. It appears from seventeenth-century spelling that "Nice" may refer to Necy or Annecy.
12. Ps 137:1-4.
13. The original text is more vivid: "This other Caiaphas or Balaam's ass. . . ."
14. Pietro Francesco Montorio (or Montoro), 1558-1643.
15. Giuseppe Ferreri, archbishop of Urbino.

gnon. He promised the penitent that he would help him to enter the austere order of the *Fate ben Fratelli*. He did so some time later.[16]

Up to now we have been quoting the words of Monsieur Vincent in a letter written from Avignon. A gentleman of Dax,[17] nephew of Monsieur de Saint Martin, found it by chance in 1658, fifty years after it had been penned. He gave it to his uncle, and he sent a copy to Monsieur Vincent. He thought that he would be glad to read of his former adventures and in his old age see his younger self. As soon as Vincent read the letter he threw it into the fire. Soon after he wrote to thank Monsieur de Saint Martin for having sent the copy but asked if he would send the original as well. Later, only six months before his death, he sent another and more urgent appeal for the original.[18] His secretary slipped in a note with this appeal.[19] He suggested that Monsieur Vincent would probably burn the original as he had the copy. He further suggested that Monsieur de Saint Martin send the original but addressed to someone other than Monsieur Vincent to keep it from being lost. He did so, sending it to a priest of the Congregation who at the time was superior of the seminary connected with the College des Bons Enfants at Paris. This letter was thus preserved without Monsieur Vincent ever having discovered the pious deception. Otherwise we would certainly never have found out about these days of his slavery. This servant of God made strenuous efforts to conceal the graces and gifts he had received from God and all that he had accomplished for his glory and in his service. All who knew him well recognized this trait in him, and it is hard to believe to what lengths he would go to avoid honor. So true is this that in this present book we can read only what his humility was unsuccessful in hiding from sight. If on some special occasions his charity obliged him to reveal some small detail of his past, he did so with extreme reluctance. Even afterwards he would beg pardon of his audience for having spoken of himself. When it was possible to speak in the third person without obviously referring to himself, he did so adroitly.

Besides all the facets of his stay among the infidels, such as his constancy and firmness in professing the faith of Jesus Christ, his perfect confidence in the divine Goodness in the midst of total abandonment by others, his fidelity to his self-imposed regime of pious exercises, his devotion to the most holy Virgin among the impious of Barbary, his gift of touching the hardest hearts and inspiring respect and affection for our holy religion in the minds of those deeply opposed, and for his other virtues and gifts of God which appeared during his forced exile, all of which we leave for readers to

---

16. The "Do-good Brothers," a popular name in Italy for the Brothers of Saint John of God, taken from the formula, "Do good," used by the founder and the brothers to beg alms.
17. Cesar Saint Martin d'Ages.
18. *CED* VIII:271.
19. Brother Bertrand Ducournau. For this letter, *CED* VIII:513-15.

reflect on to their own edification, two particular points remain which merit our closest attention.

The first is Monsieur Vincent's extraordinary virtue which moved him to suppress all knowledge he had acquired from the doctor of alchemy of the secrets of nature and art during his year as his slave. We are aware of how much he picked up from the letter to Monsieur de Comet, quoted above, which even then is only an extract of the full letter. The same information is contained in a second letter he wrote after arriving in Rome.[20] Had he wished he could doubtless have found many opportunities to use his skill, for many unusual types were to be found in that great city. He could have gained great personal advantage from making use of his knowledge when he was in great financial need, but he felt it unworthy of a priest of Jesus Christ. Not only did he not use this art, but even more remarkably, after his return to France from Rome he was never heard to say a single word about this, either to those of his own Congregation or to any of his closest friends. Furthermore, he never spoke about any of the events of his forced stay in Barbary. He had hundreds and hundreds of occasions to do so, since he had taken on the care of the slaves. He was heard to speak about some of the more humiliating events of his life, but nothing of his stay in Tunis, for in some way these events would turn to his own praise.

The second thing to consider in the slavery of Monsieur Vincent is his spirit of compassion toward the poor Christians whom he saw languishing miserably in irons under the barbarian yoke, bereft of consolation or help, either bodily or spiritual. They were subject to great cruelty, unbearable forced labor, and what is worse, exposed to the danger of losing their faith and their salvation. God so willed it to engrave this sorrowful sight on his soul that one day, in other circumstances, he might help these poor abandoned slaves. He was later able to do this by sending some of his missionaries to Tunis and Algiers. They were to comfort, strengthen, and encourage them, to administer the sacraments, and to provide all sorts of services and help to both body and soul, and to help them experience to some degree in their pains and in their irons the infinite care and mercy of God.

---

20. Dated February 20, 1608; *CED* I:13-17. His arrival in Rome was October 30, 1607.

CHAPTER FIVE

Monsieur Vincent's Return to France; His First Stay in Paris

MONSIEUR VINCENT stayed in Rome until the end of 1608 at the kindness of the vice-legate, who gave him board and lodging. He wrote thirty years later to one of the priests of the Congregation in Rome:[1] "I was pleased to find myself in the city, the center of Christianity, the home of the head of the Church militant, burial place of Saints Peter and Paul and so many other martyrs and saintly persons who shed their blood and spent their lives for Jesus Christ. I felt privileged to walk where so many great saints had trod before me. This grace moved me to tears."

These sentiments of spiritual consolation did not diminish his love of learning. The pains and troubles he had experienced did not interfere with his efforts to refresh the theological learning he had acquired at the University of Toulouse. While in Rome the vice-legate introduced him to Cardinal d'Ossat. The cardinal met with Monsieur Vincent several times, and came to have a positive opinion about the qualities of Monsieur Vincent. He so impressed the cardinal that he selected him to bear a secret communication to King Henry IV, which did not permit of taking the risk of a written letter. He could find no one more trustworthy than Monsieur Vincent to deliver the message verbally to the king. The cardinal had complete trust in his fidelity and discretion.[2]

On this occasion Monsieur Vincent showed once more his solid virtue and righteous spirit. He looked to God alone and had no other objective but to please him alone and to render him his faithful and pleasing service. Once he had arrived in Paris, he had an open door to the monarch, known to be an excellent judge of character. In this circumstance Monsieur Vincent's prospects looked promising in a worldly sense, but he thought little of a situation that some others would have taken every possible step to bring about.

---

1. Francois du Coudray. Letter dated July 20, 1631. In this letter he wrote "thirty years ago, when I was in Rome." These words indicate that the saint's first trip to Rome took place around 1600 after his ordination, on the occasion of the jubilee year. See also references in his conferences to the Daughters of Charity of his having seen Clement VIII, who died March 5, 1606. Conferences of May 30 1647 (*CED* IX:316-17), and of September 19, 1649 (*CED* IX:468).
2. This mission probably never took place, as the cardinal died March 13, 1604, four years before Vincent's move to Paris. In his second edition of 1667, Abelly rewrote this passage as follows: "During his stay in Rome, the vice legate discovered more and more the excellent qualities of his spirit, and he had him [Monsieur Vincent] introduced to several highly placed persons, from whose favor he could in the future receive considerable worldly advancement. He also gave him [Monsieur Vincent] the opportunity, when he returned to Paris, to see King Henry IV on a secret matter which had been confided to him."

Monsieur Vincent, in contrast, feared that the favor of an earthly king would obstruct the graces of the King of Heaven, to whose service he was absolutely committed. He resolved never to appear in court again. Once he had acquitted himself of his commission he withdrew, all the while keeping in his heart a sincere regard and resolve to obey and remain faithful to his prince. He left court and set about leading a truly clerical life, devoting himself completely to fulfilling the demands of his calling.

His first lodgings in Paris were in the faubourg Saint Germain, where he met some of the chief officers of the late Queen Marguerite.[3] Among these was Monsieur Du Fresne,[4] secretary of Her Majesty, with whom he formed a close friendship because of the virtue and good qualities Monsieur Vincent saw in him. These qualities gained the notice of the de Gondi house, where Monsieur Dufresne became secretary. He later became steward of [Philippe] Emmanuel de Gondi, count of Joigny and general of the galleys of France. He said of Monsieur Vincent: "At that time Monsieur Vincent seemed humble, charitable and prudent, doing good for everyone. He was no trouble to anyone, circumspect in his words, ready to listen to others and never interrupting. He often visited the sick poor in the charity hospital, serving them and speaking with them."

During this first stay in Paris a curious incident occurred which God allowed to prove Monsieur Vincent's virtue. It became known only after his death, through the testimony of Monsieur de Saint Martin, canon of Dax, who gave the following account. In 1609, while still living in the faubourg Saint Germain, he shared a room with a judge from the town of Sore, a village of the Landes, in the Bordeaux district. Monsieur Vincent was falsely accused of having stolen four hundred *ecus* from the judge.

The judge rose early one morning to take care of some business in the city but forgot to lock the cupboard where he had left his money. Monsieur Vincent remained in bed, indisposed, awaiting some medicine to be sent to him. Meanwhile, the boy from the apothecary shop brought the medicine and, while looking for a glass, found the money in the cupboard. Without saying a word, of course, he put it in his pocket and left, verifying this maxim: opportunity makes the thief.

When the judge returned he was surprised not to find his money. Monsieur Vincent did not know what he was talking about except that he had not taken it nor seen anyone else take it. The judge furiously demanded restitution for his loss. He forced Monsieur Vincent to leave the apartment and spoke against him everywhere as a thief and a liar to anyone who knew him

---

3. Marguerite de Valois, whose marriage to Henry IV the pope declared null. She died in 1615. Henry IV then married Marie de Medici. Vincent's name as one of her chaplains appears first in a document dated May 17, 1610, *CED* XIII:8.
4. Charles Du Fresne, lord of Villeneuve.

or had any contact with him. He knew that Monsieur Vincent was in the habit of consulting Father [Pierre] de Berulle.[5] He was then superior general of the Congregation of the Priests of the Oratory and later became a cardinal of the Holy Roman Church. The judge took the occasion one day to find Monsieur Vincent in Father de Berulle's company, together with several other distinguished guests. He publicly berated Monsieur Vincent, calling him a thief and formally serving a writ upon him, requiring him under threat of excommunication to testify before an ecclesiastical court. The man of God showed no resentment at this affront, took no great pains to justify himself, but said calmly, God knows the truth. Monsieur Vincent preserved his composure under this shameful attack, much to the edification of those present, who were struck by his self-control and humility.

But what was the outcome of this shabby affair? God allowed the boy who had stolen the money to be arrested some years later in Bordeaux for another crime. He came from that area and was known to the judge spoken of earlier. Stricken by remorse, the thief asked the judge to visit him in prison, where he admitted that he had taken the judge's money. He promised to make restitution, hoping that God would not punish him for this miserable crime. On the one hand, the judge was glad to get his money back, which he never expected to see again. On the other, however, he was chagrined to realize that he had calumniated such a worthy cleric as Monsieur Vincent. He immediately wrote to Monsieur Vincent, seeking pardon for his actions and asking him to send the pardon by letter. He went on to say, however, that if Monsieur Vincent refused to grant his request he would come to Paris in person. He would throw himself on his knees at the priest's feet and beg forgiveness with a rope around his neck.

We find a confirmation of this story in the report of a conference Monsieur Vincent gave at Saint Lazare on the question of how best to give and receive corrections. Among his recommendations he referred to this episode in the third person, and not as something which had happened to him personally.

What he said in that conference is well worth considering. "If we are not guilty of the fault of which we are accused, remember that we have many other failings for which we should be ashamed. We should not attempt to justify ourselves, much less feel angry or resentful toward our accuser." He added:

> I know of someone accused of having stolen some money from a friend. He replied simply that he had not taken it, but his friend continued to berate him. He then turned the other cheek, saying to God, "What shall I do, my God? You know the truth." With full confidence in God, then, he refused to reply further to the charges

---

5. Vincent must have met Berulle in 1609 or 1610.

against him even though they went so far as a summons before an ecclesiastical court for stealing. By God's good pleasure, six years later, at a distance of one hundred and twenty leagues from here, the thief who took the money was found. See how God cares for those who abandon themselves to his Providence! The man recognized the harm that his angry calumny had done toward his former friend, and wrote to ask pardon. He said he was so sorry for his actions that he would gladly come in person to ask forgiveness on his knees. We must recognize, gentlemen and my brothers, that we are capable of all kinds of evil. We must leave to God the question of revealing the secrets of consciences.[6]

---

6. *CED* XI:337. Abelly's version differs from that of Coste.

CHAPTER SIX

Monsieur Vincent Appointed Pastor of Clichy

ALTHOUGH MONSIEUR Vincent had resolved to devote himself completely to God and his service in the clerical state, false accusations served only as a goad for further progress. The good use he made of them drew down upon him new graces to help him still more to fulfill his good resolution. He realized that living among lay people, as he was obliged to do upon first coming to Paris, was not conducive to carrying out his God-given desire for the life of a clergyman. His reputation for virtue gave him an entree to the fathers of the Oratory, who kindly received him into their house. He had no intention of joining the community, as he himself later said. He wanted only to shut off social engagements and give himself a better opportunity to discern and follow God's designs for him. He was well aware that we are all blind in our own affairs. He knew, too, that the best way to know God's will is to have a visible guardian angel to lead us, that is, a wise and virtuous spiritual director to serve as a guide. As a result, he decided to choose such a person for himself. He selected the person who led this saintly community of the Oratory with such wisdom and blessings, Father de Berulle,[1] whose memory as we have already shown is held in the highest veneration. Monsieur Vincent opened his heart to him. This quickly made his guide, one of the most enlightened men of the century, see him as one destined by God for great deeds. He reportedly told Monsieur Vincent at that time that God would use him for a great service to the Church by establishing a new religious community of priests. They would have God's blessing upon them and produce much fruit.[2]

Monsieur Vincent remained around two years in this retreat, until Father Bourgoing,[3] pastor of Clichy, decided to resign his charge and enter the Congregation of the Oratory.[4] As it turned out, he later was to become the superior general of this community. Father de Berulle prevailed upon Monsieur Vincent to accept the care of the parish and begin his active work in the

---

1. Pierre de Berulle, 1575-1629, founder of the Oratory of France, and later named a cardinal by Pope Urban VIII. Despite his early support of Saint Vincent, he tried to prevent the approval of the Congregation of the Mission by the Roman Curia.
2. This testimony was given by De la Tour, the sixth general of the Oratory, in his letter to Clement XI supporting the canonization of Vincent de Paul.
3. Francois Bourgoing, third superior general of the Oratory of France.
4. The foundation of the Oratory took place after Bourgoing's resignation.

Lord's vineyard. By a spirit of obedience Monsieur Vincent accepted this post.[5] He was pleased to take on the humble position of pastor of a simple country place in preference to some of the more honorable opportunities available to him. Some two or three years earlier, the king, upon recommendation of Cardinal d'Ossat,[6] had offered him the abbey of Saint Leonard de Chaume in the diocese of Maillezais, now La Rochelle.[7] In addition, Queen Marguerite had heard of his reputation for holiness and took him as her ordinary chaplain and added him to her official family. This humble servant of God preferred to renounce these honors. He chose rather, in imitation of the prophet, to live humbly in the house of the Lord than to dwell in the tents of sinners.[8]

Once he had taken possession of his parish of Clichy[9] as pastor of the flock the Providence of God had confided to his care, he resolved to fulfill faithfully and carefully all the duties of this office. He strove to follow the norms of the sacred canons and in particular the directions of the last general council. As a good shepherd he made it his first care to know his flock, then to provide good pasturage for their souls, turning to God by prayer and sacrifice for the graces they needed. He broke the bread of truth for them by his sermons and his religious instruction. He led them to the fountain of grace by offering the sacraments and in every way possible offered them his help and consolation. This charitable pastor was ever occupied in advancing the welfare of his flock. He would visit the sick, console the sorrowing, help the poor, reconcile enemies, preserve peace and harmony in families, recall the lax to their duty, encourage the good, and in sum make himself all to all to gain all to Jesus Christ. Above all else his own example and his life of virtue was a constant sermon. This had such an effect that not only the people of Clichy but even some people from Paris with houses in the area respected him and regarded him as a saint. The neighboring pastors also developed an esteem and sense of confidence in him. They sought out his company to hear from him how best to fulfill their own functions and to carry out their duty as pastors.[10]

On one occasion he was absent briefly from Clichy because of some other duty. His assistant wrote to give an account of the parish, and then added, among other things, "The pastors of the neighboring areas anxiously desire your return. The people are equally anxious to have you come back. Hurry then, to take the lead of the flock you have set on the right path, for all await your presence."

---

5. May 2, 1612. *CED* XIII:17-18.
6. Arnauld d'Ossat, who had negotiated the reconciliation of Henry IV with the Holy See.
7. Saint Vincent held this abbey from June 10, 1610 to November 4, 1616. *CED* XIII:8-13.
8. Ps 84:11.
9. Then a little parish located outside the city gates of Paris. *CED* XIII:41-43.
10. For the saint's testimony as to the happiness of his stay at Clichy, see *CED* IX:646.

A doctor of the University of Paris, a religious of a celebrated order who occasionally preached at Clichy, gave this testimony.

> I rejoice that at the beginning of this happy institution of the Mission, I often heard confessions in the little town of Clichy of the one chosen by God to begin that small spring which has since watered the garden of the Church. It has turned into a flood, a thousand times more fruitful than the mighty Nile in this spiritual Egypt. While he laid the foundations of such a great, holy, and sanctifying work, I offered to preach to these good people of Clichy, whose pastor he was. I found them living like angels, so much so that I felt as though I was attempting to bring a candle to the sun.

The praise of this doctor for the flock shows the vigilance and zeal of their pastor and his care for their instruction and their formation in the virtues and other practices of a truly Christian life.

At the beginning of his tenure as pastor he found the church itself in poor condition and the vestments and sacred ornaments unsuitable for divine service. He carried out a plan for restoration.[11] It was completed, it must be said, not at his own expense or even at the expense of the parishioners. He himself was poor and gave all his assets to those in need, and the people were not too well off either. Some of his friends in Paris helped him. They were glad to help him carry out his plans.

He saw to the establishment of the Confraternity of the Rosary in the parish as well, so that by the time he left he had rebuilt and refurbished the church, leaving it in a very good condition.[12] Besides, he left it purely and simply, without taking anything for himself, in the hands of a worthy successor, Monsieur [Jean] Souillard.[13] Among his other parochial duties, the new pastor instructed several young clerics sent to him by Monsieur Vincent and prepared them to be faithful servants of the Church.

---

11. This section of the church still stands.
12. This confraternity required its members to give alms, and Vincent's experience of this could well have influenced his foundation of the Confraternity of Charity in Chatillon.
13. Monsieur Vincent did not give up the parish completely for another nine years, in 1626, all the time receiving a pension from his successor. The record of the pastoral visitation by the archbishop, dated October 9, 1624, lists Master Vincent Pol [sic] as pastor. (See *Annales CM* 94 (1929):729-30.) *CED* XIII:85-86.

CHAPTER SEVEN

His Associations with the de Gondi House

AROUND 1613 Father de Berulle suggested that Monsieur Vincent accept the position of tutor to the children of Emmanuel de Gondi, count of Joigny and general of the galleys of France,[1] and of his wife, Dame Francoise Marguerite de Silly, a woman of excellent reputation.[2] She was all the more praiseworthy because at that time piety was a rare possession among members of the court. The choice of Monsieur Vincent for this position was no small proof of the judgment of the first superior general of the Oratory about his merit and his good qualities of mind, for he was going to one of the most pious and most illustrious houses of the kingdom. Three young princes of great promise were confided to his care and instruction. The oldest was a duke and peer of the realm. The second later became a cardinal in the Church. The third, gifted in mind and body, God called prematurely from this world at the age of ten or eleven years to receive in heaven a more wonderful inheritance than he would have received on earth.[3]

Monsieur Vincent spent twelve years in this illustrious household.[4] He conducted himself with such wisdom, moderation, and reserve that he won the esteem and affection of all with whom he came in contact. He never came into the presence of the general or of Madame unless sent for. He did not meddle in anything not directly connected with his responsibility. Outside the time devoted to the care or instruction of the three princes, he lived in this busy house as in a Carthusian monastery. He went to his room as though it were a cell and did not come out unless called for or unless charity dictated that he do otherwise. He adopted the maxim that the only way to appear in public amid the moral dangers so prevalent in the great city of Paris without danger to his soul was to remain in retirement and silence unless called upon

---

1. Philippe Emmanuel de Gondi, count of Joigny, General of the Galleys of France. When he became a widower, he joined the Congregation of the Oratory. He died in Joigny, June 29, 1662.
2. 1580-1625.
3. The eldest son was Pierre de Gondi, who became the duke of Retz, and succeeded his father as the captain general of the galleys. The middle son was Jean Francois, later the second Cardinal de Retz, and the youngest, Henri, who died as a young man in a hunting accident.
4. His first stay can be dated from September 1613 to July 1617, when he left for Chatillon les Dombes. Abelly is probably counting the period from 1613 to March 1, 1624, when Monsieur Vincent was named the principal of the College des Bons Enfants. On February 28, 1614, Saint Vincent was named the pastor of Gamaches in the archdiocese of Rouen, a village to which Philippe Emmanuel de Gondi had the right of presentation. The next year, May 27, 1615, he became a canon and treasurer of the collegiate chapel of Ecouis in the diocese of Evreux. Monsieur de Gondi likewise had the right to make these chapter appointments. *CED* XIII:19-24.

by charity to go out or to speak. When called to offer some service to the neighbor for the good of his soul, however, he voluntarily left his cloister. On these occasions he acted with great charity to do for them all the good he could. He settled disputes and dissensions, promoted union and concord among the house servants, visited them in their rooms when they fell ill and provided the most careful services for them on these occasions. When the major feasts of the Church approached he gathered the domestic help for religious instruction, especially in regard to the reception of the sacraments. He used to slip in topics of some significance at table to forestall useless conversations. When Monsieur or Madame would go with their children to their holdings in Joigny, Montmirail, Villepreux, or elsewhere, his singular pleasure was to use his free time in providing religious instruction for the peasants. He would preach to the people, give exhortations, or administer the sacraments, particularly the sacrament of penance, with the bishop's approval and with the agreement of the local pastors.

His manner of acting was so prudent and virtuous that he soon gained the affection of all who came in contact with him. Madame especially was so taken with his modesty, discretion, and charity that after one or two years in her service she decided to have him as her spiritual director. She requested Father de Berulle to intercede for her to have this wise and virtuous priest direct her conscience and offer advice in her Christian living. Out of respect for his own spiritual guide whom he held in such veneration, Monsieur Vincent accepted this new responsibility but with much confusion, caused by his own humility of spirit.

This virtuous lady deeply loved promoting the welfare of her family and her subjects, and was moved at the grace of God which had given her a priest who was all she could hope for as a spiritual guide. Besides the other sterling qualities she recognized in him, his wisdom and charity were so evident that she could in all confidence place herself under his direction.

To understand better Monsieur Vincent's way of acting during the time he was serving this illustrious house we must allow him to speak for himself. He did so on two occasions. On the first he used the third person in a conference he gave to some clergymen assembled at Saint Lazare when he spoke of the manner of best fulfilling the office of chaplain in noble houses. He said, among other things:

> I know a person who gained much for himself and others as well in the service of a noble lord by looking upon him always as though he were Jesus Christ himself, and seeing the holy Virgin in his wife. This resulted in his retaining always a reserve and a modesty in all his words and actions. This earned the affection of the lord and his

lady, and even the domestics, and provided the basis for much good that was done in the family.

The second time he spoke more openly to a young Parisian lawyer, a man both learned and pious, who was considering joining the house of Retz as steward.[5] This young man requested advice on how one could maintain his religious disposition amid the inevitable distractions and countless business matters his position would entail. Monsieur Vincent replied that since he had lived in that sort of situation he could speak. "God had given me the grace to recognize in the person of Monsieur de Gondi, general of the galleys, our Savior himself, and in the person of Madame, the Blessed Mother. I recognized in the officials, servants, domestics and others of the household the disciples and followers of our Lord Jesus Christ."

This is how Monsieur Vincent kept himself constantly united to Jesus Christ. He honored him in the true reflections of his divinity found in all people, and guided all his activities, both internal and external, by this view. From reading and meditating on this mystic book, ever open before his eyes, he drew the lessons of virtue which marked his life.

Despite the great respect he had for the general of the galleys he was able to speak openly to him when the good of his soul seemed to demand it. Even then he was a model of moderation and circumspection. His zeal for promoting the good and his horror for the least hint of evil, either in himself or in others, was tempered by prudence. If he was strong he was also discreet. As an example of this trait we can cite the case that arose on one occasion when the master of the house planned to fight a duel, in keeping with the damnable custom of the time. Our great monarch, like a Christian Hercules, has happily in his earliest years with a single blow cut the tentacles of this Hydra.[6] He said once in a conference given to some clergy at Saint Lazare,[7] speaking in the third person:

> I knew a chaplain once who became aware that his lord was about to fight a duel. After celebrating mass, he went to the lord who had remained kneeling in the chapel and said to him, "Monsieur, allow me, if you will, just a word. I am aware that you plan to fight a duel. I declare to you on the part of the Lord whom I have just worshiped and you have just adored in the holy mass, that if you do not renounce this evil design the Lord will carry out his justice toward

---

5. Martin Husson joined the household of Pierre de Gondi in 1650. Husson later became consul in Tunis. On his return to France, he accepted a position in the household of the duchess of Aiguillon. He died in December 1695.
6. Under the influence of Vincent de Paul and Jean Jacques Olier, Queen Anne of Austria influenced her son, Louis XIV, to issue an edict banning duels. See also *CED* V:618-20, a request to the pope on the same issue.
7. September 24, 1643.

you and all your posterity." The chaplain said this and left. You will notice, my friends, the opportune moment he seized and the words he used, which you must imitate in like circumstances.[8]

---

8. *CED* XI:25-28.

CHAPTER EIGHT

A General Confession Made by a Peasant Occasions Monsieur Vincent's First Mission, and This in Turn Leads to Others

MADAME DE GONDI felt joy and indescribable consolation in having Monsieur Vincent in her house. She regarded him as a second guardian angel who each day drew down new graces upon her family by his zeal and prudent conduct. Her ambition was to advance unceasingly along the way of perfection, and he in turn as a wise director helped her by all means at his disposal to fulfill this earnest wish. These two souls, animated by the same Gospel spirit, devoted themselves to various charitable works. The virtuous woman gave generous alms, particularly to the poor peasants on her own lands. She visited the sick and served them with her own hands. She had a particular concern that her officials exercise justice correctly and carefully, and to ensure this, she was careful to make good appointments to this position. Not content with this, she strove to settle lawsuits among her subjects, appease quarrels, and above all saw to the protection of widows and orphans, making sure they were neither oppressed nor treated unjustly. She used all her energy to see to it that God was served and honored in every place she had any influence. In all this she was seconded by her husband's piety, and aided by Monsieur Vincent's presence and advice. In turn, he too was not remiss in exercising his charity and zeal on these occasions. He visited and consoled the sick, instructed and exhorted the people by public preaching and by private interviews, and used every device possible to win souls to God.

Around 1616 he went to Picardy with Madame, who owned some land in the region. They stopped at the chateau at Folleville in the diocese of Amiens, which he used as a base for works of mercy, as was his custom.[1] One day he was asked to go to the village of Gannes, about two leagues away, to hear the confession of a dying peasant who had requested the last sacraments. He was a good man and had an excellent reputation. Monsieur Vincent, however, thought that it might be well to have him make a general confession as a greater security toward the salvation of his soul. From later events it appears that God directly inspired this thought to show his mercy to this poor soul.

God wished to use his faithful minister to withdraw this man from the precipice. Despite his reputation his conscience was burdened with several

---

1. The chateau of Folleville is presently in ruins. The church, which still exists, contains the pulpit from which Vincent preached his famous sermon.

mortal sins he was too ashamed to confess. As he himself later publicly stated, he had never mentioned them in confession. When in her charity Madame came to visit him on his sickbed he said: "Madame, were it not for this general confession I would have been damned. I was guilty of several grave sins which I had never dared reveal."[2]

These words showed the true contrition that moved the sick man and the sentiments he carried to the end. Death came three days later at age sixty, and he owed his salvation after God to Monsieur Vincent. This is how he spoke of these events to members of his Congregation at Paris:

> Shame prevents some of the good country people from confessing their sins to their pastors, but this leaves them in serious danger. Some time ago one of the most renowned persons of our day was asked if these people could be saved, should shame prevent them from confessing their serious sins. He replied that if they were to die in that state they would surely be lost. Alas, my God, (I said to myself) how many may be damned? How important the general confession is, if it is accompanied with true contrition, as it usually is. This man admitted he would have been damned, because he was truly moved by a spirit of repentance. When this takes possession of a man he conceives such a horror of sin that not only does he confess to a priest but to the whole world, if that will assure his salvation. I have seen people who after their general confession wanted to proclaim their sins before everyone, and I've had difficulty restraining them. Despite my refusal to allow them to do this, they say to me, "No, Monsieur, I will tell them to everyone. I am good for nothing, I deserve death."
>
> You can see in that, if you please, the power of grace and the strength of sorrow. I've known several in this state, for it is frequent enough. Yes, when God enters the heart he makes the person realize the enormity of the offenses he has committed, and he is willing to announce this to anyone who will listen. Touched by a spirit of compunction he has no hesitation in saying aloud: "I am an evil man, because on this or that occasion I did such-and-such. I ask pardon of God, of the pastor and all the parish." We notice some of the greatest of the saints have acted in the same way. Saint Augustine in his Confessions revealed his sins to the whole world. Saint Paul declared and published in his epistles that he had blasphemed and persecuted the Church, to show forth more abundantly God's mercy toward him. This is the effect of grace when it fills the heart. It replaces every other sentiment.

---

2. *CED* XI:2. See also XI:169-72, XII:7-9.

God's grace working in the soul of this peasant, in the presence of Madame de Gondi whose vassal he was, made him admit publicly his sacrilegious confessions and the great sins of his past life. This struck this virtuous lady with astonishment. She said to Monsieur Vincent:

> Alas, Monsieur, what is this? What have we just heard? This is the way it must be with most of the people. Alas, if this man with his good reputation was really living in danger of damnation, what must we think of others who live less righteously? Alas, Monsieur Vincent, how many souls are lost! What shall we do about this?

Monsieur Vincent said:

> It was January 1617, when all this happened, on the feast of the Conversion of Saint Paul, the twenty-fifth of the month. This lady asked me to preach in the church of Folleville to persuade the local people to make a general confession. I did this, pointing out the importance and usefulness of this practice. I showed them how to do so worthily. God had such regard for the confidence and faith of this good lady (for the great number and enormity of my sins stood in the way of my effecting any fruit) that he blessed this sermon. All those present were moved by God, and came to make their general confession. I continued my instruction, disposing them to receive the sacrament well, and then began to hear their confessions. Even with the help of another priest who was with me, however, the press of those waiting to receive the sacrament was too great. Madame sent to request the Jesuit Fathers of Amiens to come help us. She wrote to the rector, who came himself, but not having enough time available he sent another Jesuit, Father Fourche, to help us in hearing confessions, preaching and catechizing. By the grace of God, these occupations kept us busy.
>
> We next went to other villages in the vicinity which also belonged to Madame, to do the same as we had done in the first. We had large crowds, and God gave us his full blessing. This is how the first mission was accomplished. That it took place on the feast of the Conversion of Saint Paul was due solely to God's design.[3]

This mission in Folleville was the first given by Monsieur Vincent and has always been considered as the seed for all the others to follow. Every year, on the twenty-fifth of January, he and his Congregation thanked God for all the graces given in his infinite bounty to this first preaching. He always wanted this feast of the Conversion of Saint Paul to be regarded as the founding date of the Congregation of the Mission, although it was to be eight more years before this first seed grew and multiplied. He never thought that

---

3. *CED* XI:4-5.

this tiny mustard plant would serve as the basis for the establishment of a new Congregation in the Church, as later came about. This is why the missionaries of the Congregation celebrate the feast of the conversion of the apostle, in memory of the way this new Paul, their father and founder, happily completed on this day his first mission.[4] This first one was to be followed by so many others, leading to the conversion of a large number of souls, and contributing so strikingly to the growth of the kingdom of Jesus Christ.

Madame de Gondi recognized clearly by the success of this first mission the necessity of general confession, particularly among country people. She saw how a mission could help bring this about among the people. She conceived the idea of giving a foundation of sixteen thousand *livres* to any community willing to undertake the giving of a mission every five years in all her territories. She charged Monsieur Vincent with carrying out this project. He appealed first to Father [Etienne] Charlet, provincial of the Jesuits, who said he would need to consult Rome before accepting. The answer was unfavorable. The Fathers of the Oratory also received the offer, but they too refused. Lastly, not knowing where to turn, she wrote her will, which she reviewed yearly. In it she gave the sixteen thousand *livres* to set up this project. It would be arranged in the time and place judged appropriate by Monsieur Vincent, or to use the language he himself used, it was "put at the disposition of this wretched man."

---

4. Vincent himself established this celebration. *CED* XI:169-172; XII:7-8.

CHAPTER NINE

Vincent Secretly Withdraws from the de Gondi House

THE GOOD opinion of all those who knew Monsieur Vincent grew abundantly. God bestowed great blessings on his charitable enterprises and everyone came to recognize that he was filled with the Spirit of God. Both the general and Madame shared this opinion, which they showed publicly on occasion, much to the confusion of Monsieur Vincent who sought only abasement and lack of recognition. This situation concerned him so that, in imitation of many the saints, he saw no other remedy than to flee from the danger of vanity. More than one person before him, despite a life of virtue, had been seduced by calm seas and a favorable wind.

Saint Ambrose had written of Moses of old: "He fled from King Pharaoh's court. He feared that the favors he had received would tarnish his soul and that the power and authority he had acquired would bind him to the place he was. He fled, not from the lack of resolve or courage, but to find the path of innocence, the road to virtue and the freedom to express his piety."[1]

Although the de Gondi household was one of the best managed of the court, and Monsieur Vincent did nothing contrary to true piety, the honors he received and the signs of affection which he experienced were enough to cause him anxiety. He felt that the influence he exercised over the minds and hearts in this illustrious family were only traps that would prevent his progress in the way of perfection so appropriate to his station in life. He therefore closed his eyes to all natural influences, to all worldly prospects, and resolved to leave this position so that he could give himself more perfectly to God.

Another reason which suggested itself to Monsieur Vincent that he should leave the service of Madame was his recognition that she was becoming too dependent upon him. She was troubled by scruples and other interior trials, brought about by God to add the crown of patience to that of charity. She had developed such an esteem and confidence in his spiritual direction that she feared losing his service. She was convinced that she would never be able to replace him with anyone with his grace and understanding who could calm her troubled soul, lighten her fears, and lead her in the way of true and solid virtue. She was so afraid of losing him that on those occasions he was forced to be away she could hardly bear his absence. She feared that hot

---

1. PL 14:579.

weather might make him ill or that he might meet some accident. Surely all this was an imperfection in an otherwise virtuous woman. When Monsieur Vincent became aware of her obsession, he tried to help her by occasionally directing her to see a Recollect priest for confession.[2] He was a well-known director of souls, and Monsieur Vincent judged he would be acceptable to Madame. This proved to be the case. It gave Monsieur Vincent the opportunity to convince her that God could just as well lead her by another as by himself, if only she would put all her trust in his infinite goodness.

These sentiments were not strong enough to overcome what she saw as the necessity of having someone as prudent and charitable as he to accompany her on her trips to the country where she owned much property. She was obliged to visit these holdings frequently, often for a good part of the year. Yet she felt unable to bring herself to seek the help of the priests of the small towns to resolve her personal difficulties. Monsieur Vincent considered her situation and her wish that no one else have the least thing to do with her direction, plus the fear he had of seeing the esteem people had for the "wretched man," as he imagined and described himself. Added to this was his fear that this excessive attachment might block the spiritual progress of an otherwise virtuous soul. Instead of being an indispensable help to her he feared he might actually prevent her advancement along the way of perfection. Thus he finally concluded that he must leave the service of the de Gondi family.

Since Father de Berulle had persuaded him to accept this position in the first place, Monsieur Vincent now presented this plan to leave for his approval. He said only that he felt an interior movement of grace to go to one of the distant provinces to devote himself to teach and serve the poor country people. Father de Berulle did not object to this. He had seen in Monsieur Vincent a man so committed to God and so enlightened by his grace that he felt he could propose nothing better than what had been suggested.

He left the de Gondi house in July of 1617, using as pretext that he was only making a short trip. He was well aware that there would likely be adverse judgment on his leaving like this, even accusations of ingratitude for the honors and good treatment he had received during his service in this house. He undoubtedly was sensitive on this point, for he was by nature thankful for all that was done for him, and yet he rose above all human considerations. He renounced personal interest and opened himself to criticism. Yet he felt that he was being faithful to God and was acting for the greater benefit of the virtuous soul confided to his spiritual direction.

---

2. Probably a Franciscan Recollect, a reformed branch in the Franciscan family.

CHAPTER NINE

Although the means he used were extraordinary they show his lack of self-interest and his commitment to God alone.

When Father de Berulle realized that Monsieur Vincent was set on leaving the de Gondi house but had no particular place to continue his priestly work, he suggested that he might look into the region of Bresse where there was a serious lack of Gospel workers. He suggested the parish of Chatillon les Dombes, where his zeal could reap a great harvest.[3] Monsieur Vincent followed this recommendation. One of the first things he did upon arriving at Chatillon was to gather together the five or six clergymen he found in the area. He formed them into a sort of community to make their ministry more effective for God and his Church.[4] This arrangement lasted for a long time, to the great edification of all the parish. He applied himself with his usual zeal to instructing the people and converting sinners by his effective preaching and exhortations in both public and private. He did not neglect the sick and poor. He visited them and consoled and helped them in all kinds of ways. God blessed his efforts to bring back to the faith some heretics, as we shall see later in this book.

Up to this time nothing was known in the house of the general of the galleys of these events, for Monsieur Vincent had told no one his intentions except one or two confidants in Paris. Sometime after his arrival he thought he ought to inform the general, who then was in Provence, of his reasons for leaving his service. He asked him to approve his departure, saying that he lacked the capacity and the grace to serve adequately as tutor of his children. He included the remark that he had told neither Madame nor anyone else of his intention of not returning.[5] The general was so struck and saddened by this information that he immediately informed his wife in the following letter:

> I am in despair at a letter I have just received from Monsieur Vincent. I am sending it to you to see if whether something can be done to prevent his loss to us. I am astonished that he did not discuss this with you and that you had no hint of this. Please use every means to make sure we do not lose him. Although his position may

---

3. This parish, in the ancient province of Bresse, was located near the principality of the Dombes. Today it is the chief town of the department of Ain. The church of Saint Andrew in Chatillon was dependent on that of Saint Martin in Buenans, a village close to Chatillon. Officially speaking, Vincent de Paul was named as pastor of Buenans. He took canonical possession of both of these churches August 1, 1617. The canons of Lyons were the temporal lords of Chatillon. Appalled by the condition of the parish, neglected by previous benefice holders, they appealed to the newly founded house of the Oratory in Lyons. This request came to the attention of Berulle, its founder. Since no one in Lyons was willing to care for these parishes, he turned to Vincent. CED XIII:43-44.
4. Monsieur Vincent was assisted by Louis Girard, a doctor of theology, who later served as his vicar and then as his successor. CED XIII:47, 52, 53-54, 439.
5. CED I:21.

be true (his alleged incapacity,) it makes absolutely no difference to me. Nothing is more important to me than my own salvation and that of my children, which I know he can greatly help, or the fulfillment of the resolutions that I have often spoken about to you.[6]

I have not yet replied to him. I will await more news from you. Do you think the intervention of my sister, Madame de Ragny, who is not far from him, would make any difference?[7] I doubt if anyone has more influence over him than Father de Berulle. Mention to him that although it may be true that Monsieur Vincent may be weak when it comes to teaching the young, we could easily supply a tutor to work under his direction. Emphasize that I am extremely anxious that he return to our service. He may lead his own life, and I shall be a right-thinking man myself only if he stays with us.

This letter was written in September 1617 and was received by Madame on the feast of the Exaltation of the Holy Cross. This was truly a cross for her, a sword of sorrow which pierced her soul. After receiving this letter she did not stop crying, and could neither eat nor sleep. She wrote to a confidant in this vein:

I never would have thought that Monsieur Vincent's charity toward my soul would allow him to leave me like this. But, God be praised, I do not blame him. I believe that nothing ever happens but by God's special providence as inspired by his holy love. Nevertheless his leaving is strange. I admit I cannot understand it at all. He knows the need I have for his direction and for the business affairs I have taken up with him. He is aware of the pains of mind and body I must bear without his help and the good I wish to accomplish in my towns which I will not be able to do without his advice. In short, I am in a sorry state. You can see how disturbed the general is by what he writes. The children are depressed, and the good accomplished in my house and in my lands and for these seven or eight thousand souls shall be no more. What? Are not these souls as much redeemed by the precious blood of our Savior as those of Bresse? Are they less precious?

In truth, I don't know what Monsieur Vincent intends, but these matters are so important to me that I must do all I can to see him again. He acts only for the greater glory of God. I certainly do not want to act contrary to his holy will, but I will pray with all my heart for his return. I pray to the holy Mother of God and would pray even

---

6. Probably his desire to retire to the Oratory. This resolution was fulfilled after the death of his wife.

7. Hippolyte de Gondi, who married Leonor de la Madeleine, marquis of Ragny.

more earnestly if my own personal interest were not so intertwined with those of the general, my children, my family, and my subjects.

These were the sentiments of this virtuous lady. She wished to use the most efficacious means at her disposal to reverse this decision, and so turned to prayer, both by herself and by all those whose piety she could count on. She recommended this intention to the prayers of all the leading religious communities of Paris. Several times she visited Father de Berulle. She opened her heart to him, exposing the great pain and affliction she suffered. Her tears and pressing arguments convinced this great servant of God of her need for the presence and counsel of Monsieur Vincent. He agreed that she could in all good conscience do everything possible to bring about his return, for he saw that amid her acute suffering she retained a complete resignation to God's good pleasure. She was disposed to suffer all rather than go against his holy will. To her great consolation he assured her that he would use his good offices with Monsieur Vincent to persuade him to return.

This was balm for her soul. She later said that Father de Berulle was the most consoling man in the whole world. She could not rest at ease, however, for she was well aware that Monsieur Vincent was not a person to do things by halves. He had undoubtedly already thought of whatever she might do or say, before leaving. All this did not prevent her from taking every measure she could to convince him to return. She wrote several times, after showing her letter first to Father de Berulle. She sent him the letter her husband had written to her and asked him to weigh well the great hope he expressed of having Monsieur Vincent come back under whatever conditions he might impose. In one of her letters which will allow us to see her state of mind in regard to him she wrote as follows:

> I was not wrong to fear losing you, as I expressed to you many times, for it has come about as I dreaded. The anguish I experience would be insupportable were it not for an extraordinary gift of the grace of God, which I do not deserve. If this were only temporary I would not mind it so much, but when I consider all the occasions when I need your help, your guidance or your advice, whether in life or in death, my sorrow knows no bounds. Can my soul and body long endure these trials? I do not look for or receive any help from elsewhere, because you know well that I cannot open my soul to many. Father de Berulle promised he would write to you. I, too, beseech God and the holy Virgin to return you to our home for the salvation of our entire family and for many others who will benefit from your charity. I beg you once more to do this for us for the love you bear for our Savior. I submit to his will, although I do not know for how long. If you refuse me, I shall place at your feet all that shall

befall me and all the good I shall not be able to do for want of your aid. You will be responsible for my often being deprived of the sacraments during my travels and for whatever suffering I endure, for you are aware of how few can help me.

You see that the general has the same hope as myself, by the mercy of God. Do not refuse to do what you can for his salvation, for he in turn can do much good to others. I know that my own life is useless, since I live, it seems, only to offend God. It would not be of great consequence to put my life in danger, but at least my soul should have some help at the hour of death. Recall the anxiety I experienced the last time I took sick in one of the villages. I fear that something worse will befall me and the very thought does me such harm I do not see how I can avoid dying from it.[8]

Before leaving this matter we should reflect on the admirable way God acts toward those called to a high degree of virtue. He disposes the various events and accidents of life as elements in their advance along the road of perfection. What shows the wisdom and power of God is that often those very things which seem most contrary to his divine plan are the ones that contribute best to fulfilling it. God's good pleasure, without a doubt, had given Monsieur Vincent to Madame de Gondi to serve as a faithful guide in the pilgrimage of life. Her great progress in the path of virtue and the ardent charity which inflamed her heart and flowered in such marvelous deeds, were evident signs of God's blessing upon the direction of her wise counselor.

For his part, Monsieur Vincent found new occasions every day to exercise his zeal for building up the kingdom of Jesus Christ. However, God had brought it about that Monsieur Vincent and Madame de Gondi would be associated for his service and their mutual sanctification by works of piety and charity. In the same way, he caused their separation, which at first glance seemed so contrary to all the desirable results already attained and so harmful to this virtuous lady, to prepare them both for still more graces. By their resignation and acceptance he prepared them to receive still greater blessings. They would be worthy instruments for his all-powerful mercy in cooperating more completely in the salvation of a great number of souls. We shall see this later in this book.

God willed that Madame, his faithful servant, should make several acts of heroic resignation. She had to sacrifice her Isaac, her support, her counsel, her consolation, her help deemed so necessary to both her own advancement in virtue and even her own salvation. For Monsieur Vincent, God willed that he make several heroic acts of perfect detachment from those dearest to him,

---

8. *CED* I:21-22.

to whom he had been led by divine grace to esteem with a pure and sincere charity.

Beyond doubt, he was obliged to make a great effort to overcome his natural inclination when he left this house without even saying a word to anyone. Another renunciation was called for when he received this letter from Madame, not to succumb to the reasons, recriminations, prayers and entreaties it contained. A person less enlightened or less united to God than Monsieur Vincent could easily have been taken unawares by the recital of the pain, the distress, the great need she had of his help, the language she used to implore him to reconsider, and the recollection of the esteem, respect, and good will she expressed.

Since he had committed himself completely to God and wished to conform himself totally to his good pleasure, the first thing Monsieur Vincent did upon receiving this letter was to raise his mind to God. He then renewed his promise of inviolable fidelity to his divine Majesty and offered the sacrifice of all human inclination and consideration. He asked for the light and grace to know the divine will and to have the strength to follow it. After some reflection in God's presence he felt that he was not being asked to change the decision he had taken. He accordingly wrote to Madame, expressing his sympathy for her suffering but urging her to submit to the designs of God's holy will.[9]

She had already been assured that she might in good conscience pursue the possible return of Monsieur Vincent. This letter did not in the least hinder her efforts to bend his spirit. She persuaded people of all different classes and occupations to write to him. He received letters from her children, from Cardinal de Retz, her brother-in-law then bishop of Paris, from her close relatives, from the chief officers of the household, from several pious persons. They all requested and urged his return.[10]

Father de Berulle wrote also, as he had promised he would, but he wrote in a style worthy of his great prudence and piety. He merely pointed out the extreme discomfort of this virtuous lady, the dangers threatening her, and the wish the general harbored for his return. He said nothing more. He left it to the discretion and charity of Monsieur Vincent to consider if the will of God were sufficiently manifest. He was persuaded that Monsieur Vincent was more than capable of discerning the designs of God in his own regard and able to carry out this divine purpose with no need of outside advice or persuasion.

---

9. *CED* I:23.
10. During Vincent's stay in the de Gondi household, three members of the family were in turn bishops of Paris: Pierre, uncle of the general of the galleys; Henri, brother of the general, and the first Cardinal de Retz; and Jean Francois, another brother. This latter named his nephew and namesake his successor, and he became the second Cardinal de Retz.

Since all these remonstrances seemed to have no effect on Monsieur Vincent, one of his closest friends, Monsieur Du Fresne, the general's secretary, was sent to Chatillon in October 1617 to speak to Monsieur Vincent.[11] He succeeded in persuading him to consider whether God was really calling him to remain longer in that place. This was enough to make Monsieur Vincent uncertain of just what the will of God for him really was. In an affair of this importance he did not want to act solely by his own lights.

In imitation of the apostle Paul he sought his own Ananias, that is, he took counsel of a wise and virtuous person. He suggested that Monsieur Vincent accompany him to Lyons, where he could consult Father Bence, superior of the Oratory.[12] After considering all these issues, he suggested that a return to Paris would allow Monsieur Vincent to consult with those who had known him for a long time. He would be able to discern with more light and assurance God's exact will for him.

After receiving this advice he wrote to the general who was then in Marseilles, saying that in two months he hoped to make a trip to Paris where he would search out the designs of God for him. He wrote much the same thing to Monsieur Du Fresne but without committing himself in any way. Some time later, at Chatillon, he received the following reply from the general, on October 15 of the same year.

> Two days ago I received the letter you wrote from Lyons, informing me that you will be coming to Paris toward the end of November. I am exceedingly happy to hear this news. I look forward to seeing you there, in the hope that you will answer my prayers and accept the advice of all your good friends. I will not now say anything more about this, for you have read the letter I wrote to my wife. I ask you only to consider the thought that possibly God wills you should contribute much to making the father and his sons worthy gentlemen.[13]

Monsieur Vincent left Chatillon, to the great sorrow of the people there, who regretted losing one who had served them so well, and reached Paris on December 23.[14] Here he met with Father de Berulle and some other enlightened advisers. Encouraged by their counsel he finally returned to the service of the general of the galleys on Christmas eve. The whole family

---

11. Du Fresne had previous been a secretary to Queen Marguerite de Valois, and was responsible for the saint's introduction to her household. Vincent returned the favor by recommending Du Fresne to the Gondis.
12. Jean de Bence, one of the first companions of Pierre de Berulle. One of Bence's companions, Paul Metezeau, gave Vincent a letter to introduction of Jean Beynier, a Huguenot, who provided hospitality to the new pastor. Beynier would later be converted by Vincent.
13. *CED* I:23.
14. His official resignation was dated January 31, 1618; his successor, Louis Girard, assumed the pastorate July 10 of that year.

rejoiced, particularly Madame, who received him as an angel from heaven. She regarded him as sent by God to guide her along the right path leading to her salvation and her own perfection. Fearing that he might leave a second time, she made him promise that he would continue in her service until her death, which he did. God willed it so that this good woman would be his instrument in helping bring about the foundation of the Congregation of the Mission, as we shall see later in this book.

CHAPTER TEN

The Beginnings of the Confraternity of Charity for the Sick Poor

WHILE MONSIEUR Vincent was still at Chatillon, as he was about to mount the pulpit one feastday, a lady of a noble house in the neighborhood[1] said a few words to him. She asked him to recommend to the charity of the parish a family whose children and servants had fallen sick on their farm about a half league from Chatillon. They needed help urgently. He felt obliged to speak about them in his sermon. In it he spoke of the duty we have to help the poor, especially the sick, and in particular this family which had been recommended to them.

God so blessed his words that after the service a large number of people visited the sick family, carrying bread, wine, some meat, and several other provisions. After vespers, he himself went with some of the people of the parish, unaware that others had already gone. He was astonished to meet a number on the road returning in large groups, and even some sleeping under the trees, since it was so warm. The Gospel text came to mind: "These are as lost sheep, with no shepherd to guide them."[2]

He said:

> This undoubtedly shows that these people have great charity, but is it well organized? The poor sick family will be overwhelmed with so much in such a short time, most of which will spoil. Afterward they will be no better off than before.

The following days he met with several zealous and wealthy women of the parish to seek ways of establishing greater order in the way the sick poor of the moment and those who would call for help in the future could be helped. He found these women well disposed toward this project and was able to work out with them a plan for action. He drew up a few regulations which they promised to observe and which would encourage these virtuous women to give themselves to God through this practice of charity. Thus began the Confraternity of Charity for the corporal and spiritual help of the sick poor. They chose several officers from among their own number and met under Monsieur Vincent's chairmanship every month to report on progress.

He himself said on several occasions that he was due no credit in the beginning of this good work. All was accomplished with no planning on his

---

1. Mademoiselle de la Chassaigne.
2. Matt 9:36

CHAPTER TEN

part and with little thought of what significant developments these small beginnings would become, by the grace of God.[3]

The Confraternity of Charity which Monsieur Vincent began at Chatillon was the first, the mother confraternity, of a great many others he and his Congregation have since established in France, Italy, Lorraine, in Savoy, and elsewhere.

After Monsieur Vincent returned to the de Gondi house, as we have related in the previous chapter, his zeal would not leave him idle but led him to undertake many missions for the poor people in the countryside. Previously he had worked in the various territories belonging to Madame. He was now determined to extend his charity to all the other regions belonging to the de Gondi house. In keeping with this resolution, he gave a mission at Villepreux and the villages which depended on it.[4] He had the help of two clerical counselors of the Parlement of Paris, Fathers Berger and Gontiere, with Monsieur Cocqueret, doctor of theology of the college of Navarre, and several other clerics as well.[5] Here, on February 23, 1618, he established the Confraternity of Charity of the Sick Poor, under the authority of Cardinal de Retz, then bishop of Paris, who approved its rule. This was the second begun by Monsieur Vincent, and by God's grace, it has continued, like the first, to this day. The third was established in the town of Joigny, and the fourth in Montmirail.[6] God blessed these beginnings to such an extent that the confraternity began in more than thirty parishes in lands depending on the general of the galleys or on his wife.

---

3. *CED* IX:208-10, and 242-44.
4. A small town located near Paris.
5. Jean Coqueret was one of the most esteemed and learned priests of the age. Together with the other theologians, Louis Bail and Nicolas Cornet, he took part in the conferences held at Saint Lazare to determine strategy in the struggle against Jansenism. *CED* III:318-32.
6. See the rules for the confraternities in *CED* XIII:461-75.

CHAPTER ELEVEN

The Conversion of Several Heretics whom Monsieur Vincent Brought Back to the Catholic Church

WHILE MONSIEUR Vincent was at Chatillon, God used his zeal and prudence to influence several people who had fallen into heresy. He was able to bring them back to the path of truth.

We will recount here the events surrounding the conversion of only two of these heretics. They owed their conversion, after God, to the zeal of Monsieur Vincent. He was responsible for their regaining the gift of faith which they had lost in their defection from the Church.

The first was a young man from Chatillon named Monsieur Beynier, born into a family that had instructed him thoroughly in their heretical doctrines. He was an only son and had inherited a sizable estate from his parents. Under the evil liberty of his false religion, however, he led a dissolute and scandalous life. Monsieur Vincent, moved by his zeal for the glory of God, wished earnestly to snatch this prey from the hands of the devil, to return him to Jesus Christ. Little by little he gained the friendship of this young man, despite his reputation for leading a debauched life. He often visited him and engaged him in conversation, much to everyone's astonishment. In so doing, he aroused the jealousy of the Protestant pastors of the locality. They were indifferent to his dissolute life as long as he remained committed to their religious sect.

These pastors began to object when they noticed that he was becoming more reserved than before. This was the first step recommended by Monsieur Vincent to help him recognize and embrace the truth. Finally, at a time willed by God, his eyes were opened and his heart moved. He abandoned both his life of debauchery and his heresy. He gave himself so completely to the practice of the Christian virtues that he resolved to embrace perpetual celibacy. He even forgave the debt of two or three persons whom he felt his father had treated unfairly, although they had not registered any complaint on this score. As for the rest of his worldly goods, he used them as a source of alms and other pious works. As a legacy he endowed several religious houses, particularly the foundation of the Capuchin Fathers at Chatillon. We owe the following account to Father Desmoulins of the Oratory who was well aware of these events, since he was superior in Macon at the time.

What appeared most remarkable in this conversion of morals and beliefs is the part played by Monsieur Vincent, whom God used for the purpose (these are his exact words.) Monsieur Vincent assigned all the credit to those who had merely received the abjuration and given absolution. He could have claimed this honor for himself, following the suggestion of Archbishop de Marquemont of Lyons, were it not that his personal humility preferred it be assigned to others.[1]

The second heretic Monsieur Vincent regained for the Church was Monsieur Garron, who later moved to Bourg, the capital city of Bresse. We learn of his conversion from a letter of thanks he wrote to Monsieur Vincent dated August 27, 1656, some forty years after his conversion.

> Behold, one of your children in Jesus Christ again has recourse to your paternal goodness. He benefited from it before when he was engendered in the Church by your absolution from heresy in the church of Chatillon les Dombes in 1617. You taught me the principles and the beautiful maxims of the Apostolic, Roman Catholic religion. By God's mercy I have persevered in it, and I hope to remain in it for the rest of my life. I am that little Jean Garron, nephew of Monsieur Beynier of Chatillon, in whose house you stayed while you were there. Please give me some advice now to help me carry out God's designs. I have an only son who, now that his schooling is ended, has decided to become a Jesuit. This son is blessed above all others in this province in worldly goods, but I do not know what to do.[2]

He presented reasons for and against this proposition and finally concluded: "I am afraid of erring in this matter. I beg of you most humbly to advise one of your children what course to follow. You will be happy to know that the pious association of charity for the sick poor is still alive in Chatillon."[3]

We do not know what Monsieur Vincent said in response to this letter. Its contents nevertheless confirm our opinion that God had given him the grace of discerning hearts, teaching the truth, and inspiring the love of true virtue and solid piety. Here is a father of one of the richest families of his province. His only beloved son wished to leave home and deprive him of one of the greatest of human consolations. He did not listen to flesh and blood but turned to him, to whom, after God, he owed the life of his soul, to ascertain God's will in this matter. He was ready, if it proved to be the divine will, to sacrifice his Isaac, so deeply had Monsieur Vincent planted piety and the love of God in his soul that its growth forty years later produced such heroic fruit.

---

1. Denis de Marquemont, archbishop of Lyons, 1612-1626.
2. Monsieur Vincent was responsible also for the conversion of Garron's three brothers. *CED* XIII:49,51.
3. *CED* III:29. Coste incorrectly assigned a date of August 26, 1646.

This same letter was, no doubt, a source of great joy to Monsieur Vincent. It let him learn in his old age that God by his grace had preserved this first Association or Confraternity of Charity which he had begun forty years before in Chatillon. It had been an inspiration and model for the establishment of many others in various places where the sick poor, suffering members of Jesus Christ, could receive such gracious help for both body and soul.

CHAPTER TWELVE

The Marvelous Change Brought About in the Life of a Noble Person under Monsieur Vincent's Spiritual Direction

MONSIEUR VINCENT'S reputation during his stay in Bresse spread in the vicinity, leading the count of Rougemont, a resident in that province, to visit him for spiritual direction. He was so pleased with his talks with Monsieur Vincent that he decided to place himself completely under his guidance. He was formerly a noble of Savoy, since retired in France after King Henry annexed Bresse to the kingdom. He had been raised at court and had assumed all its values and practices. At the time one of the most deplorable evils was dueling, by which gentlemen proved their valor or defended their honor. He had gained notoriety as one of the leading duelists of his time.

By the marvelous effects of divine grace, God used the words of Monsieur Vincent to convince him of the evils of this practice and the spiritual danger in which he lived. He was so touched that not only did he give up forever his dueling, but all other misguided elements in his life as well. To atone for his past excesses he adopted the most heroic of Christian practices.

First, having sold his estate of Rougemont for more than thirty thousand *ecus*, he used a good part of the proceeds for the founding of monasteries and the relief of the poor. His meditations on the sufferings of Jesus Christ led him to ask how many blows were borne by the Son of God in his scourging. He wanted to give a like number of *ecus* to the Oratory at Lyons. In a short time he so progressed in virtue under the guidance of his prudent director, that he became an example to all. Mental prayer became his usual occupation, and he was often seen to spend three or four hours in meditation, kneeling with no support and head uncovered. His home, the chateau of Chandes, became almost a hospice for religious and a hospital for the poor, both sick and well. They were received here with an almost unbelievable charity for the relief of their bodily and spiritual needs, for which he provided priests.

Not a sick person lived in his domain whom he did not visit and serve in person. On those rare occasions when he had to be away, he had his household staff visit them.

Father Desmoulins of the Oratory is the source of the following information.

I write nothing but what I have seen with my own eyes. This

good nobleman seemed almost ashamed to own so much, even though he looked like a simple farmer and used his wealth in favor of the poor. One day, with tears in his eyes, he said to me: "Alas, Father, what is to happen to me? And why am I treated as a lord, and why do I own so much?" (Monsieur Vincent, as his spiritual director, reportedly kept him in that condition.) "It is Monsieur Vincent's responsibility. If not for him, Father, I assure you that in less than a month the count of Rougemont would not own a single bit of land!" He was astounded that a Christian could hold anything on his own, seeing that the Son of God deprived himself of everything during his stay on earth.

What a remarkable lesson for the great of this world on how to make use of their wealth and with what detachment they ought to own their worldly goods. They should remember the words of the holy apostle that "they should use their earthly goods as if they did not use them, for the form of this world passes away."[1]

This view also consoled the poor. They saw their condition respected and even sought for by a great lord in an effort to conform more closely to Jesus Christ. It gave an occasion for the sons of Monsieur Vincent to thank God for having given such graces to this nobleman through the prayers and efforts of their wise founder. He himself never spoke of these matters, except in a conference he once gave on detachment from creatures. He cited the example of the count of Rougemont, but without referring to the part he himself had played in this story. Here are his own words, preserved in the minutes of this conference:

> I once knew a gentleman of Bresse, Monsieur de Rougemont, an avowed duelist. He was well placed and had often had occasion to be challenged or to challenge others who had offended him in some way. He told me himself that he could hardly remember the number of persons who had challenged him because of some quarrels or whom he had challenged as his adversaries. He told me he had struck, wounded, and killed an unbelievable number. But God so touched his heart that he entered into himself and saw what a sorry state he was in. He decided to change his life, and with God's grace he did so.
>
> After some little time in his new manner of living he went to request from the archbishop of Lyons the privilege of keeping the blessed sacrament in his chapel as a mark of respect for our Savior and as a way of furthering his well-known piety. When I visited his house, he told me what practices of devotion he was observing,

---

1. 1 Cor 7:31.

mainly his detachment from worldly goods. "I feel sure", he said to me, "that if I am bound to nothing in this world I will be able to give myself completely to God. Therefore I know that if I allow the friendship for a lord or a relative to hold me back, or if my own self-love hinders me, or if my worldly goods or my vanity, my passions or my love of ease do me spiritual harm, I must pray, break these bonds, and leave this place. This is what I commit myself to."

He then told me something I have often thought about. He related how he was on a journey one day, thinking of God, as he was his custom. He wondered where, since the time of his conversion, he had held back anything. He reviewed his business dealings, his associates, his reputation, the various movements of the human heart, both great and small. He went round and round in his mind considering these things.

All at once his eyes fell upon his sword. "Why are you carrying it? Why? Abandon this sword which, after God, has delivered you from a thousand dangers? If you are attacked once more, you would be lost without it. You might come across some disturbance and you will not be able to restrain yourself if you still carry it. You will again offend God. What, O God, should I do? What should I do? Such an instrument of my shame and my sins is still dear to me? This sword alone still stands in my way. Oh that I was not so cowardly to hold on to it!"

Just at that moment he found himself near a large rock. He got off his horse, took his sword, and immediately broke it on the rock into a hundred pieces. He then remounted his horse and rode off. He told me that this act of detachment, this breaking the iron chain which held him captive, gave him such a sense of liberty that great as his love was for that sword, he never again felt attracted to any object but God alone.[2]

We can see by this example how a heroic act of virtue and a victory won by force over oneself can lead in short time to great progress in sanctity. Also, we see how important it is to renounce attachment to the least things of this earth to be united perfectly to God.

---

2. *CED* XII:231-33.

CHAPTER THIRTEEN

Different Works of Piety that Monsieur Vincent Was Involved with After His Return to the de Gondi Household

TRUE CHARITY is never content to sit idly by. Once it possesses one's heart perfectly, it is ever on the alert to do all it can to further God's glory and bring about the salvation and sanctification of souls. Since Monsieur Vincent was so endowed with this virtue, he showed its fruits wherever he was. No sooner had he returned to the de Gondi household than he undertook duties similar to those he had done in Chatillon and the other places he had lived. After the missions at Villepreux and its surrounding villages, which we spoke of in a previous chapter, he began other missions in all the villages which depended on the de Gondi family. These produced unbelievable fruits, often aided by Madame de Gondi who, though unwell, would go in person to distribute alms or help in other ways. She visited and consoled the sick living on her or her husband's lands, healed long-standing arguments, and brought lawsuits to an end. She also supported by her own authority all the good that Monsieur Vincent and his team attempted to accomplish for the suppression of abuse and scandal and for the advancement of the kingdom of Jesus Christ. Finally, after returning to Montmirail, Monsieur Vincent took up again his usual routine, teaching catechism to the poor and to children, promoting frequent confession, and visiting the sick poor. Once, speaking in one of his sermons of the special devotion all Christians ought to have for the Mother of God, he had the children begin a hymn in her honor on a Saturday. This practice continues still. The older people who survived Monsieur Vincent spoke after his death of how the people from that time on always thought of him as a saint.

During 1620, while Monsieur Vincent was so occupied at Montmirail, Madame de Gondi learned that three heretics lived in the vicinity. She requested that Monsieur Vincent undertake their conversion. She invited these gentlemen to her chateau, where Monsieur Vincent would spend two hours in instructing and in answering their various objections. This lasted for a week, after which God opened the eyes and touched the hearts of two of these men, but not the third. He was a bit conceited, given to dogmatizing, but not noted for the personal probity of his life. Although convinced of the truth presented by Monsieur Vincent, he was not yet persuaded. He looked for subtleties, and always had a few new doubts. Once, as Monsieur Vincent later recounted in his edifying talks, this person seemed on the verge of abjuring his errors but raised a final objection.

> Monsieur, you have said that the Holy Spirit guides the Church of Rome, but I have trouble believing this. You see Catholics in the countryside abandoned by their evil and ignorant shepherds. They are not taught their duty and for the most part scarcely know what Christianity is all about. If, on the other hand, you look at the cities, you see them filled with do-nothing priests and monks. In Paris alone there are perhaps ten thousand who leave the peasants in lamentable ignorance, leading to their damnation. And yet you would have me persuaded that the Holy Spirit is behind all this? That I will never believe.

This objection raised by the heretic deeply impressed Monsieur Vincent. It renewed his conviction of the great spiritual needs of the people of the countryside, and the obligation of helping them, all of which he knew from personal experience. Without admitting this, he replied to the heretic:

> You are mistaken in what you say. Many parishes have good pastors and vicars. Among the clergy and religious in the cities, many go into the country regions to catechize and preach. Some of these religious are given to prayer, chanting the office both day and night. Others serve the public good by writing books, teaching sound doctrine, or in administering the sacraments. If some do nothing, these are individual men subject to error and are not the Church. When we speak of the Church as being led by the Holy Spirit, we refer to the Church as a whole, when she is assembled in council. Also, the Holy Spirit is present in the faithful when they act by the light of faith and follow the path of Christian justice. Those who do not resist the Holy Spirit. While they are still members of the Church, they live (as Saint Paul put it) according to the flesh, and shall die.[1]

Although this response should have been enough to answer this heretic, he remained obstinate in his error. His mind was so deeply impressed with the ignorance of the peasants and the little concern of the priests for their welfare that he regarded it as an infallible argument against the Church being led by the Holy Spirit.

The following year Monsieur Vincent returned to Montmirail together with several priests to present missions in this town and the surrounding villages. One was Monsieur Feron, then bachelor in theology and later doctor of the Sorbonne and archdeacon of Chartres. The second was Monsieur [Bernard] Duchesne, also doctor of the Sorbonne and archdeacon of Beau-

---

1. Rom 8:13.

vais. Several other priests and religious who were his friends accompanied him. All the region benefited so much from these missions that the obstinate heretic of whom we spoke was moved by curiosity to investigate what was happening. He attended the catechetical instructions and sermons. He saw for himself the care being taken for the instruction of the peasants in what they needed to know for their salvation. He witnessed the way in which even the slowest and crudest were treated to help them understand what they must believe and do. He saw the effects in the hearts of even the most hardened sinners bringing them to conversion and penance. All these things impressed him so strongly that he sought out Monsieur Vincent to say to him: "Now I can see that the Holy Spirit truly guides the Church for I see how much care is taken for the instruction and salvation of these poor villagers. I am now ready to enter the Church, if you would be pleased to receive me." When Monsieur Vincent asked him if any doubts still remained in his mind, he replied, "No, I believe all you told me. I am now prepared to renounce publicly all my past errors."

Monsieur Vincent asked him several other questions on the main truths of faith to see if he remembered well what he had been taught. Since he was satisfied with the answers, he directed him to appear the following Sunday at the church in the village of Marchais, near Montmirail, where a mission was in progress. Here he would make his abjuration and receive absolution for his heresy.

He appeared as arranged. In the presence of the official witnesses who had been notified, Monsieur Vincent called him by name at the end of the morning sermon to come before the congregation. He was asked if he still wished to renounce his heresy and enter the sheepfold of the true Church. He replied, pointing to a statue, "Yes, I am still of this mind, but I still have one difficulty. I cannot believe that any power resides in this crudely fashioned stone statue of the Blessed Virgin here."

Monsieur Vincent answered: "The Church teaches that no special power resides in material things, unless it be on those occasions that it pleases God to confer this power upon them. He did this, for example, with the rod of Moses, the source of so many miracles. Even children understand this." Thereupon he called upon one of the better-instructed children to explain what we ought to believe about sacred images. The child replied, "They are good to have, and we respect them, not because of what they are made from, but because they represent our Lord Jesus Christ, his glorious Mother, or the other saints in paradise. They have triumphed over the world, and now these silent images urge us to follow them in their faith and good works."

This reply so pleased Monsieur Vincent that he repeated it. He pointed out to the heretic that there was no reason to delay at this difficulty, once he understood Catholic belief. The same was true of all the other points of doctrine. All the same, he thought he was not yet ready for his abjuration and put it off for another occasion. In fact, he later did present himself again, abjured his heresy before the whole parish, and publicly professed the Catholic faith to the edification of the entire region. He has persevered in this belief ever since.

These events surrounding the conversion of this heretic, and particularly the reason for leaving his error to embrace the Catholic faith, that is, the care taken in the education of the country poor, led to Monsieur Vincent's speaking of it to his Congregation in a conference he once gave: "What happiness for us missionaries to witness to the guidance of the Church by the Holy Spirit, by our work for the instruction and sanctification of the poor!"[2]

---

2. *CED XI:34-37.*

CHAPTER FOURTEEN

After Appointment as Royal Chaplain of the Galleys, Monsieur Vincent Visits Provence and Guienne to Provide Physical and Spiritual Help to the Convicts

WHEN THE GENERAL of the galleys had seen the blessings brought about through the efforts of Monsieur Vincent in working for the salvation of souls, he wished to widen the arena for the exercise of his charity, that is, to the convicts condemned to serve in the galleys.[1] He requested the late king of glorious memory, Louis XIII, to appoint him as royal chaplain of the galleys, which he agreed to do.[2] This new office required Monsieur Vincent to travel to Marseilles in 1622. He had to see for himself the condition of these poor convicts and to provide for their needs as much as he possibly could.

On his arrival there, he saw a sight as pitiable as could be imagined. These poor creatures were doubly weighed down, by the weight of their sins and by the more tangible weight of their chains. They were overwhelmed by pain and misery that destroyed any thought of their salvation and were given to constant blasphemy and despair. It was an image of hell. They mentioned God only to deny or to curse him, and the evil dispositions of these poor unfortunates rendered useless all their sufferings. Monsieur Vincent was so touched by what he saw of the convicts that he resolved to do all in his power to help them. By encouraging them, he hoped to lift their spirits and to dispose them to be receptive to the spiritual good he hoped to provide. He listened to their complaints with great patience, sympathized with their sufferings, embraced them, kissed their chains. He did all he could by entreaty and protest to the officers of the galleys to have the convicts treated more humanely. In so doing, he gained their confidence, disposing them to be more open to God.

He wrote something like this to a priest of the Congregation who used rude and harsh words in speaking to peasants. He pointed out that if the priest wished to win over any of these poor souls he should deal with them in a spirit of meekness, the true spirit of Jesus Christ.[3]

---

1. The galley slaves were sentenced to servitude in the fleet and in times of war they took part in naval battles. The galley slaves were, however, under a separate jurisdiction from the navy, with a general named by the king. This title was suppressed in 1748.
2. *CED* XIII:55. The date of his appointment was February 8, 1619.
3. See *CED* IV:53 which gives the text of this fragment.

He desired to serve these poor convicts and bring a greater number of souls to heaven. This led him to accept this appointment as royal chaplain of the galleys. In this position he would have charge of the other chaplains, and thus be in a better position to succeed in his charitable designs. This was in keeping with the ardent love burning in his heart. It impelled him to undertake whatever might procure the salvation and sanctification of souls, particularly of the most abandoned.

After some time in Marseilles, he was obliged to return to Paris, where God wished to use him on other occasions for his glory. The trip to Marseilles was important for him, for it allowed him to see at first hand the wretched state of these poor convicts. He could then devise some relief from their great sufferings and some hope for their spiritual welfare. He was able to move in this direction by assigning some priests of the Congregation of the Mission to take care of the hospital for the galley prisoners. They also conducted missions on the galleys themselves, as we shall recount in a later chapter of this book.

On his return to Paris he made it a point to visit felons newly condemned to the galleys. He found these prisoners in an even worse state than those he had left in Marseilles. They were kept in the dungeons of the Conciergerie or other prisons, sometimes for extended periods. They were infested with vermin, overwhelmed by weariness and poverty, and entirely neglected in both body and soul.

Seeing these prisoners in such misery, he approached the general of the galleys, pointing out that these poor creatures were his responsibility. While they were awaiting their assignment to the galleys, his charity should see to it that some decent care be taken of these men. In fact, Monsieur Vincent proposed a plan to benefit the convicts, both physically and spiritually. The general of the galleys approved and gave Monsieur Vincent full authority to carry out his plan. This involved renting a house in the faubourg Saint Honore, near the church of Saint Roch, where the convicts would live under guard. As a result of great efforts the house was readied to receive the prisoners in that same year, 1622.[4] Here Monsieur Vincent could give free rein to his charity, to provide all sorts of services for these poor abandoned people. He visited them often, taught them, sympathized with them, prepared them for general confession, and administered the sacraments to them. Not content with these spiritual aids, he looked after their bodily needs as well. Sometimes to be of great service to these convicts he would stay with them, even during a time of dangerous contagion. In his love for them he forgot himself and his own safety, preferring to give himself completely to them.

When he was obliged by other duties to leave them, he enlisted the help

---

4. The correct date is 1618. Coste, *Life* I:115, n. 1.

of two other clerics, both good and devoted men. One was the late Monsieur Portail.[5] He had joined Monsieur Vincent several years before and, on his advice, had received the priesthood. He was always obedient to the wishes and orders of this wise director. He persevered until 1660, when death separated these two friends in anticipation of a more perfect union in heaven. The second was the late Monsieur Belin, chaplain of the de Gondi house at Villepreux. Both lived in the prison hospital and celebrated mass there. God so blessed this work of charity begun by Monsieur Vincent that in his Providence he has allowed it to continue to this day.

The poor convicts have been housed, helped, and cared for in both body and soul these many years, first in the faubourg Saint Honore and later near the Saint Bernard gate of the city.

The chaplain of the galleys had begun so well that the general was most pleased. In the following year, 1623, the galleys of Marseilles were moved to Bordeaux because of the war against the heretics.[6] As a result, he heartily agreed that Monsieur Vincent should go to Guienne to bring the same help to the convicts in that province as he had done in Marseilles and Paris.

On his arrival in Bordeaux he contacted several other religious orders for help in this work. He was able to assign two chaplains to each of the galleys, where they were able to conduct a mission for the prisoners. These were helped to reconcile themselves to God by making a good general confession, submit themselves to his divine will, and patiently accept their sufferings as satisfaction for their past sins. In Bordeaux, Monsieur Vincent was able to bring a Moslem into the Church. He brought him back to Paris with himself, where he presented him to the general, who graciously received him. He was given the name Louis at his baptism. Now that he is still alive he is ever mindful of the thanks he owes to Monsieur Vincent, to whose charity, after God, he owes the grace of his salvation.

---

5. Antoine Portail, 1590-1660. He came as a young man to Paris to study at the Sorbonne. He met Vincent de Paul in 1612, and became one of his first companions. He was ordained in 1622. He was employed among the galley slaves, and gave missions in the countryside and worked for the ordinands. He was chosen first assistant general, and director of the Daughters of Charity in 1642, spending most of the rest of his life at Saint Lazare.

6. In 1622 the Huguenots rose in revolt against the king. From their fortified center at La Rochelle, their survival depended on receiving supplies by sea from England. Louis XIII massed his navies to blockade the city, and thus the galley slaves were transferred from Marseilles, on the Mediterranean, to Bordeaux, on the Atlantic, where they were evangelized by Monsieur Vincent.

CHAPTER FIFTEEN

He Provides for the Physical and Spiritual Necessities of the Poor of Macon, with Excellent Results

SINCE THE FIRE of charity burned ever more brightly in the heart of Monsieur Vincent, God provided other opportunities for the development of this virtue. Once, passing through Macon he became aware of the many poor people who suffered even more in soul than in their physical needs.[1] What is worse, they seemed to have no sense of the deplorable state of their spiritual welfare. They were unaware of the most elementary things concerning salvation and lived in a spirit of irreligion and horrifying impiety. No one seemed able to bring about any relief to this problem.

These doubly stricken people walked the streets or frequented the churchyards, begging alms, unmindful of the laws of the Church or even the commandments of God. They almost never went to mass. They did not know how to confess their sins or to receive any of the sacraments. They passed their lives in profound ignorance of God and of what concerned their salvation and descended to lives of filth and vice. Monsieur Vincent had such great sympathy for these suffering people that even though he had not planned to stop in Macon, he decided to stay. As a good Samaritan, he looked upon these poor people as travelers robbed and beaten by the enemies of their salvation. He hoped to bind up their wounds and provide some sort of help to them. He set up a system whereby the men of the town helped the poor, while the women looked after the sick.[2] Here is the account written by Father Desmoulins, then superior of the Oratory in Macon:

> I did not learn of the condition of the poor through others but saw it myself with my own eyes. From the beginning of this project, all the poor who received help came to confession on the first of the month. Other confessors and I came upon older people of sixty or more years who openly told us they had never gone to confession before. When we spoke to them of God, the Blessed Trinity, the birth, passion, and death of Jesus Christ, and other mysteries of our religion, they said that they had never before heard these things. Through this Confraternity of Charity these disorders were addressed, and the corporal and spiritual needs of the poor were

---

1. September 1621. *CED* XIII:497.
2. It was his practice, later followed by his Missionaries, to found Confraternities of Charity in each parish in which they preached a mission.

quickly met. His Excellency, Louis Dinet, then bishop of Macon, approved Monsieur Vincent's plan of action. The members of the chapters of the cathedral and of Saint Peter, all of noble birth, supported it. Monsieur Chambon, dean of the cathedral, and Monsieur de Relets, provost of Saint Peter's, were among the directors, and Monsieur [Hugues] Foillard was lieutenant general. They carried out the directions given by Monsieur Vincent, that is, that a list be kept of all the poor of the town, who should be given alms on particular days. If found begging in the churches or going from door to door, they would be fined. In addition, the townspeople were forbidden to give them anything in these circumstances. Those passing through the city would be allowed to stay a single night, then would be sent on their way with two *sous* as a parting gift.

The sick poor would be helped by food or medicine, just as in other places where the Confraternity of Charity had been established. This whole enterprise began with no public funds to support it, but Monsieur Vincent was so adept at organizing things that many contributed to its success. One gave money, another gave food, each according to his or her ability. In all more than three hundred poor were housed, fed, and reasonably cared for. After giving the first contribution, Monsieur Vincent left the town.[3]

But how did he leave? We can learn from what he himself wrote in 1635 to Mademoiselle le Gras. On his advice she had gone to Beauvais for a similar project but needed some encouragement.[4]

I spoke well when I warned you that you would have great difficulty in Beauvais. Blessed be God, you have succeeded. When I first began the Confraternity of Charity in Macon, people made fun of me. They said I could never bring it off. Tears of joy greeted its establishment. When I was about to leave, the authorities of the town were prepared to do me such honor that I was obliged to leave secretly to avoid their congratulations. This is one of the better of these Confraternities of Charity. I hope that the trouble you have experienced at the beginning will in the end turn into consolation and that the enterprise will become more stable.[5]

The fathers of the Oratory were good enough to offer him lodging for the three weeks he remained in Macon. They became aware that he removed the mattress from his bed, preferring to sleep on the straw underneath. He had begun this practice some years before, and continued it right up to the time

---

3. *CED* XIII:494-95.
4. July 21, 1635, but Coste holds for 1634. *CED* I:239-40.
5. *CED* XIII:833-34.

of his death, that is, for over fifty years. Since these fathers found out about this only on his last day with them when they came early to his room to say goodbye, he passed it off lightly, with some innocuous comment.

CHAPTER SIXTEEN

He is Chosen by the Blessed Francis de Sales, Bishop of Geneva, and by Mother de Chantal as the First Spiritual Father and Superior of the Religious of the Visitation of Saint Mary in Paris

IT HAD BEEN several years since God had brought into being the saintly order of religious of the Visitation as a new flower spreading the odor of sanctity in the garden of the Church. God used Blessed Francis de Sales, bishop of Geneva, to begin and to cultivate this mystical plant, which he did with all the care suggested by his incomparable charity.[1] Mother de Chantal, whose memory is held in benediction, had been sent to Paris by Blessed Francis to found a monastery of the order.[2] She worked with such zeal and prudence that despite opposition, contradictions, and persecutions, the walls of this new Jerusalem and home of peace were raised.[3] Several souls, mindful of their salvation and their perfection, came to seek a refuge against the vanity and temptations of the world. Modesty, meekness, patience, obedience, charity, and all the other virtues of these spiritual daughters of Jesus Christ were the admiration of all who came to know of them or who heard of them.

It now became a question of finding a spiritual father and superior for this religious community, that is, a visible guardian angel. By his charity and prudent conduct, and by his vigilance and fidelity, he would preserve the primitive spirit which Jesus Christ had given them, through the ministry of their holy founder. He would have to be able to render all help necessary to have the sisters pass from virtue to virtue along the way of perfection.

As this holy prelate had said in his book *Philothea* [*Introduction to the Devout Life*][4] speaking of a spiritual director for an individual, "For my part

---

1. Francis de Sales, bishop of Geneva, was born on August 21, 1567 near Annecy, and died in Lyons, December 28, 1622. Francis de Sales and Vincent de Paul admired one another greatly. Vincent spoke at the beatification process of his friend. He was beatified in 1661, canonized in 1665.
2. Jeanne Francoise Fremiot, born in Dijon, January 23, 1572, had four children from her marriage to the baron of Chantal. After his death, she placed herself under the guidance of Francis de Sales, and with him established the Order of the Visitation. She lived in Paris from 1619 to 1622, where she became acquainted with Vincent de Paul, whom she requested from Jean Francois de Gondi, archbishop of Paris, as ecclesiastical superior of her daughters. Until her death, December 13, 1641, she kept in close contact with Monsieur Vincent, whom she consulted both as a spiritual director and as an advisor in the business matters of the monastery of the Visitation. She was beatified in 1751, and canonized in 1767.
3. On May 1, 1619, the first house opened.
4. Part I, Ch. 4.

I say choose one out of ten thousand. Even then you will find fewer than you would like who are capable of this office." This being so, we can imagine how difficult it would be to find a true spiritual father and a worthy superior for this holy congregation. Each day it was growing both in numbers and in virtue. It demanded as much light and grace as is possible in the one charged with its direction since the religious life is the more sublime; its life of perfection more important, and its failure more disastrous for the Church. For these reasons the holy founder required qualities beyond those needed for personal direction. He looked for a man of great virtue and great charity joined to learning and experience. This meant, in a word, a man endowed with all the virtues, capable of leading souls called by God to the highest perfection.

With these desirable qualities in mind, it is a tribute to the high virtue and the other gifts of mind and heart of Monsieur Vincent that he should be chosen from among all his learned and pious contemporaries. Blessed Francis de Sales had a singular gift of discerning spirits, and Mother de Chantal a clear understanding mind. They judged Monsieur Vincent to be the best qualified and most capable person for this responsibility, to assume charge of those they held most dear and most precious in all the world.

In Paris there were persons of learning and piety older than Monsieur Vincent: pastors accomplished in their work, noted doctors of the colleges of Sorbonne, Navarre, and the other colleges of the noted university of the first city of the kingdom. There were also renowned spiritual directors. Despite all this, after long consideration, prayer, and consultation with the saintly superior the blessed bishop felt he could not make a better choice for this important position than Vincent de Paul. He found in him all the qualities so necessary for the first spiritual father and superior of this religious congregation at its birth.[5]

If what was said by an ancient author be true, "It is a special grace to be praised by one himself worthy of praise;[6] the excellence of virtue in the one who speaks gives weight to what he says in honor of the other,"[7] we must admit that Monsieur Vincent could not have received a more significant endorsement than he did from the saintly bishop of Geneva. We know from the results that the bishop's judgment was correct.

From this time on, Monsieur Vincent served as superior of the sisters,

---

5. He became superior of the Visitation sometime before December 22, 1622. He was not the first but the second superior, succeeding Charles de la Saussaye who died September 21, 1621. Saint Vincent, however, made the first regular visitation of the convent and was noteworthy for his care of the nuns.
6. Cicero, Letters, Book 5, 12.
7. Panegyric of the emperor Julian, by Claudius Mamertinus.

under the authority of Cardinal de Retz, then bishop of Paris,[8] and of his successors. In Book Two[9] we shall see the way this wise superior guided the houses established in Paris and elsewhere as well. God's blessing remained upon his leadership, which lasted thirty-eight years, until the end of his life, despite his efforts to resign several times because of the pressure of other work. Besides, he doubted that as a member of the Congregation of the Mission, committed to the direct service of the most abandoned poor, especially those in the countryside, he should be involved in this sort of work.

---

8. Henri de Gondi, the first Cardinal de Retz, and uncle of Jean Francois Paul de Gondi, the second Cardinal de Retz.

9. Ch. 7. The original edition reads Book Three, clearly an error.

CHAPTER SEVENTEEN

He is Appointed Head of the College des Bons Enfants, and Later Makes the First Foundation of the Congregation of the Mission

MADAME DE GONDI, as we have already said, saw both the need and the success of the missions. She had conceived the idea some years before of endowing a foundation of priests or religious to give some of their time to providing missions on her lands. She grew more and more anxious about this project, especially each year when she reviewed her last will and testament. Her plan was to contribute sixteen thousand *livres* toward this undertaking, and her wish was that Monsieur Vincent would be the one to carry it out.

Monsieur Vincent looked everywhere for the means and the occasion for complying with the wishes of this virtuous lady. He spoke several times with superiors of various orders and used all his powers of persuasion to have them accept the foundation. However, he found none willing to take up the project for his own community. Each one had his own reason, but the fact was that none judged it proper to do so, for all felt this foundation was destined by God to be Monsieur Vincent's arena of service. Providence directs all things to their proper end and often makes use of secondary agents to effect its design. This is how it came about, in this instance, that the foundation became Monsieur Vincent's concern.

Madame de Gondi became aware of the refusal of the religious communities to take up this work.[1] She also was aware that doctors and other clerics helped Monsieur Vincent in the work of the missions. She thought that if they had a house in Paris they might possibly come together in some form of community. This might even attract others to this same work, and so perpetuate the work of the missions she had so much at heart. She spoke of this to her husband. He not only approved the idea but wished to become a co-founder with her of this foundation. The two spoke to His Excellency, Jean Francois de Gondi, the general's brother, the successor to Cardinal de Retz as leader of the Church in Paris, and later its first archbishop.[2] He heartily approved their plan, since his diocese would likely win many advantages from it. He proposed that on his part he would make available

---

1. *CED* XI:170-71.
2. This Jean Francois was brother both to Philippe Emmanuel and Henri de Gondi. In 1622 he succeeded his brother, the first Cardinal de Retz, as the first archbishop of Paris, raised to an archdiocese by Gregory XV in that year.

the College des Bons Enfants, which was then at his disposition, as the residence for these priests.[3]

The three together considered who might be best suited for bringing this project to a successful conclusion. All three decided to meet with Monsieur Vincent to overcome all objections his humility would raise and to have him accept. All this came about as they hoped, chiefly because Monsieur Vincent's great respect for all three of these persons led him to do all they asked of him. He agreed to their proposition, first, to take over the direction of the College des Bons Enfants and the priests who might come to live there to help out in the giving of missions; second, to accept, in the name of these priests, the foundation given by the de Gondis; and third, to select personally those he thought proper and disposed to participate in this holy work.

Once they had agreed on these matters, a formal deed was drawn up. On March 1, 1624, the archbishop sent him his appointment as head of the College des Bons Enfants.[4]

On April 17 of the following year, the general of the galleys and his wife delivered the contract of foundation, written in a fashion worthy of their piety.

It declared, in the first place:

> God, having for some years inspired in us the desire to honor him in our own lands and elsewhere, and we, having now considered how it has pleased his divine Majesty to provide in his infinite mercy for the spiritual needs of the residents of the cities by many doctors and good religious who have preached and catechized, and who have preserved in them a spirit of devotion, only the poor of the countryside now remain, and they alone are neglected. It has seemed that this evil might be remedied by a pious association of clerics, learned and devoted and of known ability. They should renounce all the conveniences of the towns and all benefices or other Church dignities. Under the guidance of the bishops they would give themselves entirely and solely to the salvation of these poor people, going from village to village at their own common expense. They would preach, instruct, exhort, and catechize those poor people and bring them to make a good general confession of their past lives, without taking any recompense in any manner

---

3. This residence, nearly three centuries old, was one of the oldest of the university, but almost abandoned and dilapidated. It occupied some sixteen acres. It took its name, "Good Youth," from the type of upper-class students expected there. Students, whether foundation scholars or paying borders, were provided with shelter and sleeping quarters.

4. At this same time, Vincent acquired rights to the priory of Saint Nicolas de Grosse Sauve in the diocese of Langres. *CED* XIII:56-57. The document is dated February 1624. He may never have exercised these rights, however.

whatsoever. In this, they would give freely what they have freely received from the hand of God.

To help arrive at this, the said lord and lady, in thanksgiving for the gifts and graces they have received and continue to receive from the divine Majesty, to contribute to the salvation of the souls of the poor in honor of the mystery of the incarnation of our Lord and of the life and death of Jesus Christ our Lord, for the love of his blessed Mother, and to obtain the grace to live the rest of their lives worthily and come with their family to eternal glory, the said lord and lady have contributed a sum of forty thousand *livres* into the hands of Monsieur Vincent de Paul, priest of the diocese of Dax, with the following clauses and charges, To wit:

The said lord and lady confide to Monsieur Vincent the right to select and choose within the year a certain number of clerics to live at the expense of the foundation. These men will have the learning, piety, good conduct, and integrity of life necessary to engage in this work for the remainder of their lives under the direction of Monsieur Vincent. The said lord and lady expressly understand and order that because of the confidence they have in him and because of the experience he has had in the missions, so blessed by God, he should guide this undertaking. Nevertheless, it is understood that Monsieur Vincent will continue to live in the de Gondi household to continue to provide the spiritual help he has given these many years past.

That the said clergy and others who might in future wish to join in this holy enterprise devote themselves solely to the welfare of the poor country people. For this purpose they promise not to preach or administer the sacraments in any city where there is an archiepiscopal or episcopal palace or regional court, unless it be a case of unusual necessity.

That the said clerics live in common, under obedience to the said Monsieur de Paul or his successors after his death. That the name of this community be the Company or the Congregation of the Mission. That those who join this community have the intention of serving God in the manner spoken of above and promise to observe the rules which shall be given. That every five years they serve all the lands of the said lord and lady by preaching, hearing confessions, catechizing, and doing the other good works spoken of above. That they render spiritual help to the poor convicts so they many benefit from the corporal sufferings they may have to undergo, although the general recognizes no obligation on his part to do so. That this charity be continued in the future by the said clerics to the said convicts for good and just considerations. Finally, the said lord and lady remain jointly founders of this good work. As such, they and their heirs enjoy and retain in perpetuity all the rights and privileges accorded to patrons in the sacred canons, except the right of assigning persons to positions of responsibility, which right they have renounced.[5]

Some other clauses in this contract had to do with the good order to be observed by the priests, or the frequency of the missions, or their own development. These are too long to cite here, but what has been given suffices to see the origins of this first of the houses of the Congregation of the Mission. It also allows us to see how exalted and agreeable to God, whose greater glory alone motivated this action, was this foundation for the salvation of most abandoned souls, such as the poor of the countryside.

It is particularly noteworthy how disinterested the benefactors were. They imposed no obligation of masses and prayers for themselves, neither in this life or after their death. Freed from this obligation, the priests of the Congregation could act with greater liberty. They could give themselves completely to the functions of their ministry and work more diligently for the missions. These charitable founders voluntarily deprived themselves of all the spiritual suffrages they might have had, in favor of the poor and to the greater glory of God.

Shortly after the execution of this contract, the general of the galleys went to Provence, and Madame remained in Paris. They were both greatly consoled that their offering to God had been accomplished. They were greatly relieved to know their new foundation was off to a good start by being placed in the care of Monsieur Vincent, in whom they had such complete confidence. They knew for sure that, like the servant in the Gospel who had received the ten talents, he would devote himself completely to making good use of them. In this they were not to be disappointed, for under the prudent and faithful direction of Monsieur Vincent this first foundation, by the blessing of God, led to many others, as we shall see in this book.

---

5. *CED* XIII:197-202; for the act of approval by the archbishop of Paris, April 24, 1626, see *CED* XIII:202-03.

CHAPTER EIGHTEEN

Madame de Gondi Passes from This Life to a Better One. Monsieur Vincent Goes to the College des Bons Enfants

THE FOUNDATION of the priests of the Mission was the one dearest to the heart of Madame de Gondi. She recognized the great fruit it could produce in the Church for the salvation and sanctification of many souls. After God had allowed her to put the finishing touches on this project, it seemed, like another Saint Monica, she could say in her heart that her work on earth was at an end. God heard her prayers, calling her to himself to receive the crown prepared for her because of her great service to his divine Majesty.[1]

Only two months after signing the contract of foundation, she was stricken with an illness that soon brought her to the last extremity. Her previous sicknesses and the fatigue brought on by her life of zeal and charity left her with little strength to resist the progress of her latest sickness. On the eve of the feast of Saint John the Baptist in 1625, she passed from this life to her eternal home.[2] This death must have been precious in God's sight, for it was preceded by a saintly life that would fill an entire volume were it set down in writing. Monsieur Vincent was the one person with the most complete knowledge of her excellent qualities and her rare virtues, but he kept a close silence on all her actions in which he had any part. He never spoke of these things so as not to reveal his own part in them. Since this holy and virtuous woman had done almost nothing for the service and glory of God without the cooperation of Monsieur Vincent, her works could not be spoken of without attracting attention to himself. He feared this more than anything and did all he could to avoid it.

After the last respects were paid to Madame de Gondi, her body was taken to the Carmelite monastery on the rue Chapon as she had requested. Monsieur Vincent left soon afterwards for Provence to bring the sad news to her husband. He knew well that this news and the painful separation it involved would deeply affect the general of the galleys. He at first concealed his reason for coming, speaking instead of the obligation the general had to thank God for the special graces he and his family had received. This thanks to God is shown by a perfect spirit of dependence on God and a desire to conform ourselves to his holy will in all things without reserve. Finally, he

---

1. PL 32:775.
2. June 23. She died in Paris, at age forty-two.

came little by little to the sad news he bore. After his first shock, the general was consoled by Monsieur Vincent with all that the Holy Spirit suggested as consolation in the face of the sad news and as a help to him in bearing this affliction, which he felt so deeply and so sharply, with peace and tranquility of spirit. We can truthfully say that among the special graces Monsieur Vincent had received from God was his gift of consoling the sorrowful and assuaging the interior sufferings of others. Our Lord Jesus Christ had given him this grace by a special outpouring of his Spirit. This enabled him to say in imitation of the Lord, "The Spirit of the Lord is upon me, to evangelize the poor, to console the afflicted, and to cure those wounded in heart."[3]

This gift of Monsieur Vincent had often been experienced by the saintly departed woman, who suffered much from the interior pains God saw fit to send her. In this state she could find no surer consolation than that offered by Monsieur Vincent. She recognized in him such a concern for the true good of her soul and a source of such graces for her family that she never wanted him to leave her household. She regarded him as the Ark in the house of Obededom, attracting God's blessing by his very presence. All this explains why in her last testament she begged him, "for the love of our Savior Jesus Christ and of his holy mother, never to leave the household of the general of the galleys, nor, after his death, the home of her children." In addition, the testament continued by asking the general to retain Monsieur Vincent for himself and the children, to remember and practice his wise recommendations. She was well aware that if they did, they would benefit greatly from his prudent direction.

Monsieur Vincent was not satisfied to remain in this house, for though well run, it had too much of a worldly atmosphere about it. Considering what God was calling him to, he preferred to obey that call rather than fulfill what his patroness has so earnestly desired. He ardently besought the general to assent to his leaving to take up residence in the College des Bons Enfants. He finally obtained this agreement and moved to his new home.

In 1625, the general, this faithful servant of God who had sailed on the stormy sea of the outside world, came by a singular gift of divine Providence to that sure harbor where he was to lead a truly apostolic life. He renounced all honors, dignities, and other worldly goods to commit himself to work at his own spiritual perfection and the salvation of others through the practice of the virtues taught and lived by Jesus Christ.[4]

---

3. Isa 61:1; Luke 4:18.
4. He spent a year arranging his temporal affairs and providing for the future of his sons, and then retired to the Oratory, where for thirty-five years he lived a most courageous and edifying life. He continued to support the charitable works of Monsieur Vincent. The saint wrote to his former benefactor to take his leave as his life was coming to an end; see *CED* VII:435-36. Father de

It was here that he laid the foundations of his Congregation of the Mission, committed as were the first disciples of Jesus Christ to follow that first missionary, come down from heaven to live among us. He dedicated himself to the same mission as did Jesus during his mortal life.

To appreciate God's designs in regard to this new Congregation of the Mission, it is necessary to know the one chosen by the infinitely wise Providence as its founder. We must see how God gave him all the qualities of mind and heart so necessary to succeed in this project of such importance to the glory of his name and the good of the Church. It certainly will not be easy to discover what his humility so carefully concealed. What charity or obedience obliged him to reveal we can know but we cannot know the main facets of his disposition. These were interior and of a spiritual nature. In the following chapter we can present only a superficial and imperfect sketch of his character. Yet this will be enough to give some indication of the person we will speak of in the remainder of this work.

Gondi died at Joigny, June 29, 1662.

CHAPTER NINETEEN

Monsieur Vincent's Dispositions of Body and Soul

MONSIEUR VINCENT was of medium height and well proportioned. His head was somewhat fleshy, large enough, but well suited to the rest of the body. His forehead was broad and stately, his face neither too full nor too pinched, his appearance mild, his look penetrating, his hearing acute, his bearing grave but benign, his countenance relaxed and open, easy to approach, his disposition kindly and good.[1] His temperament was sanguine and bilious. His constitution was strong and robust yet he was more subject to the bad weather than one would have thought. This left him open to developing fevers.

His spirit was broad, composed, circumspect, capable of great things, and difficult to take unawares. He was not a quick learner, but when forced by circumstances to do so, he could penetrate quickly to the heart of the matter. He looked into all the circumstances both great and small. He foresaw the difficulties in a course of action and the likely outcomes. Unless forced to take quick action, he would seek counsel before deciding. He looked into the reasons for and against and was happy to consult with others. When asked for his advice, or when obliged to come to some decision, he outlined the problem at hand in such clear order that he astonished even the most expert in the field, above all in matters spiritual or ecclesiastical.

He never rushed into business matters. Neither the magnitude of the question nor its problems bothered him. With determination and force of mind he would undertake a project, applying himself with order and insight and would bear its burdens with patience and tranquility.

When a question of some issues arose, he would listen respectfully, never interrupting the speaker. By contrast, when he himself was interrupted he would stop at once and later take up again the thread of his argument. When he gave his opinion on some matter, he did not speak at length. He would express his thought in few words, with his natural eloquence. He could not only explain his perspective clearly and solidly but also touch his listeners by his affective language when he thought it proper. Both prudence and

---

1. He always refused to have his portrait painted, even at the repeated requests of those closest to him like Mesdames Goussault and de Lamoignon. His confreres also tried to persuade him to allow a portrait to be painted. Finally, a painter was secretly brought to Saint Lazare to study his proposed subject, and he produced a portrait. The details of this were preserved by Brother Bertrand Ducournau, the saint's secretary.

simplicity marked his speech. He said sincerely just what he thought. He kept quiet on some matters when he saw it could cause some hurt if he spoke. He was ever present to himself, careful never to say or write anything showing anger, rancor, or disrespect toward anyone.

His mind was not given lightly to changes. His maxim was: if things are going well, do not easily change them to try to improve them. He suspected new and extraordinary propositions, whether merely speculative or practical. He held to common usages and customs in matters of religion. He used to say: "The human mind is quick and restless. The most active and most creative minds are not always the best, if they are not accompanied with discrimination. Those walk most securely who travel the same path as most of the wise."

He did not stop at mere outward appearances, but penetrated to their nature and end. By his own excellent common sense, he was able to distinguish the true from the false and the good from the bad, even though they often appear under the same guise.

His heart was tender, noble, generous, and free. He easily developed an affection for what was good and in keeping with the holiness of God. Nevertheless, he had an absolute control over his natural tendencies. Reason so controlled his passions that it was hard to know he had any.

We cannot say he had no defects, for holy Scripture says otherwise. Even the apostles and other saints were not preserved from faults. All the same, scarcely anyone in this final age was so involved in all sorts of situations, meeting all types of people, and participated in a large variety of enterprises and who met with less criticism than Monsieur Vincent did. God had given him the grace to be fully self-possessed, so nothing seemed to surprise him. His viewpoint was ever directed toward our Savior Jesus Christ and so his words and actions were influenced by this divine model. In this way he acted with great circumspection and reserve toward the great and with kindness and affability toward the least. His life was not only above reproach but worthy of the universal and public approbation he received.

Since there are ever those who do not follow the general opinion, some spirited types took exception that he took too long to make up his mind and carry out his decisions. Others objected that he spoke too poorly of himself and too well of others.

There is something in these two points, but most people fall into the opposite defect. We might say of Monsieur Vincent what Saint Jerome wrote about Saint Paula: "Her faults would be considered virtues in others."[2]

As to the first charge, Monsieur Vincent was slow and deliberate in making decisions because of both his nature and his understanding of what was proper.

---

2. PL 22:898.

His own understanding gave him an extensive view of a question, which required some time to resolve, and often left him in a sort of indecision. His spiritual viewpoint was that we must never anticipate divine Providence. He had a most sensitive conscience on this point. He was convinced that God could accomplish what he wished just as well with him as without him. What God does of his own accord is done better and with greater assurance.

On the other hand, people often do more harm than good. They contribute some of their own frailty or passion. He used to say: "Nothing is more common than the poor success of things done too precipitously."[3] Experience proves that Monsieur Vincent's deliberate way of acting did not hinder any good work. On the contrary, he did more of the most varied and important things and stuck to his projects better than most other people, as we will have occasion to see during this book. It seemed that God wanted to convince everyone that ardor and haste were not the key points. The earth, solid and heavy as it is, is what brings forth trees and flowers. The vivacity of fire, if not well regulated, is suited more to destroy.

As to the second point, the world is so given to self-praise and pulling down the reputation of others that if he conformed to this way of acting no one would ever have said a word of reproach. But since he did just the opposite, there were complaints. His usual practice was to praise virtuous people, but speak disparagingly of himself, as being in a long line of sinners. In so doing he was following the example of the greatest saints, and even the Saint of Saints. He said by the mouth of a prophet that he was a worm and no man.[4] Although Jesus was just and innocent, or rather Justice and Innocence itself, he passed for a sinner among men. He presented himself before his heavenly Father loaded down with the sins of the people.

Monsieur Vincent had so taken to heart this practice of humility and self-deprecation that he seemed to see only vice and sin. When he requested prayers to help him bless God, it was not to thank him for the singular graces his goodness had bestowed upon him, but to praise the patience with which divine mercy bore his sins and, as he used to say, supported him even in his abominations and infidelity.

Only in the secret of his heart did he express his thanks to God for his great favors and the evident gifts he had received from his hand. He never spoke of these things, fearing to attribute any of this to himself. He looked on the graces he had received as belonging to God and on himself as being unworthy of them. He did not think of these gifts as belonging to himself but as coming from God and belonging to him. He imitated the apostle in boasting only of his infirmities and concealed all the rest.

---

3. *CED* I:434.
4. Ps 22:7.

CHAPTER NINETEEN

On the other hand, in closing his eyes to the weaknesses and faults of others, particularly in those he was not actively directing, he gladly praised the good he perceived in them. He did so not so much to attribute these good qualities to the other person but so as to glorify God, the sovereign author of all good. He said once: "Some always think well of their neighbor, as much as true charity will allow them to do so. They cannot witness virtue without praising it nor virtuous persons without loving them." He was himself an example of this maxim, but always with the greatest prudence and discretion. He seldom praised the members of his own Congregation publicly, and then only when he judged it would be expedient for the greater glory of God and the greater good of all. For others, he rejoiced openly with them for the graces they had received from God and the good use they had made of his gifts. He spoke this way to encourage them to perseverance in the good they had begun.

Lastly, to express in few words what we will say more fully in Book Three on the virtues of Monsieur Vincent, he had taken Jesus Christ, our divine savior, as the only exemplar of his life. He had so imprinted the image of Jesus Christ upon his mind and was so penetrated with his holy maxims that he spoke, thought, and acted only in view of God. The life of our divine Savior and the lessons of the Gospel were the sole rule of his life and actions. They were his book of morals and his book of politics, and they guided him in all the matters that passed through his hands. They were, in a word, the sure foundation on which he built his entire spiritual edifice.

We can say in truth that without realizing it, he left us a miniature portrait of his whole life and a sort of motto, when he said one day: "Nothing pleases me except in Jesus Christ."[5] This was the source of his unshakable constancy and firmness in doing good and of his being able to stand unmoved by any consideration of human respect or his own personal interest. This source enabled him to support the contradictions, to endure the persecutions, to put his life on the line and, as the wise man says, to defend to the death justice and truth. Toward the end of his life Monsieur Vincent spoke in these remarkable words: "Whoever speaks of the teachings of Jesus Christ speaks of an unshakable rock: eternal truths, which infallibly produce their proper fruit. They should rather expect the heavens to fall than find the truths of Jesus Christ to fail."[6]

To impress this truth more firmly in the minds of others, he would sometimes use the following story:

> Our good peasants know that the moon changes. It causes eclipses of the sun or the other stars. They often speak of these

---

5. This statement and a few other slight corrections on one page of this chapter were added to a second printing of the first edition in 1664.
6. *CED* XII:116.

events, and observe them when they occur. An astrologer looks at these same things from afar in another way. By his art or science he can say that on such and such a day, at such an hour, at such a minute, we will have an eclipse. And this is true not only of astrologers in Europe but in China or elsewhere. Looking into the obscure future they can predict what will happen in the heavens a hundred, a thousand, four thousand or more years ahead. They know the rules which govern the motion of the heavens. If these people have this kind of knowledge, how much more should we believe that divine Wisdom penetrates into the least circumstances of the most hidden things. The truth of his maxims given in the teachings of the Gospel, although unknown to many in the world, are clearly seen after they occur, ordinarily only at the hour of death. Alas, why are we not convinced that these same truths as proposed by the infinite charity of Jesus Christ will never be proved wrong? The truth is that we are not convinced and quickly turn to human prudence as our guide. Do you not see that we are to blame if we trust in human reasoning rather than the promises of eternal Wisdom, to the deceitful disappointments of the world rather than the love of our Savior, who came down from heaven to show us the right path?[7]

Monsieur Vincent was not content to fill only his own mind and heart with the truths and maxims of the Gospel. He used every opportunity to persuade others, and particularly those of his own Congregation, of these same truths. This is what he said, on one occasion, on this subject:

> The Congregation must give itself to God to be nourished by this heavenly ambrosia, to live the way our Savior lived, to direct our actions to him, and to mold our lives on his example.
>
> He made it his first maxim always to seek God's glory and justice, always and before all else. How beautiful this is, to seek first the reign of God in ourselves and in others! If any group accepts this precept of working for the glory of God, how great will be its own happiness! What reason to hope that all will turn out well! If it pleases God to give us this grace, our happiness will be beyond compare.
>
> In the world, when someone takes a trip, the first concern is that he is going the correct way. How much more those who have professed following Jesus Christ in the practice of the teachings of the Gospel (particularly seeking the glory of God above all things else) should be aware of why they are acting as they do. They must

---

7. *CED* XII:121-22.

ask themselves, why am I doing this? Is it because I feel like it? Is it because I have an aversion to something else? Is it to please some unworthy creature? Or could it be to fulfill the good pleasure of God and seek his justice? What a noble life that would be! Would it be a human life? No, it would be an angelic life, since I do what I do purely for the love of God and leave aside what I do not do for the sake of this love.

If you add to this the practice of seeking to do the will of God, which ought to be the soul of the Congregation and a practice you should keep close to your heart, you will have a means of perfection that is easy, excellent, and infallible. Our actions will be more than human, even more than angelic, and in some way divine, for they will be done in God by the movement of his Spirit and by his grace. What an excellent way of life such a way of acting would be! What a way of life that of the missionaries would be, if it embraced this practice.

Next comes simplicity, which causes God to take delight in the soul in which it dwells. Look around our own group to consider those in whom this virtue is particularly noticeable. Are they not the most lovable? Does not this candor appeal to us when we speak with them? Who should not strive for this virtue, since our Lord himself was so pleased to be with the simple?

Well regulated prudence also makes us agreeable to God since it leads us to those things conducive to his glory and makes us avoid what is opposed. With prudence we do not simply avoid duplicity in word and action but act with wisdom, circumspection, and rectitude. We reach our goals by the means suggested by the Gospel, not just once, but forever. How blessed we would be, ourselves and our Congregation, if we walked this path.

If you add to these virtues meekness and humility, what would be lacking? They are two blood sisters, just like simplicity and prudence. Our Savior Jesus Christ taught us this lesson when he said we must learn of him because he was meek and humble of heart. Learn of me, he said. What words! What an honor to be his pupils, to learn this short but powerful lesson, which would be so impressive if it were to make us like himself. O my Savior, shall you not have the same influence over us as the philosophers had over their students, who were so strongly attracted to their statements that it was enough to say, The Master has said . . . , to gain their belief? What will we say in response to our Lord who has taught us so much, if we have learned so little? But do you want to know what happiness will be ours if we embrace these virtues born so nobly in the heart of Jesus Christ? They will lead us to that furnace of love whence they took their birth. O my God, who of us would not be all in love with you!

What can we say of him who would seek the kingdom of God, would embrace the holy practice of seeking his most holy will, who tries to be simple and prudent and practices the meekness and humility of our Lord? What would we all be if we were to act this way? What sort of Congregation would the Congregation of the Mission be? God alone could reveal this to you. For my part I do not have words enough to express myself. Tomorrow at mental prayer think about this, about what such a person and such a Congregation would be.[8]

To all this Monsieur Vincent added two other important maxims, which he professed himself, and which he strove to inculcate in his followers.

The first was not to be content with an affective love for God, nor to have exalted notions of his goodness and great wishes for his glory. These sentiments must be expressed in action or as Saint Gregory says, "to give proof of your love by your good works."[9] On this matter he one day spoke thus to his community:

Let us love God, my brothers, let us love God, but let it be in the strength of our arm and in the sweat of our brow. Sentiments of love of God, of kindness, of good will, good as these may be, are often suspect if they do not result in good deeds. Our Savior said that his Father was glorified in our bearing much fruit. We should be on our guard, for it is possible to be well mannered exteriorly and filled with noble sentiments toward the Almighty in our minds and yet stop there. When the occasion for action arises, such people fall short. They may be consoled by their fervent imagination or content with the sweet sentiments they experience in mental prayer. They may speak like the angels, but when it is a matter of working for God, of suffering, of mortifying themselves, of teaching the poor, of seeking out the lost sheep, of rejoicing at deprivations, of comforting the sick or some other service, oh, here they draw the line. Their courage fails them. No, no, we must not deceive ourselves: *totum opus nostrum in operatione consistit* ["all our work consists in action"].[10]

Monsieur Vincent often repeated these words, which he said he had first heard from the lips of a great servant of God on his deathbed, when asked for some final edifying words. He had replied that he saw clearly in this last

---

8. *CED* XII:182-84.
9. PL 76:1220.
10. *CED* XI:40-41.

hour that what some people took as contemplation, ecstasy, or an overwhelming experience of God were not evidence of divine union but were mere smoke. This feeling proceeded either from idle curiosity or the natural inclination of a mind inclined to the good. All this was far from that good and perfect action which characterizes true love for God.

Monsieur Vincent said:

> That is so true, that the holy apostle declares that our good actions alone will accompany us to the next life. Reflect on this, especially so because there are those in our time who seem virtuous enough, and perhaps are. However, they are inclined to an easy and soft life rather than to a solid and laborious one. The Church is compared to a great harvest that needs workers, but workers who actually labor. Nothing conforms more to the Gospel than to take the light and strength one finds in his soul in mental prayer, in spiritual reading, or in solitude, and bring this spiritual nourishment to others. This is what our Lord did, and his apostles also. This is to join the Martha's role to Mary's. This is to imitate the dove that takes but a part of its food for itself, while bringing the rest to the nest for its young. This is what we should do, how we should prove by our works that we do love God: *totum opus nostrum in operatione consistit* ["all our work consists in action"].[11]

The second maxim of this faithful servant of God was always to see our Savior Jesus Christ in others, to inspire our charity toward them. In the Holy Father, the pope, he saw our divine Savior as pontiff and head of the Church. The bishop he saw as Jesus the bishop and prince of pastors. He saw the doctors of the Church as Jesus the doctor, priests as Jesus the priest, all religious as Jesus the religious, the king as Jesus the sovereign ruler, gentlemen as Jesus the noble one, magistrates, governors, and other officers as Jesus the judge and all-wise ruler. In the Gospel the kingdom of Heaven is compared to a merchant, and so it was that he looked on traders. He saw Jesus the worker in the artisans, Jesus the poor man in the poor, Jesus suffering in the sick and dying. He looked on all states in life, seeing in each the image of his sovereign Lord who dwelt in the person of his neighbor. He was moved, in this view, to honor, respect, love, and serve each person as our Lord, and our Lord in each individual. He wanted his followers and all those with whom he spoke to enter into these same sentiments, to make their charity toward the neighbor more constant and more perfect.

This is a sketch of the mind of Monsieur Vincent, traced out for the most part by his own hand, without his being aware of doing so. His constant effort was to remain in the background, to cover the gifts and grace he had

---

11. *CED* XI:41.

received with the veil of silent humility. God willed it so that he unwittingly revealed much of the graces and excellent qualities poured into his soul, to make him a worthy instrument of his glory, and to use him in those great enterprises for the good of his Church, as we shall see in this book.

To summarize in a few words what has been said in this chapter about Monsieur Vincent, we can say without fear of contradiction:

(1) He was a saint ever directed toward God and leading others to him, as well and directing all things to God as to their final goal.

(2) He was humble, mistrustful of his own lights, quick to take counsel in his doubts, and attentive to the Holy Spirit as his guide and teacher.

(3) He was mild in his way of acting, understanding the weaknesses of others and accommodating himself to events and persons.

(4) He was firm in his accomplishment of the will of God and whatever concerned the spiritual development of his own community. He was not swayed by opposition or cast down by difficulties.

(5) He was straightforward, never allowing himself to be turned aside from the ways of God by any consideration of human respect.

(6) He was simple in his behavior, rejecting all pretense, duplicity, artifice, or prudence of the flesh.

(7) He was prudent, choosing the best means of accomplishing the end he ever proposed to himself, which was to do what he considered most pleasing to God. As much as it was in his power he took care in carrying out his designs that he would not shock or sadden anyone, and either avoided difficulties or overcame them by his patience and his prayers.

(8) He was circumspect, not speaking of matters before their time or to those with no right to be informed. He used to say, "The demon rejoices in needless publicity given to good works. These then become trivial and without effect."

(9) He was reserved and circumspect, not given to levity, not pushing himself to the fore.

(10) Lastly, he was disinterested, not seeking honors or personal satisfaction for himself, or any temporal gain. His sole goal, in imitation of his divine Master, was the glory of God and the salvation and sanctification of souls.

CHAPTER TWENTY

The Birth and Establishment of the Congregation of the Mission

WE COULD truthfully say that this Congregation in its beginnings was that small mustard seed spoken of in the Gospel: although the least of all the seeds, it becomes a great tree in which the birds of the air build their nests. Nothing was so small as the Congregation at its commencement, not only in external things, but in the mind of Monsieur Vincent and the first priests associated with him. They thought of themselves as the least of all those engaged in Church ministry. They committed themselves to the humblest tasks, serving the lowest and least appreciated in the common opinion of the world, such as instructing and catechizing the poor, particularly in the small villages and the most abandoned places. They would help, assist, and aid the sick poor, and disposing both the poor and the sick to make good general confessions. They thought of themselves as servants of the pastors and other priests, but also of the villagers, the galley slaves, or any other person in need. They were of a mind to do this gratuitously, with no recompense whatever. They considered it an honor to serve Jesus Christ in the person of the poor and accepted it as a favor that pastors would allow them to carry out these works of charity in their parishes.

It pleased God to pour out abundant blessings upon these small beginnings, and there soon developed a large community which happily has expanded to many other places, as we shall describe below. This community has contributed, and continues to contribute, with special benediction, to the advancement of the kingdom of Jesus Christ.

As has already been said, in 1625 after the death of Madame de Gondi, Monsieur Vincent moved to the College des Bons Enfants, which had been obtained to him through the archbishop's efforts, supported by Madame and the general, to carry out the purpose of their foundation. Monsieur Portail, of whom we have already spoken, and who had already spent twelve or fifteen years with Monsieur Vincent, now saw a new opportunity to devote himself to God. He moved to the College des Bons Enfants with Monsieur Vincent, deciding to join the new company of priests and to commit himself to the missions. He persuaded another priest to join him in this decision, promising him fifty *ecus* each year for personal expenses.[1] The three went

---

1. Adrien Gambart, priest of the diocese of Noyon. Among other works he published *Le Missionnaire paroissial*, 10 vols., Paris, 1668, which reflects the method of preaching recommended by Saint Vincent.

from village to village, catechizing, exhorting, hearing confessions, and performing the other exercises of the mission with simplicity, humility, and charity, all at their own expense, not asking for anything for themselves. They worked first in those places where the missions had already been set up, but gradually moved to other parishes, chiefly in the diocese of Paris. Since they did not have the means to engage watchmen to live in the College des Bons Enfants, in their absence they left the keys with one of the neighbors.

Who would have thought that from such modest beginnings great progress would be made, such as we now see? Or that two poor priests going out to the smallest villages and other forgotten places would actually be laying the foundations of such a large spiritual edifice which God was pleased to raise up in his Church? Monsieur Vincent spoke of this marvel one day to his community at Saint Lazare:

> We went plainly and simply, sent by their lordships the bishops, to evangelize the poor, just as our Lord did. That is all we did. And for his part, God accomplished what he had foreseen from all eternity. He so blessed our work that other clerics joined us, asking to be received into our Company, not all at once, but from time to time. O Lord, who would ever have thought we would develop to our present state? If anyone had said as much then, I would have thought he was mocking me. And yet, that is how God began the Company. Oh well, would you call that human which no one even thought of? Neither myself nor Monsieur Portail ever did. Alas, we were far from that![2]

The archbishop of Paris, Jean Francois de Gondi, later gave official approbation to the institution of the Congregation of the Mission, by a decree dated April 24, 1626, in the same style as he used in the contract of foundation. Two good priests from Picardy, Fathers Francois du Coudray[3] and Jean de la Salle,[4] came to Monsieur Vincent and offered to join Monsieur Portail in living and working under Monsieur Vincent's direction. He received them and associated them with himself in executing the foundation set up for the purpose, by an act certified by two notaries of the Chatelet on September 4, 1626.

The late king, Louis XIII, of glorious memory, by letters patent of May

---

2. *CED* XII:8-9.
3. Francois du Coudray, 1586-1649, joined the Congregation in 1626, whose only other members were the founder and Antoine Portail. Vincent chose him to go to Rome to negotiate the approbation of the Congregation; he remained there from 1631 to 1635. He served in many houses: Paris, Toul, Marseilles, La Rose, Richelieu. His theological knowledge was marred by some unorthodox opinions, and Vincent took steps to prevent him from spreading errors.
4. Jean de la Salle, 1598-1639, a gifted biblical expositor (see *CED* XII:293), came to Monsieur Vincent in 1626. He was the first director of the internal seminary (novitiate), 1637.

1627, at the recommendation of the general of the galleys, confirmed and approved the contract of foundation allowing the association or Congregation of the priests of the Mission to live in common, to reside in various parts of the kingdom of France as shall seem good to them, and to accept all legacies, alms, or other gifts which shall be made to them.[5]

God thus blessed the beginnings of the Congregation of the Mission by the special gift of his merciful Providence. By this same Providence he allowed it to increase and multiply. For this purpose he inspired several other clerics to work with Monsieur Vincent at the harvest of souls. Four other priests joined, besides the three already mentioned, that is, Jean Becu of the village of Brache in the diocese of Amiens,[6] Antoine Lucas of Paris,[7] Jean Brunet of the village of Rion in Auvergne in the diocese of Clermont,[8] and Jean Dehorgny of the village of Estrees in the diocese of Noyon.[9]

These seven thus associated themselves and joined Monsieur Vincent to live and die in the Congregation of the Mission, promising God to remain faithful their entire life in working for the salvation and sanctification of the poor country people. This they faithfully accomplished. We could say these men were like the seven priests of Joshua. Their trumpets broke down the walls of Jericho, and their example, zeal, and virtue attracted several others to this holy army.

By a papal bull of Urban VIII dated January [12,] 1632, this pious Company was raised formally to the status of a Congregation, the priests of the Congregation of the Mission, under the direction of Monsieur Vincent.[10] The pope gave him the authority to set down regulations for the good order of the community. To further the work of the institute, the king gave new letters patent, dated May 1642, approved by the Parlement of Paris in September of that same year.[11]

The bull of Urban VIII gave the name Priests of the Congregation of the Mission to those of this community. By this name they are distinguished from all other communities, even those who work at the same sort of mission

---

5. *CED* XIII:225-26.
6. Jean Becu, 1592-1667, ordained a priest in 1616, came to the Congregation in 1626. Two of his brothers followed him, and one of his sisters became a Daughter of Charity.
7. Antoine Lucas, 1600-1656, entered the Congregation in 1626, and was ordained two years later. He was known for his zeal and talent for preaching. He died a victim of his zeal for the plague-stricken.
8. Jean Joseph Brunet, 1597-1649, joined Vincent in 1627. He died a victim of his zeal for the plague-stricken.
9. Jean Dehorgny (or d'Horgny), ?-1667, joined Vincent in 1627, and was ordained a priest a year later. He directed the College des Bons Enfants on three occasions. He was assistant to the superior general twice, superior of the house in Rome twice, and director of the Daughters of Charity from 1660 to 1667. Several of his conferences to them are still extant.
10. *CED* XIII:257-67. By contemporary reckoning, the year was 1633, since the papal year began not on January 1 but on March 25.
11. *CED* XIII:286-87.

as those of Monsieur Vincent. We have thought it necessary to underline this to avoid possible misunderstandings, if this distinction is not kept in mind.[12]

---

12. Alexander VII completed the work of Urban VIII by the approving the constitution of the company, 22 September 1655 (*CED* XIII:380-85). By this brief he approved the taking of vows, while explaining their exact nature for the Congregation of the Mission. He further legislated the exemption of the congregation from the jurisdiction of bishops in matters of internal administration, but respecting their jurisdiction in those things regarding the missions to be given in their dioceses. The first vows were taken by Monsieur Vincent and some of his confreres September 8, 1629.

CHAPTER TWENTY-ONE

Some Remarkable Statements of Monsieur Vincent Regarding the Spirit of Humility and the Other Virtuous Dispositions He Wished to See as the Foundation of His New Congregation

MONSIEUR VINCENT saw that God's hand was with him and his fellow priests, and that God had blessed the beginnings of this new enterprise. He wanted this new structure of the Congregation of the Mission to have a foundation proportional to the heights it one day might attain. Like a good architect he wanted an absolutely firm foundation on which to build. His choice was nothing less than the virtue of humility. He realized that among the temptations and distractions the Missionaries would be exposed to in their work, the best means of safeguarding their souls and their salvation was to hold fast to a low opinion of themselves. They must become despised and abject in their own eyes to be great and estimable before God. There was nothing to fear in humility, however well developed it might be. What was to be feared, even abhorred, was the least glorification to which they might come by presuming on themselves. This is why, from the very beginning of the Congregation, he sought to inspire its members with a spirit of abasement, humility, deprecation, and contempt of self.

He led them to think of themselves always as the least of all those who worked in the Church and to judge all others as superior to themselves. We know of no better way to convey his sentiments than to quote what he said once when a new priest recently received into the Congregation had referred to it as "this holy Congregation." This humble servant of God stopped him and said:

> Monsieur, when you speak of our Company, we ought never use the terms "this holy Company" or "this holy Congregation," or any such terms. Rather, we ought to say "this poor Company," "this little Company," or some such expression. We should imitate the Son of God, who called the company of his apostles and disciples "little flock," or "little company."
>
> How I wish that God would give this grace to this wretched Congregation that it might be well-grounded in humility, that it might be founded and built upon this virtue, and that humility would ever remain part of its structure. Gentlemen, be not deceived. Without humility, we have nothing. I speak not only of exterior humility but mainly of humility of the heart. This leads us to believe

truly that no one on earth is more wretched than you and I, and that the Congregation of the Mission is the most wretched of all the congregations, the poorest in numbers and in quality of its members. We ought to be at ease when people speak about us this way. Alas, what is it when we want to be regarded differently, to wish to be treated differently than the Son of God? It is insupportable pride. When the Son of God was on earth, what did people say of him? What did they think of him? He was regarded as a fool, a seditionist, a bumpkin, a sinner, though he was none of these. He even allowed Barabbas to be preferred to him, a robber, a murderer, a very evil man. O Savior, O my Savior, how your humility will confound sinners, especially miserable me, on the day of judgment! Be on your guard when you go on mission, you who speak in public. Often enough people will be so touched they will be moved to tears by what you say. They will even say, "Blessed is the womb that bore you, and the breasts that nursed you."[1] We have occasionally heard such things. Nature is pleased and vanity born if we do not turn from these vain praises and if we work for anything else than the glory of God and the salvation of souls. To do otherwise is to preach ourselves and not Jesus Christ.

And what about someone who preaches for applause, praise, esteem, and reputation? What shall we say of this person, this preacher? What, a person who uses the word of God, who speaks of divine things to acquire honor and a reputation, yes, it is a sacrilege. O my God, give the grace to this poor little Company that none of its members falls into this unhappy fault. Gentlemen, we shall never be properly disposed to fulfill our duty toward God if we do not have a profound humility and an entire disregard for ourselves. No, if the Congregation of the Mission is not humble, and if it is not persuaded that it can do nothing of value of itself and will spoil everything rather than succeed, it will never do any good. But if it lives in the Spirit, then, gentlemen, it will be a fitting instrument in God's designs, for through such people God accomplishes his true and great deeds.

Several doctors who explain today's Gospel[2] teach that the parable of the five wise and five foolish virgins ought to be understood as applying to people who have entered religious communities. If it be true that half of these persons will be lost, alas, have we nothing to fear? What of me, first of all? Should I not wonder? Let

---
1. Luke 11:27.
2. November 25, Feast of Saint Catherine.

us, gentlemen, encourage one another, and not lose heart. Let us give ourselves to God completely, renounce ourselves, our personal satisfactions, our ease, and our vanity. We should recognize that our greatest enemy is ourselves. Yet let us do all the good we can and do it with all possible care. It is not enough to help our neighbor, to fast, to make mental prayer, to work on the missions. All that is good, but not enough. We must do all this in the same spirit as did our Savior and in the way he did, humbly and purely, so that the name of God be glorified and his holy will accomplished.

Plants cannot produce more excellent fruit than that dictated by the nature of the stock on which they grow. We are like the stock of those who would come after us, whose perfection is determined by us. If we have done well, they shall do well, following our example. Those who stay will teach those who follow them the way the first members of the Company practiced virtue, and these in turn will teach others, all aided by the grace of God merited by the original members. How is it that we see in the world certain families in whom the fear of God dwells? I have one such family in mind, whose grandfather and father I knew, both good men, and even today I know that the children carry on this same tradition. Where does this come from? Chiefly from their parents, who have merited this grace from God by their good and holy lives, according to the promise of God himself that he would bless such families to the thousandth generation.[3] On the other hand, we see husbands and wives leading good lives, but who nevertheless seem to lose everything, and nothing succeeds. Why is this? Because their parents have earned God's punishment by the faults they have committed. This punishment has been passed on to their descendants, according to what is written, to the fourth generation. Although these punishments are understood to refer chiefly to material things, we can apply the thought to spiritual things as well. If we are exact in observing our rules, if we practice well the virtues appropriate to a true missionary, we will merit in some way this same blessing for our children, that is, to those who will succeed us. They will be able to live good lives following our example. If we do ill, it is to be feared that they will do the same and even worse, because nature is inclined always to disorder and seeks after the self.

We ought to consider ourselves as the fathers of those who will follow us. The Company is still in its infancy, it has only just been born. It has been just a few years since it began. Is that not to be in

---

3. Exod 34:7.

infancy? Our successors in the next two or three hundred years will look on us as the fathers of the Company, even for those who have joined later. They too will be counted as fathers of the community, for anyone in the first hundred years will be so regarded.

When you look up a passage from some Father of the first centuries, you say, "This passage was from the pen of a Father of the first or second century." In the same way, they will say at some later day, the first priests of the Congregation of the Mission did this or that. They lived this way, and they observed such and such virtues. Because things are like this, gentlemen, do we not have a duty to leave a great example to our successors, since the good they do depends in some way on us? If it is true, as some Fathers of the Church say, that God allows parents in hell to see their children's evil as an added torment, then the more these children sin, the more blameworthy are the parents who have caused their children's evil deeds by the bad example given them.

Saint Augustine says, on the other hand, that God allows fathers and mothers in heaven to see the good their children do upon earth, for their greater happiness. In the same way, gentlemen, what a consolation and joy for us when God allows us to see the good our Company accomplishes, abounding in good deeds, faithfully observing the daily schedule, living in the practice of the virtues, and giving good example everywhere. How miserable I am, that I do not act this way! Pray for me, gentlemen, pray to God for me, my brothers, that I may be converted.

Let us all give ourselves to God and to everything that is worthwhile, working, helping the poor country people who await us. By God's grace some of our priests are almost always engaged in our work, some more, some less, in this or that mission, in this village or some other. I remember formerly when I was returning from one of the missions, as I approached the gates of Paris I felt they would fall upon me and crush me. Rarely did I return from a mission but this thought came to me. The reason was, I heard a voice saying within me, "You have gone out to such and such a village, but others await the same help as you brought them." Again, I seemed to hear it said, "If you had not been there, probably many persons would have died in their miserable state and would have been damned. If you have found such and such sins in the one parish, do you not think you would probably find the same in the neighboring parishes? And yet you leave, with people dying in sin, and you will in some way be responsible for their loss. You should fear that God will punish you for this." This is how my spirit was troubled.⁴

On another occasion he said to his followers:

The state of the Missionary conforms to the Gospel maxims. These essentially are to leave all, following the example of the apostles, to follow Jesus Christ and to imitate his manner of living The devil alone could find something to complain of in such a life, as someone once said to me. Nothing is more Christian than to go from village to village, helping poor people in working out their salvation, even at the cost of fatigue and inconvenience. This is how several of our confreres now work in a village of the diocese of Evreux, where they must sleep on straw. Why? To help souls reach paradise, by teaching and by suffering. Does this not resemble what our Lord came to do? He had only a stone on which to lay his head. Yet, he went from place to place to gain souls to God and even gave his life for them. He could not make us comprehend any better how precious these souls are to him, nor persuade us more effectively to spare no pains in teaching them his doctrine and washing them in the fountain of his precious blood. Would you like to know how to receive this grace? Devote yourselves to the virtue of humility, for the more one is humble the greater shall be his love for his neighbor. Charity is the paradise of communities. It is the soul of the virtues, but it is humility which adorns and guards them.

Congregations which are humble are like valleys, which attract all the life-giving waters flowing down from the mountain. If we are empty of ourselves, God will fill us with himself, for he does not wish anything to go empty. Humble yourselves, then, my brothers, so that God may glance at this little Company committed to serving the Church. Can we say Company when we speak of a mere handful of men, lowly in birth, knowledge, and virtue, the dregs and the outcasts of the world? Every day I pray two or three times to ask God to finish us off if we are not contributing to his glory. What! gentlemen, would we want to continue if we were not pleasing to God and did not procure his greater glory?⁵

These then are the foundations upon which Monsieur Vincent wished to build the spiritual edifice of his Congregation, that is, humility and charity.

Apropos of this, the late Father de Condren, general of the Oratory,⁶ whose memory is held in benediction, said one day to Monsieur Vincent:

---

4. *CED* XI:439-45.
5. *CED* XI:1-2.
6. Charles de Condren, second superior general, 1588-1641.

How happy you are, Monsieur, that your Congregation bears the marks of a foundation of Jesus Christ. In founding the Church he delighted in choosing the poor, the unlettered, and the crude to spread his message throughout the whole world. He used the humblest means to show forth his almighty power, refuted the wisdom of the philosophers by poor sinners, and resisted the power of kings by the weakness of these simple men. It is the same with you. Most of those called to your Congregation are persons of the lowest class, at best rather ordinary. They do not have much learning, but as such are fit instruments to fulfill the designs of Jesus Christ. He uses them to destroy pretense and vanity.[7]

---

7. *CED* XI:132.

CHAPTER TWENTY-TWO

The Establishment of the Priests of the Congregation of the Mission at Saint Lazare

THIS MYSTIC JERUSALEM began little by little to develop into a new city, built from living stones shaped by the practice of the appropriate virtues. It is true, however, that the College des Bons Enfants furnished neither the space nor the revenue to support any except a few persons. God came to the rescue in a manner that will surprise the reader, but in keeping with his infinite wisdom. While the good priest missionaries were occupying themselves solely with extending the kingdom of Jesus Christ and gaining souls for it, God's providence arranged things to enable the community to establish itself in the house of Saint Lazare near Paris.[1]

This was an ecclesiastical manor, seat of high, middle, and lower courts, in which besides a large expanse of land, buildings, and yards, all services and means of support for the new foundation could be obtained. The circumstances surrounding this transaction clearly show God's hand. This was especially so since it took place contrary to all human expectations and even in the face of situations which, humanly speaking, should have made it impossible.

We cannot better realize what occurred than by the account given by Monsieur Vincent,[2] and confirmed after his death by the leading actor in this affair. His virtue and position as doctor of the Sorbonne and pastor of a parish in Paris merit credence. This individual was the late Monsieur de Lestocq, doctor of the faculty of the Sorbonne and pastor of Saint Laurent in Paris. He left us a written record in his own hand of these events.[3] We see in them how admirable was the guidance given the Congregation of the Mission, and how pure and disinterested was the part played by the one destined by Providence to bring this about.

---

1. Saint Lazare was situated north of Paris on the road from the city to Saint Denis, in what is today the faubourg Saint Denis. It was probably on the site of the ancient abbey which Saint Gregory of Tours mentioned in Book 6, ch. 11 of his history, the abbey governed by Saint Domnolus. It was eventually transformed into a leprosarium at the time of the Crusades, when this disease was spreading quickly through Europe. By the seventeenth century, there were no more lepers interned there, and the house was occupied by some canons of Saint Victor, religious who followed the rule of Saint Augustine.
2. *CED* V:533-34.
3. Guillaume de Lestocq was the pastor of Saint Laurent, the parish neighboring Saint Lazare, from 1628 until the day of his death, May 9, 1661. He was the main instrument in achieving the union of the Congregation of the Mission with the Priory of Saint Lazare.

An account of the events leading to the establishment of the Congregation of the Mission in the house of Saint Lazare near Paris, written and signed by the late Monsieur de Lestocq, doctor of the Sorbonne and pastor of Saint Laurent[4]

Father Adrien Le Bon, religious of the order of Canons Regular of Saint Augustine and prior of Saint Lazare, had some difficulties with his religious in 1630. These led him to think about changing his position for another benefice. Several were offered him, abbeys or other significant benefices, but his friends convinced him that it would be preferable to resolve the dispute within his own community. A conference among them, in the presence of four doctors, was proposed. He agreed to this, and the religious also agreed to attend. This conference was held at the home of a well-regarded and saintly doctor. The prior aired his complaints, and the religious replied, speaking through the sub-prior. It was agreed to draw up a formal rule of life for the future, governing their behavior. The prior persisted in his wish to leave his office. Hearing of the priests who devoted themselves to the missions under the direction of Monsieur Vincent, whom he did not know, he thought that perhaps they could be invited to the priory. In this way, the monks would share in the good being done in the Church.

As his neighbor and friend, I was invited to go along to meet with Monsieur Vincent to discuss this possibility. I pointed out to him how this thought must have come from heaven, for these good priests work for the welfare of the country people, so much in need of help, by instruction and help in confessing their sins. It seems they were ordinarily unable to do so to the parish clergy, either through ignorance or shame. I was able to speak this way of their work and reassure him, for I had seen it at first hand. Besides, I assured him that he would see a man of God among them, referring of course to Monsieur Vincent.

Together, then, we went to the College des Bons Enfants near the gate of Saint Victor to inform Monsieur Vincent of the reason for our visit. We told him that we had heard great things of the Congregation and of the work it did in favor of the poor peasants. The prior said he would gladly contribute to such a charitable work and proposed for this purpose giving the house of Saint Lazare to Monsieur Vincent for his use.

---

4. *CED* XIII:244-48.

This generous offer astounded the humble servant of God, with the same effect as an unexpected clap of thunder. Upon seeing this, the prior remarked to Monsieur Vincent, "Monsieur, you tremble." "Yes," he replied, "your offer does astound me, for it appears so far beyond us that I dare not think of it. We are simple, poor priests. We live humbly, with no other purpose than to serve the poor country people. We are much indebted to you, Monsieur, for your good will and we thank you most humbly."

In a word, he showed no inclination to accept the offer and seemed to suggest that any further discussion was out of the question. However, the pleasant and affable way he was received so touched the heart of Monsieur Le Bon that he did not give up. He said only that he would give Monsieur Vincent six months to think it over.

After this he again asked me to go with him to see Monsieur Vincent to make the same offer. He stressed that God was moving him to give up the priory in favor of the Congregation of the Mission. For my part, I begged Monsieur Vincent not to let this opportunity pass, but this did not change his mind. He gave as his reasons the small number of priests in the community only recently founded, that his move would be talked about and that he did not relish the publicity, the notoriety, and lastly, that he did not deserve such a favor of the prior.

At this moment, Monsieur Le Bon heard the dinner bell ring. He asked Monsieur Vincent if he and I might dine with Monsieur Vincent and the community. The modesty of the priests, the reading at table, and the sense of good order everywhere so impressed Monsieur Le Bon that he continued to press Monsieur Vincent. This continued for more than twenty separate meetings in the space of the next six months. As a good friend of Monsieur Vincent I felt free enough to say that I thought he was resisting the Holy Spirit, that he would have to answer to God for his refusal, seeing that it gave him an opportunity to establish and perfect his Congregation.

I can not begin to tell you how insistently we acted. Jacob did not show greater patience in his quest for Rachel or insist so strongly for the angel's blessing than did the prior and I to have an affirmative answer from Monsieur Vincent. We besought him more earnestly than the Canaanite woman did the apostles. Finally, a year later, the prior said to him: "Monsieur, what sort of man are you? If you do not want to discuss this business any more, will you at least tell me of someone whose advice you respect? Someone you have confidence in? What friend do you have in Paris whom we could speak with? I have the agreement of all my religious, but only yours is lacking. No one who wishes you well is advising you against accepting this offer."

Monsieur Vincent then mentioned that Monsieur Andre Duval, doctor of the Sorbonne, a holy man who had written the lives of several saints, was a friend of his.[5] "We will do what he advises."

The prior went to see him, explained the matter, agreed upon all conditions, and finally drew up the accord between the prior and the religious of Saint Lazare on the one hand and Monsieur Vincent and the priests of the Congregation of the Mission on the other, dated January 7, 1632.[6] Monsieur Vincent had at last given in to all the importunities, by myself among others, and could have said on this occasion: *Raucae factae sunt fauces meae* ["My throat is parched"].[7] I would gladly have carried on my own shoulders the father of the missionaries to Saint Lazare and force him to accept. He, however, did not look at the exterior or the advantages of the place and all the outlying buildings and property. During the negotiations he had not even come to inspect the property. It was not the good location that attracted him but only God's will and the spiritual good to be done there.

After all conceivable objections, he finally accepted it for that reason alone. The following day, January 8, 1632, he came, and all passed off with gentleness and to the satisfaction of the whole house.

It will then be seen that *digitus Dei hic est* ["the finger of God is here"],[8] and that it was the promised land to which Abraham had been led. Monsieur Vincent was that true Abraham, great servant of God, whose children were destined to fill the promised land, and whose family would live for the ages.

The pastor of Saint Laurent sent the foregoing account to the successor of the late Monsieur Vincent,[9] the superior general of the Congregation of the Mission, accompanied by the following letter, dated October 30, 1660:

Monsieur, the wish you expressed to have an account of the

---

5. Andre Duval, 1554-1638, was a doctor of the Sorbonne, author of several learned works, friend and advisor of Saint Vincent, who never took important decisions without consulting him. He was so upset at seeing his portrait in one of the rooms at Saint Lazare that he insisted that Vincent remove it. See J. Calvet, "Un confesseur de Saint Vincent," *Petites Annales de Saint Vincent* 4 (May 1903):135.
6. *CED* XIII:234-44.
7. Ps 69:4.
8. Exod 8:19.
9. Rene Almeras, 1613-1672, nephew of Madame Goussault, and a civil lawyer, left everything to enter the Congregation in 1637. He was ordained a priest in 1639. The saint entrusted him with many important positions, such as director of the novitiate, and superior in Rome.

events leading Monsieur Vincent and his Congregation to Saint Lazare, together with my respect for his memory, have led me to prepare an account, which I enclose. Monsieur, I recount only the hundredth part of what took place, for I cannot detail all the pious conversations between the prior of Saint Lazare and me with the late Monsieur Vincent for more than a year and on thirty separate visits. We had thousands of occasions to discuss various objections and dispose him to accept Saint Lazare.

Most other persons would have been delighted to accept such an offer, but he refused. That is the way it is with many good projects. Moses refused to go to Egypt, or Jeremiah to the people, but despite their excuses God chose them and sent them on their mission. Their vocation was divine and miraculous, in which nature had no part. My account cannot do justice to this affair, of which God was the author and finisher. I could only sketch out these events. Let he who would, supply for my silence. Believe me when I say that I venerate the memory of the late Monsieur Vincent and count it a blessing to have been known and loved by him.

Such is the authentic testimony, having many details which the pious reader will be able to judge with the weights of the Hebrew Temple. It shows the degree of virtue and perfection to which the grace of Jesus Christ had raised Monsieur Vincent. We can see how his heart was detached from all self-interest, all human respect. He looked to God alone in all his activities, considering only those propositions most advantageous to his glory and most in conformity to his holy will.

One circumstance we ought not pass over. It will allow us to see not only the perfect detachment this great servant of God had from all temporal things and material advantages but also the exactness and fidelity which he and his confreres maintained, ever towards the least things that might contribute to the good order of their Congregation and to the quality of the service he proposed to render to God.

Once the main articles of agreement had been worked out, one remained which seemed small enough, but not to Monsieur Vincent. The prior hoped that his religious would share the dormitory with the Missionaries. He thought that it would cause no harm to the one group, but be a source of edification to the others by the good example his religious would have in the practice of the virtues and in the regularity of Monsieur Vincent and his followers. This wise superior would not agree, foreseeing the many problems that would arise, leading to the loss of the good order established among the Missionaries. He asked the pastor of Saint Laurent to inform the prior that the priests of the Mission remained in silence from night prayer until after dinner the following day, at which time an hour of conversation followed. Again, they observed silence until after supper, to be followed by another hour of conversation. After this, they spoke only when it became necessary, and then in a low voice. He was convinced that if silence were taken from a community, disorder and confusion would surely come in to take its place. He remarked once to someone, if you see a community which observes silence exactly, you may be sure it observes the rest of the regulations equally well. On the contrary, where silence is not observed it is almost impossible for the other rules to be followed. It is likely that the religious would not want to be bound by such a strict rule of silence. This, in turn, would almost surely lead to the loss of this practice among the Missionaries.

Thus Monsieur Vincent requested Monsieur de Lestocq to present his thoughts to the prior, as we find in one of his handwritten letters.[10] He continued by proposing a compromise, that the religious should live apart from the dormitory. He stated his position clearly in these remarkable words: "I would prefer to remain in our deprivation rather than depart from the designs of God upon us."

He remained so firm in this position that the provision had to be stricken from the agreement before he would consent to the other articles. He preferred to lose all the great temporal advantages that might come to him rather than agree to something which would block the spiritual progress of his Congregation. What made him firm and even inflexible on this point was his esteem and love for solitude and interior recollection. The Missionaries needed this especially, since they were exposed by their vocation to all sorts of distracting influences. He used to say on this subject, "True Missionaries ought to be like Carthusians in their houses and like apostles outside them."

After signing the agreement by which Monsieur le Bon ceded the priory, the house, and dependencies of Saint Lazare to the Congregation of the Mission, the archbishop of Paris conferred it as a benefice under his control, by letters dated December 31, 1631.[11] Our Holy Father, Pope Urban VIII, confirmed this by a bull, March 15, 1635, but it was not drawn up until April 18, 1655.[12]

The provosts of merchants and magistrates of Paris also approved the establishment of the Missionaries in the house of Saint Lazare. The king gave his approval by letters patent, which were given to the Parlement for its consent. However, a certain well-known religious community opposed

---

10. *CED* I:137-41.
11. *CED* XIII:271-76. Abelly's text reads 1632, a typographical error.
12. On January 8, 1632, the first decree of union was approved by the archbishop of Paris, and by letters patent signed by the king. *CED* XIII:248-54, 254-57. This union was confirmed by Alexander VII in 1655. *CED* XIII:372-80.

the move, alleging that the property belonged to them.[13] This position was rejected by an official decree, so that the letters of the king could be registered on September 17, 1632. We should not fail to remark that while the case was being heard in court, Monsieur Vincent remained calmly in prayer in the Sainte Chapelle at the palace. He was totally indifferent as to the outcome of the affair.

This is what he wrote to a virtuous friend in whom he had complete confidence:

> You are well aware that the Religious of N. N. are disputing our accepting Saint Lazare. You would hardly believe the way I have treated them, in keeping with what the Gospel ordains. They have no case, as Monsieur Duval has assured me, along with others who know the situation. By God's grace I remain as indifferent to this as to anything else I have ever been involved with. Please thank God with me for this grace.[14]

Another matter connected with this case is still worthy of comment, for it shows the marvelous detachment of this great servant of God. Upon taking possession of Saint Lazare he accepted the care of three or four mentally disturbed persons committed by their families to be housed in the priory. It is impossible to overstate the charity with which Monsieur Vincent looked after, by himself or others, these persons who offered so little natural satisfaction. They were incapable of recognizing the care being taken of them and in fact were usually unclean, embarrassing, and occasionally even dangerous. Seeing the possibility of his eviction from the house of Saint Lazare by the opposing religious community, well-regarded and with friends in the right places, he began to prepare as was his custom for whatever outcome the trial might bring. He set himself to consider what do, as he told a confidant later. Yet he thought nothing of the new home, an ecclesiastical manor house, so commodious and advantageous to his Congregation, situated at the gates of Paris. His only concern was for the mentally disturbed persons he would have to leave behind. He thought more of the service he rendered them, or rather Jesus Christ in their person, than he did of all the other advantages of the house, which he looked on with complete indifference. How different his sentiments from those of worldly people, and how much more elevated his thoughts than those of ordinary men. He regarded it as foolish to be attached to earthly things and regarded serving them as the highest wisdom. He regarded service given from love of Jesus Christ as a great treasure he hated to lose and thought nothing of losing what he had just begun to enjoy, and which was so suitable for the upkeep and support of his

---

13. The religious of Saint Victor. *CED* I:148-49.
14. *CED* I:151-52.

new Congregation. What good reason the holy apostle had to say that God was pleased to confound the wisdom of the world! To be wise in the eyes of God it sometimes becomes necessary to become foolish in the eyes of men.

Acquaintances of Monsieur Vincent could testify that he saw as fully and clearly as could be hoped for from a person in his position. There was no frivolity or undue vehemence in his person. His conduct was founded not on simple human reasoning but on the maxims and truths of the Gospel. These were engraved on his heart, and he took them as the foundation of his life and had them ever present to his mind. He conformed himself in all things to the doctrine and example of Jesus Christ, and in keeping with this as much as humanly possible he fled from all vainglory or ostentation. On the contrary, he embraced with enthusiasm humility, abjection, contempt, and self-denial, and similar practices. He did this to resemble more closely him who was God by nature yet made himself a man, subject to the opprobrium of men and rejection by the people.

In this spirit Monsieur Vincent obtained the peaceful possession of Saint Lazare and wished to continue this service of humility and charity, although he was under no obligation to do so. He continued to receive in the house those rejected by the world, whom no one wanted to care for. He looked on them as the sick members of Jesus Christ, and in this view he provided them with every service and every corporal and spiritual help of which they were capable of receiving.

CHAPTER TWENTY-THREE

Account of the Great Good Accomplished in the Church by the Founding of the Congregation of the Mission, of which Monsieur Vincent Was the Prime Mover; First, the Establishment of the Confraternity of Charity for the Corporal and Spiritual Help of the Sick Poor

IT IS ASTOUNDING and almost unbelievable, were it not for the accounts of so many people who knew Monsieur Vincent, that a person who thought so humbly of himself and who regarded himself as the last of all priests, would be at the head of a newly founded Company daily growing larger. He was a poor and simple priest, seeking always to remain in the background. Despite himself, he became involved in many significant activities for the service of the Church and the glory of God, as we shall see in this book. But as a holy Father of the Church said, Charity has no measure! It never says "enough," and when it takes possession of a soul it makes the person untiring in his efforts, to the extent prudence allows, to undertake anything that might contribute to the great glory of his divine Savior. It seems to him that all things are possible because of the one who strengthens him.

If we know a tree by its fruits and charity by its good works, we can say with assurance that God had blessed Monsieur Vincent with special graces to enable him to do so much. The charity with which the Holy Spirit filled his heart was so plentiful that it seemed the world was too small to measure up to his desire that God be better known, loved, and glorified.

We will give in this chapter, and in others to follow, a summary account of some of his works which date from the very beginning of the Congregation of the Mission. We will follow approximately the chronological order of these events but occasionally will interrupt this order to discuss related matters. In Book Two we will enlarge upon our treatment of these works of charity.

We will begin in this chapter with the establishment of the Confraternity of Charity for the help of the sick poor. Their corporal and spiritual sufferings so touched the heart of Monsieur Vincent that he became very sensitive on this point. After seeing the good results of the first of these assemblies or Confraternities of Charity which God had established through him in Bresse, as we have noted in one of the preceding chapters,[1] he decided to extend this

---
1. Ch. 10.

good work wherever possible. Wherever he gave a mission himself or his priests gave them, he set up this confraternity for the relief of the sick poor. God so blessed his efforts that there was hardly a place where a mission had been given that the Confraternity of Charity was not established.

Since it is not enough just to begin good works without trying to sustain and perfect them, Monsieur Vincent considered carefully what had to be done to maintain the confraternities. These were composed mostly of simple village women who needed help and encouragement in their works of charity, in which occasional contradictions would arise. They needed advice, especially in their help for the sick.

Although he had given well thought-out regulations for their guidance and visited the various confraternities as often as he could or had his priests visit them, they became too many to visit as often as he wished. Divine Providence, which watches over all, then inspired a virtuous lady to devote herself, under the guidance of Monsieur Vincent, to this charitable work. Because she contributed so much to these Confraternities of Charity and cooperated with Monsieur Vincent in other activities of which we will speak later, it is important to say more about this good woman.

She was Mademoiselle Louise de Marillac,[2] widow of Monsieur le Gras, secretary of the queen mother, Marie de Medici. God had bestowed upon her all the virtues and dispositions suitable for success in all the activities he had destined for her. She was notable for her good judgment, strong virtue, and universal charity, which allowed her to display an untiring zeal for helping her neighbor, particularly the poor. In God's providence she was greatly troubled by interior trials and was very uncertain as to her own deportment about how she might best give herself totally to God, as she wished. For several years she had been under the spiritual direction of the late bishop of Belley.[3] Following his advice she finally took Monsieur Vincent as her spiritual director. He did not usually take on the responsibility of personal spiritual direction of others for lack of time and because it would take him away from other works of greater importance for the service of the Church. Nevertheless he deferred on this occasion to the wishes of this great prelate to accept the direction of this virtuous lady. He did so under the inspiration of the providence of God, for the great good he had in store for her, as shall appear later in this book.

---

2. Saint Louise de Marillac, 1591-1660, illegitimate daughter of Louis de Marillac and an unknown mother. She married Antoine le Gras, February 5, 1613, and lost him in death, December 21, 1625. They had a son Michel. She placed her confidence in her spiritual director, Vincent de Paul, who eventually used her in his charitable works. She was canonized on March 11, 1934, and on February 10, 1960, was named patroness of all those who devote themselves to Christian social work.

3. Jean Pierre Camus.

This faithful servant of Jesus Christ felt herself strongly moved in her prayer to give herself to the service of the poor. Upon requesting the advice of Monsieur Vincent, she received this letter in reply:

Yes, certainly, Mademoiselle, I agree. Why not, since our Lord has given you this holy thought? Receive communion tomorrow and prepare for the review of life you propose to make. Later you can begin the prescribed retreat. I cannot tell you how anxious I am to see you and know how all goes with you. But I must deny myself for the love of God, which must be your sole wish also. I can well imagine how touched you were by the words of today's Gospel, for they are powerful for a soul loving with a perfect love. You must have appeared in the eyes of God as a beautiful tree, for by his grace you have borne such good fruit. I beseech him, by his infinite goodness, that you shall ever be that tree of life bearing the fruit of true charity.[4]

It was providential that Monsieur Vincent had moved to the College des Bons Enfants, as we said earlier, after Madame de Gondi died in 1625. She had contributed so much to the first missions and to the establishment of the Congregation of the Mission. God willed that Mademoiselle le Gras move to the vicinity of the college to be of service to Monsieur Vincent in all his efforts in favor of the corporal and spiritual welfare of the poor.[5] He found her in such good dispositions and of such tried virtue that at the beginning of 1629 he proposed that she devote herself completely to our Lord to honor his charity toward the poor and to imitate him in the weariness, fatigue, and contradictions he had endured for their sake.[6] He suggested that, following the example of this loving Savior, she would go from town to town, village to village, to oversee the way the meetings and Confraternities of Charity were progressing.

She agreed to do this, motivated by a spirit of obedience and her zeal and her love for the poor. Who can say how great was the blessing and fruit she brought to these visits? She re-established those fallen on difficult times, encouraged the women who made up these meetings, increased their membership when they were too few to carry out their tasks, gave them fitting advice, trained them in caring for the sick, distributed dresses and other clothes she had brought with her, supplied medicines, and suggested other possible ways they could help in the care and salvation of the sick poor.

Ordinarily she would remain in a parish, and beyond the time she gave

---

4. *CED* I:51-52. The original text is more vivid: "Oh! what a tree you have appeared to be today in God's sight, since you have borne such a fruit! May you be forever a beautiful tree of life bringing forth fruits of love."
5. She left the parish of Saint Sauveur and went to live in that of Saint Nicolas du Chardonnet.
6. *CED* I:73-74.

to the Confraternities of Charity, she would, with the approval of the local pastor, bring together in a private home the young girls of the region. She would catechize and instruct them in the duties of a true Christian. If a schoolmistress lived in the parish she would give her some hints about how best to fulfill her function. If no teacher was available she would seek out someone suitable for the office. The better to show her how to teach, she herself would hold class in the presence of the prospective schoolmistress.

For several years she gave herself to these duties in the dioceses of Beauvais, Paris, Senlis, Soissons, Meaux, Chalons in Champagne, and Chartres, with outstanding success. She had a hand-written directive from Monsieur Vincent, regarding her activities.[7] From time to time she wrote him giving an account of her efforts, and made it a rule to do nothing extraordinary without his advice. She traveled and gave alms at her own expense, always accompanied by other pious women and a servant. After spending most of the year in these activities, she ordinarily returned to Paris to pass the winter season but continued her same service to the poor. She was not satisfied to serve them simply by herself but sought as much as possible to enlist other virtuous women in her charitable activities, first by giving themselves to Jesus Christ, and then serving him in his members, the poor. What makes her activities the more remarkable is that she was of a delicate constitution, subject to frequent illnesses, but these did not hold her back from her charitable activities.

We give here an extract from the beginning and the ending of a letter written to her by Monsieur Vincent:

> Thanks be to God you have arrived in good health. For the love of God and his poor members, take care of yourself, and do not try to do too much. The devil often uses this ruse to trap worthy souls, to get them to do more than they can, so he can succeed in having them do nothing. On the other hand, the Son of God invites us quietly and calmly to do what we reasonably can, so that we can continue to serve. Do the same, Mademoiselle, and you will be following the inspiration of the Spirit of God.

> When you are looked upon with favor and praised, unite yourself to the contempt, mockeries, and affronts the Son of God endured. A truly humble soul is humbled as much in honor as in dishonor. Act like the bee. It makes its honey from the dew that rests on bitter absinthe just as well as from the dew on the rose. I hope you can do the same.[8]

---

7. See Book Two, ch. 9.
8. *CED* I:95-98. This letter was sent to Beauvais where Louise had gone to establish eighteen Confraternities of Charity. On her return from there, she received extraordinary expressions of gratitude, not only from the women but also from the men who had furtively come to listen to her instructions.

From the start Monsieur Vincent had conceived of these Confraternities of Charity as established in the small towns and villages with no hospital. Often the sick poor were left with little help, cut off from care or remedy in their illnesses. The late bishop of Beauvais,[9] became aware of the great good these Confraternities of Charity were doing in both the bodily and spiritual care of the poor. As a result, he wished to set them up in all eighteen parishes of his city. In the same way, several devoted women of Paris, seeing the good results of the Confraternities of Charity in the villages, thought of establishing the same in their parish, Saint Sauveur. The year 1629 saw the first of these confraternities in Paris, set up by Monsieur Vincent with the cooperation of the pastor of the parish. The following year Mademoiselle le Gras joined five or six women of her acquaintance in the parish of Saint Nicolas du Chardonnet, where she lived, to serve the sick poor. She wrote to Monsieur Vincent, then away on mission, to tell him of her progress in this charitable work. He suggested they follow the regulations already set out for the Confraternities of Charity, adding some specific directions for her parish, just as he had done earlier for the parish of Saint Sauveur.[10] She observed these rules faithfully, and God was generous in his blessings. Several other women joined the first group for the continued service of the poor under the wise direction of the pastor.

In that same and the following year, 1631, the confraternity was established in the parishes of Saint Merry, Saint Benedict, and Saint Sulpice, with the approval of the archbishop of Paris and the cooperation of the pastors. A little later the confraternity was established in the parishes of Saint Paul, Saint Germain l'Auxerrois, Saint Eustache, Saint Andre, Saint Jean, Saint Barthelemy, Saint Etienne du Mont, Saint Nicolas des Champs, Saint Roch, Saint Jacques de la Boucherie, Saint Jacques du Haut Pas, Saint Laurent, and in practically all the parishes of the city and suburbs of Paris.

Messieurs Descorde and Lamy, masters and administrators of the Quinze-Vingts Hospital,[11] requested Monsieur Vincent to found a Confraternity of Charity there, which he did.

We should not omit here the account of the first years of Mademoiselle Le Gras, working with the Confraternity of Charity in her parish of Saint Nicolas du Chardonnet. One day a young woman who had contracted the plague came to see her. When Monsieur Vincent heard of it, he wrote to her:

> I have just learned of the accident that has occurred to the girl whom your guardians of the poor have rescued and that you had

---

9. Augustin Potier de Gesvre, consecrated in Rome on September 17, 1617. He renewed his diocese with the help of Monsieur Vincent, Adrien Bourdoise, and the Ursuline nuns. He served in a great many important positions in both Church and state. He died June 20, 1650.
10. *CED* XIII:523-31.
11. Literally "fifteen twenties," for a total of three hundred, the capacity of the hospital.

visited. I must say, Mademoiselle, that I was so upset that were it not the middle of the night I would have come right away to see you. But the goodness of God toward those who have given themselves to the service of the poor in the Confraternities of Charity, in which no one up to now has been stricken with the plague, gives me total confidence that no harm will come to you. Believe me, Mademoiselle, for not only did I visit the late subprior of Saint Lazare in his last illness when he was afflicted with the plague, but I heard his last sigh. Yet, neither I nor those who attended him in his illness, suffered any harm. No, Mademoiselle, do not fear, for God wishes to use you for his greater glory, and I think he will preserve you for that. I will celebrate holy mass for your intention. I would go to see you tomorrow were it not for a meeting I have with some doctors at the Madeleine about the affairs of that establishment.[12]

In regard to the subject of this letter, Monsieur Vincent proved to be correct. This charitable lady, despite all her work and her own constant illnesses, lived thirty years after receiving this letter. God wished to use her services not only for the good of the Confraternities of Charity but also for the founding of an entirely new community of virtuous women. The confraternities were helpful to the sick poor, and the women would contribute so much to these confraternities and render many other services to the Church, as we shall see in the following chapter.

---

12. The plague erupted in France in 1628 and ravaged the country. See *CED* I:185-86.

CHAPTER TWENTY-FOUR

The Establishment of the Daughters of Charity

IF IT BE TRUE, as the prophet says, that "abyss calls to abyss,"[1] we can say even more truly that blessing attracts blessing, and charity, which is the source of all virtues, in accomplishing one goal, begins to seek another. This was the case here. The Confraternities of Charity spoken of in the preceding chapter led to a new Company of women bearing the same name and calling themselves Daughters of Charity. God had called Monsieur Vincent to found a Congregation of men to evangelize the poor. He willed that he would also be the father and founder of a new community of women for the service of these same poor people, particularly the sick. This new work has to be attributed to God's providence, since Monsieur Vincent did not originate the idea and did not think it proper to become involved in a new undertaking such as this. This is how things came about.

When the Confraternities of Charity had first been established in the villages, as we have said, the women gave themselves to the service of the sick. They would go one after another to visit them and help them however they could. When these same Confraternities of Charity were established in Paris, the women, moved by the same charitable spirit, wished to visit the sick in their homes and give them the same services as their country counterparts. Soon these confraternities multiplied and enrolled several noblewomen, who could not for one reason or another, such as their husbands' opposition, perform the usual services for the poor: bringing them food, making their beds, preparing medicines, and other such things. Since they themselves employed servants in their own homes for taking care of these chores, they were unable or unwilling to do them personally. They perceived that it was absolutely necessary to have some servants only for handling services for the sick poor. They would distribute food each day, or the required medicines.

This situation was brought to Monsieur Vincent's attention in 1630. He considered the matter carefully before God and recognized the need for some remedy for the situation. He recalled that in the villages were some good women who did not want to marry or who did not have the necessary dowry to become religious. Among these women some would be glad to give themselves to the service of the sick poor for the love of God. God's

---

1. Ps 42:8.

providence so arranged things that at his next missions he found two women who agreed to what he proposed, and were sent, one to the parish of Saint Sauveur,[2] and the other to the parish of Saint Benedict. Later, others came, and were sent to Saint Nicolas du Chardonnet and elsewhere.

Both Monsieur Vincent and Mademoiselle Le Gras offered advice as to how they were to comport themselves in regard to the noble ladies on the one hand and to the sick poor on the other. These women came from a wide background and did not communicate among themselves or any central authority other than the ladies of the parish were they lived. Because they had no training in how to minister to the sick, some could not measure up to what was expected. These would have to be sent away, but since few came to take their place, the ladies and the poor alike fell into their original difficulties.

This made it obvious that a larger number of young women was needed to serve in all the sections of Paris in which the Confraternity of Charity had been established. They needed to be taught how to care for the sick, how to get and prepare medicines, but beyond this they needed to be taught to pray and to live a spiritual life, for it would be impossible to stay long in such a painful service to the poor and to conquer the natural repugnances of their position without a solid foundation of true virtue.

Monsieur Vincent recognized the great need, and besides, he was importuned by the ladies concerned to undertake the formation of these countrywomen. He found it difficult to agree to do so. Since he was not a man to jump at a first idea, he was content to have recourse to God in prayer until Providence would make known how to answer this need. He was not mistaken in this, for soon afterwards some other young women came. He chose three or four whom he sent to Mademoiselle Le Gras at her home in the parish of Saint Nicolas du Chardonnet. He had alerted her beforehand to receive, lodge, and maintain them in her house, so that she could train them to be worthy of the vocation to which Providence had called them.

This took place in 1633[3] solely as an experiment, but God so blessed these beginnings that the number of women increased. They then began a small community which served as the nursery of the Daughters of Charity, Servants of the Sick Poor in the parishes, hospitals, and wherever else they were invited.

Seeing the way God blessed this small community, and moved by her love for the poor, Mademoiselle le Gras began to devote herself more and more to their formation. She appealed often to Monsieur Vincent to know whether she should dedicate herself to this particular work and if she should

---

2. Marguerite Naseau, the first Daughter of Charity.
3. November 29, vigil of the Feast of Saint Andrew. For the first rules see *CED* IX:1-14.

follow this inclination as divine inspiration. His reply was in keeping with his usual thought, that in new and extraordinary things, we ought first try them out, a little at a time.

> Please, once and for all, do not even think of this occupation until our Lord manifests his will. Often we desire something that seems to come from God but in reality does not. God permits these desires to prepare our souls for what Providence has in store for us. Saul sought his lost donkeys but found a kingdom. Saint Louis set out to conquer the Holy Land but overcame himself, gaining thereby a heavenly crown. You wish to become the servant of these poor women, but God wishes you to belong to him alone, and perhaps of more people than you would be in that way. May your heart, Mademoiselle, honor the tranquility of the heart of our Lord, for then it will be prepared to serve him. The kingdom of God is found in peace in the Holy Spirit. It will reign in you if you remain at peace. Do so, please, and thus honor the God of peace and love.[4]

In another letter, he wrote:

> I do not see clearly yet what God wishes in this matter. I am not able to discern his will. Mademoiselle, please pray to God for this purpose during the holy season when he pours out the graces of the Holy Spirit most abundantly.[5]

By these letters and others he wrote on this matter, we can see how hesitant he was in discerning the true vocation of this virtuous woman in regard to the formation of the country girls. Not only did he judge her capable of greater things than that, which at the time appeared insignificant, but he did not want to put limits on the talents and graces she had received from God. His own humility would not allow him to think that God would use him to direct one so favored by Providence as Mademoiselle. He kept her two years in this uncertainty, refusing to give a definite answer. He would exhort her to place her trust uniquely in God, assuring her that she would never be deceived.[6] His own humility made him wish that God would act without involving himself. He thought he was good for nothing except to thwart the designs of Providence. It seemed, on the contrary, that God wished to use his faithful servant despite himself, to begin and to lead this work so important for his glory.

Lastly, his repeated recommendation to Mademoiselle Le Gras that her

---

4. *CED* I:113-14.
5. *CED* I:200.
6. Convinced that it was God's will that Monsieur Vincent approved of her desire, Louise pronounced the formula of her consecration on March 25, 1634. From this time on, March 25, the feast of the Annunciation, is the day when the Daughters of Charity renew their own consecration.

confidence in God would never be deceived was verified in time by the extraordinary blessing God bestowed upon her first efforts which she had undertaken and continued only through her spirit of obedience. We could say that Monsieur Vincent was deceived, for he thought only of training a small group of young women to help in the parishes of Paris. God so multiplied this company in numbers and in grace that Monsieur Vincent and this virtuous Mademoiselle had the consolation of seeing in their own lifetimes its expansion to twenty-five or thirty places in Paris, into more than thirty other villages, hamlets, and towns in various provinces of France, and even into Poland, where the queen, by her zeal and charity, wished to aid the poor of her realm.

We see what fruits Monsieur Vincent's humility produced, even if he did not think of founding this new community of women. God was pleased to bestow such a dew of blessings and graces upon them that they were sought for everywhere, to such a point that they could not be fully trained. These women were (if we may speak this way) plucked up from the seed-bed almost as soon as they were planted there, before they had been fully formed. God in his mercy helped them to such an extent that their frugality, industry, love of poverty, patience, modesty, and charity served to edify people wherever they were sent.

The first foundations of their community were laid in the house of Mademoiselle Le Gras in the parish of Saint Nicolas du Chardonnet. Later, on the advice of Monsieur Vincent, she transferred the community to another house half a league from Paris in the village of La Chapelle.[7] This was thought to be a more suitable place to house, feed, and clothe in country fashion the candidates destined to serve the poor. Finally, around 1642 they returned to a house in the Saint Lazare section of Paris, where they remain to this day.[8]

Monsieur Vincent prescribed rules and constitutions for them, which were approved by the archbishop of Paris. By his authority he constituted them a Company or Congregation under the title Daughters of Charity, Servants of the Sick Poor, and under the direction of the superior general of the Congregation of the Mission. The king confirmed and authorized their establishment by letters patent, confirmed by the Parlement of Paris.[9]

Besides their service to the sick poor, they devoted themselves in several places to the education of young girls, teaching them to know and serve God and to fulfill the principal duties of the Christian life.

---

7. La Chapelle is now a part of Paris, and nearly adjacent to Saint Lazare.
8. The new house was directly across the street from Saint Lazare.
9. *CED* XIII:578-87.

This enterprise seems small to the eyes of the world, which judges things only by appearance and glitter. Those who reflect how precious works of mercy and charity are in the sight of God, and how strongly they are recommended by our Lord, know that this institute, so small in our eyes, is great in the eyes of God. It is the more meritorious in its activities in that Jesus Christ has expressly declared that he regards as done to himself what has been done in favor of the poor. Besides, charity toward the poor is the purer and more perfect, for the only thanks received from those served is often contradiction, complaints, and ingratitude.

Using the humility and charity of Vincent de Paul, God brought this small community to birth. It produced in the past, and continues to produce today, the fruits of humility, patience, charity, and the other virtues most pleasing to the Son of God, and most recommended in the Gospel, as we shall see in Book Two.

CHAPTER TWENTY-FIVE

The Ordination Retreats for the Benefit of Those Wishing to Receive Holy Orders

SAINT PAUL'S advice to the bishop Saint Timothy, not to impose his hands lightly on those seeking to receive holy orders,[1] is important not only to the bishop who must not share in the sins of others, as the apostle says, but to the whole Church. According to a Father of the Church, it ordinarily is threatened more by its own ministers than by outsiders. We may truly say that the persecutions of tyrants have not caused so much difficulty to the salvation of souls as the scandalous lives and pernicious conduct of bad priests.

This concerned many bishops who wanted to fulfill worthily the responsibilities of their office. On the one hand, given the large extent of their dioceses and the large number of parishioners they saw the necessity of having a large number of priests and other ministers. On the other hand it was practically impossible to know who among their many candidates would have the requisite qualities and virtues for such a holy ministry. No matter how carefully the bishop examined the candidates and considered their moral qualities, it was difficult to be sure who among them would make a good priest. The bishops were often deceived.

The late Augustin Potier, bishop of Beauvais, whose memory is held in benediction because of his zeal, pastoral vigilance, and his other virtues, often considered this situation and its possible remedies.

He recognized that God had conferred his Spirit upon Monsieur Vincent to minister to the spiritual needs of the people by the missions he had given in most of the parishes of the diocese and by the Confraternities of Charity he had established. He thought this holy priest would have the light and grace to help him reform his clergy. Because he appreciated Monsieur Vincent's virtue and especially his charity, the bishop opened his heart to him, telling him how worried he was in regard to this matter. He often called Monsieur Vincent to Beauvais or came himself to Paris to discuss what best might be done.

One day this good prelate asked Monsieur Vincent what could possibly be done to put an end to disorders among the clergy and bring them to appreciate their sacred calling properly. This wise and experienced mission-

---
1. 1 Tim 5:22.

ary responded that it was practically impossible to reform bad priests who had grown old in their faults, or to redirect pastors who had begun poorly. To have any hope of success in working to reform the clergy it was absolutely necessary to go to the root of the problem and apply the remedy there. Since changing the older priests was so difficult, the proper plan must be to see to the formation of good ones for the future. In the first place, only those should be admitted to orders who had the requisite knowledge and other signs of a true vocation. Second, those who wished to become priests must be trained in their obligations and taught a true priestly spirit which they could then bring to the parishes.

The bishop of Beauvais was pleased with these reflections. One day in July of 1628, while traveling, he was conversing with Monsieur Vincent in his carriage, when he abruptly closed his eyes and said nothing, turning over something in his mind. Those with him remained quiet, thinking perhaps he was dozing. He opened his eyes to say he was not sleeping but only thinking what could be the quickest and most effective way of preparing candidates for holy orders. He further said that he had resolved to bring the candidates into his own house for several days. During that time he would arrange some suitable exercises to instruct them in what they should know and the virtues they should practice in their calling. Then Monsieur Vincent, who previously had spoken to him in general of the necessity for such preparation, wholeheartedly approved of his initiative and said, "Oh, Your Excellency, surely this is a thought come from God. This is an excellent means for bringing order, step by step, to all the clergy of your diocese."

Encouraged thus to put the plan into immediate execution, this virtuous prelate resolved to do so at once. Before leaving Monsieur Vincent he said he would begin preparations, but asked him to think over what would be appropriate for such a conference and the timetable for the retreat to follow. He invited Monsieur Vincent to come to Beauvais fifteen or twenty days before the next scheduled ordination, which was to be the coming September. Monsieur Vincent was careful to fulfill the bishop's request. As he said, "I was more convinced that God wished this service of me, asked for by the mouth of a bishop, than if it had been delivered by an angel from heaven."

Upon his return to Beauvais, the bishop examined the ordinands, and himself opened the retreat and the conferences. Monsieur Vincent and two doctors of the faculty of Paris, Fathers Messier[2] and Duchesne,[3] then continued the program. It was similar to that which later was followed in the ordination retreats, and which remain in usage up to the present. Monsieur Vincent undertook to speak on the decalogue. He did it so clearly and with

---

2. Louis Messier, archdeacon of Beauvais; *CED* I:65.
3. Jerome Duchesne, archdeacon of Beauvais and doctor of the Sorbonne.

such feeling that many of the ordinands were moved to make a general confession. Even Monsieur Duchesne, a theologian who had given some of the conferences of the reatreat, was so moved that he asked to make a general confession of his entire life to Monsieur Vincent, much to the edification of all the ordinands.

Later, the bishop of Beauvais came to Paris to meet with the archbishop. He told him of the great fruit these retreats had begun to effect in his diocese and pointed out their importance, their usefulness, and even their necessity. He was so convincing that from the beginning of 1631 this good prelate ordered all candidates for ordination in the archdiocese of Paris to report first to the priests of the Congregation of the Mission ten days before ordination. They would learn from them the dispositions required in the priesthood, and, he hoped, would begin to acquire them.

In keeping with this decree, Monsieur Vincent began in the following Lent to receive the ordinands into the College des Bons Enfants, for he had not yet moved to Saint Lazare. The retreats were conducted as prescribed, and this arrangement has continued until the present. From this first house of the Congregation of the Mission, this holy practice of providing a retreat and spiritual exercises for the ordinands has, through the zeal of Monsieur Vincent. They spread to several other dioceses in France and Italy, and even to Rome itself, with a fruit and blessing better observed in its effects than attempted in words. We have reserved for Book Two a detailed account of the order of the retreats, the fruits they have produced, and the main reasons why these ordination retreats were so important and necessary for the good of the Church.

CHAPTER TWENTY-SIX

Spiritual Retreats for Various Groups of People

A PROPHET OF OLD said that the land was desolate because no one had reflected and meditated in his heart.[1] Exterior things preoccupy us, and we allow our minds to be taken up with all sorts of sensible objects. We hardly ever enter into ourselves, or rarely think of God, or consider the reason we have being and life, and the way to achieve our salvation. From this comes the blind spirit, the disordered heart, and finally the loss of salvation for the greater number of those who are damned.

The great saints have often spoken against this state of affairs and have exhorted the faithful to enter into themselves by the practice of meditation. In these latter days, Saint Charles Borromeo, Saint Ignatius, Blessed Francis de Sales, and many other saintly persons have favored spiritual exercises to bring souls to the practice of this vitally important recollection. Although these have been successful, lack of facilities and other difficulties have limited the number of people who could profit by them, particularly among the laity. This consideration led Monsieur Vincent to open the door of his house at Saint Lazare, and even more the door of his heart, to accommodate those persons wishing to pass some days in the exercises of a holy retreat. This faithful servant of God spoke more with his heart than with his mouth in imitating his divine Master so that everyone burdened with sin and vice should come to him to be comforted.[2]

After beginning this charitable work in the College des Bons Enfants, he continued the practice in all the houses of the Mission, particularly those in Paris and Rome. The priests of the Congregation of the Mission (who themselves make an annual retreat following the example of their father and founder, who never failed to make his retreat, no matter how busy he might be) received with open arms all those who came to participate in these retreats, no matter what their class or condition. The rich and poor, clergy and laity, professors and illiterates, nobles and artisans, masters and servants, all were welcome. They sat at the same table and received all kinds of help and services for the good of their souls. They were helped to prepare for a good general confession, aided in committing themselves wholly to God either by adopting a rule of life suitable to their situation or possibly by choosing an entirely different state in life, or were aided in discerning God's designs for them.

---

1. Jer 12:11.
2. Matt 11:28.

In the house at Saint Lazare it was remarked that there might be at any one time in the refectory nobles wearing the cordon-bleu, people from the palace, artisans, hermits, domestics, all making their retreat at the same time, not to mention some clergy as well. Monsieur Vincent remarked occasionally, with that gentle gaiety he knew how to employ, that the house of Saint Lazare was something like Noah's ark, housing all sorts of animals, great and small.

We shall see in Book Two the great fruit and admirable effect these retreats produced on many occasions. Monsieur Vincent was particularly thankful that God in his goodness had chosen him and his confreres to effect the blessings of his mercy and grace. For this reason he had a particularly strong wish that the practice of these retreats be preserved in the Company. He called them a gift of heaven, although they were a serious drain on the resources of the community, for he supported the larger number of retreatants who each year came to Saint Lazare or other houses of the Congregation. No foundation or other regular source of funds existed to defray the costs of the retreats. This great servant of God had no thought of the expenses when it was question of working for the salvation of souls, redeemed at such a price by Jesus Christ. It seemed to him, as was said by the Holy Spirit in the Canticle of Canticles, that when he had used all the substance of his house in such works of charity, he had as yet done nothing compared to what this divine virtue demanded of him.[3]

If it were not enough that men of all classes and condition found in the houses of the Mission all help in their progress in sanctity, his charity, not knowing the meaning of the words "that's enough," arranged that women and young girls would find similar help for the spiritual welfare of their souls. He arranged for them to go to Mademoiselle Le Gras' house. There they were received with open arms to benefit in every way from her generous disposition, which seemed never to be satisfied with what she had already contributed.

We give here an extract of a letter written by Monsieur Vincent to her on this topic.

> Madame Goussault and Mademoiselle Lamy have gone to your house for their retreat. I would ask you to give them the outline of subjects of meditation which I gave you, to have them report to you in each other's presence what good thoughts they have had in their prayer, and to have reading at table during meals so they may be relaxed and at ease. The subject might be of thoughts they have had in their recollection periods or possibly what they read in the lives of the saints. After meals they should walk a bit, but other than these

---
3. Cant 8:7.

two times they should observe silence. It would be good if they kept a journal of the principal inspirations of their mental prayer. They should plan on making their general confession on Wednesday. Their spiritual reading should be from the *Imitation of Christ* by Thomas a Kempis. They should take time to reflect on each section. They might also read several chapters of the Gospel as well. It would be good on the day of their general confession for you to give them for their prayer Granada's *Memorial*,[4] which is calculated to move them to sorrow for sin. For the rest, be careful that they do not become too intense. I pray our Lord will give you his Spirit in all this.[5]

Another lady, on another occasion, made a retreat at the Daughters of Charity. She gave Mademoiselle Le Gras a copy of what she had written of her reflections and resolutions so that she might send them on to Monsieur Vincent. This wise and experienced director replied in a letter to Mademoiselle le Gras:

I am returning the resolutions of Madame N., which are good, but it strikes me they would be even better if she would come down a bit to particulars. It would be good to apply this remark to all who make the retreat at your house. Otherwise it is only an exercise of the mind. There is a danger that having these good thoughts and having a certain consolation in thinking about a virtue, a person would begin to flatter herself that she has become virtuous. To acquire solid virtue practical resolutions have to be taken, and faithfully carried out. I am afraid without this, it would not be solid virtue, but simply imagination.[6]

---

4. Luis de Granada, *Memorial de la vida cristiana*.
5. *CED* I:381-82.
6. *CED* II:190.

CHAPTER TWENTY-SEVEN

Spiritual Conferences for Clergy

SPIRITUAL CONFERENCES have ever been in vogue in the Church, especially for those who want to progress in virtue. The fathers of the desert regarded them as an excellent means for mutual encouragement as they walked the narrow path of evangelical perfection. Entire volumes have been preserved reporting what they discussed in these holy assemblies. These fathers always considered Jesus Christ to be present in these meetings because of his word in the Gospel, that when two or three are gathered in his name, he would be in the midst of them.[1]

Monsieur Vincent was well aware through his own experience of how useful these conferences were, for he had used them with great blessing from the beginning of his Company. He seized the opportunity offered him by God to extend these conferences to other priests, as we shall see in what follows.

Several pious clergymen who had attended the ordination retreats and received many graces in the exercises, had felt a great desire to lead a life worthy of their sacred calling. They hoped to preserve this holy disposition and continue in the way of sanctification. For this purpose they consulted Monsieur Vincent, asking him for his advice on how best they might correspond faithfully to the grace they had received at their ordination.[2]

Monsieur Vincent was the soul of charity and was filled with an ardent zeal for whatever might contribute to the spiritual good of the clergy. Among other things he proposed they should meet once a week to discuss matters pertaining to their state, such as the virtues proper to priests, the functions of a genuine ministry, and other similar matters, all calculated to be most useful for the good of their souls. These conferences would serve to develop a union of hearts among themselves in the service of Jesus Christ and his Church, as a support and mutual encouragement and as a help in their holy ministry.

This proposal seemed to the priests concerned as though it came from heaven itself through Monsieur Vincent. Tuesday was chosen as the meeting day for the conference, which was immediately inaugurated with the blessing of the archbishop of Paris in 1633.[3] It has continued to the present with

---
1. Matt 18:20.
2. *CED* I:203-05.
3. It has become commonly known as the Tuesday conferences.

much success not only for the personal development of those attending but for the good of the entire Church, as we shall see in Book Two.[4]

Although this first meeting of priests was small in numbers at the beginning, God blessed it. As a result, it soon became a sacred nursery serving to produce for France several archbishops and bishops worthy of their office and a large number of vicars general, ecclesiastical judges, archdeacons, canons, pastors, and other clergy who most worthily fulfilled their benefices, offices and dignities in the Church. They have spread out to all the dioceses of the kingdom, where all have benefited from their good example, their zeal, and their efforts for the advancement of the kingdom of Jesus Christ.

These priests certainly did not come to the clergy conferences for any temporal advantage or for hope of receiving a benefice. On the contrary, of all the dispositions stressed for the participants, one of the most often emphasized was total lack of self-interest, with the corresponding intention of purely and simply giving oneself perfectly to the service of God in perfect fidelity to one's vocation. This wise and zealous director ordinarily stressed nothing so much as love of humility, of contempt, of poverty and suffering, after the example of Jesus Christ, their divine Master. They were to imitate him by their service to the poor, visiting them in hospitals, prisons, and other such places. When invited by Monsieur Vincent they were to accompany the priests of the Congregation of the Mission to the parishes and villages, to serve the poor country people. They were to undertake the lowest and least esteemed priestly tasks.

God exalts the humble and rejects the proud, and confirms their humble service by raising them up. These clergy conferences produced such a change in priestly lives in Paris, even among some priests of noble birth, that they began to devote themselves with such zeal to diverse works of charity that they edified the city. Cardinal Richelieu heard of these developments.[5] As a result, he summoned Monsieur Vincent to explain what was happening in these assemblies and conferences and to talk about the work of the priests of the Congregation of the Mission. He was most satisfied and from this time on developed a high esteem for the person and virtue of Monsieur Vincent, whom he had not known before, as he told his niece, the duchess of Aiguillon.[6] On several later occasions he met Monsieur Vincent, exhorting

---

[4]. Ch. 3. Jean Jacques Olier, Louis Abelly, and Jacques Benigne Bossuet and nearly three hundred other priests were received as members of the Tuesday conferences during the saint's lifetime.

[5]. Armand Jean Duplessis, Cardinal Richelieu, 1585-1642. As bishop of Lucon he acted as a spokesman for the clergy at the Estates General of 1614. Raised to the cardinalate in 1622, he entered the council of the king (1624) and quickly became its head. He guided both foreign and domestic policy. He was the author of royal absolutism, destroying the power of the nobles and of the Huguenot minority. Louis XIII followed his deathbed advice to appoint Mazarin as his chief minister.

[6]. Marie de Wignerod de Pontcourlai, 1604-1675, whose husband died in 1622, after two years of

him to continue the good works he had begun, and stating that he thought that his Congregation would do great good for the Church, and promised him every protection and support.

The cardinal wanted to know which priests came each week to Saint Lazare, the purpose of these assemblies, what they discussed, the charitable works they supported. When he received a satisfactory response to all these questions, he let it be known that he had a particular interest in having good bishops in the Church in France, who would have all the qualities required in such a high office. He asked Monsieur Vincent who might he think worthy of the episcopate, who might then be proposed to the king for nomination to vacant sees in the kingdom. Monsieur Vincent gave him the names of several. This wise and zealous minister immediately took pen and paper and wrote in his own hand the names in the order they had been given.[7]

What should be mentioned is that all this took place so discreetly that Monsieur Vincent never said a word about it. The priests of the clergy conferences never knew a thing of it during his lifetime. Monsieur Vincent was taken up in inculcating a spirit of humility, simplicity, and evangelical disinterestedness, without ever breathing the least word that he had anything to do with their appointment to high office. Rather, he exhorted them incessantly to flee what appeared grand and mighty and instead to seek their own abnegation.

We shall see more in detail in Book Two[8] the great good God drew from these assemblies at Saint Lazare, for the sanctification of the clergy and for the service of the whole Church. One of the benefits was that the clergy conferences begun at Paris soon appeared in other dioceses. By the solicitude of the prelates, the pastors, benefice holders, and priests of the towns and villages began to come together to discuss matters concerning the ecclesiastical state and the obligations flowing from it. All of this proved most helpful not only to reform the clergy but also to edify the people. The year 1642 saw an occasion when Monsieur Vincent was able to establish a second clergy conference in the College des Bons Enfants.

The women of the Association of Charity of Paris, of whom we will speak later, had requested some priests, besides those who lived in the hospital, to help tend the sick. In keeping with his usual charity, Monsieur Vincent

---

marriage. The cardinal voided her entrance into the Carmelites, and then saw to her worldly advancement and appointment as a duchess. She was a great and consistent benefactress of the Congregation of the Mission, the Daughters of Charity, and other congregations. She was president of the Confraternity of Charity at Saint Sulpice, her parish. After Monsieur Vincent's death, she had a silver-gilt reliquary made in the shape of a heart surmounted by a flame to enclose his heart.

7. *CED* II:386-88. Richelieu kept his word, and after his death, Louis XIII appealed again to Vincent, asking him to recommend suitable candidates for the episcopacy.

8. Ch. 3.

welcomed the six at Saint Lazare who were to engage in this work, to prepare themselves by a spiritual retreat. He exhorted them to do well this work of charity and to preserve the spirit of piety and fraternal union among themselves. To help in this he offered some suggestions, chief among which was to meet every week at the College des Bons Enfants for clergy conferences much like those held at Saint Lazare. These good men willingly accepted this suggestion but chose Thursday as their meeting day rather than Tuesday because Thursday was ordinarily not a class day. This allowed those studying theology to come to these weekly meetings without missing any of their classes. Thus it was that this second clergy conference began. It has continued up to the present. It allowed several priests to join the study of virtue to that of knowledge. Thus they would make themselves more capable of serving the Church and giving greater glory to God.

CHAPTER TWENTY-EIGHT

The Establishment of the Hospitals in Paris and Marseilles for the Galley Slaves

MONSIEUR VINCENT'S pity for the poor galley slaves had its origin in his own experience, as we have described earlier.[1] The charity of his heart did not allow him to forget these poor people, even among all the other important affairs calling for his attention. His thoughts often turned to the hospice he had provided for them near the church of Saint Roch, but lack of time prevented him from visiting them as often as he would have liked. He realized that this state of affairs could not go on for long unless there was some source of funds and a house of their own. Their present house was simply rented. He resolved within himself to work at this, with the help of divine Providence, to bring a solution to these difficulties.

He first requested help from the late king, Louis XIII of glorious memory, and the magistrates of Paris, to assign him the ancient tower between the gate of Saint Bernard and the river, to shelter these poor convicts. This was granted in 1632, and for several years only the alms from some charitable donors kept the house going. For his part, Monsieur Vincent looked after their spiritual needs by sending priests of the Congregation of the Mission who lived in the College des Bons Enfants to say mass, hear confessions, instruct, and console. On occasions he brought some well-born and virtuous persons to visit, as a help to the prisoners.

Mademoiselle le Gras was among those who helped out, both personally and by her alms. She was then superior of the Confraternity of Charity in the parish of Saint Nicolas du Chardonnet. The thought came to Monsieur Vincent that perhaps she might propose to these women to give some part of the alms at their disposal to these poor galley slaves since they lived in the same parish. He wrote to her about this proposal in a short note:

> Charity toward these poor convicts is of great merit in the eyes of God. You were well advised to help them, and you will do well if you continue to do so in any way you can, until I can have the happiness of seeing you, in two or three days. Consider whether your Charity at Saint Nicolas might not assume responsibility for them, at least for a time. You could help them with the money you

---

1. Ch. 14. To call these persons slaves is common but inexact English usage. They were, instead, convicts condemned to the galleys, often for a limited sentence.

have left over, but then what? It is difficult to say, but that is why I throw out this thought for you to consider.[2]

For several years he remained the chief provider for these poor unfortunates. He provided lodging, and what physical and spiritual help he could, until divine Providence inspired a certain wealthy man, who died around 1639, to leave in his will an income of six thousand *livres* to this work. His daughter and heir, aided by the counsel of several priests, would administer it for the express purpose of helping convicts condemned to the galleys.

Only after much difficulty, and over the objection of her husband, was Monsieur Vincent able to arrange the investment of a large enough sum to provide the income as called for in the will. The late Monsieur Mole, then procurator general, helped him in these negotiations. His intervention was most helpful in assuring this income. Monsieur Vincent had alerted this good lady to the deplorable state of the convicts, to convince her that a permanent endowment was essential. She consented, after several discussions with Monsieur Vincent, that the procurator general have in perpetuity the temporal administration of the investment. Later she had the Daughters of Charity appointed to care for the convicts, especially the sick, and provided an income for them from the same six thousand *livres*. Because these prisoners lived in the parish of Saint Nicolas du Chardonnet, the priests of the parish were made responsible for administering the sacraments and burying the dead. Monsieur Vincent pointed out the heavy financial burden this was, and supported by the intervention of several ladies, these priests were granted an income of three hundred *livres* on condition they would say mass, give sermons and catechism lessons and other spiritual help, all of which they have done with great charity. From time to time Monsieur Vincent would come to these poor convicts, especially when they became numerous or were about to be shipped off to the galleys. He provided a Missionary for them, to console them, and dispose them to make good use of their sufferings.

It might seem that he could do nothing more for the convicts. A heart less motivated by his sincere charity would be content with having provided a house and seen to their temporal and spiritual needs. His love, however, would not allow him to think he had done enough or to be content to see them sent away. Instead, he accompanied them to Marseilles, where he unfortunately found conditions worse even than in Paris. The convicts who had fallen sick remained chained to their benches in the galleys. They were covered with vermin, full of sores, and nearly smothered in rot and infection. His tender heart was deeply troubled, seeing these men, made in the image of God, reduced to such misery, Christians condemned to die like animals. He resolved to appeal to Cardinal Richelieu, then general of the Galleys, and

---

2. *CED* I:166.

to the duchess of Aiguillon, the cardinal's niece.³ He reported on the horrible condition of the convicts and the absolute necessity of a hospital for them where they might be taken when sick. He successfully received authorization to construct one with the help of the late bishop of Marseilles, Bishop Gault,⁴ whose memory is held in benediction, and the late chevalier de Simiane de la Coste, a most charitable gentleman from Provence.⁵

Just to have an institution is not enough. It must be supported. So it was that after the death of King Louis XIII, when Monsieur Vincent was called to Paris by the queen regent to help in administering the ecclesiastical affairs of the kingdom, she saw to it that the king, her son, was nominally designated as the founder of the hospital in Marseilles. This was confirmed by letters patent in 1645. The queen mother thereby authorized an annual income of twelve thousand *livres*, drawn from the Provence salt-tax. She specified that the priests of the Congregation of the Mission who had come to Marseilles, as we shall describe later, should have the spiritual direction of the house in perpetuity, in keeping with the concession made by the bishop of the city. The hospital's temporal administration was likewise put into the hands of the priests of the Mission, but together with four of the leading zealous citizens of the city.

To assure good chaplains for the galleys, Her Majesty in these same letters patent ordained that the superior of the mission of Marseilles should have the right to appoint and to dismiss, should the need arise. These chaplains could be obligated to live in community when the galleys were in port, to be better prepared by community exercises to fulfill their duties as chaplain. Her Majesty also specified that priests of the Congregation of the Mission be designated as royal chaplains. This appointment would give them more status to work for the salvation of the convicts with better results.

The chevalier de la Coste had the welfare of this hospital so much at heart that he went to Paris expressly to hasten the letters patent. He finally obtained them through Monsieur Vincent's recommendation.⁶ In a letter of 1645, he wrote:

> I am reporting on the progress of the hospital, to which you have contributed so much. In my last letter I told you how, after much difficulty, we finally, with the help of our Lord, have been able to bring the sick galley slaves here. I am sure I could not express the joy felt by these poor convicts when they saw themselves trans-

---

3. See Book One, ch. 46.
4. Jean Baptiste Gault, bishop of Marseilles, 1642-1643, a man highly regarded for his holiness and apostolic zeal.
5. Gaspar de Simiane de la Coste, 1607-1649, devoted to a great number of good works, and particularly to the relief of the convicts in Marseilles.
6. *CED* XIII:310-12.

ferred from their hell to this hospital they call paradise. No sooner did they come in than they were healed of half their illnesses, for they were cleaned of the vermin which covered them, their feet were washed, and they were taken to a bed a bit softer than the wooden benches they were accustomed to. Everyone was delighted to see themselves put to bed, served, and treated with a bit more charity than they were used to in the galley. We were able to cure a number who otherwise would have died. We can surely say that God has blessed this work, for we have seen the conversion of some lapsed Christians and even have witnessed some Moslems requesting baptism.[7]

After this time, most of the galleys were transferred from Marseilles to Toulon.[8] Care for the sick was also moved. A house was rented for the care of the sick, and a priest of the Mission was regularly on hand to render spiritual services to the convicts, and see to all that could be done for their cure.

---

7. *CED* II:525-27.
8. This transfer took place to avoid a plague from 1649 to 1655.

CHAPTER TWENTY-NINE

The Founding of a Group of Women to Serve in the Hotel Dieu Hospital of Paris and for Other Works of Charity in Paris and Elsewhere

THE MANY ILLS in this valley of tears forces charitable souls to expand their care and increase their ways of meeting the diverse needs of so many suffering people. Monsieur Vincent, as a person totally taken up with this virtue, was ever on the alert to hear of special needs, and his heart was ever disposed to respond. He held to the maxim of never pushing himself into new enterprises. He believed in waiting for a manifestation of the will of God, usually through others, especially superiors, rather than acting by his own initiative. His humility made him diffident about his own perceptions and alert to the possibility that he might be mistaken, especially when it came to knowing the designs of God in unusual enterprises.

This explains why he listened with such great interest and with such respect to those who proposed something that ought to be done, especially when it came from persons with a reputation for virtue. In this spirit he considered a proposal made to him in 1634 by Madame Goussault.[1] Her memory is held in benediction because of her great charity. This lady had been widowed in the flower of her age. Although all avenues were open to her, because of her gifts of nature and fortune she renounced all prospects to commit herself to Jesus Christ. She generously resolved to devote herself solely to serve the poor, particularly the sick among them. She often went to the hospital of Paris, the Hotel Dieu, to visit, but did not find things well run there, such as they later became. She appealed to Monsieur Vincent to extend his charity to these poor people and asked advice on how best to bring about some needed changes in this large hospital.

In keeping with his usual prudence and discretion he felt it best not to use the scythe in another man's field. That is, he did not wish to meddle, whether spiritually or temporally, in the hospital already under the direction of those he thought capable of bringing about any necessary changes.

Madame Goussault tried for a long time to persuade him to take an interest

---

1. In 1613 Genevieve Fayet married Antoine Goussault, a royal councillor and president of the Chamber of Accounts. Her husband died in 1634, and she then dedicated herself to works of charity. She had the idea of an association of ladies for the relief of the sick in the Hotel Dieu in Paris, and was their first superior. She saw that the Daughters of Charity were called to the hospital of Angers. Her name occurs frequently in Saint Vincent's correspondence. She died September 20, 1639.

in this project, but finally was convinced that she was not going to change his mind. Instead, she contacted the late archbishop of Paris, who informed Monsieur Vincent that he would be happy to see him consider the proposition of this virtuous lady that an assembly of women should be formed to look after the sick in the hospital. The archbishop asked Monsieur Vincent to think how best to bring about this new organization of women.

Monsieur Vincent recognized the will of God in this order of the archbishop and accepted his suggestion. He first brought together several women to discuss the matter. He spoke so effectively that on the spot they agreed to give themselves to this good work. The names of these first women were the following, as we learn from a letter of Mademoiselle Le Gras:

> Yesterday a meeting was held at the home of Madame Goussault. Present were Mesdames de Villesavin, de Bailleul, du Mecq, Sainctot and Pollalion. The proposal as presented was accepted, and we agreed to meet again next Monday. Meanwhile, we will pray for God's blessing and receive communion for this intention. Each of us will speak to our women friends about this. Madame de Beaufort will take care of this. We need you and your daughters, perhaps four of them. We will also have to think of some way to get some servants.[2]

The second assembly was better attended than the first. Among those present were the wife of the chancellor,[3] Madame Fouquet,[4] Madame de Traversay, and several other virtuous noble ladies, who joined the first group. Three officers were elected by the group, a superior, an assistant, and a treasurer. Madame Goussault was the first superior, and Monsieur Vincent was designated the permanent director of this company. The virtues and example of these first women attracted several others, so that soon more than two hundred women had enrolled, even some from the nobility, such as presidents' wives, countesses, marchionesses, duchesses and princesses, and all considered it an honor to offer themselves to God to serve the poor, recognizing them as the living members of his Son, Jesus Christ.[5]

This company, under Monsieur Vincent's direction, began in that year, 1634, a fruitful service to the Hotel Dieu hospital which lasted all his life and even after his death. The women provided both corporal and spiritual aid, which this father of the poor urged them to add to the past usage of the

---

2. *CED* I:229-31. The foundation of the Ladies of Charity at Hotel Dieu has to be dated to about June 1634.
3. Coste, *Life* I:322, note 60, corrects the identification of this person from Elisabeth d'Aligre to Madeleine Fabri, the wife of the chancellor, Pierre Seguier.
4. Marie Fouquet
5. The noble ladies of the court wanted a group of their own Ladies of Charity in imitation of those in the parishes of Paris. Queen Anne of Austria, whose own piety and support of Vincent de Paul were well known, wanted to be part of this group. *CED* XIII:821-22.

hospital, either because of insufficient care or lack of certain facilities. It held a thousand or even twelve hundred patients, with this number increasing to over two thousand later. There was a constant coming and going of these poor sick people. Some remained for a week or two, and others stayed longer, for a month or more. On some days, fifty, sixty or eighty, were admitted, and sometimes a hundred. Each year at least twenty to twenty-five thousand passed through the hospital. Some were cured, some died. In either case a harvest of souls was ready for the reaping. It offered a favorable occasion for reforming their lives by a general confession and a conversion of morals, or possibly by preparing themselves to crown their life by a happy death.

Monsieur Vincent did not experience much difficulty in bringing together these women or in having them work for the poor. The question of working in the Hotel Dieu hospital was otherwise. From his first talk to them, he pointed out the likelihood of their service being misunderstood, for their charitable service would emphasize the deficiencies in the administration of the hospital, leading to obvious difficulties. He had spoken of the great good they could do, but at the cost of great opposition. The women should prepare themselves well, he said, and consider carefully how best to carry out their ministry. He himself thought it best to contact the administrators of the Hotel Dieu to alert them to the good intentions and virtues of these charitable women, as well as to inform them of the directive he had received from the archbishop. To their credit, the administrators agreed to allow the women to come into the hospital, to serve the sick in many different ways.

After appointing those who would begin these visits and others to follow, he provided a set of practical recommendations: (1) Each day, before entering the Hotel Dieu hospital, they should invoke the help of our Lord, the true Father of the poor, and the intercession of the Virgin Mary and of Saint Louis, the founder of the hospital. (2) They should present themselves to the religious sisters in charge of the hospital, offering to work with them in serving the sick, to participate in their merits before God. (3) They should esteem and respect these religious as visible angels and speak of them with kindness and humility, always with an entire deference. (4) Should their good intentions not be appreciated, they should be understanding, seek to appreciate their perspective, and never try to get the better of them.

He said to them:

> We say we are trying to help the poor and to aid them in their search for salvation, but we will do neither without the help of these good religious in charge. We must show them every respect, as mothers of the poor, as spouses of our Lord and as the ladies of the house. The Spirit of God works gently. This is how we must act if we hope to succeed in our mission.

In this spirit, then, Monsieur Vincent began this holy work and directed wisely and prudently these good women as they began to serve the poor in the hospital. They found easy access to all departments because of their kindly and respectful attitude toward the sisters in charge. This extended not only to the services the sisters provided for the sick and convalescent but also even to their relatives when occasion arose. They were free to go from ward to ward, from bed to bed, consoling the sick, speaking to them of God, and bringing them to make good use of their sufferings.

So as not to come to these poor with empty hands, the ladies worked out with Monsieur Vincent that they would bring some sweets between dinner and supper, to supplement their words of consolation and edification. They rented a room near the hospital to prepare and store the fruit, jellies, or other small items suitable for the sick. They also asked the Daughters of Charity to buy and prepare these things, and help in their distribution.

Monsieur Vincent was away when the Daughters were invited to help. When he learned of it, he wrote to Mademoiselle Le Gras, "God bless you, Mademoiselle, for sending your Daughters to the hospital, Hotel Dieu, to help out. Be careful of your health, for you know how much you are needed."[6] Because this good Mademoiselle was so zealous for the service of the sick poor, she ever feared she was not doing enough to cooperate with the designs of God upon her, although she was doing everything humanly possible. Monsieur Vincent wrote to her:

> It is not helpful to remain at the hospital, but to come and go would be all right. Do not fear to do all the good that comes your way, but do fear the wish of undertaking more than you are able, and more than God gives you strength to accomplish. The thought of going beyond this makes me tremble with fear, for it seems to be against the designs of Providence. I thank our Lord for his grace to your Daughters which makes them so generous and so well disposed to serve him. There is good reason to believe his goodness, as you said, will supply for whatever might be lacking on your part when you are obliged to attend to other things, such as directing the company.[7]

With this rented room and the Daughters to help, the ladies prepared soups appropriate for the often numerous sick, and distributed these each morning. About three o'clock in the afternoon they would then bring a snack for everyone. It consisted of white bread, cakes, jelly or preserves, raisins or cherries in season, and in winter tea, cooked pears or sugared toast. Later they had to stop the bread, cakes, and tea because of the expense, and also

---

6. *CED* I:371.
7. *CED* I:304-05.

the soup because the hospital itself began to supply it. Each day four or five of the ladies would go to distribute this snack. Putting on an apron, each would go to a particular room, where she would go from bed to bed, distributing what she had brought. This service was given to these poor sick people, or rather to Jesus Christ in their person, to help them in their bodily needs.

To help them spiritually, they would speak to the sick with great kindness, with compassion for their suffering, and with a recommendation to accept their state with patience and submission to God's will. When they came across women or girls not well enough informed about things necessary for salvation, they would gently bring them to understand what must be believed and done to assure salvation. They helped prepare them for a good general confession if it appeared they would benefit from it. If it seemed the illness was mortal, they would help prepare them for a happy death. In those cases where a cure was hoped for, they would try to bring them to resolve to live good lives in the future.

To help out in this charitable service Monsieur Vincent had printed a short tract containing the main points for the instruction of the sick. This booklet contained four recommendations for the ladies: (1) This booklet should be held in the hand when the poor were spoken to, to show that the conversation was not to be general or about themselves, but only of what was in the booklet. (2) They should dress as simply as possible on those days they went to the hospital, or at least keep from vain and fancy clothes so as not to cause difficulty to these poor people. Seeing the excesses and extremes of the rich, they ordinarily think more of the things they do not have than of those things which they need. (3) They should treat the poor with great humility, meekness, and affability, speaking to them in a familiar and cordial manner, the better to gain them to God. [4] He then spoke of the best way to prepare the sick for making a general confession, in simple, colloquial language, which will show the reader the charity that filled the heart of this father of the poor.

> My good sister, has it been a while since you have gone to confession? Would you be willing to make a general confession if you are shown how to do it? I have heard how important it would be for my own salvation to make a good confession before dying. This would remedy faults I may have had in making my ordinary confessions and help me have a greater sorrow for my sins, seeing all I have committed in my whole life and the great mercy of God who has put up with me and has not condemned me or sent me to hell even though I deserved it. Instead, he has waited for my confession to pardon me and give me paradise if I turn to him with my whole heart, as I hope to do with the help of his grace. You may

have the same reasons as myself for making a general confession and giving yourself to God by living a good life. If you want to know what to do to recall your sins and to confess them, I was told to examine myself like I will tell you... etc. I was also told how to have true contrition for my sins, by making acts of contrition, ... etc. I was also taught to make acts of faith, hope, and love of God, ... etc.

This is how the virtuous and charitable ladies, following the advice of their wise director, handled this matter in dealing with the sick poor, to teach them and prepare them for making a good confession. They did so in such a way that there were no complaints, but rather much edification at their good example.

Some two years after the establishment of this company, Monsieur Vincent thought it appropriate to designate every three months a certain number of these ladies to be particularly responsible for the instruction and spiritual consolation of the sick poor. They would leave it to the others to take care of their physical needs. Experience had shown that it was difficult for those who worked at one of these tasks to be competent at the other. Those who had shown a greater aptitude for the spiritual works of mercy were chosen to devote themselves entirely to this aspect of the work. The company was called together in assembly, where they approved this organization and immediately put it into execution. Fourteen ladies were chosen to carry out this plan for three months.[8] The next day a delegation called on the canons of Notre Dame, who were responsible for the direction of the hospital, and then began their visits, two each day of the week, to visit, console, and instruct the sick. Every three months, at the rogation days, another group would take over. The group finishing their tour would meet with those about to start in the presence of Monsieur Vincent and the other officers of the company in their rented room near the hospital. They would hear how the others had carried out their assignments, and which ones seemed to have God's special blessing. What succeeded became the rule for the following group, and they took great encouragement from the successes reported. When appropriate, Monsieur Vincent added a word of advice as to what should be done or avoided, especially in their relationships with the religious of the hospital and the sick.

After the patients had been instructed and disposed to make a good general confession, the ladies would ask several religious priests to follow up, but this led to some difficulties. With the approval of the superiors, two other priests were asked to be available with a decent stipend as encourage-

---

8. They were called the "Assembly of the Fourteen," or the "Little Assembly," to distinguish them from the general assemblies. See *CED* II:283; XIII:762-67, 789, 826.

ment. One of these priests spoke several languages, which made it convenient for those patients from outside France. The two priests were not able to attend to all the poor, since the number of patients increased noticeably. The ladies were overburdened in their efforts to instruct them all. Further, it was not fitting for them to work with the male patients in preparing them for making a good general confession.

All these considerations led them to ask the superiors of the Hotel Dieu if six priests might be assigned there to instruct the men, and hear the confessions of both men and women. These priests would replace those already in residence at the hospital who were obligated to attend the divine office in choir, and so could not give enough time to the sick. These six priests would have as their sole responsibility the spiritual help of the poor with no obligation to attend the public recitation of the office. Before beginning their service in the hospital, the six priests were to make a retreat at Saint Lazare, where Monsieur Vincent lived, to dispose themselves to exercise their charity worthily toward the sick. Each year they were to return to Saint Lazare to renew their dedication to their charitable duties. The ladies gave each priest a stipend of forty *ecus*, arranged for them to say their mass at Notre Dame, and provided room and board for them at the hospital.[9]

To understand better the great good the company of women had produced for the salvation and sanctification of the sick poor, we should remark that previously it had been the custom to have the sick person make his confession upon admittance to the hospital. Ordinarily they were poorly prepared and ill disposed, not to mention their discomfort, depending on which sickness had brought them to the hospital. As a consequence, many of these confessions were null or sacrilegious, not to mention that some heretics among the sick would not reveal their religious affiliation for fear of being sent away. They would go through the appearance of confessing, just like the others. One result of this great abuse was that there were few true conversions. No one spoke to the patients of general confession, nor of any other kind, unless it were at the approach of death. Even then, many did not know how to make a good confession.

The goodness of God met these deplorable conditions by raising up this company of women. By their charitable and zealous dedication, all directed prudently by Monsieur Vincent, they brought a remedy to all these ills. More than this, they contributed much to the salvation and sanctification of these sick poor. Only God knows what great good was effected through his grace. He alone knows the number of those helped to die as a Christian or to begin to lead a new life of virtue. We can say the number must have been large if we judge by the number of persons converted to God in the Catholic Church.

---

9. These six priests were the first to take part in the Tuesday conferences mentioned in ch. 27 above.

In the first year alone, not to speak of the ones following, God's blessing was so manifest upon this enterprise that more than seven hundred sixty persons, estranged from the true faith, renounced their errors and returned to the Church.[10] Whether Lutherans, Calvinists, or even Moslems, some of whom had been wounded, captured at sea, brought to Paris and then to the hospital, all embraced the Catholic faith. The extraordinary blessing of God upon this charitable work in the hospital earned it such a reputation, that when a certain lady in Paris fell ill, she asked to be taken at her own expense to the hospital for the poor, for she preferred to receive the attention and help given to the poor to what she would receive elsewhere. Her wish was granted.

Monsieur Vincent had the consolation of seeing these marvelous fruits for more than twenty-five years. They continued after his death, thanks to God's constant blessing. One day he invited the ladies of the company in their assembly to thank God for having chosen them as the instruments of so many blessings.

> Ladies, how you should thank God for his inspiration to care for the bodily needs of the poor. By helping them this way, you caused them to begin to consider their salvation. Most would never have been so well prepared for death were it not for your help. Those who recovered from their illness would not have changed their lives if you had not cultivated in them such good dispositions.[11]

---

10. Coste believes this number to be exaggerated; *Life* I:285, n. 25.
11. *CED* XIII:803-04.

CHAPTER THIRTY

The Establishment of a Foundling Hospital

PAINTERS WISHING to depict the virtue of charity often use the image of a woman with many breasts and several children in her arms and in her lap. If we wanted to represent the charity of Monsieur Vincent we could use the same symbol, for it is appropriate to the subject of this chapter. We shall see this saintly man as father provider, saving a great number of neglected and abandoned children, earning the right to be credited with saving countless lives. He provided a substitute for those cruel and inhuman mothers who abandoned and exposed their children in the persons of other charitable women who stepped in to rescue and nurture these poor unfortunate infants. This truly Christian undertaking began in this way.

The city of Paris is exceedingly large with an almost countless number of inhabitants. Of necessity there are a certain number of disorders among the people, not all of which can be prevented or remedied. One of the most pernicious of these is the abandonment of newly-born infants, whose life and even salvation is put in jeopardy. The unnatural mothers or others who are responsible for this crime against these innocent creatures, are not concerned about having them baptized into the state of grace.

It has been stated that every year at least three or four hundred abandoned children have been found in Paris or in its immediate suburbs. The commissioners of the Chatelet of Paris are responsible for picking up these children, reporting where they were found, and their condition.

They were first brought to a house called La Couche ["the bed"] in the rue Saint Landry, where a widow and one or two servants received them and attempted to look after them. She was unable to attend to such a large number, nor was she able to find wet-nurses for all or to care for and raise those who were weaned. The cost of the enterprise was so much for her, that a large proportion of the children died of neglect. Sometimes the servants gave a drug to stop the children from crying, but this caused some to die. Those who survived were either given to whomever would come to claim them or sold for the trifling sum of twenty *sous*. They were bought to be nursed by women past the appropriate age, and their unhealthy milk caused the children to die. Others were to substitute for children in families who used them for evil purposes. On other occasions these children were bought for diabolic and magical rites. All these poor innocents seemed condemned to death, or worse, because nobody was seriously concerned about them.

What is worse, some died without baptism. The widow who first took them in stated that she had neither baptized any children herself nor had them baptized by others.

This strange disorder in a city as prosperous as Paris, one well policed and Christian, deeply touched the heart of Monsieur Vincent when be became aware of the problem. Not knowing what course to take, he spoke to the Ladies of Charity. He encouraged them to go to the house which received these children, not so much to see if such evil existed, but rather to see if some way existed to remedy the sad situation. They were deeply moved at the sad plight of these poor innocents who in truth were more to be pitied than those massacred by Herod. Unable to take responsibility for all, they considered taking some at least, to save a few. They first agreed to care for twelve, but not knowing the designs of God upon any of them, they chose them by lot to honor divine Providence. In 1638, they were taken to a rented house outside the Saint Victor gate of the city, and placed under Mademoiselle le Gras' care, helped by several Daughters of Charity sent by Monsieur Vincent. At first they were fed with goats' and cows' milk, and later wet-nurses were provided.

These virtuous ladies took in others from time to time as their resources and devotion would allow, always by lot as in the beginning. Their burning charity made them hope to serve all the other children, but the expense of feeding and educating so many was beyond their resources. The impossibility of carrying out this desirable task confined it for the moment to their noble hearts, without their actually being able to carry it out.

After much prayer and lengthy discussion, a general assembly of the women was called at the beginning of 1640.[1] Monsieur Vincent spoke in terms born of his zeal, of the importance and necessity of this good work and the great service to God it would be to practice excellently a virtue so agreeable to him. A general resolution was adopted to undertake the nurture and education of these children.[2] To avoid haste, following the advice of their wise director, they resolved to begin slowly. This would be an experiment, with no formal obligation to continue, since they had only twelve hundred to fourteen hundred *livres* yearly of assured income. Later the king assigned them the alms of five of his large farms, which amounted to twelve thousand *livres* yearly, thanks to Monsieur Vincent's intervention with the queen mother. Nevertheless, since their expenses came to nearly forty thousand *livres*, the Ladies found it difficult to meet this obligation and feared they would be overwhelmed.

This caused Monsieur Vincent to call another general assembly about

---

1. *CED* XIII:779-85.
2. *CED* II:6-7.

1648 to decide if the Ladies ought to conclude their involvement or continue to care for these children. They were at liberty to take this decision, for no other obligation bound them except their own charity. He proposed reasons for and against. He recalled that they had been responsible for saving some five or six hundred children. Without their intervention, they would surely have died. Some of these children had learned a trade and others were about to. All had been taught to know and serve God. To judge by the past, it could be well imagined how great the fruit of their charity would be. Then, raising his voice, he finished with these words:

> Your compassion and your charity, Ladies, has led you to adopt these children as your own. You have been their mothers according to grace, since their natural mothers have abandoned them. Do you too now want to abandon them? Do you want to stop being their mothers, to become their judges? Their life and their death is in your hands. I am now about to collect your vote. Now is the moment to read their sentence to see if you no longer want to have mercy on them. If you continue to care for them they will live, but if not, if you abandon them, they will surely die. You know from your own experience that this is the truth.[3]

His tone of voice gave no doubt of his own sentiments. The women were so moved by his words that they unanimously agreed to continue this charity no matter what the cost. The only question remaining for them was how to find the necessary means for carrying out this project.

Following this assembly the ladies obtained from the king the chateau of Bicetre, where they housed the children for a time but later moved out.[4] Perhaps because the air was unhealthy or for some other reasons, the women brought the children back to Paris where they rented a large house in the Saint Lazare section of the city. The infants were cared for by ten or twelve Daughters of Charity. Several wet-nurses were engaged to live in this house to nurse the most recent arrivals, while awaiting other women from the country to come to take children home with them.[5] These women received a monthly stipend for this care. Once the children were weaned they were returned to the house, and the Daughters of Charity took care of them. They were taught to speak, to pray to God, to know him, to love him, and to serve him. When they were a little older they were allowed to go to a small workshop. They would thus avoid idleness and await the day when divine

---

3. *CED* XIII:801. Coste corrects the date to 1647.
4. Located near Gentilly, this house had been built under Charles V and restored under Louis XIII to serve as a hospital for wounded soldiers.
5. In his solicitude Vincent did not abandon these poor children. He arranged for the Daughters of Charity to visit them and their nurses, and, in 1649, sent a brother of the Congregation on a six-week tour to bring aid to these nurses in the villages where they lived.

Providence would bring about some way for them to leave the house, ready to earn their own livelihood.

These then are the fruits of this charitable work which has continued for more than twenty-five years under the wise direction of Monsieur Vincent and by the care and service of these virtuous women. Their charity has been so favorable and advantageous to the children that it could be said that they were happier in their abandonment than if they had been raised in their own families. We can presume these must have been either very poor or possibly very wicked. It seemed that God wished to confirm by the support of his grace the first principle of the entire enterprise. This had been said long ago by a prophet, that even if unnatural mothers would abandon their own children, God's paternal Providence would look after them. He would provide other better disposed mothers to love them and supply abundantly what their natural mothers failed to do.[6]

---

6. Isa 49:15.

CHAPTER THIRTY-ONE

The Founding of Several Seminaries for Clergy

GREAT RIVERS always flow toward the ocean, ever being swelled by the waters of brooks and streams along the way. So too with the charity of Monsieur Vincent. It was ever directed to God, but grew each day, not so much from what he received from others, as from what he gave away as divine Providence presented various opportunities to him.

We have seen in several preceding chapters how Monsieur Vincent's zeal moved him to work for the revival of the priestly spirit among the clergy. He instituted the ordination retreats, the clergy conferences and retreats to further this ideal. Although all these were helpful, they still did not bring about in the clergy all the change desirable. He felt the remedy must go to the source of the clerical state, to the formation of young men, who showed signs of a true vocation, in the seminaries envisioned by the holy Council of Trent.

This is why, after moving to Saint Lazare about 1636, he used the College des Bons Enfants as a seminary to train young clerics in letters and morals to prepare them for the state to which they aspired. He realized, however, that it would take a good while before the fruits of this seminary would be seen because of the years it would require before the candidate would be of sufficient age and disposition to receive holy orders.[1] He was also aware of the pressing need the Church had of good priests who could be employed almost immediately in various clerical positions.

His zeal led to the desire that it would please God to supply this need, perhaps by the creation of seminaries for those who had already received holy orders or wished to. In them, the candidates could acquire the proper priestly spirit and be formed in the duties of their state. For him to think of himself as having a part to play in this holy enterprise was contrary to his personal humility. Divine Providence brought it about that he had occasion to mention his ideas to Cardinal Richelieu. Monsieur Vincent occasionally met with him and had spoken several times about how the glory of God might be furthered through reform of the clergy. Monsieur Vincent spoke to the cardinal about the ordination retreats and the clergy conferences already established in several places.

He then described his vision of seminaries in the various dioceses, not so

---

1. *CED* V:563-64.

much for young clerical students, as for those already ordained or about to be in the next ordination class. During one or two years these men would be trained in virtue, prayer, divine service, the rites of the Church, chant, the administration of the sacraments, the catechism, preaching and all other ecclesiastical functions, including cases of conscience or other necessary parts of theological studies. In a word, these men would be helped, not merely to develop their personal spiritual life, but to lead souls into the ways of justice and salvation. Unless something of this sort were done few priests would have the qualities needed to serve and edify the Church. Instead, it would be reasonable to expect that a large number of evil, ignorant, and scandalous priests would continue to be stumbling blocks for the people.

The cardinal heard this description with much appreciation, and urged Monsieur Vincent himself to set about this projected seminary. To help him begin, the cardinal assigned one thousand *ecus* to support the first group of clerics received by Monsieur Vincent in the College des Bons Enfants in February 1642.[2] These men were housed and taught for two years in all things appropriate to their calling. Several other clerics came later, offering to pay their own board, to benefit from the spiritual and academic program. Thus it was that the seminary of the Bons Enfants began under the wise direction of Monsieur Vincent with the permission and encouragement of the late archbishop of Paris.[3] This good prelate had already allowed the priests of the community of Saint Nicolas du Chardonnet to begin another such seminary. God showered many blessings upon it through these priests and especially by the incomparable zeal of Monsieur Bourdoise. Our Lord had conferred on him the true clerical spirit from his youth, joined with a great desire to extend this spirit to others.[4]

Several years after the establishment of this seminary at the College des Bons Enfants the number of clerics increased to such an extent they all could not all be conveniently housed. Monsieur Vincent transferred the young people who had been studying the humanities to another house, located at the edge of the enclosure of Saint Lazare outside the city. He named it the seminary of Saint Charles. The priests of the Congregation of the Mission have continued to teach the humanities there and form in virtue those young men who show some sign of having a clerical vocation.

Since then, many prelates of the kingdom have considered forming similar seminaries in their own dioceses for their young priests. Some of

---

2. *CED* II:223-26.
3. It was later called the seminary of Saint Firmin, and it continued until the French Revolution, when, on September 2, 1792, one of the bloodiest massacres of priests took place there.
4. Adrien Bourdoise, 1584-1655, one of the most zealous reformers of the clergy of his day. He founded a community of priests at the parish Saint Nicolas du Chardonnet. He and Vincent de Paul shared a mutual esteem.

them, in fact, have given over the direction of them to the priests of the Congregation of the Mission. This was the case at Cahors, Saintes, Saint Malo, Treguier, Agen, Montauban, Agde, Troyes, Amiens, Noyon, and several other places not only in France but also in Italy and other foreign provinces. Just as the success of the missions given by Monsieur Vincent and the priests of the Congregation led others to begin missions in their own territory, so the sight of these seminaries established by Monsieur Vincent, whose necessity, utility, and feasibility were shown, led to others in various dioceses of the kingdom. They have contributed greatly to the welfare of the clergy in France, and by God's mercy, the kingdom has begun to regain its original splendor. It could be said this splendor had been tarnished a bit during these last few centuries.

CHAPTER THIRTY-ONE (BIS)

Monsieur Vincent's Collaboration with Father Olier[1]

GREAT SERVANTS of God, animated by the same spirit, should be fittingly associated with each other and help each other in their charitable enterprises. Such was the case with Monsieur Vincent and the late Father Olier, a great servant of God, whose memory is held in benediction, and who was endowed by God with a truly apostolic spirit.[2]

Monsieur Vincent had a special appreciation and respect for the person and the sanctity of Father Olier. The feeling was mutual, for in his turn Father Olier looked upon Monsieur Vincent as his spiritual father and would often say to his seminarians that "Monsieur Vincent is our father." Monsieur Olier often showed his esteem for the virtues he practiced and on occasion would quote Monsieur Vincent's maxims as a stimulus for their own life of virtue. We learn this from those fortunate enough to have been under Monsieur Olier's charge. He was among the first to come to the ordination retreats, which prepared ordinands for the reception of holy orders, as we have already pointed out. From these exercises he drew his inspiration for the true priestly spirit which was so characteristic of him. He was among the first of those, in the exercise of this spirit, to attend the spiritual conferences held every week at Saint Lazare under the personal direction of Monsieur Vincent. Later, he joined some priests of the Congregation of the Mission in the giving of missions. In January 1635 he worked on a mission at Crecy, and in the following year, during the Lenten season, he volunteered to help in the mission given in the hospital of la Pitie in the faubourg Saint Victor.

Seeing at first hand the benefits of these missions for the conversion and sanctification of souls, he wished to bring them to the parishes that depended upon his abbey of Pebrac in Auvergne. He was able to do so after Lent of that same year. Two priests of the Congregation of the Mission helped him, and several other devoted priests who joined him in this work. This first mission was given at Saint Ilpise. It was reported to the clergy conference at Saint Lazare by an edifying letter in which Monsieur Olier speaks of the

---

1. This chapter was intended for inclusion by Abelly, but was published only in 1841 after it was recovered from the Sulpician archives.
2. Jean Jacques Olier, 1608-1657, was one of the main restorers of ecclesiastical discipline in the seventeenth century. He was ordained in 1633, and then worked on the missions, often with the priests of Saint Lazare, whom he edified by his zeal and humility. He continued to seek advice from Saint Vincent. Vincent assisted at his death, and consoled Olier's community afterwards. For his words on that occasion, see *CED* XIII:166-67.

success of the mission and of his own thoughts about the efficacy of this particular form of religious devotion. For the edification of our readers, we will give this letter in detail in Book Two of this Life.[3]

This worthy priest, following the success of the missions, obtained the authorization of the bishop of Saint Flour[4] for a mission to the priests of the diocese. It would be given in his abbey of Pebrac, along with ordination retreats such as were conducted at Paris. He wrote again in October of that same year to the priests of the clergy conference at Saint Lazare in Paris. He sought their help in what he considered to be the reformation of an entire diocese. In February 1637 he wrote again, after a fourth mission, when about to begin an important fifth one in La Motte, near the city of Brioude. He spoke in this letter of what had already been accomplished by the priests of the city of Le Puy, whom he had put in contact with the clergy conference of Saint Lazare in Paris.

About this same time, Monsieur Olier was well aware from his own experience how greatly the missions helped the welfare of the people, and he realized the need for working to reform the clergy. He decided to give himself to this task. He agreed to accept the charge of a parish in Paris to give the example of what a well-organized parish, a devoted pastor, and a committed clergy could contribute to the welfare of the people. He discussed this with Monsieur de Fresque, the pastor of Saint Sulpice, and was able later to establish a community of priests which proved to be most successful, as all are now aware. In a short time the parish became the admiration and the talk of all Paris, so great was the change brought about. This did not happen without serious troubles raised by the enemy of all humanity, to the extent that upon a misunderstanding having arisen between the former and the present pastor, some neighbors of the faubourg Saint Germain took up arms to dislodge Monsieur Olier and his priests from the parish.

During these troubles, Monsieur Vincent, always so devoted to the good priest, did all he could to defend and support him by his prayers to God, by his advice, and by his influence at court. It should be remarked that Monsieur Vincent himself was blamed by some as causing the troubles because the people called the community of priests at Saint Sulpice "missionaries" although they were not so. This happened possibly because Monsieur Vincent was thought of as their superior. Some short while before he had sent some priests from the clergy conference of Saint Lazare to the faubourg Saint Germain for a mission, and this led to the confusion.

One day in the Council for Ecclesiastical Affairs of the kingdom, when the subject of this disturbance came up for discussion, Monsieur Vincent was blamed for all the troubles. Rather than defend himself by stating, as

---

3. Ch. 1, sect. 2, part 3.
4. Charles de Noailles, bishop from 1610 to 1646.

was true, that the priests of Saint Sulpice did not belong to his Congregation and had no allegiance to him whatsoever, as he did on many other occasions when their good deeds were praised, he said not a single word in his own defense or to disabuse his accusers. On the contrary, in humility, and to express his esteem for Monsieur Olier and his priests, he took their side completely. He defended their interests more energetically than he would have defended his own. When they were blamed and condemned, he became their apologist, speaking of all the good they did and the happy results of their zeal. To preserve their reputation he endangered his own, allowing his own Congregation to be blamed, in an effort to protect Monsieur Olier and his priests and to enable them to live in peace and tranquility.

This stance of Monsieur Vincent ran so contrary to human prudence that it astonished some of his friends. When they asked why he acted so, he replied that he thought all Christians would have done the same. In acting as he did he felt he was simply following the maxims of the Gospel. His esteem for the virtue of Monsieur Olier gave him this opinion. He looked upon Monsieur Olier's work, not simply as an isolated good deed, but as a public service demanding the support of all persons of good will.

Some time later, Monsieur Olier expanded the field of his zeal to encompass the founding of a seminary which served then, and up to our own time, to train clerics of all classes of society for the benefit of the Church in whatever part of the kingdom they later served. They brought, to the great advantage of the Church, the graces and blessings which they had drawn from that sacred spot.[5]

Because of Monsieur Olier's contributions of which we have spoken, and the great virtues with which God had endowed him, Monsieur Vincent looked upon him as a saint.[6] He did not hesitate to speak everywhere of this conviction. When it pleased God to recall this great servant to himself, Monsieur Vincent attended him at his last illness and death.[7] He was among the many who grieved over the great loss to the Church in the person of this saintly priest. In his remaining years Monsieur Vincent continued to serve the priests of Olier's community. He would meet with them, together with some others of great reputation, to find ways of perpetuating the excellent work begun so worthily by Monsieur Olier.[8]

---

5. Here too Monsieur Vincent was able to help Monsieur Olier. This can be seen by the praise that he gave of Saint Sulpice to a priest and a pious woman desirous of helping their seminary. See Book Three, ch. 11, sect. 5.
6. *CED* VIII:330.
7. *CED* VI:275.
8. Vincent presided at the assembly of April 13, 1657, called to select a successor to Olier. He was authorized for this by Henri de Bourbon, bishop of Metz and abbot of Saint Germain, the ecclesiastical superior of the community of Saint Sulpice. Vincent signed the official notarized record of the proceedings.

CHAPTER THIRTY-TWO

Some Help Given by Monsieur Vincent to the late Commander de Sillery and to the Order of Saint John of Jerusalem, commonly called the Knights of Malta

THE LATE Monsieur Noel Brulart de Sillery, commander of the Temple of Troyes, of the Order of Saint John of Jerusalem, had served in the embassies in Italy, Spain, and other distant lands.[1] He had undertaken other important affairs for the king, always with honor and to the entire satisfaction of His Majesty. He was moved by grace to give himself totally to God by separating himself from court and from all worldly distractions to consecrate his life to God's service and to the sanctification and salvation of his soul. From his days at court he had heard of Monsieur Vincent and had formed a high opinion of his virtue. This led him to seek his counsel in his plan to change his style of life. His disposition was so good, and his willingness to follow the advice of his wise director so marked that in a short time a decided change was noted in his person and in his behavior.

Recognizing the vanity of luxury and the cost of living in the grand style, he left his home, the Hotel de Sillery, with all its sumptuous and magnificent fittings which were appropriate to the many high offices he held. He dismissed the larger part of his entourage after paying his servants in proportion to their years of service. He sold his most costly furniture and distributed large sums to various works of charity. He then was inspired to consecrate himself more completely to God by entering the priesthood. He did so after taking advice from Monsieur Vincent and disposing himself to receive this great sacrament worthily by suitable practices of piety. He began to live[2] in a manner befitting his sacred calling, giving himself to the practice of the virtues. He resolved to put himself under the spiritual direction of Monsieur Vincent and to regulate his life completely under his guidance. This is what he wrote in one of his letters:

My reverend and dear Father:

I have no doubt that you were well aware of how much your friendly and cordial letter would delight your wretched son. Not only was your letter cordial beyond what all others might be, it also spoke to me as master and superior, which I willingly acknowledge,

---

1. His title, commander, derived from the order of military knighthood, and entitled its lay bearer to income from a benefice. The name Temple was given to the order's house or church.
2. At Saint Lazare, March 1634. *CED* I:234-35.

in asking me to dispose of my weapons. I would be rude and rustic if I did not respond to your charity so lovingly displayed toward me, from a worthy and thoughtful father toward an unfeeling son. There is no other remedy for this than to accept willingly and humbly the confusion I feel at all the failings you know only too well, for which I beg pardon with reverence and submission. I promise you, with the help of our Lord's grace, my most dear father, that I will correct myself. Yes, Father, I have never been so determined as I am now. If only we can work together in amending the many ills your reverence knows so well I am completely filled with, I would be overjoyed in consolation. Should this happy outcome not develop so soon or so completely as your goodness desires, I entreat you, my worthy Father, *per viscera misericordiae Dei nostri in quibus visitavit nos oriens ex alto* ["through the deep mercy of our God, the rising sun has visited us"].[3] not to despair, and not to leave your poor son. You know well he will be poorly guided if he is left to his own devices.[4]

In this letter it is difficult to say what is the more praiseworthy, the humility and simplicity of a man who had passed the greater part of his life among the intrigues of court and in the conduct of important business for the king, or the wise and helpful direction of Monsieur Vincent which had, by the grace of God, gained such ascendancy over the mind and heart of this noble person.

After such a change in his status and in his daily routine, the Commander de Sillery was moved by his zeal to contribute to the spiritual progress of the religious and pastors of his order, members of the Grand Priory of the Temple. He received a commission from the Grand Master of Malta to visit the houses and spoke with Monsieur Vincent as to the best way to make these visits fruitful. They agreed that missionaries would accompany the commander to give missions in the parishes at the same time they were visited. This would both help the people and give the religious and pastors responsible for the parishes a good idea of the problems and remedies appropriate to the situation. They carried out these visits with great success. When this came to the attention of the grand master of Malta, he was so pleased he wrote the following letter to Monsieur Vincent to thank him:

> Monsieur, I have been informed that the renowned bailiff of Sillery selected you to help in the visits to the churches and parishes which depend on the Grand Priory and that you have already begun to devote yourself to instruct those who need it so much. This leads

---

3. Luke 1:67-68.
4. *CED* I:41-42.

me to write these affectionate lines to thank you and to ask you to continue this service for no other reason than the greater glory of God and the honor and reputation of this order. I beg the goodness of God with all my heart to repay your zeal and charity by his graces and blessings, and to bestow on me the ability to convey to you the depths of my gratitude. Yours, . . . etc.

Grand Master [Paul] Lascaris of Malta, September 17, 1637.[5]

The commander considered that it was not enough to tidy up the stream if the source was not cared for, and so felt unsatisfied at simply making the visits well. Besides, he wanted to assure good priests for the Temple at Paris and to choose candidates recognized as called by God to service in this community. He wanted to assure that those who received the habit of the order would likewise be clothed in its spirit. He hoped that from their number worthy men would be chosen to serve as pastors, and so little by little the face of this great order would be renewed.

Unfortunately, this pious wish did not succeed as much as he had hoped, although Monsieur Vincent had a hand in the enterprise and had spent some time in the Temple. Monsieur Vincent was not permitted to carry out his ideas, and so the results were disappointing. He wrote to one of his confidants:[6]

I was shocked at the hastiness of the Temple affair, which I fear did not have the success I had hoped for. I spoke out over and over again, but no one listened. Humility obliged me to defer, but my head told me things would not go well. *In nomine Domini* ["In the name of the Lord"]. I know of nothing so common as the poor success of things done in haste.[7]

We learn from another letter of the grand master of Malta that Monsieur Vincent had written several times about the Commander de Sillery and to recommend his own projects to his prayers. He obtained the authorization of the order for the disposal of the commander's large fortune in favor of different charitable works. Chief among these, in recognition of his obligations to Monsieur Vincent and in consideration of the great good his Congregation had contributed and could still in future be expected to contribute to the Church, were benefactions in favor of the Congregation of the Mission. He gave a large sum for the foundation of a house and seminary for the city of Annecy in the diocese of Geneva, helped out in the foundation in Troyes, and provided for the upkeep of Saint Lazare, motherhouse of the Congregation. He gained the eternal gratitude of the community for his

---
5. *CED* I:389-90.
6. Louise de Marillac.
7. *CED* I:434-35.

charity.[8] God recompensed him by the many graces he conferred upon him, not only in life, but especially at his death, which was precious in the sight of his divine Majesty. In his last hours, Monsieur Vincent gave him every possible help and was able to say later that he had never seen a person die so filled with God as was this virtuous and charitable gentleman.[9]

---

8. *CED* I:498-99.
9. *CED* II:142-43.

CHAPTER THIRTY-THREE

Missions Given in the Army in 1636, and the Rules Given by Monsieur Vincent to the Missionaries for this Service

THE INVASION of Picardy by foreign troops in 1636 and their first success at the city of Corbie still live vividly in memory.[1] This army was so large and its advance scouts so active that real concern was created, especially since no force seemed available to stop their advance. The royal armies were engaged either outside the kingdom or in the most distant provinces. Nevertheless, the late king, Louis XIII of glorious memory, raised a new army in a short time. He chose the house of Saint Lazare as one of the places to enroll the recruits and to train them to defend the nation. The Saint Lazare community was given the opportunity to show its obedience and affection for the service of His Majesty by carrying out this responsibility. This is what Monsieur Vincent wrote to one of his priests then in Auvergne, giving a mission with the late Monsieur Olier.

Paris is threatened with a siege by the army now ravaging Picardy, whose advance elements are within ten or twelve leagues of the city. Most of the people from the region have come to Paris for refuge. Paris itself is so threatened that some of its inhabitants have sought shelter in other cities. The king has raised an army to oppose our enemies, for his other forces are either out of the kingdom or are engaged in our most distant provinces. The site for mustering and equipping the soldiers is in our very house. The courtyards, the stable, the woodshed, and the cloister are filled with arms, and the courtyards are teeming with soldiers. The holy day of the Assumption was no exception to the tumult and confusion, for a drum started beating before seven o'clock in the morning. In the last eight days more than seventy-two companies have passed through here.

While all this was going on, our little Company continued its retreat except for three or four who are on the point of leaving the community. I have written to Monsieur Olier that I may be able to send him four or five of our priests. I will send others to the bishops of Arles and Cahors,[2] and I hope they can get off before things get more hectic here.[3]

---

1. The Spanish, marking the beginning of the French period of the Thirty-Years War.
2. Jean Jaubert de Barrault, bishop of Arles, 1630-1643; Blessed Alain de Solminihac, bishop of Cahors, 1636-1659.
3. *CED* I:339-41.

This letter allows us to see not only the marvelous spirit of Monsieur Vincent but also the extent of his virtue and the ardor of his zeal. In the midst of the noisy tumult of an army, with his house filled with soldiers, with arms and other weapons on every side, with the sound of drums in the air, he remains in great peace and tranquility. His priests are on retreat and are making their usual spiritual exercises. While allowing his house to be used for training the soldiers for the service of state and king, he busies himself with preparing missionaries for new fields of service to God and Church. His house has become a training ground for preparing soldiers of Jesus Christ for their battle against the devil. In what country? He thinks, like the prophet Habakkuk,[4] of sending some helpers to the bishops mentioned in his letter. Suddenly he is carried off, as it were, to Babylon, among the lions. The chancellor[5] sent him an order from the king that he should send twenty priests to the army to give missions among the soldiers.

Such a thing had never been heard of before, and it promised to be most difficult. Monsieur Vincent could say, in imitation of the prophet, that he did not know the way to this Babylon, for he had never before been in any army. He allowed himself to be taken by the hair of his head, that is, he submitted his own judgment to the king's and showed by his response that his obedience and affection for His Majesty was in keeping with all his other virtues. At once he sent fifteen priests, not having any others available, to the army in camp, where they began to take up the work for which they had been sent.[6]

Monsieur Vincent went at this same time to Senlis, where the king had retreated, to offer his and his Congregation's service to His Majesty. After this he left a priest with the court to receive any orders the king might think proper to give and to relay them to the superior of the priests serving with the army.[7] Later he bought a tent for the priests and sent along some furnishings and some food in a cart drawn by a mule, which they were to keep for their use. He also gave them a set of rules and regulations about what they were to do and say while serving on this mission.

The priests of the Congregation of the Mission who serve the army must remember that our Lord has called them to this holy service: (1) to offer their prayers and sacrifices to God for the happy outcome of the king's plans, and for the welfare of his army; (2) to aid the soldiers who may be in a state of sin to leave this sad condition, to help those in the state of grace to remain so, and

---

4. The prophet Habakkuk of Dan 14:36.
5. Pierre Seguier, *CED* I:343-44.
6. Only Fathers du Coudray, Lambert, Grenu and Mulan, and Brother Alexandre are named.
7. Robert de Sergis. The plague was rampant in the army, and Monsieur Vincent did not hesitate to recall a priest in the service of the king to send him to those stricken soldiers. *CED* I:351-52.

especially to do all in their power to help the dying leave this life in a state of grace.

They should cultivate a devotion to the name of God, given in the Scripture as the God of the Armies, and to the sentiments of our Lord who said: *Non veni pacem mittere, sed gladium* ["I came not to bring peace but the sword"],[8] but said this to give us peace, the end of war.

They should reflect that they can hardly eradicate all sin from the army, but perhaps God will give them the grace to diminish the number. This is as though one were to say that our Lord must again be crucified a hundred times, but perhaps we can reduce this to ninety. If a thousand souls by their evil dispositions are headed for damnation, we must see if, by God's merciful grace, we cannot reduce this number.

The virtues of charity, fervor, mortification, obedience, patience, and modesty are necessary for us to achieve this. We must continually be attentive to this, both interiorly and exteriorly, and give special attention to accomplishing the will of God.

They will celebrate mass each day, or at least communicate, for these intentions.

They will honor the silence of our Lord at the usual hours and will not speak of affairs of state. They will speak of any troubles they may have to their superiors only or to him who shall be appointed to hear them.

If called to hear confessions of those afflicted by the plague, they shall do so from afar and with all necessary precautions. They shall leave the care of the sick in the hands of those Providence has destined for this service.

They should meet together often, after reflecting before God of what should be discussed, for example, (1) the importance of having priests help the army, (2) what help should be given, (3) how best to carry out this help.

They might treat in the same manner other subjects appropriate to their assignment, such as help for the sick, what to do during battles and combats, the virtues to be practiced in the army service, such as humility, patience, and modesty.

The smallest rules of the Mission should be observed as closely as possible, especially in what concerns the hours of rising and retiring, prayer, the divine office, spiritual reading, and the various examinations of conscience.

---

8. Matt 10:34.

The superior shall apportion assignments to each one, to one the care of the sacristy, to another the hearing of confessions and the reading at table, to another the sick, to another to serve as procurator and to prepare the food, to another the tent and its furnishings to see to its being taken down and put up again at new locations. The priests shall be assigned to preaching and the hearing of confessions as the superior will judge proper.

As much as possible the priests shall live together. If they should be assigned to various places, such as the advance guard, the rear guard, or into the main body of the army, the superior will assign the various ones to each position. If possible, the priests should live in tents.[9]

Such were the regulations Monsieur Vincent gave to these missionaries. Their faithful observance drew down upon them and their works the greatest blessings, as we learn from a letter he wrote to one of the priests:

Blessed be God for the blessing he has given your work, Monsieur, which seems to me to be so great. What? To have done your part in having three hundred soldiers receive communion so devoutly—soldiers going off to death! Only those who reflect on the pains of hell or on the price of the blood of Jesus Christ for even one soul can appreciate the value of what you have done. Even though I do not know these truths sufficiently myself, I understand them somewhat, enough to appreciate what you have done for these three hundred penitents. This past Tuesday nine hundred soldiers went to confession during our missions with the army, not counting yours or those made since. O God, Monsieur, how this has surpassed my fondest hopes! We must humble ourselves, praise God, and continue with courage, for as long as we are not assigned elsewhere.[10]

He wrote in another letter to Monsieur Portail, on September 20, to excuse himself for not sending the missionaries he had promised to Father Olier:

It is impossible to send the missionaries you expected, for the ones we had prepared have been ordered to report to the regiments of the army in Luzarches, Pons, Saint Leu, and La Chapelle Orly. Already almost four thousand soldiers have appeared before the tribunal of mercy with every sign of true repentance. I hope God will be merciful to many because of this service, and perhaps favor the armies of the king.[11]

---

9. *CED* XIII:279-81.
10. *CED* I:344.
11. *CED* I:346-47.

After these four thousand confessions, the missionaries were obliged to follow the army and camp with it. At each stop, besides the spiritual help the priests gave the soldiers, several people in the dioceses through which they passed also came to confession and communion, in keeping with the express permission of the local bishops.

One of the Missionaries in charge of a group of priests wrote to Monsieur Vincent that they worked constantly for the spiritual welfare of the sick, whether soldiers or civilians, and for the refugees from Picardy. Many of the sick died, but not before receiving the last sacraments from them. Six weeks later a first group of Missionaries returned to Saint Lazare, while others remained with the army until November, when it returned triumphantly from its encounters with the enemy.

CHAPTER THIRTY-FOUR

The Establishment of the First Internal Seminary, at Saint Lazare, for the Congregation of the Mission

THE FATHERS of the desert followed a well-known maxim of receiving no one into their congregations unless he were well known and of proven virtue. This maxim has since been observed in all communities, both secular and regular, which have been established from time to time in the Church. As one of the most experienced of these ancients said so well, gold should not be worked or finished until it has been tested.[1] Aspirants to the perfection of the religious state, to which they feel called by God to dedicate themselves to his service, ought to pass various tests both to know themselves better and to dispose themselves better to work for the goal they proposed to themselves.

During the first years, when Monsieur Vincent began to work on the missions he did not yet realize the designs of God nor what God may have wanted to accomplish with him and by him. He did not specify any definite program of training for those who wished to join him in his efforts. He was satisfied with the good will that brought these first members to him. At best, he invited them to make a retreat both to strengthen their own resolution and to implore the help of divine grace. Some time later he felt some spiritual exercises ought to be added to the retreat, which was prolonged somewhat more than was usual at the time. Gradually seeing his Congregation take form, and knowing the importance of admitting only well-intentioned subjects called by God, he decided that those who came must first pass some time in a seminary[2] under a director who would form them in the practices of the virtues and introduce them to the spiritual life.

The first director chosen was Monsieur Jean de la Salle, one of the three priests who had first joined him, whom he supplied with a daily timetable and a few general regulations. This seminary was begun in June 1637 in the house of Saint Lazare, where it has remained ever since, always blessed by God. Ordinarily there were about thirty or forty seminarians, both priests and clerics. This was the first seminary exclusively for the priests of the Congregation of the Mission. The others, mentioned earlier, were for ecclesiastics who were not members of the Congregation. Monsieur Vincent referred to it as *spes gregis* ["hope of the flock"] and as the nursery of the

---

1. John Climacus, PG 88.
2. I.e., novitiate for the Congregation of the Mission.

missionaries. His confidence in the paternal Providence was such that he never doubted about adequate numbers of applicants for the seminary. He took as a maxim that God would choose and call whom he would. Just as the first missionaries of the Son of God, his apostles, did not choose themselves but were selected by this divine Savior who called those he wished, so too those who would give themselves to God to work, in imitation of many great saints, at instructing and converting the people must be chosen and called by this same Lord.

For this same reason Monsieur Vincent never wanted to say a single word to anyone to attract him to the Congregation. He forbade his confreres to persuade anyone to enter. This is what he said on this matter:

> Ordinarily, God chooses the weak to do his great deeds. We have in our own Congregation some who were admitted with much difficulty and misgivings because they offered little hope, but today we see them as good laborers in the vineyard of the Lord. Some are superiors who direct their missions with prudence and grace. We must praise God for them and admire his influence over them. Oh, gentlemen, be careful when you receive people into the house for their spiritual retreat that you never say anything which would tend to attract them to our Company. It is up to God to call them and provide the initial inspiration. Even more, when you see they are inclined this way, be careful that you do not decide for them that they are to be Missionaries, either by your counsel or by your exhortations. Say only they must turn more and more to God to seek his will and to think over carefully such an important matter. Point out to them the hardships they can expect if they embrace this state in life and how they must be prepared to work and suffer for the sake of God. If they still persist, they should be referred to the superior to speak more fully about their vocation. Leave this to God, gentlemen, and remain humbly in expectation and in dependence on the good pleasure of his Providence.
>
> By his mercy, this is what we have done in the Company up to the present, and we can say that whatever has come to us has been sent by God. We have sought neither men, goods, nor foundations. In the name of God, keep it like this and allow God to sustain us. Follow his initiative, please, and do not attempt to anticipate his direction of us. Believe me, if the Congregation follows this path, God will bless us.
>
> If you see that any of the retreatants have the thought of going elsewhere to serve God in some other community, O God! do not prevent them, lest the anger of God fall upon our Company for

trying to arrange something contrary to his holy will. And tell me, if you will, if the Company up to the present has not acted this way, in never trying to persuade others to join us, no matter how promising, unless they were sent to us by God and have been considering this vocation for a long time. The Carthusian priests and other religious communities have sent us several young men to make a retreat when they have applied there. They are cautious.

What then? Here is a young man with the thought of becoming a Carthusian. He was sent here on retreat to consider before the Lord what he is being called to, and you try to persuade him to remain here! What is that, gentlemen, if not trying to hold on to what does not belong to us? Or to enter a Congregation which God does not call him to, or which he has not even given a thought to? What would be the effect of this, other than to draw down the curse of God upon our Company? O poor Company of Missionaries if you ever fell into this sad plight! But by the grace of God you have not, and never will. Pray to God, gentlemen, pray to God to confirm this Company in the grace he has given us up to now of seeking nothing but his holy will.[3]

Another day Monsieur Vincent received a letter from a priest of the Congregation.[4] It informed him of a most virtuous ecclesiastic whom he thought a good candidate for the life of a Missionary. This person even seemed to show some inclination toward the Congregation. Monsieur Vincent replied:

I have not sent your letter to Monsieur N. [Serre],[5] for it persuades him to enter our Company, but we have a contrary maxim, never to ask anyone to join our community. God alone will choose whom he will, and we are well convinced that a missionary called by him will do more good than many others without a true vocation. We must pray that he send good laborers for the harvest, and live so our good example will attract many others, if God so wills.[6]

This is the way Monsieur Vincent spoke, and this is the way he acted. Some people spoke or wrote to him, each in his own way:

Monsieur, I am putting myself totally into your hands to do whatever you consider God is calling me to. Tell me, then, what should I do? Should I quit the world for this or that state? I am convinced that God sent me to you to know his will. I am indifferent to what I should do, so I will follow your suggestion as a most assured manifestation of the will of God.

---

3. *CED* XI:425-27.
4. Jean de Lestang.
5. Louis Serre later joined the Congregation.
6. *CED* VIII:286-87.

There were many such cases, but this humble and wise servant of God almost never would suggest or prescribe the state of life they should embrace. As he used to say, he feared he would be anticipating God's Providence and presuming on the direction of his sovereign will rather than humbly and faithfully following it.

> The solution of your uncertainty is a matter that must be resolved between God and yourself. Continue to pray for his inspiration about what you are to do. Make a retreat for several days for this purpose and be persuaded that the resolution you come to in the presence of the Lord shall be most agreeable to his divine Majesty and most helpful to yourself.

For those who came to him after deciding to leave the world, but remained undecided about which of two well regulated communities to join, he would send them away to have them consider before God which to choose. If the Congregation of the Mission was one of the two, he would say, "Oh, Monsieur, we are a poor Company unworthy to be compared to this other congregation. Go, in the name of the Lord. You will be much happier there than with us."[7]

For those who came determined to enter the Congregation, he was most hesitant to accept them. He would ask, "How long have you been thinking of this? How and on what occasion did this thought first come to you? What is your occupation? What motive leads you to seek to be a Missionary? Are you disposed to go wherever you might be sent, even to the most remote foreign lands? Are you ready to endure all hardships?" He would point out the difficulties likely to come about in their new state.

He would send them away several times without giving any decision, and even with little hope of being accepted, to test their vocation and virtue. He would put them off for a long time, obliging them to come back several times to get to know them better. He would never give them a definite answer no matter how satisfied he was of their dispositions and their perseverance until he had them make a retreat to discern God's will. If they persevered in their first objective he would have them meet some of the older members of the community. If these men judged them suitable for the Congregation he finally would accept them for the internal seminary. There they would receive two years of training in humility, mortification, devotion, recollection, punctuality, and other practices conducive to a life of virtue, and to honor, as he used to say, the infancy of our Lord. He hoped they would become prayerful to prepare themselves for the unction of the Spirit of God, which would preserve in them the fire of charity in their hearts among all the trials and labors of the missions.[8] After successfully completing the

---

7. *CED XII:316.*
8. See *CED* XI:126-28; XII:63-64.

seminary program the candidates were finally admitted to the Congregation. If they had not completed their studies, they did so to have the requisite learning befitting their state.

He wrote out in his own hand a short summary of the dispositions they should possess as a member of the Congregation of the Mission.

> One who wishes to live in community should resolve to live as a pilgrim upon earth, making himself a fool for Jesus Christ. He should be converted, mortify all the passions, seek God alone, submit himself to everyone as the least of all, be persuaded that he has come to serve and not to govern, to suffer and work, not to live in ease and laziness. He should realize that a person is purified like gold in the furnace and that he cannot persevere unless he humble himself before God. In doing so he should be persuaded that he will achieve true contentment in this life and eternal happiness in the next.[9]

In these few words the saintly man touched on many things. We can safely say he preserved the community from those who, not finding their ease or satisfaction in the world, hope they might settle down to a life of peace and repose in the Congregation of the Mission.

Here is yet another word on the dispositions he desired to see in his confreres, which he spoke to his community on an occasion when word was received of a missionary maltreated in a foreign country.[10]

> Please God, my brothers, that all who come to the Company come with the thought of martyrdom, with the desire to suffer death and to consecrate themselves totally to serve God either in a foreign land or here at home or wherever it shall please God to use this poor little Company. Yes, with the thought of martyrdom. Oh, how often we should ask this grace of our Lord! Alas, gentlemen and my brothers, is anything more reasonable than to give one's life for him who has so freely given his for us? If our Lord has loved us so much as to die for us, why do we not have the same affection for him and show it, should the occasion present itself? We see a list of popes who one after the other have been martyred. Isn't it astonishing to see businessmen, for a little profit, cross the seas and run a thousand risks? Last Sunday I met a man who said he had been persuaded to go to the Indies. When I asked him if it were not dangerous, he admitted it was. He knew one merchant who had returned, but another who had not. I then said to myself, if this person, for a few precious stones and a trifling gain, is willing to risk so many

---

9. A nearly literal translation from Book 1, ch. 16, of the *Imitation of Christ*.
10. Jean Barreau, consul at Algiers.

dangers, how much more we should be willing to do so to gain the precious jewel of the Gospel and to win souls to Jesus Christ?[11]

---

11. *CED* XI:370-72.

CHAPTER THIRTY-FIVE

Monsieur Vincent Devotes Himself to the Poor of Lorraine during the War and Takes Particular Care of Some Gentlemen and Ladies, Refugees in Paris

SAINT AUGUSTINE says rightly that God is so good he allows no evil from which he cannot draw a greater good. We could appeal to an almost infinite number of examples to illustrate this truth. We do not have to go farther afield than the last war in Lorraine, when it seemed that God permitted the extreme sufferings of this formerly blessed province to draw forth greater spiritual good. The war provided the opportunity for many virtuous persons, among them Monsieur Vincent, to show heroic charity in the service of the needy. He showed these poor suffering people to what degree charity can rise in this last age, when, according to the prediction of Jesus Christ, because of the iniquity which has abounded on all sides, charity has grown cold.[1]

When Monsieur Vincent was alerted in 1639 to the deplorable state to which Lorraine had been reduced by war,[2] he immediately resolved to offer help. He took some alms at his disposal, added some of his own, and gave them to his confreres to distribute. These alms were soon exhausted. Those who had gone to distribute them returned with almost unbelievable stories of what they had seen with their own eyes. This so affected Monsieur Vincent and several other persons in Paris to whom he related the sad story that all resolved to aid these unfortunate people at whatever cost. These good people donated great sums to the cause which Monsieur Vincent sent by one of his religious to be distributed to those in the greatest need. He did so not only in the villages but also in the larger cities. One would think them nearly untouched by war, such as Metz, Toul, Verdun, Nancy, Bar le Duc, Pont a Mousson, Saint Mihiel, and others, yet in these deplorable times people of all classes were reduced to direst necessity. Mothers reportedly crazed by hunger ate their own children. Girls and young women were ready to give themselves in prostitution to avoid death. Even reformed religious broke their cloister to seek bread, to the peril of their virtue and the scandal of the Church.

The enormous number of people of all classes and of both sexes, reduced

---

1. Matt 24:12.
2. The last period of the Thirty-Years War. In this period, Charles V, the duke of Lorraine, was defeated by Richelieu's political and military strategy.

to extreme necessity, soon exhausted even the abundant alms sent to them. A charity less than what Monsieur Vincent had would have lost heart and judged the situation hopeless, especially because of the other pressing problems in Paris and in the rest of France. But what can a heart not do which loves God and trusts in him completely? "I can do all things in him who strengthens me," says the apostle.[3] Monsieur Vincent could say the same. God so blessed his efforts in coordinating the contributions of many that he sent at various times nearly 1.6 million *livres* to Lorraine. The queen mother gave a part, and the Ladies of Charity in Paris had contributed significantly to this sum.[4]

During the nine or ten years of this sad state of affairs, people knew that a brother of the mission had made fifty-three trips to Lorraine to bring the money collected to the needy.[5] He carried at least twenty thousand *livres* each time, and sometimes twenty-five or thirty thousand *livres* or even more. What is miraculous is that by God's protection he passed through regions occupied by the army and through places threatened by soldiers and exposed to their pillaging. Yet he was never robbed or searched, but always arrived safely at the place destined to receive the alms.

To be of even greater service to the poor and to stretch out what he was providing, Monsieur Vincent instructed the Missionaries serving in Lorraine to provide a daily distribution of bread and soup and to be mindful of the sick as well. At the same time as the distribution of food, the fathers were not to forget spiritual blessings as well, by instruction, consolation, and encouragement so that the care of souls would accompany concern for bodily needs.

Who can count the number of persons this faithful provider had helped in body and soul through the urgings of his immense charity? How many did he rescue from the depths of despair? He was well aware that God was the prime author of all these benefactions and we will see more particularly in Book Two more of what was involved in this marvelous undertaking.[6]

Even this is not the whole story. The providence of God provided a new opportunity for this father of the poor to show the extent of his charity. The continued misery in Lorraine and the war obliged a group of inhabitants of the region to leave to seek refuge in Paris. There they found themselves under Monsieur Vincent's care as the assured refuge of the poor and needy. He found housing, food, and clothing for them in various places. When he found some among them who had not received the sacraments for a long time,

---

3. Phil 4:13.
4. King Louis XIII, a few days before his death, also contributed from his personal funds. Coste, *Life*, II:371.
5. Mathieu Regnard, 1592-1669.
6. Ch. 11.

because of the troubled times or because of the absence of their pastors through death or flight, he organized two missions for them. These were held during the Easter season for two consecutive years[7] in a village church about half a league from Paris called La Chapelle. Many distinguished people came from Paris, either to attend the mission or to help out in some way. The exiles received the spiritual help of the exercises, as well as the corporal help they so badly needed. The former group served the latter, and these latter were enabled to make their way in the world.

Among the refugees from Lorraine were several noble men and women forced to come to Paris by the events of their homeland. They gradually sold all they could rescue from their belongings and were reduced to a sad state made worse by their shame at having fallen so far from their former condition. They seemed to prefer to suffer silently rather than advertise their extreme poverty.

A person of some standing alerted Monsieur Vincent to this situation and suggested the thought that some way should be found to help these people. Monsieur Vincent responded, "What joy you give me, Monsieur. Yes, it is right to help these poor nobles, to honor our Lord, at once most noble and yet so poor." He then recommended this undertaking to God, considering within himself how he might secure some help for these poor unfortunate people. He felt this particular project might appeal to some more fortunate noble persons. He contacted seven or eight such people, among them the late baron of Renty, whose saintly life has been written and published since his death as a perfect model of those souls whose virtues truly ennoble them.[8]

Monsieur Vincent called these gentlemen together and he spoke so effectively of the importance and merit of this work of charity that they resolved to band together to help these distressed members of the nobility. Several were appointed to visit the refugees in their lodgings so as to form a clearer picture of their needs, to take their names, and to find out the exact number in each family. This information was presented to their next gathering, where these gentlemen arranged to provide subsistence for the next month. They continued on the first Sunday of each month to meet at Saint Lazare, where they again arranged to support these poor refugees for the following period. Monsieur Vincent was among the contributors, sometimes doing more than he should have. Once the collection of alms was two hundred *livres* short of what was necessary. He called the procurator of the house and taking him aside, asked him quietly what money was available. The response was that just enough remained for the expenses of the com-

---

7. 1641, 1642.
8. Gaston de Renty, 1611-1649, who left the military life for one of religious and charitable work in Paris. He had frequent contact with Vincent de Paul, and was his principal help in providing assistance to the nobles of Lorraine who had fled to Paris. See also Book Two, ch. 4, sect. 4.

munity for the next day. "And how much is that," asked Monsieur Vincent. "Fifty *ecus*," was the reply. "Is there nothing else in the house?" asked Monsieur Vincent. "No, Monsieur, we have only fifty *ecus*." "Please bring them to me, Monsieur." With that he gave this to make up, almost, what was lacking to maintain the refugee nobility for a month. He preferred to deprive himself and to be forced to borrow to feed his own household rather than allow these people to suffer want.

One of the nobles present heard the reply of the procurator and so admired the generosity of Monsieur Vincent that he reported it to the others present. The following morning one of them brought a small bag with one thousand *francs* to Saint Lazare as an alms for the community.

This service to the displaced nobility of Lorraine continued for almost seven years. During that time they were supported in their temporal needs, but in addition they were visited regularly, shown all marks of respect, consoled, and helped in their business affairs as much as was feasible. After Lorraine returned to some semblance of normality, some of the refugees returned home. Monsieur Vincent provided funds for their trip and gave them something to tide them over until they could re-establish themselves in their old surroundings. He continued to assist those remaining in Paris.

No activity of the virtue of charity so completely filled the heart of Monsieur Vincent that he was not open to something new. As he was helping the nobility of Lorraine, he found out about some English and Scottish gentlemen forced because of their Catholic faith to take refuge in Paris. He spoke to the same group of gentlemen helping the Lorraine nobility and had them help this new group of noblemen as well. He continued this aid up to the time of his death. The following is an extract from what one of the gentlemen wrote of these events:

> Monsieur Vincent always was the first to give. He opened his heart as well as his purse. If anything was lacking he contributed what he had, depriving himself of what was necessary to achieve his goal. On one occasion, to reach a certain sum, three hundred *livres* was needed. He gave it at once, but it was known that he had just been given this money to buy a horse better than the one he had, which was old and feeble and had fallen under him several times. He preferred to run the risk of injury rather than to leave those in need unassisted.

This assembly of nobility continued for about twenty years. It should be ranked among the major works associated with Monsieur Vincent. As author and promoter, together with the charity and zeal of the illustrious people who composed it, he brought relief to an great number of ills and provided a great number of benefactions to many.

CHAPTER THIRTY-FIVE

We must not omit here an episode about Monsieur Vincent at this time. He was so aware of the evils of war, the horrible sins, sacrileges, blasphemies, profanation of sacred things, murders, and all the violence and cruelty against even innocent persons, not to mention the devastation of entire provinces, and the ruin of many families, that his heart was torn with sorrow. He decided on a step contrary to all hope and opposed to what human prudence might suggest, to attempt what at best would be considered doubtful and possibly prejudicial to his own interests.

We have discussed in another place the high regard Cardinal Richelieu had for him. Monsieur Vincent decided to approach him not for personal gain, but for the public good. He paid a visit one day and spoke with great respect of the extreme suffering of the poor, and the other disorders and sins caused by the war. He then threw himself at the cardinal's feet and said: "My lord, give us peace. Have pity on us: give peace to France." He repeated this with such feeling the cardinal was moved. He accepted the appeal willingly, but stated that he was working for peace and that peace did not depend upon him alone. It depended on many others, both within and outside the kingdom.[9]

Had he consulted some prudent person living in society he would certainly have been advised against this manner of speaking to the prime minister. He ran the risk of being shut out from any more contact with the cardinal. Charity removed his fear and closed his eyes to all human respect, to all except the service of God and the good of the Christian people.[10]

Once he spoke on a similar topic:

> Once I went to see Cardinal Richelieu to help poor Ireland at the time England was at war with the king. He said to me, "I am sorry, Monsieur Vincent, the king has too much to do now." I reminded him the pope urged this and had promised one hundred thousand *ecus*. He replied, "One hundred thousand *ecus* is nothing for an army. You would need one hundred thousand soldiers, equipment, arms, and convoys to transport them. An army is a big machine! It doesn't move too easily!"

Although his prayers were not heard then, and what he proposed was not done, we can nevertheless see how his affection and zeal were always prepared to further religion and the true good of Catholics.

---

9. This event can be dated only between 1639 and 1642; no more definite date is known.
10. Vincent had favored turning the war from Catholic Austria to the English puritans. He intervened in the two incidents described above, even though they opposed the foreign policy of Cardinal Richelieu. This opposition was shared by the *dévot* party, scandalized that Catholic France was supporting Protestant nations, and opposing Catholic ones.

CHAPTER THIRTY-SIX

Services Provided by Monsieur Vincent to the Late King, Louis XIII of Glorious Memory, in His Last Illness, for the Spiritual Good of his Soul

THE DIGNITY of kings lifts them so far beyond that of others that the Bible calls them gods, seeing they are vicars and living images of God upon earth. This same passage, however, after giving them such a sublime and glorious title, warns them in the same text they must not forget they are mere men, and as such must pay the same tribute to nature by dying just as other men do.[1]

This law is inflexible and encompasses the wisest and most virtuous prince as well as others who are not so, but with an important difference. The death of the good king, as the Church reminds us, is a happy exchange of a temporal and earthly sovereignty for a heavenly and eternal one. For bad kings, on the contrary, death marks the end of their vicious lives and the beginning of the punishment the power of God has destined for them.

The virtues and royal qualities of Louis XIII of most happy memory gained him the reputation during his life as one of the greatest monarchs on earth, but his piety became even more apparent at the time of his death. This is not the place to recall all this truly Christian prince did and said during his last illness. Yet they revealed how much his royal heart was detached from earthly things, or how zealously he hoped for the conversion of heretics and sinners, and how he wished to bring about, as much as was possible to him, that God be better known, honored, served, and glorified throughout his realm. It is enough to say this good king had heard of the virtues and holy life of Monsieur Vincent and all the charitable enterprises he had undertaken for the spiritual good of his subjects. He ordered him to come to Saint Germain en Laye at the beginning of his last illness to be helped by the priest's good and salutary advice. He wanted to tell him of his pious hopes, particularly directed toward the conversion of the heretics of the city of Sedan.[2]

The first remark Monsieur Vincent made to His Majesty was to quote the words of the wise man of Scripture: "Sire, *Timenti Deum, bene erit in*

---

1. Ps 82:6.
2. Brother Robineau notes that "Monsieur Vincent was called to the bedside of Louis XIII at Saint Germain en Laye at the request of Anne of Austria and with the consent of Father [Jacques] Dinet, the king's confessor." *Robineau,* 75. He arrived on April 23.

extremis." ["To the one who loves God, it will go well at the last."] His Majesty, with his usual piety nurtured by frequent meditation of the Scriptures, replied by completing the verse, "*et in die defunctionis suae benedicetur*" ["And on the day of his death he will be blessed"].³

On another day, as Monsieur Vincent spoke with His Majesty on the good use of God's gifts, the king reflected on all the singular gifts he had received, especially the royal dignity to which Providence had raised him and the great honors and privileges attached to this office, chief among which was that of naming the bishops and prelates of his kingdom.

"Monsieur Vincent," the king said, "if I recover, bishops will spend three years with you,"⁴ thus wishing to convey the thought that he would require those named to the episcopal office be properly disposed and adequately prepared. He showed by this wish high regard for that office and the appreciation he had for Monsieur Vincent's projects for the training of clergy, hinting they would be equally useful for the preparation of those called to the high dignity of bishop in the Church.

Monsieur Vincent remained at Saint Germain about eight days. During that time he often had the honor of approaching the king to speak with him words of salvation and eternal life, which the king seemed to appreciate.

Finally, the king's sickness worsened despite all remedies employed. This most Christian prince, seeing that God was calling him from this world, sent for Monsieur Vincent to help him in this final passage to the next life. Monsieur Vincent returned to Saint Germain to remain with him the last three days before his death.⁵ He was almost constantly in the king's presence, helping him raise his mind and heart to God and make those interior acts of piety appropriate to prepare his soul for that final moment upon which eternal happiness depends.

This great prince completed his life by a most Christian death on May 14, 1643. Seeing the queen in such a distressed state, beyond any human consolation, Monsieur Vincent returned to Saint Lazare to pray for Their Majesties. He lamented the loss of so just and pious a prince, but was consoled by the excellent dispositions he had seen in him at the time of death and which crowned a truly Christian life by an equally Christian death. The following day he held a solemn service in the church of Saint Lazare, attended by all the priests of the house, for the repose of the king's soul.

---

3. Sir 1:13. The king's response is all the more remarkable since the verse did not form part of the prayers for the dying.
4. *CED* XI:132.
5. He returned May 12.

CHAPTER THIRTY-SEVEN

Monsieur Vincent is Appointed to the Council for Ecclesiastical Affairs of the Kingdom During the Regency of the Queen Mother

KING LOUIS XIII of glorious memory left the regency of the kingdom to the queen mother[1] during the minority of his son and most worthy successor. Considering the extent of this great monarchy and the importance of its ecclesiastical affairs, this wise and virtuous princess thought it expedient to form a Council for Ecclesiastical Affairs composed of four persons, that is, Cardinal Mazarin,[2] the chancellor,[3] Monsieur Charton, penitentiary of Paris,[4] and Monsieur Vincent. She decided to confer no benefice dependent on her nomination except with the council's advice.

Although Monsieur Vincent was committed to rendering all sorts of services to Their Majesties, he saw himself called to court only with great regret. To assume a position on the council was as disagreeable to him as it appeared honorable in the eyes of the world. His humility made him look on honors always as part of his burdensome cross. He did all he could to obtain the grace, as he called it, of being dispensed from this responsibility. The queen refused absolutely to hear of this, aware as she was of his virtue and ability.

He began this service in 1643, out of deference to the wishes of Her Majesty. He did so with a great fear, not that he might somehow lose the worldly honors whose vanity he knew only too well, but that he might not be able to leave as soon as he hoped. He wanted always to devote himself to the care of his Congregation and the practice of humility and the other virtues which he preferred to all the grandeur of the world. He prayed incessantly to God to deliver him from this burden. He told one of his confidants that he never said his mass without asking for this grace. Once,

---

1. Anne of Austria, mother of Louis XIV. Anne was a Spaniard, being the daughter of Philip III of Spain, but since he was of the Austrian Habsburg family, she is commonly known as Anne of Austria.
2. Jules Mazarini or Mazarin, 1602-1661, a veteran of the papal army and diplomatic corps, came to know Richelieu in 1630. He received tonsure but never became a priest. The pope appointed him nuncio in France, where he demonstrated his abilities. He became a French citizen in 1639, and a cardinal in 1641. Recommended by Richelieu to Louis XIII, he became principal minister during the regency of Anne of Austria. He was absolute master of France until his death, the year of the accession of Louis XIV.
3. Pierre Seguier, 1588-1672, chancellor from 1635 until his death. As chancellor, he was the most important official after the king.
4. Jacques Charton, an opponent of the Jansenists.

when he was out of the city for a few days, word went around that he was in disgrace and had been dismissed from the court. After his return, a priest friend congratulated him on having retained his position on the council. He merely lifted his eyes to heaven and struck his breast, saying, "Ah, wretched man that I am, I was not worthy of so great a grace."

God ordained that he remain at least ten years in this position, which was so disagreeable for him, for most of the matters of the council fell to him to resolve. He was given the petitions made to Her Majesty and looked into the motives and qualities of those who applied either for themselves or for others to prepare a report to the full council. The queen particularly wanted to be informed of the abilities of the petitioners so as not to be surprised. It was a matter of great admiration to see this servant of God preserve a serenity of spirit amid the ebb and flow of personalities and affairs, and possess his soul in peace under the press of distractions and importunities. He received all who wished to see him, always with the same calm demeanor, giving himself to each, making himself all to all to gain all to Jesus Christ.

If we reflect on all the cares of this new position, joined to the direction of his own Congregation and the other communities depending upon him, the establishments and assemblies we have spoken of in previous chapters, it would seem that he would have to be divided into an infinity of parts and preoccupations, looking after all, working night and day to fulfill the charges obedience or charity had placed upon him. By the grace of God this was not the case. He was always recollected within himself, united to God, and so self-possessed in peace and tranquility that it seemed he had no concerns. He was ever ready to listen to those who approached him. He rebuffed no one, but gave satisfaction to all and showed no impatience no matter how inconsiderate his visitors might be. He received with the same affability both the small and poor as he did the great and wealthy. We might say of Monsieur Vincent in his conduct of public business what the holy apostle says of himself, that he became a spectacle to the world, to men and to angels.

The court was a sort of theater where the virtues of this faithful servant of God appeared in full light. His humility won out over the vain plaudits of the courtiers. His patience was proof against their losses, troubles, and the vices of envy and malice. His constancy supported the interests of God and the Church, and there he showed himself free from all fear and human respect. On this stage he bore witness to his inviolable fidelity and constant affection for Their Majesties, his respect and submission to the prelates of the Church, the esteem and charity he preserved in his heart for all orders of the Church, and for all ecclesiastical and religious communities. His great desire to banish ambition and avarice from those who sought benefices, as well as his hope to remedy the abuses in the use of Church goods, not to mention the usual means employed to obtain benefices and other ecclesiastical dignities, will be spoken of at greater length in Book Two.[5]

What should be remarked mainly is that the queen was inundated with requests from all sorts of petitioners, eagerly seeking various charges, benefices, or other positions in the Church. What shows Monsieur Vincent's disinterest perfectly is that he never asked, or had others ask for him, anything for himself or for his Congregation, although he was as close to the source of these benefits as one could be. Had he asked, the queen would almost certainly have been happy to confer anything upon him in recognition of his merit.

There was some speculation during a short time that he was to be given the cardinal's hat. Some of his friends went so far as to congratulate him on this appointment. We do not know if Her Majesty had this in mind. Yet if she did propose this to Monsieur Vincent, his humility would have been eloquent enough to dissuade her.[6]

---

5. Ch. 13.

6. Vincent often opposed Mazarin's views in the proceedings of the Council of Conscience. He was supported by a group of important bishops and nobles. Mazarin, however, got around his opposition by rarely convening this Council. Fortunately, the Queen Mother, Anne of Austria, regularly consulted Vincent on episcopal appointments. The saint retired from the Council, but the date is unknown; it was at least before October 1652; see *CED* IV:491.

CHAPTER THIRTY-EIGHT

Monsieur Vincent's Help in Establishing the Congregation of the Daughters of the Cross and for the Spiritual Good of its Members

SINCE MONSIEUR VINCENT'S charity did not limit itself to any single outlet but extended universally to whatever he saw as contributing to God's glory, he approved and esteemed whatever tended to this end. He offered his counsel and even his intervention when he saw it might help, such that there was scarcely any public work of piety of his time that he did not have some part in. His advice was sought or his active involvement was asked for, as the following example among many others which could be cited will show.

A woman of great piety, Marie Lhuillier, widow of the late Monsieur de Villeneuve, had occasionally received into her home some virtuous women from Picardy who had occasion to come to Paris on business.[1] She recognized that these good women wanted to help other young women, especially younger girls, by instructing them in all that might help them lead a good Christian life. She felt moved by the same spirit and offered her help in any way she could. Since people in small towns and country places are ordinarily more in need of help than those in the larger cities, she moved into the country to ease the work of her guests. She even sent some of these ladies to other places where they offered effective instruction. This in turn motivated other women moved by the same sense of charity to join them. By this brief experience Madame Lhuillier recognized the great good to be accomplished through the instruction of young girls in the knowledge of God and of good manners. She also became aware of how few in the smaller towns and villages were capable of giving this instruction. The Ursuline Sisters and others devoted to education could not manage to reach into these smaller places. Also, the pious women or widows who wanted to help out in the smaller schools were simply not able to do so. In fact, in many of these smaller places there were no women teachers. The young girls of the region were left without instruction in piety. They either had to live in ignorance or perchance had to go to schools with boys, with the sad consequences that experience only too well confirms.

---

1. Marie Lhuillier d'Interville, widow at age twenty-three of Claude Marcel de Villeneuve, became associated with Mademoiselle Lamoignon and Mademoiselle le Gras, and under the leadership of Monsieur Vincent headed several charitable enterprises. She founded the first establishment of the Daughters of the Cross in 1641. Saint Vincent served as her spiritual director. She died January 15, 1650, aged fifty-two.

Considering all this, this pious widow decided to bring a more fundamental solution to the problems presented. She persuaded these good women who were so well disposed toward her to continue their own education. Beyond this, she persuaded them to choose from among themselves some others who would agree to live in various country places to serve effectively and in a Christlike way as schoolteachers. Since it is almost a universal law that pious works inspired by God are met with contradictions and difficulties, this was the case here as well. Someone remarked that these women were well named as Daughters of the Cross, a title they have retained with great affection, since it reminds them to remain united to Jesus Christ crucified whom Saint Paul calls the power and the wisdom of God.[2] They drew from this source the light and strength necessary to correspond worthily to the designs of Providence in their regard. They were thus able to devote themselves to the service of young women, destroying among them the two great obstacles to a truly Christian life, ignorance and sin.

This virtuous lady did not want to rely solely upon her own inspiration in an undertaking of such importance. Rather she spoke to several well-known religious people, among whom was Vincent de Paul, whom she particularly esteemed and appreciated. She conferred often with him about this matter. He in turn offered advice either to encourage her to undertake this good work or to help her in the spiritual formation of the women living with her. Afterward the number of those living with her increased to such an extent that she sought and obtained the approbation of the archbishop of Paris and later the establishment of this community of women as a formal religious congregation, under the title of Daughters of the Cross. This new community in the Church received letters patent from the king and recognition by the Parlement. The duchess of Aiguillon recognized the great good this new congregation could bring to the Church. Motivated by her own charity, she therefore contributed significantly to help bring the community to her city of Aiguillon and elsewhere as well.

Several years passed before the congregation had developed enough to stand alone. The almost constant illnesses of Madame Villeneuve finally resulted in her death before she could complete her plans for the community. Her sisters were left orphaned at the loss of their mother. This loss occurred at just the moment that Satan attacked the new congregation (permitted by God for his own greater glory) just as had been the case with the apostles at the beginning of the Church, as foretold by Jesus Christ.[3] It must be said that though many important people wished the congregation to succeed, the various difficulties that arose convinced many of these same people that

---

2. 1 Cor 1:24.
3. Luke 22:31.

dissolution of the congregation was the only possible remedy. They believed, at least, that the community should give up its own identity and join some other more firmly established order.[4]

Monsieur Vincent was consulted, and he presided over several meetings at which it seemed to appear that humanly speaking the community could not survive. Despite his usual reluctance to take a definite stand in matters of this nature and the difficulty he had in approving new undertakings, he firmly and absolutely gave his opinion, as though inspired by God, that every possible effort must be made to sustain this community. Despite everything which might be said he held firm in his opinion. He persuaded a virtuous woman of his acquaintance, Madame Anne Petau, widow of Monsieur Renauld, lord of Traversay, counselor to the king and the Parlement of Paris, to become the protector and guardian of these orphaned sisters. She responded to Monsieur Vincent's request with great affection and zeal, and by her help and mainly through the goodness of God, the congregation was preserved for its mission of serving the Church.

Not content with saving this community that seemed on the verge of ruin and obtaining the help of Madame Petau as patron with the authorization of the archbishop of Paris, Monsieur Vincent even persuaded a promising priest[5] to serve as the canonical superior of the new community. This was done to help these women acquire the perfection of their state and to supply what had not yet been worked out at the time of Madame Villeneuve's death. Monsieur Vincent gave some useful advice about the government of the community, which since then has been blessed by God in bringing salvation and sanctification to many souls. The Daughters of the Cross not only prepared as Christian teachers those who came to join the community but also participated in all sorts of other works of charity, especially those in favor of the poor. The doors of their houses and even more so the gates of their gardens were open to receive the poor. They wanted to offer them all kinds of spiritual help, either through instruction in all that is needed for salvation or in how to make a good general confession or on occasion even receiving them into their houses for several days to make a retreat, all according to whatever needs they might have.

After God it was Monsieur Vincent who offered his hand to save the congregation from a fall from which it probably never would have recovered. Since his counsel assured their continued progress, the sisters recognized him if not as their father and founder at least as their savior. They thanked God for all the temporal and spiritual help which they had received from his charitable hand.

---

4. The Daughters of Providence, founded by Marie de Lumague, Mademoiselle Pollalion.
5. Abelly himself.

CHAPTER THIRTY-NINE

Monsieur Vincent's Experiences During the Troubled Times of 1649. What Occurred During Several Trips He Made at that Time

THE KINGDOM enjoyed a great calm during the first years of the regency of the queen mother. She struggled to establish peace within the kingdom and to use the army to defeat the efforts of those ill-disposed toward us. But whether because of our sins or some other reason of which we are ignorant this calm was followed by one of the most violent storms France had to endure in many years.[1] Toward the end of 1648 as this tempest began, Their Majesties were obliged to flee to Saint Germain en Laye in January of the following year. Troops came to block the approaches to the town so that it was quickly reduced to extremities.

Monsieur Vincent's first reaction was to have his community beseech God in prayer to avert the calamity which would prevail if this civil disturbance lasted much longer. Beyond this, he felt it his duty to do all in his power to bring whatever remedy he could to the situation. He resolved to offer his services to Their Majesties at Saint Germain. He would represent to the queen with respect and all possible humility what he thought in the sight of God was most likely to bring back peace and tranquility to the realm. Therefore he left Saint Lazare on the thirteenth of the same month of January.

He took the precaution of leaving a letter addressed to the first president in the hands of the superior at Saint Lazare. In it he recounted the inspiration of God which had led him to go to Saint Germain to do what he could to bring about a peaceful settlement to the present difficulties. He did not have the opportunity to see the first president in person.[2] He assured the queen in this letter that he had consulted with no one else in this undertaking. He took this precaution for several reasons, first to assure the court that he had no communication with the rebellious party, and second to further the opportunity to speak effectively when she would be aware that he was acting solely through God's inspiration. To appease the Parlement he felt he had to show why he had left the city and what he proposed to do.

Leaving Paris in early morning he arrived at Saint Germain around nine or ten o'clock, not without some difficulty because of the heavy flooding and the presence of the military everywhere. After being presented to the

---

1. The troubles referred to here are those of the Fronde, eventually put down under Cardinal Mazarin.
2. Mathieu Mole, 1584-1656, first president (chief justice) of the Parlement of Paris for many years.

queen he spent nearly an hour with her. Afterwards he met with Cardinal Mazarin for a long time. He was well received by both, who appreciated his sincerity and his upright intentions. His intervention did not have the desired result, that is, peace and the re-establishment of unity in the kingdom, for circumstances were not yet favorable. But he at least had the satisfaction of having done all in his power in service to Their Majesties to procure the public good and relief of the poor. Although the least culpable, they were the most likely to suffer the most from the approaching storm.

When he finished his business in Saint Germain he left for Villepreux,[3] preferring for several reasons not to return to Paris. From Villepreux he went to a small farm in Beauce, two leagues from Etampes, in a poor hamlet called Freneville in the parish of Val de Puisseaux. Madame de Herse[4] gave this farm to the house of Saint Lazare to support its works. He stayed here for a month. He lived on the bread of tribulation and the water of anguish, for the weather was extremely cold and the housing primitive. It lacked all conveniences and was open to all sorts of trouble, given the unsettled times. Monsieur Vincent lived during this time as another Jeremiah deploring the misery of the kingdom, offering to God his tears, his sufferings, and his penances as pleas for mercy. He was another Job sitting on a handful of straw, awaiting the fulfillment of God's designs, but submissive to his will. During his stay in this poor cottage he learned that other farms near Paris which belonged to Saint Lazare and served as the main resource for his community had been pillaged by soldiers, the furniture removed, the flocks driven away, and eighteen or twenty *muids* of wheat stolen.[5]

The house of Saint Lazare itself had many vexations of its own, for six hundred soldiers were quartered there. They took the doors of the house and barns, and according to one official he had been charged by Parlement to seize the wheat and flour for transport to the public market. This order proved later not to have been given by the Parlement, and the soldiers were withdrawn and the keys returned, but the damage to the property was not repaired. Every day Monsieur Vincent was advised of some new loss or pillage, but his sole response was "God be blessed, God be blessed."

To understand better the situation of Saint Lazare at this time and to see how the patience of Monsieur Vincent was tried, we may quote from a letter of a pious priest, a frequent visitor to the priests of the Mission.

---

3. To the home of Father de Gondi, former general of the galleys.
4. Charlotte de Ligny, wife of Michel Vialart, the president de Herse. She was a relative of Monsieur Olier, and was associated with all of Saint Vincent's works, particularly the ordination retreats. She died in 1662.
5. The farm at Orsigny, near Versailles. Monsieur Vincent accepted this farm December 22, 1644, from Jacques Norais and his wife. Their heirs contested this after their death, and the Congregation lost this farm, the principal support of the house of Saint Lazare. It returned to the community only in 1684.

We have witnessed the persecution suffered by the community at Saint Lazare. They have lost their possessions and goods during the war and the unrest in Paris, brought about by the animosity of some ill-intentioned persons and even of some of the leading magistrates. Under pretext of making an inventory of available foodstuffs in the house and barns, they searched and nosed about everywhere as though they were seeking hidden treasure. Besides, they billeted a regiment of insolent soldiers who behaved unbelievably badly, and even burned all the wood in the woodshed. I saw the embers still smoking when I went to see Monsieur Lambert whom Monsieur Vincent had left in charge. This noble missionary accepted all these affronts and suffered this persecution with his usual serenity and tranquility. He was happy to share in the loss of his spiritual father and to see the loss (since God willed it so) not so much of their own goods but that of the poor for whom these things were destined, for it was their custom to distribute these goods freely and charitably during the year. *Et rapinam bonorum vestrorum cum gaudio suscepistis* ["You joyfully assented to the confiscation of your goods"].[6]

It could be said to those who conducted an armed search of Saint Lazare for supposed hidden wealth what Saint Lawrence replied to his persecutors who sought the riches of the Church in his day: the poor alone are the living treasures hidden in the vaults of the church. *Facultates quas requiris, in coelestes thesauros manus pauperum deportaverunt.* ["The hands of the poor have carried off to heavenly storehouses the riches you seek."]

Monsieur Vincent was a new Lot, saved from this scene of destruction by an inspiration as though from an angel from heaven when, having gone to Saint Germain en Laye to speak with Their Majesties, he decided not to return to Paris but instead to visit several houses of his Congregation. These places benefited by the blessing of his presence, to our privation and loss.

Monsieur Vincent remained then at this poor cottage of Freneville, suffering greatly from the severe cold, as well as from the limited amount of wretched food available in this poor region. He had only a bit of green wood to ward off the cold, and his bread was made of a mixture of rye and beans. Not a word of complaint fell from his lips. Rather he endured all in a spirit of penance. He believed it his duty as a priest to implore God's mercy to mitigate the effects of his anger being felt everywhere more and more in the kingdom.

---

6. Heb 10:34.

He preached to the peasants of this unhappy place, urging them to use their present afflictions well. He exhorted them to penance as a most efficacious means of appeasing the wrath of God. He prepared them for the sacrament of penance, and he, the pastor of the parish, and another priest of his Congregation heard their confessions.

After a stay in this neglected region he left for Le Mans despite the rigors of the season. He planned to visit a house of his community situated on the outskirts of this town.[7] From there he set out for Angers, but near Durtal he escaped from an accident which might have proven fatal were it not for some prompt help from others. His horse slipped while wading a small stream, and threw him into the water. After his rescue he remounted his horse soaked to the skin, but showing no emotion on his face. With some difficulty he found along the way a small cottage where he could dry himself, but as it was the Lenten season he did not eat until he had reached a small inn for the evening. The proprietress remarked that Monsieur Vincent, as was his custom, began to instruct the servants of the inn in their religion. She set off at once to gather the neighborhood children and had them go to Monsieur Vincent's room. He thanked her for this courtesy and immediately divided them into two groups to be instructed, one by himself and the other by a priest traveling with him.

He remained five days at Angers, taking the occasion to visit the Daughters of Charity who served in the hospital. He then set out for Brittany, but as he neared Rennes he had another accident which almost cost him his life. He was crossing a wooden bridge between a mill and a deep pond when his horse shied at the mill wheel. The horse seemed about to throw him into the pond, for his hind legs were already off the bridge. By a sort of miracle God saved him from sure disaster. Later when he was out of danger Monsieur Vincent admitted that he had never before escaped such disaster. He blessed God for such evident and miraculous protection and besought his traveling companion to join him in blessing the divine goodness.

On all his trips Monsieur Vincent paid no visits of mere civility, either at Orleans, Le Mans, Angers, or anywhere he visited. He intended to do the same at Rennes, to pass unrecognized through the town on the way to a house of his Congregation at Saint Meen some eight leagues beyond the city. Notwithstanding this, he was recognized as he entered the town, which at that time was in the same state of agitation as Paris itself. An authority of the town informed him that he was under suspicion because of his connection with the royal family. He was told that he would be arrested and it was suggested that he leave town immediately. Monsieur Vincent was disposed to follow this advice. Yet at the very moment he was saddling his horse

---

7. Notre Dame de Coeffort.

another guest staying at the same inn recognized him. He said angrily that Monsieur Vincent was likely to be shot in the head within two leagues of the town. The canon theologian of Saint Brieuc who had learned about Monsieur Vincent's visit and had come to the inn to meet with him, heard the threat. He persuaded Monsieur Vincent not to leave but rather to complain to the first president and some others, who received him well.

The following day he was preparing again to leave the inn when the one who had threatened him with death reappeared. The story went around that this man had waited in hiding along the road for the chance to carry out his threat. The faithful servant of God relied completely on God's providence. He seemed always ready to die, even desiring death after the example of the apostle that he might be united with Christ. He seemed unconcerned about his personal safety, but his friend the canon theologian of Saint Brieuc was not so trusting. He insisted on accompanying Monsieur Vincent all the way to Saint Meen, where he arrived on Tuesday of Holy Week. He remained there two weeks, spending most of his time in the confessional to benefit the poor of the region. They came on pilgrimage to this holy place and sought to be cured of their infirmities as God often granted such favors in response to the intercession of the patron saint of the town.

Monsieur Vincent then went on a charitable mission to Nantes, then to Lucon with the intention of proceeding to Saintes and then to Guienne, just to visit the houses of his Congregation. However, he received a direct order from the queen to return to Paris where the king also had returned. He went at once to Richelieu but fell sick there. When the duchess of Aiguillon heard of this she sent a small two-horse carriage and a coachman to bring him to Paris as soon as he would be well enough to travel. Some time before, he had been given the use of this same carriage because of trouble with his legs, but he had never wished to use it.

In every house of his Congregation he visited on this long trip he greatly consoled his spiritual sons, besides being such an example of humility, cordiality, meekness, and all other virtues he displayed. Finally he returned to Paris in July 1649 after an absence of six and a half months. He returned the carriage and horses to the duchess of Aiguillon with thanks, but she in turn sent them back saying that they were a gift to help him in his work. He refused once more, protesting that the difficulties with his legs were increasing so greatly that he could travel neither by foot nor by horse, that he was resolved to spend the rest of his life at Saint Lazare rather than ride in a coach. When the queen and the archbishop of Paris heard of this, they ordered him formally to use the carriage. He acquiesced in this but not without pain and confusion, calling the carriage, which in reality was quite ordinary, his "ignominy." He wanted the horses put to useful work in the fields when he was not using them to go to the city. At that time he was seventy years of age, suffering much from his legs which pained him especially when he tried to stand after sitting for some time.[8] He used this poor carriage only out of obedience and necessity. Nevertheless it enabled him to attend to some important affairs in service to the Church which he otherwise could not have done.

---

8. Abelly here shows that he believed that Vincent was born in 1580, not in 1576 as he wrote in ch. 1.

CHAPTER FORTY

Monsieur Vincent Works for the Relief of the Poor of the Frontier Regions Devastated by the War, Especially Champagne and Picardy

SCRIPTURE TRULY says that it is hard to cure long and degenerating illnesses, and likewise that a physician is inclined to abandon those with untreatable illness. It is the same for the poor. Those who work to relieve them grow tried and listless in their works of charity. The misery and needs of the poor grow day by day especially during civil wars such as have been the lot of France in recent times. After his return to Paris Monsieur Vincent was informed of the deplorable state of affairs, especially in the frontier provinces of Champagne and Picardy, and the almost limitless number of poor of all ages, sexes and conditions who desperately needed help. It must be added that a heart less moved by charity than his own would have lost courage and succumbed under the weight of this new burden. It would have believed it impossible to find a way to bring help to so many in need.

Precisely at this trying time this saintly man showed his great virtue. Just as the palm tree grows more vigorously the more it is buffeted, so he, relying on God's all-powerful bounty, resolved to undertake this charitable work just as he had done in so many other cases. After imploring the divine mercy whose treasures are inexhaustible he appealed to the Ladies of Charity who had committed themselves to just these kinds of works of mercy. They, like everyone else, had suffered greatly from the misery of the times and had lost some of their most promising members. Because of this they had been forced to give up some of the projects in which they had been involved. Nevertheless these good women closed their eyes to all human considerations and regarded Monsieur Vincent's request as an expression of God's holy will for them. They undertook to work for the relief of the poor of the devastated provinces and organized a collection of alms for their aid. Monsieur Vincent in turn sent several of his priests to aid in distributing these alms. God blessed this effort, which lasted for a full ten years until the signing of the treaty of peace.

Contrary to all hope and human judgment, the value of alms given to the poor exceeded six hundred thousand *livres* in money, food, clothing, medicine, tools, seed for sowing, and other necessities to sustain life. All this was done at the direction of Monsieur Vincent who sent the missionaries of his Company into the regions where they knew the poor were reduced to the last extremity, and there they stayed. These fathers served in all that part of the country, especially in the cities and surrounding areas of Reims, Fismes, Rethel, Rocroi, Mezieres, Charleville, Donchery, Sedan, Sainte Menehould, Vervins, Laon, Guise, Chauny, La Fere, Peronne, Noyon, Saint Quentin, Ham, Marle, Ribemont, Amiens, Arras—in a word into every city, town, and hamlet where the ruined poor, so worthy of compassion, were to be found. By this charitable help many were saved from dying of cold and hunger. This was especially true of the most neglected, the sick, the elderly, and orphans. These generally suffered frightfully, lying upon their bed of putrid straw or upon the bare earth, exposed to the rigors of the winter weather because the homes of many of them had been pillaged and burnt and they themselves were left with but a single garment to cover their nakedness. They lived in hovels daily awaiting their only deliverer, death itself.

During the early years when this desolation was so extreme, the help given by Monsieur Vincent was likewise exceptional. He sent between eight and ten of his priests of the Mission together with several Daughters of Charity to help. While the sisters tended to the sick poor the priests helped distribute bread and other necessary things to those in need. The priests crisscrossed the countryside, visiting parishes where pastors had disappeared, bringing spiritual pasturage to poor lost sheep, instructing them, administering the sacraments, consoling them in their losses, and repairing their churches as best they could, for many of them had been pillaged and profaned by the soldiers.

We shall see in Book Two[1] how these charitable and fervent missionaries were guided by the orders of their esteemed father in the practice of their works of charity. We shall see how the churches, the priests, religious communities of men and women, the impoverished nobility, women in distress, children, and abandoned sick—in a word all sorts of needy persons received both help and consolation in their distress.

If previous centuries have certainly seen such distress and misery, nowhere do we read in history that anyone responded so nobly, so promptly, and so universally as Monsieur Vincent. All this was done through the goodness of God and the ministry of a poor priest, aided by a small group of devout women inspired by his charity and guided by his counsels.

---

1. Ch. 11, sects. 2, 3.

CHAPTER FORTY-ONE

The Death of the Prior of Saint Lazare. Monsieur Vincent's Appreciation of Him

MONSIEUR ADRIEN le Bon, the prior of Saint Lazare, was the instrument in God's hand, as we have said, for bringing Monsieur Vincent and his priests to Saint Lazare. Not only did he agree that Monsieur Vincent should come but rather he was insistent on the point. For more than a year he persisted in trying to convince Monsieur Vincent to accept the house and priory, even using intermediaries to persuade him. The example of the relationship between these two servants of God is perhaps unique in our times. The only conflict between the two was about who was the more virtuous: Monsieur Vincent's humility was matched by the prior's charity. The love of poverty of the one was in competition with the generosity of the other. Perhaps the only way this contest could be ended was in consideration of Monsieur Vincent's disposition to be receptive to the inspiration of God to which he was always so attentive. On this particular occasion perhaps the greatest virtue was to give in to one who might be said to be inferior to him, rather than take another course of action which would have been less advantageous to the development of the Congregation of the Mission.

The charitable prior retained his rooms in Saint Lazare, as did his religious also. It is impossible to exaggerate the satisfaction and consolation he enjoyed for the rest of his life in observing these good missionaries and especially Monsieur Vincent. For his part, Monsieur Vincent looked upon him as the benefactor and support of the Missionaries living at Saint Lazare. He was shown all the respect, kindness, and assistance possible, in a spirit of sincere filial appreciation. This lasted for twenty years, until 1651 when it pleased God on the very day of Easter[1] to call this good and charitable prior to taste in heaven the fruits of his charity.

Just as Monsieur Vincent had honored, loved, and served this friend during his long life, he did so especially at his passing. He did all that a sincere love could suggest to help the prior in his last hours. He called together all the priests in the house to gather about the bed of the dying man to recite aloud during his lengthy agony the prayers for a departing soul, together with other prayers as well.

When the prior, aged seventy-five, had breathed his last, Monsieur

---

1. April 9.

Vincent spoke to those assembled around the bed: "Now, my brothers, our esteemed father is before God." Then, raising his eyes to heaven he prayed:

> O God, may it please your goodness to apply to the soul of your servant the merits of the good works and the small services we have been able to do in the Congregation. We offer them to you, O Lord, beseeching you to apply them to his benefit. Perhaps some of you, my brothers, were in need. The prior provided for your wants. Be on guard that you never fall into the miserable sin of ingratitude toward him or the other older priests of the house, for we are like children who must respect them as our own parents. Be grateful to them for the good they have done and strive to remember the prior and pray for him.[2]

The funeral was worthily celebrated. Monsieur Vincent himself offered many masses for his intention and had other priests do the same, both in Saint Lazare and elsewhere. He wrote to all the houses of the Congregation:

> It has pleased God to make all the members of the community orphans by calling to himself our father, the prior of Saint Lazare. He departed this life on Easter day, fortified by the sacraments and in such conformity to God's will that the least trace of impatience never appeared either in his entire last sickness nor in any previous illnesses. I beg all the priests of your house to offer masses for his intention and have the brothers receive communion.[3]

Monsieur Vincent had a fine epitaph placed in the choir of the church of Saint Lazare near the tomb of the prior as a permanent memorial. He further stipulated that on the anniversary of his death, April 9, a solemn service in his memory was to be held in the church of Saint Lazare.

---

2. *CED* XI:155-56.
3. *CED* IV:168-69.

CHAPTER FORTY-TWO

The Help Given by Monsieur Vincent to the Poor of Paris and Several Other Places During the Troubled Times of 1652 and Later

WE HAVE SPOKEN in an earlier chapter of the charity rendered by Monsieur Vincent to the poor of Lorraine, Champagne, and Picardy. New troubles arose in the kingdom in 1652, and these gave new opportunity for much wider scope to his charity.[1] God willed that the merits of his faithful servant should be increased, as well as those of all the other virtuous people who cooperated in obtaining the spiritual good and the corporal relief of the poor. Here is how these things came about.

The stationing of the army near Paris caused great desolation and misery everywhere. The town of Etampes suffered particularly because it had been under siege for a long time, and would be again several times afterward. The people of the town and neighboring villages were in a pitiable state of depression and poverty. Most were sick and were reduced to skin and bones. No help was to be found, no one to offer even a glass of cold water. To add to the troubles of the town, it had been taken and retaken until finally the plague struck. This happened chiefly because of the corpses thrown on the dung heaps. The rotting flesh of both men and women, mingled with that of horses and other animals, gave forth such a stench that no one dared come near.

Monsieur Vincent became aware of the miserable condition of the town and its environs. He immediately contacted the Ladies of Charity, who responded with their usual generosity, and he sent several members of the Congregation to provide spiritual and physical help to these poor and abandoned people. One of the first things they did was to bring in some strong helpers with wagons, to clean up all the dung heaps and sweep up the city. All this cost a good bit, as can be imagined. In addition they gave a decent burial to the poor half-decomposed bodies and then perfumed the streets and houses so that they could again be lived in. They set up soup kitchens in Etampes as well as in some other nearby towns which the Missionaries judged to have been badly treated by the army or where the people were in the worst straits. Besides Etampes, Guillerval, Villeconnin, Etrechy, and Saint Arnoult sent their needy to be fed. At Palaiseau the soldiers had been particularly vicious, and this required a soup kitchen there

---

1. The battles of the second phase of the Fronde, occasioned by the return of Mazarin to the court, December 1651. The battles came to the area around Paris.

as well. Many of the parishes were without pastors, who had either died or perhaps had fled. The priests of the Mission could not manage both the spiritual and corporal help so badly needed. Monsieur Vincent sent the Daughters of Charity to handle the soup kitchens and other bodily help, including the care of a great number of poor orphans of the region. These latter were housed together in a building in Etampes. Meanwhile, the fathers crisscrossed the area, visiting and consoling the poor, saying mass for them, giving instruction, and administering the sacraments, all done with the approval of the superiors.

All this activity in favor of the poor was given at a price. There was the extreme fatigue, not to mention the danger of contracting the very illnesses they were seeking to alleviate, due to the ever-present danger of infection. And so it happened. Several of the Missionaries fell ill and soon succumbed.[2] Who could doubt that their death was precious in the eyes of the Lord? These men who had striven so courageously for his glory, who had persevered in an inviolable fidelity to his holy will by their prompt and perfect obedience, and who had then happily finished their course, would certainly have received their crown of justice from the God of all mercy.

Several Daughters of Charity, after much suffering brought about by their service to the poor, also offered their lives with great courage to God and undoubtedly shared the glory of the same crown as the priests.[3]

While Monsieur Vincent was thus occupied with these matters, God allowed another situation to arise which gave him further opportunity to exercise his charity. The armies descended upon Paris, causing havoc in all surrounding villages and towns. When it was reported to this "father of the poor" that the people of Juvisy and the surrounding country were in a desperate state, he immediately sent some of his priests with alms to distribute to the most needy. When it became apparent that the desolation was widespread, for the region had been pillaged and the people very badly treated by the soldiers, and that most of the inhabitants were in a very grave and even extreme condition, Monsieur Vincent and several other men and women joined forces to help these poor people. In view of the great expense involved in providing what was needed, their charity, or rather the God of all goodness, suggested to them that they should organize a storehouse for goods. People of all conditions were invited to bring furniture, clothing, tools, provisions, and whatever else they could spare. It was almost impos-

---

2. Jean David, who died at Etampes, Francois Labbe, and Edmond Deschamps, were taken to the chateau of Basville near Etampes, and cared for by president Lamoignon. Jacques de La Fosse, the other missionary, was carried back to Saint Lazare on a stretcher by his companions. Others are mentioned in the saint's letters.
3. In particular, Sister Marie Joseph, mentioned by Monsieur Vincent in a conference to the Daughters of Charity, June 9, 1658, *CED* X:510.

sible for most families to donate money, for it was a time when money was very difficult to obtain.

We should not fail to mention that it was particularly Monsieur du Plessis Montbard who should receive credit for this Charity Store. He was the first to propose the plan, and he saw to it that it was carried out.[4] We shall speak more of this in Book Two.[5]

These storehouses were an endless source of help to them for six or seven months. All manner of goods were distributed: clothes, linen, furniture, utensils, tools, medicines, grain, peas, butter, oil, fruit, and other things necessary for life. Even such things as vestments, chalices, ciboriums, liturgical books, and other sacred ornaments and linens were given out because many of the churches had been looted. All these items were centrally collected and then distributed in an orderly fashion. The fathers of the Mission went from village to village in wagons loaded with food and used clothing to be given according to each one's needs. Also, it should be added that a daily distribution of soup helped save the lives of innumerable starving families who did not even know how to begin to find bread to live.

The exertions of the Missionaries were so extreme in this dedication to the poor, and the illnesses they contracted so serious, that four or five died and several others were sick for many years.[6] Although Monsieur Vincent felt these losses deeply, for these good fathers were his spiritual sons, he nevertheless praised and blessed God that they had worked and suffered so much for the members of the body of Christ with such courage. They had completed their lives gloriously on the field of battle, their arms in hand. He knew full well that such a death is not death at all but entrance into a new and happier life in full possession of Him who is the source and principle of all true life.

Besides the help to those who lived in the villages outside of Paris, others were fleeing before the army and had come to the capital for refuge. Among these were many women and young girls, and even some religious women. Monsieur Vincent found a way to group a certain number of them together and to find places of refuge for them. He requested some Ladies of Charity to undertake this work with one group of women in each house. After seeing to their bodily nourishment Monsieur Vincent urged that those who cared for the displaced persons should use the opportunity to conduct a sort of

---

4. Christophe Duplessis, baron of Montbard, a lawyer of the Parlement of Paris, one of the most active members of the Company of the Blessed Sacrament, and one of the most charitable men of his time. He contributed greatly to various hospitals. He died May 7, 1672. His *Magasin charitable* was also the title of a publication designed to inform the public and encourage contributions to this work. *CED* IV:540.

5. Ch. 11.

6. *CED* IV:432-36.

mission for them. In it they would receive instruction, badly needed by some, on what was required for salvation and how to make a good confession, and how to put themselves in a worthy state to offer prayers for peace and tranquility in the kingdom. He advised also that a retreat for religious should be given as well. On this question he wrote of all the troubles of the times to a doctor of theology of the University of Paris, who at that time was in Rome:[7]

> I have no doubt that you are aware of how things are. I want simply to tell you about carrying the relics of Saint Genevieve in a solemn procession to beseech God to bring a halt to all public suffering through the intercession of this saint. This ceremony brought together more devout people than have ever before been seen in Paris. The result of this was that on the eighth day the duke of Lorraine, who already was in the city and whose army was at its gates, turned about just as the king's army was about to fire upon his men, and withdrew to his own lands. Meanwhile the discussions with other princes[8] continue on the question of peace, and we hope, through the goodness of God, that these talks will be successful. We devoutly wish that his justice will be appeased by the great charity shown to the bashful poor of the city as well as to the poor country people who have taken refuge here. Every day fourteen or fifteen thousand people are fed who otherwise would have died of hunger. Besides, eight or nine hundred young girls have been gathered together in several houses. Some poor women religious refugees are being placed in houses also, even in some suspected places, it is said. A monastery is being used for this purpose where they will be well looked after. That is the news, Monsieur, and although it goes against our agreement to put nothing in writing, how could I not publicize the grandeur of God and his mercies![9]

We must not forget that it was the Daughters of Charity who distributed the soup, while the Ladies of Charity took an active part by their alms, sharing in all the great works of charity. Since the poor were spread out to all parts of Paris, especially the outlying districts, Monsieur Vincent had a particular concern for the welfare of those who lived near Saint Lazare. These people, some seven or eight hundred, came every day to his door both in the morning and afternoon to receive food and to participate in the same practices that are followed on the missions. After preaching to them, the men and boys were brought into the cloister of Saint Lazare and then divided into

---

7. Jerome Lagault.
8. The Prince of Conde and the duke of Orleans.
9. *CED* IV:400-03.

nine or ten groups or "academies." A priest was assigned to each group for instruction, while at the same time other priests spoke to the women and girls in the church. Monsieur Vincent himself participated in this work and shared in catechizing the poor.

It pleased God to shower his blessings on all these charitable activities begun by Monsieur Vincent, so much so that they have continued when other troubles arose, even after the death of this great servant of God. He seemed, like another Elijah, to have left his mantle not only to the members of his own Congregation but also to all the other virtuous people who joined him in fulfilling his mission of charity. Such an occasion arose in the beginning of 1661 when it was decreed that lace making would no longer be allowed. Previously, this had been a source of livelihood for many. Now, with its prohibition, many were reduced to great want and suffering. At the same time the price of wheat shot up. Also, in July and August of the same year an epidemic developed in the countryside which made it impossible for many to work at the harvest. As a consequence the price of bread and other foodstuffs increased significantly. The vicars general of Paris commissioned several priests of the Congregation of the Mission to make a survey of the entire diocese on the condition of things. They found that there were more than eight thousand sick in the eighty parishes they visited, and similar conditions existed elsewhere. These people, consequently, were mostly without any means of subsistence. Entire families were stricken and the scarcity of food was evident everywhere. In face of this, the same remedy was applied as during the lifetime of Monsieur Vincent. The Ladies of Charity led the way in collecting food and other necessities, and with the help of the alms they received they were able to aid the poor everywhere.

The famine of 1661 continued during the following year as well, not only near Paris but also in several other provinces: Maine, Perche, Beauce, Touraine, Blaisois, Berry, Gatinais, and elsewhere. The Ladies of Charity felt in their hearts the same sentiments that had moved Monsieur Vincent to undertake the relief of the poor in all sorts of circumstances with indefatigable charity. These holy women carried out these projects, especially the feeding of the hungry. God blessed their efforts so that they, together with the help of the missionaries of Monsieur Vincent, rescued from death a large number of the poor of every age, gender and condition. Without it, they otherwise would surely have been lost. The alms they distributed from 1660, the year of Monsieur Vincent's death until now, 1664, came to more than 500,000 *livres*.

CHAPTER FORTY-THREE

Monsieur Vincent in Service to the King and Kingdom during the Troubled Times Beginning in 1652

IN DEALING with wrongs, it is not enough to be concerned with effects, the causes also must be addressed. All the charitable efforts of Monsieur Vincent during the war certainly alleviated much of the suffering of the poor. Yet, to deliver them permanently from this scourge and to avoid the unspeakable disorders and enormous sins committed during such times of trouble and division this great servant of God saw that a more fundamental remedy was necessary. Filled with prudence and zeal as he was, he understood that there would be no hope for success unless the root of the evils, that is, division and war, were attacked. An assured peace was the remedy, and this could come about only by the complete submission and obedience of subjects to their sovereign. The union of head and members, established by God for the body politic as well as in nature, was the path to order, and this to peace, which according to Saint Augustine, is simply the tranquility of order.[1]

Monsieur Vincent realized that the conflagration was spreading to every region of the kingdom. He foresaw the enormous ills in store for the state and for religion itself should this evil go unchecked. He resolved, then, to use all his efforts to extinguish this unholy fire. First he had recourse to God. He invited all well-intentioned people he knew to do the same. He hoped that by their prayers, alms, fasts and other works of penance they might appease the divine justice, make reparation for the sins committed against his divine majesty, draw down his mercy, and gain peace. At the house of Saint Lazare he established the practice that every day three of his Missionaries fasted for this intention—a priest, a cleric, and a brother. The priest celebrated mass on this occasion, at which the other two received communion. He himself took his turn at this devotion, although he was over seventy years of age at the time.[2]

Once, when leaving the chapel after reflecting on the horrors of war not only in France but in several other Christian countries, and having just finished his mental prayer on the subject of the utility of suffering, he was moved to speak to his entire community:

Once again I repeat the recommendation I have so often made

---

1. PL 41:640.
2. *CED* XII:458 gives a different total: two priests or clerics, and two lay brothers.

to pray for peace. May it please him to bring together the hearts of Christian rulers. Alas! we see war on all sides and everywhere: war in France, war in Spain, in Italy, Germany, Sweden, in Poland, where they are invaded from three directions, in Ireland where the poor people are driven from their lands into the mountains and nearly inaccessible rocky regions. Scotland has fared no better, and everyone knows how bad things are in England. War everywhere and misery everywhere! In France such a multitude of people in such a deplorable state! O Savior, O Savior, how many suffer? If for the four months we have experienced the war here we have seen it bring such misery to the people who have flocked from all parts of the kingdom to Paris, the heart of France where we have provisions in abundance, what shall we say of those poor people who live in the frontier provinces, and over the space of twenty years have felt the scourge of war? If they sow, who knows who will reap? The armies come to harvest, to pillage and take away all. Anything the soldiers do not take the officers pick up. How can anyone go on? They are left to die. If any real virtue exists, it is found mainly among the poor. They have a lively faith, they believe simply, they are submissive to God's will, they have an extraordinary patience in their sufferings, and they endure all that the war brings upon them. Even in their ordinary occupation they work hard, exposed to the sun and all kinds of weather. These poor farmers and vine dressers live by the sweat of their brow, expecting that at least we others will pray to God for them.

Alas my brothers, while they wear themselves out in their labor, we seek the shade and take our rest. In our missions we are protected from the weather by our churches. We are not exposed to the wind, to the rain, nor to the rigors of the seasons. We who live off the labor of these poor people and with the patrimony of Jesus Christ ought to think each time we go to the refectory for our meals whether we have really earned the bread we are about to eat. For myself this thought has often given me much consternation, and I have said to myself, you poor creature, have you earned your bread today? This bread which comes from the work of the poor? At least, my brothers, if we have not earned it as they do, let us pray for them. Let no day pass that we do not beseech him to bestow the grace upon them that they will profit from their sufferings.

As we have said these past days, God is particularly attentive to the priests to stop the course of his anger. He waits for them to do as Aaron did, to take the censer in hand interposing themselves between these poor people and his own wrath. Like Moses they should become the intermediaries before God to avert the consequences of their sin and ignorance which perhaps could have been avoided if they were better instructed or had worked more toward their own conversion. We owe to these poor the exercise of charity, both to fulfill our office as priests and to thank them for what we receive from their labor. While they suffer and work hard against so many obstacles it is our duty, like Moses, to have our arms raised continually in prayer for them. If they suffer for their ignorance and sin, we ought to intercede for them before the mercy of God. Charity obliges us to do this. If we do not spend ourselves to teach them and aid them in this perfect conversion to God, even at the cost of our life, we are in some way the cause of all the ills they suffer.[3]

This is how Monsieur Vincent urged his own family to pray, work, and suffer to banish ignorance and sin, as the chief causes of all the evils they experienced. In this way they would obtain from God a true and lasting peace. This was the surest remedy for all the evils of the times. He never stopped recommending to his community to continue their prayers to God for peace. He had the custom of praying the litany of the Holy Name of Jesus every morning. When he came to the words "Jesus, God of peace," he pronounced them more piously and with more devotion, and always repeated the invocation. Besides, he took every occasion that presented itself to recommend to everyone he knew to offer their prayers, their alms, their pilgrimages, fasts and mortifications and penances to obtain from God the peace so necessary and so much desired.

An older priest associated with Monsieur Vincent at Saint Lazare gave the following testimony of him.

> If his charity was so great in his help to the poor ruined by the war, his zeal was no less to remove the root cause of all this suffering. While the Ladies of Charity and other helpers worked so hard at collecting alms and other contributions to aid the devastated provinces, we know with what zeal and tenderness of heart he recommended that they join to these works of mercy their vows, prayers, fasts, mortifications, and other exercises of penance, their devotions, their pilgrimages to Notre Dame, to Saint Genevieve, and other patrons of Paris and of France, their confessions and communions, masses and other sacrifices, to draw down God's mercy and appease his anger. We know how some women of delicate constitution followed his advice to mortify their flesh by hair shirts and disciplines and other instruments of penance. In this

---

3. *CED* XI:200-02.

way, they joined his own penances and those of his community to obtain the peace so much longed for and which we happily enjoy today. Who can express his distress at the disorders of the army? How he was moved at the outrages committed everywhere and against all sorts of people, and sacrileges and profanations of the blessed sacrament and churches, all brought about by the army. How often has he said, speaking to the clergy, "My friends, if the Lord is to receive fifty lashes, strive to save him from some of them. Do something to atone for the outrages committed against him so that he will have at least some to console him in these persecutions and sufferings."

Besides his prayers and practices of penance, Monsieur Vincent felt it to be his duty to do all he could to influence those in power to work for peace. The way to this, he felt, was to have the authority of the king recognized by all subjects of the realm. There must be entire and perfect submission to his authority in all parts of the kingdom. This is the only way the civil war could end. Although he had always avoided political action, through either his humility or possibly his Christian prudence that suggested he concentrate his efforts on what concerned the service of God and the good of souls, in the present situation in which France would come to ruin if the wars continued, he felt it his duty to act otherwise. He was aware that love of country is a duty of charity and the service of the king is in some way service to God. As a result of these reflections he resolved to serve his country and his prince in this important and pressing matter.

His first efforts in this direction focused on bishops, several of whom were well disposed toward him. He wrote to persuade and encourage them to remain in their dioceses during these troubled times so that by their example and teaching they might confirm their people in their duty and oppose those who strove to weaken their allegiance to the king.[4] He wrote to several prelates in similar terms, to some to congratulate them for having refused to let the towns of their diocese welcome the rebels. To others he wrote in the hope of dissuading them from appearing at court to seek redress from damages suffered from the army. He thought that this was not the appropriate time. He suggested instead that they remain in their sees to console their people and to further the interests of the king, who would be mindful of their fidelity and make good any losses they may have sustained. We shall give here three extracts from such letters. One was addressed to the late bishop of Dax,[5] the diocese from which Monsieur Vincent originally came.

---

4. A reference to Conde, a refugee in Guienne, who broke with the queen, and led the province into revolt.
5. Jacques Desclaux, named bishop of Dax in 1639, consecrated that same year in the church at Saint Lazare. He died in Paris, August 4, 1658, at age sixty-five.

I must say, Your Lordship, that I was very pleased to see you in Paris. Yet I must also say with regret that I think your visit here will have no worthwhile outcome in these unhappy times, in which the troubles of which you complain are almost universal throughout the kingdom. Wherever the armies have passed, the same sacrileges, robberies, and indecencies have occurred as has happened in your diocese, not only in Guienne and in Perigord, but also in Saintonge, Poitou, Burgundy, Champagne, Picardy, and in many other places, not excluding the environs of Paris itself. As a rule the clergy as well as the people have suffered the same fate, so much so that they have been sent out of Paris to the provinces to look for clothes and to seek alms just to keep alive. Only enough priests have remained to administer the sacraments to the sick. It is fruitless to request a reduction in tithes from the clergy for the official reply will surely be given that most dioceses will ask for the same thing. Everyone feels the effects of the war, and upon whom could this tax be transferred? God has pleased to lay this universal scourge upon the whole kingdom. And so, Your Lordship, you can do no better than to submit to his justice, awaiting the time his mercy shall bring an end to such terrible sufferings. If you should be elected to the general assembly of 1655 you will then have an opportunity to obtain some relief for your clergy. Meanwhile they will be consoled by your presence which is of such benefit to them and even for the service of the king.[6]

This letter shows the deplorable state to which France had sunk and the efforts being made to help save the clergy so that there would still be those committed to God's service. Meanwhile the devil sought to bring the clergy to ruin. We can see the prudent efforts Monsieur Vincent was making to dissuade this prelate from coming to Paris and to convince him to remain in his see. He could be of greatest utility there to the service of his Church and his king.

He wrote another letter to Jacques Raoul, bishop of La Rochelle, on the same subject:[7]

I received your letter as a blessing from God. It consoled me greatly in these troubled times. If those who threatened the peace of your diocese have not succeeded, I believe that after God the

---

6. *CED* V:90-91.
7. Jacques Raoul de la Guibourgere was named bishop of Saintes in 1632. On the advice of Monsieur Vincent in 1646 he was transferred to the see of Maillezais, to arrange for the suppression of this see and to make way for the erection of the see of La Rochelle, formerly a Huguenot stronghold. That same year he became its first bishop. He died in 1661 at age seventy-two.

storm has been averted because of your wise direction in service of the king. I thank God for this and for the many other services you have rendered both in your episcopal city and elsewhere which have confirmed your people in their duty toward God, their Church, and their prince. Even the heretics observing your manner of acting cannot help recognizing the excellence of our holy religion and the importance and influence of the office of bishop when it is administered as it has been by your sacred person. I pray God, Your Excellency, to give us many prelates like yourself who work so hard for the spiritual and temporal welfare of the people.[8]

It was Monsieur Vincent's practice, in writing to those in authority, to proceed by way of encouragement and of congratulations rather than by exhortation. This was because of his great respect for them, but also because it was more effective in influencing their thinking.

A third letter written to a bishop who is still alive shows better than the other two the appreciation Monsieur Vincent had for the service of the king and the prudence with which he expressed himself in this regard.

> I am really disturbed that our unhappy times have deprived you of the benefits of your abbey. I cannot tell you how pained I am not to be able to help you, because of our troubled times. However, Your Excellency, it seems to me that you ought to put off your visit to the court until things have clarified. You are not alone in the troubles you experience. Many bishops join you in this. Monsieur N.,[9] for example, has not only lost his regular revenue but also the provisions he has been setting aside for a long time. Even though he was well regarded at court, he received no satisfaction when he appeared there. Bishop N., who remained in his see, had the happiness of seeing his episcopal city return to its obedience to the king, even though it had at first gone over to the other side. He has received great praise from the court and has opened the way for some recompense for his losses. Even though you may not have the occasion to render the same service to His Majesty, your presence will aid notably in calming your region because of the esteem and confidence people have in you. This is greatly to be desired and will surely not go unnoticed. I most humbly beg you to accept my sincerity and promise of obedience.[10]

Monsieur Vincent wrote several other similar letters to other bishops.
Mindful that Saint Bernard and some other saintly persons who had led

---

8. *CED* IV:429.
9. Nicolas Sevin, bishop of Sarlat; *CED* IV:429.
10. *CED* IV:334-35.

a life even more retired than his own had left their solitude and retreat to appear in the courts of emperors and kings when it was a question of healing division among princes, Monsieur Vincent resolved to do all in his power to bring about the reunion of the king and his nobles. He preferred the service of the king and the good of France to all personal advantage. He closed his mind to all mere human reasoning that might turn him from this course. What he actually did in this regard is not well known, for he acted in strictest secrecy. What is certain is that he appeared several times at court and conversed with the princes and delivered messages to them from the king. He also brought back their responses. After his death there was found the draft of a letter to Cardinal Mazarin, who at the time[11] was with the court at Saint Denis. We get some idea of his activities from this document.

> I humbly beg Your Eminence's pardon for not coming to see you yesterday evening, as you had requested. Unfortunately I was not well. I have just received word from the duke of Orleans that he will send Monsieur d'Ornano[12] who will give me an answer which he wanted me to deliver to the prince [of Conde]. I told the queen yesterday that I had met both separately, and that both were respectful and gracious. I told Her Royal Highness that if the king's authority was to be recognized, a decree ending the civil strife would have to be issued.[13] This would satisfy both sides.[14] To bring these agreements about, it is difficult to negotiate through intermediaries. It must be done by those who have mutual respect and confidence, and who will discuss matters face to face. By word and gesture he assured me he was in agreement and assured me that he was going to discuss the matter with his council. Tomorrow morning, God willing, I hope to be able to bring his reply to Your Eminence.[15]

The results of these negotiations are not known in detail, for nothing further was found in Monsieur Vincent's papers about the outcome of these secret plans. God must have blessed the matter, however, for shortly afterward this important issue was settled.[16]

The troubles in the kingdom were thus brought to a close through the mercy of God. At the house of Saint Lazare Monsieur Vincent continued to offer prayers, masses, communions, fasts and other penitential practices that

---

11. The beginning of July 1652.
12. Henri Francois Alphonse d'Ornano, secretary of the duke of Orleans.
13. By Cardinal Mazarin.
14. If Mazarin were to leave.
15. *CED* IV:423.
16. Mazarin left. Vincent wrote an important letter to Mazarin on the subject, September 11, 1652. *CED* IV:473-78.

he had previously ordained. Some tried to persuade him to bring them to a close for these practices wore heavily on the community. Besides, the civil war and public division which had occasioned the penances were ended. Monsieur Vincent replied, "No, no, we must not stop now, we must beseech God for universal peace." In fact these continued until this peace[17] so greatly desired was finally achieved in 1660, eight years after these prayers began and six or seven months before his own death. God willed to give him the great consolation of seeing the fruit of his prayers, his fasts, and of his perseverance.

---

17. The Peace of the Pyrenees, signed November 7, 1659.

CHAPTER FORTY-FOUR

Monsieur Vincent's Opposition to the Errors of Jansenism

THE SAINTS have always considered it an honor to live in humble dependence not only to the will of God, but also to the Church to which they have professed their submission. They have pledged their exact obedience to its laws, their reason itself to a belief in the truths proposed to them, and their understanding in honor of Jesus Christ, the Church's sovereign head.

Everyone acquainted with Monsieur Vincent acknowledges that he excelled in his submission to and dependence upon the Church. Once she had spoken either to establish some regulation or to define some truth or to condemn some error, he had nothing more to say. He did not dispute or even reason. He had ears only to hear and a heart to submit sincerely and perfectly to all that had been set forth.

This is what he did when the errors of Jansenism began to appear, and more so when the sovereign pontiffs condemned its doctrines.

When Jansenius's book *Augustinus* first appeared[1] its novel opinions created a sensation among many learned persons. The faithful and prudent servant of God recalled the apostle's advice not to believe in any spirits before they had been tested and seen as coming from God. He was cautious in the face of this new doctrine, especially so because he was well acquainted with one of the originators of the Jansenist sect.[2] This man's spirit and actions gave good reason to make anyone hesitate. This particular point will be discussed in Book Two.[3]

When Monsieur Vincent became aware that the Church had condemned these doctrines through the constitutions of Innocent X and Alexander VII[4] and the magisterium of the hierarchy in France, he felt that he not only was

---

1. Louvain, 1640.
2. Jean Duvergier (or du Verger) de Hauranne, the commendatory abbot of Saint Cyran, 1581-1643. He struck up a friendship with Saint Vincent about 1622, and may have had some role to play in the Community's possession of College des Bons Enfants and Saint Lazare. Their frequent meetings decreased after 1632 and ceased from 1634 on. The saint tried several times to reconcile his former friend with the Church. Saint Cyran was imprisoned in 1638 at the chateau of Vincennes, on the outskirts of Paris. Among his papers was found a copy of a letter from him to Vincent. Richelieu had the saint summoned to a lay court, but he refused to testify. Later testimony, published by the Jansenists, seems to be altered or incomplete. Saint Cyran was freed in 1643, but died scarcely eight months later. He is buried in Saint Jacques du Haut Pas in Paris.
3. Ch. 12.
4. May 31, 1653 and October 16, 1656 respectively. Saint Vincent explained his opposition to the Jansenists in letters. *CED* III:318-32, 362-74.

obliged to submit to this judgment of the Apostolic See but also to do so formally and publicly. Putting aside all human considerations of political prudence he declared his entire opposition to the condemned errors and to those who obstinately sought to defend them.

He took this course of action with vigor and courage but also with prudence and moderation. He never spoke with dissimulation, but he spoke only when he considered it helpful. Perhaps he did so to strengthen those who had submitted to the Church's judgment or to win back those who had not or even to persuade those wavering in their loyalty to the Holy See. Whatever these reasons, the one guiding principle he followed was ever to seek the truth. He showed his great dedication to supporting the declarations of the sovereign pontiffs and dissociating himself from those who strove to prevent the execution of their decrees. Nevertheless, he still was able to distinguish between the error and the person holding the mistaken doctrine. He kept in his heart a true and sincere love for all people no matter what their beliefs. He spoke of them only with great reserve and compassion rather than with holy indignation. He even took steps, when occasion presented, to reconcile these people to the Church. After the proclamation of the constitution of Innocent X he visited Port Royal itself to enter into honorable communication with the dissenters. It must be said that the results of these initiatives were not as favorable as he had hoped.

He was particularly careful that the members of his own Congregation be free of these condemned errors, even that there should not be the least suspicion in this regard. If some lacked humble and sincere submission to Rome, he obliged them to leave the community.

His vigilance and charity extended to other sectors of the Church which he saw needed help or at least warning against these new errors. He was aware that those who were of this mind would try to insinuate themselves and their doctrines into monasteries and communities of women under the guise of the greater good. He knew also that these false prophets (as Jesus Christ warned us in the Gospel) would use every artifice to disguise their pernicious doctrines. Consequently, he did his utmost to protect these religious men and women. He saw to it that these wolves in sheep's clothing would make no inroads into this privileged portion of the flock of Jesus Christ. He forbade them to have any access to the monasteries or convents, especially those under his direct care.

He exercised the same precaution in preventing any surprise in the Council for Ecclesiastical Affairs, lest any of those infected with this condemned doctrine, or even those rightly suspected of holding such views, should accept any office or benefice in the Church.

His zeal for unity in the Church and for the triumph of sound doctrine led him on several occasions to alert certain members of the hierarchy, to encourage them to be on their guard against these errors, or to advise how to combat this threat. In Book Two we will quote several letters he wrote in which we will see how this great servant of God respected the dignity of the bishops to whom he wrote. We will also see how anxious he was to serve these prelates. Humility, discretion, prudence, and charity marked his words as well as his deeds.

All efforts of the creature will have little effect if God on high does not sustain and bless them with his help. He put his principal trust in the goodness of God, offering constant prayers for this intention and had others do the same. He prayed that the Lord would look down with the eyes of mercy upon his Church and not permit the spirit of evil and lies to spread havoc among the faithful. He used to say that the best defense against the errors of the time was mental prayer and the faithful practice of the virtues contrary to the sentiments of the heretics. Profound humility and submission of mind must be opposed to pride and presumption of one's own independence. A love of abnegation and rejection must be preferred to vain praises and flatteries. A straightforward and simple heart must contrast with the deceits, falsehoods, and trickery used by the heretics to disguise their errors and conceal their real purposes. Finally, an ardent charity was required that would counteract all contradictions, slanders, and calumnies the evil spirit customarily uses to suppress the truth.

He was often heard to say sorrowfully that he feared that the corrupt morals and the dissolute life of Christians, so opposed to the maxims Jesus Christ left us in the Gospel, had caused this plague afflicting the Church in our kingdom. If we did not amend our ways and appease the just anger of God he feared that ours would be the same fate as the Jews, as recorded in the Gospel. The kingdom of God would be taken from us and given to others who would respond more satisfactorily. We must tremble with fright at seeing how other great kingdoms once so flourishing in religious matters, such as England, Denmark, Sweden, and the greater part of Germany, were allowed to fall into heresy through the just judgment of God. The ills of our neighbors ought to warn us that faith is a gift of God, purchased for us by the blood of Christ. We must appreciate it and do all in our power to preserve it.[5]

---

5. *CED* III:34-36, for example.

CHAPTER FORTY-FIVE

*The Home for the Aged Poor Begun at Paris by Monsieur Vincent;
The General Hospital for the Poor Begun by Him in that Same City*

MONSIEUR VINCENT'S charity seemed like a burning fire, ever ready to spread when the conditions were right. It probably would be preferable to say that he was consumed by that heavenly fire which Jesus Christ came to bring upon the earth, to respond to everything having to do with the glory of God and the salvation of souls. This faithful servant of God did not let any opportunity pass to serve the Church or work for the good of his neighbor. Despite his advancing years and the infirmities ordinarily accompanying old age, he still bore the principal burden of the many pious works he had established. Notwithstanding this he was always ready, even anxious, to begin new ventures for the glory of God. Rather than being overwhelmed by the burdens of new projects, on these occasions his vigor and strength seemed to increase.

This is illustrated on the occasion in 1653 when divine Providence used him for a new expression of charity. This led to one of the most significant developments in the Church in many years. This was the establishment of the general hospital for the sick poor at Paris, of which we can say without taking anything away from the many other virtuous people who contributed to its origin that Monsieur Vincent laid the first stone. Rather we should say that God used him without his being aware of the designs of Providence. Since its very inception, other zealous workers have generously participated in building this marvelous structure which flourishes even today.

This is a summary of events leading to the building of the hospital.

A citizen of Paris was moved by the desire to do something in the service of God. He went to see Monsieur Vincent, whose charity was well known to him. He stated that he wished to devote a large sum for works of charity totally at the judgment of Monsieur Vincent, but on condition that his gift remain completely anonymous. He wanted to do this solely for God's glory, without his identity being known to anyone besides God and Monsieur Vincent.

Monsieur Vincent received the gift as a legacy for the poor, since he did not think he could refuse. After mature deliberation before God he prayed for light to discern what good work would be most suitable. He discussed the question with the donor until the two agreed that the gift should be used to found a home for poor workers who because of age or infirmity were no longer able to earn their livelihood. It was his experience that those reduced to begging often neglected their own salvation. By founding a home for these poor people he would be doing a double service for them: taking care of their bodily wants and at the same time looking after their spiritual welfare. He proposed this idea to the generous benefactor, who agreed wholeheartedly. He did so only on condition that the spiritual and temporal administration of the hospital would forever remain in the hands of the superior general of the Congregation of the Mission.

To carry out his project, Monsieur Vincent bought two houses and grounds in the faubourg Saint Laurent in Paris. He furnished these houses with beds, linens, and everything else deemed necessary. He had a small chapel constructed, and even with this had enough left over to set up an investment that yielded an annual return. He was able to receive forty poor persons in the hospital, twenty men and twenty women, whom he housed and fed, and this has continued to the present. The income fell off these last years. A reduction in the number of guests would have been necessary had divine Providence not provided help from elsewhere. The forty poor were housed in two separate buildings, one for men and one for women. They were, however, so situated that both groups could attend the same mass, listen to the same reading during meals, but the tables were so arranged that the two groups were entirely separate, with neither able to see or speak with the other.

He bought tools and set up workshops so the forty could occupy their time and talent to the limit of their reduced strength. He wanted to avoid their falling into idleness. He commissioned the Daughters of Charity to care for these poor people and designated one of his priests of the Mission to celebrate mass, instruct them in the word of God, and administer the sacraments. He himself was among the first to offer this instruction. He recommended especially union among themselves, piety, and above all a gratitude toward God for having provided such a peaceful home where their bodily needs and the salvation of their souls were attended to.[1]

He called this foundation the Hospital of the Holy Name of Jesus.[2] He applied for approval to the king, without, however, naming the chief benefactor, and this was given by letters patent. The archbishop of Paris approved of these matters, granting the entire direction of the hospital to Monsieur Vincent and his successors.

As soon as one of the poor patients died, another was brought in to take his place. All lived in great serenity, esteeming themselves happy to be cared for in life as well as in death. Their chief care was to live such a Christian

---

1. *CED* XIII:156-63.
2. This building had probably already been known as "Holy Name of Jesus."

life that their death would be peaceful. Their well-ordered style of life appealed to others who hoped to succeed them in the hospital, so that soon there was a wait of several years before they could be accommodated.

Once he had established and organized this new hospital, Monsieur Vincent received visits from several representatives of the Ladies of Charity of Paris and other virtuous women of some standing. They visited all parts of the establishment only to be thoroughly edified at the good order and excellent management they saw. Everywhere peace and union prevailed. Murmurings and slander were unheard of, as were all other vices. The poor, busy in their small workshops, fulfilled their religious duties as much as their condition would allow. The whole hospital seemed to recall the life of the early Christians and seemed to be a convent or monastery rather than a home for seculars.[3]

The sight of such a well-run enterprise gave rise in the minds of those who had visited the hospital the plight of the many poor who begged in the streets or in the churches of the city. These people for the most part live a disordered life, marked by vice and dissipation, but until now no one seemed able to help them. Several of the Ladies of Charity had the thought that perhaps Monsieur Vincent could rescue these poor from the streets. He possibly could do on a larger scale what he had so well accomplished on a smaller. God's grace and blessing could be relied on, and at Saint Lazare and with the Daughters of Charity some were available to help out, if only a place large enough could be found to receive these poor people.

The women who first thought of this mentioned it to several others who had visited Monsieur Vincent's hospital. Then one of the visitors gave fifty thousand *livres* to begin the building of a general hospital. Another woman gave an investment worth three thousand *livres* for the same purpose. On the day of the periodic assembly of these Ladies of Charity, at which Monsieur Vincent presided in keeping with his usual practice unless prevented by some unforeseen difficulty, they surprised him greatly, as he himself said, when they endorsed the project wholeheartedly. He could not help admiring the zealous charity of these good women for which he praised God and congratulated them. However, he stated that the matter was of such importance that it should be considered further and prayed over at great length.

At the next meeting these women appeared even more determined than before. They assured Monsieur Vincent that money for the project would not be lacking, for they had contacts with several other wealthy persons who had promised considerable help. They pressed Monsieur Vincent to give his consent. He still hesitated, but his reluctance was no match for their ardent

---

3. This hospital survived the French Revolution, with various names and locations in later years.

desire to begin this enterprise. A large enough house and grounds would obviously be required to house the number of poor they were considering. Someone proposed that the king be asked for the property known as the Salpetriere, near the river, opposite the arsenal. At the time the building and grounds were not being used. Monsieur Vincent spoke to the queen regent, who agreed and gave him the deed to the property. Some person claimed that he had an interest in the property, but was satisfied when one of the Ladies of Charity promised him an annual investment paying eight hundred *livres* to compensate his losses.

After all these matters had been taken care for, it seemed to the Ladies of Charity that it remained only to get started. Some of the more fervent were disappointed that the poor were not immediately gathered up and brought to the home. They let Monsieur Vincent know how they felt about the delay. Monsieur Vincent and the women could not agree about how the poor were to be enticed to come to this new home nor about how it was to be run. This led him to the painful position of having to slow down the project, for it was going far too fast for his taste. This explains what he said, in an effort to moderate their zeal:

> The affairs of the Lord ordinarily develop little by little. They begin slowly and only then develop. When God wished to save Noah and his family he directed him to build the ark. This could have been completed quickly, but Noah was told to begin building a hundred years before the rains began and to work little by little on its construction. In the same way when the Lord planned to bring the children of Israel to the promised land he could have done so in a short time. Instead, forty years passed before they entered into Canaan. When God sent his Son to redeem mankind did he not delay three or four thousand years? God is never rushed. He does all things in their own good time.
>
> When our Savior came upon earth he could have come at a perfect age to effect our redemption. He did not have to spend thirty years in a hidden, even superfluous, life at Nazareth, but he chose to be born an infant and grew just like other men to full stature. Did he not say on occasion that his hour had not yet come? This was to teach us not to be too hasty in those matters which depend more on God than on ourselves. He could have established his Church throughout the world in his own lifetime. He preferred, however, to lay the foundation and leave the rest to his apostles and their successors. According to this way of acting it does not seem expedient to attempt to do everything at once or even to think that we have to act immediately to keep the good will of those who are

anxious to start. What should we do, then? Go gently, pray much to God and act in union of heart.

He added:

It seems to me that we first ought to experiment with taking one, or even two hundred poor people, and afterward only those who want to come. If they are well treated there will be no lack of applications, and we can adjust the number we take to what resources Providence provides. We won't lose by following this plan, but if on the contrary we use compulsion and act precipitously, we run the risk of thwarting the designs of God. If the work we propose is from him it will succeed and endure, but if it is solely a human enterprise it will not do much good, nor will it last long.

Thus Monsieur Vincent expressed his opinion to the Ladies of Charity, who responded by tempering their zeal for the project. But what restrained them even more was that some of the leading civil officials would not approve the project, thinking it not well enough planned.[4] The years 1655 and 1656 passed with no real progress, except that several proposals were made to solve the practical problems of administering the proposed hospital. Finally a group of well-placed and zealous persons worked out a plan of administration which included a board of directors, and with God's blessing this plan was accepted. The Ladies of Charity, who under the wise guidance of Monsieur Vincent had first conceived the project, were greatly consoled to see it finally approved by public authority, and willingly gave their support to the newly created board. Monsieur Vincent for his part turned over the Salpetriere to them, as well as the chateau of Bicetre which had been given him several years before as a home for abandoned children.

Besides turning over these buildings in favor of the poor, the Ladies of Charity contributed notable amounts of money, a quantity of linens, beds, and other furniture, even some made in the shops of Saint Lazare, to prepare the hospital for its opening. The whole enterprise was not carried out as an experiment, as Monsieur Vincent had suggested, nor would it depend on a choice made by the poor. Instead, to put an end to begging, all the poor of Paris were offered the choice—either work to earn their livelihood or else go to the general hospital.

Monsieur Vincent wrote the following in March 1657 to one of his friends:

Begging is outlawed in Paris, and the poor are being brought together in suitable places where they may be helped, instructed,

---

4. The most opposed was the first president Pomponne de Bellievre, who had succeeded Mathieu Mole at his death, in January 1656. He was won to the cause before his death, and he provided generous gifts to the new establishment. Guillaume de Lamoignon succeeded him, and continued his charitable efforts.

and given something do to. It's a fine scheme but difficult. It has begun well, and thanks be to God, has won the everyone's approval. Many people have helped by giving generously, and others have donated their services. We have already collected ten thousand shirts and other things in proportion. The king and Parlement have powerfully supported the project even without our asking. They have even appointed the priests of our Congregation and the Daughters of Charity to serve the poor under the authority of the archbishop of Paris. We have not yet undertaken the actual work for we do not yet know for sure if it is the God's will for us. If we do begin this work it will at first be an experiment to see how it goes.[5]

Monsieur Vincent learned that the priests of his Congregation would be in charge of the spiritual ministry to the poor of the hospital, but in a matter of this importance he felt it should be thoroughly considered before God. Even though he was advised that it would be expedient to accept this appointment, he prayed and then called together the priests at Saint Lazare to discuss the matter fully. He pointed out the pros and cons of the case, and then they, for several great and serious reasons, decided to excuse themselves from this responsibility. Letters patent had already been issued assigning this right exclusively to the priests, so a formal legal document was drawn up which renounced this right, to enable other clerics to take up the work.

Since the hospital was just about to open, and the directors and administrators were anxious to begin as soon as possible, Monsieur Vincent persuaded one of the priests, who came regularly to Saint Lazare on Tuesdays, to accept the assignment as rector of the general hospital.[6] This was done to avoid any delay in the opening of the hospital which might have resulted from the refusal of Monsieur Vincent to take over the spiritual care of the poor there. It would also ensure that the poor were adequately provided for right from the beginning. After serving for some time with other priests of the Tuesday conference of clerics giving missions in the various parts of the hospital with others from various churches of Paris, the rector was forced by illness to resign from the difficult position he had assumed. He submitted his resignation to the vicars general of Cardinal de Retz, archbishop of Paris. He appointed, in turn, another priest of the Tuesday conference, a doctor on the faculty of the University of Paris. He has served as rector of the general hospital for some time with great success, offering missions in all houses of the institution as an expression of his dedication to the poor.[7]

---

5. *CED* VI:245.
6. Abelly himself.
7. This hospital annually housed twenty thousand poor. Abelly's successor was Thomas Regnoust. (*CED* VIII:128.)

CHAPTER FORTY-SIX

A Census of the Houses of the Congregation of the Mission Founded During the Lifetime of Monsieur Vincent

GOD PLANTED the Congregation of the Mission in his Church as a mystic vine which was to bear fruit though his grace to sanctify a large number of souls. He willed that it extend its branches everywhere. The new growth was in the establishment of other houses, which in truth should be attributed to the will of God rather than to any human intervention. The one most responsible for cooperation with this design of God was Monsieur Vincent, but only after he was convinced that not to do so would be to resist the action of God.

We have already spoken of the three houses in Paris, that is, the College des Bons Enfants, Saint Lazare, and Saint Charles.

The first house outside of Paris began in Lorraine in the town of Toul at the invitation of Charles Chretien de Gournay, bishop of Scythia. At the time, he was administrator of Toul and afterwards became its bishop. This mission was established in 1635 in the house of the Holy Spirit with the approval of the religious who lived there. It was formally joined to the Congregation of the Mission, and this action was authorized by the king with letters patent and ratified by the Parlement.

Three years later, in 1638, Cardinal Richelieu, as a memorial of his piety and as a sign of his esteem for Monsieur Vincent and his institute, founded a house of the Congregation of the Mission in the city of Richelieu. This foundation bore the obligation of having missions preached not only in the diocese of Poitiers in which the city of Richelieu is located but also in Lucon, where he formerly was bishop.[1] While awaiting the coming of other priests of the Congregation to Lucon the priests fulfilled the obligation of giving missions and were able to offer various other services. The cardinal completed his gift by leaving a sum of money for their maintenance.

Some time later, after the purchase of a house in Lucon around 1645, Monsieur Vincent sent three or four of his priests in response to the earnest request of Pierre de Nivelle, bishop of Lucon, who gave them full faculties to work in his diocese. They have remained there since, to the credit of the

---

1. Armand Duplessis, Cardinal Richelieu, was bishop of Lucon from 1607 to 1624. Named cardinal in 1622, he resigned his diocese to give himself entirely to affairs of state. He died December 4, 1642, at age fifty-eight.

missionaries of Richelieu, who gave them a small sum to help in their upkeep, and thus enable them to serve many souls more fully.

In the same year, 1638, another house of the Congregation was founded in Troyes, in Champagne, by the good offices of its late bishop, Rene de Breslay and of the late Commander de Sillery.

In 1640 Monsieur Vincent sent several priests of his Congregation[2] to work in the diocese of Geneva in Savoy. This was in response to the earnest request of Juste Guerin, bishop of Geneva, coupled with the insistence of Mother de Chantal, foundress and first superioress of the Visitation Sisters, in the city of Annecy. The bishop hoped to preserve in the diocese by means of the missions the great blessings brought by Blessed Francis de Sales. Commander de Sillery, moved by a singular dedication to the memory of this prelate, set up a foundation for the support of the missionaries, who have remained there up to the present. Besides giving missions for the sanctification of the country people, their commitment has been to reform and train the clergy. They did this by the usual ordination retreats and by founding a seminary. It began in October 1641 to train the clergy in knowledge and virtue.

In the same year, 1641, Dominique Seguier, bishop of Meaux, authorized a house of the Congregation in the city of Crecy in Brie, to conduct missions in his diocese. This was founded in the king's own name by Monsieur [Pierre] Lorthon, counselor to the king.

The following year, 1642, saw the foundation and establishment of another house in Rome through the generosity of the noblewoman Marie de Wignerod, duchess of Aiguillon, niece of Cardinal Richelieu. She was zealous for God's glory and charitable toward her neighbor, especially the most neglected poor no matter where they lived. This virtuous woman had a special esteem and affection of Monsieur Vincent, who in turn greatly appreciated her help and friendship.

This same duchess arranged to support seven priest missionaries to give missions in her territory of Aiguillon and in the counties of Agenais and Condomois. The bishop of Agen[3] arranged for them to start a house at Notre Dame de la Rose in his diocese, near the town of Sainte Livrade.

This same lady was responsible for supporting the new establishment in 1643 in the city of Marseilles, chiefly for the benefit of the poor unfortunates condemned to the galleys of France. The priests were to do all their usual good works in favor of the poor. Several years later the work was expanded by the duchess in favor of the Christian slaves of the Barbary pirates.

In the same year, 1643, Alain de Solminihac, the late bishop, baron and

---

2. To Annecy
3. Barthelemy Delbene.

count of Cahors, whose memory is held in such veneration in all the Church because of the eminent virtues with which his life was graced, brought the Congregation of the Mission to his diocese.[4] He himself was noted for his pastoral vigilance, his zeal for the glory of God and for the salvation of the people of his diocese. He was sensitive to the singular graces he recognized in Monsieur Vincent and in his institute. He judged he would do a great service to his diocese by inviting the Congregation of the Mission to open a house in Cahors.

The late king, Louis XIII of glorious memory, acquired sovereignty over the Sedan region, but unfortunately it was deeply infected with heresy. He requested Monsieur Vincent to send some members of his Congregation to conduct missions that would instruct and confirm Catholics in their faith. For the most part these people were poorly educated and in constant danger of losing their faith because of their frequent contact with heretics.

To further this project His Majesty ordered that a large sum be given to Monsieur Vincent to underwrite the work of the missions. After the death of this great monarch, Louis XIV, his successor now gloriously reigning, upon the advice of the queen regent, his mother, preferred that the remaining money should serve as a foundation for a permanent house of the Congregation of the Mission. This was done finally by Eleonor d'Etampes de Valencay, archbishop of Reims.

The house at Montmirail, a small village in Brie in the diocese of Soissons, was founded in 1644 by the duke of Retz.[5] Monsieur Toublan, his secretary, contributed some of his inheritance to this foundation.

Jacques Raoul [de la Guibourgere], then bishop of that city, established the house at Saintes that same year with the help of the diocesan clergy for the purpose of missions and a seminary.

The following year, 1645, another house was set up in the city of Le Mans, at the insistence of the bishop, Emeric de La Ferte, and the cooperation of Monsieur Lucas, head of the collegial church of Notre Dame de Coeffort, a royal foundation in the city. This was done with the consent of the canons, who turned over the church, the house and its appurtenances to the Congregation of the Mission. This was confirmed by royal letters patent, and ratified by the authorities of the town.

In the same year, 1645, Achille de Harlay [de Sancy], bishop of Saint Malo, requested priests of the Congregation to work in his diocese. Monsieur

---

4. 1593-1659. Born in Perigord, he became abbot of Chancelade near his home town. He worked strenuously for the reformation of that abbey and of others. He was named bishop of Cahors in 1636. He established a seminary for the formation of his clergy and entrusted it to Vincent de Paul. He died in 1659, at age sixty-seven. Pope John Paul II beatified him in 1981.

5. Pierre de Gondi, the eldest son of Philippe Emmanuel de Gondi, a former student of Monsieur Vincent.

Vincent sent several, and they were soon given the abbey of Saint Meen to live in. It should be remarked that the bishop was also abbot of this monastery, and the religious there agreed to the invitation. In fact, the house and its benefice was ceded to the missionaries. This transaction was authorized by letters patent from the king and later was approved by an apostolic bull of our Holy Father the pope, Alexander VII.[6]

We must not neglect to mention the foundation made in 1645 and the two following years in several remote locations. Having been pressed by the requests of some zealous and virtuous persons, but more so by his own charity, he sent some of his priests to remote places for various works of mercy, after obtaining the necessary approvals from the Apostolic See. He sent men to Tunis and Algiers for the spiritual and temporal care of Christian slaves who, whether well or ill, were in great need. He sent others to Ireland to instruct and encourage the poor Catholics of this region oppressed by their heretical masters from England. His zeal put no limits on his charity. He sent other priests all the way to the island of Madagascar then called Saint Lawrence, located below the equator. Here the people lived either in idolatry or with no religion at all. This is a vast region covered with brambles that this steward of the Gospel sought to reclaim by the indescribable labor of his followers, several of whom have already succumbed. We should mention that Monsieur Vincent displayed a remarkable firmness and constancy in supporting these apostolic efforts, particularly in this infidel island and in Tunis and Algiers. This took place despite the enormous difficulties in these missions, with the accompanying losses he suffered. We shall refer in Book Two[7] to the blessings God has poured out on these foreign missionaries and to the fruits they reaped, aided by his grace.

In the same year 1645, Cardinal Durazzo, the esteemed archbishop of Genoa in Italy, learning of the services rendered to the Church by Monsieur Vincent and the Congregation of the Mission in various places, chiefly Savoy and Rome, set about procuring the same benefit for his diocese. In response to his earnest request to have some priests of the Congregation in the city of Genoa, Monsieur Vincent sent several, and they were warmly received. The archbishop, with considerable help from local priests, Baliano Raggio and Giovanni Cristoforo Moncia, and from the local nobility, underwrote the enterprise.

In 1650 the Congregation of the Mission was set up in the city of Agen by the bishop. He also had the priests assume the direction of his seminary.

In 1651 Monsieur Vincent sent some priests of the Congregation to Warsaw in Poland in response to the invitation of the pious and generous

---

6. *CED* XIII:387-95. April 4, 1658.
7. Ch. 1, sects. 7-9.

queen. In Book Two we shall see what remarkable things took place in this foundation that reveal Monsieur Vincent's generosity, his truly apostolic zeal, and his personal self-abnegation.[8]

In this same year, 1651, Monsieur Vincent sent some of his priests to the Hebrides Islands to serve the abandoned poor of this region, located to the north of the kingdom of Scotland.

The following year, 1652, the Congregation of the Mission was established in the diocese of Montauban where Bishop Pierre de Berthier handed over to them the direction of the seminary besides the missions to be given in his diocese.

The house in the city of Treguier in lower Brittany, in 1654, was due to the kindness of Balthazar Grangier [de Liverdi], count and bishop. He was aided in this by Monsieur [Michel] Thepant, lord of Rumelin and canon of the cathedral church of Treguier, who endowed it.

In the same year Monsieur Vincent sent several of his Company to the town of Agde in Languedoc at the request of the count and bishop Francois Fouquet, who later became archbishop of Narbonne.

The same year also, Monsieur Vincent sent priests to Turin, capital of Piedmont, at the request of the marquis of Pianezza, prime minister of the duke of Savoy. This latter was a man of singular piety and had a great desire to further the glory of God and the salvation of souls by establishing a house of the Congregation in Turin.

In 1657 the court was in Metz. Moved by her usual concern to further the public good, the queen mother thought that inviting Monsieur Vincent to send some Missionaries to the city would be the most effective way to achieve this goal.[9] Accordingly, she returned to Paris, summoned Monsieur Vincent, and told him of her wishes. She also told him she wanted him to send missionaries to give a mission in Metz. He replied:

> Your Majesty is perhaps not aware that the Congregation of the Mission was founded solely for service to the poor. Our community is in Paris or other episcopal cities only to direct seminaries, to prepare young ecclesiastics about to be ordained, or to serve as a base for missions into the countryside, and not to preach, catechize, or hear the confessions of its citizens. However, another group of clerics who meet regularly at Saint Lazare can, if Your Majesty wishes, fulfill your wishes better than ourselves.

The queen replied that she was unaware that the priests of the Congregation of the Mission did not serve in the larger cities. As she had no desire to turn them from their proper goal as an institute, if the priests of the Tuesday

---

8. Ch. 1, sect. 10.
9. See *CED* XII:4.

conference of Saint Lazare were to come, she would find this satisfactory. This actually occurred in the Lenten season of 1658. Monsieur Vincent chose more than twenty priests, all capable men. He then requested the late Father de Chandenier, a man of singular virtue and of good repute, to take charge of this mission.[10] He was successful in this, carefully following the advice given him by Monsieur Vincent. He observed all the usual practices of the missions to guarantee success. When this virtuous priest reported the condition of the house to Her Majesty, she was so pleased that she decided to found a house of the Congregation of the Mission in Metz itself, but this did not happen until after the death of Monsieur Vincent.

In 1659 he sent several of his priests to Narbonne at the request of the archbishop, Francois Fouquet, who founded the house there.

The late Father de Sery of the Mailly family of Picardy had informed Monsieur Vincent several times in the past that he wished to contribute to the foundation of the Congregation of the Mission in Amiens. However, before this project could be completed, this holy priest had passed from this world. The mission was eventually established, however, by Francois Faure, bishop of Amiens, who gave the priests the perpetual direction of his seminary. The good priest survived Monsieur Vincent only a short time, having requested that he be buried near him in the church of Saint Lazare.

The late Henri de Baradat, count and bishop of Noyon and peer of the realm, wished to have the Congregation of the Mission in his diocese and wrote to Monsieur Vincent with this intention. Monsieur Vincent did not think it appropriate at the time to accede to the request. Divine Providence reserved the fulfillment of this wish to his worthy successor, Francois de Clermont. He was not long in his diocese before he followed up on the request to have the Congregation of the Mission come. This was accepted, and when the priests arrived, they were given the perpetual direction of the seminary of the diocese. This occurred in 1662.

It should be remarked that other prelates besides those in France itself wished to have the Congregation of the Mission in their dioceses for giving missions, working with those about to be ordained, and directing seminaries. Monsieur Vincent could not honor all their requests, either for lack of personnel or for other good and sufficient reasons. He did not care to attempt anything before the moment willed by God or beyond his own capabilities.

The priests of the Congregation of the Mission reaped the fruit of their labors, even here in this life. They saw their numbers increase like the stars of heaven, and the Congregation quickly became rooted in short time in various parts of the world.

Since the most ardent desire of the heart of Monsieur Vincent was that

---

10. See below, ch. 49. The total was probably less; see *CED* VII:76, 92.

God should be glorified and that souls redeemed by the blood of Jesus Christ should be saved, he was moved to profound gratitude that Providence had used him, a poor and miserable creature (as he believed himself to be) to bring about these things. The thought of all the works in which his Congregation was engaged did not give him a sense of accomplishment but rather one of deeper and deeper self-abasement. He continually offered his thanks to God that notwithstanding his own unworthiness and lack of ability he had been chosen as the instrument of divine mercy to bring about such blessings upon the world.

CHAPTER FORTY-SEVEN

Monsieur Vincent Gives the Rules to his Congregation. What He Said on this Occasion

IN 1658 MONSIEUR VINCENT finished his work on the rules and constitutions for his Congregation. His advancing years and nearly uninterrupted infirmities had made him realize that in all likelihood he would not have too much time remaining to complete this task. Just as he was ever moved by love for his confreres in life, he hoped before his death that he might give them a token of his affection by leaving his spirit embodied in his rules and constitutions.

On Friday evening, May 17, 1658, Monsieur Vincent assembled his community of Saint Lazare and spoke most paternally and affectively on the matter of obedience to the rules.

Several of those present recalled his words on that occasion. We give a few extracts to show the spirit that animated Monsieur Vincent and the prudence, moderation, charity, and zeal with which he had prepared the rules of the Congregation.

He began by speaking of the reasons why his Congregation should appreciate and observe the rules.

> It seems to me, that by the grace of God the rules of the Congregation of the Mission preserve us from sin and even from imperfections. They help us to procure the salvation of souls, to serve the Church, and to give glory to God. Whoever observes them as they should be observed avoids sin and all vices. He puts himself thereby in a state as required by God to be useful to the Church and to render to our Savior the glory due Him. What motives, gentlemen and my brothers, to avoid vice and sin, as much as human frailty will allow, to glorify God, and contribute to having Him loved and served upon earth. O Savior, what happiness! Words fail me.
>
> Our rules appear ordinary, but they will bring him who observes them to a high degree of perfection. Not only that, this observance will help destroy sin and imperfections in others as well, just as it has done in ourselves. If the Congregation has progressed at all in virtue, or if anyone has been freed from sin or advanced along the road to perfection, has it not been because of its observance of the rules? If by the mercy of God the Congregation has produced any good in the Church through giving missions and by service to the

ordinands, is it not because we have followed the customs inspired by God and now formalized in these rules? What motives do we not have to observe them scrupulously, and how happy the Congregation of the Mission will be if we are faithful to them.

Another reason to live faithfully according to the rules is that they are drawn almost completely from the Gospel, as you can see. It will help us to conform our lives to the life our Savior led on earth. It is said that our divine Savior came and was sent by his Father to preach the Gospel to the poor: *Pauperibus evangelizare misit me*.[1] *Pauperibus*: to announce the gospel to the poor, just as by the grace of God our humble Congregation attempts to do. It is a great subject of humiliation and confusion that we have never had any other purpose than to announce the gospel to the poor, and the most neglected of the poor. *Pauperibus evangelizare misit me*. Yes, that is what we were founded for. Yes, gentlemen and my brothers, our portion is the poor. What happiness for us, to do just what our Savior said he had come from heaven to earth to do, and through which we hope some day to find our way from earth to heaven. To fulfill our ministry is to continue the work of the Son of God, who went out to the countryside to seek out the poor. Our institute attempts to do the same, to serve and help the poor, whom we must recognize as our lords and masters. Our simple but blessed rules oblige us to leave the major cities to imitate the action of Christ by going out to the villages and towns in search of the poor. See the happiness of those who observe these rules and so conform their lives and all their actions to those of the Son of God. O Lord, what motives do we not have to observe our rules faithfully, which leads us to such a holy and desirable end.

You have awaited these rules for a long while, gentlemen and my brothers, and we have deferred long in giving them to you, in part to imitate our Savior who began to do and then to teach: *Coepit Jesus facere et docere*.[2] He lived virtuously during the first thirty years of his life and spent only the last three in preaching and teaching. So also the community has striven to imitate him, not only in what he did but also in the manner in which he did it. The Congregation could say that it first had done and then had taught: *coepit facere et docere*. It has been a good thirty-three years or thereabouts since we began, by God's help. All during that time, by God's grace, the same rules have been observed as those we give

---

1. Luke 4:18, citing Isa 61:1.
2. Acts 1:1.

you today. You will find nothing new in them which you have not already been observing, with much edification. If you were given rules you have not already been observing you might expect great difficulty, but as it is you will find only what you have already been doing, with much fruit and consolation, for many years. For the future you will find the rules equally useful and helpful. We must imitate the Rechabites spoken of in holy Scripture. They were so faithful to the traditions handed down by their fathers, even though nothing was actually written. Now that we have a written and published text, the Congregation has only to continue what it has observed for many years and bring the same fidelity to the future as it has displayed in the past.

If we had been given these rules right from the start, before we had a chance to practice what they prescribed, it would have been said they were more human than divine, more the fruit of human design than a work of divine Providence. Gentlemen and my brothers, these rules and constitutions have come, I don't know how, little by little, without plan or forethought. Saint Augustine's maxim was that if you couldn't trace the origin of a good thing you ought to ascribe it to God, recognizing him as the source and author. According to this, should not God be considered as the originator of all our rules, which came into being, I know not how, nor can we say when or why? O Lord, what rules! From whence do they come? Have I thought them up? Never, I assure you, gentlemen and my brothers; I never thought of our Company, nor even of the word "Mission." The Lord has done all that; men have had no part in it. For my part, when I consider the way it has pleased God to form our Congregation in the Church, I am beside myself. It all seems like a dream.

No it does not come from us. There is nothing human in it, but it comes exclusively from God. Would you call man-made what never entered into the mind of man to conceive, or what was never planned in any way whatsoever? Our first Missionaries thought no more of this than did I. In fact, it turned out differently from our expectations and hopes. Yes, when I think of all the various occupations of the Congregation of the Mission, I think it all a dream.

When an angel took the prophet Habakkuk to the far-off lion's den to console Daniel, and then brought him back to the place he originally was, did Daniel not think that it all had been a dream? If you ask me how the various practices of the community have started, or how the exercises and commitments have come about, I have to say that I do not know and cannot understand. Monsieur Portail, like myself, has seen the beginning of the Congregation. He can testify that we never thought of these things. Everything came about of itself little by little, one thing after another. Our numbers began to increase, and as they did, each new member strove to live a life of virtue. Gradually pious practices were introduced into our common life, and we began to observe a certain uniformity in our ministry. These practices were honored by all, and even to this day are respected, by the grace of God.

Finally, it was considered appropriate to put these matters down in writing, to become our rules. I hope the Congregation will regard them as coming from the Spirit of God, *a quo bona cuncta procedunt* ["from whom all good things come"],[3] and without whom *non sumus sufficientes cogitare aliquid a nobis, quasi ex nobis* ["It is not that we are entitled of ourselves to take credit for anything."][4]

Gentlemen and my brothers, I am so astonished at seeing myself here giving you the rules when I don't know what has led me here. I seem to myself to be back at the beginning. The more I think of the rules the more they seem to me foreign to all human intervention, and the clearer it is that God alone inspired them for the Congregation. If anything at all comes from me, I fear that it will be just those items that will not be observed in future, nor will they produce the fruit we hope for.

After all this, gentlemen, what remains for me? I must imitate Moses, who gave the law of God to the people and then promised all sorts of blessings for those who observed it: blessings in their bodies, souls, goods, everything. Just so, gentlemen and my brothers, we must hope for all sorts of graces and blessings for those who observe these rules which he has given you: blessings on your person, in your thoughts, on your projects, in your ministry, in your guidance of others, in your comings and goings. In a word, blessings in all things. I hope that the fidelity with which you have observed these rules and your patience while awaiting its written form will obtain from God's goodness the grace to observe them more easily and more perfectly in the future. O Lord, give your blessing to this small volume. Bestow on us the unction of your Holy Spirit so that all those who read it will be kept far from sin, detached from the world, committed to virtue, and united to you.[5]

---

3. From the collect from the Fifth Sunday of Paschaltide.
4. 1 Cor 3:5.
5. *CED* XII:1-14.

When he finished speaking, Monsieur Vincent had the priests come up to receive from his hand a small printed copy of the rules. Out of devotion they accepted the book on their knees. He preferred to put off until the next day distributing copies to the other members of the community, for it was already late.

When the distribution was completed, the assistant superior of the house[6] once more knelt and begged his blessing upon the entire Congregation. Monsieur Vincent in turn knelt and said in an affecting tone of voice the following words, revealing the depth of his concern for those present:

> O Lord, you are eternal and unchangeable law. You govern the universe by your infinite wisdom. You are the only true source of all guidance, laws, and rules of right living. O Lord, bless those who have accepted them as coming from you. Give them, O Lord, the grace to follow them always and inviolably, even till death. In full confidence in your help and in your name, despite my total unworthiness as a poor sinner, I pronounce the words of blessing over our entire Congregation.

These, in part, were Monsieur Vincent's remarks on this occasion. He spoke them in a moderate voice, humbly, gently, and devoutly, but they touched the hearts of all who heard him. It seemed to them that they were with the apostles listening to the last discourse of our Lord on the eve of his passion, at which he too gave a rule—the great commandment to love perfectly.

It is easy to gather from what was said, and ever more so by reading the rules of the Congregation of the Mission, that it began from three chief motives: first, to work at one's own sanctification by practicing the virtues taught us by the words and example of our Lord; second, to preach the Gospel to the poor, particularly to the most abandoned country people; third, to help the clergy acquire the knowledge and virtues appropriate to their calling. These are the goals of the Congregation of the Mission, expressed in the rules which Monsieur Vincent rightly said came from God, since they prescribed only what already was in the Gospel. Monsieur Vincent insisted that he could not explain how the rules came into being, but the members of his Congregation were well aware that Monsieur Vincent himself was a sort of living rule, for they saw in him a true reflection of Jesus Christ and of his precepts. They strove to imitate his example and walk in his footsteps. The rules had been observed long before they were written down, for he practiced them before committing them to paper, and his goodness and example led others to imitate him.

---

6. Rene Almeras.

CHAPTER FORTY-EIGHT

Other Works of Piety in Which Monsieur Vincent was Involved Besides His Usual Duties

PEOPLE WELL acquainted with Monsieur Vincent, aware of his zeal and the many opportunities brought about by divine Providence to exercise this virtue, can truly say that for thirty or forty years there were few important works of piety or charity especially in Paris in which he did not play some part by his advice or cooperation.

The house of Saint Lazare was a sort of magnet drawing anyone wanting to begin some new venture in service to the Church. Here Monsieur Vincent could be found to advise, help, or offer the cooperation needed for success.

This great servant of God was consulted almost continually by various people anxious to become involved in charitable works. His concerns were not confined to Paris, which alone would have given him ample scope for his work, but extended to many other places as well. He received many letters, some from people totally unknown to him, but who had heard of his virtue and especially his charity. This often gave them confidence to write. Besides the ordinary meetings he held at Saint Lazare at least three times a week, which he was most faithful in attending, he was often called to other meetings, whether of the bishops, theologians, or religious superiors, or others, of all sorts and types. Sometimes these meetings were held to resolve some pressing problem or to organize some activity, or to bring a remedy to a difficulty. In short, they sought to find a way to further the glory of God and the good of dioceses, communities, or families.

He was called upon to help restore peace within several religious houses, whether of men or of women, or to intervene in disputes and even lawsuits between individuals or entire communities.

His charity urged him to visit the sick or sorrowing. Sometimes he was invited, and other times he went of his own accord to extend his sympathy or consolation.

He was in charge of the monasteries of the Visitation of Saint Mary, established in Paris and Saint Denis as we have shown in an earlier chapter of this book.[1] He took this obligation seriously, making periodic visitations and looking after all the spiritual needs of the sisters.

To all the foregoing we must add his constant solicitude for the welfare

---

1. Ch. 16.

CHAPTER FORTY-EIGHT

of all the houses of the Congregation. He received many letters every day from all over which he was obliged to answer. Despite all his duties and the unusual interruptions to his routine, he regularly arose at 4:00 A.M. He went to the church where he remained for nearly three hours, sometimes longer, to make his mental prayer, offer mass, and recite part of the breviary. He was remarkable for the serenity of soul in his preparation and in his thanksgiving after mass. No matter what the press of business he never shortened this period of prayer, or if he did so rarely, it was because of some extraordinary circumstance.

During the day he was overwhelmed with visitors, but evenings were reserved for interviews with those living with him. He listened to each one with great kindness and with such attention, as though he had nothing else to do. He had to go out on errands of charity nearly every day, sometimes twice a day, from which he returned late. As soon as he got back he would fall on his knees for the recitation of the office. He recited it always in this posture when was home, as long as his health permitted. Afterwards he received those in the house who wished to speak to him, then he would read the daily correspondence or attend to other business. All this forced him to retire late, but he remained faithful to his usual hour of rising, provided he was not sick or indisposed.

Every year he was careful to make a spiritual retreat, despite all other preoccupations he had. He was persuaded before all else to look to his own salvation and the sanctification of his soul. He encouraged others in this same practice to which he was faithful, both to help them by his own example or to stimulate himself to continue faithful. He wished to draw from the heart of God the light, strength, and graces necessary to accomplish worthily all the great enterprises he was responsible for. In this he imitated Moses of old. Among all the cares of leading a whole nation, he had no more secure place of refuge than the sanctuary where he was secure from the importunities of the people. Here he could devote himself to pleading before God for the people for his divine help and protection.

This is how the days and years passed for this great servant of God. We can truthfully say, in the language of holy Scripture, that his days were full. Indeed they were full. We should even say they overflowed with his virtues and merits.

Whoever would cast a glance at the countless works of charity, which God inspired Monsieur Vincent to initiate and which continue to this day, cannot help being impressed. The houses of the Congregation of the Mission set up in so many places. The countless missions given, the seminaries where his priests labored, the retreats for ordinands, conferences and retreats which contributed so much to the development of the clergy and the laity, the founding of the Daughters of Charity, the establishment of the Confraternities of Charity in so many city and country parishes, the activities of the Ladies of Charity in favor of all sorts of good works, the creation of hospitals, the care of the abandoned poor, especially in the provinces overrun by war—whoever, I say, considers all these activities must realize that no one could possibly do all this. The hand of God was ever with his faithful servant to bring about these works of mercy.

Although all glory is due to God who ever remains the first and principal author of all good, we must honor and esteem his gifts and graces in his servants, who have cooperated so faithfully in his goodness. Although we confidently affirm that Monsieur Vincent was so worthy of esteem and praise, in his own eyes he was so unworthy. In everything he sought his own abasement and abjection. When he was congratulated for initiating so many marvelous works of mercy, his humility led him to answer that he was the vile and contemptible mud that God formed into the mortar used in cementing the stones of his structures.

CHAPTER FORTY-NINE

A Reflection on the Pains and Afflictions Endured by Monsieur Vincent

IT IS ESSENTIAL, as the holy apostle says, that those who wish to live virtuously in the service of Jesus Christ must endure contradictions and suffering. They must be identified with him in sharing his cross and crown of thorns to be worthy to be called his follower. Those who reign with him in eternity must have suffered with him here below.

Monsieur Vincent, who devoted himself with such fidelity to serve the King of glory and strove to imitate his Lord in all things, could not rightly be deprived of the honor of sharing in the sufferings of the cross. We do not speak here of the austerities and mortifications he imposed upon himself which shall be discussed in Book Three.[1] Instead we will take up here what he had to endure at the hands of other people, or possibly because of a singular disposition of divine Providence.

Because Monsieur Vincent was such a model of prudence, caution, deference, humility, and charity in his actions, and involved, we venture to say, beyond anyone else of our time in all sorts of charitable undertakings, he caused less opposition than would normally be expected. He could not avoid all poisonous criticism and even calumny, however, because it is not always possible to please both God and man at the same time. Also, he served in the royal council as dispenser of benefices, in which office he was obliged occasionally to refuse or even oppose the unjust pretensions of some petitioners. This, of course, aroused the wrath of those who were unsuccessful and who took great offense at this. This led to complaints, murmurings, reproaches, and sometimes downright threats and injuries, even in his own house. Complaints and calumnies were spread abroad in many quarters against his reputation and his honor. All these things were not the chief cause of pain for him, since from being broken by them one of his greatest joys was to be allowed to suffer affronts and injuries for the love and service of Jesus Christ.

More than once he experienced great loss and damage, chiefly during war time, when he witnessed Saint Lazare and all the small farms depending upon it overrun by the soldiers. They drove off the farm animals, stole provisions of wheat and wine, and still he counted this as gain, for he

---
1. Ch. 19.

recognized this as in the designs of divine Providence. He was happy to sacrifice all exterior things to conform his spirit more thoroughly to the holy will of God which was his main, or better, his only treasure.

These persecutions and annoyances, attacking either his goods or his honor, were painful to human nature but these did not cause him the most pain. It was rather the sight of France and nearly every other country in Christendom ravaged by war. War was the source of murders, violence, sacrilege, profanation of churches, blasphemy, and attacks against the person of Jesus Christ in the blessed sacrament of the altar. Within the Church schisms and divisions arose among Catholics because of the Jansenist heresy, and this gave great comfort to the enemies of the Church. In a word, the impieties, scandals and crimes he saw committed everywhere were as arrows which pierced his heart. Since the ills of his time seemed to be spread over the whole world we can well imagine how his soul was plunged into a sea of bitter sorrow.

Another source of sorrow for him to which he was very sensitive was the death of fellow servants of God, men committed to the spread of the kingdom. The number of such people was limited, and the Church's need so great, that he appreciated nothing so much as a valiant servant of the Gospel. The loss, therefore, of some of the best missionaries of the Congregation, either in France or elsewhere, touched him deeply. Many of these men were of an age or disposition such that they could still be expected to give great service to the Church. Five or six died in Genoa attending the stricken during an outbreak of the plague; four died in Barbary where they had gone to minister to the Christian slaves; six or seven died in Madagascar in their efforts to convert the infidels of that island; two died in Poland, where they had been sent to preach the Catholic religion. We do not mention the losses incurred during the wars when, tired out by their services to the poor in Paris and in the frontier regions, several succumbed.

The most regrettable losses to him in 1660, a little before his death, were the passing of three of his closest friends. The first of these was Monsieur Portail, a gift of God to him for almost fifty years. He was the first to be associated with him in the work of the mission, the first priest of the Congregation, later his secretary and first assistant. He was the one most involved in the government of the Congregation and the one in whom Monsieur Vincent had the greatest confidence.

Another loss was Mademoiselle Le Gras, foundress and first superioress of the Daughters of Charity. God had favored her with great graces of salvation and of concern for the neighbor. She had a special regard for Monsieur Vincent and had a great confidence in him, and he in his turn appreciated her virtues and especially her insights about the poor. He used

CHAPTER FORTY-NINE 247

to write often to her about matters touching the Daughters of Charity, but seldom saw her, except when necessary. She was of uncertain health and almost always ill. Monsieur Vincent used to say that for her last twenty years she had survived only by a miracle. She feared dying without having had the opportunity to receive the last rites from his hands. Yet God did not allow this to happen, either to test her virtue or to increase her merits. At the time Monsieur Vincent himself was so feeble he could hardly stand. She asked him at least to send a few words to console her in her last hours, but he preferred not to do so. Instead, he sent one of the priests of the Congregation as a living letter with the words that she was going to heaven before him, and he hoped soon to see her there. She died soon after.[2]

Though he was sorely afflicted by her passing, he had been so prepared by previous experiences of great trials that he was able to accept her death with submission to the will of God and with serenity of spirit. He had always delegated the supervision of the Daughters of Charity to Monsieur Portail, even though he himself was the founder and superior. After these two deaths the direction of that Congregation again fell to him, at a time when he could no longer go out or do much work. This caused him even more worry.

The third person whose death that same year caused him much grief was Louis de Rochechouart de Chandenier, abbot of Tournus. He had retired to Saint Lazare several years before to be with his brother, the abbot of Moutier Saint Jean.[3] These two had been received at Saint Lazare in return for some weighty considerations, even in face of the resolution previously taken by the community not to accept boarders to live with them. The exception to this rule was for those houses where a seminary was attached. The two brothers were the worthy scions of the family of their uncle Cardinal de Rochefoucauld, whose memory is still held in such benediction in all the Church.[4] These two priests were privileged by birth, but more so in their exemplary lives. The modesty of the one still alive does not allow us to speak with the same freedom as we do of his older brother. This priest served as a living example of the reformed commendatory abbots of the kingdom: mental prayer was his ordinary nourishment, humility his ornament, mortification his delight, work his repose, charity his usual occupation, and poverty his favorite companion.

He was among the clergy who came each Tuesday to Saint Lazare for the weekly conference. He had helped out in several of the missions in favor of the poor and had been in charge of the one established in Metz at the

---

2. March 15, 1660. Soon after, the saint presided at two conferences on her virtues; *CED* X:709-36.
3. Claude Charles de Rochechouart de Chandenier, who died May 18, 1710.
4. Francois de la Rochefoucauld, born in 1558, became bishop of Clermont, a cardinal in 1607, and later was named bishop of Senlis. He resigned his see to work to reform monastic life. He died in 1645, attended by Vincent.

invitation of queen mother in 1658. He also was visitor general of the Carmelites in France. Several bishops spoke to him about their wish to cede their dioceses to him, with the thought that his promotion to the episcopate would be advantageous to the Church. He expressed his gratitude but felt that God was not calling him to this exalted state. He preferred and actively sought to be at the beck and call of others rather than to rule over them.

The two brothers committed a good part of their revenues to the many poor of their region. They were aware, however, that holding multiple benefices was neither in keeping with the sacred canons nor conformable to the mind of the Church. In keeping with this thought, both surrendered all except one benefice apiece to provide for the poor. They would thus give an example so rare in our day yet so worthy of imitation.

These two worthy brothers joined two priests of the Congregation of the Mission on a trip to Rome toward the end of 1659, as arranged by Monsieur Vincent. Our Holy Father the pope, Alexander VII, was pleased to receive them, and the entire Roman court was edified at their modesty and virtue during their three or four months in Rome.

At this moment, the abbot of Tournus, who had decided even before this trip to present himself to the Congregation of the Mission as a candidate for membership, fell sick. He urged the superior of the Mission in Rome[5] to receive him into the Congregation. He feared the priest might die before having the happiness of being numbered among the missionaries. His request was not granted, however, because of his state of health. It was thought better to have Monsieur Vincent receive him in Paris, if he could manage to return there. He seemed a little better toward August of the following year, 1660. He took leave of His Holiness and, with his brother, left for Paris with the resolution of persuading Monsieur Vincent to accept him into the Congregation. God rewarded this holy and generous resolution to leave all for his service. He developed a new fever on the way and had to break his journey at Chambery in Savoy. His condition worsened, and in a few days he was in extreme danger. Finally, God called him from this world by a saintly death, to bestow upon him the crown of life.

Here is what the priest of the Mission[6] who accompanied him wrote to Monsieur Vincent:

> I had alerted you earlier to the sickness of Monsieur de Chandenier, abbot of Tournus, and the grave danger he faced. I now must tell you that it pleased God to call him to himself yesterday, the third

---

5. Edme (or Edmond) Jolly, 1622-1697, entered the Congregation in 1646 after experience in the French diplomatic corps. With his experience in Rome before and after his ordination, he rendered immense services to the Congregation by his negotiations with the Holy See. The general assembly of 1673 elected him as the third superior general.
6. Thomas Berthe.

of May, about five in the afternoon. His end was fashioned by his life, that is, saintly. I will fill in the details later when I have a little more time. I will tell you only, Monsieur, that he insisted several times that I should receive him among our number and give him the consolation of dying as a member of the Congregation of the Mission. In any case he planned on entering the Congregation once he had returned to Paris. I could not refuse him, and so I gave him the cassock of our Congregation in the presence of the abbot of Moutier Saint Jean, his brother.[7]

Let us hear Monsieur Vincent on the same subject. He wrote to one of his priests in Barbary:

Six or seven years ago the two brother priests, the Fathers de Chandenier, retired to Saint Lazare. This was a blessing for the Congregation, for they were marvelous in their edification. A month ago it pleased God to call to himself the older of the two, the abbot of Tournus, a man more filled with the Spirit of God than anyone I know. He lived as a saint and died as one of us, a missionary. He had gone on a trip to Rome with his brother and two of our priests. On his way back to Paris he died at Chambery, but not before insisting that he be received into the Congregation. This was done. Previously he had made the same request to me several times, but as his status and virtue were above us, I did not accede to his wish. We were not worthy of the honor. Only our heavenly home is suitable to receive him as a missionary. Our houses on earth have inherited the example of his saintly life, to be both admired and imitated. I don't know what he saw in our poor Congregation that made him want to appear before God clothed in our wretched rags, bearing the name and attire of a priest of the Congregation of the Mission. But it is as such that I commend him to your prayers.[8]

The body of the virtuous abbot was brought to Paris through the good offices of the abbot of Moutier Saint Jean, who cherished and honored him more as a father than as a brother and who had been such a consolation to him. He was buried in the church of Saint Lazare, where he awaits the general resurrection. No doubt his death was a great loss for the Church, for the Congregation of the Mission and especially for Monsieur Vincent. So true was this that he wept, a thing he rarely did. Thus God crowned the merits of his servant in the last years of his life by sending him these great sorrows, or rather three great occasions to heighten his virtue, in taking from him the three persons he loved so tenderly, so religiously, beyond all others.

---

7. *CED* VIII:288.
8. *CED* VIII:302-03.

CHAPTER FIFTY

Monsieur Vincent's Illnesses and the Saintly Use He Made of Them

TO PERFECT the holocaust of the life of this holy priest and to consume all in him that was not for the honor and glory of his sovereign Lord, bodily sufferings had to complete the sacrifice begun in his spirit. Having permitted him to be subject to different infirmities during his life, God sorely afflicted him in his last years to show his great patience and to give the crown of life to his perseverance and his love.

In one of the earlier chapters[1] we mentioned his having a robust physique, but one subject to several afflictions dating from the time he served in the de Gondi household. He fell ill while there with a chronic swelling of his legs and feet, which continued to bother him periodically until his death.

Besides, he was sensitive to changes in the atmosphere, which brought on a rather constant low fever lasting three or four days, and sometimes two weeks or more. This did not affect his ordinary routine, however, for he rose at 4:00 A.M. as did the others, made his meditation in the church, and tended to his usual duties and business as though he were in perfect health. He called this ailment his little fever. It was helped only by severe perspiration for several days running, especially during the summer. During the hottest times, when even a sheet was too much cover at night, he was obliged to sleep under three blankets. He also had two metal tubs filled with boiling water at his side, and he spent the entire night this way. In the morning his bed was soaked in sweat, but he insisted on changing it himself, not allowing anyone else to touch it.

The remedy was doubtless not quite so bad as the disease, but it still was most inconvenient to Monsieur Vincent, who bore it with courage. The brother who watched over him felt the treatment was excessive because it kept Monsieur Vincent awake the whole night, and because the excessive heat during the already oppressive summer weather was most painful to endure.

These long sweats and lack of sleep, which he never made up during the day, weakened him considerably. This in turn caused him to fall asleep even while speaking to visitors, sometimes to people of a high station. He did violence to himself to resist this tendency, but instead of speaking of its cause, the lack of sleep during the night, he would attribute it simply to his miserable nature, a term he ordinarily used.

---

1. Ch. 19.

Besides this low fever, he also experienced a quartan fever once or twice each year.[2] During these times God used him for some of his greatest deeds, as we have already reported. Instead of resting in an infirmary, he worked with even greater application and blessing in the service of the Church and for the benefit and salvation of the poor.

He had a serious attack in 1645. During this illness his devotion led him to receive communion every day. The severity of the fever caused several hours of delirium during which he repeated words from the abundance of his heart, which showed the dispositions of his devout soul. Among others, he repeated these words often: *In spiritu humilitatis, et in animo contrito, suscipiamur a te, Domine.* That is, Deign, O Lord, to receive us, who come to you with a humble spirit and a contrite heart.[3]

One event during this serious illness deserves mention. Monsieur Dufour, a priest of the Congregation from the diocese of Amiens, was sick in the same house.[4] Learning that Monsieur Vincent was in danger of death, he prayed the same prayer as did David for Absalom his son, that God would take him in place of the father of his soul. We mention simply that as Monsieur Vincent began to get better, the illness of this good priest took a turn for the worse, and shortly after he died.

On the night this priest died, those attending Monsieur Vincent heard, at midnight, three knocks on the door of his room but, going to see who was there, found no one. Monsieur Vincent called a cleric of the Congregation, asked for his breviary, and then had him recite a section of the Office of the Dead, as though he were aware of the priest's death, although no one had said a word of this to him.

When he was in Richelieu in 1649, he suffered from a tertian fever,[5] but did not allow it to interfere with his usual duties, despite the long and violent attacks.

In 1656 he had another illness, which began with a fever that lasted several days but which ended by a swelling of one leg, confining him to bed for some time. He had to stay in his room for nearly two months. He was unable to stand and had to be lifted in and out of bed to be near a fire. Only in this sickness could he be persuaded to accept a room with a fireplace, which gave him some relief in his sickness.

From this time on, that is, from 1656 until his death in 1660, he had frequent attacks of fevers and other sicknesses. One Lent he was especially

---

2. A fever, probably malarial, occurring approximately every seventy-two hours.
3. Vincent used these words in response to Father Jean Baptiste Saint Jure, S.J., a close friend, who had come to visit him in his illness.
4. Antoine Dufour, born at Montdidier, was received as a young priest into the Congregation of the Mission at Paris, December 31, 1639.
5. A fever occurring approximately every forty-eight hours.

ill, hardly being able to eat at all. In 1658 he developed an eye infection which would not clear up. He tried several remedies without effect, until the doctor finally suggested his putting the blood of a freshly killed pigeon upon his eye. When the brother surgeon of the house of Saint Lazare brought a pigeon, Monsieur Vincent would not allow it to be killed despite all remonstrances. He said that to him this innocent animal represented his Savior, and besides, if God wanted him to be cured he certainly knew how to do so. This indeed is what happened.

About the end of 1658, as he was returning from the city together with another priest, the axle of the carriage in which he was riding broke, throwing him to the ground, where his head struck the roadway. He was incapacitated for a long time, and to make matters worse the fever returned several days after his fall. This reduced him to a state in which he himself thought he might be in danger of death.

So as not to weary the reader with a listing of all the other illnesses suffered by Monsieur Vincent from time to time to prove his virtue, it is enough to say there were few sicknesses he did not experience. God so willed it to increase his sympathy for his neighbor, especially his spiritual children. He never failed to visit the sick in the infirmary, edifying, consoling, and making them happy at his every visit. When he came upon someone who was discouraged or, because of the length or nature of his sickness, feared he was going to die, he would say a word of edification to help him raise his mind to God. Then Monsieur Vincent would ordinarily say, especially to the younger men:

> Do not be too concerned, brother. I had this same illness in my youth, and I survived. I had shortness of breath, but no longer; I suffered from rupture, but the Lord has cured me; I had headaches, but they have passed; difficulties with my lungs and a troubled stomach which I have overcome. Have patience (he used to say), your troubles will pass and God will find use for you. Let things develop, and resign yourself to him in peace and tranquility.

We might call the most serious of all the maladies of Monsieur Vincent a sort of martyrdom which finally claimed his life. Yet it brought him closer to Jesus Christ in imitation of his sufferings as he always had been in imitation of his virtues and good works. This condition was the swelling of his feet and legs, which troubled him for forty-five years. Sometimes the pain was so severe he could not stand or walk, and at other times his legs were so inflamed he was obliged to keep to his bed. At this time, in 1632, when he began to live at Saint Lazare, he acquired a horse because Saint Lazare was some distance from the city, and at this time he began to be involved in a multitude of enterprises which continued until his death. This

horse served him well until 1649, when the trouble with his legs increased greatly. It was brought on by the long trip he had made to Brittany and Poitou, and it became impossible for him to mount or dismount. He would have been forced to remain at Saint Lazare, as he had resolved to do, were it not for an order of the late archbishop of Paris which obliged him to use a small carriage.

This swelling of the legs increased, affecting even the knees by 1656, so he could stand only with great pain and walk only with the help of a cane. Later, in 1658, one of his feet developed an ulcer and this added to the difficulty with his knees, preventing him from leaving the house from 1659 on. For some time he continued to come down from his room for the prayers of the Church and to celebrate holy mass, as also to attend the Tuesday conferences held at Saint Lazare. As to the mass, it came to the point that he could no longer mount the steps of the altar. He was obliged to put on and take off the vestments at the altar itself. This led him to remark with a smile that he had become a great lord, for only prelates vested at the altar.

Toward the end of 1659 he was obliged to offer mass in the infirmary chapel. By 1660 his legs became so bad he was no longer able to offer mass. He continued to attend, however, until the day of his death, despite the pain he felt in going from room to chapel, walking with the help of crutches.

His strength lessened daily, for he ate almost nothing. He did not want anything special brought to him, especially anything fancy. His doctor and some well-placed and pious friends persuaded him to take some broth and chicken they had brought. After one or two times, however, he said these things did not agree with him, and that he preferred not to have them brought in future. All the same he continued to tend to business, and looked after all things according to his custom.

This good servant of God was reduced to walking only with the help of crutches and with indescribable pain. There was always the danger of falling, for he could hardly move his legs. In July 1660, he was urgently requested to allow the room next to his to be made into a chapel so he could hear mass without leaving his room. He would not hear of it and gave as his reason that such domestic chapels must never be created without overriding necessity, which he did not admit to in his own regard.

He was prevailed upon to allow a chair to be made in which he could be carried from his room to the infirmary chapel to avoid such great pain of walking and to obviate the possibility of falling, as he went each day to attend mass. He resisted the suggestion of the chair until August, when he was no longer able to walk, even with crutches. He finally consented to having the chair made. He began to use it on the feast of the Assumption of the most blessed Virgin and continued to do so for about six weeks, until his death.

He regretted the inconvenience he caused the two brothers who carried him, and he never wanted them to carry him any farther than the chapel, about thirty or forty paces away.

Certainly, if this venerable old man had no other illnesses than having to remain seated every day from morning till evening for two years, and especially the last year, practically without being able to ease his pains, it would have been enough to try his patience. If we add to this the trouble he experienced with his swollen knees and the ulcerated feet for which there seemed to be no relief we can appreciate the true martyrdom he endured. Besides all these difficulties, God allowed still another problem to make him resemble even more his Master, a man of sorrows. He experienced a great difficulty in passing his water during the last year of his life, and this caused him much suffering and inconvenience. He was unable to rise from bed or use his legs. His effort to rise by pulling on a rope attached to a bracket in his room caused him much pain. He was never heard to utter any complaint, but only some aspirations to God, such as "Ah my Savior! My blessed Savior!" or other like expressions which he pronounced devoutly, casting his eyes upon a small wooden crucifix placed near his bed to console him.

Amid all the suffering he endured throughout his hard and austere life, he never wanted to sleep on a soft bed. He preferred a straw mattress to pass five or six hours of the night, not so much to take his rest as to find a new source of suffering. Fluid drained from the ulcers on his legs during the day in such abundance that it sometimes left stains on the floor. At night it would settle in his knees, causing him great pain and leading to his increasing weakness.

Even in this condition he continued to apply himself to the direction of his Congregation and to the other groups he was responsible for. He had his priests represent him at meetings when he was too weak to attend, but he would instruct them in what they were to do and say. He received a large number of letters which he read and answered. He called together the officers of the house and his assistants to speak with them, either all together or in private as the situation demanded. He asked how things were going and deliberated with them and gave orders as he saw they were needed. He sent his priests to the missions, but not before calling them together to discuss how they were to make themselves useful and efficacious in their new assignment.

With all these efforts to continue his activity, and with his sufferings, his strength lessened so that he could apply himself and speak only with much pain. Despite this, he would still talk for a full half hour or more with such vigor and grace that those who heard him were astonished, they said later, for they had never heard him speak with such order and energy. What is most remarkable is that in the case of both his own confreres as well as those from outside who came to see him, he received them politely, with a smile and with agreeable words, just as though he were in perfect health. If asked about his illnesses he would make light of them, saying they were as nothing compared with the sufferings of our Lord, and much less than he deserved. With this he would turn the conversation to any ill his visitor might have, showing more concern for them than for his own difficulties.

CHAPTER FIFTY-ONE

His Preparation for Death

BOTH MONSIEUR VINCENT and his confreres were well aware of his approaching end, but with quite different sentiments. His brethren and all who loved him dreaded this separation and felt a deep regret at seeing it so near. On the other hand, this saintly old man, like another Simeon, awaited his last hour with joy. He showed this by his serene and even joyful countenance, accepting his sufferings in a spirit of penance and humility. He longed for that life in which he hoped to possess his God, invoking his aid in his heart and uniting himself interiorly to his holy will. He put his body and soul into God's hands to dispose of according to his good pleasure for time and for eternity. His whole life was a constant preparation for dying well, by his practice of the virtues, his exercises of piety, and the works of charity that filled all his days. These were steps along the way, leading to the final blessed hour of his death.

He had over a long period adopted the custom of reciting the prayers for the dying after his daily mass, preparing himself in advance for his own departure from this life. He made use of this practice every morning, as a remote preparation for death, and he did something similar in the evening, as the following episode will show.

Shortly before his death, a priest of the house of Saint Lazare wrote to another priest of the Congregation. He told him that Monsieur Vincent had not much longer to live, and it appeared likely that he would pass away soon. Without more thought he gave this letter to Monsieur Vincent to read before sending it off, as was the custom in the Congregation. Monsieur Vincent took the letter, saying he would read it later, which he did. He wondered why the priest would put this about his coming death in a letter he was sure to read. A person other than Monsieur Vincent would have focused on the imprudence of the author, but Monsieur Vincent thought perhaps this priest was attempting to do a good office toward him in alerting him to his condition. He even considered, in his humility, that he may have given the priest some reason for writing so, without knowing when or how. He called for him, thanked him for this warning, and begged him to have the charity to alert him to any other of his faults. The priest replied that he was not aware of any other. Monsieur Vincent responded:

> As to the warning you gave me about my approaching death, I must tell you simply that God has given me the grace to think little

of this matter. I must tell you not to be scandalized in not seeing me make any extraordinary preparation for death. For the last eighteen years I have never gone to bed without putting myself into the disposition to appear before God that very night.

This priest once more excused himself for his indiscretion. He assured Monsieur Vincent he had no intention of warning him of his approaching end, but only that he had not thought of what his letter contained when he gave it to him. He reported on all that had passed between the superior and himself at a later time. He knew too well the virtuous life of Monsieur Vincent to have any doubts that he would be perfectly prepared for death, just as he was of his acceptance of God's will in all things. Since these events, a letter was found in Monsieur Vincent's own hand, written twenty-five years before, containing these sentiments:

> I had a serious fall two or three days ago, enough to make me think about death. By the grace of God I adore his holy will, and I accept it with all my heart. Examining myself to see if I had any regrets, the only thing that came to mind was that we have not yet written our rules.[1]

As stated in the Gospel, Monsieur Vincent anticipated the coming of his Lord by having, for a long time, his loins girt and a burning torch in his hand. His last hour was almost constantly before his mind. Several years before his death he used to say to his confreres, "One of these days the miserable body of this old sinner will be put in the earth where it will return to dust, and you will walk upon it."

When he spoke of his many years he would say:

> For how many years have I have abused the grace of God! *Heu mihi quia incolatus meus prolongatus est!* ["Woe to me that my dwelling has been prolonged."][2] Alas, O Lord! I have lived such a long time because there has been no amendment in my life. The number of my sins has kept pace with the number of my years.

When he would announce to his community the death of one of his missionaries, he would usually add: "You leave me, O my God, and you call your true servants. I am those weeds which spoil the good grain of the harvest, and yet see me taking up space uselessly (*ut quid terram occupo*) ["Why should I clutter up the ground?"][3] But not my will, O God, but yours be done."

He often spoke to his confreres about death as a salutary thought, and exhorted them to prepare for it by their good deeds. He assured them that

---

1. *CED* I:291.
2. Ps 120:5.
3. Based on Luke 13:7.

this was the best and surest means to ensure a happy death. He wanted this thought of death to be joined to a great confidence in the goodness of God, far from any anxiety or worry. This was the advice he gave to a person deeply troubled about death, and who had it constantly in her thoughts. He advised, in a letter he wrote on this matter:

> The thought of death is good, and our Lord counseled and recommended it, but it must be moderated. It is neither necessary nor expedient that you have this thought constantly in mind. Two or three times a day would suffice, without dwelling too long a time even then. If you find yourself upset, you should not dwell on the thought at all but gently turn your mind away.

His long and serious illness became known in Rome, and also that even in this condition he continued to recite the breviary. As a result, the Sovereign Pontiff, Pope Alexander VII, aware of how much this great servant of God meant to the entire Church, sent an Apostolic Brief dispensing him from this obligation, even though he had not requested it. At the same time Cardinals Durazzo, archbishop of Genoa, Ludovisio, grand penitentiary of Rome, and Bagni, formerly nuncio to France, all whom were in Rome at the time, wrote urging him to take care of himself, showing the esteem they had for the person of Monsieur Vincent.

We give here only the letter of Cardinal Durazzo, because it was the first one received, and the others are much the same as his.

> The activities of the priests of the Congregation of the Mission in favor of the neighbor derive from their following the directions and example of their superior general. For this reason all right-minded persons will pray God to prolong his life and give him perfect health to prolong the great good he has done. And since I take such keen interest in the happy progress of this holy institute and I have such a tender affection for your person, being informed of your age, trials, and merits, please take full advantage of the dispensation of His Holiness to give over the government of your dear confreres and to leave off all preoccupations which might prove harmful to your valued life and continued service of God. From Rome, September 20, 1660.[4]

All these precautions came too late. The victim was about to be consumed. God willed to relieve this faithful servant of all the pains and troubles he had experienced in rendering all honor and service to his divine majesty during his long life. Before finally calling Monsieur Vincent from this life, he gave him the grace of leaving the Congregation of the Mission and all the other companies he had established in the best possible condition.

---

4. *CED* VIII:456-57.

CHAPTER FIFTY-TWO

Events Surrounding the Death of Monsieur Vincent

THIS FAITHFUL servant of God in his lingering illness awaited, like another Simeon, the happy hour when his divine Redeemer would deliver him from this body of death that held his soul in captivity. If this was deferred, it was only to fill up his merits by continuing to exercise his patience and other virtues he practiced so worthily, and to complete the crown prepared for his faithful life. When this was accomplished, the Father of mercies and the God of all consolation willed to give him the supreme prize, the death of the just. To put it better, this would end his dying here below to begin the true life of the just with the saints in a blessed eternity.

Sacred history tells us that when God called Moses to the summit of Mount Nebo, he commanded him to die there. The holy patriarch submitted to the will of God. He died that very hour, not through any sickness but purely through his obedience. "And he died," says holy Scripture, "by the mouth of the Lord,"[1] that is to say, receiving death as a singular favor, a kiss of peace, from the mouth of his Lord and God.

If it be permitted to compare the graces God gave to his saints to what he gave his dearest servants, leaving aside any judgment about their merits, we may say that by a special mercy he conferred a similar gift upon his faithful servant Vincent de Paul, who had ever lived in entire and perfect dependence on his holy will. His death was not so much the result of fevers or other serious illness but rather a sort of obedience and submission to the divine will. His death was so peaceful and tranquil that it seemed a gentle sleep rather than a death. To express what occurred with this holy man, we might say he fell asleep in the peace of his Lord, who willed to anticipate the choicest blessing of his divine compassion and to place on his head a priceless crown of glory. This was the reward God wished to give for his life of fidelity and zeal. He had consumed his life in the cares, labors, and fatigues of God's service, but completed it happily in peace and tranquility. He voluntarily deprived himself of all repose or satisfaction during his life to procure the coming of the kingdom of Jesus Christ and the advancement of his glory. In dying he found a true repose by entering into the joy of the Lord. This is how it came about.

Seeing his end approaching, Monsieur Vincent disposed himself inte-

---

1. Deut 34:5.

riorly for this last passage by continuing to practice those virtues he considered most agreeable to God. This was detachment from all created things, as much as charity permitted, to raise his heart more perfectly to the Source of all good. On September 25, toward noon, he slept in his chair, something that was happening now more often because of his lack of sleep during the night, as well as his great weakness, which seemed more pronounced. He thought of this sleep as a sort of advance guard of his approaching death. When someone asked why he slept so much he remarked with a smile that it was the brother coming to meet the sister, by which he meant sleep as the brother awaiting sister death.

On Sunday, September 26, he had himself carried to the chapel for mass and communion, as he did every day, but when he returned to his room fell into a deeper sleep than usual. The brother attending him awakened him after some time, spoke to him briefly, but saw that he immediately fell into the same deep sleep. He alerted the director of the house, who had the doctor called, but he found Monsieur Vincent in such a weakened state he felt no further remedy would be effective. The doctor advised the administration of the sacrament of extreme unction, but before leaving he was able to awaken his patient. In his usual way he responded with a smiling and affable countenance, but was so weak he could say only a few words, but unable to finish what he wanted to say.

Later, one of the principal priests of the Congregation came to see him, asking for his final blessing upon all members of the community, both those present and those absent. He attempted to raise his head and said the first part of the blessing in an audible voice, but it trailed off in the second. Toward evening, as he became increasingly weaker and apparently lapsing into the last agony, he was administered the sacrament of extreme unction. He passed the night calmly, in almost constant communion with God. When he lapsed into unconsciousness only a word addressed to him could rouse him, while all other words seemed to have no effect. Among the pious aspirations suggested to him from time to time, he seemed to respond best to these words of the psalmist: *Deus in adjutorium meum intende*, ["God come to my assistance"] which were often repeated. He would respond *Domine ad adjuvandum me festina* ["Lord make haste to help me"].[2] He continued to do this until his last breath, imitating the great saints, fathers of the desert, who regularly used this same short prayer to show their dependence on the sovereign power of God, the constant need they had of his graces and mercy, their hope in his goodness, and the filial love which moved their heart. They proved their desire to seek God always as their good Father, never fearing to weary him by their insistent prayers, but showing a great and perfect confidence in his infinite love.

---

2. Ps 70:2.

A virtuous priest of the Tuesday conference, a great friend of Monsieur Vincent, was at Saint Lazare at the time on retreat.³ He heard of the extremity to which Monsieur Vincent was reduced and went to visit him in his sickroom shortly before he expired. He asked for a blessing upon all members of the conference, to leave his spirit with them, and to obtain from God that their group never depart from the way of virtue inspired and communicated by Monsieur Vincent. The response was in his usual humble way, *Qui coepit opus bonum, ipse perficiet* ["He who has begun the good work in you will carry it through to completion"].⁴ Shortly after, he quietly passed from this life to a better one with no agitation whatsoever.

On Monday, September 27, 1660, at 4:30 A.M., God called him to himself, just at the hour his confreres were beginning their meditation to attract God to themselves. This was the very hour and the very moment he was accustomed, for over forty years, to invoke the Holy Spirit upon himself and his confreres. At that hour, this same adorable Spirit brought his soul from earth to heaven, as we so confidently hope from the infinite goodness of God, considering his holy life, his zeal for the glory of God, his charity for the neighbor, his humility, his patience, and all the other virtues he practiced right up to the time of his death. His life gives us good reason to believe in the infinite goodness of God. This faithful servant of his divine majesty could well say in this hour of his death, in humble thanks for his graces, and in imitation of the holy apostle, that he had fought courageously, had completed his course, had preserved an inviolable fidelity, and there remained only that he receive the crown of justice from the hand of his sovereign Lord.

After breathing his last, his appearance did not change. He retained his usual gentle and serene expression, seated in his chair as though sleeping. He had been sitting there, fully clothed, the last twenty-four hours of his life, for those present felt there would be more harm done if they attempted to move him.

He died without a fever, without any single significant event, but by a seeming gradual weakening of nature, like a lamp going out as the oil is used up. His body did not become rigid but remained pliable as before. An autopsy removed all the principal organs, all of which were found to be healthy. A growth, the size of an *ecu*, had formed in his spleen, which the doctors and surgeons found quite extraordinary. This suggested an intervention of divine Providence in his favor, for this growth was spongy and soft, serving as a reservoir for melancholic humors. Normally, when these discharge, they release such vapors to the brain that the imagination is flooded with illusions,

---

3. Father Le Pretre, one of the most zealous members.
4. Phil 1:6.

and sometimes the judgment is adversely affected. God, who destined Monsieur Vincent for such signal services to his Church, seems to have exempted Monsieur Vincent from this natural process. God never allowed false lights or erroneous impressions to influence him. He was above all such weaknesses. He had a sound judgment and knew well how to discern in all things the good and the evil, the true and the false, the certain and the doubtful, as we saw throughout his life.

He was waked the next day, September 28, until midday, in the meeting hall and then in the church of Saint Lazare, when the divine service as celebrated, followed by his interment. In attendance were the Prince of Conti, Archbishop Piccolomini, papal nuncio and archbishop of Caesarea, and several other prelates, several pastors of Paris, and a great number of priests and many religious of various orders.[5] The duchess of Aiguillon and several other lords and ladies honored his memory by their presence, not to mention a large crowd of the people. His heart was preserved in a silver urn, given by the duchess. His body was placed in a leaden coffin, enclosed in another of wood, and was buried in the middle of the choir in the church of Saint Lazare. This epitaph was placed on the stone: *Hic jacet Venerabilis Vir Vincentius a Paulo, Presbyter, Fundator seu Institutor, et primus Superior Generalis Congregationis Missionis, nec non Puellarum Charitatis. Obiit die 27. Septembris anni 1660. Aetatis vero suae 85.* ["Here lies the venerable Vincent de Paul, priest, founder or institutor and first superior general of the Congregation of the Mission and of the Daughters of Charity. He died September 27, 1660, at the age of eighty-five"].

The priests of the Tuesday conference of Saint Lazare whom Monsieur Vincent brought together and directed for so many years, held a solemn service some time later in the church of Saint Germain l'Auxerrois at Paris. Bishop Henri de Maupas du Tour, formerly of Le Puy and now of Evreux, had a special veneration and affection for the great servant of God and gave the funeral oration with as much zeal as learning and piety. He was listened to with a singular admiration and edification by all his audience, composed of a large group of prelates, clergy, religious, and an enormous gathering of other people. He could not say all he wanted, even though he spoke for over two hours. As he said himself, his subject was so vast he would have required a whole Lenten series to do it justice.

Several cathedral churches, Reims among them, offered solemn masses for his happy repose, as did many parish churches and religious communities. Many individual priests of Paris and other places in France also offered

---

5. Among these were Jacques Benigne Bossuet and Armand de Montmorin, archbishop of Vienne. This latter requested permission to look one last time on the saint's face before the slab was fixed on his tomb. As he did so, he kissed Saint Vincent's hands.

masses in appreciation of his charity and in thanks for what he had given to the entire Church.

End of Book One

The Life of the Venerable
Servant of God
Vincent de Paul

Si tu veux dans un seul visage
Voir le Portrait de deux grands Saints:
Icy Paul et Vincent sont peints;
Mais pour l'Esprit, lis cet ouvrage

The Life of the Venerable Servant of God
Vincent de Paul

Founder and First Superior General
of the
Congregation of the Mission

(Divided Into Three Books)

by
Louis Abelly, Bishop of Rodez

BOOK TWO

New City Press

edited by
John E. Rybolt, C.M.

translated by
William Quinn, F.S.C.

notes by
Edward R. Udovic, C.M. and John E. Rybolt, C.M.

introduction by
Stafford Poole, C.M.

index
translated and edited
from the Pémartin edition of 1891,
with additional annotations, by
Edward R. Udovic, C.M

Published in the United States by New City Press
86 Mayflower Avenue, New Rochelle, New York 10801
©1993 Vincentian Studies Institute

Library of Congress Cataloging-in-Publication Data:

Abelly, Louis, 1604-1691.
    [Vie du vénérable serviteur de Dieu, Vincent de Paul. English]
    The life of the venerable servant of God Vincent de Paul : founder
and first superior general of the Congregation of the Mission :
(divided into three books) / by Louis Abelly ; [edited by John E.
Rybolt ; translated by William Quinn ; introduction by Stafford
Poole].
    Includes bibliographical references and index.
    ISBN 1-56548-052-X : $49.00
    1. Vincent de Paul, Saint, 1581-1660. 2. Christian saints—
France—Biography—Early works to 1800. I. Rybolt, John E.
II. Title.
BX4700.V6A48 1993
271'.7702—dc20
[B]   93-9446

The original edition of Abelly contained as a frontispiece an engraving by René Lochon, based on the portrait by Simon François de Tours of Vincent de Paul in choir dress. Below the portrait is a quatrain, the translation of which is:
    If you wish to see in a single face
    the portrait of two great saints
    Paul and Vincent are depicted here;
    but for his spirit, read this work.

CONTENTS

PREFACE 9

BOOK TWO. His Main Works and the Great Results Which Came From Them 11

CHAPTER ONE. The Missions of Monsieur Vincent 13
    SECTION ONE. His Missions in General 13
        PART ONE. Some Remarkable Words of Monsieur Vincent About
            the Missions 15
        PART TWO. Monsieur Vincent's Convictions about the Virtues
            Most Needed by the Missionaries, and How They Should Preach 17
        PART THREE. The Order Which Monsieur Vincent Observed and
            Wanted to be Observed by the Members of His Congregation . . 20
        PART FOUR. The Advice of Monsieur Vincent to His Missionaries
            on How They Should Deal with Heretics when on Mission 25
        PART FIVE. The General Results of the Missions Given by
            Monsieur Vincent and the Missionaries of His Congregation . . . 27
    SECTION TWO. The Most Notable Fruits of the Missions Given in
        Various Parts of France 30
        PART ONE. The Diocese of Paris 30
        PART TWO. The Diocese of Saintes 32
        PART THREE. The Dioceses of Mende and Saint Flour 35
        PART FOUR. The Dioceses of Geneva and Marseilles 38
        PART FIVE. The Dioceses of Reims, Toul, and Rouen 42
        PART SIX. Various Places in Brittany 45
        PART SEVEN. Various Places in Burgundy and Champagne 47
        PART EIGHT. Various Other Places in France 50
    SECTION THREE. Further Discussion of the Fruit of the Missions
        Given in Italy 55
        PART ONE. In Various Places Near Rome 55
        PART TWO. In the Dioceses of Viterbo, Palestrina, and Other Places 59
    SECTION FOUR. Missions Given in the State of Genoa 66
    SECTION FIVE. The Missions Given on the Island of Corsica 69
    SECTION SIX. The Missions Given in Piedmont 76
    SECTION SEVEN. The More Remarkable Events in the Missions of
        the Barbary States 84
        PART ONE. The Beginning of the Missions in Tunis and Algiers, in
            the Barbary States 85
        PART TWO. The Main Work of the Missionaries in Barbary 89

PART THREE. Persecutions Suffered by the Consul at Algiers 92
PART FOUR. Other Vexations of the Missionaries in Tunis 97
PART FIVE. An Account Given by Monsieur Vincent to His
  Community of the Martyrdom of a Young Christian Burned to
  Death in Algiers for His Faith in Jesus Christ. 99
PART SIX. Various Directives Given by Monsieur Vincent to the
  Missionaries of Barbary Regarding Their Personal Behavior and
  Their Way of Acting Among the Infidels. 102
PART SEVEN. Various Employments and Sufferings of the Poor
  Christian Slaves in Barbary, and the Help and Services
  Rendered Them by the Missionaries 105
PART EIGHT. Continuation of the Same Topic 109
PART NINE. Help Given to the Poor Slaves of Bizerte and of
  Several Other Places 112
PART TEN. The Conversion of Several Heretics and Apostates
  Brought About by the Priests of the Congregation of the Mission
  Whom Monsieur Vincent Sent to Barbary 116
PART ELEVEN. The Remarkable Example of the Constancy of Two
  Young Slaves, the One from France, the Other from England . 118
PART TWELVE. Various Other Charitable Activities of the Priests
  of the Congregation of the Mission Whom Monsieur Vincent
  Sent to Barbary for the Relief of the Poor Christian Slaves . . . 120
SECTION EIGHT. The Missions in Ireland 126
SECTION NINE. On the Mission to the Isle of Saint Lawrence, Other-
  wise Known as Madagascar 134
PART ONE. Letter from Monsieur Vincent to Monsieur Nacquart,
  Priest of the Congregation of the Mission, About This Mission . 134
PART TWO. The Departure of the Two Priests of the Congregation
  of the Mission, and Events that Occurred on Their Journey . . . 138
PART THREE. Description of Madagascar and its People 139
PART FOUR. The Arrival of Two Priests of the Congregation of the
  Mission in Madagascar, and Their Initial Activities 142
PART FIVE. The Death of Monsieur Gondree, One of the Two
  Priests of the Congregation of the Mission, and the Later Work
  of Monsieur Nacquart, the Only Remaining Priest on the Island 144
PART SIX. Letter of Monsieur Bourdaise, Priest of the
  Congregation of the Mission, About the Missions of Madagascar 149
PART SEVEN. Letter of Monsieur Vincent to Monsieur Bourdaise,
  to Whom He Sent Five More Missionaries 159
SECTION TEN. The Mission to Poland 163
SECTION ELEVEN. The Mission to the Hebrides Islands 173

CHAPTER TWO. The Spiritual Exercises to Prepare for the Proper
  Reception of Holy Orders 183
  SECTION ONE. The Pressing Need of Clergy Reform at the Time
    Monsieur Vincent Established the Ordination Retreats 183
  SECTION TWO. The Beginning of the Ordination Retreats 185
  SECTION THREE. A Summary of What is Done During the Ordination Retreats, and the Regulations that Govern Them 188
  SECTION FOUR. Monsieur Vincent's Thoughts on the Ordination Retreats 191
  SECTION FIVE. Some Examples of the Blessings Brought About in
    France by the Ordination Retreats 200
  SECTION SIX. The Ordination Retreats in Italy, and the Great Results
    Produced by Them 203

CHAPTER THREE. The Spiritual Conferences for Priests 210
  SECTION ONE. The Beginning of the Spiritual Conferences for
    Priests Established at Saint Lazare 210
  SECTION TWO. The Progress of This Company, and the Successes It
    Enjoyed 215
  SECTION THREE. Missions Given by the Priests of This Company in
    Several Hospitals and Other Places in Paris 218
  SECTION FOUR. The Remarkable Results of Two Missions Given by
    Priests of this Company 220
  SECTION FIVE. The Company of Clergy Who Met at Saint Lazare
    Fostered Similar Companies in Other Dioceses 225

CHAPTER FOUR. Spiritual Retreats 229
  SECTION ONE. The Utility of Spiritual Retreats 229
  SECTION TWO. The Zeal of Monsieur Vincent to Provide the Opportunity to All Sorts of Persons to Make a Spiritual Retreat 231
  SECTION THREE. Some Remarkable Comments of Monsieur Vincent
    About the Spiritual Retreats 235
  SECTION FOUR. The Opinions of Some Others Concerning These Retreats, and Several Examples of Happy Outcomes 241

CHAPTER FIVE. Seminaries 249

CHAPTER SIX. Delinquents and Disturbed Persons at Saint Lazare . . . 259

CHAPTER SEVEN. The Help Given by Monsieur Vincent to the
  Convents of the Religious of the Visitation of the Blessed Virgin
  Mary of the Diocese of Paris While He Was Their Superior and
  Father 266

CHAPTER EIGHT. The Confraternities of Charity in the Parishes 285

CHAPTER NINE. The Founding of the Daughters of Charity, Servants of the Sick Poor 291

CHAPTER TEN. The Assemblies of the Ladies of Charity of Paris 303

CHAPTER ELEVEN. The Help Given by Monsieur Vincent to Different Provinces Devastated by Wars 316
SECTION ONE. Help Given to Lorraine 316
SECTION TWO. Help Given to the Provinces of Picardy and Champagne 331
SECTION THREE. The Remarkable Effects of the Help Given to the Provinces of Picardy and Champagne 336

CHAPTER TWELVE. The Efforts of Monsieur Vincent to Combat the Errors of Jansenism 346

CHAPTER THIRTEEN. Monsieur Vincent's Service to the King in the Council of His Majesty and Elsewhere During the Time of the Queen Mother's Regency 372
SECTION ONE. The Appointment of Monsieur Vincent to the King's Council for Ecclesiastical Affairs 373
SECTION TWO. Rules for Awarding Benefices, Adopted on the Recommendation of Monsieur Vincent 374
SECTION THREE. The Care and Impartiality with Which Monsieur Vincent Acted Concerning Ecclesiastical Benefices 375
SECTION FOUR. His Zeal in Combating Abuses in the Awarding of Benefices 377
SECTION FIVE. A Remarkable Example 380
SECTION SIX. His Great Affection for the Service of the Prelates of the Church 382
SECTION SEVEN. Some Important Services Given by Monsieur Vincent to Several Religious Orders 385
SECTION EIGHT. Other Help Given by Monsieur Vincent to Various Abbeys and Convents of Women 391
SECTION NINE. Various Other Activities of Monsieur Vincent While on the Council of the King 393
SECTION TEN. Monsieur Vincent Preserved Always an Inviolable Fidelity to the King and a Constant Devotion to His Service, Even During Most Perilous and Difficult Times 395
SECTION ELEVEN. Monsieur Vincent Served the King With an Entire Disregard for All Personal Self-interest 397
SECTION TWELVE. Monsieur Vincent's Prudence and Circumspection In His Service of the King 400

PREFACE

Although we spoke in Book One of the great works that engaged the virtue and zeal of Monsieur Vincent, we had to do so succinctly, not interrupting the flow of his life story by too frequent or too extended digressions. This is why we have judged it necessary to include a more ample account, here in Book Two, so that the readers will not be deprived of the consolation and spiritual advantage that may come from a more extended treatment. By this they may be moved to admire the wisdom of God in his directing his servant for the salvation and sanctification of a great number of souls, to thank him for the abundant graces he lavished in this last age by the ministry of Monsieur Vincent, and to draw lessons for their own edification and imitation for those occasions when they too may participate in similar good works. Holy Scripture says that the way of the just shines forth like the light, growing to perfect day, enlightening all who would follow. It is perfumed with the good odor of Jesus Christ, which they spread by the practice of virtue, which consoles and strengthens those who would walk in their footsteps. To praise God perfectly for his presence in the saints means to recall the noble actions of their lives, to study their virtues, to imitate their piety, to perpetuate the good works they began, and to try to glorify God on earth as they did, and as they will do eternally in heaven.

It is true that this second book may appear a bit long, and those who appreciate brevity may not savor its length or the development given in some of the chapters. If these persons would consider the nature of the things discussed, and the end proposed in writing, they would see that we could not be dispensed from doing otherwise.

We are trying to make known in more detail the great deeds God accomplished through Monsieur Vincent, the motives that inspired him to undertake them, the means he used to bring them to a successful conclusion, and the great fruits which these charitable works produced. Our hope is to inspire our readers to thank and glorify God, and provide them with the thought of undertaking something similar should the occasion present itself for helping their neighbor. This could come about only if we go into considerable detail. If we stick only to general terms much less light would be thrown on these marvelous enterprises.

If it should be the case that our readers do not have sufficient time to read what is given in this second book an appreciation of the life and virtues of

Monsieur Vincent could be derived readily from Books One and Three alone.

BOOK TWO

His Main Works and the Great Results Which Came From Them

CHAPTER ONE

The Missions of Monsieur Vincent

SECTION ONE

His Missions in General

IT SHOULD not be necessary to speak at length to have the reader appreciate the necessity and utility of the missions which Monsieur Vincent and his followers conducted. Forty years' experience bears out their value. Were one not persuaded of this, he would need only to cast a glance at the deplorable condition of most people before the missions began, particularly those of the countryside. They seemed engulfed in the darkness of a profound ignorance about their salvation, and as a result, given to all sorts of vices. On the other hand, think of the good results produced by the missions of Monsieur Vincent, especially the wonderful conversions which occurred. These make us recognize and confess that the hand of God was with his faithful servant. Among other exterior means for the salvation of souls, his mercy made particular use of these missions in recent years. These were one of the most efficacious ways of helping people and upon them he lavished an abundance of divine blessings.

A noted virtuous priest who had helped Monsieur Vincent and even had worked on a mission in a large village in the province of Anjou, wrote to him more than twenty years ago:

> Among all who have made their general confession there are more than fifteen hundred who have never made a good one. Besides, many people have committed enormous sins over ten, twenty, or even thirty years, which they have not confessed to their pastors and ordinary confessors. Ignorance is widespread, but malice is even worse. Their shame is so great they have not confessed all their sins even in the general confessions they made to the missionaries. But moved by their sermons and catechetical instructions given on the mission they have finally come and openly confessed their sins, with groans and tears.[1]

---

1. *CED* II:40.

Another prelate, Jacques Lescot, bishop of Chartres, whose name is held in benediction, wrote to Monsieur Vincent in 1647 on this same subject:[2]

> I could not have received better news than that you would like to continue your mission in my diocese, if I agree. There is no diocese in France where you will be more welcome. I don't know of anywhere the mission is more necessary and useful, for the strange ignorance I encounter in my visits horrifies me. I give no directives, neither place, time, or faculties. Everything is up to you. To use Abraham's words, *Ecce universa coram te sunt* ["Behold, all things lie before you"],[3] and so I am in truth, and from my heart, etc.[4]

Another prelate, whom we shall not identify because he is still living, wrote to Monsieur Vincent in 1651:

> The mission is one of the greatest goods I know of, and one of the most necessary. In my diocese there is the greatest ignorance you can imagine among the poor people. If you could see the extent of this ignorance, you would be moved to compassion. I can truthfully say most of those who are Catholic are so in name only, because their fathers were before them, and not because they have the slightest idea of what it means to be a Catholic. What gives me great pain is that we cannot establish any order in the diocese among people who would just as soon go hear a Protestant sermon as come to mass.[5]

Monsieur Vincent was only too well convinced by his own experience of the extreme need the people had of being instructed in what was required for their own salvation, and of being encouraged to make a good general confession. And since it was in the missions that one could fulfill these duties of charity with the greatest fruit and success, he applied himself to them with all his power. Insofar as he could, he recruited for the work those whom he judged to be suited, both of his own Congregation and of others. In the following section we will give a summary of a brief familiar instruction he gave one day to his community on this matter. From it we can gauge his feelings on the necessity and utility of missions.

---

2. Jacques Lescot, a doctor of theology of the Sorbonne, and Cardinal Richelieu's confessor. Named bishop of Chartres in 1641, he was consecrated in 1643. He died in 1656 at the age of sixty-three.
3. Based on Gen 13:9.
4. *CED* III:180-81.
5. *CED* IV:284.

PART ONE

Some Remarkable Words of Monsieur Vincent About the Mission

One day, speaking to his community, he said:

We have the duty of working for the salvation of the poor country people because this is what God has called us to. Saint Paul urges us to be faithful to our vocation, to correspond to the eternal designs of God upon us. This work for the poor is the foundation of our Congregation, all the rest is accessory. We would never have worked with the ordinands nor with the seminaries for priests if we had not judged them necessary to preserve the people in good condition and to maintain the good results of the missions, by providing good priests for them. In this we imitate military conquerors who leave garrisons in their conquered territory lest they lose what they won with such difficulty. How happy we are, my brothers! We live the very vocation of Jesus Christ. Who imitates his life on earth better than our Missionaries? I speak not only of our own members, but those apostolic workers of all different orders who give missions both within and outside the kingdom. Those are the great workers, while we are only in their shadow. Look at how they go to the Indies, to Japan, to Canada, to advance the work of Jesus Christ who remained faithful to his call from the first moment his Father had sent him.

Imagine his speaking to us: Go forth, Missionaries! Go where I send you. These poor souls await you, for their salvation depends in part on your preaching and your catechizing. We ought to think hard about this, my brothers, for God has destined us to work in this particular place, this time and with these people. In other times he chose prophets in the same way, to preach in a certain place, and to certain people, not expecting them to go anywhere else. What will we answer to God if by our fault some of these poor people die and are lost? Will we have nothing to worry about, if we in some way are responsible for their damnation by not having helped them as much as we could? Should we not fear that we will be held to account at the hour of our death? If on the contrary we cooperate with the grace of our vocation, will we not have reason to hope that God will increase his grace in us every day, strengthen our Company by new members of such character that they will act in his spirit, and bless all our efforts? All those souls who attain eternal salvation through our ministry will be our advocates before God in heaven.

How happy they will be at the hour of their death who will see accomplished in themselves these beautiful words of our Lord: *Evangelizare pauperibus misit me Dominus!* ["the Lord has sent me to bring glad tidings to the poor"].[6] See, my brothers, how it seems our Lord wants to tell us by these words that one of his main concerns was to work for the poor. Cursed shall we be if we fail to serve and help them. After we have been called by God and have given ourselves to him for this purpose, he relies in some way upon us. Remember the words of a holy Father of the Church: *Si non pavisti, occidisti,* ["If you have not fed them, you have killed them."] which applied to corporal things, but could equally be said of the spiritual, and with even greater justification.

Think if we do not have reason to tremble if we fail on this point, if by age, or because of some infirmity or indisposition, we pull back and lose our first fervor. Despite my years, even I do not feel excused from the service I owe the poor. What could hinder me? If I cannot preach every day, what about twice a week? If I am not strong enough to reach all my congregation from great pulpits, could I not speak from small ones? If my voice is not strong enough for even that, what prevents my speaking simply and familiarly to these good people, like I am doing at this very moment, with them gathered around, just like you are now?

I know of some older persons who on the day of judgment may rise against us. Among others there is a good Jesuit of saintly life who used to preach at court. When he was sixty years of age he became ill, and came within a hair's breadth of death. God made him aware of how vain and useless his polished and studied sermons were, to such an extent that he was filled with remorse. When he recovered he sought permission to catechize and preach to the poor country people. He spent twenty years in this charitable work until his death. On his deathbed he asked that the pointer he used in his catechism lessons be buried with his body. As he said, it would be a symbol of his having left the court to serve the Lord in the person of the poor country people.

Perhaps some wish to live a long life, and so fear that work on the missions will shorten their days and hasten the hour of their death. They may seek to exempt themselves from this work as though it were an evil to be avoided. I would ask those who think like this if it is an evil for one who has been traveling in a strange country to come back to his native shores? Is it an evil for the sailor

---

6. Luke 4:18.

to arrive safely at his port? Is it an evil for a faithful soul to see and possess God? Is it an evil for missionaries to rejoice in the glory merited for them by the suffering and death of our divine master? What? Do you fear this day which should be so highly prized, and which can never come too soon?

What I say to the priests here, I say as well to those who have not been ordained, to you brothers. No, my brothers, do not think that because you do not preach you are excused from working for the salvation of the poor. You do so in your own way, perhaps more effectively even than the preachers, and certainly with less danger to yourselves. You are obliged to it because you form a single body with us, just like the various members of the body of Jesus Christ. All his members participated in their own way in the act of our redemption. The head of Jesus Christ was crowned with thorns, but his feet were pierced with nails and attached to the cross. After the resurrection of Jesus, the head of Christ was crowned with glory, but the feet too participated in his triumph.[7]

PART TWO
Monsieur Vincent's Convictions about the Virtues Most Needed by the Missionaries, and How They Should Preach

This great servant of God was filled with a truly apostolic spirit. As a result, he knew well what virtues were most suitable for missionaries, since he had possessed and exercised them himself in a most eminent degree, as we shall see in Book Three. It was not simply from his mind, but from his own experience, that he concluded the most needed virtue was that of a profound humility and distrust of self. This meant not attributing to one's own labors or solicitude the conversion of souls or other benefits of the mission. They should refer all to the glory of God, save their own faults and failings. The Missionaries ought to have a great faith and confidence in God, not allowing the difficulties and contradictions they were sure to meet in their work to discourage them. They needed the virtue of charity, of course, and zeal for the salvation of souls, to search them out, to help, and to serve them. They should have meekness and patience to attract their hearers, and simplicity and prudence to lead them to God.

They should be detached from worldly goods to become freer in the works they undertake for God, and be able to inspire others to hunger for the goods of heaven. The Missionaries should be mortified in both body and spirit, so

---

7. *CED* XI:133-37.

that the movements of nature would never impede the operations of grace. They should be indifferent about position, place, time, or persons, having no other motive than to do in all things the will of God. Those who preached were to be ready to cede the pulpit to others, even in the midst of a mission, if this should be ordered by a superior.

He insisted that the Missionaries defer to religious or other preachers in the parishes, especially when these others had some standing there. They should willingly give up the pulpit to them and show them every respect. He wished his followers to be prayerful and edifying, being convinced they would produce more fruit this way than by any knowledge or eloquence they might display. Prayer would attract upon themselves an abundance of grace and interior unction, and their good example would dispose their audience to receive what they themselves had been given by God.

Monsieur Vincent wrote to one of his priests in 1633 about how to preach:

> I have heard from several sources the blessing it has pleased God to shower upon your mission at N.[8] We were most pleased to hear this, because we know these blessings come from God, who bestows them especially upon the humble, those who appreciate that any good they do comes from him. I pray God with all my heart to give you the spirit of humility in your work. You must believe most assuredly that God will take away from you this grace should any thought arise in you to take complacency in your work, and attribute to yourself what belongs to God alone. Be humble then, Monsieur, remembering that even Judas received greater graces than you, and these graces were more effective in him than in you, and yet he was lost. What would it profit the greatest preacher in the whole world, endowed with the greatest talents, if after he received the plaudits of an entire province and even converted countless souls to God, he were to perish?
>
> I do not write this, Monsieur, because I fear this defect in you or in your helper, Monsieur N.[9] I do so only to warn you that if the demon attacks you from this angle, as he will, you must be on the alert to reject his suggestions, and instead honor the humility of our Lord.
>
> In my recent conference to the community I have taken as my theme the simple style of life our Lord led upon earth. He preferred this common and abject way of living, just like so many other persons of his time. He abased himself as much as possible (O marvel, surpassing all human understanding) although he was the uncreated wisdom of the eternal Father. His manner of expounding

---

8. Probably Mortagne sur Gironde (Charente Maritime).
9. Lambert aux Couteaux, or Robert de Sergis.

his teaching was even more simple and direct than his own apostles. Please read some of his teachings and compare them with those of Saint Peter or Saint Paul, and the other apostles. This would lead you to believe he was a person without learning, whereas the apostles appear to be better instructed than he. Even the success of his teaching was astonishingly less than that of the apostles, for in the Gospel we see him persuading his apostles and disciples one by one to join him, and that at a cost of much effort. Saint Peter, on the other hand, converted five thousand at his first sermon. That single incident gave me more understanding of the great and marvelous humility of the Son of God than any other consideration I have ever had on this subject.

Every day at mass we say the words, *in spiritu humilitatis,* etc. ["In the spirit of humility."] A holy person told me once that he had learned from the lips of the blessed bishop of Geneva that this spirit of humility, which we ask for in each of our masses, consists chiefly in a continuous attitude of humbling ourselves, on all occasions, both interiorly and exteriorly. But, gentlemen, who can give us this spirit of humility? Our Lord alone, if we ask it of him, and if we remain faithful to his grace, and exercise this virtue in ourselves. Please do this, then, and let us remind each other of this when we say these words at the altar. I hope in your charity you will do this.[10]

Speaking one day to the priests of the Congregation of the Mission on this same topic he said:

> The Company must give itself to God to explain the truths of the Gospel in familiar comparisons in our work in the missions. Pay close attention to forming your own mind to using this method, in imitation of our Lord, who, as the evangelist says, *Sine parabolis non loquebatur ad eos* ["He spoke to them in parables only"].[11] Do not use quotations from the profane authors, unless you use them as stepping stones to the holy Scripture.[12]

He also recommended to the missionaries not to become too emotional in their preaching, nor speak too loud. He preferred that they speak to the people simply, with moderate voice, both to make their words more acceptable, and to conserve their strength and health. Having to preach every day of the entire year, and sometimes twice a day, they run the danger of destroying their health. By their shouting they would ruin their voice and their lungs.

One day he wrote to one of his priests:

---

10. *CED* I:181-84.
11. Matt 13:34.
12. *CED* XI:50.

I have learned that you put too much of yourself into your preaching, and have suffered some bad effects. In the name of God, Monsieur, take care of your health by moderating your voice and your emotional involvement in your preaching. I have spoken before of how our Lord blesses sermons spoken in familiar and simple language, because this is the way he himself taught and preached. This way of speaking is more natural, less draining than a forced way of speaking. The people like it better, and respond more readily. Believe me, Monsieur, the actors in the theaters realize this. They have changed and no longer use the elevated tone they used to employ in reciting their parts. They now speak with a moderate tone of voice, as though they were conversing familiarly with their audience. This is what I heard from an actor who happened to be speaking with me within the last few days.

If the desire to please the world has led these people to change, what a subject of confusion it would be for those who preach Jesus Christ if their love and zeal for the salvation of souls would not have the same result? I was sorry to learn that instead of teaching the longer catechism lesson in the evening, you have substituted a sermon in its place. This ought not to be done: (1) because the morning preacher might have trouble preparing the evening talk. (2) The people need the catechism lesson, and will profit more from it than from a second sermon. (3) We honor better the way Jesus Christ set out to teach and convert the world. (4) This is our tradition, to which it has pleased Our Lord to give many blessings, and using this method we find more occasion to practice humility.[13]

PART THREE

The Order Which Monsieur Vincent Observed and Wanted to be Observed by the Members of His Congregation

Since all things coming from God are done with order, as the apostle teaches,[14] and since order leads us to God, according to Saint Augustine,[15] it is not surprising that the missions were well organized and regulated. The missions were works of divine grace helping souls return to God when they had been estranged by sin. Each group of Missionaries was like a company of well-trained troops, or like a small army, whose organization and efficiency made it terrifying and formidable to the enemies of Jesus Christ.

---

13. *CED* VI:378-79.
14. Rom 13:1.
15. PL 32:976-77.

From the beginning Monsieur Vincent prescribed a definite order for the missions, which he wanted all his priests to observe in the following manner. First, the Missionaries were never to begin a mission unless the bishop of the diocese had invited them, and they had then presented themselves to the pastors before beginning any service in their parishes. They sought their blessing on their work, or that of their vicar if they were absent. If they were refused the Missionaries simply retired. They would humbly take their leave in imitation of the acceptance of the rebuffs our Lord had received in similar situations, as reported in the Gospel.

After the invitation of the bishop and the consent of the pastor of the parish where the mission was to be given, a priest would give the opening sermon on a feastday or a Sunday to alert the people to the coming of the missionaries. The services they hoped to render the people were explained, then they were exhorted to penance, and to dispose themselves to making a good confession. On the same day, after vespers, a second sermon would be given. This one discussed how to make their confession, especially on how to examine their conscience. It explained briefly the more common sins committed against the commandments of God, or other serious sins, to move them to sorrow for offending God.

Several days later, when the other priests who were to work on the mission had arrived, they began the usual functions and exercises of the mission. These consisted mainly in preaching, hearing confessions, the longer and shorter catechetical instructions, reconciling those estranged from one another, visiting and consoling the sick, admonishing hardened sinners, remedying abuses and public disorders. It general they devoted themselves to all the works of mercy and charity possible to them, and which providence brought to their attention. Meanwhile, the priests attended to their own spiritual exercises, such as mental prayer, the divine office said in common, the holy sacrifice of the mass, examens, both general and particular, and other similar spiritual practices.

All their activities were regulated, the hour for rising, retiring, meals, meditation, mass, divine office, and the other exercises of which we have spoken, such as preaching, catechism lessons, confessions and the other aspects of the mission, all done with great attention and devotion.

Ordinarily each day there were three public functions. The missionaries preached early so that the poor country people might attend, then a short catechism lesson around midday, and lastly a more extended catechizing in the evening, after the peasants had returned from their work.

The usual subjects of the sermons, besides the two we have already spoken of at the opening of the mission, were the various aspects of the sacrament of penance, the last things, the enormity of sin, the rigors of divine justice, hardness of heart, final impenitence, false shame, relapse into sin, slander, envy, hatred and enmity, swearing and blasphemy, intemperance in eating and drinking, and other similar sins most often committed by country people. Also, the topics chosen might include patience, the good use of adversity and poverty, charity, the good use of time, how to pray well, how to receive the sacraments and how to assist devoutly at the holy sacrifice of the mass, the imitation of our Lord, devotion to his most blessed mother, perseverance and other virtues and good works appropriate to people in their state of life.

The order and topics of preaching were changed according to circumstance and needs. Sermons were added or curtailed depending on the length of the mission, which in turn depended on the number and disposition of the people. Ordinarily the mission continued until all the people of the region were sufficiently instructed and put on the road to salvation through their general confession, to which they were encouraged by all possible means.

The evening catechism lessons ordinarily took as subject the principal mysteries of religion, the Trinity, the incarnation of our Savior, and the blessed sacrament of the altar. Then the commandments of God and of the Church, the articles of the Creed, the Our Father and Hail Mary. All this was done in consideration of the length of the mission, as explained above. If the mission did not last long enough to cover all these matters, only the most important and necessary were treated, according to the capacity of the hearers.

This longer lesson ordinarily took place in the pulpit for the benefit of the hearers. It normally began with a short repetition of the previous lesson, on which the instructor asked the children questions for about a quarter of an hour. Following that, he explained the main topic. At the end the instructor made some applications to daily life, to join instruction with edification of his hearers.

The shorter catechism lesson was held at one in the afternoon for the instruction of the children. The first day began with a short exhortation in a familiar style to urge them to attend, and to behave well. On the following days they gave instruction on the faith, the main mysteries of religion, on the commandments of God and other topics covered in the principal catechetical instruction of the evening, but presented in a more familiar style and suited to the mentality of the children. This catechism lesson was given with the instructor moving among the children instead of mounting the pulpit. He had the children sing the commandments of God to impress them more firmly on their minds.

Toward the end of the mission, those children capable of doing so, but who had not yet made their first communion, were carefully prepared to do so. Besides the other instructions given during the mission, an exhortation was given on the eve of their communion to dispose them better for receiving the sacrament. Immediately before receiving, another talk was given in the presence of the blessed sacrament to excite the children to greater devotion and reverence toward this adorable mystery. After vespers a solemn procession was held, in which the blessed sacrament was carried. The children who had made their first communion walked two by two before the blessed sacrament, each carrying a candle, followed by the clergy and people. Following the procession another brief exhortation was delivered to children and adults, and finally a Te Deum was sung to thank God for his graces.

On occasion a mass would be sung early the next morning to thank God for his gifts, and a sermon given on perseverance, if one had not been given the previous day. Monsieur Vincent also had the practice of looking into the establishment of a Confraternity of Charity, composed of the women and girls of the region to look after the spiritual and corporal needs of the sick poor. Toward the end of the mission, sermons were preached on the subject of charity toward the poor, and on the rules and practices of this confraternity.

Near the end of the mission, when most of the work was done, the missionaries saw to hearing the confessions of the children not yet old enough to receive communion, but with enough discernment to commit sin and offend God. To dispose the children to respect this sacrament, and to teach them how to confess well, some instructions were given suited to their situation. They sought to remedy two abuses which had crept into most of the country parishes. In some places, the children made their confession publicly, in front of everyone. In other places no confession at all was practiced, or at least not until the children were at an age to receive communion.

During the mission the sick, and especially the poor, were visited and helped as much as possible, both spiritually and corporally. They were urged to make a good general confession as an assurance for their salvation.

The Missionaries visited schoolteachers and gave them advice and instruction on how best to fulfill their ministry of cultivating virtue in the children, and inspiring them to piety.

Monsieur Vincent himself observed one more practice, and took care that his priests did also. All the instruction and services of which we have spoken were to be given free of charge. They accepted lodging and the use of those utensils which could not conveniently be carried. The priests of his Congregation have scrupulously observed this practice up to our own time.

Besides all these services given to laity, Monsieur Vincent was anxious that his Missionaries do what they could for any clergy in the area. He used spiritual conferences for this purpose. In them he discussed with them the obligations of their state, the faults they should guard against, the virtues they should practice as most fitting their state, and other similar topics.

As we said in another place, Monsieur Vincent was most assiduous in giving missions because he recognized their necessity and the good reception they had among the people. When he had to return to Paris, it seemed to him, as he said several times, "that the gates of the city would fall upon him" for turning to other duties when the salvation of so many poor people depended upon his help.

He soon recognized by his own experience that this type of activity was most tiring, and took a toll on even the strongest. It was impossible to continue without some relaxation, which he proposed to give his priests each year. It appeared the best time for this would be the harvest and vintage time, when the peasants were so taken up with their harvest they could not participate in the exercises of the mission without great inconvenience. Monsieur Vincent gave his Missionaries this time to study and prepare the sermons and catechism lessons they were to give in future missions. After they spent themselves completely for others they were now to take time for themselves. They were to give themselves with greater leisure and tranquility to recollection and prayer, just as our Lord did with his apostles when they returned from their preaching, and reported to him all they had done. He said "Come apart to a solitary place, to spend some time in rest and tranquility."[16] This is what Monsieur Vincent hoped to provide his Missionaries. During this time they made their annual retreat, their annual confession, and looked to the renewal of their interior life.

It happens often enough that those who work for the salvation of others, and are concerned with apostolic undertakings, themselves need to be restored by interior recollection, after so much exterior dissipation, just as the great clocks which serve the public need periodic repair. In this connection Monsieur Vincent said several times, "The life of a Missionary ought to be the life of a Carthusian in the house, and an apostle in the countryside. The more he cares for his own interior development the more his labors for the spiritual good of others will prosper."[17]

In a letter he wrote in 1631 to one of his priests, on this same question, he said:

> At Paris we lead a life almost as solitary as the Carthusians. We neither preach, nor catechize, nor do we go to the city for confessions, and almost no one comes here on business. We, in turn, have no business of our own. This solitude makes us long for work in the country, and the work makes us long for this solitude.[18]

---

16. Mark 6:31.
17. See, for example, *CED* III:346-47.
18. *CED* I:122.

PART FOUR
The Advice of Monsieur Vincent to His Missionaries on How They Should Deal with Heretics when on Mission

Since heretics lived in places where missions were given, particularly in such provinces as Guienne, Languedoc, Poitou, and others, where the weeds had taken root more deeply than elsewhere, Monsieur Vincent was deeply concerned about them. His limitless charity was such that he hoped for their salvation as much as for anyone else's. He wanted his Missionaries to bring about their conversion, if possible. To succeed in this he laid down several rules of conduct that experience proved to be effective.

First, he felt that contentions and disputes in matters of religion, particularly those carried on in an argumentative spirit with sharp exchanges, were totally unsuitable for encounters with heretics. He recommended to his confreres to avoid absolutely all invective, all reproach. In this connection he said that the learned can gain nothing in dealing with the devil through pride, since he is better equipped than they in this regard. On the contrary, humility easily overcomes him, because he does not have this weapon in his arsenal. He added that he had never seen or heard of a single heretic being converted by subtle arguments, but only by kindness and humility.

Although Monsieur Vincent did not want his Missionaries to dispute with heretics, he still wanted them to be prepared in the theology of the contested points. They should be ready to give a reason for the faith they held, according to the maxim of the prince of the apostles. This study would enable them to sustain the truth and refute the contrary errors. All the while they would deal amicably with the heretics, replying gently to their objections, and more to convert them than to confound them. He directed his priests to attend conferences on these points and to make a special study of current heresies. This is what he wrote, in 1628 from Beauvais to the priest he had left in charge of the College des Bons Enfants during his absence.

> How are things going with the Company? Are all in good disposition, and happy?[19] Are the regulations well observed? Are the students studying the points of theology which are in such dispute? Are you following the schedule? I beseech you, Monsieur, pay attention to this. Take care that your students learn the matter in the shorter Becanus very well, for I cannot tell you how useful this little book is.[20]
>
> I must tell you how God used this miserable person (this is the

---

19. The original letter reads: "Is everyone in a good mood? Is each one happy?"
20. An abridgement in Latin of the famous and influential *Manuale Controversiarum* by the Belgian Jesuit, Martin Becanus (or van der Beeck).

way he referred to himself) to convert three heretics since I left Paris, using the most basic arguments of kindness, humility, and patience in dealing with these poor unfortunate souls. It took two days to bring one around, the other two, less. I wanted to say all this to my own confusion, so the Company can see that if God has used the most ignorant and most wretched of his flock to do this, how much more can we expect from the others.[21]

It was his maxim to join to teaching and study of the controversies the virtues of humility, gentleness, and patience when one conversed or conferred with heretics. He wanted them to be treated with respect and affection, not to flatter them in their mistaken beliefs, but more readily to win over their hearts. Above all, he felt that the virtuous and exemplary lives of Christians, especially of priests and missionaries, were more powerful arguments than any others in leading them to renounce their errors and return to the true religion. He often spoke of this in his letters, such as in this one, written to the superior of the house at Sedan:[22]

When the king sent you to Sedan, he did so on condition of your never disputing with the heretics, neither from the pulpit nor in private. He knows that this does little good, and often produces more noise than fruit. A good life and the good odor of the Christian virtues attract people to the right path, and confirm Catholics in their beliefs. This is the way our Company can profit from its stay in Sedan. It will add to good example the carrying out of our usual functions, instructing the people in our usual way, preaching against vice and bad morals, speaking of the virtues, showing their necessity, their beauty, their practice, and the means of acquiring them. This is what you should do. If you wish to speak on the issue in dispute, do so only if the day's Gospel gives you occasion to refer to this. You can then speak of the truths denied by the heretics, but do not mention them by name nor even refer to them.[23]

A brother of the Congregation of the Mission, trained as a surgeon, offered to contribute his skill and charity to evangelize the island of Madagascar. Monsieur Vincent sent him to La Rochelle in December 1659, together with several priests of the Congregation to embark on their mission. This brother learned that several Huguenots were also embarking on that ship for the same destination. He was most distressed at this news, which elicited this reply to his letter to Monsieur Vincent.

I was grieved to learn several heretics will accompany you on

---

21. *CED* I:66.
22. See also *CED* I:295.
23. *CED* VIII:526.

your voyage to Madagascar, and that you anticipate great difficulty in traveling with them. God is the Master of all, and he has allowed this to come about for reasons of his own which we do not know. Perhaps it was to compel you to be more reserved in their presence, more humble, and more devoted to God and charitable toward your neighbor, so that seeing the beauty and sanctity of our religion they may be inspired to return. You must carefully avoid any sort of dispute or argumentation with them. Show yourself always patient and well-mannered toward them even if they murmur against you or argue against our beliefs and practices.

Virtue is so beautiful and so lovable that they will be forced to admire it in you if you practice it well. It would be well not to distinguish between Catholics and heretics in the services you give to God on this ship, for by this they will know you love them in God. I hope your good example will benefit both groups. Take care of your health, please, and that of our missionaries with you.[24]

PART FIVE
The General Results of the Missions Given by Monsieur Vincent and the Missionaries of His Congregation

The Gospel maxim recalls that we know the tree by the fruit it produces. There is no more assured way of judging its vigor and fertility than by examining what it brings forth. In a similar way, we can judge the excellence and usefulness of the missions and the labors of the Missionaries by looking at the great good they have engendered in all the Church. We will speak first of these results in general, and then in more detail, but simply and without exaggeration. We are not writing a panegyric, but a simple recital of events. The reader will derive greater satisfaction and even edification from this seeing that what is reported is done so with sincerity and without any attempt at cleverness.

We have already spoken in Book One[25] of how, even before he founded the Congregation, Monsieur Vincent had begun the first missions in 1617, and continued to give them up to 1625, not only in the towns and villages of several dioceses but also in the hospital of the Petites Maisons in Paris and in the galleys at Bordeaux. Several learned and pious priests, and even some of noble birth, helped him in this work. We do not know the number of missions given by Monsieur Vincent himself during these seven or eight

---
24. *CED* VIII:182-83. Letter to Brother Philippe Patte, born 1620 at Vigny in the diocese of Rouen. He was received into the Congregation in 1656. He died in Madagascar in 1664.
25. Ch. 8.

years. He gave them, however, in almost all the territory of the house of de Gondi, including that which belonged to the wife of the general of the galleys, in the villages, towns and hamlets which number close to forty, not to mention those he gave elsewhere.

Since the beginning of the Congregation in 1625 until 1632 when it moved to Saint Lazare, either he or his confreres gave more than one hundred forty missions. From 1632 until the death of this great servant of God, the house at Saint Lazare alone hosted nearly seven hundred, at some of which he himself participated, with great blessings. If we add to these the missions preached by the other houses of the Congregation, established in more than twenty-five dioceses both inside and outside the kingdom of France, who can conceive the extent and the diversity of benefits they reaped, tending to the glory of God and the good of his Church?

Who can count the number of persons in blameworthy ignorance of the truths of salvation who were instructed in the truths they were obliged to know? How many others had lived their entire lives in a state of sin, from which they were freed through a good general confession? How many sacrileges committed by receiving the sacraments unworthily have been redeemed? How many enmities and hatreds and cases of usury have ended? How many bad marriages and other scandals have been rectified? How many pious practices and charitable enterprises have been encouraged? How many good works and virtues have been begun in places where they were scarcely known? How many souls were sanctified and saved, who now glorify God in heaven? Without the help they received in the missions they might otherwise have died in their sin, and might now be blaspheming and cursing God with the demons in hell. God alone knows the extent and number of all the good his grace effected through his faithful servants, and which will one day be revealed to his own greater glory. To put all this in few words, it seemed his merciful Providence wished to use the missions to accomplish the ends which brought about the incarnation of his Son, and which were foretold by the prophet: "to banish iniquity, destroy and exterminate sin, and reestablish sanctity and justice."[26]

While awaiting eternity, when God will reveal all that was accomplished, we will give in the following chapters some small samples of the effects of the missions. First, however, we must say a few words about them.

We must first say that the Missionaries did not make an accounting of their successes. They were too busy in doing good to spend time writing about it. What we have learned, almost by chance, comes from extracts from letters written by the bishop of the diocese in which the missions had been given, or possibly from superiors writing to Monsieur Vincent to tell him of

---

26. Dan 9:24.

what had occurred on the mission they were responsible for. If it had been possible to examine every letter, undoubtedly even better things would have come to light, but the recital would have been too long. The little we will mention will enable us to judge all the rest.

Our second remark is that Monsieur Vincent did not want his Missionaries to conduct the missions in haste or on the run. He wanted them to take all the time necessary to accomplish all they had set out to do, that is, instruct the people, convert sinners, sanctify souls, and reestablish the service of God. When working in a particular place they would not leave until all the people had been well taught, their status rectified, using for this all the time necessary.[27] In the larger places the missionaries would remain for five or six weeks, but in the smaller towns or villages they might stay three weeks or so. For even smaller places, two weeks might suffice.

Monsieur Vincent set down as a rule that all who would give themselves to God to serve him in the Congregation must be free from all business or financial obligations. If so, they could devote themselves completely to the work of the missions, in imitation of the Son of God who went from town to town preaching the Gospel to the poor.

Although Monsieur Vincent's main care was meeting the extreme needs of the poor of the countryside, and he was chiefly committed to them, he was also mindful of people in the larger cities. He encouraged other virtuous priests, especially those who attended the Tuesday Conferences at Saint Lazare, to undertake missions in the larger cities of the kingdom, and even in Paris itself. Partly because of his charitable advice and directions, these missions were abundantly blessed.

Even in other provinces, a large number of other priests recognized the good effects of the missions given by Monsieur Vincent and his confreres and grouped together. They founded companies to give missions and work for the instruction and salvation of the poor. Some did this in imitation of his zeal, while others were moved, perhaps, by a spirit of emulation. But the great servant of God, animated by a truly apostolic charity, approved, appreciated, and highly praised these works undertaken for the service of God, whatever their motivation. It made no difference to him, as long as Jesus Christ was preached, his holy name known and glorified, and souls, redeemed by his blood, were sanctified and saved.

---

27. See *CED* VII:56.

SECTION TWO

The Most Notable Fruits of the Missions Given in Various Parts of France

PART ONE
The Diocese of Paris

We learn from Monsieur Vincent himself the great fruit of a mission given in a village of the diocese of Paris, when he reported the success to his community to have them give thanks to God for it.

I beg the community to thank God for his blessing on the exceptional missions we have just finished, especially the one at N. There had been a marked division in this parish between the pastor and his parishioners. On the one hand they had a strong aversion to the pastor, and on the other he had a deep resentment at the bad treatment received from the parishioners. He had gone so far as to begin a lawsuit against them, and had succeeded in having three or four of the ringleaders put into prison for having laid a hand on him in the church, or on some of his relatives. Most people not only did not want to attend his mass, but would leave the church when they saw him approach the altar. The affair had gone so far out of hand that I never saw the like. They protested that under no circumstance would they ever go to confession to him, and they preferred not to receive communion even at Easter time.

Things had grown so bad that several of these people came to us a while back to ask that a mission be given in their parish. We did so, and by the mercy of God, they all returned to their religious duties. What moves us ever more to bless and thank God is that the parishioners have become perfectly reconciled to their pastor, and a great peace and union has come to the parish. Both sides are pleased and grateful. Ten or twelve came, speaking for the whole parish, to thank us, telling us how much the mission had accomplished among them. I was embarrassed to hear what they had to say.

Who was responsible for this, gentlemen? God alone. Was it within the power of man to bring about this union of hearts? Even an entire Parlement would not be able to bring a solution to a situation where people were so divided, except for policing the parish to avoid criminal activity. God alone was the author of this outcome, and it is to him we give thanks.

Gentlemen, please give thanks to him with all your hearts. Ask him in his divine goodness to confer on this Company the spirit of union which is no other than the Holy Spirit himself. We should be so united that we can bring about this union among others. We were founded to reconcile souls to God, and man to man.[28]

Another brief mission was conducted in the parish of N., near Paris, having in all only three hundred souls in the entire village. However, we can remark nine different outcomes worthy of comment. Although these things refer to this particular parish, much the same will be encountered in almost any of the places where missions are given.

(1) Two church wardens were elected each year, but for ten or twelve years they had never given an account of their office. They kept for themselves some of the money belonging to the Church, but since they had been challenged on their administration they made a report and made good the money they had held back.

(2) Several persons had kept papers and documents belonging to the Church for many years. They have now turned them over, and they have been stored in the parish strongbox.

(3) Some concubinage has been rectified, with the guilty parties separating or leaving the parish.

(4) The entire population, men, women, and children, received the seed of God's word. They were so responsive to the mission that with marvelous attention they attended every morning and evening sermon, and even the midday catechism lesson.

(5) Although poor, they made a tabernacle and presented a ciborium and silver chalice to the parish. The previous ones were only tin.

(6) They repaired their church, which was in imminent danger of collapse. They decided to rebuild it completely, although the cost would come to at least twelve thousand *livres*.

(7) All lawsuits and differences were settled, so that there remained not a single one of which anyone was aware which was not resolved. This was done in such a Christian manner that the parties in dispute fell to their knees, asking pardon of each other.

(8) All the sick poor were visited, consoled, and helped, both corporally and spiritually.

(9) Each person in the parish made a good and praiseworthy general confession. They acquitted themselves so well during the mission that they

---

28. *CED* XI:5-6. Jacques Tholard directed this mission, which took place in 1655; the village is not identified. See *CED* V:360.

were well instructed and strengthened, not only in the faith, but also in the disposition to lead a Christian life in future.

We will not speak in such detail of other missions, for that would take much too much time, and be repetitious. We will recount only some significant events which we learn from the accounts of the missionaries themselves, or from other persons worthy of credence.

PART TWO
The Diocese of Saintes

Monsieur Vincent had sent the priests of his Congregation to present a mission in the diocese of Saintes around 1634. A pious person wrote the following account:

> Our Lord blessed in an unbelievable way the mission at Saintonge. Many conversions took place in morals and even in religion. What was so praiseworthy in the work of the missionaries was that they made the people see the beauty of the Catholic religion in their usual way, without dispute. This in turn led several heretics to return to the Church. Madame de N. told me that she thought of these missionaries as the apostles of the primitive Church, in the way in which they accepted all who came to them, whether Catholic or heretics.

Monsieur Vincent sent other priests of the Congregation of the Mission to this same diocese in 1640 at the urgent invitation of the late Bishop de Raoul, who with his clergy welcomed them for their missions.[29] It pleased God to bless their work, for they produced much good, according to the reports of the superiors, confirmed by several letters of this good prelate.

In one of his letters, a missionary said:

> We are at the end of our mission in N., which has lasted seven weeks. I hesitate to tell you of all the blessings we have received, for fear of vainglory. It will be enough to say that this parish, which had the reputation of being the worst in Saintonge because of its enmities, discords, and even murders, not to mention other abominations, is now, by God's mercy, completely changed. It has made public reparation for scandals given. A large number of people attended every service of the mission, even the short catechism instruction. Quarrels have been settled, spite has disappeared, and reconciliations have been achieved even without our active intervention. We attribute all these graces to the goodness of God and

---

29. Jacques Raoul de la Guibourgere.

to the merits of the holy family of our Savior, to which we dedicated this mission. The people of another parish some distance away requested their pastor to bring a mission there. When this proved impossible they asked him to preach each morning, teaching them how to pray, and how to serve God well. He has begun to do this with much success.

Another priest wrote of a mission in another parish of the same diocese.

This mission has received many blessings, some most extraordinary, by the grace of God. Some important reconciliations took place between certain persons of considerable standing, which in the past even the bishop had not been able to bring about. For a long time there had been much bitterness and deep divisions within the parish. This in turn led to angry lawsuits, but now by the mercy of God these have ended, and the persons involved have become perfectly reconciled.

Although we found the parish completely divided, we leave it united in great peace, by the mercy of God. He has conferred other singular graces as well, in favor of noted public sinners who have been converted. These have, both privately and publicly, made restitution for their wrongs. God has touched the hearts of several converted heretics.

Another Missionary reported on the mission in 1647 at Gemozac, in the same diocese, at which, besides the more usual fruits of the mission, a group of seven or eight heretics were converted. Several others seemed disposed to make this same change, but hesitated for fear of added taxes because the board which imposed them were all heretics. Most of them were pleased at the king's order obliging all to go to mass, for this provided a release for the human respect which had kept them away.

One of those converted was an old man whom we had exhorted several times, but without effect. Just before leaving, seeing that we had made no headway, the thought came to us to have recourse to the blessed Virgin Mary, to obtain the conversion of this poor soul. We had barely finished reciting the litany on our knees for this intention when the man came to tell us that he now recognized the truth and that he wished to abjure his heresy. We received his profession of faith, had him make a general confession, and then gave him holy communion. In saying farewell to us he earnestly begged that he be recommended to the prayers of all Catholics.[30]

The superior of the mission in Saintes stated in one of his letters that, after working for a solid month in the village of Deniat, he and the missionaries

---

30. *CED* III:164.

with him were so overwhelmed by the crowd of people from all the surrounding areas that they were forced to end the mission ahead of time. They were so weak they collapsed in the confessional. With regret, they had to leave a large group of people without the usual closing services of the mission. He added in his letter that more than four hundred reconciliations had been effected, and a hundred lawsuits ended.

These good people earnestly desired to make their confession. Since they knew that we would not give absolution to those not reconciled or at least to those who had not made every reasonable effort to be so, they went from door to door, seeking out those who might have something against them. On the eve of our departure a large crowd gathered in the church for evening prayers. The pastor announced the missionaries would be leaving the next day, and took the occasion to exhort the people to make good use of the instructions they had received during the mission. The people were deeply moved, and began to cry and weep so much that not a word could be understood of what the pastor was saying. The Missionaries did not find it easy to leave, for the people did not want to let them go.

Almost the same thing happened in the town of Usseau, near the village of Niort. After working for a month there, the Missionaries were so worn out and so weakened that they had to close the mission, leaving a large number yet to confess their sins. These people were so upset they tearfully begged the Missionaries to stay, and cried so loudly that no heart was left untouched. A large number of reconciliations took place here also, but in the beginning the Missionaries experienced great resistance, especially in their attempt to abolish the public dance held on the feast of Pentecost. It had occasioned many disorders, including the kidnapping of young girls and even murders. The sermon for Pentecost dealt with this abuse, but even so several of the townspeople went to the dance in the evening. The superior of the mission was alerted, and he and some other priests went to the scene, whereupon all the revelers fled. The next day a strong sermon was given before a large group of people, during which the violin used at the dance was broken into bits. The effect on the hearers, by God's grace, was such that all who had attended the dance were moved to repent. They came to throw themselves at the feet of the preacher, and asked pardon for their sin. The people conceived such a horror for dancing and all the evils accompanying it that they banished it entirely from their parish.

Another benefit of this mission took place at a meeting of the priests of the region, numbering seventeen pastors. The conferences there were so effective they all resolved to lead a more truly priestly life, in both their exterior demeanor and their interior spirit.

The missions of this diocese had been so blessed and had produced such good results that the late bishop of Saintes wrote to Monsieur Vincent in 1642 to tell him the people had come to thank him for arranging them.[31] In another letter of the same year, he said: "I have had your Missionaries come to this city to take a bit of rest. For the past six months they have worked with such devotion that I am astonished they could manage it. I went myself to invite them here."[32] In another letter of 1643 he wrote: "I have spent the feast of Pentecost with your Missionaries, who work with such marvelous zeal. They have the consolation of seeing the blessing God gives to their work. I cannot thank you enough for what they have accomplished."[33]

PART THREE
The Dioceses of Mende and Saint Flour

The diocese of Mende in the Cevennes was overrun by heretics. On several occasions Monsieur Vincent had sent his missionaries, either to attempt to bring the heretics back to the faith or to strengthen the Catholics and prevent them from falling into error. This worthy superior of the mission decided to go himself to the region in 1635. At the time one of his priests at Rome, well versed in Hebrew and Syriac, had been asked to work on a translation of the Syriac Bible into Latin. Monsieur Vincent thought it would be better if he came to help him on the mission in the Cevennes. He wrote to him as follows:

> Monsieur, please do not accept the proposal made to you, to work on the translation of Scripture. I know well it would satisfy the curiosity of some, but would not contribute to the salvation of the souls of these poor people to whom the Providence of God, from all eternity, has called you. It ought to be enough that by the grace of God you have spent three or four years learning Hebrew. You now know enough to defend the cause of the Son of God in the original language and to confound his enemies in this kingdom.
>
> Think of those thousands of souls who raise their arms to you and say: "Alas, Monsieur, God chose you to help in our salvation. Have pity on us, and give us a hand to draw us from the pitiable state in which we find ourselves.[34] Come to draw us from the ignorance in which we live, unmindful of the truths necessary for salvation, and living in sin which through shame we have never

---

31. Jacques Raoul de la Guibourgere. *CED* II:266.
32. *CED* II:267.
33. *CED* II:397.
34. The original text of this sentence is shorter: "Have pity on us."

confessed. Without your help we are in great danger of losing our souls."

Besides the cries of these poor souls, appealing to the charity within you, listen, Monsieur, if you will, to what my heart says to yours. It feels called to work and die in the Cevennes, and it will, if you do not come at once to these mountains. The bishop cries for help, and says that this region, once the most flourishing of all the kingdom, is now in sin and the people die of hunger for God's word.[35]

Monsieur Vincent sent other missionaries several years later to work in the same diocese. This led the late Bishop de Marcillac to write: "I assure you I esteem the work of your missionaries in my diocese more than if you had given me a hundred kingdoms. I am delighted to see my people responding so well. My pastors derive much profit from the Conferences your priests have set up with such success and blessing."[36]

In a letter of the following year, 1643, this same prelate wrote:

Your missionaries have left here to report to you on their activities in the Cevennes, in my diocese, where I have just made my visitation. I have received thirty or forty Huguenots who have recanted their errors, and I expect an equal number of others will do the same in the next few days. We had the mission here with unbelievable success. And as these blessings come from God, with your help, I know of no one, other than these good priests, who could give you a more accurate account of all that took place.[37]

In 1636, the late Father Olier, who later became the founder and first superior of the seminary of Saint Sulpice, a great servant of God of renowned virtue, and whose name is held in such benediction, requested of Monsieur Vincent several priests of his Congregation to give missions in the lands of his abbey at Pebrac, in the diocese of Saint Flour.[38] He, together with several other priests, accompanied them to the first of these at Saint Ilpise. The priest was so taken by the evident signs of grace on this occasion that he wrote the following letter in June to Monsieur Vincent and the priests of the clergy conference at Saint Lazare, of which he was a member.

I cannot remain long absent from you without writing to tell you what has happened here. The mission began the Sunday after Ascension, and lasted until the fifteenth of this month. The people came at first the way we hoped they would, that is, as many as we

---
35. *CED* I:251-52, addressed to Francois du Condray.
36. Sylvestre de Crusy de Marcillac became bishop of Mende in 1628; died October 20, 1659. *CED* II:266.
37. *CED* II:405-06.
38. These priests were Antoine Portail and Antoine Lucas.

could manage in the confessional. These people were so manifestly influenced by grace that we could tell where the priests were hearing confessions by the sobs and sighs of the penitents. Near the end of the mission the press of people was so great it became almost impossible to manage. From dawn to dusk they remained in church without eating or drinking, awaiting their turn to go to confession. Even so we had to extend our catechism lessons to over two hours to take care of the strangers who came. They left the service with as much hunger for the word of God as when they first came. We had to use the pulpit because of the crowd. There was no other place in the church for the priest to stand. The people crowded the church to the windows and doors, all eager to listen to the instructions. The same thing happened at the morning sermon and the evening instruction. I don't know what to say about all this except blessed be God, who reveals himself with such mercy and generosity to his creatures, especially the poor. We have noticed that he resides mainly in them, and he seeks our cooperation in helping them. Do not refuse, gentlemen, this service to Jesus Christ. It is such an honor to work in his vineyard, and to contribute to the salvation of souls, and to the glory he will receive from them for all eternity.

You have begun well, and your first successes made me leave Paris to work here, in this location. Continue in this divine work, of which earth can show no equal. O Paris! You distract many who could with the grace of God convert a multitude of souls. Alas! How many there are in Paris who work with nothing to show for it! How many apparent conversions, and how many pious sermons given which fall on deaf ears because of the poor dispositions in those who attend! Here, a single word is a sermon, and the poor, poorly taught as they are, find themselves blessed with an abundance of God's grace.[39]

In another letter written February 10 of the following year, he said:

Our fourth mission was given two weeks ago. More than two thousand people made general confessions, although we had only six priests, and eight toward the end of the mission. We were overwhelmed with people who came from distances of seven or eight leagues from here despite the frigid weather and the remoteness of the location, a true desert. These good people would bring their provisions for three or four days, sleep in the barns, and often talk together about what they had heard in the sermons and the catechism lessons. We see peasants and their wives here who in

---

39. *CED* I:332-34.

their own homes continue the mission. Shepherds and farmers chant the commandments of God in the fields, and question each other on what they had heard during the mission.

In fact, the nobility, for whom it seemed we were not speaking, using so coarse a language as we were, after they did their Christian duty in an exemplary manner, they took their leave of us with eyes moistened with tears. Five Huguenots abjured their heresy at this last mission. Previously four of them had avoided us, but now came of their own accord to seek us out. They taught us, gentlemen, a lesson you have often given, that the work of conversion of souls is a work of grace which we often hinder by our own interference. God works always in and by our nothingness, that is to say in and by those who recognize and acknowledge their own powerlessness and uselessness.[40]

PART FOUR
The Dioceses of Geneva and Marseilles

We cannot better show the fruits the missionaries from Annecy achieved, through the grace of God, than by calling upon His Excellency Juste Guerin, bishop of Geneva, who wrote to Monsieur Vincent in June 1640.

Would to God you could look into my heart, for I truly love and honor you with all my affection. I acknowledge myself obligated to your charity more than to any other human being in the whole world. I cannot express the blessings and fruits your missionaries, your dear children in the Lord, have produced in our diocese. They would not be believed by anyone unless he had witnessed it for himself. I saw these results with my own eyes on the occasion of the visit I made after Easter.

The people love the missionaries, they cherish them without exception and speak their praises. Certainly, Monsieur, their doctrine is holy, as is their conversation. They are very edifying in their manner of living. When they finish their work in one village to go to another, the people weep and say as they accompany them, "O good God, what will become of us, now that our priests have gone?" For several days they go to the other village to see them once more. Persons from other dioceses come to confess to them, and many admirable conversions have been attributed to their ministry. Their superior has great gifts from God, and has a marvelous zeal for the

---

40. Dodin, *Supplément*, 14.

glory of God and the salvation of souls. He preaches with much fervor and fruit.[41] We are much obliged to Commander de Sillery for underwriting this mission. How admirable divine Providence is to have so gently inspired the heart of this noble person to provide these evangelical missionaries for us! The good God has done this without any human intervention but simply because of our great need, situated as we are in the shadow of that wicked city, Geneva.[42]

In a letter of October 1641, he said:

> I must tell you I am ever obliged to you and to your dear sons, the priests of the Mission. You have continued to succeed, and have won more and more souls for heaven. Indeed, Monsieur, I never cease to admire the care divine Providence has taken of this diocese in sending us these good workers from your great community. I never cease to thank him, and you too, for I would be truly remiss if I did not do so. Alas, we have to our great regret lost Commander de Sillery, our great benefactor.[43]

This same prelate wrote again, in August 1644:

> Your missionaries continue to enrich paradise with souls set on the path of salvation. They showed them the way through instruction, catechism lessons, exhortations, preaching, and the administration of the sacraments. Add to this the good example of their exemplary lives wherever they give the mission. The only regret I have is that they are so few compared with the vast extent of our diocese, which has five hundred eighty parishes. Alas, if our Lord would give me the grace of seeing the mission given in every locale, I would say with all my heart, and with great consolation: *Nunc dimittis servum tuum Domine, secundum verbum tuum in pace* ["Now, Master, you can dismiss your servant in peace; you have fulfilled your word"].[44]

The missions given at Marseilles and in Provence are of two kinds, one given at sea, the other on land. The first has to do with the convicts of the galleys, and the second with the peasants in the countryside, both blessed by God.

The mission for the galleys began in 1643, to the great satisfaction of Jean Baptiste Gault, the worthy bishop of Marseilles, who died soon after in the odor of sanctity. He wrote on March 6 to the duchess of Aiguillon, who took an interest in this mission because her nephew, the duke of Richelieu, was

---

41. Bernard Codoing, superior at Annecy, 1639-1642.
42. *CED* II:52.
43. *CED* II:199.
44. Luke 2:29. *CED* II:473.

the general of the galleys.[45] She had earlier asked Monsieur Vincent to assign some of his priests to this work.

Although it has not been long since I wrote you about the arrival of the missionaries whom you caused to be sent to work in the galleys, I must tell you of what has happened since, and of the satisfaction all experienced who work at this difficult task.[46] I, too, rejoice with them at their success, and I know you will share this happiness. We began the mission in the galleys with eight priests from Provence, two to a ship.[47] The priests who came directly from Paris have gone to the other three ships. I have tried to help out where I could, especially in regard to the many Italians in the galleys. The results of the missions surpass anything we could have hoped for. It is true that at first not only were persons ignorant of their religion found there, but many who were hardened in their sin. They did not want to hear things of God spoken of, being hardened to the highest degree by the miserable condition in which they were. Little by little, by the grace of God and the work of these missionaries, their hearts were softened to such a degree that they show contrition equal to their previous defiance.

You would be astonished, Madame, if you could see the number of those who had passed three or four years or even ten without going to confession. Some who had been away for twenty-five years even said they would not do anything about it as long as they remained in their cruel punishment. Finally our Lord conquered and chased Satan from these souls over whom he had exerted such power. I praise God for inspiring you to make it possible for these missionaries to come. Since their arrival I have resolved to work at this mission, which before I might have hesitated to do. It is to be feared that some among them will die in the unhappy state in which they are. I hope we will be able to reap the same fruit in the other galleys. I cannot tell you, Madame, how deeply these poor convicts appreciate the aid they have received, and which has proved so helpful for the good of their souls. I am looking for a way to perpetuate the good dispositions in which they now are. I am on my way to give absolution to four heretics who were converted while serving in the galleys. Others plan to return, for the extraordinary events of the mission have moved them deeply.

---

45. Armand de Wignerod. At the death of the cardinal, he inherited his title of duke of Richelieu. He also inherited the title of the general of the galleys from his father, Francois de Wignerod de Pont Courlay, who in turn had succeeded Philippe Emmanuel de Gondi when he retired to the Oratory.
46. Vincent sent five missionaries, led by Francois du Coudray.
47. These were the missionaries founded by Christophe d'Authier de Sisgau.

Two or three months later Monsieur Vincent received a letter from the superior of the missionaries at Marseilles, telling him the sad news of the death of this holy bishop. He reported plans for further work:

> We still have one more mission to give on one of the galleys, but that will finish up for this year. The work is trying, but what helps us bear it is the completely satisfactory change we perceive in these convicts. Yesterday I taught catechism to seven Moslems from various galleys whom I had brought here. God in his mercy has blessed this enterprise, which I recommend to your prayers. Another Moslem was baptized on board a galley, since he was gravely ill. Besides this man, about thirty heretics made their abjuration.[48]

This same priest wrote to Monsieur Vincent again on June 1 of the same year:

> Yesterday the feast of the most holy Trinity, nine Moslems were baptized in the cathedral church, in a public ceremony before the people of Marseilles. The streets were filled with people blessing God. We chose to make such a display to encourage some other Moslems who seemed unsure of themselves. Today two new ones came to tell me they would like to become Christians. They came with another who had been baptized ten days before. We teach them catechism in Italian twice a day, to strengthen and affirm them as much as in our power. Otherwise they would be in danger of relapsing into Islam.[49]

Since that time Monsieur Vincent continued to support the Missionaries at Marseilles, who continued to offer their services to the galleys, even when the home port of the galleys was transferred to Toulon. These missions continued to do much good for the salvation of the souls of these unfortunate convicts.

Besides these services to the convicts, these missionaries gave their missions in the countryside with equal success. This is what one of them wrote in 1647:

> We have just finished a five-week mission. It has kept us chained to the confessional and the pulpit and to the settlement of disputes. It has been so successful that I can say without exaggeration that we could not have hoped for anything better. We have rectified nine or ten marriages, and have settled twenty-five or thirty disputes involving either large sums, affairs of honor or other matters. Most of these were settled face to face, without anyone else involved. Some were arranged publicly in the church, even during the sermon, with such tearful feeling that the preaching was interrupted.

---

48. *CED* II:395.
49. *CED* II:398.

It happened also that a man of some modest standing had angrily replied to one of our priests, and had even publicly blasphemed at the door of the church. Some two weeks later he came to his senses, and as a penance imposed upon himself, gave a hundred *ecus* for the repair of the church that had witnessed his blasphemy.[50]

PART FIVE
The Dioceses of Reims, Toul, and Rouen

Among the missions in the diocese of Reims, one of the most important was the one given by order of the king in the city of Sedan in 1643. Following is the letter of the superior of the mission to Monsieur Vincent.

I must say, Monsieur, that since it has pleased God to form the little Company of the Mission, it has never worked so usefully or so importantly as it has here. Heretics continue to be interested and come to the sermons, which they loudly praise. We must work with the Catholics almost as neophytes, for since the time four or five years ago when the town was opened to all preachers, nearly everyone is taken up with controversies. Few enough, however, trouble themselves about religious practices and exercises. We have run across some who frankly admit they have never thought it necessary to confess all their sins. The same sort of abuse exists with the blessed sacrament and other things as well. We have to begin from the first principles of religion. This is not to say this work is without consolation, for the people listen with pleasure to what we have to say and faithfully put it into practice. They cannot admire enough the graces God has given them, nor can they begin to thank him as much as they would like.[51]

We may judge the great fruit of this mission by the evident needs of the people. The late Archbishop d'Etampes of Reims thanked Monsieur Vincent in a special letter which he wrote to the superior of the Congregation.[52]

Several other missions were given in other places in the same diocese, among others at the village of Sillery, after the war. The superior wrote to Monsieur Vincent that only eighty persons still lived in the village, since all the others had died from the dire conditions of the times. These few survivors showed such good dispositions that nothing more could be hoped for, especially in those who came to the altar to receive communion.

---

50. *CED* III:159-60.
51. *CED* II:425-26.
52. Eleonor d'Etampes de Valencay, archbishop of Reims, 1641-1651.

> They communicated with such feeling that their tears were a tribute to the real presence of their divine Savior, who took possession of their hearts. They were so converted to the Lord that not only did they renounce sin, but resolved to suffer with patience and submission and out of love for him alone, whatever would please his divine will. This is how they themselves spoke, often repeating, "All for the love of God."[53]

This same priest wrote to Monsieur Vincent some time later from the village of Ludes, where he had given a mission.

> All has gone here as you wished. That says it all. One of the fruits of the mission was the completion of the church, which would never have been accomplished unless the mission were held here. The taverns have closed, and the evening parties stopped. The people have done away with swearing, and they speak the holy name of God only with great respect. We see people in their houses falling on their knees to ask pardon of those they have offended.[54]

He wrote again from the village of Fontaine, in the same diocese.

> God blessed the previous missions, and seems to have increased his grace for this one. Concubinages which have lasted twenty-five years have ended; lawsuits are settled; many people, both from this village and surrounding area, who have been away from the sacraments for twenty, thirty, or thirty-five years have recognized and repented their sins. People from the town have called their relatives even in distant places to come and share in the fruits of the mission. Some gentlemen have come from as far away as seven, ten, or fourteen leagues, mostly from the region of Rethel.[55]

Lastly, this good missionary worked in the town of Ai in the same diocese. He reported as follows to Monsieur Vincent:

> We arrived here to find that some of the leading people of the town had spoken against us, and had persuaded the people not to accept us. After several days of patience, God, who sent us here by the orders of our superiors, so changed the hearts of the people that never did a mission start better. The people confessed very exactly, with all signs of a true contrition. They repaid what they owed, went to ask pardon of one another in their homes, prayed both morning and evening, and resolved to change their way of living to a truly Christian behavior. They could not hear enough of the word of God.

---

53. *CED* VI:616-17.
54. *CED* VII:164.
55. *CED* VII:151-52.

The minister who lived here has fled. The few heretics in town, unlettered vine dressers, have attended all our sermons.[56]

Monsieur Vincent had sent priests of the Congregation to the diocese of Rouen several times to conduct missions with the same happy results, by God's grace, as in other dioceses. To avoid repetition, we will be content to cite a letter of the archbishop of Rouen to Monsieur Vincent, written in 1656, which expresses his appreciation of the missionaries and their work.[57]

I do not hesitate to write to you, for you have been unstinting in your help for us. The help the diocese has received through the saintly workers you have sent is evidence enough. How I thank our Savior to see his spirit so abundantly poured forth upon the priests whom you have formed by his grace. I could have no greater wish for the Church and for the glory of his sacred name, than that all priests have the same ability and the same fervor. I return your valiant Monsieur N. and his generous troops who have fought so bravely against sin. I hope on other occasions they will again enlist under the standard of the primate of Normandy. He appreciates their virtue and admires their zeal, and remains without reserve, in the army of the Lord, your very humble, etc.[58]

The Missionaries established themselves in the town of Toul, in the diocese of the same name, despoiled by the ravages of war. They received God's blessings upon the missions they gave there. The superior of the group wrote as follows to Monsieur Vincent at the conclusion of three missions:

I cannot fully express the goodness of God toward us. We have heard around five hundred general confessions with no relief for a full month. The harsh winter weather left the roads covered with snow up to two feet deep. Yet this did not keep these poor people, rich in faith and eager for the word of God, from showing their attachment to the kingdom of heaven despite the annoyances they had to put up with from the soldiers. All we hoped for has come about, and we may rightfully say that Jesus Christ has graciously spread everywhere the good odor of his Gospel.[59]

In another letter written some time later, he said:

We have just finished a mission in the large village of Charmes. After working five weeks there we have finished. We are somewhat worn out, but our hearts are filled with joy and consolation because of the blessings God has showered upon us and all the people of this parish, and even of neighboring parishes. The pastor is a devout

---

56. *CED* VII:154-55.
57. Francois Harlay de Champvalon, archbishop of Reims, 1651-1670; later archbishop of Paris.
58. *CED* V:577-78.
59. *CED* V:553.

man, and everyone in the parish, from himself to the least person, came to make their general confession, no one excepted. These confessions were so well made, in such sentiments of true conversions, that I do not remember any in the last twenty-five missions at which I have participated where the people have seemed so moved as in this one. After being reconciled to God and to their neighbor, each one seems committed to following our counsel about living in the grace of God. There is a monastery of religious in the town,[60] the members of which, particularly their superior, a true saint, were completely astonished to see so many miracles.

All these glorious triumphs of grace which our Lord has won over once-rebellious hearts, who now give him glory by their true repentance, demand that we give him most humble thanks. I realize I must work more than ever before, for I recognize how the missions are such a great means of aiding souls. I have returned from this mission with this thought and resolution.[61]

PART SIX
Various Places in Brittany

The missions in Brittany were as successful as those in the other provinces. The superior of the missionaries headquartered at Saint Meen in the diocese of Saint Malo wrote to Monsieur Vincent in 1657.[62] He said that at a mission in Pleurtuit, three thousand persons had gone to confession. Further, if the priests should return, they would need more than twenty confessors to satisfy the great number of people who would come for confession. Among other things he said that upon leaving the church, a respected person of the parish fell to his knees in the cemetery before his fellow parishioners. He asked pardon from those he had offended, to the great consternation of all at this demonstration. Another person, upon leaving the confessional, went of his own accord eight leagues away to ask pardon of someone he had offended in some rather slight way.[63]

In another letter from 1658, he reported to Monsieur Vincent several remarkable events which occurred at the mission of Mauron.

Every day, even on working days, more than twelve hundred people came for the catechetical instructions. The leading people of the town came to hear the sermons. Several men and women

---

60. Capuchins.
61. *CED* V:620-21.
62. Louis Serre, superior at Saint Meen, 1655-1665.
63. *CED* VI:281.

servants even left their employment because their masters or mistresses would not give them time off to attend the services. They preferred to lose their wages rather than miss an opportunity to hear the word of God. We saw mothers, after they had made their own general confession on the mission, take the place of their daughters in service, to give them the opportunity to do likewise. Other servants requested permission to come to the instructions, even at the cost of losing their wages for the time they would not be at work.

On Quinquagesima Sunday and the two following days, such a crowd of people wanted to receive communion that it took until seven o'clock in the evening to satisfy them all. Since the closing the mission, I have been told that, of all the taverns there, not a single one remains, for in one of our sermons we had mentioned how difficult it was for inn keepers to keep from sin in giving people drink to excess, a vice prevalent in this region. In addition, in the dealings they have with one another, instead of sealing an agreement by a drink, as is customary in this region, they now give money to the Confraternity of Charity, which we were able to set up in the locality for the sick poor.[64]

The following year this same superior wrote of another mission:

Our mission in Plaissala is now completed by the grace of God. He showered his blessings in such abundance that all who worked on it agree they have never seen one which accomplished so much good.

We noticed people from seventeen surrounding parishes. Several men who came to confession remarked they had waited ten days in the church. I believe the same thing could have happened to five hundred others as well. Major disputes have been settled, particularly among the nobility, helped along by the Baron du Rechau. He has a house in this parish, where he came from Saint Brieuc, his ordinary residence. After hearing our first sermon, he came to our house with his wife, to tell us he was going to stay here the entire mission. I asked him to help us settle the frequent disputes in this region, and to bring reconciliation, especially between gentlemen. He succeeded to an extraordinary degree.

The carnival days were taken up in exercises of piety. On Monday we had a solemn procession, in which the bishop of Saint Brieuc carried the blessed sacrament.[65] The people attended with devotion and modesty, walking four by four in the procession which

---

64. *CED* VII:115.
65. Denis de la Barde.

lasted nearly two hours in an almost continuous rain, and only a few dropped out. The same prelate conferred the sacrament of confirmation the next day, Tuesday, in the cemetery, in the midst of wind and rain, for the church was not large enough to hold all the people.[66]

The bishop of Treguier had a mission given at Guingamp, after another at Morlaix in 1648.[67] He wrote of them to Monsieur Vincent:

Your letter has found us busy in the mission, from which I expect a great deal. One of your priests preaches admirably and devoutly in the evening service. Another gives the main catechetical instruction at one o'clock in the afternoon, to the satisfaction of all. Another priest teaches the shorter catechism lesson, and my theologian preaches in the morning in the native dialect. In a word, everyone is working, even myself, for I preach twice a week. With God's help, we will begin the confessions tomorrow. The people of the area are not used to missions, but are astonished at what takes place, and each expresses his thoughts differently, but all with respect. I hope that all will work out well with the grace of God.[68]

In another letter, written in 1650 about another mission, he said:

I thank you for the faithful service of four of your priests in the mission they have given here. Their ability, their zeal, their care in preaching and hearing confessions have been so great that they have reaped abundant fruit. I may say the residents of this region, men and women of all ages and conditions, have been converted. I praise God that through you we have such good laborers in this vineyard. Monsieur N. exerts such energy in his preaching that no one can resist him. I have already engaged him for the mission next year at N.[69]

PART SEVEN

Various Places in Burgundy and Champagne

In 1642 Monsieur Vincent sent several priests of the Congregation to give a mission in the parish of Saint Cyr in the diocese of Sens. The lord of the region wrote, after the completion of the mission:

The efforts of your priests, joined with their piety, have made such a difference in the life of my peasants that they are hardly recognizable by their neighbors. I hardly know them either, and am persuaded God has sent me a new colony to people my village.

---

66. *CED* VII:469-70.
67. Balthazar Grangier de Liverdi.
68. *CED* III:269-70.
69. *CED* III:630.

> These gentlemen who came here found such rustic types they could never be changed, except by the grace that accompanied your missionaries, especially those you sent for the conversion of my people. This is a result of the mercy of God and of your prudence that those you sent were so suited to our needs. After my thanks to you, I must pray fervently that God will endow your Company with blessings, for I judge it to be one of the most devoted to his glory of those in the Church today.
>
> I fear these poor people, for lack of a good pastor to support them in the good resolutions taken during that helpful mission, will forget or neglect to put into practice what has been so carefully taught them. Since you have not agreed to give us a pastor, I nevertheless believe that you, as their new father in Jesus Christ, must obtain one for us by your prayers, which I earnestly solicit.[70]

Madame de Saint Cyr was just as thankful as her husband, as she explained in a letter to Monsieur Vincent:

> I realize I am incapable of thanking you sufficiently for the honor and good you have done for our parish, yet I still must affirm that after God you are, in some way, our savior, by sending us the missionaries who have worked such marvels here. They have so gained the appreciation of Monsieur de Saint Cyr that I fear he may fall ill at seeing them leave. For myself, I cannot tell you how I feel, for I am too sad to express myself.[71]

Monsieur Le Boucher, vicar general of the abbey of Moutier Saint Jean, wrote to Monsieur Vincent about the mission given in Burgundy in 1644.

> You do good everywhere, and you render great services to God, to the Church, and to our holy religion. I have returned from Tonnere where I met your dear children, priests of the Mission, led by a man of God. I must add, Monsieur, that these good priests have worked marvels by their teaching and example. They reconciled many souls to God and to their neighbor.[72]

One of the missionaries who worked in this province in 1650 wrote to Monsieur Vincent:

> I must tell you the results of your prayers and sacrifices have been equally great in Joigny as at Longron, where we now are busy with a mission. I have nothing special to say of the people of Joigny, except to admire their faithfulness to the sermons and catechetical instructions, and their care about rising in the morning. Sometimes

---

70. *CED* II:242-43.
71. *CED* II:243.
72. *CED* II:451.

we began our sermons at two o'clock in the morning, and even so, the church was full.

I must say in truth I find greater blessings in the countryside than I do in the cities. I see there more marks of true and sincere penitence, and also the signs of uprightness and simplicity marking primitive Christianity. These good people present themselves to their confessor bathed in tears. They judge themselves the greatest sinners in the world and ask for even greater penances than those imposed upon them. Yesterday, a person who had confessed to another priest came to me to ask for a more severe penance than the one he had received. He suggested I order him to fast three times a week for the rest of the year. Another asked for the penance of walking barefoot in the snow. Another man came to tell me: "I heard in the sermon the best way to overcome swearing is to throw yourself on your knees before those who heard you swear, and that's what I've done. As soon as I realized I had sworn "my faith," I fell to my knees, asking God's mercy upon me."[73]

About two months later this same priest continued his report of events in the missions of Burgundy:

If it is right that the one who plants the tree should enjoy its fruit, just so you should know of the blessings God has given in such abundance to your little flock. I can assure you that in the missions we have given since Joigny, I don't think anyone failed to make his general confession. It is wonderful to see how much the people were affected. Because of this, I limited myself to speaking of truths that would lead to repentance to the first few days because of their tender consciences. I feared I would otherwise excite their imagination too much.[74]

We should remark that the priest with this gift of moving the people to repentance was a noted penitent himself. He practiced what he preached.

Among the missions preached in Champagne, one of the most notable took place in 1657 at Nogent, in the diocese of Troyes. The bishop sent two of his priests, and came himself, to work on the mission for several days. The mission lasted six weeks. God greatly blessed it, for which the people were most grateful to their bishop. All possible blessings which a mission might accomplish were fulfilled in this one. The vicars general were in admiration. They said that the time of priests was wasted if it was not devoted to the salvation of souls, and that the most effective way of assuring success was to preach and catechize according to the method used by the Mission-

---

73. *CED* III:621-22.
74. *CED* IV:26.

aries. The people were so faithful to the sermons and catechism lessons that the pastors stated they had never seen so many people in church, even on the feast of Easter, as they saw during the mission.

The bishop of Chalons sur Marne requested several priests of the Mission from Monsieur Vincent in 1658 to conduct missions in various places in his diocese.[75] He had several of his pastors attend the exercises to learn how best to instruct their parishioners. One of the missionaries wrote this account to Monsieur Vincent:

> Our mission at Vassy received all the blessings we could have hoped for. Four pastors and another priest, all able and virtuous, helped us. Two of them learned our method so well that, even though formerly they were uneasy speaking in public, they now were quite capable and as good as any I have seen. Catholics influenced by heretical doctrines have recanted, have been confirmed in their faith, and have been launched on a truly Christian way of living. Not only did we serve the people of this town, but others came as well from four or five leagues away.
>
> We are now at the mission in Holmoru, where even more good is expected from the many people in attendance. The appreciation of the pastors is so great that today twelve of them came from three or four leagues away to help out and learn our method of instructing the people.[76]

PART EIGHT
Various Other Places in France

From the time when Monsieur Vincent had first sent his priests to work outside the diocese of Paris to most distant parts of the kingdom, a noted abbot wrote a letter of congratulations in 1627, on what he had observed.

> I have just returned from a long trip into four of the provinces where the good odor of your holy institution which works for the instruction and salvation of souls of the countryside has been noted. In truth, I believe that in the Church of God none is more edifying and praiseworthy among those who have received the character and the order of Jesus Christ than your priests. We must pray God to bestow his spirit of perseverance upon a work so advantageous to the good of souls, to which so few of those consecrated to the service of God give enough attention.[77]

---

75. Felix de Vialart.
76. *CED* VII:100.
77. *CED* I:35-36.

Monsieur Vincent sent two priests to the diocese of Montauban around 1630 to strengthen Catholics in their faith. Living among heretics, they ran the constant danger of falling into their errors. After two years of constant effort he recalled them. Although they had been sent mainly to work with the Catholics, God allowed them to convert twenty-four heretics while there.

Several years later the late Bishop de Murviel of Montauban wrote to Monsieur Vincent about several sorcerers who had appeared in his diocese, and his difficulties in eradicating their influence.[78]

> The priests of the Mission are most necessary in this diocese, for the places they formerly worked show no signs of either sorcerers or sorceresses. This shows what good the catechetical instructions and general confessions have brought about. They put the people in such a good state the devils can make no headway by their charms and spells, as they can with those sunk in ignorance and sin.[79]

In 1634 Monsieur Vincent sent other Missionaries to work in the diocese of Bordeaux. They wrote to tell him people came from far away to the mission with such devotion that many passed entire weeks living where the mission was being given, awaiting their turn to make their confession. Some fell to their knees and openly confessed their sins to receive absolution. Others said they would rather die than return home without making their general confession.[80]

In 1638 several priests of the Mission were sent to work in the diocese of Lucon. Three years later one of them wrote to Monsieur Vincent about the mission they had given:

> It is hard to imagine how much our labors have been rewarded by the consolation sent by God to encourage us. These souls of Poitou, who seem hard as rocks, have caught the fire of devotion so ardently that it seems it will not be easily extinguished.[81]

Another priest wrote in 1642 from the mission at Essarts, stating that seven heretics had been converted, and that wonderful changes had been brought about among the nobility and the officers of the law.[82]

Still another priest wrote from the mission of Saint Gilles on the coast. He reported that dissensions and quarrels had been settled, hearts reconciled, difficult lawsuits ended, appropriate restitutions made when necessary, the poor aided, and the sick poor consoled and helped by the Confraternity of Charity. Catholics were strengthened in practicing the true religion.[83]

---

78. Anne de Murviel, bishop of Montauban. Richelieu had captured this city from the Huguenots and reestablished Catholicism. Murviel, who had been chased from his see, was also reestablished there. The following year he asked for missionaries to evangelize his diocese.
79. *CED* II:429.
80. *CED* I:289-90.
81. *CED* II:168.
82. *CED* II:266.
83. *CED* IV:108.

The late Bishop de Nivelle of Lucon wrote to Monsieur Vincent in 1642 about the mission which the priests of his Company had presented in his diocese.

> If it shall please God to preserve the institute of the priests of the Mission in the Church for many years, we can expect much fruit from it. The diocese of Lucon in which, by your appointment, your priests have worked for the last three or four years, has received such blessing that I am infinitely grateful to Cardinal Richelieu for arranging to have them come, and to yourself for having sent them. Their superior, especially, has worked hard and earnestly. He has the gifts needed in his position, especially his zeal, to everyone's admiration. His only fault is that he perhaps works too hard, if it be possible to be excessive in working to gain souls to God.[84]

Other priests of the Mission went to the region of Angouleme in 1640. A noble woman there had wished to have them give a mission in the village of Saint Amand which belonged to her. She received the following letter from one of her officials:

> I imagine I could not begin my letter on a matter more agreeable to you than by telling you the happy success of the mission you arranged in your territory of Saint Amand. It was so blessed that not only your dependents but thirty or forty neighboring parishes shared in its marvelous fruits. The Minims and the Capuchins were no less zealous, and their example attracted a large part of the leading people of Angouleme. I assure you, Madame, that according to common report, the missionaries have never labored so successfully for the glory of God. They have converted five or six of the leading Huguenots of Montignac, and the Duke de la Rochefoucauld is so pleased he will ask Monsieur Vincent to arrange a mission next spring at Verteuil and at Marcillac. The lords, N. and N., who attended this mission were so touched that one decided to give up his paramour and the other has married the woman who was living with him.

Monsieur Vincent sent other missionaries to the diocese in 1643, but we know no details of their work. Nevertheless it seemed so useful to Bishop du Perron of Angouleme that he wrote in January of the following year as follows:[85]

> Although I have already thanked you for sending your missionaries into this diocese, I felt I could not send off this letter to our

---

84. *CED* II:244.
85. Jacques Noel du Perron, the nephew of Cardinal Jean Dovy du Perron, archbishop of Seus.

little Conference without expressing, however feebly, my appreciation of the great fruit this diocese has received from your charitable hands.[86] My happiness will ever be incomplete, Monsieur, until that day when we shall have a permanent mission in this diocese, which needs it so much more than other places. When I learn that you can do us this favor, I shall do all in my power to find the means of making this establishment. I believe this will contribute much to the glory of God and will aid the Church in its mission for the salvation of souls. I know it is the sole motive you have in view in all your efforts.[87]

This letter was followed two weeks later by another, written to Monsieur Vincent by a priest from Angouleme.

> I am just about to leave by horseback for Blansac, with the money you sent me for the needs of your missionaries who have been working there. Once again, please let me repeat my humble prayers in favor of this poor and desolate diocese. It begs you to send permanent workers to tend to its extreme spiritual needs. These can be remedied only if persons of an impartial charity and zeal such as your priests of Saint Lazare come to take charge. I know well, Monsieur, that the providence of God can use a thousand other means to help us, should it please him. Yet it seems clear enough that he has chosen you among these thousands to help the poor dioceses of this kingdom, but especially those that seem to be the most abandoned of all.[88]

The late Archbishop de Montchal of Toulouse wrote to Monsieur Vincent in 1640:

> I cannot allow these two priests you sent to us to leave without thanking you, as I do with all my heart, for the great service they have rendered to God in my diocese. I cannot adequately express the pains they have taken, nor the fruits they have reaped for which I am especially grateful since they work in my stead. One of them learned the language of the region to the admiration of those who speak it, and has shown himself untiring in his labors. When they have recovered a bit I wish you would send them back, for I am thinking of establishing the ordination retreats, and I will need their help. All will work out for the glory of God if you will help us.[89]

In 1648 the superior of the mission at Richelieu wrote to Monsieur

---

86. This was a conference of ecclesiastics, founded on the model of the Paris conference.
87. *CED* II:441-42.
88. *CED* II:443-44.
89. *CED* II:88-89.

Vincent to tell him three Missionaries had given a pair of missions in Bas Poitou. Among the graces God had given through their ministry, not the least was the conversion of twelve heretics.[90]

It is proper to note an important consideration in the conversion of heretics, such as those we just mentioned, and in the great number of others effected from the time of the first missions of Monsieur Vincent until the present. Their conversion was not brought about in arguing with them, nor was it accomplished by helping them, finding them jobs, or by other temporal favors. By God's special favor, the instruction and good example of the missionaries made them see Christian verities in their true light and attracted them to the Catholic religion. The appeal was the stronger the more removed it was from any mere human consideration.

About this time, the same Missionaries gave their services to the parish of Sache in the diocese of Tours. They wrote to tell Monsieur Vincent that, although only six hundred people lived in the parish, twelve hundred participated in the general communion. They told him the mission had produced many reconciliations, restitutions, true conversions, and other similar fruits. The pastor, his vicar, and five other priests had made their general confession. One of the richest men of the parish, a miser, was so touched by this that he told the preacher that in future he would distribute bread three times a week to any of the poor who would present themselves at his door.[91]

After this mission another was given in the village of Villaine, in the same diocese. The same blessings seemed to be upon it also, in the number and devotion of the people, in the conversions of sinners, and in the reconciliations of enemies, thirteen or fourteen of which were significant. The general communion was made in an atmosphere of much feeling. At the procession of almost two thousand people, the eighty-eight-year-old pastor wept for joy at the sight of such graces given to those under his care. He had never seen such devotion in his church as he saw on that occasion.

There was yet another mission in 1650 in this same diocese of Tours, in the parish of Cheilly. Besides the graces God ordinarily bestowed on the people, four or five notable reconciliations took place. One occurred between the pastor and one of the villagers who had insulted him. Another took place between the churchwardens who managed the goods of the parish the previous five years, and the one now in charge. This settlement was advantageous to the church, which was very poorly furnished. The third was between several officers of justice, who for five or six years had lived in

---

90. *CED* III:302.
91. *CED* III:269.

great enmity. The fourth was between two noblemen over something or other. The fifth was between a landowner and his tenant over some accounts, much to the disadvantage of the worker.

We omit mention of a great many other situations which occurred in various parts of the kingdom. If reported, they would be repetitious and besides would require several volumes to recount. The few we have given may serve as a sketch of how it pleased God to bestow his great blessings on the work of Monsieur Vincent throughout the kingdom. I use the words "great blessings" advisedly, measuring them by what they cost Jesus Christ. He in turn taught us the way we should value the conversion of sinners and all that contributes to it. He said in his Gospel "that there will be great joy among the angels of heaven upon one sinner being converted, and doing penance upon earth."[92] We can well believe these wise and enlightened spirits rejoice at what is truly worthwhile.

SECTION THREE

Further Discussion of the Fruit of the Missions Given in Italy

PART ONE
In Various Places Near Rome

We now move from France into Italy, accompanying the Missionaries sent by Monsieur Vincent to establish themselves in the first city of Christendom. Since the sovereign pontiff, Urban VIII of happy memory, received them favorably, they were able with their usual zeal to fulfill the orders given them by His Holiness, by the ordination retreats, spiritual conferences, retreats, and other services offered to priests, especially in Rome. They were able, also, in various other places near the city and elsewhere in Italy, to present missions for the people.

We will speak first of an extraordinary form of mission which was as difficult as it was charitable. They began it more than twenty years ago and still maintain it today, that is, the missions for the shepherds and cowherds of the countryside.

So that those who have not been to Rome will better understand what we

---
92. Based on Luke 15:10.

are describing, it should be pointed out that this great city lies in a sort of desert, so that within four or five leagues there are neither villages nor towns. This is not because the soil is not arable, but because the quality of the air is poor. It is difficult to find people willing to live in the area and to till the soil since they cannot survive there. Since the ground is not cultivated, there is abundant pasturage for cattle. Flocks and herds from everywhere are brought here to spend the winter, after which they are led back to the kingdom of Naples, or wherever else they came from.

The shepherds and cowherds remain five or six months in this deserted countryside. They almost never attend mass or receive the sacraments, and they do not regret it, because for the most part these are rough people, poorly instructed in their Christian duties. During the day each one goes his separate way to pasture the animals. At night they come together in a common area where they set up portable huts for themselves which sleep ten or twelve persons and sometimes even more.

Monsieur Vincent was always particularly concerned about the souls of the most neglected poor. Knowing of the condition in which these shepherds passed the better part of their lives, he directed the priests he sent to Italy to relieve and help the poor, to minister to these poor people while they were caring for their flocks. He had great compassion for them and wanted to help them. He devoutly honored their work as shepherds. Though it was abject and base in the sight of men, it was nevertheless one of the greatest attributes of the Savior of the world. In the Gospel, Jesus calls himself above all the Good Shepherd. He transmitted this attribute to those to whom he confided the care of his flock, the Church, particularly to him who is the first and the head of the faithful, that is, the sovereign pontiff.

These good Missionaries received this commission from their spiritual father and, moved by their own zeal, thought of how best to instruct these poor shepherds. It was obvious that they could not be brought together in a church for sermons and catechism lessons, as was done in other missions, since they could not leave their flocks unattended. It was unreasonable to expect them to come together, in view of the difficulties of the situation. Charity suggested that the best course of action would be to meet these poor shepherds in their huts. They would pass the night with them, taking whatever opportunity presented itself to speak with them and teach them as best they could. It seemed that Lent would be the most appropriate and fruitful time to begin. Following this plan, the Missionaries went out, one to a hut, awaiting the return of the shepherds in the evening. There they first attempted to win over their hosts by pointing out that they did not come to ask for anything, but only to offer their help. At first they asked only to pass the night with them in their humble quarters.

While the shepherds prepared their evening meal, the Missionaries spoke with them about what was necessary and useful for their salvation, of the main truths of faith, and of the proper dispositions for worthily receiving the sacraments, particularly penance and the eucharist. They also spoke of how a person ought to live as a good Christian, and how to fulfill the obligations of this calling. When the hour for sleep came, they helped them pray to God, then took their rest on a sheepskin or upon the bare ground.

They continued these instructions at irregular intervals. When they saw that the shepherds were sufficiently prepared, they administered the sacrament of penance, and helped them in their general confessions, either in the evening or during the day, as was most convenient for them. When they had ministered in this way to all the huts in the area, they had all the shepherds assemble on a feastday, or a Sunday, in the nearest chapel, if there were one in the open countryside. There they celebrated mass, gave a sermon, and distributed holy communion to all. Afterward, these poor shepherds, in imitation of those who came to adore Jesus Christ in his crib, returned, praising and glorifying God, thanking him for the graces his mercy had given them through the ministry of the good Missionaries. They continued from time to time to render this charitable service to them.[93]

Although these charitable efforts in favor of the poor shepherds, together with all their other work in the city of Rome, took up most of their time, they still managed to exercise their zeal in all the surrounding area, in neighboring dioceses, and even in several more distant ones. They gave missions in these places, with no fewer blessings than those given in France. We do not intend to speak of all of them here, nor even of the twentieth part of them, but rather only of a few of the more remarkable ones. We hope to give the reader some idea of the spiritual advantages which the people of these regions received and continue to receive up to our own time, by the grace of God, and the zeal of Monsieur Vincent, and the efforts of his spiritual sons.

In 1642 the superior of the Missionaries of Rome wrote to Monsieur Vincent:

> We gave a mission in a place which I will not name, a walled town of about three thousand souls, on the road between Rome and Naples. During the month the mission lasted we had our share of troubles and encountered terrible disorders. Most of the men and women know neither the Our Father nor the Creed, much less the

---

93. The first of these missionaries was Louis Lebreton, sent by Monsieur Vincent from France in 1638. Also sent was Jean Baptiste Taoni, a priest of the diocese of Nice, who had entered the Congregation. What these missionaries did for the shepherds in the Roman countryside they also did for the poor sailors and fishermen of the Italian coastal dioceses. Urban VIII was pleased with their efforts and authorized the Congregation to establish a house in Rome in 1641. Louis Lebreton died from an illness while evangelizing the diocese of Ostia on October 17, 1641.

other things necessary for salvation. There were many profound enmities among them. Blasphemies were not only common, but they were such as to make your hair stand on end. Some people of every class live in concubinage. Prostitutes openly seduced the young. Along with all these disorders, we ran into much opposition and resistance, with the evil spirit leveling violent attacks against us, even from those who should have been supporting us. In short, this mission has been almost a constant source of grief for us.

There seemed no way to win over the hearts of these people. They considered it a point of honor not to allow themselves to be taught or converted. The only way to make peace with them was to stop preaching or hearing confessions. However, after two weeks of patience and perseverance in the ordinary exercises of the mission, the people began to open their eyes and recognize their condition. In the end God's grace won out. Many reconciliations were effected, enmities ended, and blasphemies stopped. Four street women have been converted. One of the most obstinate mistresses has been converted. She had lived fourteen years in public adultery and caused much difficulty in the family involved, not to mention scandal in the town. She gave up her life of sin, and has removed herself from the scene.

Another completely unexpected fruit of the mission was that they gave up an abominable sin which shall not even be mentioned, to which they were much given. They made a general communion in good dispositions, and all were touched to hear their weeping, and groaning and to see their tears. This mission was finally brought to a close with great blessings, despite all the efforts of the evil one to undermine it.[94]

Another priest of the Mission of Rome wrote to Monsieur Vincent in 1654 of several missions given in the diocese of Sarsina in Romagna. After telling him of all the most interesting aspects of these missions, he continued:

In the last mission, which took place in the high mountain regions of the Apennines, we found a general state of disorder. This is common enough in Romagna, but is much worse in these isolated places. The young men and women interact with much familiarity, even when they have no intention of marrying. They never confess these faults, much less the dangerous consequences which follow, since they spend a good part of the night together. This happens especially on the eve of feastdays. Because of their wicked attraction for each other, they have little respect for the churches. They often go

---

94. *CED* II:319-20.

only to be seen, or to leer at the others and make immodest gestures. Besides the bad thoughts and other interior ills, this conduct sometimes results in scandalous affairs. This still does not restrain the others, or make their parents more careful to prevent such things.

When we became aware of these abuses and their dangerous and sorry consequences, we spoke in our sermons as strongly as possible in attempts to stop them, but with little success. They used all sorts of sophistries to justify their conduct, to our great chagrin. At length, by God's grace, we were able to bring a remedy to this evil by refusing absolution to those not firmly resolved to renounce absolutely this amorous behavior. This had the desired effect, for almost all changed their ways.

I had read to them in Italian a chapter of the book *Philothea*,[95] which treats of this matter. They heard their behavior described as though the author had written it expressly for them. Several tearfully resolved to repent the past and improve in the future. May God give them perseverance in their good dispositions.

Lastly, Monsieur, although the pastors of the locality at first took us for spies, and had put it into the minds of the people that we were suspect, they too eventually came around. When they saw the simplicity with which we acted, how we deferred to them and behaved during the missions and, above all else, when they saw that we had no selfish interest, they came to appreciate us. I might say that we carried away their hearts, as some told us with tears.

I should not fail to mention here another extraordinary event. An evil priest had publicly boasted that he would never come to any of our services. Shortly after, by God's just judgment, on the very spot he had made this boast, another evil priest killed him. The victim had told me in fine words that he was about to change his life, but this had no effect.[96]

PART TWO

In the Dioceses of Viterbo, Palestrina, and Other Places

A priest of the Mission in Rome wrote to Monsieur Vincent, in December of 1655, about a mission given in the diocese of Viterbo.

Cardinal Brancaccio did us the honor of calling us to his diocese of Viterbo.[97] He sent us to Vetralle, a large town in the diocese about

---

95. *Introduction to the Devout Life* by Saint Francis de Sales.
96. *CED* V:133-34.
97. Francesco Maria Brancaccio, successively bishop of Capua and then Viterbo. He became a cardinal in 1633, and died in 1675.

two days journey from Rome. Once we arrived there, we had some difficulties in beginning our mission. Nevertheless, we ended by having seventeen hundred persons come to make their general confession, with all the signs of repentance one could wish for.

The most ordinary things seem to have moved these people the most, as for example, (1) the explanation we made every morning after the first mass of what it means to be a Christian; (2) the instruction on the main mysteries of the faith, and the way to confess well; (3) the general examination of conscience, which we performed aloud with the usual prayers in the evening services after the sermon. What seems to have made the greatest impression upon the minds and hearts of the people is the powerful warning given by our preacher at the end of his exhortation about preparation for communion. He said, speaking in the name of God, that no one should dare approach the holy table without first being reconciled with his enemies. I am convinced that this vigorous sermon, filled with the spirit of our Lord, has been more effective than all the rest of the mission, particularly in regard to reconciliations among those living in mortal hatred of each other. Since this sermon we have seen and heard practically nothing else but many reconciliations and tearful mutual pardons, not only in the privacy of their homes but publicly in the streets and particularly in the church before everybody. The same thing happened with the restoration of ill-gotten goods, and the repayment of long-delayed debts. This was done publicly and courageously, without any regard for one's reputation.

If I were to tell you all the details of these events, I would never finish. I will limit myself to three or four of the main ones. The first occurred during the procession, where one of our priests had arranged for the men to walk two by two. Divine Providence was pleased to bring it about that two of the local people with a long and deep-seated hatred for one another found themselves walking side by side without knowing who the other was. Once they realized who their neighbor was, they were both touched by grace and found their enmity turned into friendship. Before the entire assembly they embraced and asked pardon of one another in a way that caused the admiration and consolation of everyone.

The second case involved another local resident who owed four hundred *ecus* to someone else. He had made no effort to repay what he owed, either at the insistence of the law or by the sentence of excommunication passed against him. His creditor no longer had any hopes, but this debtor changed suddenly. Not only did he repay the entire four hundred *ecus*, but they became and have remained friends ever since.

The third concerned a wealthy, avaricious man. He owed a poor working man one hundred *ecus*, but had failed to make any payment for such a long time that all hope of his ever doing so had been given up. Nevertheless, God so moved him that on his own, not pressed by anyone, he imitated Zacchaeus. He repaid three or four times what he owed and, even more, gave the poor man a house and part of a vineyard to enable him and his small family to live well.

Lastly, the fourth case was of a father who had a mortal hatred against a man who had attempted to kill his son and, though the attempt had failed, he had wounded him, leaving one of his arms useless. The father had spent a large sum in hopes of restoring its function. Despite his resentment, he did two things worthy of a true Christian: he pardoned from his heart the man who had attempted to kill his son, and he gave up all claim to the money he had already spent to heal the injury. Before the mission, several persons had failed to reconcile these two gentlemen.

These are but some of the fruits of this mission, whose effects we can truly say came from the all-powerful hand of God. The priest on the mission were themselves incapable of effecting the marvels reported here. This makes us say as was said of Moses when he worked his marvels in the presence of Pharaoh: *Digitus Dei est hic* ["The finger of God is here"].[98] The hand of God works these marvels, and not human eloquence, learning, or power. Perhaps for this reason divine Providence did not allow our great prelate and eminent cardinal to attend our mission as we had hoped, for a wheel of his carriage fell off while on the way here. If he had given us the honor of his presence we might have attributed the marvels which occurred to his presence and his authority rather than to God alone, to whom the glory is due.[99]

This same priest recounted the success of another mission given the following January.

In the mission we gave at Breda we noticed the faithfulness of the people in attending our sermons and catechism lessons. Their attitude was so good that everything they heard made a strong impression upon them. We noticed, after the instructions, that they continued to urge one another to practice the virtues we had recommended. The whole morning of the general communion passed in

---

98. Exod 8:15.
99. *CED* V:481-84.

reconciliations and in their embracing one another. This showed the power of God's grace, for the most eminent men and women of the parish, disdaining all human respect, humbled themselves before everyone and asked pardon of all they might have offended.

When it came to the sermon immediately before communion, hearts were so moved that several persons fainted away. The preacher was obliged to interrupt his sermon twice, and stop talking altogether, to arrest the tears and sobs of these good people. After the sermon, a priest of the region came to the altar to prostrate himself. He asked pardon first of God and then of the people for the scandalous life he had led. The congregation was so touched at this example that they raised aloud the cry, "Mercy!"

The devil envied the success of the mission, and attempted to disrupt the good order and the good dispositions of the people in the procession held after vespers. This had to do with the question of precedence among several of the Confraternities of Penance established in the parish. God in his goodness prevented any disunity by reminding someone that the preacher had said that the penitents clothed in white were to have the preferred places. The great respect they had for his word made them give way without more discussion. When this was settled, the procession took place with much piety to the edification of everyone.

I also should not omit one more thing: after urging the people to buy a silver cross for the church, each one wanted to share in the purchase to such a degree that a hundred *ecus* were collected, more than enough for the project.[100]

As to the see of Palestrina, the report made of the missions given there in 1657 states that the first mission was given in a large town of twelve hundred souls. The town, filled with enmities, had a violent, even bloody, reputation, with frequent homicides committed there. In the previous three years there had been seventy. The people, though cruel and given to passion, responded to the word of God and faithfully attended the exercises of the mission, which lasted a full month. Almost everyone made a general confession and were reconciled to God and to their sworn enemies. Some had lived ten or fifteen years without speaking to their enemies, but now began to do so. A widow there, whose husband had been slain, had refused to forgive his murderers despite the request of Cardinal Colonna, lord of the region.[101] She was so moved by one of the sermons that she called the pastor and a notary to announce joyfully her forgiveness to all.

---

100. *CED* V:528-29.
101. Girolamo Colonna, 1603-1666.

Another widow, who showed herself equally unforgiving toward a man who had killed her husband, was also moved to reconciliation on this same occasion. Afterward, she remarked that she had never in all her life experienced such consolation. When some of her relatives remonstrated with her that such prompt and complete forgiveness reflected a meager love for her departed husband, she replied that only by such forgiveness could her own soul be saved. She added that if it had to be done all over again, she would most willingly do so.

A young man who had lost his arm in an attack wanted to have nothing more to do with his assailant. Leaving a sermon one day, he met the man on the public square, threw himself on his knees before him, and embraced him with such affection and cordiality that his example and words served to motivate several others to forgive the injuries they had received.

The most important of all the reconciliations brought about during this mission which reflected most perfectly the grace of God was that between two of the chief families of the town. Members of the one family had killed a member of the other and seriously wounded his brother. This led the surviving brothers to swear to exterminate the family of the murderers. For three years, this feud had resulted in the slaying of ten innocent victims. It was most difficult to bring about this hoped-for reconciliation, for the offenses were recent and those who planned their revenge ranged the countryside during the day to avoid the authorities, returning home only during the night. It was difficult even to speak with them and they were so determined that there seemed no way their hearts could be swayed. One of them even used to say that he would never rest until he had killed everyone of the other family.

Despite all these difficulties, and after several attempts, it pleased God in his goodness to allow this effort to succeed. The preacher of the mission managed to meet these desperate men in a secluded place, and to speak to them for a short while. He begged them in the name of our Lord Jesus Christ, embraced them cordially, and urged them to pardon and restore peace. Suddenly, the leader among them, touched by these entreaties, lifted his cap and raised his tearful eyes to heaven, to say, 'I promise God and your reverence to make peace, and I shall do so.' Having said this, he withdrew to allow his tears greater freedom to fall. After this, the reconciliation was to be finished the next day, but unfortunately such new difficulties arose that it seemed impossible to resolve them. Someone suggested that they invoke the most holy Virgin, and thanks to her powerful intercession all obstacles were overcome. This peace was received with such blessings that most of the residents came to the church to celebrate. They all wept for joy and blessed God at the sight of the two families embracing each other with much affection. An old man remarked to a younger man of the other family whom he had recently hated so fiercely, 'From now on, I will take you for my son.' The other replied, 'And I, I will take you for my father.'

It would take too long to recount all the accomplishments and reconciliations of this mission. Family feuds were almost universal in the region, for an offense of anyone against another was taken as an insult against the entire family. The enmity of one single person for another extended to the relatives of the other, so that they no longer talked or extended greetings. By the mercy of God, at the end of this mission not a single person remained at enmity with others. Each one had been truly and sincerely reconciled to everyone else.

Another group of Missionaries went to work in the parishes dependent upon the abbey of Subiaco. There they conducted four missions upon which God showered many blessings, mainly by effecting reconciliations, breaking up immoral liaisons, and tending to several public scandals. To avoid repetitions, we will report here only what occurred in one of the parishes. Three women there, public sinners, asked pardon in church before all the people for the scandal they had given in the past. Everyone resolved to avoid the unhappy sin of blasphemy, much in vogue in the area. Several parishioners agreed among themselves that if one of them should swear while gambling he would automatically lose their turn. Others agreed if they swore they would be fined a certain amount, which would later be given to the poor. Others took the resolution to give up gambling completely, a better and surer course.

Feast days caused problems for the people, for they seemed not to know what to do with themselves. They accepted willingly and gratefully the suggestion given by the missionaries to buy a psalter and antiphonary to use in singing vespers in the church on Sundays and feasts. They also recommended several books, such as the lives of the saints, the works of Granada, and other similar ones, so that on these days they could come together in the church for an hour of spiritual reading.

Another report sent by the superior of the priests of the Mission at Rome spoke of the missions given in some places that he did not specify. It mentioned that God blessed them with his usual blessings: scandals ceased, concubines sent off, public sinners converted, and frequent occasions of sin in the region removed. So many differences were settled, both in civil and criminal cases, that on a single one of the missions a notary was kept busy for a whole week drawing up the settlements. Certain other usurious contracts were abrogated, as were some alienations of Church property which had been unjustly arranged. Not only were vices and disorders rectified, but a love for virtue was planted in receptive hearts, and all sorts of good works began, especially those in favor of the poor, of which we will give a few examples.

At the end of one of the missions, a physician, moved by charity, offered to take nothing for his services for three years, provided that the measure of grain which each house of the town was obliged to give him each year would instead be put in a common store to benefit the poor. The townspeople willingly agreed to this proposal.

In the same town, one of the officials saw that the children were poorly instructed for want of a good teacher. He offered to pay the salary of an instructor by contributing a good part of his own wages.

The local council of this same town elected two people to serve as Protectors of the Poor. Their job was to see that the poor tenants were not unjustly charged by their landlords for supposed damages. Also, a storehouse for furniture was set up to protect the property of those put in prison, for otherwise it was almost always lost.

This has been a short sketch of the excellent results of the missions which Monsieur Vincent established from Rome through the ministry of the priests of the Congregation. We have spoken of events in seven or eight of these. Yet, more than two hundred were given during the first twenty-two years that the missionaries worked in this capital city of all Christendom. We have judged the few we have spoken of to show sufficiently the abundant grace God was pleased to shower upon the enterprises of his faithful servant, and upon those whom God called to labor under his direction. We will end this chapter by citing a letter written to Monsieur Vincent by Cardinal Spada from Rome in 1651.[102]

> The institute of the Congregation of the Mission, of which you are the founder and superior, each day merits more and more esteemed reputation in this locality. I have seen its extraordinary effects among the people in my city, and in the whole diocese of Albano. Your good priests have worked for them with such care, charity, selflessness, and prudence, that all have been most edified. It remains for me to thank you, which I do. I assure you that I have a special regard for your community. I shall not fail to proclaim the merits and benefits of this holy institute on any occasion that shall present itself.[103]

---

102. Bernardino Spada, nuncio to France, 1623-1627, made a cardinal in 1626, bishop of Albano, 1646-1652. He died in Rome, November 10, 1661.
103. *CED* IV:170-71.

SECTION FOUR

Missions Given in the State of Genoa

We know of no better way to introduce the topic of the missions in Genoa than to cite the letter written by the worthy archbishop of Genoa, Cardinal Durazzo, to Monsieur Vincent, in August 1645:[104]

> This past month, Monsieur N. [Bernard Codoing] passed through here. I learned he was a member of the Congregation of the Mission. I prevailed upon him to exercise his ministry in several parts of my diocese. He did so with much success and blessings for the service of God, the salvation of souls, and to my personal satisfaction. When he told me he was obliged to return to Paris by orders of his superior, I agreed, since you have sent other priests to continue the work he so happily began.[105] We hope to establish a similar institute here, for the greater glory of his divine majesty. I wanted you to know how encouraged we have been in this regard.[106]

To appreciate the effects of grace on these missions, we will cite several of the letters written by the missionaries sent by Monsieur Vincent.

A priest of the Mission of Genoa wrote to his superior to tell him what had happened on the mission:

> God blessed our mission, particularly the last one at a place called Chiavari, for besides the reconciliations of many individuals, three entire parishes which previously had been divided against each other came together in peace.

The superior of the Mission of Genoa reported the success of another mission he did not name, in a letter to Monsieur Vincent in July 1646.

> We had up to eighteen confessors, and more than three thousand general confessions, and a large number of reconciliations of major importance. These ended animosities which had caused twenty-four or twenty-five murders. Most of those involved, having obtained in writing the pardon of those offended, were able to secure a favorable verdict from the prince and have since returned to full favor in the town.[107]

---

104. Stefano Durazzo belonged to an illustrious Venetian family which had provided many doges to Venice and prelates to the Church. He was closely associated with the work of the missionaries, and followed their rule in his own personal life. He was a holy and energetic bishop for whom Vincent had a profound veneration. He died in 1667.
105. Four priests and a brother. Etienne Blatiron was superior of this mission.
106. *CED* II:544.
107. *CED* II:609.

The same superior, in another letter to Monsieur Vincent written around the same time, mentions a detail which deserves attention:

> When I last wrote about our mission, I forgot to tell you what we do to instruct the people and help the confessors. We have two young priests who, other than during the catechism time, go over the principal mysteries of religion for those who wish to go to confession. When they are sufficiently instructed, they are given a note which they present to their confessor. This paper assures him that the penitent knows enough necessary Christian doctrine, and thus does not have to be questioned. This allows the confessors to move more quickly, so those waiting to go to confession do not have to wait so long.[108]

In a letter dated May 6, 1647, this same superior wrote again.

> We have just returned from the mission at N., involving five parishes besides the rest of the area. We were able to bring about a large number of conversions and general confessions despite the obstinacy of the people. They are so hard to influence that we almost lost courage at the beginning of the mission. But our Lord consoled us at the end by letting us see hardened hearts moved, and poured his grace upon these people to such an extent that those who did not even want to listen to us came around to not wanting to see us go. On the day of our leaving, we went to the church to receive the pastor's blessing. All the people gathered, weeping and pleading, as though in leaving we were taking away their very lives. We had great difficulty in getting away.
>
> Many of the nobility came here from Genoa to attend the mission, at which they were most edified. The archbishop of Genoa came to give the sacrament of confirmation. Afterward, at a reception for him and some gentlemen who had accompanied him, he presented a gift from a noble of the region, but this was declined when he learned that the missionaries never take anything for their services.[109]

In a letter of December 16, 1647, this same superior wrote of another mission in which seven brigands had been converted. Also, a Turkish servant of one of the gentlemen of the region had asked for baptism. This was granted only after he was well instructed and had his faith carefully examined.[110]

In a later mission several other brigands likewise were converted after being pardoned by the relatives of those they had killed. Several of these bandits threw themselves at the feet of those they had harmed, only to be accepted with

---

108. *CED* II:609-10.
109. *CED* III:186-87.
110. *CED* III:257.

great charity and emotion from both parties. This mission took place in the town of Sestri. After they had attended the mission with such care and diligence, the people did not want to see them leave. Hearing they were about to depart, they surrounded their house in a sort of siege for two or three days, forcing these good missionaries to slip away under cover of darkness.

By a letter of December 10, 1648, he reported on a mission in Lavagna at which several brigands were converted, being restored to grace and forgiveness.[111]

In another mission given in January 1650, although the people were very poor, they willingly accepted the suggestion of establishing a Confraternity of Charity for the sick poor in their parish. They made such sacrifices to contribute to this enterprise that five hundred *livres* in cash was collected, not to mention seven hundred additional *livres* in pledges.

Another confraternity or company for men was set up, called the Company for Christian Doctrine. Its aim was to teach the Our Father and Hail Mary and the principal mysteries of the faith to those needing this instruction. Another task was to round up children to attend the catechism lessons given in the town.

On a trip from Paris to Italy in December 1650, one of the older priests of the Congregation stopped at a mission being given at Castiglione. He wrote to Monsieur Vincent about his experiences.

> I have seen the exercises of the mission given in this parish, and in eight or nine others in the vicinity. The people are careful to attend the sermon and catechism lessons, and keep the confessors busy. I must say the people here are in no way inferior to those of other regions, and even surpass them in some respects. Two persons living in adultery publicly admitted their sin in church during the sermon, in the presence of a large congregation. Several usurers agreed in writing before notaries to restore what they had unjustly exacted from some poor people who had borrowed money from them. The Confraternity of Charity has been set up in this parish and the others mentioned above. The superior of the mission gives a conference each Monday to ten or twelve of the local pastors. I attended one of these, and all went well, giving hope that much benefit will come to these priests and to their people.[112]

In a letter which the superior of the Mission at Genoa wrote to Monsieur Vincent on February 6, 1659, he said:

> We have just finished two small missions which God has blessed, especially the last. The parish has but two hundred forty

---

111. *CED* III:393.
112. *CED* IV:117-18.

members in a remote location, and nevertheless at the general communion there were more than seven hundred here, who had come from all the surrounding area.

Among the reconciliations effected here, a notable one concerned a father whose eldest son had been killed accidentally in his sleep just a short time before. Several important people of the area tried to persuade the father to forgive the murderers, and the day before he had refused me when I had made this same request to him. In fact, he asked me never to speak of it to him again. But God by his grace did what man could not do by his recriminations and exhortations. The following day I took the chance of again urging him, with prayers and tears, to bestow his pardon and peace on these murderers, for the love of our Lord. All at once he changed and granted what I asked, with such Christian sentiments it drew tears from all those present.[113]

In another mission in the same year, a man was reconciled whose seventy-year-old father had been murdered. During the mission he could not overcome the violent feelings of revenge he felt, to forgive the one responsible for the murder. After the mission and the departure of the priests, however, the seed of the word of God sown in his heart during the sermons and exhortations took effect, and finally produced their fruit. Although this came a little late, it was soon enough to show the magnitude of God's mercy toward him.

SECTION FIVE

The Missions Given on the Island of Corsica

This island lies in the Mediterranean, as a dependency of the republic of Genoa.[114] In 1652 Monsieur Vincent was asked for some priests of his Congregation to give missions in the area. Seven priests were sent to work in various places on the island, aided by four other ecclesiastics, and by four religious supplied by Cardinal Durazzo, archbishop of Genoa.[115]

The first mission was given at Campo Lauro, the usual residence of the

---

113. *CED* VII:450-51.
114. It belonged to France after 1768.
115. Etienne Blatiron was superior.

bishop of Aleria. At the time, however, the see was vacant. Two vicars general were governing it, one named by the Congregation *De propaganda fide*, and the other elected by the cathedral chapter. These two vicars had difficulty getting along, and often found themselves on opposite sides of every question, so much so that what one did the other undid. For example, when the one would pronounce a sentence of excommunication, the other would absolve from the censure. This resulted in the clergy and people being in a most troubled and divided state, and caused many disorders throughout the country.

The second mission was given in a place called Il Cotone, the third at Corte, in the center of the island, and the fourth and last at Niolo.

To understand fully the outcome of these missions, we must realize that lack of instruction was widespread among the people. It caused the vices of impiety, concubinage, incest, stealing, lying, and above all else revenge, which was almost universal. They often treated one another barbarically, never pardoning or even wanting to discuss reaching an accord, until they had satisfied their thirst for vengeance. Not only did they treat the one who had done them the injury in this fashion, but also their entire family, down to the third degree of kinship. It was therefore necessary that everyone remain on guard since, because of something that one of their relatives had done, they would automatically be considered as accomplices. This happened even though they themselves were innocent and even unaware of their relative's act. As a result, everyone went about armed. At the least word their honor was threatened and would have to be avenged by a killing. As a consequence, although this kingdom of Corsica is a beautiful and fertile land, it is sparsely settled.

By the grace of God, the missions were quite successful. This came about, first, by the conferences and spiritual exercises which the Missionaries gave each day in the church to the canons, pastors, and other priests after the other people had been dismissed. The superior of the Mission presented a series of exhortations on the obligations and duties of priests, and suggested subjects for meditation. He prepared them for making their general confessions, and by this means rectified several past scandals. Good resolutions were taken to fulfill their obligations toward God and their neighbor. Some among the clergy were so moved with regret for past failings they publicly asked pardon for the bad example they had given. There were several pastors who thus publicly confessed their faults, as did an entire chapter through the voice of one of the canons, speaking in the name of all.

The missions were successful in resolving many conflicts and effecting many reconciliations. One person pardoned the death of his brother, another of his father, his child, his wife, a parent, etc. Others forgave those who had falsely accused them, or testified falsely against them in lawsuits, overlooking all that might be due their honor or their interest. They embraced their former enemies cordially, those who shortly before sought to take away their honor or even their very lives. What is even more remarkable, these important reconciliations were numbered not by twos or threes, but by fifties and hundreds everywhere.

A third area of blessings was the cessation and correction of many concubinages, a frequent occurrence on the island, and the large number of loose women who publicly asked pardon for their disorderly conduct. Their repentance moved many others. Remorseful at giving such scandal by their sins, they rose from their places in the crowd and cried aloud to God for his mercy and pardon from the people. Their words were accompanied by such signs of true repentance for their sins that it moved the entire assembly to tears.

Lastly, the establishment of the Confraternity of Charity not only provided help for the sick poor, but gave an outlet for other good works for members of the Confraternity. All these added to the edification of their families and to others who witnessed their good example.

To appreciate better the extent and importance of the outcome of these missions, on which God poured out grace abundantly on Monsieur Vincent, we will give here a somewhat lengthier account of the last of these missions. It follows the report sent by the superior of the Mission to Monsieur Vincent.

> Niolo is a valley about three leagues long, by a half league wide, surrounded by mountains, with access and roads as limited as any place I have seen elsewhere, even including the Pyrenees or those in Savoy. This results in the region being infested with bandits and riffraff of the island, who commit their robberies and murders with no fear of the hand of the law. There are several small villages in the valley, and about two thousand inhabitants, all told, in the surrounding regions. In all Christendom I do not know of any people more neglected. There are hardly any vestiges of the faith, except some few who say they were baptized. There are a few churches, but these are in bad repair. They are in such ignorance of matters concerning their own salvation that only with great difficulty could you find a hundred persons who would know the commandments of God or the Apostles' Creed. To ask them if there is one God or many, or which of the three Persons became man for us, is to speak Arabic to them.
>
> Revenge is the vice which passes here for virtue. Children learn it before they learn to walk or talk. For the least offense, vengeance is the proper response, and no one will tell them anything else. This is the traditional lesson learned from their own parents, and this vice

has taken such roots in their hearts they are not able to conceive anything to the contrary.

There are some here who have not been to mass in seven or eight months. They have gone three, four, eight, or ten years without going to confession. There are some young people of fifteen or sixteen who have never confessed, and with that, some vices are prevalent among these poor people. They are given to stealing, and have no scruple about eating meat during Lent or other forbidden times.

They treat one another like barbarians. If there is question of an enemy, they do not hesitate to accuse him falsely before the courts of great crimes, with as many false witnesses as you care to see. On the other hand, the one accused, whether guilty or not, produces as many "witnesses" as he needs to support his innocence. Thus it comes about that justice is a commodity no one expects. It is left up to each to defend himself, which they do, often killing one another in the process.

Besides this, another source of difficulty concerns the sacrament of marriage. They seldom receive it unless the parties have previously lived together. Ordinarily, when the couple are engaged, the girl moves in with the future husband, and remains in this state of concubinage for two or three months, and sometimes two or three years, before getting around to marriage. Even worse, many of these marriages take place between close relatives, with no thought of dispensation from the impediment of consanguinity. They continue to live in this state eight or ten years or even fifteen years or more. If they have children, and the husband dies, they are abandoned as bastards, with the woman marrying another, often enough one of her own relatives. We have seen cases of a woman with three husbands with whom she has lived in concubinage and incest. Sometimes, after living together for a while, some come to lose their mutual affection, even when children are involved, and leave each other to seek new partners.

There is another great abuse here, in that most parents cause their children to be married long before the proper age. Some are married at age four or five, and there is even a case of a one-year-old girl being married to another child, five years old. Another disorder comes from this, that these children often have no affection for one another, cannot get along together, and not only get a divorce, but often develop hatreds. This leads to attacks and even murders against the other party.

In this single valley we discovered one hundred and twenty

concubinages, of which about ninety were incestuous as well. Among these were about forty who had been denounced and excommunicated because of it, but this did not prevent their neighbors from dealing and conversing with them as freely as if the Church had not censured them. Most of the people of the region had become involved in this, one way or the other, either by the original excommunication or by incurring this same punishment themselves for continuing to associate with those who had been denounced.

This is the deplorable state in which these poor people lived when the priests were sent here to give the missions. Here is how we began to bring some remedy to these disorders:

In the first place, we used all our energy to instruct the people in what was required for their own salvation. This took us about three weeks.

(2) We then separated the concubines, at least those we knew about and who lived in the area. Then on the feast of Saints Peter and Paul, patrons of the local church, all the concubines, convinced of the evil state in which they were living and moved by a true spirit of penance, fell on their knees at the close of our sermon. They publicly asked pardon for their scandal, and promised on oath to separate. Those who had really left each other's company approached the tribunal of the confessional.

(3) The excommunicated who showed signs of a truly humble and contrite heart were gathered together at the door of the church to be absolved from their sentence. They were told the seriousness of the offense, and were obliged, one after the other, by a public oath, to promise to remain separated, and never to enter the house of the other party for any cause or reason whatsoever. Then they were absolved. They were then received in confession, and later given communion. Even some priests in the region had contributed to these disorders by their own bad example, and had committed incest with nieces or close relatives. It pleased the mercy of God to touch their hearts, too, either by the charitable warnings made to them, or by the spiritual conferences which they had attended. All these made their general confession with all signs of true repentance, adding thereto public reparation for the scandal they had given.

The most difficult part of our work was our efforts for effecting reconciliations, and I could rightly say *hoc opus, hic labor*, ["this is the task, this is the toil"][116] because the greater part of the people

---

116. Virgil, Aeneid, 6,129.

lived in enmity. We were fifteen days with no signs of progress, except for a young man who forgave an assailant who had shot him in the head. All the others remained adamant, unmoved by all we could say. Even so, this did not prevent a crowd of people at our sermons, given both in the morning and evening.

The men come to the sermons fully armed, a sword at their side and a firearm at their shoulder, their customary attire. The bandits and criminals, besides these arms, had in addition two pistols and several daggers in their belt. These people were so occupied with thoughts of hatred and vengeance there was nothing we could say to cure them of this strange disease, or to make any impression upon their troubled minds. When we spoke of the forgiveness of enemies, several left the sermon. We all were perplexed about how to proceed, especially myself more than the others, since I was chiefly responsible for resolving these difficulties.

Lastly, the eve of the day for general communion, as I finished my sermon, I once more exhorted the people to pardon one another. God inspired me to take my crucifix, and invite anyone who wished to pardon his enemies to come and kiss it. I spoke of our Lord holding out his arms to them, saying that those who would come and kiss the crucifix would give a sign that they were willing to pardon and were prepared to be reconciled to their enemies. At these words they began to look at one another, but no one stirred from his place. As I prepared to leave, I covered up the crucifix, conscious of their hard hearts. I told the congregation they were not worthy to receive the grace and blessings our Lord was offering them.

At this, a Franciscan stood up, and began to shout: "O Niolo! O Niolo! Do you wish to be cursed by God? Do you not want to receive the grace he is sending you through these missionaries, who have come from so far away for your salvation?" While this good religious was speaking these words, a local pastor whose nephew had been killed, with the murderer in the church listening to the sermon, came forward and asked to kiss the crucifix. At the same time he said in a loud voice, "Let him, the murderer, come forward, and I shall embrace him." After this, another priest did the same in regard to his enemies who were also present, and many others followed. For an hour and a half the church witnessed a whole series of reconciliations and embraces. As a precaution, the major settlements were put in writing for the town notary to legalize.

The next day was the general communion day. We arranged a day of general reconciliation, in which the people asked pardon of

God and then of their pastors, and in turn the pastors asked the same of the congregation. All this happened with much edification. I then asked if anyone at all still was not reconciled with his enemies. At once one of the pastors called out several by name. They came before the exposed blessed sacrament, and with no hesitation offered their hand to their former enemies. O Lord, what happiness on earth and what joy in heaven to see fathers and mothers pardoning out of the love of God those who had killed their son or daughter, women whose husbands had been slain, children their parents, brothers and close relatives their own family members, in a word, all reconciled to one another. In some other countries it is not unusual to see penitents weep at the feet of their confessors, but it is a small miracle to see this in Corsica.

The day following the general communion we received instructions to go to Bastia, where a galley sent by the senate of Genoa awaited us. However, we still delayed two days, which we used profitably in tying up some loose ends. On Tuesday we gave a sermon on perseverance, at which so many people attended we had to hold the service outside the church. Promises and resolutions were repeated, together with commitments to lead truly Christian lives and to persevere until death. The pastors promised to be faithful to teaching catechism, and to carrying out their other duties as well.

The rain that began at the end of the sermon prevented our leaving that day. In the evening I went to a remote place to speak to two people who had not attended the mission for fear of being moved to forgive their enemies, who had murdered their brother. The pastor had persuaded them to agree not to retaliate for this killing, at least until after they had spoken with us. They agreed to this, and by the grace of God their hearts were moved to pardon the murderers. On Wednesday morning we heard their confessions and gave them communion, and then we left together with several priests and other leading citizens. As a sign of their happiness and as a token of thanks to us for the little services we had rendered, they fired their guns and pistols as a salute as we were boarding the galley for Genoa.[117]

---

117. *CED* IV:411-16.

SECTION SIX

The Missions Given in Piedmont

A mission was given in April 1656, in a large town called Scalenghe, near Pinerolo. The superior of the Mission of Turin described it to Monsieur Vincent:[118]

> Four or five thousand people attended. What edified me the most is the universal affection displayed for the word of God. Ordinarily fifty or so priests would help us at all the exercises of the mission. All the nobility of the region have taken part with extraordinary devotion. The common people showed such eagerness during the whole mission, which lasted about six weeks, that there is no doubt they wanted to profit from it. A number brought little with them, but remained eight whole days and nights in the church or nearby, to assure their having an opportunity to go to confession. All this shows the good disposition of these people, and the great good to be expected, even though we are so few, so poor, and so wretched, since God's goodness uses us to effect so much good. I say poor and wretched for I never cease to marvel how these good people put up with me, seeing I am more capable of repelling than attracting them. God alone works purely by his goodness, and would do even more if I did not put obstacles in the way by my lack of learning, my lack of spirit, and my other deficiencies.[119]

In another letter, of June 24 following, he said:

> We have just finished a mission near Luserna, where there were eight or nine thousand people at the general communion. We had to preach in the open air, in the public square. An accident occurred there which shows the effect of the word of God and the power of his grace. One of the guards, armed like most people of the region with three or four pistols and several daggers besides his sword,

---

118. Jean Martin was superior of the house at Turin from 1655 to 1665. He was born in Paris in 1620. He was received into the Congregation in 1638 and was sent with another student to take part in the celebrated mission given to the court at Saint Germain en Laye at the request of Louis XIII. His catechetical teaching so impressed the queen that she asked him to teach catechism to the dauphin, the future Louis XIV, who was still an infant. In 1642 he went to Rome to work on the missions there. He came to speak Italian fluently. In 1645, Vincent sent him to Genoa, where he worked for several years. He accompanied Cardinal Durazzo on his pastoral visitations. In 1652 he was one of the seven missionaries sent to Corsica. In 1655 he was named superior of the Turin house. He died February 17, 1694 in Rome, where he was also superior.

119. *CED* V:586.

was listening attentively to the sermon while leaning against a wall. A stone, dislodged from the wall, fell on his head, and caused a deep gash and much blood. The only words out of his mouth were, "O just God, what a time for this to happen!" To those who expressed surprise at his patience he remarked that his sins deserved this and more. Then, with his head bandaged, he returned for the rest of the sermon as though nothing had happened. This is extraordinary for someone of this region, for the people are lively, quick to anger, and much inclined to violence.

At the end of our mission here, they earnestly requested us to go to a nearby town about a league and a half from here. It had been deeply divided for the past ten or twelve years, and had experienced the murders of more than thirty people during that time. The town had become an armed camp, one faction against the other, so that they were in danger of exterminating each other. I feared our visit there would not be successful, for we had no possibility of giving a complete mission. We were so strongly urged to go we felt we must, leaving the outcome completely in the hands of divine Providence.

We stayed two days in the town. During that time it pleased God so to move hearts that after our sermons, and particularly on the feast of Corpus Christi before the blessed sacrament exposed, a general reconciliation of great solemnity took place. The leading parties on either side came to the altar, and on the Gospels swore they pardoned their adversaries. As a sign of this conversion they offered the greeting of peace before all the people, and signed a formal peace treaty drawn up by the public notary. Afterward, we sang the Te Deum in thanksgiving. All this greatly consoled the people, who for many years had seen the murders and blood of so many of their relatives in this undeclared war.[120]

In another letter, of February 3, 1657, this same priest wrote of the success of an important mission:

By the mercy of God we have completed the mission of Racconigi. It pleased his goodness to allow us to finish six weeks of continuous effort there, despite our being completely worn out by another mission immediately before. We would never have dared undertake the second of these missions in the most populated part of Piedmont were it not that the archbishop of Turin had requested it at the earnest solicitation of his clergy and people. Even though we were helped by four good priests of the city and by several religious who worked with us, we could not totally respond to the

---

120. *CED* V:641-42.

devotion of these people whose demands left us not a moment of rest. The press of people at the sermons and catechism lessons continued, and their desire for confession was so great that they came at midnight to awaken us for this service. Some remained in church several days and nights even in this severe time of winter to have an opportunity to go to confession. The good effects and the fruits of the mission correspond, by the grace of God, to their good dispositions, as we may judge from their good resolutions and reconciliations they made. The clergy themselves, consisting of around forty priests and clerics, gave the example to the people. We gave a special conference to them every week, a practice they decided to continue for themselves. We established a Confraternity of Charity for the sick poor. Those who joined have already begun to carry out their ministry with great devotion.[121]

In June of the same year, while on the mission at Savigliano, he wrote:

We are now busy on this mission, which is one of the most difficult we have yet experienced in this country. God has given it his special blessing, despite the poverty and fewness of its preachers. We are charged with a large region where the inhabitants are taken up with penance and conversion. What is even more astounding to me is that the religious of five or six monasteries come to the sermons, and all the priests have made their general confessions. The many nobility think of nothing else but acquiring a true spirit of penance. We have been obliged to ask the religious of the locality to help us in the confessional. We even had to call on those from Turin to help out.

The Providence of God has brought us here when the soldiers, quartered here for the winter, are returning to the army. We have had the opportunity before their leaving, particularly for several captains and French soldiers, to have them at our sermons and catechism lessons for an entire week. A number made their general confession with great devotion, seeing they are off to the dangers of the war. I must say I cannot remember ever having received such consolation in my life as I have had in seeing men of their profession, away from the sacraments for years, dissolve in tears at the feet of their confessor, and take truly Christian resolutions for their lives. For soldiers, they are extraordinary. This is surely the effect of the mercy of God, whom I pray you to have the goodness to join us in thanking.[122]

At the conclusion of this mission, this same priest wrote:

---

121. *CED* VI:174.
122. *CED* VI:312-13.

I told you earlier how at the beginning of our mission God had moved the hearts of many soldiers. Since then we have continued our sermons, catechism lessons, and other usual exercises at which we have had such a great crowd the church could barely hold them all, even though it is so large. This was true even during times which custom dictated were to be given over to domestic chores. By order of the authorities the stores closed at the hour of the sermons and the longer catechism instructions. On market days, all trading was suspended during these same hours to give everyone an opportunity to hear the word of God. Both religious and priests attended the mission in large numbers, and most of them have made their general confession, even though they had to confess to one another. They have made restitutions and reconciliations as elsewhere. The conclusion of the mission was held on the public square before twelve thousand persons. Also, during the whole mission, we gave spiritual conferences to the clergy. About a hundred of them attended each session.

One of the priests, a very good ecclesiastic whom we had invited from Turin to help us, worked several days in the confessional. He then fell sick, and finally died, with extraordinarily pious sentiments. His refrain, in dying, was, "humility, humility, without humility I am lost." Hardly had he breathed his last when crowds of people came to offer their condolences, and to show their affection and thanks. They wanted to celebrate the funeral solemnly, with torches and candles. All the religious were there and the burial was among the most honorable ever held in this place.

When they saw what good we had been able to do for them, the people wanted to have the priests of our Congregation stay here permanently. For this purpose they made as generous a proposal as could be hoped for. When we excused ourselves because of our small numbers, the people proposed establishing a foundation to support four or five priests, and further, they sought the intervention of the marquis of Pianezza.[123] They argued their case so persuasively that on our return he strongly urged us to accept this foundation. We had to tell him, with all due respect, that we would not be able to do so.[124]

Toward the end of that same year a mission was given in Bra which God greatly blessed. We know no better way to convey this than by citing extracts

---

123. Philippe de Simiane, the prime minister of Piedmont, became a correspondent of Monsieur Vincent, and founded a community house in Turin where he lived in his retirement.
124. *CED* VI:395-96.

of three letters this same superior sent to Monsieur Vincent. They tell of conditions before the mission, and its effects produced through the grace of God.

In the first of these, dated October 27, 1657, he wrote:

> I believe it will be necessary to put off to another time the mission which the Madame Royale has asked us to give in Bra, a town which depends upon her, because of the divisions which exist there.[125] They have developed to such a degree that the streets are barricaded, and soldiers and other armed men fill the houses. They attack each other even in the church, and are so embittered they even attack others' homes to enter by force. Each one fortifies his home as though resisting a siege. It is worth their life to leave the house.
>
> It was hoped a sort of armistice could be worked out for the time of the mission, and that by the sermons, exhortations, and remonstrances, some relief could be brought to the tense situation, and even some reconciliations effected. The people were so severely divided that not even the leading ministers of the state, sent by the Madame Royale, could bring this about. It seemed to us that not only was it useless to have a mission in a place where no one could come to the services, but it would be dangerous for those few who would dare to attend. We have enough other places where we can give our services.[126]

Despite this, the superior wrote another letter from the same place on February 6, 1658:

> It has been a month since we began working in Bra, where it has pleased God to inspire the people to become reconciled with each other. This came about mainly by His Highness expressing his displeasure at their animosity, and then by the mission which sought to change their attitudes. Persons from both camps came to our sermons and other exercises of the mission in the same church, which at first seemed difficult to achieve, if not hazardous. As soon as the people gathered in church, they were persuaded to lay aside their arms, which they always carried with them everywhere. Their faithfulness to the sermons and catechism lessons, coupled with the good sentiments inspired in them by the grace of God, brought about their complete reunion. They even exchanged greetings of peace in the presence of the blessed sacrament, while mutually asking pardon. Some of the leading persons of the town were

---

125. Christine of France, sister of Louis XIII, duchess of Savoy. She governed Savoy during the minority of her son, Charles Emmanuel II.
126. *CED* VI:568.

publicly reconciled in the main square. They showed such happiness at this turn of events that it gives great hope this reunion of hearts will endure.

The people are consoled at seeing former enemies, who shortly before were seeking ways to kill each other, now walking and talking together as if there had never been trouble between them. Before, the streets were filled with armed men, but now we see none. All seem preoccupied in how best to be reconciled to the majesty of God by a worthy spirit of penance. When the Madame Royale heard the good news of these events, she deigned to write to us of her satisfaction. The marquis of Pianezza also wrote to tell us of his enormous consolation at the way things have turned out. We are busy now with confessions. Although we have asked all the priests and religious of the area to help us, the crowd of penitents is so great I do not know when we will finish.[127]

Lastly, in his third letter, dated March 9 of the same year, he wrote:

We have finished our mission at Bra where God showered his graces in great abundance upon the poor souls there, who for such a long time lived in the deplorable state I described in my earlier letters to you. We spent seven weeks there during the time when the carnival is usually celebrated, but for the inhabitants of Bra it was time for penance, a time of one continuous feastday, celebrated with great devotion. There were around nine or ten thousand general confessions with such evident fervor in the people that several spent the entire day and a good part of the night in the church, despite the cold of this time of the year, to be sure to have an opportunity to get to confession. It pleased God to diffuse peace and charity in their hearts so abundantly that the residents there were astonished to see such complete reconciliations. They cannot recall seeing such union and cordiality. They reported all this to the Madame Royale, to whom I went yesterday to report on all that had occurred, and on the hope I had for total perseverance among the people. She was so happy and consoled, and her heart so moved, I noticed tears in her eyes. To crown all this good news and to erase all memory of the unhappy past, she issued a general pardon for all wrongs of the past, and for all excesses committed during the time of contention.

As one act of mercy and favor usually draws down still another coming from God's goodness, it pleased him to extend the same blessings he had given the people of Bra to another nearby town. For the past forty years or so, discord and division had made such

---

127. *CED* VII:73-74.

a mark there that the place was nearly destroyed. Many persons of both parties had been killed, some houses destroyed or damaged, and many had to go elsewhere to live. The senate of Piedmont had several times sought to end the disputes, but without success, and all other efforts to heal the divisions had ended the same way.

Lastly, when the lord of the place, one of the leading men of Piedmont and a most wise and virtuous person, had considered the mission held at Bra at which some of his people had attended, he thought it proper to summon all parties to a meeting. He wanted to see if some way might not exist to bring peace to his town, as had been accomplished with their neighbors. For just three or four days we gave some of the sermons and exercises of our mission. It pleased God so to move hearts that in the presence of the blessed sacrament a large number of people of the region offered a gesture of peace to one another. They pardoned each other, and swore on the holy Gospels they would live in eternal peace. As a sign of this union, they invited one another to join in a meal, at which they showed such union and charity as befitted brothers. Her Highness had the goodness to grant the same grace and absolution as she had done for Bra, so all could return to their homes, and cultivate their lands in peace.[128]

On the following March 26, another mission was given in Cavallermaggiore, a village of four or five thousand inhabitants. Although there were not the same serious disorders as in the previous places the missions had been given, several disagreements and resulting lawsuits left us not a minute of peace. The divinely inspired confidence these people had in us led them to put all disputes, whether civil or criminal, into our hands for settlement. We have hopes of bringing them all to an end during Lent.[129]

In still another letter, dated July 6, he wrote:

We are leaving Fossano, a small but densely populated town, where we have just finished a mission. It pleased God to bestow many blessings on this work, in keeping with the needs we discovered there. The crowds at the exercises were so large that the church, large as it is, could not hold all the people who came to the sermons and other services. Not only were the lay people in attendance, but the clergy and religious were also present.

Besides the usual blessings of the missions, in which evil practices are ended and hatreds resolved, we were able to introduce

---

128. *CED* VII:100-02.
129. *CED* VII:113-14.

several practices for the future: (1) the evening prayers we began will be continued in the church of the fathers of the Oratory of Saint Philip Neri, which many people attend each evening; (2) the canons have agreed to hold a general communion every three months, to help preserve the present sentiments of piety in the people; (3) these same canons and all the clergy are to continue the spiritual conferences we began for ecclesiastics. We hope, with God's blessing, that these will be most helpful in re-establishing and preserving among them a true priestly spirit, to which several among them seem much inclined. This region now seems to be totally renewed in its Christian life, which we trust will be continued through the ongoing growth of the grace of God.[130]

In a letter of March 12, 1659, he spoke of several missions given near the city of Mondovi of which the main result was the cessation of many murders and homicides. In just one of these small places, forty bandits repented their crimes like the others. In the presence of the blessed sacrament they gave abundant signs of their conversion of heart immediately before receiving holy communion.[131]

Lastly, in a letter of July 12 of the same year, 1659, he wrote:

We have come back from our mission at Cherasco, which lasted a bit longer than the others because of the crowds which come from surrounding regions. To satisfy the people completely we would have needed twenty priests, and they would have been kept busy for two whole months or more. It pleased God to bestow as many blessings as anyone could hope for. Many quarrels and differences have been resolved. Among the blessings I must mention is a large neighboring village where the people were so divided one against the other that, on the eve of the very day we arrived, four people had been killed. Nevertheless, by God's mercy, peace has been reestablished. This did not take place without difficulty, however, for it took forty days of preaching and negotiations. At the end all worked out for the consolation of the people and with much edification, in the presence of the blessed sacrament which had been exposed expressly for this purpose. Most importantly, after their reconciliation these people came to confession with excellent disposition.[132]

These are the extracts of letters written to Monsieur Vincent. If we were to report in detail all the similar results of missions in Piedmont, bestowed

---
130. *CED* VII:198-99.
131. *CED* VII:468.
132. *CED* VIII:22-23.

by God's grace, we would need another whole book, and we would be forced to repeat ourselves many times. We have given enough to allow the readers to judge the rest for themselves, and to suggest a reason for thanking God for all the graces he gave these people. We should remark that in this service of his divine majesty, in the conversion of so many, in the reconciliations and other great and admirable works, we are speaking of only four priests of the Congregation of the Mission, for Monsieur Vincent could not send more for the missions in this country. God showed his power in that the instruments he used seemed so inadequate to the task before them. He pitted a group of men, small and weak in the eyes of hell, to oppose the prince of darkness and to vanquish him in the lives of so many where sin had long reigned, and to establish the empire of his Son, Jesus Christ, to whom alone forever be the praise and blessing.

SECTION SEVEN

The More Remarkable Events in the Missions of the Barbary States

Although the missions authorized by Monsieur Vincent in France, Italy, and surrounding areas were greatly blessed, as we have seen in the preceding sections, we must affirm that the ones given in more distant regions have also borne their fruit. These successes may not have been as great as the ones on European soil, but they were equally appreciated and valued. These strange and savage lands were made fertile by the labors, but even more so by the blood of the missionaries. Several of them gave their lives by their untiring labors in the service of Jesus Christ. It was one of the most ardent desires of the worthy father of the missionaries to go himself to preach Jesus Christ among the infidels, and to risk martyrdom in confessing his holy name.

Other obligations imposed on him by divine Providence, however, made this impossible. He was heard to say, "Ah, miserable man that I am. My sins have made me unworthy to preach the word of God to peoples who do not know him." Speaking to his confreres, he said, "How happy is the Missionary who has no limit in this world on where he can go to preach the Gospel. Why then do we hesitate and set limits, since God has given us the whole world to satisfy our zeal?"

He showed a special veneration for Saint Francis Xavier, who had carried the Gospel all the way to the Indies with such courage and blessings. He appreciated the religious of his order, and all others who worked on the foreign missions. When any of them returned and had occasion to visit Saint Lazare, he would assemble the entire household to hear of their work, with the hope of inspiring his own Missionaries to imitate their zeal. He would have their printed accounts read in the refectory, and did what he could to help their missions in foreign lands, as we shall see in the following pages.

He recognized, in keeping with the words of Jesus Christ in the Gospel, that the harvest of souls was great in foreign and barbarous lands, yet the workers were few. Thus he offered his confreres to Jesus Christ for the instruction of the poor and most abandoned, not only in Christian nations but also among the infidels and barbarians.

He inspired this same zeal and dispositions among the members of the Company. When someone would volunteer to go on the foreign missions he would rejoice with him because of the grace of the courage that God had bestowed upon him. Despite this, he never sent his men out haphazardly. His great maxim was never to push himself or his own ideas, but to wait simply and patiently for the manifestation of the will of divine Providence.

In beginning to speak of the missions given in foreign lands under the direction of Monsieur Vincent, among the infidels, heretics, or other enemies of our religion, we will begin in this section with those in the Barbary States. We will see how the missionaries worked and suffered to serve Jesus Christ in the persons of the poor Christian slaves. In later sections we will speak of the more remarkable events that took place in the other foreign missions.

PART ONE
The Beginning of the Missions in Tunis and Algiers, in the Barbary States

The experience of slavery that God allowed Monsieur Vincent to endure in 1605, as recounted in Book One,[133] gave him a first-hand opportunity to realize the evils which these slaves endured in their bodies and the danger they ran of losing their souls. These experiences engendered a great compassion in his heart. He saw in this slavery an image of the human misery which had led the Son of God to come to earth to ransom those enslaved to sin and Satan. In this he saw an opportunity to imitate the Savior, by visiting, consoling, and helping these poor abandoned captives. He was so inflamed with the love of God that he was anxious to help, but he remained steadfast in his usual practice of awaiting the orders of divine Providence before

---
133. Ch. 4.

embarking on this work. He prayed to know God's will, and for the grace and means to carry it out in a way most pleasing to him.

This prayer was not in vain, for around 1642, God inspired the late king, Louis XIII, of glorious memory, with the desire of helping these poor slaves.[134] His eyes fell upon Monsieur Vincent, whom he judged was most able to carry out this task. The king asked him to send some of his missionaries to Barbary for the corporal and spiritual relief of these poor captives. He supported this request with a sum of nine or ten thousand *livres*. God alone can say with what joy this charitable priest received this commission, since he had prayed for so long that something would be done for these poor afflicted slaves.

He gave some thought to the best way to carry out this complicated enterprise, for the Moslems were not anxious to have priests among them, unless they happened to be slaves themselves. He recalled that a treaty had been worked out between France and the sultan to develop commerce between the two regions. The king was to be permitted to send consuls to the seaport cities, to look after French commercial interests and the conditions of the Christian slaves. The consuls, in turn, were to be allowed to have a priest as chaplain in their homes. In 1645, this permitted Monsieur Martin, then consul in Tunis, to invite a priest of the Congregation of the Mission to this office. Father Julien Guerin and a brother named Francois Francillon were sent.[135]

After working zealously for two years, and seeing that the harvest was beyond his own unaided efforts, Monsieur Guerin resolved to see the dey, a sort of king in the country, to ask if another priest might be allowed to come to help him in his work. God touched the heart of the dey, for he replied that this would be agreeable, and that if one additional priest were insufficient, he might then invite two or three. He promised that he would serve as his protector, and would grant him anything he asked, for he appreciated his example of doing nothing but good for everyone he met.

In reply to this request for an additional priest Monsieur Vincent sent Jean

---

134. It has been estimated that there were 20,000 in Algeria and another 6000 in Tunis.
135. Julien Guerin was born in 1605 at Selles, in the diocese of Bayeux. He entered the Congregation of the Mission, January 30, 1640. In his youth he had been a soldier. This experience made him fearless. While he was stationed at Saintes, some travelers stopped him on his journey and pointing a pistol, asked him: "Who goes there?" Without any concern, he presented his crucifix and said, "It is he who goes there." The thieves, taken aback by his answer, allowed him to pass. When he learned that he would be going to Tunis, he was filled with joy as if he was going to a victory rather than to a place where he would be in imminent danger of death. Brother Francois Francillon, born at Ceaux in the diocese of Poitiers, entered the Congregation of the Mission at Paris in April 1645. After serving the slaves in Tunis for many years, he was martyred. When the fleet of Louis XIV was bombarding Algiers in 1688, Brother Francois refused to renounce his faith to save his life. On July 6, he was executed by being tied to the mouth of a cannon. The day before, Michel Montmasson, a priest of the Congregation and vicar apostolic at Algiers, met the same fate.

Le Vacher.[136] He arrived in Tunis in the beginning of 1648 at a most opportune time, for the plague had broken out, and it affected a large number of the Moslem natives and slaves alike. Both priests worked strenuously in this critical situation, but unfortunately Monsieur Le Vacher himself was stricken in May of the same year and was soon near death. It pleased God, however, to deliver him from the danger to enable him to give life to the many souls whom he served, and to continue to minister in that country.

Monsieur Guerin wrote to Monsieur Vincent about the plague:

> It is impossible to express the depth of the sufferings and tears of the poor slaves, merchants, and even the consul, and what consolation we received from everyone here. The Moslems themselves come to visit us in our distress, and the leading people of Tunis have offered their help and service. I am convinced, Monsieur, that we must serve God faithfully, for in this tribulation he even inspires our enemies to help his unworthy servants. We are scourged by war, the plague, and famine, and have no funds, but despite how severely we are tried our courage has not faltered. We treat the plague as though it did not exist. The joy that our brother and I experienced at the recovery of Monsieur Le Vacher has made us as strong as mountain lions.[137]

Soon after Monsieur Le Vacher recovered and returned to work, Monsieur Guerin, that man of God, himself fell victim to this dread disease. His zeal had made him disregard the dangers of death all around him, and forgetting himself, worked for the relief and salvation of those stricken by the plague. He was not taken by surprise, and prepared for death not simply with patient endurance but with an entire conformity to the good pleasure of God. He accepted death as the crown of his labors, and the beginning of the life of glory he hoped for from the mercy of God.[138] We cannot adequately describe the sorrow of the Christians for whom he had given his life, nor the sorrow of Monsieur Vincent who lost in this good missionary one of his dearest and most worthy sons. The consul died soon after, leading the dey to order Monsieur Le Vacher to fulfill the office of consul until the king of France should send another to take his place.

While thus occupied with the spiritual care of the five or six thousand slaves in Tunis, and sometimes with their temporal relief as well, as we shall see later, his attention turned to the needs of the slaves at Algiers, a much larger city. There were usually more than twenty thousand enslaved Christians there. They were very poorly treated by their masters in comparison with those of Tunis.

---

136. Jean Le Vacher was born at Ecouen, in the diocese of Paris, March 19, 1619. He was received into the Congregation, October 5, 1643.
137. *CED* III:300.
138. May 13, 1648.

It was impossible for the priests to do much unless they had the full cooperation of the consuls. If the consuls paid more attention to their own interests and convenience and failed to help in the salvation and relief of the poor captives, the goals of Monsieur Vincent could hardly be attained.

Aided by the duchess of Aiguillon, who indemnified the consul of Algiers, it was arranged that in 1646 he would be replaced by the king's appointment of Monsieur Jean Barreau.[139] A native of Paris, he was zealous for the service of God and of the poor slaves. He had no greater ambition than to cooperate with the designs of Monsieur Vincent, as he did during several years of service.

Before the consul left for his post, Monsieur Vincent gave him the following advice:

> At the heart of your activity must be the intention of promoting the greater glory of God. Remain in a constant state of interior humiliation at not being able to accomplish much in the circumstances in which you work. Practice submission to the judgment and will of the priest of the Mission given you as your counselor. Do nothing without informing him, unless obliged to answer some matter on the spot. Jesus Christ was the sovereign Lord, and yet during the time he lived with Mary and Joseph he did nothing without their advice. I would ask you to honor this mystery by acting accordingly, so that God will lead you and aid you in this position, to which his Providence has called you.[140]

Later Monsieur Vincent sent three good priests, veteran missionaries, to the city of Algiers, Messieurs [Boniface] Nouelly, [Jacques] Le Sage, and [Jean] Dieppe. All three gave their lives in courageously devoting themselves day and night to those stricken by the plague which gripped the city in 1647 and 1648. They served the poor Christian slaves who had fallen ill, who, had it not been for them, would have been abandoned like wild animals. These good priests showed at the approach of their own deaths the spirit which had dominated their lives, and the charity for their neighbor which animated them.

Monsieur Dieppe died with a crucifix in his hand, with his eyes fixed upon it, repeating during the half hour of his agony these words: *Majorem charitatem nemo habet, quam ut animam suam ponat quis pro amicis suis* ["There is no greater love than this: to lay down one's life for one's friends"].[141] These three priests were followed by Monsieur Philippe Le Vacher, the brother of Monsieur Le Vacher who was at Tunis. Like his

---

139. Jean Barreau was received into the Congregation, May 14, 1645. Vincent believed that Barreau would be more effective as consul in Algiers if he were not a priest. Barreau agreed to delay his ordination, and left for his new post in 1646.
140. *CED* III:42-43. Abelly's text differs in many respects from the original letter.
141. John 15:13.

brother, he served God for many years in the persons of the poor slaves in this city whose inhabitants, with the demons of hell, seemed to have no other preoccupation than to persecute the Christians.

Monsieur Le Vacher, at Tunis, continued to hold the office of consul, and this prevented him from the usual duties of the missionaries of Monsieur Vincent. It came about that a Monsieur Huguier, in charge of the temporalities at the Chatelet in Paris, was appointed to this post. He put himself under the direction of Monsieur Vincent, to give himself completely to the service of God and to the glory of his name. When he arrived in Tunis he proved unacceptable to the Moslems, who refused to allow him to serve as consul. He stayed for some time in the city, however, helping Monsieur Le Vacher in the position. He later returned to France, where he received holy orders, following the advice of Monsieur Vincent. He was sent later to Algiers, not only as a priest of the Congregation of the Mission, but as missionary apostolic. He worked earnestly for the poor slaves until the month of April of 1663, when he succumbed to the plague in very saintly dispositions of soul.

Monsieur Vincent was unhappy to see Monsieur Le Vacher in Tunis burdened with the office of consul. It prevented him from carrying out his ordinary missionary duties. Also, he did not like to see him hold a secular office, even though it provided him opportunities to help the Christian slaves. He arranged that a lawyer of the Parlement, Monsieur Husson, a native of Paris, be appointed by the king as consul at Tunis. He was a person of high virtue. Monsieur Vincent wrote about him in a letter at that time:

> He is wise, impartial, pious, prudent, and as able as any man I know of his age. He acts solely for the service of God and the slaves, and despite the tears and arguments of his dear parents, finally won their blessing on his ministry. He acts together with Monsieur Le Vacher as though he were a member of our Congregation, although he is not.[142]

He left for Barbary in 1653, and has remained there serving very successfully as consul for several years.

PART TWO
The Main Work of the Missionaries in Barbary

Monsieur Vincent first used his influence to have consuls appointed in the two cities, Tunis and Algiers. They were to cooperate with the priests of the Mission in the spiritual and corporal works of mercy serving the Christians there, both slaves and others. It only remained for each to carry out these good intentions.

---

142. *CED* IV:625.

To understand better the great good that Monsieur Vincent hoped the priests in Barbary would accomplish, we must realize that in these cities not only French citizens whether slave or free lived there under the protection of the king of France, but also citizens of other nations, except the English. They all turned to the French consul for protection and help against the insults of the barbarians. These other nationalities included Italians, Spaniards, Portuguese, Maltese, Greeks, Germans, Flemish, and Swedes. The boats and crews engaged in trade obtained their passports through him. When the pirates captured a ship and its merchandise, it was up to the consul to try to seek its release. He would complain to the dey or to the pasha, and to the customs officer, of the injustice of these seizures, or of the bad treatment of the sailors.[143] He negotiated the release of the slaves, and as often as he could had them returned to their own country. He attempted to settle the disputes which arose between the merchants of all these nations, and those among the slaves themselves. He attempted to make sure no Christian merchant carried any contraband material banned by the church or the king, to the Moslems. These banned items included sails, rope, iron, lead, and weapons, since they could be used by the Moslems in their wars against the Christians.

The priests of the Mission were as much taken up with their spiritual ministrations as the consuls were in temporal matters. They were apostolic missionaries, under the authority of the sovereign pontiff, who gave them all the faculties and powers they needed for their work. They were vicars of the archdiocese of Carthage, upon which these two cities of Tunis and Algiers depended. With these powers, they had jurisdiction over all enslaved priests and religious, who sometimes were very numerous. They were the pastors of both the merchants and slaves, who together numbered twenty-five or thirty thousand, with more coming in all the time.

These missionary priests worked primarily to maintain the Catholic religion and to practice it publicly and privately in those very places where it was oppressed and persecuted. They did so in imitation of Jesus Christ who had said to the Jews that he honored his Father while it was they who dishonored him. In the same way these sons of Monsieur Vincent sought to honor this same Savior, and have him honored and served in the midst of an infidel land where he was dishonored by the most cruel enemies of his holy name.

Besides, they sought to confirm and strengthen the faithful in their beliefs. They supported the weak, and prevented them from being lost. They brought back those who had strayed. They administered the sacraments to the sick

---

143. The dey was the ruling official. He and the pasha were accountable to the sultan in Constantinople, the head of the Ottoman empire.

and healthy both in the cities and in the fields. They consoled the poor slaves in their pains and afflictions. They preached, instructed, worked, endured, and finally gave their lives for this poor suffering Church, just as our Lord did for the entire Church at its beginnings.

These were the main occupations of the priests and consuls in Barbary to which they completely devoted themselves. They worked closely together, hoping to succeed in the work of the salvation of souls and the greater glory of God, their one shared goal. Monsieur Vincent strongly recommended that they often consult together, sharing advice and other forms of aid. This is what he said in a letter he wrote at this time:

> I have learned of the bonds of charity that exist among you. I bless God every time the thought comes to me, so much am I moved to thanksgiving for such a great blessing which surely comes directly from the heart of God. From this union among you will come all sorts of good things for his greater glory and for the salvation of a great number of souls. In the name of God, Monsieur, do all in your power to strengthen these bonds in every way. Recall the words of the epistle to the Romans which remind us that by union and prudence all things will work out well. Yes, union among you will bring the work of God to a happy end, and nothing except disunion can stand in its way. This work is an exercise of charity such as is not seen anywhere else in the whole world, although it is not well known.
>
> O God, Monsieur, what vision we need to see the full excellence of apostolic work. How happy we should be to be called to it, and how we should respond to the demands of this ministry. Ten or twelve missionaries with this insight could bring about incredible fruit in the Church. I have heard of the battles which have cost you flesh and blood, but this must happen, for the evil spirit will not let you continue without a fight. Blessed be God that you have stood firm against all attacks. Heaven and earth rejoice at your happy task, to honor in your work the incomprehensible charity of our Lord who descended from heaven to rescue us from our slavery. I imagine that there is not an angel or saint in heaven who does not envy you this happiness, if indeed their glorious state allows them to feel the pangs of envy. Even though I am the most miserable of sinners, I must say that if it were allowed, I too would envy you.
>
> Humble yourself, and prepare to suffer at the hands of the Moslems, or the Jews, or from false brothers. They may do you harm, but do not be surprised. They will not do you any ill other than what our Lord allows. What he sends will be solely to prepare

you for some special favors which he has in store for you. You are well aware that the grace of our redemption must be attributed to the merits of the Passion. The more the works of God are resisted, the happier are the results, if only our resignation and confidence do not falter. Rarely is any good done without suffering. The devil is too subtle and the world too corrupt not to attempt to stamp out a good work at its very beginning. Courage, then, Monsieur. God himself has called you to the place and the work you are now doing. If you have God's glory as your only end, what is there for you to fear, or better, what should you not hope for?[144]

PART THREE
Persecutions Suffered by the Consul at Algiers

With good reason Monsieur Vincent prepared his confreres for sufferings and exhorted them to constancy. Living as they did among these barbarians and working for Jesus Christ they were sure to suffer persecution and feel the effects of their rage and cruelty. In fact they were threatened with fire and the rope, and other tortures. They felt that the attacks, of which we give here only one example, show that those who strive to serve Jesus Christ among the infidels are continually exposed to harassments and bad treatment, and will have to have a most ardent charity to support them in their efforts to evangelize.

Monsieur Barreau, the consul in Algiers, felt the cruelty of these barbarians, since he had been tyrannized and persecuted because he had refused to give them money. One of their practices is that when they have suffered a financial loss they look for some way to make it up, always from the most innocent, and particularly from Christians. They use forgeries and false witnesses, and employ violence and injustice beyond all reason. They call this procedure the "affront," and should someone seek justice or the protection of the more powerful, it must be bought by expensive presents, equal almost to what was demanded in the first place. The ones who act this way do not work themselves, but live on what they extort from others, especially from Christians. They are never satisfied with what they have, for many of them are rich enough, but they always seek to have more.

The consul was imprisoned in 1647 solely because he refused to pay the money unjustly demanded of him. Shortly afterward, Monsieur Nouelly, priest of the Congregation of the Mission fell victim to the plague. The consul decided to pay his ransom to be able to help the priest in his illness.

---
144. *CED* IV, 364-66.

The priest died, however, leaving the consul in danger of being returned to prison. He alerted Monsieur Vincent to these two situations, and he replied in a letter, as follows:

> I received yesterday the sad but happy news of the passing of Monsieur Nouelly. I shed many tears of regret, but also of thanksgiving for the goodness of God toward our Company for giving us one who loved our Lord so completely and who died such a holy death. How happy you must be that God has chosen you, in preference to so many other persons, for your saintly role. You have become a prisoner of charity, or to say it better, of Jesus Christ. What happiness to suffer for this great monarch, and what a crown awaits you if you persevere until the end.[145]

In 1650 this same Monsieur Barreau was again imprisoned. This led to the following letter and many other similar ones, which show how Monsieur Vincent looked upon all things in the light of our Lord. He expressed his happiness at seeing how others strove and suffered in imitation of the Lord, for the glory of God and the service of the poor.

> I learned with great sorrow the sad state in which you find yourself, and the entire Company shares my sorrow. I am sure this is a source of great merit in the sight of God, since you suffer innocently. I was consoled beyond measure to see with what sentiments you have received this new trial, and the good use you are making of your imprisonment. I thank God, with my heart full of gratitude.
>
> Our Lord came from heaven to earth for the redemption of men, and was imprisoned for them. What happiness for you, Monsieur, to be treated in the same way! You left France, a place of joy and rest, to go help and console the poor slaves of Algiers. And now it has come to pass that you have become like one of them, with some differences, to be sure. The more our conduct reflects what Jesus Christ did in this life, and the more our sufferings resemble his, the more pleasing we are to God. Just as your imprisonment honors heaven, I pray that he will reward your patience, too.
>
> I assure you that your letter has touched me deeply, and I shall use it to inspire the entire community. I have already told them of the persecution you suffer, and the resignation you display, to urge them to pray to God for your quick release from prison, and to thank his divine goodness for the grace of your indomitable spirit.
>
> Continue, Monsieur, to preserve your holy submission to the good pleasure of God. In this way you will see accomplished in

---

145. *CED* III:240.

yourself the promise of our Lord that not a hair of your head will be lost, and that by your patience you will possess your soul. Have great confidence in him, and remember what he endured for you in his life and in his death. He said that the servant is not greater than his master, and that if they have persecuted him they will also persecute you. Blessed are those who are persecuted for justice's sake, for the kingdom of heaven is theirs. Rejoice then, Monsieur, in him who will be glorified in you, and who shall be your strength, in the degree to which you shall be faithful. This is what I pray for so earnestly.

I beseech you, by the love you have for our Company, to ask of God for us the grace of bearing the cross in all things, great and small, so that we might become worthy children of the cross of his Son, who displayed such love for us on it, and by which we hope to gain eternal happiness. Amen.[146]

Another letter from this father of missionaries, dated January 15, 1651, predicted the early release of the consul.

Your last letter of the month of October has given us much joy and consolation. It tells us of your unfailing patience, and your acceptance of your present sufferings and of all that God will be pleased to allow in the future. We have already thanked him for giving you such a great grace, and we shall continue to pray fervently for your deliverance. The king has been away from Paris for six or seven months, and since his return we have taken steps to obtain his help.

It was finally decided that he would write to Constantinople to complain of your imprisonment. He will insist that the articles of peace and alliance signed by Henry IV with the sultan in 1604 be observed. This treaty called for the end of raids upon French shipping, and for the release of the slaves. Should this not be done, the king will then threaten reprisals. We will follow this initiative, God willing. It is up to Providence to do the rest, but I hope all will go well if we abandon ourselves to him with confidence and submission, which you do so well, by the help of his grace. Perhaps God will be so good to us as to deliver you from prison quicker than through our contacting Constantinople. Maybe the pasha will relent, or some other change will come about that will produce this happy outcome.[147]

It seems that God gave Monsieur Vincent a presentiment of what was

---

146. *CED* IV:81-82.
147. *CED* IV:140-41.

going to happen, by what he referred to in the last sentence of his letter, for the pasha, Murad, learned he was to be succeeded by another named Mohammed. He preferred to tell the consul that he could buy his way out of prison, rather than wait to allow his successor to gain the revenue. At the end of seven months he accepted 350 *piastres*, which was much less than he had first demanded.

The letter Monsieur Vincent wrote to him after his release from prison allows us to gauge his sentiments on the question of suffering and persecution.

> God alone, who knows the depths of the heart, can make you aware of the joy we felt at the long-awaited news of your deliverance. We have thanked him for this, and for all the other good we have received from his bounty for such a long time. I gave the news to your father, who was greatly consoled. I told him, too, of the good use you had made of your days of captivity. I never think of this without remembering your meekness, your submission to God, and your patience in suffering, as most beautiful and admirable. I cannot tell you, Monsieur, how fortunate you are to have suffered for our Lord Jesus Christ, who called us to Algiers. In fifteen or twenty years you will understand better the value of what you have contributed, and you will understand even more when God shall call you to your reward in heaven. You have reason to appreciate the time you so religiously spent in prison. As for myself, I look upon it as an infallible sign that God wishes to lead you to himself, since he has allowed you to walk in the footsteps of his only Son. May he be forever blessed, and lead you further in the school of solid virtue to which sufferings contribute so much, without which even good servants of God have reason to fear.
>
> I beg his divine bounty, in the lull you now enjoy, to flood your soul with peace. The storm did not overwhelm you, and I now pray that the calm may endure for as long as it allows you to fulfill perfectly God's designs upon you. In borrowing the one thousand *livres* you did nothing that I would disapprove of. I regard this sum as insignificant when compared with the value of your liberty, which is more precious to me than anything else.[148]

The saddest and cruelest of all the persecutions suffered by Monsieur Barreau happened in 1657, when a merchant of Marseilles went into bankruptcy in Algiers. His creditors complained to the pasha, who contrary to all reason and justice, obliged the consul to pay the debts of the merchant. He refused to do so, saying that he had no responsibility to do so, and that, even

---

148. *CED* IV:224-25.

if he wanted to, he did not have the means to pay. This inhuman and barbarous tyrant, in violation of the rights of the innocent, decided to try to force his compliance by torments and curses. He forced him to lie on the ground. Then, in keeping with the cruel custom of the country, he had him beaten on the soles of his feet so violently that he fell unconscious. When the pasha saw this he feared the consul would die, so he ordered a stop to the beating. His avarice and barbarity were so great that he threatened him with another torture, placing long needles under his finger nails. The consul, half dead, believing he had the obligation of preserving his life for the service of the poor Christian slaves, finally agreed to pay the full sum demanded of him.

Monsieur Vincent wrote to him after he learned of this latest suffering:

God's holy name be blessed. He has found you worthy of suffering, and suffering for justice, since, thanks be to God, you had never given any cause for this evil treatment. It is a sign that our Lord wishes to give you a larger share in his passion, since he puts on you the burden of the faults of others. I have no doubt, Monsieur, that in this incident you see the paternal hand of God, wishing to submit to his honor and good pleasure, rather than to the evil will of men, who know not what they do. Thus I hope that this trial will serve to your sanctification. Nothing like this has yet happened to any one of the Company. My hope is that it will attract new graces for the salvation of the neighbor.[149]

The consul had committed himself to pay twelve thousand *livres* to the pasha, but was confined to his house recovering from his torments when four soldiers of the ruler came with the demand for either immediate payment or death. If he did not pay, he was to be brought, directly from his bed, to the presence of the pasha, where he would be killed. This poor man had merely a hundred *ecus*, much less that what he was being asked to deliver. Not knowing what to do or what to say, he abandoned himself into the hands of God for whatever would be his will, even death itself.

The poor Christian slaves learned of the violence done him, and of the extreme danger that the consul was in of being put to death. They were so moved at it that they did what little was in their power, and brought twenty, thirty, a hundred, or two hundred *ecus*, to help him pay this unjust ransom, and thus save his life. They had saved these small sums to help them regain their own liberty, should the occasion present itself, but nevertheless, in thanksgiving and in charity they gave freely to help him who had done so much to aid them regain their liberty.

It seemed that God, having seen the affection of these poor slaves in this

---

149. *CED* VI:322.

instance, had revived in them the spirit of the first Christians. They had brought their goods with such devotion to the feet of the apostles to feed and help the poor. They collected so much that the consul was set free. When Monsieur Vincent heard of this, and realized that the money they had offered so willingly had been saved for their own ransom, he sought alms and gifts from friends to send back to Algiers to be given to the slaves, who themselves were ransomed later.

God blessed the charity of those who had preferred the deliverance of the consul to their own liberty. They later returned happily to France in 1661, accompanied by Monsieur Barreau, because at the request of the successor to Monsieur Vincent as superior general of the Congregation, the king had sent a replacement as consul to Algiers. Monsieur Barreau brought back seventy slaves with him, who had been ransomed by alms collected by Monsieur Le Vacher and himself for this purpose.

PART FOUR
Other Vexations of the Missionaries in Tunis

Although the missionaries at Tunis were not treated so inhumanly as those in Algiers, they also had to drink from the chalice of Jesus Christ and carry some small portion of his cross. In 1655 a false report reached the dey. He summoned Monsieur Le Vacher to complain that he was preventing Christians from embracing the law of Mohammed and becoming Moslems. For this he was to be banished from the city, and prohibited from returning. Obedient to this order, the good priest left to go to Bizerte. It seemed that God's providence had directed him there, for on his arrival he found two ships crowded with Christian slaves, whom he prepared for the sacrament of penance. The captain of the ships allowed these slaves to be unchained, at least for a while, during these functions.

When Monsieur Vincent reported this to his community, he made this reflection: "Who knows, gentlemen, if this was not in the designs of God to allow this disgrace to befall Monsieur Le Vacher, to give him the opportunity to serve these poor Christian slaves, and restore them to grace?"[150] He added that Monsieur Husson, the consul, remonstrated with the dey, pointing out that the missionary served only the Christian slaves, and that he never interfered with the Moslem religion. He requested that the priest be recalled, and this was granted. The dey ordered the governor of Bizerte to send him back to Tunis in a month's time, knowing well he would be thought of as fickle for having exiled a person for such a charge if he were to come back sooner.

---

150. *CED* XI:306.

But neither this good missionary nor the consul were to enjoy peace for long. Another storm soon broke that involved both of them. This is the way Monsieur Vincent reported it to his community:

I have already told you how the dey of Tunis wanted the consul to go to the sail makers of France to obtain some sailcloth. The consul excused himself from this commission. It not only was against the laws of the kingdom, but it had been expressly forbidden by bulls of the Apostolic See, under pain of excommunication, to export to the Moslems any war material that might be used against the Christians. Seeing himself thwarted, the dey had recourse to a merchant from Marseilles, based in Barbary, who agreed, despite the protests of the consul. He pointed out the disservice to God and to the Christians, as well as the harm to himself, not to mention the punishment he would merit if the king of France ever got word of his actions. Since these warnings had no effect, the consul drew up an account of the affair, and sent it here to France. The king gave orders to officials of all the ports of Provence and Languedoc to be especially careful of any contraband destined for Barbary. This action came to the attention of the dey, who once more became exasperated with the consul and with the missionary.

He decided to use the "affront" against them, a technique for demanding money in a sort of extortion. He summoned Monsieur Le Vacher, and said to him, "I want you to pay me the 275 piastres owed me by the Chevalier de la Ferriere. You belong to a religion where things both good and bad are held in common, so I come to you for payment." Monsieur Le Vacher explained that Christians are not responsible for the debts of others, and he should not and could not be expected to pay the debts of a Knight of Malta and a merchant captain, such as this gentleman, de la Ferriere. He explained that he had scarcely enough to live on. He was a marabout of the Christians (that is, a simple priest, in their way of speaking) who had come to Tunis expressly to help the poor slaves. "Say what you will," the dey said, "I will be paid." With that he used various measures against him to compel him to pay this money. This was only the beginning of the story, for if God did not change the heart of the dey he would surely have resorted to harsher treatment very shortly. We may say that the consul and the priest now began to be more truly Christians, as they began to share in the sufferings of Christ, as was remarked by the martyr Saint Ignatius of Antioch, when threatened with martyrdom.

And we, my brothers, we will become disciples of Jesus Christ when we have the grace to endure persecution or some wrong for the sake of his name. The world will rejoice, the Gospel for today says. Yes, the people of this world will seek their own pleasures, and strive to avoid anything that contradicts their natural impulses. God grant that I, miserable man that I am, will not do the same, and will not be among those who seek sweetness and consolations in the service of Jesus Christ, rather than accepting tribulations and the cross. If it comes to that, I surely will not be a Christian. To become one, God will provide the opportunity for suffering, and will send it to me when he wills. We must all have this disposition if we wish to be true servants of Jesus Christ.[151]

Some time after this, the dey, who had always retained resentment in his heart for the refusal of the consul, Monsieur Husson, to obtain sailcloth from France, found a new pretext to persecute him. In 1657 thirteen Moslems had been captured at sea by ships of the grand duke of Florence, and had been taken to Livorno.[152] When the dey heard of this, he called Monsieur Husson, and demanded the return of the prisoners. When he replied that such a request was beyond his power, since the Moslems were in the hands of an independent prince with no connection with the consul, the dey was overcome with rage. Refusing to listen to reason, the dey banished him from the city of Tunis. It seemed that the same treatment would be given to the missionaries, but it pleased God to move his heart to allow them to stay, to continue their ministry of charity and religion. Some time later the dey even allowed Monsieur Le Vacher to become consul once again, because of what he had done for the poor slaves.

PART FIVE

An Account Given by Monsieur Vincent to His Community of the Martyrdom of a Young Christian Burned to Death in Algiers for His Faith in Jesus Christ.

All the acts of virtue and piety practiced by the Christian slaves might well be considered as fruits of the missions given for them under the direction of Monsieur Vincent. They were the effect of the instructions, preaching, and other works of charity of the missionaries. The word of God announced among them was a seed sown in their hearts, awaiting the hour of grace, when it would bear fruit worthy of eternal life.

Among all the various activities undertaken for the slaves, one stands out as heroic. One day, Monsieur Vincent recounted it to his community at Saint

---
151. CED XI:333-35.
152. CED VI:340.

Lazare in few words, but in a way that showed the zeal that ever burned in his heart.

I cannot begin to tell you how touched I was by the accounts of the death of this young man, who, as I told you before, was put to death in the city of Algiers. His name was Pedro Bourgoin.[153] He was born on the island of Majorca, and was twenty or twenty-one years old. His master planned to sell him into service on the galleys of Constantinople, from which there was little hope of ever getting out alive. In his fear he went to the pasha to ask him to have pity on him, and not allow him to be sent to the galleys. The pasha agreed, but on condition that he accept the turban as a sign of his accepting Islam. He used all possible persuasions, adding threats to promises, until he finally persuaded the young man to become a renegade.

This poor boy nevertheless preserved in his heart sentiments of love and respect for his religion, but fell into his apostasy by fear of the cruel slavery that awaited him if he did not defect. He let it be known to some of the Christian slaves who reproached him, that although he outwardly appeared to be a Moslem, he inwardly remained a Christian. Little by little, as he reflected on the great sin he had committed by renouncing his religion, he was touched by a spirit of repentance. Since he could not expiate it except by his death, he chose to die rather than enjoy a long life as an infidel. After he spoke of his intentions to some of his intimate friends, he began to speak openly before many Christians and some Moslems of his preference for the Christian religion and his disregard for Islam. He lived in fear of the cruelty of these barbarians, and trembled at the thought of what he might have to endure for his faith. "All the same", he said, "my hope is that the Lord will help me. He died for me, and it is only just I should die for him."

Moved by remorse, and with the hope of repairing the scandal he had given, he sought out the pasha to say to him: "You seduced me in making me give up my religion, which is the one and only true one, to join yours, which is false. I now declare to you that I am a Christian, and as a sign of my belief I reject the turban you gave me, and I throw it to the ground." He added, "I know you can put me to death, but that does not bother me. I am prepared to suffer torments for Jesus Christ my savior."

The pasha was so angry at these words that he immediately condemned him to be burned alive. He was stripped, and then with a chain around his neck he was laden with a large stake, to go to the

---

153. Also known as Borguni, or, more properly, Bouruny.

place of execution. As he left the pasha's house he saw it surrounded by Moslems, renegades, and even some Christians. He raised his voice and said, "Long live Jesus Christ, and the Catholic, apostolic, and Roman faith. There is no other in which we can be saved!" As he said this, he went courageously to the fire to die for the faith of Jesus Christ.

What moved me most is what this brave young man said to his friends. "As much as I fear death, I feel something here (putting his hand to his forehead) that tells me that God will give me the grace to endure the torments prepared for me. Our Lord himself dreaded death, and yet he voluntarily accepted the greatest sufferings. My hope is in his strength and goodness." He was bound to the stake, the fire was lit, and he gave his soul to God like gold refined in the crucible. Monsieur Le Vacher was present, though at a distance.[154] He lifted the excommunication that the former renegade had incurred, and gave him absolution at an agreed-upon sign, in the midst of his sufferings.

Here, gentlemen, is the way a Christian is made. Here is the courage we must have to suffer, and even die if necessary for Jesus Christ. Ask this grace of God, and pray to this young man to intercede for us. He was such an apt pupil of so courageous a teacher, that in three short hours he became his true disciple and perfect imitator by dying for him.

Courage, gentlemen and my brothers. We hope that our Lord will strengthen us to bear whatever crosses he sends us, if he sees that we accept them with love and confidence in him. We say to whatever ills that should come, to interior or exterior pains, temptations, and to death itself, Welcome heavenly favors, graces of God and holy trials, that come from a paternal and loving hand! I receive you with respect, submission, and confidence in him who sent you. I accept what you bring, for love of him. Gentlemen and my brothers, enter into these sentiments, trusting as this new martyr did, in the help of our Lord. We ask you to recommend to him, please, these good missionaries of Algiers and Tunis.[155]

This conference of Monsieur Vincent reveals well his guiding spirit, and how much he wanted to instill this same mind in his confreres, this spirit which is none other than the spirit of martyrdom. He wanted to fortify them from the attacks of the world and of hell, and even against the movements of their own nature, to make them worthy of the self-renunciation of carrying their own cross, walking in the footsteps of Jesus Christ.

---

154. Philippe Le Vacher, brother of Jean Le Vacher. He was vicar apostolic of Algiers, 1651-1662.
155. *CED* XI:389-92.

After the fire had burned itself out, Monsieur Le Vacher went in full daylight to retrieve the body of the young man, to give it a decent burial. He wrote an account of the martyrdom, and had a painting made of it. He brought the painting to Monsieur Vincent on his return to Paris in 1657. He brought with him the remains of the martyr, burned to death for the faith, as one of the most excellent fruits that the grace of God began to produce in these barbarous and infidel lands.

PART SIX
Various Directives Given by Monsieur Vincent to the Missionaries of Barbary Regarding Their Personal Behavior and Their Way of Acting Among the Infidels.

The mortal hatred which the Moslems bore the Christians was so strong that they believed it was enough that they should kill a Christian to gain an assured place in paradise. All the same, our Lord had permitted almost eighteen years of service by the priests of the Congregation of the Mission in Algiers and Tunis without the loss of a single one. This happened despite their frequent failure to observe the law that forbade anyone, under pain of death, to speak against their religion, or to aid those who wanted to abandon it in any way. They did not feel obliged to heed this unjust prohibition when it was a question of serving Jesus Christ and obtaining the salvation of souls redeemed by his blood.

It is true that they lived in such modesty, prudence, and charity, following the directives of Monsieur Vincent, that not only did the Moslems spare their lives, but several among them willingly witnessed to their virtuous lives. For example, the local ruler of Tunis one day met a missionary whom he often saw coming and going in the city and surrounding areas, on his rounds aiding and helping the poor Christian slaves. He turned to his entourage to remark, pointing to the priest, "There goes a true papa." On another occasion when this same priest sought permission to leave the city to visit and help some poor Christians, he was given leave to go wherever he pleased. On still another occasion the ruler provided one of his officers to accompany him to a distant place where it was dangerous to travel alone.

Monsieur Vincent also recommended that they act always with great moderation and discretion, not exposing themselves needlessly to danger for fear lest in seeking an apparent good they would lose the opportunity for real ones. This is what he wrote on this matter to one of his priests in Barbary, whose zeal was ardent but who needed a rein more than a spur.[156] This letter

---
156. Philippe Le Vacher.

contained several important pieces of advice, and served as a model for others he later wrote.

I praise God for the appropriate way you have acted in having yourself recognized as the apostolic missionary[157] and vicar general of the archdiocese of Carthage. If you have acted wisely in this, you must now carry out this task even more prudently. You must be careful not to lash out against certain abuses, if you can foresee that this will lead to still greater ones. Seek to attain your goals with the priests and enslaved religious, merchants and other captives, by mild measures. Never use severity except in cases of extreme necessity, for fear that all they already suffer in their captivity, joined to the rigor you might show because of your authority, will lead them to despair. You are not responsible for their salvation, as you may think. You were sent to Algiers to console afflicted souls, to encourage them in their sufferings, and to help them in persevering in our holy religion. That work is your chief duty, and not your office as vicar general, which you accepted only as a means to take care of those primary obligations.

You cannot be rigorous in exercising your office without increasing the suffering of these poor slaves, and without making them lose patience, not to mention that you yourself will also lose patience. Above all, you must not attempt to reform things long established among them, even if they are evil.

Recently, someone showed me a beautiful passage from Saint Augustine. In it he says we must be careful about opposing a deeply rooted vice in a certain place, because not only will you not be able to drive it out, but you will shock the minds of the people in whom the evil is found. As a result, you will make it impossible for yourself to do any further good for them. You should be able to accomplish something, if you were to attack the problem from another angle. I would ask you, therefore, to consider as much as you can the weakness of human nature. You will gain more from the ecclesiastical slaves by compassion than you ever would by rebuke and correction. They do not lack understanding. They are weak, and you will remedy their weakness by kind words and good example.

I do not say that you ought to authorize or permit disorders, but I do say that your remedies must be mild and kind in whatever condition you find yourself. These remedies must be applied with

---

157. A formal title formerly given to missionary priests by the Holy See, granting them special authority in mission areas.

great prudence because of the site and conditions of your ministry, and because of the harm they might do if they are unhappy with you. They could also harm the consul, and God's work, as well, by complaining to the Moslems, who would never want to hear from you again.

You must avoid another pitfall among the Moslems and renegades. In the name of our Lord, have nothing to do with these people. Do not expose yourself to the dangers that might ensue, for in exposing yourself to these dangers you risk everything. You would do great harm to the Christian slaves if you acted so as to take away all possibility of helping them. You might slam the door for the future on the liberty we now have of doing some good for them in Algiers and elsewhere. Look at the evil that you might cause in seeking an apparent good. It is far easier and more important to prevent the loss of many slaves than to convert a single renegade. A doctor who protects the health of a group deserves more praise than the one who cures a single sick person. You are not responsible for the souls of the Moslems and the renegades, and your mission is not to them, but to the poor Christian captives. If for some good reason you find it necessary to deal with the people of the country, do not do so, I beg of you, except in concert with the consul, whose advice I ask you to follow, as closely as you can.

We have much reason to thank God for the zeal you have for the salvation of these poor slaves, but zeal is not good if it is not tactful. It seems that you have attempted too many new projects, such as giving a mission at the penal colonies, or wanting to move there, or introducing new devotional practices among these poor people. That is why I ask you to follow the customs of our deceased priests who preceded you.

It often happens that we spoil our good works by proceeding too quickly. When we act according to our inclinations, these hinder our mind and spirit because they rely on human reason. Things don't work this way, and this becomes obvious when in the end such haste does not succeed. The good that comes from God comes almost of itself, without our even thinking of it. Remember how our Congregation came into being, how the missions, the clergy conferences and the ordination retreats began. Remember how the Ladies and Daughters of Charity were founded for the help of the poor in the hospitals of Paris for the relief of the sick in the parishes, for the relief of the abandoned children, and all the other works we are responsible for. All these things came into being, and not one was planned by us. God, who willed these things, imperceptibly led us to follow his inspirations. This is why we must always follow, never pushing ahead any more than we did when we began these enterprises. O God, Monsieur, how much do I wish that you would moderate your enthusiasm, and weigh these things at the foot of the sanctuary before taking action. Be patient rather than agitated, and God will accomplish through you alone more than what many men together, acting without him, could ever accomplish.[158]

PART SEVEN
Various Employments and Sufferings of the Poor Christian Slaves in Barbary, and the Help and Services Rendered Them by the Missionaries

To understand better the help which the missionaries of Monsieur Vincent gave to the Christian slaves in Barbary, we should be aware of the inhuman ways they were treated by the Turks, the exhausting work they had to do, and the excessive pressures brought to induce them to abandon the faith of Jesus Christ, and to embrace Islam.

At sea, the pirates of Tunis and Algiers captured Christians from all parts of the world. They took men and women of all ages and condition to be brought back to these two cities for sale as slaves. These captives were brought to the market like beasts. Since so many were captured, the Moslems in Barbary had a great number of slaves, who lived in places they called Bagnes.[159] In Tunis and Bizerte the slaves were chained together, and guarded day and night, but in Algiers they were chained only during the night.

Imagine huge stables, each housing two hundred, three hundred, or even four hundred horses. This gives you some idea of the places where the Christians lived. The difference is, however, that horses are much better fed and cared for than the slaves. They lived in filth, misery, and total abandonment, mainly because of their religion, which the Moslems detested. Besides, having to depend on the whim or ill humor of their owner or of the guards, the slaves were beaten unmercifully, sometimes fatally, or crippled for the rest of their lives.

These poor slaves left these places only to go to work in the fields or to other hard labors, or possibly to serve in the galleys or join the crews of some other vessels that were so often at war with the Christians. They suffered all sorts of hardships, fatigue, blows, contempt, and unbearable pains. As a rule

---
158. *CED* IV:120-23.
159. Penal colonies.

they rowed or worked completely nude, except for a loincloth, exposed to the burning sun in summer and to the cold in winter. When they returned entirely exhausted from their labors, half-dead, they were returned like beasts to their stables, not to rest, but rather to languish.

Monsieur Guerin, priest of the Mission, wrote to Monsieur Vincent:

> We expect a large number of sick upon the return of the galleys. If these poor people have suffered so greatly at sea, those who remained behind have had their own troubles. They have had to work all day in the hot sun, cutting marble. The best comparison I can give for their work is that it is like a heated furnace. It is astonishing to see both the work and the heat they endure, enough to kill a horse. Yet these Christians endure both, losing only their skin to the sun and heat. You can see them with their tongues hanging out like poor dogs, because of the terrific heat in which they work.
>
> One day in winter an older poor slave felt sick and unable to work. He asked to be excused, but the only response he received was to be forced to work at splitting stone. I leave it to you to imagine how these cruelties moved me and caused me such sorrow. These poor slaves suffer these ills with an unbelievable patience, and they bless God even amid all the cruelties visited upon them. I must tell you that the French bear these things better than peoples of other nations. We have two very sick persons at the moment, who look like they will not recover. We administered all the sacraments to them. Last week two others died as true Christians, of whom it could be said, *pretiosa in conspectu Domini mors sanctorum ejus* ["Precious in the eyes of the Lord is the death of his faithful ones"].[160]
>
> My compassion for these poor people who work at cutting the marble leads me to bring what small refreshments I can, especially to those who are sick. Some others, who are not so badly treated, stay in the homes of their masters. They serve various functions, such as baking bread, taking care of commercial correspondence, preparing meals, or other household work. Some others are given assignments out of the house. Others are even free to work at whatever they like. They pay their patron a certain amount each month from what they manage to save from what they earn.[161]

Besides the slaves in the cities, a large number lived in the countryside. Some passed their entire lives here, never coming into the cities. They

---
160. Ps 116:15.
161. *CED* III:138-39.

worked as farmers or woodcutters. They made charcoal, or hauled stone from the quarries, or worked at other similar occupations. After working hard all day they were usually locked up for the night. We have described all these various situations concerning the slaves to give the reader a better understanding of the work of the missionaries in Barbary.

In the cities of Algiers, Tunis, and Bizerte, there were about twenty-five penal colonies. In each of them was a sort of small chapel, where amid their sufferings and pain these poor Christian captives might have the happiness of hearing mass and receiving the sacraments. One of the priests of the Mission there wrote in a letter:

> In this arrangement, we see the hand of Providence and the goodness of God. He has changed their prisons into churches to give the suffering members of Jesus Christ a way of persevering in the truth of the faith through the free exercise of all the sacraments. In these chapels the divine Savior himself has become a slave with the slaves, for each time mass is celebrated the sacred species are preserved. In this way, the truth of the words are borne out by which he promised to be with the faithful in their troubles: *Cum ipso sum in tribulatione* ["I will be with him in distress"].[162]

Among the large number of slaves, some captive priests and religious were always to be found. The missionaries interceded with their masters asking that they not be given manual labor, nor be chained. They backed up their request with monthly payments. As vicars general of the archdiocese of Carthage they then appointed these priests as chaplains in the penal colonies, watched over their conduct, corrected them, transferred them or removed them from their office as it appeared necessary. This was one of the greatest of the blessings Monsieur Vincent had brought to this place, for previous to the coming of the Missionaries all was in disorder and confusion. The slaves contributed what they could, some more, some less, for the support of these chaplains, and for lighting and furnishing the chapels. This was done freely on their part, out of personal devotion, without constraint, and there were many totally unable to give anything, since they owned nothing save the bit of black bread given them each day for their sustenance.

Besides the chapels in the penal colonies, other chapels in the houses of the consuls served as the parishes of the Christian merchants, those who came on business to these cities, and for those resident there. The consuls and the Missionaries staffed, decorated, and maintained these chapels. The one at Algiers was under the patronage of Saint Cyprian, bishop of Carthage, and the one at Tunis was dedicated to Saint Louis, king of France, whose death sanctified this land and this infidel city. The feasts of these saints were

---

162. Ps 91:15.

celebrated with all possible solemnity, as were the main feasts of the year, to the great edification of all Christians who lived there.

Who can say how consoling it was for Monsieur Vincent to receive letters written from Algiers and Tunis, relating that the divine services were performed there with a solemnity rivaling that of Paris itself. High mass and the divine offices were celebrated on Sundays and feasts. Various organizations were established, and confraternities started in each of these churches and chapels to relieve the souls in purgatory or to help the poor slaves, or to honor particular saints on their feast days. The holy Mother of God was especially honored by confraternities of the rosary or scapular, with sermons and processions on appropriate days. In the churches and chapels of the missionaries the blessed sacrament, marked by lighted candles, was reserved day and night. The blessed sacrament was brought to the sick in the penal colonies with torches and candles, while other marks of respect were shown to this holy sacrament. Every year on the feast of Corpus Christi and during its octave, the blessed sacrament was exposed, and carried in procession in the chapels and churches, with all the attendants carrying candles in their hands.

It is a common belief among the saints that our sufferings erect a throne to the mercy of God. We might add that the miseries of these poor captives not only erected this throne, but another as well to the charity and holiness of the sons of God in these barbarous lands that they might say with the psalmist: "Triumph, O Lord, amidst your enemies."[163] Certainly, the Lord would not now be adored in these infidel lands, if Providence had not allowed Christian slaves to be taken, and the priests of Monsieur Vincent to be sent to them as their missionaries.

Monsieur Guerin added another remarkable point in the letter to Monsieur Vincent:

> You will be pleased to learn that on every Sunday and feast day, we sing in our chapels and churches the *Exaudiat* and other prayers for the king of France. Even the other nationals have respect and affection for him.[164]
>
> It is edifying, too, to see with what devotion these poor captives pray for their benefactors, who for the most part are in France. It is no small consolation to see peoples from all countries, in irons and chains, praying to God for the French.[165]

Besides all the services given by the missionaries to the Christian slaves,

---

163. Ps 110:2.
164. The *Exaudiat* refers to Ps 20 (19 in Vulgate), a prayer for the king before battle. This was followed by a few versicles and responses and concluded by a collect for the king. This votive formulary could have been positioned after the Our Father or at the end of mass.
165. *CED* III:169.

by their preaching, instructions, administration of the sacraments, celebration of the divine office, and other such daily ministrations, another service was provided, no less important for their salvation. This was the consolation they offered these poor slaves in their sufferings, and the effort to soften the resentment felt because of the barbarous treatment they received, which led them to come within an inch of despair. This despair in turn brought some to the decision to put an end to their sufferings and unhappy lot by taking their own lives. Some cut their throats, some hanged themselves, some slashed their wrists. Others in fury attacked their masters, with the penalty of being burned alive for their troubles. Still others sought relief in denying their faith in Jesus Christ, incurring eternal damnation in their efforts to escape temporal sufferings.

It was an important duty of the priests of the Mission in Barbary to console these poor afflicted souls in every way possible. They encouraged them to make a good use of the sufferings they endured, and provided whatever aid was possible for them. The all too numerous sick were visited and helped. In keeping with the spirit of Monsieur Vincent, those who received the greatest attention were those who were the most abandoned.

PART EIGHT
Continuation of the Same Topic

The power of virtue to move even enemies to admiration and love is so great that the charity which the missionaries extended to the poor slaves attracted the attention, esteem and veneration of even many Moslems. This gave the missionaries the liberty to go into the houses where the slaves lived, or into the places where they worked. Since at first there was considerable opposition, one of the Missionaries used an artifice suggested by his charity. When there was sick slave in a place closed to him, he would first send a Christian pharmacist to visit. This man would report to the master that he could no nothing until the doctor had visited. The priest would assume the guise of a doctor. In this disguise he would visit the place where the sick were, to speak with them, hear their confessions, administer the sacraments even in the presence of the masters who would not understand what was going on. They thought that these religious rites were part of the medical art.

The way the blessed sacrament was carried to these poor slaves was for the priest to place it in a small silver gilt box, which in turn was put in a silk purse hung about the neck. A small stole was sewn into the cassock, and then covered and hidden by a cloak. A Christian would walk ahead, carrying under his mantle or hood a lighted candle in a small lantern, a bit of blessed water in a tiny bottle, a folded surplice, a ritual, a tiny corporal and a purificator. The priest and companion would greet no one along the way. This gave a signal by which the Christians would understand what they were doing. If they were free they would follow the priest, as their devotion suggested. In the city of Algiers, it is true, the Christian slaves would not follow the priest carrying the blessed sacrament, for fear of the unhappy consequences that might follow. A single priest in a penal colony of Algiers once gave communion to sixty sick slaves, after he heard their confessions, and a similar thing happened on several other occasions.

Another concern of the Missionaries was to preserve among the poor slaves a spirit of peace and union, a true mark and distinguishing mark of Christianity. To our shame we have to admit that the Moslems sometimes taught us a lesson in this. Monsieur Guerin wrote in a letter to Monsieur Vincent:

> I must not hesitate to tell you what a Moslem told me recently, of his impressions of some badly disposed Christians. I was attempting to reconcile two Christians who were at odds. As this Moslem saw that I was having difficulty persuading them, he spoke to me in his own language, "Father, among us Moslems, we are not allowed to remain angry with one another longer than three days, even though the other might have killed one of our close relatives." I have seen this often enough among them. After fighting one another they would quickly come to terms, embracing each other in friendship.
>
> I cannot say if this reconciliation is purely exterior or not, but for Christians there is no doubt these infidels will hate them until the day of judgment, resisting any reconciliation, either exterior or interior. They retain this hatred in their hearts, boasting of it, and they glory in the vengeance they have taken or wish to take on their enemies. Nevertheless, these people we call barbarians look upon it as a great shame if they hold hatred in their hearts against any of their own, or if they refuse to be reconciled with anyone who had done them evil.[166]

Besides what has already been said, several other extraordinary occasions arose in which it seemed that God wished to pour out his grace more abundantly upon these poor slaves. This was especially noticed at the time of some special jubilee, or at the celebration of the Forty Hours. On these occasions the priests of the Mission did not spare themselves in their service to the captives. Sometimes they would pass the entire night in the penal colonies for confessions, since there was no other time that this could be done. The masters would not allow the slaves to take time from their work during the day.

It happened once that a priest went six or seven nights without sleep. The

---

166. *CED* III:225-26.

consul alerted Monsieur Vincent, who gave directives to the priest to moderate his zeal lest he succumb. Another occasion of grace was when the priests of the Mission would urge the captives to make their general confession. Most of them did so, with signs of true repentance. At this special time of grace, the most hardened sinners would recognize their miserable state and turn to God after being away ten, twenty, thirty years or more, from confession. At these times of mercy and pardon many renegades from various nations, French, Italians, or Spaniards, would decide to renounce their apostasy and return to the Church. In order to effect this renunciation, it was necessary to escape to their native land, but this could be done only at great peril to their very lives.

Because of God's blessing and the instruction and exhortation of the priests of the Mission some of these Christian slaves, after their general confession, began to lead a truly Christian life, and to practice extraordinary virtue. They preserved an inviolate fidelity to Jesus Christ amid the most severe persecution, and suffered cruel torments with a marvelous constancy, even to death itself, rather than offend God by sin. Two examples of this may be given. Monsieur Guerin reported the first in a letter to Monsieur Vincent, in August 1646:

> I must tell you that on the feast of Saint Anne, a second Joseph was sacrificed in this city of Tunis for the preservation of the virtue of chastity. He resisted the lewd suggestions of his mistress for over a year, but received horrible beatings when this she-wolf falsely accused him. He finally gained his victory by dying for refusing to offend God's law. He was heavily chained for three days. During that time I was able to visit him, to console him, and to exhort him to suffer all possible torments rather than fail in the fidelity he owed to God. He confessed and communicated, and then said to me, "Monsieur, no matter what they do to me, I wish to die as a Christian." When they led him to his execution, I again heard his confession, and I had the consolation of attending his sacrifice, although this is usually never permitted by these barbarians. The last words he spoke, in raising his eyes to heaven, were: "O God, I die innocent." He died courageously, giving no sign of impatience at the cruel sufferings he had to endure. We managed to give him honorable burial.
>
> His wicked and lewd mistress did not long enjoy her crime. When the master of the house came back from a business trip, he strangled her in a fit of rage. This saintly young man was Portuguese by birth, and was twenty-two years old. I invoke his help. As he loved us in life, I hope he will continue to do so in heaven.[167]

---

167. *CED* III:14-15.

The other example happened in the city of Algiers, where a young slave was solicited to commit an unmentionable sin by his master, but refused courageously. In the act of defending himself from the master's anger, he struck him in the face, which enraged his master exceedingly. This slave was then charged in front of a judge of attempting to kill his owner. Instead of the master being punished for his cruelty, as he deserved, the slave was condemned to be burned alive. He suffered this cruel death as a valiant Christian.

PART NINE

Help Given to the Poor Slaves of Bizerte and of Several Other Places

The priests of the Congregation of the Mission had been sent by their superior general, Monsieur Vincent, to help and serve the poor slaves in Barbary. They did not limit their charity to the cities of Algiers and Tunis, although the number of slaves there gave them ample occasion to exercise their zeal. They extended their care to all places where the poor captives languished in irons, and were in need of their services. This led Monsieur le Vacher, who ordinarily lived in Tunis, to go as far as Bizerte, a port city about ten or twelve leagues away, with five penal colonies of slaves, to offer consolation and services helpful for their salvation. Here is what he wrote to Monsieur Vincent:

Slavery is so evil that it causes many other evils. Among the slaves here, besides the ones in the penal colonies, I found forty locked up in a small stable, so small and crowded that they could hardly move. The only air comes from a small window, covered with an iron grill, located high up in the wall. The slaves are chained two by two, and permanently locked up. Yet they have to work at grinding wheat with a hand mill. Their quota is beyond what their strength allows. These poor people in truth are fed with the bread of sorrow, and can say that they eat by the sweat of their brow, in a place so stuffy, and at work so demanding.

Shortly after I began my visit I heard the confused cries of women and children, mingled with groans and tears. I raised my eyes to the tiny window to see five poor young Christian women slaves. Three of them had small children with them, and they were all in desperate condition. They had heard the noise of greetings to me when I had come to visit the men, and had rushed to the window to see what was afoot. When they realized I was a priest, their sad state moved them to break down in cries and tears. They asked to share in the consolation I had attempted to bring to the men in their prison.

I must admit that I was almost overcome with sorrow at the sight of these poor slaves loaded with chains, and at the lamentations of these poor women, mingled with the cries of their innocent children. The youngest of these women had been greatly persecuted by her owner, who sought to have her deny her faith in Jesus Christ so that he could marry her. Oh, that a small fraction of the enormous sums spent by Christians on superfluous vanities and delicacies could be used to relieve these poor souls from their grievous sufferings. Aided by God's grace, I attempted to help these poor men and women as much as lay in my meager power. We live in a country where we have to pay large amounts just for permission to do good for the unfortunate. To get authorization just to speak to the slaves, you have to pay off their masters, as you must also do to have the slaves on the galleys unchained when they are preparing to leave port. I attempt to take the slaves, one crew at a time, to the penal colonies, to give them an opportunity to go to confession, hear mass, and receive communion. By God's mercy this has been quite successful.[168]

In another letter, written by this same priest, he said:

Two galleys left port yesterday, each carrying more than five hundred Christian slaves. By the grace of God all had been given the sacraments. How sad that day was, and how many blows were rained upon their backs by those infamous renegades in charge of the crews! I know the convicts in the galleys of France are not treated any better, but at least these convicts suffer for their crimes, while the Christian slaves of Barbary suffer solely because they are Christian and faithful to God. On the day these poor people received communion and were returned to the galleys, I was able to provide a slight celebration, at which I provided two steers, and five hundred loaves of bread. Besides, I was also able to give each galley a hundredweight of white bread, to be given to any among them who would fall sick during their time at sea.

From there I went to visit the slaves at Sidi Regeppe. I found them unchained, in keeping with the promise their master had made to me the last time I was here. I found six young men among them, aged sixteen to eighteen years, who had been slaves for the past four or five years. Since they were not allowed out of the house, they had not been able to receive the sacraments as the others had. After preparing them, I heard their confessions. Then I asked them to prepare their poor dwelling as decently as they could, for I would

---

168. *CED* IV:371-72.

> come back the next day with the blessed sacrament, as I would usually do in bringing communion to the sick. The next day, in fact, I celebrated mass in the penal colony in the chapel of the Annunciation. Then, accompanied by all the Christians I met in the streets of Bizerte, I sought out these poor slaves. O God, with what tenderness and devotion these young men received their Lord. The tears of joy and consolation which filled their eyes caused all present to weep also, not from their own miseries, but from their happiness. I heard the confession and gave communion to a seventh young man, who fell ill the next evening. I gave him the sacrament of extreme unction, but he died soon after. I used the remainder of my time in the service of the sick in the penal colonies.[169]

This is how the King of Glory, Jesus Christ, made use of the missionaries. He came himself, with unbounded charity, to visit, console, and vivify the souls redeemed by his blood. They were sought out even in the darkest prisons where they lived in the shadow of death. It was not an insignificant favor that he had inspired Vincent de Paul as the instrument of his mercy and grace in favor of these poor slaves. To him, after God, they owed all the consolation, aid, and helps for salvation given by the missionaries of his Congregation.

Monsieur Guerin, another of the priests of the mission, visited the same place, and gave a report to Monsieur Vincent of his trip to Bizerte, in a letter of 1647.

> I was advised on Easter Sunday that a galley had just come from Algiers to Bizerte. At once I set off to visit the poor chained Christians, numbering about three hundred. The captain allowed me to conduct a sort of mission for ten days. I had another priest with me who helped with catechizing and hearing confessions. We managed to help all, except for several Greek schismatics. O great God, what consolation to see the devotion of these poor captives, most of whom had not been able to receive the sacrament of penance for many years. Among them were some who had not confessed for eight, ten, or even twenty years. I was able to have them unchained while I took them to a place apart to receive communion, after celebrating holy mass. After the mission I treated them to a small celebration, ending by giving them fifty-three *ecus* worth of foodstuffs.
>
> During the time of the mission I stayed in the house of a Moslem, who would not take any payment for my stay. He said, "We must be kind to those who are kind to others," which is a remarkable

---

169. CED IV:443-44.

statement, coming from an infidel. What would amaze you even more is that almost all the Moslems of the locality were so taken and edified at the mission that some showed marks of respect to me, and kissed my hand. I have no doubt your heart would have been filled with joy at the sight. If the fruit of this mission of Bizerte was sweet, the road to it was difficult enough. I did not want to take a military escort in coming here, but I was waylaid by some Arabs who beat me. One of them took me by the throat so violently that I thought he was going to strangle me. Since I am such a miserable sinner, our Lord did not judge me worthy to die in his service.[170]

Besides the slaves in the cities of Algiers, Tunis, and Bizerte, some were kept in country places because of their work. Some of these would from time to time come to the cities, where they would manage to receive the sacraments, but others never came, or only very rarely. These, too, the missionaries attempted to visit, in the wild and deserted places where the slaves worked, often enough at very difficult tasks. The Missionaries of Tunis, particularly, were active in going into the country. They would visit what they called the Maceries (the work places and habitations in which they live), in Perriere, Cantara, Courombaille, Gaudiene with its seven streams, Tabourne, Morlochia, Hamphya and Mamedia. Their places are three, six, eight, ten or twelve leagues from Tunis, and some are in high and arid mountainous regions, more suited to the native lions than to humans.

On the first such trip made by Monsieur Le Vacher, he came upon some Christians who had not been to the sacraments for twelve, fifteen, or eighteen years. Some had lost nearly all remembrance of Christianity by being deprived for so long of any of the practices of our religion. Here is what he wrote to Monsieur Vincent:

> By giving some money to the owners or guardians of these poor slaves, I was able to bring them together for instruction and the sacraments, and by God's grace I was able to confirm them in the faith. Once I had selected the most decent place I could find, I celebrated mass, at which all communicated. Every one of these poor slaves was filled with the consolation it pleased God to bestow, amid the misery of their captivity, which is beyond the imagination of persons who live in freedom. The joy and consolation they experience in their pains could only be the gift of the grace of God. I embraced all, and to give them some small token of my esteem, I provided a celebration for them, as much as my poverty would permit. Besides that, I gave each of the very poorest a quarter *piastre*.[171]

---

170. *CED* III:196.
171. *CED* III:358.

The paternal heart of Monsieur Vincent filled with joy upon receipt of such accounts. He could see his spiritual sons animated with the spirit of the good shepherd of the Gospel, seeking lost sheep in the most remote places, in bringing them back, in a way of speaking, in their arms and upon their own shoulders, to Jesus Christ, their true shepherd. What consolation for him to learn that his missionaries had rescued some of these poor slaves from the deplorable lapse into apostasy brought on by their despair, and had treated them with mildness and charity. Many recognized their fault, and regretted deeply their infidelity to God. They tearfully threw themselves at the feet of the missionaries, accepting the penance given them for their sin. It is impossible to express the joy in the heart of the father of these missionaries at such consoling news. He joined the angels in heaven in their rejoicing at the sight of a single sinner doing penance for his sin, and being converted to God.

PART TEN
The Conversion of Several Heretics and Apostates Brought About by the Priests of the Congregation of the Mission Whom Monsieur Vincent Sent to Barbary

An admirable example of the wisdom and goodness of God was his using the captivity of several heretics who had fallen into the hands of the Moslems, to bring about their deliverance from the slavery into which the devil had led them by their adherence to error. He used the iron and chains that oppressed their bodies to free them from the chains that bound their souls. In losing their personal freedom they recovered the true freedom of the children of God. This happened many times on the missions of Barbary where there were slaves infected with the heresies of Calvin and Luther. When they saw the miserable state to which they had fallen and had been instructed by the missionaries, at length, with the help of God's grace, they recognized the truth, abjured their errors, and rejoined the sheepfold of Jesus Christ.

We do not know exactly how many heretics were converted in the missions of Barbary, but it is certain that the number was considerable. One priest wrote to Monsieur Vincent of eighteen who returned. We can well imagine the other priests being no less successful, and possibly even more so.

Among all the converts, a young Englishman is particularly noteworthy. He was only eleven years old when captured by the pirates off the coast of England, and was brought to Barbary to be sold into slavery. Monsieur Guerin wrote of this young man in a letter to Monsieur Vincent, in June of 1646:

> Two Englishmen have converted to our holy faith, and they have been an example to all the Catholics. There was a third, only eleven

years old, a more beautiful child you could not find. He was as fervent as you could wish, and very devoted to the Blessed Virgin. He invoked her continually for the grace of dying rather than renouncing or offending Jesus Christ. This, unfortunately, is the aim of his owner, who keeps him solely for this purpose, and uses every inducement to achieve his goal. If we could somehow receive two hundred *piastres* we could buy his freedom. There is good reason to hope that he would one day, with the grace of God, become a second Bede, such is his spirit and virtue.

There is nothing of the child in this young man. He made his profession of the Catholic faith on Holy Thursday, received communion the same day, and now receives the sacraments often. He has already been beaten twice to try to force him to deny Jesus Christ. The last time he told his owner during a beating that he could cut off his head if he wanted, but he was a Christian and would never be anything else. Several times he spoke to me about his resolve to die rather than renounce his faith in Jesus Christ. His entire conduct is admirable in one of his tender age. I can truly say that he is a temple of the Holy Spirit.[172]

Besides the conversion of heretics, many apostates were brought back to the fold by the priests of the Mission, aided by the grace of God. One of the priests wrote to Monsieur Vincent:

There is a large harvest here in this country. This is aided by the presence of the plague, for besides the conversion of some Moslems we prefer to keep quiet about, others at the approach of death have opened their eyes to recognize and embrace the truths of our holy religion. There were three apostates who received the sacraments, and went to heaven. There was one recently who had received absolution for his apostasy. Yet at his last hour he was surrounded by his Moslem friends who urged on him his usual blasphemies. He would not give in, but rather, with his eyes fixed on heaven and a crucifix in his hands, died while giving signs of true repentance.

His wife, a former professed religious, had also denied the Christian faith. She too had repented, and had been absolved from her double apostasy, showing as good dispositions as could be hoped for. She is now living in a secluded place. She never goes out, and daily makes the two hours of meditation which we imposed as a penance. We also ordered some bodily mortification besides those required by her rule. She was, however, already practicing some by her own initiative, so moved by regret at her sins that she would have wanted

---

172. *CED* II:597-98.

to suffer martyrdom as an expiation, were it not for the two young children in her care. We baptized these, and she in turn is raising them in keeping with her duty as a true Christian mother.

Another apostate who lives close by died, ending his days as a true penitent. Every day I prepare some Moslems for baptism. They are well instructed in our religion, often coming to see me at night and in secret. There is one among them who holds considerable rank in the country.[173]

In regard to both the Moslems and the apostates, the priests of the Mission were most prudent and circumspect in matters of conversion, lest there would be adverse effects on the good they sought to do among the infidels. Because of this, they spoke little of these events in their letters to France, and often used ambiguous language, for fear that these letters would be intercepted. Only God knows what they accomplished in their ministry to these unfortunate souls.

In a letter from one of his priests to Monsieur Vincent, wishing to speak of the conversion of two apostates, he used this circumlocution, "Our Lord has given us the grace of recovering two precious jewels that had been lost. They were most costly, and of a beauty beyond compare. I am most happy at the outcome."[174]

PART ELEVEN
The Remarkable Example of the Constancy of Two Young Slaves, the One from France, the Other from England

This account is tragic, but nevertheless considerably edifying. It enables us to see the great fruits which the priests of the Congregation of the Mission, animated with the spirit and zeal of Monsieur Vincent, gathered in these infidel lands. We owe our information to a letter written by Monsieur Le Vacher to Monsieur Vincent in 1648, of which the following is the substance.

There were in the city of Tunis two young boys of around fifteen years of age, one French, and the other English. Pirates had captured both of them, and brought them back to Barbary for sale into slavery. Although they were in two different households, they lived near each other. Their closeness in age and their common fate brought about a close friendship that bound them together as closely as brothers.

The English boy was a Lutheran, but he was won to the Church by his friend, a good Catholic. He was instructed by Monsieur Le Vacher, abjured his heresy, and became a member of the Catholic Church. Then some

---
173. *CED* V:397-98.
174. *CED* III:449.

English merchants, Protestants themselves, came to Tunis to ransom the slaves of their nation and religion. This young man boldly announced that he was a Catholic by the grace of God, and that he preferred to spend his entire life as a slave rather than secure his freedom by denying his faith. He courageously refused the offer of liberation, so ardently desired by all who endured slavery among the Turks. He judged it preferable to be maltreated and afflicted in fidelity to Jesus Christ, and to suffer all the ills of slavery rather than to fail in faithfulness to his Savior. This was the admirable effect of the grace of Jesus Christ in these two young men, who had received the word of God sown in their hearts by this good priest of the Mission. They displayed fruits ordinarily not seen, even in those who have passed their entire lives in the practice of virtue.

Continuing in their slavery, the two continued to see each other often. They encouraged each other to fidelity in their faith in Jesus Christ, regardless of whatever might be done to them to force them to renounce their beliefs. It seemed that God was preparing them for their trial, since their owners, moved by the evil spirit, redoubled their efforts to have them deny their faith in Jesus Christ. They carried their evil designs to such an extent that several times they beat the young men inhumanly, and left them on the ground nearly half dead.

One day the English boy stopped by for a visit, as he often did, since they lived so close to one another. They often spoke together for mutual support and consolation, in recounting what they had to endure for the sake of the Lord. He came upon his friend lying on the ground. He called to him by name, to see if he were dead or alive. The first words he said when he regained enough strength to speak, were, "I am a Christian, and I shall remain so for the rest of my life." The English boy kissed the torn and bloody feet of his dear friend, but while doing so some Moslems came in to ask what he was doing. With fortitude, he answered, "I honor the limbs which have suffered for Jesus Christ, my Savior and my God." The infidels were so irritated with him that they beat him, and forced him to leave, to the regret of his friend who had been so consoled by his visit.

Some time later, when the French boy had recovered from his wounds, he went to visit his friend, only to find him in the same state in which he himself had been a short while before. He was lying on a reed mat, half dead from the beating he had been given, surrounded by some Moslems and even his owner who had taken part in the torture. The French boy was so moved by the sad spectacle, and so influenced by grace that he boldly came into the room, approached his friend, and in the presence of the infidels asked him if he preferred Jesus Christ or Mohammed. The poor English boy, even in his sufferings, answered in full voice that his preference was, of course, Jesus Christ, that he was a Christian, and that he hoped to die as one.

The Moslems were very angry with the French boy. One of them, wearing two daggers at his side, threatened to cut off his ears. As he came closer, this little champion of Jesus Christ seized the initiative. He grabbed one of the daggers and cut off one of his own ears, showing these barbarians that he had no fear of their threats. Holding the bloody specimen in his hand, he had the boldness to ask if they wanted the other ear as well. He was ready to cut it off, also, to show his esteem for his beliefs, and resolve to die rather than to give up his faith. The dagger, however, was wrenched from his hand.

The courage of these two young Christians so greatly astonished these infidels that they lost all hope of making them abandon their faith in Jesus Christ. Because of this, the Moslems never spoke to them again about it. The next year, after they proved their fidelity and constancy, God called them both to himself, on the occasion of a plague. This completed the purification of their souls, and made them ready for the crown prepared for them in heaven.[175]

PART TWELVE
Various Other Charitable Activities of the Priests of the Congregation of the Mission Whom Monsieur Vincent Sent to Barbary for the Relief of the Poor Christian Slaves

It would tire the reader if we detailed all the activities which the priests of the Mission, animated with the spirit of their spiritual father and under his direction, contributed toward the aid of the poor Christian slaves of Barbary. They did everything humanly possible to aid them, whether in body or in soul. In these last paragraphs, we will speak only of some things not touched upon in the previous sections.

One of the most important services the missionaries rendered was to use all their influence to prevent some additional Christians from being forced into slavery, and to secure the release of others already held in ways that violated the customs of this country. Even in that violent and inhumane country, there was some sense of legality among the authorities. In a letter of January 1653 Monsieur Vincent wrote to Monsieur Le Vacher in reply to letters he had received:

> I thank God that by your intercession several Frenchmen cap-
> tured at sea and taken to Tunis have been preserved from slavery,

---
175. *CED* III:337-38.

and that you have been able to secure the release of some already in chains. In rendering this service to these persons, you render great service to God. May God in his goodness grant you the grace to act forcefully and efficaciously with the authorities in these matters.[176]

It is true that sometimes the violence and injustice proved too great for all the efforts of their charity. Despite their efforts or their money they were sometimes unable to stay the hands of these barbarians from harming the poor slaves they saw in grave danger. Monsieur Le Vacher wrote to Monsieur Vincent about such a case.

A young and attractive woman from Valencia, about twenty-five years old, was brought to Tunis after capture near her native city. She was put up for sale in the public marketplace, at which I attempted to ransom her by bidding up to 330 *ecus*, which the merchants had lent me, but a wicked Moor outbid me when I came to the end of my money. He already had two wives, this one making the third. This poor creature wept three days without a stop. They did not cause her to abandon her faith until she had been raped. Even some religious, captured from their convent located near the seacoast, suffered the same fate. Alas! If some charitable persons would contribute funds which could be used in similar situations, I am sure they would be richly rewarded.[177]

There was another act of goodness we cannot sufficiently praise. The zeal which burned in the heart of Monsieur Vincent and the priests of his Congregation, prevented many of these poor Christian slaves from denying their faith, especially when they saw them being tortured and on the point of succumbing. We might give several examples of this, among many others.

Monsieur Guerin wrote to Monsieur Vincent from Tunis in 1646:

We have rescued a French woman from the hands of an apostate from her own country. All the merchants contributed something, and I, myself, was able to give seventy *ecus*. The two other women are deeply troubled, but I thought it best to save the one who seemed in the greatest danger. There are other young and beautiful women in great peril if they are not rescued. One would already have been lost, if I, at great effort, had not secured an option of three months in which to ransom her, and had I not put her out of reach of her owner who surely would have violated her.

Not long ago one woman was beaten with more than five hundred blows to force her to deny Jesus Christ. Not satisfied with this cruelty, two of her torturers, as she lay half dead on the ground,

---

176. *CED* IV:544.
177. *CED* IV:575-76.

trampled upon her, and crushed her shoulder. She ended her life gloriously confessing her faith in Jesus Christ.[178]

The same priest wrote in June, 1647:

> We have done much with the money you sent, including the ransom of a poor French woman who had suffered so long at the hands of her Moslem owner. It is a true miracle to have saved her from this tiger, who would take neither gold or silver for her. One day he asked me to come to see him. During our visit we agreed upon a price of three hundred *ecus*. I paid this at once after I obtained the official release from slavery, and immediately I took the woman to a safe place. Two hours later, this miserable man regretted his action, but it was too late, by the grace of God.
>
> We also redeemed a boy from Sables d'Olonne, who was on the verge of renouncing the faith. I think I wrote before of how we tried to prevent this. He cost us 150 *ecus*, of which I was able to give 36, the rest coming from wherever we could manage. I was also able to ransom the young Sicilian woman, a slave at Bizerte, whose husband had become a Moslem. During three years she had suffered indescribable torments rather than join in the apostasy of her husband. I wrote to you around last Christmas of finding her in a pitiable state, all covered with wounds. She cost 250 *ecus*, which came from alms, including a part from myself.[179]

In still another letter, this same priest wrote:

> We have here a young boy from Marseilles, aged thirteen. Since his capture and sale by the pirates he has been beaten with more than a thousand blows to force him to deny his faith in Jesus Christ. Even more cruelly, the skin of one arm was stripped off, like you would do to a piece of poultry before putting it on the grill. This was followed by a choice of four hundred more blows, meaning death itself, or becoming a Moslem. I went at once to see his owner, and three or four times threw myself at his feet. I begged to ransom the boy, and he finally agreed to the price of two hundred *piastres*. I had no money, but borrowed a hundred *ecus* at interest, with a merchant supplying the rest.[180]

Monsieur Jean Le Vacher wrote in one of his letters to Monsieur Vincent:

> A French vessel was shipwrecked on the coast of Tunis. Six of the crew were saved from drowning, but fell into the hands of the Moors, who took them to Tunis to be sold into slavery. Some time

---

178. *CED* II:585-86.
179. *CED* III:203.
180. *CED* III:222.

later the dey forced two of them, under torture, to deny their faith. Two others died under this treatment rather than imitate this infidelity. Since the dey was set on inflicting this same cruelty on the remaining two, we felt obliged to ransom them if we could. Six hundred *piastres* was agreed upon as a price, of which I contributed two hundred. For myself, I would rather suffer anything in this life than have anyone deny my divine Master. I would willingly give my blood and my life, even a thousand lives if I had them, rather than see Christians lose what our Lord purchased by his death.[181]

We learn from other letters of Monsieur Philippe Le Vacher, his brother, written from Algiers to Monsieur Vincent about a young boy of Marseilles, only eight years old. Pirates had captured him, and he was now under duress to become a Moslem. He was ransomed, and returned to his own country. On another occasion he found three young women, sisters, natives of Vence in Provence, who had been captured by pirates and sold into slavery in Algiers. One of the sisters had fallen into the hands of the governor, who had her richly dressed, for he wished to make her his wife. Monsieur le Vacher redeemed all three at a cost of a thousand *ecus*, since this was the only way he saw to save them from this danger to their salvation. Another time he ransomed a mother and daughter and her small son, who were from the island of Corsica. All were in great danger because their owner wanted to have the younger woman deny her faith, so that he could marry her.

The priests of the Congregation of the Mission could not ransom all those whom they saw in danger of renouncing their faith because their resources were quickly exhausted. They often found themselves committed beyond their resources. This did not hinder them from continuing their preaching. By the sacraments they administered to these poor slaves in their sufferings they helped to strengthen and encourage them in their sad plight. Many of these slaves persevered courageously in their confession of belief in Jesus Christ despite all the violent persecution brought against them.

This spiritual help especially enabled ten women to remain faithful who had been badly treated for their beliefs among the many other slaves in Tunis in 1649. Their owners guarded these women closely, and did not allow them to leave their homes. They still managed to slip away long enough to attend mass, go to confession, and receive communion. They were so strengthened by the grace they received that not only did they suffer beatings and other indignities with patience, but even when they fell sick and could not be visited by a priest, they remained firm in their faith despite the efforts of the Moslem ministers who tried to force them to deny their allegiance to Jesus Christ. To understand better the inhumanity with which these poor slaves

---

181. *CED* IV:618.

were treated to make them apostatize, and the strength of virtue they needed to resist, we must realize that these Moslems had the false conviction that anyone who could cause a Christian to become one of them had an assured place in paradise, no matter what sins he may have committed.

With his understanding of the sad condition of the slaves, Monsieur Vincent took great pains to encourage his missionaries in their charitable service to them. In one of his many conferences, he said:

> This ministry is so great and so holy that it has given rise to several orders in the Church of God. These orders have always been greatly esteemed, since they are devoted to the slaves. One such order is the Religious for the Redemption of Captives, who attempt to ransom the slaves and return them to their own country. Among the vows they take is one to commit themselves to the redemption of Christian slaves. Is this not excellent and holy, gentlemen and my brothers?
>
> It seems to that me there is something even greater than going to Barbary to ransom the captives. It is to go there to live among them, to help them at every moment, in body and in soul, to look after their needs, to lend them a helping hand, to bring them every sort of help and consolation in their great afflictions and sufferings. Oh, gentlemen and my brothers, consider well the grandeur of this ministry! Do you know enough about it? Is there anything closer to what our Lord himself did, when he came to earth to deliver men from the captivity of sin, and to teach them by his word and example. This is the example all missionaries must follow. They must be ready to leave their country, their conveniences, their rest, to imitate our confreres in Tunis and Algiers who are so completely given to the service of God and neighbor in these barbarous and infidel lands.[182]

To support all the charitable and holy projects these missionaries in Barbary were offering, Monsieur Vincent collected alms. From time to time he sent considerable sums, and added some of his own, when what he collected was not sufficient. These sums were spent mainly in rescuing those Christian slaves in imminent danger of losing their faith, either by ransoming them outright, or by giving them some alms by way of encouragement in their sufferings.

Monsieur Vincent also sent money to ransom some French priests and religious who had been taken captive by the Moslems.

On many occasions he sent the entire ransom money for several slaves. By the time of his death he had rescued, through the priests of his Congre-

---

182. *CED* XI:437.

gation sent to Barbary, either by their own charity or as agents for others, over twelve hundred slaves who later returned to their own country. What was spent in these ransoms and in other works of charity in these infidel lands came to nearly 1.2 million *livres*. In writing to one of his priests who had sent him an account of what he had spent, he said:

> I have read over your account book. O God, what consolation I have received in reading it! I assure you it gave me more satisfaction than anything I have seen for a long time, because it records what you and your charity have accomplished for so many poor slaves of all nations and of all ages, afflicted with all sorts of miseries. Certainly, even though you could never be able to do more than you are already doing, what you have done is infinitely precious, and worthy of drawing immense blessings upon you. May it please the divine goodness of God to bless your work.[183]

Monsieur Vincent also sent some money to the city of Algiers to set up a small hospital for the poor sick slaves, abandoned in their illness by their heartless owners. It was mainly through the generosity of the duchess of Aiguillon that this project began. Another service of Monsieur Vincent to the poor slaves from France was to serve as a clearinghouse for letters to and from the slaves. Not only did this allow the slaves to send news of themselves to their relatives, mothers, fathers, brothers, wives, and children, but to receive letters from them as well. This consoled them greatly in their unhappy state, and sometimes allowed them to work out their release. Before Monsieur Vincent introduced this service, the slaves from diverse regions, Picardy, Poitou, Guienne, Normandy, Brittany, Languedoc or other provinces, had little hope of receiving any response to their letters, for the mail to Marseilles and Paris was most unreliable. This added greatly to their desolation. Monsieur Vincent applied an effective remedy, almost without precedent. To appreciate it fully, the plight of the poor slaves would have to be recalled, where their total isolation from families added immeasurably to all the other sufferings of their captivity.

This then is a short sketch of what Monsieur Vincent did for the poor slaves during his lifetime, and which the members of his Congregation continued after his death. I say short sketch, for only God is aware of all that was done. This humble missionary hid, as much as he could, what he did in the service of the divine majesty, in order that the glory should be given totally to his name and not to himself. If he had done nothing else, aided by his confreres, than to establish and preserve the public exercise of the Catholic religion in this land of the Turk, even in the face of cruel persecution, this would have been a triumph in the service of Jesus Christ. The Lord

---

183. *CED* V:490.

had strengthened the arm of his faithful servant to raise a shrine to his most holy name in these two infidel kingdoms, even in the midst of its enemies. Christian charity triumphed in these places where it had seemed that even human dignity had disappeared, and where injustice and violence were everyday occurrences.

SECTION EIGHT

The Missions in Ireland

In 1646 our Holy Father, Pope Innocent X, advised Monsieur Vincent that the danger to religion in Ireland had come to his attention, because of the people's lack of instruction and the efforts of heretics.[184] He wished him to send some priests of his Congregation to do what they could to remedy this. At once this humble servant of God took steps to obey him whom he recognized as the head of the Church, and vicar of Jesus Christ upon earth. He chose eight missionaries of his Congregation, among whom were five priests of Irish extraction, all trained in the giving of missions. He instructed them before their departure:

> Be united, and God will bless you, but this union must be the love of Jesus Christ within you. Any other source of harmony, not being cemented by the blood of Jesus Christ, will not endure. It is in Jesus Christ, by Jesus Christ, and for Jesus Christ that you must be united with one another. The spirit of Jesus Christ is a spirit of union and peace. How could you expect to attract other souls to Jesus Christ if you were not united among yourselves? This cannot happen. Have the same sentiments, therefore, the same will, or else you will be like those horses pulling a plow who pull in opposite directions. They spoil everything. God calls you to work in this vineyard. Go therefore, having but a single heart and a single intention, and in this way you will bear much fruit.[185]

He also encouraged them to enter into a spirit of obedience toward the sovereign pontiff, the vicar of Jesus Christ. They were going to a country where some of the clergy were negligent on this point, and were not giving

---

184. This request from Innocent X was communicated to Vincent by Cardinal Francesco Barberini, the pope's nephew and prefect of the Congregation for the Propagation of the Faith. *CED* II:505.
185. *CED* III:82-83.

:ry. He advised them how
hey arrived. He suggested
ission, so that later they
he wise counsels and the

is in 1646 for Nantes, but
ed this time in visiting and
r, and similar good works,
officials. They also gave
Charity of the parishes on
lord Jesus Christ.

Nazaire, which is near the
there. They found several
were able to offer a sort of
scheduled to travel on was
lish gentleman, who chose
a singular example of the
a mortal wound. Seeing
od for having called him to
entiments of thanks for this
sins of his past life, that it
atly.

foresaw the Missionaries
all he could to hinder their
on land and on sea, but the
ial protection. They were
inevitably destined to cause

gin their work. Some went
They began by catechism
exhortations, for Monsieur
amiliar instructions to teach
ons of Christianity, and then
uncing sin by penance, and
their state of life. This way
n all the surrounding coun-
. When the nuncio to Ireland
ated the missionaries, urged
d religious of the country to
ng.[186]

It is difficult to tell how great were the fruits of the mission, whose exercises were almost unknown in that country, and how great was the devotion of all the Catholics who came from the surrounding region. Some even came from far away to attend the catechism lessons and to make their general confession. They had, at times, to wait an entire week for a confessor, so great was the crowd. Even more remarkably, the pastors and other priests of the places where the missions were given were usually the first in line to make their general confession. They were anxious to learn the new method of catechizing and preaching, so that they could maintain the good already accomplished in their parishes by the missions.

The effects of the missions became evident during the bloody persecution Cromwell raised against the Catholics of this poor kingdom.[187] Not a single pastor in the places where the missions had been given abandoned his flock. They all remained to help and defend them until they were either put to death or banished for their confession of the Catholic faith, as happened to them all. In one case, one of the bravest of the pastors sought out the priests of the Mission who were living in a hut at the base of a mountain, to make his annual confession. He was delayed because he administered the sacraments to a sick person, arriving only the following night. The soldiers of the heretical party captured him and put him to death. His glorious death crowned an innocent life, and fulfilled his desire of suffering for our Lord, as he had expressed a year before during a retreat he had made at Limerick with the priests of the Mission.

Since the persecution of the heretics continued to increase, it became necessary to stop giving the missions, and by orders of Monsieur Vincent several of the priests returned to France. Before leaving they called upon the archbishop of Cashel, on August 16, 1658. He gave them a letter addressed to Monsieur Vincent, written in Latin, but given here in translation:

> The departure of your missionaries gives me the opportunity to render my humble thanks and appreciation for what you in your charity have done for the flock entrusted to my charge, through your priests. Not only was the time ripe for this service, the occasion was most appropriate. By their efforts and their example they have aroused the devotion of the people, which increases day by day. Even though your good priests have suffered much inconvenience since arriving in our country, they have not ceased to apply themselves to the work of the missions as tireless laborers. Aided by the grace of God, they have gloriously extended and augmented the worship and glory of

---

187. Charles I of England was executed on February 9, 1649. Ireland proclaimed his son, the Prince of Wales, as King Charles II. Irish Catholics were persecuted by Cromwell with particular ferocity because of both their religion and their support of the Stuart cause.

God. I hope this same God, who is all good and all powerful, will himself be your recompense and theirs. For myself, I shall pray that you will be preserved for a long time, for you have been chosen for the good and for the service of his holy Church.[188]

The bishop of Limerick wrote a letter at the same time to Monsieur Vincent:

It is only proper, Monsieur, for me to thank you with all my heart for the good I have received from your priests. I must also tell you of the great need we have of them in this country. I may confidently assure you that they have produced more fruit and converted more souls than all the rest of the clergy put together. What is more, most of the upper class, men and women alike, by the good example and efforts of your priests have become models of devotion and virtue. This did not happen before your missionaries arrived among us. The troubles of the times and the army have hindered their work. Nevertheless the memory of spiritual things and salvation are so imprinted on the hearts of the people of the cities and country that they bless God in adversity as well as in prosperity. I hope, through their help, to work out my own salvation.[189]

The violence of the persecution increased more and more in this country, forcing Monsieur Vincent to recall all but three of his Missionaries. These continued to work for the salvation of the people with great success and blessing, by the help of the grace of God, notwithstanding the difficulties and dangers they encountered. They experienced that having but two or three gathered in the name of the Lord was enough to feel the effects of his divine presence. They undertook a task far exceeding their own strength, but succeeded by a special gift of divine goodness. The mission in Limerick continued, as the bishop wished, but it was no longer possible to go to the countryside, since the heretics controlled it. Also, poor Catholic villagers had taken refuge in the city. The Missionaries were greatly encouraged that the bishop himself wanted to help in the work of the mission. There were nearly twenty thousand communicants in the city, and they all made their general confession. Some were in grave sin, but gave all the signs of a true conversion. The entire city took on a penitential atmosphere to attract the grace of divine mercy. The magistrates of the city also contributed their part. Besides the good example they gave in attending the various exercises of the mission, they used their authority to root out all vice, and exterminate scandals and public offenses. Among other things, they legislated against swearing and blasphemy, with the happy result that these detestable vices were entirely eliminated from the city and surrounding areas.

---

188. *CED* III:357.
189. *CED* III:356-57.

God himself seemed to confirm these measures by two incidents that occurred. The first was at Thurles, where in the open market a butcher blasphemed the holy name of God. A priest of the Mission who happened to be passing by, admonished him. The correction had such a good effect upon him that he came to himself to say to the missionary that he deserved and was willing to be put in chains for his sin, but asked the Missionary to accompany him to the place of punishment. On the way, he met one of his relatives who attempted to dissuade him, out of respect for the family honor, but the Missionary insisted he should go through with his plan to satisfy the justice of God and to repair the scandal he had given. This relative then went into a rage, and picking up some stones threatened to harm the priest if he did not persuade his relative not to go through with his act of penance. On the spot, God struck this miserable man with a strange malady which left his tongue so black and swollen, that he could not withdraw it into his mouth. This lasted until prayers were said for him and holy water was sprinkled upon his tongue, which then returned to normal. He recognized his fault, begged pardon of the Missionary, and joined the butcher in doing penance for his sin in the stocks.

The other incident happened at Rathkeale when a gentleman in company of some friends cursed and swore in the public streets. One of his friends suggested he ought to kiss the ground at the very place the oaths had been uttered, but he was mocked for his efforts. In turn, he took to his knees on the spot, and as reparation, kissed the muddy road on behalf of his friend, who continued to mock him. When he returned home, God allowed him to fall from his horse, and so injure himself. He came to his senses, and recognized the sin he had committed. With great remorse of conscience he resolved to make a general confession of his whole life to one of the priests of the Mission, and afterward he lived so virtuously and gave such good example that he was the cause of several other conversions.

While the Missionaries worked in Limerick, the bishop wrote the following letter to Monsieur Vincent, by which we can see the great blessing God showered upon this mission:

> I have often written to Your Reverence about your missionaries in this kingdom. To speak the truth as it is before God, I must tell you that never in the memory of man have we seen such great progress and advancement of the Catholic faith as we have lately seen by the industry, piety, and faithfulness of your priests, especially at the beginning of this present year when we began a mission in this city of more than twenty thousand believers. This has been done with such fruit, and such appreciation by all the inhabitants that I have no doubt most have been delivered from the clutches of

Satan by the remedies brought for so many invalid confessions, drunkenness, blasphemies, adulteries, and other disorders which have been abolished completely. The city has changed complexion. It was brought to penance by the plague, famine, war, and other dangers from all sides, which we receive as manifest signs of the anger of God. Although we are his unworthy servants, his goodness has granted us the favor of being engaged in this work. It was indeed most difficult at the beginning and for some beyond our hopes, but God used the weak to confound the strong of this world. The authorities of the city have been so assiduous at the preachings, sermons, and other exercises of the mission that the cathedral itself was hardly able to hold the people. We know of no better way to appease the anger of God than to eradicate sin, the cause of the evils which have befallen us. We of ourselves are finished, if God does not offer his hand. We look to him to have mercy and to pardon.

Father, I acknowledge that I owe the salvation of my soul to your confreres. Send them some few words of consolation. I know of no other mission under heaven more useful than that of Ireland, for if a hundred be given elsewhere there will be none that accomplish so much with so few laborers. Our sins are grievous. Who knows if God will not uproot us from this kingdom, and give the Bread of Angels to the dogs, to our blame and shame.[190]

We join to this letter of the bishop, one written by Monsieur Vincent in April of 1650 to the superior of the missions at Limerick, to encourage him in the possible difficulties he might have to endure:

Your letter has greatly edified us, seeing two excellent fruits of the grace of God. By the first, you give yourself completely to God, remaining in the country despite the dangers, exposing yourself to the threat of death rather than fail in your help to the neighbor. The second grace is your care of your confreres, in returning them to France to escape the perils in which they live. The spirit of martyrdom moves you to the former, prudence to the latter. In both you follow the example of our Lord, who was willing to suffer the torments of the cross for the salvation of men, but protected his disciples by saying, "let these go away, and do not harm them."[191] You have acted like a true child of this true Father. I thank him for the infinite graces he has given you, to enable you to act with such charity, the summit of all virtues. I pray that you may be filled with this, everywhere and always, to share it with those who lack it. Since

---

190. *CED* III:420-21.
191. John 18:8.

the other priests with you are in the same disposition to remain, despite the dangers of war and pestilence, we agree they should be allowed to do so. Who knows what God has in store for them? He truly did not inspire such a holy resolution in vain.

O God, how inscrutable are your ways! Here we have a mission as successful and necessary as any we have ever seen. Yet it seems you withdrew your mercy toward a penitent city, to allow the scourges of war and pestilence to fall upon it. This is to reap the harvest of souls, and to collect the good grain into your eternal barns. We adore your holy will, O Lord.[192]

Monsieur Vincent spoke correctly, as if he foresaw the future. The mission which accomplished so much was providentially to prepare the people for two great afflictions, to try their patience and their faith. The first of these was the plague which struck the country, especially in the city of Limerick, where over eight thousand people died, including the bishop's brother. He had joined the missionaries in visiting the sick, consoling them, and looking after their needs. It was marvelous to see how these poor people supported this trial, not only with patience, but even with peace and tranquility of spirit. They said they died content because they had left the burden of their sins in the sacrament of penance during their general confession. Others said they did not complain, because God had sent the holy priests (so they referred to the priests of the Mission) to purify their souls. Others in their sickness asked for nothing except to share in the prayers of their confessors, whom they felt were, after God, responsible for their salvation. In a word, both the healthy and the sick expressed their thanks and their praiseworthy dispositions. When their bishop heard and saw this, he could scarcely restrain his tears, nor refrain from repeating often, "Alas, if Monsieur Vincent had never done anything else for the glory of God but what he has done for these poor people, he would have to be regarded as blessed."

As a further trial and a new affliction, this poor city of Limerick was besieged and finally taken by the heretics.[193] They cruelly put to death many of the inhabitants, because of the Catholic faith they professed, notably four of the leading men of the town. These men showed on this occasion how much they had benefited from the instructions and exhortations of the missionaries, and from the spiritual retreats made in their house. They displayed an invincible zeal for the defense of the Catholic faith, especially Sir Thomas Strick, who at the end of his retreat was elected mayor of the city. He openly declared himself opposed to all enemies of the Church. When he received the keys of the city he immediately placed them at the feet of

---

192. *CED* IV:15-16.
193. November 19, 1651.

the most holy Virgin, whom he implored to take this city under her protection. Afterward, he led a procession of the people to the church, where many religious ceremonies were carried out. Next the mayor addressed the people to encourage them to have an inviolable fidelity to God, to the Church and to the king, offering to give his own life for such a just cause.

God accepted this offer, for shortly afterward the enemy captured the city, and conferred martyrdom upon him and the three other leading men of the town, who had lately shared the spiritual retreat with him. All four endured their suffering not merely with constancy but even with joy, dressing themselves in their best clothes to show this externally. Before being executed they spoke to the people, and drew tears from the eyes of all, even the heretics. They testified before heaven and earth that they died for the confession and defense of the Catholic religion. This greatly strengthened the other Catholics to persevere in the faith, and to suffer any torture rather than fail in the fidelity they owed to God.

One of the three missionaries remaining in Ireland gloriously finished his life in his labors for the mission. The other two remained during the plague and siege, but left after the city was captured. In disguise and at great risk, they were finally obliged to return to France in 1652, after serving in Ireland for six years.[194] They and their companions had worked ceaselessly at giving missions, always at the expense of the house of Saint Lazare, and supported by the limitless charity of Monsieur Vincent. He did not want to impose this charge on anyone else, but he did have some help from the generosity of the duchess of Aiguillon to cover the cost of the voyage of the priests, and of some necessary religious articles.

We are aware there were more than eighty thousand general confessions in these missions in Ireland, and other benefits beyond measure, but we cannot speak of them in detail for, out of humility, Monsieur Vincent wished to keep them under the cloak of silence. When the superior of the mission returned, he asked the superior general if he might compose a short account of the mission to Ireland. He replied:

---

194. These two missionaries were Gerard Brin and Edmund Barry. After the fall of Limerick to Cromwell's forces, they left the city in disguise together with over a hundred other priests and religious. They mixed with the retreating soldiers who had been allowed to withdraw from the city by the terms of the surrender. The night before they had prepared themselves for death since it was well known that Cromwell showed no mercy to captured Catholic priests. Fortunately they were not recognized the next day, and their escape was successful. The two confreres separated to increase their chances of escape from the country. Brin fled the country with the vicar general of Cashel. Barry took to the mountains where he was hidden by a charitable woman for two months. Eventually he managed to get on board a ship bound for France and arrived at Nantes. Vincent was overjoyed at their escape since he believed that they had been killed in the Limerick massacre. A laybrother, Thady Lee, was not so fortunate. Cromwell's troops discovered him, and horribly massacred him in front of his mother. He became the Congregation's first martyr. (*CED* IV:343.) Why Abelly omitted this account is unknown.

It suffices that God knows all that has been done. The humility of our Lord requires that the little Company of the Mission hide itself in God to honor the hidden life of Jesus Christ. The blood of martyrs will not be forgotten by God, and sooner or later will bring about a new generation of Catholics.

SECTION NINE

On the Mission to the Isle of Saint Lawrence, Otherwise Known as Madagascar

PART ONE
Letter from Monsieur Vincent to Monsieur Nacquart, Priest of the Congregation of the Mission, About This Mission

We know of no better way to begin our discussion of this important mission than by quoting from a letter written by Monsieur Vincent to the late Monsieur Charles Nacquart.[195] He was a priest of the Congregation of the Mission, a native of the diocese of Soissons, and the first one chosen for this mission. He happily spent his life in the service of the Lord, working for the conversion of these poor infidels. Monsieur Vincent wrote to him in April of 1648, from Richelieu where he was at the time.

> For a long time our Lord has given you the desire of doing something special for him. When at the meetings at Richelieu, the proposal was made to open missions among the pagans, it seemed to me that the Lord made you feel you were being called, as you wrote me, together with several others of the community at Richelieu. This seed of divine vocation has begun to grow. In speaking for the Congregation for the Propagation of the Faith, of which the Holy Father is the head, the nuncio has chosen our Company to serve God in the isle of Saint Lawrence, also called Madagascar.
>
> Our Company, in turn, has turned to you as the most precious offering it can make, as homage to our sovereign Creator, to go there

---
[195]. Charles Nacquart was born in 1617 at Trelon in the diocese of Soissons. He died in Madagascar May 29, 1650.

with another priest of our Company. O dearest Monsieur! How does your heart respond to this news? Is it filled with shame and confusion at receiving such a grace from heaven? This is a vocation equal to that of the greatest apostles and the greatest saints in the Church of God! An eternal design of divine Providence, accomplished now in you! Only humility, Monsieur, is capable of accepting such a grace. You have only to abandon all you are or could be with overwhelming confidence in our sovereign Creator. Generosity and great courage are essential for you. You must have faith as profound as Abraham's, charity as complete as Saint Paul's, and the zeal, patience, deference, love of poverty and solitude, discretion, probity of life, and the same desire to consume yourself completely for God that inspired the renowned Saint Francis Xavier.

This island lies under Capricorn. It is four hundred leagues in length, and about one hundred sixty leagues wide. Its poor inhabitants live in ignorance of God, but they are simple, of good disposition, and quite capable. You must cross the equator to reach the island.

The first thing you must do is to model yourself on the great saint, Francis Xavier, in his trip to the East. You must serve and edify the ship's company, arranging public prayers if possible. Have regard for the inconveniences of others, and put yourself out as much as you can to accommodate yourself to the others. Make this voyage, which may last for five or six months, a happy one by your prayers and the practice of all the virtues, just as the sailors do by the performance of their duties. Always show the officers a great respect.[196] Come what may, remain faithful to God and his interests, never betraying his trust in you for any consideration whatsoever. However, take care not to spoil by too great haste the designs of the good God, who takes his time and knows how to wait for the right moment.

Once you have arrived at this island, you must adapt yourself as best you can. It might be necessary to separate, to serve in different locations, but even then you must arrange to meet as often as you can for mutual support and consolation. In regard to the French colonists and any of the natives who shall be converted you must keep all the parish records. Follow the directives of the Council of Trent in all things, and make use of the Roman Ritual, not allowing anyone to introduce any other. If it should be that another ritual is already in vogue, strive gently to replace it by the Roman Rite. You will need at least two copies of the Roman Ritual.

---

196. The directors of the Company of the Indies.

Your main concern, once you see to your own maintenance, must be to live in gentleness and in good example among the people you have come to serve. Make these poor people, born in darkness and in ignorance of their Creator, come to know the truths of our holy faith, not by arguments drawn from theology but by reflections taken from the world around them. You must begin this way, leading them to understand that you are simply developing the signs God has left in them of himself, which gradually have grown dim by reason of their sins. To accomplish all this, Monsieur, you must often invoke the Father of Lights, and repeat what you say every day in the office: *Da mihi intellectum, ut sciam testimonia tua* ["Give me discernment that I may know your decrees"].[197] You will see all this by meditation on the insights he will give you.

You must prove the truth of a sovereign and first Being, and how this is related to the mystery of the Trinity, the necessity of the mystery of the Incarnation, wherein a new perfect man came to redeem us from the sin of the first man. You must make these people appreciate the weakness of human nature which they themselves recognize since they have laws and punishments. It would be good to have some books which treat of these questions, such as the Catechism of Granada, or some others which I will try to send you.[198] I do not have to repeat, Monsieur, that meditation will be the best teacher: *Accedite ad eum et illuminamini* ["Look to him that you may be radiant with joy"].[199] giving yourself over to the Spirit of God who will teach you in these encounters.

Ah, may it please his divine bounty to give you the grace of cultivating the seed of Christianity which is already there, and enabling them to live in true Christian charity. If you do that, I do not doubt, Monsieur, that our Lord will use you in these distant isles to prepare an abundant harvest for the Company. Go then, Monsieur, sent by God as his representative here below to these people. Cast the net boldly!

I am aware of how much you are devoted to purity of heart. You will need to make good use of this virtue, for the people there offend in many ways in this regard. The infallible grace of your vocation will be your safeguard. We will look forward to hearing news from you, and will send you news from home. We will send you a complete mass kit, two Roman Rituals, two small bibles, two Acts

---

197. Ps 119:125, said at least on Sundays at Sext.
198. *Introducción al símbolo de la fe.*
199. Ps 34:6.

of the Council of Trent, two books of moral theology, and pictures of all the main mysteries which will help your people understand and which they will be pleased to see. We have a young man here from Madagascar, about twenty years of age, who will be baptized today by the nuncio. I used these pictures to teach him, and they seemed to serve the purpose well.

You will have to bring the irons for making the hosts for mass, and the holy oils for baptism and extreme unction. You will each need Busee's book for your meditations,[200] copies of the *Introduction to a Devout Life*, and lives of the saints. We will send a letter giving you full authority from us, and one from the nuncio, who has this project very much at heart. For the rest, I give myself entirely to you, if not to follow you, which I am unworthy to do, at least to offer prayers every day for you, should God continue my days upon earth. If it should please him to show his mercy to me in my seeing you only in eternity, I shall see you among those called apostles, by reason of your present calling. I finish this letter by throwing myself at your feet. I beg you to commend me to our common Lord that I may remain faithful, and that in his love I may walk the path that leads to eternity. I remain, Monsieur, yours in our Lord.

The one we are sending with you is Monsieur Gondree, whom perhaps you met in our community at Saintes while he was still a cleric.[201] He is one of the best candidates of our Company, and has preserved the devotion he brought with him when he joined us. He is humble, charitable, cordial, exact, and zealous. In a word, he is someone I cannot say enough good things about.

Several merchants will leave here Wednesday or Thursday for La Rochelle. Monsieur Gondree will go with them to meet you at Richelieu, while they go on ahead where they will await you, around the fifteenth or twentieth of next month, before setting sail. Monsieur, please be ready. We will add to the books already mentioned the Life and Letters of the Apostle of the Indies. Don't say anything about all this just yet. Wait until we have announced this from here.

One of the gentlemen engaged in trade with the Indies will join you on this voyage. He has paid your passage. We will send you something for your own expenses when you arrive. What more can

---

200. A volume of meditations, *Enchiridion piarum meditationum*, by the Jesuit Joannes Buys (or Busaeus), which Monsieur Portail had edited and translated for the use of the Congregation at Saint Vincent's request.
201. Nicolas Gondree was born in 1620 at Assigny in the diocese of Amiens. As a subdeacon he was stationed at Saintes. Saint Vincent recalled him to Paris for his ordination to the priesthood, and his assignment to the Madagascar mission. He died in Madagascar in May of 1649.

I say, Monsieur, except that I pray that our Lord will give you some share in his charity, and his patience. There is nothing I desire more upon this earth, if it were permitted, than I might be your companion on this mission in place of Monsieur Gondree.[202]

PART TWO
The Departure of the Two Priests of the Congregation of the Mission, and Events that Occurred on Their Journey

Monsieur Nacquart had no sooner received this letter from Monsieur Vincent than he immediately began to put its directives into effect, considering it as showing not the will of a man, but of God himself. After Monsieur Gondree's arrival they set off together for Richelieu on April 18. They had to remain at La Rochelle for nearly a month, awaiting the completion of preparations of the ship that was to carry them to their new mission. With the bishop's permission, they used their time to catechize, to hear confessions, and to provide other services for the poor, particularly those in the hospital or in prison.

On the twenty-first of the following May, the feast of Our Lord's Ascension, the anchor was raised and the sails set for departure. During the first days the two good missionaries spent their time with the passengers, numbering about one-hundred twenty, helping them make their general confession. They did so because of the graces and indulgences of the Jubilee granted by our holy father, the pope.

They stopped first at Cape Verde to take on fresh water. There they met a ship bound for the island of Saint Christopher, to whose passengers the missionaries were able to provide the same opportunity for general confession.[203]

Their journey continued well until they approached the equator. Here the winds became so strong and contrary that they entertained the thought of turning back. The two missionaries exhorted the crew to turn for protection to the holy Virgin. Following their suggestion, all made a public vow to God in honor of the queen of heaven to confess and communicate on one of the days preceding the feast of the Immaculate Conception, and to build a church on the island of Madagascar. The storm ended, and the winds became favorable, so that on the eve of the feast they found that they had crossed the equator. During the remainder of the voyage they experienced the help of the Mother of God on several other occasions. As they approached the Cape of Good Hope they were delivered from a particularly dangerous problem.

---

202. *CED* III:278-85.
203. Saint Kitts, in the Caribbean, which had French colonists from about 1625.

Then they cast anchor in the bay of Sardaigne,[204] where they spent eight days. Finally, after six and a half months at sea, they arrived at the island of Saint Lawrence.

During all this time the Missionaries did not remain idle. They had realized that several of the sailors and some of the passengers needed instruction, and so they provided it three or four times a week. They gave catechetical instruction on the main mysteries of the faith, and other matters of importance, using the method employed on the missions. A question period followed the instruction. During it, the youngest present were asked what had been taught.

As was customary in a ship so crowded, there always were some sick among the passengers, and the missionaries served them as diligently as they could. One would visit them in the morning and the other in the afternoon. Public prayers were offered both mornings and evenings, and mass was said daily, weather permitting. For those who were well the priests organized groups of three or four, where one would read from a good book such as the *Imitation of Christ*, the *Introduction to a Devout Life*, or other similar books. This helped the passengers avoid idleness, the source of many evils, and enabled them to use their time profitably.

The priests also persuaded many of those on board to attend spiritual conferences two or three times a week on topics appropriate to their state, especially on temptations and other occasions of offending God, and also on the ways to resist or avoid the suggestions of the evil one. On these occasions the words of our Lord, who promised to be with two or three gathered in his name, were sensibly felt. At the end of the talk one of the priests would summarize what had been said, add some thoughts of his own, and conclude with some examples from holy Scripture or from the lives of the saints.[205]

PART THREE
Description of Madagascar and its People

Before speaking of what these two good priests of the Congregation of the Mission accomplished in this country, and to be able to understand it better, we should briefly describe the island and the people who live there. We will follow in this the account given by Monsieur Nacquart when writing to Monsieur Vincent.

The island of Madagascar, otherwise called Saint Lawrence because of its discovery on the feastday of this great saint,[206] is about six hundred Italian

---

204. Saldanha, near Cape Town.
205. *CED* III:547-51, the author's summary of Nacquart's lengthy report to Saint Vincent.
206. August 10.

miles in length, and two hundred miles, or in some places three or four hundred, in width. Its circumference is around eighteen hundred miles.[207] It has a warm climate, but is not unbearable. It is divided into several counties or provinces, separated from one another by high mountains. Those who have traveled widely in the island put its population at more than four hundred thousand.

Each county or province has a ruler who is accepted as the master or lord. He has several vassals, sometimes numbering up to three or four thousand or even more. The wealth of these rulers consists in the herds of animals they own, or in the tribute of rice or roots which their subjects provide. The natives are either blacks, with kinky hair, the original inhabitants of the country, or the light-skinned, whose long hair is like what we are familiar with in France. It is believed these people first came to the island from Persia, about five hundred years ago, and gradually made themselves masters in the land.

The people live in small villages. They have neither cities nor fortresses. Their houses are made of wood, and covered with leaves. Their beds and chairs are simple planks. They eat seated on reed mats.

The ordinary food of the country is rice and poultry, beef and mutton. They have no wheat or wine, but do have a drink made from honey. They also have some beans and melons, and some roots which are good to eat. Lemons and oranges abound. The rivers provide fish, but are dangerous because of the many crocodiles which frequent their waters.

Nothing seems to be fixed or stable in their religion, for in the entire island there are neither temples nor priests. Some very superstitious rites and ceremonies are based on false and impertinent notions, but some others are closely related to the truth.

They recognize one god, master of the whole world, whom they call *Senhare*.[208] He lives in heaven, they say, like a king in his kingdom. In other places they recognize neither god nor the devil, unless it be merely by name. They honor the devil in their sacrifices, and offer him the better part, reserving the remainder to him whom they call god. Why they do this is not known, unless it is that they fear the one more than the other, or maybe because of some misfortune they have experienced in the past.

There is one group among the people called *Ombiasses*,[209] that is writers, because they know how to read and write.[210] They are the guardians of the ceremonies, customs and superstitions of the country. The people fear and respect them because of their ability to read and write, but they do not have much learning or doctrine. The best they can do is quote a few sentences

---

207. The original has "fourteen hundred."
208. Zanahary, in modern spelling.
209. Ombiasa, in modern spelling.
210. The original adds "in Arabic."

from the Koran, a book first brought to the island by the early Persians. They draw from the Koran a certain number of superstitions, which they believe will enable them to cure the sick, predict the future, and find people who have become lost.

They practice the custom of circumcision of children everywhere, but not through any religious motive. This is strictly a traditional observance, from purely human motives.

The light-skinned observe a sort of fast two months of the year. This consists in not eating anything from sunrise to sunset, but at night they eat to provide strength for the next day. They do not eat beef or drink wine, but poultry and spirituous liquors are not forbidden. If it happens that someone does not want to fast, he can arrange to have someone else fast in his place.

Of all the superstitions practiced on the island the one most opposed to the honor of God and the most difficult to eradicate is the worship given by the leaders of the country and their servants to the idols, which they call *Olis*.[211] The Ombiasses make these out of wood, roots, or other base material, and sell them. They are carved crudely, often in human form. These they hollow out, fill with a mixture of oil and a certain powder which the natives believe makes the idols alive and able to respond to their prayers. They think the idols can produce good weather, good health, victory over enemies, etc. These idols are in every house, and are carried upon their person when they travel. They have recourse to them in all needs, and seek their counsel in their doubts.

The people believe that the first thought that comes to them after recourse to the idol has been suggested by the Olis. When they are about to cross a river they invoke these same idols to preserve them from the crocodiles. They even pray to the crocodiles themselves, beseeching them in a loud voice to do them no harm. They confess their misdeeds aloud, such as stealing, and promise to repay what they have taken. Then, after they throw water and sand to the four corners of the earth, they imagine they can confidently cross the river. If, despite all these superstitious precautions crocodiles catch and devour them, they explain it by saying their Olis did not do their duty.

This superstition is so ingrained in the spirit of these people that they will not allow anyone to question the practice or even speak to them about it. By the grace of God, since the arrival of the priests of the Mission several among them have had their eyes opened to the truth, and have recognized the deception of the Ombiasses and of their Olis.

Another horrible custom of these people is to reject as cursed those children born on the night between Saturday or Sunday, as likely to bring

---

211. Now spelled Ody, a charm.

disaster upon the family. They abandon these children to die, unless, as may happen, someone takes compassion on them, and rescues them from certain death.[212]

PART FOUR
The Arrival of Two Priests of the Congregation of the Mission in Madagascar, and Their Initial Activities

The French quarter of Madagascar is a section of the island near the latitude of the Tropic of Capricorn. It is called in the language of the country *Histolangar*, and a fort has been built there called Fort Dauphin.[213] The two priests, Fathers Nacquart and Gondree, after a long voyage of six and a half months, landed happily on December 4, 1648. The French there received them joyfully, and participated devoutly in singing a Te Deum and at the solemn mass of thanksgiving. It had been nearly five months since they had been able to have mass.

One of the first concerns upon their arrival was to look to the spiritual care of the French themselves, and to help them profit from the Jubilee. They then applied themselves to studying the language of the country, which proved very difficult. The interpreters and intermediaries could not find words appropriate to explain the virtues and mysteries of our faith in a country where matters of religion are never discussed.

As soon as they could stammer a few words of the language they began to instruct the natives. They found much greater docility among the blacks than among the light-skinned, who thought of themselves as sufficiently informed and preferred not even to listen when matters of the faith were discussed. If they listened at all, they did so merely through curiosity, with no intention of being taught or converted.

Six days after his arrival Monsieur Nacquart heard of one of the lords of the island named Andiam Ramach.[214] In his youth he had visited Goa and had lived there for three years. Monsieur Nacquart learned from this man himself that he had been baptized and instructed in our holy religion. To prove his point he made three signs of the cross on his forehead,[215] and recited the Our Father, Hail Mary and the Creed in Portuguese. This led Monsieur Nacquart to ask if he might not teach these same truths to his subjects, and help them to pray to God, just as Monsieur Ramach had done.

---

212. *CED* III:552-59, the author's summary of Nacquart's lengthy report.
213. Now called Tolagnaro.
214. Andriandramaka.
215. This action is explained by referring to the original, which reads: "He made three signs of the cross on his forehead, mouth, and heart, and said [in Latin] 'By the sign of the holy cross deliver us from our enemies.'"

The response to this request was favorable, and the lord agreed to attend the sessions himself, together with the leading men of the region who stated that they were well pleased that their children would receive instruction. All this obliged this good missionary to apply himself even more diligently to the study of the native language to profit from such a favorable opportunity for the propagation of our holy religion among these poor unbelievers.

On the following feast of the Epiphany, commemorating the call of the gentiles to the faith, Monsieur Nacquart and his companion began to baptize several children. Monsieur de Flacourt, governor of Fort Dauphin, offered to be the godfather of the first child baptized. He named him Peter, as the first spiritual stone in the Church beginning to be built on this island.

Continuing to study the language, and gaining a little fluency, they began to travel from place to place to teach those they found disposed to listen. On Sundays they would present a sort of catechism lesson to the youth of the area.

One day, on returning to their usual place of residence, the French fort, they met one of the chiefs of a small village who had fallen sick. He begged the missionaries to come to his house to pray to God for his cure. Monsieur Nacquart explained to him that God often allowed sickness of the body to bring about the salvation of souls. In any case, he added, God was powerful enough and good enough to cure him, if he would abandon his superstitions and give himself to God in professing the true faith. He asked on the spot if he might be taught this true religion. Monsieur Nacquart assembled all the people of the village so that they too might profit from his instruction of the sick man. In their presence he explained through an interpreter the most important and necessary articles of the faith.

The sick man listened attentively to the instruction. He said his heart was consoled to hear this message, and that he believed all he had heard. He asked if Jesus Christ was truly powerful enough to restore his health. Yes, the missionary replied, provided you believe with all your heart, and your soul is cleansed from all sin by baptism, and you accept from divine Goodness whatever he will be pleased to send you. At once the sick man had a child bring water, and insisted the priest baptize him at once.

Fearing that he sought the health of the body more than that of the soul (as was later seen to be the case) Monsieur Nacquart thought best to defer the sacrament. He said that the patient must prove that his resolution to serve God and become a Christian was truly sincere. This would be shown, if after his return to good health, which he sincerely hoped the Lord would grant, he would have his entire family instructed in the faith. The wife of the sick man was present for this exchange. She told of how, long before the French arrived on the scene, she had prayed to God. She told how once while working at the rice harvest, she was moved to raise her eyes to heaven, saying to God: "You cause the rice I harvest to grow and to mature. If you have need of it, I shall give it to you. I would want to give some to whomever has need of it." This shows how even amid the darkness of infidelity God allows some rays of his grace to fall upon people to prepare them to know and to serve him.

All those attending the instruction of the sick man showed their satisfaction with all they had heard. They judged this knowledge more precious than gold or silver, which could be taken from them by force while no one could deprive them of the gift of knowing and serving God. After this, Monsieur Nacquart and his confrere bade farewell. They left the sick man with hope of a cure and the others with the expectation of being more fully taught in the future.[216]

PART FIVE
The Death of Monsieur Gondree, One of the Two Priests of the Congregation of the Mission, and the Later Work of Monsieur Nacquart, the Only Remaining Priest on the Island

Although the judgments of God are inscrutable, as the holy apostle says, and his ways often unknown, we are still obliged to submit ourselves to his holy will and recognize and confess that all he does is for the best.

The two good priests of the Mission made good progress in their facility with the language and of their knowledge of many places on the island. They began to see the fruits of their work in the instruction and conversion of these poor unbelievers. Yet in the midst of their zealous optimism and hopes for the future, Monsieur Gondree was stricken with a fever which, together with some other complications, carried him off in a short time.

Monsieur Nacquart wrote to Monsieur Vincent:

> At the time of the Rogation Days,[217] Monsieur de Flacourt, the governor, asked one of us to accompany him on a visit he was about to make to different parts of the island. Monsieur Gondree went with him, but suffered greatly on the journey because of the heat and the small amount of food he took so as not to break the eucharistic fast. He ate only a little rice cooked in water. In this weakened state he was stricken with a fever which caused much pain in all his joints. Amid his suffering he displayed great constancy and exhibited truly Christian sentiments.
>
> The feast of Pentecost came, and although I was terribly concerned about the sickness of this good servant of God, our Lord gave me the strength to minister to the French and to the catechu-

---
216. *CED* III:564-65, Nacquart's lengthy report, summarized by Abelly.
217. The three days before Ascension Thursday.

mens. I heard confessions and preached twice a day, sang the office, and looked after the instruction of these poor people. Among others, I received two adult women into the Church. They later married two inhabitants of the region who had already been baptized.

Monsieur Gondree's sickness grew worse, so I administered holy viaticum and extreme unction, which he received devoutly. He said that his only regret was to be leaving these poor unbelievers. He recommended to the French the fear of God and devotion to his blessed Mother, to whom he was so devoted. He asked me to write to you, Monsieur, to thank you most humbly in his name for the grace of accepting him into the Congregation, and above all for having chosen him among so many others more capable than himself to preach the Gospel of Jesus Christ on this island. He asked that the members of the Congregation would join him in thanking God for this grace. He also said that I ought to prepare to suffer much for our Lord in this country, and he repeated this warning twice. After passing a part of the night in continuous aspirations to God, he died in peace and tranquility. Thus he gave back his soul into the hands of his Creator on the fourteenth day of his illness.[218]

The next day he was laid to rest, mourned by all the French. A large group of poor unbelievers was also present. They said that until our arrival they had never seen men who never became angry or irritable, or who taught them heavenly things with such affection and gentleness as our dear departed.

You can well imagine the feeling in my poor heart at losing one I loved as myself, and who was, after God, my entire consolation. I begged our Lord Jesus Christ to give me a portion of the graces he had given to the poor deceased, so that alone I might accomplish the work of two. After his death I felt the result of these prayers in a double strength of mind and body to work to convert these poor islanders, and for all that would contribute to advancing the kingdom of God in this country.

After this, afraid that death might overtake me, I felt driven to work on what I considered most necessary: composing a catechism in the language of this country treating of what is most necessary to believe and do for eternal salvation. I did this to make myself more aware of these things, and also to leave for the use of those who might come after me, should God call me from this life.[219]

---

218. May 26, 1649.
219. This catechism, the first book in the language of Madagascar, was eventually published. *Petit*

After I had put this catechism in some order, I began to assemble the people of the neighborhood on Sundays and feasts. They were astounded to see how much of their language I had learned in such a short time, but in reality I was able only to stammer what I had picked up as necessary for their instruction. Among my hearers were the children of a chieftain of a region about two hundred leagues away, who had come here to conduct some business. They faithfully attended my catechism lessons, and on the point of leaving for their homes they assured me they would report to their father what they had heard of our religion, which they found very acceptable. I gave them reason to hope that in time I might be able to visit them. After their departure I learned that their part of the country is better and more densely populated than the region where we now are. The people there are anxious to attend the prayer services of the French who go there on business. All this gives me reason to think that there may be a great profit to be gained in that area.

I take every opportunity to preach Jesus Christ, by myself or by others, either to the blacks who come here or to those from more distant lands where the French have visited. Among these latter (after I exhort them to confess and communicate before leaving, and recommend that they avoid offending God at all costs and have a great concern to give only good example to the unbelievers) I ask those I find to be the most intelligent to let no opportunity pass when they might speak of our faith to the unbelievers. I give them written instructions on how to carry out this task.

Since the death of Monsieur Gondree, my dear companion in charge of our house here, I have not been able to take as many lengthy trips as I did before. I have to be here on Sundays and feasts to celebrate mass and the divine office, and preach to the French and the inhabitants of the region. My trips now last only five or six days.

Last August I went to the nearest mountains where during the day I instructed those whom I met in the small villages. In the evening I would repeat the same instruction for those who returned from their work. I was very consoled at the docility of these poor unbelievers, who stated that they believed with all their hearts what I had taught. Tearfully I wondered *quid prohibet eos baptizari?* ["What is to keep them from being baptized?"][220] But, fearing they

---

Catechisme avec les prieres du matin et du soir, que les missionnaires font et enseignent aux Neophytes et Cathecumenes de l'Isle de Madagascar, Le tout en Francois et en cette Langue. Contenant trente Instructions. Paris, 1657. Reprinted: Antananarivo, 1987.

220. Based on Acts 8:37.

were not yet sufficiently grounded in the faith, and without a priest to develop their Christian piety they would possibly abuse their baptism, I put all into the hands of the Providence of God. I would have baptized their infants, but again I feared that with time they would become indistinguishable from the others, especially since they move about so much. It seemed to me there should be some discernible way to tell the baptized and the unbaptized apart. I was well enough acquainted with those who lived near the fort to baptize them. They began to be called by their Christian names, such as Nicholas, Francis, etc.

I would test your patience if I recounted all the trips I have made, the names of the places and the peoples I have visited, to announce our Lord Jesus Christ, and all the events that have happened to me along the way. I can tell you that you could not wish for better dispositions for receiving the Gospel. All those I meet complain that for as long as the French have been in the country no one has ever spoken to them of the faith. They have a holy envy of those who live near us, since they may hear more of our holy religion.

I will recount here only what happened in November, in a visit I made to a distant village, to which I brought a large picture of the general judgment. Paradise was represented at the top of the picture, and hell at the bottom. On my arrival in each village, I would call out that I had come so their eyes could see and their ears hear things important for their salvation. After I explained what they should believe and do to assure their eternal happiness, I would display the picture to let them see the two eternal dwellings. I would urge them to choose either the one or the other, paradise or hell. These poor simple people cried out that they did not want to go with the devil, but that they wished to dwell with God. They complained that their Ombiasses never spoke to them of God, and never visited them except for some personal gain, or to deceive them. As for myself, I visited and taught these people completely at my own expense.

I went also, some time ago, beyond the mountains, to a region called the valley of Amboul [Ambolo], where I showed my picture to the lord of the region. I told him God would punish for all eternity those who kept several wives, since I knew well that he himself had five in his house. He was visibly affected, and I noticed that his face changed color. He composed himself somewhat and asked me to come to teach him. He also promised me that he would have his servants receive the Gospel.

Last Christmas I visited the region called Anos [Anosy], which has a population of about ten thousand persons. I visited almost all the surrounding villages to give the people their first knowledge of Jesus Christ. I attempt to prepare his way, *in omnem locum, in quem ipse Dominus est venturus* ["to every town and place the Lord himself intended to visit"].[221] I press ahead so that those who will come after me will find the ground at least a little prepared.

There is nothing more to say, Monsieur, except that these poor people whom I have begun to instruct await nothing more than *aquae motum* ["the movement of the water"],[222] and the hands of several good workers to lead them to the pool of baptism. How many times during my preaching in the countryside have I not heard these poor people cry out, "Where then is this water that bathes our souls, as you have promised? Bring it to us, and say the prayers." But I continue to delay, fearing that they make this request like the Samaritan woman in the Gospel. To save herself the trouble of coming to the well, she asked our Lord for that thirst quenching water, as yet unaware of the water that extinguishes the fires of concupiscence and engenders eternal life.

When we arrived here we found five children baptized. It has pleased God to add another fifty-two. Although there are many adults well disposed, still I hesitate to administer baptism until I can confer the sacrament of matrimony immediately after baptism, to remedy a vice which is all too common in this country. Still, I take great care that none of those sufficiently prepared will die without baptism. Some time ago I did baptize a poor aged woman who had become grievously ill, and God inspired her to show her thanks for his goodness toward her. She was the first of the county to pass to eternal blessedness, and her body was the first to be buried in the French cemetery.

I will await the help and the directives you will be pleased to send. If I cannot manage to do much more, I will at least strive to maintain what has begun. Alas! Where and who are the doctors and learned persons, as Saint Francis Xavier used to say, who waste their time in the academies and universities while so many poor unbelievers *petunt panem, et non est qui frangat eis* ["they cry for food, but there is no one to give it to them"].[223] May it please his sovereign majesty in his goodness to provide for the harvest. Unless

---

221. Based on Luke 10:1.
222. John 5:7.
223. Lam 4:4.

we have enough priests to teach and to reap the fruit of their instruction, we will not be able to do too much more.[224]

PART SIX
Letter of Monsieur Bourdaise, Priest of the Congregation of the Mission, About the Missions of Madagascar

Words cannot express the grief of Monsieur Vincent when he learned of the death of Monsieur Gondree. He grieved not only at the loss of such a good worker for the kingdom but for the anxiety he felt for Monsieur Nacquart, the only priest left on the island. He feared that he might succumb to the burden of the labors his zeal would entail. After he blessed God and abandoned himself completely to his holy will, he considered sending other priests to help their confrere in the development of this new Church. He thought first of Monsieur Toussaint Bourdaise, then of Monsieur Francois Mousnier, both priests of the Congregation and both quite capable of this apostolic mission.[225] In view of the opportunities offered by this mission which suggested the need for even more workers, he followed the appointment of the first two missionaries with the appointment of three others. Fathers [Claude] Dufour, [Nicolas] Prevost, and [Mathurin] de Belleville were all of proven virtue and experienced in their missionary work. All poured out their lives in working for the advancement of the kingdom of Jesus Christ in this infidel land. Since Monsieur Bourdaise survived the others, and worked the longest in this new Church, we cite here a letter he wrote in 1657 to Monsieur Vincent after the death of all his confreres. In it he recounted all that had occurred in these missions of Madagascar.

> Monsieur, I cannot express the grief of my poor soul. God alone knows the regrets and tears we experienced when on first arriving on the island we found only the ashes of Monsieur Nacquart.[226] We had hoped he would be another Joseph to receive his brothers in a

---

224. Excerpted and summarized from *CED* III:569-77, Nacquart's report, dated February 5, 1650.
225. Toussaint Bourdaise was born in 1618 at Blois. He entered the Congregation in 1645. Several times as a student he had almost been sent away as not having the necessary talent for the work of the Congregation. Providentially, he would become the true apostle of Madagascar. Jean Francois Mousnier was born at Saintes in 1628. At age eighteen he entered the Congregation. He was assisting in the distribution of alms in Picardy when Monsieur Vincent recalled him for assignment to Madagascar. He died in Madagascar, May 24, 1655.
226. It took three years for the news of Nacquart's death to reach Paris. He was the only remaining priest on the island. When he sensed his death approaching, he encouraged the native Christians to remain faithful, and to continue to show respect to the blessed sacrament, which he left reserved in the church, being unable in his agony to consume it. He asked that the body of Gondree be exhumed and that they be buried together in the same tomb at the foot of the altar. He died May 29, 1650.

strange land, or a Moses to lead us in the frightful deserts of this desolate place.

The loss shortly after of Monsieur Mousnier, whose zeal consumed him in less than six months, was all the more grievous to me because I had to bear the sorrow alone. This wound has continued to bleed in my heart. The hope of welcoming other missionaries alleviated my sorrow somewhat, except that the long delay in their arrival concerned me. What is most regrettable is that just when I was about to rejoice at the accomplishment of a good so long desired and anticipated, all was snatched from me. I have lost everything, and have no other resources. I now find myself, my dear father, in extreme desolation. I have nothing to hope for and nothing more to lose, since this ungrateful land devours so cruelly not its own people but those who have come to set it free. You understand, Monsieur, what I have to say, and what I would wish I could suppress, to spare your tears and my sobs. Monsieur de Belleville, whom I knew only by name and by his merits, has died on the way here. Monsieur Prevost did not survive the fatigues of the voyage, and also died. Monsieur Dufour, whom I knew here only long enough to realize the value of what I was to lose, is dead.

All those you sent to Madagascar are dead, and I alone, your miserable servant, remain to give you this sad and distressing news. Yet I cannot refrain from giving you cause for joy and consolation in recounting the holy lives they led on board ship and here on land, and the blessings God bestowed on all their activities since leaving France. I will attempt, Monsieur, to give you a brief account of these happenings.[227]

God alone knows the sorrow felt by Monsieur Vincent on the occasion of these losses, in a place where their presence and health were so very desirable. Let us hear Monsieur Bourdaise speak of this need. After we hear of his great disappointment, we will take note of the causes for joy with which he consoled Monsieur Vincent.

I had hoped that if there were two or three priests here, within a year we could have baptized almost the entire vast Anos [Anosy] country. In this region, there are many small villages. I cannot go very far afield and also care for those who come to our church here. The chiefs of these villages say they would willingly be baptized if they could have someone to help them pray to God. I attempt, at least, to arouse the desire for baptism, to have them act as though

---

227. *CED* VI:194-95.

they were baptized, in the hope that this baptism *in voto* ["of desire"] would suffice in this case.

In order to explain the doctrines of our faith to these people, I have asked a Frenchman who is expert at the language of the country, to help me by translating our small catechism word for word into their language. He has done so for me, and this has proven to be very useful. I no longer use an interpreter. They are attracted more and more to our holy faith, and I see new persons every day, coming to learn the Our Father, Hail Mary, and the Creed, which I teach and explain. All the women of Histolangar wish to be baptized and married in the Church.

When Fathers Dufour and Prevost came, and were still on the tiny isle of Sainte Marie, not far from here, I had already planned to have one live here and another there.[228] This would allow me to travel to the surrounding areas to instruct the people. In order not to be a burden to anyone, I had planned to store some food in one of the main houses in the interior. In this way I could stay eight or ten days in one place, until I had taught someone in the village to pray to God and how to teach others to pray as well. These people were to help the others learn to participate in morning and evening prayers, just as we do here in our house. These plans pleased me very much. I often assured these poor blacks I would soon come to them, to teach them to know God and how to pray to him, all of which they greatly desired. I told them of my confreres who had come to help me, which pleased them greatly. God, however, wished otherwise.

I taught these good people who had received baptism how to confess, and I hoped all would confess before the feast of Easter, if it would please God. They were very faithful to the morning and evening prayers, and even those at midday. Those who felt shame, and the very old, I had come to our house, where I taught them privately.

Several wanted nothing more than to be baptized, but I preferred that they first learn how to pray. During this time I would test them, and check their behavior.

Many people told me that one of the things that held them back was fear that the French would not remain on the island. Others feared the light-skinned natives would murder them.

---

228. A larger island, also called Sainte Marie, lies just off the northeast coast, some six hundred miles north of Fort Dauphin. Some other place is meant.

I make myself available at all hours for those who want to learn. I have obliged them all to pray aloud in the church. They sit in good order, both the young and the old. May it please God, Monsieur, that all our confreres hear the sweet harmony of so many different voices, the young and the old, men and women, the poor and the wealthy, all united in the faith of the one God.

I have recently baptized five families of blacks, the husband, wife, and children. I have presided at a dozen marriages of Frenchmen and native women. They have been the first to come to pray to God, the first to be baptized, and the first in their zeal for the honor of God. These women are examples for all the rest.

We have had much trouble in getting rid of the women of the streets. I have had to go into the cafes with a whip to drive them away, but I have done this only after my prayers and requests were to no avail. Fear alone drove them away. Before doing this I had the approval of the governor.

Four blacks baptized and married by the late Monsieur Nacquart, but who were later separated by the wars, have been reunited with their wives, at the cost of much effort.

Besides all this, we have celebrated a dozen marriages between blacks, and twenty-three between Frenchmen and women of the country. This number increases little by little. Each one goes back to their own home, coming back on the major feasts of the Church.

I am attempting to learn to read and write the native language, and to help me I have the aid of one of the most renowned and most learned of the Ombiasses. We have instructed four young cowherds, sons of four of the most important men of the country, who sent them to us. One has already been baptized privately. I await the arrival of the French to be their godparents, so that all may be baptized. They greatly desire this. They have cast away their Olis which they used to wear around their neck, and have replaced it with the cross.

I talked to a farmer, whose two oldest sons I baptized some time ago. I urged him and his whole household to be baptized, together with his father and brother, kings like himself. He is very close to a decision. He left his youngest son with me, and has agreed he may be baptized. This is important for a chieftain, for if he allows himself to be baptized there will surely be many who will follow his example.

The oldest son of another king named Dian Masse has also been baptized. He is one of the most courageous men of the island, and is both strong and intelligent. Every day he prays publicly, and has promised me he will teach his wife and family our holy religion.

I have here with me two children of two of the chiefs of the island, together with their slaves. Both want to receive baptism, which we will administer, God willing, with the greatest possible solemnity for the honor of God. We will do so that the people, particularly the leading men and women among them, will be encouraged to follow the good example these two will give. We must admit that the interests of our religion are advanced more by the conversion of a single nobleman and great lord than by a hundred of the lesser ones. Experience confirms this opinion.

Last year I was alerted that three of the most powerful rulers of all the country were unwell. The most important of them was sure to die within a few days. I was most disturbed, since I knew these men were strongly attached to their superstitions. I felt an inspiration of God to go see them. God gave them the grace of opening their eyes when I spoke to them of the truth of our faith. I assured them that no one could be truly happy or avoid the eternal flames after death unless he were baptized. At once they asked for the sacrament, and for the favor of being buried as a Christian after their death. I agreed to both requests, provided they would leave their superstitions and their Olis, which they carried on their persons. They did so at once, and I administered baptism. After their deaths I saw to it they were buried fittingly in our cemetery. I cannot pass over in silence the joy and edification these blacks gave me on this occasion. They gathered in large numbers to see these men buried whom just a while before they had regarded as gods. They gave a thousand praises to the Catholic religion, which buried so honorably those who before baptism wished us nothing but ill. You can see how ready these natives are for conversion, and how much influence the nobles have over them.

I have taken on three small French children together with two sons of the king of Mavaubouille, all around two years old. This is the age at which you can be sure they still have preserved their innocence, above all their chastity. This virtue is rare here, beyond what you can imagine. It is no wonder, for fathers and mothers do not even wait for the age of puberty to teach their children of either sex to lose their purity. What is worse, they themselves excite their children. This deplorable state shows how much these poor people need to be instructed.

I also have taken in hand four other young boys now seven or eight years old. They give me much satisfaction and I hope that I shall see them one day contributing to the conversion of their own people. My hopes are principally on two of them, who already know how to read and to serve mass.

These poor natives come to me when they are sick, and thanks be to God, I have been able to help. As soon as anyone hurts himself or falls sick they send for me to come or to give them some remedy. This is important, for at such times the people are disposed to listen to me. On these occasions I have baptized several small children who died soon afterward, and as a result they went straight to heaven. We buried them with the usual ceremonies, with children of their own age carrying lighted candles.

When I went to see the lord of Imours, an old man in the last extremity of sickness, all his subjects gathered, alerted to my coming. I spoke to him of the other world and of the greatness of the Christian faith. I told him that if he consented to be baptized as a Christian he would be numbered among the children of God. This good man gathered all his remaining strength to tell me he indeed did wish to become a Christian. His illness was such that I thought it best to baptize him immediately in the presence of all the assembly. Afterward I exhorted them, and then returning to the sick man I gave him several cloves to strengthen him, for he had no more himself. He asked me if I would give him some French wine, which I promised to do.

He wanted to give me a present, but I refused with thanks. I told him that baptism was something of such worth that nothing in the world could repay its reception. Seeing him so well disposed I returned and gave him a bit of a panacea I had and a portion of hyacinth. At the end of three days he was cured. In this I owe thanks to the divine Goodness. By blessing these simple remedies for the body I find these good people are ready for the healing of their souls.

During the war a village near us was raided during the night, and about twenty men under the protection of the French were killed. They beat a woman with fifteen blows of their spears, and after ten days she was brought to me with a very high fever. Her wounds were so infected that the odor alone drove all away. The poor have no way of getting help from the Ombiasses, and their wounds are not treated. I gave her an ointment which quickly cured her by the help of God, even though she remained very nervous. When she recovered she brought her two sons to be baptized, and wanted to give them to me as slaves. I would not accept them on these terms, explaining to her that in our religion we do not have slaves.

An Ombiasse recently came to see me about a man of his village who had not been able to sleep for the past three months. He suffered greatly from an abscess on his thigh which had become large and inflamed. The skin was so hard that it could not be pierced, but when I saw it I lanced it with my scalpel. The resulting discharge of the infection was the marvel of all the poor souls who saw it. He was cured three days later. He had a similar infection on his shoulder which I lanced in the same way. Soon he was entirely relieved of this ailment.

A persistent malady among the natives here is a form of dysentery, or gray flux, which they call *sorac*.[229] It comes from lack of proper nourishment, and is usually prevalent three months of the year. This sickness is usually fatal in eight days, and they have no medicine to cure this condition. I gave them some of the panacea I had, which did cure this illness. More than a hundred were saved by God's mercy, so that all come to me when they are afflicted. It is to be hoped that the bodily cures will dispose them to accept the spiritual ministration, as happened with the apostles and our Lord himself, who cured bodily ailments before converting souls.

There is a soothsayer here named Rathy, about sixty-nine years old, short of stature, simple in appearance, and of few words. This man has somewhat of a reputation because of his predictions, most of which have come to pass. Even the French pay attention to him. In 1654 he predicted that in less than six months ships from France would appear. This turned out to be true, for soon after, those sent by the Marshal de la Meilleraye arrived.[230] Another time, on being asked if Monsieur de Flacourt, who was returning to France, would arrive safely, he said, "Yes, but as he approaches the coast of France he will run into three enemy ships." It happened as he predicted, as Monsieur de Flacourt can tell you himself. He has proven true in other cases, also, as I can testify. This makes me wonder if this is not a true gift of prophecy from the hand of God, as he gave earlier to the Sybils, as a recognition of their moral virtue. He appears to be a good man, simple and naive.

Since he often comes to see me, I once asked him if he talked to the fairies, the imps, and forest creatures. He naively replied that he did, and often. I asked him where these spirits lived, and where they come from. He said they live in the high mountains, and appear to be all belly, though they do not eat; some among them speak, while

---

229. The symptoms are those of a form of cholera.
230. Charles de la Porte, duke of La Meilleraye, 1602-1664. It was he who gave Monsieur Vincent the idea of sending missionaries to Madagascar.

others do not. I asked him if he dreamed of what was going to happen in future. He said, no, he just spoke what came into his head at the moment he was asked. I believe him, for he has answered questions immediately, with no time to consult the devil, such as when a person asks him if his father was alive, or how many brothers and sisters he had. With no possibility of knowing the right answer beforehand, he has replied correctly.

I asked him if this gift benefited him, and if it was good to pray to God. He replied very ambiguously, whether from doubt about what to say or because he was afraid to say no, and I did not press him further on this question. I asked him only if the spirit that moved him loved the priests. He stated the spirit feared rather than loved them, which led me to believe that the spirit was one of the evil sort. He predicted other things too, but we do not yet know the outcome, for example, that the whole island would be converted and baptized. Whether this prophecy is from the good or evil spirit I cannot say, it being God's will which will determine its fulfillment. We have reason to hope for this, if my sins do not prevent it.

Another of his predictions is just on the verge of being fulfilled: that he, his wife, and children will one day be baptized. He has promised to present himself soon. He comes to prayers every day, and tells me that once he has learned to pray he will accompany me to the villages, to teach the others. He no longer responds to those who ask him something about the superstitions of the people. He excuses himself on the plea that he is afraid of me. This man could do much to move the people away from their idols, for he is one of the most respected of their authorities on the Olis.

The famine here has become so serious that several of the blacks have died from hunger. I have prepared something for both the baptized and unbaptized children, who are delighted to have a bowl of soup every day. I present a catechism lesson myself at midday, at which they are very attentive and modest. Mothers come also, and bring their tiny children with them. I am very pleased at this for they take this spiritual milk with much eagerness, and seeing the fruit produced I am persuaded to continue the practice. Besides this usual feeding, I see to it that the older persons are taken care of, and also the children abandoned by their mothers, who have almost nothing to eat.

You see then, Monsieur, the rich and beautiful opportunities for extending the kingdom of Jesus Christ in this large island. At least six hundred of the inhabitants have already received the light of the

Gospel, and the number of those who await baptism is much greater. If we can judge from the favorable dispositions and the lack of resistance of these first converts how the others of the island may react, we can have great hopes for the remainder of the people of the island. We are speaking of the 400,000 inhabitants, plus the unnumbered multitude of those future generations who will owe their faith to this generation of converts. However, though I am a poor, small useless servant, if something should happen to me, alas, what would become of this poor Church? What would become of these people who live in ignorance, without the sacraments, and lacking all direction? God, who makes me aware of this pressing necessity, inspires me in spirit to throw myself at your feet to say on behalf of so many souls, with all humility and all possible respect, *Mitte quos missurus es* ["Send those whom you are going to send"].[231] Send us missionaries, for those who have died on our shores were not destined to serve in Madagascar. They were called to pass this way on their journey to heaven. No place on earth needs your Congregation more than here.

I end this letter with some news, both joyful and sad, that happened recently. The mother of Dian Machicore, one of the greatest lords of the country, who was more than a hundred years old, died after earnestly requesting baptism. I was not able to answer her request because of the great distance of her home from mine. In truth, I was much put out that I had not been called earlier to help her in her last passage. There is good reason to hope that her fervent desire will supply for what was lacking, for surely she received the interior baptism of the Spirit. This thought gave me much consolation, and I am sure she should be numbered among our neophytes.

Other men and women are probably also among their number because of this same spiritual baptism, since they find it impossible to receive the sacrament. We must fear that the number of those who will be lost is much greater, for lack of someone to bathe them in this mystic pool. This is what gives me pain, above all when I picture to myself their guardian angels saying to me, *si fuisses hic, frater meus non fuisset mortuus* ["If you had been here, my brother would never have died"].[232] O Missionary! If you had been here to help this man or this woman they would not have died this eternal death.

O my dear father, how often I wish those capable priests in

---
231. Based on Exod 4:13.
232. John 11:21.

France who live in idleness, would come to know of the great need of workers in the Lord's vineyard, and then would reflect carefully that our Lord addresses this reproach to each of them individually: *O sacerdos! si fuisses hic, frater meus non fuisset mortuus*, O priests, if you had been here on this island several of my brothers redeemed by my blood, would not have died in their sin. Beyond doubt this thought would move them to compassion and possibly to fright, if they reflect carefully that having neglected to provide this spiritual help, Jesus Christ will one day address these terrible words to them, *Ipse impius in iniquitate sua morietur, sanguinem vero ejus de manu tua requiram* ["The wicked man himself will die in his iniquity, and I will hold you responsible for his blood"].[233] If the priests, doctors, preachers, catechists, and others with talent and a vocation to the foreign missions would consider this, and would reflect on the account they will have to render for all the souls lost for lack of their help, I have no doubt they would be more attentive than they are. They would seek out the lost sheep to lead them back to the sheepfold of the Church.

Since this fervent Missionary thought that Monsieur Vincent might lose courage in the face of the death of the most excellent workers of his Congregation, he returned to his appeal.

Send us other workers, I beseech you, my dear father. If these unfortunate events make you doubt that this is properly the vocation of our Company, consider Saint Bernard in preaching the crusade for the recovery of the Holy Land, or the Israelites fighting against the city of Gibeon. Both these attempts failed, even though God had supported the first by a miracle and the second by direct revelation. The sad outcome of sending your priests here ought not to suggest that God did not call them, for other signs show his blessing. You know well, Monsieur, that God tears down and builds up according to his good pleasure. Thus we can hope that other workers whom your charity will send will succeed better than those who preceded them. This is what happened to the Israelites of whom I spoke earlier. After the Gibeonites had beaten and repulsed them twice, they were finally victorious on the third assault. It is true, my dear father, that you have lost many valuable members. Yet please, for the love of Jesus Christ, do not be discouraged, nor abandon so many souls redeemed by the Son of God. You can be sure that if so many good missionaries have died, it is not the climate of the country that brought this about. The fatigues of their voyage, their

---

233. Based on Jer 31:30 and other passages.

excessive mortification, or the excess of work, which will always be the case here with too few workers, were undoubtedly the cause of their early deaths.[234]

PART SEVEN
Letter of Monsieur Vincent to Monsieur Bourdaise, to Whom He Sent Five More Missionaries

The sad news of the loss of so many good workers deeply grieved Monsieur Vincent. This no doubt wounded his paternal heart, since it was so sensitive to the welfare of all his confreres. In this, as in all things, he remained perfectly submissive to the will of God. He was committed to his glory, and to God he had offered and continuously sacrificed of his life and that of all his spiritual family. After these shocking events, he certainly had reason to question whether God wished him and his Congregation to serve in such a distant mission. It seemed presumptuous, perhaps, to pursue an undertaking which it appeared divine Providence did not favor. This was the opinion of some of his friends, guided by the light of human prudence. Yet human prudence is always a risky thing to follow in a matter of apostolic undertakings.

This man of God, enlightened by the Holy Spirit, recognized that all these reverses signified God's approval rather than his disfavor. This is why, like the palm tree flattened by the storm, he decided to continue what he had begun with the help of God's grace, in which he placed all his trust. He wrote:

> The universal Church has been established by the death of the Son of God, and strengthened by that of the apostles, popes, and bishops martyred for the faith. She increased through persecution, and the blood of martyrs was the seed of Christians. God's usual way of acting was to test his followers, especially when he had a great work in store for them. His divine Goodness has revealed, now, as always, that his name should be known, and the kingdom of his Son be established in all nations. It is evident that the island people are well disposed to receive the light of the Gospel, for more than six hundred have already received baptism by the ministry of a single Missionary. It would be against all reason and charity to abandon the single Missionary God has preserved, and to abandon these people who ask only to be instructed in the faith.[235]

All these and other similar considerations led him to decide to send five other Missionaries to this distant island, four priests and a brother.[236] These

---
234. *CED* VI:194-202.
235. Letter of April 19, 1659, cited in Collet, *Vie*, I:456.
236. The missionaries for this fifth expedition were: Nicolas Etienne, Pierre Daveroult, Pasquier

men, disdaining danger and death, offered themselves to him, to work in this perilous and difficult mission. Before their departure he gave them the following letter addressed to Monsieur Bourdaise, in which we can read, as if it were written about himself, a description of his own zeal and virtue.

I must first tell you, Monsieur, of our uncertainty whether you are still in the land of the living. The short time that those who preceded, accompanied, and followed you survived in this inhospitable land which swallowed up those sent to cultivate it, has given us concern. If you are still alive, how great our joy will be to hear from you. You would have no trouble realizing this if you knew the esteem and affection I have for you, which is as great as it is possible for one person to have for another.

Your last report to me has allowed us to see the strength of God working in you, and to hope for extraordinary fruit from your missionary labors. We shed tears of happiness because of you, and of thanksgiving to the goodness of God. He has taken such admirable care of you and your people whom you evangelize by his grace with such zeal and prudence on your part, and such admirable dispositions on their part to become children of God. We also shed tears of sorrow at your loss in the deaths of Messieurs Dufour, Prevost and de Belleville, who found rest rather than the occupation they expected, and who increased your concerns where you had expected relief. This sudden separation was a sword of sorrow for your soul, just as the deaths of Messieurs Nacquart, Gondree and Mousnier were earlier.

You expressed such distress at their loss, in giving us news of their deaths, that I could sense your extreme affliction at these heavy losses. It seems, Monsieur, that God is treating you just as he treated his Son. God sent him into the world to establish his Church by the passion, and in the same way it seems he wishes to bring the faith to Madagascar by your sufferings. I adore his divine guidance, and I pray that his designs will be accomplished in you. It may be he has some special good in store for you, since among so many missionaries sent to the island, you alone survive. It would seem the good that they desired to accomplish will be fulfilled by you alone, whom God has preserved in life.

Be that as it may, Monsieur, we have greatly lamented the loss of these good servants of God. Yet we have good reason to admire in this surprising turn of events the incomprehensible scope of his

---

Desfontaines, Francois Feydin, and Brother Philippe Patte, a surgeon.

guidance. He knows that we devoutly kiss the hand that strikes us, submitting ourselves humbly to what touches us so deeply. Still, we cannot know the reasons for this sudden death of such promising men in the midst of a people pleading for instruction, and after so many signs in them of a vocation for evangelization.

Despite these latest losses, neither the earlier losses nor the accidents that have happened since will weaken our resolve to help you. The four priests and a brother who were attracted to your mission and who have long requested to be sent, have not slackened in their resolution.

(Here Monsieur Vincent included a description of the good qualities of each of the missionaries, and then continued:)

I do not know who will rejoice more at their safe arrival in Madagascar, you who have awaited them for such a long time, or they themselves, who have a great desire to be with you. They see our Lord in you, and you in our Lord. With this perspective they will obey you as they would the Lord himself, with the help of his grace. Please agree to be in charge of them. I hope God will bless your direction, and their submission.

You would not have had to wait so long for reinforcements if it were not for unhappy incidents on two different occasions. In one case the ship carrying two of our priests and a brother, foundered at Nantes with a loss of nearly a hundred persons.[237] It was only a special protection of God that saved our confreres. The second ship left last year, but Spaniards captured it, and the four priests and a brother aboard were returned here. It pleased God that no aid or consolation would come to you from us, but from himself alone. He will be your first and last hope in this apostolic work to which he has called you, to show that the establishment of the faith is strictly his work and not a human enterprise. This is the way it was at the beginning of the Church, when he chose only twelve apostles. They soon separated to go to the four corners of the earth, to announce his coming and his doctrine to the whole world. This holy seed of the Word began to increase, and Providence allowed the number of laborers to increase. Your Church will also grow little by little, and will in time have priests to develop and extend it.

O Monsieur, how happy you are to have laid the first foundations of this Church. It will lead so many souls to heaven who otherwise

---

237. For this fourth expedition, the priests were Charles Boussordec and Francois Herbron; the brother was Christophe Delaunay. For Vincent's account of these events, see *CED* XI:372-80. Boussordec died on a later voyage in 1665.

would not have entered there, if God did not pour out on them the principle of eternal life through the teaching and sacraments which you have administered. May you continue, with the help of his grace, for a long time in your holy ministry, and serve as an example and an encouragement for the other Missionaries. This is the prayer the whole Company frequently offers, for it has your person and your work very much at heart. I feel this deeply.

In vain will we ask God to keep you safe, if you do not cooperate. I beg of you, Monsieur, with all my heart, to take care of yourself and of your confreres. You know from your own experience how important this is, especially in that region. Your own intuition that our dear departed hastened their end by their excessive work must lead you to moderate your zeal. It is better to have some strength in reserve than to exceed your limit. Pray to God for our little Congregation. It needs both men and virtue for the many and diverse harvests we attempt to reap on all sides, among the priests or among the people. Please pray to God for me also. I feel I do not have much longer to live, given my age, now above eighty, and my bad legs no longer can support me.[238] I shall die in peace if I know that you are still living, and if I am informed of the number of children and adults you have baptized. If it should be that we no longer meet in this world, I hope to see you in the presence of God. I remain faithfully yours.[239]

These five Missionaries left France near the end of 1659, but Providence decreed they were to return to Paris after eighteen months. The ship on which they were sailing was shipwrecked at the Cape of Good Hope, but thanks be to God, all aboard were saved. These good Missionaries stayed there until a Dutch fleet called at the port ten months after the shipwreck, and kindly brought them back to France.

By the time news of this terrible accident was received, Monsieur Vincent had died. Undoubtedly he would have been greatly distressed. By now, nineteen or twenty members of the Congregation had been sent to Madagascar at various times to work for the conversion of the people of the island, to establish among them the empire of Jesus Christ. Of these, seven had died in this effort, including Monsieur Bourdaise, the last of those on the scene.[240]

---

238. Abelly perhaps altered this expression, since the saint would have turned eighty in 1660, as other letters of his clearly show. Perhaps the original read "now turning eighty" or "going on for eighty years."
239. *CED* VIII:156-60.
240. Eighteen men were sent in six expeditions: *First*, (1) C. Nacquart, (2) N. Gondree; *Second*, (3) F. Mousnier; (4) T. Bourdaise, (5) Bro. R. Foret; *Third*, (6) C. Dufour, (7) N. Prevost, (8) M. de Belleville; *Fourth*, (9) C. Boussordec, (10) F. Herbron, (11) Bro. C. Delaunay, also on the fifth expedition; *Fifth*, (12) C. Leblanc, (13) I. Arnaud, (14) P. Desfontaines, (15) P. Daveroult; *Sixth*,

The others, by the secret and incomprehensible order of divine Providence, had to return to France without being allowed to cultivate the fertile field of this poor struggling Church.

The superior who succeeded Monsieur Vincent[241] immediately sent five missionaries in December, 1662, to continue this work. They had to wait at Nantes until May of the following year. They finally embarked then for Madagascar with the same wish to work and suffer for the glory of God among these poor infidels which animated all the others who preceded them in this mission. We have since learned that by the grace of God all have happily arrived at their destination.[242]

SECTION TEN

The Mission to Poland

Her serene highness, the queen of Poland, moved by an earnest desire to obtain the spiritual good of her people, and to have Jesus Christ reign in their hearts, saw the great need they had of receiving instruction and help in their spiritual development. As a result, in 1651 she requested Monsieur Vincent to send priests of the Mission to her country. This good servant of God wanted to correspond to the designs of this virtuous princess. Since he knew the great need which the vast reaches of her realm had of the type of help his missionaries had produced in other places, he decided to send some of his priests for this work. Among those he sent was the late Monsieur Lambert, his assistant at Saint Lazare.[243] He was his right arm in the administration of the Congregation, a man of good health, energy, and sound judgment, and one for whom Monsieur Vincent had a special esteem and affection.

Nevertheless, by a heroic act of virtue and by an entire detachment from all created goods, even from him to whom he was so closely attached for the welfare of the community, he willingly surrendered this faithful collaborator

---

(16) F. Feydin, (17) N. Etienne, (18) Bro. P. Patte. The seven who died en route or in Madagascar were Nacquart, Gondree, Mousnier, Bourdaise, Dufour, Prevost, de Belleville. This listing generally follows Coste, *Life*.

241. Rene Almeras.
242. The five were N. Etienne, M. Manie, Bro. P. Patte, and Bro. G. Lebrun. They were joined by a secular priest, Fr. Frachey.
243. Lambert aux Couteaux, who zealously worked for twenty-two years, and died January 31, 1653.

together with all the help he might expect from him. In doing so, Monsieur Vincent offered a perfect sacrifice of all things, including himself, to our Lord. He sent this worthy missionary as superior of the new venture.[244] By the grace of God he arrived safely with his little band in Poland. He found not only enough to do there, but also, in imitation of the patriarch Isaac, enough to suffer in carrying out the will of God in perfect obedience. From the time he and his band of missionaries arrived there, God allowed the kingdom to be afflicted by war, plague, or famine, sometimes even by all three of these scourges together. This is what the queen of Poland herself wrote to Monsieur Vincent in September 1652:

> Monsieur Vincent, I am obliged to you for so many signs of your regard, especially the joy you had to hear good news of the king's health and mine, for which I thank you.
>
> That good priest, Monsieur Lambert, saw the dread the Polish people had of the plague, and wanted to go to Warsaw to reorganize the relief for the poor. I gave orders to house him in the castle, in the king's own rooms. Every day I had news of him, and every day I urged him not to expose himself to contagion. He has everything he needs to return here as soon as the arrangements he had made in Warsaw are on a sound footing. I have urged him to return here as soon as possible. Except for this illness, which has upset our plans, we would have completed them in Warsaw. Two days ago the Daughters of Charity arrived, with whom I am very satisfied. They seem like good women.[245]

One of the first tests God had prepared for the virtue and zeal of Monsieur Lambert and his confreres was to tend to the spiritual and corporal relief of the poor of the great city of Warsaw, in desperate condition because of the plague which ravaged the region. This is what Monsieur Vincent wrote to the superior of one of the missions, relating what he had heard from there:

> The missionaries in Poland have worked with great blessings. I do not have the time to tell you everything in detail, but will tell you simply that the plague has gripped the city of Warsaw, where the king ordinarily lives. All the inhabitants who can, have fled the city, so that just as in other stricken places, there is almost no semblance of order, but only complete disarray. Even the dead are not buried. They are left in the streets, and dogs feed on the corpses. As soon as a person is stricken by this disease, the others put him into the streets to die, for no one brings them anything to eat. The poor

---

244. Four confreres accompanied Monsieur Lambert to Poland: Father Guillaume Desdames, the subdeacon Nicolas Guillot, a cleric, Stanislaus Zelazewski, and Brother Jacques Posny.
245. *CED* IV:487.

artisans, men and women servants, the poor widows and orphans are entirely abandoned. They can find no work, nor can they even beg their bread, for all the wealthy have fled the city.

Monsieur Lambert was sent this sad situation to bring relief to all these miseries. By God's grace, he has managed to bury the dead, bring the sick to places where they could be helped in both soul and body, and he has even taken care of other sick people who do not have a contagious disease. He has found three or four different houses, separated one from the other, to be used as hospices or hospitals. There he has gathered the poor who are not sick, men to one side, women and children to the other, all helped by alms and other benefits from the queen.[246]

This is the short sketch of great works accomplished by this virtuous priest with his confreres in that country, where his zeal found new persons and new opportunities to help every day. Divine Providence, however, seeing his past services and the ardent desire to continue in his service, judged his course completed and his crown prepared. In January, 1653, while reaping a harvest of souls, God called him from this life to give him eternal rest in the next. Monsieur Vincent spoke of him in the circular letter he sent to the houses of the Congregation in the following March, in which he revealed his sense of loss of such a missionary.

May the consolation of our Lord be with us all, to accept with love the huge loss the Company has suffered in the person of the late Monsieur Lambert, who died on January 31 of this year. He was sick only three days, but of such a painful illness that despite his great patience he said himself he could not long endure the pain. He died after receiving the sacraments from the hands of one of our priests of the Congregation. The confessor of the queen of Poland wrote to tell me he is universally lamented. According to the people it would be hard to find a priest more gifted and devoted to the service of God. He added that he should be called *Dilectus Deo et hominibus, cujus memoria in benedictione est* ["Dear to God and men, his memory is held in benediction"].[247] He was, he told me, a person wholly given to God, and never was anyone seen to rise so quickly in the favor and esteem of the king and queen as he. Neither was there anyone who gained such universal approval, for wherever he went he left the remembrance of his virtues. These are the thoughts of the chaplain of the queen. His Majesty himself wrote a long letter in his own hand in which he expressed his appreciation

---

246. *CED* IV:533-34.
247. Based on Sir 45:1.

of Monsieur Lambert's contributions, and the regret he felt at his loss. He concluded by the words, "if you do not send us another Monsieur Lambert, I do not know what we shall do."

I have no doubt, gentlemen, that this loss which has saddened the entire Company has touched each of you individually. But consider: the hand of God in human affairs is adorable, and we must accept it with love. That is what we must do in this situation, persuaded that the dear departed will be more useful to us in heaven than he was on earth. We will consider someone to take his place, to continue our efforts in support of that kingdom where the needs are so pressing. The priests there need a strong personality to help them. May God be pleased to give us such a person.[248]

The one whom Monsieur Vincent chose to send to Poland as a replacement was Monsieur Ozenne, an older priest of the Company and a respected missionary.[249] He worked for several years blessed by God, and finally succumbed to the difficulties of the work, dying in that distant mission.[250]

The plague continued to afflict the city of Warsaw, and to add to its woes, war broke out against the Poles. The Swedes invaded from the one side, and the Russians from the other. When the queen realized the city of Warsaw was suffering these two scourges of war and pestilence, she ordered all but two of the Missionaries to leave for safer regions.[251] The two who remained suffered much from their dedication to the poor, particularly to the most abandoned. They remained steadfast at their post during several years, despite the troubles brought on by the war and the plague. They persevered in their service of the poor, administering the sacraments to both the healthy and the sick, providing all sorts of help with a courage and charity which deeply touched Monsieur Vincent's heart. One evening, at the end of a conference he had given the house, he recommended these two priests to the prayers of the community, and encouraged them by the example of their constancy in their sufferings.

> One of them had a serious stomach problem, brought on from the poorly treated illness of the plague.[252] I was told that he was treated by having fire applied to the putrefied flesh of his side, but his patience was so great he did not complain. He suffered the treatment with peace and tranquility of spirit. Another person there might have complained at being sick three or four hundred leagues from his own country.

---

248. *CED* IV:560-61.
249. Charles Ozenne, 1613-1658, a missionary in Poland from 1653 to his death five years later. (See *CED* II:147.)
250. August 14, 1658.
251. Guillaume Desdames and Nicolas Duperroy.
252. Nicolas Duperroy.

"Why did they send me so far away? When will they call me back? What, are they forgetting me entirely? Others are at their ease in France, and I am left to die in a strange land."

This is a sensual man speaking. He is moved by purely natural reasonings, and does not enter into the sufferings of our Lord, who found happiness in his sufferings. This is a good lesson for us, to love what divine Providence sends us. Look at the first man, who has worked so long in peace of mind and with wonderful confidence, not deterred by his long stay or the difficulties he encounters, nor concerned by its dangers.

Both our priests were indifferent to death or to life, humbly resigned to whatever God ordained for them. They gave no sign of impatience or of murmuring. On the contrary, they seemed ready for even more sufferings. And what of ourselves, gentlemen and my brothers? Are we ready to accept what God sends, repress the movements of nature, to live only the life of Jesus Christ in us? Are we ready to go to Poland, Barbary, the Indies, to sacrifice our own satisfaction and our very lives? If so, let us bless God. If on the contrary we fear any inconvenience, or complain at any item that may be lacking, or wish to be changed from house to house because the climate is not good, or the food is poor, or because we are not free enough to come and go as we please, if in a word, gentlemen, if we are still slaves of nature, given to sensual pleasures like this miserable sinner who speaks to you, who at the age of seventy is still so worldly, let us see ourselves as unworthy of the apostolic vocation to which God has called us. We should be ashamed at seeing our brothers fulfill this ministry so worthily, while we remain so far from their courageous spirit.

What do our men have to bear in that country? Famine? Yes. The plague? Yes, both, and more than once. War? They are surrounded by armies, and have experienced living amid enemy soldiers. God has tried them by all these scourges. And we live here like shut-ins, without heart and with little zeal. We see others braving dangers in the service of God, while we are as timid as wet hens. O misery! O wretchedness! Look at twenty thousand soldiers who go to war and suffer all sorts of ills. One will lose an arm, another a leg, and some their very lives, all for uncertain hopes. Yet they have no fear, and set off as though they were going after a treasure. To gain heaven, gentlemen, scarcely anyone will lift a finger, and those who say they are seeking to gain heaven, lead a life so lazy and sensual it is unworthy not only of a priest or a Christian, but even of a rational man. If there are any such among us they would be merely the corpse of a missionary. O God, be forever blessed and glorified for the graces you have given to those who abandon themselves to you. Praise be to you for giving your grace to these two priests of ours in Poland.

Let us give ourselves to God, gentlemen, to go to the whole world to carry his holy Gospel. Wherever he leads us, let us remain at our post, faithful to our customs, until we are recalled, at his good pleasure. May difficulties not deter us when there is question of the glory of the Eternal Father, the fruitfulness of his word, or the passion of his Son. The salvation of peoples, and our own, is a good of such magnitude it deserves to be bought no matter what the price. It matters not if we die in the fight. Only let us die with our weapons in our hands, and happy, for by our death the Company will not be the poorer, because, *Sanguis martyrum, semen est Christianorum* ["The blood of martyrs is the seed of Christians"].[253] For one Missionary who gives his life out of charity, God will raise up others who will do the work he left behind. May each of us resolve to resist the world and its maxims, to mortify our flesh and its passions, to submit to God's orders, and to spend ourselves in the duties of our state and in the accomplishment of his holy will, wherever in the world he wills. Let us now together take this resolution, in the spirit of Jesus Christ, with perfect confidence that he will help us in our needs. Do you not wish to do so, my brothers in the seminary? Do you, my brothers, students, wish to do so? I do not ask this of the priests, for without doubt they already have this disposition of heart.

Yes, my God, we all wish to cooperate with the designs you have for us. This is what we together, and each of us in particular, propose to do with the help of your grace. We will not be so much in love with our lives, our health, our comfort, and our ease, for one relationship over another, nor for anything else, not for anything in the world which might hinder you, O gracious God, from granting us this grace we all ask, one for another.

I do not know, gentlemen, how I came to say all this, for I did not think of it before. What I had heard of our two priests in Poland and the graces God had given them so moved me that I could not resist sharing my feelings with you.[254]

We can judge the spirit that motivated Monsieur Vincent from these

---

253. This famous statement is found in various ancient authors, among whom is Tertullian; PL 1.1:535.
254. *CED* XI:410-14.

words, and from how he strove to influence others. We can appreciate the joy he felt when he saw the priests of the Congregation of the Mission ready and disposed to undertake any mission, courageous in the face of danger, and ready to embrace confidently the suffering of the cross, to further the kingdom of God and the salvation of souls. Among these, the ones for whom he had a particular concern were the most afflicted and the most abandoned. He strove to bring them as much aid as was in his power, as was evidenced in the great kingdom of Poland, stricken by war and pestilence, and subject to both ancient and modern heresies. He was not satisfied to send laborers from his Company, but had recourse to prayers and frequent reminders of the sufferings of these people, both inside and outside the house. Here is how he spoke to his community of Saint Lazare, in August 1655:

> The queen of Poland has such good will for our Company that she has requested in all her letters that we should pray to God for her poor suffering kingdom. May God have pity on it, for it is under attack from all sides.[255]

In September 1656, he said:

> We must humble ourselves before God, since he has allowed (if rumors are true) the good we have prayed for so to be delayed. Undoubtedly our sins have caused this. There is unconfirmed word that not only have the troubles of the kingdom not come to an end, but that the king, with an army of one hundred thousand men has given battle, and has been defeated.[256] A nobleman of the court of Poland wrote me that the queen has gone to find the king, and has come within two days travel of the army. Her letter is dated July 28, and the battle took place on the thirtieth. This means she herself was in danger. Oh, gentlemen and my brothers, how concerned we should be that our sins have moved God to delay answering our prayers. We must grieve that this vast and great kingdom is so grievously attacked, and is on the point of being lost, if the news we have is true. We must grieve for the Church which will be lost in that country if the king is defeated. Religion cannot endure unless the king is saved, for the Church will fall into the hands of its enemies.
>
> The Russians already occupy a hundred or a hundred and twenty leagues, and the Swedes threaten the rest. This gives me much reason to fear the outcome predicted by Pope Clement VIII, a holy man, esteemed not only by Catholics but by heretics as well. They

---

255. *CED* XI:303-04.
256. King Karl Gustav of Sweden, had invaded Poland with an army of 60,000 men. At the end of July 1656, aided by the elector of Brandenburg, he marched against Warsaw. The king, John Casimir, remained with his troops. The queen was separated from him and the enemy by the Vistula river. Warsaw fell to the Swedes on August 1.

recognize him as a man of God and of peace, and even his enemies praise him. I have heard that even Lutherans praise and admire his virtue. This holy pope received two ambassadors from some ruler of the Orient where the faith had begun to grow. Wishing to thank God publicly, he offered mass in their presence for the intentions of this new Church. While at the altar, during his *Memento* he began to cry, sob, and weep, to their enormous astonishment. Afterward they asked why, on an occasion which should have been a joyous one, he had shown such distress. He said, yes, he had begun the mass with much satisfaction and contentment, because of the progress of the Catholic faith, but soon afterward all this turned into sadness because of the losses and harm which come upon the Church every day from the hands of heretics, so much so that there was reason to fear God willed to remove the Church to other lands. We ought, gentlemen and my brothers, to join in his concern and fear that the kingdom of God will be taken from our midst. We see this deplorable situation enacted before our very eyes, where six kingdoms have expelled the Church, that is, Sweden, Denmark, Norway, England, Scotland and Ireland. Besides, there is Holland and large parts of Germany, and several of the larger Hanseatic cities. O Lord, what a loss! And now we are on the verge of seeing this great kingdom of Poland lost, if God in his mercy does not save it.

Indeed, God has promised to be with his Church until the end of time, but he has not promised his Church would last in France, Spain, or any other specific country. He has said he will never leave his Church, and that it will endure till the end of time, wherever it might be, but not here or not there. If there ever was a country where you would have thought the Church would endure, surely it would be the Holy Land where he was born, where he began the Church, and where he worked so many of his miracles. And yet it was from this land, for which he had done so much, that he took the Church to bestow it upon the Gentiles. Formerly, the children of this same land lost the Ark. God allowed it to be taken by their enemies, the Philistines, as though God preferred to live a prisoner in the Ark among his enemies than to remain with his own people who continued their evil ways. This is how God acted, and continues to act, towards those upon whom he has bestowed so many graces, and yet continue to offend him, as we do ourselves, miserable creatures that we are.

What a curse to those people to whom God says, "I will have

nothing to do with you. Your sacrifices and offerings, your devotions and your fasts no longer please me, I want nothing to do with them. You have soiled everything by your sins. I abandon you. Go, you shall have no part with me."[257] Alas, gentlemen, what unhappiness! But, O Lord, what happiness to be among those God uses to bring his blessings and his Church! Think of this comparison of an unfortunate nobleman who sees himself pressed on every side by war, by the plague, the burning of his houses, and by the shame of seeing the desertion of a prince. Amid this desolation he sees some come to his help, offering to serve him and to help him salvage what he can save. What a consolation and happiness for this gentleman in his misfortune! Then, gentlemen and my brothers, what joy will God experience in seeing amid the ravages of his Church made by heresy, or by the fires of concupiscence, some few persons who will offer themselves to carry off the remains of the Church, if I may speak this way, or to preserve it where it remains? O Lord, what joy to see such servants, either to preserve what is good on the spot, or to go anywhere to gain new lands for you!

O Lord, what joy will be yours to see such zealous servants defend for you what remains here, while others go off to gain new grounds for you! Oh, gentlemen, what a reason for rejoicing. You are aware that conquerors leave a portion of their troops to guard what they already have gained, while they send off others to win new territory for their empire. This is what we must do, maintaining courageously the goods of the Church and the interests of Jesus Christ, and still working for new victories, and making him known even to the most distant peoples.

One day a heretical author said to me:[258] "God has finally grown weary of the sins of all these countries, and his anger has withdrawn the faith of which they are unworthy. Would it not be rash to oppose the designs of God, and to seek to defend the Church which he has resolved to destroy? As for myself, I would prefer to further God's design by working for this plan of destruction."

Alas, gentlemen, perhaps what he said is true, that God might wish to destroy the Church because of our sins. Yet this author of heresy is wrong in saying it is an act of rashness to work against this decree, to use one's energies to conserve and to defend the Church. God asks this of us, and we must do it. It is not rash to fast, to suffer, to pray, to appease his anger and fight to the death to

---

257. Based on such passages as Isa 1:13.
258. The Abbe de Saint Cyran.

sustain and defend the Church wherever it is found. If our efforts up to the present seem to be fruitless because of our sins, or at least it seems this way, we must not stop because of that. We must rather humble ourselves profoundly, and continue our fasts, communions, our mental prayer in union with all other faithful servants of God who pray unceasingly for this same intention. We must hope that God in his mercy will relent and hear our prayer. As much as we can, let us humble ourselves then, because of our sins. But we must have confidence, great confidence, in God who wills that we continue in prayer for this poor kingdom of Poland which is so tried, all the while acknowledging that all depends on him and his grace.[259]

Up to this point we have seen by the words of Monsieur Vincent his ardent zeal and his desire that his confreres share this same virtue. It seemed this faithful servant of God was so moved by a holy confidence in his infinite mercy that he sought at any price to gain what he sought, that is, the protection of God for the kingdom of Poland and the preservation of the Catholic religion threatened with imminent peril. Therefore he urged his confreres to humble themselves, to offer to God their prayers, communions, and penances. For several years, and at almost every community gathering after mental prayer or his conferences, that is, two or three times a week, he would speak on this topic, never growing weary of repeating the same thoughts. Who can say how many were his sighs and tears before God, the mortifications he practiced, and the recommendations he made in any gathering he attended to obtain this grace from God. After his death a virtuous priest recounted that he was present at an assembly at which Monsieur Vincent spoke. He described the misery of this poor kingdom of Poland with such feeling, to urge his hearers to pray for this intention, that he drew tears from all eyes.

A little before his death it pleased God to give him the consolation of seeing the king of Poland reestablished in all the provinces of his realm. The Swedes and the Russians were driven out, and most powerful enemies were obliged to sue for peace. The Church and the Catholic religion were preserved, despite all the efforts of those who sought to destroy them.

---

259. *CED* XI:351-56.

SECTION ELEVEN

The Mission to the Hebrides Islands

If the most reliable sign of perfect charity is the preference of the interests of Jesus Christ over one's own, or to say it better, complete forgetfulness of self and total commitment to Jesus Christ, then we can truly say Monsieur Vincent had this virtue in an eminent degree. In all his undertakings he put his personal advantage and that of his community out of mind, and always looked to the glory of God and the service of his divine Master. The missions discussed in previous chapters are proof of this. The one presented in this chapter will show more clearly the motive of pure charity which animated him to begin it, for there was no semblance of earthly gain in it.

We must realize that there are many islands in the Hebrides, but they are not large. Since they lie to the north of Scotland in a cold climate, they are infertile. The inhabitants are so poor that even those who pass for nobles and the most wealthy are reduced to eating oat bread. Most of the people have only straw for furniture, for both bed and table, and for some it serves as tablecloth and napkin as well. We can easily deduce the poverty which must be the lot of the ordinary people.

Once the Catholic religion had been barred from the region by the separation of England from the Roman Church, and the priests had been driven away, few ministers or other preachers of the new sects were willing to live in this forbidding region. The lack of spiritual help to most of the poor inhabitants of these islands was such that persons could be found, eighty or a hundred years old or more, who had never been baptized. One can easily imagine how it was with others. Most of those poor people did not know if they were Catholics or heretics, since hardly any religious practices remained in use among them.

In face of these extreme conditions, Monsieur Vincent needed no further motivation to help these poor islanders than his own charity. It was enough for him to know the extremity of their spiritual state to decide to send some of his priests, sparing neither cost or anxiety. We could apply to him these words: *Sufficit, ut noveris; neque enim amas et deseris* ["It is enough that you know; for what you love you will never be able to leave."][260] He proposed to several Irish and Scottish priests of the Congregation that they might go work with their brothers. They accepted willingly, notwithstanding

---

260. Augustine, PL 35:1749.

the great danger to which they would be exposed because of the repressive laws in force against all Catholic priests. He selected two Irish priests for this mission to the Hebrides, and another priest, Scottish by birth, to work in Scotland.[261]

They left in 1651, dressed as merchants to escape the notice of the heretics. For this same reason they went first to Holland to embark. There they happily came in contact with a Scottish laird named Glengarry, as noble in virtue as in his birth.[262] He had recently converted to the Catholic religion. He took the missionaries under his protection, and continued to be of service to them.

They sailed for Scotland with him, but had scarcely landed when an apostate priest who had become a Protestant minister recognized them. He wrote letters to places throughout Scotland, alerting people there to the presence of these missionaries. God in his goodness saved them from this danger by striking the body of this miserable apostate, causing him great suffering and the loss of his hearing and his sight. He finally recognized the hand of God in this malady, and that his sins had caused his sufferings. Touched by divine grace, he decided to convert, and he did so. He made a long journey to find Monsieur Duggan, one of the missionaries, to beg pardon for his fault, and to receive absolution for his apostasy. He threw himself at the feet of the missionary with evident marks of contrition, and begged him to accept his abjuration and to receive him once again into the Church. The priest of the Mission did so, in virtue of the special powers he had received from the sovereign pontiff.

We know of no better way to present the fruits of this mission, and the sufferings entailed in exercising their ministry, than by citing two letters written to Monsieur Vincent by Monsieur Duggan. The first was dated October 28, 1652:

> God gave us the grace soon after our arrival in Scotland to help in the conversion of the father of the laird of Glengarry. He is an old man of ninety years, brought up in heresy from his youth. We instructed him and reconciled him to the Church during a severe sickness which soon brought him to the tomb. And before he received the sacraments, he expressed his regret for having lived so long in error, but also his unspeakable joy at dying as a Catholic. I also reconciled several of his servants and friends, but did so in secret.

---

261. The two Irish priests were Francois Le Blanc and Germain Duiguin, as they were known in France, and referred to by Vincent. Their English names were Francis White and Dermot Duggan. The Scottish priest was Thomas Lumsden, originally from Aberdeen, who was received into the Congregation at Paris, October 31, 1645. Lumsden arrived one year after his two Irish confreres.

262. Scottish names and terms in this chapter have been corrected and updated from Abelly's original text.

That done, I said goodbye to my companion, leaving him here in these mountains of Scotland to reap great spiritual fruit, and to attend to all the good that needs to be done here. I left for the Hebrides Islands, where God by his all-powerful mercy has worked marvels above anything we might have hoped for. He so moved hearts that the laird of Clanranald, master of a good part of the isle of Uist, converted, together with his wife, the young prince his son, and all his family. All his gentlemen and their families too, came into the Church.

I also worked with the people of this island, and then went to those called Eigg and Canna, where God brought about the conversion of eight or nine hundred persons. They were so poorly instructed in religion that no more than fifteen knew anything of the mysteries of the Christian religion. I hope the others will soon give glory to God. I have found thirty or forty persons here of advanced age, of eighty, or a hundred or even more, who have never been baptized, who died soon after receiving the sacrament. Beyond doubt they are now praying for those who brought them this great blessing.

A large number of the inhabitants were living in concubinage, but thanks be to God we have been able to bring some relief, marrying those who wished, and separating those who did not. We have taken nothing for the services we have given the people. Besides, I have had to hire two men, one to row me from one island to the other and to help carry my vestments and clothing, for I sometimes have to walk four or five leagues by poor roads to offer mass. The other man helps me teach the Our Father, Hail Mary, and the Creed, and serves my mass, for he is the only one available capable of doing so, once I taught him how.

Ordinarily we eat only once a day, a barley or oat loaf, with some cheese and salted butter. Sometimes we go a whole day without eating, since we find nothing to eat, particularly when we cross the deserted and uninhabited mountains. We almost never eat meat, but occasionally it is available in places far from the sea, especially in gentlemen's homes. But the meat is so bad and so filthily prepared that our hair stands on end when we see it. They throw it on the ground on a bit of straw which serves for table and chair, for tablecloth and napkin, for plate and saucer. To purchase a piece of meat to cook as we do in France is impossible because there are no butchers in these islands. Only a full steer or sheep can be bought, but we cannot use these, for we are constantly on the road to administer baptism or the other sacraments.

There are fish in the sea surrounding the islands, but the people are not skilled in catching them, since they are lazy and not industrious. It would be a great service to God to send good Gospel workers here who could speak the language, and know how to suffer hunger, thirst, and be able to sleep on the ground. Also, they ought to have an annual income if they are to get along.[263]

In the second letter sent, in April 1654, he said:

We are infinitely grateful, and thank the divine goodness for the blessings he has showered upon our work here. I can tell you some few things, for it would not be possible to tell you all that has happened.

The islands I have visited are Uist, Canna, Eigg, and Skye; on the mainland the regions I have visited are Moidart, Arisaig, Morar, Knoidart, and Glengarry.

The isle of Uist belongs to two lairds, one called the captain of the Ranald clan, and the other of the MacDonald clan. The part belonging to the first has seen the conversion of all the inhabitants except for two men without any religion, and who seem to want to be free to sin as they please. About a thousand or twelve hundred souls have returned to the fold of the Church. In the other part of this island, belonging to MacDonald, I have not yet visited, although I have been invited. A minister wanted to engage me in controversy by letter. I responded to him, and hope for some good from the exchange. The nobility have asked me to come, and the laird agrees. I am inclined to do so for I know the minister is fearful, and has tried to prevent my coming. The two servants he sent to me have returned home Catholics, by the grace of God. I heard their general confessions after I had prepared them for the sacrament.

Most of the inhabitants of the small island of Canna have been converted, as well as some from Eigg. The island of Skye is ruled by three or four lairds, one part by MacDonald and his mother, another by MacLeod, and a third by MacFimine.[264] In the first two parts, several families have been converted, but as of yet I have not been able to do anything in the third part of the island.

As to Moidart, Arisaig, Morar, Knoidart and Glengarry, all have been converted, or are prepared to receive instructions when we have time to visit their villages. There are six or seven thousand

---

263. *CED* IV:515-16.
264. Probably a typographical error for a name variously spelled: MacSimon, MacSymon, MacShiomoun.

people in these places, very remote from one another, difficult to reach on foot and inaccessible by horse.

At the beginning of spring I went to another island called Barra, where I found the people so devout and anxious to learn that I was thrilled. It was enough to teach a child of each village the Our Father, Hail Mary, and the Creed, and in three days the whole town would know it, the great and the simple alike. I have received the leading people of the town into the Church, including the young prince and his brothers and sisters, with a hope of receiving the older laird at the first opportunity. Among those converted was the son of the minister who greatly edified the region where he is known. Ordinarily I defer communion to my converts for some time after the general confession, so the people can be better instructed, and better disposed by a second confession, and also to arouse in them a greater desire and stronger affection for communion.

Among those who received communion five did not seem to have proper dispositions, for having put out their tongue to receive the sacred host they did not draw it back. Three remained so long in this attitude the host was picked off their tongue. Later they confessed once more in a much better disposition, and then received the bread of life with no more difficulty. The other two have not yet come back, and God has given the other Christians of the locality something to think about when they approach this divine sacrament, by the extraordinary signs he permitted to occur. In the same way, some marvelous things were seen by the use of holy water, enough to induce a sense of piety in these poor people. We baptized many infants and some adults, thirty, forty, sixty, or eighty years old and more, who insist they never before have been baptized. An evil spirit troubled some of them. They have been entirely delivered from his influence after receiving baptism, so much so that there is no more evidence of his activity among the people.[265]

The virtuous and zealous missionary planned to visit the island of Pabbay, once he had cleared it with the governor of the locality. This is what he wrote to one of his confreres, March 5, 1657:

I plan to leave here the tenth of this month for Pabbay. I have not spoken of this before lest the danger and difficulties should cause you some anxiety, for this is truly a forbidding place. We have hope of rescuing some stray sheep and returning them to the sheepfold of our Lord. Our trust in his goodness, together with the hope that the inhabitants have not been infected with heretical opinions, leads

---

265. *CED* V:116-17.

us to believe they will, with God's grace, come to hear and persevere in the word of God and the truths of our holy religion. This makes me disdain the perils, even death, and we shall go with God's help, submissive to his holy will. This is why I ask you not to delay in coming. But be careful not to reveal my intentions to anyone, except Monsieur Nouelly, because for several reasons I want it to remain secret and hidden.

This good missionary was not destined to carry out this plan, for he fell sick shortly after sending this letter, and died on May 17, 1657, to the great grief of all those for whom he had worked so hard.

After speaking of the missions to the Hebrides, we must now speak of those in Scotland, where Monsieur Lumsden worked so zealously. This is what he wrote to Monsieur Vincent, in 1654:

God has greatly blessed the missions given in the lowlands. I might say that all the inhabitants whether rich or poor have never, since the time they fell into heresy, been better disposed to recognize the truth and of being converted to our holy faith. Every day we receive some who come to abjure their errors, some of high station. Besides these activities, we seek to confirm Catholics in their belief by instructing them in the word of God and by administering the sacraments. On Easter day I was in the house of a laird where more than fifty people received communion, among whom were twenty recent converts. The success of our mission inspires great jealousy among the Protestant ministers, who lack the power but not the desire to do us harm. We trust in the goodness of God, who shall, if it please him, always be our protector.[266]

By another letter, in October 1657, speaking of the same subject, he wrote:

The people of these northern regions are much better disposed to receive the truth than they have ever been before. The grace of God has not been idle this past summer. By its influence I have been able to bring back to the Church some highly placed people who have abjured their heresy. I have continued to confirm the faith of Catholics by the instructions I have given, and by the sacraments I have administered. I have even taken a trip to the Orkney Islands, and visited the regions called Moray, Ross, Sutherland, and Caithness, where they have not had a priest for several years, and where practically no Catholics remain. As I began to work, I received into the faith a good man from Caithness. He had invited me to come spend some time in that province, where he hoped for many

---

266. *CED* V:124-25.

conversions. I was obliged to leave hurriedly, for the enemy of our salvation had raised up a new persecution against Catholics, at the instigation of the ministers who had obtained an order from Protector Cromwell addressed to all judges and magistrates of the kingdom of Scotland. It stated that many people, especially in the northern provinces, had gone over to papism, and to stop this abuse they were required to search carefully, especially for priests. These latter were to be put in prison, and punished according to the laws of the kingdom. Since the minister of Bredonique was particularly hostile to me, and sought to have me taken, I had to flee to seek some haven until we could see how this persecution was to turn out. I cannot write in greater detail for fear that our letters will fall into the hands of our enemies.[267]

Not without reason did this virtuous missionary take precautions against falling into the hands of the heretics. It was not the fear of prison or even death, but the risk of depriving Catholics in this poor kingdom of the help and consolation he was able to bring. Beginning in 1655, on the occasion of a similar order from Cromwell, issued at the request of the Protestant ministers, the English authorities had hunted down Catholic priests. They found three in the castle of the marquess of Huntley, one of whom was his confrere, Monsieur White. He had been imprisoned in the city of Aberdeen since February of that same year.

When Monsieur Vincent heard the news he spoke to the community on the trials and persecutions missionary priests would meet in their ministry, and the constancy they should show in these situations.

> We recommend to God one of our priests, Monsieur White, who worked in the mountains of Scotland. The English heretics have imprisoned him, together with a Jesuit priest. They have been taken to the city of Aberdeen, where Monsieur Lumsden is. He does not fail to visit him and help him. There are many Catholics in that region who visit and console the suffering priest. Yet, seeing this good missionary threatened with martyrdom, I do not know if we should be happy or sad. On the one hand God is honored by his detention, for it comes from love of him. The Company could be blessed if God would find him worthy to become a martyr. He would be happy to suffer for God's name, and to offer himself for whatever it shall please God to ordain concerning his person and his life. What acts of virtue are called forth in his present situation, of faith, of hope, of love of God, of resignation, and of self-offering,

---

267. *CED* VI:530-31. The identification and location of Bredonique is unknown. Joseph Leonard, the translator of Coste, has suggested Brechin. Coste, *Life*, II:39, n. 13.

by which he prepares himself to receive such a crown! All this brings much joy and thanksgiving to God.

On the other hand, our confrere suffers and should we not suffer with him? For myself, I admit that according to human nature I am deeply afflicted and I feel it most keenly, but thinking of this according to the spirit, I believe we must bless God for a special grace. This is the way God acts after someone has rendered outstanding services to him: he places the cross upon his shoulders, then adds sorrows and afflictions. Oh, gentlemen and my brothers, there must be something the mind does not understand, in the cross, in suffering, since God usually sends them to those who have served him so well. He adds afflictions, persecutions, prison, and martyrdom, to raise those who give themselves so perfectly to his service to a high degree of perfection. Whoever wishes to be a disciple of Jesus Christ ought to expect this, but he should also hope, when these occasions arise, that God will give him the strength to support these afflictions and overcome these troubles.

Monsieur Le Vacher once wrote me from Tunis of a rough and ready priest from Calabria. He developed a desire to suffer martyrdom for the name of Jesus Christ, such as animated Saint Francis of Paula, but which did not occur since God had destined him for other things. This priest was so obsessed by this holy desire that he crossed the sea to seek martyrdom in Barbary where he was finally discovered, and where he died in confessing the name of Jesus Christ. May it please God to inspire us with this same wish to die for Jesus Christ however it shall please him. What a blessing this would attract upon us!

You are aware there are several forms of martyrdom, not only the kind we have been speaking of, but there is another kind too, of constantly mortifying our passions, and even another, to persevere in our vocation in the accomplishment of our duties and our exercises. Saint John the Baptist, for his courage in reproving the king for his sin of incest and adultery, was put to death for his pains. Yet he is honored as a martyr, even though he did not die precisely for the faith, but for the defense of a virtue against which the king had sinned. Dying in defense of a virtue is then a kind of martyrdom.

A mortified and obedient Missionary who does his duty well, and who lives in keeping with the rules of his state in life, makes it evident by the sacrifice of his body and soul that God alone deserves to be served, and that God should be preferred absolutely to all advantages or pleasures the world has to offer. To do so is to demonstrate the truths and maxims of the Gospel of Jesus Christ, not by words, but by the conformity of one's own life to that of Jesus Christ. Giving testimony to his truth and his sanctity to both Christians and infidels, to live and die in this effort, is another form of martyrdom.

Let us return to our good Monsieur White, to consider how God dealt with him after a life of dedication as a missionary. Here is a marvel, what some would call a miracle. A certain inclemency of the weather happened to affect the fish of the region with sterility, resulting in much suffering for the people. He was asked to lead prayers and to bless the sea with holy water, for it was felt that spells of some sort caused this difficulty. He did so, and God willed that immediately after, the difficulty passed and the fish returned. He wrote of these things himself in a letter to me.[268] Others have told me of the great work he did in the mountains to strengthen the faith of the Catholics and convert heretics, the constant dangers he braved, the hunger he endured, eating only bread made from oats. Only a person who deeply loved God would do and suffer so much in his service. Should God permit still greater crosses to come and that one become a prisoner of Jesus Christ, ought we not adore God's ways, submitting ourselves lovingly to them? Ought we not offer ourselves to him in order that he accomplish his holy will in us? Let us then ask this grace of God to thank him for this latest test of the fidelity of his servant. We should beg of him, if it is not yet in keeping with his will to deliver him, at least to strengthen him to bear the ill treatment he is suffering or will suffer in the future.[269]

According to all appearances, this virtuous prisoner was in danger of his life, since he was in the hands of his cruel enemies who wished for his death, but it pleased God that he be released after five or six months in prison. According to the laws then in effect against Catholics, there was insufficient evidence against him to convict him of having celebrated mass or performing other functions of his ministry. Someone testified against him, but unconvincingly. When challenged, he took back what he had said, stating that he did not want to be responsible for the condemnation of the accused. Monsieur White's parole was granted under the strange condition that if he preached, instructed, baptized anyone, or administered any of the sacraments, he would be hung without any further trial.

When Monsieur Vincent heard news of his release, he spoke to the community:

---

268. This letter no longer exists.
269. *CED* XI:173-76.

We thank God for having delivered the innocent, and that someone among us has been found to suffer so much for the love of his Savior. This good priest, disdaining the threat of death, went back to the mountains of Scotland to work as before. What reason we have to thank our Lord for having given one of our Company the spirit of the martyrs! The light, the grace to see how glorious, how great, how divine, to die for the neighbor, in imitation of our Lord! We thank God and we pray that he will give each of us that same grace to suffer and to give up his life for the salvation of souls.[270]

---

270. *CED* XI:304-05.

CHAPTER TWO

The Spiritual Exercises to Prepare for the Proper Reception of Holy Orders

SECTION ONE

The Pressing Need of Clergy Reform at the Time Monsieur Vincent Established the Ordination Retreats

IN THE PREVIOUS chapter we have seen the abundant blessings God had poured forth on the missions of Monsieur Vincent and his Congregation. We can judge from their fruits how appropriate they were for converting souls to God, dispelling ignorance, helping them leave their sinful ways, and leading them to take up the practice of Christian living. Our Savior Jesus Christ planted faith and other virtues in all parts of the earth through the ministry of his apostles, the main and first of the Missionaries, which is what the title apostle means. In the same way he also used Monsieur Vincent and all those who share his spirit to restore that same faith in many souls, and even to augment it and make it more fruitful.

Although this may be true, we must admit that for most people their weakness and inconstancy in doing good makes it difficult to preserve the fruits of the missions. They need shepherds and priests available to them, who will devote themselves to cultivating the good seed.

Thus it was that Monsieur Vincent earnestly besought God to supply a remedy to this pressing need. He said, speaking of this matter:

> Conquerors build forts and supply garrisons for the places they have captured. In the same way, the Missionaries, who rescue souls from the power of Satan, must see to it as well as they can, that the parishes have zealous pastors and good priests to help the people persevere in the good dispositions awakened in them by the missions. Unless this is done, the devil, driven from their souls, will retake his ground with little opposition.

Experience showed Monsieur Vincent only too well that few of the clergy were committed to this role. He saw everywhere what abuses existed among the clergy in the greater part of the places where he had worked. Had he been unaware of these things from firsthand observation, the complaints and lamentations coming from all sides, sometimes from great and respected prelates, would convince him of this.

This is the way a certain priest of noble birth and known piety, and now a canon of a cathedral church, wrote him of the situation in 1642.

> In this diocese the clergy are without discipline, the people without respect. Priests lack devotion and charity, pulpits lack preachers. Learning is not respected, vice is not punished, virtue is oppressed. The authority of the Church is either hated or defied. Personal interest is the law of the sanctuary, while the most scandalous are the most powerful. In short, flesh and blood have supplanted the Gospel and spirit of Jesus Christ. When you see the condition of our diocese, I am sure you will do what you can to help us. *Quis novit utrum ad regnum idcirco veneris, ut in tali tempore parareris?* ["Who knows but that it was for a time like this that you obtained the royal dignity?"][1] The humble prayer I make to you to consider this seriously before the Lord is worthy of your charity, for it comes from one of the first of your sons.[2]

A worthy prelate told him one day that he and his vicars general worked as hard as they could for the welfare of the diocese, "but with little success because of the large number of ignorant and evil clergy. Neither word nor example would move them to amend their lives. I am horrified when I think that in my diocese nearly seven thousand drunken or immoral priests approach the altar daily, lacking any semblance of a true vocation."[3]

Another prominent prelate wrote to him on this same subject in 1643. "The extreme desolation of the clergy in my diocese and the impossibility of remedying the situation obliges me to turn to your zeal. Everyone knows your reputation and your strong dedication to restore ecclesiastical discipline where it has been seriously weakened or entirely lost."[4]

Another prelate wrote, among other things: "Except for the canon theologian of my church, I do not find among all the priests of my diocese anyone qualified for ecclesiastical office. You may judge from this how great the necessity is for us to have help. Please allow your missionary to help us prepare our candidates for ordination."[5]

From these samples we may judge the state of affairs of the clergy in most

---

1. Esth 4:14. This alludes to the fact that at this time, Vincent began to be consulted by Louis XIII, Anne of Austria and Cardinal Richelieu regarding the appointment of bishops.
2. As a member of the Tuesday conference. *CED* II:282.
3. *CED II:428-29.*
4. *CED II:372.*
5. *CED VI:53.*

of the dioceses of the kingdom, and the pressing need to bring about a reformation. This is why Monsieur Vincent recognized, as we said in Book One, that no other remedy would be effective if the root of the evil were not attacked. It was essential that those in future preparing to receive priestly orders must bring the appropriate dispositions of soul to this great sacrament. This was Monsieur Vincent's constant goal in all that he did with such great devotion to the ordination retreats he established. In the following chapter we will follow the steps he and his priests took to bring this about, and the results they achieved.

SECTION TWO

The Beginning of the Ordination Retreats

We read in Book One[6] how Monsieur Vincent began the ordination retreats at Beauvais in September 1628, under Bishop Augustine Potier. These proved beneficial not only to this devoted prelate, who, with the help of Monsieur Vincent, continued them to the advantage of his clergy, but also to many other bishops of the kingdom and elsewhere. They established the retreats in these various dioceses with most happy results.

First, His Excellency Jean Francois de Gondi learned of what Monsieur Vincent had done in Beauvais, and decided to imitate it in Paris. For many years he had recognized Monsieur Vincent as a gift of God to the whole Church. The archbishop invited him to begin these same retreats for the candidates to the priesthood. They started in Lent of 1631 in the College des Bons Enfants, where his small Congregation was then housed. These ordination retreats were a tiny spring whose waters were destined to irrigate the whole field of the Church. Paris was the source from which several bishops and some other influential clergymen learned of the value and utility of the ordination retreats. This led them to have these retreats introduced into their localities.

Monsieur Vincent wrote two years later about this:

> The archbishop, following the ancient practice of the Church in which the bishop confers with those who wish to receive orders, decided that henceforth in his diocese the candidates had to come

---

6. Ch. 25.

to the priests of the Mission ten days before each of the orders to make a spiritual retreat. They would also learn the art of meditation so necessary to the clergy, make a general confession of all their past life, review their moral theology, especially in what related to the sacraments, and learn all the rites and functions proper to the clergy. They receive room and board during this time. This happens with such fruit, by God's grace, that those who have made the ordination retreats continue to lead an exemplary life, and for the most part have committed themselves publicly to works of Christian charity.[7]

On another occasion he spoke to his community about how their various services did not come from their own planning but from the direct intervention of divine Providence: "Did we plan to give the ordination retreats, the richest source of grace the Church has put into our hands? No, that never came into our thoughts."[8]

In 1631 there were six ordination ceremonies in Paris. On each occasion Monsieur Vincent received the candidates into his house to have them make their retreats. Things continued this way until 1643, when the archbishop thought it best to stop the mid-Lent ordination, for his council thought time was too short between each ordination for the candidates to bring to the next one the proper dispositions. It should be noted that up to 1638 only candidates from Paris attended the ordination retreats. At that period some pious women noted the remarkable changes brought about among the clergy of Paris and thought to suggest to Monsieur Vincent that he might admit candidates from other dioceses as well, from among those who already had come to Paris for ordination.

To cover the expense of such a program, a pious woman, the wife of the President de Herse, offered to provide a thousand livres for each group for five years. Since then, she and others among the Ladies of Charity of Paris have continued to support this enterprise. The Marquise of Maignelay, sister of the archbishop of Paris, a woman of great piety and virtue, had a particular esteem for Monsieur Vincent.[9] She contributed to Saint Lazare to defray the great expenses of the candidates. The queen mother herself, at the beginning of the regency, attended a lecture in the church of the College des Bons Enfants, given by Monsieur Perrochel, the bishop-elect of Boulogne.[10] She

---

7. *CED* I:179-80.
8. *CED* XII:9.
9. Charlotte Marguerite de Gondi, the wife of Florimond d'Halluin, the marquis of Maignelay. After her husband's death, she dedicated her life and great fortune to charity. She died in 1650.
10. Francois Perrochel, a cousin of Jean Jacques Olier, and a student and companion of Vincent in the work of the missions, was ordained a bishop June 11, 1645, in the church of Saint Lazare. He was bishop of Boulogne for thirty-two years. He resigned his see in 1677 and died five years later at age eighty.

was convinced of the usefulness of this practice for the Church. Several ladies encouraged her to support it with a royal grant, which she did after the five-year subsidy from Madame de Herse had run out. She contributed financial help for two or three years. However, for the next eighteen years, the entire cost of this service fell upon the house of Saint Lazare which had no source of funds to support the large number of persons attending the ordination retreats. This was accomplished only at the cost of much inconvenience, especially since 1646 even those receiving the four minor orders were obliged to follow the exercises. The purpose was that before advancing to sacred orders they might have the light to discern if God had truly called them, and if he had, to prepare themselves more thoroughly.

Much as the financial obligations surpassed the resources of Saint Lazare, Monsieur Vincent never uttered a single word of complaint about the great expense of continuing the ordination retreats. He remained silent, abandoned to God's good pleasure, and preferred always the glory of his name and the good of his Church to any temporal interest of his Congregation.

The number of those at each session of these exercises was seventy, eighty, or ninety or more, and they all lived at Saint Lazare for the eleven days of each meeting, making fifty-five days each year. Not a *sou* was asked in payment, so that they would more willingly come, seeing that nothing was being spared to prepare them better for serving the Church.

We recall here the testimony of a priest of great reputation on this question:

> It is impossible to express adequately the care taken by Monsieur Vincent to assure that everything be well done during the ordination retreats. The expense did not seem to matter, although it was far beyond the resources of Saint Lazare, which must have run into great debt because of this. I recall that during the troubled times in Paris, several important persons, well aware of how difficult it was for Monsieur Vincent to continue to support the ordination retreats, suggested that he no longer subsidize these programs. He refused to listen to this advice, despite the shortages of both food and money. He continued to spend freely for the upkeep of the candidates during their eleven-day stay, and thought little of the temporal when it was a question of spiritual good. He looked upon perishable goods as useful only to the extent they contributed to the glory of God.
>
> He often spoke to the members of his community as the time for one of these ordination retreats approached about the excellence of the priesthood, exhorting them to render whatever service or help they could to the candidates. He exhorted them to use all the strength

of body and soul to encourage the growth of the clergy in holiness. His words were like burning darts, penetrating the heart. They are worthy of preservation, even in writing. If not, it would be an incomparable loss.

SECTION THREE

A Summary of What is Done During the Ordination Retreats, and the Regulations that Govern Them

Those who wish to receive ordination come to the house of the priests of the Mission ten days before the Saturday on which they are to be ordained. Upon arrival their names are recorded, their ecclesiastical rank, degrees, etc. Some priests of the house are present to receive their guests, to take their cloaks, to show them to their rooms or around the house, to wait on them, to encourage them, and to explain the order of the retreat. They also recommend recollection, silence, and modesty and the exact observance of all the usages of the exercises so they would gain the maximum profit from them, and prepare themselves to receive orders worthily. A director of the ordination retreats is charged with the general responsibility of the program. The candidates are answerable to him. His chief care is to see that all who serve the candidates and those who make the exercises are animated with the same spirit.

Each day two conferences are given, the first in the morning on the principles of moral theology and on practical matters a clergyman should know. The other conference is given in the evening on the virtues, qualities and functions proper to those in holy orders.

There are ten different topics for these talks. The order of the topics for the mornings on moral theology is:

On the first day, the general censures of the Church.

On the second, particular censures, such as excommunication, suspension, interdict, and irregularities.

On the third, the sacrament of penance; its institution, its form, effects, and the conditions necessary for the confessor to administer the sacrament well.

On the fourth, dispositions for receiving the sacrament of penance well, i.e., contrition, confession, satisfaction; and indulgences.

On the fifth, divine and human laws. Sins in general; their kinds, circumstances, causes, effects, degrees, and remedies.

On the sixth, the first three of the ten commandments, which include the duties of man toward God. The three theological virtues, the virtue and acts of religion.

On the seventh, the other seven commandments, which refer to the neighbor.

On the eighth, the sacraments in general; confirmation, and the eucharist as sacrament.

On the ninth, the eucharist as sacrifice; extreme unction; marriage.

On the tenth, the Apostles Creed, emphasizing what a priest should know about each article, and the way to teach the creed to others.

The order for the evening conference:

On the first day, mental prayer is spoken of, with reasons why clerics should practice it. Then an explanation of mental prayer, the method to be used, and how to pray well. This is chosen as the first evening topic because during the retreat some time each day is reserved for this kind of prayer.

On the second, the vocation to the ecclesiastical state. The necessity of being called by God to this state before accepting orders. What this vocation consists in, how a person may recognize the call, and how he may correspond well to this grace.

On the third, the true ecclesiastical spirit is discussed. The obligation of acquiring this spirit; its signs, the means of acquiring it, and how to perfect oneself in this spirit.

On the fourth, orders in general; their institution, necessity, matter, form, effects, differences among them, dispositions required to receive them profitably.

On the fifth, the clerical tonsure; the doctrine behind this ceremony; obligations imposed, qualities it should have, dispositions to bring to its reception, response to objections, and several difficulties about the tonsure.

On the sixth, the minor orders: definition, matter, form, function, and virtues required to exercise these functions with profit.

On the seventh, the subdiaconate; the virtues proper to this order, especially chastity.

On the eighth, the diaconate, and the virtues proper to this order, particularly charity toward the neighbor.

On the ninth, the priesthood; the knowledge proper to priests to acquit themselves worthily of this order.

Lastly, on the tenth day, a conference is given on the life of an ecclesiastic, in which it is explained that the life of a cleric ought to be much more holy than that of laymen. Various ways are suggested to help them lead such a life.

Each day following the conferences, the candidates are divided into groups, each composed of from twelve to fifteen persons. The groups are formed of those having similar backgrounds, presided over by a priest of the Mission, to discuss among themselves what had been said. This helps fix the matter and their own reflections more surely in their memories.

Each day about a half-hour is given for mental prayer, and afterward the discussion groups meet to help those unacquainted with this form of prayer. It is explained how to make the considerations, arouse the affections, and arrive at practical resolutions.

Each day they have the opportunity to practice the particular rite of the order they are to receive, and the rites of both private and solemn masses.

They recite the divine office together, with close attention paid to the pauses and periods of reflection.

Special attention is given to encouraging everyone to make a general confession of their entire life if they had never made one before, or at least of the time since their last general confession, if they had done so previously. It was for this reason that the subject of general confession had been discussed in the conference on the things a cleric should be aware of in his calling. The day following their confession, a Thursday, all receive communion at the high mass.

Seven and a half hours are given to sleep, and two hours a day to holy and upright conversation after meals, at which there are readings from holy Scripture and the book on the dignity and sanctity of priests, by Molina the Carthusian.[11]

In a word, the candidates are introduced to a well-ordered life, not too free and not too austere, but well suited to their calling as ecclesiastics, which they might continue to live after leaving Saint Lazare.

The Sunday after ordination they return home after high mass, at which all receive communion in thanksgiving for the grace of ordination.

This, then, is a summary of the ordination retreats begun and since continued by Monsieur Vincent, and carried on by his Congregation for the welfare of the whole Church.

He strongly recommended that those who gave the conferences follow carefully the notes drawn up for each talk. These had been well prepared, covering just those points most necessary and most important for the candidates, and in a sequence most suited for attaining the goal of the exercises.

When a bishop himself would give these conferences, Monsieur Vincent strongly commended their contributions, as father to his children, solid in their spiritual doctrine, and showing the active role of the Spirit of God in their life and teaching.

Monsieur Vincent said to his priests, "Simplicity impresses the candi-

---

11. Antonio de Molina, 1550-1612(?), *Instrucción de sacerdotes*. A Latin version existed in Vincent's day, but a French version did not appear until 1676.

dates. They are very happy with it, and they are not looking for anything else here. Presented in this garment, truth will be well received, and will be most effective in an unadorned modesty." One day, when someone gave a conference in a fashion other than in the spirit of the Mission, he fell on his knees before him, and begged him earnestly to be simpler and more devout.

SECTION FOUR

Monsieur Vincent's Thoughts on the Ordination Retreats

Before speaking of the development and the results of the ordination retreats, it would be appropriate to recall the way Monsieur Vincent looked upon them, and how he exhorted his confreres to devote themselves to them.

Once he said, "To devote yourself to fashioning good priests, as a secondary efficient and instrumental cause, is to do what Jesus Christ did. During his mortal life he strove to raise up twelve good priests, his apostles, by having them live with him, by instructing them, and by forming them to their divine ministry."[12]

Another day, during a conference to his community on this same matter, after which he had invited others to comment, he ended by saying:

> Blessed are you, Lord, for the good things which have been said, for you have inspired those who spoke. But, my Savior, all this will come to nothing, if you do not supply your helping hand. Your grace alone will bring about all that we have spoken of, and will bring us that Holy Spirit necessary for anything we do. How can we, miserable as we are, know what we should do? O Lord, give us the spirit of your priesthood which your apostles and the first priests who followed them had. Give us the true spirit of that sacred character that you conferred on poor fishermen, artisans, low-born, in those latter days. By your grace, you bestowed on them your divine Spirit. For, O Lord, we too are these wretched people, poor workmen, peasants. What comparison exists between our miserable selves and our holy, eminent, and heavenly calling? Gentlemen and my brothers, we ought to pray earnestly to God for this pressing need of the Church. In many places the Church teeters on the brink

---

12. *CED XI:8*.

of disaster because of the evil lives of priests, and there are many who fit this description. It is only too true that the depravity of the clerical state is the chief cause of the ruin of the Church of God.

I attended a meeting recently at which seven bishops were present, to discuss the disorders that have become evident in the Church. It was publicly stated that the clergy were chiefly to blame.

It was the priests. Yes, we are the cause of this desolation which afflicts the Church in so many places. It has practically been destroyed in Asia, Africa and even in a large part of Europe, such as in Sweden, Denmark, England, Scotland, Ireland, Holland, and the other United Provinces, and in large sections of Germany. How many heretics do we not see in France herself? Look at Poland, already deeply affected by heresy, and now threatened by the invasion of the king of Sweden, to be lost completely to the Church.

Does it not seem, gentlemen, that God is about to transport his Church to some other country? Yes, if we do not change radically we may fear that God will abandon us completely, as we see powerful enemies of the Church force their way in. In less than four months the notorious king of Sweden has invaded a good part of this great kingdom. He may be a scourge from God raised up to punish us for our sins. These people are the same whom God raised up in other times to afflict us: the Goths, the Visigoths, and the Vandals, all come from that same region. God used them, over twelve hundred years ago, to punish the Church of those times. What is happening now, as unusual as it has ever been, ought to put us on our guard. A kingdom as vast as ours, invaded out of nowhere, in the space of four months! O Lord, who knows if this powerful conqueror will stop there? Finally, *Ab aquilone pandetur omne malum* ["From the north evil will boil over"],[13] from there came the evils our ancestors had to endure. That's the region to fear.

Look to the restoration of the clerical state, for evil priests are the cause of all these woes, and bring such disasters upon the Church. These good bishops have recognized this from their own experience and have spoken out openly, in the sight of God. Yes, Lord, we are the ones who have provoked your anger. Our sins have brought about these calamities.

Yes, the clergy and those aspiring to that state, the subdeacons, deacons, and priests, yes, we priests, have brought about this desolation in the Church. What now, O Lord? What can we do, humbled before you, now that we have resolved to change our lives?

---

13. Jer 1:14.

Yes, my Savior, we desire to do all in our power in satisfaction for our past sins, and to restore the clerical state. We are assembled here for that purpose, and we implore your grace upon us. Ah, gentlemen! What can we not accomplish!

God has given us the grace to work for the rehabilitation of the clerical state. God has not confided this task to doctors of theology, nor to any other communities renowned for knowledge and holiness, but to this wretched, poor, and miserable Company, the last of all, and the most unworthy. What does God see in us for such a great task? Where are our great triumphs? Where are the mighty deeds we have done? What prospects do we offer? Nothing of all this. God has solely by his own will confided this task to a miserable group of men, to try to repair the breaches made in the walls of his kingdom, and to reform the ecclesiastical state.

Oh, gentlemen and my brothers, let us preserve this grace God has conferred upon us in preference to so many learned and holy men more deserving than ourselves. If we fail by our negligence to carry out his purposes, God will take it from us to give to others, and punish us for our infidelity. Alas, which of us would want to be the cause of such a misfortune, and deprive the Church of such a blessing?

Could I ever be so awful? Let each of us look into his own conscience and say to himself, never could I be so deplorable. Unfortunately, it takes only one such as I am to turn the favors of heaven away from a whole community, and make the curse of God fall upon it. O Lord, who see me weak and filled with sin, do not withhold your grace from this little Company! Grant that it may continue to serve you with humility and fidelity, and may cooperate with your will, so that by its ministry it may re-establish the honor of your Church.

But how can we do this? What shall we do for the success of the next ordination retreat? We must pray much, since we lack so much. We must offer our communions, our mortifications, our mental prayer and all other prayers for this intention. We must do everything for the edification of these candidates, treating them with respect and deference, never arguing with them, but serving them graciously and humbly. These must be the weapons we missionaries use. If we use them we will succeed. In humility we must truly look forward to our own self-effacement. Believe me, gentlemen and my brothers, believe me when I repeat the infallible maxim of Jesus Christ that a heart must be empty of itself to be filled with God. Then God will live and act in us, and this wish for self-effacement will empty our hearts. Humility, holy humility, will bring this about, and then it will no longer be ourselves who act but God in us, and all will go well.

Those of you working directly with the ordination retreats must have the spirit of the priesthood, and inspire those who do not. You who have these souls confided to you to receive this holy and sanctifying Spirit, look solely to the glory of God. Have simplicity of heart toward him, and great respect for the candidates. Be persuaded that by these means you will accomplish much. Any other course will be fruitless. Humility and the pure intention to please God have made these ordination retreats succeed up to now. I recommend also the ceremonies, and I pray that all the Company will observe them carefully. These ceremonies are but the shadow of the underlying truth, but they should be performed with as much care as possible, with religious silence, and much modesty and gravity. How will the candidates observe these practices if we ourselves do not do them well? Let us sing with moderation and recite the psalms with devotion. Alas, what shall we reply to God when we render an account, if we have done them poorly?[14]

On another occasion, Monsieur Vincent spoke as follows:

Gentlemen and my brothers, we are now on the eve of another of these days when we begin the ordination retreats. Tomorrow, O God, you providentially send us those whom you wish us to form to a better life. What! Gentlemen and my brothers, here is surely a large mouthful—to form clerics to a better way of life. Who could fully appreciate the significance of our task? What state is equal to the ecclesiastical state? Principalities and kingdoms do not compare with it. You are aware that kings cannot change bread into the body of our Lord, nor remit sin, nor perform the other services which are so far superior to temporal power. Yet these are the people being sent to us to sanctify. Could there be anything like this? O poor and wretched workmen, how unfitted we are for this task. But since God does us the honor to assign this responsibility to our small Congregation, the last of all and the poorest, we on our side must use all our energy to see that the retreats are fruitful. We must prepare our candidates for sacred orders, and inspire them to acquit themselves well of their duties. Some will be pastors, some canons, some provosts, abbots, bishops, yes bishops. These are the ones we will be receiving tomorrow.

This past week the bishops met to consider the problem of the drunkenness of priests in a certain province, a thing strictly forbid-

---

14. *CED* XI:308-12.

den. Holy doctors say that the first step for someone wishing to acquire virtue is to control the mouth. What shall be the result if a person gives in to his every desire? What disorder! They become servants, slaves, unable to control themselves. Nothing is so base, so deplorable as to see most of the priests of a certain province so given to this vice that bishops had to call a meeting to search for some remedy for it. What shall happen to the people?

What should we not do ourselves, gentlemen, to give ourselves to God to rescue his ministers and his spouse from this disorder, and the many others we are aware of? Not that all priests are guilty. No, O Savior! There are some holy men among the clergy whom we see here on retreat, pastors and others who come from far away to look to the state of their soul. And don't forget the many good and saintly priests of Paris. Among the priests attending the clergy conferences here not a single one was not edifying in conduct. They all work with exceptional success.

There are evil clergymen in the world, and I happen to be the worst, the most unworthy, the greatest sinner of them all. On the other hand, some give great glory to God by the sanctity of their lives. What happiness for us that not only has God called such poor persons as ourselves, without learning or virtue, to help in the reformation of a fallen and disordered clergy, and even to contribute to the development of the virtuous, as we have seen happen. How happy you are, gentlemen, to further by your dedication, meekness, affability, modesty, and humility, the growth of the Spirit of God in the souls of these priests. You serve God in these great servants of God. How happy you are, you who give such good example at the conferences, the exercises, in choir, in the refectory, everywhere. How happy we shall all be if by our silence, discretion, and charity we fulfill the purpose for which God sent them to us. We must be on the lookout to notice anything they may need or want. We must be attentive to all their wishes. By serving them we will surely edify them. We must ask the grace from our Lord to do all this. I ask the priests to offer mass for this intention, and the brothers also to have this same intention when they attend mass.[15]

On another occasion, he said:

Now that we have an ordination retreat about to begin, we must pray that God give his Spirit to those who address the candidates in the conferences and the discussions. Above all, be attentive to act with humility and modesty. Our learning will not make us success-

---

15. *CED* XI:8-11.

ful, nor will the brilliant things we say to them. They are much more learned than we are. Several have their bachelor's degree, others have the licentiate in sacred theology, some are doctors in the law, and only a few do not know philosophy and perhaps theology as well. They are used to disputations. Practically nothing we could say to them is new or what they haven't heard before. They themselves say that these things do not impress them here, but what does impress them is the virtues they see practiced here. Be humble, gentlemen, considering such an honorable position as that of helping make good priests. What could be greater? Be humble at our own unworthiness, we who are uneducated, poor in understanding, poor in our position in society. Why has God chosen us for such a great service? Because God, as a rule, chooses only the basest things for the marvels of his grace. The sacraments bear witness to this, where he uses water and a few words to confer his greatest graces.

Pray for these candidates, yes, but pray, too, for ourselves so that God would turn away from us anything that might hinder the working of God's Spirit, which he seems to want to send upon our Congregation. Have you ever been on pilgrimage to one of the holy shrines? Ordinarily upon entering the shrine some feel ecstatic, others are suddenly moved by devotion, others are filled with respect and reverence for the holy places, and still others feel other pious sentiments. Where does this come from? This comes about because God's Spirit is there, moving the hearts of those present. We must look forward to the same thing in regard to the candidates, if the Spirit of God abides in this house.

We must make our moral preaching practical, relating it to actual situations so that the principles will be well understood. We ought to aim at having the candidates carry away exactly what was said to them in the conferences. Be on your guard lest the evil spirit of vanity should show its face, urging us to speak of high and mighty things. This would only destroy rather than edify. They will carry away what has been spoken of in these conferences, if we speak simply after impressing this point upon them. We should speak only of this, and not of other things, for many good reasons.[16]

Once, when a brother spoke during repetition of prayer about his mental prayer, and how he prayed that God would send good priests to his Church, Monsieur Vincent used the occasion to say:

God bless you, brother, for asking God to provide good bishops, good pastors, and good priests. This is something we should all pray

---

16. *CED* XI:11-12.

for. "Like priests, like people." The officers of an army get either the credit or the blame in a war, and we can say the same thing in the Church. If the ministers of the Church are good and do their duty, all will go well. On the contrary, if they do not, they bring about all sorts of disorders. God calls us all, in the state which we have embraced, to work at producing a masterpiece. What greater masterpiece could there be than to form good priests, in comparison with which we can think of nothing greater or more important. Our brothers can contribute to this by their good example and by their temporal work. They can offer the divine office for the intention that God will be pleased to bestow his Spirit to these candidates for ordination.

Let each of us do the same, and be on the lookout to edify these gentlemen. We should anticipate their wishes as much as we conveniently can. Those with occasion to speak with them or to help at their discussions must raise their minds to God to know what to say to them. God is the unlimited source of wisdom, of light, and of love. We must draw inspiration from him for what we say to them.

We ought to deny our own spirit and our own personal feelings to be open to his grace, which alone enlightens and warms the heart. We must leave our own selves to enter into God's designs, turning to him to learn his thoughts, and pray that he will speak in us and by us. In this way it will be his work, not spoiled by what we are or do. In conversing among men, Our Lord did not speak of himself, but as he himself said, "the words that I speak are not my own, but come from him who sent me."[17] This shows how much we must have recourse to God so that it is not we ourselves who speak and act but rather God in us.

God may possibly bless our work with some success. It could well be that this is attributable to the prayers of a brother who has not even talked to the candidates. He could be taken up with his ordinary work, but often raising his mind and heart to God, invoking his blessing upon these ordination retreats, and it might well be that God will answer his prayer because of the dispositions of his soul. There is an expression in the Psalms, *Desiderium pauperum exaudivit Dominus* ["The Lord hears the desire of the poor"].[18]

Monsieur Vincent stopped at this point, not remembering the rest of the verse. He asked how the rest of it went. His assistant completed it: *Praepa-*

---
17. John 7:16.
18. Ps 10:17. This psalm was used at Sunday Matins.

rationem cordis eorum audivit auris tua ["Strengthening their hearts, you pay heed."] "God bless you, sir," Monsieur Vincent said to him in a spirit of joy, being taken by its beauty, and having repeated it several times in a devout and touching manner, he then continued:

What a marvelous way of speaking, worthy of the Holy Spirit. The Lord has heard the sighs of the poor. He has understood the wishes of their heart to make us see that God responds to hearts well disposed even before they cry to him. This is a great consolation. It ought to encourage us in our service of God, despite our own wretchedness and poverty. Do you recall that fine reading we heard at table yesterday? We heard that God conceals from the humble the treasures of grace he has given them. A few days ago one of you asked me about the virtue of simplicity, although he already possessed this treasure. He did not think he even had this gift, although he is one of the most ingenuous of the Company.

It was reported to me that some have been in certain places where many clergy lived, but these were almost all ineffective. They did recite the breviary, celebrate mass, and administer the sacraments, however poorly, but that's all. Even worse, they lived in vice and disorder. If it please God that we become thoughtful and recollected, we may hope that God will use us, wretched as we are, to effect some good, not only for the people generally but more importantly for the sake of the clergy. Even if you do not say a word you may touch hearts merely by your presence, if only you are wholly taken up by God. The two Fathers de Chandenier and others who came to give the mission in Metz in Lorraine, went in surplice from their house to the church, then back again without saying a word. Their recollection was so remarkable that it made a strong impression on those who saw them, never having experienced the like. Their modesty was a silent sermon so efficacious, I am told, that it may have contributed more than anything else to the success of this mission. What we see influences us much more than mere words, for we believe our eyes beyond what we merely hear. Even though faith comes by hearing, *fides ex auditu*,[19] virtues we see in operation impress us more deeply than those we are taught.

All physical things are distinguished by their specific differences. Each animal and even man differs from each another, and can be told apart. Likewise, the servants of God are distinguished from sensual men by a certain exterior deportment, humble, recollected, devout, which comes from the grace within which influences

---

19. Rom 10:17.

the soul. There are those so filled with this grace that I can never look on them without being moved. The painters of the saints often depict them surrounded by rays of light, to represent to us the aura coming from the just who live such saintly lives.

Such grace and modesty marks the images of the holy Virgin that it strikes all who look on them with reverence and devotion. This appears even more noticeably in our Lord, and in due proportion with the saints. All this, gentlemen and my brothers, makes us aware that if we are committed to acquiring virtues, and if we are filled with divine things, and strive to perfect ourselves, each one in particular and without ceasing, even if we have no special talents to contribute, God will use our presence to enlighten the minds and strengthen the wills of the candidate for ordination, and so make them better.

May it please God to grant us this grace. This work is so difficult and so exalted that God alone can help us. That is why we must pray incessantly that he will bless the small services we render, and the words we say to them. Saint Teresa saw in her time the great need the Church had for worthy ministers. She besought God to inspire good priests, and counseled the sisters of her order to pray often for this intention. Perhaps the changes for the better in the condition of the clergy which we have begun to notice are due in part to the devotion of this great saint. God often uses the weakest instruments for carrying out his greatest designs.

Even in the beginning of the Church did he not choose poor and unlearned rustics? Yet our Lord used them to overthrow idolatry, subject to the Church the princes and powers of this world, and extend our holy religion throughout the whole world. He can use us, wretched as we are, for the progress of the clergy toward a life of virtue. In the name of our Savior, gentlemen and my brothers, let us give ourselves to him completely, by our service, our good example, our prayers, and our mortifications.[20]

These simple and touching exhortations are but samples of the many which Monsieur Vincent gave on this subject. On the one hand they serve to show the great need the Church had of good priests, and the absolute necessity of a worthy preparation for this office. On the other hand they show his devotion to those who aspired to this vocation, and the care he took to inspire the same spirit in his Congregation, demonstrating the appropriate means to success, namely, humility, meekness, respect, penance, prayer, interior life, and purity of intention. He urged these virtues by his words, but

---

20. *CED* XII:14-19.

still more by his example. He was a master at joining practice to persuasion. This is seen even in his talks where he humbled himself. Urging others to prayer, he lifted his own soul to God, and gently attracted others to do the same. Lastly, the correctness and purity of his own intentions inspired the same sentiments in the members of his Congregation.

SECTION FIVE

Some Examples of the Blessings Brought About in France by the Ordination Retreats

The first testimony we will cite is Monsieur Vincent himself. In 1633 he wrote a letter to a priest of the Congregation who was in Rome, in which he spoke from the depths of his heart of the blessings which God had bestowed upon the ordination retreats from their beginning.

I must tell you, if I haven't already done so, that it has pleased the goodness of God to bestow a very special and unbelievable blessing on the ordination retreats. All those who have participated in them, or almost all, are leading lives becoming their station as good and perfect priests. Some among them of noble birth, or gifted in some other way by the goodness of God, live as regular a life as we do ourselves. Some even are more recollected than many among us, especially myself. They schedule their time, make mental prayer, celebrate mass, examine their conscience every day as we do. They regularly visit the hospitals and prisons, and even the colleges, where they catechize, preach, hear confessions, all with the evident blessing of God. Among others, twelve or fifteen in Paris live this way. These are respectable men, who are becoming known to the people.

A few days ago, one of these priests suggested that perhaps those who had attended the ordination retreats might form some sort of assembly or company. This took place, to the great satisfaction of all the others. The purpose of the assembly is to look to their own perfection, and to lead a life pleasing to God, to make him known and served in society, and to procure his glory in the clergy, and among the poor. All this is done under the guidance of someone here, where they meet every week. In imitation of some of the pastors of the diocese making retreats with us, these gentlemen thought of doing so too, and have actually begun. God will, we hope, be pleased to give his blessing to all this, which I recommend especially to your prayers.[21]

These are the first fruits of the ordination retreats which Monsieur Vincent had the happiness of harvesting from the first services he rendered the ordinands. Later they were to produce abundant advantages for the entire Church, not only in Paris but in the dioceses of France and Italy as well. These exercises were started in Rome itself by priests of the Congregation of the Mission. Inspired by the spirit of their holy founder and guided by his counsel, they succeeded in filling his Church with good priests. This same thing happened in many other places where the priests of the Mission were not yet established, or where the bishops themselves set up ordination retreats according to the model furnished by Monsieur Vincent and which his community has continued wherever they worked.

Let us add to the testimony of Monsieur Vincent that of some other clergy. Henry Louis Chastaignier de la Rocheposay, bishop of Poitiers, sent his candidates for ordination to Richelieu, where the priests of the Mission offered the same ordination retreats as at Paris. The superior of the house there wrote to Monsieur Vincent in June of 1642:[22]

> We received only forty-three candidates. Their modest demeanor has begun to produce a marvelous edification, so much so that the people seeing them at the divine office could not restrain their tears of appreciation at the sight of their good order, modesty and devotion. These good people seemed not to see men but angels from paradise. To God alone be the glory. To Cardinal Richelieu, who brought us here, be the merit and reward. To ourselves be shame and embarrassment before heavenly and earthly powers at daring to serve in such a lofty ministry.[23]

In December of 1643, Monsieur Vincent received a letter from the bishop of Angouleme in which he, among other things, asked to have a house of the Congregation of the Mission established in his diocese. He referred to how God had blessed the ordination retreats which he had begun that same month. That blessing had been so great, he said, that everyone in the city of Angouleme praised and blessed the name of God, and prayed for the continuation of such a good work.[24]

In the same year, 1643, Eleonor d'Etampes, archbishop of Reims, had written to Monsieur Vincent requesting priests of the Mission to offer the

---
21. *CED* I:203-05.
22. Abelly's text reads 1649, a typographical error.
23. *CED* VIII:523.
24. *CED* II:430.

ordination retreats to the first group of candidates to be ordained in his diocese since his installation.

> I do not know how to thank you for the favor you did me in sending your missionaries to conduct the ordination retreats for my candidates. I assure you they were badly needed, and could not have been sent to any place where they were more needed. They themselves will send you an account of the success of this retreat.[25]

In the same year, 1643, the ordination retreats were begun by the priests of the Mission in the city of Noyon. The clergy of the local conference wrote to Monsieur Vincent as follows:

> If our thanks should match the blessings received, our Company would fail in its duty to thank you sufficiently for the magnificent edification received from your priests in the direction and instruction of our ordinands. We have waited a long time for this blessing from you, but now that our group has experienced for itself the happy results of this service, we find that we lack words to express the sentiments we feel.[26]

From the pen of a pious member of this same Conference comes a personal letter to Monsieur Vincent:

> I would like to be able to find the proper terms to express the consolation and edification we felt at the sight of the candidates, but also of the members of the conference, and particularly the conferences which Monsieur N. of your Congregation gave. He so touched hearts that the gentlemen of the Conference could not stop speaking of it. Among the ordinands, many let it be known beforehand that they wanted nothing to do with the making of a general confession, and especially not to one of your priests. After hearing the conferences they were so moved they openly admitted their bad intentions, and contrary to their original resolution, stated their desire to make their general confession, and to one of the missionaries. This they all did, so moved to tears were they. In my own name, I thank you for your great charity toward us, and in addition I write in the name of these gentlemen. They asked me to tell you how pleased they were at the retreat.[27]

In May 1644, Monsieur Vincent sent two priests of his Congregation to Chartres at the invitation of Jacques Lescot, then bishop of that city. So blessed was their work for the ordinands that the bishop wrote his thanks in these words:

---

25. *CED* II:39.
26. *CED* II:398-99.
27. *CED* II:399.

The two Missionaries you did me the honor of sending for the Pentecost ordinations are fine representatives of the clergy. They are upright, learned, capable, careful, and zealous. Thanks be to God, their work was blessed abundantly, for which I and the entire diocese are infinitely obliged to you. The people here are well disposed. But we need the help of your charity. Please, Monsieur, I am counting on it, since your charity is so universal and great that you can refuse no one.[28]

In March 1645, the bishop of Saintes wrote to thank Monsieur Vincent for the priests of the Congregation he had sent for these same retreats. "Our ordinands make them with exceptional blessings, but there is such a demand for places now that we will be hard pressed to accommodate all who want to come."[29]

It would take entire volumes to relate in detail all the benefits these retreats produced wherever they were offered, or to speak of all the graces and blessings received by those who put no obstacle in the way of grace. This appeared even in their exterior deportment after their ordination in their changed life and in the practice of all the priestly virtues. It is enough to say that because of lack of workers Monsieur Vincent was unable to respond to each of the bishops of the kingdom for priests to conduct the ordination retreats in their dioceses. This general approval is an obvious tribute to the excellence and usefulness of the retreats.

SECTION SIX

The Ordination Retreats in Italy, and the Great Results Produced by Them

Since the nature of goodness is to communicate and diffuse itself, we should not be surprised that the ordination retreats, which were so effective and beneficial, expanded readily outside of France to other countries, including Italy. They had the same blessing and success there as they did in France. We will recount here the events in only two of the leading cities in Italy, as characteristic of what happened in many others.

The first is Genoa, where Cardinal Durazzo, the archbishop, had estab-

---

28. *CED* II:461.
29. *CED* II:506.

lished a house of the priests of the Congregation of the Mission for the instruction of his people and the reform of his clergy.[30] He determined that every ordination in his diocese be preceded by the candidates' making the ordination retreats. This produced marvelous results in the clergy who took part in this grace. The superior of the Mission at Genoa wrote to Monsieur Vincent on this subject, and we can suppose the same fruits were reaped in other places as well.[31]

Our ordination retreat was small in number, but rich in blessings. God was generous in the gift of his grace. They followed the regulations faithfully, and the silence and modesty of the ordinands especially during meal times was so evident it seemed they had been formed in one of our own houses. The grace of God was even more evident during mental prayer and the discussions which followed. I don't think it possible these exercises could be attended to with greater fervor than these gentlemen brought to them. During the time of mental prayer and even during the discussions some were in tears. Others publicly thanked God for the grace of participating in the ordination retreats, with its insights of knowing well the state they were about to embrace, and how to live in keeping with God's designs upon them as true priests.

Among others, one was making his farewells at the end of the retreat, and told me with great emotion that he had prayed to God to send him a thousand deaths rather than let him offend his goodness. When this was repeated yesterday to Cardinal Durazzo, the archbishop, he wept with joy and appreciation. His heart could not contain the emotion he felt at the blessings God had bestowed upon this ordination retreat.[32]

The second city we speak of is Rome, where the sovereign pontiff, Urban VIII of happy memory, had received the priests of the Congregation of the Mission in 1642. The following year they began to receive in their house those who came on their own initiative to prepare themselves to receive holy orders. The success of these first efforts was reported after several years to His Holiness, who in November 1659, directed the cardinal vicar of Rome to order that all who aspired to sacred orders should make the ordination retreats with the priests of the Congregation of the Mission. This was done under the authority of our holy father, Pope Alexander VII.

When this order was first given, the superior of the Mission in Rome wrote to Monsieur Vincent as follows:

---

30. Stefano Durazzo, archbishop of Genoa from 1635 to 1664.
31. *CED* VIII:294.
32. *CED* IV:601-02.

> In our weakness we are preparing ourselves to serve the candidates for ordination. Our confidence is in God, who shows himself ever more the author of this good work, seeing that we do not know how this order came about, nor who promoted it. I can rightfully say: *a Domino factum est istud* ["By the Lord has this been done"],[33] and so there is reason to hope that *qui coepit ipse perficiet*[34] ["He who has begun the good work, will carry it through to completion"].[35]

Monsieur Vincent was pleased to see used in the Church during his lifetime the ordination retreats to which God willed that he give himself from the beginning and which he began. He was also especially gratified to see them established in the mother city of all Christendom. What is more, his own priests were charged with giving these retreats in Italy, although they had done nothing to promote them outside of France.

This first ordination retreat was given in December 1659. Divine Providence arranged that the Fathers de Chandenier, nephews of Cardinal de la Rochefoucauld, had gone to Rome at the time, and were housed with the priests of the Mission when the ordinands were received.[36] God so disposed it that these two virtuous priests contributed by their saintly deportment to the edification of all who saw them, for it would be impossible to find two models of modesty better suited to show the ordinands what their exterior behavior should be. The older of the two brothers celebrated high mass daily in the chapel of the Mission, at which all the ordinands attended. He displayed his usual gravity, devotion, and recollection, while his brother humbly filled the role of acolyte and thurifer. Two Italian priests of the Congregation of the Mission gave the conferences in the morning and evening, and all went so well that a favorable report was given to His Holiness, the pope. He referred to this in a consistory held soon after, in which he stated that he was most pleased with the ordination retreats. Cardinal Santacroce[37] informed the superior of the Mission of this, and he in turn wrote to Monsieur Vincent, who asked for some additional details. His reply to Monsieur Vincent was as follows:

> Monsieur, you requested information about the ordination retreats, and whether there seems to have been a carryover for the ordinands. As to the retreats themselves, and to all the particulars of the rule observed in France, we have tried and are still trying to

---

33. Ps 118:23.
34. Phil 1:6.
35. *CED* VIII:183.
36. Claude Charles de Chandenier and his brother Louis were both devoted to Saint Vincent.
37. Cardinal de Sainte Croix, in Abelly's text. Marcello Santacroce, 1619-1674, was the cardinal protector of Poland.

have them observed in the same way as in Paris. We schedule each day and hour according to the memorandum we received from Saint Lazare. The ordinands declared they were very pleased, and not only ourselves, but some outsiders have reported the fruits some of them have taken by God's grace from the retreats. We even have some taking part in a second program in which we are now involved, in this first one for this Lent. These men are giving good example to the others. It seems that God in his infinite goodness wishes to bestow his blessing upon these retreats, and to confer his graces upon the priests of this country as he has done elsewhere.[38]

At the end of each session this superior informed Monsieur Vincent of how things had gone. We report here only a few extracts from his letters.

By the mercy of God, the fruits of previous retreats are in evidence. Several of these gentlemen who have made the retreats come here to visit us from time to time, telling us of their perseverance in their good resolutions. One of them, a person of some standing, who has attended three of these sessions, came here yesterday to celebrate his first mass, after making a short retreat to prepare himself for this occasion.[39]

In another letter the same superior told Monsieur Vincent that "some cardinals and other prelates had come to hear the conferences. Among the ordinands were several from highly placed families, among others a canon of Saint John Lateran and nephew of Cardinal Mancini, a canon of Saint Peter's named Count Marescotti, and others of high standing. The pope was firm in insisting that no one was to be exempt from attending the ordination retreats."[40]

He said in another letter:

The ordinands we had at the beginning of Lent and those we have at the moment have been faithful to the retreats. Their devotion has astonished us. I might say, in regard to modesty and silence, that they could not have done better. Our Lord makes us realize by this that he alone is the source of all the good done here.[41]

In still another letter, he said:

We had in the last ordination retreat a Spanish gentleman, a doctor from the diocese of Piacenza, whose bishop is now the ambassador extraordinary of the king of Spain. This good gentleman had planned to receive holy orders, and so came with great sentiment to take part in the retreat. However, after hearing the

---

38. *CED* VIII:244-45.
39. *CED* VIII:302.
40. *CED* VIII:294.
41. *CED* VIII:275.

conferences, he recognized the importance of not receiving holy orders unless one were called by God. In addition, he realized the great obligations assumed by the one who does take orders. These considerations raised great fear in him, and left him in a confused state of mind. At length, he resolved his uncertainties, and received orders with fine dispositions. The changed style of life in himself and in many others after the ordination retreats gives reason to hope he made a good decision.

After the retreat, he told his bishop of his experiences. The bishop in turn asked to speak to us, and we went to see him this morning. We found a zealous prelate who had arranged several missions in his own diocese much like the ones we of the Company give, except they are somewhat briefer. He himself preaches, hears confession, and catechizes, but this emphasis on forming good priests delights him. He asked if he might come here to our next session, to observe what we do, and asked if, on his return to Spain, we might give him one of our priests. While awaiting these developments, he would like to alert his diocese to what we do in the ordination retreats, so they might be introduced there.[42]

This good prelate came to the following session not simply to learn about the ordination retreats in theory, but to follow all the exercises so he could bring the practices back to his own diocese.

After Monsieur Vincent received this news, he felt that the priests in Rome were moving too quickly on the question of sending a priest of the Company to Spain. He was ever on his guard about any human activity which would lead to the extension of his Congregation. He alerted them by letter, the tenor of which we can gather by the reply the Roman superior sent him.

> As to the bishop of Piacenza, ambassador of Spain, God has given us the grace, according to your wishes, not to return to his house to speak further about the ordination retreats. According to your orders we will do nothing, God willing, to seek new jobs or to push ourselves. Even if we are pressed we will always refer everything to you for decision. We hope to be faithful in this.[43]

Since the best and holiest activities are the ones most open to jealousy and contradiction, the fruits of the ordination retreats and the comments heard in the city of Rome led some religious persons, convinced they were rendering service to God, to attempt to remove the priests of the Mission and substitute their own community in the direction of these retreats. This is an account of these events, written by this same superior to Monsieur Vincent in May 1660.

---

42. *CED* VIII:269.
43. *CED* VIII:285.

I must alert you, Monsieur, to some opposition that has recently arisen about the continuation of the ordination retreats. First, a while ago the cardinal vicar told me that another religious community had asked to be put in charge of the ordination retreats, and that the ordinands should be sent to them and not to us. The cardinal absolutely refused the request. I had previously been informed of this move, and told which community was involved.

Second, I was advised that on the occasion of the examination for sacred orders, Father N. had said that since so many distinguished people came to Rome to be ordained, it was not proper to oblige them to keep attending the ordination retreats, and that he would speak to the pope about this. I have learned that he did speak to him, and tried his best to persuade the pope not to oblige the ordinands to come to us. His Holiness is well informed of what is done in the ordination retreats, and paying no attention to the remonstrances, remains firm in his commitment. You see, Monsieur, how we are under the special protection of our Lord and of his holy Mother.[44]

Since that time many attempts have been made to abolish the ordination retreats. Both the pope and cardinals were appealed to in complaints that the retreats had to be made with the priests of the Mission rather than elsewhere. They seemed to be of the opinion they could not be well made except in their own houses. All this made no impression on the mind of the pope. He remained persuaded that all should observe the brief he had published earlier. He also published a second one in 1662 on his own authority.[45] It approved and confirmed all he had said on the question, but added the obligation not only that every person of whatever nation or class who was to be ordained in Rome should make the ordination retreats, but that those of the six suffragan dioceses should do so likewise. He was so convinced of the efficacy of the ordination retreats in the formation of the clergy that he reserved to himself the power of dispensing from this obligation. Even those who were dispensed, to receive orders *extra tempora* ["outside the canonical time"], he obliged to make a spiritual retreat with the priests of the Mission before ordination.

All these graces and favors could rightly be attributed to the protection of God and to the great purity of intention that motivated Monsieur Vincent. Because of this he was not overly disturbed by all the storms raised against the retreats. He recognized that God had originally given them to the missionaries, and that God was good and powerful enough to look after

---
44. *CED* VIII:290-91.
45. Alexander VII, "Apostolica sollicitudo," August 7, 1662.

them, as long as the priests of the Mission would be faithful to their obligations. He was aware that failing in this, they would deserve to be deprived of them.

It would seem that so many efforts against the ordination retreats would surely reduce their success, but the contrary was the case. These attacks seemed to attract new blessings, or to publicize the retreats. For example, a single ordinand from the kingdom of Naples who had attended one of the sessions returned home and persuaded his archbishop to have all the ordinands of the archdiocese attend the retreats before receiving holy orders.

Cardinal Barbarigo heard about the happy fruit of the ordination retreats, and called the priests of the Mission of Rome to his city of Bergamo, in the state of Venice, of which he was the bishop.[46] Recognizing the importance of the ordination retreats, he began them with the intention of continuing them in future. When he returned to Rome the following year, 1663, he attended one of the conferences, at which several other cardinals happened to be present as well. His presence visibly impressed the ordinands and greatly edified the other cardinals.

Several other cardinals attended the following session, that is, Cardinal Albizzi,[47] and Cardinal Santacroce, to the great approval of the other cardinals, bishops, prelates, generals of orders and other notables in attendance.

The same superior remarked in several of his later letters that by God's grace the good effects of the retreats on the clergy were evident. This good result extended even beyond Rome itself, for among the ordinands there were, besides those from Italy, some from other countries.

These are some examples of the happy fruits of this enterprise established in the Church by the all-encompassing zeal of Monsieur Vincent, and by the blessing of God given for his own greater honor and glory.

---

46. Gregorio Barbarigo, 1625-1697, was canonized by Pope John XXIII in 1960.
47. Francesco Albizzi, called Albici in Abelly's text, died in 1684.

CHAPTER THREE

The Spiritual Conferences for Priests

SECTION ONE

The Beginning of the Spiritual Conferences for Priests Established at Saint Lazare

A BOND among the virtues not only causes one virtue to lead to another, but in those rightly disposed, attracts other entirely new virtues as well. The same thing may be said of grace, the source of the virtues and generally of all God's gifts. These always increase beyond measure in those who do not resist nor put any obstacle to God's sovereign goodness, its source.

God had wished to inspire Monsieur Vincent to begin his work with the missions, and with them the ordination retreats, both of which were everywhere successful. Then in his divine goodness he moved Monsieur Vincent to begin another service for the Church. This not only preserved and confirmed the grace received in ordination, but helped priests to exercise all the functions of their sacred ministry with dignity and fruit. This is how this came about.

This great servant of God witnessed the good effects of the ordination retreats. This filled him with joy and led him to give continuous thanks to God. Aware of the weakness and inconstancy of the human heart, he feared that the priests at the conclusion of these retreats would return to their worldly ways. Since, as the apostle says, they were obliged to live among a wicked and perverse generation,[1] they were in danger of little by little losing their first fervor and perhaps the graces they had received. This led him to reflect on what might be done to warn and strengthen them in such a way that their own weakness or the wickedness of the world would not trouble or lessen the saintly resolutions they had taken.

Despite his insights on the problem, his humility always made him hesitant of his own lights. One of his maxims was never to push himself ahead of the designs of God. He felt, therefore, the best course of action was to invoke the Holy Spirit, awaiting a manifestation of his holy will. During this wait, a virtuous priest who had attended the ordination retreat at Paris

---
1. Phil 2:15.

came to see him. He proposed the formation of some sort of group for priests. They had already come to Saint Lazare to prepare for ordination, and now wished to meet there periodically to discuss among themselves matters pertaining to their sacred ministry.

Monsieur Vincent looked upon this proposal as coming from God himself. He recognized the good effect such spiritual conferences had among the fathers of the Egyptian desert in former times. They defended them against the attacks of their hidden enemy, and helped their progress in the way of perfection. As a result, he judged it would be no less helpful to the clergy of his own time in their life amidst the dangers of the world. After mature reflection and prayer to the Lord, and after receiving the approval of the archbishop of Paris, he looked around to find the right ones to begin this project. The providence of God provided just such an opportunity, as we shall see.

Several priests who had attended the ordination retreat realized their debt to Monsieur Vincent for the good dispositions God had given them through his help. As a result, they came to offer themselves to him to work at whatever ecclesiastical function he might judge most useful. Monsieur Vincent responded by asking them to organize a mission to the masons, carpenters, and others who were building, near the Saint Antoine gate in Paris, the church of the Visitation of Saint Mary, whose superior and spiritual father he was. At the beginning of June 1633, these good priests began their work with great affection and ingenious charity in such a way they did not interfere with the progress of the construction.[2] They found a way to give the usual instructions and exhortations every day, and prepared the workers to make a general confession and to lead a good Christian life, according to their particular state.

While the priests were working on this mission, Monsieur Vincent observed the zeal for the salvation of souls which motivated them, and the union of hearts which reigned among them. He thought it appropriate to begin what he had in mind. On the eleventh of that same month, the feast of Saint Barnabas, he went to speak to each one privately of his thought of bringing them together for mutual support. He found them receptive to his plan, leaving all in his hands as he might think best for their own advantage and for the greater glory of God. He asked all to come to Saint Lazare on a particular day, when he outlined in more detail what he had in mind. He spoke of the need of persevering and cultivating the holy dispositions God had inspired in them and the graces they had received in their ordination. He then exhorted them strongly to give themselves completely to his divine majesty, to continue for their entire life what they had begun so well. In this way, he said, they would meet the obligations of the state in life they had

---

2. See *CED* I:204.

embraced, and so it would never be said of any of them that he had begun well, but failed in courage to complete the building. Since they had been honored with the sacred character of the priesthood and raised to a truly holy state, they should give themselves entirely to the service of God. It should never be said of them what the prophet Jeremiah deplored in his day, that the gold had become dim, had lost its shine and beauty, and that the precious jewels of the sanctuary had been scattered among the stones on the streets.[3] All this happens when those whom Jesus Christ has chosen as his ministers in the Church begin to fail in the charity and perfection which should mark their state in life. Those who are closest to the sanctuary and who are the dispensers of its mysteries allow themselves to walk the highways of the world, and become blameworthy by their dissolute life.

He explained to the assembled priests that he did not expect them to separate themselves from the world, to live together in the same house. This would give rise to many difficulties. They were to continue to live in their own homes or possibly with their relatives. They should be united by a special bond of charity, a life of virtue, and ecclesiastical dedication. He proposed to draw up a rule of life whose observance would preserve them from worldly corruption and help them fulfill perfectly the obligations of their calling. In short, what one of the prophets said could be said of them: *Stellae dederunt lumen in custodiis suis, et vocatae dixerunt, adsumus; et luxerunt illi cum jucunditate, qui fecit illas* ["Before whom the stars at their posts shine and rejoice; When he calls them, they answer, 'Here we are!' shining with joy for their Maker"].[4] They would be in the Church as so many brilliant stars, spreading the light of their good example in their families. They would be always ready to go wherever and work at whatever they were called to, so that Jesus Christ, the author of the priesthood, would be honored in their service.

The priest who had first proposed this assembly to Monsieur Vincent was not present on this occasion, since he was working on a mission away from Paris. For that reason Monsieur Vincent wrote this letter to him:

> God be blessed, Monsieur, for all the graces and blessings he showers upon your mission. Does it not occur to you that so many idle workers could be well employed in the great harvest at which you are working? Those who know the need of the master of the harvest for workers are guilty of the blood of his Son, which remains without effect if it is not applied. How well the clergy have received the plan you did me the honor of explaining a while ago, all as a group, and each one in particular. We met two weeks ago, and

---
3. Lam 4:1.
4. Bar 3:24-25.

agreed to all you had suggested to me, with a union of spirit which can come only from God. I began my talk to them by what you had said to me, but without mentioning your name until I had to name you to save a place among them. They are to meet again today. How much good we can anticipate from this company! You are the mover, and you are interested in its success. Please pray for it, Monsieur, and especially for me.[5]

These priests came together once more, on the ninth of July, to organize this conference, choose their officers, and set the Tuesday of each week as the most convenient day to assemble to discuss the virtues and functions of their ministry. Monsieur Vincent chose as the subject of the first of his conferences with them, on July 16, the spirit of the ecclesiastical state.[6] He divided it into three parts: first, the reasons and motives which priests and other sacred ministers have to acquire the ecclesiastical spirit; second, what this spirit consists in; and third, the means to acquire and preserve it, and to bring it to its full development. One of the members of the Company took notes of this first conference, as well as later ones. These notes are the source of much of what we have written.

The members have continued to meet every week, and take as their topic of conference the matters suggested by Monsieur Vincent. These were always on the virtues or functions proper to their calling. Their manner of speaking in these conferences was humble, simple, and familiar, in keeping with the spirit of their director, his suggestions, and his example. He had a special grace which was effective and grace-filled when speaking of the virtues or other pious topics. His language was simple and without display, but vigorous and from the heart.

Ordinarily he did not prepare himself by any special study, but used his time in prayer in God's presence. He shared the lights he received in prayer with his hearers. His talks were founded on principles derived from holy Scripture, particularly the examples and words of the Son of God found in the Gospels, whose intent he penetrated in a way all his own. Often he added little or nothing to what had already been said by someone else. He was satisfied to share a good thought, or to comment on what had been said. In so doing he added a new force to it, for he had an extraordinary way of treating the most common and ordinary things. He used expressions which moved people, often producing good results, showing that our Lord Jesus Christ spoke with his lips, and inspired his words and his heart.

Among the other good results he had on his hearers, was that of leading

---

5. *CED* I:202-03.
6. Since July 16 was a Saturday that year, the probable date is July 19, the mistake caused by an inverted numeral.

others to speak the same way as himself, with humility, simplicity, and sincerity. In the meetings no one strove to present learned discourses or to be admired for his erudition. The honor and glory of God, the spiritual welfare of the audience, and their own humiliation was the sole motive of the speakers. He advised the clerics to prepare themselves for their talks, but by way of prayer rather than by study, if the subject did not demand a more detailed treatment, or did not require the reading of some good book, as for example when it was question of ecclesiastical offices or positions, or other similar topics.

To draw down greater blessings upon this ecclesiastical company, Monsieur Vincent thought it proper to set down a series of regulations for it. It began by a formal statement of its foundation:

> To preserve the good dispositions it pleased God to give them during their ordination retreats, the priests concerned have resolved, with the blessing and approval of the archbishop of Paris, to come together, to attend conferences at the house of Saint Lazare, to honor the life of our Lord Jesus Christ, his eternal priesthood, his holy family, and his love for the poor. They propose to model their lives upon his, and to procure the glory of God in the ecclesiastical state, in their families, and among the poor, not only in the cities but in the countryside as well, as dictated by the devotion of each of them.
>
> This company shall be composed only of clergy raised to sacred orders, who shall be received only after long scrutiny of their life and morals, and after a spiritual retreat, which they shall strive to make annually if possible.
>
> They will gather on Tuesday of each week to confer on topics which shall be assigned, which ordinarily shall be the virtues, functions, and works proper to their ministry.
>
> They shall recognize that our Lord has gathered them together with a new bond of love, to keep them perfectly united in himself, and for this purpose they shall cherish one another, visit and console each other in their difficulties and illnesses. They shall attend the funeral services of any of the members who die. The priests among them shall each offer three masses for the departed, while the others will offer their communions.[7]

Besides this document, he drew up a brief daily schedule, which prescribed the following, among other things:

> They should set the time for rising daily after enough sleep. Each morning they should spend a half hour in mental prayer. They

---

7. *CED* XIII:128-32; the manuscript edition of this document differs in many details from that quoted by Abelly and it is much longer.

should celebrate mass, and then read a chapter of the New Testament, while kneeling and with head uncovered, all the while making three internal acts: (1) adoration of the truths contained in the chapter which had been read; (2) entering into the spirit of these same truths; and (3) the application in practice of the things taught by the passage. Next, they were to study something in keeping with their duties. Before dinner they were to make a particular examination of their conduct, and after dinner they were to read some good spiritual book. The time remaining was to be used in study or in other exercises suitable for their state.[8]

SECTION TWO

The Progress of This Company, and the Successes It Enjoyed

This Company, begun so well under the wise guidance of Monsieur Vincent, continued to enjoy new blessings, which God conferred upon it through the hands of his faithful servant. Among the first fruits was the growth of the Company, which happened quickly, for more than two-hundred and fifty priests became members during the lifetime of Monsieur Vincent. Among the members were some notable persons, distinguished by their birth or by their learning, for there were more than forty doctors of the faculty of Paris. All this occurred contrary to the wish of Monsieur Vincent and its members not to make this happen, but rather to honor the hidden life of our Lord. They sought to remain unknown as much as possible. They worked humbly in the least esteemed positions, yet in those most useful and advantageous to the salvation of souls, particularly among the poor, catechizing and hearing confessions in the hospitals, prisons, and villages. God did not allow this little city, built on the mountain of charity by the hand of his servant, to remain hidden for long. On several occasions, as we shall see, he brought to light the works it accomplished. Besides, his Providence allowed twenty-two prelates to be members, both archbishops and bishops, for the benefit of their dioceses. We should add that the membership included vicars general, canonical judges of the dioceses, archdeacons, pastors, canons, seminary directors, superiors, and visitators and confessors of

---
8. *CED* XIII:129-30.

religious, all of whom as members of the Company spread everywhere the good odor of Jesus Christ through the example of their virtues.

It should be remarked that it was due chiefly to the head of their Company, Monsieur Vincent himself, that must be attributed many of the blessings upon its members, for they shared in the salutary influence he exercised over his own Congregation. From the beginning he had introduced this same practice of holding periodic conferences to discuss the virtues and the duties of the ecclesiastical life. After he had seen for himself the success these spiritual conferences had for the interior advancement of the members of his Congregation, he felt the same sort of conferences would be equally beneficial for priests from elsewhere. This led him to establish the conferences, as we have indicated above in Section One.

One day, speaking to his community at Saint Lazare, he said:

> If anyone ought to attend and appreciate spiritual conferences, surely it ought to be the priests of the Congregation of the Mission. God has entrusted to this Congregation the introduction of such conferences among clergy, in which the practice of virtue is discussed. When I came to Paris, I never saw such conferences, in which the virtues proper to one's state in life were discussed, and how to live well in one's own vocation. In the academies, of course, points of doctrine were presented, and sometimes cases of conscience were thrashed out. About fifty years ago, Cardinal de Sourdis introduced into his diocese of Bordeaux this way of handling some points of moral theology.[9] He would assemble his pastors and other priests to instruct them better on these points, and he was quite successful at it. But concerning the virtues proper to their state in life, for ecclesiastics or clergy like ourselves, nothing was available at all, at least as far as I was aware, or had ever heard of.
>
> Some religious have this practice, just as the monks of former times did. In our times, however, God has been pleased to entrust to this miserable Congregation these conferences for priests, who in their service to souls must live amid the corruption of the world. We must help them to become better equipped for their ministry. God has inspired the Congregation of the Mission with much appreciation to begin these conferences which contribute to the growth of virtue. In them we treat of the motives for acquiring them, their nature, their practice, and the particular acts which relate to

---

9. Francois d'Escoubleau, Cardinal de Sourdis, archbishop of Bordeaux from 1598 to 1625. Saint Vincent saw him and appreciated his work on his first trip to Bordeaux in 1605, and then in 1623 when he returned there to evangelize prisoners. The cardinal was considered one of the holiest and most courageous prelates of his time.

them. We treat also of the obligations of our state in life, toward God and the neighbor. There you see the point of these conferences. What do you think, if we were to be the first to neglect them? What account would we give to God if we neglect such useful and efficacious means used so assiduously by the ancient fathers and anchorites, as reported in the book written by the monk Cassian?[10]
I must say from my personal experience nothing so touching, so moving, of all that I have heard, read, or seen, equals these conferences.[11]

Besides these first results of the spiritual conferences, which were limited to the clergy who gathered at Saint Lazare, others became evident in a wider sphere. Chief among these was the effect of the good example of the priests of the Company that began to be noticed among others, for the members of the Company were significant in their positions, whether by their learning, or by the responsibilities and benefices they occupied in the Church. Their example influenced others greatly, leading them to imitation, either by their modesty in dress or in the way of wearing their hair, or in their avoidance of worldly gatherings and mannerisms. On the positive side, their devotion to works of charity or other functions proper to their calling attracted many to do and act the same, which in many places was a source of much edification.

As a second result Monsieur Vincent often asked the ablest and most pious of the priests to address the ordinands following the exercises at Saint Lazare. Their exhortations, joined to the example of their lives, were powerful influences on the ordinands, gathered in Paris from all the dioceses of France. On the one hand they saw the perfect models of what they should become, and on the other, heard from their own lips what they must know and do to imitate them. In this Monsieur Vincent imitated the God of nature, who uses the fruit of a tree to produce new trees of the same species, or like the children of their father who become in their turn fathers of other children. This Company of clergy was the result of the first ordination retreats, and now, in their turn, they were helping the participants in these same exercises.

As a third result the priests were often sent or called to other dioceses to help in the ordination retreats, or in spiritual retreats which the bishops had organized for their pastors, vicars, and other clergy of their dioceses. When some had to go into the country on business, they took the occasion to gather the priests of the region to help them organize conferences among themselves touching on their functions and duties, or to urge them to mental prayer, or to the practice of the virtues proper to their calling. Since one of

---

10. John Cassian, *Conferences*, PL 49-50.
11. *CED* XI:13-14.

the aims of their Company was to do what they could for the spiritual good of priests, they often contributed to the education of poor priests, or those who were not fulfilling their office worthily. Many were helped to a true conversion, and so removed a source of scandal in the Church.

SECTION THREE

Missions Given by the Priests of This Company in Several Hospitals and Other Places in Paris

Among all the possible services which the ecclesiastics might render, the missions were always thought of as the most useful and advantageous for the salvation of souls. Monsieur Vincent willingly accepted the offer of some among them to join priests of his Congregation, with his approval, to aid in the work of the missions. Consequently, several of them received his permission and went with the priests of his Congregation to help in their missions. What is more, their Company requested several of their number to give missions in other dioceses, with the permission and approval of the bishops. This happened principally in the larger cities where the priests of the Mission did not go. In their humility they preferred the poorer places in the country, as we have earlier shown. It pleased God to give such blessings to these missions that conversions were often seen that both astonished and edified all, and were marked by restitutions, reconciliations, and other extraordinary effects which followed.

Besides these missions given over the course of thirty years in many cities and regions of the kingdom, others no less fruitful were given in Paris itself.

Before the general hospital was established for the poor beggars from the streets of Paris, many of these were brought together to receive some alms, and to be taught how to prepare themselves for making a good general confession, and how to lead a more Christian life than in the past. The priests of the Company were particularly successful in their work with refugees from Lorraine living in Paris, as described in Book One.[12]

The soldiers of the King's Guard were also brought together in appropriate places, with the approval of their captains, for a mission. At various times and places in the city, missions were given for the workers in the factories

---

12. Ch. 35.

and shops. These produced good results for the masons and unskilled workers. They for the most part never attended the instructions or catechism lessons in the parishes, and lived their lives in neglect of things conducive to their salvation. So as not to take them away from their work, instructions and efforts to prepare them for their general confession were given during their rest periods.

The members of the Company gave missions in several hospitals of the city. They began in 1633 in the hospital of Quinze-Vingts,[13] then in the hospital for the blind and their families, and for people of the neighborhood who wanted to attend. Several times they gave missions to the poor of the hospital of La Pitie. They also gave missions at the Refuge, a prison for fallen women and girls, who were much in need of spiritual help. Monsieur Vincent himself had a great compassion for these poor miserable women. He not only urged the priests of the Company to give missions to them from time to time, but often went himself on Sundays and feasts to administer the sacraments and preach the word of God to them, always with the permission and approval of the archbishop.

A mission was given also in the hospital des Petites Maisons. Besides the mentally ill who could not be helped by the preaching, many poor families, together with some people of the neighborhood, took part. It was on this mission that a pamphlet called "Duties of a Christian" was drawn up and prepared on a single page in a succinct and familiar style, so that even the most untutored could read and understand. It pleased God to give it such a blessing that it was circulated quickly throughout France and elsewhere in the millions of copies, with unbelievable benefit to the poor and to other persons of whatever state.[14]

Several missions were given in the hospital of the galleys in the Tournelle, the place [in Paris] where these poor criminals were kept until they were sent off to the galleys. Just as their spiritual needs were extreme, so the instructions and other spiritual helps they received from these priests were of great profit.

These same priests gave spiritual help to the sick poor of the Hotel Dieu of Paris, for one of the principles of their Company was to work for the spiritual good of the poor. Scarcely any could be found where they could be helped more than in this hospital, for the poor were there in large numbers. They first resolved to go there in a body to dispose the sick poor to make a good general confession. Then they appointed some of their number to visit each day to continue their charitable interest. Every Friday some of the

---

13. Literally "fifteen twenties," or three hundred, for the number of patients who could be accommodated.
14. See *CED* II:366.

priests would go to preach and conduct catechism lessons for the sick. Finally, with the advice and in cooperation with Monsieur Vincent, they gave an entire mission, in 1639, in keeping with the wishes of the superintendents of the hospital, the sick themselves, the officials and staff, and of the religious in service there, to whom the priests gave spiritual conferences three times a week.

The poor beggars of Paris had been confined to the General Hospital not only to put an end to begging and its attendant abuses, but also to see to the spiritual good of those confined and contribute to the salvation of their souls. The rector,[15] himself a member of the Company, together with the administrators and directors appointed by the king, thought it useful from the beginning of this enterprise and even necessary to have missions given in all departments of the hospital. The priests of the Company worked at this with great zeal and much blessing. Since every day saw new poor brought to the hospital and others released, the missions were often repeated. Besides the help the priests of the Company gave during the year in all the parts of this hospital, they ordinarily went on Sundays and feasts to preach and hear confessions. On other occasions they were called by the successor to the original rector, likewise a member of their Company. As a result, scarcely a year passed that a mission was not given, according to the judgment of the rector about the needs of the poor people confined there.

SECTION FOUR

The Remarkable Results of Two Missions Given by Priests of this Company

As an example of the blessing God showered upon these priests, working under the direction and in the spirit of Monsieur Vincent, we will recall here only what occurred on two of their missions. We will leave aside the others, so as not to annoy the reader with the inevitable repetitions that would otherwise result.

Several years ago these priests gave a mission in a large market town, which for the most part housed either officers of the law or tavern keepers. They found the disorders shared by both groups. The tavern keepers were

---

15. Abelly himself.

in the habit of serving drink and promoting drunkenness, even on Sundays and feasts during the hours of divine service. The abuses of the officers of the law approached scandalous proportions. The judges ate and drank in the taverns with those to be tried before them. The attorneys would meet their clients only in the same setting, but still conscious of their rights of office. They employed all sorts of trickeries to prolong the legal process, so that a poor peasant often found all his funds exhausted there before his case ever came to judgment. Almost always these judgments were not given in open court, but were remanded to arbitrators to extract still more money from the plaintiffs and to use up the funds for their expenses.

The court attendants were no less a source of disorder and injustice. The officers of the courts were so venal the courts themselves were described in a common proverb of the region as a "pillar of hell."

The members of this Company, then, or rather God working through them, sought to remedy this sad state of affairs. They first preached strongly against the abuses and disorders in the taverns, especially on Sundays and feasts. Afterward, they persuaded the chief of police to issue a regulation and set fines appropriate for the case. He was to visit the tavern himself on these days, and punish by fines or other penalties the innkeepers, as well as those they met there while divine services were in progress.

Later they went to see the provost, the chief magistrate of the locality. They held several sessions with him, in which they pointed out that besides the glory of God and the dictates of his conscience, he owed it to his own reputation and to his own interest to bring an end to all these disorders and injustices, and to take strong measures to root them out. Finally they persuaded him to use his authority to impose fines or other penalties upon the attorneys, sergeants, or other officers of justice who failed in their duties. They were to be forbidden to frequent the taverns with their clients, nor were they to prolong cases through technicalities, and were to give judgment in open court whenever possible without more delays unless absolutely necessary. After this, since some of those working on this mission were related to presidents and counselors of Parlement, they saw to it that in case of appeal against the regulations or the penalties enacted, someone would be appointed to assure that these regulations would be maintained and supported by the higher courts. This person promised to see to this, and be firm and constant in the matter should it arise in the future.

The priests brought together all the attorneys of the locality, and in a conference, showed the necessity of bringing a remedy to the abuses and disorders which had been allowed to develop. They could not at all be sure of their own salvation if these things continued. Besides, the sacrament of penance could not be administered to them either licitly or validly if they did not take a firm and complete resolution to change their customs and obey the regulations set down in these matters. Lastly, they exhorted the lawyers to do with good will and for the love of Jesus Christ what the provost had ordained by his authority. Those present acquiesced in these demands, and with good heart promised to comply.

A similar assembly was held for the sergeants of the courts, when a long list of some twenty-five or thirty articles set forth their principal duties and the way they should be carried out. The sergeants agreed to everything, and as a sign of this drew up a formal document, which each one signed.

After these meetings, and after they had agreed on the resolutions, these members of the court came to the sacrament of penance, to the great edification of the people. Since then, it has become known that they have well observed all these points, to the extent that the provost fined his own father, an attorney, for attempting to delay a case by some tricks and useless formalities.

The second mission of which we speak in this section has to do with the one given in the Saint Germain des Pres neighborhood of the city of Paris, in 1641, at which the priests of the Company worked with much success. This neighborhood at the time was the sewer of all Paris, even of all France, as the home of libertines, atheists, and others living in impiety and wantonness. The impossibility of remedying the situation, in the minds of many, led to all sorts of debauchery and vice, carried out with complete impunity.

A woman of great virtue,[16] moved at the sight of so many offenses against God, opened her heart to Monsieur Vincent. She was well aware of the good the missions had accomplished elsewhere, by the grace of God, and therefore proposed that a mission should be given in this neighborhood, as well. Monsieur Vincent had to explain that his Congregation was not to give missions in the episcopal cities. In addition, he saw almost insurmountable obstacles and difficulties in attempting such a project in this place where such disorder reigned and where the people were so poorly disposed toward religious matters. This lady was not put off by this, but redoubled her entreaties with such strong insistence that finally Monsieur Vincent felt it was God himself inspiring her to act. He spoke of it to the Company of priests gathered at Saint Lazare, with the proposal that they should undertake this mission.

This aroused much resistance and the Company represented to Monsieur Vincent the strong reasons that they should not attempt an enterprise which, to all human appearances, was doomed to failure. Nevertheless, Monsieur Vincent, after recommending this project to our Lord by long prayer, persisted in his own opinion. He said there was good reason to believe that

---

16. The duchess of Aiguillon.

God was asking this service of them, and that his grace and blessing would enable them to overcome all obstacles and draw much good from it, despite the efforts of the devil and evil men against them. Seeing that his earnestness hurt some of the opposite opinion, he dropped to his knees, and begged pardon of the entire Company, that he, so wretched and miserable, had spoken so strongly of what he felt. He then said that he had been forced to act by an interior light that God was asking this service of their piety and their zeal.

The great humility of this saintly man so affected them that even those once most opposed to the mission were now agreed it should be given. By a common agreement and in a spirit of submission, they resolved to undertake it. Before beginning, however, they discussed with Monsieur Vincent what exactly must be done, with the thought of being guided completely by his advice and orders. When he was asked about how to preach and teach catechism, seeing that the people of this section of the city were so different from those of the country, and that they would be subject to the criticisms of many, this great servant of God replied that the method and style they should use was the same simple direct method they used in their previous missions, which God had so blessed. The spirit of the world, which filled the neighborhood, could not be fought and conquered with greater success than by the spirit of Jesus Christ. They should try to enter into his sentiments, and seek, like him, not their own honor and glory but solely the glory of God. They must be prepared, like him, to suffer objection and contempt, and even contradiction and persecution, should this prove to be the will of God. They must preach and speak as he did, simply and familiarly with humility and charity. In this way they could be assured that it was not themselves, but Jesus Christ speaking through them. He would use them to serve as his instruments of mercy and grace, to touch the hardest hearts, and convert the most rebellious spirits.

These gentlemen received all this advice as though it were Jesus Christ speaking to them through the mouth of his servant. They began the mission, therefore, in perfect acceptance of the will of God, and with great confidence in his goodness. It pleased him to pour out his extraordinary blessings upon it, and to shower his graces in such abundance and so effectively that almost miraculous conversions took place. Even those who worked on this mission were astonished at them, seeing the disproportion between the means used and the results attained. Besides the large crowds at their sermons and catechism instructions which they presented in the simple and familiar style suggested by Monsieur Vincent, they were filled with admiration at their results. They saw inveterate sinners, hardened usurers, fallen women, libertines who had spent their entire lives in crime, in a word, people without faith in God or anyone, throw themselves at their feet, their eyes bathed in tears, their hearts moved with sorrow for sins, begging mercy and forgiveness. It could rightly be said: *digitus Dei hic est* ["The finger of God is here"],[17] or *Non manus nostra; sed Dominus fecit haec omnia* ["Not our hand, but the Lord has done all these things"].[18] It is certain that if we had to report in detail all the good done on this mission, the conversions, the reconciliations, the restitutions, etc., it would require a whole volume all by itself. A single incident will suffice to recall what happened toward the end of the mission.

A merchant of Paris was devout enough to attend the various activities of the mission, and seeing the great good effected by God was moved by the experience. One day he came to the house where the priests took their meals, and asked to speak to the head of the band. He announced himself as a widower, having lost his wife and children. He was now coming to offer his temporal goods, amounting to over seven or eight thousand *livres* annual income, and himself, too, to serve for the remainder of his life. All this, if only the priests would remain together and continue to devote themselves in other places to the same work they had done in this neighborhood. He added that he knew of no way he could render greater service to God, or obtain a greater good for the Church, or better use his personal gifts and possessions. He was thanked graciously for his gesture of good will, but those who had worked on this mission were indeed resolved to serve God throughout their lives in similar activities, yet they for many good reasons were not called to live together in the way he hoped. They assured him that God was most pleased with his good will.

The Providence of God made use of this mission not only for the immediate good done by it, but as a preparation for the blessings and graces he wished to bestow upon that area in the immediate future by the ministry of Father Olier, who shortly afterward was called to be the pastor of Saint Sulpice, where with members of his community and his seminary, he not only conserved but increased and perfected the good accomplished through this mission.[19]

---

17. Exod 8:19.
18. Not a direct quotation from Scripture, but reminiscent of passages such as Isa 66:2 and Acts 7:50.
19. Olier accepted this parish in the following year, 1642. At the beginning of his ministry, he highly praised the missionaries who had preceded him, particularly Francois Perrochel, the future bishop of Boulogne, who had preached with a remarkable simplicity and effect.

SECTION FIVE

The Company of Clergy Who Met at Saint Lazare Fostered Similar Companies in Other Dioceses

Since it is a quality of charity to diffuse itself, these good ecclesiastics were so animated with this virtue wherever they happened to find themselves, that they were moved to extend the same sentiments God had inspired in them, through Monsieur Vincent, to others whom they met. Several among their number had gone to other dioceses on personal business, or to work on one of the missions, or to fulfill some charge or benefice. They were anxious on all occasions to have the local clergy meet, with the permission and approval of their bishop, in assemblies like their own of Paris. These were to be formed to discuss the virtues and everything else about the duties proper to their calling. Some bishops were already aware of the great advantages these conferences might contribute in their own diocese. They established them not only in the episcopal city, but in various other places in their diocese for the pastors and vicars of the country places.

To have a brief sketch of the fruits these assemblies and conferences produced outside of Paris where they were established, we will give here some extracts from several letters written on this matter.

The late Father Olier, one of the first members of the conference at Saint Lazare, went to give missions in the regions depending upon his abbey of Pebrac, in Auvergne, together with several priests of the Congregation of the Mission and other members of the company in 1636 and with others of the company of priests. He convinced the canons of the cathedral church of Le Puy to form a similar company, and gave them the same regulations as those of Paris, but modified to suit their role as canons. He wrote of this to the company at Paris, telling the priests of the abbot of Pebrac learning of their company at Paris, and wishing to form a similar one for the priests of his area. The regulations of their association were modeled upon those of Paris, except for some modifications made necessary by their own conditions. He was sending along a copy which he asked the priests to read and to make appropriate changes, if they thought they were needed, and to associate this new group to their company, to share in their prayers and sacrifices.

The abbot of Pebrac wrote to the members of the Paris company about the newly-formed association in Le Puy:

Our Lord established you in Paris, as a light set upon a lampstand to enlighten all the clergy of France. You will be encouraged to learn the great fruit and spiritual profit the new company of clergy of Le Puy has produced. The members display virtues which edify the entire province. They give catechism lessons throughout the city, frequently visit the prisons and hospitals, and prepare missions for all the regions depending on this chapter. I am humbled by their zeal, especially in their asking me to open their mission, even though I am so poorly gifted to do so.

The canons of the cathedral church of Noyon also formed a similar company through the efforts of Monsieur Bourdin, doctor of theology and archdeacon of this church, and a member of the Paris company. They wrote to the Paris group in November of 1637 as follows:

> Gentlemen, here is a little stream returning to its source. We take the liberty to speak thus, for our tiny assembly owes its birth, after God, to no other source or being except your venerable company. Its renown, practice of charity and piety, the gifts you have given to the Church, and the incomparable benefits enjoyed by the priests fortunate enough to be its members, have led us to establish a similar association among ourselves. We have met several times, and have drawn up the regulations we now send you. We have attempted to model them after yours as closely as we could, taking into account our obligations as canons, or our other duties. We would humbly ask you do us the charity to examine these, to add, subtract, or modify what you think proper. When it meets with your approval, we shall follow it with greater assurance and security.
>
> We do not know how to thank sufficiently the divine goodness for inspiring us with such a helpful wish, and you, gentlemen, for having provided us with such a beautiful example, and clearing the way so favorably to enable us to fulfill the duties of our calling. We shall bless his eternal Providence, with the help of God, and attempt to recognize by our prayers the singular blessings we have received from you. Permit us, gentlemen, to take the liberty of asking you for a written report of one of your conferences, especially on the spirit of your company, so that we might be clothed with this same spirit, without which we surely will not succeed in our undertaking. We ask one thing more of your charity to assure us of your union with us, and to make us part of your holy prayers and sacrifices, *ut qui coepit in nobis opus bonum, ipse perficiat solidetque* ["that he who has begun the good work in us, will bring it to perfection and make it firm"],[20] for which we will ever be much obliged.

---

20. Based on Phil 1:6.

The priests of the town of Pontoise organized a similar association. One of their principal members wrote to Monsieur Vincent, in May of 1642, as follows:

> The assembly of the priests of Pontoise has asked me to write to you, to tell you of our satisfaction with our little group. I must confess that at first we did not appreciate fully what was involved, but now we realize more and more each day the grace and blessing God has poured upon us. We see clearly all the good that can come to each of us, and to the whole body of the Church. It is to you, Monsieur, after God, that we are obliged for all we have gained by our association with your good and virtuous company of Paris. Our company received its first instructions from you, a seed which has continued to grow, and to which God has given his blessings. We would ask one more favor, since we are as children in virtue and do not have enough strength to direct ourselves. Please allow some of your priests of Paris to visit us, to help us walk with greater surety in the path we have begun with such courage. We expose our weakness to you to encourage you to help us.[21]

A similar company was begun in the city of Angouleme. One of its members wrote to Monsieur Vincent in 1644, in the name of all the others:

> Our company feels we must not long delay in paying our respects, and in telling you it recognizes itself as unworthy of the honor you have done us in all that concerns our growth and development. This company begs you most humbly, Monsieur, that it may regard you as its grandfather, since it was one of your sons whom God used to bring us into existence. You would add another obligation of gratitude to the first, by looking upon us not as strangers, but as your grandchild. You have allowed the beautiful and illustrious company of Paris, which is like your elder daughter, to accept us as her sister, although we are so far beneath her in every respect.[22]

We will not quote from similar letters from Angers, Bordeaux, and other cities of the kingdom,[23] and even from Italy, where similar associations and conferences were formed according to the example of the one in Paris. We will finish this chapter by relating the sentiments of Monsieur Godeau, then bishop of Grasse, now of Vence, which he wrote in 1637, shortly before he left his see:[24]

---

21. *CED* II:252.
22. *CED* II:455.
23. For example, Bossuet wrote from Metz to Monsieur Vincent telling him of the establishment of a Conference there. See *CED* VII:155-56.
24. Antoine Godeau, named bishop of Grasse in 1636, moved to the diocese of Vence in 1638. He was known both for his learning and piety. He died April 17, 1672.

Gentlemen, I had hoped even today to visit you to say adieu, but the press of business prevented my having this satisfaction. Please remember me in your sacrifices, for I regard it as a singular blessing to have been received among you. The memory of the good example I saw, and the excellent things I heard, will rekindle my zeal when it shall fade, and you shall be the model upon which I shall strive to form good priests. Continue, then, your activities in this same spirit, and respond faithfully to the designs of Jesus Christ upon you. He surely wills to renew the grace of the priesthood in his Church through you.

CHAPTER FOUR

Spiritual Retreats

SECTION ONE

The Utility of Spiritual Retreats

THE PERFECTION of clergy in their state of life is an undertaking which requires much help, both interior and exterior, because of the obstacles found in the world in which they have to live. Not only conversations and business affairs, but other dangerous occasions and the frequent temptations to which they are exposed, threaten too often and sometimes overcome the best resolutions they have taken, if priests are not sustained and affirmed by powerful reinforcements. Indeed, the ordination retreats help greatly in establishing them in the true spirit of their vocation, and spiritual conferences contribute much to their sustenance. Yet through his long experience, Monsieur Vincent knew only too well the feebleness and inconstancy of the human will. He felt that still another means was required to strengthen priests in their practice of the virtues. He thought of nothing so effective as spiritual retreats. They dispose the soul to receive a new increase of grace, and prepare it to be clothed by power from on high, as our Lord said to his apostles when he directed them to await the coming of the Holy Spirit after his ascension into heaven.

What inclined Monsieur Vincent to do all he possibly could to help spiritual retreats even more, was that he realized that their benefits could be extended even beyond the clergy to laity of all classes as well, as a help to them in leading a life in keeping with their obligations as Christians. Because so few give enough consideration to these obligations, or are guided by the truths and maxims of the Gospel of Jesus Christ, largely because of insufficient reflection, he believed he would perform a service agreeable to God, advantageous to the Church, and helpful to souls if he were to encourage the practice of spiritual retreats. His efforts were directed toward reestablishing a true spirit of Christianity among the faithful, as we read in a note he left, written in his own hand:

> By the expression spiritual retreat or spiritual exercise, we understand a separation from all temporal cares and occupations, to

consider seriously one's interior state, to examine one's conscience, to meditate, contemplate, and pray. In this way, we prepare the soul by purification from all sin and from evil attractions and habits, to be filled with the love of virtue, and ready to seek out the will of God, and once having discovered it, to submit to it, to embrace it, and by union with the plan of God move toward and finally attain one's own proper perfection.[1]

By these few words we understand the mind of this great servant of God, that these spiritual retreats had no other end than the complete renovation of the interior self. One was to be purified from sins, from all evil habits, unlawful attractions, uncontrolled passions, and all other faults and imperfections, so that with the eyes of the soul being opened, the particular obligations of one's state in life might be more clearly seen, and the virtues needed would be appreciated and practiced. One could be grounded in true charity, which unites the heart and all the powers of the soul to God, that we might be ready to say with the holy apostle, "Now, it is no longer I who live, but Jesus Christ who lives in me."[2]

Because of this the times and exercises of these spiritual retreats were established: the various meditations and spiritual readings, the examinations of conscience, and the making of a good general confession, if not of one's whole past life, at least one going back to the last general confession. Resolutions were taken, not only to avoid sin and the occasion which might lead to it, but more especially to put into practice the virtues and activities proper to one's particular calling. A plan of life was set out for the future, and if a person had not yet decided upon a state in life, God was consulted in fervent prayer to know his will. In a word, the retreatant strove to acquire the dispositions necessary to lead a truly Christian life, and to acquire the perfection of one's state.

Monsieur Vincent particularly advised his confreres that they have their retreatants well understand that the aim of the exercises they followed was to help each one become a perfect Christian, whatever his particular calling. One would be a perfect scholar if he were a student, a perfect soldier if his profession was a man of arms, a perfect member of the judiciary if his vocation was to serve in the courts of law. If the person was in holy orders, he was to strive to become a model ecclesiastic. Should he happen to be a member of the hierarchy, he was to become another Saint Charles Borromeo. If those coming to the retreat came to discern their calling, or to root out a vice, or acquire a certain virtue, or for any other purpose, they must, he used to say, direct all the exercises of the retreat to this end. Those thinking of

---

1. *CED* XIII:143-44.
2. Gal 2:20.

leaving the world must be helped, but the advice given must accord with the maxims of the Gospel and not the views of human prudence. When a question would arise of choosing a particular religious community, this should be done between the person and God alone, although it would be proper to give general advice as to choosing a reformed community.

It is commonly understood that most of those who are lost lack the necessary consideration and attention to those things concerning their salvation. The main reason for sin and disorders in which so many pass nearly their entire lives is that they seldom if ever consider the end for which God gave them being and life. These people do not reflect on his goodness, nor on the teachings and example given us by Jesus Christ, nor the graces of the sacraments he instituted. The pernicious effects of sin are not considered, nor the vanity of the world, the deceptions of the flesh, the malice and deceits of the devil, the incertitude of the moment of death, the fearsome judgments of God, eternal happiness or unhappiness, and other truths so fundamental to our salvation.

Monsieur Vincent felt that spiritual retreats supplied all these lacks by the serious reflection made on all these truths, considered and weighed in the light of the sanctuary. He rightly considered that of all the means put at the disposal of people to remedy the disorders of their lives, and aid them in their progress in virtue, nothing is more efficacious or more likely to produce as noticeable, as frequent, and as marvelous results than these spiritual retreats. Sinners who are not converted by them or who do not amend their ways, stand in need of true miracles for their conversion if these spiritual retreats do not bring it about.

SECTION TWO

The Zeal of Monsieur Vincent to Provide the Opportunity to All Sorts of Persons to Make a Spiritual Retreat

Since the spiritual retreat is such a salutary means for sanctification and perfection of souls, as we have said in the previous section, God so inspired his Church from the first centuries of Christianity, that great saints retired to the deserts of Egypt and elsewhere to participate in them. In recent times many saintly persons have revived this custom. Among others, Saint Ignatius made it possible for persons living in the world to find a place of retreat, some in the cities and others in remote places, yet these places were not well attended since lay people rarely followed these retreat exercises. Moved by an ardent desire to procure the greater glory of God and the salvation of souls, Monsieur Vincent strove to extend this opportunity to all sorts of persons, either lay or clergy, and he made this practice more common than ever before.

With a wholly impartial charity, he opened the doors of his heart and his home to all those who wished to share in this good work. He would receive them kindly and paternally, with no distinction of persons. In this he was imitating the father of the family in the Gospel who accepted to his banquet all those who came: the poor, blind, lame, and the crippled, and sending out to the streets and squares of the cities, and even to the fields and most isolated areas, to invite and even compel all to attend.

We must admit that in our day this great servant of God did something similar to the astonishment and edification of all. In the refectory at Saint Lazare many other persons could be seen among the missionaries. They were of all ages and conditions, from city and country, poor and rich, young and old, students and doctors, priests and holders of benefices, ecclesiastics and prelates, gentlemen, counts, marquis, attorneys, lawyers and councillors, presidents, receivers of petitions and other officers of justice, merchants, artisans, soldiers, pages, and lackeys. All were received, lodged, and fed in this great hospice of charity to make their retreat, to find the remedy for their spiritual infirmities, or the help necessary to set them securely on the path of salvation.

This one house of Saint Lazare of Paris received, lodged, and fed every year from seven to eight hundred persons for their spiritual retreat, not to mention the other houses of the Mission which accepted as many as they could, especially at Rome where great numbers were always received. With all this taken into account, from 1635 to the time of Monsieur Vincent's death twenty-five years later, more than twenty thousand people participated in these retreats. Their general confessions and other exercises brought remedies to a countless number of disorders of family and conscience. A large number of public and secret sinners were reconciled to God. Those who had strayed from the path of salvation were returned to the right way. The just received an increase of blessings and grace, and all were given arms against their great enemies, the world, the flesh, and the devil by the helpful advice they received, to repulse their attacks and so gain glorious victories over these enemies of their salvation.

In the beginning, in fact, not many people came to make the spiritual retreats. The numbers increased only little by little. The charity of Monsieur Vincent directed that all who came should be received with open arms, at the expense of the house at Saint Lazare although there was no assured source of funds to support them. Among those who came, some who were better off left a donation which he did not refuse, since it had been freely offered. This did not happen often, because nothing was asked for, or possibly because it was simply overlooked. It was evident to all that retreatants were accepted with no thought of the expenses involved, solely through charity and zeal for their salvation and perfection.

Although the house of Saint Lazare experienced much inconvenience and accumulated a large debt on this score and by reason of the ordination retreats, they continued and will remain, God willing, as long as humanly possible. These good works for the glory of God and the consolation of the people shall always remain open for the spiritual advancement of those who wish to make their retreat there and renew their life. In this, the sons of Monsieur Vincent have shown themselves possessed of his spirit. His confreres spared no effort or expense when there was question of the salvation of souls, in consideration that our Lord had given his blood and his life for them. Monsieur Vincent was persuaded that his Congregation would never want for material support so long as they used their patrimony in works of charity.

He even felt at ease in seeing his confreres in real need on occasion, to give them an opportunity to display their absolute dependence on the Providence of God. They must have the experience of saying, amid their wants and financial difficulties, like Saint Peter in the storms and waves that threatened: "Lord, save us, we perish."[3] God preserved this tiny craft from foundering, as though by miracle, despite its being often threatened, but never enough to lessen the charity of Monsieur Vincent. In this connection, a brother of the Mission, seeing the huge number of those making the retreat, took the liberty of suggesting that perhaps too many retreatants had been accepted. Monsieur Vincent's only reply to this was, "Brother, this is because they wish to be saved."

On another occasion it was pointed out to him that the house was not able to cover the expense of all those who came to make the retreat, and was already running into debt because of this. He replied, "If we had thirty years to exist, but because of receiving so many retreatants would be able to manage only fifteen years, this must not concern us. The expense is truly great, but money cannot be used any better. If the Congregation of the Mission is in debt, God knows how to get us out. This is what we hope from his Providence and from his infinite bounty."

He also said to the one in the house charged with receiving the guests: "Give them our rooms when all the others are taken." When it was pointed

---

3. Matt 8:25.

out to him that the house could not take care of all who came to make their retreat, he offered to take over as receptionist, thinking perhaps that he might be able to cut down on the number accepted. The opposite happened, for his charity was such that he could not turn anyone away, causing the suspicion he might have taken the role of receptionist to increase the number of retreatants rather than lessen it.

One day someone said to him that among the large number of those who came, some seemed to gain nothing from the exercises. His reply was, "There is no loss if only one person gains from the retreat." When some said that some came only through pressure or to receive the corporal nourishment offered rather than the spiritual, he responded, "Well, even this is an alms agreeable to God. If you make it too difficult to come, it will surely happen that you will turn away someone God has destined to be converted on this retreat. Too great an exactness in examining motives will make you lose some who would otherwise be led to give themselves to God."

We shall finish this section by citing the opinion of a worthy priest who knew Monsieur Vincent well and who had made several retreats at Saint Lazare.

> Although Paris is filled with all sorts of people, the downtrodden and afflicted of all ranks, they all could find an asylum. Monsieur Vincent and his confreres staffed a house of consolation and help. The door, the table, and the rooms of Saint Lazare, all give witness to this. I have also seen everyone made welcome: all ranks of ecclesiastics and religious, lords and magistrates, soldiers and scholars, hermits and peasants. Monsieur Vincent refused consolation and spiritual help to no one. His house was a perpetual mission, a succession of spiritual exercises, retreats, penances, general confessions for poor sinners who wished to be converted and change their lives. This was usually for all sorts of persons, lodged and fed during their retreat, one after another, continually throughout the year. Everything was done with such good grace and charity that the hardest hearts could not help being moved. They were touched and stirred by this hospitality, goodness, and meekness, and by all the other evidences of good they saw.

SECTION THREE

Some Remarkable Comments of Monsieur Vincent About the Spiritual Retreats

This great servant of God recognized on the one hand the great fruits these retreats could produce for the glory of God and the salvation of souls, but he realized too the burden for his community in the expense as well as the difficulty in constantly caring for so many people of all different backgrounds and dispositions. He was apprehensive lest his confreres grow weary under such a heavy burden. This is why he often recommended to his community to be faithful to this responsibility with constancy and perseverance, and to take it to heart to serve and help those souls who came seeking God. He would say, "We must fear, gentlemen, that God will take this harvest from us to give his grace to others if we fail to use it as we ought."

On one occasion when he was recommending to the prayers of his community a person on retreat, he took the opportunity to exhort them to appreciate this holy enterprise.

Oh, gentlemen, how we ought to esteem the grace God gives us, to send us so many persons to be helped in attaining salvation. We even have many soldiers coming. Recently one of them said to me, "Monsieur, before I go into some situations I foresee, I want to be well prepared. I have had remorse of conscience and reason to doubt what might happen to me, but I have come to accept whatever God shall ask of me." Right now we have a good number of persons on retreat. Oh, gentlemen, what happy results that can produce if we work at it faithfully! But what a loss if this house would some day withdraw from this service. I declare to you, gentlemen and my brothers, I fear the day when we will no longer have the zeal which up to now let us receive these many people for retreats. And then what happens? We must fear that God will withdraw his grace for this particular work, and perhaps for others also.

Just the day before yesterday I was told of the Parlement humiliating a counsellor. He was brought in to the Grand'Chambre, dressed in the red robes of his office, but the president directed the marshals to strip him of his robes and cap, as being unfit to wear them and unequal to the duties of this office. The same thing could happen to us, gentlemen, should we abuse the graces of God in neglecting our duty. God will withdraw them from us because we are unworthy of our vocation, and unfit for the work he has called us to. My God, what unhappiness! To convince you of the great evil this would be if God deprived us of the honor of serving him in this way, think of those who come to the retreat to discern the will of God in their thought of leaving the world. I recommend one such person to your prayers who has just finished his retreat and who is leaving here to join the Capuchins. Other communities send us their applicants to make their spiritual retreat here, to test their vocation before entering. Others come from ten, twenty or even fifty leagues away, not only to find a place for recollection and to make their general confession, but also to choose their vocation in the world, and take proper steps to assure their salvation.

We also receive many pastors and clergymen who come from everywhere to renew themselves in their calling and to advance in the spiritual life. They come with little thought of what it will cost, knowing they will be well received no matter what their financial condition. In this connection, someone told me recently what a great consolation it was for those without money to know there was some place in Paris always ready to receive them out of charity when they come, with the thought of putting themselves right with God.

In former days, gentlemen, this house was a hospital for lepers. They were accepted but not a single one was ever cured. Now it is used to receive sinners, afflicted with a spiritual leprosy, but they are cured by the grace of God. We can say more. Those who were dead are brought back to life. What happiness that the house of Saint Lazare has become a house of resurrection! This saint, after three days in the tomb, came forth alive. Our Lord who raised him from the dead does the same to others here who, after living like Lazarus in the tomb, come forth with a new life. Who would not rejoice at such a blessing? Who would not be moved to love and thank the goodness of God for such a great blessing? What a source of shame, if we make ourselves unworthy of such a grace! What confusion, gentlemen, and what regrets would we not experience one day if, by our own fault, we were degraded in shame before God and man!

What a source of sorrow it would be for a poor brother of the Company, who now sees so many people come from everywhere to spend a few days with us to amend their lives, to see this great work neglected. We would see no one else coming. We could come to that, gentlemen, not at once, but later on. What would bring this about? If you say to a poor lax missionary, Father, would you please see to the spiritual direction of this retreatant, he would see this as a sort of torture from hell. If he does not excuse himself entirely, he does it only, as they say, with a lick and a promise. It is nearly impossible for him to give up a half hour after dinner or a half hour after supper of his usual recreation. Yet it is a question of the salvation of a soul and is the best possible use of time in the entire day.

Others complain of this work because it is so demanding and expensive. And so it is that the priests of the Mission who once gave life to the dead shall have but the name and appearance of what they once were. They will be but corpses, not true missionaries. They shall be the cadaver of Lazarus, not the resurrected Lazarus, and still less men who bring life to the dead. This house which is now a pool of healing in which everyone may come to bathe, will become a corrupt cistern brought about by the laziness and relaxation of those who live here. Let us pray God, gentlemen and my brothers, that this sad state of affairs never develop. Let us pray to the holy Virgin that by her intercession and by her interest in the conversion of sinners, she may prevent this from happening. Let us pray to the great Saint Lazarus that he may ever remain the protector of this house, and obtain for us the grace of perseverance in the good work which has begun.[4]

On another occasion he recommended a retreatant to the prayers of his community, then added:

Please thank God for inspiring so many persons to make their retreat here. So many priests of city and country leave all to come. So many apply each day to come, and some apply much ahead of time. This surely is a good reason to praise God! Some have just said to me, "Monsieur, so many times I have sought admission, but have had to be turned down." Others say, "Monsieur, I must leave [my present position], I am in charge, my benefice calls me, I am about to take over these responsibilities. Please allow me to stay." Another says he has just finished his studies and must decide what to do next. Still others say, "Monsieur, I have such great need of a retreat. If you, Monsieur, only knew how much I need one, you would surely allow me to stay." Some older men even come to prepare themselves for death.

What a great favor for God to call so many to this house to follow these holy exercises, and to use this family of ours as an instrument for their conversion. What should we have in mind except to gain souls for God? This is so especially when they come to us, for we

---

4. *CED* XI:14-17.

should have nothing else in mind than living for that alone. Alas, they have cost the Son of God so dearly, and now he sends them to us to be returned to his favor. O Savior, take good care that we not become unworthy of this choice nor take away your helping hand from us.

I would like to believe that very few do not use the retreat well, and even so, just for the ones who do not profit from them, we must not deprive others from benefiting from what gives such good fruit. Yes, even wonderful fruit. I have spoken to you of this on other occasions, so today I will give you but one example. During the last trip I made to Brittany five years ago, an excellent man came to see me. He thanked me for the graces he had received during a spiritual retreat he made in this house. He said to me, "Oh, Monsieur, I would have been lost without it. I owe my salvation, after God, to you. The retreat brought peace to my troubled conscience. It enabled me to begin a new way of life which I have preserved since, by the grace of God, with great peace and satisfaction of mind. I am so obligated to your charity, Monsieur, that I do not hesitate to tell everyone everywhere that I would have been damned except for the retreat I made at Saint Lazare. How can I sufficiently value the grace you have secured for me? Please believe that I shall be mindful of it all the days of my life."

After hearing this, gentlemen, would we not be most unfortunate if by our laziness we forced God to withdraw his graces from us? Indeed, not all who make their retreat here will profit from it like the man I just spoke of. But is not the kingdom of God on earth peopled with the good and the bad? Is it not a net that catches all sorts of fish? In the great abundance of grace that God showers upon everyone in the world, how many abuse it? And yet, though he knows who will not use it well, he does not withdraw his grace from them. How many there are who do not use the fruits of the passion and death of our Savior and who, as the apostle says, trample under foot the blood shed for their salvation. O sweet and merciful Savior! You knew well that the greater number of men would disregard your sacrifice, and yet you did not hesitate to suffer death for their salvation even considering the vast number of infidels who would mock you, and the great number of Christians who would abuse the grace you won for them.

Every pious work is profaned by someone, and nothing is so holy that some do not abuse it. This should not make us desist. We would be blameworthy before God if we relaxed in our works of charity simply because all those who participate in them do not gain all the fruit we might wish. What a loss and what unhappiness for us, if we grew weary of this favor God has given us, of choosing us among so many other communities to provide this service, and depriving his divine majesty of the glory owed him!

Yes, I say it again, gentlemen and my brothers, how unfortunate would he be who, by his laziness or for fear of losing his ease or by a desire for rest when he should be working, would slacken in his fervor in this holy exercise. Even should this happen by the fault of some individual, this must never happen to us as a group. We must have courage and hope that God who has given us this grace will preserve it in us, and even increase it. Let us place our confidence more and more in him with a heart strong against inconstancy, and have courage in the face of difficulties. Only this cursed spirit of laziness allows us to be put off at the least inconvenience, or fears difficulties, or which seeks to avoid trouble and work so often. It prefers its own personal satisfaction. This is an effect of self-love, which spoils and ruins everything it touches. This is why we must mortify ourselves and submit ourselves to the love of God.

Let us ask that in his mercy he would conserve in us what he had so freely given us. Yes, my brothers, this is a great gift he has given our Company. We must pray that he, in his goodness, will not allow any of us to become unworthy of his gift. O Savior, raise up in us the spirit of the great Saint Lawrence, whose feast we celebrate today, which made him triumph in the midst of the flames over all the infernal hatred against him. Raise up in us this same divine fire, this ardent fervor, which will make us, too, triumph over all the wiles of the devil, and our own corrupt nature, so opposed to the good. Grant us an ardent zeal to obtain your glory in all our work, so that in imitation of the great saint we may remain faithful to death. We ask you this through his intercession.[5]

On another occasion he spoke as follows:

We must thank God a thousand thousand times, my brothers, for choosing the house of Saint Lazare as the place to bestow his mercy, where the Holy Spirit continually inspires so many souls. If we could see this with our bodily eyes, how marvelous would it be! What happiness for us missionaries, that Saint Lazare is the throne of his divine action! That Saint Lazare should be the place where the King of Kings lives in the souls of those who come here with good intention to make their retreat! Gentlemen, we must serve

---

5. *CED* XI:229-32.

them, not as mere men, but as those sent by God. We show no preference for persons. The poor are as dear to us as the rich, even more so, for they live closer to the way Jesus Christ lived when he was among us. I recommend to your prayers one of our retreatants in special need. He no doubt can do much good if he gives himself wholly to God. On the other hand, it is to be feared that if he does not, he could do much harm.[6]

On another occasion, he said:

A captain is staying with us, thinking of becoming a Carthusian. As is their custom, these good fathers have sent him here to test his vocation. I beseech you to recommend him to our Lord and also to admire his goodness in inspiring a man to a state in life so different from the one he is actually living. Let us adore this merciful Providence and appreciate that God does not regard the quality of person but chooses anyone, when in his goodness he thinks it proper to do so.

We have another retreatant here who is also a captain in the army, and whom we recommend also to your prayers. Include in your prayers, too, a man recently converted from Protestantism. He is working and writing sincerely for the defense of the truths of the faith to persuade others to follow his example. We thank God for him, and beg him to fill him more and more with his grace.[7]

On still another occasion, he said:

We recently had a priest with us who came from a long way off to make his retreat. He said to me, "Monsieur, I am coming to you for my retreat and if you cannot receive me, I shall be lost." When he left, he seemed so filled with the Spirit of God that I was astonished. Three others came from the limits of Champagne, mutually encouraging one another in coming to Saint Lazare for their retreat. O God, how many come from far and near by the inspiration of the Holy Spirit. Yet how strong this inspiration must be to bring men to such a crucifixion. A spiritual retreat is a sort of crucifixion of the flesh, as the holy apostle says: "I am crucified to the world and the world to me."[8]

Here then we have given some simple accounts of happenings which show the holy ardor which motivated the heart of Monsieur Vincent to bring about the reign of God in souls by the spiritual retreat. He strove to communicate this same divine fire that burned in him to his spiritual sons to

---

6. *CED* XI:18.
7. *CED* XI:18-19.
8. Gal 6:14. *CED XI:19-20.*

enkindle in them an tireless charity and zeal for those who come to this house in search of the cure or salvation of their souls.

SECTION FOUR

The Opinions of Some Others Concerning These Retreats, and Several Examples of Happy Outcomes

A priest of Languedoc came to Paris in 1640 to make his retreat at Saint Lazare. Afterward he wrote to one of his priest friends:

> I was welcomed with such graciousness in this house by all with whom I came in contact, that I was overwhelmed. Beyond all the others, Monsieur Vincent himself received me with such kindness that I was completely taken. My heart felt this, although I cannot find words to express what I experienced. What I can say is that during the retreat I was in paradise, and now that I am no longer there, Paris seems like a prison to me. Do not think I am saying this simply as a compliment; no, I speak of what I felt. I no longer know how to continue living in the world, so my resolve is to leave it, to give myself entirely to God.

Another priest, from Orleans, wrote to Monsieur Vincent on this same topic:

> For the love of God and of the holy Virgin please allow me to make another retreat in your house. I sincerely desire this, and I hope when you realize why I ask this favor, I will receive your permission by the mercy of God and your goodness. Certainly, Monsieur, when I think of the good sentiments I had at Saint Lazare, I am carried away. My only desire is that it would please God to have every priest attend these exercises. If that were to come about, we would no longer have the bad example that some give to the great scandal of the Church.[9]

A pastor of a country parish not far from Paris wrote to Monsieur Vincent in 1642:

> The fruits which those who made their spiritual retreat with you spread such perfume wherever they went that they have aroused the

---
9. *CED* IV:108.

desire in others to gather the same fruit for themselves. One of my close relatives feels this way. I can do him no greater favor than to ask you most humbly to please receive him in your house to follow the exercises of the spiritual retreat. He hopes to receive from it the light and grace for the guidance of the remainder of his life.[10]

The late baron of Renty, as noble in virtue as he was in birth, had tried every way he knew to persuade a pastor of his acquaintance to mend his disastrous ways, but without success. He had the thought of writing to Monsieur Vincent in the hope that he would make a retreat at Saint Lazare. In the letter he wrote, he told Monsieur Vincent that he was confident that under his charitable guidance a retreat might convince this pastor to change the deplorable life he had led into one of blessing.

The superior of a reformed order in a house in Paris had the same thought about one of his religious, who held the office of pastor at a parish, but who had fallen into similar disorders in his personal life. He wrote the following letter to Monsieur Vincent:

> This good religious has a great need, as he may tell you, to amend his life, which currently gives great scandal to the souls under his direction. He has been advised to make a retreat with you as a place where he can receive help and be directed back to the path of duty. I beg of you most earnestly to take him and do all in your power what you judge proper to regain him for God.[11]

Another religious of one of the more celebrated monasteries in Paris felt he could do nothing better for a servant boy who wished to be converted than to put him in Monsieur Vincent's hands. He requested him to take the boy into his house for several days of spiritual retreat. In a letter he wrote in 1644, he said:

> I pray that God will prolong your days and years for his glory and for the good of the neighbor, for whom you work so hard. I send you a person fit for your charity, a page of the Prince de Talmont, who has been raised in the false religion of Calvin but has come to me to ask for instruction leading to his conversion. I do not think of myself as capable of this good office. Therefore I take the liberty of writing to you as the one God has given his special grace for his glory and the salvation of those in sin or who have gone astray. Please have the charity, then, my most honored father in our Lord, to accept and welcome him as a poor straying sheep but who now seeks to return and be saved from the fangs of the wolf.[12]

---

10. *CED* II:257.
11. *CED* II:437.
12. *CED* II:451.

If we had to recount here in detail all those who had recourse to the charity of this great servant of God and to list the infirmities, miseries, and spiritual necessities he was asked to attend to through the ministry of these spiritual retreats in the house of Saint Lazare alone, we would certainly need several volumes for this. We could in some sense say of the servant what the Gospel said of the Master, that people were brought to him from all sides, suffering from all illnesses and maladies, but that a power went out from him which delivered each one from his trouble and cured all.

Since it was not only in the house of Saint Lazare that the effects of the charity of Monsieur Vincent were felt but in several other places as well, we will report here the testimony and examples from some other of these spiritual retreats given by the sons of this father of missionaries.

A priest of Paris of some standing and virtue had worked on the missions with the priests of the Congregation of the Mission, and had made several retreats at Saint Lazare. He was eventually named a bishop. He immediately went into seclusion to prepare himself for his consecration and for all the various duties of his charge. Accompanied by some priests of the Mission, he then went to his own diocese. He began to put into practice there what he had observed of Monsieur Vincent and his confreres. Recognizing from his own experience the usefulness of the spiritual retreat, he convoked his pastors and other clergy to his episcopal palace, of which he consecrated a part for these exercises. In 1644 he wrote to Monsieur Vincent:

> As to news, I must tell you we continue to assemble the priests of the diocese, together with some others from neighboring places who have asked us. About thirty priests here are following their spiritual retreat in the episcopal palace with much fruit and blessing.[13]

Another great prelate, an archbishop, had for several years visited the house of Saint Lazare, and taken part in the retreats given by the Congregation. He considered that he could do nothing better for his clergy than to have them come to his palace in groups to follow the exercises of a spiritual retreat, under the guidance of a priest of the Congregation of the Mission. This priest wrote to him to give an account of these events in the following letter:

> At the beginning there was much fear and murmuring. The more timorous did not know what to think. But God, through your direction and mostly working in secret so changed hearts that they could all say: *Vere Deus est in loco isto, et ego nesciebam* ["Truly, the Lord is in this spot, although I did not know it"];[14] as time went

---

13. *CED* II:491. The writer was Nicolas Pavillon, bishop of Alet.
14. Gen 28:16.

on and the exercises unfolded, the dark and cold gradually dissipated. They then said: *Quam bonum, et quam jucundum habitare fratres in unum* ["How good it is, and how pleasant, where brethren dwell at one"],[15] and by the end of the retreat, *faciamus hic tria tabernacula* ["Let us erect three booths here"].[16] These good gentlemen, some forty pastors and vicars, seemed not to have lived except these last ten days. They wept openly, remembering their past lives and the ignorance in which they lived. The oldest among them hastened to the exercises. I can assure you that I have never before seen such fervor, nor such tangible evidence of the presence of the Spirit of God. He holds in his hand not only the kings of this world, to bend to his will as he sees fit, but kings of heaven, and priests, whose hardness of heart often resists his grace.

Each one made his general confession, most of them of their entire past life, in the belief they had done little up to now. All took strong resolutions to work at their own salvation and that of their people, saying with the prophet-king: *Dixi, nunc coepi, haec mutatio dexterae excelsi* ["This is my sorrow, that the right hand of the Most High is changed"].[17] To show you how grace changes hearts, one person came to tell me that the devil had blinded him to believe the retreat was an intolerable burden, a prison, and a kind of hell. Others told me: "Monsieur, how indebted we are to our bishop, and how we ought to pray for him and for his return. If we had the lights we now enjoy, we would never have done what we did."

In a word, Monsieur, they acted as little children. I was astonished that people who could have been my grandparents put so much trust in such a feeble instrument. *Vitulus et leo, lupus et ovis, simul accubabunt, puer parvulus minabit eos* ["The calf and the lion, the wolf and the sheep, shall lie down together, with a little child to guide them"].[18] These good retreatants have encouraged your entire city, not only by their words but more so by their modesty of demeanor. Priests who ridiculed these exercises have been surprised to see their friends and confreres change their way of speaking, and some of your chapter have asked when their turn would come. I hope, Your Excellency, that your prayers will obtain from God the fulfillment of so many holy resolutions and that in this way, your diocese will be transformed, your leaders influencing the rest of the body.

---

15. Ps 133:1.
16. Based on Matt 17:4.
17. Ps 77:11.
18. Based on Isa 11:6.

We add here the extract of another letter written to the same archbishop. It discussed further the blessings God had bestowed upon the clergy of his diocese in other retreats. In this letter the same priest of the Mission wrote:

Neither place nor time make men holy, although both may contribute significantly. Grace has its time, just as nature does. The Church calls the days of Lent days of salvation and propitiation. The experiences of this last retreat do not let us doubt this. I can assure you, Your Excellency, that if God showed himself liberal with his graces in the preceding retreats, he has shown himself prodigal in this one, which finished on the eve of Palm Sunday. Besides noticing the influence of grace in the souls of these gentlemen which softened the hardest hearts and brought light to darkness, I often heard it said they were beginning to open their eyes to the eminent dignity of the priesthood. If they had fully understood it before, they would never have embraced it so casually.

Some offered their financial help for the continuation of these retreats each year, while others wished to resign their benefices to have greater freedom to attend similar retreats. Others wanted to spend some time in the seminary, as long as their parishes could be taken care of. Each one left with such regret they were in tears, but with a total dependence upon you and your vicars general, ready to do anything or go anywhere you would be pleased to send them. In this way, Your Excellency, you can have missionaries in each parish to water what the missions have planted.

The laity praise the divine goodness and appreciate in their pastor the heart of a father in both spiritual and temporal things. I can assure you that if you had seen the marvels of the mercy of God, your joy would have been as perfect as it ever can be in this world. I almost forgot to tell you, Your Excellency, about one of the retreatants, who has not lived as a priest for several years, although he lived in several places in the diocese. He came to the exercises only to mock and to save appearances, as he later admitted, but little by little his heart was touched. He still did not want to be caught in my net, preferring to make his confession to another priest in whom he would have greater confidence. God denied him the opportunity to do so, for the night before the general communion, bothered by his conscience, he could not sleep. *Quis enim ei restitit et pacem habuit?* ["Who has withstood him and remained unscathed?"][19] He broke out in a sweat, and a trembling in his whole body seized him. He heard an inner voice saying to him, "This is the hour of grace.

---

19. Job 9:4.

You are about to die. You resist the grace of God." He called to one of his confreres sleeping in the same room to say he was dying, and asking that I be summoned. I came at once, and between midnight and four o'clock in the morning I heard his confession. He made it tearfully and full of thanks to his divine bounty for his favors known to God alone. He communicated with the others, but with such remorse, I feared both that he might lose his mind, and that the devil might be transforming himself into an angel of light to deprive him of his senses. In fact, this good gentleman was beside himself for a time. When he gained possession of himself again, he told me it was a just judgment of God, who wished his reparation to be public, just as his faults had been known to all. He left satisfied, saying, *Misericordia tua magna est super me, qui eruisti animam meam ex inferno inferiori* ["Great has been your kindness toward me; you have rescued me from the depths of the nether world"].[20]

Let us now turn to Italy where these same retreats were given, and let us begin with Genoa. The superior of the Mission of that city wrote to Monsieur Vincent in 1646, as follows:

We wrote in the name of Cardinal Durazzo, archbishop of the city, to all the places where missions had been given to advise the clergy that the exercises of the spiritual retreat would be given on such a day in our mission. All those who wished to attend should present themselves at such an hour. Several came, and have now departed, after attending the retreat. I cannot tell you adequately of the consolation they received or the abundance of graces the Lord gave, or the modesty and silence they observed, or the humility and sincerity with which they reported on their mental prayer. The same can be said of the admirable, almost miraculous, conversions that took place. Among others, one pastor said, almost publicly, that he had come to mock, by hypocrisy rather than devotion, to get a higher stipend from the cardinal for his attendance. He told me the Congregation of the Mission had no greater enemy than himself. He spoke every kind of evil against it and against His Eminence. He was given to vice, he had obtained his benefice by simony, receiving orders only to have the benefice. He had performed clerical duties, administered the sacraments, served in the Curia, all for several years. He was a man of schemes and intrigue, but God touched his heart and touched it effectively. He was converted, he wept, he humbled himself, and gave every evidence of having changed. Those who saw him at the exercises, or heard about his altered

---

20. Ps 86:13.

attitude, were very edified. We were too, but no less so for the others who benefited from the exercises, each one according to his needs.

I must tell you, Monsieur, of the joy and consolation of His Eminence. The tears which filled his eyes as he heard his priests tell him of their feelings would give you a better understanding of this than my poor words. All this became public knowledge in the city, and even in the surrounding areas, such that several other priests came to make their retreat with us.[21]

From time to time, this same superior wrote to Monsieur Vincent of the success of similar retreats, but it would take too much space to speak of them all. We will recount here the events of only this one retreat.

The pastors left here Friday, fervent and edified, marveling at the graces God had given them, which were great indeed. I must say I have never seen better disposed retreatants, nor have I seen more tears shed. I cannot even think of this without wonder and admiration. One said we were here in the Valley of Josaphat, because of the freedom each one showed in opening his heart, and as I said, this was done tearfully, in public and in private.

This was the result of God's all-powerful grace, but what a marvel that God showed himself so generous toward those who were faithful to our simple rule for a retreat, especially silence. I have seen thirty gathered together in a room, awaiting my appearance, with no one daring to say a single word, one to another. We currently have four retreatants, one of whom is a Jew who wishes to become a Christian, and whom the cardinal sent to us from Pisa.

A senator here wants to prepare for a good general confession but cannot find time from his duties to make the exercises of the spiritual retreat. He has taken the three days of the feast to come twice a day to confer with me. He has begun with much fervor. I trust he will finish the same way.

We expect six or seven priests this evening to come for the retreat. They are planning to give a mission in the city such as we gave in the country. In your charity please remember this intention in your prayers.[22]

The cardinal of Genoa himself made the spiritual exercises several times with the priests of the Mission, not with the pastors, but with the missionaries themselves, who make an annual retreat. The superior wrote about this in a letter to Monsieur Vincent, in 1649:

His Eminence the cardinal spent eight days with us in making

---

21. *CED* III:74-75.
22. *CED* IV:591.

the retreat with the ten priests of the Mission who are here. What a great servant of God! It is hard to believe the exactitude and punctuality with which he followed the order of the exercises, despite having a weak constitution. Although only fifty-six years of age, his spiritual and temporal concerns make him look older. He makes his mental prayer in the morning with the others, kneeling without moving from beginning to end, although some others sit down. For other meditations made in private in the sleeping rooms, he makes these kneeling or if he happens to be too fatigued, he comes for permission to sit, to have the merit of obedience, even though I have suggested that he remain seated when he feels tired.

When he reports on the thoughts and sentiments of his mental prayer, he does so with the simplicity, humility, and devotion of any one of us. No sooner does he hear the bell for the office or other exercises of the community, than he leaves all, and is the first in the chapel. At table he insists on being treated just like the others. After my insistence, he finally allowed some preference be shown him. He is pained to have his own bathroom, preferring to be treated like everyone else. At the end of the retreat I asked him to give us his blessing to ask perseverance of God. He refused, insisting instead that I give this blessing, but finally, after much entreaty, he relented. Oh, my dear father, what an example of virtue we have before our eyes.[23]

---

23. *CED* III:505-06.

CHAPTER FIVE

Seminaries

THE HOLY Council of Trent was aware of how important it was for the glory of God and the edification of the faithful that those promoted to sacred orders have the requisite dispositions and qualities of that state in the Church. It recognized that if virtues were not cultivated early in the hearts of the young there was good reason to fear they would never develop the deep roots required by a life of priestly service. Rather, if the necessary virtues were not cultivated, the candidates would accept benefices or ecclesiastical offices, and receive holy orders without the required dispositions. Instead of building up the Church they would serve as stumbling blocks by the evil example of their lives. For these and other considerations, the council directed seminaries to be established in each diocese. In them, young men with an aptitude and inclination to the clerical state could be trained in piety and the appropriate branches of knowledge. The poor were to be preferred, but others would not be excluded. In either case their minds and spirits were to be carefully cultivated, to make it possible for them one day to give fruitful service to the Church.

Although this decree had been most wisely adopted by the council, the corruption and evil spirit of the times prevented it from being carried out as completely as had been hoped. Many of the great prelates of the kingdom who had attended the council, did set up these seminaries in their dioceses upon their return to France. Unfortunately, as time went on, instead of the choice of students being limited to those inclined to the ecclesiastical state, and the staff being selected from among the most learned, pious, and those distinguished by their sacerdotal spirit, the opposite happened. Temporal and personal interest prevailed and all the good planning degenerated. On the one hand, the townspeople in those places where the seminaries were established saw they could avoid paying for the education of their sons by having them trained in these seminaries. This would exclude the poor, with no thought of their possible calling to the ecclesiastical state. On the other hand, the directors and teaching staff of the seminaries were not put in the hands of the most capable, but in those most able to scheme for personal advantage. All this resulted in the Church in France being deprived of the benefits envisioned by the fathers of the council.

Monsieur Vincent was aware of this abuse and it displeased him greatly. He attempted to bring some relief by setting up a seminary as the council suggested, in the College des Bons Enfants at Paris,[1] for the instruction and training in virtue and knowledge of those young men in whom some inclination and disposition to the ecclesiastical state had been noticed. His experience with this kind of seminary convinced him it was too slow in producing tangible results. It took a long time for a young boy to complete his training and enter into holy orders and the ministry of the Church. Monsieur Vincent foresaw, too, that those educated in the seminaries would not always fulfill the hopes placed in them, and that several of them would not have a vocation to the ecclesiastical state. As a result, the Church would not receive any help in the great need it had for good holy priests.

For these reasons Monsieur Vincent judged it useful and in some way even necessary to establish other seminaries for those clerics already ordained, or who were soon about to receive holy orders. They were to be taught over a long time the theology they needed, principally moral theology, the administration of the sacraments, and the various functions they were expected to know, such as plain chant, the rites of the Church, how to catechize, and how to preach. Above all, they were to be guided in the virtues proper to their state, in leading a well-regulated life, conformable to the character they bore, to be ready for whatever assignment given them by their bishop, and prepared to render useful service to the Church. He began this seminary at the College des Bons Enfants, as we mentioned in Book One,[2] but without closing the minor seminary. He moved it to a building near Saint Lazare and then renamed it the Seminary of Saint Charles. He continued this minor seminary to fulfill the wishes of the council and to use this as one more means of securing good priests for the Church.[3]

It pleased God to bestow such blessings to this seminary established by Monsieur Vincent for clerics already promoted to sacred orders, or for those about to be, that besides the fruit they produced and continued to produce, they served as models for many others in various other dioceses.

For good reason another zealous servant of God worked strenuously together with his community for the reform of the ecclesiastical state.[4] He had deplored that, whereas academies for the nobility prepared young gentlemen for their position in life, and that every occupation, no matter how humble, had its system of apprentices before allowing them to practice their trade, yet in the clerical state alone was it possible to enter the profession

---

1. In 1637.
2. Ch. 31.
3. Vincent supported making a clear distinction between what would later be called "minor" and "major" seminaries. The college of Bons Enfants became in effect a major seminary, under the name of Saint Firmin. The younger students were transferred to the newly established "Petit Saint Lazare," (Seminary of Saint Charles) in order to continue their studies in the humanities, thus in effect constituting a minor seminary.
4. Adrien Bourdoise, a priest of the community of Saint Nicolas du Chardonnet in Paris.

with little or no preparation. This was a more grievous failing in that these priests were destined for most important functions and for a ministry of divine service. At length it pleased God to remedy this serious deficiency through the seminaries, which served as schools of virtue and sanctity, where the candidates for the priesthood learned the science of the saints. So it is that in these latter days God raised up Monsieur Vincent and his Congregation to answer this holy and pressing need, and to it he gave his special blessing.

On one occasion Monsieur Vincent spoke to the priests of his community on the topic of seminaries:

> God has particularly sent the Missionaries to work for the sanctification of priests. One of the purposes of our institute is to teach them not only the subjects they must know, but also the virtues they must practice. To show them the one without the other is to do little or almost nothing. They must be able to understand how to lead a good life. Otherwise, they would serve no purpose, and even be dangerous. We must do both, then, as a duty asked of us by God.
>
> In the beginning we gave scarcely a thought to serving the clergy. Our concern was ourselves and the poor. How did the Son of God begin? He remained hidden. He seemed to think only of himself, he prayed, and did nothing special. Only later did he announce the Gospel to the poor. He finally chose his apostles, and took pains to teach them and form them to virtue. Lastly he sent his Spirit upon them, not for themselves alone but for all people upon earth. He also taught them all they needed to know to become priests, to administer the sacraments, and to acquit themselves worthily of their ministry.
>
> So it was at the beginning of our little Company. Our first concern was our own spiritual development, and then the evangelization of the poor. At times we were preoccupied with ourselves, and at other times we would go to the people in the countryside. God allowed us to begin like that, but in the fullness of time he has called us to contribute to the formation of good priests, to provide pastors for the people, and to show them what they must know and do. How elevated is this work! How sublime! How far above us is this calling! Who among us would ever have thought of the ordination retreats or of the seminaries? This thought never entered our heads, until God made known to us that we were to undertake this work. The Company has been brought to this with no choice on our part, but God expects us now to apply ourselves seriously, humbly, devoutly, constantly, corresponding to the excellence of this call.

Some might say that they came to the Congregation to work in the country in favor of the poor, and not to be shut up in the cities in a seminary. Each one of us should know, however, that what we do for the clergy, especially in the seminaries, must not be neglected under the pretext of caring for the missions. We must do both, not slight either, for we are obliged to do both by our institute. Long experience has taught us that it is difficult to preserve the fruits of the missions we give if we are not supported by the pastors whom we seek to serve by our Company. This is why we ought to do willingly what we can for their welfare.

To work for the instruction of poor people is truly a great work, but it is even better to help the clergy, for if they are ill-formed the people they lead are bound to be the same. We could ask the Son of God, why did you come upon earth? Was it not to evangelize the poor, in obedience to your Father's will? Why then did you consecrate priests? Why did you take such care to train and teach them? Why did you give them the power to consecrate, the power to bind and to loose? The Savior would respond that he came not only to teach truths necessary for salvation, but to prepare a priesthood superior to the priesthood of the Old Law. You are aware that in ancient times God rejected priests who dishonored their office, who profaned sacred things. He looked upon their sacrifices with horror, and said that he would raise up other priests. From the rising of the sun to its setting, and from south to north, they would make their voices heard: *In omnem terram exivit sonus eorum* ["Through all the earth their voice resounds"].[5] How did he accomplish this? By his Son, our Savior, who chose priests, instructed and formed them, and gave his Church the power, through them, to make other priests. *Sicut misit me Pater, et ego mitto vos* ["As the Father has sent me, so I send you"].[6] He did this to act through them in the centuries to come, to do what he had done in his own lifetime, to save all peoples by their teachings and by their administration of the sacraments.

It would be a mistake, a great mistake, for a Missionary not to help as best he can in the work of forming good priests, for there is nothing better than a good priest. Think as long as we like, we will not find anything better than to help in forming a good priest, to whom our Lord gives power over his body, both corporal and mystical. He gives the priest the power of consecration, and the power to forgive sins. O God, what power! What a dignity! These

---

5. Ps 19:5.
6. John 20:21.

considerations ought to lead us to serve the ecclesiastical state, which is so holy and so exalted. This is all the more true because of the need of the Church for good priests, to attend to the ignorance and vice with which the world is so filled, for which good people should shed tears of blood.

We may wonder if all the disorders we see in the world might not be laid at the feet of priests. It may scandalize some even to suggest this, but the subject demands that I show the extent of the evil, to point out the importance of supplying a remedy. Several meetings have recently been held on this, to seek the causes of such ills, the result of which is that the Church has no worse enemy than the bad priest. Heresies have come from them, as for example the recent great initiators of heresy, Luther and Calvin, both of whom were priests. Because of priests, heresies gained a foothold, vice reigned, and ignorance set up its throne among the poor people. This came about because of their own misconduct, their failure to combat with all their strength, as they were obliged, these three torrents which now have engulfed the whole world. What sacrifice, then, gentlemen, should we not make to help them live in keeping with the sanctity of their state, so the Church might be delivered from the sad desolate state in which she is.[7]

On another occasion, he said:

The character of the priest is a participation in the priesthood of the Son of God. He gives them the power to offer the sacrifice of his body, and to give it as food for eternal life to those who receive it. It is a divine and incomparable character, a power over the body of Jesus Christ whom the angels adore, and a power to forgive sins, a subject of astonishment and thanksgiving to them. Is there anything more admirable or greater? Oh, gentlemen, how great a good priest is! What can a good priest not accomplish? How many conversions can he not secure? Look at Monsieur Bourdoise, this excellent priest, what he does, and what he can do in the future! The well-being of Christianity depends on the priest, for when parishioners see in him a good ecclesiastic, a charitable pastor, they respect and follow his voice, striving to imitate him. How we should strive to do good for them, since this is our duty, and the priesthood is such an elevated state!

But, O Lord, if a good priest can do so much, how much evil can a bad one do if he sets himself to is! How difficult to put him on the right way! O my Savior, how we poor Missionaries should devote

---

7. *CED* XII:83-86.

ourselves to you, to contribute to the formation of good priests. This is the most difficult, the most elevated, the most important for the salvation of souls and for the advancement of Christianity.

If Saint Vincent Ferrer strove for sanctification so that God would one day raise up good priests and apostolic workers for the reform of the ecclesiastical state and for readying men for the last judgment, how much stronger reason we have in our day for working for our perfection to cooperate in such a happy restoration when we see the ecclesiastical state now returning to what it should be.[8]

These were the sentiments of this holy priest, with which he passed on to his Company the zeal God had inspired in him to restore the ecclesiastical state to its original purity and splendor. This is how he encouraged them to work in the seminaries to encourage those called to orders and to charges and dignities in the Church, to receive the spirit of Jesus Christ, so necessary for them to fulfill its obligations worthily.

The zeal of Monsieur Vincent was seasoned with a great prudence, and his various occupations and long experience had given him much light. He judged that to profit from seminary training the clerics who followed the program would require a long time if it was to be fruitful. He thought those who aspired to orders ought to spend at least a year in the seminary to purge from their spirits all bad habits they may have contracted in the world, and to strip from their hearts all undue attachment to creatures. They would thereby progress in the knowledge and love of God, to whose service they wished to dedicate themselves. This time would be required to penetrate deeply the truths of Christianity, the maxims of the Gospel which God revealed to us by his Son, and to establish solidly in their hearts the principles of sanctity and perfection through solid resolutions to follow the example of the life and virtues of Jesus Christ.

He believed this extended time was necessary to learn how to make mental prayer well, saying in this regard: "What the sword is to the soldier, mental prayer is to the one dedicated to the service of the altar." This was all the more true, since one of the main functions of the priest was to offer prayer and sacrifice to God.

He thought it best not to exempt any from this seminary experience, even the most virtuous and learned. Besides increasing both these qualities, and so making themselves more worthy of their calling, their presence among the others was most helpful, since generally the example of the strong encourages the weak, and they follow the path of virtue more easily when they see others walking it. He was convinced, too, that by making the rule

---

8. *CED* XI:7-8.

universal he would be saved from the importunities of those seeking exemptions, to their own disadvantage. He referred to the example of the late bishop of Cahors, a perfect model for prelates.[9] He took it as a principle to dispense no one of his diocese from the obligation of attending the seminary before receiving holy orders, and remaining a full year before receiving the subdiaconate, then remaining until they were ordained to the priesthood. This firm policy contributed much to putting his diocese in good condition, as he wrote to Monsieur Vincent some years before his death:

> You would be pleased to see my clergy, and you would bless God a thousand times over if you could realize the good your priests have done in my seminary. Its effects have been felt in the entire province.[10]

To appreciate more fully the great utility of the seminaries by the nature and diversity of the benefits they produced, and the powerful motives Monsieur Vincent had to exhort the priests of the Congregation of the Mission to work at this task with love and fidelity, we give here two summaries. They were written by the directors of seminaries in Paris and in Brittany. From these, we may form a judgment of what occurred in others, as well.

The report from Paris stated:

> (1) The seminary is run like a continuous mission, and we see the same fruits as those we have come to expect in the country places and cities in which the missions are given. For example, those holding benefices and other responsibilities, after leading a disorderly life for a long time in their home territory, now seem to be converted. They shed tears of regret and they ask us to be allowed to admit their sins publicly, and humble themselves on all occasions. When they speak in the conferences, they admit their past blindness, and congratulate their confreres on the opportunity they have to profit from their seminary training. If some longstanding animosities trouble them, they attempt reconciliations by most humble letters to the parties concerned. They restore large sums to the Church when this is called for. In canon law, the fathers of the earliest and even the present centuries often refer to clerics as incorrigible. By the grace of God their amendment, if it occurs, ordinarily happens in the seminary.
>
> (2) Some who have held conflicting benefices for a long time, following the custom in their province, have voluntarily stepped down.

---

9. Blessed Alain de Solminihac. See *CED* VIII:79.
10. *CED* III:343.

(3) Some priests, even elderly ones, have held significant offices, such as abbots, canons, priors, and pastors, or as counselors to Parlement or to presidents. Now, however, they serve willingly as porter, acolyte, thurifer, or cantors, happy to fulfill these humble charges, or regretting not having previously served out of disdain for these lowly offices.

(4) Several who never before bothered to instruct their parishioners, now catechize. When they return home they declare openly, even from the pulpit, and to everyone's amazement, that they have come to recognize their obligations and mean to put them into practice.

(5) Several priests, upon leaving the seminary, have formed small groups of clergy to live in common, and leave their family home, even their birthplaces. They wish thereby to continue their spiritual exercises together, the better to gain others to Jesus Christ and his Church.

(6) We have had several canons of cathedral or collegial churches, who upon their return home, have succeeded with little fanfare to work with others in restoring or sustaining discipline in their churches. We hear of the zeal and prudence with which they speak in open chapter, or in private, of ecclesiastical discipline and the obligations it entails.

(7) Some others have realized the importance of elementary schools, and have undertaken from their own pockets to help them out of pure charity. This has resulted in the great blessing and edification of the villages where this has been done.

(8) We should not fail to mention that God has given the grace to most, nearly all, of persevering in piety and in the worthy fulfillment of their obligations. We have reports of this from all sides.

(9) What is most touching is the innocence of life in the seminary, which has ordinarily made it difficult for the confessors to find enough matter for absolution.[11]

Another priest of the Mission, in charge of a seminary in Brittany,[12] discussed in these words the successes he had seen:

Among the fruits of the seminary training for ecclesiastics has been increased care for the instruction of the people, to which those who were here now apply themselves most seriously. Since they were taught how to preach practically and directly, preachers have

---

11. This report came from Jean Dehorgny, the director of the seminary at Bons Enfants in Paris.
12. Treguier.

multiplied in some dioceses to the extent that where formerly a single one might be available to preach the Lenten sermons to five or six parishes together, three or four preachers are now available. Also, after the sermons the priests are available for confessions, to the great benefit of the country people. Previously, in some places they were fortunate if they had three or four sermons the whole of Lent.

Besides, the clergy devoted to preaching, (1) are more inclined to lead an exemplary life, and (2) are more given to study as a preparation. In this way they save themselves from laziness and a host of other disorders.

Because they preach simply and directly to the people, as they were taught in the seminary, people from five or six of the neighboring parishes come to hear them.

We observe priests acquiring the spirit of zeal in the seminary for the salvation of souls. Not only do they hear confessions assiduously on Sundays and feast-days, but also on weekdays too, something almost unheard of before. The great number of the pastors of the country parishes who had been in the seminary, try to have a priest with them. They hope to continue with greater facility the exercises of piety they observed in the seminary, and so preserve more easily the good resolves they have taken.

There are entire dioceses in which before the establishment of the seminaries it was hard to find a single priest in the country places who dressed in black. Most wore gray, and after their morning mass went to work just like the usual lay person. Since the institution of the seminary, almost all wear at least a short cassock. A large number are in full cassock, with their hair cut short, and their general appearance befitting a priest.

We have seen good benefices given up to allow the priests greater freedom to catechize and hear confessions in the country parishes, where the need is greatest.

There are others who upon leaving the seminary worked chiefly at inspiring this same zeal in rural priests. Sometimes, up to fifty of these priests live in a single parish, apart from one another, a league or more from the church. An attempt was made to bring them together gently once a week for a spiritual conference, not only for these poorly prepared priests, but also for the sick poor whom they help in their illnesses.

We have seen many rural priests much taken with the good example of those who came from the seminary. They made many changes in their own lives, and this edified the entire diocese. Some came from as far away as twenty-five leagues to make a retreat, to solidify their good resolutions.

Ordinarily, the clergy of the country assemble now on the vigil of a feast to plan the liturgy, so it will be celebrated with greater devotion and edification for the people. They write to us for suggestions about this, showing the appreciation they have had for the divine offices since the establishment of the seminary.

In some nearby dioceses, catechism never used to be taught, but now there is practically none in which it not taught well, and most devotedly.

Before finishing this chapter we should not fail to mention that Monsieur Vincent was not satisfied to give instructions and all possible spiritual help to those in the seminary of the Bons Enfants which was the responsibility of his Congregation. Besides that, he saw to it during these first years that some who were unable to pay their board but who gave promise of profiting from the exercises there, were supported by the Congregation, aided by gifts and alms from others.

Monsieur Vincent's goodness inspired other pious persons to contribute to other seminaries as a help to needy students. Among others, a noted and pious priest sent over the space of ten or twelve years a large sum each year to the seminary of Troyes in Champagne, and to Annecy in Savoy, for the support of poor students.[13] This enabled them to be prepared for useful service to the Church in their dioceses. No doubt such alms were agreeable to God, especially because such good results could be hoped for from them, for the glory of God and the good of his Church. A good priest is capable of doing such good that this led Monsieur Vincent to say several times: "What a great thing to be a priest! What can he not accomplish! But, with the grace of God, who can say what he can do?[14]

---

13. Monsieur Chomel, the vicar general of the diocese of Saint Flour. He came from Lyons, and was a councillor at the Paris Parlement. He had been a student of Monsieur Vincent at Bons Enfants, and he later supported with his zeal and fortune the works of the saint, and several houses of the Congregation, particularly those at Lyons, Troyes, Annecy, Angers, and Saint Flour.
14. *CED* XI:7.

CHAPTER SIX

Delinquents and Disturbed Persons at Saint Lazare

AFTER DISCUSSING the missions in Chapter One of Book Two, we spoke in the four following chapters of the four great works which Monsieur Vincent, fortified by the spirit of God, labored at with such zeal and blessing for the service of the ecclesiastical state. We refer to the ordination exercises, the clerical conferences, spiritual retreats, and the seminaries. We may call them four mystic rivers. They flow from the same source and continue flowing to water and nourish the garden of the Church. We will now turn to those other activities he undertook, moved by this same Spirit, who extended his influence far and wide.

We will begin with one that might seem the least esteemed in the eyes of men, but very useful to the general welfare of society. Also, it is most precious in the sight of God, since humility and charity are virtues most pleasing to him. In this work they shine forth in a special way. This humble and charitable work of which we speak, adopted by Monsieur Vincent from his first days at Saint Lazare, was to receive at Saint Lazare two special sorts of persons. The first concerned delinquents who had become the sorrow of their parents by their unruly behavior, the disgrace and ruin of their families by their association with bad company. They were often given to all sorts of vice, licentiousness, and debauchery, and ended miserably.

Their families used every effort to bring them back to reason, but finally decided the only recourse was to deprive them of the liberty they had used so poorly. They were shut up in Saint Lazare, with the consent of the local magistrates at the charge of their parents. They were not allowed to see anyone from outside, except with the consent of those who had committed them. Their fate was not divulged to anyone, except to those obliged to look after them. The brothers of the Congregation took charge of their physical needs, while the priests cared for their spiritual needs. The brothers took care of their meals and other exterior wants. The priests visited, consoled, and exhorted them to change their way of acting, to abandon vice, and to give themselves to good and to virtue.

The priests pointed out the evil consequences of a disorderly life, both in this life and the next, and the corresponding advantages of honor and salvation to obedient sons, of wise men who feared the Lord. Their isolated and humble condition helped to open their eyes to their state, as did the good spiritual reading given them.

These delinquents were usually confined until some signs of a true conversion appeared in them, such as a disposition to live better and behave themselves more reasonably in the future. Even so, before leaving they had to attend spiritual exercises, to prepare themselves for making a good general confession, and to receive worthily the sacred body of Jesus Christ in communion. Several managed to lead a good Christian life, and employed their time well. Some profited from this stay at Saint Lazare so much that upon their release they rose in the legal profession to judgeships or other offices of importance, and with the grace of God, succeeded well.

Let us hear a priest of singular piety, well informed on these matters:

> I have always considered it as an illustration of the great graces given by God to this saintly man that the late Monsieur Vincent in his zeal opened the doors of his house at Saint Lazare to all sorts of persons, to win them for God. This included debauched and incorrigible young men, to the great relief of their parents, who otherwise would have had no place to send them. He received them and treated them with such respect and consideration that they were soon living almost like religious, in a building of their own, following a regular program of activities. Some profited so much that upon leaving, they went to monasteries to embrace the religious life.

Besides these delinquent youths, others at Saint Lazare were mentally deranged. These were a burden on their parents and a shame to their families, but Saint Lazare was without doubt doing a great service to the public. At a reasonable cost, these delinquents could be housed, fed, and cared for with great charity. Monsieur Vincent took special care of the delinquents and for the mentally disturbed who were in his care as superior of Saint Lazare. This is how he once spoke to his community on this matter:

> I recommend to the prayers of the Company the boarders we have here, both those troubled in mind, and those not. Among others, there is a priest who was in some mental difficulty, but recovered. Unfortunately, he has relapsed once again. This difficulty comes from an excess of black bile, which sends acrid vapors to his brain. He is so weak that he falls victim to this disorder. This poor man feels his sickness coming on (as he told me himself). It begins always with a deep depression which he finds he cannot overcome. Those in this condition surely deserve our compassion. They are certainly not capable of sinning, for they are not in command of themselves, and have neither judgment or freedom. They should be happy if they are stricken while in the state of grace. If on the contrary they should happen to be in a state of mortal sin, they are greatly to be pitied.

The others here, who have their faculties but who use them poorly, give me the opportunity to remark there are many rebellious and debauched youth in the world today. A short while ago an official of a sovereign court[1] complained to me of a nephew of his. He is an unruly young man who several times threatened to kill him if he did not give him some money. When a judge in the city suggested he be sent to Saint Lazare, where he would be taught his duty, he stated he had no idea we took such people here. He thought there ought to be four such places in Paris like Saint Lazare to take care of all who should be confined.

We must thank God, gentlemen, for confiding the care of the mentally ill and the delinquents to the care of this Community. We did not seek this service. It was given us by God in his Providence, just as he has given us everything else in our Company. I must tell you that when we first came here, the prior was caring for two or three mentally disturbed people. As we took over the house, these persons became our responsibility. In those days there was a lawsuit that would decide whether we would have to leave Saint Lazare or not. I remember wondering what, if we had to leave here, would most bother me about it and what would most displease me. It seemed to me then, it would be losing the opportunity to care for and serve these poor unfortunate people whom we had inherited when we came.

My brothers, it is no small thing, as some think, to take care of the afflicted, for this is pleasing to God. Yes, it is one of those services most pleasing to him, this taking care of the mentally deranged, because there is little natural satisfaction in it. It is done quietly, for even those we serve are hardly aware of what we do for them. Let us pray God to give the priests of the Company a taste for this sort of work when they are assigned to it, and that he strengthen our poor brothers and help them by his grace in the work and care they expend for our boarders. Some are sick in body, the others sick in mind; some are dull, and others flighty; some are insane, and others vicious. In a word, all have needs, but the one group through infirmity, the other through vice. The one group of boarders come here in the hope of a bodily cure. The other group is sent here to amend their evil ways.

Have courage then, my brothers. Did you know that in former times there were popes who cared for animals? Yes, in the times of the emperors who persecuted the Christians in their head and in the

---

1. A general name for a court of last resort.

members, they forced the pope to look after the lions, leopards, and other such beasts kept for the amusement of the unbelieving princes. These beasts were fitting images of their own cruelty! The popes took care of these beasts. The men you have charge of are certainly not animals, but in a way they are worse than animals because of their debauchery.

God willed these saintly persons, the fathers of all Christians, to experience these humble and extraordinary trials to make them sympathetic to the abject sufferings of their spiritual sons and daughters. When anyone has endured weaknesses or suffering himself, he is so much more sensitive to the troubles of others. Those who have lost their belongings, their health, or their honor, are much better prepared to console others in trouble than those who have not experienced these losses themselves.

I recall someone telling me once of a great and saintly person, a man of a strong and steady disposition. He was gifted in mind, feared no one, and was hardly ever tempted. For all that, however, he found it difficult to support the weak, console the sorrowful, and help the sick, for he had never experienced these things himself.

You are aware that our Savior took all miseries upon himself. "We have a high priest," Saint Paul says, "who knows how to sympathize with our weaknesses, for he has experienced them himself."[2] Yes, O Eternal Wisdom, you took all our poverty upon your innocent self! You must know, gentlemen, that he did that to sanctify all the afflictions to which we are subject, and to serve as the prototype of all states and conditions of humankind.

O my Savior, you who are Wisdom uncreated, you have accepted and welcomed our miseries, our confusions, our humiliations, our infirmities, save only ignorance and sin. You willed to be a scandal to the Jews, and foolishness to the Gentiles. You even allowed yourself to appear as a fool, yes, our Lord permitted himself to be regarded as insane, for it is reported in the Gospel that some felt he had become mad. *Exierunt tenere eum; et dicebant quoniam in furorem versus est* ["They came to take charge of him, saying, He is out of his mind"].[3] The apostles themselves sometimes looked upon him as giving way to anger, for he appeared so to them, leading them to declare he had compassion on all our infirmities, and sanctified all our afflictions and weaknesses. He thus taught them, and us also, to be compassionate toward those who suffer these same afflictions.

---

2. Hbr 4:14.
3. Mark 3:21.

Let us bless God, gentlemen and my brothers, and thank him for having called us to care for these poor people, deprived of sense or of right conduct. In serving them we become abundantly aware of the extent and variety of human misery. We become better able to serve our neighbor, for we will better fulfill our obligations to them if we know from personal experience what they suffer. I beg of those in this service to our boarders to continue with much care for them. I beg the Company to pray often to God for them, and to appreciate any occasion you have to exercise your patience and charity toward these poor people.[4]

Perhaps some would say, Monsieur, we have plenty of other work without taking on this. Indeed, we have nothing in our rule about receiving the mentally deranged at Saint Lazare, or those other troubled spirits who can be such little devils.

To this I would reply that our rule must be the example of our Lord, who willed to be surrounded by lunatics, demoniacs, the crazy, the tempted, and the possessed. These people were brought to him from everywhere to be delivered and cured, which he did with great goodness. Why then would we be blamed if we attempted to do the same thing that he found so fitting? If he received the outcasts and possessed, why should we not do so too? We do not go out looking for these people, they are brought to us. Who knows whether his Providence might not wish to use us to cure the ills of these poor people. The Savior was so sympathetic that he seemed to be numbered among them, as I just mentioned. O my Savior and my God, give us the grace to look on these things in the same light in which you saw them.[5]

A priest, an official of the house, one day reported to Monsieur Vincent that one of the delinquents seemed to be making no progress in reformation, although he had been in the house a long time. He felt it would be better if the boy were returned to his parents, rather than that he be kept any longer. He was threatening to do harm, and he was bound to do something bad, sooner or later.

Monsieur Vincent quickly silenced the priest:

You must recall, Monsieur, that the main reason we have taken these boarders into our house is to exercise our charity toward them. Now will you tell me, is it not a great charity to keep this man? If he were let go, he would simply cause trouble to his parents all over again. He was sent here with permission of the courts, for he is a

---

4. *CED* XI:20-24. Abelly adds the following section from another conference.
5. *CED* XII:88.

bad influence they could do nothing with. He was sent here to give a bit of peace in their family, and to see if God would use us to bring about his conversion. To release him now, in his present disposition, would be to cause trouble in his family all over again. For the moment they are enjoying some respite from his evil ways. His threats must not be taken too seriously, for by the grace of God no harm has come to the Company because of him, and we hope none will come in the future. Remember, Monsieur, this boy blames his father and mother for his being here. He knows they sent him, and not us.

Monsieur Vincent often asked his community to pray to God for this undertaking, and for those who worked in caring for the boarders. One day he said, "Otherwise, God will punish us. Yes, we could expect his curse to fall upon the house of Saint Lazare if we neglected the care we should show to these poor people. I recommend above all that we should feed them well, at least as well as we do our own community."[6]

The prayers and charitable concern of this gentle priest for these men lacking in either their behavior or their judgment gained the consolation of seeing many happy results of his care. The public noticed the improvements in a certain number of these boarders. Besides the relief enjoyed by the families in seeing these persons cared for at Saint Lazare, protected from the dangers or the temptations of the world, some were converted from their evil passions, such as drunkenness, impurity, or other serious failings. After a certain time at Saint Lazare, some acquired an abhorrence of these vices, chose to renounce their life of debauchery, and began to live wisely and circumspectly. Several joined the more austere religious orders to lead a life of penance as reparation for past failings. Others joined other communities devoted to the service of God and the neighbor. Still others became secular priests, or undertook public service as laymen. Lastly, some entered the business world or other secular pursuits, where they began and continue to live exemplary lives.

Some left off their stealing, their assaults, their blasphemies or other horrible crimes, and by the mercy of God were converted, and have since lived virtuously. Among others, one, who became a religious, returned often to Saint Lazare to express his appreciation for what had been done for him.

Others had stolen from their own homes, and hidden their spoils in a secluded spot. These had freely and frankly revealed where they had hidden their ill-gotten goods, out of sorrow for the trouble they had caused their parents, and with a resolve to amend themselves.

Some so forgot themselves as to have struck their parents, both father and

---

6. *CED XI:331.*

mother. Some others had even attacked their parents, or had threatened to kill them. Upon leaving Saint Lazare they appeared in tears before them, begging forgiveness for their crime, and in future lived up to their good resolutions.

Several young men who had forsaken their schoolbooks for a life of debauchery were committed to this school of penance. Afterward, they returned to their regular classes with much success.

It is extraordinary that several had almost a complete change of heart when they were sent to Saint Lazare. The charitable care they experienced enabled them to leave in an entirely different frame of mind, as good as new. They are today good members of society.

All these good things happened with a large number of people, most of whom came from the upper classes of society, and this over thirty years or more. It seemed that God was pleased, and is still pleased, to grant his mercy and grace through the mediation and charity of his servant, Vincent de Paul. In imitation of Jesus Christ he consorted with sinners and the weak to hasten their cure of both soul and body. Monsieur Vincent could well be called, as a distinguished person once did, the "refuge of sinners." But at this the humble priest protested that this name belonged to the Son of God alone, and to his merciful mother.[7]

---

7. As in the Litany of Loreto, recited in honor of Mary.

CHAPTER SEVEN

The Help Given by Monsieur Vincent to the Convents of the Religious of the Visitation of the Blessed Virgin Mary of the Diocese of Paris While He Was Their Superior and Father

THE HELP and services which the religious of the order of the Visitation of Saint Mary of the diocese of Paris received from Monsieur Vincent for the thirty-eight years he was their superior and spiritual father deserve to have a place in this second book. This work not only shows the extent of his charity but also how enlightened he was from on high in discerning spiritual matters, and what prudence, meekness, firmness and other excellent virtues he possessed for the guidance of others.

We do not intend to give more space to this than it deserves, but simply to report what we have garnered from some reports furnished us, mostly from religious of this holy order.

Blessed Francis de Sales, bishop of Geneva, founder of this order of the Visitation of Saint Mary, and the Venerable Jane Frances Fremiot, foundress and first superior of this order, and superior of the first convent of the Visitation in the city of Paris, learned and recognized the rare qualities of Monsieur Vincent as a wise and saintly director. They earnestly besought him to accept the office as superior and spiritual father of the houses of this holy institute in Paris.[1] Also in 1622 the late Cardinal de Retz, then bishop of Paris, asked him to accept this office and take over the direction of these virtuous women.[2]

The venerable mother, their foundress, soon realized the gift God had given in the person of this worthy superior. She developed such an appreciation for him that she turned nowhere else for advice in the management and progress of her institute. Her successors in office did the same, not seeking guidance elsewhere except from him. This resulted in great blessings from God, for preserving union and regularity for the community, and for the progress of the individual religious and the spread of their houses.

A second convent opened soon after, and a third soon followed. The one

---

1. In 1619, Saint Jane Frances Fremiot de Chantal arrived in Paris from Bourges with three sisters to found the first monastery of the Visitation in Paris. Saint Vincent's relationship with the Order of the Visitation began then and continued until his death. The first monastery was established in the Hotel du Petit Bourbon on the rue de la Cerisaie. In 1628, the sisters purchased another residence, on the rue Saint Antoine, not far from their first monastery. Saint Vincent served as the director of these houses in Paris.
2. See *CED* XIII:84-85.

was situated in the faubourg Saint Jacques, and the other in the village of Saint Denis. Monsieur Vincent, directed them both, and God funneled his graces as abundantly through him as he had done for the first convent. After some time the convent of Saint Jacques led to yet another convent in Paris, situated on the rue Montorgueil. It too came under Monsieur Vincent's direction with equally happy results. In this way, he was responsible for these four convents up to the time of his death, in all thirty-eight years of service to this institute. He acted with so many blessings and successes that from the first two of the houses in Paris about twenty others have come in various cities of the kingdom. The daughters of this wise superior spread the good odor of their virtues and testify to the spirit of their blessed founder. They thereby attract many other women to the service of their divine Spouse.

Blessed Francis de Sales had met Monsieur Vincent in Paris several times. He said he had met no one so wise and virtuous as Monsieur Vincent. The late Monsieur Coqueret, doctor of theology of the faculty of Paris, at the college of Navarre, reported that he had heard this judgment himself from the lips of the bishop.[3] This blessed prelate was called to heaven soon after he had confided the direction of the daughters of the Visitation in Paris to Monsieur Vincent. He was happy to have put in his capable hands the pious enterprise he valued more than any other he had accomplished.

The venerable mother superior survived Blessed Francis by nearly twenty years. Because she was obliged to travel on business affairs and for the general good of her Congregation, she often wrote to Monsieur Vincent. She placed herself and her institute under his guidance, and received great light and consolation from him. In November 1627, while he was away working on a mission, she wrote him about her interior state. This shows the confidence she had in this wise counselor, and we report it here for the edification of the Christian reader:

> You are working, my dear father, in the province of Lyons and so we will be deprived for a long time of seeing you. We have nothing to say when God acts, except to bless him in everything, which I do, my dear father. I take the liberty you have given me to speak my confidences to you, and I do so simply. I made four days of the retreat, not more, because of some business matters which came up. I recognized that I must work at the virtues of humility, and of care for the neighbor. These are virtues I chose last year, and our Lord has given me the grace to practice them to some extent, but I owe all to him. He will help me again, if it pleases him, since he provides me so many opportunities to practice them.
>
> As to my inner state, I think I am in the frame of mind to accept

---

3. Jean Coqueret, 1592-1655, a friend and counselor of Monsieur Vincent.

whatever God will ask of me. I have no desires or goals. Nothing matters but to let God direct my steps. I do not yet see where I am being led, but in the depths of my soul I am ready. I have no agenda or plan. I do at the moment what seems needed, without troubling myself about the future.

Often, in the lower part of my soul there is revolt, which causes me much suffering, but I realize that in patience I shall possess my soul. Also, I have much annoyance in my responsibilities, for my spirit is not adapted to action, and being compelled to act in necessities, my body and spirit are beaten down. On the other hand, my imagination troubles me greatly during the spiritual exercises, to my chagrin. God also allows many exterior difficulties so that nothing in this life pleases me except the will of God who wants me here. I ask you most earnestly to beg that God may have mercy on me. On my part I shall pray, as I do with all my heart, that he will strengthen you in the role he has assigned to you.[4]

In another letter, written about several matters, she began in this way:

May I never experience any other emotion but sorrow if I forget the charity you showed me the day of your departure. My heart is consoled in difficulties and strengthened in the troubles it meets, coming from whatever quarter. I prostrate myself in spirit at your feet, asking pardon for the pain I caused you by my lack of mortification, now embracing lovingly the humiliations which come to me. To whom can I reveal my weaknesses but to you, my dear father, who understands so well? I hope that in your goodness you will not grow weary of me.[5]

During her visit to Annecy, in some hope of seeing Monsieur Vincent, she write to him as follows:

Alas, my true and dear father, would it be possible for God to give me the grace to meet you in this region? This would be the greatest consolation I could receive in this world. This would be for me, I dare say, a special gift of God's mercy for my soul. It would be greatly consoled in relief of an interior trial I have borne for more than four years, in a sort of martyrdom.[6]

Monsieur Vincent visited the houses in Paris and Saint Denis from time

---

4. *CED* I:34-35.
5. *CED* I:313-14.
6. *CED* II:53. This took place in 1640. The complications which arose in the work with the foundlings made it impossible for Vincent to make the trip mentioned in the letter. In the following year, Jane de Chantal visited Paris. She saw Vincent for spiritual direction for the last time during this visit. This visit restored the inner peace of Jane Frances, who had been experiencing a long period of spiritual suffering. She died in December 1641.

to time to look to their general progress, and to the welfare of each individual religious. He sought to lift them up from falls common to humanity, and to encourage them in perfection. He displayed such humility, recollection, prudence, and charity that he was evidently led by the spirit of God. He acted so prudently among the sisters that they would clearly see that his ardent zeal was a fruit of the Holy Spirit working in him. This made his visits profitable and successful. The community seemed anointed with his devotion, filled with the desire to strive for perfection, but an effective and firm desire appeared in the various spiritual exercises of these religious. He stimulated their love of their vocation, and led them to embrace the spirit of their holy institute. He inspired them especially with the maxims of the Gospel and the precepts of their blessed founder contained in their rules and constitutions. He drew from this source the good advice he gave, and the practices he recommended, knowing that this fidelity to rule was the secret of the perfection of their state.

He strongly recommended the other writings of their blessed founder and of their worthy mother foundress, for which he had such a high opinion. His esteem for these writings was so marked that he could never read them without being moved. He was seen to be in tears while reading the book *Responses* by the venerable foundress, from which we cite the extract of a letter written to her devoted superior in September 1631.[7]

> You are always admirable in your humility, from which I always receive such special consolation. I am especially pleased to hear of your satisfaction in your visit to our house in the faubourg. The superior has written also, saying she and the sisters were most pleased with your visit. Blessed be God, praised and glorified always. May he give our dear father a glorious crown for his troubles and the charity he shows in dealing with our sisters. Alas, my dear father, how good you are. I was convinced of this in seeing the tears you shed in reading our recent *Responses*.[8]

After citing these letters of the venerable mother foundress, we will turn to others written by the older and principal religious of the convents of this holy order at Paris. They knew Monsieur Vincent particularly well.

> We can say with assurance that several times almost miraculous things occurred during his visits or immediately after. From the first time he came, he set free one of our sisters from a troubled mind that was so strong it affected her whole body, making it impossible for her to give any service to the convent. She aroused the sympathy

---

7. *Réponses... sur les Règles, Constitutions et Coustumiers de notre Ordre de la Visitation*, Paris, 1632.
8. *CED* I:121-22.

of all who saw her, but since her cure she has been able to exercise various offices for several years, including that of mistress of novices, and even superior. At length, by the grace of God she died peacefully.

Several other religious troubled by pains and serious temptations found they were entirely delivered in speaking of their difficulties to this charitable father. Others had a decided change in conduct by the help of the abundant grace which flowed from him. In fact, all were renewed at each of his visits, and walked more joyfully on the road to perfection than ever before. We might add that his blessings extended even to temporal things following his visits.

The special graces this humble servant of God had received to enlighten, console, and strengthen souls was seen on several occasions, especially in regard to the late Mother Helene Angelique Lhuillier.[9] She was led to God through the severe interior trials she endured. She was severely troubled by various extreme ailments of body and soul, but she found no relief, after God, except in this dear father, who had such a gift of consoling tortured souls. On one occasion, when it was thought that perhaps he was being bothered too much, he said that he deemed nothing more important than to be of service to someone in this sad state. He spoke agreeably to these suffering ones, often using light and joyous expressions to divert them from their sadness and sorrow.

His charity for the consolation of his neighbor was a source of much suffering for him, when his own infirmities prevented him from attending the sick religious who asked him to visit. He was not satisfied to offer some words of consolation to those in difficulty. He did all he could to alleviate their sufferings. One day a domestic sister, whose virtue he much appreciated, took sick and developed a high fever. She said she was at peace and ready to die. "O my sister," he replied, "your time has not yet come." He made the sign of the cross upon her forehead, and at the instant the fever left her, and she later experienced neither fever nor pains.

As he had experienced all the facets of human existence himself, infirmities, humiliations, and temptations, he would console those in similar circumstances by saying he had come through the same, and God had delivered him, and would do the same for them. "Have patience," he would say, "accept whatever is the good pleasure of God, and meanwhile, use this or that remedy." Once a good domestic sister mentioned she was too rustic to apply herself to spiritual

---

9. 1592-1655, several times superior of the Visitation in Paris and Chaillot.

things, because in her own region she had looked after the animals on her father's farm. He said to her, "My sister, this is the first thing I did myself—I looked after the pigs. But if this serves to humble us, we will be all the better prepared for the service of God: Courage!"

Another sister spoke of a temptation which troubled her. He took the occasion to tell her that he had experienced a similar temptation for several years, but this never gave him matter to confess. He thereby made her realize the distinction between temptation and sin, and that she should not be concerned, for she had not consented in any way. He spoke of this about himself despite his great care never to speak of the graces God conferred upon himself, unless it clearly benefited someone else, as in this instance.

He did not think it useful or expedient that the religious should have too frequent or too familiar communications with superiors. If some wished to speak with him and he saw no great necessity, he would make them wait a long time to oblige them to weigh well what they were to say.

He used to say one thing to be avoided at all costs was for the religious to instigate petty intrigues against the rule of the mother superiors. This had harmed many, and ruined many houses. If one or several religious complained of the superior, he would look into the matter carefully, and judge prudently if it was a natural impulse or motivated by a true zeal. If he found the complaint justified, he would provide a remedy and speak to the superior about it. He would never align himself with malcontents against their superior, but would seek to excuse her, if he could do so in justice, to maintain her reputation and authority, knowing that this was necessary for the smooth running of the community.

He was most concerned that the houses in Paris and the others founded by them be careful of the clergy who visited, lest they be infected with the new opinions prevalent in clerical circles. "For," he said, "those who have adopted a false doctrine strive to spread it everywhere. They do not immediately show their hand. They are wolves which come meekly into the sheepfold to ravage and destroy."

On his advice the late Mother Helene Angelique Lhuillier, superior of the first convent in Paris, refused a large sum of money from a noble lady. She had offered it to the community for her retirement, but on condition that on occasion several Jansenists would be allowed to come visit her at the grille.[10]

---

10. Anne Hurault de Cheverny, a widow from the second marriage of the marquis of Aumont.

When a religious or a group of religious would request his blessing, he would fall to his knees, recollect himself, and convey the sense of his own unworthiness and the majesty of God. He would say a devout and touching word or two, invoking a blessing upon the work and their person, always with some word of encouragement.

Despite his incomparable meekness, he still was firm in facing up to serious failings, but his prudence dictated that he await the proper moment for his corrections to be well received. Once he was asked to rebuke a young woman for some fault she had. He responded: "You give medicine to those with a fever only in cases of great necessity," for she was not yet disposed to accept this remedy. He taught the superiors to use their admonitions with much circumspection and charity if they were to be helpful. For himself, he acted so when he had to give penances, for evidently it would have been easier for him to do the penance himself than to impose it on others.

He once met a group of religious, who, in a spirit of holy liberty, criticized those more exact in their observance of the rule. He quickly put an end to their pretensions. He made them see that only in the mastery of their passions found in perfect mortification would they attain the perfect liberty they sought.

He had a marvelous facility to bring down the haughty without their being aware of what was happening. His zeal was reserved even more for those who disobeyed in something serious. He would reprimand them so severely they would be humbled, and would think of what it would be like before God on the day of his fearsome judgment, since the word of a mere man abased and humiliated them so severely.

He was beyond compare in supporting the weaknesses of others, whether of soul or body. His very presence commanded respect, but rather than repel, hearts opened up to him. No one inspired greater confidence than he, or received the most secret thoughts or the weaknesses most difficult to disclose. He supported and excused everyone, like a tender mother making excuses for her child.

One of the most enlightened and capable of the mother superiors of the entire order excused herself from speaking of Monsieur Vincent, for her house had already sent several reports from the other sisters.[11] She added this:

Since what has already been written says what I had in mind, I

---

11. Probably Marie Henriette de Rochechouart.

find I can add little. I would not want to speak in generalities, however admirable, and only of what his profound humility could not hide. As to certain particular events, I am sure you have already received accounts of those. I prefer to honor the silence I observed in him on a thousand occasions, to our great admiration. I often marveled at the depth of his mind, hardly ever leaving his presence without sensing my own superficiality, seeing him penetrate to depths I could scarcely follow. By the grandeur of the lights I saw in him, which he revealed only by degrees, I felt the poorest and most incapable person in the world.

He inspired in hearts a confidence that led people to speak to him of the most painful things, but this confidence was coupled with a most profound respect for him. His words had a marvelous effect upon the soul, whether to calm those in trouble or put others at peace.

His tolerance for the failings of others was extreme, but this did not detract from his firmness. He held to the exact balance when forced to correct someone. If he could be said to lean to one side more than the other, it was always on the side of those two great virtues, humility and charity, which he held so dear. I have fallen into the very pit I wanted to avoid, for I speak from the abundance of my heart, which preserved for this saintly man greater esteem, love, and respect than can be expressed or imagined.

Monsieur Vincent was without human respect. He stood firm for the interests of God and for the spiritual good of the religious houses he was responsible for, despite any objections or temporal disadvantages he was threatened with. This was particularly shown by the way he handled requests for visitation rights, often from noble women, even from princesses. Some of these were curious about what went on in these communities, or out of devotion wished to pass some hours with the sisters. Some, whether of high or low estate, who had run into some misfortune, felt they had a right to be received. He generally but politely refused all such unjustified requests, explaining the reasons he could not accord this permission, sometimes using conscience as his argument. Some ladies were granted this privilege. Occasionally he gathered the superiors and principal sisters of the convents to see which ones were founders or major benefactors of the religious, and who had a right to such visitations. Once they established this list, he had it put in writing and made it a rule to exclude all others. The religious were forbidden to go against this list, because when they made exceptions, the grand ladies refused entrance complained. He feared greatly that the spirit of the world would penetrate the convents. He feared that after these ladies left they would leave the religious less devoted for having seen and spoken with secular persons, who often displayed their vanity in the cloister and even during the exercises of piety.

He was firm even in dealing with the queen mother of the king, while still respecting the honor due Her Majesty. She wanted one of her ladies of honor to be received in the original Paris convent. When he had to refuse such requests, he never hid behind the religious, but spoke up himself in their place and for them.[12] A noblewoman to whom he had refused entrance to the Saint Denis monastery in turn refused him permission to conduct missions on her lands. In 1658 he received word that Madame Payen, the mother-in-law of Monsieur de Lyonne was at the gate of the monastery on the rue Saint Antoine demanding that she be allowed to enter to see the dying granddaughter of the minister. Vincent responded: "I am the very humble servant of Madame Payen, and I very much desire to be at her service, but my rule is to permit no such visits. I have refused Madame de Nemours, Madame de Longueville, and the Princess de la Carignan. They have never forgiven me and what would they say if they were to learn I had made an exception? To do anything else would go against my conscience."[13] On other matters, he preferred that nothing extraordinary be done if it were a matter of some consequence, without first seeking the advice of the superiors and councillors, so as to act in union with them and with a common understanding. Even then, his chief recourse was the oracle of truth, for before responding to any proposition he would seek the guidance of the Spirit of God within himself. In seeing his evident recollection the sisters accepted his advice as a light from heaven. His frequent practice of beginning his remarks by his customary words *In nomine Domini* ["In the name of the Lord"] emphasized this view.

If we put down here in detail everything written in the reports of these good sisters in praise of their superior, this chapter would be far too long. We will simply append to what we have already said some remarks sent by the religious of the convent at Saint Denis.

> His behavior always seemed to us to be so unselfish, looking always to the glory of God alone, in everything he did.
>
> From the moment he recognized something as the will of God he would be thoroughly committed to it, saying with a marvelous serenity, "In all things we must believe in his divine Providence."
>
> In the advice he gave upon matters presented to him, he acted with great prudence and with a judgment so profound and enlightened that no circumstance escaped his notice. This became evident

---

12. Vincent's refusal to allow these visits resulted in some rancor and opposition.
13. See *CED* VII:476.

in several complicated matters referred to several enlightened persons, and even to some learned doctors, but the questions remained unresolved. After Monsieur Vincent had recourse to this worthy father, he wrote with such clarity and justice, penetrating to the heart of the question, that we were able to arrange the solution without harming the community or failing in charity for our neighbors. This caused several people to remark that only the Spirit of God could provide such an equitable discernment to satisfy all parties. Also whatever the question, he would never give an answer before entering into himself, seemingly invoking the grace of the Holy Spirit.

We were always pleased with his way of acting, recognizing the fullness of God in him, and the evangelical spirit in his calm yet persistent zeal, on fire for the glory of God. He had a mild persistence in maintaining the observance of our rule. He often asked if we had failed in any one of them, and spoke of our blessed founder and worthy mother to encourage us to their faithful practice. He gave as much attention to the smallest observance as to those of greater moment. He never used his own authority to introduce any change in the rule. On the contrary, he attempted to confirm and maintain it.

We had a good example of his edifying firmness in his efforts to preserve the exact observance of the cloister, despite any human consideration or selfish interest. He refused entry even to influential people whose position and wealth could have benefited both him and us financially. He preferred the incomparable good of our solitude to all the vain hopes of the world.

In his own visitations he spared no pain to make them useful, doing everything with thoroughness, serenity, and attention. He had a kindness reflecting the spirit of God, listening to the newest novice of the house with the same patience as he did for the oldest religious. When he reproved any faults, he prepared and disposed the minds of those concerned with such charity and meekness that the grace of his words was remembered long after the sting of the correction, so great was his gift of leading souls to God.

To know and recognize our faults, he used to have us enter into judgment with God (to use his way of speaking) and with ourselves. He used to say the lightest faults were serious, considering the designs of God and his expectations of us.

We noticed that although extreme charity and understanding always accompanied his admonitions, when it was a question of failings in reciting the divine office he seemed to take on a new personality. His holy zeal moved him to speak with such vigor and strength that it impressed on our hearts the fear and respect for the majesty of God, as one who dwelt in unspeakable glory. He wanted even the least ceremonial directives to be observed, saying that God directed his people to preserve his rites and his commands. He threatened those who failed to observe the rites just as he did against those who disobeyed the law. He suggested that we read our rule and directories often, as well as what pertained to our institute. He wanted us to imitate the Israelites, who after their captivity, wept tears of contrition while reading the law, at the remembrance of their failures in observing it.

During his visits he recommended union with our superiors, but it should be, he said, union of hearts, deferring to their wishes even in indifferent matters. He recommended respect and cordiality among us, especially for the older sisters, in whom we were to honor the Ancient of Days. When reproving us for any failure in charity, he would recall the spirit of meekness of our founder. He taught us to honor the silence of the divine Word upon earth by our own silence. He said we were to give ourselves to God by a perfect practice of obedience to God, to our rule and to our superiors. Since we had vowed obedience, we had surrendered our own personal direction.

He wanted an account of the visit to be composed, which should be read from time to time in chapter. "This reading will attract the grace of God upon you," and in fact it did give us the blessing of renewing the dispositions of fervor, exactitude, and recollection that we had experienced in the visits.

He led the houses he directed to a great simplicity and perfect self-denial. He taught us to avoid all show, all love of creatures, and everything that would lead the religious to have communication with lay persons. He made us see the blessing it was to be located outside Paris, separated from high society. He urged us to shun all curiosities, such as books and meetings with spiritual persons possibly tainted with the dangerous opinions of the day. He counseled us to confine our reading to the writings of our blessed father, for whom he had a special veneration.

In this spirit of self-denial he respectfully refused the request of the Ursuline sisters who lived next door to break through the wall separating the two communities. The reason for the request, which had been approved by their ecclesiastical superior, was blood sisters in the two communities, and the communities themselves, might visit. He told us "Religious are dead to the world, and should no longer even recognize their own relatives."

He spoke little, but we realized that one of his words had greater effect than entire sermons, through the spirit of God which spoke through him and the respect we had for his holiness. A sister told us that when she made her confession to him, he said in four words just what she needed to hear in her troubled state. That astonished her as much as it satisfied her.

To another sister he counseled the exercise of the presence of God. He mentioned that since adopting this practice he had never done anything in secret he would not have wanted to be known on the public square. He said, "The presence of God ought to have greater influence over our minds than the presence of every living creature of the whole world, assembled together."

From a large number of examples of his charity from which we might choose, we select one from when time was so valuable to him, near the end of his life, when he was weighed down with infirmities and cares. He came here several times to speak with the poor extern sister who was asking to be dispensed from her vows so she could marry. This holy man felt in making the change she would put her salvation in danger. He presented reasons why she should remain in such a touching way it could have softened a heart of steel.

He treated matters of charity with such care that there never was the least hint of self-interest. When it became necessary to reveal a fault of someone in the interests of truth, he made a special effort to seek out the good qualities of the person, to erase any bad impression that had been formed.

He was most serene in handling business matters, to which he gave all the time necessary to understand them thoroughly. His equanimity of disposition made him accessible to all, even allowing him to amuse the sick and afflicted persons he dealt with, for whom he had an incomparable charity. His generous nature accommodated itself to their weaknesses whether of body or mind. It could be said of him, with Saint Paul, that he made himself all to all, to gain all to God.

His deference and respect for all sorts of persons was admirable. His efforts to speak only good of everyone was equaled only by his habit of speaking poorly of himself as a sinner and lowering himself in the sight of all, for the greater glory of God and the edification of the neighbor.

These are the testimonials about their superior from the religious of the Visitation, or at least the principal ones they sent. For the sake of brevity we have left out some others containing some spiritual advice Monsieur Vincent gave to these religious on various occasions, either in general or in particular cases. These generally dealt with the virtues most suitable for them. They were, especially, the union and charity that should reign among them, obedience to their superiors, fidelity to the observances of the community, interior recollection, mental prayer, preparation for reception of the sacraments, purity of intention, love of poverty, the necessity of mortification, perseverance, and other similar topics.

Monsieur Vincent had a heart totally inflamed with charity toward the neighbor. Consequently, it was only natural that he should communicate some spark of this ardor to his dear daughters and that he should lead them to give themselves to the salvation of souls as much as their situation would allow. They hoped to do this, not only by their prayers, but also by some more practical help, which they believed to be in the spirit of their institute and conformable to the intentions of their blessed father and founder. They felt that it was not enough to exercise their charity among themselves, but that this divine light and fire should extend to others outside, to help them achieve good order, regularity, union, and all sorts of other spiritual goods. These ideals had inspired the superior, Monsieur Vincent, to agree that the religious of the Visitation should work with other convents in need of reform. We will give here but a single example. It will suffice to show the saintly dispositions of this charitable spiritual father, and of his virtuous daughters also, in extending their charity to those outside their convent.

Several years previously the piety and good will of the late Marquise de Maignelay, whose memory is held in benediction, and with the help of many other like-minded persons, founded the convent of Sainte Madeleine, near the Temple in Paris.[14] It was to serve as a sort of refuge for girls and women who wanted to leave their lives of vice and become converted to God. From its first days, the management of the convent was recognized as its greatest weakness. Those who came had no experience in directing a house, nor the other qualities necessary for such a position. After thinking about how to remedy this problem, it was suggested that the religious of the Visitation might be asked to take over the administration of this new convent, since they seemed to be more capable than any others. The spirit of their institute, which obliged them to the twin virtues of charity and meekness, seemed most suitable to win the affection of the poor souls and to bind them with bands of love to Jesus Christ.

This had been discussed with the blessed bishop of Geneva. He agreed

---

14. The Temple was the former headquarters of the Knights Templars, a military order.

that it might well be undertaken one day, but for the moment the time was not yet ripe. Some years later, when the suggestion was made to Monsieur Vincent, he considered before God the importance and necessity of this venture. He was persuaded that the religious of the Visitation ought to undertake it. He spoke with Mother Helene Angelique Lhuillier, superior of the first convent, and she in turn discussed it with her community. Notwithstanding the apprehensions she and her sisters felt at such a difficult undertaking, they agreed to do so. They were encouraged by the great good to be effected in this work and by the help they hoped for from God.

In 1629 Monsieur Vincent chose four religious of the first convent of the Visitation to move to the convent of Sainte Madeleine as prioress, director, and porter, with the blessing of the archbishop of Paris. From time to time these sisters were replaced because of the trying nature of the work. Their direction was so successful that soon good order reigned in this large house. For more than thirty years all has gone well, even to the extent that this convent led to two others, in Rouen and in Bordeaux. Monsieur Vincent contributed much by his wise counsel and charitable care, either going to visit it in person or by writing often to the sisters there. He helped especially in obtaining good confessors who could maintain peace, obedience, and good order in all that concerned the worship of God.

Since the beginning, many obstacles to its realization marked this work. Because many regulations had to be adopted, Monsieur Vincent, with his usual prudence, held several meetings with doctors or other pious people to discuss ways of meeting the difficulties of the enterprise and to resolve doubts which arose. This enabled him to act with greater assurance in a matter of this importance, affecting the relief and edification of the public and the spiritual good of so many poor creatures who found in this new enterprise a safe harbor amid their stormy lives.

Ordinarily around a hundred or a hundred and twenty girls lived in the house. Some of them took the three vows of religion, others not, but they remained of their own free will, and all lived a regulated and well-ordered life. Some others were there under duress, but God who is rich in mercy gave the grace to some of these to pass from this third group to the second, and some even to the first. They were helped in this by the charitable care they received from the sisters of the Visitation, who undoubtedly found much difficulty in guiding this house. God gave them the grace to surmount all these sufferings by their humility, patience, and meekness. By these virtues they were able to overcome the contradictions, persecutions, and calumnies raised by the devil and the world against them. Monsieur Vincent helped them greatly. He encouraged them to persevere, showing them how much their patience and their charity redounded to the glory of God. They merited grace and attracted blessings for the entire order by their devotion. It was a great honor for them to do what the apostles did, and what Jesus Christ himself came upon earth to do, to convert souls to God. This is what he wrote to Mother Anne Marie Bollain, the first superior sent to the convent of Sainte Madeleine, where she worked successfully for several years.

> Our Lord who always calls us to what is most perfect would prefer you to continue your services to Sainte Madeleine than to do anything else. The grace of perseverance is the most important of all, the crown of all the others. Death that would find us arms in hand for the service of our divine Master would be the most glorious and the most desirable. Our Lord ended his life as he lived. His life had been hard and painful, his death severe and agonizing with no human consolation. For this reason some of the saints wanted to die alone, totally abandoned by all, in the hope of having God alone as their comfort. I am convinced, my dear sister, that you seek him alone, and when presented with a choice you always prefer what is for his greater glory, and not your own personal interest.[15]

Among all the other considerations referred to, which Monsieur Vincent extended with such affection to the sisters of the Visitation in this undertaking, and which have continued to this day despite all the difficulties that have arisen, he dwelt on one subject more than on any other. He feared that if these religious withdrew from this enterprise, the venom of novel errors would enter this house, for it had a way of spreading everywhere. He would say that besides the harm it did to faith and religion, it introduced dangerous seeds of ill feeling into the community. It was a source of division which the enemy sowed secretly to destroy it if great care were not taken, as experience only too well confirmed.

Before ending this chapter, we have felt that for the edification of the reader, it would be well to include two accounts written in Monsieur Vincent's own hand about the two great servants of God who founded the saintly institute of the Visitation. These show the extraordinary and remarkable graces it pleased God to bestow on his faithful servant. They also manifest the sanctity of Blessed Francis de Sales, founder of the order, and of the Venerable Mother Jane Frances Fremiot, its foundress. Here is what he wrote, in the first of these pieces:

> It pleases the goodness of God to work miracles through the saints, to show forth their sanctification. I write of one, of which I was witness, in the person of sister M. M. of the Visitation of Saint Mary, in the convent in the faubourg Saint Jacques, in Paris.
>
> About six years ago this religious was seized with a horrible

---

15. *CED* VIII:252.

temptation of aversion against God, the blessed sacrament, and all the exercises of our holy religion. She blasphemed against God, and cursed him as often as she praised him, or rather as often as she heard the other sisters praise him in the divine office. In choir, she blasphemed and cursed aloud, in the hearing of all those around her. When her superior asked her to make an act of devotion toward God, she replied that she had no God but the devil. She had such anger and fury against God's divine majesty she was on the verge of killing herself, the better to be in hell, as she herself said, where she could curse God eternally. This is what she wanted.

The reverend mother superior had her see various persons who might help, such as bishops, priests, and others familiar with such internal matters. In keeping with their advice she was sent to medical doctors. They prescribed various remedies, but all without effect. Finally, the superior thought if she would apply a piece of the surplice of the blessed bishop of Geneva she would be cured. She did this, and a short time later the cure followed instantly. She lost the troubled spirit which so bothered her, and became completely at peace. Her weakened body regained its strength, and her appetite and sleep returned to normal. All this happened in an instant, and all has remained well in both mind and body ever since. She recovered so completely that she was able to take on some of the principal responsibilities of the house, and is now serving as mistress of novices.

What makes me believe in the miraculous nature of this cure is that it followed the application of the surplice of the blessed bishop of Geneva, and this only after all human remedies had failed. Her ailments increased at the moment of application of the surplice, something that usually happens in miraculous cures, but the cure came suddenly, justifying the faith of the mother superior. She is as convinced as if she had seen and touched him that our Lord did this miracle in favor of the blessed bishop, and by the application of his surplice. I write these things after talking to the sister during her illness and after her cure. I learned all the circumstances from the mother superior and from the religious herself immediately after her cure, which happened on the day I went to make my visitation of the convent, on the authority of the most illustrious and most reverend archbishop of Paris.[16]

After this account by the humble servant of God, there is no room to doubt this extraordinary and miraculous cure. It came about through the merits of

---

16. *CED* XIII:64-66.

the blessed bishop of Geneva, founder of the order of the Visitation, source of so many miracles since that time. This holy bishop should rightly be regarded as its true author, after God, who will be all the more honored and glorified in his saint. Nevertheless, some circumstances which accompanied or followed this miraculous cure involving Monsieur Vincent, make us think God wished him to play some part in this event.

We must remark, in the first place, that it pleased God to give this grace to the worthy superior whose visits to the house of the Visitation sisters usually produced such striking graces. Among others is the case of several of the religious suffering great pains or enduring most grievous temptations, who were entirely freed from them after he had spoken with them.

Second, the visit of which he speaks in this account was the first he made in the second convent of the Visitation at Paris, around 1623.[17] He was still in the service of the late general of the galleys, some years before the foundation of the Congregation of the Mission.

Third, having seen in this visit this good religious obsessed as she was and tormented with such pain, he was moved with much compassion. In an effort to be of help, he prayed for her. Afterward the religious was suddenly delivered. As we have already said, the glory of this cure belongs, after God, to Blessed Francis de Sales, bishop of Geneva. By his intercession we believe God delivered this good religious from such horrible pains and temptations. However, without taking away anything from the honor due this holy prelate, may we not say it was also at the intervention of Monsieur Vincent, whom he greatly respected and loved in life, that he was moved to intercede before God in favor of him who was rendering him such faithful and helpful service in the person of his dear daughters?

The second document contains the following words:

> We, Vincent de Paul, most unworthy superior general of the Congregation of the Mission, certify that for twenty years God has given us the grace to know the deceased, our very worthy Mother de Chantal, foundress of the holy order of the Visitation of Saint Mary. I had frequent contact with her by word and by letter. It pleased God that I met with her from the time she first came to this city, twenty years ago. I have met her other times, during which she did me the honor to put herself under my spiritual direction. It appeared to me she was gifted with many virtues, especially faith, although she was tempted her whole life long by contrary thoughts. She had great trust in God, and a generous love of his divine bounty. Her spirit was just, prudent, temperate, and strong, to an eminent degree. She possessed humility, mortification, obedience, zeal for

---

17. The date should be 1626 or later since the house was not founded until 1626.

the sanctification of her order and for the salvation of the souls of the poor, all in a superlative degree.

In a word, I never saw in her any imperfection, but rather the constant exercise of all the virtues. Although she appeared calm and peaceful, characteristic of souls who have reached a high degree of virtue, she truly suffered great interior pains. Several times she wrote or told me directly that she was so troubled by all sorts of temptations and obsessions that she could scarcely look into her own interior. She could not bear the sight of her own soul, filled with horror to such an extent that it was the image of hell for her. Despite these pains, she never lost her serenity of countenance, nor did she relax in the fidelity due God in the exercise of the Christian and religious virtues, nor in the prodigious solicitude she had for the welfare of her own order. I can say without hesitation that she was one of the most saintly souls I ever met on the face of the earth and that surely she is now among the blessed in heaven. I have no doubt that some day God will bring her sanctity to light, as I hear he has already done in some parts of this kingdom in various ways. I will recount one example of this. I learned it from a person worthy of belief, who would rather die, I assure you, than to report a falsehood.

This person,[18] having heard of the serious illness of our dear departed, fell to his knees to pray to God for her.[19] The first thought which came to him was to make an act of contrition for any sins she may have committed, or was in the habit of committing. Immediately after, there appeared before him a globe of fire which raised itself above the earth. This was joined by another, more luminous and larger. It united with the first, rising still higher, until this was absorbed into still another globe, infinitely greater and more luminous than the others. He heard an interior voice which told him the first globe of fire was the soul of our worthy mother; the second, that of our blessed founder, and the third the divine essence itself. The two souls were united, and together were absorbed into God, their sovereign principle.

Moreover, this same person, a priest, offered holy mass for our worthy mother, overwhelmed with sadness after hearing the news of her passing. When he was at the second *Memento*, the prayer for the dead, he thought it would be good to pray for her, since she might be in purgatory for some light words she may have said that

---

18. Vincent himself; see *CED* II:212.
19. Jane Frances de Chantal died at Moulins on Friday, December 13, 1641, at age sixty-nine.

possibly were venial sins. At that moment he again saw the same vision as before, the same globes and the same union. He preserves an interior conviction that this soul was truly among the blessed, and had no need of prayers. This thought has remained imprinted on his mind, so much so that he cannot think of her without recalling it.

What might lead to some doubts about this vision is this priest has such a high regard for the sanctity of this blessed soul that he could never read her book, *Responses*, without weeping, so convinced is he that God had inspired her with its contents. Perhaps this vision was an effect of his too vivid imagination. What makes me think it was a true vision is that he was never known to have others, except the one related here.

As proof of this, I have signed this with my own hand, and affixed my seal.[20]

Monsieur Vincent made this declaration in 1642. He speaks of himself in the third person when he speaks of the vision of the globes. God revealed to him the blessedness of the holy foundress of the devout institute of the Visitation, but before he wrote or spoke to anyone he went to see the late archbishop of Paris, to whom he related what had occurred. He told him simply and exactly what had happened, so as not to be deceived. He spoke also to Dom Maurice, a Barnabite, whom he met at the convent of Saint Mary in the faubourg Saint Jacques, on the day following the death of Madame de Chantal, to have an assurance that the devil was not deceiving him. Both these advisers told him the vision had all the marks of a vision coming from God. They advised that he might safely relate this event to certain members of the order, who were so deeply moved by the loss of their dear mother. He did so, describing the details of the vision, and later put them into writing to preserve the memory.

---

20. *CED* XIII:125-28. The testimony of Vincent de Paul and Francis de Sales was considered to be of such importance in the process for the beatification of Jane Frances that at the ceremony for her beatification, November 21, 1751, her image was placed between those of Francis and Vincent, "her two fathers and her two witnesses."

CHAPTER EIGHT

The Confraternities of Charity in the Parishes

AMONG THE SIGNS our Lord gave of his divine mission and his role as messiah and redeemer of the world, when the holy precursor John the Baptist sent two of his disciples to him, the last and principal one was *Pauperes evangelizantur*, that the poor would have the Gospel preached to them.[1] As he said in another part of the Gospel, all his works gave testimony to who he was. The marvelous cures he wrought by his word were undeniable proofs of his identity as Son of God and savior. Nevertheless, after referring to giving sight to the blind, speech to the mute, hearing to the deaf, life to the dead, he added one more proof, more compelling than the others: *Pauperes evangelizantur*, the poor would have the Gospel preached to them.

Beyond any doubt charity is the true mark of the children of God, but the surest sign of the presence of true and perfect charity, free from all self-interest and personal satisfaction, is its exercise in favor of the poor. If it be permitted to extend this thought, added luster is given to the precious pearl of this virtue when it is given in service to the sick poor. In the double handicap which they suffer, poverty and sickness, their corporal and spiritual needs are tended to; their body is given the food and medicine it requires, and their souls the consolation they need. In these conditions charity shines forth even more than usual, because of the benefits it confers, the efforts it demands, and the natural repugnances which ordinarily have to be overcome in these situations.

The corporal and spiritual help to the poor, especially to the sick and afflicted among them, allows us to appreciate the degree to which Monsieur Vincent possessed this virtue of charity. We have already seen this in Book One[2] and in Chapter One of Book Two. We spoke there about the missions and the great results they produced, especially for the poor. Besides all these benefits there is still another that we have put off until this chapter, the establishment of the Confraternities of Charity for the help of the sick poor, a creation of Monsieur Vincent. God used him for the creation of this great work, which cannot be praised enough, not only for the bodily relief of a multitude of the sick poor, but even more for the salvation of their souls. Were it not for him, in many places they would have lived and died abandoned. They were often in danger of being lost were it not for the

---

1. Matt 11:5.
2. Ch. 8.

spiritual help he gave them, especially in preparing them to die a happy death.

We appreciate the charity of those who contributed to the support of the hospital for receiving and treating the sick poor. If some rich person were to use part of his wealth to found one, this would undoubtedly be approved and applauded by everyone. What do we think then of a poor priest, working alone, who was able to do what the richest and most powerful with all their resources were not able to accomplish? I do not speak of the founding of one hospital, or of ten, or of a hundred, but of a thousand and more. Making something out of nothing, with five small loaves feeding thousands of people, this is something that only God could do. Surely this would be seen as an undertaking beyond human power. We can say that Monsieur Vincent was this poor priest whom God used to work this marvel, not in building hospitals to receive the sick poor, but in establishing the Confraternities of Charity for their care. This was something even more advantageous for them than the hospitals would have been, as they themselves agree.

If, for example, fifty or sixty sick poor of a parish in Paris, helped by the Confraternity of Charity, were asked if they would have preferred to be taken to the Hotel Dieu, the answer would have been unanimous: they appreciated being left in their poor homes under the constant care of the members of the Confraternity of Charity.

We saw in Book One[3] the origin of these Confraternities of Charity, in 1617 when Monsieur Vincent was at Chatillon in Bresse. It was there he began for the first time to gather some good and virtuous women to help the sick poor of the parish, to provide the food and medicines and spiritual help for them in their own homes, without separating husband and wife, or mothers and children.

This great servant of God had never heard anyone speak of this way of helping the sick poor, as he himself has told us. The thought came to him only on the occasion of finding some sick persons in his parish deprived of every resource, and he wondered how he might help out. His charity was so cordial and tender toward the poor that his ingenuity suggested this novel and saintly innovation. He started it as an experiment but its immediate success showed decidedly that the inspiration had come from God. He blessed this first Confraternity of Charity so manifestly that it has continued for more than fifty years, even though Monsieur Vincent was called away to other duties and occupations and could not give it his personal attention.

Since the beginning of this first confraternity, it pleased the bounty of God to shower so many graces upon the father of the poor that he was able to spread this holy institution in innumerable parishes throughout France,

---

3. Ch. 10.

Italy and elsewhere. His spiritual sons continue to this day in the parishes where missions are given, inside and outside the kingdom, to organize these Confraternities of Charity with the approbation of the Holy See, and the permission of the prelates and pastors of the locality.

Someone may ask how these Confraternities of Charity are supported, since most have no source of fixed income. It would have to be admitted that indeed they are founded, but only on the Providence of God. He has not allowed any one of these confraternities which has faithfully followed the regulations to be cited shortly, to lack what was needed to serve the sick. Generally, a collection would be taken up in the parish on the occasion of the establishment of the first confraternity. From this a small income, smaller or larger depending on the place, would be generated. Also, a collection of furniture, clothing, and household utensils was organized. Collections were taken up in the churches on Sundays and feasts. This proved enough to support the work, above all when the officers followed the directions they had received for the good government of the confraternity, and when the pastors of the parishes supported the undertaking.

Since good order preserves things as they should be, and since as the apostle says, all that comes from God is well ordered, Monsieur Vincent felt it desirable from the very beginning of these confraternities that some organization of them was necessary. He drew up a set of regulations, therefore, which we append to this chapter. They were followed wherever the confraternities were established. It is written in simple and direct language, in few articles, but enough to show the truly Christian prudence of its author.

Monsieur Vincent planned originally to set up these confraternities in the villages of the countryside, for the care of the sick poor where the need was usually most pressing. However, some noble ladies with lands in the diocese of Paris or elsewhere, and who had hosted the missions, saw the Confraternity of Charity established with happy results for the sick poor. They realized that many similar cases existed in Paris, and believed these same Confraternities of Charity should be formed in the parishes of Paris and in the outlying districts. Many of the poorer families could barely manage on the wages from their work. When sickness overtook the breadwinner, the family fell into great distress. Many, through shame or for some other reason, did not want to go to the Hotel Dieu, but this left them and their families in utter desolation.

These women spoke to the pastors, and they in turn consulted Monsieur Vincent. He agreed to help in setting up these confraternities in the parishes which needed them. They have continued there to our own day, greatly blessed by God. The Ladies of Charity of each parish were independent of the others, but for twenty-five or thirty years have provided the same care and concern for the sick poor as was done in the Confraternities of Charity in the country places, and sometimes even more. At their own expense the women took turns in preparing soup and meat and other needed items for the sick of the parish.

Since that time, in imitation of those of Paris, these confraternities have spread to many other cities of the kingdom, and even into the villages and to foreign countries, so that today their number can hardly be counted. We can well imagine how thousands of poor people are helped every day, in body and soul. After God, they owe so much of this charitable help, and for many the healthy state of their souls and perhaps even their eternal salvation, to the charity of this great servant of God. By this alone, not considering all his other activities, he has earned a glorious crown in heaven, ever increasing because of those who are saved daily because of him. On earth he merited the title of Father of the Poor, and this will draw down upon all his enterprises an infinity of graces and blessings.

REGULATIONS OF THE CONFRATERNITIES OF CHARITY

The Confraternity of Charity is established to honor our lord Jesus Christ and his holy mother, to help in body and in soul the sick poor of the place where it is established, by providing food and drink and medicines in time of sickness. Spiritually, these persons are helped to receive the sacraments of penance, holy eucharist, and extreme unction. Those about to die are helped to leave this world in good conscience. Those who are cured are helped to resolve to lead a good life in the future.

The confraternity shall be composed of a certain limited number of women and girls, with the consent of their husbands or of their fathers and mothers, as the case may be. They shall hold an election, in the presence of the pastor, for three officers, every two years. This shall take place on the day after Pentecost. The first of these officers shall be called the superior or director; the second, treasurer or first assistant; the third, the storekeeper, or second assistant. These three officers shall have the complete direction of the confraternity.

With the advice of the pastor, a pious and charitable layman of the parish shall be elected to serve as procurator.

The superior shall take care to see that the present regulations are observed and that all members of the confraternity do their duty well. She shall accept the sick poor of the parish for treatment, and shall discharge them with the advice of the other officers.

The second person shall serve as a counselor to the superior. She shall keep the funds of the confraternity in a safe, locked with a lock having two different keys, of which she shall hold one, and the other shall be held by the superior. She shall keep no money on her person, except a single *ecu*, for current expenses. She shall give an account at the end of two years to the newly elected officers, to the other members of the confraternity, in the presence of the pastor and interested parishioners.

The storekeeper shall also be a member of the council of the superior. She shall keep the linens of the confraternity, wash and mend them, and shall supply the sick poor with needed items upon orders of the superior. Like the treasurer, she shall give an account of her services at the end of the two years.

The procurator shall hold the funds raised in the collections in the parish and the gifts from individuals. He shall furnish receipts for gifts. He shall provide for a storehouse and see that it be well supplied with needed items. He shall aid in drawing up the treasurer's report as needed. He shall keep a record book in which these present regulations will be copied, and the act of foundation of the confraternity shall be included. This same record should hold the names of the women and girls accepted as members of the confraternity, the day of their joining, and the day of their death; the election of officers shall be recorded; the summary of the reports of the officers shall be included; the names of the sick poor helped by the confraternity, the day of their reception, the day of their death or discharge, and in general, all that has happened that is most significant or remarkable.

Each day the sisters of the confraternity shall serve the sick poor accepted by the superior, bringing to their homes the food and drink prepared for them. They shall all take their turn at seeking alms at church and in the homes of the people, on Sundays and the main solemn feasts. They shall deposit these alms with the treasurer, and give a report to the procurator of what was collected. They shall gather for a mass at the altar of the confraternity the first or third Sunday of the month, at which they shall communicate, after going to confession, if this is convenient. On this same day they shall attend the procession held between vespers and compline, when the litanies of our Lord or of our Blessed Mother are chanted. They shall do the same each year on January 14, feast of the name of Jesus, their patron.

They shall mutually cherish each other as those called and bound by the love of our savior, often visiting and consoling one another in their afflictions and sicknesses. They shall attend as a group the wake of anyone who shall have died, and receive communion for her intention at a high mass to be celebrated for her.

They shall do the same for the pastor and for their procurator, if they should die. In the same way they should attend in a body the funeral services for any of the sick poor they had cared for, and have a low mass said for the repose of their soul. All the above shall not bind under pain of sin, either mortal or venial.

At each meal for the poor they shall give the sick enough bread to eat, and five ounces of veal or lamb, a soup and a *demi-setier* of wine in the Paris measure.

On fast days, besides bread, the sick should also be given wine, and soup, two eggs, and a bit of butter. For those unable to eat solid food, they should be given some bouillon, and some fresh eggs, four times a day. When death approaches, if there are no relatives to help, the sisters of the confraternity should offer this service.[4]

---

4. *CED* XIII:419-22. This rule served as the model for all the other charities founded by Vincent de Paul, although he made modifications if necessary to adapt it to the particular circumstances of a new confraternity.

CHAPTER NINE

*The Founding of the Daughters of Charity,
Servants of the Sick Poor*

WE WILL NOT repeat here what has already been said in Book One[1] about the origins of the Daughters of Charity, Servants of the Sick Poor, and the circumstances which brought about their foundation. We will not develop further the thought that Monsieur Vincent brought to this enterprise only his fidelity to the designs of God's providence. This led him to become, almost without conscious effort on his part, the originator of this charitable organization, and the spiritual father of these virtuous women.

We will speak here only of some things worthy of remark not reported in Book One about this devoted community, since raised to the status of a congregation by the late archbishop of Paris by the following letter of incorporation:

> Because of the blessings God has bestowed on the work of our beloved Vincent de Paul to further this pious enterprise, we have confided to him and commissioned him by these present letters to undertake the guidance and direction of this society and community for as long as he shall live. We extend this commission to those who, after his death, shall succeed him as superior general of the Congregation of the Mission.[2]

Later, the king confirmed this appointment, and the Parlement of Paris confirmed and registered it.

Seeing himself thus charged so providentially with the care of this work, he gave it his full attention and concern to perfect it as much as he could.

---

1. Ch. 24.
2. *CED* XIII:572. The first approbation of the Daughters of Charity, given by the archbishop of Paris in 1646, was somehow lost, together with the royal letters patent. Vincent thus had to present a second request in 1655. This approval is the one Abelly cites here. An important modification was introduced in this new request: that the Daughters of Charity be placed under the perpetual direction of Vincent de Paul and his successors as superiors general of the Congregation of the Mission. Vincent, who characteristically had feared anticipating divine Providence, had himself been reluctant to agree to this provision. Louise de Marillac perceived that leaving the choice of director after Vincent to the authority of the archbishop of Paris would eventually lead to the community's withdrawal from Vincent's spiritual family. She was unshakeable in this conviction, and worked long and hard to convince Vincent. See *CED* III:254-55; IV:220-22. He finally agreed at her continued insistence, and Cardinal de Retz, the archbishop of Paris, gave his approval on January 18, 1655. See *CED* XIII, 569-72, 572-77. The somewhat revised statutes, approved by the archbishop, were confirmed in the name of the pope by his legate, Cardinal de Vendome, June 8, 1668.

His first thought was to propose to these virtuous women that they should regard as their primary objective the service of Jesus Christ spiritually and corporally in the persons of the sick poor, whether men or women, despite their shyness or the urgency of their needs. To make themselves worthy servants of their Lord in such a holy service they must work strenuously at their own sanctification. They should give all their service in the spirit of humility, simplicity, charity, and in union with our Lord Jesus Christ, excluding all vanity, human respect, self-love, and natural satisfactions.

He strongly recommended several other virtues he judged most necessary in their condition, such as obedience to their superiors and to the pastors of the parishes; indifference about the place, work, and persons with whom they worked; poverty, as a means to acquire a love for the poor as their servants; patience, to bear willingly and for the love of God the inconveniences, contradictions, mockeries, calumnies, and other mortifications which would surely befall them, even for having tried to do good, regarding all this as a sharing of the cross of Christ upon earth, so as to live gloriously one day with him in heaven.

It will not be necessary to go into much detail about their rule. It sought to encourage mental prayer, frequent reception of the sacraments, annual retreats, spiritual conferences, union and mutual charity among themselves, common life in dress and activities, and a most careful modesty.

Besides the rules common to all, Monsieur Vincent left others written for each particular office. These pointed out what should be done in whatever place they happened to be, in the cities or in the villages, or in their contacts with the ladies, or others for whom they worked, and in regard to the poor themselves whom they sought to serve and teach. There were six of these special rules, the first for the sisters who served the sick in the parishes; the second was for those who taught school; the third for those who took care of abandoned children; the fourth for those who helped the ladies who served the poor in the Hotel Dieu in Paris; the fifth for the sisters who served in the hospital reserved for convicts condemned to the galleys; the sixth for those who served the sick in other hospitals of the kingdom. These rules stressed the dangerous situations they should avoid, the precautions they must take, and the attitudes they must have so as to do and say, even in the least circumstances, whatever would help them do their duties well: feeding, bandaging, dosing, cleaning, edifying, consoling, and reprimanding the poor of all sorts, old and young, well or sick.

It could be said these rules of Monsieur Vincent were definitive, for he was in no hurry to produce them. He wanted God alone to be their author, and human considerations to have no importance, except in their observance.

They were the fruit of long experience, aided by the most enlightened advice of Mademoiselle le Gras and always with service to all sorts of poor people as the primary objective.

These rules assured that the Daughters of Charity served the poor to the satisfaction of everyone, and they were soon being requested from all sides. Several cities among the major ones of the kingdom asked for them, as did many lords and ladies who wanted them to come to their lands. These requests were satisfied as much as the growth of this Company allowed, which was great, by God's mercy. The Congregation provided an excellent opportunity for widows or other women who wished to withdraw from the world, to assure their own salvation by these works of charity for others. This was chiefly so for those who wished to become religious, but who did not have a dowry. The Daughters of Charity had no such requirement. The only thing asked of them, besides their first dress, was a worthy disposition of body and soul to respond to such a holy calling. This calling cannot be appreciated by those lacking in charity, but Monsieur Vincent extolled it in these words:

> A Daughter of Charity has greater need of virtue than even the most austere religious. No other congregation asks more of their members than does theirs. They must work at their own perfection like the Carmelites and other similar orders. In the care of the sick they serve like the religious of the Hotel Dieu of Paris, or of other nursing communities. In the education of poor girls they are as devoted as the Ursulines.[3]

We cite here several sections of the rule of Monsieur Vincent for sisters working for the sick poor in the parishes:

> They must remember that, although they are not properly called religious, because this state is not suitable for their particular calling, they are much more exposed to dangers than cloistered religious living behind their grilles. Their convents are the houses of the sick. Their cells are the sickrooms of the poor, and even these are often rented. Their chapel is the parish church. Their cloister is the street of the town. Their enclosure is holy obedience. Their grille is the fear of God and their veil, holy modesty. For all these reasons they must have greater virtue than if they were professed religious in one of the orders. This is why they must try to act wherever they are with such reserve, recollection, and edification as true religious do in their own convents. To obtain this grace from God they must strive to attain all the virtues recommended and stipulated in their rules. This is particularly true of the virtue of profound humility, perfect obedience, and a great detachment from creatures. Above

---

3. *CED* X:143-45.

all else, they must use every precaution to preserve perfect chastity of body and heart.

They should think often of why God has sent them to this parish, which is to serve the sick poor, not only in body by feeding them and giving them their medicines, but spiritually as well, seeing that they receive the sacraments in time. Those about to die should be helped to die in good grace, while those who recover should be helped to resolve firmly to lead a good life in the future. To help them attain these spiritual benefits, the sisters should do what they can in the little time they have, depending on the condition of the sick persons they serve. They should strive to console, encourage, and teach the sick what is required for salvation, helping them make acts of faith, hope, and charity toward God and the neighbor, and of contrition, urging them to forgive their enemies and to ask pardon of those they have offended. They should help the sick to resign themselves to God's will whether it be to suffer or to recover, to live or to die, and other similar acts, not all at once, but a few each day, and as concisely as possible so as not to weary the sick ones.

Above all else the Daughters should help their patients make a good general confession of their entire lives, especially if there is danger they will die from their illness. They should point out the importance of making this general confession and how to make it. Among other things they should tell them to confess not only their sins committed since their last confession, but those of their entire lives, even though they may have been confessed before. If they are not in a condition to make this confession of all their past, they should at least have a sorrow for all their sins, with a firm purpose of preferring death to sinning again, helped by the grace of God.

If the sick recover but then suffer a relapse, they should be urged to receive the sacraments again, even extreme unction, and the sisters should help them do so. If they are about to die, the Daughters should help them to die well, using some of the acts mentioned before, and praying to God for them.

Should the sick be cured, the Daughters should urge them to profit from their sickness and their cure. They will point out that God allowed their sickness of body to bring health to their souls, and has restored them to well-being to enable them to do penance and lead a good Christian life. Good resolutions are required to do all this, so they should help them make strong ones or renew those they made when they first recovered. They should suggest some practices to help them, depending on their dispositions, such as praying to God while kneeling morning and evening, confession and communion several times a year, avoiding the occasions of sin, and so forth. All this should be done briefly, simply, and humbly.

To avoid any difficulty which these spiritual ministrations might cause by delaying the bringing of food or medicine to the other sick, they should be careful to regulate their time and exercises according to the number and needs of the sick. Since their duties are usually less pressing in the evening than in the morning they might use this time in teaching their patients or in exhorting them to the spiritual exercises spoken of, particularly when bringing them some medicine.

In serving the sick they should have God alone in view, accepting praise and blame with the same equanimity. They should interiorly reject the praise, but accept the blame in honor of the abuse heaped on the Son of God upon the cross, even from those he had so blessed and favored.

They should accept no present from the poor they serve, no matter how small it might be, remembering they are obligated to this service to the poor. They owe them still more, for the small services they render must be given with affection, rejoicing the angels of heaven, who one day will receive them into the eternal kingdom. Even in this life they receive more honor and true happiness than they could ever have dared hope for, especially because of their own unworthiness.

These were the main regulations Monsieur Vincent gave these virtuous women, from which we can judge the spirit he engendered in them and the high degree of perfection to which he called them. We see, too, the spirit with which he himself was filled, and how abundant were the lights and graces given him by God for the direction of others.

He gave the Daughters some good advice also in regard to their contacts with certain other persons in particular, as for example, the priests in the parishes where they lived. He recommended they have a great respect for them, but not to visit with them or speak with them outside the confessional, except out of necessity. They were never to go alone to their houses nor receive them in their own houses. They were not to tend to them in their sicknesses nor provide medicines for them. They were not to take care of washing the surplices, albs or other altar linens, nor to clean or decorate the church and altars or other similar things. Although these were good and holy services, they were not in keeping with the goals of their institute and would detract from their care of the poor.

In regard to laity of whatever rank, he recommended that the Daughters not visit them unless it were necessary, nor to waste time or become too familiar with them. If they fell sick, the Daughters were not to tend to them or care for their children, servants, and domestics. They were not to become involved in their affairs, their household, or in giving them medicine. All this was contrary to the spirit of their institute, which was to be devoted to the poor and not to the rich. All these recommendations were more important than they first appeared, because the occupations he forbade were ordinarily easier, more agreeable, and more honorable in the sight of others, and were more attractive to the natural inclinations of the Daughters. If the Daughters followed them, they would little by little depart from what our Lord was asking of them, and for which their little Company was founded.

Besides the parishes in which these good women worked for the sick poor, five hospitals in Paris gave the same services: (1) The Hotel Dieu, where they helped the ladies who visited the sick. (2) The foundling hospital, where there was much opportunity for them to show their charity, for each year three or four hundred of these children were cared for admirably. (3) The hospital for those condemned to the galleys, where they had occasion to practice the works of mercy most abundantly, for the patients were as miserable in soul and body as could be imagined. The sisters sent to work here required extraordinary graces of God to succeed in this attempt. Monsieur Vincent wrote a set of suggestions for them to help in this difficult assignment. (4) The hospital of the Petites Maisons, where they looked after, cleaned and fed those poor who were unsound in mind. These were numerous, both men and women, some of whom were sick, but all were treated most considerately and charitably. The administrators of this hospital acknowledged that the Daughters had put an end to many disorders, including the serious financial loss of the institution, but especially the lack of care of the patients themselves. The administrators were most edified and satisfied with their contribution to the welfare of the hospital. (5) The hospital of Name of Jesus, where these charitable women housed and cared for aged men and women.

Besides these hospitals in the city of Paris and all the parishes where they worked either in Paris or in other places in France, they served the poor in many other hospitals, such as those of Angers, Chartres, Chateaudun, Hennebont, Saint Fargeau, Ussel, Cahors, Gex, etc., and in Poland, in the city of Warsaw. In all these places they served the poor with much blessing from the hands of God. We will give here only one letter from Monsieur Vincent to Mademoiselle le Gras, discussing sending three Daughters to work in Poitou:

> I pray that our Lord will bless our three dear sisters, and make them share the spirit he has given the saintly ladies who accompany

them, and who cooperate in his solicitude for the sick poor and for the instruction of children. O good God, what happiness for these good Daughters to go where they are sent, to continue the charity which our Lord displayed when he was on earth! How the heavens must rejoice at this! The praises they shall receive in the next life are admirable! With what holy confidence they will appear before the throne of judgment after so many holy works of charity![4] It seems to me the crowns and empires of the earth are but of clay in comparison with the merit and glory we confidently expect they will receive one day as their crown.

It remains only that, in the spirit of the holy Virgin, they travel and do their work, having her ever before their eyes and doing always what this most blessed Lady would have done in their place. I hope they will reflect above all on her love and humility. I hope they will be humble toward God, cordial among themselves, agreeable to all, and edifying to all who meet them. I trust they will be faithful to their morning prayers, if they can do so before the stage leaves, or along the way, if not. They must say their rosary, and carry some book of piety they might read. They should contribute to conversations which refer to God, but have nothing to do with worldly talk, especially with those who are too free. They must be adamant against any men who would strive to be too familiar with them.

After arriving at their destination, they should first visit the blessed sacrament, and then see the pastor to receive his directions in regard to the sick and the children of the school. They will do what they can to benefit the souls of the sick poor while they are treating their illnesses. They shall follow the orders of the charity officials, and be careful to esteem and practice their own regulations. They should go to confession every eight days. Following all these suggestions, they will see they have led a saintly life, and although they are but poor women upon earth, they shall become great queens in heaven. This is what I pray for to God.[5]

Since in all the hospitals in which they served there were often a great number of sick and usually there were only a few sisters in each, the sisters were often overburdened. One of them wrote of this in a letter to Monsieur Vincent:

> Monsieur, the work is overwhelming us, and we surely will succumb if we are not relieved. I am writing to you in the evening

---

4. The original text of this sentence is shorter: "How they will go, with head raised, to the day of judgment."
5. *CED* I:513-14.

> while looking after two dying persons, because I have no opportunity to do so during the day. While watching at their bedside I am attempting to write. I say to one, "My dear friend, raise your heart to God, and beg his mercy." Then, I write a line or two of my letter, then go to the bedside of the other to say, "Jesus, Mary, My God, I trust in you." Then I return to my letter, and so I come and go, writing snatches to you, divided in spirit. I write to ask you most humbly to send us another sister to help us.[6]

Monsieur Vincent, reading this letter, admired the spirit of this woman, who in her natural eloquence expressed her need so forcefully that she persuaded him to send some help.

What put the finishing touches to the charity of these good women was the work they undertook in obedience and with sincere affection, not only in the places of which we have spoken, but also in the hospitals of the armies to which their charitable and zealous superior sent them. There they took care of the wounded soldiers and other sick, such as at Rethel during its siege, and later at Calais during the siege at Dunkirk, where two of the sisters gave up their lives in their dedication to charity.

Monsieur Vincent recommended these good women to the prayers of his community on one occasion:

> I recommend to your prayers the Daughters of Charity whom we have sent to Calais to care for the wounded soldiers. Four of them went, but two have died, the two most robust and strongest of the group have fallen under the burden. Imagine if you can, gentlemen, these four poor women among the five or six hundred wounded or sick soldiers. You can see something of the goodness of God and his providence, that in these times he has raised up such a congregation. Why? To help the poor in body and spirit, by saying a word or two to bring them to think of their own salvation, particularly the dying, to help them die well by making acts of contrition and trust in God. In truth, gentlemen, this is touching. Does it not seem to you to be a great thing that these women with such courage and resolution go among the soldiers to relieve them in their needs and contribute to their salvation? They go in face of enormous obstacles and despite such dangerous illnesses, and even in the face of death, for the benefit of these men exposed to all the dangers of war, for the good of the state.
>
> We can see how much these poor women are filled with zeal for the glory of God and for assistance to their neighbor. The queen has done us the honor to write us to ask us to send others to Calais to

---

6. *CED* IV:389.

help the poor soldiers. Today, we sent four to help out. One of them, about fifty years of age, came to see me last Friday at the Hotel Dieu to tell me she had just heard of the death of two of her sisters at Calais. She offered to go in their place, if I would agree. I told her I would think about it. Yesterday she came to learn what I had decided.

You see, gentlemen and my brothers, the courage of these women, to offer themselves this way, and to offer their very lives as victims for the love of Jesus Christ and the good of their neighbor. Is that not admirable? As for myself, I do not know what to say, except that on the day of judgment these women will be my judges. Yes, these women shall be our judges, if we like them are not willing to risk our lives for God. Since our own Congregation has a connection with theirs, in that God used the Congregation of the Mission to begin their congregation, we must thank God for all the graces he has given them. We should pray that in his infinite goodness he will continue his blessings in the future.

You can hardly believe how greatly God has blessed these good Daughters, and how many places have asked for their help. A bishop asked for sisters to staff three hospitals, another for two, and a third asked also only three days ago, pressuring me to send some. But how? We cannot, for we do not have enough. Just the other day I asked a pastor with some sisters in his parish how they were doing. I dare not report to you the good things he said about the sisters. Some are better than others. It is not that they have no faults. Alas! Who does not have some? But that does not prevent them from showing mercy, that beautiful virtue of which it is said that it is the nature of God to be merciful.

We too exhibit mercy, and we should do so for our entire lives, corporal mercy, spiritual mercy, mercy in the countryside on our missions, serving the needs of our neighbor, mercy in the house for those on retreat here, and in regard to the poor, and on all other occasions God presents us the opportunity. In a word, we should be men of mercy if we wish to do the will of God, in all and by all.[7]

We should not omit mentioning something of importance here. Just as

---

7. *CED* XII:39-40. In 1654 and 1656, the queen appealed to the Daughters of Charity to care for wounded and sick soldiers. After the Battle of the Dunes, June 14, 1658, which accompanied the siege at Dunkirk, six or seven hundred wounded or sick soldiers were sent to Calais. Anne of Austria who was present at these places was touched by what she saw, and she requested that the Daughters of Charity be sent to help them. Saint Vincent chose four sisters for this mission. See *CED* X:548-56. These events serve as the background to the saint's comments as reported by Abelly.

the first missions given by Monsieur Vincent in the parishes of the villages gave birth to the Congregation of the Mission, so too the Confraternities of Charity which he organized in the parishes developed into the Company of the Daughters of Charity. These came about by no previous design but by the secret order of divine Providence. After God, the founding of these two congregations, their development, their usefulness, their regulations, and their customs, all came from the zeal, prudence, and piety of this wise founder. He saw them come to light from his own work, and developed them by his careful guidance in the sure ways of the holy Gospel. He consecrated both to the love of God and neighbor in an effective and practical way, embracing all the corporal and spiritual works of mercy. This is the road he himself walked. This is the path he traced out for the men and women he guided if they were to acquire the perfection of their state.

To see the relationship between these two congregations, recalling the spirit of the first Christians of the early Church, we will cite here a letter he wrote to a priest of his Congregation. The priest had wondered why the missionaries, with their rule of not taking on the direction of women religious, still accepted the guidance of the Daughters of Charity. Monsieur Vincent answered at some length, in a letter of February 7, 1660:

> I thank God for the reactions he has inspired in you to my letter about religious. I am much consoled in seeing that you appreciate the reasons the Congregation has for not taking on this service, to be free to serve the poor more fully.
>
> Since you are anxious to know why we undertake the care of the Daughters of Charity, even though by rule we do not accept the direction of women religious, I reply:
>
> (1) I must say, Monsieur, that we do not have anything to do with the direction of religious. On the contrary, we praise those who give themselves to this service of these spouses of Christ who have renounced the world and its vanities to unite themselves to their sovereign lord. But what is praiseworthy for other priests is not expedient for us.
>
> (2) The Daughters of Charity are not religious but lay women. They are members of their parishes under the care of the pastor where they have been established. If we have the direction of their houses, it is because God used our Company to help bring theirs to life. You are aware that the same causes which God uses to give being to things he uses to preserve them.
>
> (3) Our little Congregation is consecrated to God to serve the poor, corporally and spiritually, and this from its very beginning. Also as it strives to work for the salvation of souls by the missions,

it has tried to help the sick by the Confraternities of Charity. The Holy See has approved this way of acting by its bull of confirmation of our Congregation.

Since the virtue of mercy has different aspects, the Congregation has exercised it in various ways for helping the poor. Think of the dedication to the convicts in the galleys or the Christian slaves in Barbary. Consider what was done in Lorraine at the time of its great trial, and later, in the ruined areas of the provinces of Champagne and Picardy, where we still have one of our members distributing alms. You yourself are witness, Monsieur, to the help we gave to the people near Paris, stricken by famine and the plague following the invasion of the armies. You played your part in this great work, and you were at the point of death. Many gave their own lives to conserve the lives of the suffering members of Jesus Christ, who is now their reward and one day will be yours as well. The Ladies of Charity of Paris are also witnesses to the grace of our vocation, in our working with them in the many good works they do, inside and outside the city.

All this being understood, Providence brought the Daughters of Charity into being to enable us to do by their hands what we could not otherwise do in serving the bodily needs of the sick poor, and saying a word or two of instruction and encouragement as helps to their salvation. We have the obligation to help them advance in virtue that they may carry out well their charitable services.

There is a difference between them and religious, in that most religious have as their goal their own perfection, but these women, like ourselves, are committed to the salvation and relief of the neighbor. In saying this I am not saying anything contrary to the Gospel, but in keeping with the practice of the early Church. Our Lord looked after some women who followed him on his journeys. We see in the Acts of the Apostles that they administered the distribution of food to the faithful and were regarded as an integral part of the Church structure.

If it should be said that it is dangerous for us to speak with these women, I would reply that we have taken care of that as best we can, by the directive not to visit them in their houses in the parishes without necessity and without the express permission of the superior. They too have a rule to make their cell a cloister and never allow men to enter.

I trust, Monsieur, that the way I have responded to your difficulties will satisfy you.[8]

---

8. *CED* VIII:237-38.

Monsieur Vincent gave spiritual conferences to these eighty or a hundred women who served in the hospitals and parishes of Paris. He called them together to the house of their superior, and alerted them in writing of the topic to be discussed so they could make their mental prayer on this same subject. He ordinarily would ask several to speak, to prepare their minds for the spiritual message he was to give, and to share with the others the good thoughts God had given them. This helped these women see better the importance of a Christian and perfect life to which he hoped to lead them. He would end by speaking for a half hour, or sometimes for an hour or more. His talk was so suited to their needs and condition, so clear and persuasive that they retained most of what he said and became more interior and spiritual by practicing what he taught. The sisters collected more than a hundred of these talks of their good father which they read and reread, awaiting the day when they could be published for the benefit of those living far from the motherhouse.

CHAPTER TEN

The Assemblies of the Ladies of Charity of Paris

WE HAVE ALREADY spoken enough in Book One[1] of the origins and progress of this devout assembly of Ladies of Charity of Paris. They have always recognized Monsieur Vincent, after God, as their founder and most prudent director. This chapter will serve merely to supplement what has already been said and will include some things that we feel should not be omitted.

We should remark first that these ladies came together to help the poor of the Hotel Dieu, but their charity was not limited solely to that work. By a singular grace from God, and through the help of their director, he led them to undertake several other important services for the glory of God, the service of his Church, and the salvation of souls. Besides what they did for the sick of the Hotel Dieu and for the orderly running of the hospital, they took in hand the feeding and education of the poor abandoned children of the city and suburbs of Paris. Previously, these children were utterly abandoned. Now they owed their lives and spiritual growth, and the possibility of leading a good Christian life and so their salvation, to the charity of these ladies.

They established the house of the Daughters of Providence to receive, educate, train and protect some young women.[2] Were it not for this refuge they would have been in great danger, since there was nowhere else for them to go in the city of Paris.

God used these same noble ladies to lay the foundation stones of the General Hospital, as described in Book One.[3] It was established at Sainte Reine, where the works of mercy owed their origin to the charity of these ladies.[4]

---

1. Ch. 29.
2. The Daughters of Providence were founded by Marie de Pollalion for the reform of wayward girls, and to provide a refuge for those whose virtue was threatened. Marie was the wife of Francis Pollalion, a gentleman of the king's chamber. Widowed after only a few years of marriage, she then resigned her position as a lady of honor to the queen, and under the direction of Vincent de Paul, adopted a simple style of life, and dedicated herself to charitable works. She was one of the most active Ladies of Charity. Dressed as a simple peasant serving girl, she accompanied Louise de Marillac to serve the poor country people. With Vincent's encouragement and help, she finally founded the work with the repentant girls. After her death on September 4, 1657, Vincent continued to help the work she had begun.
3. Ch. 45.
4. Sainte Reine, then in the diocese of Autun, but now in the diocese of Dijon. A popular place of pilgrimage at the home of Sainte Reine, virgin and martyr. A gentleman from Paris had the desire of establishing a hospital there, and asked for Saint Vincent's support. Vincent successfully

They also contributed notably to the establishment and maintenance of several missions in foreign countries, in the isles of the distant Hebrides and in Madagascar. Their zeal extended even to the Indies, where they supported the sending of several missionaries. Besides, they contributed to paying the expenses of the bishops of Heliopolis, Beirut, and Metellopolis.[5] With the blessing of the Apostolic See, these bishops set out for China and the Far East to work for the conversion of infidels and the building up of the kingdom of Jesus Christ.

They worked with tireless charity at unbelievable expense during the recent wars, helping those afflicted by the scourge of war in the provinces of Lorraine, Champagne, Picardy, and many other places, as we shall see in the next chapter.

These virtuous ladies did all these vast projects and holy works with order, humility, discretion, zeal, and admirable perseverance, under the wise guidance of Monsieur Vincent. He conveyed his own spirit to this devout company and inspired in them the same fervor and charity with which he was so filled. We shall report here, as a permanent record of his direction, what he said in a meeting with these women in an extraordinary general assembly held in the home of the duchess of Aiguillon, their superior at the time. It was taken down in secret by one of the Missionaries who accompanied him on this occasion. The reader will be consoled to see the prudence and piety of Monsieur Vincent and his way of convincing the women of the assembly. In addition, the diversity and quantity of items covered by him show how much good he was able to do for and with them.

After invoking while kneeling the Holy Spirit by the hymn *Veni Sancte Spiritus*, he spoke to them as follows:

> Ladies, there are three things we would like to speak about in this assembly. The first concerns the election of new officers, if you judge it appropriate. The second, a report on the works God has accomplished through the Company. The third, ladies, will be to consider the reasons we must surrender to the goodness of God so he may give us the grace to support and continue the good works we have begun.
>
> The elections were discussed in the ordinary assembly last Friday, attended by the officers and some other ladies. The officers were of the opinion there should be new elections, but the others thought the officers should continue to serve until Easter. Since you, ladies, have the deliberative voice in this matter, we will vote at the

---

appealed to the queen and the Ladies of Charity in its establishment. He then sent Daughters of Charity to serve the poor there.

5. These were titular sees, whose bishops had responsibilities for evangelizing in East Asia.

end of this conference to see if you prefer to keep your present officers or if we should proceed to a new election.

Concerning our present state of affairs, let us begin with the Hotel Dieu, if we may. We began our Company there and it is the foundation upon which it has pleased God to establish the other good works we are involved with. It is the source of all the other good we have done.

With these words he took in hand a report of the receipts and expenses, which he read aloud. It showed that the expenses of the food brought to the poor every day for the past year since the last general assembly amounted to 5000 *livres*, while the income was 3500 *livres*, leaving a deficit of 1500 *livres*. Then, resuming his talk, he continued:

This comes from the death of several of our members who have not been replaced by others. We have come together, ladies, to see if there are some ways we can assure the continuance of this work. It has now lasted for several years through the efforts of many, but mainly of God. He blessed it so that we have great reason to thank him.

Oh, ladies, how we should thank God for inspiring you to care for the bodily needs of these poor sick. The help you have given them has had this effect of God's grace in you, that you have thought of their eternal salvation. Most of them would otherwise never have done so, and so you have prepared them for a happy death. Those who have recovered would never even have thought of amending their lives, were it not for your efforts.

He then read the expenses of the help sent to Champagne and Picardy. From July 15, 1650 to the day of their last general assembly, 348,000 *livres* was sent and distributed to the poor. Since then, from the general assembly till today, 19,500 *livres* were sent, about the same as preceding years. He then continued:

This money was sent to feed the sick poor and to support around eight hundred orphan children, boys and girls, from the devastated towns. They were instructed in a trade, after having been clothed and educated, or taught how to serve some function in a household. Many pastors were supported in their ruined parishes who otherwise they would have had to leave for want of food. Lastly, the money was used to renovate to some degree several churches which were in such a ruined state you cannot even speak of them without shuddering in horror.

This money has been distributed to places in the towns and regions of Reims, Rethel, Laon, Saint Quentin, Ham, Marle, Sedan and Arras.

If you add to that the clothes, linens, blankets, shirts, albs, chasubles, missals, ciboria, etc., it comes to a large sum.

Certainly, ladies, we can only admire the great number of these items of clothing for men, women, and children, and even for the priests, not to mention the items for the pillaged churches. They were so damaged and reduced to such a poverty that the sacred mysteries could not have been celebrated in them without this aid. Without it, sacred places would have been suited for profane uses alone. If you had visited the homes of the ladies responsible for collecting used clothing you would have thought you were in a storehouse or in the shop of a prosperous merchant.

Blessed be God, ladies, for having given you the grace to clothe our Lord in his poor members, most of whom were in rags, and some children were as bare as my hand. The clothes of some women and girls were so scanty that no one with even the least bit of decency would have looked at them. All were threatened with death from the cold during the winter. How much you are obligated to God for having inspired you and given you the means to meet such pressing needs! How many of the sick have you saved from death! They were left by everyone, sleeping on the ground, exposed to the elements, and reduced to the last extremity by the soldiers and by the scarcity of the harvest. It is true their misery is not so great now as it was several years ago, and yet we continue to send about 16,000 *livres* a month.

Even now, in view of the danger the poor run of dying if something is not done promptly, encourage one another in your efforts to help them. However, because the times have improved this last year or two, the alms for their support have greatly fallen off. We still have nearly eighty churches in ruins, and the poor have to travel far to hear mass. Do you see where we are? We have to begin to work at this, trusting in God's Providence for our Company.

Ladies, does not the recounting of these things wring your hearts? Are you not moved to thanksgiving to God for his goodness to you and to the poor afflicted ones? His Providence spoke to some ladies of Paris to help two desolated provinces. Does that not seem strange to you? History does not tell us of anything similar happening to the ladies of Spain, or Italy, or other countries. This has been reserved for you, ladies, who are here now, and to several others who have gone to God, where they have found a full reward for such perfect charity. Eight of your number have died in the past year.

And concerning these deceased members, O Savior, who would have told them the last time they came together that God would call them before the next general assembly? What reflections would they not have made upon the brevity of this life and the importance of spending it well? How much they would have appreciated the practice of their good deeds! And what resolutions they would have taken to give themselves more than ever before, to the love of God and neighbor, with greater fervor and greater effort! Let us give ourselves to God, in keeping with these sentiments. They are now in glory, as we devoutly hope. They realize how good it is to serve God and to help the poor. At the judgment they will hear the comforting words of the Son of God: "Come you blessed of my Father, possess the kingdom prepared for you, because when I was hungry you gave me to eat; when I was naked, you clothed me; when I was sick, you visited and served me."[6] It is a fine thing, ladies, and for me too, to offer ourselves to God, to make ourselves worthy, as often as we have the occasion, of being among that happy number, and of having decided to do the good we would wish to have done, were this to be our last assembly. Just think, eight in one year! If you subtract the same number for each of the past years you would find the number remaining in the Company greatly reduced. At the beginning we had two or three hundred, but now we are reduced to a hundred and fifty. I recommend to your prayers these dear departed ones.

We turn now to the abandoned children, taken under your care. I see by the account of Madame de Bragelogne, your treasurer, that the receipts for the past year came to 16,248 *livres*, while the expenses were 17,221 *livres*. Looking at the number of these children in the care of nurses in the country or in the city, those who have been weaned, the older ones in trades or in domestic service, and those who remain in the hospital, it comes in all to 395.

It seems the number abandoned each year remains about the same, on the average about one a day. If you will, ladies, look at the order in this disorder. What great good you do in taking care of these little deserted creatures, abandoned by their own mothers to be brought up, educated, taught how to earn their livelihood, and to work out their salvation. Before you took up this work the canons of Notre Dame pressured you. Since this work was so complicated, you thought it out carefully and finally you took it up, recognizing it would be most pleasing to God, as has been borne out since.

---

6. Matt 25:34-35.

Before that, it had never been known in the previous fifty years that a single one of these abandoned children survived, dying from one cause or another. It was to you, ladies, that God reserved the grace to save a large number and to enable them to live well. You taught them to speak and to pray to God. You kept them busy, each one according to each one's own age or abilities. You looked after them, and guided them, correcting them in good time when required by their evil inclinations. They were happy to have fallen into your hands, and they would have been miserable with their own parents, who for the most part were either very poor or possibly vicious. You only have to see how they spend their day to see the fruits of your care. It is of such importance you have every reason in the world, ladies, to thank God for having confided it to you.

It remains for me to say a few words about renewing our dedication to these works of charity the mercy of God has brought to their present state. We will see their results only in heaven. We are obliged, I say, all of us here, enrolled in this holy militia, to continue and even augment our first fervor. Those not yet members of the Company should do what they can to support and develop these projects so much in keeping with what our Lord did, and recommended in favor of the poor.

The first motive for this is that your Company is a work of God and is not of human making. I have said before that others do not know how to achieve what you have done. God is involved, and in fact all good comes from God. He is the author of all these good works. Everything must be referred to the God of Virtue and the Father of Mercies. To what do we attribute the light of the stars but to the sun from which it comes? To whom do we attribute the idea of your Company but to the Father of Mercies and the God of all Consolation, who has chosen you as persons of consolation and mercy? God never calls anyone to a position if he does not see in her the qualities needed to fulfill the calling or if he does not plan to give her these qualities. God, then, by his grace has called you and brought you together. His grace brought you to these three types of service, and not your own will, but the goodness he put in you. We surely then must stir up by every means the charity within us. What? God honored me by calling me, and I must hear his voice. God has destined me for these charitable enterprises and I must devote myself to them.

He did not will, ladies, that you should, like Simeon, see the Savior, but he does will that you hear his voice when he calls, if not blindly, like Saint Paul, at least with joy and tenderness. To hear the call and not respond would be most unworthy of the grace of your vocation. I have seen the beginning of the work, I have seen God bless it. I have seen it begin by a simple meal brought to the sick, and now I have seen how it has grown in a way so mightily for his glory and for the advantage of the poor. Ha! Now I must support it. What hardness of heart, should there be anyone who would not contribute to the development of such great works as these.

The second motive is the fear that these works of charity might come to ruin at your hands. This would be, beyond doubt, a great disaster, ladies, all the greater because the grace of God has called you to this service which is something rare and extraordinary. It has been eight hundred years or thereabouts, since women have had any public office in the Church. There used to be what were called deaconesses. They preserved order among women in the churches and taught them the rites then in use. At the time of Charlemagne, by a secret decree of Providence, this custom stopped, and from that time women were allowed no public service in the Church. This same Providence today spoke to some women among us to serve the sick poor in the Hotel Dieu. You responded to this invitation, and soon other women joined the first ones. God then led them to become the mothers of abandoned children, the directors of their hospital, and the distributors of the alms of Paris for the needy in the provinces. These good souls have answered with ardor and constancy, by the grace of God. Ah, ladies, if all these works were now to fail in your hands, this would be a great sorrow. What desolation! What shame! What must we think of such a tragedy? How could it come about? Let each of you ask herself the question, is it I who have helped bring about the failure of this work? What is there in me that has made me unworthy to sustain it? Am I the cause of God withdrawing his graces? Without doubt, ladies, if we examine ourselves well, we fear we may not have done all we could to support this enterprise.

If you consider well its importance, you will cherish it as the apple of your eye or as the instrument of your salvation, and you will work for its advancement and perfection with the help of God. You will bring other women of your acquaintance too, for otherwise you will earn the reproach made to the man in the Gospel who began to build but was not able to finish. You will have laid the foundation of a work but you will have left it at that. This is all the more important if you consider your building as an ornament of the Church, and an asylum for the forsaken. If by your fault it were to fail, you would remove from the public a source of much edification and from the poor a great comfort.

The brother assigned to distribute your charitable alms told me, "Monsieur, the grain you sent to the frontiers has saved the lives of a large number of poor families. They had no seed saved for sowing and no one would lend them any. The fields were lying fallow, with many regions deserted because the people had either died or had fled away." Twenty-two thousand *livres* worth of grain have been distributed during a single year to get them through the summer and the following winter. You can see, ladies, from the good you have accomplished how great would be the suffering should you allow your project to fail.

The third motive you should have for continuing these holy works is the honor they give to our Lord. How is this? Because we honor him by entering into his sentiments, appreciating them, doing what he did, and carrying out what he has ordained. His most cherished wish was to care for the poor: he cured them, consoled them, helped them, and urged others to do the same. This was his delight. He himself willed to be born poor, to live among the poor, serve the poor, take the place of the poor, up to the point of saying that the good and evil we do to them he considers as done to his divine Person. How could he show more tender love for the poor? What love could we have for him if we did not love those he loved so tenderly? So much so, ladies, that to love him well we must love the poor. To serve him well we must serve them. To honor him as we should, we must imitate him in his care for the poor. Considering all this, what motives there are to inspire us to continue these good works, and to say from the bottom of our hearts, yes, I commit myself to God to care for the poor and to support the charitable enterprises established in their favor. I will help them, love them, and recommend them to others. After the example of our Lord, I will love those who are consoled, and will cherish those who are visited and helped. If their gracious savior is honored by our imitation of him, how much greater is our honor for being likened to him? Does it not seem to you, ladies, that this is a powerful motive to renew in yourselves your first fervor? For myself I think that we ought to offer ourselves today to his divine majesty that he would inspire us with his charity, so that henceforth we could say of us all that it is the charity of Jesus Christ that compels us.

These are motives enough for those who love God. It seems you might say to me, Monsieur, we are indeed persuaded of the importance of continuing what we have begun, for it is the end that crowns the work. We understand that we must not only serve God and help the poor, we must do so as best we possibly can. We now are seeking the means to do this, for we are resolved to do what we can to support these works and to continue our assemblies.

The first means I would present to you, ladies, is to have an interior and continuous desire to work at your own spiritual advancement and to live in as great perfection as possible. You must always have the lamp within you burning brightly, by which I mean the ardent desire to please the Lord and to obey him, or in a word, to live as true servants of God. Those in these dispositions will surely attract the grace of God, and our Lord himself, into their hearts and actions. Living this way, you will persevere in good works, because the Lord of mercy will continue to live in you. The maxims of the world are not in keeping with these thoughts. Nothing can so deprive you of the spirit of God as to live worldly lives, and the more a person does so, the more unworthy she makes herself to possess Jesus Christ. The Ladies of Charity ought to avoid this spirit of the world like they do the plague. They must declare themselves as members of the party of God and of charity. I say they must be entirely committed to God. Were someone just a bit given to this other spirit, it would not work out. God will not suffer a divided heart, he demands all. Yes, he demands all. My consolation is to be talking to souls that are fully given to him, separated from all that could harm them in his eyes.

Formerly, when we had to choose among those who wanted to enter our Company, we selected those who avoided games, the theater, or other dangerous pastimes, and who were not vain, but wished to be devoted to the service of God. We must have the faith to know that God will give his grace only to those who avoid high society and are united to him in their aspirations, prayers, and good works in such a way that everyone can see they are committed to serving God.

O Lord, are there many to be saved? There are two doors which open to the other life, one straight and narrow, the other wide open. Few go by the first, but many by the second. The saints tell us the large number refers to the worldly who follow their own uncontrolled appetites. These earn the anger and curse of God, according to what Saint Paul says: "If you live according the flesh you shall die."[7] O Lord, what a threat! We have reason to fear that we will

---

7. Rom 8:13.

be of that number, and be condemned. Yes, if we do not walk the narrow way.

The ladies who give themselves to God to live as true Christians by the observance of the commandments of God and who keep the rules of justice; the married, who live in obedience to their husbands; widows who live as widows; mothers who take care of their children; governesses who look after the serving boys and girls; all these, and those besides who do what the blessed bishop of Geneva advised, joining those companies and confraternities who strive to practice virtue, and do some exterior works of mercy or piety, leading to the mortification of the passions and to the love of God: these are the women who walk the way that leads to life. Join this company or confraternity, then, ladies, if you are not already enrolled, for it is committed to God alone to do only his will, and to serve him. If one's concern is the husband, do it for God; care of the children, do it for God; working at some business, do it for God. This is the way to pass by the narrow gate that leads to salvation.

Our Lord dealt with three groups, his apostles, disciples, and the people. These last heard him for a while, but after a time returned to their homes. This forced our Lord to ask his disciples: "And you, do you want to abandon me too?" There are those, ladies, who see you following our Lord by the narrow way of the love of God and neighbor, and wish to imitate you. It seems such a beautiful way of life, but they find it difficult and turn away. Among those who followed our Lord, there were both women and men. They were faithful even to the cross. They were not apostles but in a middle state, and they later began caring for the temporal needs of the apostles, and contributing to their ministry. It is desirable that the Ladies of Charity take these devout women as their model.

There is no position in the world that equals the calling you have. You support the workers of the Gospel but also the needy faithful. This is your office, ladies, your portion. Bless God for his having called you to this work, and live as holy women. Have the tenderness and devotion of the blessed Joanna, the wife of Chuza, and the others of whom Saint Luke speaks.[8] This is how you will enter the narrow gate that leads to life. You all will be saved, for as Saint Thomas says, no one can ever be lost in doing works of charity.

Let us put ourselves within the enclosure of this virtue, coming to the feet of our Lord, praying him to expand in our hearts his light and warmth that we may bring to a happy conclusion the work we

---

8. Luke 8:3.

have begun. Not to do tomorrow what we have done today is to slip back. In the spiritual life we must always go forward, and we do so by not putting aside the good we have been doing. May it please God to preserve you in your good deeds, to live as true mothers who never abandon their children! You are the mothers of the poor, just as our Lord is their father. He made himself like to them and came to preach to them, help them, and recommend them to our care. Do the same, visiting the holy places, I mean the hospitals, and virtuous persons, the members of your own Company, and this will be a sign of your own predestination. It will be a way for you to advance in virtue, a way to attract others, and the chosen way to make your Company prosper, to the glory of God and the edification of the people.

Another way to preserve your Company is to moderate your activities, for a proverb says, he who holds on to too much grasps poorly. It has happened in some other companies or confraternities, in several communities, and even in entire orders, that by attempting too much they have succumbed under the burden. Virtue stands in the middle, between the opposite vices of excess and defect. For example, if under the pretext of charity you would try to do every possible good for another, allowing nothing to pass when you see you could do something, you would fall into a vice, just as much as the person who would do nothing would fall into the opposite vice. Theologians tell us it is just as dangerous to fail by excess as it is by defect. Ordinarily the devil tempts charitable people to excess in their charity, knowing that sooner or later they will succumb. Have you never seen persons too loaded down who fall under their burden? It could happen that a whole company could fail, if it attempts too much.

We see this ourselves in the fourteen ladies of the Company who go two by two to the Hotel Dieu to visit and console the sick poor. They do much good and others bring some small refreshments every day to the sick. The work is divided up to console and instruct the poor women and sick girls in their beds or wherever they happen to be. It has been difficult to keep up this visitation, and there are some things hard to overcome, so that it has become difficult to get volunteers for this service.

The help given to the border regions and the invaded provinces is great. It is almost unknown that a group of women would gather together to help regions of the country reduced to such extreme necessity, by sending large sums of money and food and clothing for a large number of poor men and women of all conditions and ages. We have never before read of such persons joining forces to do what you ladies have done. We must be careful not to overburden ourselves, and so perhaps leave aside some important work, and allow the whole enterprise to fail. Someone said to me recently, God is all powerful, but we are weak. We seek virtue by doing more. But virtue is not found simply in doing more. Saint Peter converted five thousand in a single sermon, while our Lord preached several times and perhaps converted not a single person. He even said himself that those who believed in him would do more than he himself had done. He willed to be more humble in undertaking less. A loaded stomach does not digest well. A porter will lift his load first before putting it on his shoulders to see if it is too heavy for him.

We should pray to God to determine our burden, for then if our strength fails, he will help us carry it. May he give the grace to the Company to be reserved, to take up nothing but what comes from him. How much time passed before taking up the care of the abandoned children? How many requests did we have to take up that work! How many prayers, pilgrimages, and communions were made, to help us decide. You are aware, ladies, of all this, and you are aware, too, that we should always use the same caution before accepting any new obligations through an indiscreet zeal. When you see you are doing the things well that God has asked of you, have courage and bless his infinite goodness. Give yourselves to these duties with perseverance, but do not presume to try to do more.

Consider the feeding and instruction of the poor in the Hotel Dieu, the care and education of the foundlings, looking after the spiritual and corporal needs of the criminals condemned to the galleys, the help given to the frontier regions and the ravaged provinces, the contributions to the missions, to the Far East, the Hebrides, and the south. These, ladies, are the responsibilities of your Company. What? Have these ladies done all this? Yes, and for more than twenty years God has given you the grace to begin these and carry them out. Do not undertake anything further unless you consider it carefully, but do what you are now doing better and better. This is what God asks of you.

A third means of preserving the Company is to continue to invite other women of piety and virtue to join you. If new members do not come, your Company will decrease in numbers and become too weak to fulfill the heavy burdens you bear. It has been proposed that some time before their death, a sister or a friend be induced to enter the Company, but perhaps this would not appeal to everyone. A good means, ladies, would be if each of you would be persuaded of the great good in this world and the next for souls to exercise the works of mercy, spiritual and corporal, in the way you do. This undoubtedly would lead others to join you in your practice of charity, in consideration of the good you do. This conviction would have the effect of mutually encouraging each other, and this in turn would influence others by your words and example.

"Allow me, ladies, to ask your opinion." Turning to Madame de Nemours he said, "Madame, has anything come to your mind, that would be a means to help the Company?" After she spoke, he asked others. Most replied they thought the means he had suggested were perhaps the best, and others added the following:

(1) Those who die must be encouraged beforehand to leave legacies in favor of the poor. Monsieur Vincent replied: "this is a helpful suggestion, which could be made to rich people when they are visited in their sicknesses."

(2) Be more exact in observing the daily prescribed exercises. Monsieur Vincent added, "This is good advice to attract persons, and this exactitude leads to a holy life which also attracts."

(3) Each lady of the Company ought to make up the deficit of the Company, as much as she is able.

In conclusion, Monsieur Vincent said: "It remains only to find out if you prefer to have your officers remain. If not, we will proceed to a vote." He asked each one's opinion, one after the other, with the unanimous result that the officers should continue, and therefore there was to be no election at that time.

He ended the assembly with these words:

> Let us thank God, ladies, for this assembly. Let us pray that he will accept the new sacrifice we will offer him on our knees, in giving ourselves to him with our whole heart, to receive from his infinite bounty his spirit of charity. Let us pray also that he give us the grace, to each one of us in particular, and to the Company in general, to respond to his designs upon us. May he raise up this ardent spirit of charity of Jesus Christ, that we may merit to be filled with it, and that having spread this charity abroad in this world he may make us worthy to be received by his Father eternally in the world to come. Amen.[9]

---

9. *CED* XIII:802-20.

CHAPTER ELEVEN

The Help Given by Monsieur Vincent to Different Provinces Devastated by Wars

SECTION ONE

Help Given to Lorraine

WE CAN SAY without exaggeration that we will see in this and in the following two sections a masterpiece of charity seldom equaled. In these pages we speak of the help given by Monsieur Vincent to an almost limitless number of persons reduced to the last extremity by the horrors of war. The pages of history tell us of many examples of the extreme misery caused by the scourges of war. They speak of the ruin and desolation of cities, provinces, and sometimes of entire monarchies. In none of these pages do we read that amid the terror and confusion of armies, and surrounded by the violence and plunder of the soldiers, the spiritual and corporal works of mercy were widely practiced. This was not in favor of a privileged few, but to entire peoples, and not for some days, but for a long succession of years. During these times charity triumphed in those very places where justice had no voice, legitimate authority was no longer recognized, and the laws and ordinances of the sovereigns were trampled under foot.

Indeed, we must insist that in all past ages nothing of the kind had never been seen. If something similar was done, historians have not recorded it, possibly because they would find it so hard to believe, or because they would think the written records of such events were exaggerated. What we have to recount here was so public and evident, and seen over several years by a large number of witnesses, that there is no fear these accounts will be received with hesitation. Should some incredulous persons contradict what we shall say, whole provinces would rise up against them in a parade of witnesses. They owe their lives and what they value more even than life itself, to the charitable help Monsieur Vincent gave them.

The one who conceived this help by the inspiration of God, who began it, continued and sustained it over many years, and who inspired so many others to participate in these undertakings with the same charitable spirit with which he was so filled, was no other than this same Vincent de Paul.

God was pleased to enlighten, strengthen, and give him such an abundance of grace that he created a masterpiece of charity, exceeding all human industry and power.

We will begin this chapter by speaking of Lorraine, which first felt the effects of war, and which the violence of the scourge completely ruined. This province was formerly one of the most densely populated, the most fertile, and the most pleasant of all Europe. It had good rulers, and the people were faithful to them, with mutual esteem, so unlike what often happens with other countries. For many years it enjoyed peace, both inside and outside its borders, with all the blessings which flow from years of prosperity.

The abundance of worldly goods and pleasures is more apt to attach the hearts of men to earth than to raise them to heaven. Among the satisfactions and comforts of life only rarely would vices and sins occur which Providence would purge by way of the waters of tribulation. This began in 1635 with three scourges, if not at the same moment, at least one after the other, that is, plague, war, and famine. These came as a deluge, destroying everything almost, afflicting the entire province. A large number of inhabitants were stricken, and nearly all the survivors fled for their lives. Priests, nobles, and leading citizens escaped, seeking elsewhere the supports of life they could not find in their own homes. Desolation reached such a point that those who remained had to eat the half-rotten carrion of beasts to survive. They themselves became the prey of wild animals. From all sides starving wolves tore to pieces and devoured women and children, even in full daylight, and in the sight of everyone. Some of these poor creatures, grievously torn by the wolves, were carried half dead to the hospitals of the towns, where priests of the Mission tended them. The wolves were so hungry for human flesh they would come into the towns and villages. They entered houses whose doors chanced to be open. They would come into the larger cities at night through breaks in the walls, and carry off women and children, and whatever else they could find.

God is ever mindful of his mercy, even in this life in the midst of the most rigorous carrying out of his justice. Wishing to give some consolation and help to this sorely tried people, he raised up Monsieur Vincent. When he learned of the desolation of the province, he was deeply moved. He responded like another Moses in prayer: "Why, O Lord, has your anger risen against your people? Please let your vengeance cease."[1] Moved by a spirit of compassion and charity, he offered himself to the divine majesty to do what he could to relieve and console these poor people, reduced to such extremity. Shortly after, divine Providence sent him someone with money to be used for this purpose. He immediately sent it to the priests of his Congregation in Toul, in Lorraine, and these charitable missionaries began

---

1. Exod 32:11-12.

at once to use the money to house, feed, and tend the sick poor collected from the streets.[2] He sent other priests and brothers from the house of Saint Lazare to help out in other cities in Lorraine, especially Metz, Verdun, Nancy, Bar le Duc, Pont a Mousson, Saint Michel,[3] Luneville, and others.

The following letter, dated December 1639, testifies to the help he gave to the poor of Tours:

> Jean Midot, doctor in theology, archdeacon, canon and vicar general of Toul, the see being vacant, certifies and affirms that the priests of the Mission living in this city have continued with much edification and charity to help, clothe, feed, and doctor the poor for these past two years. They cared for the sick, sixty of whom they brought to their own house, and a hundred more in the suburbs. Second, they helped by their alms many other poor persons, ashamed of their condition but brought low by a great need, and who fled to this city. In the third place, they accepted into their home or brought to the Hospital of Charity many sick and wounded soldiers of the king, who were fed and cared for to the great edification of all people of good will. In testimony of which we have signed, and countersigned, and sealed.

The priests of the Mission who lived in Toul sent this certification to Monsieur Vincent, asking him to obtain similar statements from the other cities they had served. He answered: "It would have been better not to have asked this. It is enough that God knows what has been done, not to mention the poor themselves, without any need for more testimonials."

The same help was given in the city of Metz, where incredible poverty affected huge numbers of people. Sometimes four or five thousand gathered at the gates of the city, both men and women all ages. Often in the morning ten or twelve would have died during the night. Some of the older girls were tempted to sell themselves rather than starve. Several religious communities were on the verge of breaking their cloister to seek food. When Monsieur Vincent was alerted to these extreme needs he sent help to save the lives of some and the honor of others, in an effort to help all. The city magistrates wrote the following letter to Monsieur Vincent, in October 1640:

> Monsieur, you have made us your debtors in coming to the aid of the extremely poor, discouraged and sick, and especially of the poor monasteries of religious of this city. We would be remiss in

---

2. Francois du Coudray and Leonard Boucher, missionaries stationed at Toul, gathered forty poor persons into their own house, and the helped 150 outside of the city. Vincent feared that the missionaries would succumb under the weight of their labors both physically and financially. He wrote to them to preserve both themselves and their resources. Du Coudray responded: "Monsieur, either send me help, recall me, or leave me to die among the poor." See *CED* I:538.

3. Also spelled Saint Mihiel.

our duty if we did not thank you for the help you have given us. We can assure you that the alms you sent have been used exclusively for the needy poor, and especially the religious deprived of all human help. The first received nothing of their usual income because of the war, and the others received none of their usual alms, since conditions here are so bad. We must ask you, Monsieur, as we do most humbly, to continue the help you have been giving to each group. This will undoubtedly be most meritorious for those who contribute to this cause, and to you, Monsieur, who direct this effort with such prudence and efficacy, to the glory of God.[4]

The missionaries living in Verdun wrote to Monsieur Vincent:

In 1639, 1640, and 1641 we had sometimes five or six hundred poor persons to care for. At other times we had at least four hundred to whom we gave bread each day, and divided them into two groups, the younger and the older, so we could offer instruction with greater effect.

We gave soup and meat to some fifty or sixty sick poor each day, and some money to others, as the need arose. We helped about thirty poor who were ashamed to come with the others. Many peasants and farmers came asking for alms, and we gave them bread whenever they came. We clothed the naked, and gave shoes to those who needed them most.

One missionary wrote to Monsieur Vincent that he had been greatly edified and consoled at the admirable patience and unbelievable resignation he experienced among the sick and the dying. "Oh, Monsieur, how poverty has led many to paradise! Since coming to Lorraine, I have seen more than a thousand poor people die, and they all seemed perfectly ready. How many intercessors in heaven for their benefactors!"[5]

In Nancy, the following distributions were made to various categories of poor during these same years:

(1) Those in good health, four or five hundred, were given soup and bread each day. Instructions were given to prepare them to confess and communicate, usually once a month. In their charity, the missionaries housed some of these poor people in the same place they themselves lived.

(2) Besides, they kept in their own home some sick persons, whom they fed and nursed. Other sick were taken to the Hospital of Saint Joseph. Each one received linens and some money, but only after they had gone to confession and received communion. Usually thirty or forty other sick

---

4. *CED* II:131-32.
5. *CED* II:216.

persons were kept here or there in the city, to whom they gave bread, soup, and meat each day.

(3) They helped two types of people in financial difficulties, about fifty of the middle class, to whom they gave a certain amount of bread each week. The other group numbered around thirty upper class people, either priests or laity, much in need, but ashamed of their poverty. They received some money each month, depending on their condition and need.

(4) They took particular care of many poor nursing mothers, to whom they gave money, bread, flour, and soup.

(5) They took care of the sick and wounded soldiers, paying the doctors and the cost of the medicines. They even had received some inexpensive private remedies which brought great relief to many of the sick.

(6) They gave linens and clothes to all the poor who needed them. When they gave shirts to them, they would take the soiled ones to have them washed, to be given in turn to others. This would sometimes amount to six or seven dozen at a time.

We are not able to cite the most touching letters Monsieur Vincent received from this desolated province on the extreme affliction of the people, or on the extraordinary help they had received, because most of the these letters have been lost. He sent them to various places, to influence the rich to contribute, or to show those who already had contributed what good use their money was being put to. The following letter is what a virtuous priest wrote to Monsieur Vincent on this matter:

> After I saw the letter from Lorraine, which you sent to Monsieur N., and who then showed it to me, I must tell you I could not read it without tears. Sometimes I shed these tears in such abundance I could scarcely continue reading. I praise our good God for the paternal providence he has exercised toward his creatures, and I beg him to continue his graces to your priests, whom he uses in this holy work. I must tell you in closing how much I mourn the deaths of some of your charitable workers who have gone to heaven. They have helped so many others attain it also, while miserable me, I remain a useless beast, wandering over the earth.[6]

The first priests of the Mission who went to Pont a Mousson in May 1640, sent word to Monsieur Vincent they had helped four or five hundred poor people. These had suffered so much from their poverty that the missionaries had never before seen people so deserving compassion. Most were from the country, and some were so emaciated and frail that they died as they ate.

The four pastors of the village had given them a list of the sick and the most miserable of the embarrassed poor. They had visited the sick, and found

---

6. *CED* II:37.

several in their last agony. Some religious sisters were in great need. In the regions surrounding the city wolves had been attacking people, and this frightened a number from coming to seek food, particularly the children of ten or twelve years of age. A good and charitable pastor offered to bring some relief to them, aided by the alms given by the missionaries.

There were usually around a hundred sick in this town, and fifty or sixty shy or embarrassed poor, besides the many other good people reduced to hunger. The missionaries helped all in the other localities, in the same way we have described. They distributed bed linens and clothing, particularly to the sick, and shoes and tools to those still able to work, to enable them to earn their bread by their own labor.

The missionaries daily distributed food to several hundred other poor refugees. To all they offered a sort of mission to dispose them to make a good general confession, which many did in a Christian manner.

The mayor, magistrates, police and city council of Pont a Mousson wrote to Monsieur Vincent in December 1640, to thank him for his help, and to beg him to continue his help:

> The fear we have that shortly we will be deprived of the charity your goodness has bestowed on the poor of our city causes us to write to you, Monsieur, to ask you to please continue to help us as before, for our needs are as great as they have ever been. For the past two years the harvest has failed, and the animals have eaten our crops in the fields. The constant garrisoning of the troops has brought us all to begging. These motives, agonizing but true, should stir your tender heart, already so full of love and pity, to continue your kindness toward these five hundred poor. They would surely die quickly if your kindness to them would come to an end. Please do not allow this to happen, but give us the leftover crumbs from the other towns. You will not only be exercising charity toward the poor, but you will be snatching them from death and earning the eternal gratitude of the undersigned.[7]

Around the same time one of the priests of the Mission went to the town of Saint Mihiel, writing to Monsieur Vincent as follows:

> Once I arrived here, I immediately began to distribute alms. I found a large number of poor, not all of whom I could help, for more than three hundred were in direst need, and three hundred more required assistance. Monsieur, I tell you the truth. More than a hundred seemed to be mere skeletons covered with skin and so frightful I would not have been able even to look at them if the Lord did not strengthen me. Their skin was like polished marble, and so

---

7. *CED* II:145-46.

shrunken that their dry teeth appeared in their open mouths. It was the most appalling thing I have ever seen. They looked for roots in the fields to cook and eat. I very much recommend the great misery of these poor people to the prayers of our Company. Some young women die from hunger, and I fear that some among them may fall into even great disaster than anything merely temporal.[8]

In another letter of March 1640, he wrote again:

At the last distribution of bread, we helped 1,132 poor, not counting the many sick, with food and medicine. They all pray for their benefactors with such a sense of thanksgiving that many cry from emotion. Some rich people react the same way. I do not believe that these people, for whom so many prayers are being offered to God, will die. The authorities of the town praise this charity, publicly admitting that many would have died without this help, and acknowledging the debt they owe to you. Just recently a poor man from Switzerland abjured his Lutheran heresy on his deathbed, and after receiving the sacraments died a Christian death.[9]

In this same year, 1640, Monsieur Vincent sent one of the leading priests of the Congregation[10] to visit all the missionaries working at distributing alms in Lorraine. He was to suggest ways of carrying out this charity, and also to ascertain the regions of greatest need. He wrote to Monsieur Vincent from Saint Mihiel:

I must tell you, Monsieur, of the admirable things I have seen in this town which you would scarcely believe if you did not see them with your own eyes. Besides all the poor beggars, already mentioned, the greater number of inhabitants of the town, the nobles above all, endure such hunger as you can scarcely imagine. What is worse, they cannot bring themselves to ask for bread. Some do, but others prefer to die rather than beg. I have spoken myself to some of these people who could not refrain from weeping as they spoke of this situation.

Another unusual thing happened. A widow had nothing for herself or for her three children. When she saw herself threatened with starvation she skinned a snake, put it over the coals to be roasted, and ate it for want of anything else. Our confrere here heard of this, and brought something for her.

No horse dies in the town, no matter from what cause, without being grabbed and eaten. Not three or four days ago I saw a woman

---

8. *CED* II:24.
9. *CED* II:35.
10. Jean Dehorgny.

at the public distribution of bread. Her basket was filled with some of this tainted meat which she was trading off for bread with some of the other peasants.

A young woman was thinking of selling what was most precious to gain a bit of bread, and was looking for an opportunity to do so. God be blessed and thanked, she found none, and now is out of danger.

Another deplorable case concerns the priests. By God's mercy they all lead exemplary lives, but they suffer the same lot as the others, with no bread to eat. A pastor living a half league from here is reduced to pulling a plow, joining his parishioners in the traces in place of horses. Is it not deplorable, Monsieur, to see a priest and a pastor reduced to such a state? You do not have to go to Turkey to see priests condemned to hard labor. We see this at our very doors, brought about by the troubles of the times.

Our Lord is so good, Monsieur, it seems he has blessed Saint Mihiel with a spirit of devotion and patience. Amid their extreme lack of temporal things, the people seem avid for spiritual things. We see up to two thousand persons attending the catechism lessons, a lot for such a small town, where most larger houses are deserted. The poor are careful to attend and to receive the sacraments. The missionary here is greatly esteemed, for he teaches and cares for them. Those with a chance to speak to him consider themselves fortunate. He shows great charity and devotion to his work for all the people of the region. He was so overworked by the number of general confessions, and his lack of proper nourishment, that he has fallen sick.

I am amazed how with so little money coming from Paris he has been able to give so much to so many. I see in this a manifestation of the goodness of God, who has multiplied his resources. He reminds me of what the holy Scripture says of the manna in the desert: each family received the same amount, which turned out to suffice for all, regardless of the number being fed. I see here something similar, for our priests who have more poor people to help do not give any less and yet want for nothing.[11]

In 1643, the lieutenant, provost, council, and governor of the city wrote the following letter to Monsieur Vincent:

The governors and citizens of Saint Mihiel give you a thousand thanks for the care and help you have rendered by the alms and other helps you have given to the sick poor, and by helping to have a part

---

11. *CED* II:58-59.

of the garrison taken from the city. We ask you most humbly to continue your concern and your alms since this poor and desolate city has as great a need now as ever before.

By your care, a countless number have been saved who otherwise would have perished. If your help is curtailed or even stopped altogether, we must expect a large part of the inhabitants will die from hunger, or at least will leave to seek their living elsewhere. We need hardly mention the help you have given to enable the convents to survive, or the help given to so many good people, even some of the upper class, in their sickness and need. We cannot praise enough the efforts and care you have taken of us. We pray you most earnestly to continue these same helps for so many sick and needy, which undoubtedly will be a source of great merit and honor before God.[12]

The poor of Bar le Duc, eight hundred or so inhabitants and refugees, received help in both soul and body. This was a great help to the surrounding countryside and especially the city. Previously a large number of poor were to be found there. They slept on the streets, at the crossroads, and in the doors of the churches. Tradesmen were dying of hunger, of the cold, and of their illnesses and misery. One of the priests of the Mission wrote to Monsieur Vincent in February 1640 that at each distribution of bread he had to give clothes to twenty-five or thirty poor people, and then he added:

In a short time I have clothed, by actual count, two hundred sixty, but I cannot measure the spiritual good of general confessions and holy communion, in the space of the past month alone. I have counted more than eight hundred. This Lent I hope we will be able to do even more. We give the hospital a *pistole* and a half every month for the sick we send there. Since among them around eighty are sicker than the others, we give them soup, bread, and some meat.[13]

The visitor sent by Monsieur Vincent passed through Bar le Duc in July 1640. He sent this report:

First, every week our missionaries give some linens, especially shirts, to many poor. The missionaries collect the old ones to have them cleaned, so they can be given to others, or to be cut into bandages for the wounded or the ulcerous.

Second, they themselves take care of some persons suffering from a scalp disorder. There used to be about twenty-five, but only about twelve are now sick of this ailment. This disease is common

---

12. *CED* II:369-70.
13. *CED* II:21.

throughout Lorraine, in all the other cities of the province. They are well taken care of, and an effective medicine has been found which our brothers have bought.

In the third place, our priests here spend a large amount to help peasants on the move. Our Missionaries in Nancy, Toul, and other places often meet whole groups of peasants whom they help to reach France, since this town is a gateway to the kingdom. The priests give them food and some money for their journey.[14]

Of the two priests who worked in Bar le Duc, one died from his exertions, and the other became grievously sick. Father Roussel, the rector of Jesuit college where the priests stayed, wrote to Monsieur Vincent in 1640:

> You have heard of the death of Monsieur de Montevit, whom you sent here.[15] He suffered much from his lengthy sickness, but I can truly say I have never seen such great patience and more resignation than I did with him. We never heard him say a single word that showed the least impatience. All his speech reflected a rare piety. His doctor said he had never treated a sick person more obedient and simple than this man. He received communion often during his illness, including the two times he received communion under the form of viaticum. His agony, which lasted eight days altogether, did not prevent him from receiving extreme unction with full awareness. He relaxed when he received this sacrament, and lost consciousness immediately after. Finally he died as I would wish to die, and as I ask of God.
>
> The two chapters of the city joined the funeral procession, as did the Augustinian Fathers, but the greatest honor of his burial was the seven hundred poor who accompanied his body to the grave, each with a candle in his hand. Most of them wept as if they were burying their own father. The poor owed him this tribute, for he had contracted his illness in treating them and in alleviating their sufferings. He was ever among them, and breathed no other air but the tainted air of this sickness. He heard confessions with such devotion, morning and afternoon, that I could never prevail upon him to take a day off. He was buried near the confessional where he caught his sickness, and where he gathered the beautiful bouquet of merits he now enjoys in heaven.
>
> Two days before his death his companion fell sick with a high fever which put him in danger of death for eight days. He has

---

14. *CED* II:59-60.
15. Germain de Montevit, born at Cambernon, near Coutances. He was already a priest when he entered the Congregation at age twenty-six on April 19, 1638.

recovered and is now well. His sickness came from overwork, and too much attention to the poor. On Christmas Eve he went twenty-four hours without eating or sleeping, leaving the confessional only to say mass. Your priests are docile and flexible in everything, except when it comes to taking advice about taking a bit of rest. They think their bodies are not flesh and blood, and that their whole life ought to be lived in a single year. The brother is a young man of exceptional piety.[16] He served the two sick priests with as great a patience and devotion as anyone could wish for.[17]

We will not speak of all the other villages, towns, and hamlets in Lorraine which received the same charitable help from Monsieur Vincent's missionaries. He could rightly be called, after God, the father of the poor, and the provider of this desolate province, for it would be too long and repetitious. We will cite only a letter from the authorities and members of the council of Luneville to Monsieur Vincent:

Monsieur, for the several years this city has been stricken with the plague, war, and famine, which have reduced it to the extremity in which it now is. In that time, we have received nothing but hardships from those from whom we expected to receive help, and cruelty from the soldiers, who have taken by force the little bit of grain we had. It seemed that heaven had only punishment reserved for us until your sons in our Lord arrived here with their alms. They greatly relieved the effects of the ills we suffered, and rekindled our hope in the mercy of God. Since our sins provoked his anger, we humbly kiss the hand which punishes us, and receive with sentiments of extraordinary thanksgiving the gifts of his divine goodness. We bless those instruments of his infinite mercy, and those who have helped us by their gracious charity, as well as those who contributed and those who distributed these alms. We bless you especially, Monsieur, whom we believe to be, after God, the principal author of the charity we have received. To say these alms will be well used in this poor place, where all have been brought low, is something your missionary can tell you better and with less bias than we can ourselves. He has seen our desolation. We acknowledge before God the eternal obligation we have incurred, by your having come to our aid in our sorry state.[18]

When the missionary who carried the alms to Lorraine returned to Paris, he reported to Monsieur Vincent and to the Ladies of Charity that a large

---

16. David Levasseur.
17. *CED* II:23-24.
18. *CED* II:257-58.

number of noblewomen and others with no means of livelihood, nor relatives to help them, were greatly harassed by the officers of the garrison. This led Monsieur Vincent, who agreed with the Ladies of Charity, to instruct the missionary to bring to Paris all those women who wanted to come, to avoid the danger in which they were. When he announced this offer in the various towns he passed through, a large number came to take advantage of the opportunity. He had to choose those in greatest danger. He managed, over some time, to bring a hundred and sixty with him to Paris, all at his own expense. Several small children accompanied them. They were received at Saint Lazare, and placed in families as servants. Monsieur Vincent directed the young girls to the home of Mademoiselle le Gras. She made their presence known throughout the best families in Paris, so those who wanted chambermaids or servants might apply to her for their services. In this way they were placed in honorable positions, saved from the dangers to which, unhappily, they were exposed.

Besides those women and children, the missionaries in Lorraine arranged for several men and women to leave their region and find a new life in France. Most of these poor people came in droves to Paris, where they were welcomed and helped by Monsieur Vincent, both corporally and spiritually. To prepare them to make a good general confession and to live a Christian life he had them brought together in the town of La Chapelle, a half league from Paris, where he gave a mission in 1641. Other groups which came the following year were likewise given a mission, and both groups were helped to become established, and to find work in their trade.[19]

Among these refugees was a blood brother of a canon of Verdun. The canon had had to leave his cathedral church because it was unable to provide him with anything else but the bread of sorrow. Lately he had been forced to till the soil to have enough to live on, but the hard work and poor food had finally made him ill. He was no longer able to do anything, and would soon have died unless he received some help. He ended the letter he wrote to his brother with these words:

> In truth, I do not know where to turn for help except to you, my brother, who have had the good fortune to fall into the hands of one of the saintliest and most charitable men of our unhappy times. By your intercession, I hope I may receive some help from Monsieur Vincent.

His hope was not misplaced, for the charitable father of the poor provided the help he needed in his extreme situation.

---

19. The people of Paris marveled at this charity and said: "Monsieur Vincent must be from Lorraine himself, since he does so much good for the poor people there." Yet his charity also extended to Paris, where each day the poor came to receive bread.

Among the many refugees in Paris were several nobles, and others of standing, even entire families. They were not accustomed to earning their living, and even less to asking for help, and they could not survive at all. Monsieur Vincent undertook to help them, not with the alms destined for the poor of Lorraine which he sent faithfully to the thousands of poor still there, but by another organization which God inspired him to form. He gathered several lords and other people of substance living in Paris, and these he brought together once a month at Saint Lazare. He took up a collection, to which he also contributed, to amass a great enough sum to support these distressed nobles. Each month he distributed alms according the number and needs of the people in each family, and this continued for seven or eight years. We will say only a word in passing about this, for we have already spoken of this enough in Book One.[20]

Several other persons of all classes came from time to time to Paris from Lorraine of their own accord to seek help from Monsieur Vincent. He became known as the universal refuge of this poor region. Father Pierre Fournier, the rector of the Jesuit College in Nancy, said in a letter written in 1643:

> Your charity is so great that everyone has recourse to you. You are regarded here as the asylum of the needy poor. This is why some have come to me, so that I could recommend them to you, and so that they too could experience your goodness. There are two here now whose virtue and character recommend them to your charitable favor.[21]

A Missionary at Saint Mihiel came across fourteen Benedictine nuns who had come from Rambervilliers in the hope of reestablishing themselves. Because of the extreme famine, however, they were not able to do so. Upon the advice of Monsieur Vincent and the Ladies of Charity the Missionary brought them to Paris for help. God permitted, in time, that they settled in the faubourg Saint Germain, where they have since remained. From that time on they spread abroad the good odor of their saintly lives, to the great edification, not only of the faubourg, but of the entire city of Paris. They later took the name of Religious of the Blessed Sacrament.

The distribution of bread, soup, and meat ended in Lorraine in 1643. Monsieur Vincent recalled most of the Missionaries he had sent, since few sick persons remained, and the poor had received some relief from the oppression of the soldiers. The peasants were able once again to take up their ordinary work. The alms did not completely stop, but continued for five or six years for the help of the most unfortunate. Monsieur Vincent saw to it

---

20. Ch. 35.
21. *CED* II:365.

that these alms were distributed in most of the other towns of Lorraine, such as Chateau Salins, Dieuze, Marsal, Moyen Vic, Epinal, Remiremont, Mirecourt, Chatel sur Moselle, Stenay, and Rambervillers. By this means large sums helped not only a great number of the bashful poor, the ruined middle class, and the noble families who, unable to liquidate their wealth, were in a deplorable state, but also all the religious communities of men and women. These funds were given yearly, depending on the needs of each house. Some received three or four hundred *livres* each quarter, and others five or six hundred, depending on the number of persons involved and their needs. The missionary assigned to distribute alms obtained a receipt from each house for the alms given.[22]

Besides these sums, more than four thousand bolts of cloth were bought in Paris and brought to these ruined cities for the benefit of the poor religious, both men and women, the poor nobility, and several other persons and even entire families covered only in rags. The queen herself was so touched by their pitiable sight that she sent the funeral tapestries and cloths after the death of the late king, and the duchess of Aiguillon did the same.

The religious houses were given entire bolts of cloth to enable the members to sew their own habits. Those who lacked them received veils and shoes. Usually around a hundred persons, men and women, boys and girls, were brought back from each trip into the provinces. We should remark that these distributions of money and clothes continued for nine or ten years. This happened not only in the towns of Lorraine, as we have already said, but upon orders of the queen and under Monsieur Vincent's direction, in several other devastated towns conquered by the king's armies. Among these were Arras, Bapaume, Hesdin, Landrecies, and Gravelines. The priest assigned to distribute alms went from one parish to another and from house to house. He was accompanied by the pastor or some other cleric assigned by him to help distribute these clothes and money according to the needs of each, so as not to be deceived about those most in need of help.

The sums distributed in the two regions of Lorraine and Artois came to one hundred fifty or sixty thousand *livres*, for the relief of the extreme poverty of twenty-five towns and surrounding areas, and of a great number of other smaller villages and hamlets. This undoubtedly was an effect of the infinite love of God with которой the heart of Monsieur Vincent was so filled, especially in favor of the most afflicted of the people. It was shared by the

---

22. Brother Mathieu Regnard was almost always in charge of these distributions, of which more than fifty receipts dating from February 1647 still exist. He was born at Brienne le Chateau in the diocese of Troyes. He gave his account of his work at the request of Vincent's successor, Rene Almeras, in view of the anticipated canonization of the founder. Brother Regnard always attributed his own safety and the incredible success of his mission to the prayers and merits of Vincent de Paul. Brother Regnard died at Saint Lazare, October 5, 1669.

late king and the queen, and by others of standing and virtue, and particularly by the Ladies of Charity of the city of Paris whom he had brought together for these great enterprises. All these persons were inflamed by the divine fire burning in the heart and words of this saintly priest, and provided him with the alms to be distributed under his care. He used his missionaries for this purpose, following in everything the suggestions made by these Ladies of Charity in their meetings, or the orders from the queen, so that all would be done in keeping with the intentions of the donors.

The fruits of these alms were, as we have seen: (1) To preserve the life, and restore health to an almost infinite number of persons made listless and discouraged by hunger, cold, nakedness, and other miseries. (2) The instruction of many, preparing them to receive worthily the sacraments and to lead a good life. (3) Help to the dying to enable them to die well, in the grace of God. (4) To rescue from a shameful lot a large number of young women reduced to extremity by their pitiable condition. (5) To enable several religious communities to preserve their cloister, their vows, and their rules, and to continue the sacred liturgy in their houses, for without external help most would have been forced to wander among the people, seeking to preserve their lives with great danger to their conscience. We learn this from several of their letters, but it would weary the reader to report all this in detail. What has already been said will suffice to give as much information as needed.

We will add only one additional extraordinary piece of information among several others which God permitted in the carrying of large sums of money in both Lorraine and Artois. This had to do with the brother[23] who made more than fifty trips, carrying up to twenty-five or thirty thousand *livres* of gold, never having it stolen, although he had to cross through areas frequented by many soldiers, and had to avoid many robbers. He even managed to escape several times while traveling in a group that was attacked. Traveling with others on another occasion, he fortunately, by a secret design of divine Providence, became separated from them, for they were immediately afterward robbed, while he suffered no such indignity. Several times also he would go through a wooded area filled with robbers or wandering soldiers. As soon as he heard them or saw them coming he threw into the bushes his wallet, which ordinarily he carried in a beggar's pouch, and then walked fearlessly right through them. Sometimes they searched him. When they found nothing, they allowed him to go on his way, but of course, as soon as they left, he would return to find the wallet he had tossed into the bushes.

One evening, he met some robbers who took him into the woods to

---

23. Mathieu Regnard.

frighten him. When they found nothing on him, they still wanted him to pay fifty *pistoles* ransom. He replied that if he had fifty *lives* he could not ransom them with one Lorraine *gros*. He was let go.

On another encounter with some Croatians[24] in open country he had time only to slip off his beggar's pouch and to cover it with some weeds, leaving only a few sticks to mark the spot. He returned at night to find his money, but was able to locate it only the next morning. In sum, God gave him a cleverness, and favored him with a special protection, either to avoid the robbers, or to escape from them when he was taken. Even the queen was delighted to hear of his adventures, and several times had him recount his experiences and the simple stratagems he used in avoiding difficulties. For his part, he always attributed his good fortune to God's protection of him, and because of his faith and the prayers of Monsieur Vincent.

SECTION TWO

Help Given to the Provinces of Picardy and Champagne

In 1650, by a secret judgment of God, the scourge of war which for many years had afflicted the greater part of Europe began to be felt in France. It continued to do so until the concluding of a general peace in 1660.[25] Among all the provinces of the country, Picardy and Champagne were most exposed to the storm. They endured its violence longer, particularly after the enemies of the state besieged the city of Guise, and the king's army advanced to its relief. The two armies confronting each other at the frontiers caused extreme desolation. When they withdrew they left in their wake many soldiers weakened by hunger, and suffering from many illnesses. Many wandered in search of food, but others fell by the roads from sheer weakness, dying miserably, deprived of the sacraments and all human consolation.

Some witnesses to this sorry spectacle brought the news to Paris. Everyone rejoiced there at the retreat of the enemy, but few troubled themselves about the poor abandoned soldiers who died so miserably, deprived of all help.

Monsieur Vincent, so sensitive to the sufferings of the neighbor, was touched to learn the pitiable state to which these poor people were reduced.

---

24. Members of the Croatian regiment in the French army.
25. The Peace of the Pyrenees, signed November 7, 1659.

He spoke to Madame de Herse, much given to works of charity, and immediately sent two of his priests with a horse loaded down with provisions. They carried around five hundred *livres* in cash in the hope of saving those dying from hunger or readying those beyond hope for a happy death. Once the Missionaries arrived on the scene they found such a great number of these poor people dying along the hedgerows and the roads that they quickly exhausted the provisions they had brought. They had to go to the nearest villages to purchase more, but were astonished to find the same conditions prevailing in the villages as in the countryside. They quickly wrote to Monsieur Vincent to alert him to the desolation of the entire province, and that the help they had brought was completely inadequate in the face of such pressing needs. The armies had gathered in all the crops, and had left the people with scarcely the shirt on their backs. Most of the country people had left their homes to seek some means of livelihood in the towns, but no one gave them any help, for even the merchant class lacked bread. They gradually weakened, and many died terrible deaths. Once Monsieur Vincent received these letters, he alerted the Ladies of Charity of Paris, and arranged with them to send other missionaries with greater alms than before.

To understand better the magnitude of these works of mercy we must realize the extreme misery of the people in these two provinces during the ten years or so when the armies from one side or the other pillaged and ravaged, spreading desolation everywhere. We can see this better by citing the letters these same Missionaries wrote to Monsieur Vincent from various places, telling him of what they had seen with their own eyes, to provide an outlet for his great charity. This is what they wrote, from Guise, Laon, and La Fere:

> It is a great pity to see such a vast multitude of sick everywhere we turn. Many suffered from dysentery and fever. Others are covered with sores or a purple rash, or with tumors and boils. Many are swollen, either in the head, the belly, or the entire body. These troubles come from eating only the roots of plants during most of the year, or spoiled fruit, or some bread made from barley husks, scarcely fit for dogs. We hear nothing but pitiable cries for something to eat. Sick as they are they travel in the rain and by wretched roads two or three leagues distant to have a bit of soup. Many live in the villages deprived of confession and the sacraments. They do not even have anyone to see to their burial. This is so true that not three days ago, in the village of Lesquielle, near Landrecies, where we had gone to visit the sick, we found a dead man. His body was half eaten by wild animals who had entered the house. Is it not a

strange desolation to see Christians so neglected in life, and even after their death?[26]

They wrote in another letter:

We have just finished visiting thirty-five villages near Guise. We found there nearly six hundred people whose misery is so great they throw themselves upon dead dogs and horses after the wolves have satisfied their hunger. In the city of Guise alone are more than five hundred sick living in cellars or caves, more suited to house animals than men.[27]

Many poor people in Thierache for many weeks have not had bread to eat, not even the bread made from the husks of barley which is reserved for the better-off. They eat only lizards, frogs, and wild grasses.[28]

In several ruined towns, the leading inhabitants are in a shameful necessity, their pallid faces showing how great their need is. They must be helped privately, like the nobility in the countryside. Seeing themselves without bread and lying upon straw, these people suffer the shame of not being able to beg for what is needed to live. And besides, from whom can they ask help, since the war has spread its misery everywhere?

What is even more lamentable is that these people on the frontiers not only lack food, wood, clothes, and blankets, but lack a shepherd and any spiritual comfort. Most of their pastors are either dead or sick, and the churches are ruined and sacked. In the diocese of Laon alone are a hundred or so churches where mass cannot be celebrated, since they are so ruined. We do what we can, but the task is endless. We must come and go without stopping, always at risk from the hunters, to help the more than thirteen hundred sick we have under our care in this single district.

Several convents live in great poverty, and the nuns suffer from hunger and the cold. Their choice is to die in their cloister, or to break it to seek enough to sustain life.[29]

Writing from the diocese of Soissons, the priest there said:

We have visited the poor of the town, and the other villages of the valley, where the affliction we have seen surpasses anything you have been told. To begin with the churches: they have been profaned, the blessed sacrament trampled under foot, the chalices and ciboria carried off, the baptismal fonts broken, the furnishings

---

26. *CED* IV:97.
27. *CED* IV:136. Abelly joined the following several letters into one.
28. *CED* IV:214-15.
29. *CED* IV:107.

stolen. In this small region are more than thirty-five churches where it is impossible to say mass.

Most of the local people died in the woods while the enemy took over their houses. Others returned to die under their own roofs. We see only the sick wherever we go. More than twelve hundred, besides the six hundred enfeebled ones, live in the thirty ruined villages in the area. They sleep on the ground, or in houses half destroyed and open to the sky, without any help. We find them living with the dead, and small children at the side of their dead mothers.[30]

Those from Saint Quentin wrote as follows:

How can we help the seven or eight thousand starving poor, the twelve hundred refugees, the three hundred and fifty sick who should be fed with soup and meat, the three hundred families of the city or country too ashamed to beg, the young women on the verge of selling themselves, or to prevent what happened the other day to a young man about to kill himself, and who would have done so if someone had not prevented him, the fifty priests whom we should help feed before all the others? Just the other day one was found dead in his bed. He preferred to die rather than ask for himself what he needed to stay alive.[31]

The suffering of the poor cannot be expressed. If the cruelty of the soldiers drove them into the woods, hunger brought them back, and they have now taken refuge here. There are nearly four hundred sick, and the town cannot help, forcing many to leave, only to die along the roads. Those who stayed are in such rags they rise from their rotting straw only to seek us out.[32]

The famine is so great we have seen men eating the soil, grazing on grass, chewing on the bark of trees, tearing the rags covering their bodies to swallow them. What we could not dare say, if we had not seen it with our very eyes, horrible as it is, they eat their own hands and arms, and die in their despair. We have three thousand poor refugees, five hundred sick, not to mention the poor nobility and the poor of the city too ashamed to beg, whose number increases every day.[33]

The Missionaries sent to the region around Reims and Rethel wrote as follows:

No words could tell nor ears believe what we have seen since we

---

30. *CED* IV:106.
31. *CED* IV:106-07.
32. *CED* IV:257.
33. *CED* IV:300.

first came here. Churches are profaned, with what is most sacred and most adorable not spared. The fixtures have been stolen, the priests either killed, tortured, or put to flight. All the houses are destroyed, the harvest carried away, the fields lying idle, with neither tillers or sowers. Famine and death are everywhere. The dead are not buried, but left for the wolves to devour. The remaining poor are reduced to searching the fields for bits of wheat or oats which serve to make a kind of bread that is almost like dirt, so unhealthy nearly everyone is sick. They take shelter in caves or in huts where they sleep on the bare ground, without coverings unless they happen to have a sheepskin. Their faces are black and disfigured, and yet their patience is admirable. Entire districts are deserted, since those who have escaped death have themselves left to seek food. Only the sick remain, or orphans, or poor widows in charge of little children. They are all exposed to the rigors of hunger, cold, and all sorts of difficulties and misery.[34]

This, then, was the state to which the people of these two great provinces had been reduced, especially the four or five dioceses closest to the frontiers. This happened for nearly ten years, from 1650 until the publication of the general peace treaty in 1660. This great desolation was not the same everywhere, nor at the same time, except at the beginning. During the remainder of the time, however, these conditions prevailed in one or another part of Picardy and Champagne.

From the beginning Monsieur Vincent sent ten or twelve missionaries to travel everywhere and attempt to save the lives of thousands of persons reduced to the last extremity. They divided the territory among themselves, some in the diocese of Noyon, others in Laon, or Reims, or Soissons. Each one took responsibility to serve the needs of their particular district. They set up centers for the daily distribution of soup and bread, food, jams, medicines, clothes, linens, shoes, tools, seed, church furnishings, money, and so on.

The Daughters of Charity were also sent to several places, especially to look after the sick poor. Since their alms and distributions were needed so widely, the expenses during the first years mounted to ten, twelve, or even sixteen thousand *livres* a month. The price of commodities was so high and the misery so extreme and widespread that, without this help, nearly all these poor people would surely have perished.

Since spiritual help is no less important for souls, the missionaries devoted themselves with great care and almost indefatigable zeal to the poor. Since they could not be everywhere at once, they had the aid of some other priests who helped out in those parishes with no pastor.

---

34. *CED* IV:144-45.

Besides the Missionaries employed in the various dioceses, Monsieur Vincent sent a qualified priest to oversee the entire enterprise.[35] He traveled everywhere to see the actual needs of the poor, and those places which needed help most desperately. He selected persons of piety and charity in the various towns and villages where the Missionaries could not remain, to take charge of the distribution of food and other alms to the poor. This supervisor regulated the flow of aid, increasing or decreasing it according to circumstances as the number of poor and sick increased or diminished in each place. He reported all this faithfully to Monsieur Vincent by letter.[36] He in turn kept the Ladies of Charity of Paris informed. These ladies met each week with him, to advise and agree on what could be done to further this holy enterprise.

SECTION THREE

The Remarkable Effects of the Help Given to the Provinces of Picardy and Champagne

After seeing the extreme misery of these two provinces and the deplorable state to which the people had been reduced, it would be well now to consider the blessings with which God favored the charitable help Monsieur Vincent obtained for them. We can see the happy results of the alms of the Ladies of Charity and all the other virtuous contributors, and the unbelievable efforts of the missionaries who distributed them. It would not be possible to report all, but the little we will say will suffice to judge all the rest.

A month after Monsieur Vincent began to help, he received the following letter:

> The food given as a result of the alms sent from Paris to the sick at Guise, Ribemont, La Fere, and Ham has saved the lives of more than two thousand poor people. They would otherwise have been driven out of the town where they had taken refuge, and would surely have died in the fields, with no help, either spiritual or corporal.
>
> The religious women of La Fere and other towns realize that the help they received saved their lives. Thus, they pray unceasingly for those responsible for such great blessings.[37]

---

35. Rene Almeras.
36. See *CED* V:72, 92, 94, 103, 115, 119.
37. *CED* IV:88.

Other letters written from Laon, Soissons, and other places may be cited as well.

> We have given out the church ornaments, and the blankets and clothes for the sick. We cannot tell you what an effect this has had in the frontier regions, where people talk about practically nothing else except this charitable help. Our helpers have taken such care of the sick that by God's grace in the single city of Guise, of the five hundred sick we had, over three hundred have recovered. In the forty villages around Laon, so many have returned to perfect health that you can scarcely find six poor people unable to work at their own livelihood. We have felt obliged to help them in this, by supplying axes, billhooks, and spinning wheels to enable the men and women to work on their own with no burden on anyone, as long as no other misfortune occurs to reduce them again to miserable conditions.
>
> We have distributed the seed sent from Paris. It has already been sown, and God has blessed the sowing. These poor people support their ills with greater patience when they have hope the harvest will bring them some relief.
>
> We provide two hundred *livres* each month in support of several poor pastors, and as a result all the parishes of the deanery of Guise, Marle, and Vervins have been taken care of. Mass is celebrated in each parish at least once a week, and the sacraments are being administered.[38]

In letters written from Reims, Fismes, Bazoches, and other surrounding areas, we read:

> We do not have words enough to express our thanks. We are well aware the hand of God has struck this province, turning its fertility into sterility, and its joy into tears. Its once-populated villages now have only deserted hovels. Were it not for the charitable people inspired by God in Paris, there would not remain any trace of the people caught in this storm. The saved owe their lives to these generous people.
>
> The thirty-five villages of this valley and its surrounding areas give a thousand thanks to their benefactors. We have distributed items for the churches, and clothes to the poor. Many of the sick have recovered and are now able to earn their own living.
>
> We have held a meeting of the local pastors, during which we distributed to the twenty-three most needy the four hundred *livres* sent to us from Paris. This will enable them to survive and reestab-

---

38. *CED* IV:131-32.

lish their parishes, which otherwise they would not have been able to do.[39]

Letters were written from Saint Quentin and surrounding areas on the same topics, of which we give several extracts:

> We cannot tell you how many sick have been cured, how many in affliction have been consoled, how many poor people have been rescued from despair by your help. They would otherwise have been lost in both the country and in the towns.
>
> Alms you sent from Paris during Holy Week enabled us to rescue several young girls from imminent danger of losing their virtue. We spent our Lent in the country places in over a hundred and thirty villages to help the poor or to see that others help them both corporally and spiritually. We have given forty pastors ten *livres* each month, enabling them to remain in their parishes to carry out their pastoral duties.
>
> We used your gift to buy seven hundred *livres* worth of sickles, flails, and winnowing baskets and other tools to enable the poor to earn their living by working on the harvest. Our oats have come up well, thanks be to God and to the seed you sent, giving us hope for a good harvest and relief for the coming winter.[40]

These letters were written in 1651. The following were written in 1654 from Saint Quentin, Laon, Reims, and other places:

> We are threatened by roving bands of robbers, but we have visited more than a hundred villages. We have found older people and children, nearly naked, and almost frozen with the cold. Women are in despair, nearly paralyzed by the cold. We clothed more than four hundred, and gave them hemp and spinning wheels. The help we began to give to the pastors has continued. After we brought them together by deaneries we saw they were almost despoiled of everything. We gave clothes and cassocks to them, and supplied church items to them, and missals. We helped repair the roofs and windows of their churches, to protect the sacred host from the elements and to prevent the wind from blowing it away during mass. This is why we now have the holy sacrifice of the mass celebrated in a large number of churches and parishes where the people receive the sacraments, which otherwise would be deserted and abandoned.[41]
>
> Besides the four hundred poor who have been clothed, we

---

39. *CED* IV:132-33.
40. *CED* IV:181.
41. *CED* V:87-88. Abelly has joined the two following fragments with this one.

discovered in the region of the city of Laon nearly six hundred orphans under twelve years of age, in pitiable nakedness and need. The alms from Paris have enabled us to clothe and help them.[42]

Despair had brought many girls of good families living near the frontier, to the greatest danger. We thought the best remedy was to remove them from the site of greatest danger, and so we began to bring them to the community of Daughters of Saint Martha in the city of Reims. There they were taught the fear of God, and put to some useful work. We now have thirty of these young girls in this charitable home, all daughters of gentlemen of the region. Some had to be hidden in the cellars for a time to avoid the insolence of the soldiers. The expenses of this charitable effort and of bringing others to places of security are great, for besides paying for their board we had to supply clothes for them. We hope, however, that the charity of people which began so well will continue, and even increase.[43]

The Missionaries had to go from one town to another after they had cared for the most pressing needs of the priests and the churches, helped the poor, removed young girls to safe havens, seen to the care of the orphans, and provided means of earning their own livelihood to those capable of working. In order not to leave the sick or those likely to become so unattended, they set up an organization in each locality to care for them, depending on the virtue and fidelity of some charitable persons to whom they gave some money and medicines, which they renewed from time to time. In the many towns with ruined and abandoned hospitals, the missionaries worked to put them back into operation, and received many patients at the expense of six or seven *sous* per day for each one. They were careful to pay this sum regularly on orders from Monsieur Vincent, and by the generosity of the Ladies of Charity of Paris who supplied the funds.

In the city of Rethel the hospital could not receive all the many sick soldiers and peasants. More than seven hundred were sent to the hospital of Reims. Since the number of those sick increased and the expenses mounted greatly, it was thought advisable to have the brothers of the Congregation, together with some priests, bring certain medicines, especially some powders compounded by the infirmarian of Saint Lazare for dysentery, fevers, and some other ailments. God blessed these medicines so greatly that those who used them thought they were almost miraculous, for they hastened the cure of a large number of sick, who before were at the point of death. On occasion these medicines would work their wonders in twenty-four hours or thereabouts.

---

42. *CED* V:118.
43. *CED* V:95.

Not content to help the living, Monsieur Vincent extended his concern even to the dead. The following single example will suffice to show this. After the battles which took place in Champagne in 1651, near Saint Etienne and Saint Souplet, more than fifteen hundred enemy remained dead on the field of battle, prey for dogs and wolves. Once he learned of this, Monsieur Vincent sent one of his Missionaries[44] to supervise the burial of the decomposing corpses, using local labor for the purpose. He managed so well with the three hundred *livres* at his disposal that he was able to bury them all, delivering the living from a horrible spectacle and the polluted air. This good priest himself wrote about these events:

> We have finished today what Jesus Christ recommended to us in his Gospel, to love and do good to our enemies. We have given decent burial to those who had stolen our goods, ruined many of our people, and who beat and outraged them. I consider myself happy to have been able to obey your orders in a matter explicitly recommended in holy Scripture. I must say, however, that there was some difficulty in collecting these corpses spread over a large area, especially because of the thaw which developed near the end. We can see how God favored our work, by the great cold wave that occurred. If we had to do this service in the warmer weather we could not have had helpers for a thousand *ecus*, and yet it cost us only three hundred *livres* in all. These bodies which will one day share in the resurrection are now enfolded anew in the womb of their mother. The whole province is indebted to the charitable contributors to this good work, not to mention the crown God has prepared for them in heaven as a reward for their virtue.[45]

We ought not omit mentioning the help Monsieur Vincent gave to the poor Irish Catholics, exiled from their own country by Cromwell. Out of necessity they had to enroll in the army. Two regiments of these soldiers suffered much in the war at Bordeaux. The following year they were sent to the region around Arras, and after serving in these two campaigns retired to Troyes. They arrived there in a sad state. They brought with them more than a hundred and fifty orphans and a large number of poor widows, barefooted and covered only in the rags they had been able to salvage from those killed in the wars. This desolate army walked toward Troyes, gathering for their food only what the dogs themselves would disdain.

When Monsieur Vincent was informed of these conditions by the priest of his Congregation stationed there, he alerted the Ladies of Charity of Paris, and sent a priest of his household, originally from Ireland, to go to their relief.

---

44. Edmond Deschamps.
45. *CED* IV:143-44.

The girls and widows were taken to the hospital of Saint Nicolas for lessons in spinning and sewing. The orphans were given special care, and each one clothed and helped. At first six hundred *livres* was sent from Paris, with many clothes and other things so badly needed. This aid continued from time to time, as the needs developed. The timely help given to these poor exiles lifted their saddened spirits. It prepared them to receive the instruction and exhortations of the missionaries who spoke to them in their own language twice a week in Lent, to prepare them for communion at Easter. Since nothing is stronger than good example, his devotion to these poor people aroused the charity of the townspeople, not only toward these poor strangers, but also toward everyone else in their town.

After three or four years of help to the two provinces of Picardy and Champagne, at the cost of nearly three hundred thousand *livres*, things began to improve for the people because the armies moved away and because they had received help. Monsieur Vincent recalled most of his priests, leaving only a few to continue their help until the signing of the general peace treaty. These few priests continued to help the poor, to help in the repair of the churches, and to assist the priests and pastors. Moreover, one of those who remained, following the advice he received from Monsieur Vincent, formed a Confraternity of Charity of a certain number of the more charitable and better situated of the merchant class. They were to care for the sick, orphans, and other abandoned poor, under the guidance of some virtuous priests. He formed these associations in several towns, especially Reims, Rethel, Chateau Porcien, La Fere, Ham, Saint Quentin, Rocroi, Mezieres, Charleville, Donchery, and other places, after first having them carry out these services to the poor. By his guidance and the regulations he left them, he enabled them to continue this good work for the relief of the poor.[46]

We would add to what we have said only some expressions of thanks, given in letters written to Monsieur Vincent by some of the leading persons of the places which had been helped. We will cite only a few, to confirm the truth of what has already been said.

Father Rainssant, canon regular of the order of Saint Augustine and pastor of the town of Ham, wrote:

> The missionary you sent to this region has left me to look after the assembly of our pious citizens in favor of the poor. He left me

---

46. One of the missionaries remaining in Picardy after the conclusion of the peace was Brother Jean Parre. He was one of the main and most devoted distributors of Vincent's charity in the devastated provinces. For two years, Vincent wrote him weekly. These letters, filled with charity and prudence, furnish details on the distribution of the alms sent from Paris. The brother let no opportunity pass without soliciting help for the great needs of the region which he knew of. He was born at Chatillon in Dunois in the diocese of Chartres. He entered the Congregation, April 16, 1638. His death date is not recorded.

grain and money to feed and keep the orphan girls who are taught a skill to help them earn their own livelihood. I teach them catechism, while a religious sister of the hospital teaches them to pray, and has them attend mass every day. They live together in the same house.

All the sick of the town are well cared for. A good doctor visits and prescribes all that is needed. We are careful to see that nothing is lacking. Our ladies are devoted to this service. I would never have dared hope to see in this poor town of Ham what I now see with great consolation and admiration, due solely to the divine and heavenly Providence of our Lord. Just recently we regained a poor girl from the hands of the heretics. She is now doing well. This motivated a Huguenot servant to come to me to be converted, seeing the care we take of the poor and the charity we show to the sick. We have instructed him enough, and in a few days he will make his abjuration.

This same missionary of yours has left me something to help the poor orphan boys and girls, and the sick poor of the villages which depend on our town of Ham. He has obtained two good and virtuous pastors to help me in this until his return. We owe all this good work to you, Monsieur, as the prime mover, after God.[47]

Monsieur de la Font, lieutenant general of Saint Quentin, wrote the following letter on the same topic:

The aid sent by the grace of God and your care to this province and so carefully distributed by those you commissioned, has given life to thousands of people reduced by the scourge of war to the last extremity. I must render you most humble thanks for all these people. We saw last week, during the movement of the troops, up to fourteen hundred poor refugees in this city fed each day from your alms. We still have more than a thousand, not counting those in the countryside, with nothing to eat except what is given them from your charity. This misery everywhere is so great no one remains in the villages, since there was only straw to lie upon. Those previously the most affluent were unable to find enough to live on. Some who once owned more than twenty thousand *ecus* now need a piece of bread, and have gone two whole days without eating. I am obliged by my position and by the sights I have seen, to beg you humbly to continue to be the father of this region, to save the lives of so many poor. Although they are languishing and dying, they are helped so worthily by your priests.[48]

---

47. *CED* V:333-34.
48. *CED* V:377-78.

Monsieur Simonnet, president and lieutenant general of Rethel, expressed his thanks in these words:

> We may observe in the charity you show to us the original form of true Christian devotion, since in the primitive church the Christians had but a single heart, and would not allow any of their number to suffer the effects of poverty without coming to their aid. You, likewise, Monsieur, looked to the needs of the poor with such methodical zeal, using the priests of your Congregation, that you sent them to all the surrounding area. The poor there had been reduced to eating field grass and even eating dogs, as I have seen with my own eyes. These priests have saved the lives of an innumerable multitude, and have consoled and comforted others in their last agony. All this has been the fruit of your charity.[49]

Monsieur de Y, canon and later archdeacon of Reims, wrote the following letter:

> I am happy to write to you to thank you in the name of the poor of our area for your generosity to them, for without your help they would have died from hunger. To express the gratitude they have, I must tell you these poor people use the little strength they have to raise their arms to heaven, to call down on their benefactors the graces of the God of Mercy. The poverty of this province cannot be accurately described. Everything that has been said is inadequate to current conditions. You must believe the reports sent to you by your priests. Their zeal and fairness was so evident in the distribution of the alms you sent that it edified everyone. For myself, I thank you for having sent them to us and for the good example they have given us.[50]

The late Monsieur Souyn, bailiff of the city of Reims, wrote to Monsieur Vincent on this same topic:

> I trust you have been shown the report I sent to Paris on the charitable work you have accomplished here, and the corporal and spiritual help you have given to the poor of the region. You did so in imitation of our divine master and savior, whose perfect imitator you become. Two of your priests came to this city. One came to pick up some money in alms, which he could not do in his usual place of residence for it was totally without resources. The other came to pick up some grain he had bought, to be taken to Saint Souplet for the poor of that town. Both worked under your direction at the relief of the most afflicted, while you continued to inspire the

---

49. *CED* IV:233.
50. *CED* V:385.

fire of divine charity throughout Picardy and Champagne for the relief of the poor.

I await the arrival of Monsieur N., to whom you have given the general direction of this great work, who will set up our winter headquarters. Meanwhile, I am looking after the hospitals and providing assistance to some poor pastors. Our storehouse of oats, set up by your help, is busy in making distributions during these bad times. Continue your charitable care, Monsieur. It preserves the mortal life of so many of the poor, and assures them eternal happiness by all the spiritual help they are given, particularly by the administration of the sacraments. This would cease in many places in our diocese if we did not have your help.[51]

We will pass over many other letters which contain similar expressions of gratitude. In concluding this chapter it is enough to say that since the beginning of the assistance to these two provinces until the signing of the general peace treaty,[52] more than five hundred thousand *livres* in alms were sent from Paris, in money and in clothes, church furnishings, etc. At the direction of Monsieur Vincent, these alms were distributed with such order and prudence that they not only saved the lives of a countless number of poor, but also supported a large number of pastors in their parishes who otherwise would have had to leave. Many pillaged and ruined churches were made fit to celebrate mass. Many, even some of the nobility, were rescued from imminent peril to what they held dearer than life itself. A place of refuge was found for a great number of orphans, totally abandoned by everyone else.

Lastly, the priests of the Mission contributed to the eternal salvation of a great number of souls by the administration of the sacraments and by other spiritual helps when these were most needed.

One day, Monsieur Vincent reflected on these events:

We cannot think of the immense alms God inspired people to give without being filled with admiration: the alms, clothes, linens, blankets, dresses, shoes, etc., given for men, women, and children, and even for priests. Think of the number of albs, chasubles, missals, ciboria, chalices, and other church goods sent for the restoration of the churches, so ravaged that the celebration of the sacred mysteries and the other exercises of our Christian religion could never have been reestablished without this help. Many of these churches had been given over completely to profane uses.

It was surely a spectacle to see the houses of the Ladies of Charity

---

51. *CED* IV:260-61.
52. The Peace of the Pyrenees.

of Paris filled with all sorts of goods, looking for all the world like the storehouses of wholesale merchants! These women will undoubtedly have in heaven the crown of priests for their zeal and charity, to clothe Jesus Christ on his altars, in his priests, and in his poor suffering members.[53]

---

53. Dodin, *Entretiens*, 946-47.

CHAPTER TWELVE

The Efforts of Monsieur Vincent to Combat the Errors of Jansenism

IN IMITATION of the patriarch Job, this humble and faithful servant of God could say about the errors which have troubled the Church in this present century, that what he had most feared had come to pass.[1] He found himself involved in what he had always regarded as most dangerous.

He once said to his community:

> All my life I have dreaded the birth of some new heresy. I have seen the damages inflicted by those of Luther and Calvin, and how many people of all ranks have succumbed to the deadly poison after merely tasting the false doctrines of the so-called reformers. I have always feared being engulfed in the errors of some new doctrine before knowing what was happening. Yes, all my life I have feared this.[2]

He repeated this same idea many times to others, people of virtue and worthy of confidence.

Nevertheless, by a singular design of his Providence, God willed that what he feared came about. In his lifetime Jansenism appeared in the Church, and even before this new heresy appeared he became involved with one of its first apologists. This was to show most clearly his firm faith and vigorous zeal. It also established him as a pillar of iron in the Church, as a wall of granite, (as was said of an ancient prophet[3]) to maintain and defend the truth.

In preparing him and warning him against these new errors, God permitted him to form a close friendship with a priest, originally from his own province.[4] After a long stay at the university of Louvain, he returned to France. With him, he brought Jansenius, his classmate and confidant in the new doctrines which he had conceived to reform the Church in her discipline and in several points of her faith.[5]

This priest visited his own province and some others also, and realized

---

1. Job 3:25.
2. *CED* XI:37.
3. Jer 1:18.
4. Jean Duverger (or, Duvergier) de Hauranne, the commendatory abbot of Saint Cyran. He was born in Bayonne in 1581. He studied at Paris and Louvain. Around 1616 he accompanied Bishop Henry Louis Chastaignier de la Rocheposay to the diocese of Poitiers. The bishop resigned the Abbey of Saint Cyran in his favor. Duverger is customarily known to history by this name.
5. Cornelius Jansenius, to give the Latin form of his name, was born at Acquoy, a village near Leerdam in Holland in 1585. He studied at Louvain and then came to France where he became acquainted with Saint Cyran. In 1636 he became bishop of Ypres. He died two years later, 1638.

there was no place like Paris for propagating his errors. He met there some people willing to listen to him, either out of vain curiosity, or to appear to be someone special in hearing from him a new doctrine unknown, as he said, these last centuries to the scholastic doctors.

Seeing the esteem several persons had for his countryman because of his learning and other good qualities, Monsieur Vincent believed his conversations could not but be helpful to him and to his Company, which then was in its infancy. He used to visit often, and this led to a close friendship. Monsieur Vincent was that mystic bee with no other aim than to draw out that honey of good doctrine, and other fitting counsels that he felt he could take from his friend. The priest, on the contrary, wished to profit from these conversations and friendship to insinuate the venom of his errors and his pernicious maxims into the mind of Monsieur Vincent. He hoped then to influence the entire Company, and so to spread his views into many other places.

Since Monsieur Vincent was disposed to listen to him, this is why he began little by little to put forth some of his own ideas. They were based on such beautiful pretexts and interspersed with other good and holy ideas that a mind less enlightened than Monsieur Vincent's would have had difficulty appreciating them in their true light.

This faithful servant of God was at first surprised to hear such an extraordinary doctrine and such maxims. The more the Abbe went in his explanations the more these ideas began to appear suspect to Monsieur Vincent, and even dangerous. One day, as on other occasions, they were discussing together some point of the doctrine of Calvin. He was surprised to hear the Abbe take the side and defend the errors of this heresiarch. When he pointed out that the Church had condemned this doctrine of Calvin, the Abbe replied that Calvin was not so much wrong as poorly understood, adding the Latin words, *bene sensit, male locutus est* ["He understood well, but he spoke badly"].[6]

Another time, as this Abbe was heatedly supporting a proposition condemned by the Council of Trent, Monsieur Vincent felt charity demanded some response. "Monsieur, you go too far. What? Do you want me to believe someone like yourself, subject to error, rather than to believe the entire Church, which is the dove of truth? It teaches me something, and you suggest the opposite. Oh, Monsieur, how can you prefer your own judgment to that of the best heads in the world, and to so many holy prelates assembled in the Council of Trent, who have pronounced on this point?" "Don't speak to me of the council," replied the Abbe, "it was a council of the pope and scholastics, with little else but intrigues and cabals."

---

6. See *CED* III:319-20.

These rash words from a spirit intoxicated with self-esteem and beginning to leave the straight path of truth, obliged Monsieur Vincent, with his singular respect for all decisions of the Church, to exercise much more circumspection in his conversations with this man. He saw them as dangerous, and if he continued in this way he was determined to break off contact completely. He did not have long to wait, for this to happen in another encounter with his friend.

Going one day to visit, Monsieur Vincent found him in his room reading the Bible. He remained for a while not saying anything, not to disturb his reading. Finally, the Abbe turned to him and said, "Do you see, Monsieur Vincent, what I am reading? It is holy Scripture, and God has given me a perfect understanding of it, and many lights to help me in explaining it. Holy Scripture is clearer in my own mind even than it is in itself." These were his very words, which Monsieur Vincent spoke of several times.[7]

Another day, Monsieur Vincent had celebrated mass at Notre Dame, and went to visit the Abbe, whom he found shut up in his study. When he finally emerged some time later, Monsieur Vincent smilingly said to him in his usual good-natured way: "Admit it, Monsieur, you have been writing down what graces God favored you with in your morning mental prayer." After inviting him to be seated, the Abbe responded, "I must confess to you, God has given and continues to give me great lights. He has shown me that the Church no longer exists." Seeing the surprise of Monsieur Vincent, he repeated, "No, the Church no longer exists. God has made me see that for the past five or six hundred years there has been no Church. Previously, the Church had been like a great river of flowing clear water. Now, what we have been calling the Church is no more than a stream of slime. The bed of this river remains the same, but the waters have changed."

"What, Monsieur," Monsieur Vincent said, "do you prefer your own thoughts to the word of our Lord Jesus Christ, who said he would build his Church upon a rock, and the gates of hell would not prevail against her? The Church is his spouse, and he will never abandon it. The Holy Spirit will always be at hand to help her." The Abbe replied, "Indeed, Jesus built his Church upon a rock, but there is a time to build up and a time to tear down. She was his spouse, but she is now an adulteress and a prostitute. This is why he has repudiated her, and he wills another more faithful one should be substituted for her." Monsieur Vincent told him he was far from the respect he owed the truth, adding that he should be most hesitant about his own sentiments, so preoccupied as he was with bad thoughts. After some further remarks, they left each other's company.

Monsieur Vincent himself recounted all these events on several occa-

---

7. See *CED* III:318-32; IV:148-49.

sions, either to some members of his own Congregation, or to others from outside who have reported them. He always spoke of them with sorrow, and did so only when obliged by some motive of charity, to disabuse or to warn people against the surprises of these new doctrines.

He was aware from this time that his exalted opinion of his own prowess had blinded the Abbe, and he was being moved by presumption and pride. Also, the Abbe was likely to fall into the abyss of a new heresy and probably would influence many others to follow him. Thus, Monsieur Vincent felt the obligation in charity and the bonds of his former friendship to make a last effort to save him, by the exercise of fraternal correction.

With this intention Monsieur Vincent one day paid him a visit. After some usual pleasantries he began to speak of the obligation of submitting one's judgment to the Church, and of having a greater respect and deference for the holy Council of Trent than he had shown before. Coming to particulars, to some of the erroneous propositions he had advocated, Monsieur Vincent made him see that these were contrary to the doctrine of the Church. Monsieur Vincent showed him that he was making a great mistake in entering upon this labyrinth of errors, and even more, in having tried to entice him and his whole Congregation down this same slippery path. He begged him, in the name of our Lord, to retrace his steps before it was too late.

We do not know the details of this conversation, but only that Monsieur Vincent spoke so strongly to him that he seemed so bewildered as not to respond at all. However, he found it difficult to accept this intervention, which struck him to the heart. Upon returning to his abbey, he wrote a lengthy letter a month later to justify himself. We will cite here only some extracts.

> The natural humility which is part of your character leads you to believe what others tell you of holy Scripture. It helps me see nothing is easier than for you to accept what you now see as my mistakes. When I heard you in your fraternal admonitions add this fifth reproach to the four we had spoken of before, that I was interfering with you and your entire house, I felt it was not the moment to defend myself. I was happy to accept this from a person who has honored me for such a long time with his friendship, and who has the reputation in Paris of being a man totally given to doing good.
>
> What struck me with admiration was that you, who profess to be so meek and so reserved, have taken the part of those rising up against me. You joined others in their attacks, and even added the insult of coming to see me in my own quarters, something no one else dared do. I take the liberty of pointing out that none of the

prelates who haunt your house, with whom I am not in agreement, and whose approval of my opinions I do not seek when I speak with them in private, are delighted and thank me for what I have to say.

After several other intemperate expressions, his inflated opinion of himself made him reject all the charitable suggestions of his faithful friend. He ended his letter as follows:

I have put up with certain practices of yours, especially seeing how attached you were to them because of the advice of the great personages you consulted. I was always careful to keep these thoughts to myself, that God did not at all approve of what you did, for they could be justified only by a true simplicity rare indeed among Christians. I rarely agree with what a saint of our own day has said, that of the ten thousand who profess to be directors of souls, scarcely a single one is worthy of the name.[8] The only thing which excuses them before God is simplicity of mind. I had the patience to let you go on, and to accept only by condescension what I did not entirely agree with.[9]

This letter allows us to see the hope which Saint Cyran had of attracting Monsieur Vincent to his own party, and to insinuate his opinions and maxims into the Congregation of the Mission. By a singular grace, God preserved the father and children alike from this contagion and always maintained them in a faithful and sincere profession of the truths recognized and taught by the Church.

Some time later this priest, persisting in spreading secretly his evil doctrine, was put in prison by the king's order, and his papers seized.[10] Among them was found the draft of the letter we have just quoted, which came to light in this way. The judge questioned him publicly on what Monsieur Vincent had said to him to provoke his letter. It would have been hoped that this detention would humble his spirit, and open his eyes to what was happening, but this did not occur. Those of his party used their influence to have him released, but by a secret judgment of his Providence, God soon after called him from this life.[11]

---

8. Francis de Sales, beatified in 1661, canonized in 1665.
9. *CED* I:401-06.
10. Saint Cyran worked actively to spread his theological opinions. Cardinal Richelieu understood the dangers which they posed both to the Church and to the State. He formally inquired into these doctrines after many complaints and charges were leveled against Saint Cyran and his teaching, including the opposition of both Vincent de Paul and Charles de Condren, the superior general of the Oratory. Richelieu imprisoned Saint Cyran at Vincennes in 1638. He instituted a formal interrogation of the prisoner which unfortunately failed to meet canonical standards. He proceeded on his authority justifying his actions by saying that "if Luther and Calvin had been imprisoned when they had begun to teach heresy, the European states would have been spared from the troubles they caused."
11. He was released from prison after the death of Richelieu in December 1642. He himself died the

CHAPTER TWELVE

About this same time two pernicious books promoted by this Abbe appeared. The one attempted to show that Saints Peter and Paul had received from God an equal power in the government of the Church, thus striving to undermine the authority of the head of the Church.[12] The other book was *Augustinus* by Jansenius, which has since made such a disturbance and caused such division in France and throughout the Church.[13] Monsieur Vincent was well aware of the dangerous source of this new doctrine, and felt himself obliged to do all in his power to have it condemned.

To begin with, among other things he did, he wrote to a cardinal,[14] on October 4, 1646, as follows:

> I most humbly beseech Your Eminence that I might send you some pages written by one of the most learned of our theologians, and one of our most honest, but who does not wish to be named.[15] These refute the opinion of the two leaders, Saints Peter and Paul. He has learned from the Gazette of Rome that the book he refutes is being examined, and that two doctors of the Sorbonne have testified the doctrine of the book is that of their faculty. After this same faculty heard that this opinion of the two leaders was ascribed to them, they assembled, and declared to the nuncio that these two professors are in error. The faculty is of the contrary opinion. They asked him to have the next issue of the Gazette report that this doctrine was erroneously reported as being theirs.
>
> Thus it came about that this good and virtuous person brought me these writings with the request that I send them on to Rome, and help those whom His Holiness has delegated to examine the book in question. He found that the passages seeking to support the equality of Saint Peter and Saint Paul are refuted by the very authors themselves, one after the other.[16]

After this letter was sent, the Holy See censured and condemned the book on the two leaders.[17] Monsieur Vincent had the consolation of seeing in this the happy outcome of his own efforts in this regard.

Monsieur Vincent quickly realized that the book by Jansenius was a collection in bits and pieces of all the late Abbe had been speaking of in the

---

following year at the age of sixty-two.
12. This work, *De l'autorité de Saint Pierre et de Saint Paul*, 1645, was written by Martin Barcos, Saint Cyran's nephew.
13. *Augustinus, in quo haereses Pelagii, etc., recensentur* was published at Louvain in 1640. Urban VIII condemned it on March 6, 1641, particularly the "Five Propositions" extracted from it, and which summarized the erroneous doctrines of the entire work. Successive pontiffs continued this condemnation.
14. Jerome Grimaldi.
15. Nicolas le Maistre, a doctor of the Sorbonne.
16. *CED* III:65-67.
17. January 1647.

conversations he had with him. The venom of this new doctrine was the more to be feared because it claimed to be restoring theology to its original purity. This is why, with his greater awareness, he felt obliged to provide some antidote to warn others against the dangerous reading, while waiting for the authority of the Church to bring a more definitive remedy. He requested several persons of learning and piety to take up the pen in refutation of the errors of this evil book. Among others was the late Monsieur de Raconis, bishop of Lavaur,[18] whom he advised and with whom he worked to stop the spread of this evil doctrine. This has come to light by the discovery of several letters written to Monsieur Vincent by the bishop at this time, of which we will cite only one:

> Since yesterday, after I had the honor of speaking with you, I have seen the Prince of Conde on the matter of Jansenius. I found him eager and enlightened about the errors of this author. He encouraged me greatly to continue my work, and to encourage your zeal for the defense of the Church. We spoke at length, to my complete satisfaction. He had two recommendations for me. The first was to see the nuncio, to tell him that the prince,[19] for his part, would be available to meet with him to talk over this matter, and to explain the absolute necessity for the good of both Church and state to reply to this author. I took care of this at once. After a long talk, I agreed with the nuncio, that I would draw up a catalogue of the errors of Jansenius already condemned either by councils or by popes. I promised to do this. From there I returned to see the prince, who was delighted at the way this turned out. He assured me he would speak to the queen and to Cardinal Mazarin about the importance of this matter.
>
> The second recommendation he made to me was to assure you of his zeal in this matter, and his willingness to work together with you.[20]

Since this false doctrine influenced many to follow these novelties, and since Monsieur Vincent had been invited into the queen's council from the very beginning of the regency, he explained to Her Majesty and to Cardinal Mazarin the importance to religion and to the state of not offering benefices or positions to any suspected of these novelties. Knowing that the professorships and pulpits were the sources from which saving waters of doctrine and morality were drawn, he did all in his power to assure that those

---

18. Charles Francois d'Abra de Raconis, born in 1580. He taught philosophy at Paris. His exemplary life, joined to the success of his teaching and preaching, brought him a promotion to the see of Lavaur in 1639. He died in 1646.
19. Henri II de Bourbon, the Prince of Conde.
20. *CED* II:498-99.

appointed were well grounded in the common teachings of the Church. He had prayers offered for this intention, and used other means for this purpose, as his charity dictated.

He often consulted with the nuncio and with the chancellor[21] on the ways to arrest the spread of this false doctrine. Once, when he learned that someone wanted to defend a thesis suspected of Jansenism in a religious house, he used his influence to have it stopped. This is what he wrote to a worthy prelate:

> Your Excellency, a religious of this city has advanced a thesis in support of a proposition tainted with Jansenism, and which the Sorbonne has condemned. The chancellor forbade the assembly and the public defense customary on these occasions. When the superior protested, he was sent for, and told that as he contravened the order, he and his community would be dealt with appropriately. He was sent to the nuncio, who reproached him for allowing this thesis to appear. He threatened him and all those favoring this doctrine with punishment, and with being reported to the pope and the general of their order. This superior and all his community punished this religious. They declared him unable to accept any responsibility or office in the order, deprived him of his active and passive voice, and ordered him expelled from their house. This leads us to hope that if such measures are taken to prevent these abuses, this pernicious doctrine will soon die out.[22]

This faithful servant of God lost no occasion to prevent these errors from causing havoc in the Church. However, this evil continued to grow despite all efforts to oppose its progress, and it began to appear everywhere. It introduced division into the schools and even into religious communities, and sometimes into secular families. It in some way threatened the tranquility of the state. Monsieur Vincent was aware of this evil, and foresaw the deadly results that it was likely to produce. He prayed incessantly to God, and thought often within himself how the progress of this heresy might be stopped. He used many prayers and practiced many mortifications to appease God's anger, and to secure from his infinite goodness the favor of these ills from happening. His prayers and tears were not without effect. It appeared soon after that several prelates of the kingdom were moved by a holy zeal for preserving the faith and the Catholic religion. They resolved to petition the Holy See to prompt and decisive action in remedying these disorders.[23] He was very consoled, and praised their intention, all the while

---

21. Pierre Seguier.
22. *CED* III:630-31.
23. The bishops wrote a joint letter to the pope. They met at Saint Lazare under the direction of Isaac Habert, the bishop of Vabres, with Saint Vincent in attendance. The prelates then attended the

urging other prelates he knew to join their voices to the others. This is what he wrote to several, in February 1651:

> The evil results produced by some of the current opinions have convinced a good number of our prelates of the kingdom to write to our Holy Father the pope, to urge him to pronounce judgment on this doctrine.
>
> The reasons leading them to do this are, first, they hope that this will hold those to orthodox doctrine who otherwise might drift away. This happened when the censure appeared on the question of the two leaders.
>
> Second, this is a rapidly spreading evil, because it seems to be tolerated.
>
> Third, Rome believes that most of our bishops in France themselves hold the new opinions. Rome must be convinced that in reality few hold these views.
>
> Fourth, this agrees with the Council of Trent. It ordained that if opinions arose contrary to what it had decided, recourse should be had to the sovereign pontiff to decide. This is what we wish to do, Your Excellency, by the enclosed letter, in the hope you would add your signature to the forty others who have already signed it, as the enclosed list will confirm.[24]

Besides this circular letter which he sent to several bishops, he wrote personally to one, from whom he had received no reply:[25]

> Paris, April 23, 1651
>
> Your Excellency, some time ago I sent you a copy of a letter which most of the bishops of the kingdom wished to send to our Holy Father the pope. They asked him to pronounce on the new doctrine, hoping you would be good enough to sign, if you would wish to be among their number. Since I have not had the honor of hearing from you, I fear that perhaps you did not receive it, or you may have been put off by an account sent everywhere by the adherents of this doctrine to persuade the bishops not to sign. As a result, Your Excellency, I am sending you a second copy. In the name of our Lord please consider the necessity of this letter, caused by the division which the new doctrine introduces into families, cities, and the universities. It is a fire spreading daily, debasing spirits, and menacing the Church with irreparable desolation if a prompt remedy is not forthcoming.

---

meeting of the general assembly of the clergy held in Paris, where they signed the document. Monsieur Vincent sent copies of this letter to other bishops soliciting their support.

24. *CED* IV:148-49.
25. Pierre de Nivelle, the bishop of Lucon.

CHAPTER TWELVE

The present state of affairs does not allow us to await a general council. Besides, you are aware of how long it takes to bring one about, and how long the last one took. This remedy is too far off for an evil so pressing. What then is the remedy for this? Beyond doubt, it must be the Holy See, not only because the Council of Trent in its last session reserved to it the resolution of difficulties which might arise from its decisions. If the Church decides in a general council canonically assembled, as it was, and if the Holy Spirit guides the Church as we may not doubt, why do we not follow the light of this Spirit which directed us in these doubtful circumstances to have recourse to the sovereign pontiff? This reason alone, Your Excellency, urges me to count you among the sixty prelates who already have signed the letter, which is nothing but a simple proposition. Besides, some others may still sign.

If someone were to object that he ought not state his opinion so far in advance on a matter that he might later have to judge, we may respond that it seems unlikely that we will have a council for them to be judges at. But supposing the opposite, having recourse to the pope is no obstacle. Saints have protested new opinions, but this did not keep them from councils where they acted as judges and condemned erroneous opinions.

If the popes impose silence in this matter, forbidding people to speak, write, and argue about it, would this not falsify the position of the pope as head of the Church, to whom all members should be able to contact? We should be able to have recourse to him, to be assured in our doubts and worries. To whom then should we refer? And how will His Holiness know of developing troubles if he is not informed about them?

If it should be argued, Your Excellency, that a long delay in his answer or one less decisive than what we would wish, would serve only to increase the boldness of our opponents, I can assure you the nuncio has news from Rome. Once His Holiness has a letter from the king of France, and another from a representative number of the bishops of the kingdom, he will give his decision. Her Majesty has decided to write, and the First President has said only that provided the bull from the Holy See does not originate from the Inquisition at Rome, the Parlement will receive and publish it.

What will have been gained should a third objection be raised, that is, once the pope has decided, those favoring the new doctrines do not submit? This may be true of some, especially those of the party of the late Monsieur N. [Saint Cyran.] He was not disposed to submit to the decisions of the pope, nor even to those of a council. I am aware of this, Your Excellency, from my own experience. Some may be as obstinate as himself, blinded by their own importance. A few others, attracted only by what is new, or by some friendship or family, or because they have not thought these matters through carefully enough, will now draw back, rather than rebel against their own lawful father. We saw something of this in the controversy about the book on the two leaders, and on the *Catechism on Grace*.[26] Once they were censured, they were no longer talked about. It is greatly to be hoped, Your Excellency, that many souls be disabused of the errors in the rest of these new doctrines, as they were of these points, and that others should be helped to avoid these newer errors.

The example of a man named Labadie is a proof of the evil nature of this new doctrine.[27] This is an apostate priest with a great reputation as a preacher. He caused great harm in Picardy, and later in Gascony, but finally joined the Huguenots in Montauban. In a book he wrote on his so-called conversion, he stated that since he was a Jansenist, he has found the same beliefs in the new religion he has joined. Their ministers, Your Excellency, boast in their preaching that most Catholics are of their opinion, and will soon come over to their side. Since this is so, should we not do all we can to extinguish this fire which gives such assurance to the sworn enemies of our religion? Who would not attack this beast which begins to ravage the Church, and which shall devour it, if it is not crushed at birth? What would the many courageous and saintly bishops we now have, wish they would have done, if they had been in office at the time of Calvin? We can now see the mistakes in doctrine of that earlier time. They were not opposed strongly enough, and have thus caused so many wars and divisions.

At that time there was much uncertainty, but our bishops are now much better educated, and they show much more zeal for the faith. Take Bishop N. [Alain de Solminihac], of Cahors, for example. He lately wrote to tell me of a defamatory libel which appeared against our letter. It is the spirit of heresy, he told me, not to accept just correction and reprimand, and to have recourse to violent attacks and calumny. We are now at that point, as I have always thought we would come to.

Because I had expressed the hope that he would take care to

---

26. Mathieu Feydeau, *Catéchisme de la grâce*, Paris, 1650.
27. Jean Labadie. See *CED* IV:179, 471-72.

recover from an accident he had suffered, he said he would, but only to take his place in the battle about to begin, in which he hoped, with God's help, we would emerge victorious. That is what this good bishop says. We expect the same from you, Your Excellency, who are so active in preaching the orthodox doctrines of the Church in your diocese. You undoubtedly would be happy to see the Holy Father require this same doctrine to be preached everywhere, and to repress those new opinions so steeped with the errors of Calvin. This would certainly contribute to the glory of God, the peace of the Church, and I dare say, to that of the state. We see this more clearly at Paris than elsewhere. If it were not for this, Your Excellency, I would not have troubled you with such a long exposition. In your goodness please forgive me, for I dared write only in recognition of the danger.[28]

Among the other bishops to whom Monsieur Vincent wrote, two responded jointly, explaining why they did not choose to sign the letter.[29] He replied to them in a letter which follows, in which we can see his spirit and his zeal:

Your Excellencies, I have received with the respect I owe to your virtue and dignity, the letter you did me the honor to send, near the end of May, in response to mine on the questions which now trouble us. I observe many thoughts worthy of the rank you hold in the Church, which seem to incline you to keep silent in the present controversies. I take the liberty of presenting several reasons which perhaps might lead you to another conclusion, which, prostrate at your feet, I beg you to consider.

First, as to your fears that the judgment of His Holiness would not be received with the submission and obedience owed to the sovereign pontiff, and that the Spirit of God would not find enough docility in hearts to bring about a true reunion, I would willingly agree. When the heresies of Luther and Calvin, for example, began to appear, if anyone had waited until they were prepared to submit and to reunite themselves, these heresies would still be among those

---

28. *CED* IV:175-81.
29. Nicolas Pavillon, the bishop of Alet, and Francois Etienne de Caulet, the bishop of Pamiers. They argued for caution and further discussion. (*CED* IV:265-66.) Pavillon was born in 1597. He was under the direction of Vincent de Paul for a time, and helped in his charitable works and with the clergy conferences. He became bishop of Alet in 1637. He became more and more inclined toward Jansenism as time passed. Vincent was personally saddened at his position. Pavillon died in 1677. Caulet was born in 1610. He became bishop of Pamiers in 1645. Although he opposed Saint Cyran at first, he gradually became a Jansenist. He later showed his courage by strongly opposing Louis XIV in the "régale" controversy, which concerned a longstanding royal prerogative of disposing of the revenues coming from vacant dioceses during their vacancies. He also, however, strongly opposed Rome's position against Jansenism. He died in 1680.

opinions to be either accepted or rejected. They would have affected more people than they have. If then these opinions of our own day, whose pernicious effects we see in consciences, are of the same nature, we will wait in vain for those who spread them to come to agree with the defenders of the doctrines of the Church. We cannot hope for this, and it will never come about. To put off the condemnation by the Holy See gives these people time to spread their poison. Also, it takes away the opportunity for some well-placed people of great piety the opportunity to earn the merit of obedience, which they protest they will give to the decrees of the Holy Father as soon as they are promulgated. While awaiting this, they remain with the other party in good faith. They are attracted by the appearance of good and the reform they preach, but they do not recognize these are really only the sheep's clothing, which wolves always wear to harm and deceive souls.

Second, Your Excellencies say that the fervor of the two sides to sustain their respective position gives little hope for a true reunion, which is the end to be sought. I must point out that contraries can never be united when it comes to matters of faith and religion. If we are to join with others, it must be to join the pope, when a council is not in session. Those who do not look upon reunion in this way are not ready for any reunion, except for an unacceptable one. Law can never be reconciled with crime, nor lies with the truth.

Third, the uniformity you desire among the bishops is surely to be desired, if it can be achieved with no prejudice to the faith. We must not base our union on evil and on error. If this true union is to come about, the lesser part must unite with the greater, the member to the head, which is what is being proposed. Of six parts, the five hold to what the pope shall say in the absence of a council, which cannot meet because of the wars. If afterward a division remains, a schism if you will, it will be composed of those who want no judge, who do not recognize the position of most of the bishops, and who do not defer even to the pope himself.

From this comes a fourth reason in answer to what Your Excellencies were pleased to say to me, that each side is convinced that reason and truth are with them. I admit this, but you know well that heretics have always said as much, but this has not prevented condemnations and anathemas from popes and councils. Union with heretics has never been known to cure the ills. On the contrary, fire and the sword must be used, sometimes too late, as may happen here. Certainly, each side blames the other, but with this difference, that one side asks for a judge, while the other does not—truly a bad sign. It does not want a solution from the pope, I say, because they know a solution could be given. Instead, they call for a council because they know it is impossible to call one in present circumstances. If they thought a council were possible, they would reject it, just as they now reject the pope.

There will never be, to my way of thinking, a cause for ridicule by libertines and heretics, or a scandal to the faithful in seeing the bishops divided. The number of those who have not signed the letter to the pope on this matter is small. It is not an extraordinary thing in the Church to see differences in mentality. But this shows the need to have a pope to decide, for as vicar of Jesus Christ, he is the head of the Church, and the superior of the bishops.

Fifth, with wars everywhere, spreading almost throughout Christendom, they do not realize that the pope is prevented from observing all the conditions and necessary formalities prescribed by the Council of Trent for those matters referred to His Holiness. This happened in the past. As we read in the fathers and in church history, several saints and bishops regularly consulted him and referred to him in doubts of faith. To anticipate that his judgment will not be accepted is not something to be presumed or feared. Rather it is to be viewed as a way of seeing who are the true children of the Church and who are not.

As to the remedy Your Excellencies propose, to safeguard the right of either side to open discussion, I beg you most humbly to consider if this has not already been tried, and has served only to give standing to error. Seeing themselves treated on the same footing as those who possess the truth, they have taken the opportunity to spread their message. It is already too late to uproot it completely, for this doctrine is more than mere theory, and has descended into practice. Consciences can no longer support the troubles and uncertainties raised in the hearts of many by such thoughts, for example, as whether Jesus Christ really died for us. We hear of those attending the dying, urging them to have confidence in the goodness of our Lord who died for them. Yet we are also told that others have told the sick they should not believe this, for our Lord did not die for everyone.

Permit me also, Your Excellencies, to add to these considerations that those holding these novelties, who see that their threats are effective, increase them, and are preparing a more serious rebellion. They take your silence as a powerful argument in their favor, and even boast in a book they have published that you are of their opinion. On the other hand, supporters of the ancient faith are weakened and discouraged, seeing they are not universally supported. Will you not someday be sorry, Your Excellencies, that your names were used, despite your good intentions, to confirm heretics in their error and to shake believers in their faith?

To come back to the question of a general council: how could one be convoked during wartime? It took about forty years from the time Luther and Calvin began to trouble the Church before the Council of Trent could be held. Other than a council, no more timely remedy exists than to have recourse to the pope, as the council itself stated in the last session, in the last chapter of its decrees, of which I will send you an extract.

Once more, Your Excellencies, we must not fear that the pope will not be obeyed once he has decided. We see this in all heresies, but this does not mean we should allow them to go unchallenged. We also have one recent example to contradict the false notion which came from the same source, that there were really two equal rulers in the early Church. This was condemned by the pope, he was listened to, and we hear no more of it.

Certainly, Your Excellencies, all these reasons and some others you know better than I, and which I would be glad to learn, for I respect you as my fathers in the faith and as teachers of the Church, have resulted in few of the bishops of France not signing the letter in question.[30]

These letters of Monsieur Vincent, and all his other activities in this matter, allow us to see that his sole motive was the glory of God and the salvation of souls. We must admire his ardent zeal for the service of our Lord and his Church, coupled with profound humility and singular respect for the sacred office of the bishop. If on the one hand his charity moved him to speak out and to share the insights God had inspired in him, on the other hand his humility and respect led him to prostrate himself in spirit at their feet, begging them to pardon his forwardness. He then spoke more with the heart than the mouth to those he revered as fathers and doctors of the Church, from whom he was ready to learn in the matter he spoke of. He always acted this way, and by this humility and charity he was blessed, first by God, but then by the bishops who recognized his sincerity and zeal, which furthered their own position. In this he resembled several other holy persons who, though living a retired life, sometimes felt compelled to alert the prelates of the Church to dangers in the heresies threatening the tranquility of the Church.

---

30. *CED* IV:204-10.

While Monsieur Vincent was engaged in these efforts to have the sovereign pontiff give judgment about the book of Jansenius, his opponents in turn were doing everything in their power to thwart this move and prevent its execution. To further this design, they wrote a circular letter which was sent to all the bishops of the kingdom, to persuade them not to sign the previous letter addressed to the pope. However, this did not prevent more than eighty bishops and archbishops from signing this letter, sent to the Holy See.

As a result of this development, the Jansenists had recourse to Monsieur de N. [Louis Gorin, Abbe de Saint Amour], doctor of theology, and already in Rome, directing him to use all his influence to prevent the pope from pronouncing judgment on this matter. Besides that, they feared they did not have enough influence to avert the storm over the book of Jansenius, so they sent three of their doctors to Rome by coach. They were to prevent, or at least delay as much as they possibly could, the judgment of the pope.

When it became known that these Jansenists were on their way to Rome, Monsieur Vincent felt it most important that several orthodox doctors should also go there, to combat the efforts of the others. By a singular grace of divine Providence which ever watches over his Church, he found three members of the faculty of the Sorbonne willing to undertake the trip in service of the Catholic religion. These three were Fathers Hallier, Joisel, and Lagault, the first of whom later became bishop of Cavaillon, appointed by our Holy Father the pope, Innocent X, in recognition of his merits and service to the Church.

Monsieur Vincent was pleased when he heard of the plans of these three gentlemen. Since he knew them personally, he encouraged them in their project. He offered to do what he could to help, both before their departure for Rome or after their arrival there.

This is not the place to describe all these gentlemen did in service to the Church and for the defense of truth during their stay in Rome. They wrote to Monsieur Vincent from time to time, and in return received some suggestions from him for the benefit of religion. We shall cite only a letter, dated December 20, 1652, written to Monsieur Hallier on this topic:

> I thank God for the happy success he has given your efforts there. I thank you most humbly for your kindness in writing. I can assure you, Monsieur, that nothing brings me greater joy that your letters, and I pray for nothing in this world more than I do for you and your concerns in Rome. The goodness of God leads me to hope that peace will soon be restored to his Church, and that thanks to your zealous efforts truth will prevail. This is what we shall continue to ask of God. Let us know, please, how things are progressing.[31]

---

31. *CED* IV:534.

It appears from this letter that Monsieur Vincent had some inkling from Monsieur Hallier that the doctrine of the book of Jansenius contained in the five propositions sent to Rome would be condemned, and that his friend would soon be raised to the episcopal dignity. This happened, as we have already mentioned.

As to the condemnation of the five propositions,[32] the Catholic reader will have the satisfaction of reading two letters written from Rome to Monsieur Vincent on this matter. The originals of these are preserved in the house of Saint Lazare in Paris. The first of these was from Monsieur Hallier:

Last Monday I had time to send you only the news that the constitution against Jansenius greatly benefited the defense of the Catholic religion and the condemnation of error. The Jansenists left this city today to go to Loreto, where their servants have been for the last fifteen days. They promised the pope they would obey promptly. Yet I have reason to doubt this, for they have said to all their confederates they were never condemned in what they actually hold, which is also the position of Jansenius. I know they are ridiculous in saying so. Jansenius has been condemned, the propositions taken from his writings have been condemned, and even the sense given to the five propositions by the Jansenists themselves have been expressly and specifically condemned. Their interpretations have been condemned absolutely. Nevertheless, their persistence in error may still find supporters, both in this country and elsewhere. That is why we must work to disabuse the unlearned. We should do all we can to publicize the bull, and see to its ratification by the Parlement, in the dioceses, in the faculties of the universities, with the king and the chancellor and keeper of the seal, with the bishops, and the doctors.

I fear Monsieur de Saint Amour runs away with himself, and does not tell things the way they happened, by saying they were not fully heard. This has been answered several times. First, they had the opportunity to inform the cardinals of the Congregation, either orally or in writing, for an entire year. Second, they had access to our material, as they themselves mentioned in their speech to the pope. Third, there was no point to hearing them, or ourselves either for that matter. It was a question of the doctrine taken from the book of Jansenius which the pope had directed be examined most care-

---

32. The "Five Propositions" extracted from the book by Jansenius and denounced by Nicolas Cornet as containing the summary of the heretical doctrines found in *Augustinus*. Cornet, born October 12, 1592, was a doctor and the syndic of the faculty of theology of Paris. He was a friend of Vincent's. He died April 18, 1663. Bossuet, who had had him as a teacher, preached his funeral oration.

fully. It was useless to hear them, for they brought up motives in their defense all found in Jansenius. Fourth, it is not the custom when a book is condemned, to receive other information than what comes from the book itself, and from people learned in the matter treated of in the book. Fifth, when the Jansenist doctors were given the opportunity to speak before the cardinals, for two, three, four or five times, as often as might be needed, they refused. Sixth, when they furnished documents, as requested, they were beside the point. They were designed to delay the proceedings, and thus delay the pronouncement against their heresy, to give them more time to spread it further.

As to the way they seek to avoid the effect of the bull, you have only to read what they say to condemn them. They came expressly to defend the propositions sent to the pope by the bishops, and to prevent their condemnation. They wanted to prevent the censure of the faculty also, although this was mild. They wrote three apologies for Jansenius. They interpret the propositions in the sense given them by Jansenius, and the propositions have no other meaning, if words mean what they signify to the one who first used them. The pope condemned them all as heretical, and they cannot be explained away. The propositions were condemned in the meaning they gave to them, and which they presented to the pope. *Ubi lex non distinguit, nec nos distinguere debemus.* ["Where the law makes no distinctions, neither must we."]

You are aware that the nuncio has a brief for Her Majesty, in which the pope asks for the bull's publication. You see the importance of this. There is also a brief for the bishops, as well. We will remain here until we get news of how the bull has been received in France. The intention here is to condemn the apologies for Jansenius, *Victorious Grace, Everyday Theology,* and others, after we see how the bull has been received.[33]

You will see from the enclosed that all the usual niceties of style have been omitted to make our point clearer. This gracious procedure obliges us the more to a respectful obedience, and we should do all in our power to have it accepted, just as the Jansenists will do all they can to prevent its acceptance. We must inform the queen of the care, effort, work, and kindness His Holiness has devoted to this, and make clear to her that her duty in conscience, her honor, and the security of the state of the king her son, are all involved on

---

33. Noel La Lane, *La grâce victorieuse de Jésus-Christ*, 1650; and Jean Duverger de Hauranne [Saint Cyran], *Théologie familière*, 1642.

this occasion. We have been wondering if we should write to her, since the ambassador said he was not going to write, deferring to us. We have also had the thought of writing to the cardinal. In the end we decided against it, for fear it would appear we were acting in self-interest. Far be it from us to do this. But we felt it would be better that others inform him, as you shall judge best.

From Rome, June 16, 1653. Your very humble and devoted servant, Hallier.[34]

The second letter comes from Monsieur Lagault, written from Rome, June 15, 1653, as follows:

Monsieur, I did not have the time in my last letter to write adequately, for the bull against the Jansenists was finished only on the very evening the couriers were leaving. There is no better way to tell you the result than to say with Saint Paul: *Regi saeculorum immortali, invisibili, soli Deo, honor et gloria* ["To the King of ages, the immortal, the invisible, the only God, be honor and glory"].[35] God worked so manifestly in this whole affair that to him alone must we give the praise. The pope himself recognized this, saying so in the congregations, where they sometimes remained in session for five hours. Except for his compassion for the theologians who could not remain standing any longer, they would have been willing to remain for eight or nine hours. He understood all so completely that he met in the evening with Cardinal [Fabio] Chigi, secretary of state, to go over all that had been said.

The hand of God appeared, too, in the three great difficulties the pope had to overcome: the people of rank who wanted him to leave things unsettled, and the others who wanted him to forego its consideration, under the pretext that it would notably compromise his health. I do not believe that such powerful complaints ever came from your side. Time will tell us more. Despite all this, he remained so firm in his determination that he did not hesitate for a single moment. Since this matter concerned the good of the Church, he always felt that he was determined to bring it to a conclusion. He had it so much at heart that when some of his relatives came to see him by way of diversion, he could talk of nothing else.

Every care was taken to remove all pretext for complaint. After twenty-five meetings of the congregation of cardinals, he had ten meetings, lasting in all over four hours. He then invited the Jansenists themselves, since they had requested it, though he was not

---

34. *CED* IV:610-13.
35. 1 Tim 1:17.

at all obliged to do so, especially since they had refused to appear before the cardinals. They behaved so poorly before the pope that he did not agree to a second session with them, for they simply wanted to draw things out, and would need, they said, up to twenty-five sessions to present their case. They did not discuss the issue at all. Instead, they railed against the Jesuits, attempting to prove they were the authors of more than fifty heresies.

The pope recognized their scheme, and refused to go along with it. They have no reason to complain, for we have had, ourselves, but a single audience with him. Besides, since coming to Rome they have had eight or nine with him. Even after the decision they had another, lasting more than an hour, in which they promised to obey. To tell you the truth, I doubt they will do so. They are returning immediately to France, despite the heat, where it may be surmised they will work to prevent the publication of the bull.

However, we will remain here by request of the cardinals, who have thought it best we remain until we have heard how the bull was received in France. We could possibly advise on further steps, but I do not believe anything further is to be said. Monsieur Hallier told me he sent you a copy of the bull, which explains why I do not enclose one with this letter. I have written to you at length for you to disabuse some people who probably have been badly misinformed.

I forgot to tell you that already some have tried to take advantage of the fact the bull was removed two and a half hours after it was put up, and this at the order of the pope. You should know, Monsieur, that this was done by design, after it was put up in manuscript form. The pope did not want any copies made until it was first sent to the courts of Europe and to the nuncios. He instructed the police not to allow it to be copied. At nightfall, as is the custom, he had it taken down, to prove that it had really been posted. Since then it has been sent to France, with a brief for the king, and another brief for the bishops. The pope sent an express courier to Poland, since it is so far away. I hope I shall be able to send you from here a further account of what has taken place.

Monsieur, please continue to thank God for having preserved the Church in France from falling further into Calvinism. Do not forget in your masses him who is, with all his heart, your very humble and obedient servant, Lagault.

Since writing the above, we today, the sixteenth, have thanked His Holiness, who received us in audience for more than two and a half hours. He told us that we should know what he had done before coming to his decision: he had ordered prayers to be offered to God, both in public and in private; he mentioned the sessions he had held on the matter. He confirmed what I have already written, of the singular pleasure he had taken in the discussions, and the special and palpable help he had received from the Holy Spirit. Nothing theological was set forth which was not easily understood and retained. In addition, he told us the reasons the bull was given, point by point. Among other things he said that one morning, after recommending himself to God, he called a secretary, and dictated the bull in a single morning. He told us that these gentlemen whom I dare call the Jansenists (for I would like to believe there will be no more) came to thank him for his decision, and that their promise of submitting entirely to it moved him to tears. God grant they will keep this good resolution. He added that at their public audience they delivered a terrible invective against the Jesuits (these were the words he used), and nothing they said addressed the subject at hand.[36]

As soon as the constitution of our Holy Father the pope, Innocent X, was brought to France, Monsieur Vincent thought to himself how best to reap the fruit to be hoped for from its publication, which was chiefly the reconciliation and reunion of minds drawn away by the false glamour of this new doctrine. His first thought was to visit the superiors of several religious houses, and some doctors and other influential people most active in this affair, to urge them to do all in their power for the reconciliation of the vanquished party. He remarked to them that he felt they should temper public expressions of joy, and not make references in their sermons or conversations which might embarrass those supporters of the condemned doctrine of Jansenius. He feared this would only further aggravate them rather than win them over. The most expedient course would be to go out of their way to offer the hand of friendship to them in this most humiliating situation. This would also simplify their return when they saw themselves treated with such respect and charity. He assured them that for his part he would act in this way.

He did just as he had said, for he went to Port Royal to see some gentlemen who habitually lived there, to congratulate them on their submission to the pope, as they had done from the beginning, at least in appearance. He spoke with them openly for several hours, and with much esteem and affection. He later went to see some other important people of that party who also promised complete submission to the Holy See in what pertained to the condemned doctrine.

---

36. *CED* IV:607-10.

These charitable efforts of Monsieur Vincent did not have all the good effects he had hoped for. Their deeds did not conform to the fine words that they had uttered. Many of the Jansenists were at first touched and truly wished to submit to the judgment of the head of the Church. The pretexts and subterfuges of the main leaders of the sect, however, led a number to continue holding to the condemned doctrine, despite all the exterior forces and interior movements of grace which invited them to recognize and confess the truth.

Nevertheless, when the new constitution of our Holy Father, Pope Alexander VII, appeared, toward the end of 1656, confirming and explaining that of Innocent X, Monsieur Vincent, with his usual zeal, again began his visits and meetings with the leading members of the Jansenists. They showed no more submission to this new constitution than they had to the first. This led this faithful servant of God to see that nothing was to be gained in working with those so poorly disposed. He turned his thoughts and care to preserve the faith in those not contaminated, to warn them of the dangers of these new errors.

As charity demanded, he used his energy to keep the members of his own Congregation in the purity of the faith and the doctrine of the Church. He spoke several times to his community to impress upon them how much they were obliged to the goodness of God for having preserved them from these novelties, which were capable of corrupting and ruining their Congregation. He recommended that they pray for the peace of the Church, for the removal of these new errors, and for the conversion of those infected. He forbade them to read the books of Jansenius or to support either directly or indirectly their doctrine, nor any of the opinions likely to favor them.[37] After all this, if he knew of anyone who belonged to the sect in any manner whatsoever, he removed him from the community as a gangrenous member, one likely to infect and corrupt the rest of the body.

After assuring the safety and security of his own confreres, he extended his solicitude to several communities of women, preserved by his counsel and charitable intervention from the contagion of these new errors. This was particularly true in several convents of nuns who owe their preservation, after God, to his zeal and charity.

We will add to this an example of his charity which extended not only to his own community but to people to whom he extended an affectionate helping hand. He did this to preserve in them their orthodox beliefs, or to help those who may have fallen, if they gave the least sign of wanting to return.

A doctor of the faculty of the Sorbonne had embraced Jansenism, not only

---

37. See *CED* VI:88-89.

by the attachment he had for this new doctrine, but even more so by the contacts he had formed with some leading and influential devotees of this party.[38] The constitution of Innocent X had impressed him, and if it had not entirely converted him, it at least had shaken him. In his doubts and perplexities he arranged to make a retreat at Saint Lazare. He carefully examined himself on all the thoughts which came to his mind on this matter. He then finally admitted to Monsieur Vincent that he was ready to leave the Jansenists, if only the pope would enlighten him on several doubts he still harbored, which he wrote in a letter to His Holiness.

Monsieur Vincent was instrumental in obtaining a favorable response. This led the doctor to decide to renounce the condemned doctrine, but instead of following this inspiration promptly he paid too much attention to human respect, and preferred the glory of men to that which we owe to God. Monsieur Vincent was not to be put off. He urged him to act, but the reply was that he could not renounce a doctrine which God seemingly favored by miracles, which it was said were taking place at Port Royal. At this, Monsieur Vincent wrote him the following letter, and sent him the papers mentioned in the letter:

> I am sending you the new constitution of our Holy Father the pope, which confirms that of Innocent X, and other popes who have condemned the new opinions of Jansenius. I believe, Monsieur, you will no longer find any room for doubt after its acceptance and publication by the prelates of the kingdom, assembled so often for this purpose. The assembly of the lower clergy has published a tract on the matter, which I also enclose, and finally, the censure of the Sorbonne, and the letter written at the direction of His Holiness to you.
>
> I hope, Monsieur, that with all this you will give glory to God and edification to his Church, as all expect of you. If you wait longer we must fear that the evil spirit, who uses every subterfuge to avoid the truth, will imperceptibly put you in such a state you will not have the strength to return because you have not used the grace offered you for such a long time. I have never known God to have given such persuasive and powerful graces to any other of your party.
>
> To say, Monsieur, that miracles of the holy thorn worked at Port Royal seem to show the divine approval of the doctrines held there, I recall to you the teaching of Saint Thomas. He wrote that God has never confirmed error by miracles, since truth cannot have any

---

38. Jean Des Lions, doctor of the Sorbonne and dean of Senlis. He had influence over Arnauld and the duke and duchess of Liancourt.

place with error, nor light with the dark. Who cannot see that the propositions supported by that party are errors, since they have been condemned? If then God works miracles, he does so not to justify false opinions, but to enhance his own glory in some other mysterious manner.[39]

To wait for God to send you an angel to enlighten you further is useless. He sends you to the Church, and the Church assembled at Trent sends you to the Holy See for the matter at hand, as you can see from the last chapter of this council.

You cannot wait for Saint Augustine to come back to explain himself. Our Lord has told us that if we do not believe the scriptures we would not believe even the dead come back to life. If this saint were to come back, he would submit to the sovereign pontiff as he did on other occasions.

Should you await the judgment of some famous faculty of theology to decide these questions? Where would it be found? None is more learned in Christendom than that of the Sorbonne, of which you are a distinguished member.

Should you wait for a great doctor and good man to tell you what to do? Where will you find one in whom these two qualities are more evident than he to whom I speak?

It seems to me, Monsieur, that I hear you saying you should not decide too quickly, so that you might bring others of stature in with you. This is good, but the danger is that in thinking to save others from drowning you might be trapped and go down with them.[40] I say this mildly, since their salvation is as dear to me as my own, and I would willingly give up a thousand lives, if I had them, for their sake. Your example might be more effective in having them return than anything you might say. Considering all this, in the name of God, Monsieur, do not put off this step which would be so pleasing to the divine goodness. Your own salvation depends on it. You have more reason to fear for yourself than many others in the same errors, for you, unlike them, have received a special enlightenment from our Holy Father.

How displeasing it would be for you, Monsieur, if putting off your decision, you would be forced to take a stand, which is what the bishops are planning. This is why I beseech you anew, in the

---

39. At the same time that he was writing this letter, he encouraged the publication of a work, *Defense de la verité catholique touchant les miracles*. This work strongly attacked the veracity of the Port Royal "miracles."
40. This is what eventually happened to Jean Des Lions, who joined the duke and duchess of Liancourt in the Jansenist party.

name of our Lord, to take the step. Do not object that the most
ignorant and abominable of men speaks this way to you, for what
he says makes sense. If in the scriptures we read that beasts have
spoken and evil men have prophesied, I too could be saying the
truth, even though I am a beast and wicked.

May it please God to speak to you effectively, in making you see
the good you should do. Besides being in the state that God asks of
you, it is to be hoped that at your example a good part of these
gentlemen would return from their erroneous ways. On the contrary, you may be the cause of their remaining in error if you delay
your decision, and in this case I doubt if you would ever return. This
would be a severe blow to me because of my esteem and affection
for you, and having had the honor of serving you as I have, I would
be extremely sorry to see you leave the Church. I hope our Lord
would not permit such an unhappy event, and I often pray for this
intention, I who remain, in his love, etc.[41]

By his response to this letter, this doctor gave once again some hope for
his return. He waited only, it seemed, to find the time and circumstance
suitable for this step, to bring some others with him back to the Church.
Monsieur Vincent outlined a series of steps he should take. All these efforts
were in vain, however, for this doctor remained in his heresy despite all the
charitable efforts of Monsieur Vincent to bring him back.

We will finish this chapter by recalling a reply he gave to a man of honor
and merit, much impressed by some of the more wealthy of the Jansenists,
and their generosity, rather than with the more learned ones among them.
He was in a sort of suspense, not daring to condemn in his heart those who
showed themselves so generous and virtuous. This man, then, a close friend
of Monsieur Vincent, came to see him one day, to ask if in some way
Monsieur Vincent might soften his approach in dealing with the gentlemen
at Port Royal. "Why," he said, "must you push them so hard? Would it not
be better to come to some kind of agreement? They are so inclined, if only
they would be treated with more moderation, and I know of no one better
than yourself to soften the harsh attitudes on either side and so bring about
a reunion."

Monsieur Vincent replied to this by saying:

When a dispute has been adjudicated, the only course to follow
is to carry out the decision rendered. Before the gentlemen were
condemned, they used all their energies to make falsehood triumph
over truth. They took such pains in this that they could be stopped
only with the greatest difficulty, and they were unwilling to concede

---

41. *CED* VI:266-70.

anything. Now that the Holy See has decided these questions to their dissatisfaction, they have given different meanings to the constitution to avoid their effect. Although they pretended to submit to the common father of the faithful, and to receive the constitution in the true sense that condemned the propositions of Jansenius, their writers continue to support these opinions and have put out books and tracts to defend them. They have not said a single word withdrawing their condemned opinions.

What union can we possibly have with them, if they do not have a true and sincere intention of submission? What kind of moderation can we show for what has been decided by the Church? These are matters of the faith, which cannot be changed or compromised, and so we cannot adjust our thinking to these gentlemen. They must submit their minds and rejoin us in the one faith, by a true and sincere submission to the head of the Church. Other than this, Monsieur, we can do nothing but pray for their conversion.[42]

This is a brief sketch of the firmness with which Monsieur Vincent always opposed those who upheld the doctrines of the Jansenists. Since its condemnation by the Church, he always declared himself openly on the matter, and felt that all true Catholics ought to do the same. He felt it to be a great evil to deceive or to equivocate, and even worse to remain in a sort of indifference or neutrality when it was a question of faith and religion. Although he always advised that moderation govern all, and great charity mark dealings with the adherents of the Jansenists in the hope of their conversion, he wished too that this meekness be joined to firmness, and held that any new heresy must not be flattered or pampered, no matter in whom it appeared. Although it is not permitted to judge anyone, it is a greater evil through a false charity or any other unworthy motive to accept those in heresy or suspected of heresy. Not only is it not rash, but it is unjust and even impious to withhold judgment from what the Church has condemned, or even worse to support it. It is surely an evil to wish to judge the Church herself, to condemn the judgments she has given through the mouth of her head and her prelates.

Although Monsieur Vincent was moved by a true zeal against Jansenism and did all he could to oppose it, he was able to distinguish the condemned errors from laxism, which he never approved, as he showed on many occasions. He always recommended his confreres attach themselves strongly to a truly Christian morality, as taught in the Gospels and in the writings of the fathers and doctors of the Church. He highly praised the bishops and the Sorbonne who worked against moral laxity, just as much as against Jansenism. He accepted graciously what the Holy See taught on both the one and the other.

---

42. *CED* XIII:167.

CHAPTER THIRTEEN

Monsieur Vincent's Service to the King in the Council of His Majesty and Elsewhere During the Time of the Queen Mother's Regency

WE COULD WELL include among the great accomplishments of Monsieur Vincent his tenure on the king's Council for Ecclesiastical Affairs, and the services he rendered His Majesty. Besides the importance of the matters confided to him, which he always handled well, he showed on these occasions his strong character and eminent virtue. He should be the more appreciated in this, since one rarely finds in one person what was seen in him, that is, ready access to sovereigns coupled with a perfect detachment from all worldly interests. He combined political prudence with Christian simplicity, a great vigilance and active involvement in exterior concerns and an interior recollection and intimate union with God, the management of diverse matters of great importance and an uprightness never in doubt, the coming and going of all sorts of persons who came to see him, coupled with a serenity of disposition which showed itself in kindness and affability toward everyone. Lastly, he manifested a mind capable of the most important decisions in the service of his prince coupled with a will totally penetrated with the sentiments of a solid and perfect devotion to God.

These qualities of Monsieur Vincent were astonishing to those who saw them firsthand. In this chapter we will give some examples of them, even though he was reticent in speaking of his years of service to His Majesty. He held to the maxim once taught by an angel, *Sacramentum Regis abscondere bonum est* ["A king's secret it is prudent to keep"].[1] We have been able to learn from other sources some episodes of the time of service of this great servant of God, whom divine Providence had led to this important position. Since all he did was under the inspiration of divine grace, we may speak openly of it, for the same heavenly spirit mentioned earlier also said: *opera Dei revelare et confiteri honorificum est* ["but the works of God are to be declared and made known"].[2]

---

1. Tob 12:7.
2. Ibid.

SECTION ONE

The Appointment of Monsieur Vincent to the King's Council for Ecclesiastical Affairs

In 1643, after the death of King Louis XIII, of happy and triumphant memory, the queen mother [Anne of Austria] saw herself charged with the direction of this great kingdom during the minority of her son. She also recognized that to attract God's protection upon the precious child confided to her care, and also upon the entire state, she could do nothing better than to put religious matters into good order. She desired that God should rule in the hearts of her subjects, thus strengthening royal authority in the kingdom. To further this, she established a Council for Ecclesiastical Affairs, especially for granting those benefices at Her Majesty's disposition. Knowing of the virtue of Monsieur Vincent, and his other excellent qualities, she wanted him to become a member of this council.

We cannot adequately describe the surprise and astonishment of this humble servant of God at this appointment, nor the efforts he made to be dispensed from this service. It was as unbearable to him as it appeared honorable and brilliant in the eyes of others. Her Majesty persisted in her request, making it known that she was adamant in wanting him to give this service to God and to the king, her son. His humility gave way to obedience, believing that this request of the queen was a manifestation of God's will for him. This is why he renounced his own preferences in the matter, and he offered himself to God to do all that would be most pleasing to him.

He foresaw the great storms and violent shocks to which he would be exposed on this tempestuous sea of the court. He knew from experience that in sustaining the interests of justice and piety he would be the recipient of many recriminations and persecutions. He felt he could do nothing better than to abandon himself to divine Providence. He resolved to acquit himself faithfully and religiously in the position confided to him, and to preserve an inviolable fidelity to God and to the king, regardless of what might happen.[3]

This resolution was well taken. After it became known that the queen sought his advice, some persons of high rank would come often to seek his favor and his recommendation. They would have obliged him to devote all his time to their business, were it not for his practice of not going to court

---

3. According to the testimony of Louis de Chandenier, Cardinal de la Rochefoucauld convinced Vincent to serve on the Council of Conscience for the sake of God's honor and the welfare of the French Church.

unless called for, and his conviction that as a priest he ought not to become involved in worldly affairs.

SECTION TWO

Rules for Awarding Benefices, Adopted on the Recommendation of Monsieur Vincent

After being appointed to the council in the way we have described, Monsieur Vincent felt the first order of business ought to be to set out some guidelines for the awarding of those benefices which depended upon nomination by the queen.

The main ones adopted were:

(1) The queen would grant no pension for bishops and archbishops except in the only case foreseen by the law. This envisions that an officeholder, after serving for a long time, voluntarily resign from his office because of infirmity, old age, or other valid reason.

(2) The queen would give no commission for abbeys except to those who, besides the other qualities required, will be at least eighteen years of age; sixteen years of age for priors, canons of cathedral churches, and fourteen years for canons of collegial churches.

(3) No commission would be given for benefices that have devolved upon the crown, unless documents had been submitted in support of these requests. Certification must be presented regarding the life, morals, and abilities of those requesting these benefices. If the petitioners do not have the required qualities, others shall be chosen in whom these qualities do exist, and who can reestablish the devolved benefices.

(4) There would be no assistant honorary abbots, not even provisional ones.

(5) There would be no appointments to bishoprics, even as coadjutors, except for those ordained at least a year.

(6) No coadjutors would be appointed to abbeys of women, unless it be known for certain that the rule is observed in these abbeys. The religious to be appointed to this position should be at least twenty-three years old, and of at least five years of profession.

It is easy enough to take good resolutions. Keeping them is something else. Monsieur Vincent did all he could to make sure they were strictly observed. He often recalled them to mind. When he saw they were not being followed exactly, he had them reinstated. This allowed him to correct abuses which had slipped into the awarding of benefices and the handling of the administration of ecclesiastical goods. He did so freely but always respectfully. He complained only when he saw purely human considerations taking precedence over those referring to the service of God and the good of the Church.

This is not to say that he disregarded persons of birth and courage for ecclesiastical positions, and even for bishoprics, when birth and other qualities did not serve as a pretext for vanity, and if they had the competence, virtue, and other necessary dispositions.

In this connection he followed an old maxim: "Better fifty deer led by a lion than fifty lions led by a deer." He lamented before God when he saw temporal interests prevail over spiritual considerations, to the prejudice of the service of God and to the disadvantage of his Church. Nevertheless, after doing what he felt it was his duty to do, he committed the rest to Providence and remained at peace.

SECTION THREE

The Care and Impartiality with Which Monsieur Vincent Acted Concerning Ecclesiastical Benefices

Since Cardinal Mazarin had been appointed by the queen as the head of the Council for Ecclesiastical Affairs, he gave as much time to it as his other duties allowed. When he summoned the council he asked for advice on the giving of bishoprics. Monsieur Vincent gave it with both respect and freedom. He spoke his opinions, before God, about the ability or lack of it, the merits or the deficiencies, of those who had been proposed. No regular day was set for the meeting of the council, and the meeting depended on the time available to the prime minister, who was often taken up with other important matters of state. For this reason, His Eminence often decided by himself, with the queen's agreement, on the abbots and even bishops he judged would best serve the king. When he believed they presented no difficulty, he did not think it necessary to have them considered by the council.

All the same, there were many such lesser offices to be filled, either of the regular or secular clergy or many resignations or changes to be considered, and other matters to regulate to prevent abuses or to put things in good order. Because of this, Monsieur Vincent, who was responsible for these, had much to report on at each meeting of the council.

In awarding benefices he felt it proper to look to the clergy attached to the court and to the chaplains of the army in preference to others, if he found them well qualified. He felt the officials in the service of Their Majesties who lived decently among the corruptions of the court deserved special consideration. Because some were not all they should be, however, and some already were well provided for but still asked for additional benefices and pensions, sometimes the most unworthy were better off than the more qualified. To bring a remedy to this disorder, he drew up a list of the chaplains, confessors, clerks, cantors, and other ecclesiastical officials of the house, chapel, and musical department of Their Majesties, adding the amounts they already were paid, or those not paid at all. He wanted to be sure to do all he could to have the available support evenly distributed among all.

In Normandy, the king had the right of appointment to benefices which were under lay patronage, but whose patron was a minor, and thus a ward of the crown. Monsieur Vincent was careful in awarding these benefices when they became vacant by resignation or death to make sure that they were granted to the most deserving. He was convinced that those whose duty it was to name those who would receive a benefice with a care of souls, were responsible before God, not only for all the evil done by unworthy pastors, but also for all of the good which remained undone by those who were unworthy and who had been granted the benefice in place of a more worthy candidate.

At this time many gentlemen, crippled during their wartime military service, urgently requested that they be awarded pensions from benefices as a reward for their services to the king. Monsieur Vincent gladly recommended to the cardinal and the queen their requests for pensions, but he strongly objected to these pensions being drawn from ecclesiastical sources. He felt that these could only rightly be used for ecclesiastical pensions.

On the one hand, this faithful councillor had his eyes open so as not to be taken by surprise in this matter of benefices, to the prejudice of the service of God and the honor of the Church. On the other, he was careful to oversee, as much as it was possible for him, the just distribution and use of ecclesiastical goods. The Church fathers called these the patrimony of the poor, and the price of the redemption from sin.

SECTION FOUR

His Zeal in Combating Abuses in the Awarding of Benefices

We have to admit that we live in a time when we can repeat the lament of Saint Bernard against those who in his day sought benefices for unworthy motives.

> Where can we find someone who seeks, or someone who is sought out, to have ecclesiastical charges and dignities for the sole and sincere intention of offering himself to God, to serve him in true holiness of body and soul, and to work with greater fervor at his own salvation and that of others, by prayer and the ministry of preaching? On the contrary, do we not see it is ambition or the hope of enriching themselves that leads to all sorts of schemes, and sometimes of unlawful or even shameful ways to gain access to the treasury of Jesus Christ? Mothers and fathers are busy seeking benefices for their children even from their earliest years, sometimes even before they are born. Solicitations and repeated requests are made until they are heard, and often those receiving the most are the least grateful. On occasion they are downright ingrates.

In his time, Monsieur Vincent saw these same abuses and disorders, and others worse still, which deeply wounded his heart. In imitation of this great saint he was not content to complain in the sight of God, but used all his energy to combat these abuses. He opposed these disorders with no regard to human respect, nor did he trouble himself with the resentment powerful people felt, or their threats to himself and his community. The interests of God were incomparably more significant to him than any other consideration.

He was not able to hide his displeasure at the insistence with which some tried to promote their nomination to the episcopacy. They used every conceivable stratagem, making large donations to abbeys, and going to great expense to secure their nomination. This faithful servant of God, usually so sparing in his use of words, could not refrain from saying to one of his friends that he greatly feared this damnable traffic in sacred offices would attract the curse of God upon the entire kingdom.

A chaplain to the king, a good man, was urged by his relatives to speak about his years of service and his willingness to accept a bishopric. He was inclined to follow this advice, thinking that if he did not speak up or have others petition for him, he would be passed over in forgetfulness. He realized this would be contrary to the humility and modesty suitable for a priest. He would be surer of his own salvation if he would leave himself in the hands of divine Providence. He was troubled in spirit over what course to follow, and in this perplexity wrote to Monsieur Vincent for advice. This great servant of God replied in these words:

> Monsieur, I have received your letter with all the respect I owe you, and with the esteem and thanks for the grace God has put into your kindly heart. God alone, in face of the natural inclination of man to advance himself, has given you the thought of the opposite. He will give you the strength to carry out whatever is most agreeable to him. In this, Monsieur, you are following the rule of the Church, which does not allow anyone to push himself forward for ecclesiastical dignities, especially for the episcopacy. You imitate the Son of God. Though he was the eternal priest, he did not come to exercise this office on his own. He waited for his Father to send him, even though he had been awaited for such a long time as the "Desired of all the nations."[4]
>
> You give a great example to the present generation, in which few observe this rule or follow this example. You will have the consolation, Monsieur, should it please the Lord to call you to this ecclesiastical dignity, that it is truly a call from God, since it came about with no human intervention. You would be sustained with special graces of God, part of a true vocation, and if you fulfill the duties of an apostolic life, you can anticipate a blessed eternity. We see this in those prelates who have done nothing to push their own cause, and who honor God in themselves and in their work.
>
> In closing, Monsieur, you will have no regrets at the hour of death in having taken upon yourself the cares of a diocese, which otherwise would seem unbearable. Indeed, I cannot write this except with thanks to God, to see you in no way seeking this burden, and for his having given you the disposition of not wanting to push yourself forward. This is a grace which cannot be prized and cherished enough.[5]

Not only in the seeking of bishoprics, but in all kinds of other benefices, some sought so earnestly that they went so far as to commit simony or to reveal confidences. Monsieur Vincent used an extraordinary vigilance to prevent this evil. When he came upon something of the sort he would first warn the offender. If this did no good he would refuse them absolutely. Since he was aware that the human malice is ingenious in hiding under various

---

4. A reference to the Latin text of Hag 2:8.
5. *CED* IV:77-78.

pretexts, he was most careful to be on guard against the camouflages of this unholy business. When he did not see clearly what was happening in the changes, resignations, or other modifications in the benefices sought, he would send away the petitioner until he could have a clearer insight into the matter. In addition, he kept careful watch on pensions, to see there was no abuse in them, and that they were not excessive, or too great a burden on the revenues of the benefice supporting them.

There was another evil committed in the quest for benefices which he sought to remedy as much as was in his power. Some sought to profit from the property of the Church, but not being able to do so legally, sought to achieve their goal by more devious means. This scheme was to threaten to have the benefice held by someone else declared vacant, and oblige the legitimate holder to pay ransom to stop the annoyance. If these unscrupulous persons could not gain title to a benefice, at least they hoped to get some financial benefit. Because these parasites on the property of the Church ordinarily hid their specious pretexts under the appearance of good to make their designs less hateful, more often than not Monsieur Vincent had to be most vigilant. He attempted to attack the evil at its root. He obliged those appealing to the council for the devolution of any benefice, before answering their petition, to justify and prove the causes and reasons upon which they based their claims.[6] Those who could not do so he reported to the council, with the recommendation that these requests should not be honored, but should be rejected.

By this procedure he put a stop to a countless number of lawsuits at their very beginning. This prevented annoying vexations for many virtuous clergy, and even some pastors. Without this charitable protector they would have been obliged to abandon their flock and spend months, and sometimes entire years, in defending themselves in various courts from the injustices practiced against them.

Although the temporal part of benefices is not as significant as the spiritual, they still should not be neglected. They are goods offered to God, and the beneficiaries, their stewards and dispensers, are obliged to use them wisely. Nevertheless some productive abbeys were held by powerful persons content to accept the profits, but with little care for the buildings or for making needed repairs.[7] Sometimes buildings and even churches were in

---

6. Devolution is a legal claim made on a benefice on the basis of the alleged incapacity of its holder or on some default in his titles. Because of negligence like this by an inferior collator, the right of conferral of the benefice reverted after a certain amount of time to a superior collator, by "devolution."

7. The award of an ecclesiastical benefice in trust, *in commendam*, to a lay person needed a canonical dispensation from regularity. The French term *commende* (from Latin *commenda*, a protection or safeguard), was synonymous with a trust.

danger of falling into ruin. In seeing this, and wishing to remedy it, Monsieur Vincent had the king send a letter to the officials of the local Parlements, authorizing them to force the abbots, even by seizing their revenues, to make the necessary repairs.

SECTION FIVE

A Remarkable Example

Among many other examples which could be cited to show the concern of Monsieur Vincent that benefices, particularly those relating to episcopacy, be conferred only upon those worthy of the office, and who might be expected to fulfill its duties fittingly, we will speak of only one. This will enable us to see the virtue and mentality of this great servant of God.

At the time, the court was not in Paris. This occasioned Cardinal Mazarin to write the following letter to Monsieur Vincent:

> These few lines are to inform you that Monsieur [Mathieu Mole] hurried here, as soon as the bishopric of [Bayeux] became available, to ask the queen that it should be conferred upon his son. She was happy to comply, for he has the requisite qualities, and Her Majesty was pleased to find such a suitable opportunity to thank the father, through his son, for his past services and his zeal for the welfare of the state. The queen promised me she would write to you, and I thought I should write, to ask you to contact this young man, to give him the instructions and advice you think necessary for properly carrying out this office.[8]

This letter concerned Monsieur Vincent greatly, for though he greatly respected anything coming from Her Majesty or her prime minister, he knew well that this priest nominated for the bishopric did not have the qualities needed for this charge. Besides, the diocese in question, one of the largest of its province, had been neglected by its previous bishops. It now needed a pastor who would live and work for revitalizing it. This could not be hoped for in the one selected. What could the faithful and zealous servant of God do to avert this disaster?

To appeal to the queen and the cardinal was too late, for the appointment

---

8. *CED* II:563-64.

had already been made. Besides, the court was in need of the loyalty of the father. Monsieur Vincent still felt he had to do something to prevent this appointment. It would be so prejudicial to the welfare of the poor diocese and to the salvation of both the father and the son. Since he enjoyed their friendship, he believed his duty demanded that he render a charitable service for them, the more pure and impartial in that he would run the risk of losing their affection.

He went to visit the father at his own home. He showed him that his son lacked all the good qualities needed for governing the diocese, and how important it was for himself and his son not to incur the wrath of God because of the evil results of such an appointment. To convince the father that he should not proceed with this matter, he foresaw the objections likely to be raised. He responded in advance to what fatherly love was apt to suggest. This good gentleman listened attentively to these remarks, saying he agreed with what had been said. He even thanked Monsieur Vincent for his trouble, promising he would give the matter further consideration.

Several days later Monsieur Vincent returned to his home on some other business and met with these words: "Oh, Monsieur, Oh, Monsieur Vincent, what sleepless nights you have caused me." He then spoke in detail of his house and its affairs, his advanced age, the number of his children and the obligation he was under to look to their settlement before he died, not to leave them unprovided for. He pointed out that his son would have virtuous and learned priests working with him, who would enable him to fulfill his duties as bishop. For all these reasons he felt that he had done well to obtain this appointment for him.

Monsieur Vincent had already spoken against all such human considerations, and said nothing more, leaving events in the care of divine Providence. Shortly after, God showed clearly how displeasing this whole episode was to him. He called from this world the new bishop, so recently elevated to this dignity. The father was left with the regret that he had not followed the advice given by Monsieur Vincent.[9]

---

9. Edouard Mole, bishop from June 22, 1647 to April 6, 1652.

SECTION SIX

His Great Affection for the Service of the Prelates of the Church

Monsieur Vincent always displayed a singular respect for the dignity of the bishop, in whose person he recognized and honored the power and majesty of Jesus Christ. He made it a rule to obey and serve the bishops in all situations, as far as it was possible for him. Especially after his appointment to the council of the king, he was eager for opportunities to be of help, not even waiting to be asked. On his own initiative he took their part before the queen and the cardinal or other persons in authority, with greater devotion even than for the interests of his own confreres.

He strove to work out some accommodation between the two bishops, Rieux and Cupif, both of Leon in Brittany.[10] The first had been removed from his see during the reign of Louis XIII, of glorious memory, but now sought to regain his seat by ousting his replacement, Bishop Cupif. He, for his part, had the backing of both the spiritual and temporal powers, and would not budge. This affair was the source of a sad division within the diocese, and of much talk in the entire Church in France. Finally, after many meetings, Bishop Rieux regained his seat and Bishop Cupif was named bishop of Dol, leaving both satisfied, and the difficulty resolved.

He also contributed much to the moving of the episcopal see from the town of Maillezais to La Rochelle. In former days it had been the refuge of heretics, and the sanctuary of enemies of the state. It had served, however, as an unwitting memorial to the piety of the late king by being the subject of his wrath, his courage, and his power, when he reduced this rebel city to his obedience. Since that time some had thought it should be made an episcopal city, to reestablish the Catholic religion with as great a majesty and justice as the seditious heretics had disgraced it in ignominy and irreligion. However, the execution of this praiseworthy design was reserved, by order of divine Providence, for the regency of the queen. By the advice of Monsieur Vincent, she chose Bishop Jacques Raoul, then bishop of Saintes, as the first bishop of La Rochelle. Bishop de Bethune of Maillezais[11]

---

10. Rene de Rieux, the bishop of Saint Pol de Leon, had compromised himself politically and had been forced to flee the country into exile. Since he did so without royal permission, a canonical process was begun to depose him as bishop. The Holy See commissioned four other bishops to decide, and he was formally deposed on May 31, 1635. After a long vacancy, the see was filled by Robert Cupif in 1639. De Rieux contested this in a lengthy suit which was not settled until 1648.

11. The dioceses of Maillezais and Lucon were created by the division of the diocese of Poitiers.

was rewarded by the archbishopric of Bordeaux for his willingness to agree to the change, and Monsieur Bassompierre was appointed to be bishop of Saintes.[12] As part of the settlement, some of the benefices formerly depending on the now suppressed chapter of Maillezais were to be united to those of the canons of La Rochelle.

Monsieur Vincent's zeal for the service of the prelates became evident when there was need of the authority of the king and the protection of the chancellor against heretics. He invoked the help of each of these in enforcing the regulations limiting the places the heretics could meet or preach. He also did what he could to put a stop to this abuse among them: those who wished to marry a Catholic girl would feign conversion, but soon after the ceremony would return to their errors, making evident they had little faith, either divine or human. He encountered others who purchased certain important positions in various cities. They would pay two or three times their worth, and then would try to have themselves accepted at whatever price, despite edicts to the contrary. Monsieur Vincent did not hesitate to complain to the queen and the chancellor to prevent their being accepted. He also wrote, in the king's name, to the legal authorities in the provinces to stop the many activities of the heretics. He recommended to them that they be active in supporting the rights of Catholics in the various lawsuits which arose in disputes with the heretics.

It would be wearying to the reader if we were to report here all the good offices the prelates received in many different situations from Monsieur Vincent. It is enough to say that he willingly accepted any request from the bishops, and did all he could to be of help. This might take the form of sustaining their legitimate interests, or supporting their lawful wishes. It might be the obtaining of protection from the authorities against certain annoyances, or possibly the giving of good advice when asked for, or when he saw it was necessary for the good of their dioceses. In all this he used much circumspection and reserve. His extreme humility and the respect he had for the episcopal dignity often made him keep his counsel or not reveal his own sentiments, of which he was ever distrustful. He was persuaded that bishops had a purer and more comprehensive light than his own, which he considered small and limited. It is true that on certain occasions his devotion for their service would override his humility, as we can see in this example with which we will conclude this section.

The great servant of God was aware of a major abuse introduced into the

---

Henri de Bethune had been its bishop since 1630. In 1646 he was named to be archbishop of Bordeaux. He took possession of this see in 1648, and died in 1680.

12. Louis de Bassompierre became the bishop of Saintes in 1648. He was a great supporter and patron of the Congregation in his diocese. At his death in 1676 he left his estate to the community and was buried at Saint Lazare.

Church in France, by what was called the "Appeal." It had been allowed at first to make sure the canons and ecclesiastical discipline were strictly followed, and to prevent slipshod methods and practices from being followed in the ecclesiastical courts. The practical results were quite the contrary, however, for the appeal was used to render ineffective the legitimate authority of the bishops. Its use allowed those who wished to remain untouched in their vices and defiance of all law. Monsieur Vincent often prayed before the Lord for some remedy for this state of affairs, whose pernicious effects were well known to him. Seeing the evil to be too deeply rooted to be completely corrected, he strove to diminish its bad effects by the helpful advice he gave to several bishops.

He pointed out to them that the first step in preventing this abuse was to establish good order in the ecclesiastical courts. They should have virtuous and capable priests in charge, well versed in the civil and canon law, well experienced in the procedures of the courts, irreproachable in their personal lives, inflexible in their judgments, and exact in observing all the formalities in use in the kingdom.

He wrote once to one of the bishops who had sought his advice, to make him understand how important it was to have the proper person in this office. He said in his letter:

> One day I carried to the late Monsieur Mole, procurator general and first president, the complaint of several bishops. The Parlement had treated them badly for seeking to remedy the disorderly conduct of several priests. The bishops were so annoyed by the opposition that they had tearfully resolved to do nothing more, and to let things go on just as badly as ever. This wise magistrate told me that when the bishops or other officials are faulty in observing the formalities prescribed for ecclesiastical justice, the court is lenient in allowing appeals.
>
> When the bishops or other authorities are careful to follow all the procedures, they are never opposed. He gave me this example: We are well aware that the official of Paris is capable and most careful in his judgments. When we get an appeal from his judgments, we never accept it. This is what we will do to all others also, if they are as carefully handled as his.[13]

---

13. *CED* VIII:170.

SECTION SEVEN

Some Important Services Given by Monsieur Vincent to Several Religious Orders

Monsieur Vincent's esteem and appreciation for the religious state disposed him to render to its members whatever services he could, particularly when it was a question of reestablishing or maintaining good order in their houses. He was zealous for this, and seized every occasion he could in the king's council, or elsewhere, to be of help. We can say without exaggeration that even with all the orders there are in France, not one failed to experience the effects of his charity. This might be felt by the order as a whole, by some of its members, by the protection or good opinion of the king which he strove to promote, or by other services he was able to render. He was particularly anxious to support the efforts of reformers, such as those of the communities of Saint Maur, Saint Bernard, Saint Anthony, the Canons Regular of Saint Augustine, the Premonstratensians, and others. We will recall here only several examples of this, passing over many others in silence. We think it best to allow certain disorders to be buried in the tomb of silence.[14]

An abbot, a religious of great virtue, attempted to reform his order in the face of obstacles raised by some persons in authority, and even against a prince enlisted in the struggle against him. He received much help and encouragement from Monsieur Vincent, and wrote a letter of appreciation to him, in 1644, in which he said:

> It is surely necessary to look to God for the strength you show in defending the cause of God against the powers of the world. We rely solely on God and his Providence, and on your zeal, Monsieur. You are our only recourse on earth, and the sole support of our desolate order.

A non-reformed religious was elected abbot of an important foundation,

---

14. Francois de Maida, the superior general of the Minims, accorded Vincent de Paul an affiliation with his order in 1621 in honor of his services to the order. In Book One, ch. 32, there is an account of how he aided the Commander de Sillery in the reform of the houses and territories of the Order of Malta. During the canonization process, various abbots of the Premonstratensians testified to Vincent's help in the reform of their order. In the reform of the order of the Canons Regular at Chancelade, Saint Vincent provided support to Alain de Solminihac, its abbot and superior. (*CED* III:223-24.) Vincent helped Dom Gregoire Tarrisse in his reform at the Benedictine Congregation of Saint Maur. He advised Charles Fremont, the reformer of the order of Grandmont. Cardinal de la Rochefoucauld, delegated by the Holy See to reform the French religious orders, called Vincent his "right arm" in this work. In speaking of Vincent and Dom Gregoire Tarrisse, he called them "my two saints."

the motherhouse of the order, and important for the progress of the reform. He applied to the king for a confirmation of his election. Since Monsieur Vincent was well informed of the invalidity of this election, however, he did all he could to have it annulled, and to have a reformed abbot elected in his place. He wrote to a bishop friend as follows:

> About a year ago I had the honor of writing about the election of N. as abbot of the abbey of N. I asked you to come to Paris to speak to the queen of the kind of person needed for this abbey. Because you were not able to come, you were good enough to tell me of some of the reasons that this election should not be accepted. Things have dragged out, especially on the complaints of two of the electors who were informed only after it was too late to attend. This caused the Parlement to nullify the election, much against the wishes of the one chosen, who had pressed so hard to have his election confirmed. Since he has the support of some powerful persons, there is reason to fear he may be reelected. This makes it so desirable for you to be here, to say a word to the queen, and to give weight to the reasons there are to prevent this evil. I know that Her Majesty, who esteems you highly, would be happy to have you come, and the Keeper of the Seals has approved my writing to you. I do so humbly, begging you to come as soon as you can, for the love of God. I do so, knowing how close the interests of God are to your heart. Perhaps, as you said in your letter to me, the whole reform of this house depends on this, as well as the reform of the daughter houses. Perhaps the Lord will attribute to you the merit of such a happy outcome, as one of the prelates of the kingdom with such zeal for the glory of his Church.[15]

Monsieur Vincent also did what he could to initiate the reform in orders, as here, when he wrote to the general of the order,[16] enclosing a letter from the king:

> Most Reverend Father,
>
> His Majesty has written to Your Reverence because it was decided in the Council for Ecclesiastical Affairs, when one of the priories of your order in the diocese of [Lodeve] was vacant, that we consider one of your good religious by the name of Father [Fremont] for a pension. This would be on condition that the former rule be observed, as is done in some other of your houses, so that the pension should pass to his successors, according to this usage. When this was reported to Her Majesty she was pleased, and urged us to see it through.

---

15. *CED* III:631-32.
16. Georges de Barny.

It is to be hoped, Father, that the good Lord would use you to rebuild such a holy order as yours, which has been so famous in the Church and such a blessing for this kingdom. This reform has begun under your rule, regaining for your order the same reputation it enjoyed in other times, now so much desired by men of good will.

The king wants to help. It likewise seems to be the will of God, seeing he has given you this good religious, as an appropriate instrument which Your Reverence could well employ. This would be especially true if you would appoint him to look after the houses of [Epoisses], [Thiers], and [Lodeve], with power to receive novices and professed members according to the traditional observance, all under your authority and direction.[17]

I have no doubt that Your Reverence will carry out the wishes of His Majesty in something so reasonable. It tends to the glory of God and the control of an organization of which you are the leader. The Lord shall pour his own religious spirit upon you and your assistants also, so he may reign there for centuries to come. By this means your person and your zeal will be remembered to posterity, not to mention the merits Your Reverence shall have in the sight of God.[18]

When an important abbey had been conferred on a young prince, still under the tutelage of his mother, Monsieur Vincent wrote to her to persuade her to allow the reform to be introduced into the abbey, which needed it badly. He wrote as follows:

Madame,

I take the liberty of writing to Your Highness, to renew my promise of obedience, with all possible humility and submission. I accompany in spirit the good religious who seeks the honor of doing you reverence. He will tell you of the disposition of the abbey of N., for receiving the reform, and together with the appropriate means of achieving it. He is of good reputation and is of a most respectable family. I trust, Madame, that Your Highness will have the goodness to hear him, first because I know of your great zeal for the glory of God to which you are so committed that you involve even those persons who have the honor of belonging to you. Second, if you do so, Your Highness will cause Jesus Christ to be better honored and served in that monastery which should not be in the state it is now, as will be explained by the courier with this letter.

---

17. This letter had its intended effect. The reform that Fremont introduced was not limited to those three priories, but was extended to many others.
18. *CED* IV:309-11.

Third, the late bishop of N. had so much at heart the introduction of the reform into this abbey that he wrote me several times about it. I am sure he would have carried this out but for the opposition of one of the leading religious of the abbey, with much influence over the others. Unfortunately, he died before he could carry out his plans. Perhaps, Madame, God has allowed this delay, to reserve to the abbot, your son, and to Your Highness, the merit of this great accomplishment.[19]

Monsieur Vincent worked actively not only in introducing the reform, but also in restoring peace and union in those religious houses where he saw differences and divisions. He did all in his power to remedy those situations. Since he always acted with great prudence and circumspection in those cases in which he strove to unite divided parties, he arranged to have some virtuous persons, armed with the authority of the king, visit the houses to learn the truth. He would listen to both sides in disputes so as to be able to take the best means for restoring harmony, as he did on several occasions.

He arranged for some prelates to attend the general chapters of orders, when he saw this to be necessary, to hinder by their presence and authority certain religious who seemed to stir up trouble. He also wanted to make sure that each religious had perfect liberty in the voting, and that the order as a whole would take the necessary steps for the welfare of the entire group. Afterward, the prelates would report to the king that the elections and discussions were canonical in every detail. The king would then approve the elections and pay no more attention to any complaints raised against those elected.

Several times he was requested to mediate disputes between religious houses. He received letters from superiors general of different orders from Rome on three or four occasions. They thanked him for the help he had given to their communities, and for his intercession with Her Majesty in obtaining her protection. They looked on him as their guardian angel.

He was much afflicted to notice the decline of a certain order to such a deplorable state that he saw no way it could be redeemed. At this same time, a religious of another order, unhappy with his own community, wrote to ask his advice about transferring to the first one mentioned above. This is the reply he received from Monsieur Vincent:

I would never advise anyone to join the so-called religious order of N., much less a doctor, professor of theology, and a great preacher like yourself. It is in disarray, not an order, a body with no sense of direction and no head. Its members live entirely independently of one another. I once met the Keeper of the Seals in his

---

19. *CED* V:381.

library. He told me he was looking up the origin and development of this group in France, but he had been unable to find anything about them. In a word, it is a ghost of an order. It serves only as a refuge for libertines and rogues who, to escape the yoke of obedience, join this imaginary order to live under no restraints. This is why I judge these persons to be in bad conscience, and I pray our Lord would preserve you from such frivolity.[20]

This letter disabused this poor tempted religious, and opened his eyes to the precipice he was facing. He came to his senses, and resolved to persevere in his own congregation.

Another religious, noted both within and outside his order for his virtue and for his having preached in the most celebrated pulpits of the kingdom, once spoke to Monsieur Vincent of the extent of his work, the austerity of his rule, and the lessening of his strength. All this caused him to fear that he could not expect to continue long in his service to the Church. He had thought of a remedy to prolong his service. He was to be made a suffragan to the archbishop of Reims, because the dignity of bishop would dispense him from the obligation of fasting and other austerities of his order. This in turn would preserve his strength for preaching, and allow him to continue with more vigor and effect. He asked Monsieur Vincent for his advice, and if he thought well of it, to approach the king for his appointment to this position. He promised he would supply several recommendations from noteworthy friends to support his candidacy.

At once, Monsieur Vincent realized that this was a temptation for the good religious. He made this clear in the response he gave to this letter. In it he first showed the regard he had for him personally, and the esteem he had for his order. Then he congratulated him on the many talents given him by God for preaching, and the edification he had given up to this point to the entire order. He added this:

> I have no doubt that you would do marvelously well in the episcopal office if God called you to it. He has made it evident, however, that he wants you in your present position by the success he has given to your efforts, and he not suggested that you should change. If Providence would wish you to be a bishop, it would not speak to you to bring it about. It would inspire those whose responsibility it is to name people to charges and ecclesiastical dignities to choose you, although you would have made no overtures yourself. Your calling, then, would be pure and assured, whereas if you propose yourself you could not hope to have the blessing of God in such a charge. This should hardly be desired or

---

20. *CED* V:314-15.

pursued by a soul as humble as yours. Besides, reverend father, what harm you would do to your order, to deprive it of one of its chief supports, who sustains it by his teaching and example. If you open this door you will lead others to follow or at least to lose their taste for the practice of penance. They will not lack pretexts to soften and lessen it to the prejudice of the rule. Nature does not like austerities. If you ask it, it will reply they are too much, and that they must be avoided if one wants to live a long life to serve God more. Our Lord said of all this: He who loves his life shall lose it, but he who hates it shall save it.[21] You know better than I what this means, and I would not have dared write my opinions on this if you had not asked me.

Perhaps you have not thought of the crown that awaits you. O God, how beautiful it shall be! You have already done so much, reverend Father, to gain this crown, and perhaps there remains but little more to do. You must persevere in the path you have entered, for it leads to life. You have already surmounted great difficulties. You should take courage, and trust that God will give you the grace to overcome those which remain. My suggestion would be to forego preaching for a while to regain your health. You are still able to do much good for the service of God and for your congregation. It is one of the holiest and most edifying of all in the Church of Jesus Christ.[22]

Lastly, Monsieur Vincent extended his concern to the temporal affairs of religious communities as well as to the spiritual. Several times he helped in obtaining for various religious houses and hospitals the rents due them from the royal lands, which were in arrears because of the expenses of the wars. He became their advocate before the queen and the cardinal to obtain satisfactory payments for them. He took special pains to protect the hospitals on the frontiers of the kingdom, which were threatened by the soldiers, and saw to the support of several others through the gifts and privileges accorded them.

---

21. Based on Matt 16:25.
22. *CED* IV:18-19.

SECTION EIGHT

Other Help Given by Monsieur Vincent to Various Abbeys and Convents of Women

Saint Cyprian rightly remarked that the more sublime the glory of religious virgins consecrated to God, the more care should be taken of them.[23] Their loss is frequent and easy, as their sex is weak, and their constancy in good is more difficult and rarer than among men. This caused Monsieur Vincent to extend his regard for the religious life especially to the abbeys and convents of women. He sought to preserve them in their discipline if it already was in vigor, or to restore it if it had been lost.

He was particularly careful, as much as he could, to preserve the right of election in the abbeys where it was traditional, and he strongly opposed the pretensions of some religious. With no hope of being named abbess by election because of their lack of ability or merit, they hoped to attain the office through the authority of the king or the influence of their relatives. He took a position in favor of those elected for a three-year term, if this was the custom in their convent, opposing those who sought a mandate from the king for a lifetime appointment.

One day a virtuous bishop had overseen the election of a fine religious as the abbess of a convent in his diocese. In seeking the confirmation of the election by the king, he tried to persuade Monsieur Vincent of the superiority of a perpetual appointment over the three-year term. In contrast to his usual dislike for innovations going against the canonically established practices in religious communities, he argued with humility and respect that the triennial elections were much to be preferred. This was especially so for women, since they are more inclined to change and more likely to fail in major responsibilities once they saw themselves in office for life.

When an abbey of women depending on the king's nomination became vacant, schemes and intrigues ordinarily began for the choosing of women of birth or position for abbess. Not satisfied with their worldly success, but carrying their family ambition even to the holiest places, they bent all their efforts to have their daughters, sisters, or nieces placed in charge within the cloister. We read often of the strange requests made to Monsieur Vincent. He knew only too well that the good or bad discipline of religious houses usually reflects the attitudes of the superior, and he totally disregarded these pressures built on human

---

23. PL 4:443.

respect. He remained firm in insisting that only the most capable, most experienced, and most exact in regular observance be chosen abbess.

A gentleman had a daughter in an abbey where the previous abbess, her aunt, had just died. He came to Saint Lazare to complain that Monsieur Vincent was preventing his daughter from succeeding to the office, just as the aunt had succeeded another aunt before her. The patience of Monsieur Vincent served only to provoke his anger and resentment. The gentleman blamed him and scolded him, and even threatened, yelling and shouting like a man out of his head. This lasted an hour or more.

Monsieur Vincent had been told that this abbey was a sort of hereditary benefice of his house. To deny it to his daughter was, in the eyes of this gentleman, a great wrong. The husband, wife, and the entire family were accustomed to spend several periods each year in the abbey as a sort of vacation home. They lived there at the expense of the community, greatly disturbing the functioning of the abbey. All the religious murmured and complained about this, and once the abbey became vacant they insisted on having another superior, someone other than this niece. Monsieur Vincent was well informed of the qualities of the pretender to the chair. He answered the father mildly and respectfully, saying the daughter was too young. He added that he was obliged in conscience to advise the queen to choose the one most capable and most suitable for the office. After this, he listened to all the invectives of the father, letting him pour out all his pent-up anger upon him with unbelievable patience. He then accompanied him to the door, happy to have been abused and covered with opprobrium for upholding the interests of the Lord.

Often enough some abbesses with ties to their families, and who had a sister, niece, or cousin as a religious, would ask to have them appointed as assistant, under pretext of age or infirmity. Monsieur Vincent, ever on his guard against flesh and blood, was never quick to agree to this request, unless it were truly necessary. He was adamant on this, since when a vacancy developed through death the sisters were to have full liberty to choose the most virtuous and capable one to maintain good order if it existed, or to restore it if it did not.

If an abbess resigned her charge, and provided testimonial letters for the ability and good morals of the one in whose favor the resignation had been made, he would be slow to accept all that had been said. To his way of thinking, the testimonial letters could not always be relied on here. He would take steps to learn the qualities of the person being recommended. If he found the choice well made and likely to be advantageous to the abbey, he would accept the resignation, otherwise not.

At times some trouble would slip into convents of women, either division among themselves or some other trouble. He would try his best to correct the difficulty. He would often send some virtuous and experienced visitors, under royal authority, to examine the difficulty, or reestablish the cloister if it had been neglected, or take care of some other needs. He would have Their Majesties write to the superior of these convents, and to the bishop of the locality, to look into the matter.

A certain abbey was in turmoil, and the superior was not able to resolve it despite all her best efforts. When Monsieur Vincent was called upon to help, he sent as visitor an abbot of the same order, a wise and zealous man. He wrote to Monsieur Vincent that the case could not be rectified unless the women were given a different confessor, one with the gift of calming spirits and maintaining peace. Monsieur Vincent requested a highly respected and virtuous priest, gifted in the direction of religious women, to serve God as a confessor in this abbey. He did so with much blessing, little by little restoring peace, and uniting all elements of the community.

In some convents of women the evil spirit had gained a foothold under the pretext of some revelations supposedly made to the superior. The imaginations of these superiors were inflamed by the angel of darkness. They claimed that God had revealed to them extraordinary ways of leading souls to perfection, and even for reforming the Church. They proposed many other curious doctrines, many reminiscent of those of the Illuminati.[24]

When Monsieur Vincent was alerted to this, he had some meek and virtuous persons selected to visit these houses. They were to become aware of the abuses and diabolic illusions which sometimes had deceived many persons of all conditions and of both sexes. By this means the evil was brought to light, and it pleased God to stop its spread.

SECTION NINE

Various Other Activities of Monsieur Vincent While on the Council of the King

The zeal of Monsieur Vincent for everything concerning the service and honor of God made him attentive to those occasions when he might further this service or prevent anything that might oppose it. He used his good

---

24. The "Enlightened," a group of spiritual persons in Spain in the sixteenth century, characterized by a retired life of contemplation, prayer, and mystical visions. Some in the movement were doctrinally and spiritually unbalanced.

reputation in this way on the king's council, judging that day a happy one in which he could prevent some ill or promote some good.

During the war years he tried to prevent the disorders committed by the soldiers on all sides, particularly the profanations of churches and disrespect for persons consecrated to God. Seeing it was impossible to prevent this evil entirely, he tried to lessen it. When all else failed he had recourse to God in prayer and penance, invoking the help of his grace and mercy both for those who suffered these ills and for those who committed them.

Another disorder offensive to good morals was that of certain actors in the theaters who presented not only indecent, but scandalous topics. These could not be spoken, heard, or seen without offending God. When Monsieur Vincent was informed of this, he recognized the pernicious effects this license was apt to produce. His remonstrances led to their being completely suppressed.

The troubles of the times and various activities against the welfare of the state obliged the king to confine those guilty or even suspect to the Bastille. They received there everything they needed, but no provision existed there for their spiritual welfare. Monsieur Vincent persuaded a priest of the Conference of Ecclesiastics held at Saint Lazare to take it upon himself to visit these prisoners and to speak to them. Morning and evening prayers were arranged, as well as some other religious practices, to the great spiritual benefit of their souls.

The demon, the enemy of peace, spread discord and provoked war in the kingdom, and sowed the seeds of disobedience and rebellion against the service of the king. He also incited some to rebel against God himself, and to attack religion in various ways. Among other things, there were those who sought to spread the maxims and damnable errors of the Illuminati. When Monsieur Vincent saw this, which had begun to spread in many places in France, especially in Paris and the diocese of Bazas, he applied such a prompt and effective remedy that this heresy was stifled in the cradle before it could do much harm to the Church.

Many seized upon the sense of freedom during the troubled times of the Fronde to permit anyone to say what he liked about religion or the state. This opened the door to another pernicious evil. This was the writing and publishing of all sorts of libels, even against faith and good morals. Monsieur Vincent spoke against this in the council and had this abuse reproved. The order was given to search out and seize such evil books, and the printers and bookstores were forbidden to publish or sell them.

This saintly man used all his energy in speaking and advising, entreating and remonstrating, against the damnable practice of dueling. This was finally happily eradicated through the piety of the queen and by the zeal and authority of the king. He from his earliest years, like a Christian Hercules, had the strength and happiness to slay this dragon. His predecessor on the throne, Saint Louis, despite his laws and ordinances against this monster, was never able to achieve this. God reserved the glory of this victory to our great monarch, and marked the first years of his reign by this heroic triumph. It has saved the bodies and souls of thousands of French gentlemen and spared an infinity of noble families from ruin and utter unhappiness. For this they are eternally grateful to him who brought about their happiness and salvation.

Monsieur Vincent did what he could to root out blasphemy, causing the ordinances to be renewed against this detestable crime. He proposed other measures which might have stopped it entirely. Although he did not live to see the effects of these measures, he must surely have gained the merit of having attempted to prevent this evil. It is to be hoped that God will someday hear the ardent prayers he offered for this, and that he will inspire our incomparable monarch [Louis XIV] to take more effective means, even fire and the sword if he judges well of it, in imitation of Saint Louis, his predecessor, to purify the state from this infernal gangrene, which infects and corrupts it in many places, including those most important and most noble.

SECTION TEN

Monsieur Vincent Preserved Always an Inviolable Fidelity to the King and a Constant Devotion to His Service, Even During Most Perilous and Difficult Times

It does not suffice to give to God the things which pertain to God, for in keeping with the maxim of the Gospel we must also give to Caesar the things which pertain to Caesar. The same law which binds us to adore God, to obey him, and to love him above all else, also requires that we honor and respect kings. They are images of his sovereign majesty upon earth, and we are to give them the affection and service due them, and keep an inviolable fidelity to them. Christian princes have an advantage over all other monarchs who do not believe in Jesus Christ. Their subjects are attached to them, not only by the bonds of the laws, or by the fear of their sovereign power, or by the favors they might expect from their liberality, but by stronger and nobler bonds. These come from divine law, and from the tenets of their religion.

They cannot fail in their duty to the king without contravening God's will. The obedience, respect, and fidelity they give to him are not founded on him alone, but on God. He regards as being done for himself what is done for those he has established upon earth as his visible representatives in the governing of peoples. It follows that among the subjects of a Christian prince those who are the most faithful, obedient, and attached to his service are those who are the most virtuous, those most united to God by grace and charity. On the other hand, from those who are lacking in what they owe to God, we should not expect a consistent fidelity, nor a sincere attachment to the service of their prince.

With this understanding, it should not be difficult to infer from what has been said here in Book Two and even in Book One, that with Monsieur Vincent's fidelity in carrying out the will of God, and his zeal for God's honor and glory, he should have shown such fidelity to the king and such singular attachment to his service. These qualities depend upon his relationship with God. The measure of the affection and fidelity to one's prince is found in one's attachment to God.

Besides this very strong general consideration, we can produce other proofs, more particular and no less convincing if we recount how this saintly man proved himself a servant of the king during the most difficult and perilous times. He risked his material welfare, his life, and his entire Congregation, in showing himself faithful to the service of His Majesty.

The deplorable state of affairs in France during 1649, 1652, etc., are still fresh in memory. We could say of those times that by a secret judgment of Providence, God had permitted the depths of the abyss, spoken of in the holy Scriptures, to be opened and its noxious vapors spread over the entire kingdom.

It filled the minds of the French with a darkness so obscure that some among them lost all sense of the duty they owed their sovereign. Even though they may have retained an affection for him personally, their actions betrayed this sentiment. While thinking they were working and fighting for his service, their armies were disputing his authority by killing some of his most faithful servants, and despoiling and ruining all parts of his kingdom.

Just as a bright star shines the more brilliantly when surrounded by clouds which serve only to emphasize its light, we could say these troubles of the nation served to allow the perfection of his fidelity to the king and his zeal in his service to appear. During those deplorable times, confusion was so great in many places that most loyal Frenchmen and those most attached to the interests of their prince, felt they could only keep quiet and groan in silence. They knew well anything they may have said would have served only to make things worse. Prudence suggested quiet, to avoid worse troubles. Monsieur Vincent, on the contrary, always so prudent and circumspect, acted differently. He openly declared himself a servant of the king, and promised obedience to his directives. Not content with assuming this posture for himself, he strove to have others share his attitude. His voice could be heard only where he was, but his letters to various people carried his message, especially those to bishops, as was reported in Book One. In them he persuaded the bishops to remain in their dioceses and to use their influence to confirm their people in obedience to the king.

He showed his fidelity to the king and his zeal for his service when, at the risk of his own welfare and that of his Company, he went to find Their Majesties at Saint Germain en Laye after they left Paris, to offer them his services. He left his house of Saint Lazare and all his dear confreres as a prey to their enemies. After the example of their father, they, too, suffered with patience and even with joy, seeing themselves despoiled of their goods and maltreated on this occasion.

What makes his commitment to the service of Their Majesties shine forth still more clearly is his thought of giving some advice that he felt was helpful and even necessary in the affairs of state. He did so despite his fear that he would not be favorably received by those holding the reins of government. He ran the risk of losing favor at court, but he preferred this, and even disgrace in the eyes of Their Majesties, than to fail in what he saw as an opportunity to be of service. Her Majesty the queen appreciated his sincere heart and received his suggestions well. Cardinal Mazarin gave him a favorable audience, well aware that he had no other goal than to be of help. Even though they did not follow his advice, this in no way diminished the appreciation his fidelity and affection merited. It was recognized that he had the courage to risk his standing in court, rather than fail in giving a suggestion he felt was helpful for the good of the kingdom.

SECTION ELEVEN

Monsieur Vincent Served the King With an Entire Disregard for All Personal Self-interest

We in no way wish to blame those who serve the king in the hope that His Majesty would reward them for their faithful service. On the contrary, we would say it is neither just nor reasonable to blame such a person. This would benefit the state. Just as the law sets out punishments for those who rebel against the will of the sovereign, it should also sanction his favors being given to those who serve him faithfully. Just as the fear of punishment holds the dissolute to their duty, so the hope of reward is a still greater spur for the good to act in such a way as to win favors from the prince.

Although it is permitted and even praiseworthy to serve the prince faithfully in the hope of recompense from his generosity, we must admit there is an even more excellent disposition, one nobler and more perfect, that is, to have in view in serving the king only the good of his service. Even more excellent would be the attitude, in fulfilling one's duties, of seeing in the king God himself, and therefore serving him with the sole view that this service is pleasing to God. This would lead one to have as the sole motive in serving the king that this is pleasing to God and is accomplishing what one knows to be his holy will.

Would we not have reason to say with the wise man of Scripture, speaking of him who did not seek after gold, nor put his trust in riches: *Quis est hic, et laudabimus eum?* ["Who is he that we may praise him?"][25] Who is this admirable person who has mastered this most uncontrollable of all the passions? Where can we meet him, so we can praise him as he deserves? Happily, he has been found. Despite the corruption of the age, France has had the glory of producing in our day a masterpiece of virtue in the person of Vincent de Paul. It can truly be said that his heart never sought after gold, nor did he put his trust and his affections in riches. Although his duties brought him in close contact with the source of rich treasures and magnificent rewards, he paid no attention to these possibilities. He had in view only the faithful service of his king, which would in turn redound to the glory of God. This was the sole motive which led him to accept the appointment and duties assigned to him. This was the bond that held him attached to the service of Their Majesties, even in most difficult times. This motive of giving glory to God in faithfully serving his prince gave him the strength, constancy, and perseverance in his service, amid all the contradictions, calumnies, and persecutions he had to undergo, and amid the dangers his position entailed.

First, when the queen mother at the beginning of the regency did him the honor of calling him to the Council for Ecclesiastical Affairs, he accepted solely out of the obedience he felt God willed that he should give to the wishes of Her Majesty. His zeal to promote the interests of religion and to procure greater glory for God made him accept this call, despite the extreme reluctance suggested by his humility, and by all that he foresaw would disturb his peace of mind and the desire he had, at his age, to live out his days in peace.

---

25. Sir 31:9.

In his position he had favorable opportunities to advance the temporal interests of his Congregation, if he wished to do so, and as he could have done most legally. It might have seemed, even, that the charity he owed his own confreres may have suggested this. Since many benefices passed through his hands, it would not have been difficult to direct some to the houses of his own Congregation, many of which were just in initial stages of establishment, and badly in need of help. Many of them could hardly support their service to God and to the Church without help, especially since their efforts in favor of the poor were always given without charge.

Despite this need, he never accepted benefices for his own houses. He never sought, directly or indirectly, any such help for them.[26] If he did allow some benefices to be conferred on the seminaries, this was done at the insistence of the benefactors, who had the right to designate the recipients of their favors. Sometimes these charitable persons had to use as much persuasion to have him accept these gifts as some others used in attempts to obtain them. His purpose in accepting these benefices was not to enrich his houses, nor to put them at their ease, but to use the revenues faithfully for teaching and forming those called to ministries in the Church.

One of his closest friends came to him one day and offered a large sum (we know it was close to one hundred thousand *livres*) given by others, but on the condition that he would support their position in some advice that they had given to the council. This request seemed reasonable enough to them since it would not cost the people anything even if it was in some way prejudicial to the interests of the clergy. This holy man made no other reply but to raise his eyes to heaven, and sigh: "God save us. I would rather die than to say a single word on this matter."

Second, just as he never took any temporal profit from the service he gave Their Majesties, he never sought the help of powerful people who might have been able to help him. This was not because he thought it was a virtue to be rude and cruel like those who enjoy offending those in high places. On the contrary, he always treated these persons with much respect, and sought to please them even in trivial matters, but with this reservation, that God must first be pleased. If he saw that what was asked of him was in keeping with the orders and the will of God, he would agree easily and with good grace. If he saw what was asked was not agreeable to God's law, no human respect nor fear of any disgrace or evil whatever would move him. He had no regard to the position of those he refused, nor did their threats sway him.

---

26. According to the testimony of Claude Le Pelletier, Michel Le Tellier, a minister of state, said: "I have had many dealings with Monsieur Vincent. He has done more good works in France on behalf of religion that anyone I know, but I particularly remember that while he was a member of the Council of Conscience he never sought any advantage for his own personal interests, those of his Congregation, or those of the ecclesiastical houses he had established."

He thought nothing of the ills or persecution that might come, but looked solely to God whom he sought to please, and whose displeasure alone he feared.

Third, his disinterest was seen not only in never seeking advantages but still more in suffering willingly the losses which came about, as we have seen, because of his service to Their Majesties. Remarkably, for all the losses he suffered during the wars, and for the poor treatment he had received from the bad will of some who resented his devotion to the service of the king, he was never heard to utter the least complaint, nor did he ever seek the least reimbursement for his losses. What is even more remarkable is that by his unselfish charity he turned aside the gifts which the queen, in her goodness, wished to give him, in favor of others, when he could do so without violating justice and charity.

We must surely say he served his king with complete disregard for self-interest. Monsieur Vincent practiced this virtue to an heroic degree, the more admirable in that it is so rarely seen today in the courts of princes.

SECTION TWELVE

Monsieur Vincent's Prudence and Circumspection In His Service of the King

The government of the state and the service of a sovereign are of such importance that they should be confided not only to well qualified and faithful persons, but also to those alone who are prudent and discreet, of sound mind and solid judgment. They should have a background of experience equal to the importance of the things committed to their care. Also, not all those with reputations of piety have these natural qualities, but among virtuous people some have received these qualities from God. They are able to put them to good use in the service of their prince and for the good of the state. Just as it would be imprudent to think the advice of the pious man should be followed in whatever situation just because we imagine that all he suggests must be good and useful, so too it would be equally foolish, and possibly unjust, to reject or suspect the advice of a good man because of his reputation for piety, as though piety could not be found with prudence, and as though piety was somehow incompatible with serving God and one's king.

Some believe and try to persuade others that whoever performs exercises of piety and is devoted to the service of God (the so-called "devout," whom they decry so vehemently) is unfit for service of the king, or for the conduct of state affairs. Their concern for heavenly things would make them unsuitable for being in charge of mundane matters. The "devout" often are moved by a zeal, if not indiscreet at least too impetuous, and give advice based not on whether it is useful but whether it seems to them to be good. This would eventually be most prejudicial to the service of the prince and the good of the state. To their mind the man of virtue is so suspect that he ought to be looked upon as a disguised spy, or as someone in the pay of a foreign prince or an enemy of the state.

Those who wish to appear less doctrinaire might admit that a virtuous man might have a true and sincere dedication to the service of his prince, and show steadfast fidelity, and even serve him with complete lack of self-interest. Even then he would not be acknowledged as having the discretion and prudence required for important affairs, since his rules of piety might not accord with the maxims of politics.

If things are like this, as those who think this way say they are, advising a king or prince is most unfortunate. Royalty would then be reduced to excluding from their court the most virtuous of their subjects, or to be constantly on their guard against them as persons suspect, whose advice may harm the good of the state. If it be true, as we said before, that those most united to God by virtue and especially charity, have a more sincere appreciation and a more constant fidelity for the service of their prince, they would be the very ones he must exclude from his service. Instead he should commit the care of most important affairs of his realm and take the advice of those whom he trusts less.

It is not difficult to see the falsity of such a position by the example of several great princes. They have trusted in their councils and confided the direction of their realms to various persons renowned for their virtue and piety. By their experience and wisdom they have been most successful. By their advice and faithful service they have contributed greatly to the good of the state.

Not to wander too far from our subject, we have only to recall him whose memory is still fresh, the great servant of God, Vincent de Paul. He joined piety to wisdom, zeal to discretion, the science of the saints to the knowledge necessary to serve his prince. We will relate here only some scattered events which will show clearly that he had in a high degree those excellent qualities needed as counselor to the king.

Evidently, one of the most necessary dispositions to have in handling important affairs of state is a free spirit, unencumbered with uncontrolled affections and passions. These secure the understanding and prevent one from seeing the true state of affairs and likely consequences of actions. All those who knew Monsieur Vincent agree that whether by grace or by a natural disposition he seemed entirely free from uncontrolled emotion or erratic behavior, something found in few other men. If these impressions were felt by him, he had acquired such mastery over himself and all the movements of his soul that nothing appeared externally, either in his gestures, his words, or even his features. They remained calm and serene, even in the face of affronts and most trying insults. What ordinarily would cause strong reaction in others were the very occasions when he seemed most calm and most self-possessed, speaking and acting with great circumspection.

Another feature of his behavior which added to his wise and prudent manner was slowness in giving an opinion. He decided slowly, especially in matters of moment, but gave himself time and leisure to consider all the circumstances, to weigh the reasons for and against, and to foresee the consequences of decisions. This resulted in his advice being solid and assured, which could be followed with no fear of being deceived. He held to this saying from an ancient writer: "Nothing is so injurious in the consideration of great events as to proceed with too great haste. This haste prevents our seeing, and even more so, foreseeing, all that must be considered before giving good advice. We must deliberate and take resolutions with leisure, but once decided, we must act on what has been determined."[27]

After he had maturely considered something, taking into account all the reasons suggested by others and those which came to his own mind, he came to a conclusion and gave his advice accordingly. Later, if it did not turn out the way he thought it would, he did not worry, but remained at peace. He held to the principle of an ancient father, "It is proper for the wise to judge things, not by how they turn out, but by the intention and design with which they were begun. It is a common error to think that only those things that have succeeded have been well begun."[28]

Another disposition of Monsieur Vincent was noted as a sign of his prudence and something that helped perfect that virtue. This was his silence, an important trait in those who manage important affairs. He was never heard to speak of what had occurred in the council, except when absolutely necessary to divulge it. He kept under the seal of silence not only the secrets he had been entrusted with, but everything else he saw no necessity to reveal. In his familiar conversations with others when he came back from court, he spoke no more of the things that had been discussed than if he were returning from the cell of a Carthusian.

---

27. Abelly has joined two sources: Livy, Histories, 31.32.2 and 22.39.22, with Aristotle, Ethics.
28. Abelly has joined two sources: Isidore of Seville, Epistle 205, Book 3; and Boethius, *De consolatione philosophiae,* Book 1, prosa 4.

Even though he exercised this circumspection and prudence and remained firm in his advice, he was so moderate in his views that he never pushed them heatedly. He was not of the type which always finds a way to contradict the opinions of others because the idea did not originate with himself. He not only was outwardly deferential to those over him in rank, but submitted his judgment as well when he could do so with no reproach of his own conscience. He never criticized others for their way of looking at things, and never complained. After saying what he felt he had to say, he remained respectful and silent, leaving the outcome of events in the hands of Providence.

The chief foundation of his prudence was God's will, manifested by his law and in the Gospel. He held it as an inviolable principle never to take any position contrary to the divine will. As a father of the Church commented, he considered God's will as the sure guide for any advice he was to give or decision he had to make. He followed, to the best of his ability and as the nature of the business to be decided would allow, the maxims of the Gospel of Jesus Christ, which he accepted as the fountain of all true wisdom. He found in this source the light for his mind and the basis for the advice he gave to others with such notable benediction.

We could add to these various reflections many different examples of this rare and distinctive prudence that he displayed in the most trying and difficult circumstances. We could also illustrate the marvelous circumspection and moderation with which he acted while in the king's council, never failing to say what he felt was needed, yet with all the respect and submission he felt he owed to Their Majesties. We shall not do so, however, to avoid an annoying repetition. Undoubtedly each reader can supply on this subject for himself from what has been said in this last chapter and all through the two preceding books.

Monsieur Vincent was gifted by both nature and grace with a great prudence. This was a torch leading others by right and safe paths among a multitude of occupations and circumstances in which Providence had placed him. He acted with such integrity, moderation, and wisdom that during life he happily succeeded in all he undertook for the glory of God and in the service of those who represented God upon earth. After his death, his memory remains in benediction among them.

End of Book Two.

The Life of the Venerable
Servant of God
Vincent de Paul

Si tu veux dans vn seul visage
Voir le Portrait de deux grands Saints:
Icy Paul et Vincent sont peints;
Mais pour l'Esprit, lis cet ouurage.

The Life of the Venerable Servant of God
Vincent de Paul

Founder and First Superior General
of the
Congregation of the Mission

(Divided Into Three Books)

by
Louis Abelly, Bishop of Rodez

BOOK THREE

New City Press

edited by
John E. Rybolt, C.M.

translated by
William Quinn, F.S.C.

notes by
Edward R. Udovic, C.M. and John E. Rybolt, C.M.

introduction by
Stafford Poole, C.M.

index
translated and edited
from the Pémartin edition of 1891,
with additional annotations, by
Edward R. Udovic, C.M

Published in the United States by New City Press
86 Mayflower Avenue, New Rochelle, New York 10801
©1993 Vincentian Studies Institute

Library of Congress Cataloging-in-Publication Data:

Abelly, Louis, 1604-1691.
    [Vie du vénérable serviteur de Dieu, Vincent de Paul. English]
    The life of the venerable servant of God Vincent de Paul : founder
and first superior general of the Congregation of the Mission :
(divided into three books) / by Louis Abelly ; [edited by John E.
Rybolt ; translated by William Quinn ; introduction by Stafford
Poole].
    Includes bibliographical references and index.
    ISBN 1-56548-052-X : $49.00
    1. Vincent de Paul, Saint, 1581-1660.   2. Christian saints—
France—Biography—Early works to 1800.   I. Rybolt, John E.
II. Title.
BX4700.V6A48   1993
271'.7702—dc20
[B]   93-9446

The original edition of Abelly contained as a frontispiece an engraving by René Lochon, based on the portrait by Simon François de Tours of Vincent de Paul in choir dress. Below the portrait is a quatrain, the translation of which is:
    If you wish to see in a single face
    the portrait of two great saints
    Paul and Vincent are depicted here;
    but for his spirit, read this work.

CONTENTS

PREFACE 9

BOOK THREE. His Virtues 11

CHAPTER ONE. Some General Observations on the Virtues of Monsieur Vincent 13
CHAPTER TWO. Monsieur Vincent's faith 15
CHAPTER THREE. His Hope and Confidence in God 21
    SECTION ONE. Continuation of the Same Topic 25
    SECTION TWO. Continuation of the Same Topic 29
    SECTION THREE. Monsieur Vincent's Thoughts on the Confidence We Should Have in God. 32
CHAPTER FOUR. His Love of God 37
CHAPTER FIVE. His Conformity to the Will of God 40
    SECTION ONE. Continuation of the Same Topic 43
    SECTION TWO. His Perfect Acceptance of the Will of God by an Entire Resignation and Indifference 47
CHAPTER SIX. His Constant Attention to the Presence of God 56
CHAPTER SEVEN. His Mental Prayer 59
    SECTION ONE. A Collection of Some Counsels and Instructions of Monsieur Vincent on the Topic of Mental Prayer 65
CHAPTER EIGHT. His Devotion and Piety Toward God 72
    SECTION ONE. His Special Devotion Toward the Blessed Sacrament of the Altar 77
    SECTION TWO. His Special Care to Imitate Jesus Christ, and Conform Himself to His Example 83
CHAPTER NINE. His Devotion Toward the Most Blessed Virgin, the Mother of God, and the Other Saints 92
CHAPTER TEN. His Zeal for the Glory of God and the Salvation of Souls . 97
CHAPTER ELEVEN. His Charity Toward His Neighbor 106

    SECTION ONE. Some Remarkable Examples of Monsieur Vincent's Charity 111
    SECTION TWO. His Special Charity Toward the Poor 116
    SECTION THREE. His Alms 123
    SECTION FOUR. His Affectionate Regard for the Prelates of the Church 130
    SECTION FIVE. His Regard for Priests and Other Members of the Clergy 139
    SECTION SIX. His Charity Toward the Members of His Own Congregation 147
    SECTION SEVEN. His Charity Toward His Adversaries 156

CHAPTER TWELVE. His Meekness 163
    SECTION ONE. Continuation of the Same Topic 168
    SECTION TWO. Some Remarkable Words of Monsieur Vincent About the Meekness We Should Practice in Regard to Our Neighbor 174

CHAPTER THIRTEEN. His Humility 180
    SECTION ONE. Some Examples of Monsieur Vincent's Practice of the Virtue of Humility 184
    SECTION TWO. Some Thoughts of Monsieur Vincent About the Virtue of Humility 195

CHAPTER FOURTEEN. His Obedience 205

CHAPTER FIFTEEN. His Simplicity 214

CHAPTER SIXTEEN. His Prudence 222
    SECTION ONE. Continuation of the Same Subject 226

CHAPTER SEVENTEEN. His Justice and Gratitude 233

CHAPTER EIGHTEEN. His Perfect Detachment from the Goods of This World, and His Love of Poverty 242

CHAPTER NINETEEN. His Mortification 254
    SECTION ONE. Continuation of the Same Topic 263

CHAPTER TWENTY. His Chastity 268

CHAPTER TWENTY-ONE. His Even Disposition 274

CHAPTER TWENTY-TWO. His Fortitude in Supporting Good and Opposing Evil, and His Patience in Bearing Afflictions and Pain . . 280

CHAPTER TWENTY-THREE. His Patience in Sickness 289

CHAPTER TWENTY-FOUR. The Leadership Style of Monsieur Vincent . 293

SECTION ONE. Continuation of the Same Topic 301
SECTION TWO. How He Handled the Temporal Affairs of the Congregation 312
SECTION THREE. Advice Given by Monsieur Vincent to a Priest of the Congregation Before Sending Him to Assume the Direction of One of the Houses 317

LAST CHAPTER. Conclusion of This Work, in Which We Answer Why We Did Not Include Any Miracles in the Book to Prove the Sanctity of Monsieur Vincent 323

INDEX 327

PREFACE

We have already spoken fully of the virtues of Monsieur Vincent in the two preceding books, which cover his life and his main works, since we can truly say that his life was a fabric of the virtues which influenced his conduct and his most important works and activities. However, much remains to be said on the topic which did not seem suitable for any other section of this work. We have thought it necessary then to add this third book to illustrate more clearly the virtues of this holy man. We would like to present his mind and his practice, in the hope readers will draw much light for their own edification. We hope this third and final book will be no less agreeable and useful to readers serious about perfection than the two preceding ones. One of the fruits hoped for in reading this work is motivation for readers to practice these same virtues. We first should praise God for all the graces he gave to his faithful servant, Vincent de Paul, and through him to the Church. The reader will see here both examples and the motivation for them in the life of Monsieur Vincent.

Imitating the saints is one of the chief duties we owe them, and one of the happy fruits which recalling their virtues ought to produce in us. Otherwise, we would have reason to fear that this reading will cause us only confusion and even condemnation if we have before our eyes such marvelous exemplars and do not attempt to imitate them. The same is true, if seeing the path these great persons took on their way to God, we fail in our courage and do not follow them.

Pious readers who would profit from the reading of this third book ought to examine themselves at the close of each chapter to determine if they lack the virtue described there. They should see what God is asking of them according to their state and disposition. After forming good resolutions on this matter, they should then invoke the help of God's mercy in putting them into practice.

The great Saint Jerome, in writing the life of Saint Paula, invoked (as he tells us, himself) the guardian angel of his subject. It would not be amiss for those who read the life of Vincent de Paul to implore the help of the blessed spirit who was given by God as his protector, and who upheld him, helped, and strengthened him in all his activities. By his help we may hope to obtain the graces and strength necessary to follow this great servant of God who walked the path of virtue with such giant steps. We hope also to come one day to share that prize we confidently believe he has already attained, that is to say, the possession and enjoyment of the glory and happiness which shall never end.

BOOK THREE

His Virtues

CHAPTER ONE

Some General Observations on the Virtues of Monsieur Vincent

BEFORE SPEAKING in detail of the virtues of Monsieur Vincent, we have thought it necessary to make several remarks about four or five of the remarkable aspects of his practice of them.

First, Monsieur Vincent in his practice of the virtues never strove for the extraordinary or the singular. He always gave himself to the practice of those virtues considered common, such as humility, patience, graciousness, mortification, support of the neighbor, and love of the poor or other disadvantaged. These virtues are common, but his practice of them was uncommon. He embellished these precious stones of the heavenly Jerusalem by the excellent dispositions he brought to their practice. He exercised these virtues under the inspiration of grace and with the best of intentions. He looked to Jesus Christ as the exemplar of all virtue, strove to conform himself to this model, and faithfully sought the glory of God as the sole end of all his actions.

Second, his life of virtue had no limits. He had received from God a great and noble heart which allowed him to embrace all the virtues simultaneously, and to practice them in an eminent degree. What is particularly noteworthy is that in cases where the virtues seemed to be opposed to each other, he still excelled in each, as in his humility. His humility was profound and was accompanied by a great contempt of self, yet he had great courage when he had to sustain the interests of God. His strength of mind allowed him to devote himself to the greatest projects, but he also showed a marvelous adaptation toward the weaknesses of the most rustic people. He was able to join together the roles of both Martha and Mary in uniting contemplation to action without detriment to either. People often noted his serenity and tranquility. They shone forth in his countenance even in the midst of a multitude of business preoccupations or interruptions from all sorts of persons attracted by his generosity. The following chapters will enable us to see how all the virtues were united in his heart to an extraordinary degree.

Third, he was not content merely to know the definition of virtue. He sought to put it into practice. His sentiments agreed with the father of the Church who said: "The most assured way of acquiring the virtues is by work and patience. This roots them in our hearts."[1] He also went on to say: "We

---

1. Lactantius, PL 6.1:383.

easily lose those virtues which we have acquired without labor or at little cost. The virtues which have taken deep root in the heart are those battered by the storms of temptation, and practiced despite difficulty and the repugnance of nature."

Fourth, he was truly one of those who hungered and thirsted for justice. He was insatiable in his acquisition of the perfection of the virtues, and one can truly say that he was among those who continually hungered and thirsted for justice. He never believed that he had done enough for such a noble task. In imitation of the apostle he put aside all thought of what good had been done, to press on to that height of perfection to which God had called him.[2]

Fifth, although he used all his ingenuity to conceal his gifts, his life of virtue was well known to all who lived with him. He alone was unaware of his own goodness, for his humility seemed to be a veil hiding this from his own eyes. He was unlike that person spoken of in the Apocalypse,[3] for he was rich and abounding in virtue and heavenly gifts, and yet thought of himself as poor, indigent, miserable, and bereft of all spiritual gifts. In this way his most usual expression when he had occasion to refer to himself was to say "this miserable man." Although he was so innocent and holy, and even though good works filled his days, he never spoke of himself except in the most degrading terms, usually saying how great his need was for the mercy of God because of all the abominations of his life.

Here was a person who truly possessed a treasure in his virtues, and this treasure was even more secure in that it was hidden from him. He took as great pains to hide from the eyes of others, and even from himself, those gifts received from God, as vain people do to publicize the virtues they think they have, but which often exist only falsely and deceitfully in their imagination.

---

2. Phil 3:13.
3. Rev 3:17.

CHAPTER TWO

Monsieur Vincent's faith

FAITH IS the foundation of the other virtues and the strength of the spiritual edifice rests mainly on this mysterious foundation. As a result, here in Book Three, where we wish to study the admirable edifice of the virtues in Monsieur Vincent, we will begin with a consideration of faith. This wise architect placed it as the foundation of all the virtuous practices and all he did in God's service.

Just as trees buffeted by winds and shaken by storms put down deeper roots, we may say the same of Monsieur Vincent's faith. God permitted him, early in his life, to be tried with temptations and trials relating to this virtue. By the help of God's grace he emerged victorious in these struggles, fortified in his faith rather than weakened, for God allowed these trials to strengthen and perfect this virtue in him. After these temptations he became not only stronger in faith but also more enlightened (as he himself declared on several occasions), so that he possessed this virtue as fully as is given to someone in this life.

One of his most extreme remedies against temptations against faith was to write out and sign a profession of faith, and to carry this over his heart. He begged our Lord to accept his gesture, so that every time he was tempted he placed his hand over his heart, as a sign that he rejected the temptation, and that he was once again resolved to live until his last breath in the faith of the Church and to believe firmly all the truths that she taught.

Not only was his faith strong, it was pure and simple. It was not based on study or experience but rather on the first truth alone, God himself, and on the authority of his Church. He reproved those who wished to examine too closely the truths of faith either by the subtlety of their mind or in the light of their learning. He used the comparison of looking at the sun. The more directly you look at it the less you see. Those who more and more studied the truths of faith risked understanding less and less. "It is enough," he used to say, "that we believe what the Church proposes to us, and submit our minds to this truth."

For this reason he was always ready to give perfect obedience to the decisions of the Church, which he received with great respect and a sincere humility. He believed everything decided by the Church's authority. One day he said to his community:

The Church, which is the kingdom of God, inspires those who

govern the faithful, and helps them in their lives. Her Holy Spirit presides in the councils. From this Spirit comes the lights spread over the earth, forming the saints, judging the wicked, resolving doubts, proclaiming the truth, denouncing errors, pointing out the way the whole Church and each one of the faithful in particular must follow to assure his salvation.[1]

He was often said to have thanked God for preserving in him the integrity of the faith in an age known for its errors and scandalous opinions, and for giving him the grace of never having taken up any position contrary to that of the Church. Despite all the dangerous situations in which he found himself, he never strayed from the right path, but by the special protection of God he preserved the true faith.

Monsieur Vincent did not hold his faith locked up in his mind, for his perfect charity made his beliefs evident to everyone. We have earlier seen the zeal with which he catechized and preached, especially in places where the people were most in need of instruction, such as in the villages and among the poor. These people are ordinarily those least instructed in the truths of the faith. He applied here the words of the prophet: "I believed, and I have spoken, for the faith has loosened my tongue, and the knowledge of the truth which God has revealed to me obliges me to announce this to others."[2] He was not content to do this alone. He influenced all those that he could to join him in taking up this charitable work. He established a congregation completely dedicated to cultivating this faith in the most unfertile lands. By the grace of God his fellow workers in this Company have produced an abundant harvest.

The fruit of his faith was not limited to the poor who lived in ignorance of the truths of salvation. He also served many others who felt tempted against this virtue. A virtuous priest has related how his spirit was once greatly agitated because of his doubts about a particular article of the creed, and how he discussed this with Monsieur Vincent. The words of this holy man brought peace to his troubled spirit, something not achieved by the advice and exhortations of many other distinguished persons whom he had consulted.

The virtue of faith moved Monsieur Vincent to devote himself to teaching and explaining the truths of our holy religion, but he was also vigorous and courageous in opposing all errors. We saw in Book Two[3] how zealous he was in opposing the new heresy of Jansenius. One of his chief weapons in this battle was prayer, which he used always. Even before the decisions of

---
1. *CED* XII:133.
2. See Ps 116:10.
3. Ch. 12.

the Church, when questions of grace were all the rage in the salons of Paris, and the adherents of the new doctrines were publishing book after book on the subject to propagate their opinions, he had recourse to God, the Father of lights. At this time he said to one of his confidants, "For the past three months I have meditated on the doctrine of grace. Every day God gave me new insights, leading me farther and farther away from the dangerous opinions so prevalent in our world today."[4]

As we have already said, he was most vigilant that the weeds of this new doctrine not be sown in his Congregation. A superior of one of the missions has stated that from the time when Monsieur Vincent first studied theology, he had often looked into this question. His study had given him a violent distaste for these pernicious novelties. He had even removed a director of studies, as some in the Congregation are aware, because he gave reason for his orthodoxy to be suspect. Despite the pleadings of those who studied under this director, that he should be restored to his office, Monsieur Vincent never consented. When this group of students came to his room with this same request, he would not listen and sent them away with a severe reprimand.[5]

Another priest of his Congregation has told of the occasion when, without realizing it, he let a remark slip out that could have been construed as favoring the errors condemned by the Church. Monsieur Vincent summoned him privately to give him a chance to explain himself. He did so with complete satisfaction, but Monsieur Vincent spoke to him as he had spoken to others on similar occasions:

> You must realize, Monsieur, that this new error of Jansenism is one of the most dangerous in the history of the Church. One of the things I most bless and particularly thank God for is that he has never allowed those who first professed these doctrines, some of whom I knew well and who were my friends, to convince me of their thinking. I can hardly exaggerate the pains they went to and the arguments they used, but my answer was, among others, the authority of the Council of Trent, which manifestly opposed their teachings. In face of their persistence, instead of responding to them, I recited the Creed to myself. This is how I firmly persevered in Catholic belief. Even to my old age, I have always had a secret fear in my soul, and I have not dreaded anything else as much, that I might be swept away by some heresy and be drowned in some novelties of belief.[6]

---

4. During the course of the canonization investigations, Antoine Durand testified that he had heard Vincent say these words one day in a conference to the community. See *Summarium* no. 21, p. 52.
5. This confrere was a professor at Saint Lazare named Guilbert. See also *CED* IV: 355-56.
6. This quotation is an extract from a letter submitted to the investigation by Michel Caset, who

He said this on several occasions. A virtuous person, who died before he did, declared that Monsieur Vincent was the first to make him see what really was involved in the doctrine of the Jansenists. He developed a detestation of this heresy long before the errors were officially recognized and condemned.

At length, when the condemnation of the doctrine of the Jansenists contained in the five propositions was sent from Rome, and the late archbishop of Paris had it published throughout his diocese, Monsieur Vincent said to his community:

> We must thank God for the protection he has given his Church, especially in France, to purify it of the errors which threatened to throw it into such great disarray. God had given me the grace to be able to discern between error and truth, not that I have any sense of vain accomplishment in this, nor any spiteful joy in seeing that my judgment conforms to that of the Holy Apostolic See. I well recognize that this judgment comes purely from God's mercy, for which he must be given glory.[7]

Besides this purity, simplicity, and firmness in the faith in which he excelled, we must also say that he possessed the fullness of this virtue. Not only did faith inform his mind, but it filled his heart and animated his actions, words, affections, and thoughts. It made him act in everything according to the truths and teachings of the Gospel of Jesus Christ. What most Christians do by habit, by natural motivation, or by human reason, he did by the principles of faith. It is, according to the words of the prophet "a lamp to my hand to lead me and direct my steps in the paths of justice."[8] Without a doubt he received from God this special gift of applying the light of faith to all occasions and circumstances, and directing and undertaking even temporal and secular affairs only by motives inspired by faith, in the light of faith, and with the supernatural goals proposed by faith.

He was not content only to direct himself by this spirit of faith in all that he undertook. He inspired others, as much as he could, especially those under his direction, to act similarly. In this connection, Mademoiselle Le Gras, foundress and first superior of the Daughters of Charity, of whom we have spoken in Books One and Two, one day expressed a certain anxiety about this charitable institute, of which Monsieur Vincent was the spiritual father. He replied to her:

> I always see some purely human sentiments in you when you think that all is lost, or when you see me ill. O woman of little faith,

---

entered the Congregation in 1649. See also *CED* XI:37.
7. *CED* XI:156.
8. Ps 119:105.

you have such little confidence and acceptance of the direction and example of Jesus Christ. This savior of the world cares for the entire Church. You are responsible for a mere handful of women, whom his Providence has brought together, and yet you think he will forsake you. Alas, Mademoiselle, you must humble yourself before God for this lack of trust.[9]

He often said that a lack of progress in the virtues and the little success we have in the things of God comes from our not being motivated enough by the light of faith, and by relying on motives coming from human reason. He said one day:

No, no, eternal truths alone can fill the heart and lead us with assurance. Believe me, we must base ourselves solidly and confidently on one of the perfections of God, such as his goodness, his providence, his truth, his immensity. I am saying that in order to progress greatly in a short time, we must build on these divine foundations. This does not mean that we should not use sound and pressing reasons to guide our actions, but only that they should be subordinate to the truths of faith. Experience shows us that preachers who appeal to truths of faith do more for souls than those who fill their sermons with mere human and philosophical wisdom. The light of faith is always accompanied by a certain heavenly unction that diffuses itself secretly in the hearts of those who listen. From this we can judge that it is necessary, as much for our own progress as for the salvation of others, to follow always the light of faith in all things.[10]

He also held the maxim that things should not be judged solely from the outside and according to their appearance, but by what they are in the sight of God. He recalled the words of the apostle, *quae videntur, temporalia sunt; quae autem non videntur, aeterna sunt.* ["What is seen is transitory; what is unseen lasts forever."][11] He said:

I ought not consider a poor peasant, or a poor woman according to external appearances, nor according to what seems on the surface to be their disposition. Often enough, being so crude and earthy, they do not present themselves as respectable or reasonable beings. But turn the medal over and by the light of faith you will see that the Son of God, who chose to be poor, is present here in these poor people. During his passion, he seemed to be a fool to the gentiles, and a scandal for the Jews, and in all this he called himself the

---

9. *CED* II:158.
10. *CED* XI:31.
11. 2 Cor 4:18.

Evangelizer of the poor: *Evangelizare pauperibus misit me* ["He has sent me to preach the Gospel to the poor"].[12] O God, how beautiful are the poor if we see them in God, and in light of the esteem Jesus Christ had for them. If we see them only according to the flesh and with a worldly spirit, they truly seem miserable.[13]

Lastly, to understand how great and perfect the faith of Monsieur Vincent really was, we should look to all his other virtues. His faith was the root of them all. For as Saint Ambrose said: "We may judge the vigor and perfection of this mystical tree by considering the quantity and excellence of the fruits it has produced."[14] We will speak of them in the following chapters.

---

12. Luke 4:18.
13. *CED* XI:32.
14. PL 14.1.1:132-35.

CHAPTER THREE

His Hope and Confidence in God

IF WE SAY that the faith of Monsieur Vincent was great, we must also add that his hope was no less perfect. In imitation of the Father of all believers he often hoped against hope itself, by which we mean that he hoped in God when according to all human expectations he ought to have despaired. Just as his faith was simple and pure, founded on the truth of God alone, so his hope was not based on the considerations and reasonings of human nature but solely on the mercy and goodness of God.

Whenever there was a question of undertaking something for the service of God, after invoking his guidance and perceiving his will, he confidently relied on his infinite goodness. In carrying out his projects he used all the conventional human resources, yet he did not rely on these, but only on the help he anticipated from God. Once he had undertaken a project in this spirit, he expected that God would help him and his Company. Should one of his confreres, through a lack of hope and trust or because of human prudence sometimes points out the difficulty or even impossibility of achieving the purpose of the project, he would usually say, "Let us leave that to our Lord, for it is his work. It pleased him to begin it, so we must be sure that he will bring it to fruition in the way he deems best." He would sometimes encourage those who doubted: "Have courage, trust in our Lord. He is our inspiration and our help in this work we have begun and to which he has called us."

Writing one day to a superior of one of the missions of the Congregation, he said:

> I sympathize with you that your labor is so difficult, and has become even more so because of the sickness of some of your confreres. The good God has brought this about, and doubtless he will give you added strength to bear this added burden. He is your strength, and will be your reward for the extraordinary efforts you display on this occasion. Believe me, three men are worth more than ten when our Lord takes charge. He does help when human means are taken away, especially when he asks us to do more than is humanly possible. We pray, however, that in his divine goodness he will restore your sick priests to health and fill your community with great trust in his mercy.[1]

---

1. *CED* IV:115-16.

To cultivate the perfect confidence in God that he recommended so often to his confreres, he urged them to have a low opinion of themselves. They should also be convinced that they could accomplish nothing by themselves, unless it were to ruin God's designs. Thus by being so thoroughly convinced of their own powerlessness, they were to develop an entire and perfect dependence on the guidance of God and on the effects of his grace. For this gift they were to have constant recourse to him in prayer. Writing to one of his priests he said:

> I thank God that you have learned the art of humbling yourself by recognizing and speaking about your faults. You are right to think of yourself as unfit for many works, for on this foundation our Lord establishes his grace to accomplish his designs toward us. When you allow yourself to think of your own insufficiency, you then must also recall his adorable bounty. You truly have good reason to be wary of yourself, but you have even greater reason to trust in God. If you feel yourself drawn to evil, believe that God draws you even more to the good, and he can effect it in you and by you. Please meditate on this. During the day allow your mind to reflect on this principle so that, after reflecting on your own weakness, you may turn to his help. Think of his infinite mercy more than of your own unworthiness, of his guidance more than of your own weakness. Abandon yourself into his paternal arms in the hope that he will work through you, blessing the works you do in his name.[2]

When Monsieur Vincent sent his priests and brothers to the farthest and most difficult missions in foreign lands, his chief recommendation was that they fill their hearts with a true and perfect confidence in God. He said to them:

> Go, gentlemen, in the name of our Lord, for it is he who sends you. You begin this voyage and this mission for his service and his glory. He will guide, help, and protect you. We hope for this from his infinite goodness. Remain always dependent upon his guidance. Have recourse to him everywhere and in every encounter. Throw yourselves into his arms, recognizing him as your loving Father, completely confident that he will help you and bless your work.

Lastly, even in all the greatest and most difficult enterprises which caused him such trouble and cost him so much, once this holy man had ascertained the will of God he plunged ahead. He was undeterred by any obstacle, believing this truth which he often repeated, "Divine Providence will never fail us in those things we undertake by its direction." He devoted himself

---

2. *CED* V:164-65.

even more to those great undertakings which he saw as being more difficult and painful.

His confidence in God was also apparent when he saw the poverty and pressing needs of some of the houses and communities of his Congregation. Once, a superior of one of his houses wrote to tell him of the great difficulties that had arisen because of the poor crops and the resulting high cost of living. Monsieur Vincent replied to him:

> You must not be overwhelmed if there is a bad year, or even several bad ones in a row. God is abundant in riches. You have lacked nothing up to now, so why do you fear? Does he not take care of the sparrows, who neither sow nor reap? How much greater will his goodness be toward his servants? Naturally, you want to have all your supplies stored away to be assured of having everything you desire. Yet I think spiritually you would do better to find the occasion to depend on God alone, as a truly poor person, for the Lord is generous and infinitely wealthy. God wishes to have pity on his poor people who are so ready to complain at a time of scarcity, since they do not know how to use adversity well, nor do they seek first the kingdom of God and his justice. They do not make themselves worthy of those things necessary to the present life over and above what is given to them for eternal life.[3]

It became known that one day the treasurer of the house of Saint Lazare came to tell him that there was not a *sou* left in the house to cover either the ordinary or the extraordinary expenses arising during the ordination retreats about to begin. Full of confidence in God, he raised his voice: "What good news! God be blessed! Fine, now we will see if we have confidence in God." One of his priest friends spoke to him one day about the large expense these ordination retreats must entail. He thought that the house of Saint Lazare was surely put to great inconvenience and could no longer support such a responsibility. He suggested that perhaps each ordinand should be charged something for his stay at Saint Lazare. Monsieur Vincent replied, with a smile, "When we have spent all we have for our Lord and nothing remains, then we will leave the key under the door and go."

Also, some of his own community remonstrated with him on the large debts incurred because of the clergy conferences and other works of charity centered at Saint Lazare. It was pointed out to him that the community was in danger of financial ruin if he did not curtail his charities and limit the number of people who came for retreats. His reply to this was, "The treasures of God's Providence are inexhaustible, and our distrust of God does him no honor. If our Company of the Mission is destroyed, it will not be by poverty but by wealth."

---

3. *CED* VII:156-57.

He said practically the same thing to a lawyer of the Parlement of Paris who was making a retreat at Saint Lazare. He was surprised to see so many people in the dining room, besides the large number who normally lived there. His curiosity led him to ask Monsieur Vincent how he managed to feed so many. He answered, "Monsieur, the treasury of God's Providence is large. We must put our cares and concerns into his hands, for he will never fail to provide our food, as he has promised." He added these words of the psalmist he especially savored: *Oculi omnium in te sperant, Domine, et tu das illis escam in tempore opportuno. Aperis tu manum tuam, et imples omne animal benedictione* ["The eyes of all look hopefully to you, and you give them their food in due season. You open your hand and satisfy the desire of every living thing"].[4]

Once the house of Saint Lazare experienced a serious loss while he was absent. When Monsieur Vincent was informed of this, he wrote to the community:

> All that God does he does for the best, so we must hope that this loss will profit us, since it comes from God. All things work for good for the just. We have been told that the one who receives adversities from the hand of God must receive them with joy and blessing. Gentlemen and my brothers, please thank God for what has happened, for this loss, and for the disposition he has inspired in us to accept this loss for the sake of his love. It is a great loss, but he knows how to turn it to our profit by means we are now unaware of, but which we will surely see one day. I hope the way everyone reacted to this unexpected accident will serve as the foundation for the grace God will give us so that in the future, we may make good use of any troubles which he may send.[5]

Several of his friends suggested that he appeal the loss by having recourse to the legal remedy which they proposed. He refused, and among the reasons he gave in a letter to one of them, he included the following:

> We have good reason to hope that if we seek first the kingdom of God, as Jesus Christ teaches us in the Gospel, we will want for nothing. If, on the one hand the world deprives us of something, you can be sure that, on the other, God will make it up to us. This we have already experienced with this present loss, for God has inspired a friend to make a gift to us that covers almost all we lost.[6]

We should report here a remarkable letter on this same topic which Monsieur Vincent wrote to one of his priests who had taken charge of a

---
4. Ps 145:15-16, a prayer used as grace before meals.
5. *CED* VII:251-52.
6. *CED* VII:406.

certain farm. After giving him some general directions about its management, he concluded: "There you are, with many directions about temporal affairs. May it please God that they not distract you from spiritual affairs. May his Holy Spirit, which cares for the needs of all creatures of the entire world down to the smallest insect, dwell in you. Oh, Monsieur, we must apply ourselves well if we are to participate fully in this Holy Spirit."[7]

SECTION ONE

Continuation of the Same Topic

If, as we have just seen, the Monsieur Vincent's confidence in God was great in the pressing needs which he and his community experienced, it was no less firm in the reverses, difficulties, and other annoying and threatening things that happened to him. It was noticed that no matter what occurred, or in what difficulties he found himself, he was never beaten down or discouraged, but was always full of trust in God. He enjoyed a constant evenness of spirit and a perfect abandonment to his divine Providence. He seemed pleased to be put in such disturbing situations, to give himself the opportunity to put himself more completely and absolutely into the hands of divine Providence.

A superior of one of the main houses of the Congregation alerted him to some intrigues against the community that seemingly threatened to harm it. Even some highly placed persons supported the community's adversaries. Monsieur Vincent replied, in this manner:

> As to the intrigues against us, pray God to spare us from this spirit. If we blame others for harboring this defect, it is only reasonable for us to avoid the same fault. This is a fault against divine Providence which makes one unworthy of the care God has for all. Let us remain completely dependent upon him, in the confidence that if we do so, God will bring good from all that people may do or say against us. Yes, Monsieur, even when everyone works against us they will be able to achieve only what pleases God, in whom we have put our trust. Please adopt these sentiments and preserve them, so that you never even bother to think about these useless worries.[8]

---

7. *CED* I:475.
8. *CED* IV:393-94.

One more thing showed his perfect confidence in God. This was the preservation and spread of his Congregation. Even though its welfare was dearer to him than life itself, he depended entirely on God for all that concerned its development and safety. To assure himself that this dependence was absolute and his confidence complete, he never acted in any way to obtain any benefices, houses, or establishments, nor even to attract any candidates for the Congregation. He preferred to rely on Providence alone. When offered gifts he was more inclined to accept the lesser rather than the greater. When there was a question of admitting someone to the community, he hesitated more to receive persons of some distinction or of some renown in the world than he did for accepting those of the lower class. He did not make a distinction between persons, but he was most cautious of doing anything based on mere natural impulses or from a mere human respect. He feared he might be circumventing the direction of the Providence of God.

For this same reason he was on his guard in the face of anything out of the ordinary. He was uneasy even with gifted spirits, unless he saw that these people were endowed with a true and sincere humility. He felt that those not blessed with abundant natural talents, or those who had not acquired a special competence, were more apt to place their trust in God. Thus they would be better suited to the Congregation, where they would succeed with greater blessings than the other more gifted ones who were likely to trust more in themselves and less in God. A prelate who had often remarked on this trait in Monsieur Vincent, said on one occasion: "This principle, introduced by him into the Congregation, of not favoring gifts of nature or fortune unless they were joined to virtue and subservient to grace, was one of the major means by which God inspired him to preserve his Congregation in the purity of its spirit."

Monsieur Vincent often recommended to his confreres not to solicit anything for themselves or for the Congregation, whether position, comforts, or favors, but simply to accept with humility and thanks whatever God sent them. He wanted them to put out of their minds all worry or pressures about their needs or their occupations, so that, after taking a reasonable and moderate care of these things, they would leave everything to the good pleasure of divine Providence. He wrote the following to a priest of the Congregation who was substituting for the superior of the house in Rome during his absence.

> Every day you give me reason to praise God for your affection for our Congregation, and for your attention to the affairs of your house. I praise him with all my heart, and yet I am also obliged to tell you, as our Lord told Martha, that there is a bit too much worry on your part. Only one thing is necessary, and that is to trust more in God and to his direction than you now do. Anticipation is good

when it is accepting, but it goes to excess when we worry about avoiding something we foresee. We expect more from our own insights than we do from Providence. We think we will accomplish much by substituting our blindness for his light, and by putting our trust in human prudence rather than in his word. Our divine Savior assures us in the Gospel that not a sparrow, nor even a hair of our head, will fall to the ground without his permission. Yet you fear that our little Company will fail if we do not take this or that precaution, if we do not do one thing or another, so much so that you fear that if we fail to do these things others will build on our ruins. As soon as someone raises an objection against us, we must answer it. If someone seems ready to steal our followers, we must get ahead of him, or else all will be lost.

This is what I sense when I read your letters, and what is worse, your lively spirit leads you to do what you say, thinking you have enough insight yourself without needing to consult others. Oh, Monsieur, how unsuited this is to a missionary! It would be better if a hundred missions were concluded by others, rather than to have prevented a single one. If our zeal is genuine we ought to be glad to see anyone prophesy, to see God sending new workers into his Church, or to see the reputation of others grow and ours decrease. Monsieur, please have greater confidence in God, let him steer our little ship. If it is useful to him he will save it from shipwreck. Neither the might nor the multitude of the other vessels will cause it to founder. On the contrary, it will sail along with them with greater assurance as long as it keeps to its course and does not interfere with the others.[9]

At the time of the approval of the Congregation by Rome and the royal letters patent for the establishment of the community at Saint Lazare, the two approvals on which the future of the community depended but which had aroused strong opposition, Monsieur Vincent had such confidence in God that he wrote these remarkable words to one of the priests of his Congregation:

> I fear only my own sins, and not the outcome of the business at Rome and Paris concerning the success of the bulls and the affairs of Saint Lazare. Sooner or later everything will work out. *Qui timent Dominum sperent in eo, adjutor eorum et protector eorum est* ["Let those who fear the Lord trust in him; he is their help and their shield"].[10]

---

9. *CED* IV:347-49.
10. Based on Ps 115:11. *CED* I:162-65.

We should remark that he did not speak of the future success of these matters with a presumptuous certitude. He feared only his own sins and he placed no reliance on himself. He relied only on his perfect confidence that God, who had brought his small Congregation into being, would not abandon it, but would bring it to its perfection. He was often heard to say: "Once God has begun to do good to a creature he will continue to do so to the end unless it makes itself unworthy of his help."

We should add here what he said one day to his community, in the early days of the Congregation, exhorting them to have a perfect confidence in God.

> Have trust in God, gentlemen and my brothers, but have it completely and perfectly. You can be sure that having begun this work in us he will bring it to fulfillment. I ask you, who began this Congregation? Who called us to the missions, the ordination retreats, the clergy conferences, the retreats? Was it I? Not at all. Was it Monsieur Portail whom God sent to join me in the beginning? Not at all, for we never thought of these things, we never even considered them. Then who is the author of all this? It is God in his paternal Providence and his goodness. We are but wretched workmen, poor ignoramuses. Among us there are few or none of the nobility, no one powerful, learned, or capable of anything. God alone does everything, and he does it with people like ourselves, so all glory should be given to him alone.
>
> Put all your confidence in him, then. If we place our confidence in men, or on some gift of nature or fortune, then God will withdraw from us. But, someone will say, we need friends, both for ourselves and for our community. Oh, my brothers, be on your guard against such thoughts, lest you be fooled. Seek God alone, and he will give you friends and everything else besides. Would you like to know why we will sometimes fail in what we do? It is because we rely upon ourselves. When a preacher, superior, or confessor relies too much on his own prudence, learning, or his own gifts, what happens? God withdraws, and leaves him to himself, and whatever he does produces no fruit. This makes him see his own uselessness, and he learns through his own experience that no matter how talented he may be, he can do nothing without God.[11]

---

11. *CED* XI:38-39.

SECTION TWO

Continuation of the Same Topic

What made Monsieur Vincent's trust even more excellent and perfect was that he attached himself to God alone and he wished to depend solely on his Providence. In imitation of Saint Francis, he wanted God to be his all. Concerning this, it was remarked that no matter what talent or quality he saw in the priests of his Congregation, or whatever notable support or service they gave to the Congregation or to Saint Lazare, his usual place of residence, and despite the esteem, love, and tenderness he might have for them, he did not attach himself to any of them. On many occasions he would send those he most esteemed and cherished to the most distant places, or to those missions which were the most dangerous. Even though these particular priests might be the ones who seemed to be necessary or useful to the running of the house, he would willingly sacrifice their companionship when he saw they could render greater service to our Lord in some other place. He would deprive himself of their love as a sacrifice to God of what was most dear to him, in imitation of the holy patriarch Abraham. He based his hopes for the preservation and growth of his Congregation not on human means but solely on the Providence of God, in whom alone he put all his trust and on whom he wished to depend entirely and absolutely.

Monsieur Vincent once gave a talk on the sacrifice of the patriarch Abraham to illustrate the lesson of perfect confidence which the members of the Company should always have in God. This is what he said on that occasion:

> Do you recall this great patriarch to whom God had promised he would populate the whole world through the son he had given him? This same son was to be sacrificed, so the question naturally arose, if Abraham killed his son, how could God fulfill his promise? This holy man was so committed to carrying out the will of God that he prepared himself to carry out this order without troubling himself about anything else. It was as though he said to himself, it is up to God to decide about that. My duty is to obey his command, and I know he will fulfill his promise. But how? I surely do not know, but he is all-powerful. I will offer what is dearest to me in all the world, because that is his will. Is he not my only son? No matter. In taking the life of this child, will I not take from God the possibility of fulfilling his word? That may be, but he desires this, so it must

be done. God has told me, if I save my son, my heritage shall be blessed. Yes, but he has also told me to put him to death. I shall obey, come what may, and I shall hope in his promises.

Admire this trust that does not concern itself with grief about what might happen. It does not matter that he is deeply moved. His hope is that all will be for the best, since God has ordered this. Why, gentlemen, do we not have this same trust, leaving to God the care of all that concerns us, and simply do what he asks of us?

Again, in this regard, do we not admire the fidelity of the children of Jonadab, son of Rechab?[12] God inspired this good man to live differently than other men of his time, not living in a house but in a tent or shelter. He left all he had, and went to the country, where he planted no vines nor drank any wine, and he remained faithful to this all his lifetime. He forbade his children to sow wheat or other grains, to plant trees, or to lay out a garden. Here he was, without bread, wheat, or fruits. What will you live on, poor Jonadab? Do you think you and your family can live on fresh air? He said to himself, we will eat what God sends us.

This is a crude example. Even the poorest religious do not carry their mortification as far as this. All the same, this man trusted so completely that he deprived himself and his family of life's necessities in order to rely absolutely and completely on divine Providence. This family lived this way for three hundred and fifty years, that is to say, he and his children and his children's children.

This pleased God so, that, when he complained to Jeremiah of the hard hearts of the people given over to their pleasures, God said: go to these people, and tell them of a man who acts differently. Jeremiah called the Rechabites to come and manifest the great abstinence of the father and his sons. For this, he had bread and wine and goblets placed upon the table. Jeremiah said that God had ordered him to tell them they should drink the wine, but the Rechabites replied they had been ordered not to drink, and for these many years they have not touched wine, for their fathers had forbidden it.

If this father trusted and was without worry that God would see to the support of his family, if his children would remain so faithful to the wishes of their parents, gentlemen, what trust should we not have that God will provide for us, in whatever state we find ourselves? What is our fidelity to our rules in comparison with these children who, though not obliged to do so, still lived in such

---

12. A reference to Jer 35.

poverty? O my God, gentlemen! O my God, brothers! Ask his infinite goodness for this trust in all that concerns us. If we are faithful to this, we will lack nothing. He will live in us, he will guide, defend, and love us. What we do and say will be pleasing to him.

Do you not see the birds of the air that neither sow nor reap? God takes care of them, providing them with both food and clothing. His Providence extends even to the plants of the fields, such as the lilies, so clothed that not even Solomon in all his glory had the like. If God so looks after the birds and plants, why do you not rely on a God who is so good and so generous? Why do you count on yourself more than on him, even though you well know he can do all and you can do nothing? Yet you rely on your own efforts rather than on his goodness, on your poverty rather than his abundance. Oh the misery of man!

I will nevertheless say here that superiors must look after the needs of everyone, and provide what is necessary. God sees to the needs of all his creatures, down to the smallest mite. In the same way, he wills also that superiors and other officers, as instruments of his Providence, should watch to see that nothing necessary is lacking, neither to the priests, clerics, or brothers, nor to the hundred, two hundred, or three hundred or more persons both great and lowly who may be with us. But you yourselves, my brothers, must rely on the loving care of his Providence. Be content with what he sends, and do not worry if the community is lacking this or that. You must first seek the kingdom of God, and his infinite wisdom will supply all the rest.

Finally, I once asked a Carthusian, the prior of his house, if he called the house council together to discuss temporal affairs. "We call the superior and the procurator, but all the rest do not concern themselves with these things. They occupy themselves only with the praise of God, and with what obedience and our rules require." We have the same practice, thanks be to God, and we must hold to it. We are obliged to own some things to take care of the needs of all. There was a time when the Son of God sent his disciples out without money or provisions, but he later found it helpful to have something to maintain his group and to help the poor. The apostles continued this practice, and Saint Paul tells us how he worked to gather money that could then be distributed to other Christians. Superiors must look after temporal matters, but their concern must never distract them from their attention to the virtues. They must act so that the spiritual life remains in vigor in their houses, and God reigns over all. This must be the first of their concerns.[13]

---

13. *CED* XII:139-43.

SECTION THREE

Monsieur Vincent's Thoughts on the Confidence We Should Have in God

In the previous section we recalled the words Monsieur Vincent used in addressing his community on the subject of the confidence we ought to have in God. It will not be inappropriate if we now recount the way he testified to this same virtue in his dealings with the various persons he met.

He wrote one day to a person who had sent him greetings on his feast day:

I thank you for your devotion to my holy patron. I pray that God will reward your faith, which my own misery and unworthiness could not obtain for you. This very morning I was so involved with business that I could hardly make my meditation, and even when I did, it was only with many distractions. Judge from this how little you can depend on my prayers on this holy day. This does not discourage me however, for I put my confidence in God, and surely not in my own preparation or my own efforts. I wish with all my heart that you would do the same, for the throne of the goodness and mercy of God is founded on our own unworthiness. If we rely on his goodness, we will never be disappointed, as he himself assures us in the holy Gospels.[14]

In another letter to this same person, he wrote:

Put out of your mind all that can cause you pain, for God will take care of you. You cannot continue to act this way without (so to speak) saddening the heart of God, for he will see that you do not trust in him enough. Please trust him, and you shall see the fulfillment of all your heart desires. Once again, I repeat, put aside all thought of the mistrust which occasionally creeps into your mind. Why is your soul not filled with confidence, since you are, by the mercy of our Lord, his beloved daughter.[15]

In another letter to this same person, he said:

What treasures are hidden in his holy Providence! And how those who follow it and not stride before it honor our Lord. Recently I heard of one of the leading persons in the realm, who learned this lesson through his own experience. He tried to do only a few things on his own initiative, and instead of being successful they turned

---

14. *CED* II:289-90. The correspondent was surely Louise de Marillac.
15. *CED* I:90.

out to his loss. Isn't it reasonable that you would want your servant to do only what you told her, or what was in keeping with your orders? If this makes sense in one person dealing with another, how much more is it so in the dealings of a creature with her Creator?[16]

One day someone asked him if it were possible to offend by having too much of the hope and confidence we should have in God. He replied:

> Just as we cannot have too much faith in the truths of the faith, so too we cannot trust in God too much. We might, indeed, err in hoping for things that he has not promised, or in hoping for something he conditionally promised, while not fulfilling the conditions. For example, when a sinner hopes for pardon without forgiving his brother, or when someone asks for mercy without willing to undergo conversion. To hope to be victorious over temptation, while not rejecting the suggestions of the devil, would be both false and illusory. True hope can never be excessive since it is founded on the goodness of God and on the merits of Jesus Christ.

One day he came upon some of his confreres who seemed depressed and discouraged because of their imperfections. He said to them by way of encouragement:

> We have the seed of the all-powerful God within us. This should be the source of our hope, encouraging us to place all our confidence in him, despite our own poverty. No, it should not surprise us to see our own misery, for each of us has his own fair share. It is good to be aware of this, but we should not be unduly disturbed. When the thought of our imperfections tends to discourage us, we should turn it aside, and increase our confidence in God, abandoning ourselves into his paternal hands.

This holy man was so attentive to the Providence of God that in all his affairs he acted quite differently than those around him. Others seemed to bustle about, taking every possible measure to safeguard themselves from all possible accidents. They were preparing for any reverses and adversity by using letters, giving orders, making changes, and using all human resources promptly and without limit. They sought to conceal their lack of confidence and submission to divine Providence in the excuse that God acts through secondary causes. Monsieur Vincent was guided by a purer light and by a more assured principle of not having recourse to human means until the last possible moment. This allowed divine Providence to show its intention, and to bring things to the most propitious moment for action. His actions were motivated by the knowledge that God always works for the

---

16. *CED* I:68-69.

good, and that the less there is of the human in any affair, the more there will be of the divine.

When he saw the divine will clearly manifested for him to put his hand to some enterprise, he did so with complete peace and with little concern for the outcome. He left to God's guidance whatever would come about, good or bad. He did not think back about what he might have done, or worry about what had happened. He was content with the testimony of his good conscience, that he had striven to conform himself entirely to the will of God in what he had done. This left no room for regrets, but rather only for thanks and blessing to God for his goodness.

A well-placed priest of good reputation was greatly troubled by thoughts of despair. He wrote to Monsieur Vincent from the remote place where he was working in hopes of gaining some relief and some remedy. The reply he received gives us a good opportunity to appreciate his sentiments about the confidence one must have in God:

> Since writing your letter to me, I hope that God has dispersed the clouds that have caused you such pain. In this hope I will say only a word or two in passing about your difficulties. It seems that you are in some doubt whether you are among the number of the predestined. I would answer that no one knows infallibly of his own salvation without a special revelation from God. Yet, according to the testimony of Saint Paul, it is possible to know the true children of God if there are signs to show it. By the grace of God, I see these signs in you, Monsieur. In the same letter where you tell me you do not see these signs, I find many, and the long association I have had with you shows me others. Believe me, Monsieur, I know of no soul more given to God than yourself, nor a heart more separated from evil and committed to the good than your own. You will say that you don't see it this way. I will reply that God does not always allow his own to discern their own purity of heart among the movements of their corrupt nature, so that they may live in humility. Their treasure is better preserved by being hidden.
>
> The holy apostle had seen the beauties of heaven, but he was not justified by this, for he continued to experience darkness and struggle within himself. He had such confidence in God, though, that he felt nothing would ever be able to separate himself from the love of Jesus Christ. This example ought to suffice, Monsieur, to help you live in peace amid your darkness, with an entire and perfect confidence in the infinite goodness of God. To bring about your salvation, God invites you to abandon yourself into the arms of his Providence. Allow him to lead you in his paternal love. He does

love you, and he would no more reject a good man such as yourself than he would forsake an evil person who trusted in his mercy.[17]

Speaking one day to his community on this same topic, of confidence in God, he said:

> A true Missionary ought never be concerned about material things. He should cast all his care upon the Providence of the Lord, being entirely convinced that if he is moved by charity and is steadfast in his confidence he will always be under the protection of God. No evil will come upon him, nor will he lack anything, even when it seems that all is lost. This thought does not come from me, but is contained in holy Scripture, which says: *Qui habitat in adjutorio altissimi, in protectione Dei coeli commorabitur* ["He who dwells in the shelter of the Most High, will abide in the shadow of the Almighty"].[18] Whoever lives this teaching on confidence in God shall always have a special protection from him. He may be sure that no evil will come upon him, because all things will work for his good. He will lack nothing, since God will give himself to him and bringing all that is necessary for both soul and body. And so it is, my brothers, you must be convinced that as long as you remain firm in this trust, not only will you be preserved from all evil, but you will be filled with all good things.[19]

We will finish this chapter with an extract of a conference Monsieur Vincent gave to the Daughters of Charity. He sought to inspire them with this same confidence in God in the midst of all the contradictions and dangerous situations in which they might find themselves in their service to the poor.

> You will often find, my daughters, that the wrath of God comes suddenly and violently upon many sinners before they have an opportunity for repentance and conversion. You will see many innocent people die as well, but you will be saved. Yes, my daughters, God will see to your safety because you serve the poor.[20]

In the next part of his conference he reflected on the effects of this special protection of God manifested on two remarkable occasions.

> The first of these was the time in the faubourg Saint Germain when an almost new house collapsed at the very moment a Daughter of Charity was bringing something to a poor person living there. She was caught between two floors, and by all appearances ought to have been crushed in the ruins, as were the thirty people who

---

17. *CED* IV:316-18.
18. Ps 91:1.
19. *CED* XI:39-40.
20. *CED* IX:248.

lived there. Everyone died except an infant who survived with only an injury. This Daughter of Charity was saved as though by a miracle. Still clutching the heavy pot in her hand, she found a corner of a room which did not fall, though all the rest tumbled about her. By a sort of second miracle, all sorts of debris fell around her, beams and heavy stone, bureaus, tables, and other furniture, but she remained unharmed. She left these ruins, safe and sound.[21]

The second occasion was in the house of the Daughters of Charity when suddenly a beam gave way. By the Providence of God there was no one either below or above the room where this happened, although a short while before there had been several. Mademoiselle le Gras herself, their first superior and foundress, had just left the room. This was another marvelous protection God extended to her.

At this point, Monsieur Vincent raised his voice to say:

Ah, my daughters, what reasons we have for confidence in God! We have read about a man walking in the open fields who was killed by a turtle dropped on his head by an eagle. And we saw today how a Daughter of Charity walked out of the ruins of a house, safe and sound. What do you make of this? Is this not a sign of God's affection for you as the pupil of his eye? O my daughters, if you have this holy confidence in your hearts, God will preserve you no matter where you shall be.[22]

---

21. *CED* IX:247.
22. *CED* IX:249.

CHAPTER FOUR

His Love of God

THE LOVE of God has its home in the heart, and its most noble and perfect manifestations are known only to the one who practices them, and to God who by his grace is the source. Hence, it is very true that to know fully the love of God which animated Monsieur Vincent it would be necessary for us to find this out from the Holy Spirit, who alone knows which of his divine inspirations were operative in his servant, and the cooperation he gave to them. Since we will have to wait for that until the day of judgment when God will reveal the secrets of hearts, we have to be content to speak only of those few sparks of that sacred fire that appeared outwardly in his life.

According to the testimony of the beloved disciple, an assured sign of the perfect love of God is the observance of his law and fidelity to his word.[1] Using this criterion, we can truthfully say that Monsieur Vincent loved God greatly. He was so faithful to his law and so careful to follow his holy word, that those who lived with him and observed his conduct most carefully assure us that only an angel could have been more exact in this than he. He was so watchful of himself, mortified in his passions, balanced in his judgment, circumspect in his words, prudent in his conduct, exact in his practices of piety, and finally, so perfectly united to God as best we can judge from the outside, that the full extent of his love of God becomes clear. It filled his heart and reigned over all the powers of his soul and even over his body, governing all its movements and operations according to that eternal law which is the source of all justice and holiness.

One might say that his entire life was a continuous sacrifice made to God, not only of the honors, comforts, pleasures, and other goods of the world, but also of all that he had received from the generous hands of God: his special insights, affections, liberty, and everything else put at God's disposition. The greatest joy of his heart was to ponder the incomprehensible glory which resided in the godhead, God's ineffable love for him, and the infinite perfections embodied in the unity and simplicity of his divine essence.

His most ardent and constant wish was that God would become better and better known, adored, served, obeyed, and glorified in all places and by all creatures. Indeed all that Monsieur Vincent did and said tended to no other end than to engender, to the full extent of his capabilities, this same divine

---

1. 1 John 5:3.

love in all hearts, and particularly in those of his confreres. These men admired and experienced the grace of the perfect charity that was in him, and which was felt by everyone who came into his presence. This led his confreres to listen with great esteem and devotion to everything he said. They sought to preserve even his least remarks, all the while having to admit that his words as they were spoken had a totally different effect from what was merely preserved on paper. The sentiments of his heart flowed into his words. They gave them a unique force and energy, so that they became words of grace, penetrating the hearts of those who heard him.

In this regard, a person of great virtue, now deceased, was present at a conference he gave to the women of the Confraternity of Charity of the city of Paris. She was so moved by what she heard that she remarked to some others present, "Ah, ladies, can we not say, as did the disciples at Emmaus, that our hearts burned with the love of God while Monsieur Vincent spoke to us? As for myself, while I have not been too attentive to the things of God, I must say that my heart is overflowing with the truth of what this holy man has said to us."[2]

Another woman replied: "You must not be surprised, for he is an angel of the Lord. He allows the love of God which burns in his heart to appear on his lips as burning coals."[3] Another woman who was present added, "That is true, and his only goal is to have us share in this same love of God."

Another time several prelates were in attendance at a clergy conference being given at Saint Lazare. At the end of his talk Monsieur Vincent deferred to them, as was his custom whenever a prelate was present. All those present begged him to continue, but as he had excused himself, the oldest of the prelates said: "Monsieur Vincent, you must not in your humility deprive the Company of the sentiments with which God has inspired you on this topic. There is such an unction of the Holy Spirit in your words that we all are touched, and so all of us here present ask you to share your thoughts with us. A word from your lips means more than anything we might have to say."[4]

The great love that Monsieur Vincent had for God was shown particularly in the uprightness and purity of his intentions, in which he always and solely sought the greater glory of his divine Majesty. He did everything, even that which appeared trivial, with a view of pleasing God, and of doing what he believed would be most agreeable to him. He often said that God does not pay as much attention to our external actions as he does to the love and purity of the intentions with which we act. The little things done for God are not so inclined to be motivated by vanity and pride as are others which are more

---

2. Collet, *Vie* II:112, identifies her as Madame de Lamoignon.
3. Marie Louise de Gonzague, duchess of Mantua, later queen of Poland.
4. The speaker is not identified, but Collet, *Vie* II:112-13, records several similar remarks.

important, but which too often go up in smoke. He also said that to please God in great actions we must first accustom ourselves to pleasing him in lesser ones.

One day one of his confreres was accused before the community of having done something through a desire for human respect. Moved by his love of God, Monsieur Vincent said: "It would be better to be tied hand and foot and thrown into a raging fire than to do anything merely to please others." He then began to speak on the one hand of some of the perfections of God, and on the other, of the faults, imperfections, and misery of human beings. He emphasized the folly of those who fail to work for God, and who lose the merit of all their time and trouble by having only base and human motives in view. He added these worthy and remarkable words:

> Always honor the perfections of God. Let us take as our goal the perfection most opposed to our own imperfections, as for example, his meekness and mercy opposed to our anger, his wisdom as contrasted to our blindness, his grandeur and infinite majesty so superior to our baseness and vileness, his infinite goodness so opposed to our meanness. Let us strive to do all our actions to honor and glorify the perfection most contrary to our defects.[5]

He added that this intention should be the soul of all our actions, greatly increasing their price and value. He used the familiar comparison of the clothes reserved by princes and lords for special days of celebration. These were not admired so much because of the cloth they were made of, but because of the brocade, pearls, and other precious gems that adorned them. In the same way we should not be content to do good deeds, but we should enrich them with noble and holy intentions, doing them solely to please and glorify God.

This same integrity of intention which he often had on his lips and always in his heart, were the words of our Lord Jesus Christ, as expressed in the Gospel, "seek first the kingdom of God."[6] He used to say:

> O Lord, these words urge us to allow God to reign in us, and to cooperate with him in extending and increasing the kingdom of God in the conquest of souls for him. Is it not a great honor for us to be called to help in this great and important design? Do we not become like the angels, whose sole occupation is the promotion of the kingdom of God? What possible position could be more desirable than ours, to be engaged in extending the kingdom of God? What remains for us, my brothers, but to respond worthily to such a holy and sanctifying vocation?[7]

---

5. *CED* XI:63-64.
6. Matt 6:33.
7. Abelly's version differs considerably from *CED* XII:130-31.

CHAPTER FIVE

His Conformity to the Will of God

WHEN SAINT BASIL was once asked how a person could show his love of God, he responded that it was in doing all he could, and even more than he could if we may speak this way, to accomplish continually, in all things, the holy will of God with an ardent desire for procuring his honor and glory.[1] It was with good reason that he said this, since the union accomplished by love is mainly a union of hearts and wills. A person can never make his love of God more apparent than when he perfectly conforms his own will to God's.

This is what Monsieur Vincent practiced with so much holiness. As a result, it could be said this conformity of his own will to the will of God was the moving force and the overriding virtue of this holy man, shedding its light on all his other virtues. It was the master virtue controlling all the other faculties of his soul and even of his body. It was the prime motive of his exercises of piety, of all the holy practices of religion, and of all his actions. Whenever he knelt in God's presence in his mental prayer or was attentive to his presence, he could say with Saint Paul, "Lord, what would you have me do?"[2] If he was so anxious to consult God, to listen to him, and to use such circumspection in discerning the true inspirations coming from his Spirit, in contrast to the false inspirations from the demon or the disordered movements of human nature, it was to discern the will of God with more assurance, and to dispose himself better to accomplish it. If he strongly rejected the teachings of the world to embrace those of the Gospel, if he renounced himself so perfectly to embrace the cross with such affection, and if he abandoned himself to do and suffer all for God, it was to conform himself most perfectly to the will of his divine Master. He had such high regard for this disposition of soul that he once said: "Whoever conforms himself in everything to the will of God and takes his pleasure in it leads a truly angelic life upon earth. He can even be said to be living the very life of Jesus Christ."

On another occasion he said: "Our Lord unites himself continually to those virtuous souls who remain faithfully and constantly united to his holy will, to those who choose or do not choose according to his wishes."[3] Since

---
1. PG 31.3:1223.
2. Acts 22:10.
3. *CED* I:233.

he was so filled and penetrated with this important truth, and knew from his own experience all the graces and blessings flowing from this conformity to the will of God, he sought to inspire this same sentiment in others, particularly in the members of his own Congregation. He even left them a precise regulation on the point, as follows:

> Since the holy practice of doing always and in everything the will of God is an assured means of acquiring Christian perfection, each one should do all he possibly can to familiarize himself with it. It would be helpful to consider these four steps: (1) To accomplish promptly the things we have been directed to do, and to flee from those forbidden, with the thought that this command or restriction comes to us from God, the Church, or our superiors, or even through the rules and constitutions. (2) In indifferent things, choosing those things more repugnant to human nature rather than those more pleasing, unless they happen to be necessary. They were to be chosen then, not indeed because they are pleasing to our senses, but solely because they are pleasing to God. If some indifferent things come up, being neither agreeable nor disagreeable in themselves, then we should accept either one, indifferently, as coming from the hand of divine Providence. (3) As to those unforeseen things which happen to us, such as afflictions or consolations, whether bodily or spiritual, we should receive them with an equanimity of spirit, as coming from the fatherly hand of our Lord. (4) Doing everything for the sole motive of the good pleasure of God, imitating in this as far as we can, our Lord Jesus Christ, who always acted this way, as he said himself in these words reported in the Gospel: "I always do the things which my Father has commanded me."[4]

He considered this practice as a sure remedy for all ills. When he was asked how one should correct oneself of some fault, such as impatience or some other imperfection, or how to overcome some temptation, or how to preserve peace of soul in the midst of losses and sufferings, he would say that the secret was to conform oneself to the will of God. He insisted that this holy practice should be followed courageously, and that God's holy and divine will should be sought out perseveringly. He would not allow any lessening of this attitude. He wished the will of God to be the usual concern of the soul, as if it were the air it breathed, and the happiness to which it aspired. Once, speaking to his confreres on this topic, he said:

> The perfection of love does not consist in ecstasies, but in fulfilling the will of God. Whoever would be the most perfect of all is the one who has best conformed his own will to God's in such a way that no

---

4. John 8:29; Common Rules 2,3.

distinction remains between his own will and God's. Whoever would excel on this point would be the most perfect. When our Lord wished to instruct the man spoken of in the Gospel about how best to arrive at perfection, he said: "if anyone wishes to come after me, let him renounce himself, take up his cross, and follow me."[5] Now I ask you, who renounces himself more, or who carries the cross of mortification better, or follows Jesus Christ more perfectly than he who seeks to follow the will of God rather than his own will? Scripture says somewhere that the one who adheres to God is one spirit with him.[6] Again I ask, who adheres more perfectly to God than he who does the will of this same God and not his own, who wills and does nothing but what God wills? Oh what a means for acquiring quickly in this life a great treasure of grace.[7]

On another occasion, he wrote to a priest of the Congregation, a victim of a serious accident:

What can we do? We must will what divine Providence wills, and not anything else. This thought came to me this very morning in my wretched mental prayer. I experienced a great yearning to accept all that comes, whether good or bad, whether the evil around us or personal sufferings, just as God wills, and just as he sends them to us. It seems to me that this practice is most necessary for missionaries, and is likely to produce marvelous results. We must strive to acquire this disposition of having our wills conform to God's. Among the great benefits of this, surely peace of soul will not be the least.[8]

On another occasion, reflecting on the third petition of the Lord's Prayer, *Fiat voluntas tua sicut in caelo et in terra*, ["Thy will be done on earth as it is in heaven"],[9] he said:

By these words, our Lord wished to teach us that just as the angels and the blessed in heaven accomplish the holy and adorable will of God, so too he wishes those of us still on earth to apply ourselves to this same attitude with as much love and perfection as is possible for us. He gave us the example of this himself. He came from heaven to earth just to do the will of God his Father in accomplishing the work of our redemption, and he delighted in doing what he knew to be most pleasing to God, at the time and in the way he recognized as being in conformity with his will.[10]

---

5. Matt 16:24.
6. 1 Cor 6:17.
7. *CED* XI:317.
8. *CED* VI:476.
9. Matt 6:10
10. *CED* XI:313.

SECTION ONE

Continuation of the Same Topic

Monsieur Vincent showed his appreciation of and fidelity to this holy practice in an almost unique way. He never took up any work or sought any temporal advantage for his Congregation unless he clearly recognized this was in keeping with the will of God. Even then he acted only if he was strongly urged to do so by others. He was always careful to conserve the resources divine Providence had given his Company because God so willed it, but he never went ahead to seek out such benefits. He did not bother himself with these matters or seek them out. Neither did he even seek to have recruits for his community, although it would certainly have been permissible and even praiseworthy to persuade others to enter a state in which they could better serve God, provided this was being done through a pure zeal for his glory. The practice of this holy man was to await the good pleasure of God and follow it faithfully, but never to run ahead of it. This is a rare enough virtue. He was so filled with the desire that the will of God rule his heart and rule over all those dependent upon him that he took it as a maxim to spare no expense, no trouble, not even life itself, when it was a question of accomplishing this most holy will.

He found it hard to accept that those called by God to a state or profession of holiness would sometimes decide on their own, even with good or reasonable pretexts, to move on to something else. This is what he wrote to a pastor in this quandary, who had been thinking of resigning his responsibility:

> I would counsel you not to be too hasty. What you are about to do merits serious consideration. I would be chagrined if you had taken a final step without praying to God, and consulting Monsieur Duval, or Monsieur Coqueret, or both. It is a question of knowing if God wills you to leave the wife he has given you.[11]

The superiors of the houses of his Congregation have remarked that in all his letters he recommended nothing more often than this conformity in all events to the good pleasure of God. Several of them had written to him to alert him of threatened legal proceedings, or the dangers posed by malicious persons to their goods, property, and houses. His usual response was that nothing could come about except by the designs of God. God was, after all,

---

11. Michel Alix, pastor of Saint Ouen L'Aumone; see *CED* I:190.

the master, not only of temporal possessions, but of our very lives, and so could dispose of them just as he saw fit.

When suffering from spiritual aridity or bodily infirmities, he recommended that all should live in submission to the will of God. Those in this condition should be content to remain in the state in which God was pleased to place them, and they should not even desire to be relieved unless it became clear that this would be agreeable to him. He used to say it was the noblest and most excellent practice he knew of upon earth, for both lay persons and priests alike.

When one of the leading and most useful priests of the Congregation fell sick and was in danger of death, Mademoiselle le Gras, superior of the Daughters of Charity, was very affected by the possibility of his death. Monsieur Vincent wrote to her as follows:

> You must act against what causes pain, break its spirit, or soften it, to prepare the heart for what will come. It seems that our Lord is about to take his portion of our little Company. It belongs entirely to him, I devoutly hope, to use as he wills. In my own case, my greatest wish is to hope for nothing except the accomplishment of his holy will. I cannot express how far advanced our dear sick confrere is in this holy practice. It seems our Lord wants to call him where he can continue this practice throughout all eternity. May he give us a like submission of reason and feeling to his adorable will! He shall be the source of both our reason and feeling if we serve him alone. Let us pray that you and I may always have this same desire to be in union with him, since in this way we already experience paradise in this life.[12]

On another occasion, seeing a good lady in great anxiety over what was to become of her son, he wrote:

> Give both the son and the mother to our Lord, and you will both profit. Allow him to accomplish his will in you and in him. In your spiritual exercises, strive to attend to his will without wishing anything else. This is all you need to do to give yourself wholly to God. How little it takes to become holy. The highest and almost the only means is to strive always in all things to do the will of God.[13]

This same lady took sick on one occasion. She wrote to Monsieur Vincent, asking him to reveal to her the sickness of her soul, which she felt was the cause of her bodily ailment. He responded:

> I cannot tell you any other cause of your illness except that it is in the designs of God. Adore his will without trying to understand

---

12. *CED* I:586-87; he refers to Antoine Portail.
13. The recipient is Louise de Marillac; *CED* II:36; Abelly has edited the original.

why God is pleased to have you in a state of such sufferings. It is most glorious to abandon ourselves to his guidance, without seeking to know the reason for his actions. His holy will itself is his reason, since his reason is his will. Embrace this sentiment, as Isaac accepted the will of Abraham, and as Jesus Christ did that of his Father.[14]

He himself had taken this practice of conformity to the will of God so much to heart that he rejoiced to see evidence of this sentiment among his confreres. He wrote to one of them:

God be praised that you are ready to do his holy will in everything, and to live and die wherever he calls you. This is what we find in true servants of God, in truly apostolic men, who stop at nothing. This is a mark of God's true children, ever ready to respond to the designs of such a worthy Father. I thank him for you with a great sentiment of tenderness and gratitude as I ask of his divine bounty. I am persuaded that a heart as prepared as yours is, will receive heavenly graces in abundance to accomplish much good upon earth.[15]

The will of God is known in two ways: either in those events we have no control over, those which depend solely on his good pleasure, such as sicknesses, losses, or other accidents of life, or those which his commandments or his counsels reveal to us. These tell us what things are pleasing to him, but they still leave us with full liberty to respond as we see fit. The second way we know the will of God is through the interior movements of his inspirations. Monsieur Vincent made it a personal rule to respond to either indication of God's will. First, he kept himself in a disposition of submission to God's will even in the most serious accidents that might happen, since those were ordained or at least permitted by God. His disposition and resolution was to receive and accept these events. He did so, not only with patience and submission, but with affection and joy. He remained content to see God's holy will accomplished in himself, and that all God's directives would be faithfully carried out.

In those matters where he was at liberty to act, he sought always to do what he felt was most agreeable to God. He formed his intention at the beginning of each action, saying within himself: "My God, I do this, or I leave that, because I believe it to be your holy will and agreeable to you." From time to time he renewed this sentiment, so that always and everywhere he would accept the will of God faithfully and religiously. He called this practice the "treasure of the Christian," because it embodied mortification,

---
14. *CED* I:560-61.
15. *CED* IV:446-47.

indifference, self-denial, imitation of Jesus Christ, union with God, and in general all the virtues, since they are virtues only when they are agreeable to God in conformity to his will. He is the source and rule of all perfection.

Coming to know the will of God in interior inspirations is always difficult, for it is easy to be deceived. Self-love can disguise the inclinations of human nature as movements of the Holy Spirit. Monsieur Vincent used to say that we should put a pinch of salt on these movements so as not to be fooled. He meant we have to discern carefully, not trusting our own mind or inclination. This is what he once said to his confreres on this subject:

> Among the multitude of thoughts and inclinations that incessantly arise within us, many appear to be good, but do not come from God and are not pleasing to him. How, then, should one discern these? We must look at them carefully, have recourse to God in prayer, and ask for his light. We must reflect on the motives, purposes, and means, to see if all these are in keeping with his good pleasure. We must talk over our ideas with prudent persons, and take the advice of those placed over us. These persons are the depositories of the treasures of the wisdom and grace of God. In doing what they suggest, we are carrying out the will of God.[16]

Speaking one day to his community, he made some important remarks on this matter.

> I imagine that some present here have today undertaken some actions which in themselves are good and holy, but which may have been rejected by God because they were done through the natural movement of their own will. Is this not what the prophet said, speaking for God: "I do not want your fasts which you think honor me, for they do just the opposite. When you fast, you are doing your own will, and this spoils and compromises your offering."[17] We could say the same of other works of piety, in which the addition of our own will spoils our devotions, our missions, our penances, etc. For the past twenty years, I have never read this epistle in the mass, taken from the fifty-eighth chapter of Isaiah, without being very upset. What must we do, if we are not to waste our time and our efforts? We must never act through self-motivation, inclination, humor, or imaginings, but rather accustom and habituate ourselves to fulfill the will of God in everything, never just in some things. This is the effect of grace which makes the person and his actions pleasing to God.[18]

---

16. *CED* XII:436-37.
17. Isa 1:11, and 58:3-4.
18. *CED* XII:155-56.

We shall finish this chapter by considering a devout reflection which this holy man made one day on the happiness of a Christian confirmed in this practice of conformity to the will of God.

Notice the holy dispositions in which he lives, and the blessings which accompany all he does. He is committed to God, to him alone, and God leads him in everything and by everything. He could say with the prophet: *Tenuisti manum dexteram meam, et in voluntate tua deduxisti me* ["With your counsel you guide me, and in the end you will receive me in glory"].[19] God holds him, so to speak, by his right hand, and he accepts this divine guidance with complete submission. For tomorrow, the following week, the whole year, and his entire life, you will see him living in peace and tranquility, and in an uninterrupted movement toward God. Everywhere he spreads in the souls of his neighbor the happy spirit with which he himself is filled. If you compare him with those who follow their own inclinations you will see how filled with light he is, how fruitful in his work. He makes notable progress, and all his words have strength and energy. God blesses all his undertakings and accomplishes by his grace the designs God has for him. The advice he gives to others and all his actions give great edification. On the other hand, when we look at those attached to their own inclinations and pleasure, their thoughts are worldly, their words those of slaves, and their works lifeless. All this comes from their being attached to creatures. These allow nature to influence their souls, while grace acts in those who raise their hearts to God and aspire only to accomplish his will.[20]

SECTION TWO

His Perfect Acceptance of the Will of God by an Entire Resignation and Indifference

The love of God and a perfect conformity to his will appear chiefly in afflictions and sufferings, whether physical or mental. At that point, the human heart accepts whatever comes from his divine goodness, not with patience alone, but with peace, joy, and love, because such is his will and pleasure.

---

19. Ps 73:23-24.
20. *CED* XI:46-47.

This is first seen by a resignation, in which our will moves us to place ourselves entirely into the hands of God, rising above all natural repugnances and submitting ourselves perfectly to the good pleasure of his divine Majesty.

Monsieur Vincent did this in the face of all the crosses and sufferings by which God tried his virtue. In all these unfortunate occurrences his only response was: "God be blessed. May the name of God be blessed." This refrain showed the disposition of his heart, which was always resigned to the will of God. He had such a high esteem for this virtue that he once remarked to one of his confreres, on the occasion of a most serious accident affecting the welfare of the Congregation: "An act of resignation and acceptance of the will of God is worth more than a hundred thousand temporal successes."

Speaking to his confreres on this topic on another occasion, he first explained the difference between God's putting someone into a particular state, and his merely allowing something to happen.

> The first case may be considered as the will of God, while in the second case God permits the events to unfold. We may consider a loss, a sickness, a contradiction, boredom, or dryness, all of which come directly from the will of God, as an example of the first. What happens as a result of sin or disobedience to his commands comes to us with his permission. In these circumstances we must humble ourselves and do all we can, by the grace of God, to rise from the state into which we have fallen. We should also be on our guard against further relapses. The first sort of situation comes directly from God's will. We must accept it and resign ourselves to God's good pleasure, to suffer what he sends, as much and for as long as it pleases him. This, gentlemen and my brothers, is the great lesson we learn from the Son of God. Those who learn it well are in the most advanced class in the school of the Lord. I know of nothing more holy, or nothing more perfect than this resignation, which leads to an entire emptying of self and a complete indifference to all the states into which we may be led, sin excepted. Let us strive, then, to hold to this, and pray God to give us the grace to remain always in this state of holy indifference.[21]

From this conference we can see the high degree to which he practiced this spirit of resignation and how he recommended it to others. This led him to a complete indifference which united his heart perfectly to the good pleasure of God, not so much by overcoming the movements of nature but

---

21. *CED* XI:45-46

rather by a simple and loving acceptance, doing all for the love of the will of God. He willed nothing but what God willed. In this sentiment he received with equal affection whatever came from the hand of God, whether it be sickness or health, loss or gain.

He spoke of these things to his community:

> Indifference is a state of virtue which leads us to be so detached from creatures and so united to the will of the Creator that we are almost totally freed from any desire for one thing rather than another. I said a state of virtue, not simply a virtue which occurs within that state. This state of virtue is active, leading the heart to be detached from all that would hold it captive, because otherwise it would not be a virtue. This virtue is not only excellent, but is also of singular usefulness in helping us to advance in the spiritual life. It could even be said to be necessary for all those who wish to serve God perfectly. Could we seek the kingdom of God and devote ourselves to the conversion of sinners and the salvation of souls if we were attached to our own ease and convenience? How could we accomplish the will of God if we followed the movements of our own will? How could we renounce ourselves, according to the counsel of our Lord, if we sought the esteem and applause of others? How could we be detached from all things, if we did not have the courage to leave a trinket which binds us? You see, then, how much we need this holy indifference, and how much we must give ourselves to God to acquire it, if we wish to avoid becoming slaves to our own selves, or to say it better, slaves to an animal. He who allows himself to be led and dominated by his animal nature does not deserve to be called a man, but rather an animal.
>
> Indifference shares in the nature of perfect love or, to say it better, it is an activity of that perfect love which leads the will to all that is best and destroys all that stands in the way. Fire not only warms, but also destroys all that it touches. In the same way, according to the thought of one of the saints, indifference is the origin of all the virtues and the death of all vices.
>
> The soul in a state of perfect indifference is compared by the prophet to a beast of burden. This animal is just as indifferent about carrying one thing as another, by being guided by a rich man or by a poor man, to be part of a noble establishment or to be in a wretched stable. Everything is the same to it. It is ready for whatever is asked of it. It walks, it stops; it turns to the left, or to the right; it suffers; it works night and day. Gentlemen and my brothers, how detached we must become, detached from our own judgment, our own will,

our own inclinations, from all that is not of God. We must be disposed to accept all the orders of his holy will. That is the way the saints acted.

O great Saint Peter, you said it so well, and made it so evident, when you recognized your Master on the shore of the sea at the word of the beloved disciple, *Dominus est* ["It is the Lord"].[22] At once you threw yourself into the water to go to him. You did not remain in the boat, nor hold on to your shirt, or even to your life, but looked only to the divine Savior, who was everything to you. And you, great apostle Saint Paul, by the special grace given you at the time of your conversion, you practiced this virtue of indifference so admirably when you said: *Domine, quid me vis facere*? Lord, what would you have me do?[23] This statement reflects a marvelous conversion and a detachment which could be achieved only by grace. He had in a single moment separated himself from the law he had known, from his mission, from his pretensions and his own ideas, and was raised to such a perfect state that he was ready for and indifferent to all God wished from him. If these great saints appreciated and practiced this virtue of indifference, we ought to follow their example. Missionaries are no longer their own. They belong to Jesus Christ who wishes to use them as he wills, and they are prepared to suffer following his example. "Just as the Father has sent me, so I send you," he said to his disciples, and "as they have persecuted me, so they will persecute you."[24]

After all these considerations, must we not empty our hearts of all other affections but that of Jesus Christ, and our wills of everything else but obedience? It seems to me that I see you all disposed in this way, and I trust that God will give you this grace. Yes, O my God, I myself first of all hope for this. I am in great need of this grace because of my miseries and all my attachments which I seem powerless to break and which make me say in my old age, like David, "Lord, have mercy upon me."[25] You will be edified, my brothers, if I tell you of some of our older confreres who have asked to be sent to the Indies, and among those who have asked, some are sick. Where do they get the courage? Does it not come from a free heart which desires only that God be known and adored in all places? Nothing holds them back or attracts them but his holy will. And the rest of us, brothers, though we are so numerous, if we were

---

22. John 21:7.
23. Acts 22:10.
24. John 15:20; 20:21.
25. Ps 51:1.

not held back by some unhappy attachments, each of us could say in his heart, "My God, I give myself to you to be sent to any place on the earth where my superiors judge I could best proclaim your holy name. When it is time for me to die, I shall be ready, knowing that my salvation is in obedience, and obedience is your holy will." Those who have not yet accepted these sentiments ought to examine closely those things which restrain them. In this way, by a continuous interior and exterior mortification, they may, with the grace of God, come to the freedom of the children of God, which is found in holy indifference.[26]

Monsieur Vincent did not limit his exhortations to his confreres in general, but spoke personally to each one on this subject as circumstances dictated. Writing to one of them, he said:

You are aware that the Gospel says that the workers called at the later hour received the same pay as those who had worked the whole day. In the same way, you shall merit as much by awaiting in patience the will of the Master as if you were working, since you are ready to stay or to leave, all the while awaiting his will. God be praised for this holy indifference. It makes you a fit instrument for the works of God.[27]

He wrote to another:

I thank God greatly for the dispositions he has inspired in you to be willing to go into the foreign mission if you are sent, or not to go if you are asked to stay. Holy indifference in all things is a mark of the perfect. Yours gives me hope that God shall be glorified in you and by you, as I pray with all my heart will happen. I ask you, Monsieur, to beg God for the grace that we both might abandon ourselves entirely to his adorable direction. We must serve him as he wishes, and renounce our own wills, either about where we work or what we do. It is enough if we are totally given to God as his beloved children, being honored to bear the name of servants of the Gospel, by which our Lord wants to be known and served. What difference does it make how or where, as long as we act in this way? Assuredly this will come about if we allow him to act in us.[28]

He said to another confrere:

Oh, Monsieur, what a beautiful attribute holy indifference is for a Missionary. It makes him so pleasing to God, and brings the Lord to prefer him to all other workers in whom he does not find this

---

26. *CED* XII:227-44. Abelly's version differs from that of Coste.
27. *CED* V:525.
28. *CED* V:593-94.

indifference to accomplish his designs. If we finally arrive at this state of being deprived of all self-will, we would then be ready to accomplish the will of God, that holy will which the angels adore and in which human beings find all their happiness.[29]

This true servant of God was not satisfied to exhort others to practice this virtue, but practiced it himself most perfectly. It appeared on all occasions that his heart was so detached from all that was not of God and so firmly attached to his holy will, that everyone could recognize he had attained the highest degree of this heroic virtue. We will give here two examples, sketches which will enable the reader to judge his holy dispositions in this regard.

The first example is his indifference to all that affected him in his sicknesses, especially in the illness which led to his death. He approached his end well aware of his condition. He even stated that he knew he was slowly dying, but he was in such a state of perfect indifference that whether he lived or died, suffered or was cured, it was all the same to him. Neither in health nor in sickness was any of this apparent. He never said a single word to the contrary. He was even indifferent to the medicines and remedies given him. Although he mentioned those remedies which seemed to worsen his condition, he took whatever the physicians decided would be best for him. He seemed as unperturbed by the bad effects of some of the prescribed remedies as by the good effects of others which were more successful. He was seemingly content to accept whatever came about, provided only that God's good pleasure be accomplished, the only object of his desires and joy.

The second example is his indifference regarding the affairs of his Congregation, especially since the preservation of this holy work was more dear to him than his own life. He regarded the accomplishment of the will of God as incomparably superior even to this, so that he looked upon the continued existence and growth of the Congregation as desirable only in so far as God willed it so. He took no step, nor did he say a single word in its favor, except in agreement with the manifestation of the divine will.

Someone once wrote him that he could never expect his Congregation to flourish unless there was a constant supply of worthy candidates, and that this could be assured only by having the Congregation established in the larger cities. He replied in these words:

> We may not take any steps to establish ourselves anywhere if we are to remain faithful to the ways of God and to the traditions of the Congregation. Up to the present, Providence has directed us to the places where we are, with no activity on our part, directly or indirectly, to choose a place for ourselves. This resignation to God which keeps us in dependence on his direction is most agreeable to

---

29. *CED* IV:340.

him, especially because it is so contrary to mere human prudence. Under the pretext of zeal and the glory of God, those human sentiments often undertake projects God does not inspire and which he will not bless. He is aware of what is suitable for us, and will provide it in good time, if as true children we abandon ourselves to our dear Father. Certainly, if we are convinced of our own unworthiness, we will hesitate about intruding upon the harvest of others before we have been invited to do so. We should be careful not to push ourselves ahead of other workers to whom God has reserved this field of activity.[30]

Once a matter which promised to favor the Congregation was proposed to him, and one of his priests urged him to agree. He gave this response:

> I think we should allow this matter to simmer for the time being. This will allow the inclinations of human nature to lessen, even at the expense of the possible advantages of a prompt decision. It will help us develop holy indifference, and allow our Lord to manifest his will while we offer our prayers for this intention. We can be sure that, if he wishes it, it shall come about. A delay will not prevent this, and the less there is of ourselves in this, the more will he make it his own.[31]

He tenderly and cordially loved all the members of the Congregation, especially those who were working diligently and successfully in the vineyard of the Lord. When death came to any one of them he felt the loss deeply. Still, he practiced an admirable indifference on these occasions. He did not ask God to preserve their lives except when it was in keeping with his will and for his greater glory. This was evident on an occasion when several members of the Congregation were stricken with the plague. Among them was one who was most dear to him because of his great service to the Church, which he did even to the extent of endangering his own life. He recommended all the sick to the prayers of the community. Speaking of this particular confrere, he said:

> We pray that God will deign to preserve his life, but we submit entirely to his divine will. We must believe, for it is true, that his sickness and that of the others, and all else that happens to our Company, is done under God's direction and for the greater prosperity of our Congregation. This is why, in praying God to restore good health to our sick confreres, or to come to our help in any other way, it is always on the condition that it be in keeping with his good pleasure and for his greater glory.[32]

---

30. *CED* VI:308.
31. *CED* V:534.
32. *CED* XI:47-48. The confrere is not identified.

Another time, speaking of the death of a person who had greatly loved the community, he said:

> I have no doubt you have been much affected by the death of this person who was so dear to us. But God be praised, you have told me that God has done well to take him from us, and you would not have it otherwise, since this has evidently been his holy will.[33]

This almost perfect indifference shone forth most brilliantly on the occasion when the plague in Genoa, in 1654, took five or six of the best workers of the Company. This is how he announced this loss to the community. After exhorting them to confide in God, whatever the situation, he spoke of the sad news.

> How true it is, gentlemen, that we should have a great confidence in God and place ourselves entirely in his hands. We believe that his Providence arranges everything for our greater good no matter what should come about through his will or permission! Yes, what God gives us or what he takes from us is for our benefit, since it is according to his will, and his good pleasure is our hope and our happiness. In this spirit I must tell you of an affliction that has come to us. I must say in all honesty that it is one of the greatest tragedies that could happen. We have lost the main support of our house in Genoa. Monsieur N., [Etienne Blatiron] our superior there, and such a great servant of God, is dead. And this is not all. Good Monsieur N., [Nicolas Duport] who served the plague-stricken with such joy, who had such love for his neighbor, and such zeal and fervor for helping in the salvation of souls, has fallen victim to the plague. One of our Italian priests, [Domenico Boccone] a most virtuous and good missionary, has also died. Monsieur N., [Antoine Tratebas] a true servant of God, a good missionary and a man of all the virtues, is also dead. And Monsieur N., [Francois Vincent] whom you well know to be the equal in all this to the others, is also dead. Monsieur N., [Jean (Mc)Ennery] a wise, pious, and exemplary man, is dead. Gentlemen and my brothers, the contagious disease has taken all these men. God has called them to himself.
>
> O Savior Jesus, what a loss and what an affliction! It is now that we must resign ourselves in everything to the will of God. Otherwise what else could we do but lament and grieve uselessly for the loss of these most zealous proponents of the glory of God. Instead, in resignation, after allowing our tears, we must raise our hearts and minds to God, praise him, and bless him for these losses, since they come as expressions of his most holy will. Can we say, gentlemen

---

33. *CED* XI:100. Person not identified.

and my brothers, that we have lost those whom God has called? No, they have not been lost, and we must believe the ashes of these good missionaries will be the seed of others. We must hold it as certain that God will never take back the graces he has given them. He will give these same graces to those with the zeal to go to take their place.[34]

---

34. *CED* XI:428-32; Abelly's text differs considerably from Coste's, who gives both for comparison. In addition, the event took place in 1657, not in 1654, Abelly's date. The total number of confreres lost was six.

CHAPTER SIX

His Constant Attention to the Presence of God

THE GRANDEUR and perfection of Monsieur Vincent's love for God was seen not only in his perfect submission to all that he commanded, but also in the close attention he gave to the presence of his divine majesty. It is a characteristic of love to desire and to seek out the presence of the beloved, and to take pleasure in his company, in being in his sight, and speaking with him. Monsieur Vincent's dedication to God was such (as we learn from a very virtuous priest who knew him well and observed him during many years) that it is easy to see that his spirit was continually attentive to the presence of God. He was never seen to be distracted by the press of business or the duties he was obliged to attend to, but he was always recollected and self-possessed. It was remarked that he ordinarily would not respond at once when asked something, especially if it were a matter of some importance. He would instead pause briefly to raise his mind to God to ask his light and grace, so as to do everything in keeping with his will and for his greater glory.

This same priest has recalled that he had sometimes seen Monsieur Vincent contemplating a crucifix held in his hands for hours on end. On other occasions when news of some disaster was brought to him, or the happier news of some unexpected event, a serene expression appeared on his face, the sole indication of his continued absorption in the presence of God. In this connection, he used to say: "one cannot hope for much from someone who does not continually converse with God. Further, if someone does not serve the Lord as they should, it is because they are not attached enough to God, and have not asked for his grace with perfect confidence."

When he had to go to the city, he did so with great recollection, walking in the presence of God, praising him, and praying to him silently in his heart. In his later years when he had to use the carriage, he always took a companion with him. Not only did he remain interiorly recollected, with his eyes closed, but usually he pulled the curtains, so he could not see out or be seen, so as to be undisturbed in his recollection of God.

He had the pious custom of uncovering his head and making the sign of the cross whenever he heard the sound of the clock marking the hours and the quarter hours. He did this whether alone or in the company of others, in the house or in the city. He used to say this practice was helpful in renewing the recollection of the presence of God, and in reminding oneself of the resolutions taken during morning mental prayer. He introduced this practice into his Company, which has continued it to this day in places where they can do so.

Since he knew from his own experience the graces and benefits of interior recollection, and of this attention to the presence of God, he urged this practice upon others as much as he could. He put up, in various places in the cloister of Saint Lazare, signs written in large letters, GOD SEES ALL, so that the missionaries and others visiting might be reminded of his holy presence. He appreciated this practice so much that he used to say, "If a person could be found who truly understood this practice, and who was faithful in following it, he would soon reach a high degree of sanctity."

He was alert to allow the things of nature to raise his mind to God. He did not stop at considering external beauty or the particular beauty of the created object. Rather, he immediately raised his mind to the consideration of the perfection of its Creator. When he saw the fields covered with grain, or trees loaded with fruit, he immediately thought of the inexhaustible riches of God, or he praised him for his goodness in supplying by his Providence the food needed by his creatures. When he saw flowers, or any other beautiful object, he took the opportunity to contemplate the perfections and beauty of God. He would say in his heart these words later found in his own handwriting: "What then compares to the beauty of God, the source of all beauty and of the perfection of his creatures? Do not the flowers, the birds, the stars, the moon, and the sun borrow their attraction and their beauty from him?"[1]

He once told his community that he had visited a sick woman suffering from a constant headache. She endured this with such great patience that he seemed to see on her face a certain grace which revealed that God was present in her sufferings. He was so moved by the sight he could not help exclaiming: "Oh, the happy state of those who suffer for the love of God! How agreeable this is in his sight, since his own Son crowned the heroic actions of his holy life with terrible sufferings which brought him to death."[2]

He added on this occasion that just a few days before he had chanced to be in a room lined with mirrors, so much so that even a fly could not escape notice, no matter where it might go. This led him to think: "If men have found a way to see everything that happens, even to the smallest movement of a tiny insect, how much more must we believe that we are always in the sight of the divine mirror of God's all-seeing vision, especially the good works of his faithful, such as their patience, humility, conformity to the will of God, and all the other virtues."[3]

---

1. *CED* XIII:143.
2. *CED* XI:409.
3. *CED* XI:409.

We shall finish this chapter with these remarks which he made in speaking to his community.

The thought of the presence of God helps us in the practice of fulfilling his holy will. The memory of the divine presence grows in the mind, little by little, and by his grace becomes habitual with us. We become, as it were, enlivened by this divine presence. My brothers, how many persons there are, even in the world, who almost never lose their sense of God's presence? I, myself, a few days ago met a person who was aware of having been distracted only three times during the day. These people will be our judges. They will condemn us before the judgment seat of God's divine majesty for our forgetfulness, since we have no other duty but to love him and to show this love by our attention and our service of him. Let us pray that our Lord will give us the grace to say, like him, *Cibus meus est, ut faciam voluntatem ejus qui misit me*, my food and my life is to do the will of God.[4] Let us beseech him to give us always a hunger and thirst for his justice.[5]

---

4. John 4:34.
5. *CED* XII:163-64.

CHAPTER SEVEN

His Mental Prayer

MEDITATION IS like a precious manna which God gives to his faithful to preserve and perfect the life of their souls. It is like a heavenly dew, causing all the virtues to grow in their hearts. We are not surprised to learn that Monsieur Vincent had such a great esteem for this exercise, and a great desire to give himself to it and to encourage others in its practice.

First, every morning he never failed to devote an hour to his mental prayer, whatever other business he might have to do, or wherever he was. He preferred this practice to all other good works, unless the others were required or were absolutely necessary. He used this time to consecrate the first moments of the day to God, and to dispose himself to use the rest of the day well. He made this prayer in the church together with all his community. Sometimes he was unsuccessful in hiding the gifts of the Holy Spirit in his prayer, with sighs that revealed the ardor of his love of God, enough to move even the most tepid souls to devotion.

He prescribed this holy exercise for his Congregation, and wished that everyone would make his mental prayer each day. He said that even the sick could do so if they used the method he taught. In this prayer more attention was to be given to the affections of the will than to the understanding of the intellect, all done peacefully in the presence of God. Repeated acts of resignation, conformity to the divine will, contrition for sin, patience, confidence in the divine goodness, thanksgiving for God's benefits, the love of God, and similar sentiments were all to be elicited in this prayer.

Besides this scheduled morning mental prayer, he made others during the day and in the evening, depending on the time allowed by his other duties. He first felt obliged to carry out the responsibilities of his position and to serve his neighbor. He looked upon himself as a man for others, not free to use his time and person otherwise than in the fulfillment of the duties of the state to which God had called him.

After his dedication to his own salvation, he gave himself to the service of the Church and the salvation of souls. He recognized, however, that he could not succeed in this service of others or in any of his other work, except by the grace of God received in his mental prayer. When he had even a brief respite in work, or some interruption in sleep, he turned to his practice of mental prayer. He had a special devotion of praying in the presence of the blessed sacrament, where he was in such a devout posture and where he seemed so recollected that he edified all who saw him.

The masters of the spiritual life usually distinguish between two types of meditation (we are speaking here of prayer made privately and solely by use of the mind): the one, called the ordinary form of prayer, which anyone may practice, consists of considerations, affections, and resolutions. The second type of prayer is more subtle, more intimate, and more sublime. To this prayer God calls those he wills and when he wills.

This form of prayer depends on the action of the Holy Spirit rather than on the industry or efforts of the human person. We have not been able to discover exactly what form of prayer Monsieur Vincent used, whether the ordinary or the extraordinary form. His humility always hid as much as it could the gifts he had received from God. What we cannot safely say in any detail, however, we can say in general. His prayer must have been quite perfect, as we can infer from the excellent dispositions he brought to prayer and the fruits he drew from it. These are the two marks by which we may judge the quality and the perfection of his mental prayer. He respected the opinions of some modern authors on the excellence of the extraordinary way of praying treated in their books, and he spoke of the admirable influence of God in inexplicable ways upon certain elite souls. Nevertheless, he held to the maxim of the apostle not to believe too easily every spirit, but rather to test them, to see if they are from God.[1] He understood well that Satan often appears as an angel of light, deceiving many by his specious and evil suggestions.

His long experience in directing souls led him sometimes to say to his close friends that there were methods of prayer which appear elevated and quite perfect, but which in reality are mere illusions. For this reason he ordinarily advised that the more humble way should be followed. The lower was to remain the safest until God directed the soul to another method, which God would then illumine by his own light to allow the soul, as Scripture says, to arrive at a perfect day.[2] He felt that God should make this decision. It was a sign of great temerity, and a sort of presumption and even illusion, to decide for oneself to depart from the ordinary method of prayer to walk the unfamiliar path under the pretext of arriving at a higher level of perfection. Perfection, of course, does not consist in the method of praying a person follows, but in charity. Thus perfection may be greater and more fervent in a soul praying according to the ordinary method, than in another who flatters himself that he is following a more lofty method of prayer, but who neglects to work at the correction of his own vices and the acquisition of the virtues

---

1. 1 John 4:1.
2. Prov 4:18.

necessary for him. He may even spend his entire life living with some notable imperfections.

He preferred to judge the quality and goodness of mental prayer by the dispositions brought to it, and by the fruits it produced. He used to say: "the best virtues are humility, the recognition of one's nothingness before God, the mortification of the passions and the unregulated movements of nature, interior recollection, uprightness and simplicity of heart, attention to the presence of God, entire dependence upon his will, and frequent reminders to oneself of God's goodness."

As much as he recommended these holy dispositions to others, he himself put them into practice, preparing his soul to receive in prayer the lights and grace which God was ready to pour out upon him. The primary and most excellent fruits of his mental prayer are unknown to us, for he drew a veil of silence over them all. We would have to be resigned to this lack of knowledge were it not that he sometimes appeared like another Moses, if not totally radiant. He at least had the same fervor and love as Moses when he came from his encounter with the divine majesty. It would be easy to judge from the words that came from the abundance of his heart as he left this holy exercise, what must have been the effects of his prayer. Besides that, we can truly say that the virtues he practiced throughout his life, his humility, patience, mortification, charity, and in general all he did for the glory and service of God, were fruits of his prayer.

Since he knew from his own experience how profitable and salutary the holy exercise of mental prayer was to help in advancing in the spiritual life, and of perfecting oneself in all the virtues, he was very concerned to extend this appreciation to others. He recommended this exercise, and had others recommend it during the ordination retreats, to those who were about to receive the sacrament of holy orders. He believed the candidates would never succeed if they were not men of prayer. He did the same for those who came to Saint Lazare to make their retreat, since he saw that one of the main fruits they could take away with them was to have been well instructed in how to make mental prayer, and having the firm resolution of being faithful to it all their life. He showed this same enthusiasm in his clergy conferences, and with the Ladies of Charity in their meetings, not to mention his own Congregation.

He wanted his Missionaries to be men of prayer, as much for their personal advancement as for the ability to be of real service to others. He was most anxious that his confreres should progress in their practice of this holy exercise.

> Give me a man of prayer, and he will be able to do everything.
> He will be able to say with the apostle that he can do all in him who

strengthens him and who gives him support.[3] The Congregation of the Mission will continue in existence only as long as mental prayer shall be practiced. Mental prayer is the impregnable rampart which will protect the Missionaries from all sorts of attacks. It is like a mystical arsenal, a tower of David, which will be the source of their arms, not only to defend themselves, but to attack and rout all the opponents of the glory of God and the salvation of souls.[4]

He was not satisfied just to recommend this holy exercise to his confreres but he took the trouble to train them himself, despite the press of so much other business with which he was preoccupied. He arranged for them, from time to time, usually twice a week, to "repeat" their mental prayer before the assembled community, that is to share the lights and sentiments they had experienced in mental prayer. On each occasion he would call upon three or four confreres to speak for the mutual edification of all, as well as to give the newcomers not yet adept at this exercise a model of how to practice it.

He was deeply moved by these repetitions of mental prayer. He never failed to attend them and often spent many hours in this exercise. Whenever he was on a trip in the company of some lay people, he would persuade them to spend a little time in mental prayer, and then share the good thoughts and sentiments they had received during the prayer. This closed the door to useless conversations, and opened it to pious conversations in which the fruits of the meditation were shared among all the travelers. A woman of great virtue learned this practice from Monsieur Vincent, and later put it into use with her own domestic servants. She recounted once how a manservant, reporting on his prayer, told how he thought about our Lord's love for the poor. He felt that he ought to do something for them, but not having anything to give them, he felt he could at least show them greater consideration. He resolved to speak more graciously when he had the opportunity to meet any of them, and even doff his hat to them. Monsieur Vincent sometimes used this example to show that persons of all ranks could learn to meditate, and that those who were faithful to this prayer became better at it. Also, in this holy exercise God inspired virtuous actions which were often unheeded at other times.

He particularly recommended the practice of mental prayer to those obliged to preach to others, to catechize, or to give spiritual direction to souls. This is how he expressed himself, in writing to one of his priests:

> Mental prayer is the great book for the preacher. In this prayer you will descend into the depths of the divine truths of which the Eternal Word is the source, to give them to the people. It is greatly

---

3. Phil 4:13.
4. *CED* XI:83-84.

desirable that the Missionaries deeply love this holy exercise of mental prayer. Without it, they will produce little or no fruit. By prayer they will make themselves fit to touch hearts and convert souls. I pray that our Lord confirm you in the practice of this virtue.[5]

Above all, he counseled the prayer of affection and of practical application. This form of prayer results in forming good resolutions based on simple considerations, but does not stop at these, except by a positive influence of the Holy Spirit directing the soul to rest there. To convey the difference between the application of the mind made in mental prayer and the movements of grace received in it, he used the comparison of a ship powered either by oars or by sail. He said the oars were not used except when the wind failed. When the wind was favorable, the ship moved more easily and more quickly. In the same way, considerations of the mind were to be used when there was no obvious inspiration of the Holy Spirit. When this heavenly wind did blow, the proper course was to abandon oneself to its direction.

On another occasion he compared the subjects of meditation to different kinds of shops: in some, only a single kind of merchandise was on display, while others carried many different sorts of goods. In some subjects of meditation, only a single virtue is stressed while others refer to a whole treasury of virtues. An example of this would be the mysteries of the nativity, and the life, death and resurrection of our Lord Jesus Christ. To profit from these subjects, our Lord should be adored in the state in which the mystery presents him. He should be admired, praised, and thanked for the graces he merited for us, at the same time that we also present to him our misery and our needs, asking the help and grace we need to imitate and practice the virtue he has taught us.

He encouraged those who endured a dryness or sterility in their mental prayer to persevere, in imitation of our Lord who *factus in agonia, prolixius orabat*, in his anguish prayed with all the greater intensity.[6] He said we must look upon mental prayer as a gift from God, and urgently ask the grace to make it well, saying with the apostles, *Domine, doce nos orare*: Lord, teach us how we ought to pray to you.[7] We should await this grace from his goodness with humility and patience.

Once, speaking to his community on prayer, he said:

> Prayer is a sermon we preach to ourselves, to convince ourselves of the need we have to turn to God, to cooperate with his grace, to root out vices from our souls, and to replace them with virtues. In mental prayer we must particularly apply ourselves to combating

---

5. *CED* VII:156.
6. Luke 22:43.
7. Luke 11:1.

the passion or evil inclination to which we are especially addicted, and we must mortify this tendency, for when we do, the rest is easy. We must fight forcefully, but act calmly, not breaking our head in trying to force anything or to be too subtle. Though we have to lift our minds to God, we must above all listen to him speaking to us, for one single word from him is better than a thousand reasons and all the speculations of our minds. We must from time to time raise our hearts to God, conscious of our nothingness, awaiting his speaking to our heart, uttering a word which leads to eternal life. It is only what God inspires, what comes from him, that is useful for us. What we receive from God we must give to our neighbor after the example of Jesus Christ who, speaking of himself, said: "I say only what the Father has taught me."[8]

He had the custom of never failing to make an annual retreat of at least eight days, no matter what pressing business or duties he had. During this time he put the affairs of the house into other hands, so as to give himself completely to mental prayer and recollection. He did so in imitation of our Savior who went into the desert as an example to those who were later to preach the Gospel.

Once, when he asked for prayers from his confreres for some priests making their retreat, he spoke of these spiritual exercises. Although he did not speak of himself on this occasion, we can infer the esteem he had for these practices:

Let us pray to God for those who have begun their retreat, so that he may be pleased to renew them interiorly, making them die to their own selves, to be filled with his Holy Spirit. Yes, a retreat well made is a total renewal. The one who makes it well should be entirely renewed. He no longer remains what he was, but becomes a new man. Let us pray that God will give us this new spirit of revitalization, so that by his grace we may put off the old Adam to be clothed with the new, Jesus Christ, and so that in all things we might accomplish his most holy will.[9]

---

8. John 8:28. *CED* XI:84.
9. *CED* XI:94-95.

SECTION ONE

A Collection of Some Counsels and Instructions of Monsieur Vincent on the Topic of Mental Prayer

Holy Scripture, speaking of the prophet Samuel, says that not a single one of his words went unheeded.[10] We might say the same, in some sense, of the words of Monsieur Vincent. They were all animated by the Son of God and blessed by his grace, affecting all who heard them. They were heard by the ear but penetrated to the heart. For this reason we have felt the Catholic reader would be consoled and edified if we would insert here some of the counsels and instructions he gave at various times to his community on the subject of prayer. These were carefully recorded by some among them. Although the servant of God spoke extemporaneously as the occasion demanded, the simplicity with which he spoke like a father speaking to his children gave his words a particular effect, leading well-disposed souls to draw great profit from them.

Those who make their mental prayer well are recognized not only by the way they speak of it, but even better by their actions by which they show the fruit they have gathered from their prayer. We can also say the same thing about those who act unsatisfactorily, because it is easy to see that the first is making great progress, while the latter slips back. To derive profit from mental prayer you must prepare for it. Those who neglect this preparation or who come to prayer simply by habit and because the others are there are greatly mistaken. As the sage says, *Ante orationem praepara animam tuam* ["before going to prayer, prepare your soul"].[11] Mental prayer is a raising of the mind to God to present our needs to him and to implore his mercy and grace. It is only reasonable, before appearing before his sublime majesty, that you should prepare yourself. We must think to ourselves, What am I about to do? Before whom am I to appear? What do I wish to say to him? What grace am I going to ask for? Through laziness or lack of energy we may neglect to think of these things, or, on the contrary we may possibly be overly worried about other matters and so fail in our preparation. We should remedy this fault. We must also control our imagination, so

---
10. 1 Sam 3:19.
11. Sir 18:23.

prone to wander, and focus it on the presence of God, without straining to do this, however, for excess in this is not good.

Mental prayer has three parts, and everyone knows their order and method. We should follow this method. The subject may be an object of our senses or an abstraction. If it is sensible, such as a mystery of the faith, we should represent it to ourselves, paying attention to all its parts and circumstances. If it should concern an abstract subject, such as a virtue, we should think of what the virtue consists in, its properties, marks, effects, the acts which compose it, and the means of putting it into practice. It would be good to consider the reason for practicing this virtue, and pay the most attention to those motives which most appeal to us. We should think of passages of holy Scripture or the fathers which bear upon the subject. It is good to reflect upon these, but we should not seek to recall too many of these passages, for what good would it do to amass many passages and reasons, unless it were to enlighten the mind or to clarify our thought, but then this would become more a study than a prayer.

When you want to start a fire, you use a flint, and as soon as the tinder catches fire you light a candle. You would be foolish to continue striking the flint after the candle is lit. So too, when the soul is enlightened by these considerations, why seek others, and continue to strike our minds again and again for other reasons or other thoughts? Do you not see that it is a waste of time to do this? You should strive to move the will and to excite the affections by the beauty of the virtue to be acquired or the hatefulness of the opposite vice. This is not too hard to do, for the will seeks the light of understanding, and naturally turns to what it sees as good and desirable.

This is still not enough. We have to go beyond good sentiments to make good resolutions to work at acquiring the virtue, to put it into practice, and to do acts proper to it. This is the important point and it is the fruit to be gathered from prayer. We should not take our resolutions lightly, but rather repeat them to ourselves and fix them solidly in our heart. It is good to foresee the obstacles that may arise to stand in our way, and the means that would be helpful for putting them into execution. We should determine to avoid the one and be determined to practice the other.

In this regard it is not necessary and often not expedient to have lofty sentiments about the virtue we are seeking, or even the desire to have these sentiments. This desire to feel the virtues, which are purely spiritual qualities, can sometimes harm and pain the mind. Excessive efforts only upset the brain and cause headaches. In the same way, acts of the will that are repeated too often or too forcefully dry up and weaken the heart. We should be moderate in all things, and excess is to be avoided in all things but especially in mental prayer. We must act in gentle moderation, always preserving peace of mind and heart.[12]

Another time he explained the difference between thoughts that arise spontaneously and those inspired by God.

Notice the difference between the light of a fire and that which comes from the sun. During the night when a fire glows, we see objects by its light, yet we see them only imperfectly because this light is limited. The sun, on the other hand, lights the entire world, giving life to everything. It allows us to see beyond that which is merely exterior, to penetrate into the interior, and it makes all things fruitful and fertile according to their proper nature. The thoughts and considerations which come from our own reflections are feeble lights, showing us only the outside of things, and nothing else. The lights of grace which the Sun of Justice shines into our souls penetrate to the innermost depths of our heart, bringing forth marvelous fruits. We must then ask God to enlighten us himself, and to inspire in us what pleases him. All these lofty and studied considerations are in no way to be called mental prayer. We must act in moderation and gently, always preserving peace of mind and heart.

Those who stop and delight themselves in these lofty considerations are like the preacher who prides himself on his beautiful sermons. He delights in seeing the audience so taken up with what he says. Evidently the Holy Spirit is not at all present here, but instead it is the spirit of pride which enlightens his understanding and produces all these fine thoughts. To say it more accurately, in this case the demon himself inspires him and makes him speak as he does. It is much the same with mental prayer when we seek those fine considerations or those extraordinary thoughts, especially when they are sought only for the sake of impressing others when they make a repetition of their meditation. This is a sort of blasphemy, an idolatry of the mind, for when meeting God in mental prayer you are seeking only what will cater to your pride. You take up this holy time of prayer to seek your own satisfaction, and in taking pleasure in your own thoughts, you offer sacrifice to the idol of your own vanity.

---
12. *CED* XI:403-07.

Alas, my brothers, be on guard against such foolishness. We must recognize that we are all filled with misery. We must seek only what will further humble ourselves and bring us to the solid practice of virtue. We must abase ourselves in mental prayer to the point of nothingness, and in making a repetition on our prayer we must speak our thoughts most humbly. If some thoughts should come to us which seem good, we should be most cautious in accepting them lest the spirit of pride be their source, or even the demon inspire them. This is why we must always humble ourselves profoundly when good thoughts come to us in our mental prayer, in our preaching, or in our conversation with others.

Alas, the Son of God could have overwhelmed everyone by his divine eloquence, but he did not choose to do so. Instead, when teaching the truths of the Gospel he always used common words and expressions, ones that were familiar to his hearers. He preferred to be reviled and despised rather than be praised and esteemed. You see, my brothers, how we must imitate him and control the proud thoughts that come to us in mental prayer and elsewhere. We must follow humbly in the footsteps of Jesus Christ, using simple and understandable words. When God allows it, be at peace when what you say is not accepted or you are rejected or mocked. You must be convinced that without a true and sincere humility you will benefit neither yourself nor others.[13]

A member of the community gave a repetition on his mental prayer for the day. He said that he doubted that he should make any more resolutions because he was unfaithful in putting them into practice. Monsieur Vincent took the floor and said:

We must not neglect making resolutions in our mental prayer just because we have been negligent in carrying out previous ones we have taken. It is similar to eating, for we should not stop doing this even if it seems that we are not drawing any benefit from it. Making resolutions is one of the most important parts of our mental prayer, and perhaps even the most important. We must give our attention to making resolutions, and not to the reasoning or thoughts we might have. The main fruit of prayer consists of personal resolutions strongly and firmly made. They should be resolutions which you are convinced of and which you prepare to execute, taking into account the obstacles to be overcome. And yet, even this is not all we have to do.

Our resolutions are by their nature both physical and moral

---

13. *CED* XI:85-87.

actions. They have to be properly arrived at and fully accepted within our hearts, but we must also recognize that no matter how good they may be, their practice and their results depend absolutely upon God. What do you think is the most common reason why our resolutions fail? Is it not because we rely too much upon ourselves, upon our own good aspirations, and upon our own strength? This is why they produce such little fruit. This is why, after we make our resolutions, we should greatly distrust ourselves and turning to God, invoke his grace, so he may be pleased to shower his gifts upon us and bless our resolutions. Even then if we should fall short once or twice, or even fail to keep our resolutions repeatedly, still we must again renew our resolve by having recourse to his mercy and imploring the help of his grace. Our past faults should humble us, but not to the extent of making us lose courage. No matter what fault we fall into, we must not lose confidence that God wishes us to come to him. We must resolve anew with the help of his grace not to fall again, something we must earnestly ask of him. Physicians who see no result from the medicines they dispense to the sick do not stop administering them as long as there is still some hope. If these remedies for the body are continued until there is some sign of improvement, no matter how long or how extreme the illness, should we not do the same for sicknesses of our souls, since, when it pleases God to act, grace can produce such great marvels in them?[14]

In another conference, he spoke about a brother of the Company who stated that he followed a set way of making his mental prayer by dividing the subject into several parts. Monsieur Vincent said:

Brother, you did well to divide your mental prayer as you did, but when a mystery of religion is the subject of meditation, it is not necessary or expedient to stop at the consideration of a single virtue, and then to make your customary division based on this virtue. It would be better to look at the mystery as a whole, paying attention to all the circumstances, no matter how trivial they may be, for there are hidden treasures there if you know how to look for them.

I recall a recent meeting of some priests who had taken as the subject of their conversations the way to use Lent well. This is a common topic, spoken of every year, and yet such good things were said that all those present were touched, I especially. I can truly say that I have never seen a more devout conference than that one, nor one that made a greater impression upon those present. Although

---
14. *CED* XI:87-88.

several spoke on the same topic more than once, it seemed they were no longer the same people who were speaking, for God had inspired them in their mental prayer with a wholly new way of speaking. See, my brothers, how God hides such treasures of the truths and mysteries of our religion in the most ordinary things and in everyday circumstances. These grains of mustard seed become great trees when it pleases God to give them his blessing.[15]

On another occasion he spoke on the same topic.

Some have good thoughts and sentiments, but do not apply them to themselves and do not reflect enough upon their own interior state. This happens even though they have often heard the recommendation that when God gives a person a light or grace or a good thought in one's mental prayer, it should immediately be put to good use by applying it to one's own particular state in life. One's own faults must be considered, confessed, and acknowledged before God and even before the entire community as an aid to humility and self-denial, and as an incentive to the resolution of correcting oneself. There is always some benefit in doing this. Sometimes, during the repetition of mental prayer, I ask myself why this particular person or that one progresses so little in the holy exercise of meditation. I fear the cause of this is that they are not dedicated enough to mortification and they give too much freedom to their senses.

When the most noted writers on the spiritual life write about the practice of mental prayer, they unanimously declare that the practice of mortification is absolutely necessary to progress in mental prayer. For a person to be well disposed for such prayer, one must not only mortify the eyes, tongue, ears, and the other external senses, but also the faculties of the soul: the understanding, memory, and will. Mortification is the way to prepare for mental prayer, and reciprocally, mental prayer helps the person practice mortification.[16]

One of the brothers of the Company once threw himself upon his knees before the others to ask pardon for the fault of not having made his mental prayer for some time. He found it painful even to attempt it. Monsieur Vincent said to him:

Brother, God sometimes allows us to lose the taste and attraction for mental prayer, and even allows us to find it distasteful. This is usually a test that he sends, a trial for us, but it should not discourage

---
15. *CED* XI:89-90.
16. *CED* XI:90-91.

or dishearten us. Many good people have been tried in this way, even some of the saints. Yes, I know several pious persons who have felt this dryness and distaste for mental prayer. Yet they were faithful to God, and used this experience well. As a result, they derived great benefit in their advancement along the way of virtue. As we begin to practice mental prayer, it is true that when this distaste and dryness comes, there is reason to think it may come from our own negligence. You must be on your guard, my brother, that this is not your situation.[17]

Later, he asked a brother if he had a headache, and he simply replied that he had, coming from his attempt during his last retreat to reach a higher level in his mental prayer. Monsieur Vincent responded:

Brother, you must not act this way, attempting to force yourself to feel something beyond feeling. This attempt comes from self-love. In mental prayer we must act in a spirit of faith, quietly and simply meditating on the mysteries and virtues with no attempt at imagining. Instead we must apply the will to respond by affections and resolutions rather than have the mind try to respond by understanding.[18]

In the repetition of his mental prayer, another brother complained about not being intelligent enough to pray well. He could exercise only one faculty of his soul, the will. At the very beginning of his prayer and without any reasoning, he began to make acts of affection. He would thank God, or ask his mercy, or arouse feelings of confusion and regret for his sins, or would ask for the grace to imitate our Lord in the practice of some virtue, and then move on to some resolutions. Monsieur Vincent said to him, "Brother, you must not try to change any of this. Do not worry about trying to understand, even though this is ordinarily necessary to move the will. In your case, you move directly to these affections and to the resolutions of practicing some of the virtues. May God give you the grace to continue as you have been doing, and make you more and more responsive to his holy will."[19]

---

17. *CED* XI:91-92.
18. *CED* ibid.
19. *CED* XI:92-93.

CHAPTER EIGHT

His Devotion and Piety Toward God

DEVOTION IS a virtue which leads us to do with a special affection those things having to do with the worship and service of God, with a desire to honor and glorify him. It has no other limits than those imposed by charity. Since we honor and glorify God by the exercise of all sorts of virtues, Saint Ambrose has said that devotion is the foundation of the other virtues.[1] Saint Augustine assures us that true virtue cannot be found except in those who have a true devotion and piety toward God.[2]

Monsieur Vincent excelled in all sorts of virtues, as we have begun to see in the preceding chapters and we shall continue to see this in the following chapters. Hence there is no doubt he was gifted with a sincere and perfect devotion for all that concerned the worship and honor of God.

The devotion of this saintly man was founded first on his exalted view of the infinite grandeur of God and upon a profound respect for his divine majesty. His self-denial in all the acts of religion, the references full of respect and honor that he used when speaking of God, and the most affectionate way in which he strove to inculcate a great esteem and thanks for the perfections and grandeur of God, were all evident signs of the saintly dispositions he carried in his heart.

He once spoke to his community as follows:

> Make it your duty, my brothers, to conceive a great, a very great, idea of the majesty and sanctity of God. Could we but penetrate even a little into the immensity of his sovereign excellence, O Jesus, would that we could conceive the appropriate sentiments! Then we could well say with Saint Paul, that eyes have not seen, nor ears heard, nor the mind conceived anything like it.[3] He is the unlimited perfection, the eternal being, most holy, most pure, most perfect, and infinitely glorious. He is the infinite good, encompassing all that is good, and he is wholly incomprehensible. This knowledge which we have, that God is infinitely above all knowledge and of all human understanding, ought to suffice to make us esteem him infinitely, to annihilate ourselves in his presence, and make us speak of his supreme majesty with great reverence and submission. Our

---
1. PL 14.1.1:424.
2. PL 41:631.
3. 1 Cor 2:9.

appreciation of him ought to be in proportion to our love of him. This love should make us have a strong desire to acknowledge his blessings, and to form faithful adorers of his majesty.[4]

He had an incredible aversion to human pride. This vice robs God of the glory due him alone, and then with much temerity and injustice attributes this glory to a human being rather than to the Deity. Thus Monsieur Vincent waged a constant war against pride, not only in himself, but in all those over whom he had any influence, as we shall see more fully when we treat of his humility. We shall recount here only what he wrote to one of his priests serving on a mission.

> How consoled I was to read that these good people are so devoted to their duty. I cannot tell you how concerned I was that this might not be the case. To God alone be the glory, and may those who work with you give him this thanks. If their small efforts have any success and produce any good (*A Domino factum est istud*) God has done this,[5] and to him alone should be the glory. Oh, Monsieur, what an obstacle it is to the glorification of the name of God and to the sanctification of souls to attribute either of these to oneself or to think that you have had anything to do with it. May his divine goodness never allow any of the Missionaries ever to let such a thought enter his head! It would be a great sacrilege even to think this. The whole Congregation would be guilty of this same crime if it adopted this same opinion that by their efforts the confreres had converted people to God, and that they should be honored and respected because of this. How anxious I am to have this truth engraved on the hearts of us all! Those who think they are the source of any good, and have contributed even a part to it, and who take pleasure in this thought, lose much more than they gained by the good they did.

To the edification of all, the devotion of the great servant of God was most evident, in his public celebration of the divine office. When he came to the choir to chant the psalms, he did so with much recollection, and appeared to be totally taken up with the presence of God. He often recommended that his community fulfill this duty to God both with respect and piety, and to walk gravely, with eyes cast down, looking neither right nor left. Although his heart was usually gentleness itself, he would not countenance the least faults in the recitation of the divine office. On the other hand, he could hardly restrain his expressions of joy when the office was well said.

When he presided at a solemn office, he took pains to be informed of all

---

4. *CED* XI:48.
5. Ps 118:23.

the details of the rubrics appropriate to the occasion. In his later years he was much chagrined at not being able to make all the genuflections prescribed for the feasts. He believed strongly and often recommended that the objects used in sacred worship be appropriate to their sacred use. He also wanted the rubrics to be observed exactly. Whenever there was a failure in this regard, he made his displeasure known.

He extended his reverence and his posture to his private recitation of the office, which he always made kneeling, his head uncovered. He continued to kneel, except for the last two or three years of his life when infirmities compelled him to remain seated.

God had given him a great devotion for all the mysteries of our holy religion, particularly those of the most holy Trinity, the Incarnation of the Son of God, and that of the blessed sacrament of the altar. Since the most holy Trinity is the first and principal of the truths to be believed and adored, he was anxious to have it known and loved among souls, and taught on all the missions. Every morning and evening he honored this mystery with such devotion that he inspired all the members of his Congregation. He arranged to have included in the papal bull establishing the Congregation of the Mission an explicit obligation to honor daily in a special way this mystery of the Trinity and that of the Incarnation. The rule says: "We shall strive to acquit ourselves of this duty with great care, and in every possible way, but chiefly by observing three things: (1) producing from the heart, acts of faith and religion in these mysteries; (2) offering some prayers and good works every day in honor of these mysteries, and celebrating their feasts with all possible solemnity and devotion; (3) carefully striving by our instruction and example to have the people come to know, honor, and greatly respect these great mysteries."[6]

Since the Church invites us to honor these mysteries in a special way on the principal feasts, which recall them to the minds of the faithful, Monsieur Vincent showed his extraordinary devotion on these occasions. Thus he would ordinarily preside at the high mass and at vespers with such a spirit of recollection, modesty, and gravity that his internal union with God was made evident. Even though he was very devout on the days of great feasts in everything concerning the honor and worship of God, he was no less so on ordinary days.

He rose regularly at 4:00 A.M., no matter what time he had gone to bed the night before. Many nights he slept for only two hours, as he himself stated. Nevertheless, at the first sound of the bell, he rose so promptly that the second ringing of the bell never found him still lying down. With his usual humility, he never failed to begin the day by performing his morning

---

6. Common Rules 10,2.

devotions. He wrote the following in his own hand, to a virtuous woman, urging her to make good use of this opportunity to praise God:

> After rising I adore the Majesty of God. I thank him for the glory residing in him, and which he has shared with his Son, the holy Virgin, the holy angels, with my guardian angel, with Saint John the Baptist, with the apostles, with Saint Joseph, and with all the saints in paradise. I thank him also for the graces he has given his holy Church, and especially for those graces which he has granted to me personally, and especially for having preserved my life during the past night. I offer my thoughts, words, and actions in union with those of Jesus Christ. I pray that he will keep me from offending him, and I ask for the grace to accept faithfully everything that shall be most agreeable to him.[7]

After these acts of worship and thanksgiving, he made his bed. Then he went to the chapel to pray before the blessed sacrament, and despite having to wrap his swollen legs he managed to arrive within a half hour, and before many of the others. He was very happy to see the community assemble before our Lord. He strongly congratulated those most faithful in their prompt attendance, but was pained to see some arriving late for prayers.

After meditation he recited aloud with indescribable devotion the Litany of the Name of Jesus, and savored the titles of honor and praise given to the divine Savior. By his devotion to the litany he spread the balm of the sacred name in all hearts. Then allowing himself enough time for recollection, he prepared himself for mass, never allowing himself to be distracted by his many preoccupations. Often enough, he also went to confession. One of his priests wrote of him as follows: "I had the consolation of serving as his confessor while I was in Paris. I was able to see at first hand the sanctity and purity of his soul, which could not entertain even the appearance of sin."

He pronounced the words of the mass so distinctly, devoutly, and affectionately that his heart was obviously in what he did. This greatly edified those in attendance. He spoke in a moderate tone of voice, pleasantly, in a manner both devout and free, being neither too slow nor too hasty, but rather suitable to the sanctity of the occasion. Two traits united in him were rarely seen in the same person: a profound humility joined to a serious and majestic presence. He shared in the spirit of Jesus Christ who brought to the sacrifice the two differing qualities of both victim and priest. In keeping with the first, he humbled himself interiorly, as a criminal worthy of death before his judge. He recited the Confiteor, the words *in spiritu humilitatis et in animo contrito* ["in a humble spirit and a contrite heart"], etc., and *Nobis quoque peccatoribus* ["Also to us sinners"] and others with sentiments of humility and

---

7. *CED* XIII:142-43.

contrition, and as though filled with fear. As priest, he offered in union with the whole Church prayers and praise to God, and joined them to the merits and person of Jesus Christ. He did so in a spirit of worship, with respect and love for God.

He said one day to his priests on this subject:

> It is not enough for us merely to celebrate mass, for in keeping with God's will for us we should offer this sacrifice with as much devotion as is possible for us. With the help of his grace, we must conform ourselves as much as possible to Jesus Christ. While on earth he offered himself in sacrifice to his Eternal Father. We must do our best, gentlemen, as completely as our poor and miserable nature will allow, to offer our sacrifice to God in the same spirit as our Lord offered himself.[8]

One of the oldest members of the Company remarked that the extraordinary devotion of Monsieur Vincent in the celebration of mass was especially apparent when he read the holy Gospel. Others, too, noticed it when he came to some of the words of our Lord. He pronounced them with such tender love that it struck a chord in all who heard them. On many occasions those who did not know him, but who attended his mass, were heard to say, there indeed is a priest who knows how to say mass; he must be a holy man. Others said that while he was at the altar, he seemed to them to have the appearance of an angel.

Several others noticed that when he read the holy Gospel and came upon the passages where our Lord said *Amen, amen dico vobis*, that is, I solemnly say to you, he paid particular attention to the words that followed, as if he were amazed that these were the words that God himself truly used. By the affectionate and devout tone of his voice, he testified to the prompt submission of his own heart in recognizing the great mystery and importance of these words. He seemed to be nourished by the passages of Scripture like a child taking his mother's milk. He drew such nourishment for his soul that in all his words and actions he seemed filled with the spirit of Jesus Christ.

When he turned toward the faithful, the expression on his face was modest and serene. By his gesture of extending his arms, he portrayed the attitude of his heart, and the great desire he had that all present should be united to Jesus Christ.

Since he recognized the sacrifice of the mass as the center of Christian devotion and as the most important of all priestly actions, he never failed to celebrate mass each day, except for the first three days of the annual retreat, in keeping with the custom of the community. During these days of retreat the priests and brothers recalled any faults and failings they might have

---

8. *CED* XI:93.

committed. In a spirit of penance they did not approach the altar until after their annual or general confession. Except for those days, this devout servant of Jesus Christ regularly celebrated daily mass, no matter where he might be, whether in the city or in the country, or even on a trip. He made it a rule that the priests of the Company do the same. It was never known that he ever failed in this practice, as long as he was still able to stand erect. Ordinary indispositions would not hinder him. Often he said mass or went to meditation when he had a fever, which he usually called his little warmup.

He was not content with just celebrating mass every day, for he also had the devotion of periodically serving the other priests at the altar. He would do this even when overwhelmed with business affairs. He continued this practice well into his old age, even when he was more than seventy-five years old and could no longer walk without a cane, or could kneel only with great difficulty because of his inflamed legs. At this venerable age and in this sickly condition the first superior of the Congregation of the Mission continued to fulfill the office of acolyte, in serving other priests at the altar, to the great edification of all who witnessed this.

He recommended that when the clerics of his Company attended mass, they should never allow a lay person to act as an acolyte. Instead, they themselves should get a surplice and provide this ministry, for he said, "Laymen do not have the right to serve, except in cases of necessity. It is shameful that a cleric, deputed for the service of the altar, should see his office taken by those without this sacred character."

SECTION ONE

His Special Devotion Toward the Blessed Sacrament of the Altar

One of the greatest and most characteristic of the devotions of Monsieur Vincent was that toward the most Holy Eucharist, considered not only as a sacrifice, as we have already spoken of in this chapter, but also as sacrament, under the species by which the Son of God becomes truly present in our churches, and accomplishes in a true and marvelous manner what he had promised, to remain with us to the end of time.

This devotion of Monsieur Vincent was manifested first by the great respect which he displayed in those churches where the blessed sacrament was kept, and by his affection for these places honored by Christ's presence. We have an account of this from a very trustworthy person:[9]

> I several times noticed when Monsieur Vincent was in prayer before the blessed sacrament that his true and sincere devotion could be clearly seen in his exterior behavior. He always prostrated himself on both knees, with such a humble attitude that it seemed he would willingly lower himself to the center of the earth if by this he could show even greater respect for the sovereign majesty of the divine presence. In seeing the respectful modesty of his countenance, it could be said that a person was seeing Jesus Christ through his eyes. The impression made by his whole manner, so devout and religious, was capable of awakening the faith of the most tepid, and arousing in even the most unfeeling sentiments of piety for this adorable mystery.

This respect and devotion was shown not only during his prayers. He exhibited the same modesty no matter what the occasion, whenever he found himself in church in the presence of the blessed sacrament. As much as possible, he would never speak in these holy places. If he thought it necessary to do so, however, he would have the one he wanted to speak to first leave the church. He would act this way with persons of rank, even bishops, yet never failing in the respect he owed these persons.

This esteem for those places honored with the divine presence was such that on days he was not too occupied with the business of the community, or obliged to go to the city, he would go to the church, and remain there as long as he could, sometimes for hours, before the blessed sacrament. Like another Moses, he above all had recourse to the holy tabernacle and the oracle of truth when confronted with the thorny problems that arose during his administration of the community. It was noticed, especially on those occasions when he would receive letters which he felt would bring some particularly good or bad news, that he would go behind the altar in the church of Saint Lazare. He would kneel there with head uncovered, and open and read the letters in the presence of our Lord. He would do the same wherever else he was. One day he was given a letter in the court of the palace in Paris, which undoubtedly had news of the outcome of an important matter related to the glory of God. Although this happened at a time when he had much difficulty in walking, he went up the stairs to the upper chapel of the palace, where the blessed sacrament was kept. He found the chapel locked, but nevertheless he knelt at the door to read the letter. He undoubtedly did so to express more perfectly his submission to whatever would be revealed to him as the will of God manifested through the letter. He wished to sacrifice to

---

9. Brother Louis Robineau.

God any sentiments of joy or sadness which whatever its contents the letter might arouse in him.

When he was obliged to leave Saint Lazare on some business, before leaving he would go to prostrate himself before the Lord in the blessed sacrament to ask God's blessing upon his mission. Upon his return, he would again stop in the chapel, as though to give an account of his activities in the city. He would thank God for the graces he had received, and humble himself for any faults he may have committed. He did this, not in a formal or routine manner, but with a true spirit of worship and piety, remaining before the blessed sacrament in a humble and devout posture. He proposed this same practice to his community, saying it was only right for them to fulfill this duty to the master of the house.

When on his visits to the city he would come upon the blessed sacrament being carried through the streets, he would kneel, no matter where he happened to be. He would remain in this posture as long as the procession was in sight. If the procession went along the same street he was traveling, he would follow it bare headed, at a distance, because his difficulty in walking would not allow him to do otherwise.

On the trips he made to the villages and towns, he had the custom of dismounting from his horse to visit and adore the blessed sacrament in the church, if it were open. Otherwise he would do so in spirit. Once arrived at his destination for meals or for spending the night, he would first go to the local church to pay his respects and homage to the blessed sacrament.

In his serious illnesses, when he could no longer walk or support himself well enough to celebrate mass, he still communicated every day, if it were at all possible. In these daily communions he showed such affection and veneration for the presence of the Lord in this sacrament that he seemed transported outside of himself. In this connection, speaking once to his community on the effects of this divine sacrament upon those who approached it with appropriate dispositions, he said, "Do you not feel, my brothers, do you not feel divine fire burning in your breast when you receive the adorable body of Jesus Christ in communion?" He spoke these words out of the abundance of his own heart, and this allows us to deduce what he, in his own experience, tasted and felt in his communions. This appreciation led him to exhort everyone to prepare themselves well for the worthy and frequent reception of the holy communion of the body of Jesus Christ. He did not want his confreres to abstain from communion without serious reasons. When a person of piety came to him for counsel and guidance after omitting receiving the sacrament because of some interior trial, he wrote to her:

> You did not do well in abstaining from communion because of the interior trial you experienced. Do you not see that this was a

temptation, and that by doing this you laid yourself open to the influence of the enemy of this adorable sacrament? Do you suppose you will become better disposed, and more suited to unite yourself to our Lord by withdrawing from him? Surely, if you think like this you would be greatly mistaken, and would be living an illusion.[10]

On another occasion, he spoke to his community on the same topic:

You should lament seeing that this devotion to the blessed sacrament is declining among Christians, due in part, no doubt, to the new opinions. I have spoken with the superior of a saintly congregation and with another man who was a great director of souls, and I asked if there was a decrease in the number of those who came to confession and to holy communion. They told me that there was a great reduction in the number of those receiving these sacraments. The daily bread which our Lord wanted us to pray for, and which was received every day by the early Christians, has been discouraged by the new doctrines of our own times. This should not surprise us, for these doctrines appeal to our natural inclinations. Those who follow their own inclinations follow these new opinions which surround them, and which seem to dispense them from taking the trouble to put themselves in the required dispositions for receiving holy communion often and worthily.[11]

He added that he had known a good pious woman who had, upon the advice of her director, accustomed herself to receive communion on every Sunday and Thursday. Later, she put herself under the direction of a confessor who followed the new teachings. By some curiosity and the promise of a greater perfection, he limited her to receiving only once a week, then once a fortnight, then once a month. After eight months of this, she stopped one day to reflect on her life, and found things to be in a deplorable state. She was filled with imperfections, and subject to a great number of faults, given to vanity, quick to anger, impatient, and prey to the other passions. All this had come about since she had abstained from frequent reception of holy communion. She was astonished and moved by this, and said to herself, "What an unhappy state I am in! How I have fallen! How has it happened about that I am now subject

---

10. *CED* I:111. Abelly altered the original letter in several ways. For example, he expanded the final sentence; the genuine expression of the writer reads: "Oh! Surely, that is an illusion." It was addressed to Louise de Marillac.

11. These "new opinions" were those of the Jansenists. They were most popularly formulated in the work of Arnauld, *De la fréquente communion*, which discouraged the faithful from the frequent reception of the Eucharist. Vincent had already worked for the condemnation of Martin Barcos and his work, on the two heads of the Church, *De l'autorité de S. Pierre et de S. Paul*, 1645. He worked actively in the negotiations with Rome for the condemnation of Arnauld's work. When the condemnation finally came from Rome, the saint invited the community to give thanks to God. *CED* XI:321-22. See also VI:88-89.

to all these disorders and outbursts? What has brought about these changes in me? It undoubtedly has been caused by my leaving off and abandoning my original devotion, and having heeded the advice of these new directors. I now know from the unhappy results of my own experience that they are very dangerous. O my God, who has opened my eyes to recognize this, give me the grace to leave them completely!" Afterward, she left these new directors, and renounced their dangerous teachings which had so upset her and nearly brought her to her ruin. She returned to wiser counselors. They brought her back to her previous practice of the frequent reception of the sacraments with the required dispositions, and she found in them peace of conscience and the remedy for all her faults.[12]

Monsieur Vincent used this example several times to illustrate the great blessings inherent in the frequent and worthy reception of the blessed sacrament, in which our Lord gives us not only an abundance of grace, but himself as well, the source of all graces. Monsieur Vincent, this devout servant of Jesus Christ, felt very keenly the love and charity of God for his creatures. Thus, he often exhorted his confreres to thank God for such an incomprehensible blessing, by expressing themselves in their frequent adorations, humiliations and glorifications of the Son of God residing in this blessed sacrament. Because of their own inadequacies, he urged them to pray to their guardian angels to help them in rendering this homage.

In this same spirit he wanted the members of the Congregation to show all external marks of reverence toward the blessed sacrament. He would reprimand those he saw lacking in this reverence. He was so careful of this that if he saw someone passing before the main altar of the church where the sacrament was kept, and not stopping to make a full genuflection, or making it too hurriedly, he would speak to the offender in private, or even in public, if he judged it expedient. He would say that we ought not appear before God as puppets, making light gestures and reverences without soul and spirit. Once, when he saw a brother making only a partial genuflection, he called him aside and showed him when and how to make a proper act of reverence. He was always personally exact in this, and made the proper genuflection as long as he was able, even up to the time that he needed help in rising from his genuflection. When he grew older, and the trouble with his legs no longer allowed him to do so, he publicly asked pardon before the whole community. He said that his sins caused him to be deprived of the full use of his legs.

Once, as he did on many other occasions, he said with his usual humility, that he regretted that his age and infirmities prevented him from making the proper genuflection. He went on to say:

---

12. See his letters to Jean Dehorgny on Jansenism: *CED* III:318-32, 362-74. The conference is not reported in Coste.

If I should see the Company failing in this regard to show you what I would think of this, I would force myself to kneel down, no matter the cost, and not knowing how I could get up again myself. The faults committed in a community are the fault of the superior. The faults of the Congregation, in this matter, are important, because it is a duty of worship, and an exterior mark of the interior respect we must have for God. If we fail first in this matter, making only a small or half genuflection, the priests from outside who come here for retreats will feel that they too are not obliged to do any differently. Those in our own Congregation who succeed us, and will be guided by what we do, will do as they see us doing, and so all will fall into decadence. If the original is defective, what will the copies be like? Gentlemen and my brothers, please pay attention to this in such a way that our interior reverence will show in our external actions. God ought to be adored in spirit and in truth, and all true Christians should do so in imitation of the Son of God in the Garden of Olives. He prostrated himself in an attitude of profound interior humility, out of respect for the sovereign majesty of his Father.[13]

Since he so deeply believed that there should not be the least lack of even the exterior respect owed to the adorable sacrament, he was very displeased and filled with sorrow when he heard of the profanations and indignities against this holy sacrament committed by the soldiers and heretics during the wars. We cannot adequately describe his feelings, his sorrow, or the tears he shed, and how many extraordinary penances he endured to atone, as much as he could, for the disrespect shown to the person of Jesus Christ. Not content with his personal efforts, and what he was able to persuade his friends to do, such as sending ciboria, chalices, and other vessels to the devastated churches, he wanted the members of his community to join in the reparations. On pilgrimages, they would visit, in a penitential spirit, those churches where the sacrileges had been committed. The priests of the Congregation would celebrate mass, and the other members, joined by laymen, would receive communion. Afterward, missions would be given in the villages or other desecrated places. The Missionaries sought to move the people to penance, and to practice other works of piety to appease the wrath of God, and to repair, in some way, the injuries and offenses committed against his sovereign majesty.

---

13. *CED* XI:207.

SECTION TWO

His Special Care to Imitate Jesus Christ, and Conform Himself to His Example

Love implies a resemblance, or even better creates it. The beloved does what he can to transform himself into the image of the other, to render the loving union more stable and more perfect. The Son of God, wishing to witness to the depth of his love, became man to make himself like unto us. Also, those who truly love Jesus Christ seek, with the help of his grace, to make themselves like him by imitating his virtues. The greater this love, the more exact and fully achieved this modeling will be.

We have seen in the preceding section the singular devotion which Monsieur Vincent had for our Lord Jesus Christ in the blessed sacrament of the altar. His great love for the Lord did not stop at honoring this adorable mystery. He extended this love by honoring all the phases of the Lord's mortal and glorified life, and he strove to imitate the virtues which the savior practiced in every part of his life. He realized that the design of the Eternal Father, in the Incarnation of the Son of God, was not simply to give us a redeemer to draw us from the slavery of sin and hell, but also to offer a model who would show us all the virtues we might practice which would conform us to his image. He firmly resolved to follow this design of God by striving to imitate this divine model, and to reproduce in his own heart this exemplar of all virtues. He followed this plan so constantly and faithfully that it could rightly be said of him that his life was nothing else but a perfect expression of the life of Jesus Christ. In his own person he verified these words of this divine Savior: "Every student when he has finished his studies will be on a par with his teacher."[14]

In order to recount fully all his practices in imitation of the son of God would require a full account of his entire life. Therefore, in order not to be too long delayed, we will concentrate our remarks on two or three of the main traits which merit some more discussion.

First, Monsieur Vincent strove to imitate the ordinary and hidden life of Jesus Christ, a life which outwardly appeared to be in no way singular, but which inwardly was all holy and fully divine. In imitation of this incomparable master he led a life most ordinary in appearance. Nothing about him appeared on the surface to be outstanding or extraordinary, and he lived

---
14. Luke 6:40.

without any kind of show or singularity. Yet in the secret of his heart was a wealth of praiseworthy and truly heroic actions, marked by all manner of virtues.

He was neither completely withdrawn into himself nor constantly in the public eye, but in imitation of his divine model he led a life which perfectly united elements of both the active and the contemplative. He sometimes retired into solitude like Jesus Christ, but at other times he would come forth also like Jesus Christ to preach penance and to work for the conversion of sinners and the salvation of souls.

We might say that our Lord practiced the hidden life, not so much by separating himself from any human contact but rather by concealing the more excellent and divine traits of his character. He could have allowed himself to be seen and honored everywhere and all times as the true Son of God. He could have allowed the rays of his glory to shine forth in all Judea, as he did on Mount Tabor. He preferred, however, to be seen as the son of a simple carpenter and as an ordinary man. Following his example at every opportunity, Monsieur Vincent gloried in saying that he was only the son of a poor peasant. He sought to be known as a simple country priest. He hid from the eyes of all the excellent gifts of nature and grace which he had received from God, and which rendered him worthy of honor and veneration.

He had thoroughly studied theology, and even, as we remarked in Book One[15], had received his degree from the faculty of theology of Toulouse. Nevertheless, he spoke of himself as an uneducated man, and customarily referred to himself as a poor student of the fourth class.[16] He fled from any dignities with more care than the ambitious sought them. In every sort of circumstance he admired and perfectly imitated this dual public and hidden life of his divine master. Since he knew from his own experience that the treasures of grace lie hidden in the mystical field of the Gospel, he invited and exhorted others to share in them there. Here are some extracts of several letters he wrote to a person he was directing to follow this way:

> We must always honor the hidden life of the Son of God. This must be the center of our activities for the present, the future, and for ever. We cannot be mistaken. He does not want anything else from us but to imitate his way of life. Let us honor, I say, the ordinary life our Lord led upon earth, his humility, his self-denial, and the practice of the most excellent virtues of the way of life he

---

15. Ch. 3
16. The French secondary school system worked up from the sixth class to the first. The fourth class would, therefore, be the third year of secondary school, with students thirteeen or fourteen years old. In the typical Gascon style of his origins, the saint's reference seems, however, to be more an ironic allusion to the quality of his education or his style of speaking and writing than to his actual educational attainments.

chose. Let us especially honor our divine master in the moderation with which he acted. He did not always do all that he might have done. This was to teach us that there are times when it is not expedient for us to do all we can do, and that we should be satisfied to do only what charity dictates and what conforms to what his divine will desires of us.

How greatly I appreciate the generous resolution you have taken to imitate the hidden life of our Lord! Evidently this thought comes from God, since it is so foreign to the impulses of human nature. Believe for certain that this is the proper attitude for children of God. Remain firm, therefore, and courageously resist all contrary inclinations which may arise. You must be convinced by this attitude that you are in the state God asks of you. In it you can accomplish his holy will, which is what we all hope to achieve, and which all the saints have achieved.[17]

Monsieur Vincent led not only individuals to this holy practice, but also the members of his Congregation as a whole, often exhorting them to become true imitators of Jesus Christ in his ordinary and hidden life. On this topic, he was once explaining the renunciation to be made by all those who wished to follow the Lord. Among the six or seven examples of ways of practicing what he suggested, all taken from the life of our Lord, he referred to one taught by Saint Basil about renouncing pomp and show. He raised an objection to this, only to answer it then in his own way. In speaking to his community about what they must do, in this instance he allows us to see an example of his own way of acting. Here are his words:

Perhaps you will say to me, we are but poor priests who have already given up all the outward show of the world. We wear the simplest of clothes, our furniture is primitive, and nothing about us shows vanity or smacks of the luxury so prevalent in the world around us. What need is there, then, to exhort us to avoid pomp, which already is so far removed from us? Oh, gentlemen and my brothers, we must not deceive ourselves! We do have poor clothing and ordinary furniture, yet even with all this, we still might have a spirit of show and pomp. How could this be, you might ask. Well, if you take pains to prepare a beautiful sermon, and are pleased at the results and what people say about it in approval and appreciation, or should you publicize the good you have done, or even take pleasure in it, all these are marks of the spirit of outward show. To combat and crush this spirit, it is sometimes more useful to do

---

17. *CED* I:87, addressed to Louise de Marillac. The original letter differs in many significant respects from Abelly's text.

something outwardly less perfect, than to congratulate yourself on how well it was done.

Also, we must be ever on our guard not to give any opportunity to our spirit of vanity. We should renounce all the thoughts and feelings which come to us interiorly, as well as the public applause we receive. We must give ourselves to God, my brothers, fleeing from self-love and the praises of the world, which are the vanity of the spirit. In this connection, a celebrated preacher said to me just a few days ago that whoever seeks public approval when he preaches, hands himself over to the tyranny of the public. If he thinks he is making something of himself by his beautiful sermons, in reality he is enslaving himself to his vanity and to his frivolous reputation. We might add that those who adopt a pompous preaching style, featuring beautiful and rare thoughts, directly oppose the spirit and teachings of our Lord Jesus Christ. He said in his Gospel, "blessed are the poor in spirit."[18] By these words, the Eternal Wisdom showed us how evangelical workers should completely avoid any showy behavior and studied eloquence in speech. Instead, they should adopt a manner of speaking and acting that is humble, simple, and ordinary, after the example he himself gave us.

Be careful, my brothers. The demon inspires in us the desire to succeed. He persuades some of us that to speak in our simple way is too base and is unworthy of the grandeur and majesty of Christian truths. This is a ruse of the demon which we must avoid, and renouncing these vanities, we must remain faithful to the simplicity and humility of our Savior, Jesus Christ. He could have done startling things and spoken momentous words, but did not do so. Even beyond that, to confound our pride even more by his own admirable abasement, he wanted his disciples to accomplish even more than he did. Speaking to them, he said, "You will do what I have done, and even more."[19] Why was that? Because, gentlemen, our Lord wanted to show by his public actions that he excelled in the humblest and lowest, something which men no longer value.

He desired the fruits of the Gospel rather than the noise of the world. He wanted his disciples to accomplish even more than he did himself. He preached only in parts of Judea, but sent his apostles to preach the Gospel throughout the whole world. They enlightened everyone by the light of his doctrine. Though he did much by himself, he willed that his poor, ignorant and crude apostles and

---

18. Matt 5:3.
19. John 14:12.

disciples could still, if animated by the Holy Spirit and his power, do much more. Why is this? To give us the example of a most perfect humility. Oh, gentlemen, should we not imitate our divine Master? Should we not give way in everything to others? Should we not choose for ourselves the worse and the most humiliating? This assuredly is what our Lord did, and he is the perfect one we all strive to imitate. Let us resolve today to follow him.

Let us offer him the puny sacrifices of our self-love. For example, if I do something publicly and can possibly derive some benefit from it, I will not do so. I will rather refrain from anything which might give my action some notoriety and bring me a certain reputation. If two thoughts come into my head, I will mention the lesser one to humble myself. I will not mention the more polished one, and keep it in the secrecy of my heart as a sacrifice to God. Finally, my brothers, it is a truth of the Gospel that our Lord rejoiced in nothing so much as in a humble heart and simple words and actions. His spirit is found here, and you would look for it elsewhere in vain. If you want to find it, renounce all the vanities and satisfactions of life, and your desire for exterior show both in mind and body.[20]

This faithful imitator was not content to conform himself only in general to the ordinary and hidden life of Jesus Christ, but as much as was in his power he strove to model himself upon the Lord's way of speaking and acting. We have the following written testimony of a superior of one of the missions.

Monsieur Vincent's love for our Lord resulted in his always keeping the Savior in mind. He walked always in his holy presence, and modeled himself upon him in his actions, words and thoughts. I can truly say, as we all know, that he was so filled with God's spirit that he hardly ever spoke unless it was to recall a Gospel teaching or some action of the Son of God. I often admired how he would apply the words and deeds of our Lord whenever he counseled or recommended something.

Monsieur Portail had lived and worked for forty-five or fifty years with Monsieur Vincent. He is one of the oldest priests of the Congregation. I have heard him say that Monsieur Vincent was the perfect image of Jesus Christ whom he knew upon earth, and that he had never heard Monsieur Vincent say or do anything except relating to him who said: *Exemplum dedi vobis, ut quemadmodum ego feci, ita et vos faciatis* ["What I just did was to give you an

---

20. *CED* XII:211-27.

example: as I have done, so you must do"].[21] This is what Monsieur Vincent so often urged us to do. In the advice he gave me on the occasion of my leaving to take over the Mission which I now guide, he recommended that when I was to speak or to do something, I should reflect within myself and say, What did our Lord say or do in this case? How did he do or say this? O Lord, inspire me with what I must say or do, for by myself I can do nothing without your help.

One day a noted doctor asked one of the priests of the Mission who knew Monsieur Vincent well, what his chief virtue was. He replied:

It was undoubtedly the imitation of our Lord, Jesus Christ, for he always kept him before his eyes to serve as his model. Christ was his light and mirror, and in him he saw everything else. If in some particular case he doubted how he should act, to be perfectly agreeable to God, he reflected on how our Lord acted in similar cases, or what he said, or what he taught in his various sayings. Without hesitation he then followed his example and his words. He walked in the brightness of this divine light, and trampled under foot his own judgment, human respect, or the fear his actions would be unacceptable to those who found the Gospel too severe, or who wanted to accommodate Christian piety to the spirit of the times.

He sometimes said, "Human prudence fails and often leads one away from the right path, but the words of Eternal Wisdom are infallible, and its guidance right and secure."

Since he was so thoroughly convinced that our perfection and even our predestination consists in being conformed to the Son of God, and since his mind was so filled with this truth, he often spoke of it from the abundance of his heart. His responses to various consultations, or the advice he gave, were founded on this same truth, and always tended to influence the minds of those he spoke to. We could give a countless number of examples, but we will limit ourselves to but a single rather important one.

When the late king,[22] of glorious memory, called for Monsieur Vincent in his last illness, he asked him how best to prepare for death. He replied to His Majesty that it would be best to imitate the way our Lord acted when he was about to die, and that the holy Gospel tells us that one of our Lord's chief dispositions was an entire and perfect submission to the will of his heavenly Father, to whom he said: *Non mea voluntas, sed tua fiat*: may your will be done, and not mine.[23] The king replied in a manner appropriate to his

---

21. John 13:15.
22. Louis XIII.
23. Luke 22:42.

designation as the Most Christian Monarch: "O Jesus, I desire this with all my heart. Yes, my God, I say this and will say until my last breath, *fiat voluntas tua*, may it be done according to your will." This is how Monsieur Vincent always kept before his eyes this Original of all perfection and sanctity, and not content to conform himself to it in all things, he strove to have others do the same.

This holy man's constant goal was to imitate Jesus Christ and conform himself to him, not only in his manner of acting and speaking, but also in his interior dispositions, desires and intentions. In everything he desired and hoped for only what his divine Savior desired and hoped for: that God would be better known, honored, loved, served, and glorified, and that his most holy will would be entirely and perfectly fulfilled. He held himself ready at every moment to do or to suffer whatever God might be pleased to send in pursuit of these noble and just objectives. He was always ready for whatever work, fatigue, humiliation, pain, or persecution that might arise. Because of this he was never surprised at what happened to him, no matter how unpleasant it might be. He was never surprised by any bad treatment he might receive, since, in imitation of his divine Master, he was prepared for anything when it was a matter of increasing the glory of God or submitting to his will. He was prepared to do all or suffer all, to be deprived of what he held most dear in the world, even to the point of seeing his own Congregation dispersed and destroyed, if such should be the will of his divine Majesty. On this topic, he several times said to his community, "I pray God two or three times each day to destroy us if we are not useful to him in his service. My brothers, would you want to continue if you were not pleasing to God, or were not succeeding in having him known and loved by others?"[24]

He sought to conform himself, not only to the desires and intentions of the Son of God, but even to his disappointments, sorrows, and interior anguish. Who could penetrate into the secrets of the heart of this faithful and zealous imitator of Jesus Christ? He took the same attitude as his divine Master toward the innumerable sins committed against God, and was filled with an aversion for the teachings of the world, so opposed to those of the Gospel. He was saddened and troubled at the progress of heresies and for the great damage they wrought to the Church. He was keenly moved by compassion for the temporal and spiritual miseries of so many, and for the license and abandonment by which so many souls were plunged into the darkness of ignorance or infidelity. How many times he wanted to die, to give his life, to remedy these ills! Since by his mortifications and sufferings his life was a constant dying, it could be said God accepted his offer, but over a long period of time.

---

24. *CED* XI:2.

He wished his own confreres to enter into these same sentiments. In imitation of Jesus Christ they were to become living victims, immolating themselves in union with their divine Savior for the salvation of all. He spoke of this once, as follows:

> Whoever would wish to save his life, my brothers, shall lose it. Jesus Christ himself stated this, and he added, that he knew of no greater love than to give one's life for one's friend. And then? Can we have a better friend than God, and should we not love what he loves, and take our neighbor as our friend, for love of him? Would we not be unworthy of the life God gives us, if we did not use it in this worthy manner? Surely, recognizing that we have received our very life by his generosity, we would be acting unjustly if we refused to use it, and to expend ourselves, in keeping with his designs, and in imitation of his Son, our Lord.[25]

Speaking another time on this same subject, he spoke these words from the abundance of his heart:

> Those who describe a missionary speak of one called by God to save souls. Our purpose is to work for their salvation in imitation of our Lord Jesus Christ, the one true redeemer. He fulfilled perfectly the meaning of his name Jesus, that is, savior. He came from heaven to earth to exercise this function. He carried this out both in life and in death, and he continues as our savior by applying the merits of the blood he shed. While he lived on earth he thought of nothing but our salvation, and he continues this same work, for this is the will of his Father. He came, and continues to come to us each day, and by his example he teaches us all the virtues appropriate to this office of savior. We must give ourselves to him, that he may continue to fulfill this same office in us and by us.[26]

Lastly, he spoke in the same spirit to his Congregation in a letter he wrote to them which he placed at the beginning of the rules and constitutions.

> You must consider these rules and constitutions as produced not by the human mind, but rather by God's inspiration. All good proceeds from him, and without him we are incapable of doing any good by ourselves, as coming from ourselves. What will you find in these rules other than what will encourage you to flee vice, acquire virtue, and practice the Gospel maxims? We have attempted, to the extent of our powers, to base these rules totally on the spirit of Jesus Christ, and to draw them from a consideration of his life, as you will easily see. We have felt that persons called to

---

25. *CED* XI:49.
26. *CED* XI:74.

continue the mission of the Savior, which was chiefly to evangelize the poor, should adopt his sentiments and teachings, be filled with his spirit, and imitate him in all his actions.[27]

---

27. Common Rules, Introduction.

CHAPTER NINE

His Devotion Toward the Most Blessed Virgin, the Mother of God, and the Other Saints

THE GREAT Saint Bernard once said we should honor the most holy virgin Mary with the deepest affection of our hearts. Such is the will of him who has bestowed all manner of favors and graces upon us by the mediation of this incomparable Virgin.[1] This is not a pious invention of the human mind, nor a fruit of some particular devotion. It is an order established by the will of God that we give special honor to her whom he favored to the point of choosing her to be the mother of his only Son, that she in turn would receive true and perfect subjection and obedience from him.

The entire Church has always recognized this truth, and in every age has shown its respect and devotion toward the most holy Mother of God. It celebrates her feasts, venerates her images, and has always offered her solemn prayers. To this very day the Church continues to chant this praise by hymns and canticles, and by other means suggested by the Holy Spirit. All the great saints joined in this veneration and devotion toward the queen of angels and men. We have every reason to assume that Monsieur Vincent, always so careful to seek out the will of God and to follow faithfully the direction of the Church and the example of the saints, faithfully followed all the duties of piety and devotion toward the holy Mother of God. We have many proofs and reminders of this.

First, in the rules he left to his Congregation was this one. He regarded it as one of the main ones, and he often commended it to his confreres: "We should strive, all of us in general and each one in particular, to fulfill perfectly with the help of God our duty of honoring the most holy and most glorious Virgin Mary, Mother of God: (1) by honoring her with some special practice every day, as homage given to our lady and mistress, Mary, the Mother of God; (2) by imitating as much as we can her virtues, particularly her humility and purity; (3) by exhorting others at every opportunity to honor her as she so richly deserves."[2]

He always recommended and advised that each of the members of the Congregation have a special devotion to the queen of heaven, but more important than words, he used the force of his personal example. He fasted on the vigils of her feasts and prepared to celebrate them with practices of

---
1. PL 183.3-4:441.
2. Common Rules 10,4.

mortification and good works. Thus by his good example he introduced this custom among his confreres. He never failed to preside at the solemn offices of her feasts, and he did so with such devotion that the sentiments of his heart were obvious. He also loved to celebrate mass in chapels and altars dedicated to her.

He opened every conference or assembly at which he presided by the invocation of the Holy Spirit, and he was equally exact to end them always by an anthem or prayer in honor of the holy Mother of God.

He wore a rosary on his belt, not only because he used it often, which he did, but also as an exterior mark of his veneration and devotion toward the queen of heaven. By this practice he declared himself openly to be one of her most faithful and devoted servants.

Wherever he was, whether at home or in the city, and even in the presence of people of rank, when he heard bells sounding the Angelus he would fall to his knees (except in Paschal time or Sundays, when he would pray standing) to recite this prayer with the greatest possible devotion. His example moved others to follow this same practice.

Out of devotion, he often went to visit churches dedicated to God under the invocation of the most blessed Virgin. Likewise, during the troubled times of the wars he urged the members of the clergy conferences of Saint Lazare to make pilgrimages in her honor, to beg of God, through the intercession of this Mother of Mercy, peace and tranquility and the return of the subjects of the king to the obedience they owed His Majesty. He persuaded the Ladies of Charity to make similar pilgrimages to various places dedicated to this same holy Virgin, and to implore God's mercy through her intercession in this time of public calamity. He himself went to these places to offer mass and give communion to these pious ladies. He once went to the cathedral of Chartres for the express purpose of praying through the powerful intercession of Mary for a priest who had been named a bishop. He asked that the priest would receive the necessary spiritual insights to realize that God was calling him to the vocation of this sublime estate, since as a bishop he could render great services to the Church; and that he would overcome his great humility and accept this office.

The devotion of this saintly man for the Mother of God was evident in the sermons he gave on the various missions he preached. He introduced the practice among the Missionaries to instruct the people thoroughly in their obligation as Christians to serve and invoke the holy Mother of God, and to have recourse to her in all their needs. Finally, the many confraternities he established, and those he encouraged elsewhere, to honor our Lord in his love for the poor, were all put under the special protection of the blessed Mother. The various other groups and assemblies for pious works that he founded were also testimony to his devotion to this most holy Virgin, and to his zeal that she should be known and loved by others.

Since he was so filled with this spirit, and always so careful to render all honor and service to the queen of angels and men, can we be surprised that his enterprises were favored with such success, and so greatly blessed? They were all placed, in a special way, under the powerful protection of the Mother of God.

Monsieur Vincent himself was well aware, and often taught on the missions he gave, that the honor given to the Mother of God and to the other saints was ultimately directed to almighty God, whose servants they were. In this regard he particularly appreciated the apostles as those who had enjoyed the happiness of living close to the Son of God. They had drawn from the fountain of the Savior that water which springs up to eternal life. He regarded and honored them as the first and greatest of the missionaries, since they carried the light of the Gospel throughout the world and worked with God's blessings for the instruction and conversion of all peoples. Among all the apostles he particularly respected Saint Peter. He had loved the Savior more than any of the others, and had been chosen to be the first vicar of Christ upon earth, the head and sovereign pastor of the Church. He loved and venerated Saint Paul, the master and teacher of the gentiles, who had worked harder than anyone else. Since he bore his name, he also strove to imitate his virtues.

He had a special devotion toward his guardian angel and never entered or left his room without directing his attention to greet and honor him. He introduced this same custom among his confreres, in regard to their own guardian angels, whom they were to acknowledge when they entered or left their rooms.

He also had a strong devotion to his patron, the martyr Saint Vincent [of Saragossa]. Hearing once that a worthy and pious acquaintance of his had some Spanish connections, he asked him to use his good offices to find out more about this saint from the traditions of that locality than was found in the standard lives of the saints. He also honored Saint Vincent Ferrer, and it was noticed that on many of his retreats he read from the book written by this saint. He was so strongly influenced by what he had read about this saint's life and teachings that he often quoted them in the talks he gave to his community. He imitated this saint, particularly in his great zeal for the conversion of sinners and for the salvation of souls.[3]

He piously honored the relics of the saints. He spoke one day to his community about the procession which the priests of the chapter of Notre

---

3. One of the reasons for accepting the date of 1580 for the saint's birth is that his birthday would fall that year on the feast of Vincent Ferrer (also spelled Ferrier.)

Dame of Paris were to make to Saint Lazare, in which they carried the most notable of the relics of their church. "We must put ourselves in a frame of mind to receive these precious relics as if we were receiving the saints themselves, doing us the honor of paying us a visit. Thus we will honor God in his saints, and we must ask him to allow us to share in the graces he so abundantly showered upon them."[4]

Monsieur Vincent's chief intent in honoring the saints and angels was to honor in them the gifts of God and of his Spirit, whose temple they were. God was the object and end of the prayers he offered, and his expressions of piety toward them were ways of glorifying his divine majesty, and invoking their intercession to help him in this duty. He was faithful to the Church's teaching on the invocation of the saints. He saw to it that his confreres also were faithful to the teachings of this common mother of all the faithful, and submitted themselves to her guidance in all things which he recognized as inspired by him who is the author of all holiness.

Just as the fervor of his devotion led him to urge others to adopt the same sentiments as filled his heart, so too the coldness and indifference of many Christians of his time greatly afflicted him. On many occasions tears came to his eyes when he spoke of the fervor and exactitude of the Moslems in the practices of their false religion, their profound bows, their silence, modesty, and reserve in their mosques. He used to say that we must greatly fear that they will one day be our judges, and they will witness against our own laxity and lack of devotion.

We should not fail to mention his devotion for the comfort and deliverance of the souls suffering in purgatory. He often urged his confreres to do this duty of charity. He said they should consider these dear departed as living members of Jesus Christ, vivified by his grace, and destined one day to share his glory. Because of this we should love, serve, and help them to the full extent of our powers. He prayed and frequently offered the sacrifice of the mass for their intentions. He saw to it that the other priests of the Mission offered their masses for this same intention. The sacristan of Saint Lazare told how Monsieur Vincent often directed him to have the mass for the souls in purgatory said, especially for those detained there for a long time, with no one to pray for them. In all the houses of the Congregation, he directed that the *De profundis*[5] be recited three times each day, after the two particular examens before meals, and in the evening prayer.

Let us conclude this chapter with the testimony of two worthy priests regarding the devotion and piety they observed in Monsieur Vincent. The first of them said:

---
4. *CED* XI:49-50.
5. Ps 130.

Although Monsieur Vincent was deluged with business matters and had to deal constantly with many different people, conditions not usually conducive to recollection or devotion, we can say, nevertheless, that his heart was always filled with devotion. He seized every occasion that presented itself, no matter how difficult, to further the glory of God and the good of the neighbor. He showed that devotion is nothing other than charity, lovingly and promptly practiced, especially for those most abandoned and in the greatest need. His sense of devotion was such that his conversation alone moved those he spoke to. To hear him speak of God so respectfully and lovingly was to feel some spark of the sacred fire which Jesus Christ himself aroused in the hearts of the two disciples on the way to Emmaus. It was evident that this same Jesus Christ inspired his words, and all his other actions as well.

The second priest gave the following written testimony:

Concerning the devotion and piety of Monsieur Vincent, you had only to see him in choir, at the altar, or in the other exercises of piety, or even in his everyday activities, for his posture, his modesty, and his recollection, were all pencils sketching out his devotion. Several members of the clergy conference of Saint Lazare have spoken of how they came to these conferences mainly to hear him speak. When, through modesty, he would refrain from speaking, as happened now and again, they were very disappointed.

CHAPTER TEN

His Zeal for the Glory of God and the Salvation of Souls

MONSIEUR VINCENT had devoted himself to studying and imitating perfectly all the virtues of Jesus Christ. He particularly excelled, however, in zeal, reproducing in himself a living image of the divine Savior. It could well be said of him, "the zeal for the house of God had devoured him,"[1] for his life was consumed by the flames of the ardent desire to procure the glory of God. He continually looked for ways to undertake, to sustain, and to suffer everything to prevent any offenses against God, and to offer reparation for sins committed against his divine majesty, or to work for an increase in his honor and service. As Saint Augustine said so well in response to a question he posed for himself, "Who is this person, devoured by zeal for the house God? Whenever someone ardently desires to prevent offenses against God, and sees such an offense against his divine majesty, he does not rest until he has done everything in his power to offer some sort of reparation. If he cannot do so, he grieves in his heart, and feels great distress at seeing God so dishonored."[2]

The life and works of Monsieur Vincent, and what type of person he was, have been reported in Books One and Two. It could truly be said that he did not live for himself, but for Jesus Christ, whose honor and glory were incomparably more dear to him than his own life. His works can easily be used as proof of his zeal, since they were undertaken solely to destroy sin, and to help make God known, served, loved, and glorified in every place and by every person. This is what he worked so hard for in his missions, in the establishment of confraternities, conferences, and seminaries. In a word, he accomplished and suffered so much during his life until he was finally consumed in the flames of his own zeal.

To speak more specifically, the zeal of this great servant of God made him feel very keenly the offenses committed against the divine majesty. We cannot adequately express how much he was moved by this, or what efforts he made to prevent these offenses, and what penances he did as reparation for the sins committed. He was particularly disturbed when he learned about some miserable sinner dying in this sorry state, because a soul had been lost for all eternity. When speaking, if he emphasized the value of the single soul which had cost Jesus Christ so much, he drew tears from the eyes of his hearers.

---

1. Ps 69:10; John 2:17.
2. PL 35:1471.

To prevent this loss of souls, of those so dear to the divine Savior, there was nothing that he was not prepared to do or to suffer. He exhorted his confreres to cultivate in their hearts this same zeal which animated him. He spoke of these things while addressing his community on the occasion of the plague striking the missionaries working in Genoa.

By the grace of God, it was necessary that they suffer, and they were happy to suffer in their service of God by working for the salvation of souls. We must, gentlemen, have a similar disposition, and the same desire to suffer for God and for the neighbor, and to pour out our lives for this. Yes, gentlemen and my brothers, we must be committed to God without reserve, to him and to the service of our neighbor. We must strip ourselves of everything for their benefit, giving our very lives for their benefit, always prepared to give all and suffer for the sake of charity, to go where it will please God to send us, to the Indies or any other place even farther away, and finally to offer our lives willingly for the spiritual good of our dear neighbor, and to further the empire of Jesus Christ in souls.

Even as old and decrepit as I am, I should also adopt this attitude, even being ready to go to the Indies to gain souls for God knowing that I would probably die on the way. Do not think that God asks us for the strength of a healthy body. No, he asks only for our good will, and a true and sincere readiness to seize every opportunity to serve him, even at the risk of our lives. We should cultivate in our hearts a desire to sacrifice ourselves for him, even to suffer martyrdom. This desire is as effective and as agreeable to his divine Majesty as if we actually shed our blood. The Church adopts this same thought in honoring as martyrs several of the saints who were exiled for the faith, and who died in exile from natural causes. How learned in this science of suffering are our confreres working in foreign lands! Some serve the sick, even during the plague. Others serve in the armies in time of war, some suffer hunger, every discomfort, excessive labor, and sufferings. Notwithstanding, they remain firm and unshaken in the good they have begun. Gentlemen, let us acknowledge the grace God has given to this poor and wretched Congregation to have such people among us, members so faithful and constant in their sufferings for the service and love of his divine majesty.[3]

These words of Monsieur Vincent allow us to see how in his heart he desired to sacrifice his life as a martyr, or of going to foreign lands to be consumed as a Missionary. He would have done so if it was not for the

---

3. *CED* XI:401-03.

extreme pains in his legs and the other ailments from which he continually labored. He did manage, six or seven years before his death, when he was around eighty years old, to give a mission during the Jubilee.[4] He worked with much success, to the great edification of all who saw this venerable man. Despite all his infirmities, he gave himself completely to catechizing, preaching, and hearing confessions, and the other similar exercises of the mission. His age, infirmities, and other responsibilities did not allow him to continue in this holy exercise which he loved so well. Once, writing to one of his priests, he spoke of his sentiments in this regard:

> How blessed are they who give themselves to God in this way. They do what Jesus Christ did, and imitate him in his practice of poverty, humility, patience, zeal for the glory of God and the salvation of souls! In this way they become true disciples of this Master. They live purely with his spirit, spreading the good odor of his life and the merits of his actions for the salvation of souls, for whom he wanted to give his life.

In this same spirit and with this same zeal he urged his confreres in their work undertaken for the service of our Lord. This is what he wrote to one of his priests, whom he had sent to a foreign land, and who had much to do and suffer in the service of the Lord:

> Oh, Monsieur, what consolation I have to know that you are wholly devoted to God and to your vocation, which is truly apostolic! Love the happy chance that has fallen to your lot, and which will attract to yourself an infinity of graces if you respond well to it. You will undoubtedly have much to overcome, for the evil one and corrupt human nature will join to oppose the good you will attempt to do. They together will attempt to make your difficulties seem more than they really are. They will try to persuade you that grace will be lacking when you need it most, to discourage you, and break you down. They will raise up persons to contradict and persecute you. These will perhaps even be ones you think of as your best friends, and to whom you look for support and consolation. If that should happen, Monsieur, you must take courage. Take it as a good sign, for you will be more like our Lord, overwhelmed by sorrows, abandoned, denied, and betrayed by his own disciples, and seemingly abandoned by his Father. How happy are they who lovingly carry their cross, following such a master! Remember, Monsieur, and be convinced that no matter what happens, you will

---

4. See *CED* IV:589. By judging the year of his birth to be 1580 or 1581, he was seventy-two or seventy-three at this time.

never be tempted beyond your strength. God himself will be your support and strength the more completely you put your trust and hope in him alone.[5]

Writing to another missionary whom he had sent to a most laborious and difficult assignment, he said:

> Blessed be the Father of our Lord Jesus Christ, who so gently and yet strongly inspires the mission you have undertaken for the faith. Blessed also be the Lord who not only came to this world to redeem the very souls whom you are teaching, but also to merit the graces you need for your own salvation and for those you serve.
>
> These graces have already been prepared for you, and the good God who gives them desires nothing so much as to give them to those who will make good use of them. Therefore, what is he waiting for except for you to destroy all traces of the old man, and for the people themselves to leave the darkness of ignorance and sin? I would hope that, for your part, you would spare neither your labor, your health, or your life. You gave yourself to him for this, and risked the long voyage you undertook. Therefore, nothing remains but for you to begin your work earnestly. To both begin well and to succeed, you must act in the spirit of our Lord. Unite your actions to his and dedicate them to his greater glory, to give them a totally noble and divine purpose. In this way, God will shower all manner of blessings upon you and your work. You may not live to see them, at least not in their full extent, since God for good reasons hides from his servants the fruit of their labor. Nevertheless, he causes them to be effective. A farmer has to work many hours before seeing the fruit of his work, and sometimes he sees nothing of the abundant harvest his sowing has brought about. This same thing happened to Saint Francis Xavier. In his lifetime he never saw the results of his work, nor the great development which the holy works had produced after his death, nor the marvelous progress of the missions he had begun. This consideration ought to keep your heart at peace, and strongly centered in God, in the confidence that all will be well, despite everything you may see to the contrary.[6]

Speaking once to his community in this same spirit, he said:

> See what a beautiful field God has opened for us in Madagascar, the Hebrides, and elsewhere. Pray to God that he will move our hearts with a desire to serve him and to give ourselves to him to do

---

5. *CED* IV:280-81.
6. *CED* V:456-57.

with us what he will. Saint Vincent Ferrer drew courage from the thought that priests who would come to join him would, by the fervor of their zeal, convert the whole world. If we do not merit the grace from God to be this sort of priest, let us ask him at least to be the precursors and models for such persons. But be that as it may, we must hold it for certain that we cannot be true Christians until we are ready to lose everything and to give our lives for the love and glory of Jesus Christ. We should then resolve together with the holy apostle to choose suffering and even death rather than to be separated from the love of this divine Savior.[7]

On another occasion, when he told his community of some of the persecutions which the missionaries in Barbary were enduring, he continued:

Who knows if God did not send this accident to test our faith? Do merchants fail to put to sea because of the perils they might face? Do soldiers not go to war for fear of scars or of the death they may meet? Should we fail in our duty as helpers and saviors of souls because of the troubles and persecutions we may encounter?[8]

Thus, by his ardent zeal, he encouraged those of his community to continue their work in the service of our Lord. Since his zeal was truly disinterested, he rejoiced at the blessings God gave to the missions. Others accomplished what he would have liked to have done himself, had his age and infirmities allowed him. He was also very happy at the good done by other communities in the services they rendered to the Church. A person of some importance wrote of this as follows:

Monsieur Vincent always rejoiced when he heard of the great successes and progress of other religious communities. Far from harboring any envy or jealousy, he publicly proclaimed his high esteem for them, and often praised them. He would occasionally offer them help of all sorts. His zeal compared with that of Moses, saying with him *Utinam omnes prophetent* ["Would that all were prophets"].[9] and he wished to extend to others the graces he had received from God. And in truth, what did he not do either directly or indirectly to renew this apostolic and ecclesial spirit which we see flourishing in the Church today? He relied on everyone for this task—the tongue of one, the mouth of others, the favor of the wealthy, the care of the little ones, the prayers of the virtuous. In a word, his zeal was boundless, and nearly everyone felt its effects.

---

7. *CED* XI:74-75.
8. *CED* XI:75.
9. Num 11:28-29.

And it wasn't just the tiniest orphans and the aged poor who spoke about it.

Likewise, he often spoke favorably of the religious of the holy Society of Jesus, praising God for the great things they had done in all parts of the world in spreading of the Gospel and for the establishment of the reign of Jesus Christ his Son. Once, speaking to his community on this topic, and moved by his usual zeal and humility, he said:

> My brothers, let us be like the poor peasant who carried the traveling bags of Saint Ignatius and his companions on their tiring journeys. When he saw them fall to their knees when they arrived at the place they were to stop for the night, he did the same. When he saw these saints pray, he prayed too. When these holy personages once asked him how he prayed, he replied, "I pray that God will grant what you are asking for. I am like a poor beast who does not know how to meditate. I pray he will listen to you. I would like to pray like you do, but I don't know how, and so I offer him your prayers."
>
> Oh, gentlemen and my brothers, we must think of ourselves as porters for these worthy workmen, as poor ignoramuses who can say nothing worthwhile and as outcasts among men. We should think of ourselves as the gleaners who clean up after the great harvesters. Let us thank God that he agreed to accept our puny services. Let us offer our small handfuls along with the plentiful harvests gathered by others, and be ready to do all we can in the service of God, and for helping our neighbor. Since God had given such a beautiful insight to this poor peasant that he should be remembered in history, let us hope that our feeble efforts will contribute to God's being honored and served, and that his divine Goodness will accept our offerings and bless our insignificant efforts.

If Monsieur Vincent showed his ardent zeal in so many ways, he also showed his strength and constancy. He persevered in the holy enterprises which God had inspired him to undertake, despite the difficulties, opposition, losses, and all the other grievous situations which he encountered. Among all the missions he began, one of the most difficult both personally and for his Congregation was certainly the mission to the island of Madagascar, of which we spoke in Book Two. We saw how this mission had cost him the lives of many of his best workers, most of whom died soon after their arrival, before they could begin the work they had been sent to do. Others were shipwrecked on the way, and some fell into the hands of those at war with France. In sum, it seemed that nature and men united to oppose his efforts to help and instruct these poor natives. After so many accidents and losses, a person less virtuous than Monsieur Vincent would have bent under the weight of so many reverses, and would have abandoned this good work under the pretext that it was impossible.

The courage and zeal of this holy man enabled him to spring back, like the palm tree when flattened by the storm, which later stands straight again. The more he saw the opposition of creatures, the more he showed his constancy and the resolution of persevering in these good works undertaken for God's glory. Instead of these losses and opposition leading to discouragement, they provided the stimulus to encourage his confreres. They showed themselves even more anxious and more willing to go to this same mission, even knowing the fate which probably awaited them there. He wrote to one of his priests on this subject:

> Man proposes, but God disposes as he sees fit. The measures we have taken to support the mission in Madagascar have been so thwarted that it seems we cannot be sure of anything in the future. Nevertheless, it seems to me that we should do what we can to fulfill this plan, since it refers to the glory of the master, whom we serve and who often gives to perseverance the success that he refuses to our initial failures. He is also pleased to test his workers before confiding more important things to them, and to have them earn, by their faithfulness and hope, the grace to plant these same virtues in the souls of destitute people.[10]

As he said in another letter:

> We have wept at the news of the deaths of our dear deceased sent to us by the Madagascar mission. I cannot deny that this news has greatly afflicted us, and has given us the amazing opportunity to adore the incomprehensible judgments of the conducts of God. This affliction, however, cannot diminish our resolution to help this people, any more than all the previous losses, and the unfortunate accidents which have happened since we first arrived.[11]

On another occasion the superior of the mission at Marseilles reported it was becoming very difficult to continue the mission in Barbary. It seemed that it would take all the resources of the Congregation to support this single mission, and to overcome the difficulties raised by the Moslems in dealing with the missionaries. Monsieur Vincent responded that he could not bring himself to leave this work, for, as he said:

> If the salvation of a single soul is of such importance that we should risk our life to obtain it, how can we abandon so many out

---

10. *CED* VII:510-11.
11. *CED* VIII:156-58.

of fear of the expense? I would consider the men and money well spent if there should be no other good coming from these missions than to make this barbarous and cursed land see the beauty of the Christian religion. We send men there across the seas who are willing to leave their own country with its conveniences, and who open themselves to a thousand outrages. They do this to console and help their afflicted brothers. I believe that the men and money are being well spent.[12]

Zeal inspired in Monsieur Vincent the courage and strength to persevere in the holy enterprises he had begun. Thus it was a source of great pain for him to see that some among his own confreres were lukewarm, or allowed themselves to be overly influenced by natural sentiments and self-love. They would give way to discouragement and cause others to do the same. We will conclude this chapter by giving an extract of a conference he gave to his Company on this matter:

> It is impossible for a lukewarm priest and Missionary to be successful, or to come to a happy end. What sort of wrong do you think that these cowardly souls could do in the Company? What harm these lazy ones do to themselves and to others, whom they discourage by their bad example and by their impertinent remarks! "What good is done," they say, "by so many different kinds of works, so many missions, so many seminaries, conferences, retreats, assemblies, and trips made to help the poor? Just wait for Monsieur Vincent to die, and we will be done with all that! How can we support all these activities? Where will we find the Missionaries to send to Madagascar, to the Hebrides, to Barbary, to Poland? Not to mention the expenses of such burdensome and distant missions?"
>
> We must answer these questions in this way: if the Company at its birth and from its cradle had the courage to seize opportunities to serve God, and if the first Missionaries were so fervent, should we not trust that it will be fortified and grow in time? No, no, gentlemen, if God gives us new opportunities to serve him we must, with his grace, respond generously. These lazy and mistrusting ones are capable only of discouraging others, and for this reason you be on your guard against such people. When you hear them speak the way they do, speak up with the words of the holy apostle: *Jam nunc Antichristi multi sunt in mundo,* "Antichrists are already in the world,"[13] and they are these anti-missionaries who set themselves up to oppose the designs of God. Alas, gentlemen, we still feel the

---

12. *CED* VII:117.
13. 1 John 2:18.

effects of the first graces of our vocation poured out upon us. We already have reason to fear that by our laxity we will become unworthy of the blessings God has so abundantly given the Company up to now, and those he has bestowed upon the projects which his providence has confided to us. We must fear that we will fall into the unhappy state we see in some other communities. This is the greatest unhappiness that could possibly happen to us.[14]

Lastly, since zeal deals with the sanctification and salvation of souls, as well as with the glory of God, we will see in the following chapter what his dispositions were in regard to his neighbors. We will see how perfect his charity was toward them, to appreciate more fully the grandeur and extent of his zeal.

---

14. *CED* XI:193-95; Abelly's text differs from Coste's.

CHAPTER ELEVEN

His Charity Toward His Neighbor

CLOSELY ALLIED to the first great commandment of loving God with all one's heart is the second, to love one's neighbor as oneself. These two commandments are so inseparable that the first cannot be fulfilled if the observance of the second is lacking. Those who do not love the neighbor cannot say that they truly love God, no matter what feelings of fervor and zeal they might think they have for God's honor and glory.

Monsieur Vincent was totally convinced of this truth. He knew that the precept of loving the neighbor is so strong that whoever observes it fulfills the law of God. All the precepts of the law come down to love of neighbor, for according the doctrine of the holy apostle: *Qui diligit proximum, legem implevit* ["He who loves his neighbor has fulfilled the law"].[1]

Speaking one day in a conference he said:

> Show me a person who limits his love to God alone, a soul, if you will, so elevated to the heights of contemplation, so taken up with this way of loving God that he savors only this infinite source of blessedness, and takes no thought of his neighbor. Now consider a second person who loves God equally with all his heart, but loves his neighbor also, no matter how brusque, crude or imperfect, for the love of God. This person who also strives with all his strength to bring his neighbor to God. Tell me, please, which of these two loves is more perfect and the least self-serving? Beyond doubt, it is the second. This love unites the love of God to the love of neighbor or to say it better, it extends the love of God to the neighbor, fulfilling the law more perfectly than the first.

Then, applying this to his own Congregation, he continued:

> We ought to impress these truths deeply on our minds, to guide our lives by this more perfect love, and to do what it demands, for no one in the whole world is more obliged to this love than we are. No other congregation should be more committed to this than ourselves, nor more dedicated to works of true charity. Our vocation is neither to go to a single parish nor a single diocese. We are to embrace the whole world to gain the hearts of all. The Son of God

---

1. Rom 13:8.

said that he had come to light a fire upon earth, to fill hearts with his love, and we must do the same.

We are sent not merely to love God but also to make him loved. It is not enough for us to love God if our neighbor does not love him as well. We will not know how to love our neighbor as ourselves if we do not procure for him the same good we want for ourselves, to know the divine love which unites us to the one who is our sovereign good. We must love our neighbor as the image of God and as the object of God's love, and act in such a way that everyone will in turn love their loving creator. We must develop among ourselves a mutual charity, for the love of God, who loved us so much that he sent his own Son to die for us. Gentlemen, please look upon our divine Savior as the perfect exemplar of the charity you ought to have for your neighbor. O Jesus, tell us, if you will, what impelled you to leave heaven to suffer so on earth? What excess of love led you to humble yourself, and accept the infamy of the cross? What excess of charity made you take upon yourself all our miseries, to adopt the form of a sinner, to live a life of suffering and submit to a shameful death? Where can anyone find such an excellent and admirable charity?

Only the Son of God is capable of such love, of leaving the throne of his glory to take a body subject to all the infirmities and miseries of this life. He alone was capable of doing all he did to establish in us and among us, by word and example, the love of God and neighbor. Yes, this same love crucified him and produced the marvelous work of our redemption. Oh, gentlemen, if you had but a spark of that sacred fire which consumed the heart of Jesus Christ, could you spend your life with folded arms, and abandon those who call for your help? Certainly not, for true charity does not know how to live in idleness, nor of seeing our brother in need, and not to respond. Since our exterior actions show our interior dispositions, those who have true charity will show it by the way they act. Fire gives light and heat, and in the same way, love shines forth in action.[2]

He expressed this same thought on another occasion when he said to his community that they should be happy if they became poor themselves in exercising charity toward others.

You should not fear this poverty, never doubting the goodness of our Lord and the truth of his word. Even if you were forced to go to work for the pastors in the villages to support yourselves, or

---

2. *CED* XII:261-64. Abelly's text differs considerably from Coste's.

had to beg your bread, or sleep in barns, exposed to the rigors of the weather, suppose someone were to ask you: Poor priest of the Mission, what has brought you to such extremity? What happiness, gentlemen, if you could respond: Charity. How blessed this poor priest would be, before God and his angels.[3]

Once the Missionaries he had sent to Algiers to work among the poor slaves there found themselves in danger of having to pay a large amount for one of the fugitive slaves for whom they had supplied bail. Monsieur Vincent told the members of the Congregation about this in a noteworthy statement: "What is done out of charity is done for God. It is a great honor for us if we are asked to give away what we have, for charity's sake, since it was for God who gave it to us in the first place. In this case, we should thank him and bless him for his infinite bounty toward us."[4]

The charity of Monsieur Vincent was so perfect and his heart so filled with the effects of this divine virtue that we might say in some way that he anointed all who came in contact with him. It could be said of him what the apostle Paul said: Christi bonus odor sumus in omni loco, we are an aroma for Christ's sake.[5] Once he said to his community:

> Everything creates an image of itself, much like a mirror which reflects things just as they are. An ugly face appears ugly in a mirror, and a beautiful face appears beautiful. In the same way, good and bad qualities shine forth from us. This is especially true of charity which by its very nature communicates itself and produces charity. A heart truly filled and animated by this virtue shows forth its inner fire, and everything in a charitable person breathes and preaches charity.[6]

The charity of this great servant of God was not restricted or limited, but extended to everyone capable of receiving its effects. As much as possible he preserved an affectionate and cordial relationship with everyone. This virtue always led him to be united and submissive to the sovereign pastor of the Church, that is, our holy father, the pope. In the person of the pope Monsieur Vincent respected and loved Jesus Christ, whose vicar he was upon earth. When the Apostolic See became vacant by the death of a pope, he prayed incessantly and had the community pray that God would be pleased to give the Church a man after his own heart. When a new pope was elected he showed respect and affection for the person raised to this sublime dignity. Leaving aside all human consideration he saw in the person of the sovereign pontiff only the person given to the Church by God's providential will.

---

3. *CED* XI:76-77.
4. Dodin, *Entretiens*, 1001.
5. 2 Cor 2:15.
6. *CED* XI:76.

This same virtue inspired him with sentiments of love and reverence for all the bishops of the Church, as we shall see in one of the following sections of this chapter. He showed them every kindness and submission that he possibly could. He supported their plans, promoted their wishes, and maintained their authority. He wanted and did all he could that the clergy and people might regard their sacred persons highly, and deferred humbly and promptly to their directions.

He was also united to the pastors and other clergy. He honored and served them as dictated by circumstances, both as a general rule and also in each particular case. He was on good terms with the orders and communities of religious and even of seculars, and as occasions arose, met with the superiors of these groups. He showed a remarkable deference to all persons in authority, whether clergy or lay. If someone did not want to use his services, a lord in his territories, a pastor in his parish, or a bishop in his diocese, he never went over their heads to override their objections. Even in a matter which was just and reasonable, he preferred to leave a good action undone rather than do it against their will.

He was particularly noted for his open profession of sincere affection and his faithful service to the king, going so far as to risk the welfare of his community and even his own life to support the interests of His Majesty. A member of the nobility testified to this one day in the presence of the queen mother during the regency:

> I know of few people attached with such a sincere fidelity, constancy, and disinterestedness to the service of the king as Monsieur Vincent. Your Majesty knows well how during the troubles in Paris he risked the pillage of his house at Saint Lazare, and risked even his own life, when he gave refuge to your chancellor on his way to Pontoise to find the king. You are aware of how he endured slander and the hatred of some by the firm and faithful way he handled the pious wishes of Your Majesty, as you had directed him, particularly in the administration of ecclesiastical goods.

The queen acknowledged this tribute and said that it was true.

In summary, Monsieur Vincent was everyone's friend. He conserved and cultivated friendships, not simply to avoid having trouble with anyone, but rather to promote that holy unanimity of spirit that the Son of God so earnestly recommended. He was more anxious to do good than to receive any favors. We can say in all truth that he never acted to increase his own possessions or to receive honors. He acted for the good of his neighbor because of his true and sincere spirit of charity. It would not be inappropriate to cite the testimony of the religious of the first Visitation house in Paris, his spiritual daughters for over thirty-five years.

This great servant of God burned with such a love of God that he wanted everyone to share this virtue. He wanted charity to be practiced in all things as thoroughly as it could possibly be. He would not tolerate in this community anyone who showed a lack of esteem for others or who spoke to discredit her neighbor. He said that he feared that the community would be destroyed if its members were not united with one another, especially when disunity was caused by a lack of esteem, mutual support, and charity. He stressed that religious should look upon each other as spouses of Jesus Christ, temples of the Holy Spirit, and the living images of God.

This view should lead each person to have a mutual respect and love for one another. In turn, this should lead to the two following things. First, we must have recourse to the goodness of God who is all love and charity, to beg of him a share in his divine spirit. Second, we should be most anxious about our own conversion, and try to correct the faults and failings we may commit against the virtue of charity. We should use this as the subject of our particular examen, to root out of our hearts anything that might hinder the union we should have with God and among ourselves.

Another religious of this same order, who lived a saintly life in the second of the houses of the Visitation established in Paris, left us this testimony about Monsieur Vincent.

> We can truthfully say that this holy man strove to imitate the life of Jesus Christ, who did good to everyone during his sojourn upon earth. Who has not felt the charity of Monsieur Vincent in fulfilling the needs of their lives, whether of body or soul? Can anyone be found who had recourse to him and went away without receiving some help? Is there anyone who turned away from him when he spoke or consoled them? Who had a greater claim on the goods of his community than the person in need?

One more aspect of charity remains which we should not omit mentioning. Besides looking to the actual needs of both body and soul, he was most careful to safeguard the honor and reputation of everyone. Remarkably, he was never heard to complain about anyone, even when he had been treated poorly by them. On the contrary, the absent had an advocate who defended their cause and one who openly urged the virtue of charity. He spoke as well of others as the truth allowed. He would not allow anything negative to be said about anyone else in his presence, even when it concerned someone who had done him harm.

SECTION ONE

Some Remarkable Examples of Monsieur Vincent's Charity

To illustrate what we have just said of the charity of Monsieur Vincent we will in this first section give some examples, chosen from many others which filled the life of this great servant of God.

During the recent troubles in the kingdom, the people of Montmirail were distressed at the prospect of mistreatment at the hands of the soldiers. They did not know where to turn to safeguard their persons and their belongings from the ravages and annoyances of the soldiers. Monsieur Vincent wrote to the priests of this Congregation working in the region to do all they could to protect these poor people. The priests in turn pointed out that they were themselves in danger and would be at risk in attempting to help others. Monsieur Vincent replied: "We must come to the help of our neighbor in need. Since everything you own you have received from God, his divine majesty has the right to take it from you when he so wills. Rising above your fears, you are to come to the help of this poor town however you can."[7] This they did, helping the poor townspeople save most of their goods and their household furniture from the soldiers, leaving all that might happen to themselves in the hands of God's providence.

The priests of the Congregation of the Mission, who direct a seminary under the jurisdiction of the Parlement of Toulouse, became involved in a lawsuit about the seminary.[8] The Prince of Conti urged a solution to the difficulty by having the priests submit the case to arbitration in the city of Toulouse. Nevertheless, a bishop concerned with the seminary, and a supporter of the priests of the Mission, did not approve of the arbitration and ordered the priests to break it off.[9] They soon informed Monsieur Vincent, and sent him the letter which the bishop had written them. One of the priests then pointed out to Monsieur Vincent that the Prince of Conti, then in Paris, should be informed that the priests of the Mission were not the ones responsible for breaking off the negotiations.[10] Monsieur Vincent replied: "No, this course of action would reflect badly upon the bishop, which we must not allow to happen; this would give the priest reason to complain about the bishop. It is preferable that we take the blame, and let the recriminations

---

7. *CED* V:44.
8. The seminary at Cahors. The lawsuit concerned the abbey of La Fauvette.
9. Blessed Alain de Solminihac, the bishop of Cahors.
10. Guilbert Cuissot, superior of the seminary at Cahors.

fall upon us. We must never do anything to work to the harm of our neighbor."

The greatest example of charity, as our Lord pointed out in the Gospel, is to give our lives for those we love. On several occasions Monsieur Vincent, who had this virtue in the highest degree, freely risked his own life in the service of his neighbor. Some time after the priests of the Mission moved into Saint Lazare, God permitted a plague to strike the house, and the sub-prior was among its victims. As soon as Monsieur Vincent learned of this, he went to visit the priest, to console and encourage him, and to offer to render any service within his power. He approached his reeking bedside, and remained there as long as he was permitted to do so. At this same time, a young boy at Saint Lazare was stricken. Several thought that the boy should be transported to the hospital of Saint Louis, but Monsieur Vincent would not allow it. The boy was to be cared for at Saint Lazare. Monsieur Vincent saw to it that one of the brothers was assigned to take special care of the sick child.

Once, while in the faubourg Saint Martin, Monsieur Vincent came upon six or seven armed soldiers, swords in hand, chasing a man of the working class and just about to kill him. He had already been wounded and it was all to obvious that he would not escape death. None of the bystanders wanted to risk the anger of the soldiers in attempting to help the victim, but Monsieur Vincent thought nothing of risking his own life in assisting his neighbor. Moved by a spirit of charity, he threw himself among the soldiers, using his own body as a shield against their swords, allowing the man to escape. The soldiers, astonished at this display of courage and charity, allowed themselves to be persuaded by his remonstrances, and they gave up their evil intent.

Another example of this same virtue, as remarkable as it is rare, has been reported by several persons from both within and outside the Congregation, and especially by the superior of the priests of the Mission of Marseilles, who heard the story from several persons of that town. Long before he established the Congregation, Monsieur Vincent emulated the charity of Saint Paulinus, who sold himself to ransom from slavery the son of a poor widow. It happened that once Monsieur Vincent came upon a convict in the galleys who had been forced to abandon wife and children to a life of abject poverty. He was so moved by compassion at the wretched state to which these persons were reduced, that he resolved to do everything in his power to help them. He was unable to find any way to help, however. Then, moved by extraordinary charity, he thought he would take the place of the poor convict to enable him to go to the help of his impoverished family. He convinced the authorities to allow this exchange, and freely accepted the very chains of this poor man whose liberty he had secured. After some time, his extraordinary virtue manifested in this episode was appreciated, and he was released from servitude. Later, people, perhaps correctly, thought that the swelling in his legs may have come from the chains used to secure the convicts in the galleys. Once, a priest of the Congregation asked Monsieur Vincent if these things had really happened, that he had once taken the place of a galley slave. Monsieur Vincent merely smiled, but gave no answer to the question.[11]

We can surely say that this act of charity was most admirable. Yet we can say with even more certainty that Monsieur Vincent gave greater glory to God by using his time, talents, goods, and his very life in the service of all convicts, not just of the one he replaced on the galley bench. Through his own experience he knew their sufferings and needs, and he worked to secure both bodily and spiritual help, in sickness and in health, for the present and for the future, far beyond what he could have accomplished if he had remained chained among them.

It is not hard to accept the idea that he was minded to give up his personal liberty in favor of an abject slave in imitation of Saint Paulinus if we reflect upon his later years. Following the example of Saint Paul, he was willing in a certain sense to allow himself to become accursed for the sake of his brothers.[12] A remarkable example of this occurred during the time Monsieur Vincent was a chaplain of Queen Marguerite. We owe this account in part to what he said one day in a conference to his community, and in part to the recollections of several reputable persons reported after his death.

> I once knew a famous professor, who for a long time had defended the Catholic faith against heretics in the exercise of his role as diocesan theologian. Because of his learning and piety, Queen Marguerite had even invited him to court, which required his leaving his other responsibilities. Since he no longer preached or catechized he fell prey to serious temptations against the faith. Incidentally, this warns us of the danger of idleness, either of body or mind. Just as the fields, no matter how good the soil, will yield weeds and thorns if they are not cultivated, so too our souls cannot long remain at rest or in idleness without feeling the rise of passions and temptations which lead it to evil.
>
> This theologian, realizing that he was in this sad state, came to me. He admitted that he was undergoing violent temptations against the faith, and was even assailed by blasphemous thoughts against

---

11. This account is still much debated.
12. Rom 9:3.

our Lord Jesus Christ. He was in such despair that he felt tempted to hurl himself from a window to his death. He was in such a bad way that he had to be excused from reciting the breviary or celebrating mass, or even reciting any other prayer. Beginning even the Our Father raised a multitude of evil spirits to torment him. His imagination was so drained and his mind so exhausted at the effort to resist these temptations that he could no longer function. In this extremity he was advised to observe a simple practice. He should lift his hand or even a finger in the direction of Rome, or even toward any church, signifying whenever he made this gesture that he professed his faith in all that the Roman Church taught. What was the outcome of all this? God at length had mercy on this man, for when he fell sick he was suddenly delivered from all his temptations and the blindfold fell from the eyes of his soul. He began to see anew the truths of faith but with such clarity that it seemed he could almost touch them with one of his fingers. He finally died, giving thanks to God for allowing him to fall into these temptations only to be delivered by great and admirable insights into the mysteries of our holy religion.[13]

We know of this episode from a talk which Monsieur Vincent gave to his confreres on the subject of faith. He does not mention anything at all of the means he used to deliver this man from his violent temptation. Only after his death did it become known that it was by his own prayers and self-offering to God that this deliverance came about. This is how it happened, according to the written account of a very trustworthy person, someone unaware of the conference of Monsieur Vincent cited above.

> Monsieur Vincent took it upon himself to help this man who had revealed his troubled spirit. He counseled him to perform good acts to obtain the grace of deliverance. Later, it happened that this person fell sick, during which time the evil spirit redoubled his efforts to gain his soul. When Monsieur Vincent recognized his pitiable condition he feared that the man would succumb to the violent temptation of infidelity and blasphemy, and would die poisoned by the implacable hatred of the devil toward the Son of God. Monsieur Vincent prayed earnestly that God in his goodness would deliver the sick man from this danger, and in a spirit of penance he offered to take upon himself whatever sufferings divine justice might require. In this, he imitated the charity of Jesus Christ who took our infirmities upon himself that we might be cured, and who bore the sufferings we deserved.

---

13. *CED* XI:32-34.

In his hidden providence, God accepted this offer of Monsieur Vincent, and heard his prayer. He delivered the sick man from his temptation, calmed his soul, enlightened his darkened and troubled faith, and gave him such sentiments of reverence and gratitude toward our Lord Jesus Christ as he had never before experienced.

At the same time, God in his divine wisdom permitted this same temptation to trouble the soul of Monsieur Vincent. This beset him for a long time after. He had recourse to prayer and self-denial to rid himself of this trial, but these had no other effect than to allow him to bear these torments from hell with patience and resignation, always with the hope that God would pity him.

Since he realized that God wished to try him in permitting the devil to attack him so violently, he had recourse to two remedies. The first was to write out a profession of faith which he placed over his heart as an antidote to his trials. He specifically repudiated any thoughts contrary to faith, and entered into a sort of pact with the Savior that every time he placed his hand over his heart and upon this paper, as he often did, he intended by the gesture to renounce temptation, all without saying a single word. At the same time he raised his mind to God and easily diverted it from the thoughts which troubled him. In this way he confounded the devil without directly confronting him.

The second remedy he used was to do the exact opposite of what the tempter suggested, striving to act by faith in rendering honor and service to Jesus Christ. He carried this out particularly in his visits to the sick poor of the charity hospital in the faubourg Saint Germain where he lived at the time. This charitable practice is among the most meritorious in Christianity since it bears witness to faith in the Savior's words and example and to the desire to serve him. Jesus himself said that what was done to the least of his brethren he would regard as done to himself.[14] God allowed Monsieur Vincent to draw such grace from this period of temptations that not only did he never have occasion to confess any fault in this regard, but on the contrary the remedies he used were the source of innumerable blessings drawn down upon his soul.

Three or four years passed in this severe trial which bore down upon Monsieur Vincent, and he groaned before God under their weight. Yet, seeking to strengthen himself more surely against the attacks of the devil, he thought of taking a firm and unbreakable

---

14. Matt 25:40.

resolve to honor Jesus Christ and to imitate him more perfectly than ever before by committing his entire life to the service of the poor. No sooner had he done this than, by a marvelous effect of grace, all the suggestions of the evil one disappeared. His heart, which had been so troubled for such a long time, was suddenly freed, and his soul filled with such abundant light that he admitted on several occasions that he seemed to realize the truths of faith with remarkable clarity.[15]

Thus did that temptation cease. The result of his decision was that one might say that God in his grace drew forth from his servant all the great works he did for the aid and salvation of the poor and for the greater good of his Church. Besides the one who gave this account, several other worthy persons still living have told us the same thing. Monsieur Vincent had told it to them in confidence when he wished to help them overcome similar temptations in their own case. He spoke of what he had experienced in these situations to bring them to use similar remedies and to obtain relief in the trials they were undergoing.

SECTION TWO

His Special Charity Toward the Poor

After seeing Monsieur Vincent's charity in general, and some examples of this virtue in his life, we must now consider in greater detail his charity toward various groups of people. The first of these are the poor, for whom he had a tender love and a paternal care. If we consider his life, especially after he dedicated himself to God as a priest, it was a constant exercise of charity toward the poor, and his main works and most noted enterprises were in their favor. For them he founded various hospitals, established the Confraternities of Charity in so many places, and began the Daughters of Charity with their special mission indicated in their name, Servants of the Sick Poor. In their favor he held many fundraising meetings, which obliged his followers to undertake numerous trips. He used watchful care, and did everything he could think of to contribute to their help or service. We can say that he founded the Congregation of the Mission to evangelize the poor.

---

15. The authenticity of this account has been debated on chronological and psychological grounds.

He often used to say to his Missionaries, "We are priests of the poor. God has chosen us for them. They are our chief duty, all the rest is just secondary."[16]

In short, it seemed that the chief concern of this charitable priest was to serve the poor. This was the thing which usually occupied his mind or moved his heart. He carried the poor in his heart, and their sufferings touched him deeply. Knowing their needs and miseries, he felt it keenly when he could see no way to help them.

On one occasion, while walking with one of his confreres in the city, he spoke about the bad weather and crop failure which threatened the poor with famine and death.

> I worry about our Company, but to tell you the truth, not so much as I do about the poor. If we need to, we could ask for help from our other houses or appeal to the vicars in the parishes. But where can the poor turn? Where can they go? This is my worry and my sorrow. I am told that the peasants say they can live as long as they have their crops. Once the crops are gone, their only recourse is to retire to their graves and bury themselves alive. O God, what extreme misery! What remedy is there?

Another time, speaking to his confreres about the poor, he said:

> God loves the poor, and thus surely he must love those who love and serve them. When we also love someone, we love his friends and servants. The little Company of the Mission strives to serve the poor tenderly. God loves them so much, and so we have reason to hope that because of them God will love us as well. We then have, my brothers, a new reason to serve them. We should seek out the poorest and most abandoned. We must recognize before God that they are our lords and masters, and that we are unworthy to render them our small favors.[17]

Another time, while speaking with two highly placed priests, he said something which should not be forgotten: "'Those who love the poor in life will have nothing to fear in death, as I have seen on many occasions myself.' Because of this he tried to teach a love of the poor to those who were afraid of death."[18]

In one of his letters, speaking of the death of a virtuous priest,[19] he remarked:

> His death was in keeping with his life. He was committed to

---

16. *CED* XI:133.
17. CED XI:392-93.
18. Louis de Chandenier and Louis de Blampignon. This account was given by Brother Robineau, the saint's secretary.
19. Jean de la Salle, one of his first companions, who died October 9, 1639, at age forty-one.

carrying out the good pleasure of God's will from the beginning of his sickness to the end with no change in this sentiment. He had always lived in fear of death, but from the beginning of his last sickness he lost all fear. He even faced death with happiness, for he remembered what I had once said to him: "God takes away the fear of dying from those who have generously exercised charity toward the poor in their lives, even if during their lifetime they had always lived in this fear."[20]

Monsieur Vincent's love of the poor produced two effects in his heart. One was his great sense of compassion for their indigence and misery, for he had a most tender affection for them. For example, when the litany of Jesus was said, and he came to the words Jesu pater pauperum ["Jesus, father of the poor"], he pronounced them in a way that showed the sentiments of his heart. When people would speak to him about some particular misery or necessity of the poor, he would sigh, close his eyes, and hunch his shoulders like a person weighed down with sufferings. His face would reveal the deep suffering by which he shared in the misfortunes of the poor.

Once, in speaking about compassion for the poor, he said to his confreres:

> When we go to visit the poor we should so identify with them that we share their sufferings. We should have the same attitude as the great apostle who said *omnibus omnia factus sum*,[21] I make myself all to all, so completely that the words of the prophet would not apply to us: *Sustinui qui simul mecum contristaretur, et non fuit*,[22] I looked for someone to grieve with me in my sufferings, but found none. We must open our hearts so that they become responsive to the sufferings and miseries of the neighbor. We should pray God to give us a true spirit of mercy, which is in truth the spirit of God. The Church says that it is the nature of God to be merciful and to confer this spirit upon us. Ask this grace of God, my brothers, that he may give us this spirit of compassion and mercy, and that he may so fill us with it that as soon as anyone sees a missionary, he immediately will think, there goes a person full of compassion. Think for a moment of how much we ourselves stand in need of mercy, we who must exercise it toward others. We must bring this mercy everywhere, and endure everything for the sake of compassion.
>
> How happy our confreres in Poland are. They have suffered so much because of the wars there, not to mention the plague, all for

---

20. *CED* I:595-97.
21. 1 Cor 9:22.
22. Ps 69:21.

the sake of relieving, helping, and consoling the poor! How happy are these missionaries. Cannons, fire, armies, or the plague could not dislodge them from Warsaw. The misery and sufferings of others kept them where they were. They persevered and still persevere amid such perils and sufferings, only to show mercy. Oh, how happy they are to use this precious moment of their lives to exercise mercy! I say, "this moment," for our entire lives are but a moment, soon gone. Alas, the seventy-six years of my life seem now only a momentary dream. What remains now is only the regret that I have used this time so poorly. Think of what unhappiness we will have at the moment of our death if we have not used this brief time of our lives to show mercy to others. Brothers, be merciful toward everyone. Never meet a poor person without seeking to console him, or an uneducated person without seeking to help him understand, in a few words, what he must believe and do to assure his salvation. O Savior, do not let us abuse our vocation. Do not withdraw from this Company the spirit of mercy. What would become of us if you did so? Give us this, then, O Lord, together with the spirit of meekness and humility.[23]

On another occasion he said:

The Son of God could not have experienced a sense of compassion in the glorious state in which he existed in heaven from all eternity. He became man to share our miseries. For us to reign with him in heaven we should share with others his compassion for his people on earth. Missionaries above all other priests should be filled with this spirit of compassion. They are obliged by their state and their vocation to serve the most miserable, the most abandoned, and those suffering most from corporal or spiritual ills. First, they should feel in their hearts the sufferings of their neighbor. Second, this sentiment ought to appear in their features and their whole attitude, after the example of our Lord who wept over Jerusalem because of the calamity about to come upon the city. Third, we should use compassionate language to make our neighbors aware that we truly have their interests and sufferings at heart. Lastly, we must help them as much as we can to bring about a partial or complete end to their sufferings, for the hand must be directed as much as possible by the heart.[24]

The second effect of this love for the poor was that he always helped them as much as was in his power. He became a sort of general overseer of help

---

23. *CED* XI:340-42.
24. *CED* XI:77.

to the poor wherever they were, even in distant regions. He took great care to relieve their sufferings, and to provide food, clothing, shelter, and the other necessities of life. This is why other charitable persons willingly sent him their alms to distribute. He was so careful in this service that he always gave away more than he had received.

In this spirit a noble and virtuous priest who lived in a community in Paris and who had a large sum at his disposal for the relief of the poor, continued to send money to the Congregation of the Mission to distribute in remote provinces, even after the death of Monsieur Vincent at Saint Lazare. He said, "Monsieur Vincent was the true father of the poor and had a special grace and spirit to come to their aid. He has left this spirit as a precious heritage to his Congregation, who have followed his example and who walk in the footsteps of this worthy father."

We will not repeat here what was said elsewhere about Monsieur Vincent's activities on those occasions when the Seine overflowed. He took special care to have the bakery at Saint Lazare make bread, using the wheat of his community. It would then be brought by boat to a nearby town named Gennevilliers, about two leagues from Paris. There, the poor people, assailed by the flood waters and by famine, were reduced almost to utter ruin. They received this opportune and abundant help from the charity of this father of the poor. Two brothers were sent to distribute this food despite the danger. They distributed the bread with the help of the local pastor, who was aware of the needs of each family. This charitable service continued for as long as the flood waters lasted.

We will pass over in silence a great number of similar charitable activities of Monsieur Vincent in favor of the poor. One, however, would have been forgotten, as were many others, were it not for a document, written in his own hand, which he had to write during wartime to enable a wagon from Saint Lazare to pass through the gates of Paris. This wagon contained food destined for the poor suffering peasants, but the guards demanded proof of where it had come from, and to whom it was consigned. This certificate was written in these terms:

> I, the undersigned, the superior of the Congregation of the Mission, affirm to all concerned that I have learned from some pious persons that half the people of Palaiseau are ill, and that ten or twelve die every day. I have been asked to send them some priests for the corporal and spiritual help of these people, afflicted these past twenty days by an occupation of the army. We have sent four priests and a physician there to help them. Since the vigil of the feast of Corpus Christi we have sent every day, except for one or two, sixteen large loaves of white bread, fifteen pints of wine, and

yesterday, some meat. The priests have testified to the need for some flour and a hogshead of wine for the sick of the said town and surrounding areas. I have today sent a wagon drawn by three horses, carrying four *setiers* of flour, two half hogsheads of wine, for the relief of the sick poor of Palaiseau and surrounding villages. Testifying to these facts, I have signed this, at Saint Lazare lez Paris, this fifth day of June, 1652. Signed, Vincent de Paul, Superior.[25]

This document lets us catch a glimpse of Monsieur Vincent's charity. He sent four priests and a doctor to aid the poor and sick of Palaiseau, instead of the single priest he had been asked to send originally. While not forgetting the spiritual welfare of these poor souls, he first relieved their hunger and looked after their health. He did so at once, with all possible diligence. He sent his priests, provisions, horses from the community, and not waiting for other alms, he sent money from the community treasury amounting to 663 *livres*. This deprived him of all the community's reserve, so that he had to ask the duchess of Aiguillon if she might help to relieve this pressing need. She was not able to do so, but instead called a meeting of the Ladies of Charity at her home to see what could be done. He wrote her:

I have sent another priest and a brother, and fifty more *livres*. The pestilence is so virulent that the first four priests have all taken sick, and also the brother who accompanied them. I had to bring them back here, where two of them are still very sick. Oh, Madame, what a harvest to gather for heaven at this time when this misery is so close to our very doors! As scripture says, the coming of the Son of God was the downfall of some and the redemption of many. In some way, we can say the same of this war, which causes the loss of so many. Yet God uses this war to give his grace, salvation, and glory to others. We have reason to hope that you are in that number, as I pray to our Lord that you are.[26]

This charitable intervention by Monsieur Vincent to help the poor of Palaiseau was also the occasion when he helped the people of Etampes and other places near Paris, with the help of the Ladies of Charity of Paris, and some other persons of great piety. All these persons gained great merit by their involvement in these works of mercy, and their memory will never die.

This has been but a small sample of the charitable attempts of Monsieur Vincent to aid the poor as much as he could and in every way he could. When he did all that he could, and yet saw that his own resources and those of his friends were still insufficient, his last resource was the queen mother. He did not want to make a nuisance of himself, for it was well known that she was

---

25. *CED* XIII:362.
26. *CED* IV:424.

generous in many other works of piety. Yet in the case of extreme necessity he would present her with the pressing needs of the poor, confident that he would get a hearing. He was never disappointed.

This charitable princess would open her arms, but even more, her heart, to help him. When she had money available she would give it to him. If money was lacking, she would give him other things to help out. Once she gave him a diamond worth seven thousand *livres*. Another time she gave him a beautiful set of earrings, which the Ladies of Charity sold for eighteen thousand *livres*. Although, through a sentiment of Christian humility, Her Majesty requested Monsieur Vincent not to reveal the source of his benefactions, he did not feel obliged to accede to her request. He said to her, "Madame, Your Majesty will please pardon me if I no longer keep secret such a marvelous example of charity. It is good, Madame, that all of Paris and even all of France should know of it. I feel obliged to speak of it wherever I go."

Monsieur Vincent held this truth, that in helping the poor he should be partial to the most abandoned. Following this maxim, he had a special love for abandoned children, since they were most in need and least able to help themselves. He had a tender love for these poor innocents, but it was as effective as it was affective. Speaking to his community once on this subject he said:

> Is it not the duty of fathers to look after the needs of their children? Since God has put us in the place of their parents to save the lives of these children, to raise them, and to instruct them in saving knowledge, we must take care not to fail in a task so dear to him. After their own mothers have left them exposed on the doorsteps, if we too should neglect their care and education, what would become of them? Could we consent to see them all die, as used to happen in this great city of Paris?[27]

A well-respected person, aware of the efforts of Monsieur Vincent for these poor little creatures, and also aware of how even the most charitable ladies who had undertaken their care were losing heart because of the large expense involved, had this to say several years before Monsieur Vincent's death: "God alone knows how many sighs and groans Monsieur Vincent raised to heaven in favor of these small children. Who can count the number of times he asked his Company to pray for them? Who can know his efforts to feed them as economically as possible? Who can tell of his care in these last years in having the Daughters of Charity visit the wet nurses in various villages? Or the visits by a brother for the same reason for more than six weeks in 1649?"

---

27. Abelly's version differs considerably from *CED* XII:89.

Once it was reported to him that a priest of the Congregation had complained that the care of these abandoned children caused the great poverty of the house at Saint Lazare. He charged that it was in difficult straits and in danger of complete ruin, all because the alms received for the upkeep of the house were being diverted to the care of these children. He said that their needs seemed greater and more pressing than those of the community, and that those who had been contributing to the upkeep of Saint Lazare could not support both the children and the Congregation.

Monsieur Vincent replied to these complaints:

God will forgive me this failing, which is in keeping with the sentiments of the Gospel. What a lack of faith it is to believe that by looking after these poor and abandoned children our Lord will take less care of us. Don't forget, he has promised to repay a hundredfold whatever is done in his name. Since our loving Savior told his disciples to let the little children come to him, can we reject them or abandon them when they come to us? What kindness he showed to children. He went so far as to take them in his arms, and bless them with his hands. Did he not on that occasion give us this as a rule of salvation by showing us that we must do the same if we are to enter the kingdom of heaven? To love these children and to care for them is in some way to become their fathers. To see to the needs of these abandoned children is to replace their fathers and mothers, or rather God himself, who said that even if a mother should forget her child, he would never forget. If our Lord still lived among us on earth, and if he came across these abandoned children, do you think he would pass them by? It would offend his divine goodness even to have such a thought. We would be unfaithful to his grace if after having been chosen by Providence to provide the corporal care and spiritual good of these poor abandoned children we would desert them, all because they are causing us too much trouble.

SECTION THREE

His Alms

The subject of this section will perhaps trouble some readers. They will wonder how the superior general of a congregation, on his own initiative and without the consent of the members, could distribute so much of the wealth of the congregation to the poor. Even more, how could Monsieur Vincent do so? He was so humble, so deferential, and so committed to evangelical poverty, that, without the approval of the community, as we saw in Book One, he would not give even a modest sum to his own nephew who had traveled two hundred leagues to visit him at great cost to the meager resources of his family. If he had insisted on obtaining the express approval of the community for this expense, how, we wonder, could he give such abundant alms to the poor? This faithful servant of God often and generously helped all sorts of poor people at the expense of his community, as we shall see in these pages.

At first sight this appears somewhat surprising. Those favorably inclined to him might probably think that he acted through one of those extraordinary inspirations of the Holy Spirit which sometimes makes the saints in themselves more admirable in their practice of virtue rather than as models to imitate. This might be true here, and we might see in the life of Monsieur Vincent the extraordinary direction of the hand of God, which made him act with that divine prudence of Jesus Christ, so opposed to the wisdom of the flesh. Nevertheless, we still can consider some aspects of the case which make his conduct more understandable.

In the first place, we must recognize Monsieur Vincent not only as the superior general, but also as the source, the founder, and the organizer of this new congregation, founded on charity. While he lived it was still in its formative stages. After God, it was he who gave it being, form, and consistency. He prescribed its organization, employments, and functions. He accepted, taught, and perfected those who came to the Congregation. They always looked upon him as their true father and in turn Monsieur Vincent regarded them as his dear children. He could speak of them in imitation of the holy apostle: *Filioli quos iterum parturio donec Christus formetur in vobis* ["You are my children, and you put me back in labor pains until Christ is formed in you"].[28]

Since this was so, we should look upon him not merely as superior general, but rather as founder and father, using the goods of the family held jointly by him and his children. He controlled these goods during their minority and gave them away, not for any personal interests but for those of Jesus Christ, and in the service and relief of his brothers and sisters, the poor. Some rigorous legalist might point out that in any case he still should have obtained the consent of the children of the family. Yet he could be answered by saying that Monsieur Vincent possessed such a union of hearts with them

---

28. Gal 4:19.

that he never even considered the necessity of consulting them or seeking their authorization for his activities. They willed what he willed. What he did was so good, so holy, and so conformed to the designs and orders of God that it would insult their virtue to think they disagreed with him in the least.

Besides, we are speaking here of the beginnings of a new company, with both its temporal and spiritual traditions not yet fully formed. It is not enough to organize a community outwardly. The interior spirit proper to its own end must also be formed and communicated to its members. One of the community's chief ends, as we have said, was the evangelization of the poor, with the obligation of providing them all possible services and help. For this to happen, a spirit of compassion would have to be developed in the community, which would be characterized by a tenderness and love for the poor. Since the inspiration of the holy founder was that the members of the Company should expose and sacrifice their very lives, to the extent needed, to achieve the salvation of the poor, he was surely justified in distributing a good part of their temporal goods to these same poor, especially when this help contributed to their spiritual progress.

The state of public affairs at the beginning of the Congregation of the Mission was tragic: calamities and miseries of all kinds had overwhelmed most of the provinces of the kingdom and even all of Europe. The extreme poverty of the peasants of the countryside, and the villages overcome by the ravages of war and other misfortunes so moved the charitable heart of Monsieur Vincent that he did everything in his power to come to their aid. He appealed to the wealthy to show compassion and mercy. He persuaded them to contribute in proportion to the extreme conditions endured by countless poor people, many on the verge of perishing.

This prudent and faithful servant of Jesus Christ was well aware that actions speak louder than words. He could not have chosen a more powerful argument for help from others in the great works of charity which he practiced during his entire life than the example of what he himself had first done before recommending it to others. What made his example even more effective was that he went beyond what was merely reasonable. He and his followers took what they gave to the poor from their own resources. Far from lessening their commitment and love for the poor, this rather increased their determination to devote themselves completely to the spiritual help of these same poor people.

All this being true, let us examine just a small part of what this father of the poor gave to them. I say just a small part, since only God knows everything he did. His humility always sought to conceal his actions from others, since he acted solely for the love of God. He was far from imitating those whom Jesus Christ condemned in the Gospel: those who blew the trumpet before giving alms, or used other devices to attract attention to what they had done for the poor.[29] On the contrary, he used all his ingenuity to conceal his gifts. He never spoke of them, and was visibly embarrassed when others mentioned them. He incurred other heavy expenses in favor of the poor, either by sending his Missionaries to remote places to help them, or by paying the postage on letters addressed to him. These came either from distant provinces or from the poor slaves of Algiers, Tunis, Bizerte or elsewhere, and the cost amounted to great sums. He never spoke about these matters or took this expense into account. It was enough for him that God was aware of what he did and approved of it. If some of his charitable works became known, he would make light of them, saying it was simply a case of beggars giving their scraps and rags to other beggars.

He had established the Confraternity of Charity in the parish of Saint Laurent. Because this parish lay within the bounds of the Saint Lazare section of the city, he would donate two hundred *livres* each year to support this confraternity, as well as the Daughters of Charity, Servants of the Sick Poor in this parish. In addition, every Friday he would send two priests from Saint Lazare to visit and console the sick among the poor.

When poor persons living near Saint Lazare would die, even when he did not know them, he would provide a shroud for them if they did not have one. Once, after burying a poor woman at his expense, Monsieur Vincent received her husband into the house, where the man remained quite ill for a long time. He did the same for another man, caring for him until he died.

Once, meeting an almost naked man in the street near Saint Lazare, he at once gave him a garment. This was not unusual, for he often gave away shoes, a hat, or shirts, all at the expense of the house.

Each day he received two poor people at Saint Lazare. He had them dine with the community, after first giving them any spiritual instruction which they needed. Often it was observed that this friend of the poor, after greeting them with great affability, would help them up the steps to the refectory, and seat them beside himself. He would then see to it they were well taken care of, and would himself render little services to them.

Besides these two poor persons, each day he would distribute bread, soup, and meat to poor families who would come to the door of Saint Lazare. Two other practices that he had were to distribute bread and even money to poor peasants who came to the door no matter at what hour. Another distribution of bread and soup was made at a fixed hour three times a week for whomever might be passing by, regardless of where they came from. On all these occasions a short instruction would be given on some point of the catechism or on the duties of a Christian. After explaining the chief mysteries they

---

29. Matt 6:2.

should know and believe, those receiving aid were taught how to pray, how to live good lives despite their poverty, and how to bear their sufferings and deprivations with patience. All those points were in keeping with their state in life, and had been arranged by Monsieur Vincent himself.

Hundreds of these poor would always come for help, and sometimes the number reached five or six hundred. He did have to stop distributing soup two or three years before his death, because after the establishment of the general hospital for the poor of Paris he was forbidden to do so. When the poor would complain to him, "Father, did not God direct that alms should be given to the poor?", he would reply, "Yes, it is true, my friends, but God has also commanded that we should obey the magistrates." Despite these prohibitions, on the occasion of a particularly severe winter which brought many poor families to the brink of disaster, he would distribute soup and bread each day.

During the time of troubles in Paris he had this daily distribution made to nearly two thousand people, at a great cost to the house at Saint Lazare, which still remains in debt because of this charity. At that time he was obliged to be away from Paris for a long time, as we related in Book One.[30] He was informed of the pillage, thefts, and losses committed by the eight hundred soldiers quartered in Saint Lazare, but realizing the great suffering of the poor, he did not lessen his care for them. He wrote to his assistant telling him to continue this daily distribution of bread, using up to three *setiers* of flour each day, although it was then exceedingly costly. It was impossible to find wheat in Paris, no matter what you were willing to pay. The charity of this true father of the poor was above all such considerations, which would have deterred anyone less generous than he. The brother baker of the house, in charge of the wheat, has declared that in three months he used ten *muids* for making bread. We must admire God's Providence, for three months later, around Easter, the community did not have enough bread to live on, and seemed on the point of starvation. Just at that moment a settlement between the warring factions was reached, and passage to the outside countryside was again allowed. By borrowing money, the community was finally able to buy wheat. The care which divine goodness takes of those who help the poor was thus shown for all to see.

A virtuous priest testified to these events.

> We can see the great heart of Monsieur Vincent and his incomparable love for the poor by considering that when he learned of the damage done to Saint Lazare by the soldiers, and the shortages caused by the blockade of Paris, he directed the late Monsieur Lambert, his assistant, to provide daily aid to the poor. The house of Saint Lazare had to borrow sixteen to twenty thousand *livres* to

---

30. Ch. 39.

carry out these directives. Each day the missionaries distributed bread and provided two or three large cauldrons of soup for the poor, all as if the wheat cost the house nothing. This continued for several months, even after the settlement of the war, and fortunately several other communities and some rich persons have imitated it. This latter effect is not the least of the blessings owed to the charitable initiative of Monsieur Vincent for the relief of the poor. He has been their father and provider everywhere and always.

What is noteworthy is that he was not content to distribute alms to those who came to Saint Lazare seeking help. He even sent out his confreres, a priest and a brother, into the hovels and caves of Paris seeking out those in need, especially the sick. Since charity has neither measure nor limits, he directed his care to persons of all classes and nations.

In this regard, he learned of a group of Irish Catholics in Paris, exiled for their faith and reduced to great misery. He called in a priest of the Congregation of the Mission, a native of Ireland, and asked what might possibly be done to help these poor refugees. He said to the priest, "Is there no way we can bring them together, to console them in their suffering, and instruct them? They do not understand our language, and they seem so abandoned. My heart is stricken for I have great compassion for them." The priest responded that he would do what he could. "God bless you," replied Monsieur Vincent, "here are ten *pistoles*. Go in the name of God, to give them whatever consolation you can." We should remark that this help was quite apart from what he also did for some Irish priests, which we will describe below.[31]

Once, a young man, who had served as a tailor, returned to his own region from Saint Lazare. Aware from experience of the great charity of Monsieur Vincent, he took the liberty of writing to him, at a time when he was preoccupied with affairs at court, to ask him to send a packet of one hundred needles from Paris. He took this request seriously, and saw to it that the needles were sent. In no way did he show that he thought it strange to be bothered by such a trifling request.

Once when returning to Saint Lazare he found several poor women at the door asking for an alms. He said he would find something to give them. No sooner had he entered the house, however, than he was taken up with several important and pressing matters of business so that he forgot the women at the door. As soon as he remembered, however, he brought the alms himself, and falling on his knees before them, begged their pardon for having forgotten them and for making them wait.

Once a poor woman asked an alms from Monsieur Vincent. He sent her a half-*ecu*, but she complained that in her great need this was not enough.

---

31. Sect. 5.

Without further ado he sent her another half-*sou*. Such events were not unusual with him.

A poor drayman who lost his horses had recourse to Monsieur Vincent, and asked for help in making up this loss. At once his charitable benefactor gave him one hundred *livres*.

A tenant farmer of the community of Saint Lazare found himself unable to pay what he owed. Monsieur Vincent responded by giving him something himself. It is impossible to know how often he helped the farmers, tenants, or other debtors of the community who were unable to meet their obligations. He preferred to make new loans and risk losing everything, rather than to demand payment from them.

Through a long-term lease a farmer held a property belonging to a hospital, but being unable to pay his rent, he was evicted. After his death, he left his wife and children in great poverty. Monsieur Vincent took the two small boys into the house at Saint Lazare. He cared for them there for nearly ten years, and used the opportunity to have them taught a trade so they could earn their living. He also contributed to the support of the poor widow during this same time.

Monsieur Vincent's reputation as a man of great charity attracted a large number of people to Saint Lazare from Paris and elsewhere. Some had been prosperous or had come from respectable families. Some of these came to him in confidence to tell him of their problems, but others were ashamed at having to accept alms, and instead asked only for a loan. He gave something to everyone, to some more, to others less, often down to the last *sou* of the community's money. On these occasions he would borrow from Mademoiselle Le Gras, so as to have something to give to those who came to him.

There were a few others to whom he gave some money every month. One man showed up shortly before Monsieur Vincent's death, saying that for seventeen years he had been coming for these alms, which amounted to two *ecus* every month. He had come to regard it as a sum owed him, almost as a regular income.

One day while returning in a carriage from the country to Paris, Monsieur Vincent saw a poor person along the road. He was all covered with sores and had an otherwise revolting appearance. He had the poor man step into the carriage, and took him to his destination in Paris. He often did similar things, particularly during the winter when he would meet older or handicapped persons. He would have them get in the carriage with him, which through humility he called "my infamy," out of his sense that he was unworthy of this convenience. His attitude was that whatever he had, whether possessions or advantages, ought to be shared with the poor, so great was his love, tenderness, and compassion for them.

When he saw poor sick persons lying along the streets or lanes he would go up to them to find out what was wrong or what they needed, so he could provide some relief for them. When he saw they were not pretending but were really sick, he would offer to take them to the hospital in Paris. If he were not in his carriage, he would have them taken there. Not content to pay those who transported them, he would give the sick person an alms as well.

One day while riding through Paris he saw a young boy in distress. He stopped the carriage, went to the boy to find out what his trouble was. When the boy showed him that he had cut his hand badly, Monsieur Vincent took him at once to a doctor. He then waited until he was treated, paid the doctor, and in parting gave a bit of money to the poor child.

There was an old soldier people called "The Sieve" because of the number of wounds he had sustained in the war. He showed up one day at Saint Lazare knowing no one, but since he had heard of the charity of Monsieur Vincent he felt free to ask if he might stay at the house for several days. This was willingly accorded him, but several days later he fell sick. Monsieur Vincent moved him to a room with a stove. For two months he took care of him, and even assigned a brother to look after him until he was completely cured.

These are but a few samples of the charity which this holy man showed to the poor. We should not be surprised at these. Though he was extraordinarily generous in their behalf, what he gave came from his heart. He was even prepared to risk his life for the good of their souls. He wished nothing so much as to provide every sort of service to them, for the love of Jesus Christ whom he honored in them. He looked on the poor as true images of that infinite charity which led our divine Savior to forego all riches. He became poor for our sakes, so that, as the apostle says, we might become rich through his poverty.[32]

SECTION FOUR

His Affectionate Regard for the Prelates of the Church

We have already seen in Book Two some of the ways Monsieur Vincent sought to help various bishops, and at the beginning of this chapter we touched on his great love and respect for their sacred persons.[33] We must

---

32. 2 Cor 8:9.
33. Book Two, ch. 13, sect. 6.

admit, however, that all we have said or could say on this subject would fall still far short of the full extent of his efforts. We cannot find the words to express adequately his veneration, respect, and love for prelates of the Church whom he recognized and honored as collaborators on earth of Jesus Christ and the successors of the apostles. For this reason we have thought it best to allow him to speak for himself, and to let him explain his own disposition of soul in these instances. We have taken extracts from only some of the letters which have come to our attention, among the many which he wrote at various times to many bishops in various parts of the kingdom.

A bishop of great merit, since deceased, whom Monsieur Vincent had earlier recommended for the episcopacy, wrote of the first fruits of his work in his diocese. Monsieur Vincent congratulated him:

> Who could fail to recognize that it is a blessing from God for the diocese of N. to have a bishop who brings peace to souls, especially in a place that has not seen a bishop or had a visitation for a hundred years. Thus, would it be possible, Your Excellency, to esteem you enough, or to have an adequate respect for your person? May I say only that you are truly a gift from God, a bishop filled with grace, a totally apostolic man. You make Jesus Christ known to even the most desolate people. May his holy name be blessed forever, and may he confer on you many years on earth, to be crowned by a glorious eternity in heaven. There you will be received by the great army of the blessed souls who are there because of you and who will welcome you as their second savior after Jesus Christ.[34]

Another bishop was contemplating resigning from his diocese because he felt incapable of directing it. He wrote to Monsieur Vincent several times, asking him to help find a worthy successor. Monsieur Vincent replied in these terms:

> Your Excellency, your letters have awakened in me such respect and affection for you that I have, if I dare say so, your request ever before my eyes. I scarcely recognize the person you describe when you refer to me. You, Your Excellency, are as far above the one to whom you write to as the mountain is above the valley, but wishing to be at your service I must do what you request, on this as on every other occasion.[35]

He wrote to another bishop who, because of some difficulties he wished to avoid was likewise considering resigning his position:

> Your Excellency, I cannot tell you the sorrow I felt at hearing of your illness. Only God knows the tenderness of heart that I experi-

---

34. *CED* III:532-33.
35. *CED* IV:105-06.

ence in everything concerning you. My consolation is that your illness has a remedy and, I hope, a cure. I too had a similar problem some time ago. I lost feeling in one of my fingers, but this has since cleared up. May it please God, Your Excellency, that you be preserved for the good of your diocese, which I hear you are thinking of leaving. If I may say so, taking this liberty because of your kindness, it seems to me that you should let things remain as they are for fear that God will not be honored in your resignation. Where is the man who would be able to walk in your footsteps or rival you in your reputation? If such a one can be found, well and good, but in our troubled times I think it is too much to expect. You, Your Excellency, have not experienced in your episcopacy difficulties as great as Saint Paul did in his, yet he carried the burden until death. None of the apostles walked away from their responsibilities, except when finally called to receive their crowns in heaven. I would be too bold, Your Excellency, to recall these examples to you, did not God himself invite you to imitate them and if the liberty I take did not flow from the great respect and boundless affection the Lord has given me for your sacred person.[36]

On another occasion, a worthy bishop wrote, outlining some twenty outstanding difficulties on which he wished Monsieur Vincent's advice. The latter began his reply in these words:

Alas, Your Excellency, what are you doing? To write to me about so many important matters, to me who am a poor unlettered soul, hateful to both God and man because of my past sins and present unworthiness. I am unsuited for the honor your own humility has conferred on me, and I would keep quiet were it not that you have bidden me speak. Here then are my poor thoughts on the matters you brought to my attention, which I offer simply with the greatest respect. I cannot begin better than to thank God for all the graces he has granted you, begging him to further his own glory by bestowing success on you and your ministry which you carry out with such extraordinary zeal and devotion.

I am sure that you will be happy to know that your reverend brother has just finished a retreat with our priests at Richelieu. The superior there told me that your brother had greatly edified the small community there by his devotion, wisdom, and modesty. He has experienced such satisfaction at the exercises of piety that he plans to celebrate the feast of Christmas with them. Since I know well, Your Excellency, that nothing is closer to Your Excellency's heart

---

36. *CED* IV:47-48.

than that your close relatives give themselves to God, I pass along this information to you. I know that you will be pleased to hear it. I, too, rejoice with you. I realize also that since you are working so hard to bring about God's kingdom in your diocese, he is doing the same for your own family.[37]

Responding to another prelate who wrote expressing similar difficulties, he wrote:

> I have received the letter which you did me the honor of writing. I have read and reread it, Your Excellency, not to reflect on the question you raise but to admire your judgment which appears to me to be more than human. Only the Spirit of God dwelling in your sacred person could lead you to the combination of justice and charity such as you propose in this affair. It remains only for me to thank God for the sacred light he has given you, and for the regard you have shown to me, your humble servant. The problems you bring to my attention are so far beyond me that I think of them only with great hesitation. It is only because I wish to obey your request that I can bring myself to reply.[38]

On one occasion Monsieur Vincent became painfully aware that a bishop with whom he was friendly was involved in a lawsuit. He suggested a possible compromise to conclude the affair and at the end of the letter he wrote:

> In the name of God, Bishop, pardon me if I get involved in your affairs not knowing if my initiatives here are agreeable to you. Perhaps you will not be pleased. It cannot be helped because I acted only out of my regard for you, and to see you free of the cares and distraction these annoying affairs must cause you. I would very much like to see you return with tranquility of mind to the direction and sanctification of your diocese. For this grace I often offer to God my poor prayers.
>
> One thing pains me deeply, Bishop, and that is that you have been described to the council as a bishop so given to litigation that this is a common impression in many minds. For myself I admire our Savior Jesus Christ who disapproved of lawsuits. He did endure one, which he did not win. I do not doubt, Your Excellency, that if you are involved in litigation, it is only because you are defending your rights. I am sure that all the while you also preserve your interior peace amid all the contradictions of these affairs, looking solely to God and not to the world. You are committed to pleasing

---

37. *CED* IV:165-66.
38. *CED* IV:171.

his divine Majesty without regard to the remarks of others. For this I thank his divine goodness, for this trait is found only in those souls intimately united to him. But I must also tell you, Bishop, that this unfortunate opinion which the council has of you is likely to do you harm, and prevent your getting what you ask.[39]

This good bishop did not accept the compromise suggested by Monsieur Vincent in this letter. Monsieur Vincent did not argue the point, but wrote later in these terms:

Your Excellency, I humbly beg of you to allow me once more to suggest another compromise. I know well that you do not doubt for a minute the affection of my poor heart for you. Yet you may take offense at my lack of intelligence, and at my insistence in presenting a second compromise when the first has already been rejected.

Nevertheless, this compromise does not come from myself, but from the court secretary whom I have seen for the last two days to plead your cause. I spoke of the graces God has given you, and through you to your diocese. He replied that he was your humble servant, and that of all the people in the world he was the one who respected and esteemed you the most. In this spirit he asked me to tell you that if you would accept his advice you could settle all your difficulties. He gave me several reasons for this, among others that it would be to your benefit for a great prelate to settle the case in this way, especially in what relates to your clergy who are moved by a spirit of revolt and by their annoyance at petty grievances. He is aware of the sentiment of the council, and fears the probable outcome of these events. Several of the members of council are unaware of your saintly life and the noble motives which guide your decisions. They may thus decide against you and your dignity in this case. Bishop, please excuse my boldness in writing. My suggestions come not from me but from your own court advocate, one of the wisest men of the times and one of the best judges in the whole world. There are more people who come to him for advice than come even to the heads of the civil courts, and anyone would think himself happy to have him as an advocate. I pray God that he will restore peace to your diocese and contentment to your spirit. You know the influence you exercise over me, and the singular love God has given me for your service. If you think it proper to ask me to render you any help at all, I shall do so with all my heart.[40]

---

39. *CED* II:434-35.
40. *CED* II:435-36.

Monsieur Vincent wrote to congratulate a saintly bishop who had taken the trouble to attend the ordination retreats every day and to give a conference:

> I thank Your Excellency most humbly for the honor you have bestowed on your seminarians by your presence and instructions during the ordination retreats. I thank God for the favor he has bestowed on those privileged to hear you, and to see a bishop in the exercise of his ecclesiastical office. I hope they will carry the memory of this all their lives, and that they will continue to benefit from it for many years. Besides, I have received the letter with which Your Excellency honored me, first with joy because it comes from your hands, but second, with sorrow since it also speaks of what happened at your synod. In this, Bishop, I appreciate the action of God who thereby tests the virtue of one of his greatest servants, but also I admire the good use Your Excellency has made of this trial. I pray the divine Goodness to strengthen you more and more in this matter, so that your patience will bring all this to a happy end, to the shame of those who dared oppose you.[41]

Several people were complaining to the king that a certain bishop was not fulfilling the duties of his office. The king issued a *lettre de cachet*.[42] Monsieur Vincent became aware of this, and of the anguish it caused the bishop in question. He therefore wrote to console him:

> Your Excellency, I am so sorry to hear that you have received a letter from the court. I was greatly astonished to hear about it. I hope that I may find myself able to speak in your defense. Be assured that I will use every opportunity to do so when God will give me the means. I have always tried to make known, in every place and circumstance, the full esteem and reverence I have for your sacred person. Every time I consider the help you have been to our poor missionaries in their efforts for the instruction and salvation of your people I am moved anew. Our fathers are happy and content to work under your kind direction.[43]

He wrote to an archbishop on another subject:

> Your Excellency, I blush for shame each time I read the letter you did me the honor of writing, and more so at the way Your Lordship abases himself before a poor swineherd who is now a miserable old man filled with sin. I regret that I have given you cause to plan to come here by refusing your request for additional

---
41. *CED* IV:194.
42. A letter sealed by the king, giving permission for some action to be carried out without publicity.
43. *CED* V:50-51.

men. You may be assured that I wrote not from any lack of respect or submission, but solely because of the impossibility of obeying your wishes at this time. Please give us a six-month delay, and we shall then be greatly pleased to satisfy your request, which at present it did not please God to allow. In God's name, Your Excellency, please excuse our poverty. Save your visit to Paris for a more important occasion. It would be a blessing of God to receive Your Lordship, but I would be very embarrassed to have you go to all that trouble for no reason. Your Excellency knows well that no one in the world is more disposed to receive your orders than we, and me particularly, whom God has placed under your sovereign rule.[44]

He wrote to another archbishop about some of his people enslaved by the Barbary pirates:

Your Excellency, I have received your letter with the respect and reverence owed to one of the greatest and most worthy prelates of the kingdom. I have a great desire to fulfill all that you were pleased to ask of me. I thank God for your desire to deliver your people from this slavery. You show an immense charity in a work most agreeable to God, to deliver them from this imminent peril, and you give a good example to other bishops in going after the stray sheep and bringing them back safely to the flock. Many are living in this dangerous condition. For our part, we are happy to respond to your request and will send some of our priests to help ransom the slaves. I have written today to the consuls of Tunis and Algiers asking for passports so that they can go there in safety, as you have asked.[45]

Since Monsieur Vincent was so concerned about seeing the Church served by good and holy bishops, he was disturbed at seeing some persons so zealous in their commitment to those afflicted by the plague that they endangered their own lives and thereby risked depriving the Church of their services. He felt moved for the sake of the greater good of all to write to them to ask them to temper their zeal. One of these zealous bishops replied that he would not spare himself, and that he was willing to die in the ministry if necessary. Monsieur Vincent admitted his error in having suggested that he moderate his activities, and congratulated him for his fervor and zeal in his ministry.

Your Excellency, I did suggest moderation. This was only to preserve your service for a longer time and to avoid depriving your diocese and the entire Church of the incomparable blessing of your care. If my thought is not in keeping with your own ideas, I am not

---

44. *CED* VIII:320.
45. *CED* V:146-47.

surprised. The human sentiments inspiring me are far beneath the eminent state to which the love of God has brought you. I am still too earthly, but you are above nature. I think less of deploring my own faults than of giving thanks to God for the holy dispositions he has given you. I beg of you most humbly, Your Excellency, to beseech him not to give me these same dispositions but rather only some small portion of them, perhaps even a few of the crumbs which fall from your table.[46]

Before finishing this chapter we must consider another letter of Monsieur Vincent written to a holy bishop who wished to serve in person the plague stricken. He first, however, wanted to take counsel of Monsieur Vincent before becoming personally involved. He received the following response, which may serve as useful advice in similar situations:

Your Excellency, I cannot express the anguish I feel at the disease that has overtaken your city. The confidence you have placed in me overwhelms me. I pray with all my heart that God may turn away this scourge from your diocese, and fill me with his spirit in replying to your request. My humble thought, Your Excellency, is that a prelate who finds himself in this predicament ought to conduct himself in such a way as to attend to the spiritual and temporal welfare of all the people of his diocese, especially during times of public calamity. He ought not be tied down to one place or to one occupation, nor to any situation that would limit his availability to others. The reason is that he is not bishop of only this or that place but of his entire diocese. He should divide this burden as much as possible. But if it is not possible to see to the salvation of souls by the help of pastors or other clergy, then I think he is obliged to risk even his life for their salvation. He should entrust the care of the others to God's adorable Providence.

This, Your Excellency, is what one of the greatest prelates of this kingdom did, Bishop N., who urged his pastors to endanger themselves for the welfare of their parishioners. When the plague would break out in a particular place he would immediately go there to encourage his priests in their service to the people. He would advise and instruct them on the best way to alleviate the sufferings of the afflicted. He did not visit the sick in person, however, unless he found that he could not provide care for them from the local parishes. Saint Charles Borromeo acted otherwise. This appears, however, to have been by a special inspiration of God, or else because the plague was within the city of Milan itself.

---

46. *CED* IV:31.

Because it is difficult to do in a large diocese what can more easily be done in a small one, it seems, Your Excellency, that it would be good to plan on visiting the regions where the sick are, to encourage your pastors. If this proves impossible or if you are in danger of capture by the army in this time of war, you might send the archdeacons or other clergy for the same purpose. As soon as you learn of the epidemic striking another place you might send other priests there to encourage the pastors and to give some physical help to the stricken.

The queen of Poland learned that the plague had stricken the city of Krakow, and that as soon as a case of this illness was discovered, the homes of the plague stricken were quarantined. This, of course, led to both the well and the sick greatly suffering from hunger and the cold. The queen sent a large sum by two of our Missionaries, with orders to look after the feeding of the victims in their homes, but these priests were careful not to come in contact with the sick.

Some religious ran this risk by administering the sacraments to the sick. The queen may not have stopped this scourge, but at least she greatly diminished the ravages of the plague, and greatly consoled the people of that city, the capital of the kingdom. The city of Warsaw, where the king now lives, has also been stricken. One of our priests informed me that he had directed two of our Missionaries, a priest and a brother, to give the same help there.

The poor stricken people of the countryside are for the most part abandoned by all and in great need of help, particularly food. It would be something worthy of Your Excellency's piety, if you could send alms to all the stricken places, so that the good pastors could provide bread, wine, and even some meat to the poor people. They should be alerted to the time and place where the distribution will take place. If there is question about the honesty of certain pastors, the distribution could be handled by neighboring pastors, or by some worthy laymen of the parish. You can usually find some persons in every parish for this service, especially if they do not have to come in direct contact with the sick. I hope, Your Excellency, that if God blesses this work, our Savior will be much glorified by Your Excellency's life and even death, and by the edification your people will experience by all this. The one essential thing is that you must not shut yourself up out of harm's way.

The Missionaries I have sent you, Bishop, have told me that the Lord has given them the grace of committing themselves to the care of the plague-stricken, either those in their own neighborhood, or all over the city, as obedience and necessity will require. I have written them to be at your call, and I beg you most humbly to dispose of us as your great goodness will deem appropriate.

Many religious have offered to serve the sick, so I don't doubt that you will discover some in your city. Perhaps you will find enough to take care of the city itself. You might even be able to send some to the country places as well, instead of the archdeacons and priests I spoke of earlier. You will see, Your Excellency, by the broadside I enclose, what the archbishop of Paris has done to help the stricken people there. It will give you some ideas on how you might help your own people.[47]

After receiving this letter, this good prelate wrote to Monsieur Vincent as follows:

Upon receiving the offer of the services of your priests to serve the plague-stricken, I must say that since they work for the entire diocese, I shall not expose them to the danger of infection without an extreme necessity. I shall follow your advice in all points. I shall be careful myself not to risk danger unless I see clearly that such is God's will. I had put off doing anything until I had heard from you, but now the time for reflection is past, and I shall put into action what you suggest.[48]

SECTION FIVE

His Regard for Priests and Other Members of the Clergy

To appreciate Monsieur Vincent's high regard for priests and other members of the clergy we have only to recall all that he did for them, as we have made abundantly clear in Books One and Two. It is not necessary to produce any other evidence or testimony. We will, however, examine the results of the ordination retreats, the spiritual conferences, the retreats, seminaries, and all the other undertakings which this great servant of God initiated for the reformation, sanctification, and perfection of the clerical state. Besides these works in general, many particular events deserve to be

---

47. *CED* IV:520-23.
48. *CED* IV:528.

reported to help us better understand his respect and love for all those who ministered in the Church.

In this sentiment he wrote one day to the superior of one of his houses, a seminary for clerics:

> I greet you with tenderness and love for you personally and all your family. I pray our Lord will bless them abundantly and that this blessing will fall upon the seminary as well. May all those who study there, in whom you strive to inculcate the priestly spirit, be filled with this grace. I do not plead for them, for you already are well aware that they are the treasure of the Church.[49]

Speaking to another priest on the same subject, he said:

> How happy you are to serve our Lord as the instrument for providing good priests. You are a person who can both enlighten and inflame your students. You fulfill the role of the Holy Spirit, who alone enlightens and warms hearts. Rather, the Holy Spirit fulfills this function through you. He resides and works in you, not only to help you to live the divine life, but also to bring that same life to birth in these gentlemen, your students. They are called to the highest possible ministry upon earth, which is to imitate the two great virtues of Jesus Christ, worship of his Father, and charity for others. Consider then, Monsieur, if any earthly occupation is more necessary or more desirable than yours. For myself, I do not know of any, and I imagine God has favored you with this same appreciation since you give yourself so completely to your ministry. God has given you his grace to ensure success in your work. Humble yourself before him, always have full confidence in his goodness so that you may become united to him.[50]

The regard Monsieur Vincent had for the clergy can be seen by the courteous way he treated all other religious communities, and the way he tried to duplicate these in other places as the opportunity presented itself. In this regard he once received an urgent letter from a worthy priest who had set up a community of priests in his benefice in Anjou. The letter requested several priests of the Mission to help in this attempt, but Monsieur Vincent found it impossible to comply. He sent the following reply:

> The Spirit of God has evidently shed his graces abundantly upon you. Zeal and charity have taken deep root in your soul, and nothing stands in your way to work for the greater glory of God within your benefice, both for the present and future.
>
> May it please the divine goodness, Monsieur, to prosper your

---

49. *CED* V:382.
50. *CED* VI:393-94.

good intentions and bring them to a happy fulfillment. I thank you from my heart for the patience you show toward us who are unable to accept the honor or the financial arrangements you offer, nor to respond to your expectations. I hope, Monsieur, that you will be able to find satisfaction elsewhere. I don't know exactly where you might seek this help, because I doubt if the fathers of Saint Sulpice or those of Saint Nicolas du Chardonnet would give you some priests. These are two saintly communities. They do great good in the Church and produce many good results, but the first is committed to seminaries in the main cities, and the second is taken up with so many forms of service to the Church that I doubt they would be able to help you on such short notice. I think, however, that it would be good to send your request to them, since both are more suited and proper than ourselves to begin and sustain the work you have so much at heart.[51]

He once wrote to a highly placed woman to persuade her to devote to the seminary established by the priests of Saint Sulpice the revenue of a legacy left by her predecessors for the training of good priests.

If you apply this legacy here, Madame, you may be certain that it will be carried out in full accord with the wishes of the donors for the advancement of the clerical state. To be convinced of this you may see the good done at Saint Sulpice itself. You can expect the same in this new location, for the community is animated by the same spirit, and has but one goal, the greater glory of God.[52]

Not by words alone did Monsieur Vincent show his esteem for religious institutions or individuals among the clergy. He was always disposed to welcome, console, or serve all sorts of clerics, according to their status and needs. It was enough for someone to be a priest or to have the external marks of a cleric to receive a favorable reception from the servant of God. He used boundless charity in finding employment for priests who appealed to him. For some who were capable, he found positions as pastors or other benefices. Others he placed as chaplains to bishops or in noble families. For still others he was able to find positions as assistants in the parishes of smaller towns, or as confessors or chaplains of religious houses or in hospitals. For all clerics, great or small, he showed a great esteem and affection. He urged the men of his own Congregation to have a great regard for all clerics, to speak well of them, especially when in the pulpit. One day he showed how sensitive he was on this point. He traveled from Saint Lazare to a parish some five or

---

51. *CED* V:220-21.
52. *CED* VI:175.

six leagues away to beg pardon of the clerics there for the hasty words said by one of his own priests.

It was once reported that when a certain priest had fallen into some great difficulty Monsieur Vincent did all he could to straighten out the problem. He even wrote to Rome on his behalf, and provided a place for him to stay while awaiting the absolution from there. Later he found a way to provide for his future needs.

Another priest was sent to Saint Lazare because of some great sacrilege. Monsieur Vincent spoke to him so convincingly and so mildly that he was deeply moved. He was allowed to remain at Saint Lazare for several weeks at the expense of the house until he and his bishop were finally reconciled.

Another cleric took sick at the seminary of Bons Enfants, but wanted to receive a costly treatment beyond what he was able to pay for, or for that matter, beyond what he needed. The missionaries at the seminary were displeased and wanted him sent away, but Monsieur Vincent would have none of it. With his usual charity he insisted that the cleric be supplied with whatever he requested at the expense of the seminary, even though this was not strictly required by his condition.

Another priest fell sick in this same house, but quite unlike the previous priest he made no demands. He realized his inability to pay for his care, and feared that he might become a burden for the house. Monsieur Vincent heard of this, visited him, and assured him that he must not be concerned about money. There were chalices and other sacred vessels in the house which he would willingly sell rather than deprive him of anything he needed.

Another priest, previously unknown to Monsieur Vincent, was referred to him as being sick and in need. Monsieur Vincent received him with great charity, and housed and nursed him until he regained his health.

Yet another priest came to Saint Lazare to make a retreat but fell sick while there. Monsieur Vincent took every imaginable care of him. He recovered after a lengthy illness, and even received a breviary and cassock from his benefactor, together with ten *ecus* to help him over the next few days.

Another clergyman stopping by Saint Lazare for a single night's lodging was welcomed, although poorly dressed and unknown to anyone. The next morning he left without saying good-bye to anyone, having made off with a cassock and a long mantle. It was immediately suggested that he should be followed and the stolen clothes returned, but Monsieur Vincent would not allow it. Instead, he said that the man must obviously have had great need of these things if he went so far as to steal them. He further said that rather than having him bring back the missing articles, they should take others to give to him.

Another poor priest found himself needing to take a trip, but had no money to cover the expense, nor the necessary clothes. Monsieur Vincent gave the man what he asked, even a pair of boots, and twenty *ecus* besides.

Another priest told us himself that he once came to Paris on some business matters, but not knowing anyone in the city, he had to spend the night in a tavern. Monsieur Vincent found out about this, sent to find where he was staying, and brought him to Saint Lazare. He stayed there nearly a month at the expense of the community until his business was completed.

A good clergyman of the diocese of Tours was involved in a lawsuit in Paris that he felt obliged to pursue to redeem his personal honor. He contacted Monsieur Vincent as the most helpful person of all the clergy of Paris on whom he could rely. He wrote that without Monsieur Vincent's help he could not come to the city, nor hire a lawyer to plead his cause. Monsieur Vincent replied that he knew of just the lawyer to help out, and would pay for his services. He also provided lodging and board in Paris during this whole affair which lasted over a year, all at the expense of the house of Saint Lazare. The lawsuit was finally concluded in favor of the pastor, a good, honest man.

This great respecter of the priesthood of Jesus Christ helped restore, largely by his kindly attitude toward them, several clerics who had fallen into serious difficulties. He was helpful in removing them from occasions of sin, and provided for their pensions and subsistence. For several years, he even supported an Italian priest who was a bit unbalanced, and who had taught faulty doctrine in various places.

Another priest of Paris, a confessor to a group of women religious, fell sick. Monsieur Vincent had three clerics take his place during his illness which lasted three entire years, so that he could retain his rights to the stipends involved.

Another priest would occasionally come from quite a distance to seek some aid from Monsieur Vincent, since his own region was entirely devastated by the wars. The procurator urged Monsieur Vincent to tell this priest that he should no longer come this long way. Alms would be sent to him if he were in severe need. Monsieur Vincent replied: *Non alligabis os bovi trituranti* ["You shall not muzzle an ox while it treads out grain"],[53] which implied that he preferred to leave this poor priest at liberty to come as often as he wanted, to ask for help.

Lastly, the great charity he displayed toward all clerics encouraged all poor priests to come to him as their father, full of confidence in him. Since they came from all sides, from France and elsewhere, hardly a day passed that someone did not seek his aid. Those who appealed most to his heart

---

53. 1 Cor 9:9, citing Deut 25:4.

were the priests from Ireland, refugees in France because of their religion. Not only did he seek help for them from people he knew, but he also gave much from the resources of Saint Lazare for the relief of their needs. The priests of the house would often contribute something from the stipend Monsieur Vincent gave them each month. Over several years he supported a poor blind Irish priest and provided for a young boy to look after him. Besides the money he gave or solicited from his friends, he invited him and his young helper to his table whenever they came to Saint Lazare, which happened often. Moreover, he became aware of some younger Irish priests in Paris who were trying to complete their studies, even though they had no means of support. He arranged for them to transfer to some other provinces, where they could live more reasonably than in Paris. He contacted some of his friends in these outlying areas, and they helped in the support of these exiles. Besides all this, he provided the money to allow them to move to the provinces.

Monsieur Vincent's concern was not limited to the clerics who came to Paris to seek his help. He would help other pastors and priests, especially those in the regions devastated by war. He would mainly send priests of the Mission to help out in their most pressing needs, and send whatever was required for divine service, and especially for the holy sacrifice of the mass. He supplied, to sick and well alike, the clothes, cassocks and everything else required for staying alive in those troubled times. He did all this by collecting alms from many charitable people, and made it a scrupulous obligation to distribute carefully everything he had received.

Concerning this, one day a priest of the Mission was traveling in Champagne on some business when the pastor of a town met him and asked him who he was. When he learned that the traveler was a priest of the Congregation of the Mission, he publicly embraced him. Then he brought him to his home, and he recounted the great spiritual and temporal gifts the whole region had received from the charity of Monsieur Vincent. As for himself, he showed his visitor the very cassock he was wearing, and said, *Et hac me veste contexit* ["And he clothed me with this garment."] These were the same words our Lord had earlier said to Saint Martin after he had given his cloak to a poor beggar.[54]

We could add to this recital of Monsieur Vincent's charity toward clerics his regard for religious as well. He had a singular respect and love for them, which became evident whenever a religious would come to visit Saint Lazare. They would be received as an angel from heaven. He would often throw himself at their feet, asking for their blessing, and in humility would not rise until he had received it. On these occasions he showed great

---

54. Cited from the fourth lesson from matins of the saint's feast, November 11.

hospitality toward his visitors, doing them all sorts of little services. In turn, he wanted his priests to act this same way. In this matter he often recommended them to esteem and respect all other orders and religious communities. He said that they should not allow the least envy, jealousy, or any other sentiment contrary to the humility and charity of Jesus Christ to enter their minds. He wanted them always to speak of religious with respect and love. In a word he wanted his Congregation to look only for the good in other groups, and to praise publicly all the marvels they were accomplishing.

One day, when one of his priests asked him how he should act toward some religious whom he thought had behaved poorly toward himself, he said:

> You ask me, how you should act toward these good religious who have opposed you. Here is what I answer: you should try to serve them on every occasion that presents itself. Every time you meet them, show them that you are well disposed toward them. You should visit them from time to time. Never take a stand against them. Don't interfere in their affairs, except to defend them. Speak of them only on first-hand knowledge. Say nothing from the pulpit or in private that could cause them the least pain. In short, do all you can. Have others do the same, in words and deeds, to do all the good you can for them, even if they do not reciprocate. This is what I wish that we all do, and further, we should make it a duty to honor and serve them as often as we can.[55]

The charity of Monsieur Vincent toward religious was made known too by the good advice he gave when asked, as he was on several occasions. Among other incidents is the case of a religious of a distinguished order who was thinking of leaving his present situation to enter another order. He first thought was to ask Monsieur Vincent's opinion, since he regarded him as an enlightened and charitable person. The response of Monsieur Vincent was as follows:

> I have received your letter with respect, most reverend Father, but even more so with confusion. You have sent it to the person recognized by everyone as the most earthly and least spiritual of all men. Be this as it may, I send you my thoughts, not by way of advice, but only because of the solicitude our Lord wishes us to have for our neighbor. I am consoled to note the attraction you have for perfect union with our Savior, and how you have cooperated with this attraction, and with the tenderness of the divine goodness for you. I recognize the great difficulties and contradictions you have experienced, the other spiritual states you have passed through, and

---

55. *CED* VII:156-58.

finally, the great attraction you have for that teacher of the spiritual life, Saint Theresa.

With all of this, I think, Father, that you will have more security if you remain in the common life of your present order, under the direction of your religious superior, rather than pass to another, even if it should be more holy. First, because of the maxim that a religious ought to strive to acquire the spirit of his order, lest he have solely its habit and not its spirit. Since your order is recognized as being among the most perfect in the Church, you have a great obligation to persevere, to work to gain its spirit, practicing those things that will help you attain it. Second, another maxim has it that the spirit of our Savior is marked by meekness and kindness. Nature and the evil spirit, on the other hand, act harshly and shrilly. It appears to me in all that you tell me that your way of acting is just that, and that you hold too firmly to your own opinions against those of your superiors, even to what your own temperament inclines you to. All things considered, Father, I would think that you ought to give yourself anew to our Savior. You should renounce your own spirit to accomplish his will in the state to which his divine Providence has called you.[56]

Another religious, a doctor in theology, had a dispute with his congregation, and wanted to bring his complaint to Rome. He sought the help of Monsieur Vincent as intermediary, but this is the reply he received:

I am sympathetic, Father, at what you must bear. I pray that our Lord will deliver you from this burden, or give you strength to bear it. Since you bear it in a good cause you might console yourself that you are among the blessed who suffer persecution for justice's sake. Be patient, Father, and place your trust in our Lord who allows you to be tried. He will see to it that the congregation in which he had placed you, like a leaky boat, will bring you happily to port. I cannot beseech God, as you requested, that he help you pass to another order, for it seems that this is not his will. There are crosses everywhere, and your advanced age should urge you to avoid those you would find in such a change of state. As to the help you asked to obtain a rescript, that is another matter. I most humbly beg you to dispense me from the obligation of presenting your propositions to Rome.[57]

Monsieur Vincent's same respect for the religious state also made him sensitive to the plight of those women religious he encountered living

---

56. *CED* IV:576-77.
57. *CED* IV:124-25.

outside of their convents for whatever reason. He tried with great gentleness to have them return to their own houses, but if this was not possible, at least to go to some other convent or monastery. He wrote to an abbess on this matter: Madame, I make bold to ask you to receive in your abbey one of your own religious. She was the prioress of N., but now cannot live there because of the misery of the times. She is in need, subject to reproach and the ridicule of the world, and of the soldiers. Perhaps, Madame, you have reasons for not wishing to take her back, or at least it would be difficult for you to do so. Even so, I felt I must write, for charity obliges me to do so on behalf of a person like this. She hopes for your acceptance. Living outside her "center," I mean to say outside her monastery, she is not at ease, and feels unsafe. If it should be that she cannot return, I most humbly request that you contribute something for her upkeep, should we have to place her in a boarding house in this city. In God's name, Madame, forgive me for making this suggestion to you.[58]

If we were obliged to speak of all the expressions of esteem, and all the services Monsieur Vincent rendered to religious men and women, a whole volume would be needed. It suffices to say that he never let an opportunity pass to help or serve them. There is hardly any particular act or charitable function that he did not do in their favor. He made it obvious to all that he cherished, honored, helped, served, and protected them to the full extent of his ability. He covered their faults, published their virtues, and praised their state in life. By a loving humility, all the more praiseworthy because it is so rare, he portrayed his own Congregation as the least of all others, to make theirs shine forth even more. He wanted his own community to think of themselves as the least of all the congregations.

SECTION SIX

His Charity Toward the Members of His Own Congregation

We have seen in the previous parts of this book how charitable Monsieur Vincent was. Who can doubt that this virtue in him was well ordered, when we realize that the virtue which does not have this quality can hardly be called charity at all. According to the doctrine of Saint Thomas and other

---

58. *CED* IV:123-24.

theologians, charity demands that we have a special love for those closest to us, those Providence has put in our path. Monsieur Vincent had such an intimate union with those God had given him as his spiritual sons that he could say with the apostle that he had given birth to them by the Gospel in Jesus Christ.[59] He carried them in his heart and loved them most tenderly, after the example of the love Jesus Christ had for his apostles and disciples.

By imitating his divine master, he showed this love by the instructions, urgings, encouragement, and consolation he gave them, and by bestowing on them every good a child might expect from attentive parents. He often addressed them in moving talks, animated with the spirit of Jesus Christ, not only in the regularly scheduled meetings, but also on all sorts of other occasions. He would take the trouble to say a word of edification to one, sometimes after mental prayer, or on the occasion of some letter he may have received, or maybe on hearing some good or bad news, or possibly to recommend something special to their prayers. Like a good and wise father of the family he freely distributed the bread of souls, which is the word of God.

This way of acting was not limited to his Congregation in general, but was directed to each confrere in particular. He spoke sometimes to one, sometimes to another, according to circumstances. He would encourage one in his difficulties, to another he would offer sympathy in his sufferings. He would admonish someone for his failings, or give some prudent advice in times of perplexity. On all occasions he was generous in instructing and encouraging his followers about the best means of progressing along the way of perfection. When absent from them he wrote in a similar fashion, taking the trouble amid the constant flood of pressing and important affairs to carry on an almost unlimited correspondence with them. He warned, instructed, exhorted, consoled, and encouraged. These letters alone allow us to see his boundless charity for his own confreres.

Since one of the principal and most important lessons Jesus Christ gave his disciples was that they should love one another, his servant Vincent de Paul often repeated this to his own followers. He often made it the subject of his conferences with them. He has even left a handwritten copy of a talk, something he did for no other subject. On this question of fraternal charity, he said among many other things: "It is a sign of predestination, since by this virtue one is recognized as a disciple of Jesus Christ."

One day, on the feast of Saint John the Evangelist, while exhorting the priests and brothers to love one another by recalling the words of the apostle *filioli diligite alterutrum* ["Little children, love one another"],[60] he said: "The

---

59. 1 Cor 4:15.
60. Based on 1 John 4:7.

Congregation of the Mission will endure only as long as charity reigns in it." He roundly cursed anyone who would destroy the virtue of charity and thus cause the ruin of the Congregation, or even a lessening of this virtue, thereby making the Congregation less perfect than it might otherwise be.[61]

He then said:

> Charity is the soul of the virtues, and the paradise of communities. The house of Saint Lazare will be a paradise if charity is found there. Paradise is none other than love, union, and charity. The blessed in heaven are wholly taken up with the love of the divine. Nothing is more desirable than to live with those we love, knowing that we in our turn are loved as well.

He also said:

> Christian love begotten of charity is not only superior to natural inclination, a product of the sensible appetite and usually more harmful than helpful, but is beyond even rational affection. Christian love is a love by which we love one another in God, for God, and as God wills. It is an affection which makes us love our neighbors for the same purpose God loves them, to make them saints in this world and blessed in the next. As a result of this love we must see God alone, and nothing but God, in each of those we love.
>
> Those who would live in a community without support and without charity would be at the mercy of the humors and vagaries of those with whom they lived. They would be like a ship without anchor or rudder, traveling among reefs, at the mercy of wind and wave battering it from all sides and finally destroying it.

He concluded:

> The Missionaries ought not limit their mutual love to a merely interior sentiment or to their words only. They should show this by their deeds, and by coming to the aid of their confreres in a spirit of good will, being always disposed to their welfare.

He ardently desired that God would inspire this charity in the hearts of all the members of the Congregation, since, he said, "by mutual support the strong will support the weak, and the work of God will be accomplished."[62]

Because detraction is the chief enemy of charity and this vice occasionally intrudes into even the most saintly community, the charitable father of the Missionaries fought this vice to the end. To prevent it from finding a place among his Missionaries, he often exhorted them to be vigilant and on their guard. He compared this vice to a ravenous wolf seeking to destroy the flock.

---

61. *CED* XII:435.
62. Abelly's version differs considerably from *CED* XII:260-76.

He asserted that one of the greatest ills that could overtake a community was to harbor someone who slandered, murmured, and who found it necessary to speak to everyone of his own unhappiness. He said also that anyone who lent an ear to the slanderer was as guilty as the original offender, as the ancient fathers taught.

To warn his confreres against this vice, for which he had an extreme horror, he gave conferences on this theme from time to time. He referred to all the occasions and temptations which might lead to this failing. Once, he repeated this same talk on seven successive Fridays, and had the members of his community discuss it among themselves. After each talk he collected the results of these discussions in his efforts to eliminate this scandal from his Congregation. At the end of the seven weeks, he summarized in a forceful presentation all that had been said.

It was not by words alone that Monsieur Vincent expressed his affection for his confreres. In all sorts of encounters he manifested an openness of heart and a paternal affection for all, from the greatest to the least among them. He wanted all to be aware of his high regard for each of them. When anyone came to speak with him, either out of some particular need or for any other reason, he welcomed him cordially. He stopped whatever else he was doing to listen to what the person had to say. If he could not give his visitor the time he needed, he appointed another time for him to return, when he would have the leisure to hear him out. The priests and brothers openly spoke to him of their desires, sufferings, their evil inclinations, and even their faults. He listened in a way that showed his affection, like a doctor receiving a patient. He replied appropriately to each one according to his needs and expectations, always happily, for he had a special gift of knowing how to send away happy everyone who came to him. He was able to console and edify each of his visitors. He was blessed with a marvelous spirit of adaptability, becoming all to all, adjusting to the dispositions of each one who came. He would often lapse into the language of the region from which they came. He would speak Picard with those from Picardy, Gascon with someone from Guienne, Basque with a Basque, and even a few words of German with someone from that country.

This is the way he spoke with those who came to see him, but he did not limit this cordiality to these meetings. Whenever he had occasion to refer to any of his confreres, he showed his respect and esteem. He would praise them for their life of virtue, and speak honorably of even the least among them.

On this subject we recall that one day the father of one of the brothers of the community came to speak of his son. "He is much more important than I am," said Monsieur Vincent, "and many others say the same thing." On another occasion he said to one of his members who brought up the temptation he was experiencing of wanting to leave the Congregation, that he felt as bad when someone was leaving the community as if he were losing an arm or a leg. He was heard to say on several other occasions while speaking to the members of his community that he loved the vocation in which he lived more than his own life, and that when someone announced his withdrawal he felt as though he was being cut to the quick.

Once, he threw himself on his knees and remained in this posture for nearly two hours at the feet of a priest of his Congregation thinking of leaving the community. He begged him, in the name and for the love of our Savior Jesus Christ, not to succumb to this temptation. "No," he said, "I will not rise until you agree with what I am asking. I want, at least, to be as insistent on this point as is your tempter, the devil."

If he would notice that someone was depressed, he would do all in his power to bring him out of this condition, or at least do something to relieve and console him. He would sometimes say some little pleasantry to distract him, or invite him to his room as a mark of his esteem. He might assign him to some occupation suitable for the relief of his symptoms.

Once, there was a servant in the house, not a member of the Congregation, but one for whom Monsieur Vincent had a special regard. The servant unfortunately had some cross words with a brother of the house, whereupon Monsieur Vincent immediately dismissed him. It was pointed out to him that this servant was capable and even necessary for the good running the house, but Monsieur Vincent was adamant. He would not allow a servant to speak disrespectfully to a brother. Monsieur Vincent did help him find another position with the good letter of recommendation he wrote for him.

One day a brother came to Monsieur Vincent to complain that one of the officials of the house had treated him rudely. He was received with great kindness and meekness, and Monsieur Vincent said to him: "You were well advised to come to tell me this. I'll handle it. Come at any time to see me whenever you have a complaint, for you know how fond I am of you." These gentle words, according to the brother himself, calmed his spirit, and left him with further reason to admire the goodness of his superior.

Another brother came to speak about some doubts he was experiencing. He expressed the fear that he might be disturbing Monsieur Vincent, but he replied: "No, brother, have no fear that you are bothering me. You must realize that one appointed by God to be at the service of others is no more put out by the demands made on him than a father would be in regard to his children."

He wrote the following to a priest of the Congregation who feared that the information he had given about himself would diminish Monsieur Vincent's good opinion of him.

Thinking of your remark that possibly your confidences might lessen the esteem I have always had for you, I must assure you that this is not the case. I am aware that these enemies occasionally attack even the most virtuous, and that the thoughts of leaving the community are Providence's way of proving those whom he loves the most. He often leads them by ways of difficult and thorny paths to merit the extraordinary graces he has in store for them. Rather than having had the least thought to your disadvantage, I have thought of you as being even more faithful to God. This is especially so because you have resisted these temptations, and despite all your work, you have not neglected your ordinary spiritual exercises. In addition, after your letter to me explaining your case, you have willingly accepted the response I sent.

One day a priest of the Congregation was speaking of the state of his soul to Monsieur Vincent. Among other things he remarked that he had formed an aversion against him and was angry at him. At these words the charitable father rose, embraced him tenderly, and congratulated him for being able to speak so frankly: "If up to now I have not given my heart to you, I do so now, totally."

Another priest went to see him in his room. The priest was downcast, and was resolved to quit the community. He stated that his mind was made up, and he wanted to return to his own region. Monsieur Vincent smiled, and looking upon him with kindness and tenderness said to him, "When do you plan to leave? Are you going by foot, or will you take a horse?" The priest was so surprised by this response that Monsieur Vincent had given to distract him from this temptation, when he expected some sort of severe reprimand, that he was completely freed from this wish to leave.

Another of his priests who worked in a remote province wrote that the brother with him wished to withdraw from the Congregation. Monsieur Vincent replied:

I always expected that this good brother would be tempted by the demon of sloth, and he perhaps may remember that I warned him about this. Please help him, and encourage him to repel this temptation. But do it gently, by way of persuasion rather than by direction, as you know you are in the habit of doing. Those tempted in this way have a greater need of being treated, or should I say pampered, even more gently and charitably than those who have a physical ailment.

Another brother wrote several times to ask permission to leave the Congregation. Each time Monsieur Vincent wrote in a way that showed his fatherly love, and encouraged him to remain. We will record here only the ending of the last letter, to show the tenderness he displayed for the members of his community.

> No, my dear brother, I cannot consent to your leaving, for I see that it is not God's will that you do so. Also, your immortal soul, so dear to me, would be in peril. If you do not believe me, please, at least do not leave the Congregation except through the same door that you entered. I mean to say, before taking a step of such great importance, make a spiritual retreat. Choose one of the three houses closest to you. Be assured that you will be well received wherever you decide to go. The goodness of your heart has earned my love for you, with no other goal than the glory of God and your own sanctification. You are aware of this, I know, and you know also that I am entirely yours, in the love of our Savior.[63]

When he would send one of his confreres to a mission assignment, he would always send a note to the superior, asking him to take care of him. He would usually say, "I hope that he will have much confidence in you when he sees the goodness, support, and charity which our Lord has given you for those whom he now confides to your direction."

He wrote to one of his priests, who in his devotion to God had agreed to serve in a remote place:

> Reflecting on the extraordinary graces God has conferred on you, by calling you to serve the people in that distant place, I embrace you in spirit with joy and tenderness. You deserve this, as a soul chosen by God from among all the people in the whole world, and as one who has left all to follow this call, to bring a great number of these people to heaven. Who would not love a soul so detached from temporal things, from his own selfish interests, and even from the care of his own body to carry out the designs of God, his only ambition? But who would not care for the body, which serves to bring light to the blind, and raises the dead to life again? This is why I beseech you, Monsieur, to look upon your body as an instrument of God for the salvation of many, and to care for it for this reason.[64]

Another time he wrote a similar letter to several of his priests at work together in a foreign land, urging them to care for their health.

> You are aware that your health will be in danger in this new climate until you have acclimated yourselves. I warn you about going out in the full sun, and suggest that in the beginning you use your time in a study of the language. Become like little children again as you learn to speak. In that spirit allow yourselves to be

---
63. *CED* III:484.
64. *CED* V:565-66.

guided by Monsieur N., [Mousnier] who will act as a father to you, or by Monsieur N. [Bourdaise]. Please look on them as taking the place of our Lord, and as our Lord acting through them. Even should you lack the help of either the one or the other, you shall experience the special help of God himself, for has he not said "that even if a mother forget the child of her womb I will not forget you?"[65] You ought to be convinced that he will have care for you, my dear fathers, watching over you, keeping you, protecting you. You have abandoned yourselves to him and placed all your trust in his protection. Be careful, gentlemen, to love one another, and help each other. Support one another and you shall see that God, who has chosen you for his great purposes, will preserve you for carrying out his designs.[66]

Monsieur Vincent had the custom of falling on his knees to embrace those he was sending to the missions, or those who were returning. He saw to it that they were not lacking in anything they needed. Above all others, he showed his great love particularly for the sick. He would graciously ask about the state of their health, and often would suggest remedies for their illnesses. When circumstances dictated, he would send for the doctor, or for those able to be up and about, he would send them to the doctor to be examined. He saw to it that the infirmarians took care of the sick, and directed the superiors of the various houses to spare no expense in taking care of the sick. He was often heard to say that it was better to sell the sacred vessels of the altar rather than deprive the sick of anything they needed. To those who complained that the sick were a drain on the community, he would say that, on the contrary, they were a blessing on any house where they were.[67] Despite all his other preoccupations he never failed to pray for them, and to recommend them to the prayers of the community. As often as he could he visited the sick. On his various trips he would ask about them, the care being taken of them, and whether they lacked anything they required. He would not allow among his community any lack of charity or tenderness of heart for the sick.

One of his priests wrote on this matter:

> I personally experienced the charity he showed to the sick during two serious bouts of illness I had while in the house of Saint Lazare. God would have done me a favor if he had then called me from this world, for it seemed to me that I was well disposed to die by the help and prayers of Monsieur Vincent, who visited me several times. He did not want to spare anything when it had to do with the

---

65. Isa 49:15.
66. *CED* V:434-35. The missionaries were probably going to Madagascar.
67. *CED* XI:73; XII:29.

sick because, as he used to say, they deserve more because of their sufferings than others do by their work. I often heard him say that it would be preferable to sell the sacred chalices to help them. When he came to visit he would discreetly ask about the treatment they were receiving. He relieved their pain by his compassion, and during their convalescence he would tell some interesting stories for their amusement, often with a moral attached.

In keeping with his priorities, he neglected nothing in the spiritual care of the sick, besides the attention paid to their physical needs. For those not too ill, he gently and paternally suggested that they not omit their usual spiritual exercises, "lest the sickness of the body extend to the soul, and make it lax and unmortified."

Lastly, we can be sure that his solicitude for the welfare and care of the sick extended to those in health as well. We are assured of this by the account we have of a missionary working in Champagne for the relief of the poor. The missionary wrote to ask, among other things, if a cap could be sent to him. None was to be found in the house, but this charitable father took his own off his head and asked the brother, who told us of the incident, to send it to the priest. When it was suggested that perhaps someone could go into town to buy one, Monsieur Vincent replied: "No, my brother, we must not make him wait, for he may be in a hurry for it. Please send it, together with the other things he has asked for."[68]

Not content with expressing his love and appreciation toward his own, he extended this concern to their relatives in as many ways as he could. When he learned that any suffering had come to the relatives of the priests or brothers of his Congregation, he wanted all to sympathize and help the families as much as possible. He himself was the first to sense their grief and offer his consolation in the best way he knew how.

Speaking to his community, he said: "We pray God for the N. family, which has experienced such a loss. We should sympathize with the brother who suffers, for we owe this to one another." Sometimes, according to the circumstances, he would say, "I request the priests who have no particular intention for their mass to offer it for the grieving N. family. I plan to do the same in the mass I am about to celebrate, and I would like the brothers to receive communion for this same intention." Besides his prayers for the relatives of the members of the Congregation, he provided other more tangible help when they found themselves in reduced circumstances.

---

68. The brother was Louis Robineau.

SECTION SEVEN

His Charity Toward His Adversaries

When it comes to relationships with our enemies, Christian charity is most in opposition to our natural impulses. The grace of Jesus Christ alone can conquer the principles of the world by the power of the Gospel of Jesus Christ. Considering the love of our enemies, there is no more assured mark of divine adoption as true children of the heavenly Father. He causes his sun to shine on both good and bad alike, and allows his dew and rain to fall on sinners as well as the just.

Monsieur Vincent was so careful about all other aspects of the virtue of charity that it is not surprising to see that he had a high regard for this aspect of charity, especially since Jesus Christ had explicitly recommended it in his Gospel.

We have spoken at length of how this great servant of God related to all classes of people. He was full of respect and submission to the great of this world, of adaptability and charity for the lesser ones, and of justice and deference to all. Perhaps there never was a person more committed to all sorts of works of public service, and as a result, more exposed to criticism, slander and calumny than he. He met with little opposition. What difficulties did come his way divine Providence allowed to enable him to be more closely identified with his divine Master. Jesus Christ suffered great outrages and bad treatment and willed to be numbered among those who suffered for justice's sake.

Two situations were likely to arouse the displeasure of some of his associates. The first was his position at court where he had a part to play in the distribution of benefices. He was adamant in insisting on acting according to what he saw as right, but it was obviously impossible to please everyone seeking an appointment. Sometimes there were more than a dozen candidates for a single benefice. Those who were unsuccessful would sometimes complain loudly to others, often attributing things to him which were not true. In response, he would bless God, continue to greet these people when they met, and express his desire to help them. When an occasion would present itself he would do so more willingly than before.

The second instance which led to misunderstandings was his position as superior of a congregation. This obliged him to look after the goods of the community and to manage what had been given for the service of others. He regarded himself as the steward and not the owner of these things. He felt obligated in conscience to protect the right of ownership at Saint Lazare and other properties, as well as the fruits of a benefice he held. On this point he sometimes found that he had to resist those who would interfere in his affairs, if attempts at accommodation proved unsuccessful. The result would sometimes be that he was slandered and opposed. These sentiments gave him the opportunity to offer the same prayer as our Savior on the cross, a prayer for his enemies.

We will now give some examples of how this good servant of God behaved toward those who maltreated either himself or his Congregation.

A nobleman of some standing was unsuccessful in obtaining a benefice for a friend because of Monsieur Vincent's opposition in the council to the appointment. Monsieur Vincent judged the person proposed to be incapable of fulfilling the obligations of the office. Several days later he chanced to meet Monsieur Vincent in the Louvre where he began to berate him publicly, although he had never before complained to anyone. The queen, told of the incident, ordered the nobleman to retire from the court. Monsieur Vincent was so insistent that he be recalled that the queen finally relented. This is an example of how Monsieur Vincent showed such charity toward an opponent by doing more for him than he would have done for the best of his friends.

Another incident illustrates both his humility and his charity. Returning once from the city to Saint Lazare, he met in the faubourg Saint Denis a man who was aware of Monsieur Vincent's close association with the queen and her chief ministers. He publicly blamed him for the troubled times, and for the heavy taxes borne by the people. The holy priest himself customarily blamed his own sins as the cause of public difficulties. On this occasion he got off his horse, fell to his knees, and admitted that he was a miserable sinner. He begged pardon of God and of his accuser, the source of the troubles being spoken of. The person in question was so taken aback at the sight of this humble priest abasing himself and so aware of his own boldness, that he came to Saint Lazare the next day to ask pardon of Monsieur Vincent. He received him as an old friend. He was persuaded to stay six or seven days in the house, and to take the occasion to make a spiritual retreat and a good general confession. The story illustrates how charity completed what humility began.

He opposed any spite or grudges to such an extent that he not only bore no ill will to anyone, but he did not want anyone to harbor bad feelings against him if it were possible to avoid them. Once he noticed that a well-placed person seemed to have grown cold in his dealings with him, whereas before he had been quite friendly. When this continued, he went directly to him. With a smile he said: "Monsieur, I am unhappy if, without knowing what, I have given you some reason to be displeased with me. I have come to ask you to let me know what I may have done, so that I can correct myself." The nobleman, struck by his openness, admitted his displeasure: "It is true, Monsieur Vincent, that on such and such an occasion your actions have given me trouble." For his part, Monsieur Vincent imitated in his charity what the sun does by its light. He dissipated the shadows of doubt from his mind, and softened the hardness of his heart in such a way that the nobleman from that time on became friendlier than before.

Once while vesting for mass in the chapel of the College des Bons Enfants, he remembered that a certain religious of Paris had a grievance against him. He at once put off his vestments, went to find this person, and asked pardon for the trouble he had caused. He assured him that he esteemed and honored both him and his order. Only after he had done this did he return to celebrate mass.

Once Monsieur Vincent became aware that the superior of a well-known religious order in Paris was disturbed by the way he had handled a certain business matter. At once he went to see the superior, threw himself at his feet, and asked pardon for any offense he had given. Unfortunately the superior received Monsieur Vincent with coldness, and despite his efforts to conciliate the superior, he put Monsieur Vincent off with offensive words, and he had to leave. Yet he was happy to have had the opportunity to suffer rebuff for the love of his Master. Some time later, it became necessary to borrow some vestments for the chapel of the College des Bons Enfants. When Monsieur Vincent was asked if the superior mentioned earlier should be approached, he replied: "Yes, ask him for me if he would lend these things to us." The one who had asked him was astonished, but did as he was told. The superior in turn was amazed: "What! Doesn't Monsieur Vincent remember what I said to him? Is this all he can recall? Ah, gentlemen, the hand of God is here. Now I see that Monsieur Vincent is led by the Spirit of God." After lending these vestments, the superior was moved to go himself to visit Monsieur Vincent at Saint Lazare, where he was received with much joy by both.

Once, he heard from Marseilles that a certain religious had spoken ill of the Congregation in a matter of some importance. This was all the more galling because he had received some notable favors from the community. In reply, Monsieur Vincent wrote to one of his priests: "The words coming from this priest are an occasion for us to rejoice, seeing that we are innocent of the calumnies he spreads, thanks be to God. We will be blessed if we are found worthy to suffer something for justice's sake, especially if it helps us rejoice in embarrassment, and learn to return good for evil."[69]

The Congregation of the Mission had applied to the Holy Father, Pope

---

69. *CED* IV:301.

Alexander VII, at the beginning of his pontificate, to approve an important matter about the Institute. The superior of the house at Rome wrote to Monsieur Vincent to alert him that some powerful persons were working against this petition. When he received this letter he remarked to someone with him: "I understand by this letter that certain men (naming them) are against us. Even if they were to pull out my eyes I would not cease to love them, respect them, and serve them all my life. I pray that God will give me the grace to do this."[70] This is how he acted, always taking their part, defending their reputations, emphasizing their virtues, appreciating and praising their good works in general and for each one in particular. He rendered them all imaginable services, deference, and submission.

Several foreign clerics who were refugees in Paris because of the persecution in their own country found themselves in great physical and spiritual need. Monsieur Vincent requested one of his own priests from the same country and known to most of the clerics, to organize weekly meetings for their benefit. Together they could learn what was appropriate for their profession, and be prepared for future employment as a way out of their present want and idleness. Monsieur Vincent said: "We must find a way to help them when they assemble because they seem ready to prepare themselves to become more useful and more edifying than they now are. Monsieur, please look after this." The priest replied: "Monsieur, you are aware that as you requested, we tried these meetings. We even continued them for some time, but we are dealing with some difficult personalities. They were disagreeing among themselves, just like the provinces of their homeland, and we had to stop these meetings. They argue, and are jealous of one another. Despite all you have done for them they show no appreciation. They complain constantly, and have even gone so far as to have written to Rome to have you stop meddling in their affairs. It seems to me, Monsieur, that their ingratitude dictates that you no longer do anything for them." To this, Monsieur Vincent responded: "Monsieur! What are you saying? We must do so precisely because of this." He did more than simply talk. He continued to do all the good for them that he possibly could, in all sorts of situations.

Once, someone involved in a lawsuit asked him to write on his behalf to the judge in the case. Monsieur Vincent excused himself by saying that he had no influence in such matters. He would sometimes write such letters, although he preferred as a practice not to become involved in these affairs. Some time later, the one who had asked for this favor, thinking he had lost his case, came to complain bitterly about Monsieur Vincent's failure to write

---

70. See the letter to Etienne Blatiron, *CED* V:395-96. This matter concerned the approbation of the vows which came in spite of opposition from some within the community. Nevertheless, Vincent consistently and charitably defended his position in favor of the vows. *CED* I:162-65.

in his support. Monsieur Vincent not only accepted this criticism meekly, but asked pardon on his knees for having caused him such annoyance. The man discovered only later that the report of his having lost the case was erroneous. In fact, he won it. He then returned to Saint Lazare to beg pardon, for having complained and abused Monsieur Vincent so unjustly.

Several soldiers came upon two clerics from Saint Lazare, walking in the neighborhood. They seized their cloaks from them by force, but were observed by some people of the quarter. They ran after them, caught them, and had them put in the local jail. Afterward, Monsieur Vincent saw to their being fed, visited, and arranged for them to make general confessions. With their promise not to steal again, he released them without the penalty they so richly deserved.

Occasionally others would be caught in their robberies in the house of Saint Lazare or on the farms which depended upon it. These included grain stolen from the fields by night, trees cut from the woods, fruit taken from the orchards, or vegetables from the garden. Monsieur Vincent felt great uneasiness in allowing these people to be put in prison, and when they were, he would secure their release. Sometimes he would even go beyond this. He would offer excuses for them, invite them to eat with the community, and sometimes give them money to speed them on their way. There were many such cases, when Monsieur Vincent not only pardoned those who did him harm, but aided them, as well. He used to say, "How I pity these poor people!"

In 1654 a young German Lutheran came to Paris to abjure his heresy. Possibly he felt that he would find greater sympathy there than in his native country. He was recommended to Monsieur Vincent by a religious superior of a community of nuns at whose convent he was staying. She suggested that this young man might possibly become a member of the Congregation of the Mission, for he showed much promise. Monsieur Vincent received him at Saint Lazare to make a spiritual retreat of eight days. During the exercises his guest slipped into one of the rooms, took a cassock and long cloak and some other things as well. He dressed himself in these clothes, then left by a side door of the church to go to the section of the city called Saint Germain to meet the minister Monsieur Drelincourt.[71] He presented himself as a member of the Congregation of the Mission who had come to embrace the religion of the minister. He, seeing his visitor dressed as a cleric, was taken in. He led him through the streets to show off a great conquest—a member of the Congregation of the Mission who had become a Huguenot. He was taken to the homes of several of these heretics to be strengthened in his decision by their flattery and attention.

---

71. Charles Drelincourt, a Protestant minister and controversialist. He died in Paris in 1669.

While walking in the city, they were seen by Monsieur [Nicolas] des Isles, a man well versed in the religious controversy of the day.[72] Seeing the minister walking with a cleric raised some doubts in his mind, which led him to follow the pair to the first house, where they all entered together. He allowed the minister to go upstairs, while he himself remained to talk with the young man, who told him the whole story of his dealings with the minister. This false Missionary spoke of his stay at Saint Lazare, and of his deception. Monsieur des Isles left, saw the pastor of Saint Sulpice, and because of the scandal given by assuming the habit and title of the Congregation of the Mission, had the young man committed to the Chatelet prison. He also alerted Monsieur Vincent to the case. Many people in turn advised him to contact the authorities to see that this young man be punished for the robberies he had committed, and for the scandal he had given.

This charitable priest thanked those who had advised him, but said that he would do what had to be done. He did contact the authorities, not to demand justice, but rather mercy, for this unfortunate person. He took the trouble to go himself to see the royal prosecutor and the police lieutenant to inform them that the Congregation they did not wish to press charges, for it had forgiven the loss and the scandal that had been given. He requested most humbly that the prisoner be set free, remembering that God forgives, and it would thus please his divine Majesty if this poor stranger were released. He added, to the great edification of these gentlemen, that he looked upon the whole episode as simply a young man's prank. On this occasion Monsieur Vincent showed clearly that he had personally accepted the maxims of the Savior too completely to act otherwise than the Savior himself. Jesus not only said that he had come to save sinners and not to condemn or punish them, but had acted in this same spirit in forgiving the adulterous woman, and forgiving all kinds of sinners, even the traitor Judas.

In 1655 another young member of the Congregation decided to leave it, contrary to the advice of Monsieur Vincent. He joined the Swiss Guards,[73] but left a short time afterward, though not in such favorable circumstances as his leaving the Congregation of the Mission. He was apprehended as a deserter from the army, and was charged with other serious crimes as well. He was imprisoned, and later condemned to be executed. In this serious situation he had recourse to Monsieur Vincent, whose guiding maxim was always to render good for evil. Monsieur Vincent forgot that this unfortunate man had once rejected his advice, and came to his aid, and was successful in saving his life.

A poor person appeared at the door of Saint Lazare once, asking if he

---

72. See *CED* XII:295, where Vincent speaks of this person to his priests.
73. One of a troop of elite guards in the royal service, coming originally from Switzerland.

could tell Monsieur Vincent what people were saying about him. "Yes, my friend, speak." The man then said that people in Paris were blaming him for the fact the poor were being taken off the streets and placed in the city hospital. Monsieur Vincent's only response to this was to say, with his usual mildness, that he would pray to God for those who spoke this way about him.

The charity of Monsieur Vincent for those who mistreated him is shown well in the matter of a serious business loss affecting the Congregation. The loss suffered by the community was about fifty thousand *livres*, the greatest loss Monsieur Vincent ever sustained during his life. He wrote the following to a friend of the community, a man knowledgeable in these matters:

> Monsieur, good friends share in both good and bad fortune. As you are one of the closest we have in the whole world, I want you to know of the loss we suffered in this affair whose background you know. I do not speak of a misfortune which has happened, but of a grace that God has sent us, so I trust you will join with us in thanking him. I call the afflictions he sends a grace, provided they are accepted. His goodness has disposed us to accept this loss and to receive this accident with entire resignation. I dare even to say that we rejoice as much as if we had won our case. Surely this would be a paradox to anyone less sensitive to heavenly matters than yourself, and one less able to submit himself to the good pleasure of God in the adversities of life. This is a greater good than all temporal advantages. I beg of you most humbly to look on things in this way, so that we both share the same sentiments.[74]

What is most remarkable in this loss is the affection, respect, and charity of Monsieur Vincent for those involved in this matter. He manifested in every meeting a disposition to return good for evil, honor for dishonor, good treatment for bad. As he said himself, and as the Holy Spirit says in the Scriptures, he wished to heap coals of fire upon the heads of all his adversaries.[75]

---

74. *CED* VII:252-53.
75. Rom 12:20.

CHAPTER TWELVE

His Meekness

CHARITY REACHES its perfection, Blessed Francis de Sales said, "when it is not only patient, but mild and good mannered." Meekness is like the flower of this divine virtue. It reveals more and more of its beauty as it struggles with difficulty to overcome the outbursts of nature. These so often appear under the guise of zeal, but only seek to give greater freedom to the fits of human passions.

Monsieur Vincent was by temperament a bilious character. His spirit was lively, and therefore given to anger. He had so dominated this passion by the help of grace, and by the practice of its opposite virtue, meekness, that not only did he not offend, but he seemed not even to feel the first movements of anger. While he was in the household of the wife of the general of the galleys, as he himself mentioned to a confidant, he sometimes showed his bilious and melancholic temperament. This caused this good lady to wonder if perhaps there was something in the house which displeased him. It became apparent later that God was calling him to live in community where he would be dealing with all sorts of diverse personalities. "I addressed myself to God," he said, "to beg him earnestly to change this curt and forbidding disposition of mine for a meek and benign one. By the grace of our Lord and with some effort on my part to repress the outbursts of passion, I was able to get rid of my black disposition."

Monsieur Vincent never spoke of himself unless he thought it necessary to do so, or if it would help the edification of those with whom he conversed. His humility was such that even in these cases he would later beg pardon for having spoken in this way, for fear of having scandalized his hearers.

Monsieur Vincent has told us how, with the grace of God, he was able to acquire this virtue of meekness, even though it was not natural to him. He earned it by his prayer to God and by practice. Once, speaking to his community he said:

> Sometimes we see persons who seem to be gifted with great meekness, a feature of their natural disposition. This, however, is not the Christian virtue of meekness, whose proper role is the suppression of the opposite vice. A chaste person is not one who never experiences the urgings of lust, but one who resists them when they occur. We have an example right in our own community of a most truly meek person, Monsieur N. I don't hesitate to say it for he is not present.

You are aware that his natural disposition is dry and laconic. You may judge for yourself if there are two people in the whole world more crude and surly than he and I! Yet this man has so conquered himself that he has become more than he is. And how is that? It is the virtue of meekness, at which he has worked so hard, while miserable me, I have remained dry as a thorn. Gentlemen, please do not let your eyes rest on the bad example I give, but rather I exhort you (to use the words of the apostle) to walk worthily in all meekness and good manners in the vocation to which God has called you.[1]

It is not enough to have acquired a virtue. It must be preserved and cultivated. The virtue must be practiced often in real situations. This faithful servant of God did this, for, before instructing others, he always put his lessons into practice himself. We give here an abridgement of the advice he gave on this matter, and which he himself had already observed.

In order not to be surprised by those occasions when we might offend against this virtue of meekness, we must first foresee situations which might arouse our anger. We then can prepare our hearts in advance the acts of meekness we want to practice.

Second, we must detest the vice of anger, seeing that it displeases God. Yet even here we must not get annoyed nor angry with ourselves if we are subject to this vice. We must hate this vice, and love the opposite virtue, not because we are unhappy with ourselves but solely for the love of God. He is pleased by this virtue and displeased by this vice. If we act this way, the sorrow we feel for faults committed against this virtue will be calm and peaceful.

Third, when the passion of anger moves us, we must not act or speak, or even decide anything, until the passion has passed. What we do in anger is not fully controlled by reason, for passion troubles and obscures this faculty. Even if later what we do seems right, it will never be perfect.

Fourth, when we feel angry we must make an effort to ensure that no trace of this emotion appears on our face, which is the image of the soul. Rather, an expression of Christian meekness should appear. This is not against simplicity, for we do this not to appear other than what we are. We are to act through the sincere desire that the virtue of meekness, which resides in the superior part of the soul, appear in our features, on our tongue, and in our exterior actions, to please God and the neighbor for the love of God.

Lastly, in the fifth place, we must above all be careful to restrain the tongue. Despite the storm of anger and all the sentiments of zeal

---

1. Eph 4:1. *CED* XI:64-65.

we may think we have, we must use kind and agreeable language if we are to gain others to God. Sometimes it takes only a soft word to convert a hardened sinner, and on the contrary, a harsh word can upset a soul, and can cause it endless sufferings.[2]

In this connection he recalled that on only three occasions did he use harsh words in reprimanding others, believing he had good reason to do so. But each time he regretted having done so, for it proved not to be helpful. On the contrary, he never failed to obtain what he sought when he acted with kindness.

There is a big difference between true and false meekness. Meekness which is so only in appearance is soft, cowardly, and indulgent. True meekness is not foreign to firmness in doing good. It is always a part of it, for true virtues are all interrelated. On this subject Monsieur Vincent said:

No one is more constant or more firm in the good than the person who is meek and well-mannered. On the contrary, those given to anger and the passion of the irascible appetite are usually most inconstant, for they act by fits and starts. They are like raging torrents which have power only when bursting down the stream, but quiet down as soon as the flow of water stops. Rivers represent milder persons, without noise or show, flowing on without pause.[3]

One of his favorite maxims was *attigit a fine ad finem fortiter, et disponit omnia suaviter* ["She reaches from end to end mightily and governs all things well"].[4] To accomplish our end we must remain firm, yet all must be done with gentleness. He recalled the example of Blessed Francis de Sales, bishop of Geneva, who he said "was the meekest and gentlest person I have ever met. The very first time I saw him, I saw from the outset that his expression, his way of speaking and conversing with others was an expression of the meekness of our Lord Jesus Christ who had taken possession of his heart."

We could say in truth that Monsieur Vincent profited well from the example of the blessed prelate. Like him, he conveyed at first encounter a mildness and marvelous affability, and the most respectful language toward all classes of people.

One day he said to his community:

We have great need of affability because by our vocation we must often talk with one another and with our neighbor. What contributes to the difficulty of such conversation is that we come from such diverse backgrounds, in our place of origin, our temperament, and our dispositions. Dealing with our neighbor we will have

---

2. *CED* XI:66-67.
3. *CED* XI:65.
4. Wis 8:1.

much to put up with. Yet affability will ease the problems, for it is like the soul of good conversation. Affability will make it not only useful, but agreeable as well. Affability will help us converse with pleasure, with mutual respect for all. As charity is the virtue which unites us as members of the one body, affability is the virtue which perfects that union.[5]

He recommended that this virtue be particularly observed in dealing with the poor country people.

Otherwise, they will pull back, and fear to deal with us, thinking us too severe or too lordly for them. When they are treated affably and cordially, they feel otherwise, and are better disposed to profit from the good we seek to do for them. Since God has destined us to serve them, we must do so in a way that is most helpful, and therefore treat them with great affability. Each of us should take the words of the wise man in Scripture as addressed to ourselves: *Congregationi pauperum affabilem te facito*, "make yourself agreeable to the assembly of the poor."[6]

Although Monsieur Vincent was most affable in his speech, he was in no way a flatterer. On the contrary, he strongly opposed those who used such speech to insinuate themselves into the good graces of others. He said once to his community: "Be affable, but never a flatterer. Nothing is worse or more unworthy of a Christian than flattery. A truly virtuous man holds nothing in such horror as this particular vice."

Another maxim concerning this virtue of his, was that we must never dispute with others, even when trying to convert the most vicious. He wanted only mild and affable language to be used, as prudence and charity demanded. Acting on this principle he forbade his priests to enter into debates and disputes when it was a question of meeting with heretics, for he believed they were more influenced by mild and amicable words. He reported on a trip he had once made to Beauvais, when he had converted three heretics he had met. His mild manner contributed more to their conversion than anything else in their conversation. He said:

When we argue, it becomes obvious that our effort is designed to gain the upper hand over our opponent. This is why he prepares a resistance rather than a recognition of the truth. In this sort of debate, rather than finding a way to his mind, we ordinarily succeed in having him close the door of his heart to us. Mildness and affability, however, would have opened it. We have a good example of this in Blessed Francis de Sales, who though well versed in

---
5. *CED* XI:68.
6. Sir 4:7. *CED* XI:68-69.

controversy, converted heretics by his kindness and not by his teaching. On this subject, Cardinal du Perron used to say that he worked hard at convincing the heretics of their error, but the bishop of Geneva alone converted them.[7]

Recall the words of Saint Paul to the great missionary, Saint Timothy: *Servum Domini non oportet litigare.*[8] A servant of Jesus Christ ought not enter into controversies and disputes. I can tell you frankly, I have never seen or heard of a single heretic converted by the force of a debate or a subtle argument, but only by the kindness he had experienced. This virtue alone has enough strength to gain men back to God.[9]

The kindness of Monsieur Vincent was most evident in the corrections or admonitions he was obliged to make from time to time. He acted with such moderation and meekness and spoke so graciously but effectively, that the hardest hearts were softened. They could hardly resist the strength of his meekness. We will give here only a single example to show not only his kindness but also the prudence of the wise and charitable superior when he had to reprove one of his own. On one occasion he heard that a priest of the Congregation was not applying himself well to the work of the mission, even though he was capable of doing so. Also, when he did preach, he was rude to the poor people in church.

Monsieur Vincent wrote him a letter exhorting him to be committed to the work and more gentle toward the poor people before him. He did so in a manner that was kindly, prudent, yet energetic, with no show of personal displeasure, or hint of who had raised the question of his failings.

> I write to you to ask for news, and to give you news from here. How are things going with you after all your work? How many missions have you given? Do you find the people well disposed to follow the exercises and to draw from them the fruit we hope for? I shall be much obliged if you inform me about on these matters.
>
> I am in good contact with other houses of the Congregation. They all report that they have great success, thanks be to God. They don't quite reach the example of Monsieur N., who has been working in his mission only nine months, but who works without ceasing. It is a marvelous thing to see the strength God gives him and the extraordinary good he does, as I hear from all sides. The vicars general have written to me, others have either told me or have written, and even neighboring religious have written. The happy

---

7. Jacques Davy du Perron, died 1618.
8. 2 Tim 2:24.
9. *CED* XI:65-66.

success he has had is attributed largely to the care he uses to speak to these poor people with mildness and kindness. It had made me resolve more than ever to recommend to the entire Congregation to be committed more and more to these two virtues. If God has blessed our first missions we may say that it is because we have acted amiably, humbly, and sincerely toward all sorts of persons. It has pleased God to use the most miserable members of all in our Congregation for the conversion of several heretics. They themselves stated that because of the patience and cordiality shown them they were moved to return to the Church.

The convicts among whom I lived reacted the same way. When I spoke to them impersonally I spoiled everything. On the other hand, I began to praise them for their resignation, sympathize with their sufferings, and pointed out how fortunate they were to be making their purgatory in this life. I also kissed their chains, shared their sorrows, and spoke against their bad treatment. After that, they began to listen to me, give glory to God, and enter upon the road of salvation. Monsieur, please join me in thanking God for this. Let us ask him to give all our Missionaries this custom of treating our neighbor kindly, humbly, and charitably, both in public and in private, even hardened sinners, without ever using invectives, reproaches, or crude language against anyone. I have no doubt, Monsieur, that you will strive to avoid this unfortunate way of serving souls. It tends merely to annoy them and drive them away, rather than attracting them to you. Our Lord Jesus Christ is the meek master of men and of angels. By the practice of this same virtue you will go to him and bring others to him as well.[10]

SECTION ONE

Continuation of the Same Topic

The great meekness which Monsieur Vincent displayed in his correspondence and corrections came from a maxim he had learned from Saint Gregory the Great, that the faults of our neighbor ought to arouse our pity

---

10. *CED* IV:52-53.

more than our anger, and that true justice leads to compassion rather than indignation in dealing with sinners.[11] This holy man, Monsieur Vincent, often used to say that he was not surprised to see men fail. Just as it is in the nature of thorns and thistles to be prickly, so it is in the nature of fallen man to fail, since he was conceived and born in sin. Even the just man, according to the Wisdom of Solomon, falls seven times, that is, several times a day. He added that the spirit of a man is subject to indispositions just as his body is. Rather than being troubled and discouraged, he ought to recognize his miserable condition, humble himself, and say to God, as David did after his sin: *Bonum mihi quia humiliasti me, ut discam justificationes tuas.* It is good that you have humbled me that I may learn your justice.[12] He must learn to live with himself in his weaknesses and imperfections, all the while working to overcome them.

This knowledge of the common misery of men made him act with compassion and meekness toward sinners, and even cover their failings with prudence and a marvelous charity. He used to say that it was forbidden to judge anyone harshly, and it was even less licit to speak ill of anyone, since the apostle says charity must cover a multitude of sins.[13] In this regard, he quoted the word of the sage of holy Scripture: *Audisti verbum adversus proximum tuum? Commoriatur in te*: Have you heard something against your neighbor? You must let it die within you.[14] He would often refer to this virtue as being present in the person of the wife of the general of the galleys. Her tenderness and purity of conscience would not allow her to speak ill of anyone, and she would not tolerate anyone else doing so in her presence.

When several confreres withdrew from the Congregation, through temptation or for some other reason, some would gossip about the case even though they did not know the full story. Monsieur Vincent, of course, held to the maxim of never complaining of those who left and never discussing the reasons for their departure. On the contrary, when the opportunity presented itself, and he could do so honestly, he would speak to their advantage. He would provide all sorts of favors for them when he could, even though he knew some had been poorly disposed toward him. Several of the original members of the Congregation, and others who later came and persevered in the community, have said that after God they owed their perseverance in their vocations to the meekness and charitable support they had received from Monsieur Vincent.

Although he corrected the faults of others directly, it still was with an attitude of excusing and minimizing the failures as much as he could. He did

---

11. PL 76.2:1246.
12. Ps 119:71.
13. 1 Peter 4:8.
14. Sir 19:9.

so with such expressions of esteem and love for those who had offended that his reprimand in no way broke their spirit. On the contrary, it renewed their courage and increased their confidence in God. He greatly edified them by being, in his remarkable charity, the first to humble himself.

We might cite some extracts from his letters to allow us to better see his thoughts about the meekness that should accompany correction, and about the great concern he had to establish mutual support among the members of the Congregation.

Writing to the superior of one of the houses, he said:

> I praise God that you have gone yourself to take care of the matters Monsieur N. refused to do. You did well to act in this way, rather than insist that he go. There are those good and virtuous persons who fear God and do not want to offend him, but still fail in some matters. When this happens we must stand by them and not insist on our own way. Since God grants pardon in the confessional, I would judge that you would do well to act in this same spirit. Make allowances here for his failures since, thanks be to God, he is not a person of bad will.
>
> The harsh words of the other priest you wrote about may have come from a natural outburst and not from a disordered mind. Even the wisest people sometimes say things under the influence of passion which they are sorry for soon after. Others speak adversely about people or about their work, and still manage to do good. With some people, Monsieur, as you know only too well, we will always have something to put up with, but we must gain merit, too. I hope he of whom we just spoke will be won over by the charitable way in which he is handled, and that he is warned mildly and with prudence, and prayed for to God, as I do for your family.[15]

He wrote to another superior on the same subject:

> The priest you mention is a good man. He is striving to be virtuous, and had a good reputation in the world before he was received into the Congregation. If, now that he is among us, he has a restless spirit, is too occupied with external things and concerns for his relatives, and is a nuisance to the others, you must support him with patience. If he did not have these faults he would undoubtedly have others, and if you had nothing to suffer your charity would have little chance to be tested. You must make your response to him resemble the Lord's. He had to deal with his crude disciples, who lacked many refinements of personality, to teach us by his meekness and support how those in charge of others must act. Monsieur,

---

15. *CED* V:56-57.

please model yourself on this example. It will lead you not only to support your confreres but help them to overcome their imperfections. You must not tolerate evil, it is true, but you should seek to remedy it with gentleness.[16]

He wrote to a third, who worked in a distant diocese with another priest:

> I trust the goodness of our Lord will bless your work if cordiality and support for one another exists between you both. In God's name, Monsieur, please make this your first care. As you are the older and also the superior, support him who is with you with as much gentleness as you can. You must abandon any sense of superiority over him, adjusting yourself to him in a spirit of charity. This is the way our Lord won over and strengthened his apostles, and is the way you will win over this good priest. You must make some allowance for his moods. Don't scold him immediately when you first see some failing, but only later, and then humbly and cordially. Above all else, never let any division be seen between you, for you are in the public eye, and a single display of annoyance would ruin everything. I hope you will use the advice I give you, and that God will use the countless acts of virtue you practice as the base and foundation for the good he wishes to accomplish by you.[17]

In effect he recommended nothing so much by his letters and his conferences to the superiors and members of the Congregation, as meekness and mutual support to be a source of peace and a bond of perfection uniting all hearts. When the superior of a house would ask for the transfer of a sick member of their local house because he could no longer contribute to the work of the mission, he would reply that it was only just that he should remain. He had taken sick there, and it would be an opportunity for the other members of the mission to practice fraternal support and charity. If he would be asked to change someone because of his faults, he would say the others should support him because there was no one without faults. It was quite possible that the person taking his place might have even greater ones than he.

If some officers of the Congregation or other confreres would fail to follow his directives, doing something other than what he had been told, as happened more than once, he would say, "Monsieur, or, my brother, perhaps if you had done this in the way I asked you, God would have given it his blessing." On other occasions he would say nothing. He would allow his silence and patience to make the correction, if it were not an important matter, or not a case of formal disobedience that would require him to act more directly.

---

16. *CED* VII:136.
17. *CED* I:112-13.

Above all else, he had a marvelous meekness and support for the sick of mind or body. He never complained of the cost of caring for them, but putting himself in their place, he gave them the same care and treatment that he would have wished to receive if he were in their state. We should remark here that among those seeking admission to the Congregation some would occasionally be found who to all appearances ought not to have been received into the body of the Company. Monsieur Vincent would not send them away, but would provide medicines and additional rest, and use other remedies he thought proper. Although some others recommended to him that these persons be dismissed, he insisted that they be kept and supported. In many cases cures took place, and these confreres then rendered good service to God in the Congregation.

If he used a charitable gentleness toward those still on probation before being accepted into his Congregation, he was even more definite in regard to those who were already members. He would send no one away for health reasons, regardless of his illness. He looked upon the sick as those who would attract the blessings of God upon the Congregation. This is what he wrote to one of his priests who was thinking of leaving the Company because of his poor health. "Do not fear that you may be in any way a burden to the Company because of sickness, and you must be convinced you never will be. By God's grace, the sick will never burden us. On the contrary, it is a blessing to have them."[18] This was the mind and practice of Monsieur Vincent on this point, and his Company was so much of this same spirit that no one was ever sent away because of sickness.

He was especially gentle with the brothers of the Congregation, especially the most rustic and the least able. He never wanted to send them away because of their lack of skill or use to the community. He would have them speak in the conferences and spiritual colloquies of the community to open their minds. Even though they sometimes spoke too long, tediously, or off the topic, he would allow them to say what they wished without interruption. He never showed his disapproval of what they said, unless they said something untrue or erroneous that needed to be corrected. In these cases he spoke most paternally and gently not to discourage or sadden them. He would put a good interpretation on what they had said or excuse what he could, but pointed out how they might have been mistaken.

His kindness and understanding went beyond the natural faults of mind and body, and extended to those committed against the moral law. From time to time he met in his own or in other communities those who had fallen from the way of virtue. They caused more harm than good by their complaining, slander, or other failings. When these were publicly known, people

---

18. *CED* VI:491-92.

were surprised that Monsieur Vincent did not dismiss them from the Congregation, and he was sometimes urged to do so. This charitable and meek superior supported them all with an almost unbelievable charity and patience, to give the offenders time to come to their senses, but he nevertheless used appropriate means to remedy their failings.

The superior of one of the missions of the Congregation was happy to be rid of some lax confreres with difficult personalities. He wrote to Monsieur Vincent that such people should be put out of the Company. Monsieur Vincent responded to him in a remarkable way, revealing his thoughts on the subject we are discussing:

> I agree with you about the person you describe. I do not think he will improve, but on the contrary I fear he will continue to cause much trouble to this house where we have had him report. Not only do I fear this, but I begin to see it myself, and I must tell you that he and two others give us much grief. One has left, after we had put up with all we could, and it would be helpful if the others too would go away. To cut away the gangrenous members would do justice to the Company, and even prudence suggests we should do so. But because we are called upon to practice all the virtues, we must show support, meekness, patience, and charity, while hoping for their amendment. We will attempt to apply appropriate remedies, threats, prayers, admonitions, all with no other hope than what it will please God to bring about by his grace. Our Lord did not reject Saint Peter because he had denied him three times, nor even Judas, though it seems he died in his sin. I think, then, that the divine Goodness will be pleased if the Company will extend its charity to these two troublemakers, and to spare or neglect nothing to gain them for God. Only after they show no improvement should we then resort to amputation.[19]

Some timorous and scrupulous souls, a trial to themselves and bearing an almost insupportable burden, often tested the charity of Monsieur Vincent, and gave him the opportunity to practice the virtue of support and meekness. Among his confreres were some who for years were afflicted by scruples. They were the likely source of much annoyance by their incessant demands upon him, yet he never complained nor put them off. He supported them and received them graciously, to give them no cause for discouragement or sadness. In whatever company he happened to be, he would rise at once when he saw them approaching, and allow them to speak to him in a corner of the room where he was. Although they would return to speak of the same thing several times over, even sometimes three or four times in a single hour, he would receive them with the same serenity as before. He would listen to

---

19. *CED* IV:36-37.

them patiently, and reply with his customary meekness. This is what one of these unfortunate persons reported later:

Monsieur Vincent was always a great support for me, and treated me with great kindness during my depression. I interrupted him continually, even when he was preparing to celebrate mass or to recite the divine office. When I had heard his response, and left, and then came back again to speak with him several times in succession and at length, I never heard from him a single harsh word. On the contrary, he would always speak to me gently, and never scolded me, something he would have been entirely justified in doing, seeing the constant demands I made upon him. Even after he told me what I must do, I would allow new doubts to arise. He took the trouble to write out in his own hand what he had said to help me remember it, and to support this effort he would then have me read it aloud in his presence. Whenever hour I went to see him, even late in the evening, or even when he was occupied with others in matters of business, he would always receive me with the same kindness. He would listen to me, and reply with such gentleness and charity that I can hardly express it

Another confrere reported he had often tried the patience and charity of Monsieur Vincent by asking him to repeat several times what he had said. This charitable superior did so graciously with no trace of displeasure, repeating what he had said as often as requested, and each time explaining just what he meant. He would show as much interest and concern the final time as he had shown the very first. Once, as happened on several other occasions also, when he was occupied with the business of some persons of rank, he called a brother to say something to him. This brother did not understand exactly what was meant. He had Monsieur Vincent repeat it more than four times, which he did without the least sign of impatience. He spoke the fifth time with the same mildness and tranquility of spirit as he did the first, showing by a smile that he was amused rather than annoyed.

SECTION TWO

Some Remarkable Words of Monsieur Vincent About the Meekness We Should Practice in Regard to Our Neighbor

These remarks are taken from a collection of his remarks on this subject, gathered by one of his confreres from his various talks:

Meekness and humility are two sisters who go hand in hand. We are urged to study them carefully in the person of Jesus Christ, who said of himself, "Learn of me because I am meek and humble of heart."[20] The Son of God tells us, "learn of me." O my Savior, what a lesson! What happiness to be your pupil, to learn this short but excellent lesson which makes us so like yourself. Should you not exercise the same influence over us as the ancient philosophers did over their followers? They had such a reputation among them that they had only to say "the master has said" to end all discussion.

If by their reasonings philosophers could develop such committed disciples in regard to human affairs, how much more, my brothers, Eternal Wisdom deserves to be believed and followed in the things of the spirit? What would we answer at this very moment, if we were called upon to recite the lessons he has given us? What will we say at the hour of death when he will reproach us for having learned these lessons so imperfectly? "Learn of me," he said, "to be meek." If it were Saint Paul or Saint Peter who had told us to learn this lesson of him, we might have found an excuse, but it was God made man, come to point out the way we must act to be pleasing to his Father. The Teacher of Teachers had taught us to be meek. Give us, O Lord, some share in your great meekness, but we pray so gently and meekly that you cannot refuse our request.

Meekness has several aspects, but they can be reduced to three, the first of which is further divided into two parts. This first act of the virtue of meekness represses the first movements of the passion of anger. These are the first outbursts of this fire which rises to our features, troubles the soul, makes us lose control of ourselves, and changes the color of our face, making it either dark as a cloud or all inflamed. What of meekness? It stops these changes, it prevents him who has this virtue from experiencing these bad results. He does not allow the passion to influence him, but holds firm, not to be carried away. There may sometimes be a tint in the face, but this immediately goes away. We must not be surprised at this, for the movements of nature precede those of grace, but grace triumphs. We must not wonder at attacks of anger. We should rather ask grace to conquer them, being well convinced that even when we feel this revolt within ourselves contrary to meekness, we still may be overcoming it. This, then, is the first part of this first act of meekness. It is a beautiful virtue. It prevents the vice from showing itself in our physical makeup, and has its effects even on our minds

---

20. Matt 11:29.

and souls, for it not only tempers the fires of anger but eliminates the least trace of its action.

The second part of this first act of meekness consists in allowing anger to develop within us, on those occasions when we see that it is expedient that we do so. Yet even then this comes about by our conscious decision, not by the movement of natural forces. This was the case when our Lord called Saint Peter, Satan,[21] and when he said to the Jews, "Woe to you, hypocrites," not once, but several times.[22] This word is repeated ten or twelve times in a single chapter. On another occasion he chased the sellers from the Temple, overturned the tables, and gave other signs of being angry.[23] Was he carried away by anger then? No, for he possessed meekness in an infinite degree. In us, this virtue makes us masters of the passion. In our Lord, who was not ruled by any passion properly so-called, he simply allowed the acts of anger to manifest themselves as he thought best. If on some occasion he who is meek and kind showed himself to be angry, he did so to correct those he spoke to, to oppose sin and to avoid scandal. He did this to build up souls and for our instruction. What great fruit the Savior gained by acting in this way! His corrections were well received because reason dictated them and not simple inclination.

When he spoke with such vigor, it was not by reason of his anger, but solely for the good of the person concerned. Since our Lord ought to be our model wherever we find ourselves, those who lead others ought to see how he conducted himself, and be guided by him. He guided by love. Sometimes he promised a reward, but at other times he threatened punishment. We must do the same, but always under the banner of love. We are then in the same state as the prophet, when he said, *Domine, ne in furore tuo arguas me* ["O Lord, in your anger punish me not"].[24] It seemed to the poor king that God was in anger against him, and he prayed not to be punished when God was in this state. Everyone is like that. None of us wants to be corrected in anger. It is a favor granted to only a few not to feel the first emotions of anger, as I have said. The meek person quickly comes to himself and conquers anger and vengeance, so that nothing comes from him but what is ruled by love. This is, then, the first act of meekness. It represses the first signs of anger, either entirely, or in using them reasonably when this is necessary, but

---

21. Matt 16:23.
22. Matt 23:14,15, etc.
23. Matt 21:12.
24. Ps 38:1.

even then, meekly. This is why, gentlemen, now that we speak of it, any time that you are annoyed, stop at once to recollect yourself, and raise your mind to God, saying to him, "Lord, you see me tempted. Deliver me from any evil it may suggest."

The second act of meekness is to have a great affability, cordiality, and serenity of expression for everyone we meet, so as to be agreeable to them. Those who have a smiling and agreeable countenance please everyone. God gave them this grace, by which they seem to offer their hearts and invite others to open theirs. Others present themselves with a sad and disagreeable face, all contrary to meekness. A Missionary must strive to be affable, and so cordial and simple that he puts everyone he meets at ease. Hearts are attracted and gained, according to this word of the Lord, "the meek shall inherit the land."[25] On the contrary, we have seen people in authority who are so cold and grave they make people afraid of them, and we avoid them.

Since our work takes us among the poor country people, the ordinands, the retreatants, and all sorts of people, it is not possible for us to produce any good fruit if we are like arid land, capable of growing only thorns. We must be attractive to others, with a pleasant exterior that will repel no one.

I was consoled just three or four days ago at the sight of someone leaving here. He was all smiles, and said to me, "I noticed here a gentleness, an openness of heart, and a certain charming simplicity (these were his words) which touched me deeply."

Isaiah says of our Lord: *Butyrum et mel comedet, ut sciat reprobare malum, et eligere bonum.* He shall eat butter and honey so that he may know how to reprove evil and choose the good.[26] This discernment is given, I think, only to meek souls. Since anger is a passion which disturbs reason, it must be the contrary virtue which gives discernment and light to reason.

The third act of meekness consists of not reacting adversely, even interiorly, when we have received some discourtesy from someone. We say within ourselves: maybe he did not really think this, or maybe he acted too hastily, or perhaps he was surprised by a moment of passion, or anything else which might deflect thinking we have received a deliberate insult. If someone says unkind words to us, the meek person does not open his mouth to reply, but acts as though he heard nothing.

---

25. Matt 5:5.
26. Isa 7:15.

It is related of a chancellor of France[27] who one day was leaving the king's council, that he met a man who had lost his case before the court. He told the official he was a wicked judge for having fined him and ruined his family by his decision. He called down upon him the judgment of God and his punishments. The chancellor said not a word, but continued walking, looking neither to the right or left. If Christian meekness or some other quality enabled him to act in this way, I do not know. Be that as it may, we ought to be ashamed of ourselves sometimes to be carried away by trifles, seeing that the first minister of justice in the entire kingdom endured the insults of a citizen without making the least reply. What an admirable thing considering his rank and his great power to punish such disrespect.

But you, O Savior, do you not have even greater power over us? We see you practicing an incomparable meekness toward the most guilty, but we do not imitate your meekness. When will we be moved by your example and learn from the lessons we are given in your school?

Meekness does not make us simply excuse the affronts and unjust treatment we receive, but goes so far as to make us say a kind word to those who have offended us. Even if we are insulted by a slap in the face, we suffer it for God. This is the way meekness works. Yes, a servant of God who is truly meek offers the rude treatment he receives to God, and remains in peace.

If the Son of God was so condescending in his usual meetings with people, how much more so did he show his meekness during his sufferings. He carried it to the point of not saying a word of protest against the deicides who covered him with insults and mocked his sufferings. "My friend," he said to Judas, even while he was delivering him up to his enemies.[28] He overcame the treachery by this salutation, "my friend." He spoke with the same courtesy to those who came to arrest him: "Whom do you seek? Here I am."[29] Let us meditate on this, gentlemen, for we will see these are powerful acts of meekness which surpass human understanding. O Jesus, my God! What an example for us who have undertaken to imitate you. What a lesson for those who are unwilling to suffer anything; or, if they do suffer, become anxious and bitter.

After thinking of all this, should we not love this virtue of meekness by which God gives us the grace not only to stifle the

---

27. Nicolas Brulart, marquis of Sillery.
28. Matt 26:50.
29. John 18:4-5.

movements of anger, but to deal with our neighbor most graciously and to return good for evil? It enables us to endure afflictions, wounds, torments, and even death that men may cause us. Give us the grace, my Savior, to profit from the pains you endured with such love and meekness. Some have already profited from this gift of your goodness. Possibly I am the only one here present who has not yet begun to be gentle and patient.[30]

---

30. *CED* XII:182-194.

CHAPTER THIRTEEN

His Humility

THE SON of God proclaimed the truth that he who praises himself shall be humbled, but he who humbles himself shall be exalted.[1] God's providence allows us to see this truth verified every day. It also lets us recognize what a great doctor of the Church has said that nothing makes us more agreeable in the eyes of God and so acceptable to others, as when a person joins a saintly and virtuous life to feelings of sincere humility.

This was exemplified in the person of Monsieur Vincent, who was exalted by the great things God did in him and by him, and by his evident humility. The more profoundly he abased himself before God, the more he was raised up, and the more graces he received for himself and all his holy enterprises.

It is true that after his death it was said of him, as indeed it was said during his life, that his true character was not well known. He was admittedly a humble man. Yet the common opinion never regarded his humility as the main disposition which attracted the graces with which he was inundated, and which were the foundation and root of all the great works he did. Those who judged him most favorably felt that his zeal was the main source of his works, and his prudence happily guided them to a successful conclusion. While these two virtues were indeed highly developed in him and contributed much to his success, we must recognize that his profound humility drew down the plenitude of lights and graces which caused his works to prosper. To speak of this in a better way, we could say that his zeal led him to humble himself at every turn, and his prudence consisted in simply following the maxims and examples of the Son of God and the inspirations of the Holy Spirit. He kept himself in the disposition of heart of considering himself incapable of doing any good, and being without any virtue and strength. In this sentiment he often repeated within himself this lesson of humility he had learned from his divine master, saying in his heart, "I am a worm and no man, creeping upon the earth, not knowing where I am going, but seeking only to hide myself in you, O my God, who are my all in all. I am a poor blind man unable to take a single step in the way of goodness unless you extend your hand of mercy to guide me."

These were the sentiments of Vincent de Paul. He followed the example of his patron, the apostle Paul, and found no better occasion of correspon-

---

1. Matt 23:12.

dence and cooperation with the designs of God than when he was stricken to the ground in profound abasement. He closed his eyes to all human considerations, abandoned himself to the designs of his divine master, said in his heart, like this great apostle, "Lord, what would you have me do?"[2] In this spirit of dependence, he never undertook an enterprise of his own accord. He waited instead for divine Providence to show the work to be undertaken, either by the orders of those he regarded as his superiors, by the advice and persuasion of those he recognized as virtuous persons, or lastly by the contemporary conditions and needs that manifested the will of God to him, which he always followed but never anticipated.

When he spoke of the greatest of his works, the founding of his own Congregation, he always openly said that God alone called those received into the Company. He had never said a word to attract anyone. He stated he had not become a missionary through personal choice, but had been drawn in solely by God's will, hardly aware of what was happening. God alone was the author of any good accomplished in the missions, in all the activities of the missionaries, and in all the good works they were connected with. All this was done without his having planned it, and not knowing where God was leading him.

To speak in greater detail of the humility of this great servant of God is difficult because of his constant effort to keep this virtue hidden not only from others but even from himself. Nevertheless, we shall attempt to trace its main features, drawn from what we have seen and known of him, heard from his own lips or taken from the recollections of persons of great piety.

We have already said that although God wished to use Monsieur Vincent for great things, he himself thought of himself as being unsuited for even the least of these. Even more, he thought himself more likely to tear down rather than to build up. He recognized himself as a child of Adam, and therefore mistrusted himself as one attracted to evil as a result of the fall of our first parents. For this reason he had formed a great mistrust of himself. He avoided honors and praise like the plague. He never justified himself when he was accused, and by preference took the part of the accuser, even when he was the innocent party. He condemned the least faults in himself with greater exactitude than some others did with the greatest of their sins. He judged his slightest lapses of understanding or memory as though they were serious failures. Because of this attitude he did not push himself into any undertaking, no matter what, and was more pleased to see God working good through others than through himself.

In this same spirit he tried to hide, as much as he could, his special graces received from God. He would have revealed none but those he could not

---

2. Acts 9:6.

conceal without lacking in charity for his neighbor, or made necessary by some other obligation. He had a habitual attitude of concealing his gifts and activities and all he had undertaken for the good of others. He did this to such an extent that even members of his own Congregation knew only a fraction of the good works he had been involved with, and how many spiritual and corporal works of charity he had performed for all sorts of persons. Many of his confreres were astonished to read in this present work things they had never before known.

Not content to hide the good he had done, he took every occasion to abase himself, to lessen himself in the esteem of others as far as he was able, imitating the humility of the Son of God. Although he was the splendor of the glory of his Father and the image of God's substance, he submitted to the opprobrium of men and to being treated like an outcast by the people. He spoke willingly of those things likely to draw down the contempt of others upon himself. He fled with horror from anything that might directly or indirectly tend to his honor or praise. When he went to Paris, he never said that he was called "de Paul," lest this usage give the impression he belonged to some notable family. He called himself simply Monsieur Vincent, his baptismal name, as one would say Monsieur Pierre or Monsieur Jacques. Also, although he had a licentiate in theology,[3] he spoke of himself as a simple secondary school student. It was remarked about him that he tried on all occasions to appear to be mean and contemptible, and to pass as a nobody. When some issue would arise in which he would be blamed, he accepted the blame willingly and with such a joy that it was as though he had stumbled upon a treasure.

He referred to his Congregation as the "little, the very little, (or) the wretched Company." He never wanted his confreres to conduct missions in the large cities but only in the villages, especially the tiniest of them, to evangelize and instruct the poor peasants, for this duty was the least respected in the public eye. He wanted his Company to be regarded as the least and last of all the orders. Being obliged once to send some representatives from the house of Saint Lazare to a general meeting of the city, one of the recommendations he gave to the priest, one of the leading priests of his community, and to his companion representing Saint Lazare was that they must insist on taking the last place of all the clergy present.[4]

He would not allow anyone to say anything in praise of the Congregation. He always referred to it as "the poor and wretched Company", and said that he asked nothing of God for it, so much as the gift of humility. One day, speaking to his community, he said:

---

3. Actually, a licentiate in canon law. *CED* XIII:60.
4. The priest was Lambert aux Couteaux. His companion was Brother Louis Robineau, who composed the memoirs which Abelly probably consulted.

CHAPTER THIRTEEN 183

Is it not a strange thing that the members of the Company, the Peters, Johns, and Jameses, should flee honors and love rejection, but the Company and community should, they say, enjoy the esteem and honor of everybody? I must ask you, how can it be that Peter, John, and James truly and sincerely loved and sought to be badly regarded, and yet the Company which is composed of these same people should seek to be respected and honored? We must surely see that the two things are incompatible. Therefore all the missionaries should be glad, not only when they experience some occasion of rejection and disrespect for themselves, but also when the entire Congregation is so judged. This would be a sign that they are truly humble.[5]

His humility was so sincere that it could be read on his face, in his eyes, and in the posture of his body. He thus made it obvious that his humility and abasements came from the depths of his heart, where this virtue was so deeply engraved. He believed he had no right to the use of any creatures, even those necessary to conserve life or necessary to advance God's glory, much less those which were simply useful. In this sentiment he asked nothing for himself, but rather was always ready to deprive himself of everything. We are not at all surprised to hear that he refused the ecclesiastical dignities offered him, knowing that he considered himself unworthy of the least things.

Although his humility was as we have just spoken, he could still be constant and generous when it was a question of sustaining the interests of God or of his Church. On these occasions he showed that humility (as was so well taught by the Angelic Doctor) is not contrary to magnanimity, but rather that this virtue is perfected by humility.[6] Humility gives magnanimity a solid base, being solely dependent upon God and yet possessed of a just mean not going beyond what it should, and having no tie to vanity.

One day, he told his community that humility is compatible with generosity and courage. He used as proof the example of Saint Louis, whose humility led him to serve the poor with his own hands. He would go into the hospitals to seek out the most repulsive of the sick and wounded to serve them in person. Yet he was one of the most generous and valiant kings ever to bear the crown of France, as was shown in the important victories he won over the Albigensians and in the two trips he made to the holy land to battle the infidels. From this he drew the lesson that we must ask of God a generosity founded upon humility.[7]

---

5. *CED* XI:60.
6. *Summa Theologiae* IIa-IIae, q. 129, a. 3; and q. 161, a. 2.
7. *CED* XI:301-03.

SECTION ONE

Some Examples of Monsieur Vincent's Practice of the Virtue of Humility

A virtuous priest who knew Monsieur Vincent well said most correctly that he had never seen any ambitious person with greater desire of advancing his career, of being well regarded, and of arriving at the summit of honors, than this humble servant of God had of doing just the opposite. He sought to see himself abased, regarded as abject and contemptible, and ready to embrace all humiliations and confusions. He seems to have treasured this virtue, seizing every opportunity to practice it, and taking care to humble himself on every conceivable occasion.

Besides what we have already said in this chapter, we shall give several more particular examples in what follows.

He was far from parading the gifts and talents he had received from God, but on the contrary he strove, as much as possible, as we have already said, to hide them. When he had to reveal these gifts in the service of God and the neighbor, he displayed only what was strictly needed. His maxim in this regard is the more worthy of being respected as it is rare among us. Although we have written of it elsewhere, it bears repeating, for it deserves to be known and practiced by all.

> If I do a public action and can make myself look good, I will not do so. I will refrain from pushing myself forward, not doing what would likely give me a certain reputation. If two thoughts come to me about a particular topic, if charity does not require me to do otherwise, I will speak of the lesser of these, to humble myself, and retain the better as a sacrifice to God in the secret of my heart. Our Savior takes pleasure in the humble of heart, and in the simplicity of our words and actions.[8]

When he had to speak of the works which God had accomplished by him, or the blessings showered upon his direction of them, he would do so in the name of the Congregation, not of his own. He would say, for example, "God used the Congregation for this or that purpose. His infinite goodness bestowed such and such a grace upon the Company." When he spoke of what he planned to do in carrying out some project, he would speak in the plural, saying, for example, "We will seek to supply a remedy for this need, or, to

---

8. *CED* XII:222.

accomplish this purpose we will send this or that help." He spoke this way in a spirit of humility, not wishing to make it appear that he was the one responsible. He would not say, for example, "I will remedy this, or I will look to that, or I will send such help," or similar words, such as are often used by those who have some power and authority. He would say: "Please, thank you, I beg your pardon, I am responsible that these things did not work out as well as we had hoped, or that such an unfortunate situation developed," because these expressions are in some way humiliating. He wanted to save for himself whatever smacked of abjection or lack of success.

He had a marvelous ability to attribute good to others, and to turn any praise directed to himself to another. He acted as if he had taken no part in the happy outcome, giving any praise and all honor to God and to the neighbor. If there was any excess in his actions, it was in heaping too much praise on others, and too much disparagement on himself. When he referred to himself it was in such humble terms that it was sometimes embarrassing to hear him.

Once, responding to a person of great piety who recommended herself to his prayers,[9] he said: "I shall recommend you to God since you ask me to do so. Yet I need the help of good friends more than any person in the world because of the miseries that overwhelm me. They make me look upon the good opinion people have of me as a punishment for my hypocrisy, since it makes me pass myself off for other than I am."[10]

A worthy bishop, noticing that Monsieur Vincent humbled himself in all things, could not help saying that he was a perfect Christian. This humble servant of God answered: "Oh, bishop, what are you saying? Me, a perfect Christian? I should be considered as a reprobate, and the greatest sinner of the universe."

A new member of the Congregation of the Mission spoke in a conference in the presence of Monsieur Vincent. He said he was mortified in profiting so little from the marvelous good example he saw in the founder. Monsieur Vincent allowed these words to pass so as not to interrupt him. After the conference, however, he commented in public: "Monsieur, we have this practice among us not to praise anyone to his face, in his presence. I am truly a marvel, but a marvel of malice, more wicked than the demon, who has no more reason to be in hell than myself. I do not say this by way of exaggeration, but according to the way I really see things."[11]

A person given to Jansenism[12] once spoke to him in an effort to persuade him to come over to that party. When he finished speaking, but with little to

---

9. Marie Henriette de Rochechouart, superior of one of the Paris Visitation monasteries.
10. *CED* V:580.
11. *CED* XI:119.
12. The Abbe de Saint Cyran.

show for his efforts, he became angry. He reproached Monsieur Vincent, saying he was a true ignoramus, and he was astonished that his Congregation would tolerate him as superior general. Monsieur Vincent replied that he himself was astonished at the same thing, because, he said, "I am even more ignorant than you know."

Once he consoled a student of the Congregation who was tempted to despair. When he answered some difficulties troubling him against hope by urging him to have confidence in God, he added: "If the devil returns with this same evil suggestion, use the same response I have just explained to you. Say to this unhappy tempter it was Vincent, an ignoramus who never finished school, who taught you that."

A priest of the Congregation wrote to Monsieur Vincent that the superior of the mission where he lived was not sufficiently cultivated for that particular place. Monsieur Vincent replied, saying much good of this virtuous superior, and then added, "And me, what should I do: How have I been tolerated in the position I hold? I am more crude, more ridiculous, more stupid than any among whom I live. I cannot say six words in succession without showing my ignorance and lack of prudence. Even worse, I have none of the virtues of the man we are speaking of."

It was his custom in meetings of all sorts of persons, especially when there was some honorable reference to himself, to insist that he was a simple peasant, a guardian of sheep. He enjoyed saying the same thing to gatherings of the poor, to show them that he was of the same stock. In this connection, a peasant came to the door of Saint Lazare once, asking to see him, but the porter told him Monsieur Vincent was busy speaking to noblemen. This good man replied: "This could not be Monsieur Vincent, for he often said he was a simple peasant like myself."

Once, Monsieur Vincent accompanied a priest to the door at Saint Lazare, where a poor woman called out, "My lord, an alms, please." Monsieur Vincent replied, "My poor woman, you do not know me well. I am a poor pig farmer, the son of a poor villager." Another time he was met by a woman at the door as he bade farewell to some noble visitors. She begged an alms, and said she had been formerly the servant of Madame his mother. Monsieur Vincent replied, in the presence of his guests, "My good woman, you mistake me for someone else. My mother never had a servant, but was a servant herself, being the wife, and I the son, of a peasant."

A young man, the relative of a priest of the Congregation of the Mission, declined to sit beside him out of respect for him. Monsieur Vincent said, "Why, Monsieur, do you make such a big thing out of sitting next to a swineherd, and the son of a peasant?" The young man was very surprised at this.

Once he visited a person of rank, who wished to accompany him to the door at the conclusion of their business. He did what he could to dissuade him. He said, among other things: "You know well, Monsieur, that I am the son of a poor villager, and in my youth I tended the sheep in the fields."[13] The lord, a man of some learning, reminded him that one of the greatest of the kings who ever lived was David, who too was taken from this same occupation. Monsieur Vincent seemed confused and humbled by this response.

In the assemblies of piety which he attended, his humility led him always to defer to the opinion of others, and to prefer them to his own, even though his own were the more cogent. One day at an assembly of the Ladies of Charity of Paris, at which he presided, the participants deliberated on some matters of importance about helping the poor. One of the ladies in the group noted that, with his usual humility, he adopted the opinion of others. She could not refrain from chiding him gently that he was not firm enough in holding to his own view, even though it was clearly superior. He replied in keeping with his humility: "May God forbid, Madame, that my wretched thoughts prevail over those of others. I am pleased that God works his marvels without me, miserable man that I am."

The attraction he had for the virtue of humility, and the treasures of grace he found in its practice, moved him to extend to his Congregation the sentiments he had. This is why he usually referred to it in unflattering terms. In this spirit, he once replied to a priest who asked to be received into the Company, preferring it to all others, as the best route to take to the kingdom of heaven. "Your own goodness makes you say that, and makes you think this way. But the other communities are truly holy, while ours is the miserable one, and more miserable than miserable."

To another, who asked the same favor, he said, "What, Monsieur, you want to be a missionary? What makes you look to our tiny Company, for we are poor specimens?" The one he spoke to later mentioned that he was greatly edified at the humility of Monsieur Vincent, who spoke the way he did about his own Congregation at the very moment others were asking to enter.

Not satisfied with simply speaking this way, he tried to inculcate this spirit of humility into the Company from its very first days. While still living at the College des Bons Enfants, he fell to his knees before the seven or eight priests who then composed the community. He admitted in their presence the gravest sins of his past life. These priests were stunned by this action. They admired the action of grace in their superior which enabled him to overcome the natural inclination which all men have of hiding their failings,

---

13. This common saying occurs in several places: *CED* II:3, 171; IV:215; VIII:138, 320; IX:15; X:681; XII:21, 270, 297.

and to adopt rather the stance of attempting to destroy any natural esteem they may have had for him. He had the custom, also, on the anniversary of his baptism, of kneeling before the community to ask God's pardon for all the sins he had committed during the time the divine Goodness had allowed him to spend on earth. He would beg the Company to pardon the scandal he may have caused, and to pray to God for his mercy.

Besides, when he felt that something was not up to his ideals, he would humble himself. He did this even for interior failings, such as the first movements of impatience which had not manifested themselves exteriorly, or perhaps for some words lacking in meekness to an individual, or even for the least inadvertences.

Once, he suggested to one of the brothers of the house at Saint Lazare to give lodging to a poor person passing through. This brother opposed the idea with reasons and hesitations. Monsieur Vincent felt he had to speak more firmly to have him carry out his orders, but later his humility caused him some remorse. He went to the garden, where some older priests of the Congregation were gathered, to ask pardon of the Company for the scandal he continued to give, and which he only recently had given in speaking rudely to a brother of the poultry yard. One of the priests who was present for this humiliation added: "What he did was known to everyone. That same evening, however, I went to his room as was my custom, after the community's general examination of conscience. I saw him kissing the feet of that brother."

It was not on this occasion alone, but on a countless number of others that he was seen at the feet of his inferiors, even the least in the house. We will give here only a few examples.

Once, thinking he had offended a brother by having suggested too strongly that he must have patience in a matter that arose, he would not say mass until he had begged pardon of this brother. Not finding him in the kitchen, he went to the cellar to express his regrets for having caused him some uneasiness.

Once on a fast day he stopped by a poor inn during one of his trips. He asked for a bit of oil to put on some dried mussels he had been served, but almost immediately his humility made him fear that he had given bad example to his traveling companions. He immediately fell to his knees before them, asking their pardon.

Another time, traveling with three of his priests, he enlivened the time by some stories of what had happened to him some time before. His audience was deeply interested, but just as deeply surprised when he stopped in the middle of a sentence. He struck his breast and said he was a miserable sinner, filled with vainglory and pride, knowing only how to talk about himself. He changed the subject, and once they arrived at their destination he begged pardon of them, on his knees, for the scandal he had given, in speaking of himself.

When he took sick at Richelieu in 1649, the brother infirmarian from Saint Lazare was summoned to take care of him, because he was well acquainted with what had to be done. He welcomed the brother and received him with much affection, but Monsieur Vincent said that he sorry to have caused him the trouble of coming such a distance for nothing but a carcass. Later he felt that he had not been sufficiently generous in his welcome. He fell to his knees to ask pardon, not only at Richelieu, but again at Saint Lazare when he returned. In the presence of his assistant, who reported the event, he said, "Do you see this good brother, Monsieur? He came all the way to Richelieu to help me, and I was not as welcoming as I should have been. I ask his pardon, in your presence, and ask you to pray to God for me not to commit such faults in the future."

Once a nephew of his came from his native town of Dax to Paris. The porter of the College des Bons Enfants, where he then lived, alerted Monsieur Vincent that his nephew wished to see him. At this, Monsieur Vincent felt the first movement of some uneasiness at his arrival, and asked to have him shown to his room. Almost immediately, he changed his mind, and went himself to receive him humbly at the door. The canon of the village of Dax was in the College des Bons Enfants at the time, and he continued the story.

> I cannot pass over an act of virtue of Monsieur Vincent which I witnessed on the occasion of his nephew's visit. He instructed the porter to go to the street to meet the young man, dressed in the typical garb of peasants of his region, and bring him to his room. At once this good servant of God overcame his reluctance to receive him. He came down from his room to the street, embraced him, kissed him, and led him to the garden where he had called all the members of the community. He described his nephew as the most respectable man of his entire family, and had him meet all the priests and brothers. He would do the same for persons of rank who visited him. In the first spiritual exercise after this event, he accused himself publicly of having some shame at the arrival of his nephew, and of wanting to take him unnoticed to his room just because he was a peasant and so poorly dressed.

He went further in his practice of humility in the first ordination retreats held at Saint Lazare for, speaking to these candidates for the ecclesiastical state, he brought up some humiliating things from his past. He mentioned that one of his relatives had been condemned to the galleys. He repeated this on several other occasions, but the truth was this relative was distant, more than the fourth degree of kindred removed.

While he was so anxious to obtain humiliations for himself, he was equally receptive to those which came from others. One of the chief magistrates of Parlement one day was reported to him to have said in public that the missionaries of Saint Lazare hardly gave missions any more. Monsieur Vincent was astonished at this. His contact replied that the magistrate spoke without knowing that the missionaries had for a long time been giving countless missions, and even now were continuing to do so. He urged Monsieur Vincent to inform the magistrate, otherwise he might continue to berate the Congregation. Monsieur Vincent replied to this, "we must leave him alone. I will never justify myself except by letting my actions speak for me."

When a house of the Congregation had been seriously hurt, though innocent of any cause, Monsieur Vincent showed himself joyous rather than sad. He exhorted the community to thank God for this trial and to ask the grace to make good use of it. "To be treated the way our Lord was, is true happiness."

To establish the spirit of humility well in the Company, he proposed as a subject of prayer for the community once a month, for several years, a meditation on the horrors of pride. He said:

> The Congregation cannot subsist without the virtue of humility. When this virtue is lacking in a company, each one thinks of his own particular house, and this leads to partiality, schism, and destruction. If the missionaries should ask for one thing from the Lord, it is humility. They should be sad and weep when they receive applause, for our Lord has said: *Vae cum benedixerint vobis homines.* Cursed shall you be, when men shall praise you.[14]

His humility became most evident chiefly in his service in the court, for it was shown in the circumstances where honors were commonplace and well deserved for virtue and good conduct. In the beginning when he was summoned to the Council with the late Prince of Conde and several other lords, the prince invited him to sit beside him. He replied, "My lord, you do me too great an honor even allowing me to be in your presence, for I am but the son of a poor swineherd." At this, the prince quoted a verse from the poet: *Moribus et vita nobilitatur homo,* ["Man is ennobled by his morals and life,"] adding, "I did not just learn of your ability." He then brought up in this first meeting some disputed points. Monsieur Vincent responded so directly to them that the prince said, "Ha, Monsieur Vincent, you tell everyone you are an ignoramus, and yet you have given us a solution to one of our greatest problems with the Huguenots in just a few words." He then proposed several other difficult cases in canon law. Monsieur Vincent

---

14. Luke 6:26. *CED* XI:114.

answered with the same assurance. This led the prince to say he understood perfectly why Her Majesty had invited him to serve on the Council for Ecclesiastical Affairs, having to do with benefices and other church matters.

While this service at the court was most important and honorable, and brought him into immediate contact with the queen mother during the regency, he never wore a new cassock in going to the Louvre. He dressed the same as he did in preaching and instructing poor peasants, always neat, but in a simple and humble manner.

Speaking once of his position at court, he said: "I ask God that I may be regarded as a simpleton, as I am, so as not to have to continue in this position. In that way I would have greater leisure to do penance, and give less bad example to our little Company." This position weighed heavily upon him, not because of any lack of appreciation for Her Majesty, for whose service he would willingly have given his life, but because of the people he had to deal with. He accepted the difficulties which arose, and the calumnies that came his way, never seeking to justify himself, and still less to complain of his lot. Far from resenting those who caused him trouble, he humbled himself before them, and begged their pardon for any supposed failing against them. This occurred with a person of some standing who treated him with contempt, and also with a young gentleman who in an outburst called him an old fool. He knelt before both, asking pardon for having incited them to such conduct.

On another occasion he prevented the king from appointing an unfit person to a bishopric. His action caused the man's relatives to be most resentful. They then invented a calumny against him, adding just enough detail to convince the court of the truth of this charge. These things came to the ear of the queen, who at the first opportunity asked him, smiling, if he knew what people were saying. He replied quietly: "Madame, I am a great sinner." When Her Majesty retorted that he ought to justify himself, he replied: "Such things and more were said against our Lord, and he never justified himself."

During this same time he was at court, one of his friends alerted him to what a priest, who happened to die soon after, was spreading about the city. He was even reporting to one of the most qualified of people in Paris that Monsieur Vincent had bestowed a benefice upon someone, in return for a library, and a large sum of money. This good servant of God was at first moved to respond to this calumny, and took up his pen, as he later recounted, to write a justification of his actions. As he began to form the first letters, he recollected himself, and thought of what he was about to do. "O miserable one! What are you thinking of? What, you want to justify yourself? We have just heard of a Christian falsely accused in Tunis, who lived three whole days in sufferings, and finally died without uttering a word of complaint, although he was innocent of the crime he was accused of. And do you want to excuse yourself? No, it shall not be so!" He put down his pen, and took no action to justify himself.

To progress more in humility, he devised another tactic to further it. He brought together in Paris in 1641 some of the oldest and leading members of the Congregation to deliberate on some important matters.[15] After several conferences, he recalled the faults of his administration, his incapacity for governance, and the need to have someone else chosen as head of the Congregation. "Since you are now assembled, the office of superior general is in your hands. In the name of God, elect someone from among yourselves to be our superior." With that he left the place of the meeting, to a small chapel adjacent to the church, where he prayed turned toward the main altar of the church.[16]

The assembled priests were surprised at this suggestion and, seeing no reason to debate it, sent to have him return to the assembly. He was found, after much searching, in the chapel, on his knees. He was informed that no one else was willing to assume this responsibility. The members earnestly requested him to return, to resolve some of their other pressing business. He excused himself, and used new persuasions to urge them to a new election, saying he had resigned, and they must choose someone else to replace him. This was reported to the others in the assembly, but they left in a body to urge him to continue as superior. They said, finally: "You are the one whom we elected as our superior general, and as long as God preserves you upon this earth, we will have no other." He did all he could to resist, but finally he bowed his head, accepting the will of God and submitting himself anew to this burden. While retaining for himself all that was painful, he would not accept any of the honors and titles going with the office, not even using the term Superior General of the Congregation except in public acts, or in Letters Patent, when it was absolutely necessary to do so. Instead, he would add after his name, on some letters or documents, "Unworthy Priest of the Congregation of the Mission," or "unworthy superior." He wrote to some of his priests that at the beginning of their letters to him, they should leave no more blank spaces, as signs of deference, than he used in writing to them. He wanted no such signs of respect from his inferiors, in their dealings with him.

In this connection, one of the older priests of the community of Saint Lazare proposed that Monsieur Vincent should be shown some special marks of reverence as their common father and superior general. When he

---

15. This assembly took place in October of 1642.
16. See *CED* XIII:297-98 for formal minutes.

approached, all should stop, and bow or make a sign of reverence until he had gone by. When Monsieur Vincent realized this, he put a stop to it at once. When it was pointed out that this was a common usage in the other orders, he said: "I know this well, and we must respect their reasons for doing so. For my part I ought not to be compared to the least of men, I who am the worst of the lot."

The chair that was placed in the choir of the church of Saint Lazare when he officiated, was raised above the others. He would not agree to this, saying it was proper to do this for Their Excellencies, the bishops, but not for a miserable priest such as he was.

He always used the humblest vestments for the sacred liturgy. Once the queen mother, with her usual piety, presented Saint Lazare with some silver vestments on the occasion of the birth of the king.[17] Her Majesty sent them with the request to use them on the feast of Christmas, but when Monsieur Vincent saw the rich vestments ready for use he objected, and asked for the usual ones. No matter what was said his humility would not allow him to be the first to use these splendid vestments. The deacon and subdeacon, too, used the common ones, for the sake of uniformity.

He was not happy at the little services given him because of his age or sicknesses. He would thank those who helped him with such profusion he repaid with interest what he had received. On the contrary, he was delighted when he could serve others, either at table or even in the kitchen, doing the most humble tasks.

His humility went so far as to have him ask the blessing of his inferiors. This is what he wrote once to one of his priests, speaking of another who was dangerously ill. "Alas, Monsieur, I am anxious about the condition of our dear sick! What a loss for the Congregation if God should call him from this life! But may his holy will be done. If he is still alive when you get this, embrace him for me, and tell him of my sorrow, and recommend me to his prayers. Ask his blessing on the entire Company, and especially for me, who ask it prostrate in spirit at his feet."

We should not be surprised that he acted this way, in view of the low opinion he had of himself. He judged and proclaimed on all occasions that he was unworthy of the office of superior general and of the character of the priesthood. He said on several occasions that if he had not yet received orders, and knew his own unworthiness as he now did, he would never have consented to ordination. He would have chosen rather the humble condition of a brother in the Company, or even a simple farmer, as his own father was. Although he very worthily fulfilled all the functions and duties of the priesthood, his great humility had a deep effect on his spirit. Far from

---

17. Louis XIV, son of Anne of Austria and Louis XIII, was born September 5, 1638.

presuming on his own merits, he felt himself as an obstacle to good, and feared being responsible before God for heresies, disorders, and public calamities, because he had not prevented them, as he felt he should have as a priest. This he stated on several occasions, and this is what he wrote to Monsieur de Saint Martin, canon of Dax, his long-time friend. We present his letter here, because it gives us a good insight into his humble opinion of himself and his high regard for the priesthood.

I thank you for your care of my grand-nephew, whom I must say I have never thought should become a cleric, and even less that I should do anything to encourage him. This state is the most sublime upon earth, the one our Lord took and exercised himself. If I had known what was involved when I first dared enter it, as I now know, I would have preferred to be a common farmer than to enter such an exalted state. I have said this more than a hundred times to the poor peasants, when I have encouraged them to be content with their lot. I have told them I would be happy in their state. As I grow older, I think this way even more. Every day I see I am farther from the perfection I should attain. Certainly, priests of our time have good reason to fear God's judgments. Besides their own sins they must answer for the sins of their people, and must make satisfaction for them. The worst of all is that God shall hold them responsible for the scourges he has sent the Church, such as the plague, war, famine, and the heresies which attack it from all sides. We would say more, Monsieur, that the evil life of priests has brought about all these disasters which have so despoiled the bride of the Savior and so disfigured her that she is scarcely recognizable. What would those Fathers of the Church say now, who saw her in her pristine beauty, if they were to see the impiety and profanations which we see? Those fathers, in their day, thought few priests would be saved, although those of their time were in their greatest fervor.

All these considerations, Monsieur, lead me to think that it would be more suitable for this poor child to give himself to the profession of his father rather than to undertake the sublime and difficult state in which we are, for those not called are almost surely lost. Since I do not see any assured signs of a vocation, I suggest you advise him to continue to work as a peasant to gain his livelihood. Exhort him to fear God, to make himself worthy of his mercy in this life and in the next. This is the best advice I can give.

Please look into the work of Monsieur N., who said recently in a conference he gave here, speaking of a pastor in Brittany who had written a book on this subject, that today's priests, such as they are,

are the greatest enemies of the Church of God. If all priests were like you and he, there would not be so much truth in it.[18]

SECTION TWO

Some Thoughts of Monsieur Vincent About the Virtue of Humility

Although Monsieur Vincent sought to humble himself on all occasions, as we have said in this chapter, and all sorts of situations gave him opportunities for practicing this virtue, there were two main motives, like two pivots, on which his thoughts ever turned. They guided his own practice and the counsels he gave to others.

The first of these was the exalted knowledge and appreciation he had for the infinite perfections of God and for the failings of creatures. These made him regard it as unjust not to humble himself everywhere and in all things, because of the miserable condition of man and the grandeur and infinite perfections of God. This is how he spoke to his community on one occasion:

> In truth, gentlemen and my brothers, if we all study ourselves well, we will find it most just and reasonable to despise ourselves. If we consider only the corruption of our nature, the flightiness of our minds, the darkness of our understanding, the lack of control of our will, and the impurity of our affections, and besides, if we weigh in the scales of the sanctuary our works and our projects, we will find them all worthy of contempt. But you will say to me, what do you make of the many sermons we have preached, the confessions heard, the trouble taken to help our neighbor and to serve our Lord? Yes, gentlemen, if we reflect on even our best actions, we will find them ruined by the way they were done or in their motive, and in whatever way we look at them there is as much evil as good in them. Tell me, please, what would you expect from the weakness of man? What do you expect from nothingness? Who commits sin? What do we have of ourselves but nothingness and sin? You must hold it as certain that in everything and everywhere we are worthy only of rejection. We are always most contemptible because of the innate opposition within ourselves to the sanctity and other perfections of

---

18. *CED* V:567-69.

God, to imitating the life of Jesus Christ, to responding to the workings of his grace.

To persuade ourselves more of this truth, think of the natural and constant inclination we have for evil, our helplessness to achieve any good, and the experience we all have even when we think we have succeeded well in what we attempted, or things have gone as we suggested. Yet it happens just the opposite of what we expected, and God often allows us to be mistaken. If then we look into ourselves well, we will see that in all we think, say, or do, either in itself or in its circumstances, we are filled with confusion and contempt. If we do not give way to flattering ourselves, we will see that we are not only more evil than other men, but in some way worse than the devils in hell. If these unhappy spirits had been given the graces and opportunities given to us to make us better, they would have used them a thousand times better than we have.[19]

The second motive for the humility of Monsieur Vincent was the example and words of Jesus Christ. He kept Jesus Christ ever in view, and held him up for others to imitate. Speaking of this once in a conference to his community, he recalled the words of our Lord, "Learn of me, for I am humble of heart,"[20] and, "He who humbles himself will be exalted, and he who exalts himself shall be humbled."[21] He then added:

What was the life of this divine Savior but one continuous humiliation? He loved it so that he was never without humiliations during his whole life. Even after his death he willed that the Church should represent his divine person by the image of the crucifix, appearing before our eyes in a state of ignominy, as a criminal, and as suffering the most shameful and infamous death imaginable. Why is this? Because he knew the excellence of humility and the malice of the contrary vice. It not only makes other sins more grave, but even ruins other acts which of themselves are not bad. It can infect and corrupt even the good things we do, no matter how holy they may be.[22]

The mind and heart of Monsieur Vincent were filled with these two great and powerful motives of humility. We should therefore not be surprised if on all occasions he showed great appreciation for this virtue, and attempted to have it solidly implanted, sending down deep roots in the hearts of all sorts of people, especially his own dear confreres. Here is what he said to his community on one occasion:

---

19. *CED* XI:58-59.
20. Matt 11:29.
21. Matt 23:12.
22. *CED* XI:61.

Humility is a virtue so complete, so difficult, and so necessary, that we cannot think of it too often. This was the virtue of Jesus Christ and of his mother, the virtue of the greatest of the saints, and it is the virtue of all missionaries. What am I saying? I repeat, I would wish we all had this virtue, for when I said it is the virtue of missionaries, I mean it is the virtue we most need, and which we should ardently desire. This wretched Company, the least of all, was founded on humility as its proper virtue. Without it we will do nothing of value, neither for others nor for ourselves. Without humility we can expect to make no progress ourselves, nor do any good for our neighbor.

O Savior, give us this holy virtue, which is yours, which you brought to the world, and which you loved so dearly. And you, gentlemen, those of you who want to become true missionaries, you must work to acquire this virtue and advance in its practice. Above all, be on your guard against thoughts of pride, ambition, and vanity, as the greatest enemies you could have. You must flee from them as soon as they appear to put an end to them, and must watch carefully to give them no entrance. Yes, I say it once again, if you wish to be a true missionary, each one of you personally must be pleased if you are looked upon as poor and wretched, as persons without virtue, as ignoramuses, or if you are harmed and despised, or blamed for your faults, or declared to be insufferable because of your miseries and imperfections.[23]

I would go even further and say that we should be pleased when our Congregation in general is reviled as useless for the Church, composed of poor specimens. Be pleased when it does poorly whatever it tries to do, when its efforts for the poor peasants bear no fruit, the seminaries are useless, and the ordination retreats have little to recommend them. Yes, if we have the spirit of Jesus Christ, we ought to rejoice to be treated like this, as I have just said. Possibly someone will say, Monsieur, what are you saying? *Durus est hic sermo* ["This is a hard saying"].[24] I will admit it, this is hard for nature. It is difficult to persuade ourselves we have done poorly, and even harder to have others think and speak this way and blame us. But all this is easy for a truly humble soul to understand, one who has true humility and knows himself as he really is. Far from this causing him any sadness, he, on the contrary, will rejoice and be content to see God exalted and glorified through his humility and

---
23. *CED* XI:56-57.
24. John 6:61.

nothingness. I know well that our Lord has given this grace to several in the Company, to run swiftly in the pursuit of this virtue, and to animate their actions in the hope of their own diminution, and in the desire to remain hidden and unappreciated. We must ask this grace for all the rest of us, so that we may have no other ambition than to see ourselves lowered and annihilated for the love and glory of God, and to ensure that the characteristic virtue of the missionary is humility.

To make you appreciate this more, notice what I am about to say: if you have ever heard outsiders say that something good has been done by the Company, you will find that it was because they found some small bit of humility in it, and they have seen some humiliating and abject actions done, such as instructing the peasants or serving the poor. Also, if you have ever noticed the ordinands leaving their exercises edified at what they had seen in our house, if you look closely you will notice that they have been struck by the humble and simple way they have seen us act. This is something new for them, and it is this which charms and attracts everyone. I know that in the last ordination retreat, a priest who attended left behind accidentally some notes in which he expressed how much he was affected by the displays of humility he had seen.[25]

Another time, he spoke to his community on this same virtue:

Pay attention to the recommendation of our Lord in these words: "Learn of me for I am humble of heart,"[26] and ask him to give you a full understanding of them. If he gives us only an ardent desire for humility, that will be enough, even though we do not fully appreciate this virtue as our Lord did. He knew of its relationship to the perfections of God his Father, and to the vileness of sinful man. It is true that we will never see this, except dimly in this life, but we in our darkness should have confidence that, if our heart is set on humiliations, God will give us humility, we will preserve it, and it will grow in us by the acts we will do. One act of virtue well made disposes us for the next, and so the first degree of humility leads to the second, the second to the third, and so on for all the others.[27] Remember, gentlemen and my brothers, that Jesus Christ, speaking of the publican's humility, said that God heard his prayer. If he had said this of a man who had done wrong all his life, what should be our hope, provided we are truly humble? On the contrary,

---

25. *CED* XII:202-04.
26. Matt 11:29.
27. To the foregoing fragment, Abelly added the following either from another conference, or from a much different version.

what happened to the Pharisee? This was a man whose position separated him from the rest of the people, because it was like a sect among the Jews. The Pharisees prayed, fasted, and did many other good deeds, yet these did not keep Jesus from reproving him. Why was this? Because he looked upon these good deeds with pleasure, and gave way to vanity, as though they were owed to himself alone.

Look, then, at a just man and a sinner before the throne of God. Because the just man has no humility, he is rejected and reproved, along with his good works. What appeared as virtue in him turns out to be vice. On the other hand, the sinner recognizes his misery. Moved by a true sentiment of humility, he stays at the door of the temple, striking his breast, and does not dare to lift his eyes to heaven. By this humble disposition of heart, though he came to the temple guilty of many sins, he is cleansed of them. All this comes from a single act of humiliation, which for him proved to be his means of salvation. We should see from this that humility, when it is true, brings other virtues into the soul, and in humbling himself profoundly and sincerely, the sinner becomes the just. Even if we are wicked criminals but turn to humility, we shall be justified. On the contrary, if we are like the angels themselves, and excel in the practice of the greatest virtues, but lack humility, these virtues will be destroyed in us. They have no foundation because of our lack of humility, and we will become like the damned, totally deprived of all virtue.

Let us hold on to this truth, gentlemen. Let each one engrave it carefully on his heart and say to himself: though I had all virtues, and yet did not have humility I would be mistaken for thinking myself to be virtuous. I would be nothing but a proud pharisee and an abominable missionary. O Savior Jesus Christ, spread over us your divine light that filled your own soul, that made you prefer contempt to praise! Touch our hearts with these holy desires which burned and consumed your own, and which made you seek the glory of your heavenly Father in your own abnegation. Grant us in your grace that we may begin from this moment to reject all that does not lead to your honor and our own rejection. Take from us all that caters to our own vanity, ostentation, and self-esteem, that we may renounce once and for all the false applause of men and vain complacency in the success of our own efforts. O Savior, may we learn by your grace and by your example, to be truly humble of heart.[28]

---

28. *CED* XII:209-11.

One morning after meditation, he questioned one of the missionaries before the assembled community about the thoughts he had entertained in his meditation. He replied that he had experienced great uneasiness during a large part of the prayer. Monsieur Vincent took the occasion to speak to the community:

It is good to speak of such humiliating things when prudence allows us to reveal them. We can draw profit from them by overcoming the natural repugnance we have to reveal what our pride would wish to keep hidden. Saint Augustine published the secret sins of his youth in his autobiography, letting the whole world know of his errors and the excesses of his debauchery.[29] And did not that vessel of election, the great apostle Saint Paul, raised to the third heavens in vision, confess that he had persecuted the Church? He put this in his writings so that until the end of time he would be known as a persecutor of the Church.[30] Certainly, if we listened to ourselves, and did not do violence to ourselves, we would never speak of our misery and our faults. No, we would hide everything leading to our own confusion. This we have inherited from our first parent, Adam, who went into hiding after he had offended God.[31]

On many occasions I have visited various convents, where I have asked the religious there what virtue most appealed to them. I asked this question even of some I knew had little attraction for humility. Of the twenty or so I asked I found scarcely one who did not say it was the virtue of humility, so true it is that all find this virtue beautiful and attractive. How does it come about, then, that so few embrace it and even fewer possess it? This is because they are satisfied with thinking about it, but do not take the trouble to practice it. They are enthralled at speculation, but practice has a stark face. Practicing humility displeases us because it makes us choose the lowest place, after all others, even the least. It has us suffer calumnies, seek contempt, love abjection, all things for which we have a natural aversion. But we must rise above this repugnance, and make an effort to arrive at the actual practice of this virtue, or else we will never acquire it.

I am well aware that some here, by God's grace, practice this divine virtue, and do not entertain a lofty opinion of their talents, their knowledge, or their virtue. They recognize themselves as miserable creatures and are willing to be taken for such, and put

---

29. PL 32. Confessions, Book II, 8.
30. 1 Tim 1:13.
31. Gen 3:8.

themselves beneath all other creatures. I must confess that I never meet these persons without being thrown into confusion. They are a silent reproach to my pride, abominable as I am. These poor souls are always at peace, their joy appearing on their faces. The Holy Spirit dwells in them, blessing them so with his gift of peace that nothing can trouble them. If they are contradicted, they give way. If calumniated, they bear it. If forgotten, they assume that it is with good reason. If they are overwhelmed with duties, they work willingly, doing whatever they can. The more difficult a thing commanded is, the more willingly they accept it, confiding in the power of holy obedience. Temptations which come to them serve only to strengthen their humility, making them have recourse to God and bringing them victories over the devil. They have no more enemies to combat, save only pride. It gives no truce during life, but attacks even the greatest saints in various ways. It causes some to take vain complacency in the good they have done, or has others rejoice in the knowledge they have acquired. One assumes that he is especially enlightened, while another thinks of himself as better and more stable than others. This is why we have great reason to pray that God would protect us, and save us from this pernicious vice. It is to be feared precisely because we have such a natural inclination toward it.

We should, therefore, be on our guard, and do the contrary of what corrupt nature urges. If it puffs us up, we should abase ourselves. If we are inclined to self-esteem, we should think of our weakness. If we discover a desire to be known and appreciated, we should conceal what would make us noticed. We should prefer base and vile actions to those which have a certain flair and which are honorable. Finally, we should return often to our love of abjection as an assured refuge from all these disturbances which this unhappy bent for pride ever raises within us. Let us pray our Lord to attach us to himself by the merits of the adorable humility of his life and death. Let us offer him, each of us individually, and all of us in common solidarity, all that we can practice of this virtue. Let us give ourselves to this with the sole motive of honoring him and confounding ourselves.[32]

Another time, he spoke to his community of what had been said in a recent clergy conference.

These clergy who came here took as their topic of conversation last Tuesday what each had noticed of the virtues of the late

---

32. *CED* XI:53-56.

Monsieur Olier, a member of their company. Among other remarks, one of the more important was that the great servant of God often spoke of humility. Among all his other virtues this seemed to be the most prominent.

While they were speaking of this, I glanced at the various portraits adorning the walls of our room. I said to myself, Lord my God, if we could penetrate Christian truths as they are and act accordingly, how differently we would act! For example, looking at the portrait of the Blessed Bishop of Geneva, I thought that if we looked upon the things of the world in the same way he did, and if we spoke with his sentiments, and if our eyes were open to eternal truths as were his, vanity would have little room to occupy our minds and hearts.

Above all, gentlemen, if we look carefully at the most beautiful picture of all, that admirable example of humility, our Lord Jesus Christ, would we allow any good opinion of ourselves to enter our minds, seeing that we are so far from his profound abasements? Would we be so rash as to prefer ourselves to others, seeing that a murderer was chosen over him? Are we afraid of being looked upon as miserable, seeing the innocent lamb treated as a malefactor, and dying between two criminals, as if he were the worst of the three? Let us pray to God, gentlemen, to save us from this blindness. Let us ask him for the grace to tend always to the lowest, confessing to him and before men that of ourselves we are but sin, ignorance, and malice. Let us hope others will believe this of us, and will say so, and hold us in contempt. Lose no opportunity to annihilate yourself by the practice of this holy virtue. It is not enough to appreciate this virtue and to resolve to practice it, as some have done. We must do violence to ourselves to practice the acts of this virtue, which we have not sufficiently done.[33]

A priest of the Mission working in Artois, his native region, had a small pamphlet printed on his own initiative, which discussed the Congregation of the Mission.[34] When Monsieur Vincent learned of it he was greatly troubled, since it is opposed to the spirit of humility which he had attempted to inculcate in all members of the Company. He wrote to the priest in these terms:

If on the one hand I was consoled to see you return to Artois, on the other I was sorry to learn that you had published a short account

---

33. *CED* XI:393-94.
34. Guillaume Delville published this account in 1656. A translation appears in *Vincentian Heritage* 10 (1989) 71-87.

of our institute. I was so moved by this that I cannot adequately describe it, for it is something strongly opposed to humility to publish who we are and what we do. This goes counter to the example of our Lord who during the time he was on earth wrote no accounts of his words or his works. If there is any good in us and in our manner of life, it is for God to manifest it as he sees fit. We are but poor folk, ignorant, and sinners. We ought to hide ourselves as useless in accomplishing any good, and unworthy that anyone should think well of us. For this reason, Monsieur, God has given me the grace up to the present of never consenting to having anything printed which would make us known and esteemed, although I have been strongly urged to publish some of the accounts coming from Madagascar, Barbary, and the Hebrides Islands. For even stronger reasons, I have not allowed the printing of anything having to do with the essence and spirit, the foundation and growth of the Company, and the functions and end of our institute. May it please God that it stays this way, but since there is no remedy for the present situation, I will say no more. I would ask you only never to undertake anything affecting the Company as a whole, unless you first alert me beforehand.[35]

This truly humble servant of God could not help repeating and inculcating to his Company the beautiful lessons of this virtue of humility. This is how he spoke on another occasion:

God has not sent us to take up responsibilities and honorable positions, nor to speak and act with pomp and a show of authority. He sent us solely to evangelize the poor, and to perform the other exercises of our institute humbly, gently, and familiarly. This is why we are able to apply to ourselves what Saint John Chrysostom said in one of his homilies, that as long as we remain sheep by a true and sincere humility, not only will we not be devoured by the wolves, but we will change them into sheep.[36] On the other hand, as soon as we leave the humble and simple way proper to our institute, we will lose the grace attached to it. We will not find this grace in the brilliant things we undertake. Is it not right that a missionary who has made himself worthy of the blessing of heaven in his humble profession, and who gains thereby the approbation and esteem of men, should be deprived of both the one and the other when he allows himself to be drawn to works which by their splendor reflect the spirit of the world, and which are contrary to the spirit of his

---

35. *CED* VI:176-77.
36. PG 57:389.

state? Should he not fear that he would fade away in due time, and fall into disarray? Recall what is said about a servant who becomes a master. He becomes proud and insupportable.

The late Cardinal de Berulle, that great servant of God, used to say that it was good to remain in the lower place. The least positions are the surest, and there are untold perils in the higher places. This is why all the saints have fled honors. To convince us by his example and his words, our Lord said of himself that he had come into the world to serve and not to be served.[37]

Monsieur Vincent held it as a maxim that humility was the root of charity, and the more a person was humble the more charitable he was toward his neighbor. On this subject, he said to his community:

During the sixty-seven years that God has put up with me on this earth, I have thought and thought again about the best means to acquire and preserve union and charity toward God and the neighbor. I have not discovered anything better or more efficacious than holy humility to put oneself beneath all others, to think ill of no one, to regard oneself as the least and worst of all. Self-love and pride blind us and lead us to maintain our opinions against those of our neighbor.[38]

He said another time:

We should never look to see what is good in us, but study to know the evil and the defective. This is a fine way to preserve humility. The gift of converting souls, or all the other talents we have are not for us, for we are only the bearer of the gift. With all that, we could easily be damned. No one should congratulate himself nor take pleasure in himself, nor think much of himself, seeing that God operates his marvels through humility. He should rather humble himself, and recognize himself as an unworthy instrument which God deigns to use. God used the rod of Moses to work prodigies and miracles, although in itself it was only a worthless stick and a fragile rod.[39]

---

37. Matt 20:28. *CED* XI:61-62.
38. *CED* XI:152-53.
39. *CED* XI:59-60.

CHAPTER FOURTEEN

His Obedience

WE KNOW of no better way to begin this chapter on the obedience of Monsieur Vincent than to recall his words on this subject, particularly when he spoke to the religious of the first convent of the Visitation, in Paris.

These sisters have said that this great servant of God, who was their first spiritual father, often recommended the virtues of obedience and exactness in regularity, even to the smallest point. He had a special concern to have those two virtues well established in their communities. He used to say that the perfect practice of these two virtues constituted holy religion. To deepen their appreciation he used to bring them together, to speak about their excellence and beauty. He pointed out how it was necessary to perfect themselves in these virtues to please God, who takes delight in religious souls who are faithful to their practice. This divine Spouse so loved the virtue of obedience that the least delay in obeying was displeasing to him. A virtuous religious who had publicly vowed this virtue in the Church ought to be solicitous in carrying out what she had promised. One who failed in smaller observances would soon fail in greater matters.

He used to say that the good of the creature consists in the accomplishment of God's will. This is found in the faithful practice of obedience and in the exact observance of the rules of the institute. We cannot give a better service to God than by practicing obedience, for by this virtue he accomplishes his designs upon us. God's glory is found in the overcoming of self-love and one's own interests, and this is what we should chiefly aim at. This practice leads the soul to the true and perfect liberty of the children of God.

He recommended strongly that they renounce their own judgment to mortify it and submit themselves to their superiors. He used to say that obedience did not consist in simply doing what one is told on this or that occasion, but in having the disposition of soul of doing all they are commanded on all occasions. They must look on the superiors as holding the place of Jesus Christ on earth, and therefore give them every mark of respect. To murmur against them is a sort of internal apostasy. Just as exterior apostasy would involve removing the habit and leaving the religious life, so internal apostasy causes one to be disunited with superiors, rejecting them in the mind, and attaching oneself to ideas contrary to their wishes. This is the greatest of all ills that can happen in community. The religious soul will avoid these when she keeps herself in a holy indifference and allows herself to be directed by her superiors.

He also said on the topic of obedience that to have a true submission which should characterize a religious community we should consider attentively the following points:

(1) The role of superiors, who on earth take the place of Jesus Christ in our regard.

(2) The troubles which superiors endure and their solicitude to lead us to perfection cause them sometimes to pass the whole night in prayer in anguish of soul. Their subjects enjoy a peaceful rest. Their anxiety is the greater when they reflect that they will have to render an account to God of all their responsibilities.

(3) The recompense promised to truly obedient souls, even in this life. Besides the graces this virtue merits, God is pleased to fulfill the will of those who for love of him submit their wills to their superiors.

(4) The punishments the disobedient should fear. An example was given in the Old Testament of the chastisement of Korah, Dathan and Abiram for their contempt of Moses, their leader. By this contempt they had grievously offended God, who has said of those constituted in authority in the Church: "He who hears you, hears me; and he who despises you, despises me."[1]

(5) The example of obedience which Jesus Christ gave us. He preferred death rather than to fail in obedience. One would have to be truly hard-hearted to see God obey unto death for the sake of such wretched and miserable creatures as we are, and still refuse to subject himself for love of him.

He added that to practice this virtue perfectly, we must obey:

(1) Voluntarily, placing our will in the will of our superior.

(2) Simply, for the love of God, never allowing ourselves to question why our superiors commanded such and such a thing.

(3) Promptly, not delaying in carrying out what has been ordered.

(4) Humbly, not seeking any praise or esteem for our obedience.

(5) Courageously, not hesitating in the face of difficulties, but overcoming them with strength and generosity.

(6) Joyfully, doing what is ordered with pleasure, with no show of resentment.

(7) Perseveringly, imitating Jesus Christ who was obedient unto death.

It should not be imagined that what Monsieur Vincent said or taught on

---

1. Luke 10:16.

this matter was done as a lesson from a teacher, or the exhortation of a preacher, who sometimes does not practice what he teaches others. On the contrary, these lessons were the sincere expression of the deepest sentiments of his heart, and as a sort of reflection of what he himself practiced. He showed by the example of his own life what he proposed by his words.

First, Monsieur Vincent maintained a faithful and perfect dependence on God, submitting himself to all he understood would be most agreeable to him. We can truly say that God found in him a man after his own heart. He was always ready and disposed to do God's will, as we have seen illustrated in the earlier chapters of this book.

In this frame of mind, when he first came from Rome to Paris, one of the first things he did was to seek out a spiritual director, so that in following his advice and counsel he might obey God and cooperate with his designs upon him. This spiritual director was Father de Berulle, who later became a cardinal in the Church. In submission to his guidance, Monsieur Vincent accepted the post of pastor of Clichy. Later he entered the de Gondi household to be the chaplain of the general of the galleys and of his wife, and tutor of their children. When Madame wished to have him as her confessor and her own spiritual director, he would not consent except through obedience. Only when she worked through Monsieur de Berulle, did he accept this charge. He did not want to do anything of himself, but only in following the guidance of God.

Not satisfied with his obedience to God directly, he submitted himself, in keeping with the word of the holy apostle, to all human creatures for the love of God, especially the spiritual and temporal powers, in things unpleasant and humiliating as well as in those agreeable and honorable.[2]

His obedience was given mainly to our Holy Father, the pope, joyfully and without reserve. He recognized him as the vicar of Jesus Christ upon earth, and as the sovereign pastor of the whole Church. He was subject to him in all his judgment and affection.

Only through obedience did he accept the responsibility of superior general of his Congregation, for Pope Urban VIII had specified this in the bull by which he approved the Congregation of the Mission.

He insisted that all the missionaries under his direction be perfectly obedient to the Holy See, and he put into writing this rule:

> We will exactly obey each and all our superiors, looking upon them as taking the place of our Lord, and seeing our Lord in them, especially our Holy Father the pope, whom we will obey with all possible respect, fidelity, and sincerity.[3]

---

2. 1 Peter 2:13.
3. Common Rules 5,1.

We saw earlier the esteem and veneration which Monsieur Vincent had for the bishops.[4] We will now mention the perfect submission he always had toward them, and the perfect obedience he wished his Congregation to have in all that regarded them.

In approving the Congregation of the Mission, the Holy See had thought it expedient that the superior general should have the care and direction of its members, both in their interior lives, that is, for the progress of their souls in the practice of the virtues proper to their vocations, and in their exterior lives, in regard to the observance of the rules and constitutions, the domestic arrangements, the placement of personnel, and the choice of ministry. This was done to assure that all members of the one body might preserve the same spirit despite working in a variety of dioceses, and might be animated with the charisms which God bestowed upon their founder. It was most expedient that the superior general, with his intimate knowledge of the talents and dispositions of each of the members, could assign them to appropriate missions in a variety of possible places, all in furtherance of the work of the Congregation. Nevertheless, in anything having to do with assistance to the neighbor, Monsieur Vincent had seen to it that the Holy See subordinate his community to the bishops. This was done in such a way that the missions, the ordination retreats, the clergy conferences, the spiritual retreats, or the direction of the seminaries, all were carried out under the authority and with the permission of the ordinaries. He was careful himself to observe this always, and was insistent that this be observed also by all his Congregation, to the satisfaction of the bishop wherever they worked. The community is resolved to maintain this attitude, and with God's help, will do so in the future.

Around 1622, long before the establishment of his own Congregation, he accepted the direction of the religious of the Visitation of Holy Mary of the city of Paris. He did so at the request of the Blessed Francis de Sales, their founder, and at the command of the archbishop of Paris. This occasion gives us a good opportunity to see his fidelity to obedience. Being extensively burdened with the affairs of his own Congregation and with the other major activities with which he was connected, he sought to be released from this supervision.

The number of sisters so increased that they filled three convents in Paris and one outside the city, and this demanded much time and attention. Several times he took steps to be relieved of this responsibility and once did succeed in stepping down. Despite efforts by people in high places, he preferred not to reassume the post, and did so only at the request of the archbishop of Paris. Nevertheless, to protect his priests, and to allow them to devote themselves

---

4. Book Three, ch. 9, sect. 3.

entirely to their proper functions, he forbade them from accepting the direction of women religious. He made this a matter of rule, knowing from his own experience how incompatible this service was with their duties, and how unsuitable to their calling.

He wanted his priests to be obedient to the pastors when they gave a mission in the parishes. They were to do nothing, not even, as he used to say, to move a straw without their approval. In this connection he once wrote to someone outside the community: "We take it as a rule to work for the good of the people, with the concurrence of the pastors, and never against their wishes. At the beginning and end of each mission we seek their blessing to show our dependence upon them."[5]

He was faithful to this practice himself with the most marvelous humility. Although he was sent by the bishops with full authority to work in the parishes of their dioceses, he never wanted to act without the consent and approval of the pastor. He was as careful about this in the small villages as he was in the larger towns. He saw to it that his confreres acted in the same way, and remained faithful to this practice himself.

He spoke once to his community on the obedience due to kings and princes. He referred to the way the first Christians were obedient to the emperors and respected their temporal power. He then added these words:

> My brothers, following their example, we ought to have always a faithful and simple obedience to kings, never complaining about them, not murmuring, no matter what. If we should happen to be called upon to lose our goods or our very lives, let us give them away in this spirit of obedience rather than oppose their will, provided that what they ask is not opposed to God's will. We should act this way, for kings represent on earth the sovereign power of God.[6]

To show with what exactitude Monsieur Vincent obeyed the king even in the smallest things, we recall an incident so insignificant that few persons would ever have bothered themselves about it. A brother of the community of Saint Lazare happened upon a pheasant's nest. He took the eggs and had them hatched by a hen, and when the young pheasants had attained some size he brought them in a cage to Monsieur Vincent with the thought of giving him a bit of diversion. Monsieur Vincent recalled that the king had issued orders forbidding the hunting of the pheasants, and said to the brother, without showing what he had in mind, "go and see if these birds can manage for themselves." He accompanied the brother to the courtyard, and had the birds set free, happy to see them run off and hide. Seeing the brother

---

5. *CED* II:199.
6. *CED* XI:78.

somewhat saddened at this ending to all his troubles, he said, "You must realize, my brother, that we should obey the king. His directive against hunting applies to the taking of these eggs as well as to hunting the birds themselves. We cannot disobey the king in these temporal things without displeasing God."

Monsieur Vincent extended his obedience beyond his superiors to all sorts of persons, and recommended this same course of action to his confreres.

> Our obedience ought to go beyond those who have the right to give us orders. If we are to practice obedience as recommended by Saint Peter, we should submit ourselves to all human creatures for the love of God. Do this then, and look upon all others as our superiors, and place yourself below all, smaller than even the least. Make this evident by the deference, condescension, and all sorts of services for others. What a fine thing it would be if God would confirm us in this practice.[7]

He exhorted his confreres to this mutual condescension, a form of obedience, by a comparison to the members of the human body, which adjust and compensate for their common welfare and conservation, so that whenever one member suffers the others adapt as much as possible. He said:

> Thus should the members of a community act toward each other. The more learned should accept the weaknesses of the ignorant, at least in those areas where no error or sin is involved, and the prudent and wise should accept the humble and simple: *non alta sapientes, sed humilibus consentientes* ["Put away ambitious thoughts and associate with those who are lowly"].[8] In this same spirit of condescension we ought not only to approve the sentiments of others in matters good or indifferent, but even prefer them to our own. We should believe others to have natural or supernatural lights and qualities superior to our own. On the other hand, we must be well on guard against showing tolerance of evil. This is not a virtue but rather a great fault, and leads to dissolute ways or else to cowardice and mediocrity.[9]

He practiced what he preached, for he showed himself most accommodating to others in indifferent things, even to those of modest abilities. He held the maxim that it is better to accept the will of others than to follow one's own preferences. According to the account given by a priest who knew him well, he carried this practice so far as to follow the advice of all sorts of

---

7. *CED* XI:69.
8. Rom 12:16.
9. *CED* XI:69-70.

persons in the simplest matters, in things of no moral significance. This did not arise from his lack of knowledge of the matter at hand. His long experience in all things, coupled with the lights he received from God, allowed him to penetrate and discern what ought to be done. He preferred, instead, not to lose the merit of submission and obedience when the occasion arose to practice it.

This same quality was noticed in him about accepting the opinions of others, when it could be done without prejudice to truth or charity. He was never known to have contradicted or disputed with others, although he often had to discuss difficult questions on which there was often a difference of opinions. He deferred to the opinion of others, or after humbly stating his own position he would then maintain silence. Where there was a question touching on the service or the glory of God, he was adamant to the degree that he was known to refuse for years to budge on certain points he saw as contrary to the will of God. His great maxim in this regard was: "Be as polite as you can, provided you do not contravene God's will." When the glory of God, or charity toward the neighbor, or Christian prudence obliged him to refuse something, he did so with such grace, mildness, and humility, that his refusal was sometimes accepted better than a favor or benefit would have been from someone else.

In this same spirit of obedience and accommodation, he wrote to the superior of a mission experiencing some difficulties. He counseled following the advice of others rather than one's own opinion. He cited the opinion of Saint Vincent Ferrer, who recommended this practice as a means of perfection and sanctity.

In this same spirit of condescension he agreed to consider accepting the gift of a farm offered to the community of Saint Lazare. However, this offer had been made under the condition of a life-annuity so large he felt the offer ought not to be accepted. He persisted in this refusal for two years. The owner of the farm, anxious for the annuity, convinced the late prior of Saint Lazare, for whom Monsieur Vincent had the highest regard, of the advantages of the transaction. This good prior then urged and pressured Monsieur Vincent so much that by condescension he agreed to sign the contract. Monsieur Vincent first obtained the consent of his council, who assured him there was no risk involved. He paid the annual pension to the donors until their death, as stipulated in the agreement. Later a lawsuit was instituted, which resulted in the Congregation's loss of both the farm and a large sum. Monsieur Vincent was shown a way to circumvent this adverse judgment, but he preferred to lose both farm and money rather than show any lack of submission to the judges in any way, and so lose the merit of obedience to their decree.[10]

---

10. The farm at Orsigny, 1658.

Another incident shows his exactitude and zeal for the practice of this same virtue, on which occasion it seems that he could easily have dispensed himself. The queen had requested him to provide a mission for Fontainebleau. He sent two of his priests there, where contrary to their expectation they found a religious giving a series of sermons. In obedience to Her Majesty they felt they had to begin the mission. They held off their usual exercises at the hour this good religious was scheduled to preach, so that the people could have full liberty to attend his sermons. The people much preferred the instructions of the missionaries to the sermons of the preacher. He attracted only a few, but the church was filled when the missionaries presented their instructions and catechism lessons as was customary for the mission. The religious complained of this, leaving the priests of the Mission in a quandary. The maxim of Monsieur Vincent was to defer to everyone, on all occasions, but his instructions were also to obey the queen in her request to have the mission preached. They wrote to Monsieur Vincent, to inquire what course to follow. Seeing obedience to the queen involved, he felt it was of such consequence that he sent a man by carriage to present a letter from himself to the queen, who was at Notre Dame de Chartres at the time. In this letter he recounted the impasse at the parish, and recalled that the usual practice of the priests of the Mission in such cases was to withdraw. He humbly begged Her Majesty to agree to their retiring, which she did. He had the missionaries go to another place, leaving the field to the good religious, out of consideration for him.

Monsieur Vincent was equally careful that obedience be observed by the members of the Congregation, as much as he himself practiced it. He wanted this virtue to be in vigor everywhere, as one of the most important ways of ensuring its prosperity. When he came upon any failure in this regard, he was quick to offer a remedy. This is what happened one day to one of the oldest and most regular of the priests.[11] Monsieur Vincent had recommended that he remain in bed the next morning because his duties had kept him up late, and he felt this priest needed the extra rest. However, this good missionary, so punctual in making his morning mental prayer with the community at the usual hour, rose with the others. He thought that the recommendation of Monsieur Vincent was no more than a gracious wish on his part, not binding him to obedience. Monsieur Vincent, however, took another view of the matter. He called him over at the end of prayer, and in the presence of all the others, had him kneel for a good while, even though he was the oldest of the priests and the subdirector of the house, who took Monsieur Vincent's place when he was away. Monsieur Vincent remarked that this was the first fault against obedience he had ever noticed in him. He

---

11. Lambert aux Couteaux.

praised his zealous exactitude in the observance of the rule, but blamed his excessive fervor in this particular situation. He spoke at some length of the virtue of obedience. He recalled the case of Saul and Jonathan in the Old Testament, and some remarkable incidents drawn from the history of France itself to show his confreres the importance of this virtue.

CHAPTER FIFTEEN

His Simplicity

SIMPLICITY IS the more praiseworthy among those who strive to follow the maxims of Jesus Christ, in that it is so poorly esteemed by the vain and false wisdom of the world. It is the virtue which discovers the paths of true justice and leads us on the right way to God's kingdom. To phrase this better with the words of Saint Gregory, "simplicity is like the serene day of the Christian soul. It is not obscured or troubled by the clouds of fraud or deceit, by envy, or by trickery or disguise. It takes its light from truth itself, and shines with the splendor of the presence of God."[1]

This virtue was so esteemed by the great saints of the Church that Saint Ambrose, in the funeral oration over his brother Saint Satyrus, puts it among the main virtues. He stated that this noted man, coming from an exalted status in the world, developed such a love for this virtue that he became childlike in his simplicity. He showed by his manner and actions that his entire life was a perfect mirror of innocence.[2]

We may likewise bestow the same praise upon Vincent de Paul. Living in a decadent age and being deeply involved in the world, even among the great of the court, he nevertheless preserved an innocence of life, uprightness, and simplicity. His heart was like the pearl, which though immersed in the waters of the sea, takes on none of its impurities but is nourished only by the dew of heaven.[3]

Saint Bernard had great reason to say: "it is a rare occurrence to see humility preserved in the midst of honors."[4] We might add that it is also rare, and maybe ever more so, to find true simplicity of heart maintaining its uprightness and purity among the vexations and intrigues of the world. This, however, is what we saw and admired so much in this great servant of God. He seemed like a lily among the thorns and corruption which abound in the world.

Simplicity allows us to go directly to God and the truth, without pomp, evasions, or subterfuge, with no thought of personal interest or of human respect. Monsieur Vincent acted this way himself. He led us to believe that

---

1. PL 79:605.
2. PL 16.2.1:1307.
3. Pliny popularized this opinion about pearls formed in the oyster shell by dew from heaven in his *Natural History* 9, 54, 107ff.
4. PL 183.3-4:85.

much of the success which he enjoyed in his various enterprises was to be attributed to the simplicity of his character. It attracted the blessing of God upon him, and the approbation of men. Nothing so pleases God and wins the affection and respect of all sorts of persons as directness and simplicity in the heart, in life, and in one's words.

Since he esteemed this virtue so highly, he strove to cultivate it in his followers. For example, when speaking to them of Jesus Christ's words to his disciples to be simple as doves,[5] he said:

> In sending his apostles to preach the Gospel throughout the whole world, he particularly recommended this virtue of simplicity as one of the most important, to attract the graces of heaven, and to dispose the hearts of the people to hear and believe the word. He spoke not only to the apostles, but to all those whom Providence has called to preach the Gospel, and to instruct and convert souls. Therefore, Jesus Christ speaks to us in recommending this virtue of simplicity, so agreeable to God that his good pleasure is to be with the simple of heart: *cum simplicibus sermocinatio ejus* ["with the simple is his speech"].[6] Think, my brothers, of the consolation and happiness of those numbered among the truly simple. They are assured by the words of God that his good pleasure is to dwell with them.
>
> Our Lord further lets us see how agreeable the virtue of simplicity is to him by these words he addresses to his Father: *Confiteor tibi Pater, quia abscondisti haec a sapientibus et prudentibus, et revelasti ea parvulis.*[7] I acknowledge and thank you, Father, that the doctrine I have learned from you and which I have spoken to men is known only to the little ones and the simple. The learned and prudent have not understood, and the sense and spirit of this word is hidden from them.
>
> Certainly, if we reflect on these words, we ought to be appalled, we who chase after knowledge as if our happiness depended upon it. I am not saying a priest, a missionary, ought not to have learning, but it must be needed for his ministry and not simply what will satisfy his ambition and curiosity. He ought to study and acquire learning, yes, but with sobriety, as the holy apostle says. Others pass themselves off as being well informed on every subject. God leaves them without understanding of truth and the Christian virtues, just as he does for those who are so learned in worldly wisdom. To

---

5. Matt 10:16.
6. Prov 3:32.
7. Matt 11:25.

whom then does he give a knowledge of his truth and his doctrine? It is to the simple, the good people, most often the poor. This is seen by the difference between the faith of the poor peasants and that of persons who live in the world. I can say from long experience that lively and practical faith and the spirit of true religion are most often found among the poor and the simple. God enriches them with a lively faith. They believe and savor the words of eternal life that Jesus Christ has left them in the Gospel. Ordinarily, they bear their sicknesses with patience, their shortages and other ills without murmuring, and complain little and rarely. Where does this come from? God is pleased to confer an abundance of the gift of faith upon them, and other graces which he does not give to the rich and wise of this world.

We should also consider that everyone is attracted to simple and candid persons. These never resort to clever distinctions or duplicity but say simply and directly what is in their heart. Everyone appreciates them, even if they are at court. And high society appreciates and trusts such people. Even more remarkably, those who do not speak candidly or with simplicity, nor have such qualities in their mind, still admire those who do. Strive then, my brothers, to please God by acquiring this virtue, which by his mercy we see that some of our own confreres have. Their example invites us to imitate them.

To understand the excellence of this virtue better, we must realize that it brings us close to God, and makes us in some way resemble him. He is a totally simple being, an essence admitting of no composition. What God is by his essence we strive to become, as far as our wretched and miserable nature will allow. We must have a simple heart, a simple mind, a pure intention, and act simply. We must speak directly, act forthrightly, with no subterfuge or artifice, looking to God alone with the intention of pleasing him alone.

Simplicity comprises more than simple truth and purity of intention. It puts far from us all deceit, trickery, or duplicity. Since this virtue is shown chiefly in our words, we are obliged to say exactly what is in our heart. We must state simply what we have to say, with the pure intention of pleasing God alone. This is not to say that simplicity obliges us to say everything in our mind. This virtue is discreet and never opposed to prudence. It allows us to discern what should be said and what should not, and when we should keep quiet and when we should speak up. If, for example, I have something to say worthwhile and good in itself and in all its circumstances, I should express myself directly and simply. If, on the contrary, some circumstances are evil or useless, then I should keep quiet. Generally, we ought not speak of things against God or our neighbor, or which might tend toward our own glorification, or would have some sensual or temporal connotation. One must be careful not to sin against one or more of the other virtues.

Simplicity in actions causes us to act directly and forthrightly, always in view of God, in our business, our employment, or in our exercises of piety, avoiding all hypocrisy, artifice, or vain pretense. Someone, for example, might make a gift to another feigning that he is doing so through affection. In reality he hopes thereby to secure something of greater worth in return. He may be acting according to worldly standards, but this is opposed to the virtue of simplicity, which never allows us to do one thing but really mean another. Just as this virtue requires us to speak the way we think, it also makes us act with Christian frankness and directness. All must be done for God, the only end of all our actions. We may infer from this that the virtue of simplicity is not honored in those who through human respect wish to appear other than what they are, or who do good deeds exteriorly to be thought virtuous, who collect quantities of books to be judged learned, who strive to preach well to have the applause and praise of others, or lastly, those who do their spiritual exercises or pious works for unworthy motives.

May I ask you, my brothers, if this virtue of simplicity is not beautiful and desirable? Is it not just and reasonable to be on your guard against all duplicity and artifice in our words and actions? But this virtue must be practiced to acquire it. This is done through frequent acts of the virtue of simplicity by which we become truly simple, with the help of God's grace, which we must often ask of him.[8]

We have cited at some length this conference of Monsieur Vincent on the virtue of simplicity, for we believe we could not give a better description of his own simplicity than by using his own words. He was himself, and he wished his confreres to be, just what his words conveyed. It could be said in truth that he had this virtue in such a degree, by the grace of our Lord, that all the powers of his soul were influenced by it. What he said and what he did were influenced by this virtue. His external words and deportment were always in harmony with his interior. His actions truly reflected his intentions, which ever tended to the most perfect.

In this connection he said, "To make things look good on the outside while

---

8. *CED* XII:167-81. Abelly's version differs substantially from that of Coste.

being otherwise within is to be like the hypocritical Pharisees. It is to imitate Satan, who disguises himself as an angel of light." One of his maxims was: "Since prudence of the flesh and hypocrisy are so prevalent in this corrupt age, to the prejudice of the spirit of Christianity, the best way to overcome their baneful influence is by a true and sincere simplicity."

His fidelity to the practice of this virtue was obvious in all encounters, and extended to the least things. Among other examples we could cite, we might mention that he was so taken up with diverse and important matters that he sometimes forgot simple matters, such as speaking with someone, answering a letter, or doing something else which had been recommended to him. Rather than invent an explanation, he much preferred to acknowledge his shortcomings, even when it was a source of embarrassment to him. He used to say that it was good to state things just as they are, for God blessed this frankness. On this point he once remarked: "God is very simple, or better, God is simplicity itself, and therefore where one finds simplicity one finds God. As the wise man of Scripture says: 'He who walks simply walks with assurance, but he who uses cunning and deceit is in constant fear that he will be found out.'[9] If his duplicity is discovered he will never again be trusted."[10]

Once, when sending one of his priests to a certain province where rumor had it that dissimulation was a way of life, he gave this excellent advice: "You are going to a region where the people are for the most part cunning and devious. If that is so, the best way to be of help to them is to treat them with great simplicity. The maxims of the Gospel are utterly opposed to those of the world. Since you are going there to serve our Lord, you ought to carry his spirit, a spirit of uprightness and simplicity." In this same spirit, some time later he founded a house of the Congregation in that same province. He sent as the first superior a priest of his Company who had a reputation for great simplicity.

Since he worked as hard as he could to cultivate in his confreres this virtue of simplicity, he would not allow them in their words or actions to show that they had lost sight of God, who should be the sole end of all they did. He was attentive that they not allow their minds or hearts to be taken up with created things. In a reply to one of his priests who had written that he had given his heart to Monsieur Vincent, he wrote:

> I thank you for your letter and for the gift you give me. Your heart is too good to be put into my poor hands, but I am well aware that you give it to me merely to be passed on to our Lord to whom it belongs, and to whose love you must ever return. May your loving heart then

---

9. Prov 10:9.
10. *CED* XI:50.

be given from this moment to Jesus Christ, fully and forever, in time and in eternity. Please ask the grace that I may share some of the candor and simplicity of your heart. I stand in great need of these two virtues, whose excellence is beyond understanding.[11]

He wrote to another of his community who had revealed that he had acted selfishly or through human respect:

> You have done well to win the esteem of the persons you name. To tell me you did so that they might support or defend us was an unworthy motive. It is removed from the spirit of Jesus Christ, which would counsel us to do all for God alone, acting out of love for him. If on the contrary you wanted to protect our interests and use the good opinion of your friends to preserve our reputation, this is done in vain if it is not founded on truth. If our reputation is in fact based on truth, why do you fear? Another point in your letter reflects human respect, where you say that when you speak well of some people I will let their friends know of it, so that they may give him recognition. Alas, Monsieur, what are you dreaming of? Where is the simplicity of a Missionary, who ought to go directly to God? If you do not see good in these persons, don't say anything. If you find good in them, speak of it to honor God in them, for all good comes from him. Our Lord reproved a man who called him good because his intention in acting was not good. What will he say to you if you praise unworthy persons out of deference, to put yourself in good with them, or for any other unworthy motive? I am aware that you acted only out of another good intention, for you sought the esteem and love of others only to advance the glory of God. You must, however, realize that God is never honored by duplicity, and that to be truly simple we must think of him alone.[12]

If Monsieur Vincent was so careful to have his community practice the virtue of simplicity on all occasions, it was particularly so in their preaching and instructing the people that he wanted this virtue to shine forth. One day he spoke to them of the desire for praise and esteem, which often creeps into the minds of many preachers:

> They want to shine and have people talk about them. They love to be praised and to hear that they have been successful and have worked marvels. Behold this monster, then, which hides under beautiful pretexts. He insinuates his venom into the hearts of those who give him entrance. O cursed pride, how you corrupt and destroy the good, and how much evil you cause! You bring it about that

---

11. *CED* VI:141.
12. *CED* IV:484-87.

these people preach themselves and not Jesus Christ. Instead of building up the body of Christ, they tear it down and bring it to ruin.

Just today I was at a conference given by a prelate to his ordinands.[13] Afterward, in his room, I said to him, "Bishop, today you have converted me!" He responded, "How is that?" "You spoke so directly and so simply that I was deeply touched, and could not refrain from praising and blessing God." Then he told me, "Monsieur, I must confess, with the same forthrightness with which you have spoken, that I had prepared something more profound and more learned. I realized in time that in giving that talk I would have offended God."

You see, gentlemen, the way this bishop was thinking. This is the way all should act who are truly seeking God and the salvation of souls. If you act this way, I can assure you, God will surely bless what you say and give strength and power to your words. Yes, God will be with you and work through you, for he is pleased to remain with the simple. He helps them, he blesses their labors and their projects, but on the contrary it would be blasphemy to think that God would favor or help those who, filled with vanity, preach only themselves, and seek glory from others.

In their preaching these persons do not exhibit either simplicity or humility. Do you think God would help a man destroy himself? A Christian should not even think such a thing. If you would reflect on the great evil it is to use the office of preacher to present the message in any other way than that used by Jesus Christ or his apostles or many great saints and servants of God, and is still used by them to this day, you would be horrified.

I must tell you that for three consecutive days I once knelt before a priest. He was at the time a member of our Company. I begged him with all possible insistence to preach and speak simply, following the outline we had given him. I was never able to make any headway with him. He gave the conferences to the ordinands, but they produced little fruit. His fine thoughts and expressions went up in smoke. Words do not profit souls, but only simplicity and humility, and they attract the grace of Jesus Christ into our hearts.

If you want to know the truth, what draws these ordinands, theologians, bachelors, licentiates of the colleges of the Sorbonne and Navarre? It is not the learning or doctrine they are shown, for they have much more than do we. It is the simplicity and humility they see, by the mercy of God, and the way which we act toward

---

13. The bishop of Sarlat, Nicolas Sevin. See also *CED* V:571-72.

them. They come here to acquire virtue, and if they do not find this among us they will not return. This is why we must desire and pray that God would be pleased to give the entire Company, and each of us in particular, the grace of acting directly and simply, of preaching the truths of the Gospel in the same way our Lord taught them, so that everyone will understand and profit from what we say.[14]

We will finish this chapter by citing the testimony of a superior of one of the houses of the Mission about the virtue of simplicity which animated the heart of this holy man and which shone forth in his words and actions.

Monsieur Vincent, who himself spoke so humbly and simply, but with energy and efficacy, recommended this same humility and simplicity in the public and private utterances of his confreres. He wished to rid the community of anything smacking of pomposity or the vanity of the world. To convince us even better, he recalled as an example, among many other motives, how much more we are attracted to living animals rather than those which have been mounted for display. He used to say that this was the way it was for talks and conferences—the simpler and more direct they are, the better they are received, especially as compared with those affected and artificially polished.

He had an interest in helping me in many ways. The great number of my imperfections gave me the advantage of receiving much advice and helpful suggestions from him. I recall my days as a student of theology when it came my turn to speak to the assembled household. I prepared well, and spoke in a way I thought marvelous. That evening he called me, and in the presence of twenty people I regarded as my masters, dissected my talk at length. Finally, he summed up all with a graciousness which restored my spirits. He said I must strive to preach as Jesus Christ had done. As the Son of God, he could have talked about the deepest mysteries of religion in the most profound way, being the Word and the Wisdom of the Eternal Father. Nevertheless, he preached humbly and simply, accommodating himself to the people, giving us the model and the manner of teaching his holy word.

---

14. *CED* XII:22-25.

CHAPTER SIXTEEN

His Prudence

WE JOIN the discussion of prudence with simplicity because our Lord Jesus Christ spoke of them together in his Gospel when he taught his apostles, and in their persons all the faithful, especially those charged with the direction of others. These two virtues are so connected that one without the other, as Saint Augustine says, is of little or no advantage.[1] Simplicity without prudence is close to folly, but prudence without simplicity soon degenerates into craftiness and cunning. While it is unworthy of a Christian to use deceit, it is unsuitable that he allow himself to be surprised or taken in by the artifices of the wicked. All this Monsieur Vincent knew well, and he possessed and practiced both these virtues, having united them in his soul to an eminent degree.

We have already in the preceding chapter given a sketch of his simplicity. In this chapter we will speak of his prudence.

Among the many other virtues of this servant of God, this particular one appeared so clearly that he was commonly held to be one of the wisest and most enlightened men of his time. People came to him from all sides to seek his counsel, and he was asked to attend meetings where most significant matters about religion and piety were discussed. Almost every day at Saint Lazare there were to be seen persons of all classes, coming to seek advice in their doubts and difficulties. The papal nuncios, Bagno and Piccolomini, honored him by coming several times to confer about various matters concerning the good of the Church.[2] Many pastors, clerics, canons, abbots and even respected prelates consulted him in writing when they could not do so face to face. Many religious, also, sought counsel in the reform of their orders, or on other important business. Various lay people, among them the most respected and virtuous of the city of Paris, came to Saint Lazare to seek his advice. We can truly say that scarcely a project of any consequence in Paris related to religion did not have his hand in it. Even in the other provinces of the kingdom, his advice was sought by letter.

It was not without reason that this opinion of Monsieur Vincent was so universal. His mind was enlightened and capable of conceiving great ideas.

---

1. PL 40.6:1240-42.
2. Giovanni Francesco Guidi di Bagno (or Bagni) was the papal nuncio in Paris until 1631. He was an influential friend of the saint. Coelio Piccolomini, cardinal and archbishop of Caesarea, was papal nuncio in Paris, 1656-1663. He attended the saint's funeral.

He also had received such light and special graces from God that they provided a marvelous addition to his acquired prudence and attracted the blessings of heaven upon the advice he gave to those who came to him.

Before citing examples of his prudence in particular cases, it would not be amiss to hear what he had to say himself on this virtue. We can see here how the Holy Spirit had fashioned it in his soul. In a conference he gave one day to his community, he spoke of prudence in this way:

> It is the function of this virtue to regulate and direct our words and actions. It helps us speak wisely and to the point. It directs our conversation with circumspection and judgment when it is a question of things good in themselves and in their circumstances. It helps us keep quiet about anything which would offend God or harm the neighbor, or which would tend to our own praise, or to any other bad purpose. This same virtue makes us act with maturity, and with a good motive in all we do, in both the substance of the action and in its circumstances.
>
> Prudence helps us act as we should, when we should, and how we should. Imprudence, on the contrary, is unmindful of the right manner, time, or motive, and this is its failure. Prudence, on the contrary, acts discreetly, and does all with weight, number, and measure.
>
> Prudence and simplicity tend to the same end, which is to speak well and act well, in view of God. Since both must be present at the same time, our Lord recommended them together.[3] I am well aware that a rational distinction can be made between the two virtues, but in practice they are closely allied. The prudence of the flesh, which seeks honors, pleasures, and riches, is entirely opposed to Christian prudence and simplicity. These virtues avoid these false goods for those which are more substantial and enduring. These two virtues are like two inseparable sisters, both necessary for our spiritual development. A person who knows how to profit from them will undoubtedly amass great treasures of grace and merits.
>
> Our Lord manifested these virtues in the various encounters reported in the Gospel, but particularly in the case when the poor woman taken in adultery was brought to him. Not wishing to act as judge on this occasion, and preferring to rescue her, he said to the Jews, "Let him who is without sin cast the first stone."[4] In this situation he gave an excellent example of the practice of the two virtues of simplicity and prudence: simplicity in the merciful design

---

3. Matt 10:16.
4. John 8:7.

to save this poor creature and fulfill the Father's will, and prudence in the means he used to succeed in this design. In the same way, when the Pharisees tempted him by asking if it were allowed to pay tribute to Caesar, he had two choices. On the one hand he wanted to uphold the honor of his Father but not harm the people, and on the other he did not want to give his opponents the opportunity to say that he favored exorbitant taxes and oppression by the Romans. What did he reply, to avoid saying anything amiss and avoid all surprise? He asked that they show him the coin of tribute. When he heard from their lips that the image of Caesar was engraved thereon, he said, "Give to God the things that are God's, and to Caesar the things that are Caesar's."[5] The simplicity of this response corresponded to the intention that Jesus Christ had in his heart. He wanted to render to the King of heaven, and to those on earth, the honor which is their due. Prudence enabled him to avoid the trap they had laid for him.

It is then proper to prudence to regulate the words and actions we do, but it has another aspect too. It enables us to choose the appropriate means for reaching our end, which is to go to God and to take the most direct and assured way of getting there. We are not speaking of political or worldly prudence, which is directed to temporal success, and which is sometimes unjust and makes use of doubtful and most unsure human means. No, we speak of that prudence which our Lord counseled in the Gospel. It makes us choose the proper means for arriving at our goal, which is wholly divine. The means, then, must be otherworldly and appropriate.

We must choose means in keeping with our goal. We can do so in either of two ways: by our natural reasoning, which often is faulty, or by the maxims of faith which Jesus Christ has taught us. These are always true, and we should adopt them with no fear of deception. This is why we subject our reason to these maxims and make it an inviolable rule to judge things on all occasions as our Lord has judged. We make it a practice to say to ourselves, "How did our Lord look upon this or that? How did he handle this or that meeting? What did he do, and what did he say to this or that question?" This is the way we form our behavior according to his maxims and example.

Take this resolution, gentlemen, and walk on the royal road on which Jesus Christ is our guide and our leader. Recall that he said, "heaven and earth shall pass away, but my word shall never pass

---

5. Matt 22:21.

away.'"⁶ Bless God, my brothers, and strive to think and judge as he did, and do what he recommended by word and example. Acquire his spirit to learn his way of acting. It is not enough to do good, it must be done well after the example of whom it was said, *Bene omnia fecit*, that he did all things well.⁷ No, it is not enough to fast, to observe the rules, to fulfill our duties in the house. These must be done with the mind of Jesus Christ, that is perfectly, for the goal and in the circumstances as he did. Christian prudence consists in judging, speaking, and acting as the eternal Wisdom of God, clothed in our mortal flesh, judged, spoke, and acted.⁸

This, then, is the way Monsieur Vincent looked upon the virtue of prudence, and the way he practiced it. When there was question of deliberating upon some matter or of giving an opinion or decision, he would raise his mind to God to implore his light and grace before opening his mouth to speak, and even before considering the question at hand. He would be seen to raise his eyes to heaven, and then keep them closed as though he were consulting God himself on what to reply. If it were a matter of some moment he would take time to pray, and to invoke the help of the Holy Spirit. Since he relied solely on his divine wisdom and not on his own personal insight, he received grace and light from heaven. This enabled him to discern things which the unaided human spirit could never have known. He used to say, "where human prudence begins to diminish, there the light of divine wisdom dawns."

A certain person once came to him for advice, saying he wanted to retire from an occupation to give himself more completely to his own salvation. Monsieur Vincent replied that this seemed to be a temptation and that he should not listen to the suggestion. The man returned three different times but always got the same advice. He was to look upon this as a temptation, and if he would show more patience, and resist with more courage, he would be victorious over this trial. It happened as Monsieur Vincent had predicted, and this person later recognized that the evil spirit had suggested the move. After following Monsieur Vincent's advice he found all his troubles disappear.

A noblewoman had entered a state of life contrary to the advice of Monsieur Vincent. When she was, several months later, obliged to leave her position, she knew she would have been much better off if she had followed the counsel of such a wise and enlightened guide.

His prudence allowed him to foresee the consequences of things in such a

---

6. Matt 24:35.
7. Mark 7:37.
8. *CED* XI:51-53.

way that, when a project was suggested which appeared good, useful, and even necessary, he was able to foresee the likely difficulties. This happened on several occasions which showed his strength of mind and the lights with which he was favored. Where others saw no problems, his prudence discerned many, and enabled him to judge the best course of action, or even of inaction.

SECTION ONE

Continuation of the Same Subject

We have already remarked that Monsieur Vincent held it as a principle that, when asked his advice on some matter, he would not rush but would carefully weigh all the circumstances of the matter in question. When not pressed for an immediate answer, he would usually take his time to consider the matter before God, so as to give it more careful attention. We give some examples, among many others we might have chosen.

A person of his acquaintance was anxious to have a young lawyer appointed to a noble family to serve as steward and to handle the business of the family.[9] He requested Monsieur Vincent to use his influence in obtaining this position, but he replied, "we must think about it, but before doing anything definite we must keep our counsel for an entire month, to listen to God and to honor the silence Jesus Christ so often observed." In doing so he wished to repress the ardor this man displayed and the pressure he brought to bear, and also to seek out the will of God. He put him off for five or six months, but he finally took steps to have the lawyer appointed to the position. In this his manner of acting differed from the ordinary procedure of people of the world. They act promptly and use all manner of ways to move heaven and earth (as they say) to achieve their wishes.

When it was a question of giving rules and constitutions to his Congregation, without which he knew it could not survive, he waited thirty-three years before finally finishing this task, although his heart was disposed to finish this important work. He meanwhile had his Company practice them. He believed strongly that to perfect the rules to the extent possible and to ensure their stability they must first be observed, and then written down. They had to be engraved on the hearts of his confreres before being put on paper.

---

9. Martin Husson, then a lawyer with the Parlement of Paris. He entered the service of the duke of Retz in 1650.

He was very reserved and circumspect in his words, not only to avoid anything which might cause suspicion or distrust, but also to prevent what might injure anyone. He would say nothing which had not first been carefully thought out and turned over in his mind. There is reason to believe that this is why he spoke so little, and so carefully. He used to say:

> It is an attribute of prudence and of wisdom not only to speak well and to say good things, but also to say things in such a way that they will be well received and profit the one to whom we speak. Our Lord has given us the example of this on several occasions, and particularly when he spoke to the Samaritan woman who came to draw water from the well. He took the opportunity to speak of grace and inspired her to desire a conversion of life.

Once, traveling in the country, he met a young priest from a village, whom he did not know, holding a book. As a greeting, Monsieur Vincent's prudence and charity inspired him to say, "Oh, Monsieur, how good to see you commune with our Lord by good reading. You edify me greatly, and your example shows well how we engender good thoughts." Monsieur Vincent was not aware of what book the priest was reading, whether good or bad. Supposing in his charity that it was good, he wanted to encourage him by his gracious words to read well.

A noted pastor of Paris wished to appoint as his vicar a former member of the Congregation of the Mission. He wrote to Monsieur Vincent, asking why this priest had left the Company, how he had conducted himself, and whether he would recommend him for the position he had in mind. Monsieur Vincent was in doubt just how to reply. He did not want to harm this man, although he was well aware of his faults, and felt that they made him an unsuitable candidate for the office of vicar. Also, he did not want to deceive the pastor, nor to make him believe things that were not so. In an attempt to avoid either of these pitfalls, his prudence suggested that he use the following statement: "Monsieur, I am not well enough acquainted with the priest of whom you have written to recommend him to you, although he spent much time with us." An older priest of the Congregation, who was present when he dictated this response, felt free to say that the pastor would surely be astonished to have him say he did not know a priest who had spent such a long time in the Company, and under his spiritual direction. He answered, "I see that, but could I improve on what our Lord said in reproving those who had prophesied in his name, that he did not know them? This meant, of course, that he did not approve their activity. Consider it fitting, then, that I follow his example in using this same language."

While he was in the council of Her Majesty, he had no other objective than the greater good of the Church in the distribution of benefices. In awarding these to the persons he felt most worthy, he used no other method than to commend the virtues and merits of the most worthy candidates, and the likely advantage to God's service and the public good of their appointment. He would never speak against the qualities of the other candidates, to avoid doing them any harm. In these situations he was obliged to use great prudence and circumspection in his words, to promote the interests of the Church and to wound neither truth nor charity.

Those occasions when he was obliged to warn or reprove someone give us an opportunity to appreciate his marvelous prudence. He left no bitterness or anger in those whom he admonished, but rather an effort to make good use of the reproof they had been given. The examples we give will allow us to judge how prudently he acted.

Once, he was alerted to a renowned preacher who often came to see him for other business, and who seemed to be skeptical about certain truths of the faith. When this charge seemed likely from the testimony of others, Monsieur Vincent used a charitable and prudent device to bring home to him his deficiency. We learn about this from an account he wrote under an assumed name.

> Considering before God what I should do in this situation, I felt according to the rule of the Gospel that I ought to call on Damasus[10] in private, and speak to him in parables. One day, speaking informally to him, I said, "Monsieur, I have something I would like to ask you, a renowned preacher. It sometimes happens when we are working in country places that we run into people who do not believe the truths of our holy religion. We are at a loss to know how we should proceed to convince them. I would like to ask you what you think we should do in these cases, to lead them to believe in the truths of faith." Damasus asked me with some feeling why I would ask such a thing of him. I replied, "because, Monsieur, the poor approach the rich to get some help and charity. Since we are such poorly lettered persons we do not know the way to deal with things of the spirit. We come to you to beg you to favor us with your thoughts on this matter." Damasus got control of himself quickly, and replied that to teach the Christian faith he would do so first by holy Scripture, second, by the Fathers, third, by argumentation, fourth, by the common consent of the Christian people throughout the ages, fifth, by the witness of so many martyrs who have shed their blood for these same truths, sixth, by the miracles which God has wrought in confirmation of these beliefs.
>
> When he had finished, I said this was indeed well stated, and

---

10. A convention, like "So-and-so."

asked if he would put what he said in writing, simply and directly, and send it to me. He did so two or three days later, and brought it to me himself. I thanked him, saying I was much obliged to him and was happy to see such good sentiments from his own hands. Besides the use I can make of the suggestions myself, I said, I can use them for your own instruction. You may not believe what I am going to tell you, although it is true: some people think, and say, that you yourself do not agree with some truths of faith. You must acquire fully, Monsieur, what you have begun so well. After writing so well about the faith you must now give yourself to God to live in a way that will dispel all doubts from the minds of those who speak about you, and become the edification of everyone. I told him also that people in higher ranks, like himself, are the more obliged to be adorned with virtue. Those who wrote the life of Saint Charles Borromeo said that this virtue was most needed in those of higher rank. This is like the beauty of a precious stone enhanced by being mounted in a gold ring, rather than being placed in one of baser metal. Damasus agreed with all that had been said, saying that from this point on he was going to reform. Then he departed, leaving me satisfied at seeing him in such good dispositions.[11]

One day he was with several persons of some standing when one of them from long habit allowed himself to say "Devil take me," and similar curses. Hearing this, Monsieur Vincent went to him, embraced him, and said with a smile, "And I, Monsieur, will hold on to you, for God's sake." This edified the whole group, and served as a gentle and yet efficacious reminder to the speaker. He admitted his fault and promised to abstain from such curses in the future.

A respected priest reported a similar affair, although on a totally different subject, in regard to a prelate whom they happened to meet on the street. After some usual pleasantries, Monsieur Vincent said very graciously, "Bishop, please do not forget your ring." The prelate responded, laughing, "Ah, Monsieur, how you manage things." As an explanation to the priest, he explained that this bishop, with whom he was friendly, had several times protested that he would never divorce his wife, that is to say his diocese, for another, no matter how rich and beautiful she might be. He showed the episcopal ring he wore on his right hand, and quoted the words of the psalmist: *Oblivioni detur dextera mea, si non memineretur* ["If I forget, may my right hand be forgotten"].[12] He added that there was talk about this same prelate's being considered for a wealthy archdiocese. There were many

---

11. *CED* XIII:170-72.
12. Ps 137:5.

occasions such as this in the life of Monsieur Vincent which, although things were said in jest, yet showed great prudence and often had excellent results.

Another effect of prudence is to control the use of words so that they never offend anyone and never send anyone away unhappy. The superior of one of the missions said:

> In my own case, I never had the honor of meeting with him that I did not leave with perfect satisfaction, whether he had granted what I asked, or had to refuse. Even on the eve of the day I was to leave Paris to go where he had sent me, I spent a long time with him, only to be interrupted by several persons who came to speak with him. I admired then, as always, the way he sent each one on his way, perfectly happy. I remember two visitors in particular. The first, a priest, asked for the release of a prisoner who had committed murder on the Saint Denis road, in the section under the jurisdiction of Saint Lazare. Monsieur Vincent received the priest graciously. He spoke with him, and showed him every mark of respect, but since the affair did not depend on himself alone, he spoke of the Providence of God manifested in his justice as well as in his mercy, and that we must accept both the one and the other. He then spoke of the circumstances of the murder committed, and of the justice of the punishments God had allowed to be enacted for such crimes. He did this so graciously that the priest left satisfied, having nothing more to say.
>
> The second case concerned a layman who came to borrow some money. Monsieur Vincent made a thousand excuses why the house of Saint Lazare could not lend him anything, and how grieved he was at not being able to serve him on this occasion. He spoke with such gentleness and prudence that his refusal had no bad effect on his visitor, who left in peace.

On a trip he made in 1649, he visited several of his houses, among others a seminary in an episcopal city where the see was then vacant. A new bishop had been named, but the official papers had not yet come from Rome.[13] Monsieur Vincent had been opposed to this appointment, and this prompted many complaints from the bishop. Contrary to all expectations the bishop appeared in the town, leaving Monsieur Vincent to wonder how he ought to act toward him. If I go to pay my respects (he said to himself), he will surely be taken by surprise, and may be touched. If I send to ask if my visit would be agreeable to him, I do not know how he would react. Not to go, or not to send someone would surely give this good prelate reason to be angry with me, and I must avoid this. What should I do?

---

13. Philibert de Beaumanoir de Lavardin, bishop of Le Mans.

The prudent humility of this wise priest suggested a way out of this dilemma. He sent the superior of the house, together with another priest, to say that Monsieur Vincent had just arrived in the diocese. As he would not dare stay without his permission, he humbly asked if he might stay seven or eight days at the house of the priests of the Mission. The bishop received this humble request well. He stated that he might remain as long as he liked and that if he did not have a place to stay he would have offered his own home. Monsieur Vincent wanted to take advantage of such an obliging reply to thank the prelate in person and pay his respects. He was, however, prevented from doing so by the bishop's leaving unexpectedly that very day for some other place.

Monsieur Vincent took it as a rule in all his deliberations and resolutions to consult always and before all else the oracle of divine truth, that is to say, to consider what our Lord did and said about the matter under discussion, to conform himself to his example, and to submit to his teachings. This was the source from which he drew all the wise advice which he gave to others and which guided his own behavior. We are not surprised, then, that he acted with such prudence or succeeded with such blessings, since he went to the source of wisdom itself, the incarnate Word of God. It could be said of him, in the words of the wise man of Scripture, that divine Wisdom helped him, directed him, and worked in him in all his undertakings.[14]

In this connection he one day asked one of his priests for some advice on a particular matter. The reply was that the thing should be done, because of the grievous consequences if it were not carried out. Monsieur Vincent pointed out that so much attention should not be paid to the consequences of an action as to the nature of the action itself and to its relationship to the words and example of Jesus Christ.

In an effort to model himself on his divine exemplar, another of his principles was to do everything with as little fanfare as possible. He chose the most simple and humble works along with the most charitable. In this way he avoided the envy and opposition of others. When Satan raised difficulties, he was challenged solely by the weapons of humility, patience, penance, and prayer. He never justified or defended himself from malicious talk or calumny, nor made use of temporal authorities to support his undertakings, judging this to be the most prudent way to act.

The purity and soundness of his prudence and wisdom appeared in his always seeking to follow and accomplish in all things the holy will of God. He did so in preference to any other consideration, with no regard for temporal advantage. He rejected this and trampled it under foot when it was a question of the interests, of the service, and of the glory of Jesus Christ.

---

14. Wis 9:10.

This was the great and only object he had in mind in all his work, and by which he carried out faithfully and constantly what he had begun. He preferred absolutely and completely this holy will of God to every other consideration, with no exception whatsoever.

To conclude this chapter we cite the testimony of a most worthy priest who wrote his appreciation of the wise and prudent conduct of Monsieur Vincent, particularly in the replies he gave to those who consulted him or sought his advice. This is the order we follow, just as this priest often observed:

> Before all else, he raised his mind to God to seek his help, and usually asked those who came for counsel to do the same. By a short fervent prayer he would ask the light and grace to know the will of God in the matter under consideration. Then he would listen most attentively to what was asked, and consider it at length. If he thought it necessary, he would ask for greater details to be well aware of all the circumstances. He would never rush to give his opinion. If he felt that the matter required more thought he would ask for time to think about it, recommending meanwhile that it be prayed over in the sight of God. He was agreeable that others be consulted, and he himself was not loathe to seek advice. He deferred always, if justice and charity allowed, to the opinion of others, even in face of his own contrary opinion. When, finally, he was obliged to express himself, he gave his own opinion so judiciously and yet humbly, that he left the person free to decide on his own. For example, he would say that, for this or that reason, it seems it would be good to do such and such; or, if pressed to give a definite answer, he would use similar language: it seems to me it would be good, or more expedient, to do this or that. After all this, he followed two inviolable rules. First, to keep absolutely secret what he had been consulted about, unless authorized by the person concerned to speak to others because of some necessity or utility. Second, to be firm in following whatever decision he had come to. After discerning the will of God, he would not falter. He held it as a principle that it must be carried out, and that the vice of inconstancy strongly opposes true prudence, and ruins even the most saintly and solid resolution.

CHAPTER SEVENTEEN

His Justice and Gratitude

WE WILL not use the word justice in the sense that holy Scripture sometimes uses it to signify the grace that justifies and sanctifies souls, or the state of justice and sanctity. We will use the word justice to refer to a particular virtue, one of the most excellent of the moral virtues. As Saint Ambrose teaches, it gives to each what belongs to him. Not only does it not attribute to oneself the good which rightly belongs to the other, but even leaves off the most legitimate interests when the common good requires it to preserve the rights of the neighbor.[1] In this sense of the word, we can truly say that Monsieur Vincent had this virtue in an excellent degree. He practiced it on all occasions when the opportunity arose.

He often thought of and referred to the words of Jesus Christ: "Render to God the things of God, and to Caesar the things that are Caesar's."[2] Following this divine rule, he carefully rendered to God all the duties of religion in virtue of his being a reasonable man, a Christian, a priest, and a missionary. He likewise gave to his neighbor in general and to each one as an individual, according to his rank and condition, whatever justice required of him. He never detoured from the straight path of this virtue. On this topic, he often said to his confreres in his conferences: "Gentlemen, have regard to the interests of others as much as of your own. Let us be straightforward and act always with loyalty and fairness to everyone."

He was so careful to fulfill the demands of justice that he felt they superseded all other responses. In this connection, he wrote to one of his friends, saying:

> Remember to pray to God for me. Yesterday I found myself in the dilemma of having to fulfill a promise I had made, or to do an act of charity for a person who could do us a lot of good or ill. Unable to do both, I left off the act of charity to fulfill my promise, but my friend was not at all pleased. I was not so much concerned with my decision in doing this act of justice as, it seems to me, in following my own inclination in the matter.

He was careful that the community paid its bills promptly, and regretted to see some people forced to come several times to Saint Lazare for payments. When these persons came to his notice, he would tell them that there was no

---
1. PL 16:57.
2. Matt 22:21.

need to go to the trouble of coming to Saint Lazare. He would send promptly to their homes what they were owed. When the community had to borrow, they remarked that he would make a note of the time and place where repayment must be made. At the given time he would send someone from the house at Saint Lazare with the payment. When it was suggested that he ought to wait until he received a notice, or until the lender would come to collect his payment, he would not agree to such a plan. He said it was not just to force someone to come seeking what was rightly due him.

One day the coachman backed up, knocking several loaves of bread from a baker's stall, causing several to fall to the ground. At once, Monsieur Vincent, fearing the soiled loaves might not be sold, immediately paid the price asked by the baker, and brought them back to Saint Lazare.

Another time, when this same coachman backed the carriage against a large gateway fastened on the inside by a bar of half-rotten wood, the bar broke quite easily. Only the caretaker lived in this house. He could easily have fastened the door some other way, but Monsieur Vincent on his own, sent his brother companion to the carpenters. He had them make a completely new bar. It cost three or four times more than what the original one was worth.

If he felt he had offended someone by any word or deed which he felt might not be just, he would not fail to make satisfaction in full.

The mayor of a large town once asked Monsieur Vincent to do him a favor at court. The gentleman assured him that he would protect the missionaries in his town from several powerful persons who opposed their work and who had even gone to Parlement against them. Monsieur Vincent replied that if he could help, he would. He begged the mayor, however, to leave the priests of the Mission in the hands of God and the ordinary police authorities. He did not wish to have his Missionaries in any place owing to the favor or the authority of men.

In important lawsuits the Company found itself involved in, he sometimes went himself, or sent someone else, to see the judge. He did so, not so much to plead the cause of the Company, but to ask the judge to consider only the cause of justice in the case. He could be called the lawyer for the side of justice rather than the defender of his own interests. He was neither for nor against anyone, but pleaded equally for either, seeking always to have each one given what was rightfully his. He was not happy with having to be bothered with lawsuits of whatever kind. Once, a brother of the house of Saint Lazare, in charge of looking after these matters, came to ask him to visit the judge in a pending case to protect the rights of the Company. Monsieur Vincent showed his distaste for this. He said we must leave it to the Providence of God and to the court system, and besides, he did not believe these interventions did much good, especially with certain persons. He referred to the time he was at the royal court, when he paid little attention to the recommendations made to him about appointments to the various benefices. He looked only at the merits of the case, and what would be for the greater glory of God. In this way he was little influenced by solicitations in favor of anyone.

On another occasion he told this same brother that he must adopt the practice, when asked about a case, of saying everything good about the other party.[3] He should omit nothing, just as if the opponent were present to deduce his arguments and to defend himself, and had somehow failed to do so in the matter under consultation.

The Missionaries owned some properties in the provinces where they were established. They had much to put up with from the farmers and others there who abused their patience. The local people knew that they would not be badly treated, since they were used to the quibbling of the region, and feared little from their local courts. Because of this the superiors of several houses of the Congregation asked Monsieur Vincent to obtain a *Committimus*.[4] This might serve to intimidate those who would not listen to reason. But this man of God usually deflected them from this thought, telling them that they should do whatever they were able.

The house of Saint Lazare, which submitted its own cases to the courts of the Hotel or the Palace at Paris, had cases of those who lived at a distance, particularly if they were poor, also assigned to Paris. Monsieur Vincent was troubled at this, because it would cost them more to come there to plead.[5] "Is it just," he would ask, "to have these poor people come so far to plead their cause?"

As the Lord of the Manor of Saint Lazare, where he was responsible for high, medium, and low justice, he made his appointments gratis.[6] He chose capable and good men for these positions, preferring them to others who sought out these responsibilities and came powerfully recommended. He saw to it that justice was well administered, to the glory of God and to the satisfaction of those on trial.

We will speak of the virtue of gratitude here, because according to the teaching of Saint Thomas, it is joined to justice.[7] A Christian could fail in one of his greatest obligations of justice if he were not grateful and thankful

---

3. This was Brother Louis Robineau.
4. Documents by which a person's case would be sent to the palace courts immediately instead of to lower jurisdictions.
5. The Paris courts of Requetes de l'Hotel and Requetes du Palais were tribunals established to hear cases normally involving officials or those sent by the Parlement of Paris. In this, Saint Lazare had a privileged position not shared by the poor.
6. At a time when appointments to civil positions were usually sold to the highest bidder, Monsieur Vincent as the lord of the lands of Saint Lazare gave these positions to qualified persons without charge.
7. *Summa Theologiae* IIa-IIae, q.106, a.1.

for the benefits he had received, either from God, the first and principal source of all good, or from the neighbor whom the divine Bounty uses as the channel of his blessings. Monsieur Vincent was as far from the vice of ingratitude as his natural inclination and his heart, influenced by grace, were attracted to gratitude and thanksgiving toward God and his neighbor.

He used to say that nothing was so efficacious in winning the heart of God as a spirit of gratitude for his gifts and blessings. In this spirit he had the custom of thanking God often for the gifts from his bounty to all sorts of creatures, going back to the beginning of the world. He also thanked God for the good works accomplished through the inspiration of his grace, and he urged others to do the same. Coming down to particulars, he often invited his confreres to thank God for the protection and graces given to the Church and for the elements which made it up, especially the prelates, pastors, and other ecclesiastical workers engaged in its preservation and advancement. He was careful to thank God for the fruits produced by all well run companies and congregations. How can we express adequately the thanks he gave the divine bounty for the blessings he had poured forth on his own Congregation and each of its enterprises, such as the missions, the ordination retreats, the retreats, the clergy conferences, the seminaries, and the other services given to the Church? He often thanked God for the help given to the poor, for the promotion of good priests to positions of responsibility in the Church, for the happy outcome of the worthy designs of the king, for the victories he gained, for the triumphs of the king and other princes and Christian states over the heretics and schismatics, or in general, for all those events favorable to the glory of God and the good of the Catholic religion. These were the usual subjects of his thanks to God, but his own gratitude seemed to him so inadequate that he invited pious persons and even entire communities, mainly his own, to join him in his praise and glorification of God, and he asked others to offer their sacrifices and prayers for this intention.

He was often heard to say, "We must give as much time to thanking God for his favors as we have used in asking him for them." He complained vehemently of the extreme ingratitude of men toward God. He was referring to the lament of Jesus Christ reported in the Gospel on the occasion of his curing the ten lepers. He urged his confreres to practice this virtue of gratitude and thanksgiving, without which, he used to say, we make ourselves unworthy of receiving any favors from God or men.

It is not known for what particular graces he thanked God especially, since his humility kept the gifts he had received under the cloak of silence. On the anniversary of his baptism each year, however, he would ask the community to help him thank God for having supported him for so many years upon the earth. We can form some idea of his gratitude to God by the appreciation he showed to men. He accepted the favors of men as coming ultimately from the liberality of God, and in thanking them, he wanted the praise to be referred ultimately to the Creator.

His gratitude toward men was given not only for the major benefits he received and the great services rendered him but even for the least things done for him. This came from his profound humility, which made him think that he deserved nothing by right and that everyone gave him more honor and respect than he deserved. This led him to find reasons for gratitude in those trivial things that would not even have been noticed by many others.

In this spirit of gratitude he would say to those who visited or who rendered the least service: "I thank you for overlooking my old age;" or again, "for having taught me something I did not know;" or, "for the patience you have shown me;" or, "to allow me to come into your presence;" or, "for the charity God gives you, in my regard," etc. He extended his thanks even to the least of the brothers, or to the one who stayed with him in his illness, thanking him for the least services, such as lighting a lamp, bringing a book, opening or closing a door, showing that he kept account of the least things done for him and received them with a spirit of gratitude. This had the effect of making others take pleasure in rendering him some kind of service.

He was equally attentive on his trips to thank those who gave him the least help, such as helping him mount a horse, or other such small things. He would acknowledge these favors with cordiality and graciousness, even to children. Besides receiving his thanks, they would often receive some other token of appreciation as well. He was so exact in his expression of gratitude that, if the companion on his journeys was not thankful enough, or expressed himself coldly, he would remonstrate, and regard it as a failing in him.

This venerable priest, who in all things imitated our Lord, who said he held as done to himself what was done for the least of his brethren, thanked and recompensed those who gave any service to the brother who accompanied him on his trips, as generously as he did for those done to himself.

We spoke earlier of Monsieur Vincent's falling into a stream near Durtal on one of his trips from Le Mans to Angers, and that a priest who happened to be with him immediately plunged into the water to save him.[8] In due time this priest fell from his first fervor. Failing to respond to the good example around him, he decided to leave Saint Lazare and return to his own region against the advice of Monsieur Vincent. He told him that this proposal was a temptation from the devil to cause the priest to lose his vocation. He gradually lost the spirit he had at the beginning, so that far from accomplishing the beautiful projects he had envisioned, he found himself filled with boredom, surrounded by difficulties, and pressed by the enemies of his salvation.

---

8. Book Two, ch. 39.

After a year or so in this condition, his eyes were opened to his spiritual condition. Although he was comfortably fixed, he began to realize that Monsieur Vincent was right in trying to dissuade him from this venture. He realized, too, that he had made a bad mistake in leaving the Company to which God had called him. He followed the example of the Prodigal Son, deciding to return to his father. He wrote letter after letter, asking pardon for his mistake, and begging to be allowed to return to one of the houses, but Monsieur Vincent made no reply.

This priest redoubled his efforts and openly said that, unless a helping hand were extended, he would be lost. Monsieur Vincent felt it was not in the best interests of the Congregation that this man should return. His previous behavior had not given enough reason to hope he would succeed, and so Monsieur Vincent remained firm in his decision not to take him back. Finally, this priest decided to attack Monsieur Vincent from the most vulnerable avenue to his heart, that of his gratitude, knowing well that this was one of his greatest virtues. He therefore, figuratively, knocked at his door with the words: "Monsieur, I once saved your life; now you must save the life of my soul." Seeing his perseverance, and hoping he would do better, the grateful superior wrote that he was to come at once to Saint Lazare, where he would be received with open arms. With this response in hand, the priest rejoiced to be again in the good graces of Monsieur Vincent. He prepared to leave for Saint Lazare, but unfortunately fell sick and died before he could carry out his designs.

After Monsieur Vincent fell into the water, as we mentioned earlier, he went to a hut nearby, which proved to be the lodging of a poor peasant. He was grateful that he took him in and dried his clothes, as though he had been welcomed into a castle by a gentleman. He thanked him and paid him a sum beyond what was appropriate. Beyond that, when this man told Monsieur Vincent that he was bothered by a hernia, he was promised a truss to relieve his pain. When Monsieur Vincent returned to Paris, three or four months later, he did not forget his promise but bought the appliance. He sent it to the poor peasant, along with a letter of thanks for the help he had received from him in his home. Not having any assured way of getting the letter and appliance to its destination, he elicited the support of a highly placed lady, the wife of a marshal of France, who owned the lands in question, to deliver the package to the place he showed on a sketch.

He appreciated even those who expected nothing of him, for example, the people who cultivated the fields. By their labors they enabled the clergy and nobility to live according to their condition. Here is how he spoke of this, in a conference to his community:

> God serves as our provider, furnishing us with what we need and beyond. He gives a sufficiency and more. I do not know if we think

often enough of thanking him as we should. We live off the patrimony of Jesus Christ, off the sweat of these poor peasants. When we go to the refectory, we should consider whether we have earned the food we are going to eat. I often have this thought, and it causes me to blush. O miserable one, have you earned the bread you are about to eat? This bread and other food coming from the labor of others. At least, if we have not earned it as we should, let us pray to God for them. We should not let a day pass without offering them to our Lord, that they may have the grace to use their pains and suffering well and one day crown them with his glory.[9]

He was so grateful when he received a favor from someone for his Company that he publicized it widely, calling him benefactor, protector, helper, or giving him other engaging titles. He exhorted his confreres to recommend him to the Lord and would himself remember the benefits he had received whenever he met the person. A priest of the Congregation of the Mission had died in Lorraine, in the house of the Jesuit Fathers, who had him honorably buried.[10] On that occasion, Monsieur Vincent gave a conference to his own community on gratitude. He sought to move his followers to pray to God for these good fathers, and to ask for the grace and opportunity to thank them for their kindness, as he had already done in every way possible. He took the side of this holy Company whenever persecutions were raised against it. He sought to divert calumnies and to publicize both their great virtues and their great accomplishments.

He looked after the board of a poor woman for twenty-five or thirty years. He even paid the rent for her room near the College des Bons Enfants because she had tended to several of the plague-stricken priests at Saint Lazare at the very beginning of the existence of the Congregation.

Once, speaking in private with a priest of his Congregation and having said something good about a woman for some favor she had done, he reflected on the praise he had just given this person. He then said: "I have two qualities in myself, gratitude, and praising the good I see in others." It is true he had these two qualities, which he mentioned, but it was unlike his usual reticence to say anything to his own advantage without evident necessity.

He appreciated the generosity of the founders of the houses of his Congregation so much so that he set no limits on the expressions of gratitude he used. Writing to one of his priests, he said:

> We cannot have too much appreciation and gratitude for the founders of our house. God gave us the grace recently to offer to give back to a founder what he had given to us, because I felt he

---

9. *CED* XI:201.
10. Germain de Montevit, who died at Bar le Duc in 1640. See Book Two, ch. 11.

had fallen on hard times. If he had accepted, it seems to me I would have been happy. In this case the divine bounty would have become our surety, and we would have lacked nothing. Although this did not come about, still, Monsieur, what happiness it would have been to impoverish ourselves to help out someone who had done us so much good. God gave us the grace to do so once before, in giving back what he had just given to us, and every time I think of it I have such satisfaction that I can hardly express it.[11]

This letter was written in September, 1654. He wrote another to a benefactor, offering to return what he had given, for the same reason.

Monsieur, please use the goods of our Company as belonging to you. We are ready to sell all we own for you, right down to the very chalices we use at mass. In this we are observing the sacred canons, which tell us to look after our founders in their needs, since they have helped us from their abundance. What I now say, Monsieur, I do not say out of politeness, but by God's direction, and from the bottom of my heart.[12]

The truth of Monsieur Vincent's words was borne out in several other situations. When he learned of a pressing need of one of the benefactors of the Congregation, he sent him two hundred *pistoles*. The benefactor refused it, however, out of concern that this would cause too much inconvenience for the missionaries.

Another time he borrowed three hundred *pistoles* to offer them to a benefactor of the Congregation in need. This person realized that this money could not be accepted without seriously inconveniencing the Company, so he too refused, although he was urged to accept.

A person of great piety had left a sum of money in his will for the Congregation, to be used in works of the institute. When Monsieur Vincent was informed of it, he brought together the officers of the community and some of the older members. One of them said he felt many responsibilities would be placed upon the community in accepting this legacy. Also, there was nothing in the procurator's account, largely because the house of Saint Lazare was already burdened by a previous foundation set up by this same person.

When Monsieur Vincent heard this, he closed his eyes, and then opening them, looked to heaven and said:

Even if things are as you say (and let us assume they are) it is always something to have people give us the means of serving God and making him known. Therefore, we should be grateful for this and pray to God for him as we would for a benefactor. We see the

---
11. *CED* V:179.
12. *CED* V:393.

Church displaying this same gratitude toward her benefactors. It goes so far as to relax her usual regulations, and as we see in several cases, it gives laymen and women the right of patronage, although this should be reserved to priests. Why does she act this way, if not to show her appreciation for benefactions?

He was so grateful to the late prior of Saint Lazare and the religious who had preceded the missionaries in that house, that he prayed to God to apply to them the merits of the works of the Congregation as far as possible. This would make them participants in the good works they were able to accomplish because of their graciousness. He always showed great respect and deference for them, not in externals only by way of courtesy, but by a true sentiment of gratitude. He showed this spirit everywhere, whether these religious were present or not.

We would never finish if we were to give all the examples we could of his spirit of thanksgiving. We will be satisfied with what we have already said, and shall conclude this chapter by citing the words of a priest of the Congregation of the Mission:

The gratitude of Monsieur Vincent toward his benefactors was extreme. I personally witnessed the acts of virtue which he practiced in regard to the late Monsieur Le Bon, former prior of Saint Lazare. He called him "our father." He visited him often, and when he returned from a trip the first thing he would do, after adoring the blessed sacrament in the church, would be to greet this good prior. I was delighted once in meeting them to see with what respect Monsieur Vincent greeted him. I saw the assurance Monsieur Vincent gave of preserving a grateful memory of the prior's person, and his charity toward the Congregation of the Mission. He attended his last agony with great devotion. He had the entire community assemble in the sick room to receive his last blessing, which he asked in the name of all. This moved me deeply, as did all the other things he did and said on this occasion, which showed the gratitude he had toward him. I heard him say, speaking of the virtue of gratitude, that we must rejoice when divine Providence gives us an occasion of practicing this virtue. It is so agreeable to God, as he made known to us by establishing thanksgiving sacrifices in the Old Testament, and the Holy Eucharist in the New. This sacrament is named Eucharist, not only because it contains the author of grace, but also because our Lord in instituting it gave thanks to his Father. He required us to offer this same thanksgiving for the innumerable graces and blessings we have received, and continue to receive, from his bounty.

CHAPTER EIGHTEEN

His Perfect Detachment from the Goods of This World, and His Love of Poverty

"WHAT A GREAT virtue it is to despise the goods of earth! But how rare this virtue is, and how few practice it," says Saint Ambrose.[1] Few indeed have the courage to weed out of their hearts the unhappy covetousness which holy Scripture calls the root of all evil. Few, too, can say with the holy apostle: Behold, Lord, we have left all to follow you and to serve you.[2] As the Sage says, "He is truly happy who has not allowed his heart to run after gold and silver, and has not put his trust in riches nor in the goods of this world. Where is such a one that we may praise him, because he has done marvels in his lifetime."[3]

It will not take a long treatise to be persuaded of this virtuous disposition in the person of Monsieur Vincent. The whole story of his life and of his great and holy accomplishments provides ample evidence. No, we must not be surprised if we see that he possessed this virtue to an eminent degree since he had such a disregard for riches.

We will not repeat here what was already said in Book One, how this lover of the poverty of Jesus Christ imitated him on all occasions when it was a matter of his own interest or that of his Congregation. This was shown when the general of the galleys and his wife established a foundation for the support of religious works. He would not accept this for himself, but offered it first to various other communities, until he saw that this was a manifestation of the will of God for him. This too was the case when he was offered the house and priory of Saint Lazare, which he refused absolutely. He persisted in this for over a year, despite the pressure of the prior, who came to the College des Bons Enfants more than thirty times to talk to him about this. Only after taking the advice of wise and virtuous persons did Monsieur Vincent become convinced that God wished him to serve there.

These two examples alone suffice to show how his heart was detached from any love of riches or the things of this world, and how great was his love of poverty. Besides, he showed this attitude in countless other situations. We could say without exaggeration that the most avaricious person would not seek opportunities to enrich himself with such ardor as Monsieur

---

1. PL 15.1:1299.
2. Matt 19:27.
3. Sir 31:8.

Vincent would to embrace and practice poverty. His words and actions showed his great love for this virtue.

He was heard to say on this topic that, although he still had reason to be concerned about his own financial position before he felt the call of God to the mission, he already felt within himself a desire to have nothing for himself and to live in community, beginning to put into practice his love for poverty at every opportunity.

He always selected for himself a room without a fireplace, even in his later years, that is until four or five years before his death. He was then persuaded by his community to accept another room because of his illnesses. Until his eightieth year he lived in a tiny undecorated room.[4] It had no carpet, no other furniture but a simple uncovered wooden table, two poor chairs, and a wretched pallet and straw mattress covered with a blanket, and a pillow. Once, when he had a fever, some bed curtains were placed around his bed to protect him from drafts, but he would not agree to use it. He took from his room various pictures that one of the brothers of the house had put there. He kept only one, and said that having several was contrary to poverty. When the rooms were inspected, he wanted his to be visited like the others, to ensure that he had nothing superfluous.

In the room on the lower floor in which he received guests, a piece of material was hung at the door to protect the room from cold winds, but no sooner did he see this than he had it taken away. He took his meals in the refectory in the same spirit of poverty, saying within himself: "Ah, miserable man, you have not earned the bread you eat."[5] When he could, he took as his own portion the scraps left by others.

His love of poverty clearly led him to love to be poorly fed and poorly clothed. He was pleased when he lacked something, in whatever necessity. He ordinarily wore a used cassock, well patched, and his underclothes too were poor and sometimes torn. A nobleman who visited him once noticed his worn cassock, patched at the elbows. He was so touched that he reported to his friends how greatly edified he was at the poverty and neatness of Monsieur Vincent.

When he went to the Louvre to speak to the queen, or as a member of the council, he always went in his usual garb. It was poor and out of style, and he never changed into something more elegant. Once, Cardinal Mazarin took him by his frayed cincture, and presented him to the group, saying with a smile, "Look how Monsieur Vincent comes dressed for the court, and look at the beautiful cincture he wears."

---

4. By modern reckoning, Vincent died in his eightieth year. Abelly is following a flawed chronology.

5. *CED* XI:201.

If some member of the house protested that he should have a new cape, or that his hat was too old, he would make fun of it: "Oh, my brother, it is all the king can do to have a collar that is not torn and a new hat to wear."

When he needed to warm himself in winter he would put only a little wood on the fire, out of consideration for wasting the goods of the house. He said that these belonged to God and to the poor, and that we were simply the dispensers of these goods and not the owners. He remarked that we must render an exact account to God for our use of things, and therefore we must use only what was absolutely necessary and nothing more.[6]

Several times he began a trip with no money. He would be delighted at being forced by hunger to go to some poor peasant to ask for a piece of bread for the love of God. This happened to him particularly one day when he was returning fasting from Saint Germain to Paris.

The love he had for poverty was evidenced even in the church of Saint Lazare, for he wanted it to be seen even here. He had the decorations of the church, for the normal usage of the members of the community, made from the most ordinary things, except for the greater feasts. He thought the decorations of the church too elaborate for daily use. Also, he had the carpenters of the house fashion a railing separating a corner of the church of Saint Lazare into a chapel for the use of the community.

All this did not hinder him from being prodigal when it was a question of doing something for the glory of God or for the salvation of souls. In these cases he spared nothing. Money was of no significance for him. He even went deeply into debt when he found it necessary to do so for the interests of the service of God or for the spiritual good of the neighbor.

He strove to inculcate his own love of this virtue in the members of the entire Company. Speaking one day to his community, he said:

> You ought to be aware, gentlemen, that this virtue of poverty is the foundation of the Congregation of the Mission. This person who now speaks to you, by the grace of God, has never asked for anything the Company now owns. If it should ever happen that a single step or a single word could bring it about that we would be established in the provinces and in the larger cities, and involved in various significant activities, I would not say that one word. I would hope that our Lord would give me the grace never to say it. This is my attitude, to leave all to the Providence of God.[7]

He spoke once of his fear that the love of poverty might not continue to be honored in the community in some future day:

> Alas, what would become of this Company if it were to become

---

6. Cited from Remarks from Chapter, Pémartin ed., Vol. 8, p. 629.
7. *CED* XI:78.

attached to the things of the world? What would become of it, if it were to allow entry to that covetousness which the apostle says is the root of all evil? Several great saints have said that poverty is the touchstone of religious orders. We are not true religious since it has not been found expedient for us to become such, and we are not even worthy of being such although we live in common. But we can say the same thing as they, that poverty is the touchstone of communities, especially our own. This is the virtue that detaches us from all the goods of the world to attach ourselves perfectly to God. O Savior, give us this virtue which attaches us inseparably to your service. With it, we shall wish for and seek only you and your greater glory.[8]

Another time, moved by his love of poverty and his desire to see it flourish in his community, he spoke forcefully against the contrary spirit. He uttered three maledictions against those of the Company who allowed themselves to be guided by self-interest and the desire of amassing goods:

Woe, woe, gentlemen and my brothers, woe to the missionary who becomes attached to the perishable goods of this world. He will be trapped by them. He remains pierced by their thorns and captured in their bonds. Should this happen to the Company, what will happen then? How shall we live? "We have a thousand *livres* of income, we can live at our ease. Why go running about the villages and towns? Why work so hard? Let us leave these peasants to the care of their pastors. We should live in peace." This is how the spirit of laziness will follow the spirit of covetousness, being concerned only about protecting and increasing material things, and seeking personal satisfaction. We can then say goodbye to the missions, and to the Congregation of the Mission itself, for it shall cease to exist. You have only to read your history books to see countless examples of this. Wealth and an abundance of material things have caused the loss, not only of certain clergy, but of entire communities and orders, all for not remaining faithful to their primitive spirit of poverty.[9]

One of his priests once spoke to Monsieur Vincent about the poverty of his house. The reply of Monsieur Vincent was, "What do you do, Monsieur, when you lack what is needed by your community? Do you have recourse to God?" "Yes, sometimes," replied the priest. "Ah well," Monsieur Vincent said, "you see how poverty makes us think of God and helps us to raise our hearts to him. If we had everything we needed, we would easily forget him.

---

8. *CED* XI:223.
9. *CED* XI:79.

For this reason, I rejoice when I see that real and voluntary poverty is practiced in all our houses. There is a hidden grace in this poverty which we do not realize." The priest answered, "You take care of other poor people, all except your own." "I pray God to forgive you these words," said Monsieur Vincent. "I am well aware that you said this without thinking, but you must realize that we can never be richer than when we are like our Savior, Jesus Christ."

A priest of the Mission accepted a gift given to the Congregation of the Mission by a priest of great piety for the establishment of a new house of the Congregation. Monsieur Vincent wrote to him as follows: "These gifts are all the greater because they were totally unexpected and unmerited on our part. You have acted according to the good pleasure of God, and followed our rule of allowing the Providence of God to show the way, without doing anything of ourselves to bring this about. This is the way all our houses were begun, and it should ever be the way the Company responds."[10]

Writing one day on this same subject to the superior of one of his houses, he said:

> The proposal that you make to me of seeking the priory which you mention is contrary to the maxim and usage that exists among us of not seeking any property or establishment directly or indirectly. Providence alone has called us to all those foundations that we have, by means of the very same persons who had the property rights. And if the Company trusts me in this, it will keep itself inviolably in this wise manner of acting.[11]

Another of his priests wrote to ask if he should accept two benefices which he had been offered in his native region, with the thought of having them come into the use of the Company. He thanked his confrere as follows:

> I thank you, especially since your intention is solely to assure that God would be honored and the people helped more than ever before. This shows your zeal, which God always rewards. But in answer to your request, Monsieur, we ought never to seek other resources for the Company than those which it shall please God to send us independently of anything we do. We should not anticipate Providence, and I beg you to hold to this.[12]

His perfect detachment from material things was never seen better than when the queen regent called him to the Council for Ecclesiastical Affairs. As a member, he had a say in the awarding of all the benefices in France normally at the disposition of the king. He never asked anything for his own

---

10. *CED* VI:8-9.
11. *CED* VI:8-9.
12. *CED* VII:178-79.

Company nor for his relatives, no matter how greatly they were in need, nor for his friends as tokens of his friendship. On the contrary, it was known that, if some relatives asked him for a benefice, he would do nothing. He preferred that they stay in their state as peasants and gain their bread by the sweat of their brows. This was not for lack of affection for them, but from a totally disinterested attitude which is rarely or never seen. He was liberal and generous toward others, but so modest and reserved toward his own that even his best friends were astonished. Also, he was heard to say, when called to this position at court, that he had taken a firm resolution before God never to take advantage of his position to favor any of his relatives. Neither would he advance the interests of his Congregation. He held to this so completely that, if we were to judge by worldly standards, his Congregation certainly lost more than it gained.[13]

While Monsieur Vincent was on the Council for Ecclesiastical Affairs, one of the leading magistrates of the kingdom, a man of great authority, asked, through a priest of the Congregation of the Mission, that an abbey be given to one of his sons who did not have the requisite qualities. This gentleman promised that, if the abbey were given, he would see to it that the house of Saint Lazare would regain some lands and revenues that had been lost. He was well informed of how to bring this about, with no involvement of the priests of the Congregation in this issue. Monsieur Vincent was urged to seize the opportunity while he was in office, since this was a common practice with several other orders, which the priest named. When Monsieur Vincent received this proposal, he responded: "Not for all the goods of the world would I do anything against God or my conscience. The Company will never fail because of poverty. Rather, if poverty should fail, I fear that the Company will perish."

Monsieur Vincent would not ask anything for his Congregation, any more than he would for his relatives and friends. When some even tried to take from the Company what rightfully belonged to it, he showed himself so indifferent that even the judges were astonished. They could not help saying that surely Monsieur Vincent must be a man from another world, since he was so little attached to things of this one. When the possession of the priory of Saint Lazare was called into question, he was of a mind to allow it to be taken by the other community that sought it, rather than defend his rights in court.[14] However, when he took counsel of a great servant of God, it was pointed out to him that it was a question of the service of God and not simply his own particular interest, and that he should defend himself in the courts. He followed this advice, but retained a personal disposition of indifference to keep the property or lose it, just as the court would decide.

---

13. This was the testimony given by the chancellor Michel Le Tellier. See Book Two, ch. 13.
14. Book One, ch. 22.

This same thing happened with the house of the Holy Spirit in the city of Toul. He was on the verge of leaving it and recalling the Missionaries from there. He would have done this but for the advice of a person of virtue and standing which he followed, rather than his own inclination.[15]

On another occasion when he felt he had to recall his Missionaries from a certain diocese, he instructed the superior how he should act in leaving the town where he was.

> After giving an account to the vicars general of all the goods which they have given for your use, and which you are now returning to them, you must take leave of them graciously. Leave without a single word of complaint and with expressions of being at ease in leaving the locality. You must pray that God bless the town and the diocese. I beg you above all not to say anything from the pulpit or elsewhere which would show any resentment. Ask the blessing of these gentlemen upon yourself and the whole community. Ask their blessing for me, who desire to prostrate myself in spirit at their feet along with you.

Although the resolution had been taken to leave this town, God did not allow this to come about. Things changed to such a degree that this house has remained to this day.

He was equally detached from concern about the houses of the Daughters of Charity of which Congregation he was the founder, as he was about those of his own Company. He had sent these women to the villages, towns, and hamlets where they had been asked for, to serve the sick of the parishes and hospitals, even when the condition was attached that they could be sent back at any time the administrators wished. This was something almost unheard of, and yet Monsieur Vincent accepted it without question. For example, he heard that the administrators of the hospital of the city of Nantes were thinking of sending away the Daughters of Charity in favor of the Religious Hospitalers. He wrote immediately, telling the authorities that he had heard much good of these Sisters Hospitalers, and if they wanted them at Nantes they should send back the Daughters of Charity, and that this could be done without difficulty. After writing this letter he sent it unsealed to Mademoiselle le Gras, superior of the Daughters of Charity, for her information and to ask her to raise no difficulty about this withdrawal. "This was the way our Lord was treated while he was on earth. The spirit of Christianity demands that we enter into the sentiments of the neighbor, and God's glory will come from our doing so if we allow it to happen."[16]

---

15. Book One, ch. 46.
16. Dodin, *Supplément*, 171; this is cited from the second edition of Abelly, with many textual differences from that given here.

He said more to the person who brought the letter and message to Mademoiselle le Gras. He told him that one day one of the two Daughters of Charity who served the sick poor in one of the leading parishes of Paris, which he named, decided to marry, with the blessing of the pastor upon her promising to continue her service to the poor, just as she had done before as a Daughter. Without further ado, the pastor sent the other away to Mademoiselle le Gras. Monsieur Vincent advised her not to complain but to adore and bless God for his action. He assured her that all would work out for the best. This is what happened, for the new bride did not find in her marriage the same graces she had previously enjoyed, and soon left the service of the sick. The pastor was obliged to seek out Monsieur Vincent to ask for two other Daughters of Charity. He sent them and then said these beautiful words: "How much good can be accomplished if we are ready! If the Providence of God finds us responsive to his direction, things will succeed to his greater glory, the one thing we should aspire to."

Monsieur Vincent's detachment from exterior things and love of poverty appeared to an astonishing degree in a lawsuit regarding a farm which had been given to the community of Saint Lazare in return for a lifetime guarantee of income to the donor.[17] Monsieur Vincent had accepted it only at the strong insistence of the benefactor. Some time after several improvements had been made to the farm, the community of Saint Lazare was deprived of title to the farm, and with no recompense for all its improvements, amounting in all to some fifty thousand *livres*.

Monsieur Vincent announced this loss to the community. He told them that, soon after the decree of expulsion was handed down, a judge came to persuade him to appeal the order. He then commented:

> O my God, we must be careful not to do so. You, yourself, O Lord, pronounced this decree, and it shall remain irrevocable. We shall sacrifice this property to your divine Majesty. Gentlemen and my brothers, please let it be a sacrifice of praise. Let us thank this sovereign judge of the living and the dead for having visited us with tribulation. Let us give him thanks that he has not only withdrawn our attachment to earthly goods, but has taken away what we owned, and has given us the grace to accept this purification. I would like to believe that we all rejoice at this privation of a temporal good, for our Lord said in the Apocalypse *Ego, quos amo, castigo* ["Whomever is dear to me I reprove and chastise"].[18] Should we not love these trials as a mark of his affection? It is not enough

---

17. The farm at Orsigny, lost in 1658.
18. Rev 3:19.

to love them, we must rejoice. O my God, who will give us this grace? You are the source of all joy, and other than you there is no true joy. We ask you, therefore, for this grace. Yes, gentlemen, let us rejoice since it seems God has found us worthy to suffer this loss.

How is it possible to rejoice in sufferings, since they are by nature so unpleasant and we flee from them? It is like us when we take medicine which we know may be bitter, and even the best of them disturb us, but yet we take them, and why? Because we are hoping to be saved from an illness, or we seek a cure of one we already have. In the same way, afflictions which may be disagreeable to an individual or to the whole Company contribute to the welfare of a soul or a congregation. God purifies us with them like gold in the fire. Our Lord in the Garden of Olives suffered his agony and on the cross his terrible sufferings to such an extent that he seemed bereft of all human help and even abandoned by his Father. But even in this extremity, he rejoiced in fulfilling the will of his Father. Even though it was so painful, he preferred it to all the pleasures of the world. His Father's will was his food and his delight. My brothers, it ought to be our happiness too, to see his will accomplished in us by the humiliations, losses and troubles which arise. Saint Paul says: *Aspicientes in auctorem fidei et consummatorem Jesum, qui proposito sibi gaudio, sustinuit crucem, confusione contempta* ["Let us keep our eyes fixed on Jesus, who inspires and perfects our faith. For the sake of the joy which lay before him he endured the cross, heedless of its shame"].[19] The first Christians had the same sentiments, for the same apostle tells us: *Rapinam bonorum vestrorum cum gaudio suscepistis* ["You joyfully assented to the confiscation of your goods"].[20] Why should we not rejoice with them today in the loss of our property?

Oh, my brothers, how pleased God must be to see us gathered here to speak about this and to arouse this joy in ourselves. On the one hand we are made a spectacle to the world in the opprobrium and shame of this decree. In some way it labels us as unjust holders of the belongings of others: *Spectaculum facti sumus mundo et angelis et hominibus, opprobriis et tribulationibus spectaculum facti* ["We have become a spectacle to the universe, to angels and men alike because of our oppression and troubles"].[21] On the other hand, *Omne gaudium existimate, fratres mei, cum in tentationes varias incideritis* ["My

---

19. Heb 12:3.
20. Heb 10:34.
21. Based on 1 Cor 4:9.

brothers, count it pure joy when you are involved in every sort of trial"].[22] We must be convinced, my brothers, that our joy has come when we see ourselves fallen into various temptations and tribulations, judging that we have gained much more than we have lost. God has taken this farm from us, together with the satisfaction of owning it and the pleasure of going there on occasion. This innocent recreation, appealing to our senses, is a poisonous venom, a sharp blade, or a fire that burns and destroys. We have been saved from all that, by the mercy of God. By being more in need we have been thrown more completely on the Providence of God, and we have had to abandon ourselves completely to him for the necessities of life and for the grace of salvation. May it please God that this loss of temporal things be recompensed by an increase of confidence in his Providence, abandonment to his direction, a greater detachment from the things of earth, and a greater renunciation of our own selves. O my God! O my brothers! How happy should we be. I dare to hope from his paternal bounty, which does all for the best, that he will give us this grace.

What then are the fruits we should draw from this situation? The first is to offer to God all that remains of our goods and consolations, of body and of spirit. We must offer ourselves so completely, both individually and as a community, that he may dispose of us and of all we have according to his most holy will. We must be ready to leave all, to embrace inconveniences, abuses, and whatever afflictions might arise, and thus follow Jesus Christ in his poverty, humility, and patience.

The second effect is never to protest, no matter how right we may be. If we have to defend ourselves, let it be only after trying by all possible means to come to terms with our adversary, assuming our rights are clear and evident, for whoever trusts in human judgment is often deceived. We should practice the counsel of our Lord who said that we should also give our shirt to the one who demands our coat.[23] May God give the Company the grace to put this into practice. Let us hope that, if the Company is faithful in establishing this usage and firm in never departing from it, God will bless it, and that if anyone robs it on one side, God will give it back on the other.[24]

Many persons of great piety, experienced in these matters, had advised Monsieur Vincent both before and after the decree concerning the farm had been issued. They suggested that he file an appeal and assured him that the

---

22. James 1:2.
23. Matt 5:40.
24. *CED* XII:52-57.

judgment would almost certainly be favorable to him. The best they could get him to do was to consult in private a lawyer of the court who had been present for the original discussion of the case. After this consultation, he wrote the following letter to the late Monsieur Desbordes, Auditor of the Chamber of Accounts of Paris. He was a longtime friend of his Company and an honest and intelligent man. He also thought that an appeal should be made. This letter was written on December 22, 1658:

> Monsieur, we have sent our papers to Monsieur N. [Cousturier.] He has looked over them carefully, and believes that our appeal would be well received. He wishes to plead our case and promises that he will be successful. Although a thrifty man, he will take nothing for his services. He has even said that if we were to lose, he would recompense us in full for our loss.
>
> We have not been able to decide to follow this advice, (1) because the large number of lawyers we consulted together and separately before the decree all assured us of our secure rights, and there was nothing to fear. We consulted Messieurs Deffita and [Jean Marie] Lhoste, who looked into the matter exhaustively, the first because he was to represent us, and the second for having prepared our documents.[25] Both told us, as did Monsieur N. [Cousturier], that we were on secure ground. And yet, the court decided against us, as though we had stolen it. Opinions are so diverse, it is always dangerous to rely on the judgment of men.
>
> (2) One of our practices during a mission is to reconcile differences among the people. We must fear that if we appeal, a procedure used by all charlatans, God will withdraw his grace from us in working for reconciliations among the people.
>
> (3) We would give much scandal, after such a solemn decree, by attempting to overturn it. We would be blamed for being too attached to material things, a reproach often made against priests. We would cause gossip in the palace, do harm to other communities, and scandalize our friends.
>
> Lastly, Monsieur, to tell you the truth, I am filled with anxiety, as you can imagine, about going against the advice of our Lord, that those who follow him should not go to court to sue. If we have already done so, it was because in conscience I could not leave something legitimately given to the community, of which I am but the administrator, without doing all in my power to preserve it. Now that this obligation has been removed by a sovereign decree which has nullified my efforts, I think, Monsieur, we must leave it at that.

---

25. Monsieur Vincent often turned to these two lawyers for advice.

Monsieur, as you are so filled with Christian maxims, please consider all these reasons, and allow us to accept things as they are.[26]

This is how this true servant of God showed his entire detachment from the things of this world. He accepted the great loss of his property, and argued to convince his Company and his friends to accept the decision of the court, even though he was assured that he could easily win back the lost property by engaging the lawyer who was so sure that he could win the appeal. This man wanted to take on the case and argue it alone, guaranteeing that he would pay all costs, even paying for the property if he were not successful in reversing the decree against the Missionaries. It could be said that only Monsieur Vincent was capable of refusing this offer. He gave as his reason for refusing to appeal that the judges were honorable men and that if they had given such a faulty judgment he could not help thinking that God's Providence had so willed it, and he could do nothing better than to accept his holy will.

The procurator of Parlement, since deceased, who was involved with the affairs of the house at Saint Lazare, left a document in which he showed his admiration for such disinterestedness. He added that he had long admired the behavior of Monsieur Vincent in all other business matters of which he had knowledge. Monsieur Vincent always conducted himself without pressure or passion, either when acting in his own name as superior, or for the Congregation, no matter how much right he had on his side or how faulty the positions of his adversaries. On the contrary, no matter what advantage he had in court sentences or decrees, he was ever ready for compromise. He recalled several instances in which he had not carried out several judgments given in his favor which involved large sums. He gave as his reason that it would have caused the ruin of certain families. He delayed so long in carrying out these decrees, for fear of harming his opponents, that effectively he did nothing for his own advantage.

---

26. *CED* VII:404-07.

CHAPTER NINETEEN

His Mortification

"THERE IS NOTHING greater nor more elevated in the life of a Christian," says Saint Ambrose, "than to train the soul in the practice of virtue. To do so, the flesh must be mortified and reduced to submission, so that it will learn to obey and become accustomed to the direction of reason. Notwithstanding the effort and difficulty in carrying this out, the Christian must do so courageously. He should bring to fruition the good desires and holy resolutions he has conceived in his heart."[1]

With good reason the holy doctor spoke this way, for the Sage says "It is a glorious thing to follow the Lord."[2] The first thing that must be done to follow him, as Jesus Christ himself says in the Gospels, is to renounce oneself and to carry one's cross. A Christian ought to look upon self-denial and mortification as titles of nobility, and as a sign that he belongs to Jesus Christ and is in his band of followers. Monsieur Vincent always made a special profession of following this divine Savior and of walking in his footsteps, as we said in an earlier chapter.[3] There is no reason to doubt that he was clothed in the livery of the Savior, and bore in his body, following the expression of the apostle, the mortification of Jesus Christ. His life was practically a constant sacrifice of the body and every sense, of the soul and all its powers, and of all desires and movements of his heart. He spoke out of the abundance of this mortified heart as he addressed his community on the words of the Gospel, "If anyone would come after me, let him deny himself, and take up his cross."[4]

> This is the counsel given by our Lord to those who would follow him. He declared that the first step is to renounce themselves, then to carry the cross, and then to persevere in both for all time.
>
> We can well apply to this matter what our Lord said on another occasion: *Non omnes capiunt verbum istud* ["Not everyone can accept this teaching"].[5] There are few who give themselves truly to Jesus Christ to follow him under these conditions. Among the many who came to listen, nearly all abandoned him and went away

---

1. PL 16:76.
2. Sir 23:38.
3. Ch. 8, sect. 2.
4. Matt 16:24.
5. Matt 19:11.

because they were not prepared as the Savior had directed. They were not disposed as they should have been to mortify themselves and carry their cross.

For those who would wish to be disciples of this divine Master, they must renounce their own judgment, will, senses, passions, and so on. By judgment, we mean knowledge, intelligence, and reasoning. What an advantage for a Christian to submit his own lights and his reason for the love of God! What is this but to follow and imitate Jesus Christ, and to sacrifice one's own judgment? For example, if someone puts forth a question for discussion, each says what he thinks. To renounce yourself on this occasion is not to stay silent, but to be disposed to submit your judgment and reason to follow willingly the judgment of others in preference to your own.

Our Lord gave us the example of what it means to renounce one's own will during his whole life, up to his death. He was careful to do not his own will, but the will of his Father. He did always what he knew to be most agreeable to him. *Quae placita sunt ei, facio semper* ["I always do what pleases him"].[6] Oh, may it please God to give us the grace to remain always in the disposition of doing his will, obeying his commandments, the rules of our state of life, the orders of obedience, and thereby becoming true disciples of his Son. As long as we remain attached to our own will, we will never be properly disposed to follow him, to bear our sufferings, or to walk with him.

We therefore ought to mortify our senses and watch over them constantly to subject them to God. How dangerous curiosity is, to see and hear everything, and so turn our minds from God! How we should pray to God to give us the grace to renounce this curiosity, which caused the fall of our first parents.

We must renounce another passion which is strong in some. It is the immoderate desire of preserving our health, and to keep ourselves in top form. This causes them to do everything possible, and even the impossible, to preserve their health. This unregulated attention and fear of suffering any inconvenience, which we see in some, occupies all their thoughts. It directs them to the care of their wretched life, to the great detriment of the service of God. It deprives them of the liberty of following Jesus Christ. Oh, gentlemen and my brothers, we are disciples of this divine Savior, and yet we find we have become slaves. To what? To an item of health, to an imaginary remedy, to an infirmary where nothing is lacking, to

---

6. John 8:29.

a house of our taste, to a walk which will distract us, to a time of rest to satisfy our laziness. But some will say, a doctor has told me to cut down on my work, to take the air, to change location. O miserable and foolish one! Do nobles leave their domains because they feel indisposed? Does a bishop leave his diocese? A governor his palace? A tradesman his town? A merchant his shop? Do even kings do this? Rarely, and even then when they fall sick, they remain where they happen to be. The late king fell sick at Saint Germain en Laye, but stayed there four or five months until he died his truly Christian death, worthy of a most Christian king.[7]

On another occasion, he spoke on the same topic:

> Sensuality is found everywhere, not only in seeking the esteem of the world, in riches, and in pleasures, but even in our devotions, in the most saintly actions, and in books, pictures, and in a word, everywhere. O my Savior, give us the grace to rid ourselves of ourselves! Please give us the grace to hate ourselves, so that we may love you more perfectly, you who are the source of all virtue and perfection, and the mortal enemy of all sensuality. Give us the spirit of mortification, and the grace to resist the love of self which is the root of all our sensuality.[8]

Up to this point we have faithfully reported the words and thoughts of Monsieur Vincent and even more the affection and dispositions of his heart in regard to the virtue of mortification. It could rightly be said that this was one of the virtues he most constantly and universally practiced during his whole life, right up to his last breath. He certainly did not project an image of an extremely austere life. He judged that a life seemingly more ordinary would succeed better in the service of the people and the clergy to which God had called him. Such a life would also be closer to that of Jesus Christ and the holy apostles, after whom he sought to model himself and his missionaries. He felt obliged to give the example of a well ordered life, neither too free nor too strict, neither too lenient nor too rigorous. In private he treated himself more roughly, chastising his body in various ways and mortifying his interior faculties to have them both perfectly submissive to the will of God. His way of doing this was the more excellent and more holy in that it was concealed from the eyes of others. He made himself like the grain of wheat spoken of by Jesus Christ in the Gospel. It lies hidden in the earth, but finally sends forth its shoots, and produces its fruit in due season.

First, he mortified that love of honor and self-esteem which is so natural to everyone. It makes us hide anything which could cause the least lack of

---

7. *CED* XII:211-27.
8. *CED* XI:71.

regard from others. This holy priest resisted this natural inclination. He never allowed an occasion to pass when he could humble himself by speaking of his low birth and the poor status of his parents. He wrote to one of his priests in 1633:

> Oh, Monsieur, how happy we are to honor the poor lineage of our Lord by our own poor and wretched families. I spoke most happily just recently to one community that I was the son of a poor peasant, and to another that I had been a swineherd. Would you believe, Monsieur, that I might have taken vain satisfaction in so overcoming natural feelings? It is true, the devil is artful and clever, but whoever honors the poverty of the infant of Bethlehem and of his holy parents is even greater than he.[9]

Monsieur Vincent mortified his affection for his relatives. He was of a generous nature despite his tender affection for them, as he has told us himself, and he had sacrificed this affection as an offering to Jesus Christ. On this subject, he spoke once to his community on separation from relatives, as directed by this divine Savior for those who wished to follow him.

> Some who have gone back to their own region have become involved with the life of their family and its joys and sorrows. They have been trapped like flies caught in a spider's web, and have not been able to extricate themselves.
>
> I can use my own experience as witness to this truth. When I was still in service to the general of the galleys, and before the establishment of our Congregation, when the galleys were at Bordeaux, he sent me to give a mission to these poor convicts. I did so, with the help of some religious of the city of various orders, two to each galley. Before I left Paris for this trip I spoke to two of my friends. I told them I was going to my native region, but was not sure that I should visit my relatives. Both advised me to do so, telling me that my visit would be a consolation for them, and I could speak to them of God, and so forth. I hesitated because I had seen several good priests who had done wonders away from their native country, but I had noticed after a visit to their families that they returned completely changed. They became useless in their work because they were so taken up with the affairs of their relatives. They were preoccupied with that, whereas before they were not concerned with these matters but solely with what referred to the service of God, so distant is it from mere natural tendencies. I told my friends that I feared I would become too attached to my relatives after spending

---

9. *CED* I:206.

eight or ten days with them, even after speaking of the way to assure their own salvation, and to avoid covetousness, and to expect nothing from me. Should I have a treasury of gold and silver, I told them, I would not be able to give them anything, for a priest who has anything owes it to God and to the poor.

The day I left I felt the sadness of leaving my poor relatives so deeply that I wept all along the way, almost without stopping. These tears begot the thought of helping them, and making it possible for them to move to a better condition, to give this one something, another something else. I thought of what I could give of what I owned, and of what I did not possess. I say this to my own humiliation, because perhaps God allowed this to make me understand better the evangelical counsel of which we are speaking. I was three months in this state of agitation about helping my brothers and sisters. It weighed down my poor spirit.

When I came to my senses, I prayed God to deliver me from this temptation. I prayed so hard that he finally took pity on me and lifted this concern for my relatives, even though they were on the threshold of beggary, and still are. This gives me the grace to commend them to his Providence, and to recognize that they were happier than if they were well provided for.

I say this to the Company because there is something great in this practice recommended in the Gospel. It excluded from the number of the disciples of Jesus Christ all those who did not hate father and mother, brother and sister. In keeping with this, our rule exhorts us to renounce the uncontrolled affection for our relatives. Let us pray to God for them, and, if we can help them in charity, let us do so. But be careful of nature, which inclines us that way, and would turn us, if it could, from the school of Jesus Christ. Hold firm to this.[10]

A priest of the Congregation from Gascony went of his own accord to visit the relatives of Monsieur Vincent. On his return to Paris, he related how he had found them, and among other things said: "What simplicity, piety, and charity they showed, but they have nothing to live on except what they earn by their own labor." Monsieur Vincent replied to this, "Alas, are they not happy? Could they be better off than in the situation where they carry out the sentence pronounced by God that men should eat their bread in the sweat of their brow?"

Poverty was not the only virtue practiced by these good folk, for they were once defamed and denounced before a noted Parlement. Some friends of Monsieur Vincent urged him to intercede to stop the investigation. He

---

10. *CED* XII:218-20. The date of his return to Pouy was 1623.

answered: "Is it not reasonable, gentlemen, that justice be done to satisfy the justice of God? The punishments of offenders in this life will save them from the rigors of divine justice in the next." The judges later discovered that the accusations against his relatives were pure calumny and deceit. Monsieur Vincent, however, made himself the protector of the accusers, and was able to save them from the punishment they so richly deserved. This same priest said he had learned this in Monsieur Vincent's home town. Monsieur Vincent wrote a letter about these events:

> Only by a singular action of divine Providence were you defamed. God permitted this for his glory and for your good. For his glory, that you would be made like his Son, calumniated to the point of being called a seducer, ambitious, and possessed by the devil. This was allowed for your good, to satisfy the justice of God for any other sins you may have committed of which you may be unaware, but which are known to God.[11]

A relative of Monsieur Vincent, although he did not bear the same family name, was condemned to the galleys. He succeeded in obtaining the right to an appeal, through which he hoped to be restored to his legal rights against the designs of his accuser. He addressed letters to the Parlement of Paris hoping to profit from Monsieur Vincent's reputation, but this faithful servant of God wrote him several times advising him to omit several points in his appeal, so as to get a prompt hearing and decision in his case. He said:

> Would you dare to refuse this advice from so many persons trying to help you? I cannot believe it. Also, your age and circumstances will not allow you to support the long and costly trial of such a lengthy case. If you are building your hopes on my help, I must tell you that I can give none. I would rather contribute to your salvation in advising you to make some adjustments to better dispose yourself for death, than to see you squander all your resources in a long and dubious lawsuit. I hope you will think seriously of this.[12]

This man persisted in wanting to plead his case, but Monsieur Vincent continued to insist that he would not help him nor receive him into his house. He did nothing to relieve his poverty.

One of his nephews came to Paris in the hope of receiving some help to enable him to lead a life of greater ease. He was received cordially, but was given nothing when he was sent on his way, except ten *ecus*, for his trip on foot of about 180 leagues. Even then, Monsieur Vincent asked the Marquise de Maignelay for these ten *ecus*. It was the only help he gave to his relatives.

---

11. *CED* III:19.
12. *CED* V:433.

About 1650, the late Monsieur Du Fresne, a close friend of Monsieur Vincent of whom we spoke in Book One,[13] gave him a thousand francs for his relatives. He did not refuse this gift, but instead of spending the money on temporal things, preferring to see them earn their bread, he thought of using the money to further their salvation and spiritual advancement by missions to be given to them and to others of the region. The benefactor agreed to this.

He kept this money for two or three years, awaiting an opportunity to send some missionaries to the region. The rebellion of the nobles in 1652 affected the whole area, and Guienne was overrun by armies. His relatives were stripped of all they owned, and some among them even died from the depredations of the soldiers. Afterward, he heard of his relatives reduced to begging, but did not know why. After hearing this distressing news he did not complain. On the contrary he entertained sentiments of admiration and thanks toward the goodness of God for having inspired him not to spend the sum of money he had received years before, so he could now aid these people in their extreme need. He continued this praise of God over several weeks, thanking God for this special Providence.

However, since he did not want to allocate this money by himself, he consulted some members of the Company. Afterward he sent it by stage to Monsieur de Saint Martin, canon of Dax, leaving it to him to distribute the money as he saw fit. His only recommendation to his friend was to try to use the alms to help the people earn their living. He could, for example, buy a pair of oxen for a farmer, rebuild the house of one, clear a plot of land for another, or give tools and clothes to a third. He could not do much with so little, because so many of the poor had been abused.

This is the sum of all the wealth Monsieur Vincent gave to his relatives, although it would have been easy for him in his position to contribute much to them, in a worldly sense, if he had wished to use the available opportunities. He spoke to the rich and charitable persons who could help, about the needs of various provinces and of many families, but of his own region, and his own relatives, he said not a word. Must he not have been dead to the demands of flesh and blood to have acted this way?

In this connection, when he was once urged by one of his confreres to help his relatives known to be in need, he said: "Do you think I do not love my relatives? I indeed have the same sentiments of affection for them that anyone would have. My natural instinct is to help them, but I must act according to the movements of grace, and not those of nature. I should think of those poor persons who are even worse off, rather than of my friends and relatives."

---

13. Ch. 5.

Monsieur Vincent not only did not lift a finger to help any of his relatives out of their low status and poverty, but he also discouraged others from doing so. There were several well-placed people, even some bishops, who, out of consideration for him, wanted to help his nephews. They even wanted to have them raised to the clerical state or to some other honorable profession. He responded to these initiatives by saying, "We must be careful not to turn these children from the designs God has for them. It seems to me that it would be better to leave them in the condition of their fathers. Being a farmer is one of the most innocent and conducive to salvation."

He went further, for he often felt that he should establish the priests of his Congregation in his own native region to give the same services there as they gave in other parts of the kingdom. He feared, however, some trace of self-love in this, and some natural attraction toward his own. He examined himself then before God, and decided against it, saying to himself: "O miserable one, what are you thinking of? Should not all places be equally indifferent to you? Are not all souls equally worthy before God? Why then would you prefer one to another?"

Mortifying this desire, which he feared came more from a natural impulse than from an inspiration of grace, he resolved not to take a single step or say a single word in favor of such a foundation in his own region. We can judge from all we have said how much Monsieur Vincent mortified the natural love he had for his relatives and for his place of birth.

It is commonly said that from the movement of the hand of a clock it is easy to form an opinion about the mechanism of the timepiece. The control of the tongue equally gives a good indication of the condition of the soul. The passions and movements of the heart usually are the mainsprings of action, particularly of the words we use. Certainly, if we had no other proof of the interior mortification of Monsieur Vincent than this absolute control he had over his tongue, it would suffice to show us his having this virtue in a high degree. According to the word of the apostle James, "He who does not sin by his tongue may be called a perfect man."[14]

He had such mastery over this organ, which the same apostle called "ungovernable," that he never or seldom employed useless or superfluous words.[15] He never used those expressing slander, boasting, vanity, flattery, contempt, mockery, impatience, or other similar expressions of ill-controlled passions. He was so self-possessed that even in the heat of public talks, or in speaking to his own Company when he might not have prepared his remarks, he never said anything inconsiderate. When he thought of some-

---

14. James 3:2.
15. James 3:8.

thing unusual, he would often stop abruptly, as though recollecting himself, and considering before God if it would be expedient to say what he had in mind. He would then continue his talk, not according to the first inclination which came to him, but according to what he saw was most pleasing to God, and most conformable to the inspiration of his grace.

Sometimes a person would tell him something interesting or amusing but which he already knew. He would listen attentively, not giving any hint that he was already aware of what was being said. He did so as much to mortify that self-love that is quick to let others know we are already aware of what others have learned, as not to deprive the speaker of the satisfaction of relating something new.

On those occasions when he was blamed or even insulted, he restrained his tongue and imposed a rigorous silence upon himself. At those times nature moves us to justify ourselves to retaliate for an injury received. To imitate his divine Master he recollected himself, showing his strength in silence and patience, blessing in his heart him who cursed, and praying for the one who insulted him.

As head of his widespread congregation, he was responsible to see to all its needs. It often happened that he lacked what was necessary, to his constant concern. To add to his troubles, he would often receive news of serious losses to the property or farms of the Company. This would add to the burden he already carried, which normally would cause complaints and murmuring in the one responsible. In his case Monsieur Vincent would repress these first movements of impatience and so well mortify the feeling he may have had that he would remain admirably serene and in a spirit of thanksgiving for these serious and unforeseen accidents. He would say only, "God be blessed; God be blessed; we must submit to his good pleasure and accept what he is pleased to send us."

He showed how much he mortified his tongue and how well he controlled this member in the almost countless occasions when he could have spoken of his experiences in Tunis, and did not do so. It is natural to recount perils and accidents which one has survived, especially when these reflect on our ability or strength and tend to our praise. The marvelous truth is that in any situation in which he was, he was never heard to say a single word of his own captivity, or what he did or said to convert the one who held him in bondage, and who delivered him from the hands of the infidels.

Although he was obliged to speak often to his confreres about the Christian slaves held captive by the Moslems in Barbary to urge them to volunteer to go there, or to persons of means to contribute toward the relief and deliverance of the poor slaves, he never spoke of his own experiences or of what had happened to him there. This seemed to be because to do so would reflect favorably upon him and turn to his advantage. He willingly spoke of things humiliating to himself, but never of what directly or indirectly would tend to his own glorification. It is certain that he could not have achieved this mastery of his tongue if he had not first become the absolute master of his feelings and his interior movements by a constant practice of mortification. He regarded this virtue as being of such necessity, not only for perfection but for salvation itself, that he sometimes expressed it this way: "If a person already had one foot in heaven, but left off the practice of mortification for the time it takes to get the other foot there, he would be in danger of losing himself."

This is why he tried to inspire his confreres of the Company with a spirit of interior mortification. This is a stripping of all things and a detachment, a complete death, to the senses and the movements of nature, to all self-interest, to all self-love and self-seeking, to live only the life of the Spirit. He used to say:

> Hold firm, hold firm, against your own nature. If you give it an inch, it will take a mile. Hold it for certain that the measure of your advancement in the spiritual life depends on how much you progress in the virtue of mortification. It is particularly necessary for those who work for the salvation of souls. Preaching penance to others would be in vain, were we lacking in it ourselves, and did not let it appear in our actions and behavior.[16]

SECTION ONE

Continuation of the Same Topic

Concerning the exterior mortification of Monsieur Vincent, we can say truly that it equaled the interior, for he practiced it perfectly and almost without letup. He treated his body with great rigor until his extreme old age, even when quite sick. Besides the ordinary penances and mortifications which we will speak of shortly, he sought out all occasions when he could cause his body to suffer. We gave several examples in Book One, especially of his way of conducting himself during the trip he took in 1649, when he was more than seventy years of age.[17] The abstinences and vigils, the extreme

---

16. CED XI:70.
17. By modern reckoning, the saint was sixty-eight or sixty-nine. See Book One, ch. 39.

cold, and all the other inconveniences he was exposed to, caused a serious illness which finally caught up with him in Richelieu. On this subject he used to say that we must practice mortification in every situation, even holding the body in a posture that would be uncomfortable, provided, of course, that modesty was observed. We should deprive our senses of what might give them satisfaction, and should accept willingly the weather and temperature, whatever they were. He practiced this himself, glad to find any occasion of mortification. It was often noticed that, during the coldest days of winter, his hands were exposed to the cold. In time they showed the effects of this, and the other parts of his body shared in this mortification, for he wore the same shoes and clothes in winter as he did in the warmer seasons.

During the trials and extreme misery in Lorraine brought about by the wars, he often said, "This is the time of penance, for God afflicts his people. Should not we priests be at the foot of the altar, weeping for their sins? This is our obligation, but beyond this, should we not deny ourselves something we are used to, to come to their aid?" During the three or four years of this conflict he had the community of Saint Lazare served only brown bread. This was just like the time of the siege of Corbie at the beginning of the war between the French and Spanish crowns. He cut out one of the courses that had been served, and never re-established it later. He said, "Is it not right that we should cut back in some way, to sympathize with and participate in the public sufferings?"

He rescued a young woman from the danger of losing her virtue, and he supported her for two years and was resolved to continue this help if necessary. He told her that he would do all he could to help, but she would have to be careful not to offend God. However, at the end of this time she was seduced by some evil-minded persons and left her asylum. When Monsieur Vincent was told that she had fallen miserably, he said, "It seems to me that we have done all we could to prevent this unhappy result. It remains only to pray to God, and to do penance for her. Her situation must exact its toll of me!"

The infirmarian of the house at Saint Lazare had said that Monsieur Vincent suffered frequent sicknesses from the very beginning of the Company, even after it was established at Saint Lazare. Twice a year he suffered from the quartan fever, but he asked for no remedies, nor did he leave off his usual work.[18] Even though his legs were inflamed, he continued to take his trips on foot, until he had to travel on horseback because of his afflictions.

Either because of illness or some other cause, he often experienced extreme drowsiness, but rather than take a little rest he used the occasion to

---

18. A quartan fever is one which reoccurs approximately every seventy-two hours; here probably caused by malaria.

mortify himself. He stood or took some other posture, or did other violence to himself, to prevent his falling asleep. It was remarked that he never shortened his vigils because of his advanced age. He always arose at the usual hour even though he may have been the last to get to bed. He was among the first at church in the mornings, and would remain kneeling on the bare ground during the time of mental prayer, not using a pad. Ordinarily he would spend more than three hours in the church each morning, for his mental prayer and for his mass, including the time for the preparation and thanksgiving after, even during the coldest part of the year.

Perhaps he did not have too much reason to love his bed, for he slept on a bare cot without mattress, without curtains, and in a room without a fire. He did so for almost his entire life, even in his more serious illnesses, except for the last three or four years when he had to move to a room with a fireplace because of his bad legs. He was unhappy at the curtain put around his bed, but continued as before to sleep on the cot.

He was such an enemy of his own body that the late Cardinal de la Rochefoucauld once asked him to moderate his penances and austerities, to preserve his life for the good of the Church.

He observed the mortification of his senses almost continually and on every occasion. When he went into town or took a trip, instead of distracting himself with the view of the countryside or other interesting sights, he would ordinarily keep his eyes fixed on a crucifix he carried. Sometimes he kept them closed, to focus on God alone.

Once, going from one part of the house at Saint Lazare to another, he noticed some fireworks in the air, part of a public celebration of the city of Paris. His only response was to turn away, saying, "God be blessed."

He was never known to pick a flower, nor to keep one near him for its odor. On the other hand, when he went some place where there were foul odors, as in the hospital or in homes of the sick poor, his spirit of mortification rejoiced at the opportunity for self-denial.

Just as he used his tongue only to praise God, recommend virtue, combat vice, instruct, edify, or console the neighbor, so too he used his hearing only to attend to what excited one to the good, turning away from all else. As much as he could, he avoided hearing useless things, or listening to whatever might delight the ear but contribute nothing to the nourishment of the soul.

He was so mortified in his sense of taste that he never let it be known what sort of food was most acceptable to him. He seemed almost to regret having to take his meals. He did so only out of necessity, politely eating what was set before him in view of God and with much modesty. His example so influenced his confreres that several visitors of various ranks, who had been invited to the refectory, were much edified at the spirit of recollection, the great modesty and reserve, in what normally would be thought of as an occasion of dissipation.

He never left the table without having mortified himself in something, either in eating or drinking, just as he recommended to others. He was so little concerned at what he took for his nourishment that once, when he returned late from the city, and the cook had already retired, he was given by mistake two raw eggs with the mistaken notion that they had been cooked. He took them, seemingly not noticing their condition, and certainly did not complain or send them back to be cooked. This would never have been known if the following day the cook had not asked the brother who had remained to attend Monsieur Vincent if he had cooked the two eggs he had left for him. He responded that he had not, thinking they had already been prepared.

In his latter years he was urged to take some bouillon in the mornings. Once one of the priests was earnestly appealing to him to accept what he was presenting. "You tempt me, Monsieur. Is it not the demon who leads you to persuade me to feed this miserable body and this wretched carcass? Is it right to do so? May God pardon you for this."

After this time, however, he agreed to take each morning a certain bouillon made especially for him, not made with meat but with a bitter wild chicory and some oats, but without fat, butter, or oil. In a word, he paid so little attention to what he ate that it happened several times during the evening that he fainted from lack of food. On these occasions he was brought a bit of hard bread, because he wanted nothing else but what would meet his immediate need.

He hid the other austerities of exterior mortification as much as he could, but it was known that he was rigorous in the treatment of his body. The brother who tended him in his sickness found in his room hairshirts, bracelets and belts studded with copper points.[19] He kept them all hidden, but used them often. Each day upon rising he used the discipline. One of the Company with the room next to his, separated by thin walls, reported that he had done this for twelve years or so.

Besides this routine discipline, he used others on special occasions, as for example, when some disorder was reported to him about one of the houses of the Congregation. Because of this he used the discipline twice each night over the space of eight days. Only then did he work to remedy the situation, which fortunately was successfully resolved. Later he told a friend in confidence that he did this penance because his sins were the cause of the evil that had arisen. Therefore it was only right that he should be the one to do the penance for it.

---

19. Brother Louis Robineau.

We shall finish this chapter with his thoughts on the cross and mortification, expressed in a talk to his community:

> Our Lord so loved the state of affliction and of suffering that he wished to experience it. He became man to be able to suffer. All the saints embraced this same state, and those who had not received sicknesses from the Lord imposed afflictions upon themselves to punish themselves. As Saint Paul said of himself: *Castigo corpus meum, et in servitutem redigo*: I chastise my body and bring it into subjection.[20] This too is what we must do, we who are in perfect health. We must chastise ourselves and afflict ourselves because of the sins we have committed and the sins of the whole world against his divine Majesty. But what do you think? Man is so wretched and miserable that not only does he not chastise himself, he even complains of the maladies and afflictions which it has pleased God to send him, although these are for his own good.[21]

---

20. 1 Cor 9:7.
21. *CED* XII:30.

CHAPTER TWENTY

His Chastity

MONSIEUR VINCENT submitted his body to the mortification of Jesus Christ, so that, in the words of the holy apostle, the life of Jesus Christ might be in him.[1] He manifested this by a life of angelic purity and by his chastity, secure from all that might lead him astray, as was shown in his way of dealing with women of all ages. He conducted himself in a way that never gave the least cause for any calumny, but rather was always a matter of edification to all.

Since he was well aware of the necessity and the importance of this virtue especially for those who constantly worked for the spiritual good of their neighbors, as the missionaries of his Congregation did, he often gave advice about it.

> It is not enough for Missionaries to excel in this virtue. They must act in such a way that no one may be able to have the least suspicion that they have fallen into the opposite vice. This suspicion, even if not well founded, will harm their reputation. It would prejudice their success as Missionaries more than any other crime of which they might be falsely accused. We therefore must not be satisfied to use ordinary means to prevent these suspicions, but we must use extraordinary means if the occasion demands it. We should, for example, sometimes abstain from actions otherwise licit, good, and even holy, such as visiting the sick poor, when in the judgment of those who direct us, we would provide an opportunity by doing so for these suspicions to arise.[2]

A parish priest once asked Monsieur Vincent a question on this subject. It serves to show both his own naivete, and Monsieur Vincent's exactitude on this matter. The priest wanted to know if it was proper to feel the pulse of a sick girl or woman, to ascertain if she were on the point of dying, and thus ready to receive the last sacraments and the prayers for a departing soul. Monsieur Vincent replied:

> You should be on your guard in this matter. The evil spirit might well use this pretext to tempt both the living and the dying. The devil uses any weapon available for this last opportunity to harm a soul. Resist him firmly, even though bodily strength is fading. We

---

1. 2 Cor 4:10.
2. Common Rules 4,4.

should recall the example of the saint who when dying would not allow his own wife to touch him. He had separated from her by mutual consent, but said with the strength left to him, "Alas, there was still fire under the ashes." To ascertain if death is imminent, the surgeon or another person at the deathbed might be called upon, since they would be in less danger than yourself. The doctor might be asked what he thinks. Until his arrival on the scene, however, the priest should not touch the girl or woman for any reason whatsoever.

On this point he was a rigorist, even though he was understanding on all other matters.

He once wrote to a brother of the Congregation telling him to abstain from spending time with a female friend, even though his intentions were praiseworthy. "Even if these conversations are not bad in themselves, there will always be those who think they are. Besides, the way to preserve purity is to avoid any occasions which might stain it in any way."

Another brother experienced temptations against chastity because of what he saw during his comings and goings while tending to the business of the house. He thought that he could remedy this problem by leaving the Congregation and becoming a hermit. He wrote of his intention to Monsieur Vincent, only to receive this reply:

> On the one hand, your letter consoled me, seeing the candor with which you write. On the other hand, it caused me the same distress which Saint Bernard experienced when one of his religious, under the pretext of seeking greater discipline, wanted to leave his order to join another stricter one. The holy abbot pointed out to him that this desire was a temptation. The evil spirit wanted nothing better than this change to happen. He was well aware that if the monk could obtain this change, then a second change could be even easier, so that soon the person's life would be totally unsettled. And that's what happened.
>
> What I wish to say, my dear brother, is that if you are not chaste in the Congregation of the Mission, I can assure you that you will not be so anywhere else in the world. Be on your guard against the flightiness expressed in your wish to change. In this matter, after praying, the one thing necessary in all our needs, the remedy is to consider that no place on earth is free from temptation and the accompanying temptation of remedying the situation simply by changing one's location. After this consideration, reflect that God has called you to the Company where you now are. He has in all likelihood linked the grace of your salvation to it, and he may not

give it to you in some other place to which he has not called you. The second remedy against temptations of the flesh is to avoid meeting and even seeing the persons who disturb you. You should be open with your spiritual director, who will suggest other remedies. What I would advise, then, is to entrust yourself completely to the hands of our Lord, with the help of the immaculate virgin, his mother, to whom I often recommend your welfare.[3]

A pious woman once wrote an affectionate and tender letter to a friend who happened to be under the spiritual direction of Monsieur Vincent. He in turn sent it to Monsieur Vincent for his comments, which he gave as follows:

I would like to believe that the person who wrote to you so feelingly meant no evil. It must be said, however, that her letter could harm a heart not properly disposed or less strong than your own. May the Lord help you avoid the company of someone capable of unsettling your peace of soul, even slightly![4]

In keeping with this opinion, Monsieur Vincent included in his rule that his confreres should avoid speaking and writing in too affectionate terms to women and girls, even when it was a question of giving spiritual advice. He himself was very reserved on this point. He wrote and spoke well and respectfully to everyone, but never too softly and endearingly to women. What is more, he avoided the use of terms which, though perfectly proper, might conceivably lead to the least unworthy thought in the minds of those to whom he spoke. The very word "chastity" itself was too strong for him. He rarely used it, for fear of bringing the opposite vice to mind. He preferred to use the term "purity," which has a wider sense. If he was obliged to refer to or speak of a fallen woman or girl to bring about some improvement to an unhappy situation, he would ordinarily use another word than "woman" or "girl," such as "this poor creature." He would refer to her fall by more general expressions, like "her unhappiness" or "her weakness." In a word it is impossible to exaggerate his care to avoiding anything having even a shadow of impropriety about it.

His countenance reflected the modesty of his heart, and it so ruled his tongue that his words made it evident to all that the virtue of chastity was precious to him. This is why, in his rule, he included every imaginable precaution to preserve it. We have already referred to his mastery of his body by his arduous work and constant penances, by his practice of humility, and by his temperance in eating and drinking. He watered his wine so much that a person of piety, and very trustworthy, remarked that he was often

---

3. *CED* IV:592.
4. *CED* VI:348.

astonished to see an old man drink so little, even at the age of eighty or more.[5]

He was reserved in the use of all his senses, especially his sight, never looking around idly or curiously in an uncontrolled manner. He did not stare fixedly at women, or speak to them alone except within sight of others, with the door of the parlor open.

He would never visit the women of his assemblies [of the Ladies of Charity] in their homes without necessity, not even Mademoiselle Le Gras, superior of the Daughters of Charity which he had founded. This is what he wrote once on this matter when she lived in the village of La Chapelle, a quarter of a league from Paris:[6] "Should the need arise, I may soon come to see you at La Chapelle. If such a visit is necessary I ask you to tell me, if you please. Otherwise, I would prefer not to come, as we had agreed from the beginning of our association."[7] In another letter written at a time Mademoiselle had fallen ill, he wrote, "If you wish me to come to see you in your illness, please let me know. I have taken it as a rule not to visit, unless it is really necessary or useful."[8]

Sometimes he found it necessary to meet with this virtuous lady and with her spiritual daughters in his role as founder and spiritual father, especially during their annual retreat. He had to be asked in advance and urged, and even then he accepted as seldom as he could, and only often after a long delay. He always brought a companion along, and never allowed him to leave the room he was using while he talked with these women. During his conversation his companion would remain some distance apart, to insure the privacy of the interview. He always wanted to have witnesses present on these occasions when he spoke to women. This would assure that there would be no possibility of sin, and would as well put him beyond the evil suspicions of even the most small-minded persons. Even the best of men may have their reputations ruined by calumny. Even our Lord, although falsely accused of so many other crimes, did not allow himself to be accused of anything relating to his virginal purity, which shone as bright as the sun.

Once, Monsieur Vincent was counseling a family from Paris, in which the husband and wife were being divorced. The young and attractive wife was in a dangerous situation, living apart from her former husband. While speaking with her in the parlor at Saint Lazare, the brother in the room felt he ought to leave, to give them greater privacy. He left and closed the door behind him, but no sooner had he done so than Monsieur Vincent called him to have the door left ajar, which he did. He acted this same way on all occasions when he was obliged to speak to women.

---

5. Brother Louis Robineau.
6. She began residing at La Chapelle in 1636.
7. *CED* I:582.
8. *CED* I:584.

Once, he went to the city to speak to a woman separated from her husband, about some important affair that needed detailed discussion. He was surprised to find that the woman was not yet out of bed. He finished his business with her in a few words. This astonished his companion, but he understood perfectly that Monsieur Vincent had cut the conversation so short because she was still in bed, even though at the time he was more than seventy years of age.[9]

The affection he had for the virtue of chastity motivated him to help many girls and women to leave their sinful profession. First, by giving missions, he sought to take them away from the company of those who had led them into evil.

Second, in provinces ruined by war, he attempted to supply food and clothing to those tempted to lose their virtue because of the lack of these necessities. This was particularly true in Lorraine. He was able to bring to Paris some of these young women who were most susceptible of being abused by the soldiers. With the help of the Daughters of Charity these women were cared for and placed in the homes of respectable people.

Third, Monsieur Vincent used the good offices of Mademoiselle Pollalion, a member of the Ladies of Charity and under his spiritual direction, to help these young women. By her advice, service, and support, she succeeded in helping a large number to keep from perishing, such that her name became known all over Paris. One day this zealous lady brought one of these young girls to Monsieur Vincent. She was about fourteen or fifteen years of age and very beautiful. He said he was most grateful to God for having permitted her to be placed in a pious family and under the care of a charitable person who looked after her honor and her salvation. He hoped that she would be grateful and appreciate having such a place of refuge, and would make good use of this favor from God. He felt sure that our Lord would do the same for others, for he had so loved virgins that he allowed them to accompany him in his travels. He hoped that she would be happy to remember this.

Fourth, he used the good offices of his spiritual daughter, Mademoiselle Le Gras, to receive into her home some of those who had been solicited to evil, or who were in danger of falling. By her advice and spiritual retreats, she helped them re-establish themselves until they could be placed in more suitable surroundings.

We have seen elsewhere what Monsieur Vincent had done for the Daughters of Saint Madeleine.[10] A gentleman from Paris has reported that shortly before his death Monsieur Vincent had spoken of establishing a

---
9. Brother Louis Robineau, then serving as his secretary.
10. Book One, ch. 23, Book Two, ch. 7.

hospital in Paris especially for abandoned women and girls, particularly for those who had corrupted others. These men had spoken together several times about this project. Although Monsieur Vincent anticipated great difficulties in carrying out the project, he had begun to work out the details with some other devoted people. If he had lived longer, he might have been able to make it succeed, as he did with so many other enterprises he had undertaken. Since his death, his collaborators on the project have advanced it to the point that it is about ready to begin.

CHAPTER TWENTY-ONE

His Even Disposition

A N EVEN disposition is one of the surest marks, or better, one of the excellent fruits of mortification. Through mortification, a person acquires a mastery not only over exterior deportment but also over the interior movements of the soul. No matter what happens outside him, or what he feels within, nothing is able to disturb the person with this virtue. In the superior part of his soul he enjoys peace, and remains always in a quiet possession of himself. Whatever occurs, whether it be important business, or something someone might do or say, proves powerless to disturb his equanimity. The same serenity appears in his countenance, the same reserve in his actions and words, and no change occurs in the voice except in its tone. His heart, undisturbed in its peace, maintains the whole of his interior in a constant uniformity that is reflected in the exterior as well.

This small sketch, imperfect as it is, shows the state to which Monsieur Vincent had arrived, or rather to which he had been raised by the practice of all the virtues we have spoken of in the preceding chapters, especially mortification. This virtue seems to have won him a perfect control over all his passions. They seemed to have no influence over him, since his disposition remained ever the same. This was shown even in his face and in all his mannerisms.

The constancy and equanimity of spirit of Monsieur Vincent was remarkable, first in his style of life, always humble and marked by piety and charity. It was without episodes of youthful indiscretions, or laxity in the practice of virtue, even in the frailty of old age. He kept to this path in spiritual affairs, and he walked in the path of perfection in the footsteps of our Lord. He urged his confreres to remain faithful to the practice of the maxims of the Gospel and to the rules of their state in life. He himself was an outstanding exemplar of this in all places and at all times, in tribulations and in consolations, in health and in sickness, in great cold and in oppressive heat. He regarded everything as being the same in the sight of God. The same could be said of everything else he encountered in his life.

It was often remarked of him that, no matter how important and pressing the affairs he might be considering, when someone would interrupt him to speak with him, he would listen and respond with complete attention and a tranquil spirit. It seemed as though he had nothing else on his mind at the time. This, surely, was a mark of the calm with which his soul was possessed.

This appeared also in the way in which he persevered in the various enterprises he took up, in service to the poor, the instruction of the people, or the reform of the clerical state. He never turned back from what he had begun. He never left off one project to begin another. Of all the works he undertook, he left none of them before the appropriate moment. Rather, he sustained and supported them to the end with an evenness of disposition and a marvelous constancy. He did so despite contradictions, reverses, and persecution, which seemed to have the result of steeling his courage rather than weakening his resolution.

Even more admirable and rarer among mortals is that Monsieur Vincent preserved this evenness of disposition in each of the different responsibilities he held. For example, in the pervasive atmosphere of the court, scarcely any strong person remains uninfluenced. Yet, during his time as a counselor to Their Majesties, we find that the court did not affect Monsieur Vincent's spirit. He was as calm and reserved in the presence of an army of courtiers as he was among his own missionaries. He was as humble in conversation with the great as he was in speaking with the lowliest. During the several years that he was on the council, he omitted none of his usual practices of piety nor did he diminish the respect and affability he showed to everyone. A well-respected prelate who would visit him at Saint Lazare admired especially such a great humility in someone occupying such exalted and important responsibilities, and who besides was the superior general of a congregation and founder of several other companies. This prelate was led to say, "Monsieur Vincent is always Monsieur Vincent; that is, he is as humble, affable, and prompt to serve everyone as he was before being called to the court. He has falsified the proverb that says honors destroy virtue."

His composure was particularly apparent in the way he accepted the losses which he sometimes sustained of goods needed for the support of his Congregation and for the service of God. Several of his houses were supported by funds coming from royal enterprises, such as taxes, coach and carriage lines, and others as well. At times, news would reach him that these funds were being cut back by a quarter or a half, and sometimes even the whole yearly revenue would be stopped. During the wars, community farms were raided, horses and other animals stolen, and bad news would arrive of other losses or accidents. In all these situations his only words were: "God be blessed. We must submit to his will, and accept all it pleases him to send us." The greatest complaint ever heard from his lips was: "If God does not show us his mercy, perhaps we will have to hire ourselves out as assistants in the village parishes."

The loss of the farm spoken of in Chapter Eighteen gives us the opportunity to appreciate his evenness of disposition, for when the news was brought to him of this, the first words he said were, "Blessed be God." He repeated them five or six times, then went to the church to pray before the blessed sacrament. What shows his composure even more in this same loss is that he made no effort to reclaim it, even after eight of the most distinguished lawyers of the Parlement of Paris, who had been consulted on the matter, all agreed that the house of Saint Lazare had every right to the property in question.

Another episode which shows his composure was the way he received news of the sinking of the vessel sent out to Madagascar by the late Marshal de la Meilleraye. It carried several missionaries, together with sufficient clothes, furniture, and books to support them for several years. The missionaries were saved by the grace of God, but everything else perished. Despite these losses, his spirit was not shaken, nor did he lessen his resolve to support this great and important enterprise. On the contrary, it seemed that his courage was strengthened, for he sent another group of missionaries to the island, even larger than the group which had been shipwrecked.[1]

He evidenced this same evenness of disposition on the occasion of the loss of some valued confreres of the Congregation who succumbed to their labors in the service of God. When he received news of their deaths, he at first was visibly affected. He soon regained his composure, however, and he turned his mind to God, accepting with his usual equanimity this expression of the good pleasure of the divine Majesty.

This is what he wrote on one occasion to one of his priests:

> Are you aware of the heavy losses we have suffered? Oh, Monsieur, how great they are! Not only because of the number involved, ten or eleven, but because of the quality of those we have lost. They were all priests, and were among the best workers of our Company. They all died serving their neighbor in saintly and unusual circumstances. Of these, six fell victim to the plague in Genoa while serving those stricken, not to mention a brother who also died. The others gave up their earthly lives to bring eternal life to the inhabitants of the Hebrides and Madagascar. No doubt all these missionaries are now in heaven, since they were motivated by charity. Jesus Christ himself said no one has greater love than he who gives his life for the neighbor. May God be glorified, Monsieur, for the glory with which he has rewarded our brethren, as we believe, and may his holy will be the source of peace and calm for our saddened hearts. I do not speak of the sorrow with which we have received the sad reports which almost all came at the same

---

1. The shipwreck of November 2, 1656, off the port city of Nantes.

CHAPTER TWENTY-ONE 277

time. I could not express the depths of my sorrow. You who love the Company so tenderly know for yourself that we could hardly receive any worse news without being overwhelmed.²

These were his sentiments of regret at the deaths of his dear sons. Those who noticed his tender and calm tranquility say that it was admirable, and the source of much edification.

The even disposition of this man of God was shown on another occasion when great sorrow and great joy followed one another in rapid succession, but only those he told through necessity were aware of anything unusual happening. Near the end of 1659 he sent four priests and a brother to the missions of Madagascar. Arriving at Nantes, these missionaries found that the ship would leave from La Rochelle. Some traveled there by sea, others by land. Monsieur [Nicolas] Etienne, the superior, wanted to go by sea, and took the brother with him to look after some baggage they were taking to Madagascar. The ship on which they were traveling was buffeted for twelve or fifteen days, constantly in danger of capsizing. As it was, it had lost its mast, sails, and provisions, until finally the report reached Monsieur Vincent that it had sunk between Nantes and La Rochelle. Shortly after, this sad news was confirmed by two young men who had survived the sinking by escaping in a small boat when the ship ran aground on a sandbar. When they reached La Rochelle they reported that they had seen the ship founder. One of the two wrote to his mother, Madame Sauve, at Paris, and she in turn sent the letter to Monsieur Vincent.³

He had good reason to regret more than any other thing that could have happened, this loss of the superior of the group going to Madagascar. It caused him great sorrow. Far from giving way to regrets over this bad fortune or showing any other signs of sorrow, he even concealed this accident from the community. He gave strict orders to the three persons aware of the tragedy not to speak to anyone else about it. He wanted time to prepare his community for this sad news, as he did in lesser matters. This would allow the spirit of resignation to gain ascendancy over the natural movements of disordered nature in face of the trials of this life. He hoped to inculcate the same evenness of disposition in his confreres as he himself had.

He immediately spoke to another priest in private, and asked him to take the place of the one presumably dead. While the priest was at table, and Monsieur Vincent was writing a letter to the other priests still at La Rochelle to inform them of their new superior, a packet of letters was brought in. It contained two that appeared to be in the hand of Monsieur Etienne whom he believed already dead. He opened the letters to confirm by the signatures

---

2. *CED* VII:8-9.
3. See *CED* VIII:217-19.

that they were indeed from him, one sent from Bayonne and the other from Bordeaux. They told him that the ship in question had arrived at Saint Jean de Luz totally ruined, but that they had miraculously saved themselves. He and the brother with him were hastening to La Rochelle to arrive there before the ship sailed to Madagascar.[4]

Only God can know the consolation which this loving father received from these letters. He read them in the presence of his assistant and secretary, who were both aware of the matter. They now saw him pass suddenly from one extreme to the other, from a state of desolation to one of joy, yet with no external sign of any change either in his spirit or in his features. He simply thanked God, praised him and blessed him, in life as in death.

This is the way the will of God appealed to him, under whatever guise it assumed. He tried, in a multitude of ways, to teach his confreres, and in fact prescribed a rule on this point both for himself and for them, "Concerning all the things that befall us, such as afflictions or consolations, whether corporal or spiritual, we must receive them all equally as coming from the paternal hand of our Lord."[5]

In this spirit, in 1660, seven months before his death, he accepted the separation by death of his close companion, Monsieur Portail. He expressed his feelings in a letter to one of his priests:

> It has pleased God to call Monsieur Portail from us on the fourth of this month. He lived in fear of dying, but as death approached he accepted it with peace and resignation. He told me on several of my visits to him that he retained no trace of his previous fear. He died as he lived. He made good use of his sufferings in the practice of virtue, and had the desire of immolating himself in imitation of our Lord to accomplish the will of God. He was one of the two who first worked on the missions, and always contributed to the other undertakings of the Company to which he so generously gave of himself. We would have lost much in his passing were it not that God always works for the good, and we find our happiness even in what appears to be great evils. We must hope that this devoted servant of God will be more helpful to us in heaven than he was on earth. At the time of his death Mademoiselle Le Gras was also very ill. We were convinced she was going to die before him, but God preserved us from this double sorrow.[6]

We should remark that this double sorrow happened a month later, in the

---

4. Another departure of the missionaries was organized and took place January 25, 1660. This is the departure which Abelly places at the end of 1659. The ship on which these missionaries sailed was also wrecked off the Cape of Good Hope. See Book Two, ch. 1, sect. 9.
5. Common Rules 2,3.
6. *CED* VIII:248-49.

deaths of Mademoiselle le Gras, and a friend whom he esteemed, honored and loved deeply, Father de Chandenier. We are well aware Monsieur Vincent felt these losses keenly, but even so he never lost his tranquility of spirit or allowed any change to appear on his countenance.

He was able to bear with composure the loss of material things, and of persons most helpful for his Congregation, and even his own honor, his health, and his very life.

He was so self-possessed that when sharp words, injuries or calumny were used against him, as sometimes happened, he showed no agitation, but replied in his customary way with no trace of bitterness. This reaction on his part was particularly appreciated by some of those present on these occasions, who found themselves angered even though these remarks were not addressed to them.

One day during the second battle for Paris, returning from the city to Saint Lazare, he was arrested by the townspeople at the gate of the city. He had to dismount, then was insulted, and even threatened with death. He answered with his usual courtesy and moderation, unswayed by their threats. He was allowed to pass, and subsequently he solicited a pass from the duke of Orleans, which was readily accorded, allowing him to come and go freely.

He was in serious physical danger several times, particularly during a visit to Brittany. Twice he was in danger of drowning, and once in danger of assassination, but no change was seen in his disposition or even in his features.

No matter what pains he endured in his sicknesses, or how long certain annoyances lasted, or what reverses his projects experienced, he was never seen to appear to be disturbed or worried. He remained in a profound sense of peace and in an undisturbed frame of mind. The mildness of his speech and the serenity of his features testified to this. Some mistakenly believed that he had personally never suffered much, or even that he was insensitive. Yet he had only to be seen shortly before his death, so afflicted with various ills that he was watching himself dying, as he expressed it, but still with no discernible change in his exterior demeanor except for weakness and a gradual wasting away. He remained as always, seated in his chair, fully clothed, tending to the affairs of the community as was his custom. His spirit changed even less than his body, and remained calm and tranquil until the last moment. We can even entertain the doubt whether anyone's composure was ever more entire, more complete, more tested, or more consistent than that of this great servant of God.

CHAPTER TWENTY-TWO

His Fortitude in Supporting Good and Opposing Evil, and His Patience in Bearing Afflictions and Pain

THE GREAT apostle Paul understood well the strength and courage needed to remain constant and faithful in the love of his divine Master. He showed this when he had defied all that was most terrible and fearsome in nature: "Who then will be able to separate us from the love of Jesus Christ? Will tribulation, suffering, hunger, nakedness, dangers, persecutions or the sword?"[1] It is characteristic of this virtue to despise all that men fear the most. As Saint Ambrose says, "Fortitude joins in this irreconcilable war against all the vices. It makes us unbowed in our efforts, without fear in the midst of dangers. It rejects ease and comfort, and makes us unyielding in the face of all the world's allurements."[2]

Vincent de Paul always walked in the footsteps of this great apostle, whose name he was proud to bear. He became the perfect imitator of his virtues, particularly of this one, in which he excelled. Those who knew him best were well aware that neither promises, menaces, hopes, threats, nor calumnies could ever influence his firm resolve in the pursuit of good. He highly regarded everyone in authority over him. He paid great respect to their opinions, and he followed their wishes when he could do so with no harm to his conscience. When he saw that the interests of God, his service or his glory, were in question, or if he were being turned away from what God was asking of him, or if he were asked to do something contrary to the will of God, no consideration or persuasion could move him.

A virtuous priest wrote of him: "What constancy and fortitude he showed when it was a question of receiving affronts and injuries rather than agreeing to the least thing opposed to justice or right. While he served on the Council, he firmly opposed the designs of even the most powerful when they sought to obtain the goods of the Church or benefices by improper means, or for persons he deemed unqualified."

A highly placed magistrate of a sovereign court once met him on the street. He attempted to persuade him to do something in his personal interest which Monsieur Vincent did not believe to be right in the sight of God. He therefore excused himself as politely as he could, and could not be swayed, no matter how much he was urged. The judge became angry and spoke most

---

1. Rom 8:35.
2. PL 16:74-75.

unbecomingly to him, but Monsieur Vincent remained serene. He showed no emotion except to say, "Monsieur, I am convinced you try to do your duty as worthily as you possibly can. I must try to do the same in my position."

A highly placed lady once asked him to expedite the awarding of a benefice she had asked of the king for one of her sons. Feeling he could not in justice do this, Monsieur Vincent begged to be excused. This woman fell into a fit of anger. She told him that she knew how to get what she wanted in another way, and that she had been mistaken in giving him the honor of even asking him to help, and besides, he had no idea of the proper way to deal with ladies of quality. Monsieur Vincent had no other reply but to remain silent, suffering these abusive remarks rather than do anything he felt to be against his better judgment.

He acted the same way toward another lady who wished to involve him in a matter that he felt was unjust. He said in his usual modest way: "Madame, our rules and my conscience do not allow me to obey you in this. I therefore beseech you most humbly to excuse me." This lady, too, would not accept his refusal, and angrily heaped insults upon him, which he suffered with his usual patience and serenity.

He showed this same strength and fortitude in not allowing lay women to visit convents of religious of which he was the superior, when no legitimate reason existed for giving this permission. He even refused some princesses who strongly pressed their requests. When they saw they were making no impression upon him, they were upset. They called him rude and uncivil, and made their feelings known publicly. Several retained their resentment against him up to the time of his death, but still he was not to be shaken, nor was he willing to do anything he thought of as unjust.

In these encounters and others, he was victorious over all considerations of human respect, which sometimes demanded the greatest courage of him. The following episode was one in which he surpassed himself. As was said in a previous chapter,[3] he was always most grateful for everything done for him, and in appreciation he was disposed to do almost anything he could to express his grateful sentiments toward his benefactors. Among these, Monsieur Le Bon, prior of the priory of Saint Lazare, was in the first rank, and Monsieur Vincent always recognized his special obligation of gratitude to him. He had the kindest and most deferential attitude toward the prior, but a situation arose in which he was obliged to refuse something that the prior earnestly requested.

An abbess from a noble family had been imprisoned for some scandalous behavior by order of the queen regent, following the advice of Monsieur Vincent. The prior of Saint Lazare, who owed the abbess some favors, was

---

3. Ch. 17.

commissioned by her to secure her release. He set about doing this with all his power. This was ample since he held such influence over the mind of Monsieur Vincent in everything not contrary to the service of God. He asked and urged insistently that the abbess be released, pointing out that it could easily be done. Monsieur Vincent told him frankly that he could do this only by betraying his conscience, and therefore, begged most humbly to be excused.

The refusal greatly angered the prior, and he said, "Is this how you treat me, after I gave you this entire house? Is this how you thank me for all the good I have done for you, to help you and your Company?" Monsieur Vincent replied, "You have truly honored us and helped us greatly, and we certainly owe you the same duty as children do their father. Monsieur, please take all this back, since by your judgment we are so unworthy of your favors." At these words the prior fell silent and withdrew, greatly displeased. Nevertheless, several days later, he had become better informed than before about the scandalous conduct of this lady. He recognized the justice of the decision of Monsieur Vincent, and went to him. The prior fell to his knees before him, and Monsieur Vincent also knelt. The prior begged pardon for what he had said and asked him not to alter the penance prescribed for the abbess, seeing it was designed for her amendment, and said that he had been wrong in seeking to have her set at liberty. This is how the firmness of Monsieur Vincent was rewarded, and how God showed his approval of his stand.

We shall not repeat here what was said elsewhere about his fortitude and constancy in supporting the various works he began, notwithstanding the almost insurmountable obstacles standing in their way.[4] These would have discouraged others whose zeal had urged them to begin these enterprises. We saw how he supported the project of the foundlings when the Ladies of Charity of Paris were on the verge of giving up on it because the expenses seemed beyond their means. Happily he succeeded in speaking in their assembly so effectively and so filled with the spirit of God that he rekindled their fervor. He made them hope against hope itself. They decided to continue this good work at whatever cost, and continue to support it up to now.[5]

If this faithful servant of God showed such fortitude and constancy in supporting good and opposing evil, he also showed his patience when it pleased God to send him afflictions and crosses as assurances of his love. In the midst of the most violent tempests and severe storms of his times, this virtue of patience enabled him to preserve in his heart a calm and tranquility untroubled by any accident, however sad and discouraging. This same virtue

---

4. Book One, ch. 30.
5. Book Two, ch. 10.

by which he possessed his soul also made him master his feelings in the face of the pains, contradictions, and the crudest persecutions imaginable. It let him say not a word nor show the least trace of impatience or sign of a troubled spirit.

Once when he was on a trip in Brittany, he stopped in a small village at a poor little inn. He had no sooner closed his eyes in sleep after a hard day's travel than a group of peasants came to the inn to pass the night in revelry, in a place near his room. Several even came into his room, but he did not complain. On the contrary, the next day he expressed his satisfaction, thanking the innkeeper despite the noise of the previous evening, as if he had received the best treatment in the world. Besides, he distributed several beautiful Agnus Dei which he had been given a long time before.[6] The missionaries who accompanied him on this occasion, and who had looked after these objects, were surprised at this. He had never given any of them away in other places where he had been courteously received, where the children were well behaved, the servants efficient, and where he had taught catechism, but he did so to these poor people on this occasion. This led to the thought that Monsieur Vincent had done so because these people were truly poor, and had given him an opportunity to practice his patience.

On another occasion, he was cited to appear before a councillor of the Grand'Chambre of the Parlement of Paris since the community of Saint Lazare was being sued because of the complaints of a certain person. This man had a violent temper, and acted on this occasion with no respect for the magistrate, nor did he respect the place where he was. He spoke insults and atrocious calumnies against the honor and reputation of Monsieur Vincent. For his part Monsieur Vincent showed no emotion except pity for the man for behaving this way in the presence of the judge. The attorney of the community was present for this hearing. He wanted to speak in defense of Monsieur Vincent, but he restrained the attorney and excused the actions of the man as best he could. This same lawyer, a good man, spoke admiringly of these events and of such patience, which to him seemed extraordinary, for he had seldom witnessed anything like it. Those who knew Monsieur Vincent better realized this was his usual way of acting. They had often seen him endure affronts, insults, and calumnies with much peace and humility.

Monsieur Vincent showed his great patience not only on these great occasions when the spirit is usually most in command of itself, but also in those more frequent encounters of everyday life, in the eager requests, the indiscreet demands, the impertinent replies, and the other failings against

---

6. A devotional image of the Lamb of God, blessed by the pope, to which indulgences were attached.

him personally, either by inferiors or by others. In these situations he was never seen to give the least sign of impatience, nor even to raise his voice. In fact, on these occasions he acted and spoke with even more gentleness and serenity than usual.

When losses which were sometimes great occurred to the temporal goods of the Congregation, he accepted them not only patiently but even joyfully. It was once said to him that what was most serious about a large loss suffered by the community of Saint Lazare was the loss of reputation of the Company, and the opportunity it provided for some to speak ill of him. Monsieur Vincent replied that, on the contrary, this would be a good thing, for it would give him an opportunity to practice patience.

We should not be astonished if he was not filled with sadness at these unhappy events, for he spoke of being somewhat worried that God did not try the Company enough by afflictions. Once he spoke of this to the community:

> Recently I have often paused to think that the Company is not suffering. Its works are succeeding, and we are enjoying a certain prosperity. Let us say it better, God is blessing it in every way, and it feels neither reverses nor disappointments. I began to wonder at all this, knowing well that God tries those who serve him and chastises those whom he loves: *Quem enim diligit Dominus, castigat.*[7] I remember it is reported that while Saint Ambrose was on a trip he went into a certain house where the owner told him he did not even know the meaning of the word affliction. At once this holy prelate, enlightened by heaven, understood that this house, untried by any adversity, was destined for ruin. "Let us leave," he said, "for the anger of God will fall upon this house." And so it happened. No sooner were they outside than a clap of thunder flattened it, and killed all who lived there.
>
> On the other hand I see several congregations, particularly one of the greatest and holiest in the Church, being disturbed by trials. It is now very disturbed, and even at this moment is suffering a horrible persecution. I say to myself that this is how God deals with the saints, and how he would treat us if we ourselves were strong in virtue. Knowing our weaknesses, he supports us and feeds us on milk like little children. He makes everything we do succeed even if we have little to do with it. These considerations made me fear that we are not wholly agreeable to God nor worthy to suffer something for his love. He turns away any affliction from us which would test us as his true servants. Although we have had some

---
7. Heb 12:6.

shipwrecks when our missionaries set out for Madagascar, yet even then God looked after us. During the war in 1649 the soldiers caused us losses amounting to forty thousand *livres*, but this loss was not particular to us, for everyone felt the troubles of the times. Difficulties were everywhere, and we were treated just like everyone else.

Blessed be God, my brothers, for it has now pleased the adorable Providence of God to take away some of our property.[8] This is a major loss for the Company, very great indeed. We must adopt the sentiments of Job when he said: "God has given, and God has taken away. Blessed be the name of the Lord."[9] Do not look upon this as caused by human intervention. Rather, God has judged us, humbling us under the hand that strikes us, as David said, *Obmutui, et non aperui os meum, quoniam tu fecisti.* "I shall keep silence, Lord, for it is you who have done this."[10] Let us adore his justice, and realize that he has done this in his mercy. He has done so for our good: *Bene omnia fecit*, as Saint Mark says, "He has done all things well."[11]

In these perfect and elevated sentiments Monsieur Vincent endured not only the loss of his temporal possessions, but also the death of persons dear to him. He must have felt their loss keenly. In his soul, he persisted in this attitude even when he lost one of the older priests of the Congregation. He had had a special confidence in him, and considered him a pillar of the Company. At the same time he was also in danger of losing another who was ill. He wrote to one of his friends: "By the grace of God, my heart is at peace in the thought that what happens is according to God's good pleasure. Sometimes I fear that my sins may have caused these losses, but even then I recognize God's holy will, which I accept with all my heart."

One of the priests complained once of the difficulties he had in directing a house of the Company. Monsieur Vincent said:

Alas, Monsieur, would you prefer to have nothing to suffer? Would it not be better to be possessed by the devil than to have no cross to bear? Yes, for then the devil could cause no harm to happen to the soul. If you had nothing to suffer, neither your soul or body would be conformed to Jesus Christ in his suffering. But this conformity is a sign of our predestination. Do not be surprised at your troubles, since the Son of God has chosen them for your salvation.[12]

---

8. The farm at Orsigny.
9. Job 1:21.
10. Ps 39:10.
11. Mark 7:37. *CED XI:52-53.*
12. *CED* V:196.

He said to another person suffering in the cause of justice: "Is not your heart consoled to see that you have been found worthy before God to suffer in his service? Certainly you owe him special thanks, and you must ask him for the grace to make good use of these trials."

He once learned that an abbess was encountering many difficulties and opposition in her efforts to establish some sort of order in her abbey. He advised a priest to do what he could to encourage her in her efforts, and to tell her that the sufferings endured in creating any good work attract the graces needed to succeed in it.

Once, the devil raised up a storm against the missionaries to frustrate the success of a mission they were conducting. Monsieur Vincent wrote the superior:

> Blessed be God for the troubles he has been pleased to send you. On this occasion we must honor those same experiences of the Son of God while he was on earth. Oh, Monsieur, how great these must have been! Hatred for him and his teachings was so great that he was forbidden to go to certain places, and finally was put to death. He warned his disciples of this when he said that they would be mocked, scorned, and maltreated, and that parents would be set against their children, and children would persecute their parents. We must profit from these situations and sufferings, Monsieur, as did the holy apostles, and from the opposition that we encounter in the service of God. Instead, we must rejoice when these things happen, and make the same good use of them as the apostles did of their sufferings, following the example of their leader, our Lord. If you do so, be assured that the very means which the devil uses to defeat you will turn to his destruction. You will cause heaven to rejoice, and all the good folk on earth who will see or hear of your way of acting. Even those who now oppose you will finally come to bless you, recognizing you as an assistant in their salvation.
>
> How so? *Hoc genus daemoniorum non eijcitur nisi in oratione et patientia* ["This kind of demon you can drive out only by prayer and patience"].[13] Holy modesty and interior recollection as practiced in the Company may also be of help. It would be good to find out if you can what causes this aversion the people have for the missionaries, so we may avoid it in the future. We will do the very opposite, should it be appropriate. When you find out something, please let me know.[14]

He wrote to someone who complained about someone else:

---
13. Based on Mark 9:29.
14. *CED* I:226-27.

I can well believe that the person you mentioned has given you trouble, and I am sorry he has acted the way he has. You must not take what he does as coming from him, but rather as a trial sent by God to try your patience. This virtue will grow in you in the measure that you are naturally sensitive, and you have given far less offense than you have received. Show yourself a true child of Jesus Christ, who did not meditate in vain on his sufferings. Show that you have learned to conquer yourself in putting up with those things that provoke you the most.[15]

He wrote to another:

In short, Monsieur, we must go to God *per infamiam et bonam famam* ["spoken of well or ill"].[16] His divine bounty is merciful to us when he allows us to be blamed and to suffer public disgrace. I do not doubt that you have patiently accepted what has happened. If the glory of the world is nothing but smoke, the opposite is also true when it is accepted. I hope you will draw much good from this humiliation. May God give us the grace to do so, and send us many others, for by these trials we merit to be most pleasing to him.[17]

What confirmed Monsieur Vincent so strongly in this virtue of patience was his firm faith in two truths. First, even the worst ills which can happen to us come from God, for the prophet says: *Non est malum in civitate, quod non fecerit Dominus* ["If evil befalls a city, has not the Lord caused it?"][18] And second, God will never permit us to afflicted or tried beyond our strength. He will help us by his grace to use our trials for our profit and advantage, as the apostle tells us: *Fidelis Deus est, qui non patietur nos tentari supra id quod potestis, sed faciet etiam cum tentatione proventum, ut possitis sustinere* ["Besides, God keeps his promise. He will not let you be tested beyond your strength. Along with the test he will give you a way out of it."][19] Convinced of these truths, he said:

The state of affliction and pain is not an evil state, but one in which God enables us to practice the virtue of patience and to learn compassion for others. Our Lord experienced these sufferings. He is a high priest who has compassion on our infirmities, and he wished to encourage us by his example to practice this virtue of patience. [He added that] one of the surest signs that God has great plans for a person is when he sends desolation upon desolation, pain upon pain. The best time for a soul to progress spiritually is the time

---

15. *CED* IV:239-40.
16. 2 Cor 6:8.
17. *CED* V:229-30.
18. Amos 3:6.
19. 1 Cor 10:13.

of temptation and tribulation, for the way in which he receives these trials shows clearly what he will become. A single day of temptation enables us to acquire more merit than years of tranquility.

He said that "stagnant water, which has become putrid and infected with disease, is the image of a soul ever at peace. Souls tried by temptation are like rushing streams flowing over boulders and rocks. Their water is pure and refreshing."[20]

The extent of his virtue of patience gave him a special gift of communicating it to others, and to have them make good use of their sufferings. He wrote to a friend to console and strengthen her in her afflictions:

> I sympathize with you in your pains, which have lasted for such a long time. This is a cross which extends to your spirit and your body, but it raises you above the earth, which I rejoice in. You should be consoled to see yourself treated as our Lord was treated, and honored with the same marks by which he showed us his love. His sufferings were both interior and exterior, and beyond all comparison with those of others. But why do you think he tests you as he does? For the same reason that he himself willed to suffer, to cleanse you of your sins, and to communicate his virtue to you, so that the name of his Father should be sanctified in you.
>
> Remain in peace, then, and have confidence in his goodness. Never think in any other way. Be wary of your own feelings, and believe in what I say and in my knowledge of you, rather than in what you may think and feel. You have reason to rejoice in God, and to hope for everything from him because of our Lord who dwells in you. After his leading you to renounce yourself, I see nothing which should disturb you, not even sin. This is the only evil we should fear, for in the religious state you have embraced you do penance for the past, and for the future you have a great horror of everything which might displease God.[21]

---

20. Abelly added to the preceding paragraph this fragment borrowed from a repetition of prayer of 1645 on temptations; *CED XI:150*.
21. *CED* VIII:313-14. The original text reads: ". . . you do penance for the past, and you hate it too much for the future. . . ." His correspondent was a Visitation nun.

CHAPTER TWENTY-THREE

His Patience in Sickness

THE EVIL spirit knows well how weak our flesh is, and how sensitive we are to what affects our bodies whether in sorrows or sicknesses. The demon rightly said that we would willingly endure anything to escape the pains and illnesses which are the forerunners of death itself. After he had unsuccessfully attacked the patience of the patriarch Job by the loss of his possessions and his children, he promised himself victory if only God would allow him to attack him bodily by sickness and suffering. In this last and furious test, this holy man displayed his virtue to the fullest. He mastered this severe test, not only with patience, but with a perfect submission to the good pleasure of God. He blessed and praised God with an affection as great as his sorrows had been grievous and his pains severe.

We could truly say that this same test of sorrow and sickness gave the final touch to the patience of Monsieur Vincent, and crowned all his other virtues. He was robust in body and of a sound temperament, and his manner of life was so well ordered we might have expected that he would have a long life of perfect health. Nevertheless, God willed that he be tried by various frequent illnesses. Perhaps this came from what he suffered during his captivity among the Moslems, or from the violence he did to himself. Perhaps it came from the work and fatigues of the missions which he endured for many years, or lastly, from his constant worry about the great enterprises of charity and piety which were so often trying and difficult. From whatever cause, it is certain that this holy man, by a singular disposition of divine Providence, was nearly always in poor health, either with running sores on various parts of his body, or by the fevers he often experienced, or by falls or painful accidents which he suffered. The swelling and inflammation of his legs troubled him almost continually. Despite these painful ailments, he preserved a peace and serenity of spirit so great that he would have been thought to be healthy, if the evidence of his body were not so clear.

Writing once to a friend about his sufferings, he expressed his thoughts in this way:

> I hid my condition from you as best I could, and did not want you to know of my indisposition, for fear of saddening you. But, O Lord, how could we be more affectionate toward you than to share

with you the happiness of being visited in this way by God? May our Lord strengthen us to find our happiness in his good pleasure.[1]

Various members of his household, and some from elsewhere, saw him in some of his sicknesses. They were astonished at his patience and tranquility, especially in the face of the violent pains he suffered in his legs. His discharges which were so abundant that, despite his legs being bandaged, the floor was moistened by them. In this condition he could no longer rise from his chair or scarcely move. Though he was in constant pain and could not sleep day or night, not a single word of complaint passed his lips. His features retained the same gentleness and affability as he always showed in health, and he continually practiced a near heroic patience.

A virtuous priest who knew him well testified:

> The more he advanced in age, the more his body weakened. His afflictions increased so that he was no longer able to celebrate mass. Before this, it had been his joy and consolation. Because of his feebleness and sufferings, he had to remain in his chair, and even then he continued to receive a stream of visitors, both from within and from outside the house. He continued to direct the affairs of Saint Lazare and his entire Congregation. He responded to all his visitors with grace and a serenity of speech as if he were in good health and felt no pain. This affability and gentleness remained reflected in his features up to the time of his death.

One day one of his priests met him in his room when his inflamed and ulcerated legs were being treated. Seeing how painful they were, and moved with compassion, he said, "Oh, Monsieur, how terrible your sufferings are!" To this Monsieur Vincent replied, "What? You call terrible what comes from God, and what he sends to make a miserable sinner, such as I am, suffer? May God pardon you, Monsieur, for what you have just said, for this is not the language of Jesus Christ. Is it not just that the guilty should suffer, and are we not more guilty in the sight of God than we think?"

Another time this same priest remarked that it seemed that these painful conditions worsened each day. Monsieur Vincent replied: "It is true, from the soles of my feet to the top of my head I feel them getting worse. But alas, what account would I have to render before the tribunal of God I am soon to appear before, if I did not make good use of them?"

We must not be surprised if this great servant of God had such sentiments and spoke as he did of his grievous sufferings. He had long worked at acquiring the virtue of patience, and had filled his heart and mind with the perfect maxims of this virtue. He was disposed to practice it on all occasions,

---

1. *CED* VIII:427.

but especially in his illnesses. In this connection, he wrote the following to one of his confreres who was ill:

> Sickness truly reveals who we are much better than health does. In the midst of sufferings, impatience and melancholy tempt even the most resolute. But since only the weak fail, you need have no fear, for you have profited by these attacks. Our Lord has strengthened you in the practice of accepting his good pleasure, and this appears in your resolution so courageously to resist impatience and discouragement. I hope it will be seen even more clearly in your accepting your sufferings for the love of God, not simply with patience, but with joy and gaiety.[2]

He spoke once to the community on this same subject:

> It must be said that sickness is a grievous trial, almost insupportable to human nature. It is, however, one of the most powerful means God uses to recall us to our duty. It detaches us from our affection for sin, and fills us with his gifts and graces. O Savior, you suffered so much and died to redeem us. You showed us in this that sufferings can be used to glorify God and to sanctify us. Please grant us a knowledge of the great good and treasure hidden in sickness. It is in this, gentlemen, that souls are purified, and those who are weak in virtue have an opportunity to acquire it. It is not possible to find any situation so suited for practicing virtue. In sickness, faith is marvelously exercised, hope is enkindled, resignation, love of God, and all the virtues are encouraged. In sickness we discover who and what we are. Sickness is the measuring rod to tell each of us most assuredly what our virtues are, whether we have many, few, or none at all. We can never come to know just what is in a man any better than by sickness. This is the test to find out who is the most virtuous, and those who are not.
>
> All this shows us how important it is to understand fully how we must act in sickness. If we accept it as a true servant of God, our sickbed becomes a throne of mercy and of glory. A true Christian surrounds himself with the mysteries of our holy religion. Above the bed is the symbol of the most blessed Trinity; at the head, the incarnation; on one side the circumcision of our Lord; on the other, the blessed sacrament; at the foot, the crucifixion. No matter which way he turns, to the right or to the left, or raises his eyes or lowers them, he sees himself surrounded by these divine mysteries, and finds God everywhere he turns. What a beautiful picture, gentle-

---

2. *CED* II:571.

men, what a beautiful picture! If God gives us the grace to act so, how happy we will be!

We have reason to praise God for his goodness and mercy if we have infirm and sick members in the Company. In their weakness and sufferings they have the opportunity to exercise patience and all the virtues. I have said it many times before, and will say it again: we should regard those in the Company who are sick as those who bring down the blessings of God upon it.

We must think of our illnesses and afflictions as coming from God. Death, life, health, all these come by order of his Providence. Whatever they may seem to be, they are always for the good and for the salvation of a person. However, some bear their sufferings with much impatience, and this is a great fault. Others want to move about, to go here or there, to this house or to that province, back to their native place, all under the pretext that there the air would suit them better. What do you think of that? These are people attached to themselves, effeminate souls, persons who want to suffer nothing as though bodily ills were evils they must flee at all costs. Yet to run from the state God wills for us to is to run from one's happiness. Yes, suffering is a state of happiness and of the sanctification of souls.[3]

I know a man named Brother Antoine.[4] His portrait hangs in our hall. He could neither read nor write, yet he had the spirit of God in its fullness. He called everyone his brother, or a woman, his sister. Even when he spoke to the queen, he spoke to her as to his sister. Everyone wanted to see him. Once he was asked, "My brother, how do you accept the illnesses that happen? How do you manage? How do you make good use of them?" He replied that he received them as sent by God to test him: "For example, if a fever occurs, I say, My sister the fever, or my sister the sickness, you come from the hands of God. Welcome! And then I strive to fulfill God's will in myself."

There, gentlemen and my brothers, is how he used them. This is the way the servants of Jesus Christ use these things, those who are true lovers of his cross. This does not prevent them from using the medicines we have to cure each sickness, for this, too, honors God. He has, after all, given each plant its properties to bring about healing. All the same, to be too solicitous for oneself, to be too sensitive to the least suffering that comes our way, this we must avoid. Yes, we must avoid this delicate care of ourselves.[5]

---

3. *CED* XI:72-74.
4. Antoine Flandin Maillet, 1590-1629, was widely known for his sanctity.
5. *CED* XII:32-33.

CHAPTER TWENTY-FOUR

The Leadership Style of Monsieur Vincent

THE LEADERSHIP style of Monsieur Vincent has become evident in this book on his life and virtues, and his words and writings show with what rectitude and sanctity he directed all his steps. Nevertheless these items have been spread throughout this work. We have thought it best, for the edification and satisfaction of the Christian reader, to gather together what would be most appropriate in a single chapter.

In the first place, if we consider the end he proposed either for himself or others, it was always to act for the greater glory of God, and to accomplish his most holy will. This was the sole end this good servant of God proposed to himself in all his plans and enterprises. This goal dominated his thoughts, his desires, and his intentions. He strove to bring others to this same view, by his advice, counsel, exhortations, and by every spiritual and temporal help he could manage. He strove for nothing but that God's name be blessed, his kingdom advanced, and his will accomplished on earth as it is in heaven. This is the way he looked at things, and the way he strove to act throughout his life.

To achieve this, his main and nearly universal method was to conform himself entirely to the example of Jesus Christ. He knew very well that he could not walk nor lead others on a surer path than that traveled by the Word and Wisdom of God. He had engraved his words and actions upon his own mind, modeling himself in all he did and said upon the prototype of all virtue and sanctity. His holy Gospel was etched in his heart. He carried it in his hand like a great light, so he could say with the prophet: "Your word, O Lord, is like a lamp unto my feet, to enlighten my path which leads to you."[1]

Walking then in this clear divine light, he strove with the help of grace primarily for his own salvation and perfection, in imitating the virtues of his divine Master. He had learned from the Gospel that it profits us nothing if we gain the whole world but lose our own soul. He knew the truth that the proper measure for the love we must have for our neighbor is the love we have for ourselves.

After this fundamental concern for his own salvation and perfection, he next thought that he could best conform himself to his divine Savior by devoting himself entirely to the service of others. He wished to help them

---
1. Ps 119:105.

attain salvation and the sanctification of their souls, redeemed by the Savior's blood and death. He spared neither time nor effort, nor his very life, in the various works of charity of which we have spoken at length in the three parts of this work. He gave himself in such a holy and perfect manner that it was evident that this came from God, with the Holy Spirit as the true source and director of his soul. This will appear more clearly when we examine the excellent qualities and properties of his leadership.

In the first place, his leadership was always marked by a great humility, Monsieur Vincent's first and most faithful adviser. Although he had a clear and capable mind, he always mistrusted his own thoughts. He turned to God in every situation to ask for his light and help. Then he would seek the advice of others, even of his inferiors, and he advised his confreres to act in the same way.

One day he wrote to the superior of one of the houses of the Congregation on this topic:

> It is not a fault to seek the advice of others. On the contrary, it is helpful, and sometimes even necessary to do so when the matter is important, or when we are not well informed about it. In temporal affairs, we take the advice of lawyers or other knowledgeable persons. In matters concerning the house, the appointed officers are consulted, or even other members of the community, when this is judged useful. As for myself, I often ask the brothers, and take their advice in matters pertaining to their work. When this is done with the necessary precautions, the authority of God which resides in the superior is not compromised. Because of the good order that results, his authority is even more respected and loved. Please act accordingly, but remember that when it is a question of changes of personnel or of other major matters, the superior general should be consulted.[2]

He wrote in another letter to urge a superior to act similarly:

> Live together cordially and simply, in such a way that in seeing you together, it could not be guessed who the superior was. Do not take any action, in anything important, without taking their advice, especially that of your assistant. As for myself, when I have to make some difficult decision affecting spiritual things or on matters having to do with priests, I gather the community to ask their advice. If it is a case of temporal affairs, I consult with those in charge of the department concerned. I ask the advice of the brothers in charge of various parts of the house because they know their business. This helps the superior decide, and God will bless the steps he takes after

---

2. *CED* IV:35-36.

this consultation. This is why I beg of you to act this way yourself, to be more successful in your office.³

After consulting and carefully weighing what had been said, he was firm and consistent in carrying out the decisions which had been reached. He would not listen to any contrary thoughts which might come to his mind. He wrote to one of the superiors, in a letter on this topic:

> Once we have commended something to God, and taken counsel, we should remain firm in what we have decided, rejecting as a temptation all thought to the contrary. We must have confidence that God will not blame us, for we have a ready-made excuse: "Lord, I have referred the matter to you, and have taken counsel. This is all I could possibly do to determine your will."

The example of Pope Clement VIII illustrates this point. A matter of great importance had been brought to him, dealing with an entire kingdom.⁴ An entire year passed before he was ready to give an answer to the delegates sent to him. He prayed to God about the matter, and consulted with learned men in whom he had much confidence. At length, he decided in favor of the Church. However, he later had a dream in which our Lord appeared with a severe countenance, reproaching him for what he had done, and threatening to punish him. When he awoke, shaken by this sight, he mentioned the dream to Cardinal de Toledo.⁵ He prayerfully considered it, and finally told the pope that he felt he should not pay any attention to it, for it was an illusion of the devil. He had no reason to fear, for he had prayed and taken counsel. That is all anyone could do. This good pope accepted this advice, and no longer worried about it.⁶

Although Monsieur Vincent sought insight and advice from others, he did not then consider himself dispensed from using all possible attention and vigilance to work against the evil and obtain the good of those under his direction. He was ever alert to what was going on among his confreres, to be aware of what was likely to be asked of them. He acted with much prudence and circumspection, a characteristic of leadership in which he excelled. All who knew him realized how careful and considerate he was in what he said and did, especially when it had to do with directing others, or when it was a question of being obliged to give his advice on some matter. He was so reserved and circumspect in his words that he almost never gave an absolute opinion. He would state his thoughts simply, as though in some

---

3. *CED* VI:66.
4. The issue was the abjuration of Henry IV and his accession to the French throne.
5. Francisco de Toledo, created cardinal by Clement VIII in 1593; he died in 1596.
6. *CED* V:318.

way accepting the judgment of those who sought his advice. He would say, "It seems to me that this might be looked at in this way," or, "Perhaps it would be well to do this or that," or, "If you decide to do so, perhaps God will bless it," or other similar ways of speaking. He used these expressions, avoiding more forceful or categorical ways of speaking, and a manner of expressing himself that would convey his wisdom or the prudence of having sought his advice. He said nothing absolutely, "I advise you to do so and so," or rarely, "It is my advice that . . ."; he would prefer to say, simply, "There is my thought," or, "That's the way it seems to me." However, when it was a matter clearly contained in the Gospels, he did not hesitate. He took his stand absolutely with this oracle of truth.

He held it as a principle that any advice given too quickly was an expression of one's own personal judgment rather than the inspiration of the Holy Spirit, whom he preferred to consult before responding. Occasionally he was pressed to give his opinion in certain important matters which did not allow any delay. Rarely would he do so in some important cases, but even then he would not answer until he had raised his mind to God and asked his light and help. Otherwise, he would base his answer on some passage of holy Scripture, or on some action of the Son of God that had a bearing on the matter under discussion.

Once, needing to make a recommendation on a capable candidate to become consul in Tunis in Barbary, he thought of Monsieur Husson, a lawyer of the Parlement of Paris, who then lived in Montmirail, a town in Brie. He had all the qualities necessary for the post. He wrote to the lawyer, expressing his thoughts for and against the appointment, but left him at liberty to accept the appointment or not.

The lawyer wrote a letter which spoke of his uncertainty.

> To come to know what God wished of me, I went to see Monsieur Vincent. My concern was that I might be leaving Montmirail too readily, or perhaps staying out of stubbornness. To avoid either of these pitfalls, I felt I must ascertain just what God wanted of me. I saw Monsieur Vincent to clear up the uncertainty, but he at first strongly urged me to seek advice elsewhere. I insisted that I would speak only with him. Finally, on Easter Sunday, 1653, he said, "In the mass I have just said, I have offered to the Lord your doubts, pains, and tears. Immediately after the consecration I threw myself at his feet, asking him to inspire me. Then I thought about what at the hour of my death would I have wished I had done. It seemed to me that if I were to have died at that very moment I would have been happy to see you go to Tunis, because of all the good you can do there. On the other hand, I felt that I would have been very sorry

if I had dissuaded you from going. That's what I think. You can go or not go, just as you think best."

I must say this advice showed me things as clearly as if God spoke to me as I believe he did through Monsieur Vincent. He showed himself to be little attached to his own opinion and to the advice he had given, and gave it only at my strong insistence.

He did not want to choose the missionaries to work in foreign lands by himself. He considered only those who had some time before, by an interior disposition and movement from God, told him of their desire to serve on foreign shores, and who had even asked him more than once for this assignment. He felt that a man called by God was likely to be more successful than many others who did not have a true calling to this work.

To the prudence and circumspection he exercised in his leadership, he joined strength and firmness to maintain regularity and punctuality. He used to say that those in charge of others ought to be firm in maintaining the observances, and be on their guard lest they be the cause of the laxity of the community by their own lack of firmness or exactitude. Among all the things that might hurt a community, nothing is more dangerous than that a community be governed by a superior who is too soft, who wants to please others, and who seeks to be loved. He added the thought that just as a poor showing in a war is ordinarily laid at the feet of the general of the army, so the failings of a religious community can usually be attributed to the superior. By contrast, a happy community is largely the result of a good leader. He referred to the example of a very regular community which, in the space of four years, fell into disarray because of the lack of concern and laziness of the superior. He ended by these words: "Since so much depends on them, we certainly should pray for them often. They are charged with and responsible for all those under their care."

On one occasion there was a community house composed of people of different dispositions. One group was composed of those less observant of the regulations, and the other was more exact and virtuous. Monsieur Vincent wrote to the superior, who had complained of the matter:

> I am upset, and with good reason, at the conduct of the priest and brother of whom you wrote. May God give them the grace to see the dangerous position they are in by following the impulses of rebellious human nature. This is not at all in accord with the spirit of Jesus Christ. How difficult it is for those who fall, (as Scripture tells us) after they have once been enlightened, to be saved! Certainly they have reason to fear an unhappy end if they leave the path God has traced out for them. How can they hope to succeed in the world if they are not called to live there, if they are not helped by

the grace of God and by all the spiritual and temporal helps they will lack, if they are not in their proper calling? We should never be surprised at seeing people changing and leaving, for it happens even in the holiest of companies. God permits it to show us the misery of the human condition, and to warn even the firmest and most resolute. God tries the good and gives them the opportunity to practice the various virtues.

You spoke to me of the two discontented confreres who are disturbed by the observances of Fathers N. [Toussaint Lebas] and N. [Julien Dolivet], which weigh on the others. I can easily believe it about those who are less regular and less interested in their own personal advancement and in that of the community. Yes, Monsieur, zeal and exactitude are troublesome for those lacking these qualities, for the virtue of the one group condemns the laxity of the other. I admit that virtue has two closely associated vices, defect and excess. Of the two, excess is more praiseworthy than defect and should be the more encouraged. These two good Missionaries practice virtue to a degree the others cannot attain, and so the others imagine it is an excess, but it is not so before God. They blame their way of acting because they lack the courage to imitate them. May God give us the grace to see good, in our Lord, in all that is not really evil.[7]

Again, he wrote to one of his priests on a mission:

You are in charge of your companions. I pray that our Lord will give you some share of his spirit and his guidance. Undertake this obligation in this spirit. Honor the prudence, the foresight, the meekness, and the exactitude of our Lord. You will be doing much if you succeed in having the regulations well observed, for this will attract the blessings of God upon all the rest. Begin by keeping to the exact times of retiring and rising, to mental prayer, to the divine office, and to the other exercises. Oh, Monsieur, how rich a treasure is this habitual observance, while the opposite causes no end of trouble! Why is it such a hardship to fulfill your duty in this, when we see people of the world generally keeping such a tight schedule? We rarely see the court officials late in rising or failing to show up when expected. Much less the shopkeepers, who are so regular in opening and closing their businesses. It seems that only we clergy, such lovers of our ease, do things guided solely by our personal inclinations.

Monsieur Vincent extended his concern that the rules be observed beyond

---

7. *CED* VIII:28-29.

the houses of the Congregation and the missions where they worked. As many of the priests can testify, he wanted them to observe the rule as much as possible even while traveling. We will give here but one example, from a priest who wrote as follows:

> After I received an appointment from Monsieur Vincent to go to a remote province in the company of another priest of the Congregation, he received the two of us in his room on the eve of our departure. He told us what he expected of us during our trip, which would take eleven or twelve days. We were to travel with the stage to Toulouse, together with many different kinds of people. Among many other things, he had four main recommendations: (1) never to omit making our mental prayer, even if we had to make it on horseback; (2) to celebrate mass every day, if possible; (3) to mortify our eyes, especially in the towns, and practice sobriety in eating and drinking among lay people; (4) to present catechism lessons to the servants in the inns, and especially to the poor.[8]

Although he was exact even in the smallest details of the rule, and firm in maintaining this among his confreres, this was always accompanied with a mild grace. In this he imitated God himself, for as the wise man of Scripture says, "Indeed she reaches from end to end mightily and governs all things well."[9] The superior of one of the houses of the Congregation spoke of this in the following testimonial:

> Monsieur Vincent was exact and severe on himself, but was full of meekness and charity toward others. He did everything for them that could be expected. Once he reluctantly refused permission for me to go to the city. Although I sought no reason for this refusal but accepted his decision as my guide, he explained that since several others had already gone, he wanted me to be on hand in the house for whatever might turn up. The next day he called me, thinking that he may have hurt my feelings by his refusal, telling me to go wherever I wished in the city. This was the way he usually acted. He did not give orders to impress you with his position or authority. He would say something like, "Monsieur, or brother, would you please do this or that."

His custom was to invite to his room on the eve of their departure those setting out for a mission. He would speak to them as a true father, and upon their return he would receive them with open arms and with warm affection. This is what one said, and it surely could be echoed by all the others:

> I cannot admire enough the charity and goodness of his great

---

8. *CED* XI:95.
9. Wis 8:1.

heart. When I was leaving or returning from a trip, the cordial reception he gave me overwhelmed me. His words were so filled with spiritual grace, so gracious and yet so efficacious that they accomplished what he had in mind, with no sense of pressure or constraint.

When he was obliged to refuse something, he preferred that his confreres would surmise as much, without obliging him to refuse outright for fear of giving pain. When someone pressed him to agree to something he did not think proper, he replied, "Would you be good enough to remind me of this some other time?"

Once he wrote to someone who felt the loss of a person working with him: "I have no doubt that the loss of this dear companion and friend is most painful. But remember, Monsieur, that our Lord left his mother. Also, the disciples who had been so united by the gift of the Holy Spirit, separated from one another to serve their divine Master."[10]

Another superior complained to him of the vexations he experienced in his position, from people within and outside the community. He wrote to him, as follows:

> I sympathize with you in your troubles, but you should not be surprised by them, or much less let them discourage you. We meet troubles everywhere. Two people living together will find enough to bother them. Were you to live alone, you would find difficulties with yourself, enough to try your patience. So it is that our miserable life is filled with crosses. I bless God for the good use you make of yours, as I am sure you do. I have too long recognized the wisdom and meekness of your disposition for me to doubt that you will fail in these unhappy situations. If you cannot please everyone, you should not let that bother you, for even our Lord could not please everybody. How many there were then, and still are today, who have found his words and actions difficult to accept![11]

He was aware of the feelings of those he was assigning to difficult tasks or to foreign places in the service of God. Once he wrote to one of his priests:

> I am writing to ask you about your health, and what you think of a proposal I have in mind for you. We have been called to send four or five missionaries to N. We have thought of you to lead this group. I would ask you, Monsieur, to pray to God, to listen to what he has to say to you about this. Please write me soon about your health and your attitude toward accepting this assignment. I beg the Lord to give you the grace to respond always and everywhere to his holy will.

---

10. *CED* V:566.
11. *CED* VIII:100.

He acted in somewhat the same manner toward those at home, but differently according to each one's temperament. Ordinarily, he was lighthearted and cordial, as the following example will illustrate. Once he wanted to send one of his missionaries to Rome. He asked the designated confrere if he was ready to take a pleasant trip in the service of God, without mentioning where. When the priest said that he was ready, Monsieur Vincent said yes, but the trip extends beyond the kingdom. When the priest replied to this that it was all the same to him, Monsieur Vincent then said that it would also involve a sea voyage. The priest replied that to go by land or sea was immaterial to him, for he was ready to go. Monsieur Vincent smilingly said that it was a little matter of twenty-five hundred miles, thus preparing him for the assignment he was to receive. He did the same for others, as the case warranted, to prepare them gently to accept what God asked of them in his service.

SECTION ONE

Continuation of the Same Topic

The leadership of Monsieur Vincent being what it was, as we have seen in this chapter, he followed a definite priority in his concerns. First, he sought to destroy sin and the faults and failings in those under his care. He asked those who wished to be admitted to the Congregation to enter the internal seminary, established as a school of virtue, to root out their vices and evil inclinations by the practice of humility, mortification, obedience, meditation, and the other exercises of the spiritual life. After spending enough time there, if there were some who needed to study theology or philosophy he sent them on for these studies. He feared that these studies would diminish their first fervor, or possibly lead to too great a desire for knowledge, or even to curiosity. Because of this unease, he gave the following advice:

> The step from the seminary to studies is dangerous, and has caused the ruin of many persons. If there is any time we must be on our guard about our faith, it is surely when we go on for our studies. Going from one extreme to the other is dangerous. A glass that comes from the furnace into the cold runs the risk of cracking. In the same way it is most important to maintain one's first fervor, to preserve the grace received, and to prevent human nature from surprising us. If each time we enlighten our understanding we strive

to move our will, our studies will serve to bring us closer to God. We can be sure of the maxim that the more we perfect our own interior, the greater will be our capacity for serving our neighbor. This is why, in studying to be better equipped to serve souls we must be careful to nourish our own soul with both piety and knowledge. We must read good books, and avoid those which simply satisfy our curiosity. Curiosity is the pest of the spiritual life. The curse of our first parents brought death, disease, famine, war, and all the other miseries of our world. Therefore we too must be on our guard for curiosity is the root of all sorts of trouble.[12]

Not only must we banish such curiosity from our Company, but sensuality must go, too. Unhappy is he who seeks his own satisfaction. Unhappy is he who avoids the cross, for he will find it so heavy he will not carry it. Anyone who minimizes the practice of external mortification, saying interior mortification is much more perfect, makes it clear that he is not mortified at all, either outwardly or inwardly.[13]

On another occasion he said, "I have noticed that most of those who have lost their vocation have failed in two things. The first is the morning rising, which they have not faithfully observed, and the second is the appearance of their hair, which they allowed to grow too long, and which seems to lead to other similar vanities."

In this connection he wanted all the priests of his Congregation to wear their hair short. When he encountered someone whose hair came down over his collar, he would reach for a strand, and pull it a bit, smiling all the while, but letting it be understood that he preferred it to be cut. Sometimes he would say a word or two publicly, since the failing was public and for all to see.

He was aware that among religious persons, and especially those living in community, some vices were to be feared more than others, particularly rivalry and slander. To counteract any tendency toward these faults among his confreres, he used to say that "the traits of envy and detraction pierce first the heart of Jesus Christ before reaching those against whom they are aimed."

He used another device to counteract vice and the failings in the houses under his control. This was fraternal correction. But since this is something not too easy for nature to accept, he used it with such mildness and courtesy that the words of the wise man were verified in him: "The wounds of him who loves me were sweeter than the deceitful kisses of my enemy."[14]

---

12. *CED* XI:28-29.
13. *CED* XI:71.
14. Prov 27:6.

Ordinarily he did not use corrections on the spur of the moment, and never in anger. He acted in a spirit of charity, after reflecting before God, and taking into account the dispositions of the one to be corrected and how to make the admonition useful and salutary. Once he had to correct a difficult character, someone not at all disposed to receive such advice. He made his mental prayer for three days on the issue to ask God's light on the best way to handle it.

When he did make some observations to someone, it was always with such grace mixed with firmness that it was like the oil and wine of the Good Samaritan. Usually the results were good.

In the first place, he would show his regard for the person involved, and even praise him for the good qualities he recognized in him. Next he would show him his fault in all its ramifications, as it affected others, and its circumstances of time, place, and other elements. Lastly, he would suggest the proper remedy. To help in having his suggestions better received, he would then include himself into the criticism, according to the nature of the fault being discussed. He would say, for example, Monsieur, or brother, you and I both need to work at acquiring humility, or to acquire patience, to be punctual, or whatever virtue was under consideration.

He tried to make his corrections not only useful, but even agreeable to those he was admonishing. He took care never to hint at who might have complained about the fault. He preferred not to blame the offender if by doing so he would introduce some division into the community as a result. He considered that peace and unity in a community are preferable to all other benefits.

Once he spoke to the community about members not seeking any positions of responsibility:

> He who is in charge of others is responsible for their failings if he does not prevent them with humility, with meekness, and with charity. The first time you have to admonish someone you should do so mildly and graciously, and even then, only after waiting a long time. On the second occasion, you should speak a bit more severely and gravely, but still courteously, using prayers and charitable remonstrances. The third time, you must speak firmly and earnestly, telling the offender what he must do to correct himself.[15]

One day when he was about to correct one of his confreres, he first asked him if he were willing to hear something that had to be said, to which he answered that he was. This way of acting so impressed him and remained in his memory that he has assured us himself that it had a great effect upon him. He has rarely been tempted to commit this same fault again without recalling the kindness with which this wise superior had dealt with him.

---

15. *CED* XI:140.

A certain Missionary was assigned to a position of some danger, and he proved to be difficult with those for whom he worked. Monsieur Vincent prudently gave him a series of directives about what he should and should not do, but on several occasions he went beyond what he had been told. To his chagrin, God permitted him to experience some of the consequences of his fault. Monsieur Vincent sent him a paternal correction, helping him profit from his mistakes by learning from experience the consequences of disobeying the orders of his superiors. He ended his letter to him with these words:

> Monsieur, please accept simply what I am saying, and please do not be overly sad. Be like the pilots of ships. When they are caught in a storm, they redouble their courage, and steer their vessels right into the heart of the largest waves, which seem ready to swamp them.[16]

A superior of a house did not carry out an order to send a certain priest to another house. Monsieur Vincent had repeated it several times. He then felt obliged to follow up on this matter and to point out his fault to him. He did so, but in the mildest way imaginable. Instead of pointing out how this superior had failed in the obedience he owed to his superior, Monsieur Vincent simply used these words: "It seems to me, Monsieur, I see in your hesitation a shadow of disobedience."

If he surprised someone in a failing he corrected him with a mild firmness. If the guilty party was humiliated, he took this humiliation as a good sign. He neither reproached him further nor reminded him of it again, seeing that he had already been embarrassed enough by his failing.

The superior of a house of the Congregation was under the impression that someone had written to Monsieur Vincent complaining of his faults, and asking Monsieur Vincent that the superior's faults should be pointed out to him. Seeing that the superior of the house had unfounded suspicions, Monsieur Vincent wrote to him most kindly:

> You must be persuaded, Monsieur, that if I have any correction to suggest to you, I will do so directly and simply. Thanks be to God, you are doing well, and your conduct seems to me without reproach. In this regard, I do not recall that anyone has complained against you. Should they do so, I know you too well to think I would give it any credence. As much as you can, you should be on your guard about harboring suspicions, but refer everything to God.

A superior complained to him of the conduct of one of his subjects who had spoken to him disrespectfully, and had shocked him by some of his activities. Monsieur Vincent wrote the following letter in his own hand.

---

16. *CED* V:211.

Besides addressing the immediate problem at hand, this letter gives some good advice on the question of leadership.

> I share the pain you experienced concerning the matter you wrote to me about. I prefer to believe that he did this without any malice, and when he thinks a little about all the circumstances of this encounter he will see that this must not be repeated. For yourself, Monsieur, you must see this as a small trial which our Lord sends you to help you learn how to lead those confided to your care. It will help you see how great is the goodness of our Lord. He bore with the weaknesses of his apostles and disciples when he was on the earth, and suffered much from both good people and bad. You will see how superiors have their thorns to bear from time to time, and how those superiors who do their duty by word and example have much to put up with from their inferiors, not only from the lax but even from the best of them.
>
> Because of this, Monsieur, give yourself to God to serve him in this way, with no thought of seeking your satisfaction from men. Our Lord will console you if you work at having our rules more perfectly followed, and at acquiring the virtues proper to a true missionary, especially humility and mortification. It seems to me, Monsieur, you would do well to say to this good priest when he comes to see you, or in some other chance meeting with him, that you would be glad if he would tell you of any failings which he sees in you. In your position as superior you undoubtedly have a number, not to mention those you have as a missionary or as a Christian. There is no doubt that a word of impatience escapes you when the first movement of human nature overtakes you, before reason can control your animal appetites. This happened even to the greatest of the saints, but, aided by grace, they gained great benefit when they were told about their failings.
>
> It seems to me, Monsieur, that you would do well to act in the same way. Tell your community from time to time that you would be glad to hear from the confreres in the house named to do this act of charity, but you would truly be disappointed if others did not do so too. They should feel free also to write to the superior general, if they care to do so, as is done in all well-regulated communities. Tell them that you will not read either their letters nor the replies from the superior general. Oh, Monsieur, how great is the misery of human nature, and how necessary it is for superiors to have patience.
>
> I end by recommending myself to your prayers. Please offer them to God, that he would pardon the faults I have committed every

day in the office I now hold. I am the most unworthy of all men, and worse than Judas in his betrayal of our Lord.[17]

Another superior was annoyed with some confreres under his care. He wrote to Monsieur Vincent that he would prefer to take care of a flock of animals rather than these men. This holy man replied in a letter as judicious as the superior's letter was indiscreet:

> What you told me can be explained. What you say is true for those who want everyone to bow before them. They want no one to resist them, and want everyone to act according to their own viewpoints. They want to be obeyed without hesitation, and in a certain way, want to be adored by them. This is not so for those who seek contradictions and contempt. They look upon themselves as the servants of their brethren. They seek to walk in our Lord's steps. He endured from his own followers crudeness, rivalry, lack of faith, and so on. He even said that he had come to serve and not to be served. I am aware, Monsieur, that you, with the grace of God and the help of our Lord, act with humility, modesty, meekness, and patience. I am sure you used the term you did only to express your vexation, and to persuade me to replace you. And so, we will try to send someone to take your place.[18]

This superior, a good man in his own right, found this reply of Monsieur Vincent so to the point that he responded as follows: "I admired, and admire still, your letter to me, which was both beautiful and powerful. I appreciate it, respect it, and will apply it to myself."[19] In sending another priest to replace him, Monsieur Vincent included these remarks: "We are sending N. to replace you, as you requested us to do. I trust that all will see in you an example of the submission and confidence each of us owes to his superior."[20] He phrased it this way because he was to remain living in the same house as before. We should remark that the superior would often remain in the same house after being replaced by another. This gave him an opportunity to practice a perfect humility and obedience.

A priest of the Mission, a seminary professor, was most pious and zealous, but of a naturally sour disposition. This caused him to treat the seminarians with less than the desirable courtesy. Monsieur Vincent had occasion to write the following letter to him:

> I believe what you write even more than what I see. I have too many proofs of your love for the seminary to have any doubts. For this reason I reserve judgment on the complaints I have received

---

17. *CED* VII:594-96.
18. *CED* IV:174-75.
19. *CED* IV:194.
20. *CED* IV:204.

about your black disposition until I have heard from you. All the same, I would ask you to reflect on your way of acting, and give yourself to God to correct, with his grace, anything discourteous that you discover. Besides the offense to his divine Majesty, despite your own good intentions, several consequences follow from this. The first is, those who are unhappy and who leave the seminary may depart from virtue and fall into vice. They may be lost for having left this holy school too soon, all because they were not treated with proper courtesy. The second is, they may well speak against the seminary and dissuade from coming those who might otherwise have come and received the instruction and graces suited to their vocation. The third is, the bad reputation of a single house reflects on the entire Company. If it loses its good reputation, it may be hindered in its services and may be unable to do all the good it pleases God to effect through it.

If you say that you have never realized these faults in yourself, it shows you have little humility. If you had the humility which our Lord asks of a priest of the Mission, you would consider yourself to be the most imperfect of all, capable of these failings. You would attribute to a secret blindness that you do not see what is clear to others, especially after being warned of it. About the warning, I am told that you resent being told your failings. If that is so, Monsieur, you are in a sorry state, far from the way of the saints. They humbled themselves before everyone, and rejoiced when shown their faults. To act in this way is to imitate poorly the saint of saints, Jesus Christ. He allowed himself to be publicly accused although he had done no wrong, and then said not a word in his own defense.

Learn from him, Monsieur, to be meek and humble of heart. These are the virtues you and I should unceasingly ask of him. We should pay special attention to them, and not allow ourselves to be carried away by the opposite passions. They will destroy the edifice built by the virtues. May it please this same Lord to enlighten us with his Spirit. This will enable us to see the darkness in our own soul, to submit to those he has placed over us, and to animate us with his infinite graciousness that will flow out in our words and actions. This will make them acceptable and useful to our neighbor.[21]

Speaking one day to his community on the same subject, he gave an important warning in his usual humble way:

I must state that those who see the faults that would lead to the ruin or weakening of the Company and do nothing about it, are guilty of

---

21. *CED* VI:385-88.

what then happens to the Congregation. In this same spirit, I would be most grateful to be warned of any faults I have that I may correct myself. These faults would otherwise bring disorder and destruction to the Congregation. If you see that I teach or support anything contrary to the doctrine of the Church, the assembled Congregation ought to depose me, and put me out of the Company.

Another time, he replied to the superior of one of the houses regarding the admonitions the superior believed he was obliged to give publicly before the entire community:

> In only two or three cases should the warning be given to a single person before the whole community. First, do so when the evil is so ingrained in the guilty party that you judge a private admonition would be useless. For this reason, our Lord warned Judas in the presence of the other apostles, in obscure language, when he said he who puts his hand in the dish with me will betray me. Second, do so when it is a question of those weak spirits who cannot bear a correction, no matter how mild, although they are good enough people. This goodness of not publicly naming them enables them to respond to a general recommendation, enough for them to correct themselves. In the third place, do it if there is danger that others will fall into the same defects if something were not said. Outside of these cases, I would think it more appropriate to give such admonitions in private.
>
> Inferiors surely ought to be warned about faults committed against the superior himself, but two or three cautions should first be observed. First, it should never be given on the spur of the moment unless there is some pressing need. Second, it should be done mildly and be to the point. Third, it should be done with some consideration, explaining the bad consequences of the fault, and done in such a way that the superior is evidently not being moved by caprice nor because it affects him personally, but because it is for the good of the individual and for the community.[22]

Monsieur Vincent did not confine himself to remedying vice and rooting out the faults of the houses and of those under his care. He did what he could to lead them to the perfection of their state and to a most exact regularity. His chief weapon in this was the example he himself gave in imitation of our divine master, who, the Gospel tells us, began to do and to teach. This wise and zealous superior was exact in the exercises of the community, particularly to the practice of mental prayer in the morning. He rose like the others at four o'clock, even if he had slept little because of a fever or some

---

22. *CED* IV:50-51.

other reason. What is more, on the days he was bled or forced to take medicine, and on the following days, even in his later years, he did not fail to join the others at their prayer.

It is hard to believe how much the example of fervor and exactitude of this holy priest led his confreres to imitate him. It might be said that his example was one of the chief causes of the good order so much admired in the house of Saint Lazare, where the priests of the Mission had been established, and which gave such edification to those who observed it. He always wished the superiors to be the most exact in their observance of the regulations. He wanted them to be the first at all the exercises of the community, as much as their health and other duties allowed.

He spoke on this topic to the priests of his community:

> Those who are not exact in their observance, particularly to rising in the morning and making their mental prayer with the others, no matter how many talents and how bright they may be, are not suitable to be superiors of the houses or directors of the seminaries.

He added that when it was a question of choosing superiors, a consideration of great importance was their example and regularity. Otherwise they would lack one of the main qualities required in those who had charge of others.[23]

This is what he wrote one day to a superior of a seminary on the way he should act toward the clerics under his care:

> I praise God for the number of seminarians N., the bishop of N., has sent to you. You will not lack for applicants as long as you take care to raise them up in the true spirit of their vocation. This consists chiefly in the spiritual life, the practice of mental prayer, and the virtues. It is not enough to teach the chant, the rites and a bit of moral theology. The main thing is to form them in a solid piety and devotion. For this, Monsieur, you ought to be filled with these qualities yourself, for giving instruction without example is useless. We ought to be the cisterns flowing with never-failing water, and we should have the spirit we hope to engender in them. No one can give what he does not have.
>
> Ask this grace of our Lord, and let us give ourselves to him, to conform our thoughts and actions to his. Then your seminary will spread its repute inside and outside the diocese, and your seminarians will be increased in numbers and in blessings. If, on the contrary, we act simply as professors toward those in our care, it would be a great hindrance to the welfare of the seminary. This could happen if we strive to be too polished, too worldly, too well

---

23. *CED* XI:83.

treated, too anxious to be honored and well thought of, too distracted, too sparing of ourselves, and too much taken up with the outside world. We must be firm, but not crude, in our behavior, and avoid too soft a manner which serves no good end. We must learn from our Lord that our lives ought always be lived in humility and graciousness to attract hearts to him, and to repel no one.[24]

Writing to another superior, he said:

My great hope is that you would contribute much, by God's grace, to the salvation of these people. Your good example will help your confreres love this work and apply themselves to it in the place, time, and manner you shall prescribe. You should consult God, like another Moses, and receive the law from him to be given to those you direct. Remember, the direction of this holy patriarch was gentle, patient, supportive, humble, and charitable. In our Lord these same virtues appeared in their perfections to serve as a model for us.[25]

A superior of a house wrote to ask that he be replaced in his position. Monsieur Vincent wrote to him as follows:

With respect to the change you requested, please do not think more about it. I hope that under the ashes of humility that led you to request a replacement is hidden the spirit of our Lord. He himself will inspire your actions, strengthen your weakness, enlighten your doubts, and empower you in your needs. On your part, Monsieur, give yourself to him, so as not to burden anyone. Treat each person with courtesy and respect, using requests and pleasant words, but never hard and commanding expressions. Nothing is so likely to gain hearts as the habit of acting humbly and courteously, and so to attain the goal you have in mind, that God be served and souls sanctified.[26]

Writing to another confrere on the same subject, he said:

The reasons you give why you should not be made superior and that another be appointed in your place, have served rather to confirm us in our choice. Your awareness of your own failings and insufficiency should be used to humble yourself, not to discourage you. Our Lord had enough strength for himself and for us too. Let him act in you. Have no doubt that if you continue in the humble sentiments you now have and if you continue in humble confidence in him, his guidance will sanctify your own service. I trust so much

---

24. *CED* IV:596-97.
25. *CED* V:421.
26. *CED* VIII:176-77.

in his goodness, and in the good use you will make of his graces, that he will accomplish this in you. In this hope I enclose your appointment as superior of your community. Please have it read, that they may see you in our Lord, and our Lord in you, as I trust they will.[27]

Before closing this chapter we will insert here a letter of Monsieur Vincent to a Daughter of Charity. In it he gave some advice regarding those either to be received into her Congregation, or to be sent away.

The reply you should give to the good woman before she enters your Congregation is to tell her that she cannot be assured that her place is guaranteed for life. No one receives this, because there is always the possibility that someone will become negligent toward the exercises of community life, becoming a scandal to the community, and so become unworthy of her calling. If such a thing should happen, would it not be reasonable to cut off a gangrenous member so as not to infect the others? You are aware, my sister, that people are only rarely dismissed, and then only for serious faults. They are never dismissed for common or even extraordinary failings if they are not habitual. This remedy is always put off as long as possible, after long enduring such a person, and using without success the remedies appropriate to her state.

This patience and charity is shown to the newcomers of the community, and even more so to the old. If some do leave, it is usually they themselves who decide to go, either through a flightiness of character, or by having become lax in the service of God. God rejects them long before the superiors have thought of dismissing them.

To say that those who are faithful to God and faithful to holy obedience leave the community, is simply not so, thanks be to God, whether for those who are in good health or for those who are sick. Everything possible is done to save everyone, both the well and the sick, up to the time of death. If the good woman wishes to enter your community, and is resolved to die in it, she will be treated just like all the others. But tell her, please, this will be by assuring her vocation by good works, according to the counsel of the apostle Paul. She ought to rely on God alone, and hope in him for her perseverance. If she still seeks this assurance from human sources, it would seem she is seeking something other than God himself. She should then be left in peace where she is now.[28]

---

27. *CED* VII:124-25.
28. Letter to Marguerite Chetif, stationed at Arras. *CED* VIII:295-97.

SECTION TWO

How He Handled the Temporal Affairs of the Congregation

We have seen in several of the preceding chapters how great a reliance Monsieur Vincent had on the Providence of God in regard to what was required for the subsistence of the houses of his Congregation. He held it as an axiom that if the members of his Company were faithful to the rules and fulfilled the duties of their calling, this divine Providence would never fail to provide what was required for their life. In this he relied on the promise of the Son of God, "Seek first his kingship over you, his way of holiness, and all these things will be given you besides."[29]

This did not prevent him from being careful to preserve and manage the temporal goods of the Congregation. This he did because of the command that we earn our bread in the sweat of our brows, and the plan of God to use secondary causes in carrying out his designs. Just as the father of the family has the responsibility to feed his children, generals of armies to supply arms and equipment for their troops, and the heads of organizations to influence the spirit and life of their members, Monsieur Vincent saw himself as obliged to look after the needs of his community. He worked at this because God willed it, and required it for the good of souls. He had a double care, first, to make the most of what little he had, and second, to use his resources sparingly.

To make the most of the temporal goods of the community he appointed procurators and other knowledgeable people to handle these affairs, but these remained under his close scrutiny. They did nothing without his advice. He often pointed out what they were to do and say, and afterward he would require a report of what had been done. He would often ask them in the evening what they had done during the day, and then give them the next day's assignment.

So as not to neglect anything, he would often say that once something had been started it ought to be pursued to its conclusion. No matter how careful or accomplished those were who attended to these matters, he did not want them to do anything in the house or outside of it without informing him, though many things were being done. If these procurators were too inclined to go off on their own, he would replace them with others. He would do this even to superiors of the houses if they undertook some major projects,

---

29. Matt 6:33.

such as building or tearing down a structure, without informing him and obtaining his authorization. He used to say that if everyone did whatever came into their heads, the dependence ordained by God would be weakened, and the house would be marked by constant changes and disorder.

He employed the brothers of the Company to work the farms at Saint Lazare, so that it would be said that the Missionaries worked with their hands, as the apostle said, for the sake of the Gospel.[30] He employed laymen to help in the domestic work, the farm, and the animals, to provide food for the house at Saint Lazare. This was demanding work, and called on all his ingenuity to meet these needs. He took an interest in both the least and the most important things, occasionally checking the reports in the farmyard at Saint Lazare. He looked after all, cared for all, and used everything, even the trees and fruits of the garden, so that nothing would be lost or wasted for want of foresight and good management. In a word, he considered nothing beneath his dignity or unworthy of his attention.

The missions were given without charge, and he instructed his confreres to take neither money nor gifts from those they evangelized. Nevertheless, he did allow his Missionaries to receive gifts or alms, provided they were truly given out of charity, and not by way of salary or recompense. In this, they imitated our Lord's practice of receiving alms. This is what he wrote to one of his priests on this subject: "There is no problem in receiving the gift of Monsieur N. [Father de Gondi] If you have already turned him down, you may make your excuses. We have no right to refuse what is given us for the sake of the love of God."[31]

Second, to save what he could, he wanted the provisions of food and clothing to be appropriate to the times and to the places where the community was situated. He recommended to those in charge to see that nothing be lost, and that frugality be the general rule. He urged everyone to be satisfied with the clothes and food given them, even though these were of poor quality.[32] In bad years, when prices were high, he tried to see if some cutting back of the usual portion of meat or wine served at meals could be made. He sought to share in the common suffering of the people by cutting back on the expenses of the house.

Once when frost had ruined the grain and the vines, he spoke to the community to urge them to have compassion for the suffering people. His talk ended with these words:

> We must bear the burden of the poor, and suffer with those who suffer, otherwise we are not disciples of Jesus Christ. But what can

---

30. 1 Cor 4:12.
31. *CED* I:137.
32. Common Rules 3,7.

we do? Think of the people in a besieged city checking on the food they have left. How many loaves do we have? So many. And how many people are to be fed? So many. And so they decide how much bread each one may have for each day. They figure that at two *livres* a day they can hold out for such and such a time. If they see the siege is going to last beyond that time, they reduce the ration to one *livre* of bread, then ten ounces, six, or even four, to prolong the time that they can hold out. This will prevent their being overcome by famine.

And as for the sea, what happens there? Should a ship be driven off course by a storm, the food and water are examined to see if there is enough to last them to the port. The longer they are delayed the smaller the rations become, to stretch them out as long as necessary. The governors of towns and the captains of ships act in this way. Prudence suggests they do so, since otherwise all would be lost. Should we not also do the same? Are you not aware that the tradespeople are cutting back this year? Even the best households, in view of the poor vintage of this season, are cutting back their use of wine, lest they run short next year.

Yesterday, some upper class people who were here told me that some of the houses had completely stopped serving wine to the servants. They were told that there was enough to serve only the master of the house. All this, my brothers, makes us think of what we must do. Yesterday, I brought together the older priests of the community for their advice. It finally was decided to serve only a half-*setier* of wine at each meal for the rest of the year. This will cause some hardship to those who feel they need a bit more. Yet those used to submitting themselves to Providence and to overcoming their own appetites will make good use of this privation, just as they make good use of other mortifications without complaint.

Perhaps some will complain because they are so tied to their own satisfaction. They are children of the flesh, sensual, pleasure seekers who are never satisfied. They murmur at everything not in keeping with their taste. O Savior, save us from this spirit of sensuality.[33]

He avoided all superfluous expenses, spending only the least amount possible for necessities. Yet he spared nothing when it came to charity, as we have said before. He gave everything to God and to souls, but to the flesh and sensuality, to pleasure and conveniences, he gave the least he possibly could. He built no building unless it was absolutely necessary. He spent nothing on embellishments, paintings, ornaments, furniture, or niceties

---

33. *CED* XII:286-88.

which were not strictly necessary. When pressed to make so-called improvements, he always resisted these changes. He said that God's Providence was obliged to give us what was necessary, but not anything superfluous.

A superior of one of his houses requested permission to build. He even suggested that Saint Lazare should help pay for it, although it was in no position to do so. Further, he suggested that much good would fail to be done unless the building were constructed, since his community found living in the older building most disagreeable and almost impossible. The request to Monsieur Vincent brought the following prudent reply:

> You speak to me of beginning a new building. O Jesus, Monsieur, you must not even think of it. It is a great mercy of our Lord to our Company to have given us the building we now have, such as it is. We must await his divine goodness before we do anything different. We could not avoid the inconveniences you point out to me, for they did not come from us. It seems to me your condition resembles in some way God's dealings with his people. He permitted them to live in disarray for several centuries, and at the cost of an infinite number of souls. Their experiences put them in a disposition to receive the Son of God, and profit by his life, passion and death, after being prepared by so many warnings, prophecies and yearnings for his coming. If this view is not correct, I shall gladly retract it. If you have a better one, please let me know.[34]

Monsieur Vincent avoided another source of expenses, into which too obliging superiors often fall. This comes from the natural human desire for change, a desire for a change of location, for better climate or occupation, or because of the people who might be there. Some imagine that everything will be better elsewhere. Sometimes the superior becomes dissatisfied with one of his inferiors, thinking that another would surely be an improvement. According to these people, men have to be changed often, or sent on long trips at great expense. This view comes from a lack of mortification or of mutual support in bearing the defects of others.

There were few houses where these situations did not come up, but Monsieur Vincent would not agree to these transfers. He counseled those concerned to wait a while and be patient, or he excused himself on the grounds of the difficulty of finding a suitable replacement. He would say that in due time he would look into the matter, but with the hope that time would help them lose the desire for a change. He did, from time to time, change certain confreres, but only for good reasons, and never to favor their inconstancy or their personal satisfaction, against which he showed an extraordinary resolve.

---

34. *CED* V:441.

He gave this answer to a priest requesting a transfer. It may serve as an example of many others written by Monsieur Vincent in similar circumstances:

> It has pleased God to give me an understanding of the Congregation, the state and the needs of each house, and the disposition of each of its members. At present I do not see how you could be more useful to the Congregation than where you now are. In the name of God, Monsieur, hold firm, and be convinced that you will not lack God's blessings. One of the greatest consolations I have is to see you where you now are, and one day I hope to see you in heaven.[35]

He did all he could to avoid useless expenses, and in a holy fashion purchased only what was necessary for the service of God. In addition, he was most careful in his use of time. This was precious to him, because of the number of projects he was involved with both in the temporal and in the spiritual spheres. Besides his own Congregation, he directed other groups, so he strove to lose not a single moment in doing anything useless.

First, he was always taken up with praying, speaking, writing, taking or giving advice, solving difficulties and following up on agreed-upon solutions. Second, he robbed himself of sleep to devote more time to his various responsibilities. Besides retiring an hour or two later than the others, to give him time to speak to someone, to finish reading letters sent to him, or for other duties, he continually had to have his charges in mind, like a true shepherd watching over his flock. Third, the other priests of the Congregation enjoyed two hours of recreation each day, an hour after each meal, but Monsieur Vincent used this time for other duties. Fourth, although he gave full liberty for those who spoke to him to say all they wanted, especially those from outside the community, he never engaged in useless chatter or gossip. Even in pious assemblies which met to help the poor or for some other charitable purpose, he would call the discussion back to the point if the speaker digressed. He would often say, "Let us return to the question, wrap it up, and see what remains to be done. Monsieur, or Madame, do you agree we should end this?" Fifth, he paid few visits, unless they were required by some business, or an expression of gratitude or charity.

This has been a short sketch of his leadership. It is summarized in the next section in a conversation he had with one of his priests, and written down immediately after by the person concerned.

---

35. *CED* IV:380-81.

SECTION THREE

Advice Given by Monsieur Vincent to a Priest of the Congregation Before Sending Him to Assume the Direction of One of the Houses

Oh, Monsieur, how great it is to be called by God to the task of directing souls. What other vocation can compare with that of a priest of the Mission, to direct and lead others, whose interior movements are known to God alone? *Ars artium, regimen animarum* ["The art of arts is the direction of souls"].[36] This was the task of the Son of God on earth. This is why he descended from heaven, was born of a virgin, gave all his attention during life, and finally suffered a most painful death. This is why you must have a high regard for the work you are about to take up.

What means should you use to fulfill this task of leading souls to God? This, in the face of the torrent of vices among the people, or in meeting the challenge of poor seminary training. You must inspire those confided to you with Christian and priestly sentiments, to ensure their salvation and their perfection. Certainly, Monsieur, there is nothing human in this. This is not man's work, but God's. *Grande opus* ["A great work"].[37] It is a continuation of the work of Jesus Christ, which human effort can only destroy, if God does not have his place in it. No, Monsieur, neither philosophy nor theology, nor learned talks influence souls. Jesus Christ must be united with us and we with him. We must work in him, and he in us, to speak as he did and with his spirit, just as he was in the Father. We must teach the doctrine he taught, as the Scriptures constantly tell us.

You must strip yourself, Monsieur, to be clothed with Jesus Christ. You are aware that things ordinarily reproduce their own kind: a sheep creates a sheep, and a human another human. In the same way, he who would lead others, form them, and speak to them with mere human ideas and ideals, will give birth merely to the purely human in those who hear him. Despite all appearances to the contrary, he will engender merely the show of virtue, and not the reality. He will create in them the same spirit that moves him, as we see in the teachers in the schools who bequeath their maxims and mannerisms to their disciples.

---

36. PL 77:14.
37. Neh 6:3.

On the other hand, if a superior is filled with God and with the maxims of our Lord, all that he says will be fruitful. A power will go forth from him that will build up, and all his actions will serve as incentives for creating good in those who become aware of them.

To achieve this, Monsieur, our Lord himself must mark you with his own character. It is the same as we see when a cultivated stock is grafted on to a wild stock, and the wild then carries on the natural results of the cultivated. We too, miserable creatures, who are but flesh, thorns, and briars, are sealed by our Lord with his own seal. We receive, so to speak, his own spirit and grace, so that united to him as the vine is to the branch, we accomplish through him what he himself did upon earth. I mean to say we perform divine actions, engendering children to our Lord, as Saint Paul said, filled as he was with this same holy spirit.

An important task is that you should apply yourself carefully to is to remain in close touch with our Lord by mental prayer. This is the storehouse where you will find all you need, to accomplish the task you are about to assume. When you have a doubt, have recourse to God, and say to him: "Lord, the Father of Lights, reveal to me what I must do in this case."

I not only give you this advice for the difficulties you may experience, but to teach you what you are to say to those under your care. In imitation of Moses, you must hear from God what is to be communicated to his people. *Haec dicit Dominus.* ["Thus says the Lord."]

Monsieur, you should have recourse to God in mental prayer to preserve your soul in his holy fear, and in his love. Alas, Monsieur, I must tell you and you should know that often those who work for the salvation of others are in the end lost themselves. This could happen to anyone who is so taken up with others that he forgets himself. Saul was worthy of being appointed king because of his life in his father's house. Yet after being raised to the throne he fell miserably from God's grace. Saint Paul chastised his body, lest after preaching to others and showing them the way of salvation, he himself should become a castaway.

To keep from falling into the unhappy state of Saul or Judas, we must commit ourselves inseparably to Jesus Christ our Lord. We should lift our minds and heart to him and say: "O Lord, do not allow me, after preaching to others, to be lost myself. Be my shepherd, and do not withhold from me the graces you bestow on others through my intercession and my ministry."

You ought to be devoted to mental prayer to beseech from the Lord the graces needed by those you direct. You will achieve more lasting good this way than by any other practice. Jesus Christ, who ought to be your model in everything, was not satisfied by his preachings, his works, his fasts, his blood, and even his death. To all these he added his prayer. He had no need of prayer for himself. It was strictly for us, for whom he prayed so often. It was to teach us to do the same for our own needs and for those we seek to save, with his help.

Another thing I recommend to you is our Lord's humility. Say to him often, "Lord, what have I done to merit such a vocation? What works of mine have merited the task you assign to me? Ah, my God, I shall spoil everything if you do not direct my words and all my actions." Just recall all that remains in us of what is human and imperfect, and we will find enough there to humble ourselves. This will be not only before God but before others as well, and in the presence of those whom we call our inferiors.

Above all, do not take any pains to appear as being the superior and master. I do not agree with the opinion of someone who recently said that to lead others and maintain one's authority you must make it clear that you alone are the superior. O my God, our Lord Jesus Christ did not speak in this way. He taught us exactly the opposite, both in word and example. He told us that he had come not to be served, but to serve, and that he who would be the master must first become the servant of all.

Accept this holy maxim that you should live among your confreres *quasi unus ex illis* ["like one of them"].[38] Let them know that you did not come to rule over them but to serve them. If you act this way both within the community and outside of it, you will find that all will go well.

What is more, we should always credit to God any good that we do. On the other hand, we should attribute to ourselves all the ills which the community may suffer. Yes, remember that the disorders which arise in communities come mainly from the superior, who by his negligence or bad example allows laxity to creep in, so that in the end all the members suffer because the head is not in good order.

Humility ought to lead you to avoid the complacency that slips in, chiefly in works that have a certain glamour to them. Oh, Monsieur, realize how vanity is the dangerous poison even of good

---

38. 1 Sam 17:36.

works. It is an evil that ruins even the holiest of actions, and causes people to forget God. In the name of God, be on your guard against this fault, one of the greatest dangers I know of to the spiritual life and to advancement in perfection.

To avoid this vice, give yourself to God to speak in the humble spirit of Jesus Christ. Make it known that your teaching does not come from yourself but from the Gospel. Use the simple words and comparisons our Lord used in the sacred Scriptures when you speak to the people. What marvels he could have revealed! What secrets of the divinity he could have made known, of the admirable perfections of God, since he was the Eternal Wisdom of his Father! Yet, notice how he spoke in an understandable language, using the simple comparisons of a farmer, a field, a vine, a grain of mustard seed. This is how you must speak if you want to be understood by the people to whom you announce the word of God.

Another thing you should pay particular attention to is to allow yourself to be guided by the Son of God. When you must act, you should ask yourself, "Does this conform to the teachings of the Son of God?" If you find that it does, fine, then do it. If it does not, then have nothing to do with it.

Besides, when there is question of doing some good work, say to the Son of God: "Lord, if you were in my place, what would you do on this occasion? How would you teach the people? How would you deal with this sickness of mind or of body?"

This dependence should extend to those who represent our Lord for you, your superiors. Believe me, their experience and the grace given them by Jesus Christ because of their office has given them much insight for leadership. I tell you this to alert you to do nothing of importance, nor undertake anything extraordinary without alerting us. If you are pressed for time, and cannot await our reply, seek the advice of the nearest superior, asking him, "Monsieur, what would you suggest in this situation?" We know from experience that God blesses those who act in this way. On the other hand, those who act independently not only have fallen into difficulties, but have embarrassed us greatly.

I would ask you to be careful not to introduce anything singular in your direction. Nothing should be peculiar to yourself, but you should walk the *viam regiam* ["royal road"], the main highway, so as to proceed surely and without reproach. What I mean by this is that you should follow the rules and customs of the Congregation. Do not introduce anything new, but follow the suggestions drawn up for those in charge of one of our houses. Do not omit anything of what we do in our Company.

Be careful in the observance of the rules, but also, see that the others follow them, for otherwise all will go badly. Since you hold the place of our Lord, you should be, in imitation of him, a source of light and warmth. "Jesus Christ," says Saint Paul, "is the splendor of the Father,"[39] and Saint John says, "he is the light which enlightens all those who come into the world."[40]

We notice that higher causes influence the lower, as for example, the angels who are in a superior hierarchy brighten, illumine, and perfect the intelligences of the lower hierarchy. The same thing applies to a superior. The pastor and director ought to cleanse, enlighten, and unite to God the souls who have been confided to his care by God himself.

Just as the heavens shed their blessings upon the earth, those placed over others should extend to those others the same spirit which moves them. For this to happen you must be full of grace, light, and good deeds, just as you see the sun giving its full light to the other stars.

Finally, you must be the salt of the earth, *Vos estis sal terrae*, preventing corruption from creeping into the flock you shepherd.[41]

After Monsieur Vincent had spoken in this way, with a zeal and charity that I cannot express, a brother of the Company interrupted him. He came to discuss some matters about the house of Saint Lazare. After the brother left, he took the opportunity to give me the following advice:

You see, Monsieur, how we have to go from considering the things of God to temporal matters. You must understand that a superior must be concerned not only with spiritual matters but with the temporal as well. Since those he has charge of are creatures both of body and soul, he must look after the needs of both. In this, he follows the example of God himself. From all eternity he engenders the Son, and the Father and the Son give rise through their mutual love to the Holy Spirit, but besides these operations *ad intra* ["internally"], I say, he created the world *ad extra* ["externally"]. He is continually concerned for his creation. Every year he provides new crops from the fields, and new fruit from the trees. His adorable Providence extends to the least things, so that not a leaf falls from a tree without his consent. He counts the hairs of our head, and feeds

---
39. Based on Heb 1:3.
40. John 1:9.
41. Matt 5:13.

the insects, even to the smallest mite. This thought seems strong to me. It makes us realize that he must be concerned not only with spiritual things, but also since he in some way represents the power of God, he must attend to temporal things too. Nothing should be too small to be unworthy of his attention. Give yourself to God to obtain the temporal good of the house where you are going.

The Son of God when he first sent his apostles out on mission, told them to carry no money. Later, however, when the number of disciples increased, he willed that there would be one of his band, *qui loculos haberet* ["who would have the purse"].[42] He would not only give to the poor, but would look after the needs of the group. Besides that, he allowed some women to accompany him, *quae ministrabant ei* ["who used to minister to him"].[43] He told us in the Gospel that we should not be concerned with tomorrow. By this we understand that we should not be too worried or solicitous about the goods of the earth. He did not absolutely counsel us to neglect the means of life and care for our clothing, otherwise, we would never sow any seed.

I have finished what I wanted to say. That is enough for today. I repeat what I already said, that what you are about to undertake is a great work, *grande opus*. I pray that our Lord will bless your leadership. Please join me in praying he will forgive me all the faults which I have committed in the position I now hold.[44]

---

42. Based on John 13:29.
43. Based on Mark 15:41.
44. *CED* XI:342-51; the recipient of the advice was Antoine Durand, named superior of the seminary of Agde.

LAST CHAPTER

Conclusion of This Work, in Which We Answer Why We Did Not Include Any Miracles in the Book to Prove the Sanctity of Monsieur Vincent

THOSE WHO write a life of a saintly person normally conclude their work by an account of the miracles God had allowed to happen, as a testimony to the sanctity of their subject. Just as we should not lightly accept accounts of extraordinary and miraculous events, so too we should not reject them outright. The hand of God cannot be stayed, and his power is no less today than it was in preceding ages. He is the sovereign Lord of the universe, who does what he wills in heaven and on earth. Since miracles are one of the chief means he used in establishing the Church and in planting the faith in human hearts, there is no doubt he can, and does, use miracles to strengthen this same Church and reawaken the faith of Christians, which sometimes seems so lethargic.

This being so, we might well be asked why, in this life of Monsieur Vincent, no miracles have been reported. If his life was so virtuous and so holy, how could God not allow miracles in his favor? And if there were some, why were they not mentioned? According to the word of the angel in the book of Tobit, "It is an honorable and glorious thing to declare and make known the works of his power."[1]

We may respond, first, that this is not a necessary consequence that a person who had led a holy life will have this confirmed by the gift of miracles. We know of several great saints, recognized throughout the Church, who never performed a miracle. The Gospel expressly tells us that John the Baptist, declared by Jesus Christ to be the greatest of men, never performed any. Ecclesiastical history tells us of many saints, of all ages and condition, who likewise never performed any, and yet their sanctity has been confirmed. All this shows that although God never performed a miracle through Monsieur Vincent, it in no way diminishes our appreciation of his virtue or the veneration due the memory of his holy life.

We might further reply that if there has been no account of any miracles in his life, we do have the testimony from most credible witnesses of different things which happened during his life and after his death that are truly remarkable. He had, for example, predicted several events before they

---

1. Tob 12:7.

happened. He had spoken of other interior occurrences which would have been known to God alone. He eased the interior pains of many people who had for a long time suffered greatly with no relief. He obtained bodily cures from serious sickness which seemed hopeless and beyond all human remedy when these persons had recourse to his intercession.

Although we could have given many examples of such events, well founded as they are, and which deserve to be believed because of the trustworthiness of those who report them, we have preferred to hide them under the veil of silence. In this way we are exactly obedient to the wishes of the Church. It has directed that nothing be declared a miracle unless it has been recognized and approved as such by the authority of the bishops. Besides, we are thus more in keeping with the spirit of this father of missionaries, whose humility dictated that he keep secret the extraordinary graces and gifts he had received from God's Providence, until this same Providence itself would be pleased to bring them to the light of day.

If we have cited no miracle to show the sanctity of Monsieur Vincent it is only because there are other proofs so compelling that any reasonable Christian person would have no difficulty in agreeing. In this connection, there is a story of a cardinal of advanced years who attended the consistory for the reading of the life of a person who had died in the odor of sanctity. When a lengthy list of miraculous cures was read, the cardinal appeared to doze off. Later, the account was read of her being attacked on the street and badly injured, and still she treated her assailant with great patience and love. At this the cardinal opened his eyes as though awakening from sleep and said in a loud voice: "Now, that is a true miracle." He wished to show by these words that virtuous acts, heroic acts of virtue above the normal human powers, constantly practiced during life, are true and convincing proofs of sanctity.

In keeping with this maxim, anyone who reflects on all that has been said of Monsieur Vincent will find enough to convince him. If we care to call miraculous what is far beyond the ordinary human ways, which surpasses its usual strength, and exceeds the deeds of most Christians, we can say that the long life of Monsieur Vincent was almost a continuous miracle. It was a constant display of the most excellent virtues, in which he persevered for his entire life.

To clarify our point to the reader, let us consider, if we will, that God uses other means besides miracles to justify the truths and mysteries of our holy religion. God in his Providence does not always use miracles for this purpose, but uses other no less efficacious means. So it is that we see in ecclesiastical history some called to a most extraordinary holiness, or a way of living quite out of the ordinary, more angelic than human. They were venerated and admired by all the faithful. God has ordained that the sole fact of martyrdom can lead to canonization, while the learning and teaching of others have made them illustrious in the Church and respected as saints.

As to his servant, Vincent de Paul (if it be permitted to speculate on the mysteries of his Providence), it seems that God by his special and no less marvelous grace, wished to use his lowliness to exalt him, and his profound humility to render him more worthy of honor and veneration in his Church. This happened in such a way that this humble priest verified within himself what Jesus Christ had said: "Those who humble themselves shall be exalted."[2]

Certainly, if we consider on the one hand Monsieur Vincent's opinion of himself, and his constant effort to present himself as a nobody, a poor useless servant, an outcast, a miserable sinner, and then on the other hand if we look at the extraordinary and almost incredible things it pleased God to bring about by his ministry and have them blessed with such success, we can realize this could never have come from human strength. It was the direct result of the wisdom and power of God. This divine intervention was a sort of miracle of the goodness of God, a testimony to the approval of what was undertaken in his service.

Is it not a type of miracle to see the son of a simple peasant, born humbly in the lowest possible class, raised as a tender of animals, and then reduced to serve as an unhappy slave, and who always sought to remain hidden in the shadows of an abject and obscure life, and then, despite all this, suddenly appear as a new sun in the Church? As a sun he shone on an innumerable multitude of poor souls, "who languished in darkness and in the shadow of death," as the prophet put it.[3] These people spent their lives in a dreadful ignorance of God and of the things needed for salvation. Monsieur Vincent not only taught but vivified them in the fire of his zeal. He brought them from death to life, and kindled in them the fire of divine love.

What must we think of a simple priest, without a benefice, and with no material support, or with no position or authority in the Church, who was able to bring an effective remedy to the disorders among the clergy? What was he able to accomplish, for the benefit of priests, both in and outside the kingdom of France, which even the greatest and most zealous prelates with all their authority and their great resources, hardly dared undertake, even in their own dioceses or in territories depending upon them?

That a poor man, with no resources, was able to help the destitute, not of a single town, but of entire provinces, and not during a single bad year, but extending over many years, being able to provide food, clothing, and other

---

2. Matt 23:12.
3. Isa 9:1, and Luke 1:79.

necessities, what can we say? He repaired churches ruined by war, and refurnished many of them. He provided for pastors and other priests. He took pains to supply food and medicine for a huge number of the sick poor in villages all over France, Savoy, Italy, and other remote provinces for more than thirty years. He continued to support all these enterprises, as well as the Confraternities of Charity which he had established.

Lastly, that a man who never hid his lowly birth, who announced himself an ignoramus, who never showed any notable talent, who composed no books, preached in no famous pulpit, but who did all he could to remain in the background, and sought only to be forgotten, what must be the fate of such a man? How can we explain that with all we have said, this forgotten man acquired a reputation that spread through almost the entire world? That he was honored and sought after by the powerful, and even called to share in the council of the nation?

Certainly, anyone who would carefully consider these circumstances must recognize the hand of God in the affairs of his faithful servant to work these wonderful deeds. The life, the manner of living, the works, and the success of the enterprises of Monsieur Vincent were the effects of the wisdom and power of God. God is able at any time to bring light from darkness, or to bring to nothing all that is greatest and most astounding in all the world.

After all, the reader will find here ample reason to glorify and bless God for the example of virtue he has revealed in the person of his faithful servant. Saint Gregory of Nyssa, speaking of Saint Ephrem, said "God had put him on the earth as a great light to shine upon the world. He was like a living guidepost, pointing to men the way of virtue and sanctity, after the manner of the signposts erected along major roads."[4] We may say the same of Monsieur Vincent. God raised him up and gave him to the Church for many marvelous enterprises. Even more God sent him to give us the example of his holy life as a sure guide to a life of great perfection. By his example may we be moved to follow his path, walk in his footsteps, accept his direction, embrace his teachings, and above all else seek to imitate him in seeking the kingdom of God, the accomplishment of the divine will, all to the greater honor and glory of God.

The End

---

4. PG 46.3:819.

INDEX

*Translated from the 1891 Pémartin edition,
edited, with additional annotations
by
Edward R. Udovic, C.M.*

A

Aaron (Old Testament figure), **1:214.**

Abbess. Vincent asks an abbess to allow a religious who was living outside of her monastery to return, **3:147.** He opposes the release of an abbess who had been imprisoned because of her scandalous behavior, **3:281-82.**

Abbeys. Vincent works for their reform. **2:385 ff.**

Abelly (Louis), originally vicar general of Bayonne, then bishop of Rodez. Member of the Tuesday Conferences, **1:9,145.** He gives missions in the countryside, **1:9; 2:220.** Appointment as vicar general of Bayonne, **Ibid.** Pastor of Saint Josse in Paris, **1:10.** Involvement in Jansenist controversies, **1:10,15.** Ecclesiastical superior of the Daughters of the Cross, **1:10,197.** Rector of the general hospital, **1:10,229.** His resignation, **1:11.** Confessor to Cardinal Mazarin, **1:110.** Translations of Abelly's biography into other languages, **Ibid.** As an author of theological works, **Ibid.** As the author of Vincent's biography, **1:11-13.** Errors and omissions in Abelly's account, **Ibid.** Abridged edition of 1668, **1:15.** He dedicates this work to the queen mother; Anne of Austria, **1:22-23.**

Aberdeen (city in Scotland). The Missionary Francis White is imprisoned there, **2:179.**

Abiram (Old Testament figure), **3:206.**

Abraham (Old Testament patriarch), **1:122; 2:14,135; 3:21,29,45.**

Absalom (son of King David), **1:251.**

Abundance. See, *Temporal Goods.*

Abuses. How to deal with them. Quotation from Saint Augustine, **2:103.**

Accidents. Vincent almost drowns in a river while traveling from Le Mans to Angers, **1:201; 3:237.** He risks assassination, **1:202.** He takes a dangerous fall from a stagecoach, **1:252.** His calmness in these circumstances, **3:279.** A Daughter of Charity is miraculously preserved from harm in the collapse of a house, **3:35-36.** Louise de Marillac and several Daughters of Charity are providentially protected in the collapse of a floor in their motherhouse, **3:36.**

Achmed I (Sultan of the Ottoman Empire), **1:44.**

Actions. Criteria that Vincent proposes for judging these, **2:399.** The little things that are done in order to please God are not as subject to the effects of pride and vanity as are efforts in greater matters which are often ruined by these vices, **3:38-39.** Four principles which should be observed in order to insure that one's actions are done in conformity to God's will, **3:41.** The care with which all actions should be taken. Recommendation of the practice of offering them to God, **3:195.** See, *Intention.*

Actors. Vincent condemns certain performances of theirs which he considers to be immoral, **2:394.**

Acts (legal). Foundation contract of the Congregation of the Mission, **1:94-96.**

Acts of the Apostles (book of the New Testament). Citations in Abelly: 1:1-**1:238.** 8:37-**2:146.** 7:50-**2:224.** 22:10-**3:40,50.** 9:6- **3:181.**

Adam (Old Testament figure), **3:181,200.**

Admonitions. Those which are to be given to someone because of their failings. These should always be given discretely. Example of Vincent, **2:272.** What Vincent has to say relevant to them, **Ibid.** They should be given in a great spirit of gentleness. Example of the saint, **3:166-67.** Prudence of Vincent. Examples; **3:227 ff.** His recommendations on this subject, **3:302 ff.** A superior must first of all pay attention to his own failings, **3:305.** In what circumstances must the superior publicly bring to the attention of the community the failings of one of its members? **3:308-09.** The way in which a superior should admonish when the faults have been committed against him personally, **Ibid.**

The spirit with which one must receive admonitions, **1:50-51.** Advice given by Vincent to a confrere who had been hurt by being admonished, **3:307.** Those given by the superior because of the conduct of a member of the community. The obligation of making known to the superior the sorrows, temptations, and notable faults of one's confreres, **3:308.**

Examples of those given by Vincent: To a laybrother who had left the room leaving him alone in conversation with a woman, in violation of the rule, **3:271.** To a superior who had not obeyed an order from the superior general, **3:304.** To a superior who had written that he would prefer tending animals to dealing with people, **3:306.** To a confrere who failed to treat the seminarians under his care with an appropriate gentleness, **3:309.** See, *Correction.*

Affability (of Vincent). It deeply touches the prior of Saint Lazare, Adrien Le Bon, **1:121.** Vincent listens kindly with complete attention to everyone, even the least important. Of the favors asked of him, those he could do he granted easily and with a good grace, **2:399.** He always greets each of his confreres with affection, **3:150.** He always shows his confreres a great personal consideration in trying to speak to them in the dialects of their regions, **Ibid.** He is affable to them even when he has to refuse their requests, **3:230.** He speaks paternally to them, **3:300.** He acts towards them in a manner that is always happy and cordial. Example, **3:301.** Affability is the soul of good conversation, **3:165-66.** It is a necessary virtue for Missionaries, **Ibid.** Be affable but never flattering; there is nothing so unworthy of a Christian heart than flattery, **3:166.** Affability wins hearts, **3:177.** Our conduct must be both humble and graceful in order not to alienate anyone and to win all hearts to our Lord, **3:310.** See, *Cordiality, Mildness.*

Affairs (ecclesiastical). See, *Council of Conscience.*

Afflictions. The principal afflictions which God permitted Vincent to be tested by in his life, **1:245 ff.** Example of the patience of Vincent, **3:25 ff.,282 ff.** He sees afflictions as being graces from God, especially those which are received obediently, **3:162.** They contribute to the good of one's soul, and of the soul of the Congregation, **3:250.** The state of affliction is not necessarily a state which is bad since God himself uses it to test a person, **3:287.** See, *Trials, Sufferings.*

"Affront". Legal maneuver used in Barbary to extort money from the Christian slaves and the Missionaries, **2:92,98.**

Agde (city in Languedoc). The establishment of the community in this city. The foundation of a seminary there, **1:166,234**. See, *Durand (Antoine), Lebas (Toussaint)*.

Agen (city in the province of Guienne). Diocesan seminary there, **1:166**. Another foundation of the community in this diocese is made at Notre Dame de la Rose, **1:231**. The seminary here is conducted by the community, **1:233**.

Agenais (county of), **1:231**.

Ages (Cesar Saint Martin d'). Nephew of Jean de Saint Martin, canon of Dax. He discovers Vincent's captivity letter, **1:46**.

Ai (market town in the diocese of Reims). Mission held there, **2:43**.

Aigues Mortes (town near Montpellier). Vincent, escaping from captivity, lands there on June 28, 1607, **1:45**.

Aiguillon (Marie de Wignerod), duchess of, niece of Cardinal Richelieu. Biographical notice. Testimony as to her virtue, **1:230-31**. She provides a carriage and two horses to bring the elderly and infirm Vincent back to Paris. She compels him to keep them for his use, **1:202**. She establishes a house of the Congregation in her duchy at Notre Dame de La Rose, **1:231**. She founds the house of the Congregation in Rome, **Ibid.** She founds the hospital at Marseilles. The spiritual direction of the hospital is confided to the Congregation, **1:150**. She founds another house of the community in the same city, **1:231**. She asks Vincent to send some of his priests to give a mission to the galleys at Marseilles. Letter which the bishop of this city addressed to Vincent, **2:39**.
She gives several considerable donations to support the ministry to the galleys, the missions in Barbary, and those in Algeria **1:231; 2:125**. She helps to obtain the consulate at Algiers for the Congregation, **2:88**. She contributes to the expenses of the mission to Ireland, **2:133**. She arranges for a mission to be given in Paris in the faubourg Saint Germain, **2:222**.
As a benefactor of the Congregation of the Daughters of the Cross, **1:196**. As a Lady of Charity. Gathering held in her home. Conference given by Vincent, **2:304 ff.** Her charity for the devastated province of Lorraine, **2:329**. Vincent asks her to convoke an assembly of the Ladies of Charity in order to meet the pressing needs of the areas around Paris, **3:121**. At the death of Vincent she donates the money for a reliquary to contain his heart, and she attends his funeral, **1:262**.

Albano (city and diocese in Italy). Missions held there, **2:65**.

Albi (diocese of). Vincent says one his first masses in this diocese at the Church of Notre Dame de Grace, near the town of Buzet, **1:39-40**.

Albigensians. Heretics defeated by Saint Louis, **3:183**.

Albizzi (Francesco), cardinal. He preaches the conferences for the ordination retreats at Rome, **2:209**.

Alchemy. Vincent's knowledge of this science, **1:44,47**.

Aleria (diocese in Corsica), **2:70**.

Alexander VII, (Fabio Chigi), pope. Vincent announces his election as pontiff to the community, **3:108**.
His brief approving the vows taken in the Congregation of the Mission, and exempting it from the jurisdiction of the ordinaries (September 22, 1655), **1:112, 3:159**. He renews the condemnations against Jansenism. Conduct of Vincent in this instance, **1:221; 2:367**. He unites the abbey of Saint Meen in Brittany to the

Congregation of the Mission (1658), **1:233.** He orders that the ordinands for the diocese of Rome must make their ordination retreats at the house of the Congregation there, **2:204.** In the Sacred Consistory he speaks of his satisfaction with the success of these retreats, **2:205.** He does not want to exempt anyone from attendance at these, and he refuses to listen to those who want to remove the responsibility for holding these retreats from the Congregation and give it to other communities, **2:206,208.** He also obliges all those wishing to be ordained in Rome, and the ordinands of the suffragan bishops of Rome, to attend these retreats, **2:208.**

He sends a brief to Vincent in order to dispense him from the recitation of the breviary during his last illness, **1:258.**

Algiers. Vincent wants to establish a hospital in this city for the poor galley slaves. Missionaries are sent to work for the ransoming of the slaves, and to provide them with religious assistance, **2:88-89,125.**

The torture and martyrdom of two Missionaries, Michel Montmasson and Brother Francois Francillon, put to death by the Algerians, **2:86.** A young Christian slave endures death in order to safeguard his chastity, **2:111.** See, *Barbary, Imprisonment, Slaves, Le Vacher (Philippe).*

Aligre (Elizabeth d'), wife of the chancellor of France, a Lady of Charity, **1:153.**

Almeras (Rene), priest of the Mission. Biographical notice, **1:122.** He assists the poor pastors of Picardy (1653), **2:336.** He is named, after the death of Vincent, as superior general of the Congregation of the Mission (1660). Guillaume de Lestocq sends him an account of the events surrounding the original donation of Saint Lazare, **1:122-23.** Sending of additional Missionaries to Madagascar, **2:163.** He commissions and then testifies as to the veracity of Abelly's biography of Vincent, **1:12.** Role in falsifying Vincent's age and birth date, **1:13.**

Amboul (Ambolo), (valley region in Madagascar). Evangelized by the Missionaries, **2:147.**

Ambrose (Saint). Citations in Abelly. On the example of Moses, **1:63.** On the fruits of faith, **3:20.** Devotion as the foundation of the other virtues, **3:72.** He recommends the virtue of simplicity, **3:214.** Teaching on justice, **3:233.** His praise of poverty, **3:242.** On mortification, **3:254.** On fortitude, **3:280.** Vincent cites him on the manner in which a Christian must regard the trials that are experienced in this life, **3:284.**

Amiens (city and diocese of). During the war Vincent sends confreres and other assistance to this city, and surrounding areas of Picardy (1650), **1:204-05; 2:335.** The diocesan seminary there is confided to the direction of the Congregation, **1:235.** See, *Faure (Francois), Folleville.*

Amos (book of the Old Testament). Citation: **3:6-3:287.**

Ananias (New Testament figure). Consulted by Saint Paul, **1:70.**

Andiam Ramach (Andriandramaka). Chieftain on the island of Madagascar, **2:142.**

Angel. Vincent recommends imitating the holy angels who work to promote the kingdom of God by incessantly doing his holy and adorable will, **3:39-40.** Each morning Vincent prays in thanksgiving to God for his glory reflected in the angels, **3:75.**

Angel (guardian). Saint Jerome recommends praying to these angels in order to obtain the grace to imitate them, **3:9.** Each morning Vincent remembers his guardian angel in prayer, **3:75.** The special devotion of Vincent towards the guardian angels, and the devotional practices in their honor introduced by him in his Congregation, **3:94.**

Angelus. Exactitude and devotion of Vincent in the recitation of this prayer, **3:93.**

Angers (city and diocese of). Vincent visits the Daughters of Charity working in this city during the troubles of the Fronde and receives great consolation from them (1649), **1:201; 3:237**. Success of the missions held in this diocese, **2:13**. A Conference of Ecclesiastics is founded here, **2:227**. The Abbe Chomel uses his personal fortune to assist the works of the Congregation, **2:258**. Site of a hospital served by the Daughters of Charity, **2:296**.

Angouleme (city and diocese of). Beneficial results of the missions given in this diocese, **2:52-53**. The bishop asks Vincent to establish a house of the Congregation in this city (1643), **Ibid., 201**. Results of the ordination retreats, **Ibid.** Results of the Conference for Ecclesiastics. The letter of the members of this group to Vincent, **2:227**. See, *Blansac, Du Perron (Jacques), Montignac, Saint Amand*.

Anne of Austria (queen, regent, mother of Louis XIV). Her personal feelings of esteem for Vincent, **1:22**. She serves as the superior of the Ladies of Charity at the royal court, **1:153**. She obtains Vincent's assistance in the relief of the ravaged province of Lorraine (1640), **1:186; 2:329**. She names Vincent as a member of the Council of Conscience (1643), **1:192; 2:373**.

She obtains from the king a grant of 1200 *livres* for the work with the foundlings, **1:161**. She establishes a house of the Congregation at Sedan (1644), **1:232**.

Her helpful assistance in the foundation of the hospital at Marseilles (1645), **1:150**. She attends a conference at an ordination retreat and gives a donation in order to support this work, **2:186**. She agrees to the establishment of the hospital of Sainte Reine, **2:303-04**.

Vincent goes to the court at Saint Germain during the Fronde and asks the queen to dismiss Mazarin (1649), **1:198; 2:397**. The saint leaves Paris. The queen commands him to return there after the first troubles of the Fronde, **1:202**. She commands him to use a carriage because of his age and infirmities, **Ibid.** She testifies to the fidelity that Vincent had for the king, **3:109**. She dismisses a noble from the court who had insulted Vincent. The saint asks that the offender be forgiven, **3:157**.

She assists in Vincent's plan for the establishment of the general hospital (1653), **1:227**. At her command, he sends Daughters of Charity to care for the wounded soldiers at Calais, **2:298-99**.

She directs Vincent to give a mission in the city of Metz (1657), **1:234-35**. She expresses her satisfaction at the success of this mission, **1:235**. Vincent sometimes adroitly redirects the queen's generosity so that it may benefit communities other than his own, **2:400**. On one occasion she gives Vincent a diamond worth 7000 *livres* and another time an earring worth 18,000 *livres*. Vincent wants this charity to be publicized, **3:122**. She advises Vincent to justify himself in the face of a slander. The response of the saint, **3:191**. She requests that a mission be given at Fontainbleau, **3:212**.

She expresses her sorrow at the death of Vincent (1660). Abelly dedicates *The Life of the Venerable Servant of God: Vincent de Paul* to her (1664), **1:22-23**.

Annecy (city in the duchy of Savoy). The usual place of residence for the bishops of Geneva. The bishop asks Vincent for some Missionaries to work in his diocese (1640), **1:231**. The Commander de Sillery, in agreement with Saint Jane de Chantal, founds a house of Missionaries in this city, **2:38-39**.

The bishop tells Vincent of the success of the missions held there, **Ibid.**

Annunciation (Feast of the). The anniversary of the first taking of vows of the Daughters of Charity in 1634, **1:135**.

Anos (Anosy). Region in Madagascar evangelized by the Missionaries, **2:147**.

Antioch (Ignatius of), saint, martyr. The Missionaries from Tunis can say like him that they are beginning to be true Christians once they begin to suffer as Christ suffered, **2:98.**

Apologies for Jansenius. Vincent proposes that Rome should condemn these books, *The Book of Victorious Grace*, and *Everyday Theology*, **2:363.**

Apostates. Conversions in Barbary, **2:111,116-18,122-24.**

Apostles. The example of their use of temporal goods, **3:31.** Special devotion of Vincent towards them, **3:94.** As models of courage and perseverance, **3:132.**

Appeals (*appels comme d'abus*, a legal technique by which a challenge registered in Parlement to any ecclesiastical decision would temporarily suspend the enforcement of the decision.) Advice given by Vincent to some bishops on this subject, **2:384.**

Aquinas (Thomas), saint. He holds that a person cannot be lost in the exercise of charity, **2:312.** His teachings on the demands of charity, **3:146-47.** His teaching that humility is not contrary to magnanimity, **3:183.** His teaching on justice and gratitude, **3:235.**

Arisaig (region in Scotland). Region evangelized by Dermot Duggan, **1:176.**

Aristotle. Vincent has for a maxim a quote from Aristotle: "one must deliberate carefully, but once a decision has been made it must be executed diligently," **2:402.**

Armies. Missions given to the army in 1636, **1:174 ff.** See, *Soldiers*.

Arnauld (Antoine), a leading Jansenist. His book, *On Frequent Communion*, **3:80.**

Arras (city in the province of Artois). During the war Vincent sends aid and Missionaries to this city, **1:205; 2:305.**

Artois (province of). Assistance sent there, **2:330.**

Assemblies (General, of the Congregation of the Mission). The first general assembly is held at Saint Lazare in 1642. Vincent submits his resignation as superior general. The assembly declines to accept it, **3:192.**

Assembly of the Fourteen. Periodic meetings of the leadership of the Ladies of Charity of Hotel Dieu, **1:157.**

Assisi (Francis of), saint. His abandonment to God is imitated by Vincent, **3:29.**

Assistance (given to various provinces ravaged by war), **2:316 ff.** See, *Public Misery*.

Assolens (Monsieur), secretary of the University of Toulouse, **1:40.**

Attachments. The necessity of breaking free from these. The example of Monsieur de Rougement, **1:77.** See, *Detachment, Indifference*.

Auch. See, *La Mothe (Henry de)*.

Augustine (Saint). Citations in Abelly. On humility, **1:35.** He publicly confessed his sins in order to manifest the mercy of God, **1:60.** God allows no evil from which he cannot draw a greater good, **1:185.** On the tranquility of order, **1:213.** God as the source of all good, **1:239.** He said that God gave mothers and fathers in heaven the ability to see the good done by their children so that their eternal joy would be increased, **1:116.** Good order leads to God, **2:20.** He advised not attacking abuses too precipitously, **2:103.** True devotion cannot be found except in those who have a true devotion and piety toward God, **3:72.** Zeal for God, **3:97.** On simplicity and prudence, **3:222.** Interpretation of this saint's teachings are at the center of the Jansenist controversies, **2:369.**

Augustinus. Condemned work of Jansenius, **2:351.**

Authors (profane). Passages from their writings are not to be used by preachers as if they are as important as the Gospel, **2:19.**

Auvergne (province of). Missions given here, **1:167;2:36**. See, *Pebrac, (abbey of), Saint Flour, (diocese of)*.

Aux Couteau (Lambert), priest of the Mission. He ministers to soldiers during the war in 1656, **1:175**. He takes the place of Vincent at Saint Lazare during his trip from there to Saint Germain (1649). Sack of Saint Lazare by the Frondeurs, **1:200**. Vincent publicly rebukes him for an instance of disobedience, **3:212**. Superior at Warsaw. His devotion during the plague there, **2:163**. His death and eulogy, **2:165-66**.

Aversions. Conduct of Vincent towards a confrere who admitted to having feelings of aversion towards him, **3:152**. Towards some others who told him of their cool feelings towards him, **3:157-58**.

Avignon. Vincent stays with the vice legate, in this papal city, after his escape from captivity, **1:45-46**.

B

Bachelor's degree. Vincent receives his bachelor's degree in theology from the University of Toulouse (1604) **1:40**.

Bagnes. Penal colonies for Christian slaves in Barbary, **2:105-07,112-14**.

Bagni (Giovanni Francesco), cardinal. Papal nuncio to Paris. He comes to confer with Vincent on matters of importance to the Church, **3:222**. He writes a letter of consolation to the dying Vincent, **1:258**.

Bail (Louis). Anti-Jansenist theologian, **1:73**.

Bailleul (Elisabeth Marie Maillier), Madame de. One of the first Ladies of Charity at Hotel Dieu in Paris, **1:153**.

Bandits (converted by the Missionaries in various places in Italy and Corsica), **2:67-68,83**.

Bapaume (town in the Lorraine). Help sent there by Vincent during the war, **2:329**.

Barabbas. Figure in Christ's passion, **1:114**.

Baradat (Henri de), count and bishop of Noyon. He asks Vincent to send Missionaries to work in his diocese, **1:235**.

Barbarigo (Gregorio), cardinal, saint. The bishop of Bergamo in Italy. He appoints the Missionaries to give the ordination retreats in his diocese. He preaches at the ordination retreats in Rome, **2:209**.

Barbary. Vincent is sold into slavery there. It is from this experience that he conceives his life-long dedication to work for the relief of the slaves, **1:42 ff; 2:85**. See, *Captivity*. Louis XIII orders Vincent to send some of his Missionaries there. Julien Guerin travels to Tunis together with a laybrother (1645), **2:86** The painful labors endured by the slaves, **2:105 ff**.
The work of the Missionaries in Barbary, **2:84 ff., 89 ff., 105 ff., 120 ff**. Acts of heroic courage and deaths of several Christian slaves persecuted for their virtue, or for their faith, **2:111-12,116-120,122-23**. The Missionaries try to keep slaves from captivity, and try to ransom Christian slaves, **2:120**. Vincent speaks highly of the possibility of the company undertaking this work. He indicates that the work of the Congregation in Barbary will not interfere with the traditional ministry of the Trinitarians and Mathurins already working there, **2:124**. Donations given by Louis XIII and the duchess of Aiguillon for the missions in Barbary (1643), **2:88-89**. News from the Missionaries who are working in this country, **3:101**.

The endowment for the house in Marseilles is increased by the duchess of Aiguillon so that the Missionaries can send assistance to the slaves in Barbary, **1:231**. How the consulates of Tunis and Algiers are obtained for the Congregation of the Mission (1646), **2:87-88**. Advice and rules of conduct given by Vincent to the Missionaries destined for this country, **2:102 ff**. See, *Algiers, Barreau (Jean), Husson (Martin), Le Vacher (Philippe), Slaves, Tunis*.

Barberini (Francesco), cardinal. He writes to Vincent in the name of the pope asking him to send Missionaries to Ireland, **2:126**.

Barcos (Martin), Abbe, nephew of Saint Cyran. Jansenist author of, *Défense de feu Monsieur Vincent de Paul...contre les faux discours du livre de sa vie publiée par M. Abelly, ancien évêque de Rodez, et contre les impostures de quelques autres ecrits sur ce suject*, **1:38**. Also of the controversial book, *De l'autorité de Saint Pierre et de Saint Paul*, **2:351**.

Bar le Duc (city in Lorraine). During the war Vincent gathers relief for this city (1640), **1:185**. Self-sacrifice of the Missionaries working there, **2:324**. The confreres working for the relief of the Lorraine are received with hospitality in the house of the Jesuits in this city. The edifying death of a confrere, Germain de Montevit, at the Jesuit house, **2:325; 3:239**.

Barny (Georges), superior general of the order of Grandmont. Vincent sends him a letter from the king concerning the reform of his order, **2:386**.

Barra (island in the Hebrides). Evangelized by Dermot Duggan, **2:177**.

Barrault (Jean Jaubert de), archbishop of Arles. Vincent promises to send him Missionaries, **1:174**.

Barreau (Jean), cleric and then priest of the Mission. He is made consul to Algiers. Vincent gives him advice and rules of conduct for his post (1646), **2:88**.

His imprisonment (1647), **2:92-93**. He is imprisoned again (1650). Vincent advises him to use his captivity well since he thus had the happiness of being treated as Jesus Christ himself had been treated, **2:93**. He informs him of the negotiations which would be begun with the authorities in order to obtain his freedom, **2:94**. He is released after seven months of captivity. The saint congratulates him on his release (1651), **2:95**.

He is once again put in prison and tortured (1657), **Ibid**. Vincent shares in his suffering and encourages him, **2:96**. His admirable devotion to collecting funds for the ransoms of the poor Christian slaves, **Ibid**. Vincent reimburses the slaves for the consul's ransom. Barreau returns to France bringing back seventy ransomed slaves (1661), **2:97**.

Barry (Edmund), priest of the Mission. His dangerous situation after the siege of Limerick. His evasion of arrest, and his return to France, **2:133**.

Baruch (book of the Old Testament). Cited in Abelly. 3:24-25: **2:212**.

Baschet (Francoise). See, *Chassaigne (Mademoiselle de la)*.

Basil (Saint). Cited in Abelly. How a person should show their love for God, **3:40**. On the imitation of Jesus Christ, **3:85**.

Bassompierre (Louis de), bishop of Saintes (1648). His affection for the priests of the Mission, **2:383**.

Bastille (The). Vincent arranges for an ecclesiastic from the Tuesday Conferences to minister to the prisoners here, **2:394**.

Bayeux (diocese of), **2:381**.

Bayonne (diocese of). See, *Abelly (Louis), Fouquet (Francois)*.

Bazas (diocese of). Vincent supports efforts against the "Illuminati," in several places in this diocese. **2:394.**

Bazoches (area assisted by Vincent during the war), **2:337.**

Beaucaire (city near Nice). Site of an annual trade fair in France featuring goods imported from the East, **1:43.**

Beauce (region near Paris). Location of a farm belonging to the Congregation, **1:199, 212.**

Beaufort (Madame de). One of the first Ladies of Charity of Hotel Dieu in Paris. **1:153.**

Beauvais (city and diocese of). Louise de Marillac visits the Confraternities of Charity there, **1:130.** Missions given by Vincent in this diocese, **1:138.** In this city the Ordination Retreats are held for the first time (1628). Their success, **1:139-40.** Vincent writes from this city in 1628, **2:25.**

The bishop establishes a Confraternity of Charity in each of the eighteen parishes of the city (1629). Louise de Marillac visits them. Difficulties which she encounters (1635), **1:88,130.** Her success, **1:131.** See, *Poitier (Augustin)*.

Becan (Martin), Jesuit. Vincent recommends the use of the abridgment of his *Manuale controversiarum hujus temporis*, **2:25.**

Becu (Jean), priest of the Mission. One of the seven first companions of Vincent, **1:9,111.**

Bede (the Venerable), **2:117.**

Beirut (the bishop of). **2:304.**

Belart (Honore), priest of the Mission. Vincent reprimands him for lacking courtesy towards the seminarians he directed, **3:306-07.**

Belin (Monsieur), a chaplain for the de Gondi's at Villepreux. He ministers to the galley slaves, **1:86.**

Belleville (Mathurin de), priest of the Mission. He dies on the way to Madagascar. Vincent's praise of him, **2:149-50; 3:276.**

Bellievre (Pomponne de), first president, **1:228.**

Bence (Jean de), Oratorian and doctor of the Sorbonne. **1:70.**

Benedict XIII (pope). Beatifies Vincent on August 13, 1729, **1:25.**

Benedict (Order of Saint). Vincent assists in the reform of this order, **2:385.**

Benedictine (nuns). Take up residence in the faubourg Saint Germain, **2:328.**

Benefactors. Vincent's gratitude towards them, **3:239 ff.**

Benefices (ecclesiastical). Definition of, **2:379.** Resolutions suggested by Vincent and adopted by the Council of Conscience for the awarding of benefices, **2:374-75.** Vincent's zeal for fighting abuses in the awarding of benefices while a member of the Council, **2:377 ff.** Examples, **2:380-81.** Animosities which this caused against Vincent, **3:156-57.** Vincent refuses the request of a benefice for the son of Monsieur de Chavigny the Secretary of State, **3:247.**

Vincent denies permission for a Missionary to accept two benefices, even though he had the intention of one day giving them to the community, **3:246.** Vincent never solicits the granting of any benefices to his community, **Ibid. ff.**

Bergamo (city in the state of Venice). The Missionaries conduct the Ordination Retreats there, **2:209.**

Berger (Monsieur), ecclesiastical counselor of the Parlement of Paris. He accompanies Vincent on a mission, **1:73.**

Bernard (Saint). Cited in Abelly. It is a rare treat to see a humble man exalted, **1:36.** His life of solitude, **1:218-19.** His preaching of the crusades, **2:158.** Unworthy seekers of benefices, **2:377.** Honor due to the Blessed Virgin, **3:92.** It is rare to preserve one's humility in the midst of worldly honors, **3:214.** On the temptation to leave the religious life, **3:269.**

Berry, (province of). Assistance sent there, **1:212.**

Berthe (Thomas), priest of the Mission. He writes to Vincent to announce the death of the Abbe de Tournus (1660), **1:248-49.**

Berthier (Pierre de), coadjutor and then bishop of Montauban. He establishes the Missionaries as the directors of his seminary, **1:234.**

Berulle (Pierre de), cardinal. Biographical notice. After his first arrival in Paris Vincent frequents his company and takes him as his spiritual director, **1:50,52; 3:207.** He predicts that one day Vincent will found a new congregation. He persuades Vincent to accept the parish of Clichy, **1:52.** He arranges for him to enter into the service of the de Gondi family, and to provide spiritual direction for Madame de Gondi (1613), **1:55-56.** He agrees to Vincent's request to leave the service of the de Gondi's and suggests accepting the parish of Chatillon les Dombes, **1:64.** In the matter of Vincent returning to the de Gondi's he did not think that he could give Vincent any better counsel than he would, in the end, give himself, **1:65,69.** His attempt to have Vincent return to the service of the de Gondi family, **1:66-67,69-70.**

His teaching on the spiritual dangers inherent in high positions. **3:204.**

Bethune (Henri de), bishop of Maillezais and later archbishop of Bordeaux, **2:382-83.**

Beynier (Jean). Although a Protestant he provides a place for Vincent to stay on his arrival at Chatillon. He later is converted to Catholicism by Vincent, **1:70,74-75.**

Bicetre (the chateau of). Donated by the king as a residence for the foundlings, **1:162.**

Bidache (collegiate church in the diocese of Dax). Site of Vincent's reception of the minor orders, **1:38.**

Bizerte (seaport in Tunisia). Location of a slave camp. Missionaries work there, **2:97,105,107,112,114.**

Blaisois (province of). Assistance sent there by Vincent, **1:212.**

Blampignon (Louis de), prior of Montguyon. Friend of Vincent. Conference of Ecclesiastics at Metz. Mission given in this city, **2:227; 3:227.** His love of the poor, **3:117.**

Blansac (in the diocese of Angouleme). Mission given here, **2:53.**

Blasphemy. Example of the providential punishment for this sin during a mission given in Ireland, **2:129-30.** Vincent's zeal against this vice, **2:395.**

Blatiron (Etienne), priest of the Mission. Superior of the mission at Genoa (1645), **2:66-68.** Missions he gave in Corsica (1652), **2:69.** He dies of the plague. Vincent praises him. **3:54,276.**

Blessed Sacrament. Devotion to the blessed sacrament of the slaves in the prisons of Algeria, **2:108,114.** *Devotion of Vincent towards the blessed sacrament,* **3:77 ff.** Vincent kneels or follows the blessed sacrament whenever he encounters it being carried in procession through the streets, **3:79.** Exterior exercises of devotion in the churches, **3:81.** Expiations and honorable amends that he makes after learning of profanations against the eucharist in various places, **3:82.** See, *Communion, Mass, Visit to the Blessed Sacrament.*

Blessed Sacrament (religious of the), **2:328.**

Boccone (Domenco), priest of the Mission. His death in the service of the plague-stricken at Genoa, **3:54,276.**

Boethius (philosopher). Cited, **2:240.**

Bollain (Anne Marie), religious of the Visitation. Vincent asks her to accept the direction of the house of the Madeleine, **2:280.**

Bons Enfants (College des). At Paris, the birthplace of the Congregation of the Mission. This house is obtained through the intervention of the de Gondis. Vincent is named as principal (1624), **1:94,98.** He moves there after the death of Madame de Gondi (1625), **1:98.** Vincent gives the Ordination Retreats there (1631), and establishes a seminary (1636), **1:164; 2:185-86.**
Vincent establishes the Tuesday Conferences there for the theology students of Paris (1642), **1:146.** He establishes a seminary there reserving it for older students. Its rules and results (1642), **1:164-65; 2:250,255,258.** See, *Saint Firmin.*

Bordeaux. Vincent takes a trip to this city (1606), **1:42.** The galley slaves are gathered there (1622). Vincent gives a mission to the prisoners. Results of this (1623), **1:86; 3:257.** Results of the missions given in this diocese (1634), **2:51.** Conference of Ecclesiastics in this city, **2:227.**

Borguny (Pierre). He undergoes martyrdom in Algiers. Vincent's account, **2:100 ff.** He remains are brought to France and interred at Saint Lazare, **2:102.**

Borromeo (Charles), saint. He encouraged the practice of making retreats, **1:141.** His conduct during an outbreak of the plague in Milan, **3:137-38.**

Bossuet (Jacques Benigne), bishop of Meaux. A member of the Tuesday Conferences of Saint Lazare, **1:145.** He writes to Vincent to announce the formation of a Conference of Ecclesiastics at Metz modeled on that at Saint Lazare. He asks Vincent to be its superior (1658), **2:227.** He is present at the memorial service for Vincent (1660), **1:262.**

Boucher (Leonard), priest of the Mission. At Toul (1639), **2:318.**

Bourbon (Henri de), bishop of Metz, abbot of Saint Germain. Ecclesiastical superior of the priests of Saint Sulpice, **1:169.**

Bourdaise (Toussaint), priest of the Mission. He is sent to Madagascar. Account of his work there addressed to Vincent, **2:149-50,159-60.** His death and eulogy, **2:149,162.**

Bourdeilles (Francois de), bishop of Perigueux. He ordains Vincent to the priesthood, **1:39.**

Bourdin (Monsieur), archdeacon of Noyon. He establishes a Conference of Ecclesiastics at Noyon modeled on that of Saint Lazare, **2:226.**

Bourdoise (Adrien). Founder of a community of priests at the parish of Saint Nicholas du Chardonnet in Paris. He founds a seminary, **1:165.** His zeal for the sanctification of the clergy, **2:250,253.**

Bourg (capital city of the province of Bresse), **1:75.**

Bourgoing (Francois). Pastor of Clichy. Vincent replaces him in this position. He is later superior general of the Oratory, **1:52.**

Boussordec, (Charles), priest of the Mission. He leaves for Madagascar. He providentially survives a shipwreck, **2:161.**

Bra (region in Piedmont). Mission given in this area, **2:80.**

Bragelogne (Madame de). Lady of Charity and treasurer for the work of the foundlings, **2:307**.

Brancaccio (Francesco Maria), cardinal and bishop of Viterbo. He asks for Missionaries to evangelize his diocese, **2:59-60**.

Breda (parish in the diocese of Viterbo). Mission held there, **2:61**.

Breslay (Rene de), bishop of Troyes. He contributes to the establishment of a house of the Congregation at Troyes (1638), **1:231**.

Breves (Francois Savary), marquis of. French ambassador to the sultan, **1:44**.

Brie (region near Paris), **1:231-32; 3:296**.

Brin (Gerard), priest of the Mission. Dangers he faced in the siege and fall of Limerick. His escape and return to France, **2:133**.

Brittany. Vincent's trips to this region, **1:201,253; 2:238; 3:279,283**. Results of missions held here, **2:45 ff**. The establishment of a seminary in this region, **2:256 ff**. See, *Saint Brieuc, Saint Meen, Treguier*.

Brunet (Jean Joseph), one of the first seven companions of Vincent. **1:111**.

Buenans (parish in the diocese of Lyons), **1:65**.

Buglose (in the diocese of Dax). Site of Marian shrine, **1:35**. Vincent often visits here as a child establishing his deep devotion to Mary, **Ibid.**

Bull (papal). Of Urban VIII approving the foundation of the Congregation of the Mission (January 1632), **1:111**.

Burgundy (province of). During the Fronde, **1:217**. Missions held there, **2:49-52**.

Busee (Jean), Jesuit. Author of a popular book of meditations, **2:137**.

Buzet sur Tarn. Stay of Vincent there, **1:40**.

C

Cadillac (town in the province of Guienne). Residence of the duke of Epernon, **1:42**.

Cahors (city and diocese of). Diocesan seminary, **1:166**. Establishment of the Congregation in this city (1643), **1:232**. Site of a hospital served by the Daughters of Charity, **2:296**. Lawsuit over the seminary, **3:111**.

Caithness (region in Scotland). Evangelized by Thomas Lumsden, **2:178**.

Calais. Vincent sends Daughters of Charity to this city to serve the sick and wounded soldiers. Death of two of the sisters. Additional sisters are sent, **2:298-99**.

Calumnies. Vincent is accused of theft by the judge of Sore. His Christ-like response, **1:49-51**. His conduct in these situations, **Ibid.; 3:157-58,160,162**. These accusations are a cause for rejoicing, **3:189-90**. He stops himself in the midst of penning a defense, **3:191-92**. See, *Persecution*.

Calvin (John), Protestant reformer. Harm that he did to the Church, **1:31; 2:42,253,357**. Similarity of his views to those of Jansenism. Saint Cyran tells Vincent that Calvin's doctrines were not bad in themselves, but only poorly understood, **2:346-47**.

Campo Lauro (in Corsica). Mission held there, **2:69**.

Camus (Jean Pierre), bishop of Belley. Former spiritual director of Louise de Marillac, **1:128**.

Canada (the missions to), **2:15**.

Canna (isle in the Hebrides). Work of the Missionaries there, **2:175-76**.

Cantara (location in Barbary). Slaves are visited here by the Missionaries, **2:115**.

Canticle of Canticles (book of the Old Testament). Cited: 8:7-**1:142**.

Cape of Good Hope. Shipwreck of the Missionaries there, **2:162; 3:278**.

Captivity (of Vincent), **1:42 ff.** Vincent's attempts to recover the letters containing the accounts of this event, **1:46**. He never speaks of these events, **3:262**. He takes the place of a galley slave in Marseilles, **3:112-13**.

Capuchins. Jean Beynier, one of Vincent's converts, founds a house of these religious in Chatillon (1617), **1:74**. In the town of Charmes, **2:45**.

Cardinal. There is a rumor that Anne of Austria intended to have Vincent made a cardinal, **1:194; 3:183**.

Carmelites. Madame de Gondi is interred in their chapel on the rue Chapon in Paris, **1:97**.

Carriage. The duchess of Aiguillon gives a carriage to Vincent for use in his old age. Reluctance of Vincent to use it. The archbishop of Paris and the queen order him to use it, **1:202-03**. He refers to the carriage as his "infamy." He often provides the poor with rides, **3:129-30**.

Carthage. The Missionaries of Tunis and Algiers have the title and jurisdiction of vicars general of the archbishop of Carthage. Advice of Vincent on the conduct of this post, **2:90,103,107**.

Carthusians. They send those desiring to enter their community to first make a retreat at Saint Lazare, **1:181; 2:240**. Their manner of managing their resources, **3:31**. According to Vincent; Missionaries should be like Carthusians at home, and like apostles on the mission, **2:24**.

Caset (Michel), priest of the Mission. **3:17**.

Cashel (diocese in Ireland). Work of the Missionaries there, **2:127**. Letter from the bishop thanking Vincent for the work of his Missionaries, **2:128-29**.

Cassian (John), saint. His conferences. Vincent's esteem of them, **2:217**.

Castiglione (region in Italy). Mission given there, **2:68**.

Catechism. While traveling Vincent always takes the opportunity of teaching catechism to the children and servants of the inns where he stays, **1:201; 3:283**. It is to be taught during the course of missions, **2:22**. Great success of this teaching during the missions given in Ireland, **2:127**.

Catechism of Grace (a Jansenist work condemned by the pope), **2:356**.

Catherine (Saint). Vincent explains the gospel for her feast, **1:114-15**.

Caulet (Francois Etienne de), bishop of Pamiers. He refuses to sign a letter against Jansenism sent by the bishops of France to the pope. Vincent tries to convince him and refute his objections, **2:357**.

Cavallermaggiore (in Piedmont). Mission given in this area, **2:82**.

Ceremonies (liturgical). Care with which these should be conducted. They are only shadows, but they are shadows of great things, **2:194**. All of God's rites and commands should be obeyed, **2:276**.

Cevennes. Mission given in this region in 1635. Vincent himself wants to go to this mountainous area to evangelize these neglected people, **2:35**.

Chalons sur Marne (diocese of). Louise de Marillac visits the Confraternities of Charity in this diocese, **1:130**. The bishop asks Vincent to give missions in his diocese. Success of these missions, **2:49-50**. See, *Holmora, Vassy*.

Chambon (Monsieur), dean of the cathedral of Macon, **1:88.**

Champagne (province of). Frightful condition of this province; ruined and ravaged by war. Assistance organized by Vincent, **1:275 ff; 2:33 ff.** See, *Public Misery.* Results of the missions given in this area, **2:47 ff.**

Champvallon (Francois de Harlay de), archbishop of Rouen, later of Paris. Letter of congratulations to Vincent on the work of the Missionaries at Rouen, **2:44.**

Chancelade (the abbey of). See, *Solminihac (Alain).*

Chandenier (Claude de), abbe of Moutier Saint Jean. Praise of his virtue. He goes to Alet with is brother, and Vincent recommends them to the bishop of this diocese (1650). They take up residence at Saint Lazare (1653), **1:247,249.**

Chandenier (Louis de), abbe of Tournus, brother of the above. Member of the Tuesday Conferences, **1:247.** Vincent instills in him a love of the poor, **3:117.**

He leads a mission given in the city of Metz, **1:234-35,247; 2:198.** He travels to Italy with his brother and two Missionaries (1659), **1:248.** While returning from Rome to France he dies at Chambery (May 3, 1660), after having been received into the Congregation, **1:249, 3:279.** He is buried at Saint Lazare, **1:249.**

Chandes (in Bresse). Home of Monsieur de Rougemont, **1:78.**

Changes. Vincent has as a maxim that when things are going well they should not be changed easily even under the pretext of improvement, **1:101.** He generally opposes the frequent change in assignments for Missionaries, **3:315.**

Chant (liturgical). It is necessary to chant slowly and with devotion, **2:194.**

Chantal (Saint Jane Frances Fremiot de). Biographical notice, **1:90.** Together with Saint Francis de Sales she decides that there could be no better director for the Visitations in Paris than Vincent de Paul, **1:91, 2:266.** Her confidence in Vincent's spiritual direction. Letters she writes to him, **2:267 ff.** Letter thanking him for the visitation of a monastery, **2:269.**

At her insistence Vincent establishes the Missionaries at Annecy in 1640, **1:231.** Her desire to see Vincent again, **2:268.** Her death (1641). Vincent testifies to the heroism of her virtues, and his vision on this subject, **2:283-84.**

Charity (towards our neighbor). Vincent had received a particular grace for consoling the afflicted, **1:98.** He is careful never to say or write anything harsh or lacking in respect towards anyone, **1:101.** He always praises the good that he notices in anyone else, **1:103.** He says that there are those who cannot see evidence of virtue without praising and admiring those in whom the virtue resides, **Ibid.** A maxim that he practices himself and recommends to others is to see Jesus Christ in others, and thus be inspired to respect and serve them, **1:107.**

Vincent says that he consideres nothing to be more important than serving an afflicted soul, **2:270.** The example of Jesus, **2:285.** According to Saint Thomas a person could not be lost as long as they practiced charity, **2:312.** How Vincent's heart is filled with the love of God. Effects of this love, **2:329-330.**

Examples and teachings of Vincent, **3:106 ff.** 1. *Ardent Charity.* The love of God is most perfect when it is extended towards a neighbor, **3:106.** There is no one more obligated to this love than the Missionaries, **Ibid.** If a Missionary was reduced to begging for his bread and someone asked him; "Poor priest of the Mission, what has brought you to such an extremity? What happiness if you could respond: Charity!" **3:108.** His heart is so filled with charity that it spreads to all those who came in contact with him. **Ibid.** 2. *Universal Charity,* of Vincent, **Ibid.** 3. Charity full of *cordiality,* **3:109.** Just as the avaricious and ambitious never miss an opportunity to

INDEX 341

enrich themselves with goods or honors so Vincent never misses an opportunity to do good for others, **3:109**. Some remarkable examples. He instructs his Missionaries not to hesitate to risk everything to help others, **3:111**. His peace of soul in accepting the temptation against faith of a doctor of theology, **3:113-14**.

Charity (towards the poor). Vincent practices this since his childhood, **1:37**. He gives away the last money from the treasury of Saint Lazare, **1:188**. *Maxims and conduct of Vincent*, **3:116 ff**. Two effects of this love: 1. compassion; its necessity, **3:118**. 2. assistance; Vincent has a special grace for this which he gave to his followers, **3:119-20**. Some details relative to the times of public misery, **Ibid**. Care of the foundlings, **3:122**. Vincent sends needles to a tailor in need, **3:128**. He sends a truss to a poor peasant, **3:238**. He reduces the amount of food and wine served to the community at Saint Lazare during the times of public misery, **3:264**. See, *Alms, Public Misery, Poor*.

Charity (towards bishops). Loving respect that Vincent has towards them, **3:130 ff**. See, *Bishops*.

Charity (towards ecclesiastics and religious), **3:139 ff**. See, *Ecclesiastics, Religious*.

Charity (towards members of his own community). **1:243,246,252; 3:147 ff**. By his instruction and encouragement, **3:148**. By his behavior, **3:150**. In their trials and in their work, **3:150-51**. In their illnesses, **3:154-55**. Towards their families, **3:155**.

Charity (towards his enemies). The excellence of this virtue. Feelings and conduct of Vincent, **3:156 ff**. Several examples, **3:157**.

Charity (towards the slaves). Throughout his life Vincent has a great compassion for them based on his own experiences, **1:47**. See, *Slaves*.

Charity (fraternal). Charity is the paradise of communities, **1:117**. Vincent often recommends this virtue to his community, **3:148**. This is a sign of predestination, **Ibid**. The Congregation of the Mission will endure as long as it practices this, **Ibid**. See, *Friendship, Cordiality, Support, Union*.

Charity (Confraternity of). Nature and excellence of this work. Its origin at Chatillon les Dombes (1617). Its results, **1:72; 2:285-86**. Vincent establishes these in almost all of the parishes where missions are given whether in France or abroad, **1:73,87,127-28,131; 2:23,68,71,78,287-88,341**. He commissions Louise de Marillac to visit many of them (1629), **1:129**. He gives them a common rule, **2:288-90**.

Charity (Ladies of). The first Ladies of Charity at Chatillon: Mademoiselles de la Chassaigne and Charlotte de Brie. Their heroic example (1617), **2:286**.

Origins of the Assemblies of the Ladies of Charity at Paris (1634), **1:152; 2:303**. They take on service at the Hotel Dieu (June 1634), **1:153**. Second Assembly and the nomination of officers, **Ibid**. More than 200 noble women are members, **Ibid**. Establishment of an assembly of the Ladies of Charity at the royal court (1635). End of this work, and their exercises of piety, **Ibid**.

Spiritual and temporal services of the Ladies at Hotel Dieu. Advice of Vincent on this subject, **1:154 ff**. They teach the sick how to make an examination of conscience in preparation for confession, **1:156**. Assembly of the Fourteen, **1:157**. They gather the resources to hire six priests as chaplains at the hospital, **1:158**. Vincent asks them to take on the work of the foundlings. Conference given to convince them of the value of this work (1635), **1:161; 2:303**. Principal works of the Ladies in Paris, **2:303-04**. They contribute to send confreres on the foreign missions, **2:304**. Vincent speaks of the excellence of this group as a work of God, **2:308**. The mission that God has confided to them is very honorable, **2:309**. Jesus Christ himself is honored by their love and service of the poor, **2:310**. The first means for successfully accomplishing their work; personal transformation, **2:311**. The model for all of their actions is to be found in the Gospel, **2:312**. The second means; moderation and discretion in the accomplishment of their functions. Third means; zeal for the extension and the renewal of their company, **2:314**. He recommends that they make periodic pilgrimages to sanctuaries of the Blessed Virgin. He often accompanies them on these trips, **3:93**.

They furnish Vincent with considerable sums to assist *Lorraine and the other ravaged provinces* during the war (1640), **1:185-86, 2:304,329**. They contribute to the relief of the provinces of Picardy and Champagne (1650), **1:204-05; 2:332,335,344**. Vincent says that they will be rewarded in heaven for their service to the clergy and to the Church, **2:345**.

During the Fronde (1652) they assist the unfortunate in Paris, **3:121**. They provide for nuns and young girls who seek refuge in the capital, **1:210-12**.

They urge Vincent to undertake the work of the general hospital, and provide generous funds for this (1653), **1:226,228-29**. Details of other works in which the Ladies are involved, **2:303-04**. Conference given by Vincent on the state of the works of the Ladies, and the motives for continuing, **2:304-17**. Account of their work at Hotel Dieu, **2:305**. Donations for the relief of the provinces of Champagne and Picardy from 1650 to 1652. Accounting of their use, **2:305**. Expenses in 1656 for the foundlings, **2:307**. Edification of these women when hearing Vincent speaking to them, **3:187**.

The Daughters of Charity assist them in serving the sick at Hotel Dieu in Paris (1636), **1:155**.

Charity (Daughters of).

1. *Their Founding.*

God's design in this institution. Its creation must be especially attributed to divine providence, **1:133 ff**. Vincent's role in its establishment, **2:300**. He says that the Daughters had obviously been raised and assembled together by providence, **3:19**. Beginning of this Institute, **1:133 ff.; 2:291,300**. The Cardinal de Vendome, the legate of the pope, confirms the statutes of the Company of the Daughters of Charity as approved by the archbishop of Paris, **2:291**.

The first Daughters of Charity and the edification they caused, **1:136**. Deaths of several sisters caring for wounded soldiers at Calais, **2:298**. The example of a Daughter of Charity who asks to be assigned there. Four sisters are sent, **2:299**.

2. *The excellence of their vocation.*

How the Company of the Daughters of Charity is excellent in God's eyes, **1:137**. The poor that they serve are their friends in heaven and will one day welcome them there, **2:295**. They find a true contentment in their vocation which they could not have found in the world, **Ibid**. The empires and kingdoms of the world are only dust when compared to the glory with which they will one day be crowned, **2:297**. Although they are only poor women on the earth they will become great queens in heaven, **Ibid**.

3. *Their works.*

The ends for which they were established, **2:291-92**. Details of their works in 1646 and 1660, **2:296**.

The care of the poor is their principal work, with special attention paid to their spiritual care, **1:136; 2:294**.

They instruct poor young girls, **1:136**. They teach abandoned children, **3:123**.
They care for prisoners, **1:149; 2:296**. They work at the Hospital of the Petites Maisons and the Nom de Jesus, **1:225, 2:296**.
They assist the Ladies of Charity in serving the poor at Hotel Dieu (1636), **1:155; 2:296**.
They are charged with the care of the foundlings at Paris, **1:161; 2:296**.
In 1650-51 at Picardy and at Sedan they care for the unfortunate victims of the war, **1:205; 2:335-36**. They help the poor in the ruined city of Palaiseau (1652), **1:209**. Several are victims to their charity in caring for the poor at Palaiseau and Etampes, **1:209**. They distribute food to the starving in Paris in 1652, **1:211**. They are sent to Calais and Rethel to care for wounded soldiers, **2:298**.
Help that they give to poor refugees in Paris during the wars of the Fronde, **2:296**.
They are sent to other cities and other countries, **2:454**. They are requested for service in Poitou and Richelieu. Letter of Vincent, **Ibid**.
How God blessed their works and how they developed. Actual state, **1:137; 2:300**.

4. *Nature of their Institute*.

The Daughters of Charity have more need of virtue than cloistered religious, **2:292-93**. For their cloister they have only the streets of the city, etc., **2:293**. Why they are not religious, **2:301**.
The admirable perfection of their principal rules, **2:292 ff**. He asks them to share their reflections on the topics of his conferences, **2:302**.
No dowry is required for their entrance into the community. All they are to bring is their first habit, **2:293**.
They are placed under the authority of the superior general of the Congregation of the Mission, **2:291-92**. Why the Missionaries are charged with assisting in their direction, **2:300**.

Charles I (king of England), **2:128**.

Charles II (king of England), **2:128**.

Charles X (the duke of Lorraine). His defeat by Louis XIII, **1:185**.

Charles Emmanuel II (the duke of Savoy), **2:80**.

Charlet (Etienne) French provincial of the Jesuits, **1:62**.

Charleville. Vincent sends Missionaries and aid to this city, **1:205**. The Missionaries establish a Confraternity of Charity there, **2:341**.

Charmes (town in the diocese of Toul). Mission held there in 1656, **2:44**.

Charton (Jacques). Penitentiary of Notre Dame and director of the Seminary of Trente-trois. He is named as a member of the Council of Conscience, **1:192**.

Chartres (city and diocese of). Louise de Marillac visits the Confraternities of Charity in this diocese, **1:130**. Results of the missions, and the satisfaction of the bishops, **2:14**. Success of the Ordination Retreats (1644), **2:202-03**. Vincent makes a pilgrimage to Notre Dame de Chartres, **3:93**. See, *Lescot (Jacques)*.

Chassaigne (Mademoiselle de la). Noble lady at the parish of Chatillon who brings to Vincent's attention the needs of a sick family in the parish. One of the first members of the Confraternity of Charity here, **1:72**.

Chastity. The admirable examples of the young Christian slaves enduring death to preserve this virtue, **2:111**. Vincent recommends that his Missionaries be vigilant when working among faithless and corrupt people, **2:136**. *Teaching and example of Vincent*, **3:268 ff**. What their Rule prescribes for the Missionaries, **3:268**. Vincent's response to a Missionary who asks if it is appropriate to take the pulse of a dying woman, **Ibid.** Recommendations concerning the temptations relative to this virtue, **3:269.** Avoiding letters which are too tender or affectionate. Do not sustain relations with those who write these letters, **3:270.** Precautions to be taken to preserve this virtue, **Ibid.** Reserve of the saint in dealing with the Ladies of Charity and Louise de Marillac, **3:271.** When speaking to a woman in private he always leaves the door of the room open. He admonishes a brother who closes the door on one of these occasions, **Ibid.** His zeal to assist large numbers of women whose virtue is in danger, **3:272.** See, *Purity.*

Chateaudun (city of). Site of a hospital served by the Daughters of Charity, **2:296.**

Chateau l'Eveque (summer residence of the bishop of Perigueux). Vincent is ordained to the priesthood here (1600), **1:39.** See, *Bourdeilles (Francois de).*

Chateau Porcien (town in Picardy). The Missionaries establish a Confraternity of Charity there, **2:341.**

Chateau Salins (city in Lorraine). Vincent sends assistance there, **2:329.**

Chatel sur Moselle (town in the diocese of Toul). Helped by Vincent, **2:329.**

Chatillon les Dombes (town now located in the archdiocese of Lyons). Vincent is named pastor there. Good that he accomplishes (1617), **1:65.** Vincent leaves the parish to the regret of his parishoners, **1:70.**
Circumstances surrounding the foundation of the Confraternity of Charity in this parish (1617), **1:72.** This Confraternity is the first and the model for all that will follow, **1:73.** After forty years it is still operating effectively, **1:75; 2:286.**
Account of Vincent's conversion of several heretics, **1:74.** The conversion of Monsieur de Rougemont, **1:77.**

Chauny (town near Soissons). Vincent sends Missionaries and assistance there, **1:205.**

Cheilly (parish in the diocese of Tours). Mission there, **2:54.**

Cherasco (in Piedmont). Mission held there, **2:83.**

Chetif (Marguerite), Daughter of Charity. Vincent gives her instructions relative to the admission of postulants to the Daughters of Charity, **3:311.** She succeeds Louise de Marillac as superioress of the Daughters, **1:24.**

Cheverny (Anne Hurault de), **2:271.**

Chiavari (in the diocese of Genoa). Mission held there, **2:66.**

Chigi (Fabio), cardinal, secretary of state, and later pope (Alexander VII). His role in the condemnation of Jansenism, **2:364.** See, *Alexander VII.*

China. The Ladies of Charity contribute to support missionary activities here, **2:304.**

Chomel (the Abbe of). Former student of Vincent. Vicar general of the diocese of Saint Flour. He generously assists Vincent's works, especially many seminaries, **2:258.**

Christine of France, (sister of Louis XIII, and the duchess of Savoy). She has a Mission given at Bra in Piedmont, **2:80-81.**

Chrysostom (John), saint. Cited on the virtue of humility, **3:203.**

Cicero (Latin poet). Cited, **1:91.**

Clement VIII (pope). Vincent sees him at Rome, **1:48.** His apprehensions at the losses suffered by the Church, **2:169.** Eulogy of his holiness, **2:170.** Vision that he had on the occasion of the absolution that he granted to Henry IV, **3:295.**

Clement XII (pope). He canonizes Vincent on June 16, 1737, **1:25.**

Clergy. State of the clergy in France at the end of the sixteenth century, **1:31-32.** At the beginning of the seventeenth century, **2:185 ff.** Various efforts of Vincent to remedy this deplorable situation: the ordination retreats, **1:138 ff.**, the spiritual conferences for ecclesiastics, **1:144 ff.**, the establishment of several seminaries, **1:164 ff.** Dedication of Vincent when he is employed in the ecclesiastical affairs of the kingdom on the Council of Conscience during the regency of the queen mother, **1:192 ff.** Vincent desires that in the course of a mission several conferences should be given to the local ecclesiastics, **2:23.** Example of this practice in the missions given at Usseau, **2:34.** The Missionaries must greatly esteem and honor those ecclesiastics whom they serve, **2:191.** To prepare good priests is to do the work of Jesus Christ, **Ibid.** It is necessary to work with zeal because wicked priests are the cause of the problems in the Church, **2:192-93.** To form better priests is the highest task in the world, **2:194.** To produce a good priest is to produce a masterpiece, **2:197.** It is necessary to serve the clergy with eagerness and devotion; meeting their desires and their needs as much as one reasonably can, **2:188,195,197.** In order to serve them it is necessary to ask God to be filled with a spirit of the priesthood, **2:191.** Applying oneself to this work with feelings of unworthiness and humility, **2:193,196.** It is not necessary to try to teach them, but rather to give them a good example by treating them cordially and humbly, and by praying for them, **2:194.** Having respect for them, **Ibid.** Vincent complements a laybrother who had prayed that God would give good bishops and priests to his Church, **2:196.** How he began the important work of the seminaries, **2:249 ff.** Sentiments of charity of Vincent towards the ecclesiastics, **3:139 ff.** Service given to a great number of them; some details, **3:141 ff.** General rules of conduct for the Daughters of Charity with regards to ecclesiastics, **2:295.** With regards to the Missionaries, **2:301.** See, *Conferences, Church, Pastors, Bishops.*

Clermont (Francois de), bishop of Noyon. He confides the direction of his seminary to the Missionaries, **1:235.**

Clichy (parish near Paris). Vincent is named pastor of Clichy. His conduct among his parishoners and his associates (1612), **1:52.** Favorable testimony of a theologian about the faith and conduct of the people of this parish, **1:54.**

Climacus (John), saint. On testing those to be received into religious life, **1:179.**

Codoing (Bernard), priest of the Mission. His works and success at Genoa (1645), **2:66.**

Coeffort (Notre Dame de), collegiate church in the city of Le Mans is united to the Congregation (1645), **1:232.**

Coelmez (Monsieur de), chancellor of the University of Toulouse, **1:40.**

Collet (Pierre). Eighteenth-century Lazarist and biographer of Vincent. Notes from his work, **1:9,12,35; 2:159; 3:38.**

Colonna (Girolamo), cardinal, **2:62.**

Comet (Monsieur de) the elder, lawyer and judge from Dax. He entrusts Vincent with the education of his children, **1:38.** He procures for him the parish of Thil, **1:40.**

Comet (Monsieur de) son of the above, a lawyer in the presidial court of Dax. Vincent sends him the account of his captivity in Tunis, **1:43.** Vincent writes him from Rome, **1:47.**

Communion. Vincent's personal reflections on the reception of the eucharist, **3:79** His sentiments of fervor: "Do you not feel, my brothers, divine fire burning in your hearts when you receive the adorable body of Jesus Christ in communion?" **Ibid.** He tells a scrupulous woman that she had done wrong to omit receiving communion because of some interior pain, **3:79-80.** He deplores the Jansenist opinions which oppose frequent communion. Story of a pious woman led astray by the new teachers, **3:80-81.** The reading of Arnauld's book, *On Frequent Communion*, considerably diminishes the number of communicants in Paris, **Ibid.**

Communities (Religious). The requisite qualities for members, **1:182-83.** Numerous services that Vincent gives to them, **1:242; 2:385 ff.** His esteem and his love for the secular communities, **3:140.** See, *Religious.*

Compassion. Vincent's love of the poor has the effect of filling his heart with compassion, **3:118.** It is necessary that we never encounter a poor person without consoling him; if we can, **Ibid.** Example of Jesus Christ. Four effects of the spirit of compassion, **3:119.** Reasons for bearing with the faults of a neighbor rather than becoming indignant, **3:169.**

Conde (Henry II de Bourbon, prince of). He opposes Jansensism with the support of Vincent, **2:352.**

Conde (Louis II de Bourbon, prince of), son of the above. His politics, **1:211,216.** His gracious response to the humble words of Vincent, **3:190.**

Condescension. Reasons for practicing this virtue; examples from Vincent, **3:210 ff., 248-49.** Its extent, **3:210.** "Be as polite as you can, provided that you do not contravene God's will," **3:211.** May God give us the grace to see good, in our Lord, in all that is not really evil. **3:298.**

Condomois (county of). Missions given here, **1:231.**

Condren (Charles de), the second superior general of the Oratory. He tells Vincent that the humility of the first Missionaries is a sign of the divine institution of the Congregation of the Mission, **1:117-118.** His opposition to Jansenism, **2:350.**

Conduct (of Vincent). In general, **1:100 ff,108 ff; 2:270 ff.** With respect to Jansenists, **2:370.** With respect to the Council of Conscience, **2:372; 3:156-157.**
Examples and advice of the saint, **3:293 ff.** His goals and his means, **Ibid.** The characteristics of his conduct; humility, **3:294,** prudence, **3:295,** exactness, **3:297,** meekness and gentleness, **3:299.** The rules which he gives for the formation of Missionaries for his Company, **3:301;** by correction, **3:302;** and edification, **3:309.** Temporal affairs of the houses of the Congregation, **3:312 ff.** Advice of Vincent to one of his Missionaries whom he had made superior of a house, **3:317.** See, *Affairs, Counsel, Constancy, Equality of spirit, etc.*

Conferences (given by Vincent to the Missionaries and to the Daughters of Charity), **1:24,241; 2:187-88; 3:38,148.**

Conferences (given to the priests of the Mission). From the beginning Vincent gives conferences to the Missionaries. Excellence of this practice, **1:144.** He reminds the Missionaries that he is sending to be chaplains to the army to be faithful to their vocations, and he indicates to them the best way to undertake their work, **1:175-77.** The reasons that the Missionaries have to esteem the value of these conferences, **2:216-17.**

Conferences (given to the Daughters of Charity). Vincent gives the Daughters of Charity a great number of spiritual conferences, **2:302.**

Conferences (given to the Ladies of Charity). Conferences of the saint, **2:304 ff.** Edification of these ladies in listening to the words of Vincent; various accounts, **3:38.**

Conferences (of the Ecclesiastics at Saint Lazare, or the Tuesday Conferences). Origin of this group (1633). The first members. Subjects and methods of the conferences, **1:144**

ff; **2:200,210 ff.** Character of the teachings of Vincent. How the ecclesiastics enjoyed and appreciated his words, **1:145; 2:213; 3:38,96.** First meeting at Saint Lazare. Teaching of Vincent on the purpose of this association, **2:211.** He stresses simple topics, **2:213.** Rules governing the conference, **2:214-15.** Progress of this Company. The number of members who are a part of the conferences in Paris, **2:215.** Their meditations are made with great piety and spirit, **3:69.** This assembly was like a holy seedbed; it supplied France with many prelates who performed their duties with holiness. Excellent fruits of this institution, **1:145; 2:215,217.** Richelieu expresses his satisfaction. He asks Vincent for the names of its members who are qualified to be named to vacant bishoprics, **1:146.** The members of the assembly make a particular promise to help the poor of the hospitals, or of going to the country to work with the priests of the Mission, **1:145; 2:218.** Various missions given by the ecclesiastics of the conference to the refugees from Lorraine, and to the soldiers in the hospitals of Paris, **1:229; 2:218 ff.** With great success they give a mission at Metz in 1658, **1:234-35.** Remarkable results obtained by a mission given among the judicial officials, **2:220-21.** Mission given in the faubourg Saint Germain in 1641, **2:222.**

Another assembly meets on Thursday at Bons Enfants for the priests of Hotel Dieu and the students of theology (1642), **1:146.**

The practice of the conferences expands to other dioceses in France, **1:146; 2:224.** In Italy, **2:227.** Vincent would like conferences to be given to local ecclesiastics during the course of missions, **2:23.** This is practiced in France, **2:34;** in Italy, **2:68-69;** in Piedmont, **2:78-79,83.** He gives a conference on the virtues of Jean Jacques Olier (1656), **3:201-02.** An ecclesiastic of the conference asks the dying Vincent for his blessing for all the members of the assembly. They sponsor a solemn service and funeral oration for the saint in Paris in the church of Saint Germain l'Auxerrois (1660), **1:261-62.**

Confession. Vincent as spiritual director of Madame de Gondi obliges her occasionally to consult another confessor, **1:64.** Children are to receive the sacrament at the end of a mission, **2:23.**

Confession (general). Of a peasant in the village of Gannes (1617), **1:59.** Their necessity, **1:59-60; 2:13.** Their fruits among the Christian slaves in Barbary, **2:111.**

Confidence (in God). During his captivity Vincent never stops hoping that God will rescue him, **1:46.** Examples and teaching of Vincent on this virtue, **3:21 ff.** Three people are more than ten when our Savior lends his assistance; and he always helps when he asks us to do something which is not humanly possible, **3:21.** We have a great reason to distrust our own efforts, but we have an even greater reason to trust in God, **3:22.** Do not be frightened by a year of scarcity, nor by several; but trust in God who is always abundant in his blessings, **3:23.** Our lack of confidence dishonors God, **Ibid.** What should we do when faced with unfortunate events? **3:24.** The abandonment of the saint with respect to his Congregation, **3:25 ff.** He resigns himself to the deaths of his best Missionaries and expresses his reliance on God, **3:29 ff.** Example of Abraham, **Ibid.,** of the Rechabites, **3:30.** The throne of mercies of God is established on the foundation of our own unworthiness, **3:32.** He who relies on God will accomplish what his heart desires, **Ibid.** Those who live with confidence in God will be favored by a special protection on God's part, **3:35.** Providence watches over the Daughters of Charity because they serve the poor. Signs of this protection, **3:35-36.**

Confraternities. Vincent cites the advice of Francis de Sales who counseled everyone to join these, **2:312.**

Confraternities of Charity. See, *Charity, Confraternities of.*

Congregation of the Mission. See, *Mission, Congregation of.*

Consolation. Vincent had a special grace for consoling the afflicted, **1:98.**

Constancy. Example of Vincent on the occasion of the deaths of the Missionaries sent to Madagascar, **2:158-59.** He picks himself up again like a palm tree battered by a storm, **2:159.** *Teaching and conduct of Vincent,* **3:280 ff.** He says that one must reject as a temptation the thought of abandoning what has been decided upon after discernment, **3:295.** Once an affair has begun it has to be pursued until it is finished, **3:312.**

Constantinople (capital of the Ottoman Empire and headquarters of the Sultan), **2:90,94,100.**

Constitutions. See, *Rules.*

Consul. French consuls in Tunis and Algiers. The Missionaries are often required to hold these positions, **2:87 ff.**

Contempt. On how to personally profit from the contempt of the world; like the bee who is able to make honey just as well from bitter absinthe as it can from roses, **1:130.**

Conti (Armand de Bourbon, prince of), assists at the funeral of Vincent, **1:262.** His assistance in a lawsuit involving the seminary at Cahors, **3:111.**

Contradiction. Because of his humility Vincent tries never to contradict anyone, **3:231.**

Controversies. Vincent desires that theological polemics and any other controversies be avoided, **2:25.** He recommends, to this end, that the abridged version of Becanus be studied, **Ibid.** It is necessary to avoid engaging in controversy in order to promote conversions, **Ibid.**

Conversations. Affability must be the soul of conversation, **3:165-66.** Vincent would stop and reproach himself whenever he realized that he was speaking about himself, **3:188-89.** Example of our Savior, **3:227.** Example of Vincent, **3:261-62.** He never spends time in idle conversation when the time could be better spent elsewhere, **3:316.** See, *Affability, Cordiality.*

Coqueret (Jean), a doctor of theology of the college of Navarre. Vincent consults him, **1:73; 3:43.**

Corbie (city in the province of Picardy). Captured by the Spanish (1636), **1:174; 3:264.**

Cordiality. Vincent had a tender but strong and noble heart which easily conceived an affection for all that he saw was truly good and from God, **1:101.** The saint asks pardon of a laybrother who had come to take care of him and who the saint felt he had not received with enough cordiality, **3:189.** He always receives others with affection, **3:300.** See, *Affability, Union.*

Corinthians (first letter of Saint Paul to the). Citations: 2:2-**1:4**, 7:31-**1:78**, 1:34-**1:196**, 3:5-**1:240**, 9:2-**1:277**, 6:17-**3:42**, 2:9-**3:72**, 9:22-**3:118**, 9:9-**3:143**, 4:15-**3:148**, 4:9-**3:250**, 9:7-**3:267**, 10:13-**3:287**, 4:12-**3:313**.

Corinthians (second letter of Saint Paul to the). Citations: 4:18-**3:19**, 2:15-**3:108**, 8:9-**3:130**, 4:10-**3:268**, 6:8-**3:287**.

Cornet (Nicolas). A doctor of theology of the College of Navarre. He extracts from the book of Jansenius the Five Propositions which sum up the errors which were later condemned by the pope, **2:362.**

Correction (fraternal). See, *Admonitions.*

Corrections. These must always be given with a spirit of mildness. Example and recommendation of Vincent, **3:166 ff.** Without excusing the actions of the guilty, as much as possible they should be given the benefit of the doubt, **3:169-70.** While it is not necessary to be too tolerant with those in need of correction it is necessary to treat them with mildness, **3:171.** Corrections will be well received if they are reasonable and not dictated capriciously, **3:176.** If the superior admonishes someone vigorously he should not do it in an outburst of temper, **3:176-77.** It is generally agreed that no one can be effectively corrected if they are corrected in anger, **3:176.** Vincent uses correction to ensure the proper running of the houses of the community, **3:302-03.** Human nature does not like to receive corrections, but receives them more easily when they are done with mildness as exemplified by Vincent, **Ibid.**

Correspondence. Vincent is very attentive to his correspondence and never writes anything hard to understand, or anything which testifies to any bitterness or a lack of respect or of charity towards those he is writing to, **1:101.** He withholds a letter of a Missionary written to a secular priest encouraging him to enter the company, **1:181.** His reaction in reading a letter which inadvertently contained the news of his impending death, **1:235.** On avoiding expressions in one's correspondence which are too tender or too affectionate, **3:269-70.**

Corsica (island of). In 1652 the Senate of Genoa asks Vincent to give missions on this island. Extraordinary results of these missions, **2:69 ff.** Concerning the Corsican slaves who were freed from Algiers by the Missionaries, **2:123.** See, *Aleria, Campo Lauro, Corte, Cotone, Niolo.*

Corte (in Corsica). Mission held there, **2:70.**

Coste (Pierre). Twentieth-century Vincentian scholar and biographer of Vincent. Notes on Abelly's work, **1:9,12,13-15,38,85,88, 153,159,162; 2:179.**

Cotone (in Corsica). Mission held in this area, **2:70.**

Council of Conscience (or of Ecclesiastical Affairs). Vincent is named a member of this group by Queen Anne of Austria (1643). His sentiments on this occasion, **1:192 ff; 2:184, 372-73.** He fights abuses, **1:193-94; 2:373,376-77 ff.** Cardinal de la Rochefoucauld tells him that it is his duty to retain this position, **2:373.** Rules of conduct that he follows, **Ibid.** Rules of conduct that he has the Council of Conscience adopt to govern the distribution of benefices, **2:374 ff.** He asks God to relieve him of this position, **3:191.** Neither he nor the community ever benefit from his position, **3:247.** Divergences with the views of Mazarin on episcopal appointments, **2:375,380.** Services rendered to the bishops, **2:382 ff.** To the religious orders, **2:385 ff.** To various women's monasteries, **2:391 ff.** To other religious causes, **2:393.** Devotion and fidelity of Vincent to the service of the king, **2:395 ff.** His personal disinterestedness, **2:400.** Adversaries who resented his integrity in the distribution of benefices, **3:156-57,191.** Injuries that he receives because of this, **3:280-81.** Violent scene with a woman whose son he had refused to recommend for the episcopate, **3:281.** Modesty of the saint in the council, **3:190,243.** The testimony of a prelate: "Monsieur Vincent is always Monsieur Vincent," **3:275.**

Council of Trent. See, *Trent, Council of.*

Counsel. How Vincent gives advice to others, **1:100.** How he gives counsel and offers his advice, **Ibid; 2:274-75.** On never making a decision in important matters without first seeking advice. On deciding whom to consult, **3:43,293-94.** The saint voluntarily defers to the counsel of others, **3:232.** God blesses personal resolutions taken with the advice of others, **3:295,320.** Once a judgment has been reached it should be adhered to firmly especially with regard to any temptation to abandon it, **3:295.** Prudent conduct of Vincent when he is asked to give counsel, **3:295-96.**

Couroumbaille (location in Barbary). Christian slaves held here are visited by the Missionaries, **2:115**.

Crecy (city in the diocese of Meaux). Establishment there of a community house (1641), **1:231**.

Cromwell (Oliver), the Lord Protector of England. His persecution of Catholics in England and Ireland, **2:128,179,340**.

Cross. If we love others and have confidence in God it is necessary to carry the cross, **2:101**. There must be power in the cross since God ordinarily gives success to the services which are given to him in persecutions and martyrdom, **2:180**. Vincent says that it would be better to be possessed by the devil than not to have a cross to carry in life, **3:285**. Our sufferings are a cross which elevate us above the life of earth, **3:288**. Unhappiness of those who flee from the cross; because only in feeling its weight can one overcome it, **3:302**. See, *Trials, Sicknesses, Patience, Suffering*.

Cross (Daughters of the). Abelly serves as their ecclesiastical superior, **1:10**. Origins and purpose of this community. Services which Vincent gives to them, **1:195 ff.** At the death of their foundress, Madame de Villeneuve, Vincent helps in the preservation of this community, **1:196**. See, *Villeneuve (Madame de)*.

Cupif (Robert), bishop of Saint Pol de Leon, and then of Dol. Lawsuit over his first diocese, **2:382**.

Curiosity (sensual). Its dangers and the necessity of conquering it, **3:255,261,301-02**. How Vincent restrained it by mortification of the eyes and ears, **3:265**.

Cyprian, (Saint), bishop of Carthage. The chapel at the consulate in Algiers is placed under his patronage, **2:107**. His views on the care to be taken of religious women, **2:391**.

D

Daniel (Old Testament prophet), **1:239**. Citation from the Book of Daniel, **2:28**.

Dathan (Old Testament figure), **3:206**.

Daughters (of Charity). See, *Charity, Daughters of*.

Daughters (of the Cross). See, *Cross, Daughters of the*.

Daughters (of Providence). See, *Providence, Daughters of*.

Daveroult (Pierre), priest of the Mission. He is sent to Madagascar. Shipwrecks, **2:159; 3:276**.

David (Old Testament king), **1:251; 3:187**.

David (Jean), priest of the Mission. His death in the service of the poor at Etampes during the wars of the Fronde, **1:209**.

Davy du Perron (Jacques), cardinal and archbishop of Sens. Cited, **3:167**.

Dax (diocese of origin of Vincent), **1:35**. Hesitation of the saint to establish a community house in his home region, **3:261**. See, *Desclaux (Jacques)*.

Death. The preparations made by Vincent for his death. Like the apostle he looked forward to death since it would unite him with Christ, **1:202,256**. Before his death he declares that for eighteen years he had never gone to bed without first preparing himself to appear before God during the night, **1:257**. During an illness twenty-five years previously he had been prepared to die. His only disappointment at that time was that he had not yet given the community its rules, **Ibid.** He says of the sleep that comes before death, that it is the brother who comes to meet his sister death. His tranquility of soul at this time, **1:260; 3:279.** His death on September 27, 1660, at four o'clock in the morning, **1:261; 3:279.** His tomb in the church of Saint Lazare, **1:262.**

"It matters not if we die in the fight. Only let us die happily with our weapons in our hands; for by our death the Company will not be poorer," **2:168.** The most glorious and the most desirable death is that which finds us working in the service of Jesus Christ, **2:280.** The death of Jesus Christ was harsh and without any human consolation. It is in order to honor this death that many saints have had the desire to die alone and abandoned by men, in the confidence that they would have God to assist them, **Ibid.** What is the best preparation for death? Answer of Vincent to Louis XIII, **3:88-89.** Those who have loved the poor during their lives need have no fear of death, **3:117.**

How Vincent is saddened by the death of Missionaries, **1:246.** Death of Louise de Marillac, **Ibid.** Antoine Dufour who gave his life to God in return for the preservation of Vincent's life, **1:251.** Deaths of the Missionaries to Madagascar, **3:54-55,103.** See, *Madagascar.*

Defects (which Vincent was reproached for). It took him too long to make up his mind and carry out his decisions; and he spoke too poorly of himself and too well of others, **1:101-02.**

Deffita (Monsieur), a lawyer of the Parlement of Paris, **3:252.**

Dehorgny (Jean), priest of the Mission. One of the first companions of Vincent. Biographical notice, **1:111.** He visits the Missionaries working in Lorraine (1640), **2:322.** As superior of the College des Bons Enfants in 1642. He gives an account of the good work done here, **2:254.**

De la Paix (Antoine), a young Christian slave in Barbary. He endures torture and death in order to preserve his virtue, **2:111-12.**

Delaunay (Christopher), laybrother of the Mission. His heroic example in the shipwreck at Saint Nazaire, **2:161.**

Delbene (Barthelemy), bishop of Agen. He establishes at Notre Dame de la Rose a house of the Congregation founded by the duchess of Aiguillon, **1:231.** He confides the direction of his seminary to the Missionaries, **1:233.**

Delville (Guillaume), priest of the Mission. Vincent reprimands him for having published, without permission, an account of the Congregation and it works, **3:202-03.**

Deniat (village in the diocese of Saintes). Results of a mission held here, **2:33.**

Denmark. Fallen into heresy, **1:233; 2:170,192.**

De Paul (Jean), father of Vincent, **1:35-37,40.** Why the saint was simply called Monsieur Vincent, **3:182.**

De Sales (Francis), saint, bishop of Geneva. Friendship of the saint and Vincent, **1:90-91.** Agreement with Saint Jane de Chantal giving Vincent the direction of the Visitandines in Paris, **1:91; 2:266-67; 3:208.** He often recommends the use of spiritual retreats, **1:141.** Vincent cites his interpretation of the prayer *In spiritu humilitatis,* **2:19.** Miraculous healing through his intercession is attested to by Vincent, **2:280 ff.** In a vision, God reveals to Vincent the heavenly glory of the holy bishop and of Saint Jane de Chantal, **2:283-84.** He advises the laity to join confraternities, **2:312.** His teaching on gentleness, **3:163.** Vincent praises his meekness, **3:165.** He cites the example of his method of dealing with heretics, **3:166-67.** He was insensible to any sentiments of vanity, **3:202.**

Desbordes (Monsieur), viscount of Soude, auditor of accounts. Vincent informs him that the community had lost the Orsigny farm in a lawsuit. **3:24,162.** He explains to him his reasons for refusing to pursue a civil appeal against the sentence of the court, **3:252-53.**

De la Salle (Jean), one of the first companions of Vincent, **1:110.** The first director of the internal seminary of the Congregation (1637), **Ibid.**

Deschamps (Edmond), priest of the Mission. His devotion in Champagne during the war. His works and his death at Etampes in the service of the poor, **1:209; 2:340.**

Desclaux (Jacques), bishop of Dax. Vincent dissuades him from coming to the court to claim reparation for some damages that the war had caused in his diocese, **1:216.**

Descordes (Monsieur), a counselor to the Chatelet and administrator of the hospital of Quinze-Vingts. He asks Vincent to establish a Confraternity of Charity at the hospital, **1:131.**

Desdames (Guillaume), priest of the Mission. In Poland, **2:164,166.**

Desfontaines (Pasquier), priest of the Mission. Sent to Madagascar, **2:159-60.**

Desires. A constant desire for personal perfection is the light which illumines a person before others, **2:311.**

Des Isles (Nicolas). Contemporary religious controversialist, **3:161.**

Des Lions (Jean), a doctor of theology of the Sorbonne, dean of the diocese of Senlis. Letter from Vincent trying to win him back from the Jansenist party. Failure of these attempts, **2:368.**

Desmoulins (Monsieur), superior of the Oratory at Macon. His testimony in favor of Vincent, **1:74,77,87.**

Detachment (from persons). Example of Vincent on the subject of his own congregation, **3:52-53.** Relative to the persons whom he cherishes most, **3:53,285.** He is ready to consent to the destruction of his own congregation if it is the will of God, **3:89.** Relative to the Company of the Daughters of Charity and to their establishments, **3:248.** His reaction in learning of the shipwrecks and the deaths of the Missionaries traveling to Madagascar, etc., **3:276 ff.** At the death of Antoine Portail, **3:278.** At the death of Louise de Marillac, **3:279.** Vincent cites the example of our Lord who separated himself from his own mother and his apostles, **3:300.** Example of Vincent, **3:296.** See, *Disinterestedness, Evenness of Spirit.*

Detachment (from temporal goods). Vincent leaves his position as chaplain to Queen Marguerite in order to become the pastor of a small parish, **1:53.** Example of the count of Rougemont, **1:77.** The conduct of Vincent when he is offered Saint Lazare; showing his detachment from such things, **1:120 ff.** He refuses even to go and see the property at Saint Lazare after he is first asked to accept it, **1:122.** He never uses his power or position at court to obtain anything for his own Congregation, **2:399.** He submits to temporal loses which result from his loyalty to the king; and never complains of these, **2:400.** The true Missionary must never be dependent upon temporal goods, but rather should depend solely on the providence of the Lord. Some examples, **3:23 ff.** Conduct of the saint in the face of a considerable temporal loss, **3:162,249.** See, *Orsigny.* His evenness of spirit in this trials, **3:275,283.** *Examples and Teaching of Vincent* on the necessary detachment from temporal goods, **3:242 ff.** It is necessary to lovingly accept temporal loses when God permits them to happen, **3:249-250.**

Deuteronomy (book of the Old Testament). Cited in Abelly: 34:5-**1:259**, 25:4-**3:143.**

Devolution (of benefices). Legal definition, **2:379.**

Devotion (towards God). *Examples and Teaching of Vincent,* **3:72 ff.** His great esteem for the perfections of God, **3:72.** His piety in the celebration of the divine office, and towards the mysteries of religion, **3:73-74.** His piety in prayer and in the celebration of the eucharist, **3:74-75.** How he lamented the lack of devotion of many Christians, **3:95.** Accounts given of his piety and the edification of others which resulted from it, **3:96.** See, *Eucharist, Imitation of Our Lord.*

Devotion (of Vincent towards Jesus Christ). Examples and teaching of Vincent, **3:83 ff.** See, *Jesus Christ.*

Devotion (of Vincent to the Blessed Virgin, and to the saints). *His examples and his teaching,* **3:92 ff.** See, *Mary, Saints.*

Dey (local ruler in Tunis and Algiers), **2:87,90,97.**

Dian Machicore (tribal leader on Madagascar), **2:157.**

Dian Masse (tribal leader on Madagascar), **2:152.**

Dieppe (Jean), priest of the Mission. His apostolic works and his death at Algiers, **2:88.**

Dieuze (city in the province of Lorraine). Vincent sends assistance there, **2:329.**

Diharse (Salvat), bishop of Tarbes, **1:38.**

Dinet (Jacques), Jesuit confessor of Louis XIII, **1:190.**

Dinet (Louis), bishop of Macon. He approves the Confraternity of Charity established in the city by Vincent (1623), **1:88.**

Dinner. The great edification given to the prior of Saint Lazare, Adrien Le Bon, when eating one day at a meal with the first confreres, **1:121.** Vincent often reflects on whether the community really had earned the food that they were to eat, **1:214; 3:239,243.** His personal modesty and his mortification. In his last illness, he will not permit any special food to be brought to him, **1:253; 3:244,266.** His devotion to the prayers said at dinner, **3:24.** He orders a reduction in the amount of food served to the community during the time of the public miseries. Reflections of the saint, **3:264,313-14.**

Director (spiritual). A visible angel to guide us, **1:52.** Necessity of obedience to one's director. Example of Vincent, **3:207.**

Disinterestedness (of the conduct of Vincent), **1:109.** The saint never wished to attract anyone to join his institute who might be considering joining some other congregation, **1:180-82.** He never asks any favor from the Council of Conscience for himself, nor on behalf of any of his interests, **1:194.** Vincent was a perfect model of this virtue in his relations with the court and with the nobility, **2:398.** Testimony of a State counselor, **2:399.** Response of the saint to the offers of the mayor of a city, **3:234.** See, *Temporal Goods, Detachment.*

Disputes. Vincent carefully avoids involvement in them, **3:211.**

Disunity. See, *Unity.*

Divine Office. While at home Vincent always recites it while kneeling, **1:243.** He continues to recite it until his last illness. The pope sends him a brief to dispense him from recitation, **1:258.** He zealously reproves any mistakes made in the rubrics, **2:276.** He recites it with a devout spirit, **3:93.**

Dodin (André), twentieth-century Vincentian historian. His notes and remarks on Abelly, **1:13,17,19; 2:38,345; 3:108,248.**

Dolivet (Julien), priest of the Mission. Problems caused by this Missionary, **3:298.**

Donchery (a village near Sedan). Vincent sends Missionaries and aid to this area, **1:205**. They establish a Confraternity of Charity there, **2:341**.

Drelincourt (Charles), Protestant minister in Paris, **3:160**.

Dress (of the Missionaries). Simplicity and propriety of Vincent, **3:191**. Poverty and cleanliness. How he dresses at the court, **3:243**. Mortification of Vincent, **3:264**.

Duchesne (Bernard), a doctor of theology of the Sorbonne. He gives a mission with Vincent at Montmirail (1622), **1:81**.

Duchesne (Jerome), a doctor of theology of the Sorbonne, archdeacon of Beauvais. He preaches the ordination retreats at Beauvais with Vincent (1628). He makes a general confession of his life to Vincent, **1:139-40**.

Du Coudray (Francois), priest of the Mission. One of the first companions of Vincent, **1:110**. The saint dissuades him from working on a new Syriac translation of the Bible, **2:35**. He evangelizes the army in Picardy (1636), **1:175; 2:318**.

Ducournau (Bertrand), laybrother of the Mission, and one of Vincent's secretaries. He is asked to preserve and record the "holy discourses of Monsieur Vincent," **1:10,12,24**. He preserves the letter relative to the captivity of Vincent, **1:46**. His role in having Vincent's portrait painted, **1:100**.

Duel. Zeal of Vincent for the banning of dueling, **1:57-58; 2:394-95**. He converts the count of Rougemont, a famous duelist, who breaks his sword as proof of his conversion, **1:77-79**.

Dufour (Antoine), priest of the Mission. He offers God his life in exchange for the recovery of Vincent who is ill. The saint is miraculously told of the death of the pious Missionary, and recovers his health (1645), **1:251**.

Dufour (Claude), priest of the Mission. His departure for Madagascar, **2:149**. His work and death at this mission. Eulogy, **2:150-51**.

Du Fresne (Charles), lord of Villeneuve, secretary of Queen Marguerite de Valois, friend of Vincent. His eulogy, **1:49**. Later secretary and steward to Monsieur de Gondi. Testimony that he gives as to the virtue shown by Vincent while living among the de Gondis, **Ibid**. He visits the saint at Chatillon to convince him to return to the Gondis, **1:70**. He gives Vincent a sum of money to use for the relief of his family. The use made of the money by the saint, **3:260**.

Duggan (Dermot), (Duguin, Germaine) priest of the Mission. His departure for Scotland (1651), **2:174**. His letters written from the Hebrides. His apostolic work and his death in these islands. Praise of his virtue, **2:174 ff.; 3:276**.

Du Mecq (Madame), one of the first Ladies of Charity of Hotel Dieu, **1:153**.

Dunkirk (the siege of), **2:298**.

Du Perron. See, *Davy du Perron (Jacques), Noel du Perron (Jacques)*.

Duperroy (Nicolas), priest of the Mission. Work and suffering of this Missionary in Poland, **2:166**.

Duplessis (Christophe), baron of Montbard. Founder of the Charity Store (1652), **1:210**.

Duport (Nicolas), priest of the Mission. His work in Genoa. His death, and eulogy, **3:54,276**.

Durand (Antoine), priest of the Mission, **3:17**. Advice given to him by Vincent when he is named as superior of the seminary at Agde, **3:322 ff**.

Durazzo (Stefano), cardinal, archbishop of Genoa. He asks Vincent for Missionaries to evangelize his diocese (1645). Foundation at Genoa, **1:233**. His letter to Vincent thanking him for the work of his Missionaries, **2:66**. He assists with the missions (1647), **2:67**. He experiences a great consolation from the success of the ordination retreats, **2:203-04**. The Missionaries give a retreat to his clergy. Very consoling results, **2:246**. He gives a retreat with the Missionaries. His exemplary piety, **2:247**. The cardinal writes a letter of consolation to Vincent as he nears death, **1:258**.

Durtal (city located between Le Mans and Angers), **1:201; 3:237**.

Dusault (Jean Jacques), bishop of Dax, **1:38**.

Duties of a Christian. Popular pamphlet published under this title is used with great success, **2:219**.

Duval (Andre), a doctor of theology of the Sorbonne. Vincent asks him for his advice on whether to accept the house of Saint Lazare, **1:122**. The saint suggests to a priest that he seek his advice, **3:43**.

Duval (Monsieur), a canon of Treguier. See, *Treguier*.

Duvergier de Hauranne. See, *Saint Cyran*.

E

Eagerness. Vincent never hurries in his affairs, and he bears their burden with patience and tranquility, **1:100**. Nothing is more common than the failures of matters decided upon with too much haste, **1:102,172**. Was Vincent too sluggish in making decisions? Answer, **1:101-02**. The saint cites several examples drawn from the conduct of God in the ancient law, and of our Savior, **1:227**. One often spoils good works by proceeding too quickly with them, **2:104**. One must be very attentive to the will of God and not decide to undertake anything which does not come from God. Only then can we be assured of his help, **2:314**. Vincent moderates the preoccupations of Louise de Marillac, **3:18-19**. Advice to a Missionary on the same subject, **3:27**. Foresight is good when it is submissive to God, but it becomes excessive when we hurry ourselves, **Ibid**. In order to allow divine providence the time necessary to manifest the divine will one must wait as long as possible before relying on human industry, **3:31**. One cannot act with eagerness without saddening the heart of God, **3:32**. The saint delays his answer to an advantageous proposition in order to avoid the natural temptation of wanting to take immediate advantage of a seemingly favorable opportunity, **3:53**. He will not give an important answer without first pausing to pray to God and implore his light and assistance, **3:56,225**. When we observe a moderation in our actions our Savior is honored. He has taught us to be satisfied with doing his will, since it is not expedient to do everything that we would like to do, **3:85**. Vincent once delayed a decision for an entire month because the natural solution appeared to be hasty, **3:226**. He waits for thirty-three years to give rules to his Congregation, **Ibid**. See, *Affairs*.

Ecouis (collegiate church in the diocese of Evreux). Vincent receives an appointment as a canon and treasurer there from Monsieur de Gondi (1615), **1:55**.

Eigg (island in the Hebrides). Work of the Missionaries there, **2:175-76**.

Elect (the). Will many be saved? **2:311**.

Elijah (Old Testament prophet), **1:212**.

Emmaus (the disciples at), **3:38,96**.

Enemies. Charity of Vincent towards them, **3:156 ff**.

England. Fallen into heresy, **1:223**. Vincent aids the English gentlemen refugees living

356 INDEX

in exile in Paris, **1:188**. The heroic constancy of a young English slave in Barbary, **2:116-17**. Admirable courage of another young Englishman and his companion a young Frenchman, **2:118 ff**. Persecution of Irish Catholics under Cromwell, **2:128 ff**. See, *Ireland, Scotland.*

"Enlightened". Vincent actively opposes their errors which were to be found in many monasteries of women, and in various dioceses in France, **2:393**.

Envy. One of the vices to be most feared by the community, **3:302**.

Epernon (Jean Louis de Nogaret de la Valette), the duke of, **1:42**.

Ephesians (epistle of Saint Paul to the). Cited in Abelly: 4:1-**3:164**.

Ephrem (Saint). Spoken of by Saint Gregory of Nyssa, **3:326**.

Epoisses. Reform of a monastery of the order of Grandmont in this village, **2:387**.

Essarts (village in the Vendee). Success of a mission given in this area, **2:51**.

Establishments (of the Congregation of the Mission). A list of those which were founded during the life of Vincent, **1:230 ff**.

Esther (book of the Old Testament). Cited in Abelly: 4:14-**2:184**.

Etampes (city south of Paris). In 1652, Vincent helps the inhabitants of this city recover from frightful suffering. He sends Missionaries there, **1:208**. The Daughters of Charity there receive the orphans from the villages ruined by the war, **1:209**. Misery and pestilence in this city. Work and death of many Missionaries, and of many Daughters of Charity, **Ibid; 3:121**.

Etienne (Nicolas), priest of the Mission. Danger that he was in by traveling by sea from Nantes to La Rochelle, **3:277**. His work in Madagascar. He is massacred there, **2:159**.

Etrechy (village in the area around Paris). Helped by the Missionaries, **1:208**.

Even Disposition. Excellence of this virtue. Example of Vincent, **3:274 ff**. In his works, **3:274**. In the loss of goods, **3:275**. In the loss of cherished persons, **3:276**. In the loss of honor, **3:278**. In the loss of his health, and in his approaching death, **3:278-79**.

Evreux (diocese of). The good example of some Missionaries who worked in this diocese, **1:117**. See, *Ecouis, Maupas du Tour (Henri de).*

Example. Particular motives by which Vincent exhorts the first Missionaries to be models for their successors, **1:115 ff**. It is the example of our leading good lives that will attract others to work with us; if God is calling them there, **1:181**. The first Missionaries recognizes Vincent as their living rule and try to imitate him, **1:241; 3:308**. Giving good example is more necessary to produce results among the Missionaries than their learning or eloquence, **2:18**. What we see influences us much more than mere words; for we believe our eyes beyond what we merely hear, **2:198**. The efficacy of good example, **2:315; 3:108**. Vincent would like superiors to be the most exemplary and regular, **3:309**. It would be almost useless to give only instruction in the seminaries and not good example as well, **Ibid**. The saint recommends the same thing to a director of a mission for the conduct of his confreres, **3:310**.

Exodus (book of the Old Testament). Cited in Abelly: 34:7-**1:115**, 8:19-**1:122**, 8:15-**2:61**, 4:13-**2:157**, 8:19-**2:224**, 32:11-12-**2:317**.

Ezekiel (book of the Old Testament). Cited in Abelly: 34:3-**1:32**.

F

Fabri (Madeleine), one of the founding Ladies of Charity of Hotel Dieu, **1:153**.

Faith. Firmness of Vincent's faith among the infidels during his captivity, **1:46**. He distrusts all sorts of new speculative propositions or practices, especially in matters of religion, **1:101**. Submission of the saint to the authority of the Church, **1:221**. Persons who otherwise appear to be charitable and virtuous must not be excused if they do not submit to the doctrines defined by the Church, **2:370-71**. It is a great evil to conceal, or even worse, to have a kind of indifference or neutrality when it is a question of doctrines of the faith, **2:371**. Vincent declares that if he should ever teach anything which is contrary to the doctrines of the Church the Congregation should assemble, depose him as Superior General, and expel him from their midst, **3:308**. Qualities of the virtue of faith in Vincent. *Teaching and examples of his strong faith*, **3:15 ff**. See, *Temptations*. The faith of Vincent is pure and simple. His zeal to maintain this purity of faith among his followers, **3:15**. He uses the comparison of looking at the sun; the more directly you look at it the less you are able to see, **Ibid**. Vincent gives thanks to God that he has always been preserved in believing in the truths of the faith, **3:16**. How he wished that one should work to preserve and propagate the faith, **Ibid**. Proofs as to his zeal against Jansenism, **3:18**. Vincent's faith filled him and animated all of his actions, **Ibid**. Vincent takes on the temptations against faith of a doctor of theology, **3:113 ff**. See, *Jansenism, Freedom of Conscience*.

Faith (Sacred Congregation for the Propagation of the), **2:70,126,134**. See, *Propaganda*.

Family. Vincent chooses to allow his family to remain in their humble condition, **1:36; 3:247,258**. He sympathizes and takes an interest in the difficulties of families of members of the Congregation, **3:155**. He often mentions the humble background of his family, **3:257**. See, *Humility*. He exhorts them to accept a calumny against them, and dissuades them from defending themselves publicly, **3:258-59**. One of his family members, after having been convicted of a crime, asks for help to obtain letters of pardon. Vincent refuses to use his influence to help him in this affair, **Ibid**. How he uses a sum of money that had been given to him for them, **3:260**. He thinks that it would be better if his nephews remained in the humble condition of their parents, **3:260-61**. Love of Vincent for his family. Rules that he establishes for himself in expressing this love, **Ibid**. Vincent relates, on the basis of his own experience, how it can be harmful to your vocation to visit your family once you have left them for God's service, **3:257-58**. How he interprets the maxim of Jesus Christ that it is necessary to hate one's parents, **3:258**. See, *Nephew*.

Faure (Francois), bishop of Amiens. He confides the direction of his seminary to the Congregation of the Mission, **1:235**.

Fear of God. See, *God, (Fear of)*.

Feron (Monsieur), a doctor of theology of the Sorbonne, and archdeacon of Chartres. He gives a mission with Vincent at Montmirail (1622), **1:81**.

Ferrer (Vincent), saint. His view on the reform of the ecclesiastical state, **2:254**. Particular devotion of Vincent for this saint and his teaching, **3:94**. Example of, **3:101**. Recommends following the advice of others rather than trusting one's own opinions, **3:211**.

Ferreri (Giuseppe), successor to the vice legate Montorio at Avignon, **1:45**.

Fervor. This virtue has two vices which are very close to it; a lack of fervor, and the excess of fervor. Having excessive fervor is a preferable vice which must be accepted, though moderated, **3:298.**

Feydeau (Mathieu). Author of the condemned Jansenist work, *Catechisme de la grace*, **2:356.**

Feydin (Francois), priest of the Mission. At Richelieu. The saint announces to him that he has been chosen for the Madagascar mission, and gives him useful advice. His departure, **2:160.**

Firmness (in the conduct of Vincent), **1:108; 3:165,280,297.** Inconstancy ruins the holiest and most solid resolutions, **3:232.** Among those things which can cause the decay of a community nothing is more dangerous than to be governed by superiors who are too mild. Examples. **3:297.** A superior must be firm but never rude in his conduct, **3:310.** See, *Strength*.

Fisme Vincent sends Missionaries and aid to this region (1650), **1:205; 2:337.**

Flacourt (Etienne de), French governor of Madagascar. The godfather of the first Malgache infant baptized by the Missionaries (1648), **2:143.** Other details, **2:144.**

Flattery. Always be affable, but never flattering. There is nothing more unworthy of the Christian heart than flattery, **3:166**

Foillard (Hugues), lieutenant general of Macon, **1:88.**

Folleville (town in the diocese of Amiens). House and lands of Monsieur de Gondi. Stay there by Vincent in 1616, **1:59.** First sermon; the origin of the Congregation of the Mission (January 25, 1617). Its extraordinary results, **1:61-62.**

Fontaine (parish in the diocese of Reims). Missions held there, **2:43.**

Fontainebleau (city and royal residence). The Missionaries give a mission in this city on the order of the queen, **3:212**

Fort Dauphin (in Madagascar), **2:142.**

Fortitude (virtue of). Madame de Gondi observed that Monsieur Vincent was not the type of man to do something halfway, **1:67.** He had an absolute control over his natural tendencies. Reason so controlled his passions that it was hard to know that he had any, **1:101.** Jesus Christ was the source of his firmness in doing good and of his being able to stand unmoved by any consideration of human respect, or of his own personal interests, **1:103.** From the moment that he recognized something as being the will of God he would be thoroughly committed to it, **2:275.** *Conduct and examples of Vincent*, **3:280 ff.** His conduct in supporting the good and in the repression of evil, **3:280-81.** In the support of those suffering from afflictions and trials, **3:282.** See, *Firmness, Patience*.

Fossano (town in Piedmont, Italy). Mission given there, **2:82.**

Foundlings. Origin of the work of the foundlings and the devotion of Vincent to this work, **1:160 ff.** Frightful state of the abandoned infants placed at the house of "La Couche" in Paris, **Ibid.** Vincent recommends to the Ladies of Charity that they work with these little infants, **1:161.** The Missionaries must support this work of charity, **3:122.** The saint criticizes a Missionary who wants to limit this work. He cites the example of our Lord, **3:123.** New establishment near the gate of Saint Victor in Paris under the direction of Louise de Marillac and the Daughters of Charity in 1638, **1:161.** General Assembly of the Ladies of Charity of Hotel Dieu in 1640. At this meeting it is decided to take care of all the foundlings. **Ibid.** Anne of Austria obtains alms from the king to support the work with the foundlings (1644), **Ibid.** Ten or twelve Daughters of Charity are employed to take care of them (1646). They take care of three or four hundred children each year, **2:296.**

General Assembly of the Ladies of Charity in 1648. Impassioned words of Vincent asking them not to abandon the care of these little children, **1:162.** Louis XIV gives the Ladies of Charity the Chateau of Bicetre as a home for the infants, **Ibid.** It is necessary to move them from the Bicetre to a house in the area near Saint Lazare (1649), **Ibid.** Vincent arranges that the children and their nurses be assisted by the Daughters of Charity, and by a laybrother, **3:122.**

How they are to be educated. The Christian education which they subsequently receives under the care of the Daughters of Charity, **1:162.**

Fouquet (Francois), bishop of Bayonne, then of Agde, finally archbishop of Narbonne. He establishes the Missionaries at Agde (1654), **1:234.**

Fouquet (Marie), one of the first Ladies of Charity of Hotel Dieu, **1:153.**

Fourche (Monsieur), Jesuit. Assists in hearing confessions at the first mission at Folleville, **1:61.**

Fournier (Pierre), Jesuit, rector of the College at Nancy. He recommends the needs of the poor of Lorraine to Vincent, **2:328.**

France. State of the Church at the time of the birth of Vincent, **1:31-32.** All of the Christian slaves in Barbary, except the English, are under the protection of France, **2:90.** All the slaves, even the foreigners, ask the king to be their benefactor. For the most part they were recognized to be French subjects, **2:108.**

Francillon (Francois), laybrother of the Mission. He is sent to Tunis, **2:86.** Then to Algiers, **Ibid.** He is attached to the mouth of a canon by the Algerians and is thus executed (1688), **Ibid.**

Franciscans. Vincent's early studies in their school in Dax, **1:38.**

Fremont (Charles), reformer of the religious of the Order of Grandmont. Vincent praises him, **2:385,387.**

Freneville (area near Paris). Location of a small farm belonging to the Congregation of the Mission. Vincent stays there for a month during the troubles of the Fronde. He gives a mission to the inhabitants of the area (1649), **1:199-200.**

Fresque (Monsieur de), pastor of the Church of Saint Sulpice in Paris, **1:168.**

Friendship. Christian love is superior to the merely sympathetic love that exists between friends; which even though is the most prevalent can also be the most harmful, **3:149.** Detachment from loved ones; the example of Jesus and his apostles. See, *Detachment.*

Fronde (The troubles of the). Origins, **1:198 ff.** Conduct of Vincent during this time. His prayers. His meeting with the queen and Cardinal Mazarin, **1:198-99.** Pillage of the farm at Orsigny, and of the house of Saint Lazare, **1:199.** See, *Anne of Austria, Mazarin (Jules), Public Misery, Paris.*

Frugality. This virtue is universally admired in the first Daughters of Charity, **1:136.** Vincent recommends the observance of this virtue to his Missionaries. Exhortation to practice an even greater degree of frugality during the times of the public misery, **3:313.**

Funeral (of Vincent de Paul), **1:262.**

G

Galatians (epistle of Saint Paul to the). Cited in Abelly: 2:20-**2:230**, 6:14-**2:240**, 4:19-**3:124**.

Galley Slaves. Vincent experiences the life of a slave himself during his captivity in Tunis. **1:42 ff.** He begins the work with the galley slaves at Paris (1618). His mercy towards the poor galley slaves, **1:84,148.** He is named chaplain general of the galleys by Louis XIII (1619), **1:84.** He visits the galleys at Marseilles (1622). His charity, **Ibid.** Transfer of the prisoners to the faubourg Saint Honore near the church of Saint Roch. Help which he procures for them, **1:85,148.** His voluntary captivity (1622). He puts on the fetters of a galley slave, **3:112-13.**

Vincent gives a mission to the galley slaves of Paris held at the Tower of Saint Bernard (La Tournelle) in the parish of Saint Nicolas du Chardonnet (1632), **1:85,148.** Vincent arranges for their care by the priests of the Congregation from the College des Bons Enfants, **1:148.** Louise de Marillac also assists them. He recommends them to the care of the Confraternity of Charity of Saint Nicholas du Chardonnet. The Ladies of Charity at the court will also help them (1635), **Ibid.** Definitive establishment of the works with the convicts (1639), **1:149.** Mission given at Marseilles for the galleys in 1643, **2:39-40.** The priests of the Conference of Saint Lazare give many missions at La Tournelle, **2:219.** Daughters of Charity begin serving the convicts, **2:296.**

Vincent obtains for the galley slaves at Marseilles the creation of a hospital and a group of chaplains (1642-1649), **1:150.** A house of Missionaries is established at Marseilles for the care of the galley slaves (1643), **Ibid.** Louis XIV gives, in perpetuity, the title of Chaplain General of the Galleys to the superior general of the Congregation of the Mission (1644). Royal appointment as Chaplain General by Louis XIV is given to Vincent, **Ibid.** The galleys are transferred from Marseilles to Toulon. Vincent establishes one of his priests in this city to care for the needs of the convicts (1649-1655), **1:151.**

Gallus (Andre), rector of the University of Toulouse, **1:40.**

Gamaches (parish in the archdiocese of Rouen). Vincent is named pastor there, **1:55.**

Gambart (Adrien), priest associated with Vincent, **1:109.**

Gannes (village near Folleville). Vincent hears there a general confession of a dying peasant which is the occasion for beginning the work of the missions (1617), **1:59.**

Garron (Jean), Protestant at Chatillon les Dombes. Vincent brings him back from heresy to the Catholic faith. His letter to Vincent forty years later, **1:75.**

Gatinais (province of). Assistance sent there by Vincent, **1:212.**

Gaudiene (location in Tunis). Christian slaves there are visited by the Missionaries, **2:115.**

Gault (Jean Baptiste), bishop of Marseilles. He helps Vincent obtain the foundation of a hospital for the convicts at Marseilles, **1:150.** His zeal for the missions to the galleys, **2:39-40.**

Gemozac (parish in the diocese of Saintes). Letter from a Missionary giving an account of a mission given at the parish there in 1647, **2:33.**

General Hospital. See, *Salpetriere.*

Genesis (first book of the Old Testament). Cited in Abelly: 13:9-**2:14,** 18:16-**2:243,** 3:8-**3:200.**

Geneva (diocese of). Results of the missions held in this diocese, **2:38 ff.** See, *Annecy, Guerin (Juste).*

Genevieve (Saint), patroness of Paris. Solemn procession of the reliquary of the saint, and general processions throughout Paris to obtain the end of the public sufferings in 1652, **1:211.**

Gennevilliers (village near Paris). Vincent sends aid there during a flood of the Seine, **3:120.**

Genoa (city, archdiocese in Italy). Cardinal Durazzo, archbishop of Genoa, asks a passing Missionary to give missions in his diocese (1645). Results of these missions. Letter of the cardinal. He founds a house of the Missionaries, **1:233 ff.; 2:66 ff.** Success of the ordination retreats there, **2:203-04.** The Missionaries give retreats to the clergy. Consoling results, **2:246.** Ravages of the plague. Work of the Missionaries. Death of many of them, **3:54,98,276.**

Genuflections. Vincent teaches that these should always be made with great care, **3:74.** He gives example of this, despite his infirmities, **3:82.**

Germany. Fallen into heresy and lost to the Church, **1:212; 2:170,190.**

Gex (town near Geneva). Site of a hospital served by the Daughters of Charity, **2:296.**

Gibeonites (figures in the Old Testament), **2:158.**

Girard (Louis), doctor of theology. Pastor of Chatillon les Dombes, **1:65.**

Glengarry (Lord), Scottish noble. He and his father are converted by the Missionaries, **2:174-75.**

Glengarry (region in Scotland). Visited by Dermot Duggan, **2:176.**

Glory of God See, *God, (Glory of).*

God.

Conduct of God. God for good reasons hides from his servants the fruit of their labor. Nevertheless, he causes them to be effective, **3:100.**

Fear of God. It is the grille that shelters the Daughters of Charity; like religious behind their cloister, **2:293.**

Glory of God. Seeking it always is the first maxim of the Gospel, **1:104.** If you have God's glory as your only end, what is there for you to fear, or better, what should you not hope for? **2:92.** When presented with a choice always prefer what is for God's greater glory, and not your own personal interest, **2:426.** The greatest joy of his heart was to ponder the incomprehensible glory of God, **3:37.** To attribute to oneself the glory which comes from the sanctification of souls would be a great sacrilege, **3:73.** When the glory of God is in question Vincent pays no attention to any temporal interests or concerns, **3:219.** It is his goal in all that he does to seek this, **3:293.**

Goodness of God. "Once God has begun to do good to a creature he will continue to do so to the end unless it makes itself unworthy of his help," **3:28.**

Kingdom of God. The work of understanding and propagating it, **3:39.** To bring the reign of God to souls is to act like the angels who labor for this end without ceasing, **Ibid.**

Love of God. It must be not only affective but effective; different reasons, **1:106.** "Let us love God, but let it be in the strength of our arms and the sweat of our brows," **Ibid.** Outreach of the charity of Vincent, **1:127 ff.** *Examples and teaching of Vincent.* Ardent charity in his works; in his words. Various testimonies of his pure intentions of pleasing God, **3:37 ff.**

Perfections of God. The devotion which they inspire in Vincent, **3:72.** The reverential knowledge that we have of these fills us with reverence and love of the Divine Majesty, **3:72-73.** They must inspire humility in us, **3:196.**

Presence of God. The presence of God ought to have a greater influence over our minds than the presence of every living creature of the world, **2:277.** *Practice and teaching of Vincent* on the sentiment of the presence of God, **3:56 ff.** How Vincent was himself elevated to this view by natural and sensible things, **3:57.** Comparison of the mirrors, **Ibid.** Example of a person who was made conscious of having been distracted from his contemplation of this only three times in one day, **3:58.**

Providence of God. Vincent did not want to anticipate providence. This was his usual way of acting in his affairs, **1:102.** He says that he clings to the providence of God in all things, **2:274.** Providence will never fail in those things that we undertake by his direction, **3:22.** It is in times of scarcity that our true confidence in God must appear, **3:23.** There are great treasures hidden in providence, **3:32.** We honor the sovereignty of our Lord when we do not anticipate or presume on his providence, **Ibid.** Vincent undertakes nothing on his own initiative; trusting that divine providence would reveal all the works that were to be done, **3:181.** If providence finds us ready and responsive to its directions what we undertake will succeed to the greater glory of God, **3:249.**

Will of God. How excellent is the practice of conformity to the divine will. To apply oneself to this must be the aim of the Congregation, **1:105.** *Practice and teaching of Vincent* on this virtue, **3:40 ff.** Our Lord unites himself continually with those who are united to his will and not to their own, **3:40.** Whoever conforms himself in everything to the will of God and takes his pleasure in it leads a truly angelic life upon earth. This person can even be said to be living the very life of Jesus Christ, **Ibid.** Four things to be observed in order for this to be accomplished, **3:41.** "The perfection of love does not consist in ecstasies, but in fulfilling the will of God," **3:41.** Among the many benefits of conformity to the divine will, surely peace of soul will not be the least, **3:42.** The devotion of Vincent is to follow the will of God, and never to precede it, **3:43.** He has as a maxim that no effort should be spared when it is a question of accomplishing God's will, **Ibid.** The highest and almost unique means for a soul to be totally holy is to habitually do the will of God in all things, **3:44.** It is an anticipated paradise, **Ibid.** God is highly glorified by our abandonment to his will without seeking to know his reasons, **3:45.** Ways of knowing this holy will: by events, or by commandments and precepts, **Ibid.** Vincent calls this practice of conformity the "treasure of the Christian," **3:45.** An act of resignation and acquiescence to the good pleasure of God is worth more than one hundred thousand temporal successes, **3:48.** To conform oneself to this is the best preparation for death, **3:89.** Vincent is always prepared to see his own Congregation destroyed if it is the good pleasure and will of the divine Majesty, **Ibid.** Accepted in all adversities this will is one the greatest goods; greater than any temporal advantages, **3:162.** Vincent is always ready to do God's will. God found in him a man after his own heart, **3:207.** By obedience to God's will we can be seen as true disciples of Jesus Christ, **3:255.**

Godeau (Antoine), bishop of Grasse, then of Vence. Member of the Tuesday Conferences. His letter to the members of this group, **2:227.**

Gondi (Francoise Marguerite de Silly), baroness of Montmirail, dame de, wife of the general of the galleys. Her virtues. She places herself under the spiritual direction of Vincent de Paul (1613), **1:56; 3:207.** Her personal esteem for the saint, **1:59.** She asks Vincent to give a sermon at Folleville on general confession, and to give periodic missions throughout her lands (1617). She provides a donation for this purpose to

Vincent in her will, **1:62.** Her desolation at the departure of Vincent for Chatillon. Letter which she writes on this subject to a trusted friend, **1:65-66.** Letter to Vincent, **1:67-68.** At the return of the saint, whom she receives as an angel from heaven, **1:71.** She erects in her lands numerous Confraternities of Charity, **1:73.** She cooperates in the fruits of the missions by her zeal in visiting the poor (1620), **1:80.** She procures the College des Bons Enfants for Vincent (1624), and together with her husband draws up a contract of foundation for the establishment of the Congregation of the Mission (1625), **1:93 ff.** Her death (June 23, 1625), **1:109.** Vincent's praise of her virtue. She never spoke badly of any person, **3:169.**

Gondi (Henri de), bishop of Paris (1598-1622) and the first Cardinal de Retz, brother of the Jean Francois, and of the general of the galleys. **1:69,91.** See, *Retz.*

Gondi (Henri de), youngest son of Emmanuel de Gondi. His premature death, **1:55.**

Gondi (Hippolyte de), sister of the general of the galleys, marquise of Ragny, **1:66.**

Gondi (Jean Francois de), archbishop of Paris (1622-54), brother of Henri, and of the general of the galleys. Louis Abelly in his service, **1:9.** He confers the College des Bons Enfants on Vincent (1624), **1:69,93.** He approves the deed of foundation, and the first rules of the Congregation of the Mission (1626), **1:110.** He issues the necessary letters confirming the union of Saint Lazare to the Congregation of the Mission, **1:124.** He authorizes Vincent to establish the Confraternities of Charity in the parishes of Paris, **1:131.** He orders that all the ordinands of the diocese take part in the ordination retreats at Saint Lazare before each ordination, **1:140; 2:185.** He approves of the establishment of the ecclesiastical conferences, (the Tuesday Conferences) by Vincent (1633), **1:144.** He encourages Vincent to establish the Company of the Ladies of Charity of Hotel Dieu (1634), **1:153.**

He approves the establishment of a seminary at Bons Enfants (1642), **1:165.** Vincent has a vision relative to Francis de Sales and Jane de Chantal and consults with him as to judging its authenticity, **2:284.** He approves the rules of the Daughters of Charity. He erects them as a congregation under the direction of the superior general of the Congregation of the Mission (1646), **1:136; 2:291.** Together with the queen he commands that the infirm Vincent use a carriage (1649), **1:202.**

Gondi, (Jean Francois Paul de), another son of Emmanuel de Gondi, coadjutor to his uncle, and then archbishop of Paris, second Cardinal de Retz. See, *Retz, (Cardinal de).*

Gondi (Philippe Emmanuel de), count of Joigny, general of the galleys. Biographical notice. Vincent becomes the tutor of his children (1613), **1:55.** The saint dissuades him from a duel, **1:57.** His sadness at the sudden departure of Vincent. The letter that he writes on this subject to Madame de Gondi (September 1617), **1:65-66.** Additional letter written to say that he hoped he would have the joy of once again seeing the saint, **1:70.** Vincent establishes numerous Confraternities of Charity throughout his lands, **1:73.** He has Vincent named as Chaplain General of the galleys (1619), **1:84 ff.** Together with Madame de Gondi and his brother the archbishop of Paris, he procures the College des Bons Enfants for Vincent in order that he may found a society of priests (1624), **1:93 ff.** Contract of foundation for the establishment of the Congregation of the Mission (1625), **1:94-96.** Vincent travels to Provence to tell him of the death of Madame de Gondi (1625), **1:97-98.** He retires from the world to the Oratory and is ordained. His death, (1662), **1:98-99.**

Gondi (Pierre de), bishop of Paris and cardinal, uncle of the general of the galleys, **1:69.**

Gondi (Pierre de), duke of Retz, son of Emmanuel de Gondi. See, *Retz, (duke of).*

Gondree (Nicolas), priest of the Mission. At Saintes, **2:137.** He is designated to accompany Monsieur Nacquart to the Madagascar mission. His apostolic work at La Rochelle before departing, and on the vessel during the voyage, **2:138.** His arrival and work in Madagascar, **2:142 ff.** His death; the sorrow of Nacquart and Vincent, **2:144,149-50.** Praise of his virtues, **2:137.**

Gontiere (Monsieur) An ecclesiastical counselor of the Parlement of Paris. He preaches a mission together with Vincent, **1:73.**

Gonzague (Marie Louise de), queen of Poland. Lady of Charity. Her esteem for Vincent, **2:163; 3:38.** She brings the Daughters of Charity to Poland, **1:136.** She asks Vincent for Missionaries to found a house of the Congregation in Warsaw (1650), **1:233-34; 2:163 ff.** Her wise conduct during the plague in Poland. She praises the Missionaries and the Daughters of Charity, **2:164-66; 3:138.** Letter of the queen to Vincent. She asks for his prayers. Her courage during the war facing the Swedish army, **2:169-70.**

Good (The). One rarely does what is good without experiencing some difficulty and pain: "The devil is too subtle and the world too corrupt not to attempt to stamp out a good work at its very beginning," **2:92.** See, *Temporal Goods.*

Gorin (Louis), Abbe of Saint Amour. See, *Saint Amour.*

Gospel. For Vincent it is etched in his heart and he uses it as the guide for all of his conduct, **3:293.** He held absolutely to this oracle of truth, **3:296.**

Gournay (Charles Chretien de), bishop of Scythia, administrator and later bishop of the diocese of Toul. At his request a house of the Congregation is established at Toul (1635), **1:230.**

Goussault (Genevieve Fayet), Madame de, the president. Aunt of Rene Almeras, **1:122.** Biographical notice, **1:152.** She suggests to Vincent the establishment of the company of the Ladies of Charity for the service of the poor of Hotel Dieu in Paris (1634). She makes her retreat with Louise de Marillac at the suggestion of the saint, **1:142,152.** She is named as the superior of the Ladies of Charity, **1:153.**

Grace. Vincent reproaches himself for abusing the graces given him by God, **1:257.**

Grace (Notre Dame de), pilgrimage chapel in the diocese of Albi. Vincent says one of his first masses at this church, **1:39-40.**

Granada (Luis de). Vincent recommends the reading of his spiritual works, **1:143.** These are read during some missions, **2:64.**

Grandmont (Order of). Vincent assists in the reform of this order, **2:385.** The saint sends a letter from the king to the superior general inviting him to take certain appropriate measures to reestablish the primitive observance in his order, **2:386-87.**

Grand Turk (the sultan of the Ottoman Empire), **1:43; 2:86,94.**

Gratitude. Vincent has a heart that is always grateful, **1:64.** He is full of gratitude for the gifts of God, **1:102.** *Sentiments and examples of Vincent* on this virtue, **3:236 ff.** His gratitude towards God, **3:236.** He said, "we must always give as much time to thanking God for his favors as we have used in asking him for them," **Ibid.** His gratitude towards others; some traits, **Ibid.** He is characterized by his gratitude, and his inability to keep from praising the good, **3:240-41.** How this virtue is pleasing to God, **3:241.**

Gravelines (city in Lorraine). Assisted by Vincent, **2:329.**

Gregory the Great (Saint), pope. Cited in Abelly. He says that works are the proof of one's love of God, **1:106.** On dealing with the faults of our neighbor, **3:169.** Value of simplicity, **3:214.** The art of spiritual direction, **3:317.**

Grenu (Daniel), priest of the Mission. Evangelizes the soldiers of the army in Picardy (1636), **1:175.**

Grimaldi (Jerome), cardinal, archbishop of Aix. Vincent sends him a book written by a theologian against the heresy promoted by Martin Barcos, **2:351.**

Grumbling. One of the greatest evils which can exist in a community is when there are those who grumble and criticize everything, **3:150.** See, *Union.*

Guerin (Julien), priest of the Mission. Biographical notice, **2:86.** At Saintes, **2:86.** At Tunis, **2:86-87.** Letters to Vincent. He describes the sufferings of the slaves. His charity, **2:106,108,110.** He recounts the good example given by a young Christian slave who died preserving his virtue, **2:111-12.** He gives an account of his apostolic works at Bizerte, and of the perils that he encountered (1647), **2:114-15.** He recounts the heroic constancy of a young English Christian slave, **2:116-117.** Torments endured by many women and young men who were slaves at Tunis, **2:121-22.** His sufferings. Letter to Vincent. His death from the plague in service of the slaves. Praise of his virtues, **2:87.**

Guerin (Juste), bishop of Geneva. He obtains Missionaries from Vincent to preach (1640), and to begin a seminary (1641) in his diocese, **1:231.** He praises the success of the Missionaries who preached in his diocese to Vincent (1640-1644), **2:38-39.**

Guerin (Mathurine), Daughter of Charity. She testifies to the care taken by Louise de Marillac to record the words of Vincent, **1:24.**

Guibourgere (Jacques Raoul de la), bishop of Saintes, then of Maillezais, finally of La Rochelle. He establishes the Missionaries at Saintes, **1:217,232.** Vincent writes him to dissuade him from returning to the court. He congratulates him for having maintained the loyalty of his people to the king during the troubles of the Fronde, **1:217.** He obtains a promise from Vincent to give missions in the diocese of Saintes (1640), **2:32.** He writes from Saintes to Vincent on the success of the missions, **2:35.** The success of the ordination retreats, **2:203.** Vincent works to have him named as the bishop of Saintes, and then of La Rochelle, **2:382-83.**

Guienne (the province of). During the Fronde, **1:217.** Heretics there, **2:25.**

Guilbert (Monsieur), a priest of the Mission, **3:17.**

Guillerval (village near Etampes). Helped by the Missionaries (1652), **1:208.**

Guillot (Nicolas), priest of the Mission. Sent to Poland, **2:164.**

Guingamp (village in Brittany). Mission held there in 1648, **2:47.**

Guise. (city in Lorraine). Vincent collects aid for this city and sends Missionaries with this help (1650), **1:205; 2;332-33, 336-37.**

H

Habakkuk (Old Testament prophet), **1:175,239.**

Habert (Isaac), bishop of Vabres. His letter, written in the name of the bishops gathered in Paris, asking the pope to condemn Jansenism, **2:353-54.**

Haggai (book of the Old Testament). Cited in Abelly: **2:8-2:378.**

Hair. Vincent criticizes immodesty in hair styles, **3:302.**

Hallier (Francois), doctor and professor of theology of the Sorbonne, later bishop of Cavaillon. He is sent to Rome in order to fight the Jansenists, **2:361.** Vincent congratulates him and encourages him in accomplishing his mission, **2:361-62.**

Letter to Vincent announcing the condemnation of the Jansenists and letting him know of their continued activities at Rome, **2:362-63**.

Ham (town in the diocese of Amiens). Vincent sends Missionaries and assistance there (1650). Letter of the pastor of this city to the saint, **1:205; 2:305,336,341**. The Missionaries establish a Confraternity of Charity there, **2:341**. See, *Public Misery*.

Hamphya (location in Tunisia). Christian slaves here are visited by the Missionaries, **2:115**.

Health. Proper care should be taken to preserve one's health. The body is an instrument to be used for the welfare of many; it should therefore be preserved according to this purpose, **3:153**. Although an excessive concern is a great obstacle to the service of God, **3:255**.

Heart. God does not want to be offered a divided heart, **2:311**. Response of the saint to a priest who had written to him pledging his heart's devotion, **3:218-19**.

Heart (of Jesus). The source of humility and mildness. This noble source must bring us to embrace its virtues, **1:105-06**. It is a furnace of love that affects us all, **Ibid**. Vincent encourages Louise de Marillac to imitate in her own heart the tranquility of the heart of the Savior, **1:135**. "If you had but a spark of that sacred fire which consumed the heart of Jesus Christ could you spend your life with folded arms, and abandon those who call for your help?" **3:107**. "The traits of envy and detraction pierce first the heart of Jesus Christ before reaching those against whom they are aimed," **3:302**.

Heart (of Vincent), after his death it is deposited in a valuable reliquary, **1:262**.

Hebrew. The study of this language. Advice of Vincent to Monsieur Du Coudray, **2:35**.

Hebrews (epistle to the). Cited in Abelly: 10:34-**1:200**, 4:14-**2:262**, 12:3-**3:250**, 10:34-**3:250**, 12:6-**3:284**, 1:3-**3:321**.

Hebrides (Islands). Located off the western coast of Scotland. Vincent sends Missionaries to these islands (1651), **1:234**. Ideas about this country, **2:173 ff**. Departure of Messieurs Le Blanc, Duggan, and Lumsden (1651); their voyage, **2:174**. It is a beautiful field that God opened to the zeal of the Missionaries, **3:100**. The devotion of the Missionaries, **3:276**. Sufferings of the Missionaries, and the fruits of their work in these islands. Three letters from one of them, **2:174 ff**. Death of Monsieur Duggan. Praise of his virtues. He is buried in the island of Ouist (Vista), **2:178**.

Hell. "Only those who reflect on the pains of hell or on the price of the blood of Jesus Christ for even one soul can appreciate the value of what you have done," **1:177**.

Hennebont (city of). Site of a hospital served by the Daughters of Charity, **2:296**.

Henry IV (king of France), **1:32,42,44**. Alleged secret mission of Vincent to this prince, **1:48-49**. His treaty with the sultan (1604), **2:94**.

Herbron (Francois), priest of the Mission. He leaves from Nantes for Madagascar. Escape from a shipwreck, **2:161**.

Heresy. Horror of Vincent for any heresy. Why God willed that he lived in the time of Jansenism, **2:346**. Rules of conduct of the saint relative to the heretics. He spoke of the danger that in wanting to do something to bring heretics back to the faith that their would-be rescuers would instead be carried away with them, **2:369**. He opposes any compromise with them, expecting that they should submit themselves to the definitive judgment rendered by the Church, **2:371**. A new heresy is an evil that can never be accepted in whatever person it is found, **Ibid**. While it is not necessary to recklessly judge a person it is a more dangerous evil by a sense of a false charity to want to excuse those who obstinately support the heretics or who themselves are suspected of heresy, **Ibid.**

Heretics. Converted by Vincent at Chatillon (1617), **1:74 ff.** At Montmirail (1620), **1:81.** Objections raised by one of them in pointing to the religious abandonment of the peoples of the country, and of the seeming worship given to the Blessed Virgin. Responses of the saint, **1:81-82.** A large number are converted at Hotel Dieu of Paris after the reforms introduced there by Vincent, **1:159.** At Beauvais; advice of the saint on the mild and charitable manner that one must have in dealing with them **2:25.** Vincent declares that he never knew of a heretic being convinced by the subtlety of an argument, but rather only by being treated with mildness and humility, **Ibid.** If we would like them to come to belief it is necessary to love them. Recommendations to various Missionaries, **2:26.** Abjurations during the missions, **2:41 ff.** Practice of the Missionaries, **2:54.** Conversions increase among the heretic slaves in Barbary, **2:116 ff.** Vincent often claimed the authority of the king to repress their activities, **2:383.** He often must write on behalf of the king to support the right of Catholics in their lawsuits and disputes against the heretics, **Ibid.** It is by mildness that Vincent wins over and converts heretics, **3:166-68.** See, *Jansenism.*

Herod (allusion to the massacre of the Innocents), **1:161.**

Herse (Charlotte de Ligny), Madame de. She gives the Congregation of the Mission the farm at Freneville, **1:199.** By her gifts she contributes to the growth and support of the ministry to the ordinands, **2:186.** Assistance which she gives destined for Picardy, **2:332.**

Hesdin (town near Calais). Help procured by Vincent for this town, **2:329.**

Hilary (Saint). His writings against the Arian heresy, **1:31.**

Histolangar (Today Tolagnaro), a town in the south of Madagascar, **2:142,151.**

Holland. Lost to heresy, **2:192.**

Holiness (of the conduct of Vincent), **1:108.**

Holmoru (in the diocese of Chalons sur Marne). Mission given there, **2:50.**

Holy Spirit. Guiding the Church and the faithful who do not resist. And the care of the poor of the countryside, **1:81-83; 2:355.** Source of consolation, **1:98.** Movement of the, **1:105.** Source of moderation and calmness, **1:130.** The kingdom of God is found in the peace of the Holy Spirit, **1:135.** Graces of the, **Ibid.** Vincent inspired by the Spirit, **1:138.** In the Canticle of Canticles, **1:142.** The Spirit of God works gently, **1:154.** Unction of the, **1:182,240.**
Temple of the Holy Spirit found in the example of a young Christian slave in Barbary, **2:117.** Role in life and teaching of bishops, **2:190.** Waiting for the coming of the Holy Spirit after the Ascension, **2:229.** Inspiration of the Holy Spirit during retreats, **2:239-40.** Acting in, and speaking through Vincent, **2:277; 3:124,158,162,223,294.** Role of the Holy Spirit in salvation history, **3:16.** Indwelling of the, **3:25,140,201.** Only the Holy Spirit knows the full extent of Vincent's holiness, **3:37.** Self-love can disguise human inclinations as movements of the Holy Spirit, **3:46.** Gifts of the Holy Spirit in prayer, **3:59-60,63-64.** The presence of the Holy Spirit in preachers and their preaching, **3:67,86-87.** The Holy Spirit as the source of all devotion to Mary, **3:92.** Vincent always began speaking by first invoking the Holy Spirit, **3:93.** Religious should look on each other as being temples of the Holy Spirit, **3:110.**

Honors (their dangers). Constant humility of Vincent, **3:275.**

Hope. *Teachings and example of Vincent* on this virtue, **3:21 ff.** "Just as we cannot have too much faith in the truths of the faith, so too we cannot trust in God too much."

Explanation of this maxim, **3:33**. "We have the seed of the all-powerful God within us. This should be the source of our hope, encouraging us to place all our confidence in him despite our own poverty," **Ibid**. Consolation given to a person tempted to despair, **1:34**. Although it is necessary that God sometimes rejects a good man, he also will never forsake a sinner who hopes in his mercy, **1:35**.

Hospitals. Hospitals served by the Daughters of Charity in Paris, **2:296**. Letter of one of the hospital sisters to Vincent, **2:297-98**. See, *Hotel Dieu, Nom de Jesus, Quinze-Vingts, Salpetriere*.

Hotel Dieu (Hospital in Paris). Establishment of a Company of the Ladies of Charity to help the sick poor (1634). First assembly, **1:153**. Second assembly. Nomination of officers. Services given to the sick, **Ibid**. The Daughters of Charity begin their work there under the direction of Louise de Marillac (1636). Services that they provide there, **1:155; 2:296**. Organization of the spiritual service. Six priests are established to help the ordinary chaplains in the care of the sick, **1:158**. Priests from the Tuesday Conferences teach catechism. They also give a mission to the patients (1639), **2:219-20**. Detailed account of these works given in the presence of the Ladies of Charity in 1657, **2:305 ff**.

Huguier (Benjamin), priest of the Mission. His eulogy. He is appointed to the post of French consul at Tunis, **2:89**. He is called back to France and sent to Toulon, **Ibid**. Vincent gives him the mission of going to Algiers to work for the release of the counsul unjustly held responsible for the debts of a French merchant, and exposed to the affronts of the Moslems, **Ibid**. His death in the service of the slaves at Algiers (1663), **Ibid**.

Humiliations. Example of our Lord, **3:196,202**. *Teaching and practice of Vincent*. He feels that in these he has found his treasure and has profited from every opportunity of practicing them, **3:184**. Affection of Vincent for receiving them and accepting them obediently, **3:187**. It is a honor to be treated in the same manner as our Lord had been, **3:190**. When prudence permits, it is a good practice for one to speak highly of them. Examples of Saint Paul and of Saint Augustine, **3:200**. The divine will is merciful when it is pleased to permit us to take the blame and contempt in public, **3:287**.

Humility (example of our Savior Jesus Christ). It is the model that Missionaries must follow. What is the life of the divine Savior but a continual humiliation, both active and passive? **1:102; 3:196,202**.

Humility (example of Saint Francis de Sales and of many other saintly persons), **2:19; 3:201-02**.

Humility (of Vincent de Paul), **1:22**. I. *General teachings of Vincent*.
a. Some characteristics:
He speaks of his humble origins, **1:36; 2:271**. He does not speak of his studies or the degrees that he received, **1:40-41; 3:182**. He wishes to destroy the letter which contained the account of his Tunisian captivity. He keeps silent about this event throughout his life, **1:46**. Was Vincent excessively humble? Answer, **1:101-02**. How he followed the examples of humility of our Savior. How he had taken this virtue to heart, **1:102**. Humble conduct of Vincent, **1:108; 3:294**. He responded when someone spoke to him of his works that he was only "the vile and contemptible mud that God formed into the mortar used in cementing the stones of his structures," **1:244**. In the delirium of a fever he prays for humility, **1:251**. Some humble words spoken at the end of his life, **1:257**.
He speaks with humility of his failings and his infidelities, **1:102; 2:193; 3:132,185-**

88. He speaks of his incapacity, in saying that he was only a poor scholar of the fourth form, etc., **3:182,186.** He speaks of his humble origins, **3:135,186,257.** Gracious response of the prince of Conde and another noble to the humble words of Vincent, **3:187,190.**

2. *Excellence and nature of this virtue.*

Vincent says that humility and meekness are two close sisters who go well together, **1:105.** Humility alone is capable of carrying the great graces of God, **2:135.** First of all a heart must be empty of itself, then God fills it, **2:193-94.** The knowledge of our faults must be used to humble but not to discourage us, **3:310.**

3. *Examples and teaching of Vincent de Paul,* **3:14,180 ff.** It is to his humility more often than his zeal or his prudence that it is necessary to attribute the fruitfulness of all his works, **3:180.** It is said that he refused the highest ecclesiastical dignities, **3:183.** With this he came to possess all the other virtues. Humility is not contrary to magnanimity, **Ibid.** Some particularly humble actions of Vincent, **3:184 ff.** Remarkable act of humility of the saint in receiving his nephew, **3:189.** Vincent desires that this virtue be taken as a subject of prayer every month, **3:190.**

Sentiments of Vincent on humility, **3:195 ff.** Two principal motives for humility, **Ibid.** Various exhortations on the practice of this virtue, **3:196 ff.** Explanation of the parable of the pharisee and the publican, **3:199.** Prayer to obtain humility, **3:199.** It is the virtue for which religious souls have the most attraction, **3:200.** It is one source of peace, **Ibid.** It is the source of charity, **3:204.** It is the only weapon that Vincent uses to oppose contradictions, **3:231.** It is the first and the most faithful guide for all his conduct, **3:294.** II. *Particular teachings for the Congregation of the Mission.*

Humility is one of the foundations on which the Congregation is established: if we do not have this virtue we have nothing, **1:113-14.** With what humility Vincent spoke of his community, **Ibid; 117; 3:182,187-88.** It is most needed by the Missionaries, because of the praise that the people sometimes give them for their work, **1:113.** God has chosen the members of the Company as he chose at another time his humble disciples, **1:118.** The Missionary must not only accept the humiliations which are his personally, but also those that God sends to the Company in general, **3:182.** God gives to other companies whatever virtues that it pleases him to give; but for the Congregation of the Mission this virtue is humility, **3:183.** "If you have ever heard outsiders say that something good has been done by the Company you will find that it was because they found some small bit of humility in it," **3:198.** "The more one is humble the greater shall be his love for his neighbor," **Ibid.**

"Congregations which are humble are like valleys which attract all of the life-giving waters flowing down from the mountain," **1:117.** Humility in the manner of preaching, **2:18-19,190.** See, *Preaching.* At the moment that we abandon the simplicity and the humility that is fitting to our institute we will lose the graces that are attached to it, **3:203.** It is God who accomplishes the good that we do. We are only the distributors of his gifts, **3:204.** We are like the fragile rod which God himself used to work miracles in the hand of Moses, **Ibid.** It is the example of the humble and simple manner with which one acts towards them which edifies the ordinands, **3:198.** In the seminaries wanting to be effective by merely teaching those who are under our charge will be a great obstacle to the accomplishment of the end of this work, **3:309-10.** See, *Humiliations, Blindness, Vanity.*

Husson (Martin), lawyer of the parlement of Paris. Vincent obtains a position for him as a steward in the house of the duke of Retz. Wise advice that he gives him, **1:57; 3:226.** Vincent advises him to quit this position to accept the post of consul at Tunis

(1653). The saint greatly praises his virtue and his skill, **2:89; 3:296-97**. He is the object of an "affront" from the dey of Tunis, **2:98-99**. New "affront" in 1657. The dey dismisses him from Tunis, **2:99**.

I

Idleness. The idle soul becomes an infertile land which produces only useless thorns. Terrible example of an ecclesiastic, **3:113**. Example of a laybrother, **3:152**. See, *Time (Good Use of), Work, Zeal*.

Images. In the presence of a heretic Vincent asks a child what the teaching of the Church is concerning the use to be made of the images of the saints, **1:82**. The saint counsels the Missionaries of Madagascar to use images to teach the mysteries of the faith. He sends one himself for the instruction of a young Malgache, **2:137**. Pagan images used by the natives in Madagascar. The Missionaries of Madagascar use Christian images effectively in the instruction of the people, **2:147**.

Imitation (of Our Lord, Jesus Christ). See, *Jesus Christ, (Imitation of Our Lord)*.

The Imitation of Christ (Classic spiritual work). Recommended by Vincent, **1:143**. Quotations cited by the saint, **1:183**.

Imitation (of the saints). It is one of the principal purposes and one of the most salutary fruits of devotion to them, **3:9**.

Immaculate Conception of the Blessed Virgin Mary. Vincent mentions this privilege of the Blessed Virgin, **3:270**.

Imours (village in Madagascar), **2:154**.

Incarnation (Mystery of the). The manner of teaching it to the ignorant, **2:136**. The devotion professed and recommended by Vincent to this mystery, **3:74**.

Indies. Vincent cites to the Missionaries the example of a merchant who returned there, despite many dangers, for simple temporal gain, **1:183**. He is pleased that some of the aged confreres ask to be sent there, **3:50**. Foreign missions here, **2:15**.

Indifference. Definition. This state of virtue is active leading the heart to be detached from all that would hold it captive. Its necessity, **3:49**. In what sense it is the origin of all the virtues and the death of all vices, **Ibid.** Example of Jesus Christ and of his apostles, **3:49-50**.

A characteristic of Monsieur de Rougement, **1:78**. Beg God for the grace that we might abandon ourselves entirely to his adorable direction, **3:51**. Example of the saint in his sicknesses, and in his death, **3:52**. As a virtue for the Congregation, **3:52-53**.

Innocent X (Pope). Issues the bull against Jansenism (May 31, 1653). Details of this judgment, **1:221; 2:362-366; 3:18**. His request to Vincent for Missionaries for Ireland, **2:126**.

Insane. Loving devotion of Vincent for those whom he finds committed in the house of Saint Lazare when he first takes possession of it. He continues to receive them there, **1:126; 2:259 ff**. Reasons for having a devotion to their service, **2:261**. Consoling fruits which resulted from this work, **2:264**.

Inspirations. They are a means of knowing the will of God, but they must be carefully examined, **3:46**.

"In spiritu humilitatis", etc. Vincent cites the interpretation of this prayer given by Francis de Sales, **2:19**.

Insults. How it is necessary to follow the example of our Lord in receiving these. Silence of Vincent in talking about those he received, **3:178,262,279**. Vincent is threatened with injury and death at Rennes (1649), **1:201**. He is insulted by a noble at the palace whom he had refused the request of a benefice, **3:157**. On being blamed as the cause of the public miseries and food shortages, **Ibid**. He is blamed for the treatment of the poor at the general hospital, **3:162**. Injuries received from a person who falsely blamed him for the loss of a lawsuit, **3:159-60**. On the part of the abbe Saint Cyran, **3:186**. On the part of a young gentleman, **3:191**. Insults received from a magistrate, **3:280-81**. From many high-born ladies, **3:281**. On the part of the townspeople at one of the gates of Paris, **3:279**. On the part of an adversary in the presence of the judges, **3:283**. See, *Calumny, Persecution*.

Intention (of our actions). "It would be better to be tied hand and foot and thrown into a raging fire than to do anything merely to please others," **3:39**. Means of forming our intentions, **Ibid**. "We should enrich our good deeds with noble and holy intentions, doing them solely to please and glorify God," **Ibid**. "We must discern carefully, not trusting our own minds or inclinations," **3:46**. See, *Actions*.

Internal Seminary (or novitiate, of the Congregation of the Mission). Its object and its end, **1:179 ff; 3:301-02**. Its origins. What Vincent demanded as preparation for his first companions, **1:179**. Its establishment in Paris (1637). Jean de la Salle, first director of the seminary, **Ibid**. How Vincent depends on the divine providence of God to send the necessary candidates, **1:180**. It is enough for us to pray to God that he will send laborers into the harvest, and trust that the example of our good life will attract others to work with us, **1:181**. The saint never says anything to any person to attract them to the Congregation. His teaching and his recommendations on the needs of the seminary, **1:182**. The dispositions that he demands of those who ask to be received in the Congregation of the Mission, **Ibid**. His charity for the sick seminarians, **3:172**.

Introduction to the Devout Life (Classic spiritual work). This work of Saint Francis de Sales is read in public during a mission, **2:59**.

Ireland. The Holy See asks for Missionaries for this country (1645). Vincent sends eight priests of the Congregation there (1646), **1:233; 2:126 ff**. Advice that he gives them, **2:126**. Success of their work, **2:127 ff**. The persecution of Cromwell interrupts their work. Vincent recalls many Missionaries, **1:214; 2:128-29**. Consoling success of those who remained, **2:129-30, 134**. Their devotion in the middle of the double scourges of war and plague (1650), **2:132**. The capture of Limerick by the troops of Cromwell. Apprehension of Vincent about the fate of the Missionaries (1651), **Ibid**. They succeed in escaping without being harmed, **2:133**. A seminarian is massacred by the heretics, **Ibid**. The saint organizes assistance for the Irish refugees in France, **3:128**. Vincent asks Cardinal Richelieu to give armed assistance to this country and promises him the support of the pope, **1:189**. Irish refugees persecuted for their religion and living in exile at Troyes are assisted by him (1654), **2:340**. Charity of Vincent with regards to the ecclesiastics from this country who were refugees in France, **3:144**. They are mistaken about the saint's intentions. Generous sentiments of him for them, **3:159**.

Isaac (son of Abraham), **1:68; 2:164; 3:29,45,68**.

Isaiah (Old Testament prophet), **1:31,75; 3:177**. Book of the Old Testament cited by Abelly, 54:7-**1:23**, 55:8-9-**1:36**, 61:1-**1:98,238**, 49:15-**1:163**, 1:13-**2:171**, 66:2-**2:224**, 11:6-**2:244**, 1:11-**3:46**, 58:3-4-**3:46**, 49:15-**3:154**, 7:15-**3:177**, 9:1-**3:325**.

Italy. Confraternities of Charity there, **1:73**. Seminaries confided to the Congregation there, **1:166**. Missions given to the people; their results, **2:55 ff**. The Missionaries begin the work of the spiritual retreats for the clergy there. Consoling results, **2:246**. Vincent receives an Italian religious at Saint Lazare who is troubled in spirit, and who had taught heresy, **3:143**.

J

Jacob (the Old Testament patriarch), **1:121**.

James (the epistle of). Cited in Abelly: 1:2-**3:251**, 3:2-**3:261**, 3:8-**3:261**.

Jansenism. Vincent opposes Jansenism and struggles against this heresy, **1:221 ff**; **3:17ff**. He sends a cardinal in Rome a refutation of the heresy of Martin Barcos (1646), **2:351**. Insults of the Jansenists against Vincent and support of him by the orthodox, **2:371**. Vincent spends many months in his meditations on the subject of the doctrine of grace. God gives him particular lights of insight on this subject, **3:17**. He says that Jansenism is one of the most dangerous errors that has ever threatened the Church, **Ibid**. Accounts of his zeal against this heresy, **3:18**. Vincent works in the Council of Conscience to remove from office and teaching positions any ecclesiastics who were suspected of Jansenism, **1:222; 2:353**. His apprehension about the progress of this heresy among Catholics, **1:223**.

Vincent intervenes to oppose the introduction of Jansenism in a religious house, **2:353**. Letter sent to the bishops of France asking them to support an appeal to the pope asking for a condemnation of Jansenism (1651), **2:353-54**. Another letter sent to the Bishop of Lucon asking him to sign the letter to Rome. This letter refutes the arguments of its opponents and tries to show the necessity of this condemnation, **2:354-55**. He remarks on how closely Jansenism resembles the errors of Calvin, **2:356-57**. Hesitations of several bishops in signing this letter, and the renewed requests sent by the saint. Response of the bishops of Alet and Pamiers. He refutes their objections, **2:357 ff**. Resistance and intrigues of the Jansenists who were in Rome to oppose the condemnation. Vincent strongly supports sending several orthodox theologians to Rome to state the case against Jansenism, **2:361**. He encourages these theologians in their important work, **2:361-62**.

Condemnation of the doctrines of Jansenius as contained in the "Five Propositions" (1653). Letters from the orthodox theologians sent to Rome announcing this decision to Vincent, and warning of the continuing threat of the Jansenists, **1:221; 2:351,361-62**. Eagerness of Vincent to receive a copy of the papal bulls of Innocent X and Alexander VII against Jansenism (1653,1656). His forceful and charitable actions promoting their acceptance, **1:222; 2:366-67; 3:18**.

God always preserves Vincent and his followers from this heresy. Vigilant care of the saint to keep this heresy far from the Congregation, **1:222; 2:350,367; 3:17**.

Jansenius (Cornelius), bishop of Ypres. Companion at Louvain of the abbe Saint Cyran. His work, *Augustinus*, **2:351**.

Japan. Foreign missions there, **2:15**.

Jealousy. Jealousy is one of the vices to be most feared in communities, **3:302**.

Jeremiah (Old Testament prophet), **1:23,141,199; 3:30**.

Jeremiah (book of the Old Testament). Cited in Abelly: 12:11-**1:141**, 31:30-**2:158**, 1:14-**2:192**, 35-**3:30**.

Jerome (Saint). Cited, **1:101; 3:9**.

Jesuits. Vincent asks the Jesuits from Amiens to help at the first mission given at

Folleville (1617), **1:61**. Madame de Gondi offers them an endowment to give regular missions on her lands which they cannot accept, **1:62**. At Bar le Duc they charitably care for a dying Missionary. Gratitude of Vincent, **2:325; 3:239**. Vincent speaks of them with esteem, **3:102**.

Jesus Christ

Love for Jesus Christ. Vincent has as a rule of life these words: Nothing pleases me except in Jesus Christ, **1:103**. Admirable results of this love, **Ibid**. Vincent always sees Jesus Christ in others; it is this that motivates him to charity. He recommends this practice, **1:107**. *Spirit of Jesus Christ.* "The spirit of our Savior is marked by meekness and kindness. Nature and the evil spirit, on the other hand, act harshly and shrilly," **3:146**. Leading souls to God is the work of Jesus Christ which human effort can only destroy, **3:317**. Results that are received in the ministry of the superior who is filled with the spirit of Jesus Christ, **3:318**.

Imitation of Jesus Christ. For Vincent, Jesus Christ is the mystical book ever open before his eyes. He drew from there the lessons of virtue which marked his life, **1:57**. His viewpoint was ever directed toward our Savior Jesus Christ and so his words and actions were influenced by this divine model, **1:101**. It is this principle that made his conduct not only without reproach, but universally and publicly approved, **Ibid**. The life of our divine Savior and the lessons of the Gospel are the sole rule of his life and actions. They are his book of morals and his book of politics, and they guide him in all the matters that pass through his hands, **1:103**. Excellence of, and reasons for, this practice. *Conduct and maxims of Vincent* on the imitation of our Savior Jesus Christ, **3:83 ff**. In his manner of acting and speaking, **3:87-88**. In his interior dispositions and his sentiments, **3:88-89**. He recommends reflecting before acting and asking: How would our Savior have acted or spoken on this occasion? **3:88,225,231,320**. The imitation of Jesus Christ is the principal virtue of Vincent, and of a Missionary, **3:88**. It is his principal means for accomplishing his ends, **3:293**. The Congregation of the Mission is totally dedicated to following the work of this great and first Missionary who came from heaven. It proposes to imitate our Savior in all things, **1:99**. We are his students. What authority he must have over us, **1:105; 3:175**. Recommendation to the Missionaries to apply themselves to this practice, **3:90**. The rules of the Congregation have all been formed in the Spirit of Jesus Christ and in imitation of his actions, **3:90-91**.

Jesus Christ the model of different virtues:

1. Jesus Christ the model of *Charity*: in the consolation of the afflicted, **1:98**. In the love of neighbor, **3:107**. The model of the spirit of compassion, **3:119**. Devoted to the good of children, **3:123**. To the pardon of enemies, **3:156-57**. Of the spirit of support, **3:170-71**. Of patience in the midst of insults, **3:178**.

2. Jesus Christ, model in *Conversations*, **3:227**.

3. Jesus Christ, model of *Meekness*. It is necessary that we learn meekness and humility from him, **1:105**. "Our Lord Jesus Christ is the meek master of men and of angels," **3:168**. How he mixed mildness with severity, **3:176-77**.

4. Jesus Christ model of *Humility*, **1:102; 3:196-97,202**.

5. Jesus Christ model of *Mortification*, **3:254-55**. Our Lord is the mortal enemy of all sensuality, **3:256**. He teaches us patience in the midst of conflicts, **3:286-87**.

6. Jesus Christ model of *Obedience*, **3:206**.

7. Jesus Christ model of *Prayer*, **3:318**.

8. Jesus Christ model of *Silence*, **3:226**.

9. Jesus Christ model of the conformity to the *Will of God*. He teaches us to accept sufferings and humiliations, **3:250,255**. *Maxims of Jesus Christ*. See, *Maxims*.

Name of Jesus. "He fulfilled perfectly the meaning of his name Jesus, that is, savior," **3:90.** See, *Litanies.*

Joanna (wife of Chuza). Her example cited in the Gospel, **2:312.**

Job (Old Testament patriarch). **1:199; 2:346; 3:285.** Book of the Old Testament. Cited in Abelly: 31:18-**1:37,** 9:4-**2:245,** 1:21- **3:285.**

John (first epistle of). Cited in Abelly: 5:3-**3:37,** 4:1-**3:60,** 2:18-**3:104,** 4:7-**3:148.**

John (gospel of). Cited in Abelly: 18:8-**2:131,** 5:7-**2:148,** 11:21- 2:157, **7:16**-2:197, 20:21-**2:252,** 8:29-**3:41,** 21:7-**3:50,** 15:20-**3:50,** 20:21-**3:50,** 4:34-**3:58,** 8:28-**3:64,** 14:12-**3:86,** 13:15-**3:88,** 2:17-**3:97,** 18:4-5-**3:178,** 6:61-**3:197,** 8:7-**3:223,** 8:29-**3:255,** 1:9-**3:321,** 13:19-**3:322.**

John the Baptist, 3:75,323.

John Casimir (king of Poland), **2:169.**

Joigny (city in the diocese of Sens). Vincent establishes a Confraternity of Charity there, **1:73.** Mission given there in 1650, **2:48.**

Joisel (Monsieur), a doctor of theology of the Sorbonne. Sent to Rome to denounce the Jansenists. **2:361.**

Jonadab (son of Rechab). See, *Rechabites.*

Jonathan (son of Saul). His failure against obedience, **3:213.**

Joseph (Saint). Devotion of Vincent to Joseph, **3:75.**

Joshua. (Old Testament figure), **1:111.**

Judas (Apostle). His example is instructive to inspire humility. He had received great graces, and yet he was lost, **2:18; 3:318.** Jesus speaks to him, **3:178.** Warned by Jesus, **3:308.**

Judas Maccabeus. Allusion to his vision, **1:23.**

Jude (epistle of). Cited in Abelly: 8-**1:31.**

Judge. The judge of Sore accuses Vincent of theft, **1:49.** He eventually writes him to ask his pardon. Conduct of Vincent in this incident, **1:49-51.** See, *Calumnies.*

Judgment (personal). Why and how it must be renounced, **3:254.**

Justice. Sentiments and examples of Vincent on this virtue, **3:233 ff.**

Juvisy (village near Paris). Vincent provides assistance here (1653), **1:209.**

K

Kings. Seeing Jesus the sovereign ruler in them, **1:107.** Honor, respect, and obedience due to them, **2:396.**

Knoidart (region in Scotland). Evangelized by Dermot Duggan, **2:176.**

Korah (figure in the Old Testament). He grumbled and complained against Moses. His punishment, **3:206.**

Krakow (city in Poland). Outbreak of the plague there, **3:138.**

L

Labadie (Jean), apostate priest. He became a Huguenot at Montauban after having supported the errors of Jansenius. Vincent uses this example to show the affinities between the two heresies, **2:356.**

La Barde (Dennis de), bishop of Saint Brieuc. Assists at the mission given in Plaissala, **2:46.**

Labbe (Francois), priest of the Mission. In service to the poor at Etampes during the Fronde, **1:209.**

La Carignan (princess de). Vincent refuses her permission to visit the cloister of the Visitandines, **2:274.**

La Chapelle (village near Paris). Louise de Marillac goes there with the newly founded community of the Daughters of Charity to live in the greatest simplicity (May 1636), **1:136; 3:271.** Vincent gives missions there to refugees from Lorraine, **1:187; 2:327.**

La Couche (home for the foundlings in Paris), **1:160.**

La Chapelle Orly (village near Paris). The Missionaries provide spiritual assistance to the soldiers there (1636), **1:177.**

La Coste (Gaspar de Simiane de). His help in the foundation of the hospital for convicts at Marseilles. Letter to Vincent, **1:150.**

Lacour (Claude Joseph). Eighteenth-century Vincentian historian, **1:12.**

Lactantius. (Father of the Church). Cited, **3:13.**

La Fauvette (abbey of). Lawsuit concerning, **3:111.**

La Fere (town near Soissons). Vincent sends Missionaries and aid there (1650), **1:205; 2:332,336.** The Missionaries establish a Confraternity of Charity there, **2:341.**

La Ferriere (Chevalier de), **2:98.**

La Ferte (Emeric Marc de), bishop of Le Mans. He establishes the priests of the Mission in his episcopal city (1645), **1:232.**

La Font (Monsieur de), lieutenant general at Saint Quentin. Letter of thanks sent to Vincent for the help he had gathered for this city, **2:342.**

La Fosse (Jacques Corborand de), priest of the Mission. He helps the poor at Etampes during the wars of the Fronde. He becomes sick there, **1:209.**

Lagault (Jerome), doctor of theology of the Sorbonne. Vincent tells him of the misery in Paris and his hope for relief of the city (1652), **1:211.** He is sent to Rome with two other theologians to fight against Jansenism. The saint encourages this mission and congratulates him and his colleagues, **2:361.** Letter to Vincent in which he gives him the details of the condemnation of Jansenism by the pope, and brings him up to date on the activities of the heretics, **2:364.**

La Lane (Noel). Jansenist author and controversialist, **2:363.**

La Meilleraye (Charles de la Porte), duke of, **2:155.**

Lamentations (book of the Old Testament). Cited in Abelly: 4:4-**2:148,** 4:1-**2:212.**

Lamoignon (Guillaume de), first president. He cares for the Missionaries at Etampes who become sick while serving the poor, **1:209.**

Lamoignon (Madaleine Potier de), Lady of Charity. How she was affected by the words of Vincent, **3:38.**

La Mothe (Henri de), archbishop of Auch. He praises Vincent and gives his approval to the *Life* of the saint written by Abelly, **1:26**.

La Motte (village in the diocese of Saint Flour). Mission given there, **1:68**.

Lamy (Antoine), administrator of the hospital of Quinze-Vingts. He asks Vincent to establish a Confraternity of Charity in this hospital, **1:131**.

Landrecies (city near Cambrai). Assistance gathered by Vincent for this city, **2:329,332**.

Language. Zeal of the Missionaries in Madagascar to learn the language of this country, **2:142-43**. They compose instructions in this language for themselves and their successors, **2:145**. They edit a little catechism, **Ibid.**

Languedoc. Heretics in this region, **2:25**. Letter from a priest of this region after a retreat made at Saint Lazare, **2:241**.

Laon. Vincent sends Missionaries and aid to this town (1650), **1:205; 2:305,332,337-38**. See, *Public Misery*.

Larran (Esprit), Augustinian, **1:40**.

La Rochefoucauld (Francois de), cardinal. **1:247**. He urges Vincent to remain as a member of the Council of Conscience, **2:373**. He calls the saint his "right arm" in the work of reforming the religious orders, **2:385**. He tells him to moderate his austerities to preserve his life for the service of the Church, **3:265**.

La Rochefoucauld (Francois de), duke. He proposes asking Vincent for some Missionaries to evangelize various locations, **2:52**.

La Rochelle (city, port, and diocese of). Missionaries travel there to leave for Madagascar, **2:26; 3:277**. Messieurs Gondree and Nacquart serve the poor and the prisoners while waiting for their departure for the missions, **2:138**. Vincent takes part in the negotiations for the transfer of the episcopal see from Maillezais to La Rochelle, **2:382**. He recommends the transfer of the bishop of Saintes, Jacques Raoul, to the see of La Rochelle, **2:382**. See, *Guibourgere (Jacques Raoul de la)*.

La Roche Posay (Henri Louis Chastaignier de), bishop of Poitiers. He sends the ordinands from his diocese to make the ordination retreats at Richelieu at the house of the priests of the Mission, **2:201**. He resigns the Abbey of Saint Cyran in favor of Duvergier de Hauranne, **2:346**.

Lascaris (Paul), Grand Master of the Order of the Knights of Malta. His relations with Vincent. Letter to the saint, **1:171-72**.

La Tour (Monsieur), of the Oratory. His testimony in favor of Vincent, **1:52**.

La Vallette (Jean Louis de Nogaret de), duke of Epernon and Grand Master of the Order of Saint John of Jerusalem, **1:42**.

Lavardin (Philibert de Beaumanoir de), bishop of Le Mans. Vincent opposes his promotion. Skillful conduct of the saint in meeting with the prelate, **3:230**.

Law. Submission to civil laws. Lesson given by Vincent to a laybrother, **3:209**.

Lawrence (Saint). The poor were his treasures, **1:200**. It is necessary to pray for his spirit of fervor, **2:239**.

Lazarus (Saint). Raised from the dead by Jesus. Patron of the house of Saint Lazare, **2:236-37**.

Lebas (Toussaint), priest of the Mission. At Agde, **3:298**.

Le Blanc (Francois) or (Francis White), priest of the Mission. His departure for Scotland. First work there (1651), **2:174-75**. He is taken prisoner (1655), **2:179,181**. He regains his liberty. His stay in Scotland. Vincent announces that he has returned to his work (October 1658), **2:181.**

Le Bon (Adrien), religious of the Order of the Canons Regular of Saint Augustine, prior of Saint Lazare. Biographical notice. He offers Vincent the house of Saint Lazare. Affection and esteem that he has for the Congregation. His insistence that his offer be accepted, **1:120,122; 3:242.** The gratitude shown by Vincent towards him and his fellow religious, **3:241.** He asks the saint to recommend the release of an abbess who has been imprisoned because of her scandalous behavior. Refusal of Vincent, **3:281-82.** His edifying death (April 9, 1651). Sentiments of Vincent on this occasion, **1:206-07.**

Le Boucher (Monsieur), vicar general of Moutier Saint Jean. Letter to Vincent on the success of the missions held there, **2:48.**

Lebreton (Louis), priest of the Mission. At Rome (1638). He evangelizes the shepherds of the Roman countryside. Death of this Missionary (1641). His eulogy, **2:57.**

Lee (Thady), laybrother of the Congregation. Massacred by the followers of Cromwell in Ireland, **2:133.**

Le Gras (Antoine), secretary of Queen Marie de Medici. The husband of Louise de Marillac. His death. **1:128.**

Le Gras (Louise de Marillac). See, *Marillac (Louise de)*.

Le Maistre (Nicolas), doctor of theology of the Sorbonne. Vincent sends his work against the heresy of the "Two Heads" to Cardinal Grimaldi in Rome, **2:351.**

Le Mans (city of). Establishment of the Missionaries in this city in 1645, **1:232.** Vincent visits Le Mans during the troubles of the Fronde, **1:201; 3:237.** See, *La Ferte (Emeric Marc de), Lavardin (Philibert de Beaumanoir de)*.

Le Pelletier (Claude), minister of state of Louis XIV. He gives testimony as to the disinterestedness of Vincent while serving at the court, **2:399.**

Le Pretre (Monsieur), an ecclesiastic of the Tuesday Conferences. He is present at the death of Vincent, **1:261.**

Le Puy (city and diocese of). A Conference of Ecclesiastics is established in this city on the model of that of Paris, **1:168; 2:225-26.** See, *Maupas du Tour (Henri de)*.

Lesage (Jacques), priest of the Mission. His death at Algiers, **2:88.**

Lescot (Jacques), a doctor of theology of the Sorbonne, confessor of Richelieu, later bishop of Chartres. Letter to Vincent on the success of the missions in his diocese, **2:14;** and on the results of the ordination retreats, **2:202-03.**

Lesquielle (village near Landrecies). Assistance given to the population of this village during the war, **2:332.**

Lestang (Jean de), priest of the Mission, **1:181.**

Lestocq (Guillaume de), a doctor of theology of the Sorbonne and pastor of the Church of Saint Laurent in Paris. His discussions with Vincent to convince him to accept the priory of Saint Lazare, **1:120.** His work with the Missionaries in the country, **Ibid.**

Le Tellier (Michel), counselor of state. His testimony as to the disinterestedness of Vincent at the court, quoted by his brother, **2:399.**

Le Vacher (Jean), priest of the Mission. Sent to Tunis in 1648. He is attacked by the plague and is left for dead; his healing, **2:87.** He temporarily exercises the functions of French consul, **Ibid.** Vincent announces to him the departure of Martin Husson who will come to Tunis to occupy the post of consul. He greatly praises him to this young man, **2:89.** Troubles with the dey of Tunis. The ministry among the slaves of Bizerte (1655), **2:97-98.** After the return of Husson to France the dey of Tunis obliges him to exercise the functions of the consul (1657), **2:99.** With the consul, Jean Barreau, he ransoms seventy Christian slaves (1661), **2:97.** Letters to Vincent. He describes the suffering of the slaves of Bizerte and what is being done to assist them, **2:112 ff.** He gives an account of the courage of two young slaves, one French and one English, persecuted for the Catholic faith, **2:118-19.** Vincent congratulates him on having preserved many Frenchmen from captivity, **2:120.** He gives an account to the saint of his efforts to deliver slaves whose virtue was in danger, **2:120 ff.**

Le Vacher (Philippe), priest of the Mission, brother of the above. Sent to Algiers (1650), **2:88.** His collaboration with the consul of Algiers. Vincent congratulates the two of them (1655), **2:91.** He is acknowledged at Algiers as vicar apostolic and vicar general of the archbishop of Carthage. Reform of abuses, **2:102-03.**

At Algiers he assists the young Pierre Borguny dying at the stake for the faith (1656), **2:101.** He returns to France in 1657 and brings the remains of the young confessor for the faith, **Ibid.**

Levasseur (David), laybrother of the Mission, **2:326.**

Lhoste (Jean Marie), lawyer, **3:252.**

Lhuillier (Helene Angelique), a religious of the Visitation. Superior of the Monastery on the rue Saint Antoine. Vincent relieves her spiritual difficulties, **2:270.** He convinces her to refuse a donation offered by a Jansenist, **2:271.** He convinces her to accept the apostolate with repentant women at Sainte Madeleine, **2:279.**

Liancourt (Roger and Jeanne de Schomberg), duke and duchess of. They testify to their submission to the bull of Innocent X (1653). They afterwards once again adhere to the Jansenist party (1657), **2:369.**

Liberty (of Conscience). Vincent views this as a new heresy which could not be hidden in anyone who accepted it. He says that all true Catholics must accept definitive judgments of the faith, **2:371.** According to Vincent, while it is not permitted to judge anyone, it is a greater evil through a false charity or any other unworthy motive to accept those in heresy or suspected of heresy, **Ibid.**

Liberty (of the cults). Saint Cyran is put in prison at the chateau of Vincennes by the order of Richelieu. The latter said that if Luther and Calvin had been imprisoned when they first began their teaching the Church would have been spared its consequent troubles, **2:350.** Vincent also says that it had been a great mistake at the time not to have firmly opposed the errors of Calvin, and that this failure had been the cause of the subsequent wars and divisions, **2:357-58.**

Liberty (of the press). Vincent convinces the Council of Conscience to decree that evil books should be banned, and libraries forbidden to print or sell them, **2:394.**

Limerick (city and diocese of, Ireland). Vincent announces to the bishop of this city that he is sending eight priests to Ireland. Their first work, **2:127.** Letter of the bishop thanking Vincent for the work of his Missionaries (1658), **2:129.** Very successful mission held in Limerick, **2:129.** The bishop gives an account of them to Vincent, **2:130-31.** Letter of the saint to the superior of the Missionaries, **2:131-32.** Their devotion in the midst of the double plague of war and pestilence, **2:132.** Capture of the city by the troops of Cromwell (1651). Massacre of the Catholics, **2:133.** The Missionaries escape without harm, **Ibid.**

Lion. Vincent quotes the remark of Aristotle that it is better that fifty stags be led by one lion, than fifty lions be led by one stag, **2:375.**

Litany (of the Holy Name of Jesus). Devotion of Vincent to this litany. His reaction to the invocation: *Jesu, Deus pacis*, **1:215; 3:75**. His reaction to the invocation: *Jesu, pater pauperum*, **3:118**.

Liturgy. Zeal of Vincent for the liturgy, **3:73**. Exactitude of the liturgical ceremonies held at Saint Lazare, **3:77**. See, *Mass, Divine Office*.

Liverdi (Balthazar Grangier de), bishop of Treguier. He establishes the Congregation in this city in 1654, **1:234**. Letters to Vincent on the success of the missions, **2:47**.

Livorno (Italian port city), **2:99**.

Livy (classical author). Cited in Abelly, **2:40**.

Lodeve (diocese of). Letter relative to the establishment of the reform in a priory located here, **2:386**.

Lombard (Peter), medieval theologian, **1:40**.

Longron (in the diocese of Sens). Mission given there in 1650, **2:48**.

Longueville (Madame de). Vincent refuses her permission to visit the Visitandine cloister, **2:274**.

Lorraine (the province of). Confraternities of Charity, **1:73**. Extreme misery of this province during the war, **1:188 ff; 2:316 ff; 3:264**. Alms distributed by the Missionaries, **1:185; 2:316 ff.,329**. Vincent takes care of the needs of the refugees from Lorraine in Paris. A mission is given to them by the ecclesiastics of the Tuesday Conferences, **2:218,327**. He brings a large number of boys and girls from the ravaged areas to safety in Paris, **2:327**. Assistance given to a large number of young women from this area whose virtue was in danger, **3:272**.

Vincent establishes in Paris an association of gentlemen to assist the impoverished nobles from this province (1640), **1:187; 2:328**.

Help furnished by the queen and by the Ladies of Charity to Vincent for Lorraine (1643), **1:185-86; 2:304,329-30**. Principal results of this assistance, **2:330**. Providential protection of a laybrother who carried aid to the province during the wars, **Ibid**.

Lorthon (Pierre de), counselor and secretary of Louis XIII. Founder of a house of the Congregation at Crecy, **1:231**.

Lot (Old Testament figure), **1:200**.

Louis IX (Saint, king of France). Vincent comments on the mystery of this king's holiness, **1:135**. The chapel of the consulate in Tunis is placed under his patronage, **2:107**. Vincent praises his humility and generosity, **3:183**.

Louis XIII (King of France). He names Vincent as Chaplain-General of the Galleys (1619), **1:84**. He confirms by letters patent the contract of foundation of the Congregation, and authorizes it to be established everywhere within the kingdom (1627), **1:111**. He agrees with Vincent to turn the tower of Saint Bernard (La Tournelle) in Paris into a place of lodging for the convicts (1632), **1:148**. Vincent goes to see him at Senlis. The king asks him to send Missionaries to minister to the army (1636), **1:175**. A mission is given at Saint Germain en Laye, **2:76**.

He issues new patent letters in favor of the Congregation of the Mission (May 1642), **1:111**. The house at Crecy is founded in his name, **1:231**. He sends Vincent a considerable sum to give missions in Sedan and its surrounding area, **1:232**.

He is assisted by Vincent in his final illness, **1:190 ff**. The saint comforts him with the knowledge of his many works of piety, **1:191**. His esteem for the Congregation of the Mission. He declares that if he recovered his health he would not name anyone a bishop who had not spent three years with Vincent, **Ibid.** He again calls the saint to assist him in his last moments, **Ibid; 3:88-89.** Edifying circumstances of his death (May 14, 1643) recounted by Vincent, **3:256.**

Louis XIV (King of France). He signs the letters patent for the foundation of the hospital at Marseilles, and orders that the priests of the Mission are to be its directors in perpetuity (1645), **1:150.** He gives a considerable donation to the Ladies of Charity for the care of the foundlings (1645), **1:161.** He provides the Chateau of Bicetre to lodge these infants (1648), **1:162.** Queen Anne of Austria establishes, in the name of the king, a house of the Congregation at Sedan, **1:232.**

Vincent urges bishops to encourage the loyalty and obedience of the people to the king during the times of troubles, **1:216 ff.** He tries to negotiate a reconciliation of the princes (1652), **1:219.** The king gives the enclosure of the Salpetriere to serve as a general hospital (1653), **1:227.**

Louvain (university of). Saint Cyran and Jansenius study here, **2:346.**

Louvre (royal palace in Paris), **3:191,243.**

Loyola (Ignatius), saint. His esteem for the practice of making spiritual retreats, **1:141, 2:231-32.** The Missionaries should be like the poor peasant who carried the traveling bags of Ignatius and his companions, **3:102.**

Lucas (Antoine), priest of the Mission. One of the seven first companions of Vincent. **1:111.** He gives missions together with Jean Jacques Olier in the diocese of Saint Flour, **2:36.**

Lucas (Martin), provost of the collegiate church of Notre Dame de Coeffort at Le Mans. He resigns his title of pro-pastor. Union of the church to the Congregation of the Mission (1645), **1:232.**

Lucon (city and diocese of). The Missionaries from the house at Richelieu give missions in the diocese of Lucon in 1638. Beneficial results. Some confreres are established in this city in 1645, **1:230; 2:51.** Vincent travels there in 1649, **1:202.** See *Nivelle (Pierre de)*.

Ludes (parish in the diocese of Reims). Mission held there, **2:43.**

Ludovisio (Nicolas Albergati), cardinal, Grand Penitentiary of Rome. He writes a letter of consolation to the dying Vincent, **1:258.**

Luke (gospel of). Cited in Abelly: 4:18-**1:98,238; 2:16; 3:20,** 11:27-**1:114,** 22:31-**1:196,** 13:7-**1:257,** 2:29-**2:39,** 15:10-**2:55,** 10:1-**2:148,** 8:3-**2:312,** 22:43-**3:63,** 11:1-**3:63,** 6:40-**3:83,** 22:42-**3:88,** 6:26-**3:190,** 10:16-**3:206,** 1:79-**3:325.**

Lumsden (Thomas), priest of the Mission. His departure for Scotland. First works, **2:174,178.** Letters to Vincent, **2:178-79.**

Luneville. Testimony of gratitude from the inhabitants of this city to Vincent, **2:326.**

Luserna (in Piedmont). Mission given in this area, **2:76.**

Luther (Martin). How his heresy injured the Church, **2:16,253,346, 357,360.**

Lutheran. A young German of this sect commits a crime in the neighborhood of Saint Lazare while posing as a Missionary, **3:160-61.**

Luzarches (town north of Paris). The Missionaries give spiritual assistance to the soldiers there (1636), **1:177.**

Lyons (city and archdiocese of). Canons of this diocese are the temporal lords of Chatillon les Dombes, **1:65.** House of the Oratory located here, **Ibid.**

M

Mac Donald (one of the ruling clans of the island of Skye in the Hebrides), **2:176**.

Mac Fimine (one of the ruling clans on the island of Skye in the Hebrides), (error for Mac Simon), **2:176**.

Mac Leod (one of the ruling clans on the island of Skye in the Hebrides), **2:176**.

Macon (city of). How the Confraternity of Charity is established there by Vincent (1623), **1:87**. Rules of the confraternity, **1:88**. Virtues that the saint practices during his stay in this city. He is obliged to flee secretly to avoid the praise and gratitude of the people, **Ibid**. See, *Desmoulins (Monsieur), Dinet (Louis)*.

Madagascar. Vincent agrees to evangelize this island (1646). His zeal in this enterprise, **1:233; 2:158**. Morals and beliefs of its inhabitants. Messieurs Nacquart and Gondree are designated for this mission. Rules of conduct established for them by Vincent, **2:134 ff**. A young Malgache is instructed by the saint at Saint Lazare, **2:137**. Description of Madagascar and its people, **2:139 ff**. Apostolic zeal of the Missionaries during their voyage (1649), **2:138-39**. Arrival of the Missionaries on this island; their first work, **2:142 ff**. Death of Monsieur Gondree. Continuation of the work by Monsieur Nacquart, **2:144 ff**. Death of Monsieur Nacquart. Praise of his virtue (1650). Departure of Messieurs Bourdaise and Mousnier (1654), **2:149-50**. The island is a fertile field opened by God to the Missionaries, **3:100**. Admirable perseverance of Vincent in supporting this mission, **3:102-03**.

Departure of Messieurs Dufour (Claude), Prevost and Belleville (October 29, 1655), **2:149**. Their death (1656), **2:150**. Earnest prayers of Monsieur Bourdaise to Vincent not to abandon the mission. Heroic constancy of the saint in these trials, **2:158-59**. Departure of Messieurs Boussordec, Herbron and of Brother Christopher Delaunay (September 29, 1656). Shipwreck of their vessel near Nantes, **2:161; 3:276**. The saint does not want to abandon this mission, and submits to these trials, **3:276**.

Account, addressed to Vincent by Monsieur Bourdaise, of the arrival of the Missionaries and their work. He also asks for an foundation of the Daughters of Charity, and the creation of a hospital and seminary (1657), **2:149 ff**. He learns of the death of Monsieur Mousnier. Praise of this Missionary, **2:150**.

New departure of Missionaries (March 1658). The vessel is shipwrecked and captured by the Spanish. Dispersion of the Missionaries, **2:162**. Vincent announces the next departure of several Missionaries (April 1659). The departure is postponed, **2:159**. Departure from Nantes. The Missionaries are delayed by a storm at La Rochelle, **3:277**.

New departure of Missionaries from La Rochelle (Messieurs Etienne, Feydin, Daveroult, Defontaines, Parre). They are shipwrecked at the Cape of Good Hope (April 1660) and are rescued by the Dutch, **2:162; 3:278**. Vincent's successor sends new Missionaries who land at Madagascar, **2:163**. See, *Bourdaise (Toussaint), Dufour (Claude), Etienne (Nicolas), Gondree (Nicolas), Mousnier (Jean Francois), Nacquart (Charles)*.

Madeleine (Monastery of Sainte). Refuge for repentant women. Nature of this work. Vincent consults various doctors about the affairs of this establishment, **1:132**. He convinces the religious of the Visitation to accept the direction of this work, **2:278**. The different types of women who are received there, **2:279**. He encourages Mother Anne Marie Bollain to be its superior, **2:280**. Interest that the saint always had for this establishment, **3:272-73**.

Magnanimity. The virtue of humility is not in opposition to this, **3:183.** Why it is necessary to ask God for great things, **Ibid.**

Maida (Francois de), superior general of the Minims. He grants Vincent letters of association to his Order, **2:385.**

Maignely (Charlotte Marguerite de Gondi), marquise de. Biographical notice. She contributes gifts to support the work with the ordinands, **2:186.** She contributes to the foundation of the monastery of Sainte Madeleine for repentant women, **2:278.** She provides a personal service to Vincent on behalf of one of his nephews, **3:259.**

Maillet (Antoine Flandin, Brother), popular religious figure of the seventeenth century. The example of his attitude toward sickness, as well as other proofs of his piety, **3:292.**

Maillezais. Vincent takes part in the negotiations for the translation of the episcopal see of Maillezais to La Rochelle, **2:382.** See, *Guibourgere (Raoul de la)*.

Maine (province of). Assistance sent there, **1:212.**

Malta (Knights of the Order of). See, *Lascaris (Paul)*.

Mamedia (location in Barbary). Christian slaves held here are visited by the Missionaries, **2:115.**

Mamertinus (Claudius). Classical author cited, **1:91.**

Marchais (village near Montmirail). Conversion of a heretic here, **1:82.**

Marcillac (Sylvestre de Crusy de), bishop of Mende. He asks for the help of the Missionaries in his diocese, 2:36.

Marie Joseph (Daughter of Charity). Martyr of charity at Etampes, **1:209.**

Marillac (Louise de), (Mademoiselle Le Gras), foundress of the Daughters of Charity. Biographical notice. Her qualities; her virtues, **1:128.**

Louise de Marillac is first under the spiritual direction of Jean Pierre Camus, the bishop of Belley, who passes this role on to Vincent. The latter gives him some of his recommended rules, spiritual readings, and practices of piety. Vincent indicates to her the conduct to follow in his absence (1626), **1:129.** He agrees with her desire to give herself to the service of the poor, and praises her resolution to imitate the hidden life of our Lord Jesus Christ. He strengthens her in her vocation, **Ibid.** She leaves the parish of Saint Sauveur and moves to the parish of Saint Nicholas du Chardonnet, near the College des Bons Enfants, where Vincent is living (1626), **Ibid.** Vincent appeals to her when he does not have any money to give to the poor, **3:129.** Vincent again attempts to develop the vocation of Louise de Marillac. He uses her to make visitations of the Confraternities of Charity. Instructions that he gives her for this purpose (1629), **1:129,134.** She visits several dioceses. Methods that she used in these visits. Beneficial results, **1:130.** She teaches school herself and instructs the local school mistresses, **Ibid.** She overcame the weakness of her health. Vincent counsels her to moderate her zeal, **1:130.** He indicates to her how she should conduct herself in the midst of both success and failures, **Ibid.** He congratulates her for having visited a sick person stricken by the plague (1631), **1:132.**

Women make their retreats at the house of Louise de Marillac. She receives many different persons thus revealing the goodness of her character, **1:142-43; 3:272.** She assists the prisoners at Saint Bernard's tower. Letter of Vincent, **1:148-49.**

Vincent reproaches her for worrying too much about her health, **3:18-19.** At first she did not know how to balance her eagerness with patience in anticipating God's providence, **3:32.** Vincent wishes that her soul would be full of confidence based on

the knowledge that she is a cherished daughter of our Savior, **Ibid.** He encourages her to always submit herself to the adorable will of God, **3:44-45.**
Louise de Marillac attentively receives the advice and direction of Vincent, **1:24.** The saint desires that her heart would imitate and honor the tranquility of the heart of the Lord, **1:135.** She has a heart which never tired of doing good, **1:142.** Her confidence in Vincent and the esteem of the saint for her, **1:246.** Vincent later said that because of her poor health she had lived for twenty years only by a miracle, **Ibid.** He is extremely reserved in his relations with her so as not to give any cause for rumor, **Ibid; 3:271.** He thanks her for remembering his feast day, **3:32.** He criticizes her for abstaining from communion because of scruples, **3:79-80.**
Vincent predicts to Louise that God wants her to serve him in those things which were to his glory, **1:132,135.** He guides and moderates her desire of consecrating herself to the formation of daughters for the service of the poor (1632), **1:135.** She consecrates herself to this work by vow (March 15, 1634), **1:136.**
Vincent goes to Louise's home to give conferences to the first Daughters of Charity on their works and their way of life. This begins their company (1634), **1:134.** He advises Louise to accept whatever difficulties occurred in the establishment of the Daughters of Charity, **3:249.**
Together with Vincent she insists that the Company of the Daughters of Charity be officially constituted dependent on, and under the control of the superior general of the Congregation of the Mission. This is officially established (1651), **2:291.**
Louise is providentially preserved from harm in the collapse of a ceiling in the motherhouse, **3:36.**
Her last illness. Vincent, who is himself very ill, cannot assist the dying Louise, **1:247.** He sends a message to her saying that although she was going first he "hoped to see her soon in heaven." Death of Louise (March 15, 1660), **1:247; 3:279.** Vincent presides at two conferences with the Daughters of Charity on the virtues of the deceased Louise de Marillac, **1:247.**

Mark (gospel of). Cited in Abelly: 6:31-**2:24,** 3:31-**2:262,** 7:37- **3:225,285,** 9:29-**3:286,** 15:41-**3:322.**

Marle (town near Laon). Vincent sends Missionaries and assistance to this area, **1:205; 2:305,337.**

Marquemont (Dennis de), archbishop of Lyons. He authorizes Vincent to receive the abjuration of a heretic at Chatillon, **1:75.**

Marsal (city in Lorraine). Vincent sends aid there, **2:329.**

Marseilles (city, port, and diocese of). Vincent goes there to receive an inheritance. Traveling by sea he is taken prisoner by pirates and reduced to slavery, **1:42.** He visits the galleys there in 1622. Their deplorable state at the time. His charity, **1:85.** He procures the creation of a hospital for the sick convicts (1642) and of a group of chaplains, **1:150.** Mission given to the galleys with the agreement of the bishop, Jean Baptiste Gault (1643), **2:39-40.**
Establishment of the Congregation of the Mission there (1643). The superior of the Congregation is instituted as superior of the chaplains of the galleys (1644), **1:150,231.** A knight gives Vincent an account of the beneficial results of the establishment of the hospital for the convicts (1645), **1:150.** The galleys are transferred to Toulon. A confrere follows them there to continue to assist the convicts (1649), **1:151.** Results of the missions given in this diocese (1647), **2:41.** Two young men from this city who are held as slaves in Barbary are ransomed by the Mission-

aries. Horrible torments endured by one of them, **2:122**. Voluntary captivity of Vincent, **3:112-13**. A religious in this city speaks against the community. Christian response of Vincent, **3:158**. See, *Get (Firmin)*.

Marsillac (area in the diocese of Angouleme), **2:52**.

Martha (sister of Mary and Lazarus in the New Testament), **3:26**.

Martin (Jean), priest of the Mission. He goes to Turin to take direction of the house founded by the Marquis de Pianezza (1655). His letters to Vincent. Account given of the missions (1656), **2:76 ff.**

Martin (Lange), French consul at Tunis. He receives into his house the two Missionaries who have come to minister to the slaves, **2:86**.

Martyr. Vincent desires that all the Missionaries have an ambition to suffer martyrdom for the sake of Jesus Christ, **1:183**. In the life of those who have professed to serve Jesus Christ among the unbelievers there is always the possibility of this end. Example of the Missionaries sent to Barbary, **2:92**. Account of the martyrdom of a young Majorcan (Pierre Bourguny); burned alive at Algiers, **2:100 ff**. Heroic traits and deaths of several Christian slaves, **2:111 ff.,118 ff.** Vincent congratulates a Missionary who did not hesitate to expose himself to death rather than miss the opportunity of assisting someone, **2:131**. The mayor and other notables of Limerick in Ireland courageously endure death for the Catholic faith, **2:132-33**. It is a kind of martyrdom to be consumed by virtue, **2:180**. A Missionary must have the desire to suffer martyrdom for the sake of the name of Jesus Christ. Example of a priest from Calabria, **Ibid.** It is good to desire martyrdom, and to often ask God for the grace of this disposition, **3:98**.

Heroic deaths of several Missionaries. See, *Francillon (Francois)*, *Le Blanc, (Francois)*, *Le Vacher (Jean)*, *Lee (Thady)*, *Montmasson (Michel)*.

Mary (The Blessed Virgin). From his childhood Vincent has a special devotion to her. He visits her chapel at Buglose, **1:35**. He invokes her intercession during his captivity, and believes firmly that he had been delivered because of her, **1:44**. At Chatillon he establishes the custom of each Sunday singing a hymn in her honor, **1:81**. He prays at her altar at the church of Notre Dame in Paris, **2:199**. *Sentiments and examples of Vincent*, **3:92 ff.**

Model of modesty, **2:199**. The model of the manner of performing visits, **2:297**. Powerful intercession of, **3:270**.

Mary (sister of Martha and Lazarus in the New Testament), **3:26**.

Mass. Vincent's first mass. His fervor in its celebration, **1:39**. He spends considerable time in prayer to prepare for mass, and in thanksgiving afterwards, **1:243**. On the suffering endured by the Christian slaves in order to attend mass, **2:123**. The devotion with which the saint celebrates mass, **3:75-76**. The edification and admiration of those who assist him at the altar, **3:76**. He never fails to celebrate mass, **Ibid**. Until his old age he has the custom of serving other priests during their masses, **3:77**. One time before celebrating mass he goes to find, and be reconciled with, a religious who had stated that he had some reason for having a personal aversion towards him, **3:158**.

Matthew (gospel of). Cited in Abelly: 9:36-**1:72**, 11:28-**1:41**, 10:34-**1:176**, 24:12-**1:185**, 13:34-**2:19**, 8:25-**2:233**, 17:4-**2:44**, 11:5-**2:285**, 25:34-35-**2:307**, 16:25-**2:390**, 6:33-**3:39**, 16:24-**3:42**, 6:10-**3:42**, 5:3-**3:86**, 25:40-**3:115**, 6:2-**3:126**, 11:29-**3:175**, 16:23-**3:176**, 23:14-15-**3:176**, 5:5-**3:177**, 26:50-**3:178**, 23:12-**3:180**, 11:29-**3:196,198**, 23:12-**3:196**, 20:28-**3:204**, 10:16-**3:215,223**, 11:25-**3:215**, 22:21-**3:224,233**, 24:35-

3:225, 19:27- **3:242,** 5:40-**3:251,** 16:24-**3:254,** 19:11-**3:254,** 6:33-**3:312,** 5:13- **3:321,** 23:12-**3:325.**

Maupas du Tour (Henri de Cauchon de), bishop of Le Puy, later of Evreux. He preaches the homily at the requiem service for Vincent at the church of Saint Germain l'Auxerrois in Paris. He approves of the *Life* of the saint written by Abelly, **1:26,262.**

Maurice (Dom). Barnabite whom Vincent consults as to the authenticity of his vision of the souls of Jane de Chantal and Francis de Sales, **2:284.**

Mauron (in the diocese of Saint Malo). Mission given there, **2:45.**

Mavaubouille (local chieftain in Madagascar), **2:153.**

Maxims of Jesus Christ. They are for Vincent a sure rudder to guide him in the advice that he gives others, or in the personal resolutions that he takes, **2:403.** He regards them as the fountain of all wisdom, **Ibid.** When he read these words of the Gospel: "I tell you solemnly" he becomes particularly attentive. He savors these passages, like an infant drinking its mother's milk, **3:76.** Vincent forms his judgments according to them and he has no concern that his conduct is not approved by the world, **3:88.** Thus he does not hesitate to stand absolutely with this oracle of truth, **3:296.** How a Missionary must believe in them, **3:317-18.**

It is necessary to understand the maxims of Jesus Christ. Reasons that we have to follow them. The authority of the Teacher, **1:103,105-06; 3:175.** "Whoever speaks of the teachings of Jesus Christ speaks of an unshakable rock: eternal truths, which infallibly produce their proper fruit. They should rather expect the heavens to fall than to find the truths of Jesus Christ to fail," **1:103.** The Congregation must nourish itself on this heavenly food, **1:104.** Explanation of the maxim, "Seek first the Kingdom of God," **Ibid.** Principal virtues which are the object of the maxims of Jesus Christ, **Ibid.** Two other important maxims, **1:105.** Only eternal truths are capable of filling the heart and of guiding us with assurance, **3:19.** As an inviolable rule true prudence consists of conforming our conduct to these maxims, **3:225.**

Maynard (Michel Ulysse). Nineteenth-century biographer of Vincent. Note, **1:12.**

Mazarin (Jules), cardinal, minister of state. Abelly serves as his confessor, **1:11.** Biographical notice, **1:192.** His policies and opposition of Vincent to them, **1:193,208,219-20.** Member of the Council of Conscience (1643), **1:192.** Difference of views between the minister and Vincent on the choice of prelates, **2:375.** Opposition of Vincent to the promotion of one of Mazarin's candidates to a bishopric, **2:380.** He makes a remark about the poor dress that Vincent wears at court, **3:243.** Troubles of the Fronde. Vincent has an unsuccessful meeting with the cardinal, **1:199; 2:397.** The saint gives Mazarin an account of his interview with the duke of Orleans and the prince of Conde trying to achieve peace (1652), **1:219.**

Mc Ennery (Jean), priest of the Mission. His death from the plague in Genoa, **3:54.**

Meaux (diocese of). Louise de Marillac visits the Confraternities of Charity in this diocese, **1:130.** See, *Crecy.*

Medici (Marie de), queen of France. Wife of Henry IV and mother of Louis XIII, **1:42,49,128.**

Meditation. See, *Prayer.*

Mende (diocese of). The bishop pleads for assistance, saying that his diocese is dying from hunger for the word of God. Vincent sends Missionaries. Their work; their successes, **2:35-36.**

Mercy. It is the first effect of the love that one feels for the poor, **3:118.** The true nature of God is to be merciful, **Ibid.** As soon as anyone sees a Missionary he immediately should think; there goes a person full of compassion. The example of the first Missionaries, **Ibid.**

Messier (Louis), doctor of theology the Sorbonne, archdeacon of Beauvais. He preaches the first ordination retreat at Beauvais together with Vincent, **1:139.**

Metellopolis (the bishop of), **2:304.**

Metz (city of). Vincent collects aid for this city during the war (1640). Gratitude of its inhabitants, **1:185; 2:318.** Mission held at Metz (1658). Edifying conduct of the preachers and their success, **2:198.** Formation of an assembly of ecclesiastics on the model of that of Saint Lazare. Letter of Bossuet to Vincent asking him to be its superior, **2:227.**

Mezieres (city of). Vincent sends Missionaries and assistance to this city (1650), **1:205.** The Missionaries establish a Confraternity of Charity there, **2:341.**

Midot (Jean), vicar general of the diocese of Toul, **2:318.**

Minims (Order of the). The superior general of this community grants Vincent letters of affiliation to his order, **2:385.**

Miracles. The healing of various sicknesses and temptations among the Visitandines is attributed to him, **2:270-71.** Vision which the saint has at the death of Saint Jane de Chantal, **2:283-84.** Vincent raises objections to the miraculous claims of Port Royal in support of the Jansenist party, **2:368-69.**

Mirecourt (town near Nancy). Help sent by Vincent there, **2:329.**

Mission (Congregation of the). Founded by Vincent de Paul

1. *History.*

Pierre de Berulle predicts to Vincent that he will found a new Congregation (1609), **1:52.**

1617: Occasion of the foundation of the Congregation. The mission held at Folleville, **1:61-62.**

1618: The saint gives missions aided by various virtuous ecclesiastics from Paris, **1:73.** He holds that it is a great honor for the Missionaries to be able to imitate the conduct of God towards his Church in evangelizing the poor, **1:83.**

1624: The College des Bons Enfants, the birthplace of the Congregation. The saint is named as principal of the college by the archbishop of Paris, **1:94.**

1625: Contract of foundation by Monsieur and Madame de Gondi for the establishment of the Congregation of the Mission. The end of the new institute, **1:94-95.** Birth and erection of the Congregation, **1:109 ff.** Monsieur Portail, together with Vincent, arrives at the College des Bons Enfants, **Ibid.**

1626: Approval of the contract of foundation and the foundations of the new company by the archbishop of Paris, Jean Francois de Gondi, **1:94 ff.,110.** Humble and providential beginnings of the Congregation of the Mission, **1:110,237-38; 3:28.** Act by which the first three companions of the saint are formally associated with him, **1:110.**

1627: Letters patent of Louis XIII confirming the contract of foundation of the Mission and approving its establishment everywhere in the kingdom, **Ibid.** The first seven Missionaries who join with Vincent are compared to the seven priests placed under the direction of Joshua after Jericho, **1:111.**

1632: (12 February). Urban VIII by the bull *Salvatoris Nostri,* erects the Company of the Mission as a Congregation approved by the Holy See, and gives Vincent the power to establish its rule, **1:111-12.** The pontiff assigns to the company, to the exclusion of all other communities, the title of the Congregation of the Mission, **Ibid.** Conference of Vincent on the virtues of humility and charity which he sees as the foundations of the Congregation, **1:113 ff.** Establishment of the Congregation at Saint Lazare near Paris, **1:119ff.** See, *Saint Lazare.*

1637: Establishment of the internal seminary. **1:179 ff.**

1642: First assembly of the Congregation. Vincent asks it to accept his resignation as superior general. The refusal of the assembly, **3:192.**

1652: Opposition of the Oratorians to the establishment of the Congregation. Vincent outlines, for the benefit of his agent in Rome, a wise and charitable plan to counteract this opposition, **3:25,159.**

1655: (September 22nd). Brief of Alexander VII approving the vows, and the exemption of the Congregation of the Mission from the jurisdiction of the ordinaries, **3:159.** How it is to relate to the bishops, **3:208.**

1658: Distribution of the Common Rules to the Missionaries. Conference given by Vincent on this occasion, **1:237 ff.**

1660. The death of Vincent de Paul. The continuation of the work of the community in France and elsewhere, **1:212; 2:163.**

Listing of the establishments founded during the life of the saint, **1:230 ff.**

2. *Its nature and its Works.*

The rules of the Congregation of the Mission, its works, and its pious exercises are not the work of man: God alone is their author, **1:239-40; 3:181.** The three ends for which the Congregation of the Mission is instituted, **1:241.** Each of its members must, before everything else, work for their own perfection, **3:318.**

Evangelization of the poor, **1:83; 3:117.** See, *Poor.* Assistance to the Christian slaves is one of the most charitable works which the Missionaries can exercise on earth, **2:124.** Encouragement of the practice of making a spiritual retreat, **2:229,235.**

Instruction of ecclesiastics. Excellence of this work, **2:191 ff.** The laybrothers of the community can by their prayers contribute to the results of the ordination retreats, **2:197.**

Foreign Missions. The Missionaries must themselves be ready to be sent everywhere on the earth to proclaim the Gospel, **3:51.** Their vocation is to bring the entire world to recognize the love of God present in their heart, **3:106-07.** See, *Foreign Missions.* To form and direct the Daughters of Charity, **2:300.**

3. *Some General Rules.*

1. The disinterestedness of Vincent relative to the advancement of the interests of his congregation, **3:48,53.** He asks God two or three times each day to destroy the Congregation if it fails to be useful in his service, **3:89.** Intrigues against the company in Rome. The saint refuses to combat these by the same means, and instead places his confidence in divine providence, **3:159.** He says that he never would say anything to purposely attract anyone to join the Congregation, **3:181.**

2. Sentiments of humility of Vincent on the subject of the Congregation, **3:27.** The Congregation would commit a great sacrilege if it attributed to itself the glory which it received from God for the sanctification of souls, **3:73.** Humility of the saint in comparing his congregation to others, **3:102,147.** He describes it as a small and insignificant company, **3:182,187.** He explains how each of the members must esteem humility, and how the congregation must not love and search after honors, **3:182,197-98.** He blesses God for the calumnies and the contradictions that it must accept, **3:190,284.** He reprimands a Missionary who had printed a work which had advertised the spirit, the functions, and the works of the company, **3:202-03.**

3. A spirit of zeal must animate the Congregation of the Mission. The zeal of the Missionaries must be carried to everyone throughout the world, **2:85.** Ardent exhortation of the saint for this spirit, **2:170.** A Missionary without zeal would only be the corpse of a Missionary, **2:237.** No other congregation must be more dedicated to the exterior exercise of an effective and true charity than that of the Mission, **3:106-07.** The vocation of the Missionaries is to bring the entire world to accept the love of God in their hearts, **Ibid.** Excellence of the ministry of the priests of the Mission in the conduct of souls, **3:317.**

Missionaries (or priests of the Mission). The life of the priests of the Mission is a life which is in conformity to the maxims of the Gospel. There is no life which is more Christian, **1:117.** Vincent believes that there is nothing in the world more precious than a good minister of the gospel, **1:246.** Excellence and difficulty of this work, and the ways in which it must be carried out, **3:317.**

The name of the priests of the Mission is granted to them by Urban VIII to the exclusion of all other communities, **1:111.**

Vincent is their model. Enumeration of the virtues which according to the saint are the most necessary for them, **2:17-18.** In order to be effective they must, above all, be men of prayer and of good example, **2:18.** Vincent desires that they do not esteem the qualities of nature or of fortune as if they were virtues, **3:26.** The fruit of their works will depend on the spirit with which they are animated: a sheep acts like a sheep; a saint acts like a saint, **3:317.**

Works of the Missionaries. In Picardy, Champagne, Lorraine, Artois during the war, **1:204 ff,212; 2:317,329,331 ff.** They go to assist the poor of Etampes and at Palaiseau, etc. Many die there, **1:208-09.** The spiritual care of the elderly at the hospital of the Nom de Jesus is confided to them, **1:225.** See, *Mission (Congregation of the)*.

Missions (evangelization of rural parishes).

1. Of Missions in general. The necessity of missions, **2:13 ff.** They are the first object of our vocation. Neither age nor infirmities must deter Missionaries. Lively exhortation to work for the salvation of the poor, **2:15 ff.**

Order of exercises to be observed in the mission, **2:20 ff.** On preparing children for their first communion, and celebrating it with fitting solemnity, **2:23.** Visiting the sick, **Ibid.** Recommendation of Vincent on the manner of acting towards heretics in the course of the missions, **2:25 ff.** Advice on this subject to the superior at Sedan, **2:26.** Advice to a brother who had to travel with heretics, **2:27.** The work of the missions must be done only with the permission of the local pastor. Nothing is to be done, no matter how small, without the pastor's permission, **3:209.** Advice to a Missionary who encountered opposition to the exercises, **3:286.**

Vincent believes that it is necessary for the Missionaries to spend some time during the year resting from their labors, **2:24.** He desires that as much time as necessary be spent on conducting the missions in order to do them well, **2:29.**

The exercises of the mission must be given freely, **2:23.** The Missionaries may receive what is offered to them as alms, but they cannot expect to be paid anything for their work, **3:313.**

2. Of some missions in particular. Some very remarkable missions, **2:13 ff.** Vincent begins to give missions in 1617, **2:27.** Results of the missions in various provinces in 1627, **2:50.** Missions given by the first ecclesiastics of the Tuesday Conferences to the workers in Paris (1633), **2:211.**

Missions given in Saintonge (1634-1648 and following), **2:32 ff.** In Cevennes

(1635), **2:35**. In Auvergne (1636), **2:36**. In the diocese of Geneva (1640 and on), **2:38**. In Saint Germain en Laye (1638), **2:76**. Mission at Fontainbleau, **3:212**.
Great number of missions that Vincent gave or caused to be given. Results of these missions, **2:28,50,55 ff**. See, *Zeal*.
Missions to the galleys. Vincent gives a mission to the galleys gathered at Bordeaux (1613), **1:86**; **3:257**. Missions to the galleys at Marseilles, in 1643. Several seminarians from the College des Bons Enfants ask to help, **2:39**.

3. Foreign Missions. Particular esteem of Vincent for these missions. His zeal for what concerns them, **2:84 ff.,138**. Virtues necessary for those who work in these, **2:135; 3:99-100**. Manner of teaching pagans the truths of the faith, **2:136**. Concerning the older confreres who ask to be sent to the faraway missions, **3:50-51**. Encouragement for this holy disposition, **3:51**. Vincent declares that he himself is ready to depart for the missions in the Indies, **3:98**. Exhortations to support these missions, **3:99-100**. If these efforts result in bringing to these barbarous lands the beauty of the Catholic religion, and inspiring a devotion to it, the men and the money spent in the effort will be well worth it, **3:104**. Vincent would like to undertake the evangelization of all the infidel countries, **Ibid**. Our vocation is to bring the entire world to accept the love of God in their hearts, **3:106-07**. Vincent sends to the missions only those who request to be sent there, **3:297**. See *Barbary, China, Madagascar*.

Modesty (of Jesus Christ, and of the Blessed Virgin). It is the seal and the halo of the saints, **2:199**.
Vincent gives edification by his practice of this virtue in his youth and during his entire life. A testimony, **1:42; 3:56,96**. Good effects produced by the modesty of the saint and the first Missionaries, **1:121; 3:266**. Beneficial influence of this virtue in the success of the missions. It is a silent preaching, but is very effective, **2:198**. Modesty of Vincent during the recitation of the divine office, **3:73**. During Mass, **3:75**; —in Church, **3:78**; —in his dress, **3:191**. Modesty of the eyes. Examples, **3:265**. Vincent criticizes immodesty of hairstyles and other vanities, **3:302**.
The modesty of the first Daughters of Charity gives great edification, **1:136**. "They have for their veil, holy modesty," **2:293**.

Moidart (region of Scotland). Evangelized by Dermot Duggan, **2:176**.

Mole (Edouard), bishop of Bayeux. Vincent's opposition to his appointment, **2:381**.

Mole (Mathieu), procurator general to the Parlement, then first President and Keeper of the Seals. He assists Vincent in helping the convicts (1639), **1:149**. In 1649 during the Fronde when the saint is leaving to rejoin the court he warns him not to leave the city, **1:198,228**. Vincent tries to convince him to withdraw his son from consideration for a bishopric, **2:381**. Vincent quotes his advice to bishops concerning appeals to the Parlement, **2:384**.

Molina (Antonio de), Carthusian spiritual writer, **2:190**.

Moncia (Giovanni Cristoforo), priest, nobleman, benefactor of the Congregation at Genoa, **1:233**.

Mondovi (city in Piedmont, Italy). Mission given near here, **2:83**.

Monica (Saint). Madame de Gondi, near her death is compared to her, **1:97**.

Montauban (city and diocese of). Foundation of the Congregation there for the conduct of the diocesan seminary, and missions. Results of the missions held in this diocese, **2:51**.

Montchal (Charles de), archbishop of Toulouse. He thanks Vincent for the results of the missions in his diocese, and asks him to send Missionaries to conduct the ordination retreats, **2:53.**

Montevit (Germain de), priest of the Mission. Death at Bar le Duc as a victim of his own zeal, **2:325; 3:239.**

Montignac (in the diocese of Angouleme). Mission held there, **2:52.**

Montmasson (Michel), priest of the Mission, vicar apostolic of Algiers. He is executed by the Moslems by being tied to the mouth of a cannon, **2:86.**

Montmirail (village in Brie, a possession of Monsieur de Gondi). Evangelized by Vincent, **1:56.** The saint establishes the Confraternity of Charity there, **1:73.** Vincent converts many heretics there; in particular he spreads devotion to the Blessed Virgin, **1:81.** He gives a mission there in 1621, **1:81.** A house of the Congregation is founded in the area by the duke of Retz in 1644, **1:232.** Help given to the inhabitants during the public misery, **3:111.** Vincent urges Monsieur Husson, secretary to the duke of Retz, to leave Montmirail and to accept the position of consul at Tunis, **3:296.**

Montmarin (Armand de), archbishop of Vienne. At Vincent's funeral, **1:262.**

Montorio (Pietro Francesco), vice legate of the pope at Avignon. He brings Vincent to Rome, **1:45,48.**

Moral Relativism. Vincent rejects it, just as he rejected Jansenism, **2:371.**

Morar (region in Scotland). Evangelized by Dermot Duggan, **2:176.**

Moras (Bertrande de), mother of Vincent, **1:35.**

Moray (region of Scotland). Evangelized by Thomas Lumsden, **2:178.**

Morlaix (in Brittany). Mission held there, **2:47.**

Morlochia (location in Barbary). Christian slaves here are visited by the Missionaries, **2:115.**

Mortagne (city in Saintonge). Mission given there in 1633, **2:41.**

Mortification. Vincent cites the example of our Lord and of the saints with respect to this virtue, **3:267.**

For more than fifty years, Vincent slept on a pallet without any covering, **1:88-89; 3:265.** How he practiced mortification in the midst of his infirmities, **1:250,252; 3:265.** Mortification in his last illness, **1:253.** *Teaching and examples of Vincent,* **3:254 ff.** His mortification and his feelings, **3:256.** Mortification in his words, **3:261.** Mortification in his exterior actions; details, **3:263.** His later years, **3:264-65.** Cardinal de La Rochefoucauld commands him to moderate his penitential practices, **3:265.** His mortification of sight and of the other senses, **Ibid.** His use of the discipline and other instruments of penance, **3:266.**

Necessity of this virtue and its principal acts, **3:254.** "If a person already had one foot in heaven but left off the practice of mortification for the time it takes to get the other foot there he would be in danger of losing himself," **3:263.** The measure of our progress in the spiritual life is the measure of the progress that we make in this virtue, **Ibid.** One of the most excellent results of this virtue is an even disposition, **3:274.**

The Missionaries who lead sensual lives will be only the corpses of Missionaries, **2:168.** Their mortification is of particular necessity in view of their work, **2:239.** See, *Penitence, Renouncement, Will.*

Moses (Old Testament patriarch). His conduct is a model for ours, **1:63,215,259; 2:61,317.** At first he refused to go to Egypt, **1:123.** The lawgiver, **1:240.** We are, like the rod which he used; only humble instruments of the power of God, **3:204.** Punishment of those who had scorned him, **3:206.** Praise of the role and the mildness of this patriarch, **3:310**. In imitation of him you must hear from God what is to be communicated to his people, **3:318**. Vincent is compared to him, **3:78,101,243**.

Moslems. Conversion of, **2:41,67,118**. Some trading with them is banned by the pope and the king, **2:90,98**. Their hatred of Christians, **2:91,102,105,110**. Vincent outlines rules of conduct for the Missionaries in Barbary for their dealings with them, **2:97,104**. Their poor treatment of slaves, **2:105,120**. Some admire the work of the Missionaries, **2:109**. They are reconciled with their enemies more easily than are Christians, **2:110**. They admire the charity of the Missionaries, and testify to their admiration, **2:114**.

Mount Tabor. Jesus' glory is revealed here, **3:84**.

Mousnier (Jean Francois), priest of the Mission. In Picardy. His desire to evangelize the infidels. His departure for Madagascar, **2:149-50**. His work; his death (1656), **Ibid**.

Moutier Saint Jean, (Benedictine abbey in the diocese of Sens), **1:247**. See, *Chandenier (Claude de), Le Boucher (Monsieur)*.

Moyen Vic, (city in Lorraine). Vincent sends assistance there, **2:329**.

Mulan (Monsieur), priest of the Mission. He evangelizes the soldiers of the army in Picardy, **1:175**.

Murviel (Anne de), bishop of Montauban. He asks for Missionaries to evangelize his diocese. His letter to Vincent on the success of the missions, **2:51**. See, *Montauban*.

Mysteries, (of the Holy Trinity and of the Incarnation). The poor are often in ignorance of these. The knowledge of these mysteries is necessary for salvation, **2:136**. Devotion professed and recommended by Vincent towards these mysteries, **3:74**.

N

Nacquart (Charles), priest of the Mission. At Richelieu. Vincent designates him for the mission to Madagascar, and tells him what course to follow during the trip there, and in the mission, **2:134**. Apostolic works at La Rochelle while waiting to depart, and on the vessel during the voyage, **2:138**. His arrival at Madagascar and his first labors, **2:142**. His sorrow at the death of Monsieur Gondree. Course of his works, **2:144,152**. His death; praise of his virtues, **2:149**.

Name of Jesus (Holy). This feast is the patronal feast of the Confraternities of Charity, **2:289**. See, *Litany*.

Name of Jesus (Hospital of the), in Paris. Created by a considerable donation given to Vincent by an anonymous donor, (1653), **1:224 ff**.
Establishment of this hospital for the aged-poor in the faubourg Saint Laurent, **1:225**. The administration is assigned in perpetuity to the superior general of the Mission (1653), **Ibid**. Admirable organization of this hospital which becomes the reflection of the life of the first Christians, **1:226**. The example of this hospital leads to the creation of the general hospital, **1:226-27**. It is served by the Daughters of Charity, **2:296**.

Nancy (city and diocese of). Vincent procures relief for the misery of this city during the war (1640). Devotion of the Missionaries, **1:185; 2:319**.

Nantes (city and port). Missionaries leave from here for Ireland in 1646. They minister in this city while waiting to depart, **2:127**. Shipwreck of the Missionaries leaving for Madagascar in the sea off of the city, **2:161; 3:276**. New departure and another shipwreck, **3:277**.

The administrators of the hospital here propose to dismiss the sisters. Letter of submission to this decision from Vincent, **3:248.**

Naples (kingdom of). Ordination retreats held here, **2:209.**

Narbonne (city and port). Vincent attempts to return there by sea; during the journey he is captured by the Barbary pirates and made a slave, **1:43.** Establishment of the Congregation in this city in 1659, **1:235.** See, *Fouquet (Francois).*

Naseau (Marguerite), Daughter of Charity. The first who presented herself to be formed by Louise de Marillac, **1:134.**

Nehemiah (book of the Old Testament). Cited in Abelly: 6:13-**3:317.**

Nemours (Marie d'Orleans), the duchess of. Lady of Charity, **2:315.** Vincent refuses her permission to visit the Visitandines, **2:274.**

Nephew. Vincent receives a visit from one of his nephews, **3:124.** His act of humility on this occasion, **3:189.** The saint declares that he does not want any of his nephews to enter the ecclesiastical state, **3:194.** He feels that it would be better for them to remain in the humble conditions of their parents, **3:260-61.**

Niolo (valley on the island of Corsica). Mission given in this area, **2:70 ff.**

Niort (town of), **2:34.**

Nivelle (Pierre de), bishop of Lucon. Letter of thanks and congratulations to Vincent for the work of his Missionaries in his diocese (1642). At his request, a house of the Missionaries is founded at Lucon (1645), **1:230; 2:51.** The saint asks him to sign the letter against Jansenism which was to be sent by the French bishops to the pope telling him of the urgent necessity of a definitive decision from the Holy See, **2:354.**

Noah (Old Testament figure), **1:227.**

Noailles (Charles de), bishop of Saint Flour. See, *Saint Flour.*

Nobles (impoverished) in exile from Lorraine, and Scotland. Vincent establishes a committee of French nobles to help them (1640), **1:187-88.**

Noel du Perron (Jacques de), bishop of Angouleme, and later of Evreux. He thanks Vincent for the successful work of the Missionaries in the diocese of Angouleme, **2:52.** His satisfaction at the results of the ordination retreats. He asks for the establishment of a house of the Congregation in his diocese, **2:201.**

Nogent (city in diocese of Troyes). Mission given here in 1657, **2:49.**

Norais (Jacques), donor of the farm at Orsigny, **1:199.**

Normandy (province of). The king has the right of appointment to benefices which are under lay patronage but whose patron is a minor; and thus a ward of the crown, **2:376.** See, *Rouen.*

Norway. Lost to heresy, **2:170.**

Nouelly (Boniface), priest of the Mission, Sent to Algiers. His work; his death. Praise of his virtues, **2:88,92-93,178.**

Noyon (city and diocese of). Vincent sends Missionaries and assistance to this city (1650). Establishment of a house of Missionaries (1662), **1:166,205,235.** The canons of a church here form an ecclesiastical conference. They send their rule to the assembly of Saint Lazare in Paris. They write to the saint to thank him for the benefits of the ordination retreats (1643), **2:202,226.** See, *Baradat (Henri de), Clermont (Francois de).*

Numbers (book of the Old Testament). Cited in Abelly: 11:28-29-**3:101.**

Nyssa (Gregory of), saint. Cited, **3:26.**

O

Obededom (Old Testament figure), **1:98.**

Obedience. Vincent zealously represses transgressions against this virtue, **2:272.** *Teaching and example of Vincent*, **3:205 ff.** Recommendations of the saint to the religious of the Visitation; motives and qualities of obedience, **3:206.** The advantage of observing the will of God which contains all that is good for creation, **Ibid.** The practice of this virtue puts the soul in the state of the perfect liberty of the children of God, **Ibid.** God is pleased to reveal his will to those who are obedient for the sake of his love, **Ibid.** It would take a very hard heart to know that Jesus was obedient until death for us and yet refuse to be submissive to his love, **Ibid.** Vincent insists on the exact observance of this virtue on the part of the Missionaries. He publicly reproves a senior Missionary who had failed in obedience, **3:212-13.**

To whom must one be obedient? To the pope, etc., **3:207 ff.** To the king and princes. An example, **3:209.** Condescension towards inferiors, **3:210 ff.**

The Daughters of Charity need this virtue more than any other community. Obedience is their cloister. **2:293.** See, *Indifference*, *Grumbling*.

Olier (Jean Jacques), founder of the Company of Saint Sulpice. He is one of the first members of the Tuesday Conferences at Saint Lazare, **1:145,167 ff.; 2:224.** How Vincent supported him in his works, **1:167.** Mutual sentiments of esteem between Vincent and Monsieur Olier, **1:168-69; 2:36.** Monsieur Olier takes part in different missions, **1:167-68.** Missions in Auvergne, **Ibid; 2:36.** Vincent cannot send the Missionaries which he promised him because they are sent instead, by royal request, to be chaplains to the army, **1:177.** He sends an account of his missions to Vincent, and to the ecclesiastics of the Tuesday Conferences of Saint Lazare (1636), **2:36 ff.** His zeal for the good of souls: "O Paris! You distract many who could with the grace of God convert a multitude of souls," **2:37.** He establishes at Le Puy a conference for ecclesiastics. His letter to the members of the Paris conference, **2:225-26.**

He accepts the parish of Saint Sulpice in Paris (1642). Vincent defends him from criticism from other people and at the court, **1:168-69; 2:224.**

Vincent assists at the death of Monsieur Olier and at the election of his successor, **1:169.** The members of the Tuesday Conferences discuss his virtues. His humility is praised, **3:202.**

Olis (Ody). Charms or idols of the traditional Malgache religion, **2:141,152.**

Ombiasses (Ombiasa). Guardians of the traditional ceremonies, customs, and superstitions of the native people of Madagascar, **2:140-41,152,154.**

Oration, (funeral). After Vincent's death, a funeral oration is preached by Henri de Maupas du Tour, bishop of Le Puy, at the Church of Saint Germain l'Auxerrois in Paris, **1:262.**

Oratory (Fathers of the). Vincent lives among them during his first stay in Paris (1609-1611), **1:52.** Madame de Gondi first offers them the foundation to provide for regular missions in her lands, **1:62.** They give hospitality to Vincent during his stay at Macon. Their edification in seeing his holy life (1623), **1:88.** Their opposition to the approbation of the Congregation of the Mission (1652). Their opposition then to the approval of the vows of the Congregation by the Holy See, **3:158.**

Ordinands (Retreats for the). Their necessity, **1:138 ff; 2:183 ff.** The archbishop of Paris establishes them in his diocese in 1631. They are given at the College des Bons Enfants, **1:140; 2:185-86.** They are given for the first time at Beauvais in 1628 and are conducted by Vincent. Their marvelous success. Perfection of their organization,

1:140; 2:185. Summary of what is done in these retreats and of the rules that are observed in them, **2:185,188 ff.** The queen mother attends a conference given to the ordinands, **2:186-87.** Charitable persons furnish the funds for those who are being ordained in Paris to attend the retreats at the house of the priests of the Mission, **Ibid.** The expenses of this work fall again on the house of Saint Lazare. Vincent never complains of this, **Ibid.**

The usual number of ordinands in the house of Saint Lazare, **2:187.** These retreats lead to the establishment of the Tuesday Conferences at Saint Lazare, **2:200,210-11.** Of the illustrious prelates who preach there at the request of Vincent. See *Bossuet (Jacques), Perrochel (Francois), Sevin (Nicolas).*

The practice of the retreats is introduced in various dioceses in Italy and France. Some examples at Poitiers, Angouleme, Reims, etc., **2:200,203.** Fruits produced at Genoa, **2:203.** At Rome, **2:204.** At Bergamo, **2:209.**

Admirable sentiments of Vincent on these retreats, **2:191 ff.** He recommends that preaching there be done with great simplicity, and that preachers depend upon God for what they are to say to others, **Ibid., 2:196-97.** What dispositions are necessary in these; zeal and eagerness, **2:188-89,197.** Humility and self-effacement, **2:193.** Prayer, **2:193,197,199-200.** Treating the ordinands with simplicity and humility; acting with modesty and recollection. It is only this that will edify them, **2:194,198-99.** The edification that they receive in seeing the humble and simple manner of the conduct and the preaching of the Missionaries, **3:198,220.**

Orkney Islands. Evangelized by Thomas Lumsden, **2:178.**

Orleans (city of). Vincent stays in this city in 1649, **1:201.** A priest of this diocese writes to Vincent, **2:241.**

Orleans (Gaston), the duke of. His political activity, **1:211,219.** During the Fronde he issues a passport to Vincent enabling him to enter Paris freely, **3:279.**

Ornano (Henri Francois Alphonse d'), secretary of the duke of Orleans, **1:219.**

Orsigny (near Versailles). Location of a farm belonging to the Congregation of the Mission, **1:199.** Loss of a lawsuit by the Congregation relative to the ownership of this farm; reaction of Vincent, **3:24,211,249,276,285.** The part played by his community. Conference given on this subject, **3:249 ff.** He refuses to appeal against the sentence by civil petition to the Parlement, **3:252-53.**

Ossat (Arnauld d'), cardinal. Negotiator of Henry IV's reconciliation with Rome, **1:48,53.**

Ostia (diocese in Italy). The Missionaries evangelize this diocese, **2:57.**

Ozenne (Charles), priest of the Mission. At Troyes. His departure for Poland. Death of this Missionary; his eulogy, **2:166.**

P

Pabbay (island in the Hebrides). Dermot Duggan plans to travel here, **2:178.**

Palaiseau (village near Paris). Helped by the Missionaries and the Daughters of Charity in 1652, **1:208.** Testimony of Vincent relative to these efforts. Gratitude of the pastor and of the inhabitants, **3:120.** Vincent procures additional aid for this village. The Missionaries there become gravely ill, **3:121.**

Palestrina (diocese in Italy). Missions held there, **2:62.**

Pallu (Francois), bishop of Heliopolis, vicar apostolic of Tonkin. Assistance that he receives from the Ladies of Charity, **2:304.**

Pamiers. See, *Caulet (Francois Etienne de)*.

Pardon. The example of Vincent in asking pardon of the poor whom he inadvertently had made wait to be served, **3:128**. To persons who are angry with him, **3:158**. To some laybrothers, **3:188-89**. See, *Reconciliation*.

Paris. Vincent arrives in Paris in 1609. His mission to Henry IV. His first works in this city, **1:48 ff**. Louise de Marillac visits Confraternities of Charity in this diocese, **1:130**. He begins the work with the galley slaves there (1618), **1:148**. In this city he founds the Congregation of the Mission (1625), **1:109**. He also establishes the Confraternities of Charity in its parishes (1631). Louise de Marillac visits them, **1:130-32; 2:288**. He helps the inhabitants of the faubourgs during the troubles of 1652, **1:168**. His immense charities done in the city of Paris during this era, **1:211**. Benefits of the missions in this diocese, **2:30**. Vincent opposes the errors of the "Enlightened" which were beginning to spread in some places there, **2:394**. See, *Foundlings, Hotel Dieu, Name of Jesus, Salpetriere*.

Parish. The chapel of the Daughters of Charity is to be the local parish church, **2:293**.

Parre (Jean), laybrother of the Mission. His work in the ruined provinces of Picardy and Champagne, **2:341**. At Ham, **Ibid**.

Passion (of Jesus Christ). It is the great proof of the mercy of the Savior, **2:238**.

Pastors. Vincent is the model for their life and work. At Clichy, **1:52-53**. Pastor at Chatillon, **1:65**. Sentiments and devotion of the saint in their regard, **3:109**.
While on a mission the Missionaries should "not even move a straw pallet without their approval," **3:209**.

Patience. Vincent's patience in supporting others in their pains and afflictions, **3:282 ff**. Two truths were the source of this virtue of the saint, **3:287**. His patience in sickness, **3:289 ff**.
Patience is one of the virtues noted among the first Daughters of Charity, **1:136**.

Patte (Philippe), laybrother of the Mission. Sent to Madagascar. For his benefit Vincent outlines the rules to follow with regards to the Huguenots sailing on the same vessel, **2:27,160**. Danger in returning from Nantes to La Rochelle, **3:277**. His death in Madagascar (1664), **2:27**.

Paul (Apostle). He publicly confesses his sins to manifest the mercy of God, **1:60**. He urges fidelity to God's eternal designs, **2:15**. His charity, **2:135**. Struck blind, **2:309**. The Jansenist author Martin Barcos equates Saint Paul with Saint Peter, **2:351**. He gathered help for Christians in need, **3:31**. Special devotion of Vincent towards this apostle, **3:94**. A vocation is assured by good works, **3:311**. Perseverance of Saint Paul, **3:132**. He chastised his body, **3:318**. Spoken of in the Acts of the Apostles. See, *Apostles, Acts of*.
His epistles cited in Abelly. See, *Corinthians, Ephesians, Galatians, Hebrews, Philippians, Romans, Timothy*.

Paula (Saint). Her eulogy by Saint Jerome, **1:101**. Jerome writes the life of Saint Paula indicating the value of imitating her, **3:9**.

Paulinus (Saint), bishop of Nola, **3:112**.

Payen (Mademoiselle). Vincent refuses her permission to visit the cloister of a Visitation monastery, **2:274**.

Pebrac (abbey in the diocese of Saint Flour). Mission given by Jean Jacques Olier on the lands of this abbey, **1:167; 2:36**. See, *Olier (Jean Jacques)*.

Pémartin (Jean Baptiste), nineteenth-century French Vincentian scholar. Editor of the 1891 edition of Abelly, **1:17**.

Penance. Vincent believes that priests are specially obligated to practices of penance for the intention of an end to the miseries of war, **1:201**. Each day at Saint Lazare three Missionaries fast for the intention of peace in the kingdom, **1:213**. The saint exhorts his community to acts of penance to obtain peace from God for the kingdom, **1:215**. He continues the penitential practices and the prayers for peace at Saint Lazare until 1660, **1:220; 3:264**. The necessity of doing penance for the sins of others, **3:265**.

Pensioners (living at the house of Saint Lazare). Who they were. Results of the care that is given them, **2:259-60**. How they are treated. Advice of the saint on this subject, **2:260,263-64**. The reason why they are received, **2:262**.

Perche (region between Normandy and Maine). Assistance sent there, **1:212**.

Perfection. The more that a Missionary cares for his own spiritual development the more his labors for the spiritual good of others will prosper, **2:24**. Only an angel could have been more exact than Vincent, **3:37**. He knew the truth that the proper measure for the love we must have for our neighbor is the love we have for ourselves, **3:293**. Without taking care of their own spiritual perfection those who seek the salvation of others often can end by being lost themselves, **3:318**.

Perigord (province of). Scarred by warfare, **1:217**.

Peronne. Vincent sends Missionaries and assistance to this town (1650), **1:205**.

Perriere (location in Barbary). Christian slaves here are visited by the Missionaries, **2:115**.

Perrochel (Francois), bishop of Boulogne. His relations with Vincent and the Missionaries, **2:186**. He preaches to the ordinands at Saint Lazare. The queen mother attends this session, **Ibid.** He preaches a mission in the faubourg Saint Germain in Paris. His simplicity; his success, **2:224**.

Persecution. We will be true disciples of Jesus Christ when we have the disposition to endure any persecution for the sake of his name, **2:99**.

Perseverance. The grace of perseverance is the most important of all; it crowns all the other graces, **2:280**. What were the examples of this virtue in our Savior, **2:312**. You must persevere in the path you have entered, for it leads to life. Take courage, and trust that God will give you the grace to overcome those that remain, **2:390**. God often gives to perseverance the success that he refuses to our first efforts, **3:103**.

Pesnelle (Jacques), priest of the Mission. Letter to Vincent on the missions given in the diocese of Genoa, **2:68-69**.

Peter (Saint). Converts thousands by a single sermon, **2:314**. The Jansenist author Martin Barcos disputes the Petrine supremacy, **2:351**. He obeyed Jesus, **3:50**. Particular devotion of Vincent to this apostle, **3:94**. Jesus calls him "Satan," **3:176**. He recommends the practice of obedience, **3:210**.

Peter (first epistle of). Cited in Abelly: 4:8-**3:169**, 2:13-**3:207**.

Petites-Maisons (hospital of the). Missions given in this establishment in Paris, **2:27,219**. Services given to this hospital by the Daughters of Charity, **2:296**.

Pharisees, (the example of in the New Testament), **3:218,224**.

Philippians (epistle of Saint Paul to the). Cited in Abelly: 2:21-**1:34**, 4:13-**1:186; 3:62**, 1:6-**2:205,226**; 2:15-**2:210**, 3:13-**3:14**.

Piacenza (diocese in Italy). A cleric from this diocese attends the ordination retreats in Rome. He has the thought of bringing the Missionaries to introduce the practice of these retreats in his diocese, **2:206-07**.

Pianezza (Philippe de Simiane), marquis of, the prime minister of the Duke of Savoy. His eulogy. In Turin, he founds a house of the priests of the Mission (1654), **1:234**. He offers a foundation at Savigliano to the community which it cannot accept, **2:78-79**. He testifies to his consolation at the results of a mission (1658), **2:81**.

Picardy (province of). This province furnishes Vincent his first companions in the Congregation, **1:110**. It is invaded by the Spanish. Missions given to the French army, **1:174**. Desolation of this area ruined by the war, **1:204; 2:331**. See, *Public Misery*.

Piccolomini (Coelio), cardinal, archbishop of Caesarea, papal nuncio to Paris. He consults with Vincent concerning church affairs. He assists at the funeral of the saint, **1:262; 3:222**.

Piedmont (region in Italy). Missions given here, **2:76 ff**.

Pilgrimage (places of). Feelings upon entering these places, **2:196**. Sentiments and practices of Vincent, **3:93**. See, *Chartres*. It is a mark of predestination to make these, **2:313**.

Pitie (hospital of La). Mission given there in 1636, **1:167; 2:219**.

Plague. In Paris. Ravages in 1628 and during the following years. Louise de Marillac visits a person stricken by the plague. Vincent praises her, **1:131-32**. Vincent visits the sub-prior of Saint Lazare who is dying from the plague. He takes care of a young man at Saint Lazare who is sick with the same malady, **Ibid., 3:112**. At Marseilles, **1:151**. Its ravages in Poland. The devotion of the Missionaries (1652), **2:164-67; 3:138**. Advice of the saint to a prelate who wanted to personally help the plague-stricken, **3:137**. Outline for the rule of conduct to be followed by the Missionaries in case of the plague, **3:138-39**. The plague-stricken are taken care of in the house of Saint Lazare, **3:239**.

Plaissala (in Brittany). Mission held there, **2:46**.

Pleurtuit (in the diocese of Saint Malo). Mission held there, **2:45**.

Poitiers (city and diocese of). The Missionaries from Richelieu are directed to give missions in this diocese (1638), **1:230**. Fruits of the missions, **2:54**. Results of the ordination retreats, **2:201**. Vincent blocks the nomination of an unworthy candidate to this episcopal see. Turbulent scene with the mother of the disappointed candidate, **3:281**.

Poitou (province and city of). During the Fronde, **1:217,253**. Heretics there, **2:25**. Missions given in this area (1638), **2:51,54**.

Poland. The Polish queen asks for Missionaries and Daughters of Charity to be sent there; their departure for this country, **1:136; 2:163-64**. Help that they received there. Benefice given to Monsieur Lambert, the superior of the mission, **2:164**. Progress of the Russian armies in Poland (1654). Sadness of Vincent, **2:166,169**. Success of the Swedish armies (1655). Situation of the Missionaries, **2:169,192**. Devotion of the Missionaries in the middle of the double scourges of war and plague. Vincent gives the Congregation news from Poland, **2:166,169**. Conclusion of the peace. Joy that it gives the saint, **2:172**.

Political Affairs. The example of Jesus and the teaching of the Gospel are the sole rule of life for Vincent guiding all of his activities, **1:103**. He wants to abstain from political affairs, and why, **1:216**. He counsels his community against any involvement in the affairs of state. Different reasons for this practice. The example of Saint Bernard. Vincent nevertheless intervenes in these affairs on occasion, **Ibid.,1:219**. Vincent serves the king with an unwavering fidelity, **2:395 ff**; with a total disinterestedness, **2:397-98**; with a great prudence and a remarkable wisdom, **2:400**. Some principle rules of his prudent conduct, **2:400 ff.**

Vincent asks Richelieu for an end to the war in Lorraine (1641), **1:189**. Wisdom of the views of Vincent, **Ibid.** He asks Richelieu to aid the Irish armies against the English, and promises the help of the pope, **Ibid.** He joins the Council of Conscience. His rules of conduct while at the court, **2:372-73**.

Political troubles in 1649 and 1652. Many fail to recognize their duty to the king. Opposition of Vincent to the policies of Mazarin, **1:193-94; 2:396**. He exhorts Mazarin to resign for the sake of stopping civil discord, and exposing the court to disgrace (1649), **1:199; 2:397**. He takes on extra prayers and penances to obtain the end of the wars and the blessings of God on the state, **1:200,213,215,220**. In the midst of the civil wars Vincent is firmly on the side of the king and did all that he could to serve his cause. His letters in this sense to various bishops, **1:216 ff.; 2:396**. He works, by order of the queen, for the reconciliation of the dissident nobles with the king during the Fronde, **1:219**.

Pollalion (Marie de Lumague), Mademoiselle de, Lady of Charity, foundress of the Daughters of Providence. Biographical notice, **1:153; 2:303**. Her eulogy, **3:272**.

Pons (town near Saintes). The Missionaries assist the soldiers there during the war (1636), **1:177**.

Pont a Mousson (city of). Vincent gathers assistance for this ruined city during the war. Devotion of the Missionaries, **1:185; 2:321**.

Pont Courlay (Francois de Wignerod de), nephew of Cardinal Richelieu. Successor of Emmanuel de Gondi as General of the Galleys, **2:40**.

Pontoise (city of). The ecclesiastics of this city form an assembly on the model of the ecclesiastics in Paris. Their letter to Vincent, **2:227**. Stay of the king in this city, **3:109**.

Poor. Charity of Vincent towards them, **1:59,70,87**. The religious abandonment of the country poor is the objection given by a heretic against the Catholic church. Answer of the saint, **1:81**. The guidance of the Holy Spirit over the Church is proven by the church evangelizing them, **1:83**. Vincent is delivered from a terrible temptation against the faith by making a resolution to devote his entire life to the service of the poor, **3:116**. See, *Charity* particularly of Vincent towards the poor. Vincent says that their sufferings are caused by the cares of their lives and their sadness, **3:117**. Everyday he dines at his table with two poor persons, **3:126**. He kneels at the door of Saint Lazare to ask the pardon of some poor women whom he had forgotten to give alms, **3:128**. See, *Hospitals*.

They are the legacy of the mission, **1:238**. According to their exterior appearance they almost do not appear to be reasonable persons, but we see their true goodness if we see them as God sees them, **3:19-20**. It is especially for their evangelization that the company had been founded, **3:116-17**. God loves the poor and consequently he loves those who love the poor, **3:117**. They are the beloved of God, **Ibid**. Those who have loved the poor in life have nothing to fear in death. Vincent cites examples, **Ibid**. The Missionaries must consider them as their lords and masters, **Ibid**. When visiting them they are to be shown a great compassion, **3:118**. It is among them that the true religion, a living faith, and patience are preserved, **3:216**. We must pray for them since they feed us by their work, **3:238-39**.

The care of the poor is the principal work of the Daughters of Charity. Excellence of the service to the poor, **1:134-137**.

Poor Souls. Devotion of Vincent towards the poor souls in Purgatory, **3:95**.

Pope. Seeing in him Jesus Christ as pontiff and head of the Church, **1:107**. Obedience that we must give to him as head of the Church, and as the Vicar of Christ, **2:126; 3:207**. He serves as the head of the Congregation for the Propagation of the Faith, **2:134**. He is the recourse for all doubts that arise with regards to doctrine, **2:354-55**. Refutation of those who to not want to accept this means of resolving difficulties of the faith, **3:357- 58,369**. Sentiments of piety of Vincent in his regard, **3:108**.

Portail (Antoine), priest of the Mission. Biographical notice, **1:86**.

He asks Vincent for the opportunity to serve the convicts (1622), **1:86**. He lives with the saint at the College des Bons Enfants, and travels with him to give missions (1625), **1:109**. Vincent appeals to his testimony in speaking of the providential beginnings of the company, **1:240**. He gives testimony that Vincent, whom he knew for more than fifty years, was a most perfect image of Jesus Christ, **3:87**.

He gives missions in Auvergne with Monsieur Olier (1626), **1:167; 2:36**. Vincent writes him that the necessity of seeing to the needs of the army keeps him from sending the Missionaries he had promised to assist Monsieur Olier, **1:177**. He confides to him most of the governance of the Company of the Daughters of Charity. Devotion that he had for this community, **1:246**.

His death. His eulogy, **1:246; 3:44,278**.

Port Royal (abbey of). Vincent goes there to visit the heads of the Jansenist party to try to obtain their submission to the pope, **2:366**. There is something to criticize in all the books which come from this source, **2:367**. On the advice of Vincent a refutation is published against the alleged miracles performed in this house, **2:368-69**. Answer of the saint to someone who wanted to compromise with the Jansenist leaders of Port Royal, **2:371**.

Posny (Jacques), laybrother of the Mission. Sent to Poland, **2:164**.

Poverty. *Examples and sentiments of Vincent*, on this virtue, **3:242 ff**. Honoring the poverty of our Lord in the decoration of a church, **3:244**. Vincent economizes nothing and spends generously when it is a matter of the service of God, or the spiritual good of the neighbor, **Ibid**. Poverty makes us think of God and helps us to raise our hearts to him, **3:245**. The loss of this spirit has been the ruin of many communities, **Ibid**. It is not necessary to be frightened of poverty, **3:22**. If the Congregation of the Mission is destroyed it will not be by poverty but by wealth, **3:24,247**. This virtue is the foundation of the Congregation of the Mission, **3:244**. How we must manage the goods of the community, which are the goods of the poor, **Ibid**. The saint speaks out against Missionaries who lose the spirit of poverty, **3:244-45**.

The first Daughters of Charity by their love of this virtue have given much edification in all those places where they have been employed, **1:136**. See, *Detachment*.

Pouy (village in the Landes), today named Saint Vincent de Paul, Birthplace of Vincent, **1:35**.

Praise. Vincent rarely praises his followers in their presence; but he often shares with other persons accounts of the graces that they received and the good use they had made of them, **1:103**. His confusion when he is given praise, **3:185**. In what circumstances, according to the Gospel, that we should give praise, **3:190**.

Prayer.

1. *Nature and Necessity of Prayer.*

Many are content with the sweet sentiments they experience in mental prayer, but this must be joined with action, **1:106**. Vincent wants the Ladies of Charity who go on retreat to write the sentiments that they have received in prayer, **1:143**. Assiduousness of Vincent himself for this practice, **1:243**. He prescribes to the ecclesiastics of the Tuesday Conferences that they spend at least a half-hour doing this, **2:214-15**. Vincent once said; "what the sword is to a soldier, prayer is to those who minister at the altar," **2:254**.

Excellence of this exercise. *Practice and teaching of Vincent*, on this subject, **3:59 ff.** The two signs by which he believed one could judge the perfection of prayer: the dispositions that you brought to prayer and the fruits that you received, **3:59-61**. Of extraordinary prayer; what he thought of this, **Ibid**. His recommendations for this exercise: "Give me a man of prayer, and he will be able to do everything," **3:61**. Everyone is obliged to pray. Example of a servant, **3:62**. It is the great book of preachers, **Ibid**. Affective prayers, and practical recommendations, **Ibid**. Of dryness and aridity, **3:63**. "Prayer is a sermon we preach to ourselves," Some advice, **Ibid**. It is the reservoir where one finds the necessary strength to fulfill our tasks, **3:318**. It is there that you ask God for those things that you need. One receives more results from this means than by any other, **3:319**.

In order to attract an abundance of graces and blessings prayer is more necessary for the Missionaries than knowledge. Their exactitude in this practice, **2:18; 3:62**. The enumeration of all the good that a Missionary receives from prayer, **3:66-67**. See, *Repetition*.

2. On the method of.

Explanation of the method of prayer. The preparation, **3:65**. The three parts of the body of the prayer, **3:66**.

Some advice. Insist more on the affections than on the considerations, **3:66**. On the conclusion of prayer, **3:67**. The great difference between the lights that provide the subtlety of the spirit, and those which provide grace in prayer, **3:67-68**. Even if one has been unfaithful to prayerful resolutions one still must not stop from continuing to make them. How to observe them, **3:68**. Manner of meditating on the mysteries of the faith, **3:69**. The best means for doing good is personal mortification, **3:70**. Spiritual dryness, if it is used properly, can be useful in advancing in virtue, **3:71**. Recommendation to a laybrother to pray gently, humbly, and without any extraordinary effort of the imagination, **Ibid**. Encouragement to another laybrother who complained that he did not have the ability to pray well, **Ibid**.

Preaching. Vincent has a natural eloquence. He not only explains things clearly, but is able to persuade others by his strongly affective words. How he goes about this, **1:100-01; 2:213**. Testimonies given by the queen of Poland and the Ladies of Charity, **3:38**. By the ecclesiastics of the Tuesday Conferences of Saint Lazare, **3:96**. Reform introduced by the saint in the manner of preaching, **2:20**.

Advice of Vincent on preaching; follow the example of Jesus Christ who preached his doctrine in a style that was very common and clearer than that of his apostles, **2:19**. It is necessary to fear our vain complaisance, **2:18**. The use of familiar comparisons following the example of our Savior, **2:19; 3:320**. Passages from profane authors must not be used as substitutes for the Gospel, **2:19**. Speaking with a familiar and natural tone. Example of actors, **2:20**. Great success of this form of simple preaching in the missions in Ireland, **2:127-28**. Vincent kneels before a preacher at the ordination retreats and asks him to speak with greater simplicity, **2:191**. It is necessary to make preaching familiar by using simple examples, **2:196**. It is necessary to trust in God when we speak to others, **2:197-98**. Vincent recommends simplicity to the ecclesiastics who are preaching a mission in the faubourg Saint Germain in Paris. Success which they have as a result, **2:223**.

Preachers who preach based on the doctrines of faith are more effective with souls than those who fill their discourses with mere human reasoning, **3:19.** Searching for praise in one's preaching is to give oneself over to the tyranny of the public, **3:85.** It is necessary to remain faithful in the practice of the simplicity and the humility of Jesus Christ, **3:86.** In choosing between two thoughts choose the lesser and sacrifice to God the better in the secret of your heart, **3:87,184.** Preach simply and well. God always blesses those who preach in this way. Good example of the bishop of Sarlat speaking to the ordinands, **3:220.** The saint unsuccessfully criticizes a priest in order to convince him to preach with simplicity, **3:220.** Speak in the humble spirit of Jesus Christ; example of the Savior, **3:320.**

Predestination (marks of). A person cannot be lost in the exercise of charity, **2:312.** Making pilgrimages to the places of the saints is a sign of this, **2:313.** There is a probability in these marks that should not be doubted, **3:34.** Conformity to the suffering Jesus Christ is the mark of our predestination, **3:285.** See, *Elect.*

Prelates. Seeing in them Jesus the bishop and prince of pastors, **1:107.** Loving respect of Vincent towards them, **3:109,130 ff.** See, *Bishops.*

Premonstratensian (Order). Vincent works for the reform of this order, **2:385.**

Presence of God. See, *God, (presence of).*

Prevost (Nicolas), priest of the Mission. At Sedan. He is sent to Madagascar, **2:149.** His work and his death on this island, **2:150-51; 3:276.**

Pride. This vice causes us to have feelings that are the cause of division in communities, **3:204.** See, *Humility, Contempt.*

Priesthood. Ordination of Vincent. His sentiments on this dignity, **1:39.** Difficulty caused to the salvation of souls by the scandalous lives and pernicious conduct of bad priests, **1:138.** Priests because of the dignity of their calling are even above kings, **2:194.** See, *Priests.*

Priests. The holiness of their state. The means for persevering in it, **2:212.** Grandeur of their ministry, **2:251-53.** The disorders which reign in the world must be attributed to their failings, **2:253.** Bad priests are the greatest enemies of the Church, **Ibid.** How "a good priest is a great thing," **2:254,258.** They have the highest possible ministry on earth; which is the exercise of the two greatest virtues of Jesus Christ, worship of the Father and charity towards humanity, **3:140.** Vincent himself works to introduce needed reforms in the life and preparation of priests, **3:142-43.** Their condition is the most sublime on earth, **3:194.** The saint says that if he had known what it meant to be a priest he never would have consented to become one, **Ibid.** The ancient Fathers said that in their day they thought few priests would be saved, even though those of their time were very fervent, **Ibid.** See, *Ecclesiastics, Priesthood.*

Prisoners. Vincent procures spiritual assistance for those who are sick at the Bastille, **2:394.** See, *Criminals, Galley Slaves.*

Progress (in the spiritual life). In the spiritual life it is always necessary to continually advance, **2:276.** One advances when one does not forsake good practices, **Ibid.** The measure of our progress is indicated by our personal mortification, **3:263.** See, *Perfection.*

Propaganda. See, *Faith, (Sacred Congregation for the Propagation of the).*

Provence, (region in France). Vincent travels there to inform the General of the Galleys of the death of his wife, **1:98.** Missions given here, **2:39-40.**

Proverbs (book of the Old Testament). Cited in Abelly: 4:18-**2:60**, 3:32-**2:215**, 10:9-**2:218**, 27:6-**2:302**.

Providence of God. See, *God, (Providence of)*.

Prudence. Vincent had a great spirit which was circumspect and difficult to surpass, **1:100**. The human spirit is quick and restless. The most active and most creative minds are not always the best if they are not also discrete, **1:101**. How this virtue properly understood makes us agreeable to God, **1:105**. On the prudent conduct of Vincent, **1:108; 2:274-75,400; 3:295 ff.** *Teaching and examples of Vincent*, **3:222 ff.** He is known as one of the wisest and shrewdest men of his time, **3:222**. Prudence must be united with simplicity, **3:222-23**. Teaching of the saint on this virtue; its object, **3:223**. He exercises this before responding in important matters, **3:225**. Where human prudence fails there begins to dawn the light of divine wisdom, **3:225**. How he avoids natural eagerness. Some examples, **3:227**. Principles of Christian prudence, **3:231**. Practical rules of prudence observed by the saint, **3:232**.

Psalms (book of the Old Testament). Cited in Abelly: 127:1-**1:37**, 137:1-4-**1:45**, 84:11-**1:53**, 22:7-**1:102**, 42:8-**1:133**, 82:6-**1:190**, 120:5-**1:257**, 70:2-**1:260**, 116:15-**2:106**, 91:15-**2:107**, 110:2-**2:108**, 119:125-**2:136**, 34:6-**2:136**, 10:17-**2:197**, 118:23-**2:205**, 133:1-**2:244**, 77:11-**2:244**, 86:13-**2:246**, 19:5-**2:252**, 116:2-**3:16**, 119:105-**3:18**, 145:115-16-**3:24**, 115:11-**3:27**, 9:1-**3:35**, 73:23-24-**3:47**, 51:1-**3:50**, 118:23-**3:73**, 130-**3:95**, 69:10-**3:97**, 69:21-**3:118**, 119:71-**3:169**, 38:1-**3:176**, 137:5-**3:229**, 39:10-**3:285**, 119:105-**3:293**.

Public Miseries. In 1643 they are principally experienced in Lorraine. Immense charity of Vincent and the work of the Missionaries in relieving the province, **1:185; 2:316 ff.; 3:264, 313-14**. The saint asks Cardinal Richelieu to bring peace to France, **1:189**. State of the provinces of Picardy and Champagne ruined by war (1650), **1:204; 2:331**. Meeting of the Ladies of Charity to decide on the best means to aid Champagne. A charity store is established in Paris, **1:210; 2:336**. Work of Brother Mathieu Regnard, **2:330**. Missionaries who work for the relief of the inhabitants of the two provinces of Lorraine and Champagne, **2:332**. Daughters of Charity aid the people of Picardy during the ravages of the war (1650-1651), **2:335**. Assistance gathered by Vincent for the Irish Catholic refugees residing in exile in France, **2:340**. See, *Ireland*. Work of Brother Parre in Picardy, **2:341**. The Missionaries establish Confraternities of Charity before withdrawing from the devastated provinces, **Ibid.** Charity of Vincent for destitute priests during these times. The effusive gratitude expressed by a pastor of Champagne to a passing Missionary, **3:144**.
Results of the assistance given to the provinces of Champagne and Lorraine, **2:336 ff.** The amount of alms distributed to these two provinces; their results, **2:344**.
The misery in Paris and the surrounding areas in 1652. The efforts at relief, **1:209; 3:120 ff.** In Guienne, Saintonge, and Poitou, **1:210**. In 1657, Vincent gives an account to the Ladies of Charity of the amount of money spent, and how it was put to use, **2:305**. A person publicly accuses Vincent of being the cause of the miseries of the time. The humble and charitable conduct of the saint in response, **3:157**. See, *Champagne, Lorraine, Picardy*.

Purity. The Daughters of Charity must take all possible precautions to preserve perfect purity of body, and of the heart, **2:293**. See, *Chastity*.

Q

Quinze-Vingts (hospital of the). Vincent establishes a Confraternity of Charity there at the request of the administrators, **1:131**. Mission given there in 1633, **2:219**.

R

Rachel (Old Testament figure), **1:121**.

Raconigi (in Piedmont, Italy). Mission held there, **2:77**.

Raconis (Charles Francois d'Abra de), bishop of Lavaur. Vincent urges him to write against Jansenism. Letter of the prelate to the saint, **2:352**.

Raggio (Baliano), priest, noble, from Genoa. Benefactor of the Congregation of the Mission at Genoa, **1:233**.

Ragny (Hippolyte de Gondi), Madame de. Sister of the General of the Galleys, wife of the below, **1:66**.

Ragny (Leonor de la Magdelaine), marquis de. Brother-in-law of Emmanuel de Gondi, **1:66**.

Rainssant (Rev.), Augustinian canon, pastor of Ham. Letter of thanks to Vincent, **2:341**.

Rambervillers (town in Lorraine). Aided by Vincent, **2:329**.

Ranald, (ruling clan on the isle of Uist in the Hebrides), **2:176**.

Raoul (Jacques), bishop of La Rochelle. See, *Guibourgere (Jacques Raoul de la)*.

Rappiot (Monsieur), merchant of Marseilles. He declares bankruptcy in Algiers, and escapes to Marseilles. This is the reason for the imprisonment of the Missionary Jean Barreau who is the French consul, **2:95**.

Rathkeale (in Ireland). Account of a blasphemer converted during a mission here, **2:130**.

Rechabites (Old Testament figures). Their fidelity to the traditions of their ancestors, **1:239; 3:30**.

Rechau (the baron of), **2:46**.

Recollection. See, *Interior Life*.

Reconciliation. Example of the Moslems, **2:110**. Examples cited by Vincent with regard to those whom he may have offended, **3:157**. Before celebrating mass he goes to find a religious who had testified to having an aversion towards him, **3:158**.

Recreation. Vincent uses this time to continue working, **3:316**.

Redemption. Only those who reflect on the pains of hell, or on the price of the blood of Jesus Christ for even one soul can appreciate the value of the conversion of souls, **1:177**. It is necessary to have the same zeal to win souls for Jesus Christ as the merchants who, regardless of the dangers, go to the Indies to search for treasures, **1:183**.

Redemption of Captives, (Order of the Holy Trinity for the), or the Mathurins, **2:124**.

Reform (of religious communities). Vincent works for this with all his power, **2:278**. Details, **2:385**.

Refuge (House of). Mission given in this home for fallen women, **2:219**.

Regnard (Mathieu), laybrother of the Mission. Biographical notice. His travels throughout Lorraine to assist the poor, **1:186; 2:329-30**.

Regnoust (Thomas). Abelly's successor as the rector of the general hospital of Paris, **1:229.**

Reims (city and diocese of). Vincent sends Missionaries and assistance to this city, ruined during the war, **2:305,334,337-39.** Fruits of the missions in this diocese, **2:42.** The Missionaries establish a Confraternity of Charity there, **2:341.** Letter of thanks from the archdeacon and bailiff for the aid that has been received, **2:343.** See, *Public Misery.*

The clergy celebrate a solemn memorial service there at the death of Vincent, **1:262.** See, *Ai, Valencay (Eleonor d'Etampes de), Fontaine, Ludes, Sillery.*

Relets (Monsieur de), provost of Saint Peter's cathedral in Macon, **1:88.**

Relics. Devotion that Vincent had for the relics of the saints, **3:95.**

Religious. Seeing Jesus Christ in them, **1:107.** Vincent has a great esteem for the religious state, **2:18,385.** Services that he gives to various religious orders, **2:385 ff.** He deters a religious from transferring from his order to a less rigorous order, **2:388.** He deters another famous religious from aspiring to the episcopate, **2:389.** Charitable sentiments of the saint towards those religious who complained about him, **3:25,158,212.** Examples of the esteem and services provided by the saint for religious, **3:145 ff.** Vincent encourages many to persevere in their vocations, **3:145-46.**

Religious Orders. Important services rendered by Vincent to many of them. Details, **2:385,391.**

Religious (Women). How Vincent directs them. His conduct of the Visitandines, **2:269 ff.** Why the Missionaries are not to undertake the direction of any religious, but are to provide this service to the Daughters of Charity, **2:300; 3:208-09.** Services rendered by Vincent to various monasteries of women, **2:390.** He prefers that their superiors be elected periodically, **2:391.** Disorders which survived in certain monasteries. Salutary intervention of the saint, **2:392.** His charity. Letter in favor of an erring religious living outside of her monastery, **3:147.** He strictly enforces the rule of cloister, **3:281.** See, *Visitation, Religious of the.*

The reasons why the Daughters of Charity are not to be considered as religious, **2:300.**

Remiremont (city in Lorraine). Help sent there by Vincent, **2:329.**

Rennes (city in Brittany). Vincent travels through there in 1649, **1:201.**

Renouncement (of self). Explanation of the doctrine of Jesus Christ on renouncement, taken from Saint Basil, **3:85-86.** It is an essential condition for following Jesus Christ, **3:254.** This virtue understood as the renouncement of one's own judgment, will, and family, **3:254 ff.** See, *Attachments, Detachments, Indifference.*

Renty (Gaston de). Biographical notice. He helps Vincent by using his influence and his alms for the assistance of the impoverished nobility of Lorraine (1641), **1:187.** He refers a priest who desired to make a spiritual retreat to Vincent, **2:242.**

Repetition (of Prayer). Vincent recommends and spreads this practice, **3:62 ff.**

Resignation. Vincent presents the first General Assembly of the Congregation of the Mission with his resignation as superior general (1642), **3:192.**

Resignation (to the will of God). Nothing could be holier or of greater perfection, **3:48.** See, *Cross, God (Will of).*

Respect. A superior must treat each of his subjects with mildness and respect, **3:310.**

Respect (human). Vincent has no concern for human respect, but fears that he will be weakened by it, **2:399.**

Rethel (city near Reims). Vincent sends Missionaries and aid to this city. Letter of thanks from the governor, **1:205; 2:305,334,339,343.** The Daughters of Charity take care of sick soldiers there **2:298.** The Missionaries establish a Confraternity of Charity there, **2:341.** See, *Public Misery.*

Retreats (for ecclesiastics). Vincent desires that priests participate each year in a spiritual retreat. Many ecclesiastics and religious come to make these at Saint Lazare. Testimonies of their gratitude, **2:241 ff.** It is the most appropriate way to strongly affirm them in the good, **2:229.** The practice of these exercises spreads into other dioceses. Many prelates express their satisfaction, **2:243 ff.** In Italy. Marvelous results at Genoa, **2:246.**

Retreats (of the priests of the Mission). All the Missionaries make an eight-day retreat each year, **1:141.** Vincent never fails to make his annual retreat, in spite of his pressing business. Esteem that he has for this exercise, **1:141,243; 3:64.** He advises the practice of writing the principal spiritual sentiments that one receives in prayer, **1:143.** He recommends not hurrying too quickly through the retreat exercises, **Ibid.** The Missionaries make their retreat at Saint Lazare in the middle of the tumult caused by the troops that are stationed there in 1636, **1:174.** Vincent says that a time of rest and retreat is a necessity each year for apostolic workers, **2:24.** He advises a Missionary who is tempted to quit his vocation not to leave the Company except by the door through which he had entered; that is to say, by making a retreat, **3:153.**

Retreats (spiritual). Utility and excellence of this practice. **1:141; 2:237 ff., 241 ff.** Vincent works to spread this practice. Retreats held at the College des Bons Enfants (1630), **1:141; 2:232.** Retreats at Saint Lazare, **1:141; 2:232,239,243.** Retreats at Rome, and in the various houses of the Congregation, **1:141.** The retreats are given freely at Saint Lazare, despite the cost to the house, **2:233-34.** Testimony of the edification and the fruits that the retreatants received. **2:235,241 ff.** Remarkable words of Vincent on the retreats. He recommends to his followers that they sustain this work with constancy and perseverance, **2:235.** How the Missionaries must conduct themselves towards the retreatants, **2:236-38.** Vincent gives a retreat to a man who had insulted him, **3:157.** See, *Retreatants.*

Retz (Henri de Gondi), first Cardinal de, bishop of Paris (1598- 1622). Brother of Emmanuel de Gondi, the general of the galleys. He writes to Vincent to procure his return to the house of de Gondi, **1:69.** He approves the rules of the Confraternity of Charity of Villepreux, **1:73.** He approves Vincent as the Director of the Daughters of the Visitation in Paris, **1:91; 2:266.**

Retz (Jean Francois Paul de Gondi), Cardinal de, coadjutor then archbishop of Paris (1654), another son of Emmanuel de Gondi, **1:55.** He approves the rules of the Daughters of Charity (January 18, 1655), **2:291.**

Retz (Pierre de Gondi, duke of), oldest son of Emmanuel de Gondi, **1:55,57; 3:226.** He establishes a house of the Mission at Montmirail, **1:232.**

Revelation (book of the New Testament). Cited in Abelly: **3:17-3:14, 3:19-3:249.**

Ribemont (village near Amiens). Helped by Vincent during the war, **1:205; 2:336.**

Richelieu (Armand Jean Duplesis), Cardinal de. Biographical notice, **1:230.** He expresses his satisfaction to Vincent for the Tuesday Conferences established at Saint Lazare. He asks him for the names of worthy ecclesiastics to be named to vacant bishoprics, **1:146.** He agrees to the creation of a hospital at Marseilles for the convicts, **1:149.** He consults the saint on matters of interest for the Church and the clergy, **1:164.** He sends him a considerable gift for the instruction of ecclesiastics at the seminary of Bons Enfants, **Ibid.** Vincent, saddened by the ruins caused by the war, asks the cardinal to give peace to France (1641), **1:189.** He asks him to send an army to help the Irish, and promises him the assistance of the pope, **Ibid.** The cardinal founds a house at Richelieu, **1:230; 2:52.** He imprisons Saint Cyran at the chateau of Vincennes, **2:350.**

Richelieu (Armand de Wignerod), duke of, nephew of the cardinal, **2:39.**

Richelieu (village of). Cardinal Richelieu founds a house of the Mission there (1638), **1:230; 2:134.** Strength of the heresy in this area. Conversions of heretics, **2:53.** Success of the retreats given to the ordinands of the diocese of Poitiers in 1649, **2:201.** Vincent writes to a bishop to tell him that his brother had made a retreat there, **3:132.** Additional visit of the saint during the troubles of the Fronde (1649), **1:202; 3:264.** He becomes ill, **1:251; 3:189.**

Daughters of Charity are requested for an establishment in this city. Advice of the saint as he sends them here, **2:296.**

Rieux (Rene de), bishop of Saint Pol de Leon. He assumes his episcopal see, **2:382.**

Rinuccini (Giovanni Battista), papal nuncio in Ireland. He tries to convince the clergy of this country to adopt the evangelistic methods of the Missionaries, **2:127.**

Rising (At four o'clock). How Vincent is faithful to this practice, **1:243; 3:74,265,308.** It is at this hour when for over forty years he had begun his day in prayer that he dies, **1:261.**

Ritual. Vincent wants the Missionaries of Madagascar to use the Roman Ritual and not to allow the establishment of anything to the contrary, **2:135.**

Rivet (Jacques), laybrother of the Mission. He is tempted against his vocation. Advice of Vincent, **3:152-53.**

Robineau (Louis), laybrother of the Mission. Secretary to Saint Vincent and source of first-hand reminisces used by Abelly, **1:12,190; 3:78,117,155,182,235,266,271-72.**

Rochechouart (Marie Henriette de), superior of a monastery of the Visitation in Paris, **2:272; 3:185.**

Rocroi (town near Charleville). Vincent sends Missionaries and assistance there (1650), **1:205.** The Missionaries establish a Confraternity of Charity there, **2:341.**

Rodez (diocese of). See of Louis Abelly, **1:11.**

Romagna (region in Italy). Missions in this region in the diocese of Sarsina, **2:58.**

Roman (Jose Maria), twentieth-century Spanish biographer of Vincent, **1:15,39.**

Romans (epistle of Saint Paul to the). Cited in Abelly: 8:13-**1:81;** 2:31, 13:1-**2:20,** 10:17-**2:198,** 7:15-25-**3:34,** 8:35-39-**3:34,** 13:8-**3:106,** 9:3-**3:113,** 12:20-**3:162,** 12:16-**3:210,** 8:35-**3:280.**

Rome. Vincent stays there after his captivity and continues his studies, **1:45,48.** His emotion in entering the city. This is a memory that he always preserves, **1:48.** Beginning of the ordination retreats, **1:140.** Foundation of a house of the Missionaries in Rome. Donation given by the duchess of Aiguillon. Permission is given by the pope (1642), **1:231; 2:55,57,204.** The Missionaries evangelize, with great success, the shepherds of the Roman countryside. Death of Monsieur Lebreton, **2:55 ff.**

The pope orders that all those who are preparing to be ordained in Rome must make the ordination retreats at the house of the Priests of the Mission there (1659), **2:204-05.** Edification given by the Abbes de Chandenier during the retreats. The pope expresses his satisfaction, **2:205.** The success of the retreats given by other religious who want to replace the Missionaries in this work. The pope refuses to consent, **2:208**. He issues a new brief (1662), also obliging the ordinands of the suffragan bishops of Rome to make these retreats, **Ibid.**

Room (of Vincent). The simplicity and poverty which characterizes it, **3:245,265**.

Rose (Notre Dame de la), in the diocese of Agen. Establishment of the Congregation of the Mission in this place (1637), **1:231**.

Ross (region of Scotland). Evangelized by Thomas Lumsden, **2:178**.

Rouen (diocese of). Results of the missions held in this diocese, **2:44**.

Rougemont (count of). History of his conversion by Vincent at Chatillon. His good example of detachment, **1:77**.

Roussel (Jacques), Jesuit. Letter to Vincent on the edifying death of a Missionary, **2:325**.

Rubrics. Vincent desires that they should be observed exactly, **3:73**. See, *Ceremonies, Mass, Divine Office*.

Rules.
1. *Observance of the rules*. Vincent exercises an edifying firmness in ensuring the observance of them, **2:275-76**. He cites the example of a community which declined for some years because of a laxity in the observation of the rule, **3:297**. How rich a treasure is the habitual observance of the rule; while the opposite causes no end of trouble, **3:298**. Observe them as much as possible while traveling, **Ibid**. The superior must give example, **3:309**. See, *Obedience*.
2. *Rules of the Congregation of the Mission*. After his near fatal illness of 1635 Vincent says that the only thing he would have regretted not finishing had he died were the rules of the Mission, **1:257**.
Distribution of the Common Rules (May 17, 1658). Conference given by the saint on this occasion, **1:237 ff**. Why it took so long to give them to the Company, **1:238-39; 3:226**. Vincent reproves a Missionary who had published an abridgement without authorization, **3:202-03**.
Motives for practicing them faithfully, **1:237**. The first Missionaries thank Vincent for living their rule for them before it was written, **1:241**. They are based in the spirit of Jesus Christ and modeled on the actions of his life, **3:90-91**.
3. Rules of the Daughters of Charity. Common rules of the Daughters of Charity, and rules of particular offices, **2:292**. Excellence and perfection of these rules, **2:292-93**. Remarkable nature of these rules, **2:293**.

Rumelin, (Michel Thepaut), Lord of, canon of Treguier. Founder of a house of the Mission in this city, **1:234**.

S

Sables d'Olonne (city in the Vendee). A young man from this city held as a captive in Tunis is ransomed by a Missionary, **2:122**.

Sache (parish in the diocese of Tours). Mission given here, **2:54**.

Sacrifice (spirit of). We will be unworthy of being what God calls us to be if we refuse to lead our life according to his will, **3:90**. Example of our divine Savior, **Ibid**. See, *Martyrdom, Mortification*.

Sainctot (Marie Dalibray). One of the first Ladies of Charity of Hotel Dieu in Paris, **1:153**.

Saint Amand (village in the diocese of Angouleme). Mission held there in 1640, **2:52**.

Saint Amour (Louis Gorin, abbe de), ardent Jansenist. His opposition to Rome, **2:361-62**.

Saint Andre (parish in the city of Paris). Establishment of the Confraternity of Charity there, **1:131**.

Saint Andre (parish in the town of Chatillon les Dombes). Vincent is pastor here, **1:65**.

Saint Antoine (faubourg of Paris). The first monastery of the Visitation is established in this faubourg, **2:211,266**.

Saint Antoine (religious of the Order of). Vincent aids in the reform of their community, **2:385**.

Saint Arnoult (village near Paris). Helped by the Missionaries in 1652, **1:208**.

Saint Augustine (Canons Regular of). Vincent contributes to the reform of this order, **2:385**.

Saint Barthelemy (parish in the city of Paris). Establishment of the Confraternity of Charity there, **1:131**.

Saint Benedict (parish in the city of Paris). Establishment of the Confraternity of Charity there, **1:131**. Daughters of Charity work here, **1:34**.

Saint Bernard (religious of the Order of). Vincent helps in the reform of this Order, **2:385**.

Saint Brieuc. The canon-theologian of this diocese meets with Vincent at Rennes, **1:202**.

Saint Charles (seminary of). In Paris. Vincent establishes this seminary for young clerics to study the humanities, **1:165**. It is located within the enclosure of Saint Lazare. See, *Saint Lazare*.

Saint Cyr (parish in the diocese of Sens). Results of the mission there in 1642. Letter of thanks addressed to Vincent by Monsieur and Madame Saint Cyr who are the lords of this place, **2:47-48**.

Saint Cyran (Jean Duvergier de Hauranne, Abbe de). Biographical notice. His first relations with Vincent. Knowledge which the saint has of the true nature of the doctrines of this sectarian, **1:221; 2:346,356**. He admits to the saint his belief that it is God's plan to destroy the Church, **2:171,348**. In the presence of the saint, he agrees with Calvin's criticism of the Council of Trent, **2:347**. What he says to Vincent on the subject of holy Scripture. He believes that after five or six years there will no longer be any church, **2:348**. Visits of the saint to him to try to bring him back to the truth, **2:349; 3:185**. Letter of this priest to Vincent. Discussion on this subject, **2:349**. This sectarian collaborates with the works of Barcos and of Jansenius, **2:351**. Vincent eventually regards him as a heretic and treats him as such, **3:18**.

Saint Cyran is put in prison at the chateau of Vincennes by the order of Richelieu. Some details of his interrogation on his relations with Vincent, **2:350**. He is released at the death of the cardinal (1642). His death (1643), **2:350**.

Saint Denis (faubourg of Paris). Vincent is insulted here, and publicly accused of being the cause of the public misery, **3:157**. See, *Saint Laurent, (parish of)*.

Saint Esprit (Order of the). Union of a house of this order at Toul to the Congregation of the Mission, **1:230; 3:248**.

Saint Etienne (area in Picardy). Helped by Vincent during the war, **2:340**.

Saint Etienne du Mont (parish in the city of Paris). Confraternity of Charity established there, **1:131**.

Saint Eustache (parish in the city of Paris). Establishment of the Confraternity of Charity there, **1:131**.

Saint Fargeau (city of). Site of a hospital served by the Daughters of Charity, **2:296**.

Saint Firmin (seminary of, formerly the College des Bons Enfants), **1:165; 2:250.**

Saint Flour (diocese of). Missions given in this diocese by Monsieur Olier and priests of the Mission, **1:168; 2:36 ff.** Monsieur Olier gives a mission to the pastors of this diocese at the abbey of Pebrac, **1:168.** Results of the missions in this diocese, **2:36 ff.** See, *Chomel (Monsieur).*

Saint Germain (faubourg of Paris). Vincent takes lodging in this area when he first arrives in Paris, **1:49.** Mission given here by the priests of the Tuesday Conferences, **2:222 ff.** Vincent visits the sick in the charity hospital there, **3:115.** The Protestant minister Charles Drelincourt encounters a German Lutheran who disguised himself as a Missionary, **3:160.**

Saint Germain en Laye (city and royal residence). Vincent goes there to assist the dying Louis XIII, **1:191; 3:256.** He goes there to speak with the queen and Mazarin at the beginning of the Fronde (1649), **1:198; 2:397.** Mission given here, **2:76.**

Saint Germain l'Auxerrois (parish in the city of Paris). Confraternity of Charity established there, **1:131.** At the death of Vincent the members of the Tuesday Conferences celebrate a requiem service here, **1:262.**

Saint Gilles (village in the diocese of Lucon). Mission given here. Foundation of the Confraternity of Charity, **2:51.**

Saint Honore (faubourg of Paris). Vincent finds a house here where the convicts can be better housed (1618), **1:85.**

Saint Ilpise (village in Auvergne). Mission given here in 1636, **1:167; 2:36.**

Saint Jacques (faubourg of Paris). A second monastery of the Visitation is founded here, **2:267.**

Saint Jacques de la Boucherie (parish in the city of Paris). Establishment of the Confraternity of Charity there, **1:131.**

Saint Jacques du Haut Pas (parish in the city of Paris). Burial place of Saint Cyran, **1:221.** Establishment of the Confraternity of Charity here, **1:131.**

Saint Jean (parish in the city of Paris). Establishment of the Confraternity of Charity here, **1:131.**

Saint Jean de Luz (French port), **3:278.**

Saint John of God (brothers of), **1:46.**

Saint Jure (Jean Baptiste de), Jesuit. He comes to visit the dying Vincent, **1:251.**

Saint Landry (street in Paris), **1:160.**

Saint Laurent (island of Madagascar). See, *Madagascar.*

Saint Laurent (parish in the city of Paris). Establishment of the Confraternity of Charity there, **1:131.** Louise de Marillac transfers her home and that of the Daughters of Charity here in order to be near Saint Lazare which is located in this parish (1641), **1:136.** Vincent establishes there the hospital of the Name of Jesus (1653), **1:225.** Assistance given by Vincent, **3:126.** See, *Lestocq (Guillaume de).*

Saint Lazare les Paris. (Ecclesiastical lands and priory of the canons regular of Saint Augustine). Notice, **1:119; 3:235.** How this priory came to be offered to Vincent, **1:120 ff.** Shock of the saint in hearing of this proposition, **1:121.** Negotiations for the establishment of the Congregation of the Mission in this house. Hesitation of the saint in accepting it, **1:121; 3:242.** Vincent is installed there by the archbishop of Paris, Jean Francois de Gondi (January 8, 1632), **1:122.** How the union with the Congregation of the Mission was done and under what conditions. First agreement,

1:123. The archbishop of Paris unites Saint Lazare to the Congregation of the Mission by letters of December 31, 1632, confirmed by a decree of Urban VIII (March 15, 1635), and by letters patent of Louis XIII, **1:124.** Opposition of the religious of Saint Victor. Lawsuit. Sentiments of Vincent on this occasion, **Ibid; 3:247.** The opposition is defeated, **1:124.**

Devotion of Vincent for the insane who are kept in the house of Saint Lazare. He continues to receive these unfortunates, **1:124; 2:259.** A great number of retreatants are received there. Vincent calls it "a Noah's Ark," because of the great diversity of all those who come there. It is also called a "house of divine actions," because of the great spiritual benefits which are produced there, **1:141-42; 2:239-40.** The ordinands on retreat are also received there freely. The great expenses of the house. The generosity of Vincent, **1:142; 2:187.** The Commander de Sillery gives the house of Saint Lazare a considerable donation for the beginning of an internal seminary (novitiate), **1:172.** Great number of missions given from this house, **2:28.** Influence on retreatants. Sentiments of edification expressed by many priests and religious on their retreats at Saint Lazare, **2:241 ff.** Ecclesiastical Conferences, or Tuesday Conferences established there (1633), **2:210 ff.** Bishops meet there to plan strategy in the battle against Jansenism. Meetings of theologians opposed to Jansenism also are held here, **2:353.**

Vincent has posted in various places of the cloister of Saint Lazare these words: "God Sees All!" **3:57.** Alms given to the poor. Vincent dines with two poor persons each day at his table, **3:126.** General alms for the poor, both ordinary and extraordinary, were distributed from here, **3:127.**

The house of Saint Lazare is transformed into an army camp during the Spanish invasion of 1636, **1:174.** Meetings are held there to collect assistance for the ruined inhabitants of Lorraine. The procurator gives Vincent the last money in the house treasury to give as alms (1641), **1:188.** Gratitude and submission of Vincent with regards to the prior, Adrien Le Bon, **1:206.** This house serves for all as a center of finding ways to further the glory of God and the good of dioceses, communities, or families, **1:242.**

The house of Saint Lazare is pillaged by the Frondeurs (1649). It suffers a loss of 40,000 *livres*, **1:199; 3:285.** Death of Adrien Le Bon, prior of Saint Lazare (April 9, 1651). On this occasion Vincent writes a circular letter to the houses of the Congregation, **1:207.** During the Fronde, everyday seven or eight hundred poor are fed and catechized from this house (1652), **1:211.** Vincent orders prayers and fasting there for the intention of the reestablishment of peace in France, **1:213,220.** The house of Saint Charles or Little Saint Lazare becomes a seminary for younger students (1642), **2:250.**

Saint Leonard de Chaume (abbey in the diocese of Maillezais). Vincent receives this benefice in 1610, **1:53.**

Saint Leu (village near Paris). The Missionaries give missions there to the soldiers during the war of 1636, **1:177.**

Saint Livrade (town in the diocese of Agen), **1:231.**

Saint Louis (hospital of). Located in Paris, **3:112.**

Saint Malo (seminary in this diocese), **1:166.** See, *Saint Meen.*

Saint Martha (Daughters of), community of religious in Reims, **2:339.**

Saint Martin (faubourg of Paris). Vincent saves the life of a man pursued by soldiers here, **3:112.**

Saint Martin (Jean de), canon of Dax. His relations with Vincent, **1:6,42,46,49.** He recounts an example of the humility of Vincent which he witnessed, **3:189.** His account of a visit by one of Vincent's nephews to Saint Lazare, **3:193.** Vincent entrusts him with the distribution of a sum of money which he had received specifically for the benefit of his family, **3:260.** He asks him to send him the letter which contained the account of his captivity in Tunis, **1:42.**

Saint Martin (parish in the village of Buenans). Vincent is named pastor here. The parish of Chatillon is attached to this benefice, **1:65.**

Saint Maur (Congregation of the Benedictines of). Vincent helps in the reform of this congregation, **2:385.**

Saint Meen (city in the diocese of Saint Malo). Ceding of the abbey of Saint Meen to the Missionaries by the religious. In 1645, the Congregation is established there by the bishop in order to direct a seminary. Union of the conventual resources to the Congregation of the Mission by Pope Alexander VII in 1658, **1:232-33.**

Vincent visits this house in 1649, **1:201.** Missions given from this house in the diocese of Saint Malo (1657), **2:45.**

Saint Merry (parish in the city of Paris). A Confraternity of Charity is founded there (1631), **1:131.**

Saint Mihiel (town in Lorraine). Vincent procures assistance for this town. Details of the horrible misery which reigned there (1640), **1:185; 2:321 ff.,328.**

Saint Nazaire (city near the mouth of the Loire River). The Missionaries who are leaving for Ireland give a mission to the other passengers waiting there (1646), **2:127.**

Saint Nicolas de Gross Sauve (priory in the diocese of Langres). One of Vincent's benefices, **1:94.**

Saint Nicolas du Chardonnet (parish in the city of Paris). Vincent transfers the convicts from the faubourg Saint Honore to this parish, **1:86.** Louise de Marillac comes to live in the same parish, near the College des Bons Enfants, **1:129.** Establishment of a Confraternity of Charity, **1:131,148.** Louise de Marillac serves a girl who is sick with the plague there. Vincent congratulates her, **1:131.** Daughters of Charity work here, **1:134.** The saint recommends the convicts to the care of the Confraternity of Charity of this parish, **1:148.** He procures a yearly revenue from the clergy of this parish in order to provide for the spiritual assistance to the convicts, **1:149.** Establishment of a seminary in the parish through the zeal of Monsieur Bourdoise, **1:165; 3:141.**

Saint Paul (parish in the city of Paris). Establishment of a Confraternity of Charity here, **1:131.**

Saint Quentin (city of). Vincent sends Missionaries and assistance there (1650), **1:205; 2:305,334,338.** The Missionaries establish a Confraternity of Charity there, **2:341.** Letter of thanks from the Lieutenant General of this city to Vincent, **2:342.** See, *Public Misery. Parre (Jean).*

Saint Roch (parish in the city of Paris). Establishment of a Confraternity of Charity there, **1:131.** Vincent searches in this parish for a house large enough to house the convicts, **1:85.**

Saint Sauveur (parish in the city of Paris). Louise de Marillac first lives in this parish, **1:129.** The first Confraternity of Charity established in the capital is in this parish (1629). First rule for the Charities of cities, **1:131.** Daughters of Charity established there, **1:134.**

Saint Souplet (village in Champagne). Assisted by Vincent, **2:340.**

Saint Sulpice (parish in the city of Paris). Establishment of the Confraternity of Charity here in 1631, **1:131.** Community of priests founded by Monsieur Olier. Vincent praises them, **1:169; 3:141.** He advises a person to establish a foundation to support the seminary directed by the Sulpicians, **Ibid.** See, *Olier (Jean Jacques).*

Saint Victor (Canons Regular of). Their opposition to the change of possession of Saint Lazare, **1:124.**

Sainte Croix (Marcello de Santacroce), cardinal. And the ordination retreats in Rome, **2:205,209.**

Sainte Genevieve (abbey of). Vincent is employed there to assist in its reform, **2:385.**

Sainte Marie (island near Madagascar). Evangelized by the Missionaries, **2:151.**

Sainte Menehould (town near Chalons). Vincent sends Missionaries and assistance there, **1:205.**

Sainte Reine (in the diocese of Dijon). Hospital founded in this city with the assistance of Vincent, **2:303.**

Saintes (city and diocese of). The Congregation of the Mission is established there in 1644, through the zeal of the bishop and by a contribution of his clergy. Diocesan seminary. Vincent proposes to visit this house in 1649, **1:166,202,232.** Success of the missions given in this diocese in 1634, **2:32.** Missions in 1640 and 1642; gratitude of the bishop for the Missionaries who work in this diocese, **2:35.** Good example given by a Missionary from Saintes; Monsieur Julien Guerin, **2:86.** Letter of the bishop to Vincent on the success of the ordination retreats (1645), **2:203.** Vincent supports the choice of Jacques Raoul de la Guibourgere, bishop of Saintes, for the newly established see of La Rochelle, **2:382.**
Nomination of Louis de Bassompierre to this bishopric. His affection for the priests of the Mission, **2:383.** See, *Deniat, Gemozac, Guibourgere (Jacques Raoul de la), Mortagne, Usseau.*

Saintonge (province of). During the war (1652), **1:217.** Success of the missions in this province, **2:32.** See, *Saintes.*

Saints. The motives for imitating their virtues, **3:9.** The devotion of Vincent towards them, **3:94.**

Salpetriere (general hospital of the). Origin and necessity of this establishment (1653), **1:226.** The enclosure of the Salpetriere is given by Louis XIV in order to serve as a general hospital (1653), **1:227.** Vincent did not want the poor to be sent there forcibly, **1:228.**
Vincent announces to the duchess of Aiguillon and to Monsieur de Mauroy that the Company has decided not to accept the spiritual direction of this establishment, **1:229.** Abelly accepts the position as rector of this hospital, **Ibid; 2:220.** The priests of the Tuesday Conferences give many missions and serve the poor there, **2:219.**

Salve Regina. This antiphon to the Virgin is chanted by Vincent during his captivity, **1:45.**

Samaritan woman (New Testament figure), **3:227.**

Samuel (Old Testament prophet), **3:65.**

Samuel (first book of). Cited in Abelly: 3:19-**3:65**, 17:36-**3:319.**

Sancy (Achille de Harlay de), bishop of Saint Malo. He brings the priests of the Mission to his diocese and establishes them at Saint Meen (1645), **1:232.**

Sarlat (diocese of). The bishop of Sarlat restores his city to obedience to the king during the war (1652). Vincent cites him as an example, **1:218.** See, *Sevin (Nicholas).*

Sarsina (city in Italy). Mission given in this city, **2:58.**

Satan (the evil spirit, the devil, the demon). "The demon rejoices in needless publicity given to good works," **1:108.** Attacks the Daughters of the Cross, **3:196.**
As the enemy of humility, **2:18.** Works through pride, **2:25.** The Lord conquers him in the souls of the galley slaves, **2:40.** Subtlety of the devil in attacking a good work, **2:92.** Missionaries delivered by God's protection from his attacks, **2:127.** Those saved from his clutches as a result of the missions given in Ireland, **2:131.** Honored by the native Malgache religion, **2:140.** And a soothsayer on Madagascar, **2:156.** Missionaries rescue souls from his power, **2:183.** Efforts of the devil to block the good, **2:223.** His malice and deceits, **2:231.** Sometimes disguised as an angel of light, **2:246; 3:60,218.** He attacks the works of the Convent of Sainte Madeleine, **2:279.** Diabolic possession of a Visitandine, **2:281.** Diabolic revelations, **2:393.** The enemy of peace, and the source of war, **2:394.**
Temptation of a Missionary to leave the Congregation, **3:151.** Jesus refers to Peter as Satan, **3:176.** Source of all temptations, **3:186,225,266,268-69.** Source of all difficulties which meet our attempts to do good, **3:231.** Jesus was falsely accused of being possessed, **3:259.** Knows how to prey on our weaknesses and sensitivities, **3:289.** Tempts Clement VIII in a dream, **3:295.**

Satyrus (Saint), brother of Saint Ambrose, **3:214.**

Saul (Old Testament figure). He searched for his lost donkeys but found a kingdom instead, **1:135.** Was worthy of being appointed king because of his life in his father's house, yet after being raised to the throne he fell from God's grace, **3:318.**

Savigliano (city in Piedmont, Italy). Mission given in this area, **2:78.**

Savoy (duchy of). Confraternities of Charity in this duchy, **1:73.**

Scalenghe (town in Piedmont). Mission given there, **2:76.**

Schools. Louise de Marillac establishes these in various places, especially when she visits the Confraternities of Charity, **1:130.** They are visited by the Missionaries during the course of a mission, **2:23.**

Scotland. Vincent helps the Scotch noble refugees living in exile in Paris (1641), **1:188.** Vincent sends three Missionaries to Scotland, Messieurs White, Duggan and Lumsden. Their work in this country, **2:173-74, 178 ff.** News of the persecution in this country. **2:178,181.** See, *Hebrides (Islands of).*

Scruples. Why God sometimes permits them, **3:34.** Mildness of Vincent in dealing with those who were afflicted with them, **3:173.**

Secret. "The demon rejoices in needless publicity given to good works. These then become trivial and without effect," **1:108.** Vincent faithfully guards secrets, **3:232.**

Sedan (city of). The dying Louis XIII communicates to Vincent his desires for the conversion of the heretics of Sedan, **1:190.** The king founds a house of the priests of the Mission, **1:232.** The saint instructs the superior of this house on how he must handle himself with regards to the heretics in order to bring them back to the Church, **2:26.** Results of the missions, **2:42.**
Vincent sends Missionaries and assistance there during the war (1650), **1:205; 2:305.** See, *Cabel (Pierre), Coglee (Marc).*

Seguier (Dominique), bishop of Meaux. He authorizes the establishment of a house of the Mission at Crecy (1641), **1:231.**

Seguier (Pierre), chancellor of France. He transmits to Vincent the order of the king to send twenty Missionaries to the army to give a mission, (1636), **1:175.** Member of the Council of Conscience (1643), **1:192.**

Seminaries. Vincent regards them as necessary for applying and realizing the intentions of the Council of Trent on the reform of the priesthood. Previous unsuccessful attempts to establish them; the cause of this lack of success, **1:164 ff; 2:249-50.** The saint establishes a seminary at the College des Bons Enfants; later called the Saint Firmin seminary (1634), **1:164; 2:249-50.** He regards as very useful the creation of major seminaries distinct from schools for younger students. He petitions Cardinal Richelieu, **1:164; 2:250.** He establishes one at Annecy (1641), **1:166,231.** The work of the company in seminaries is imitated by others and they multiply in France and in Italy, **1:166.** Beneficial results of their establishment in France: at Cahors, Paris, etc., Ibid; **2:255 ff.** One must spend a sufficient amount of time there in order to be fully formed in the ecclesiastical virtues, **2:254.**

One of the principal ends of the Congregation is the instruction of ecclesiastics in the seminaries, **2:250.** Excellence of this work, **2:251.** It is a great deceit not to want to be employed in this work, **2:252-53.** There is no work more necessary in the world than that of the seminaries. The ecclesiastics who are formed there are the treasure of the Church, **3:140.**

The principal end of the education of ecclesiastics is to form them in the interior life, prayer, recollection, and union with God, **2:254; 3:309.** Reprimand given to a seminary director who was known to be harsh towards his seminarians, **3:306.** General advice for the conduct to be followed by the seminarians. The principal end of the work is to form them in a solid devotion and piety, **3:309.** The greatest obstacles to teaching those under our charge is to neglect or disedify them, **3:309-10.** See, *Ordinands.*

Senhare (Zanhary). Traditional Malgache word to designate the deity, **2:140.**

Senlis (city and diocese of). Louise de Marillac visits the Confraternities of Charity of this diocese, **1:130.** Vincent goes to this city to meet with Louis XIII who asked for Missionaries for the spiritual assistance of the army, **1:175.**

Sens (diocese of). Results of the missions given in this diocese, **2:47.** See, *Joigny, Longron, Moutier Saint Jean.*

Sensuality. Pride and sensuality can destroy the vocation of a Missionary, **3:204.** Sensuality is found everywhere; in pleasures as well as in devotions, **3:256.** Vincent wants to ban this from his community, **3:302.** See, *Mortification.*

Sergis (Robert de), priest of the Mission. He gives spiritual assistance to the soldiers during the war of 1636, **1:175.**

Serre (Louis), priest of the Mission. His vocation to the Congregation, **1:81.** Letter to Vincent on the missions in Brittany, **2:45.**

Sery de Mailly, (Abbe de). His desire to found a house of the Missionaries at Amiens, **1:235.** He wishes to be buried near Vincent in the church of Saint Lazare, **Ibid.**

Sestri (market town in the diocese of Genoa). Mission given in this area, **2:68.**

Seville (Isidore of). Cited in Abelly, **2:402.**

Sevin (Nicolas), bishop of Sarlat, then of Cahors. He gives a conference at the ordination retreats of Saint Lazare with great simplicity, and with great success, **3:220.**

Shepherds. Those of the Roman countryside are evangelized by the confreres, **2:55 ff.**

Sick. Vincent always visits them, **1:242.** His charity for them, **2:277.** He helps them and receives them into his house when they are poor, **3:130,142**. His mildness and his care in their regard, **3:172**.

The sick of the parish should be visited during the time of a mission, **2:23**. Those tempted by the spirit of sloth have a greater need of being treated even more gently and charitably than those who have a physical ailment, **3:152**. The sick are a blessing for their houses, **3:154**. A blessing for the Company, **3:172**. They merit more by their sufferings than others do by their work, **3:154**.

Attention and charity of Vincent for Missionaries who are sick, **1:252; 3:154**. For those who are not too ill he gently and paternally suggests that they not omit their usual spiritual exercises, "lest the sickness of the body extend to the soul, and make it lax and unmortified," **3:155**. It is only reasonable that the house which received the services of a Missionary should take care of and support him when he becomes sick, **3:171**.

Sickness. Various infirmities of Vincent. The holy usage that he makes of them, **1:250 ff.** It is during the years that he is afflicted by a fever that Vincent accomplishes the better part of his great works, **1:250**. While in a delirium from a fever he manifests sentiments of great piety, **1:251**. He has a grave illness in 1645, and a Missionary offers God his own life in exchange for the preservation of his, **Ibid.** His heroic courage and the marks of his spirit of faith in his last illness, **1:253 ff.** His submission and his holy indifference, **3:52,279**. His mortification, **3:265**. Receiving sicknesses as coming from God, **3:267,291**.

Patience of Vincent; *his teaching and his example*, **3:289 ff.** He did not want to call the sick "unfortunate" since their illnesses were part of God's plan for them, **3:291**. They make us appreciate our own good health. How virtues can be practiced in sicknesses, **Ibid.** Means of sanctifying them. Example of a servant of God, **3:292**. Example of Brother Antoine; how he accepted his illness, **Ibid.**

Sidi Regeppe (in Tunisia). Jean Le Vacher goes there to console the slaves, **2:113**.

"Sieve" (the), an old soldier given shelter by Vincent at Saint Lazare, **3:130**.

Silence. A community which observes it exactly observes the rest of the rule. On the contrary, in a community where silence is not observed it is almost impossible that the other rules will be observed there, **1:123-24**. Example of our Lord, **3:226**.

Sillery (Noel Brulart de), Commander of the Temple of Troyes of the Order of Saint John of Jerusalem. He gives himself to the service of God and places himself under the direction of Vincent, **1:170**. He prepares himself to enter the priesthood, **Ibid**. His ordination in the house of Saint Lazare. Letter to the saint, **1:170-71**. He visits the houses of his order. Vincent cooperates in the success of these visits by simultaneously giving a mission in parishes attached to these houses, **1:171**. Letter of thanks addressed to Vincent by Paul Lascaris, the Grand Master of the Knights of Malta, **Ibid**. The Commander makes large donations for establishments of the Congregation (1638), **1:172,231**.

Foundation of a house of the Mission at Annecy (1640), **1:231; 2:39**. Praise of his piety, and of his generosity, **1:172; 2:39**.

Sillery (Nicolas Brulart de), marquis, chancellor of France, brother of the above. He gives a good example of the virtue of gentleness, **3:178**.

Sillery (village in the archdiocese of Reims). Mission given in this place, **2:42**.

Simeon (New Testament figure), **1:256,259**.

Simonnet (Monsieur), lieutenant general at Rethel. His gratitude for the assistance given there by the Missionaries, **2:343**.

Simplicity. The charm of this virtue wins hearts, **1:105.** It is one of the characteristics of the conduct of Vincent, **1:108.** God conceals from the simple the treasures of grace he has given them, **2:198.** "As soon as we leave the humble and simple way proper to our institute we will lose the graces promised to it," **3:203.**
Teaching and examples of Vincent, **3:214 ff.** Praise of simplicity, **3:214.** Exhortation of Vincent on the practice of this virtue; motives, definition, **Ibid.** Everyone loves persons who are found to have simplicity and candor, especially by those who do not have this virtue themselves, **3:216.** It must be united with prudence, **Ibid.** Examples and advice of the saint, **3:217 ff.** Cultivating the friendship of a person in order that it will sustain us when we are spoken ill of is a base motive and very far from the spirit of Jesus Christ, **3:219.** Simplicity in preaching. Advice of the saint, **3:220.** See, *Preaching.* As natural beauty has more attraction than artificial beauty; simple discourses are better received than those which are artificially polished, **3:221.** Vincent recommends: "Let us be straightforward and act always with loyalty and fairness to everyone," **3:233.** He preserves this virtue while at the court. Testimony of a prelate: "Monsieur Vincent is always Monsieur Vincent," **3:275.** See, *Prudence.*

Singularity. Never desire to be singular in your conduct, but always follow the *viam regiam.* This is what Vincent taught about this vice, **3:320.**

Sins. In serving as military chaplains the Missionaries should reflect that they can hardly eradicate all sin from the army, but perhaps God will give them the grace to at least diminish their number, **1:175.** Vincent laments the prolongation of his life into old age because of his feeling that his sins had also multiplied with the number of his years, **1:257.** He says that his only fear are his own sins, **3:27.**

Sirach (Ecclesiasticus, book of the Old Testament). Cited in Abelly: 1:13-**1:191,** 45:1-**2:165,** 31:9-**2:398,** 18:23-**3:65,** 4:7-**3:166,** 19:9-**3:169,** 31:8-**3:242,** 23:38-**3:254.**

Skye (island of the Hebrides). Work of the Missionaries there, **2:176.**

Slanders. The absent always had in Vincent an advocate who defended their reputation, **3:110.** The saint fights against this vice, **3:149 ff.** A slanderer in a community is like a wolf who desolates and destroys the sheepfold, **3:149.** Vincent gives a conference on this vice for seven Fridays in a row, **Ibid.** He cites various authorities against the vice of slander, **3:169.** It is one of the vices to be most feared by communities, **3:302.**

Slaves. Love that Vincent conceives for them during his own captivity, **1:47.** The saint undertakes the work of corporal and spiritual assistance to the slaves of Barbary, **2:84 ff.** Excellence of the charitable ministry that the confreres exercise among the slaves of Barbary, **2:89 ff.** Its results. Martyrdom of a young Marjorcan at Algiers, **2:100-02.** Advice and rules of Vincent for the Missionaries who were going to Barbary (1646-47), **2:102 ff.** Wise counsel given to a Missionary on his way to minister to the slaves, **2:103.** Sufferings and labors of the slaves. Services which are given them by the Missionaries in Barbary, **2:105 ff, 120 ff.** Their heroic constancy and the death of many of them for their faith, **2:111,123.** The conversion of many heretics and renegades among the slaves are brought about by the priests of the Mission in Barbary, **2:116 ff.**
During the life of Vincent the Missionaries ransomed more than 1200 slaves, and spent for this purpose more than 1.2 million *livres*, **2:125.** The saint gratuitously serves as an intermediary to facilitate the correspondence between the captives of Barbary and their families, **Ibid; 3:126.** He encourages a bishop who wanted to ransom some people from his diocese who were held as slaves in Barbary, **3:136.**

Sleep. Vincent's penitential practices; sleeping on a straw pallet, **1:88-89.** Edifying conduct of some confreres, **1:117.** Examples of the mortification of Vincent, **3:265,283.**

Soffores (Monsieur de), treasurer of the University of Toulouse, **1:40.**

Soissons (diocese of). Louise de Marillac visits the Confraternities of Charity of this diocese, **1:130.** Vincent sends Missionaries and assistance to this area devastated by the war, **2:333,337.**

Soldiers. Vincent sends Missionaries to the army to assist the soldiers. Directions of the saint. Success of this ministry, **1:175-77; 2:299.** Missions given to the regiments of the king's guards by members of the Tuesday Conferences, **2:218.** Officers come to make their spiritual retreat at Saint Lazare, **2:240.** Vincent works to remedy the ruins and the disorders caused by the soldiers during the war, **2:394.** The saint saves an artisan whom some soldiers are about to kill, **3:112.** He pardons those who had robbed some of the seminarians, **3:160.**
Vincent sends Daughters of Charity to serve the sick soldiers at Rethel, Calais, etc., **2:298.**

Solminihac (Alain de), first abbot of Chancelade, then bishop of Cahors. Vincent helps him introduce the reform in the abbey of Chancellade, **2:385.** This prelate establishes a house of the Mission at Cahors in 1643, **1:174,232.** He clearly declares himself against the Jansenists. Vincent cites his example, and sends him a copy of the bull of Innocent X, **2:356.** He wants the seminary at Cahors to give up a lawsuit over a complicated affair. Generous behavior of Vincent with regard to this prelate, **3:111.**

Sorbonne (theological faculty of the University of Paris). It disavows two of its doctors who support the heresy of the *Two Heads of the Church*, **2:351.** Vincent praises its zeal for defending the faith and morals, **2:371.**

Sorcerers (in the diocese of Montauban), **2:51.**

Souillard (Jean), Vincent's successor at the parish of Clichy, **1:54.**

Sourdis (Francois Escoubleau de) cardinal, archbishop of Bordeaux. He introduces the ecclesiastical conferences into his diocese, **2:216.**

Souyn (Monsieur), bailiff of Reims. Letter of thanks to Vincent, **2:343.**

Spada (Bernardino), cardinal. Letter to Vincent. He thanks him for the good done by the mission given in the diocese of Albano. **2:65.**

Spain. Possibility of a foundation of the Congregation in this country, **2:207.**

Spiritual Dryness. If one puts it to good usage it cannot help but assist one in advancing in virtue, **3:70-71.** If it is to be feared it should be feared that it will come about through some negligence on our part, **Ibid.** See, *Consolation, Devotion, Trials.*

Stenay (town in Lorraine). Assisted by Vincent, **2:329.**

Store (Charity). Creation of this charitable storehouse to aid the poor in the area of Paris (1652), **1:210.**

Strick (Thomas), mayor of the city of Limerick, massacred by the English, **2:132.**

Students (of the Congregation at Saint Lazare). Advice Vincent gives them, **1:182.** He refuses to agree to keep as their theology instructor someone suspected of being a Jansenist, **3:17.** The passage from the novitiate to the studies of the seminary is dangerous. Comparison of the fragility of glass which passes from the heat of the furnace to a cold place. Advice of the saint, **3:301-02.**

Studies of Vincent. His diligence and his modesty. He continues them after his ordination, **1:38,40-41.**

Study. Its importance for the Missionaries. The end that they must have for their studying, **3:301.**

Subiaco (Benedictine abbey, in Italy). Missions given in the parishes dependent on this abbey, **2:64.**

Sufferings. Vincent having suffered in many ways cites his own experience to those who are being tried, **2:270.** The acceptance of suffering is the great lesson we learn from the Son of God. Those who learn it well are in the most advanced class in the school of the Lord, **3:48.** "Oh, the happy state of those who suffer for the love of God! How agreeable this is in his sight, since his own Son crowned the heroic actions of his holy life with terrible sufferings which brought him to death," **3:57.** Conformity to the suffering Jesus Christ is a mark of our predestination, **3:285.** Encouragement to an afflicted person, **3:288.** See, *Afflictions, Cross, Hope.*

Superior General. It is out of obedience to the pope that Vincent accepts this position, and later continues to hold this office in his Congregation, **3:192,207.** The obligation of the councillors to give advice to the superior general, **3:294.** Missionaries are always free to write to the superior general, **3:305.** The saint declares that if he himself was found with some scandalous fault that he did not correct, and which threatened the destruction of the Congregation, a general assembly should depose him, **3:307-08.**

Superiors

1. *Rules of conduct* addressed to the superiors for the direction of their house, **3:294 ff, 309 ff.** They must show that they themselves easily receive admonitions by requesting their admonitor to fulfill his work well, **3:305.** They must give an example of regularity, **3:309.** Particularly in rising in the morning, **Ibid.** Advice given by Vincent to a Missionary in sending him to a house as superior, **3:317 ff.** Above all do not have a passion for appearing superior, **3:319.** They must be models for the community of the imitation of Jesus Christ, **3:320.** They should exercise their influence in the community like angels, **3:321.**

2. *Importance and dangers* of this office. Our Lord and the saints had shunned these honors. Words of Cardinal Berulle, **3:204.** It is a duty to pray for them often, **3:297.** The faults of the community are imputed to its superior, **3:297,319.** Answers given to various superiors who asked to be relieved of their positions, **3:306,310.**

3. *Duties and Functions* of superiors. The superior must look after the needs of everyone, and provide what is necessary, **3:31.** Under what circumstances he must inform the community of the faults of one of its members, **3:308.** He must understand that his care of temporal things is in imitation of God who created and governs the world, **3:321.**

The superiors must exercise goodness, support, and charity towards those who are under their direction, **3:153.** Conduct to be followed towards difficult confreres, **3:169 ff, 297-300,306.** Support with patience any affliction which comes to the community in view of what our Savior suffered on behalf of those who were his, **3:170,285,305.** The position of superior has its pains like all other positions and superiors who want to do their work properly must be prepared to suffer, **3:305.** Superiors must treat each person with mildness and respect; using amiable words and never rude or imperious words, **3:310.**

Superiors (of Religious Women). Vincent feels that a three year term for superiors is preferable to a life term in houses of these religious, **2:391.**

Support (mutual). Living in community without this support would be like being a vessel without an anchor in the middle of the shoals, **3:149.** It will always be difficult to live with some persons but there will also be merit in this struggle, **3:170.** Encouragements given by considering the example of our Lord who chose to live in the midst of his imperfect disciples, **Ibid.** Our Lord will give his blessing to our works if there is mutual support and cordiality among us, **3:171.** It is a source of peace and a bond of perfection, **Ibid.** "Two people living together will find enough to bother them. Were you to live alone, you would still find difficulties to try your patience," **3:300.**

Sutherland (region of Scotland). Evangelized by Thomas Lumsden, **2:178.**

Sweden. Fallen into heresy, **1:212; 2:170,192.**

T

Tabourne (location in Barbary). Christian slaves here are visited by the Missionaries, **2:115.**

Tarisse (Dom Gregory), Benedictine, friend of Vincent. He works for the reform of the Benedictine Order, **2:385.**

Temple (House of the Order of the Knights Templar), in Paris. Vincent stays there to assist in its reform, **1:172.** The haste with which this reform was undertaken against the advice of the saint; and its subsequent failure, **Ibid.**

Temporal Goods. In what ways and with what spirit the superiors, as instruments of divine providence, must take great care of them, **3:31,312 ff.** Example of our Lord's practice, **3:31,322.**
Care taken by Vincent over the temporal goods of his houses, **3:142,156,312.** He pardons those who have stolen from the community, **3:160.** His resignation in the face of considerable loses, **3:161,283.** See, *Orsigny*. Two things which must be done by those who are in charge of supervising temporal goods, **3:312.** See, *Benefices*, *Detachment*.

Temptations. Resisting them roots virtues in the heart, **3:14.** Vincent tempted against the faith, **3:15,17.** He consoles a person tempted to despair, **3:34.** He takes upon himself a trial against the faith of a doctor of theology, **3:113-16.** His charity for those who are being tempted, **3:152.** Answer to a Missionary who believed that he had lost the esteem of Vincent because he had told him of his temptations, **Ibid.** Some advice on temptations against purity, **3:269-70.** Vincent profits from the conviction that we are never tempted beyond our capacity to resist, **3:287.** "Souls tried by temptation are like rushing streams flowing over boulders and rocks. Their water is pure and refreshing," **3:288.** Do not be overly saddened by these temptations; "Be like the pilots of ships. When they are caught in a storm they redouble their courage and steer their vessels right into the heart of the largest waves which seem ready to swamp them," **3:304.**
Temptations against vocation. Vincent is saddened by those who are tempted to leave their vocations, **3:151.** Conduct of the saint towards Missionaries who are thus tempted, **3:151 ff.** See, *Vocation*.

Teresa of Avila, (Saint). She asked her sisters to pray to God to give the Church good priests, **2:199.**

Testament, (New). The members of the Tuesday Conferences must read it each day. The dispositions that should accompany this practice, **2:215.**

Theologians. They are like the public wells where one can find the healthy and refreshing waters of doctrine and morals. Vincent turns away from those whose teaching is not orthodox, **2:353; 3:17.**

Thierache (region in Picardy). Aid given to this country ravaged by the war, **2:333.**

Thiers (city in Puy de Dome). Reform of a monastery of the Order of Grandmont in this city, **2:387.**

Tholard (Jacques), priest of the Mission. He gives a successful mission near Paris, **2:31.**

Thurles (town in Ireland). Results of mission held there, **2:130.**

Tilh (parish in the diocese of Dax). Vincent is named as its pastor, **1:39.**

Time (the good use of). Example of Vincent. His regulated life, **1:242.** "Our entire lives are but a moment soon gone. Alas the seventy-six years of my life seem now to be only a momentary dream," **3:119.** How he saved time, **3:322.** See, *Idleness, Work.*

Timothy (first epistle of Saint Paul to). Cited in Abelly: 5:22-**1:138,** 1:13-**2:200,** 1:17-**2:314.**

Timothy (second epistle of Saint Paul to). Cited in Abelly: 2:24-**3:167.**

Tobit (book of the Old Testament). Cited in Abelly: 12:7:**3:323,372.**

Toledo (Francisco de), cardinal. He consoles Pope Clement VIII afflicted by a diabolic vision, **3:295.**

Toublan (Louis), secretary to the duke of Retz. He contributes to the foundation of the house of the Mission at Montmirail, **1:232.**

Toul (city and diocese of). Establishment of a house of the Mission in this city, **1:230.** Results of the missions in this diocese, **2:42.**
Vincent relieves the misery of this city during the war, **1:185; 2:317.** Charity of the priests of the Mission and gratitude of its inhabitants, **2:318-19.** See, *Charmes, Gournay (Charles Chretien de), Saint Esprit, (Order of the).*

Toulon (city and port of). The galleys from Marseilles are transferred here (1649-55). A Missionary goes there to reside and assist the convicts, **1:151.**

Toulouse (city and archdiocese of). Vincent studies in this city, **1:39.** He receives the degree of Bachelor of Theology there, **1:40-41.** He edifies everyone there by his modesty, **1:42.**
Results of the missions in this diocese (1640), **2:53.** Letter of the archbishop to Vincent. He gives testimony to the success of the missions and asks for Missionaries to give the ordination retreats, **Ibid.**

Touraine (province of). Assistance sent there, **1:212.**

Tournus (city and abbey of the order of Saint Benedict), **1:247.** See, *Chandenier (Louis de).*

Tours (diocese of). Results of the missions in this diocese, **2:54.** A pastor who has a lawsuit in Paris has recourse to the charity of Vincent, **3:143.**

Tours (Martin of), saint. Example of this saint, **3:144.**

Tratebas (Antoine), priest of the Mission. His death, **3:54.**

Traversay (Anne Petau, Madame de). Lady of Charity, **1:153,197.**

Treguier (city and diocese of). Establishment of the Congregation here. The diocesan seminary, **1:166,234.** Results of the missions in this diocese, **2:47.** Admirable results obtained at the seminary, **2:256.**

Trent (Council of). Vincent believes that in order to remedy the state of the clergy seminaries needed to be created according to the intention of the Council of Trent, **1:164.** He recommends to the Missionaries in Madagascar that they follow carefully all the prescriptions of this Council, **2:135**. The declarations of Saint Cyran against the Council, **2:347**. Vincent recalls that the Council trusted the pope with settling any difficulties which would arise on the subject of the faith, **2:354-55,360,369**.

Trials. Those which God sent to Vincent, **1:245 ff.** Rarely is anything good done without suffering. Two reasons for this, **2:92**. Vincent says that he never had anything to do which he thought as important as that of helping a soul tried by interior afflictions, **2:270**. Submitting oneself to trials according to the will of God is the most excellent practice of a Christian, **3:43**. Vincent blesses God for those trials which had been experienced by his Congregation, **3:284**. Those which are endured for a good purpose attract the graces needed to successfully endure them, **3:286**. Advice to some confreres on living through trials, **3:286 ff.** The means used by the devil to fight us and get us to fall, **3:286**. One of the most certain marks of God's great plans for a person is when he sends him desolation upon desolation and pain upon pain, **3:287**. The best time to recognize the spiritual growth of a soul is during a time of temptation and tribulation, **3:288**. See, *Affliction, Devotion, Aridity, Sufferings, Temptations*.

Trinity (Mystery of the Most Holy). Never let an occasion pass without teaching this mystery to the poor people. The knowledge of this mystery is necessary for their spiritual welfare, **2:136**. Devotion professed and recommended by Vincent for this mystery, **3:74**.

Trips. Advice give by Vincent to Louise de Marillac, **1:130; 2:297**. He has the custom of visiting the blessed sacrament before, during, and after trips, **3:79**. Advice given to the Missionaries: four principal rules to observe while traveling, **3:299**. Affectionate greeting given by the saint to those who were leaving or returning, **3:299-300**.

Troyes (city and diocese of), in Champagne. House of the Congregation of the Mission founded in 1638. Diocesan seminary, **1:166,172,231**. Missions given in this diocese with great blessings (1657), **2:49**. An ecclesiastic gives a considerable donation for the seminary, **2:258**. The priests of the Mission assist the Irish persecuted for their religion and living in exile at Troyes (1654), **2:340**.

Tunis. Vincent is held as a captive in this city, **1:43; 3:262**. Monsieur Julien Guerin, priest of the Mission, is sent there with Brother Francillon. Their work and the perils they experienced (1645), **2:86 ff.** Arrival of Monsieur Le Vacher (1648), **2:87**. All of the Missionaries here contract the plague. Death of Monsieur Guerin. Praise of his virtues, **Ibid.** Messieurs Jean Le Vacher and Huguier, consuls, **2:87,89**. Monsieur Martin Husson, consul (1653), **2:89; 3:296**. Testimony of the admiration of the dey for the charity of the Missionaries, **2:102**.

Martyrdom endured by a young Christian slave to preserve his chastity, **2:111**. Heroic constancy of a young English slave to preserve his Catholic faith, **2:116**. Admirable courage of two other young slaves, one French the other English, **2:118**. Torments inflicted on many women and a young man from Marseilles, **2:121-22**. See, *Barbary, Husson (Martin), Le Vacher (Jean)*.

Turin (city in Piedmont, Italy). Establishment of the Congregation in this city (1654), **1:234**.

Tutor. Vincent's work as a tutor, **1:55**.

U

Uist (in the Hebrides). Evangelized by Dermot Duggan, **2:175-76**.
Union with God. See, *Interior Life*.

Union. Advice to remember the maxim from Romans that "by union and prudence all things will work out well," **2:91.** Exhortation of Vincent on this subject. The love of Jesus Christ must be the bond of this union, **2:126.** Two means of procuring it, **3:110.** Vincent says that he does not know of anything which is better and more efficacious for procuring this than holy humility, **3:204.** See, *Fraternal Charity, Cordiality*.

Urban VIII. Approves the Institute of the Mission and erects it as a Congregation (January 12, 1632), **1:111.** He confirms the union of Saint Lazare to the Congregation (March 15, 1635), **1:124.** He praises the zeal of the Missionaries and their agreement to establish themselves in Rome (1641), **2:55,57.** He condemns the *Augustinus* of Jansenius, **2:351.**

Usseau, (village in the diocese of Saintes). Mission given in this parish, **2:34.**

Ussel (city of). Site of a hospital served by the Daughters of Charity, **2:296.**

V

Vabres (diocese of). See, *Habert (Isaac)*.

Valencay (Eleonor d'Etampes de), archbishop of Reims. At Sedan he establishes a house of the Congregation founded by the king (1644), **1:232.** He thanks Vincent for the results of the missions, **2:42.** Also for the success of the ordination retreats, **2:201.**

Vanity. God will remove his grace from us if we allow a spirit of vain complacency to enter our lives, **2:18.** It would be a great sacrilege to attribute to ourselves the glory which belongs to God for the conversion of souls, **3:73.** "Realize how vanity is the dangerous poison even of good works. It is an evil which ruins even the holiest of actions and causes people to forget God," **3:319-20.** It is a most dangerous fault in the advancement in the spiritual life, **3:320.**

Vassay (town in the diocese of Chalons sur Marne). Mission given here, **2:50.**

Vence (city in Provence). Three young women from this city, held as captives in Algiers, are ransomed by the Missionaries, **2:123.** See, *Godeau (Antoine)*.

Verdun (city of). Vincent procures relief for this desolated city (1640), **1:185.** Devotion of the Missionaries and gratitude of its inhabitants, **2:319,327.**

Vernon (city near Evreux). The pastor of the parish of this city is a benefactor of the Congregation. Gratitude of Vincent, **3:239.**

Verrone (Alexandre), laybrother of the Mission. Sent to serve the army in Picardy, **1:175.**

Verteuil (town in the diocese of Angouleme), **2:52.**

Vervins (town north of Laon). Vincent sends Missionaries and assistance there, **1:205; 2:337.**

Vetralle (market town in the diocese of Viterbo, Italy.) Mission given there, **2:59.**

Vialart (Felix de), bishop of Chalons sur Marne. He requests Vincent to give missions in his diocese. Success of these missions, **2:49-50.**

Villaine (village in the diocese of Tours). Mission held there, **2:54.**

Villeconnin (village, near Etampes). Helped by the Missionaries (1652), **1:208.**

Villeneuve (Marie Lhuillier d'Interville), Madame de, foundress of the Congregation of the Daughters of the Cross. She takes the advice of Vincent for the foundation and the governance of her community, **1:195.**

Villepreux (village near Paris). On the lands of Monsieur de Gondi. Evangelized by

INDEX 423

Vincent (1613), **1:56**. The saint gives a mission there in 1618, aided by many virtuous ecclesiastics, **1:73**. He establishes a Confraternity of Charity there (1618), **Ibid**. Vincent returns there in 1649 to visit the Reverend de Gondi, **1:199**.

Villesabin (Isabeau Blondeau, Madame de). One of the first Ladies of Charity of the Hotel Dieu in Paris, **1:153**.

Vincent (of Saragossa, saint and martyr). Patron saint of Vincent, **3:94**.

VINCENT DE PAUL Founder of the Congregation of the Mission and the Company of the Daughters of Charity:

1. *His Life.*

1580/81-1588. His birth and early years, **1:35 ff**.

1588-1592. Studies with the Franciscans in Dax, **1:38**.

1592-1596. As a tutor in the house of Monsieur de Comet, **1:38**.

1596. He receives tonsure and minor orders, **1:39**.

1596-1604. His theological studies at Toulouse, **1:39**. His tutoring at Buzet and at Toulouse, **1:40**.

1600. He is ordained a priest, **1:39**. He says his first Mass, **Ibid**. Continuation of his work as a tutor, **1:40**. He travels to Rome, **1:47**.

1604. He receives his Bachelor's Degree in Theology, **1:40**.

1605-1607. His captivity at Tunis. His deliverance, **1:42 ff**.

1607-1609. His stay at Avignon and Rome, **1:45,48**.

1609. His mission to Paris and Henry IV, **1:48**. He is named chaplain to Queen Marguerite, **1:49**. His visits to the Charity Hospital, **Ibid**. The judge of Sore calumniates him. Reparation, **1:49- 50**.

1610. He receives the benefice of the abbey of Saint Leonard de Chaume, **1:53**. His dispositions of body and spirit. The characteristics of his conduct, **1:100 ff**. He takes on the temptation of a doctor of theology, **3:113-16**.

1611. His stay at the Oratory of Paris, **1:52**.

1612. He is pastor of Clichy, **1:52,54**.

1613-1617. His entrance, his stay with, and conduct in the house of the de Gondi, **1:55 ff**. How he obeys and respects Monsieur and Madame de Gondi, **1:56**. His efforts to procure the abolition of duels in France. He deters the General of the Galleys from a duel, **1:57-58; 2:394-95**.

1615. He receives a canonry in the collegiate church of Ecouis in the diocese of Evreux, **1:55**.

1617. Mission given at Folleville, **1:59 ff**. Vincent leaves the house of the de Gondi, **1:63**. He is named pastor of Chatillon les Dombes, **1:65**. His works in this parish, **Ibid**. He establishes the first Confraternity of Charity there, **1:72**. He converts his hosts, and the count of Rougemont, **1:74,77**. He returns to the house of the de Gondi, **1:70**.

1618. He expands the Confraternities of Charity, **1:73**. He gives missions aided by many virtuous ecclesiastics of Paris. Missions at Villepreux and at Montmirail. Conversions of Protestants, **1:73; 2:28**. He begins the works with the galley slaves in Paris, **1:84**.

1619. He is named Chaplain General of the Galleys, **1:84**. He is chosen by Saint Francis de Sales and Saint Jane de Chantal to be superior of the Visitation of Paris, **1:90; 2:266; 3:208**.

1622. He visits the galleys at Marseilles, **1:84**. His voluntary captivity, **3:112-13**.

1623. His missions in Marseilles and in Bordeaux, **1:84,86; 3:257**. He establishes the Confraternity of Charity at Macon, **1:87**. He visits his family. Impressions and preoccupations that he reported, **3:257**.

1624. He is named principal of the College des Bons Enfants, **1:94**.

1625. He founds the Congregation of the Mission, **1:94-95,109; 3:27-28**. He assists Madame de Gondi at her death, **1:97**. He retires to the College des Bons Enfants, **1:98**. His first companions and their works, **1:110-111**. His first relations with Saint Cyran, **2:346**.

Continuation of the work of the missions. He is reproached in a dream for reentering Paris to rest while so many villages in the countryside remained in need of evangelization, **1:116-17**.

1626. He signs a contract of association with his first companions, **1:110**. His relations with Louise de Marillac, **1:128-29**.

1627. The Congregation of the Mission is approved by the archbishop of Paris and by the king, **1:110**.

1628. He establishes the ordination retreats. First retreat is held at Beauvais, **1:139**.

1629. He employs Louise de Marillac to visit the Confraternities, **1:129**. Services rendered to the Convent of the Madeleine, **1:132; 2:278 ff; 3:272-73**. Mission given in Montauban, **2:51**.

1630. Negotiations relative to Saint Lazare, **1:119**. Origin of the Daughters of Charity, **1:133-34**. Their spirit, their rules, their works, **1:136; 2:291**.

1631. Ordination retreats in Paris, **1:140; 2:183**. Regulations for these retreats, **2:188**. Their spirit; their results, **2:191**.

1632. The Congregation of the Mission is approved by the pope; Urban VIII, **1:111; 3:28**. He takes possession of Saint Lazare, **1:122**. Establishment of the spiritual retreats, **1:141; 2:229**. See, *Retreats*. Establishment of hospitals for the convicts, **1:148**.

1633. The Daughters of Charity are established as a Community, **1:134**. Establishment of the Ecclesiastical Conferences, **1:144 ff; 2:210 ff**. See, *Conferences*.

1634. Louise de Marillac makes her vow for the service of the poor, **1:136**. Institution of the Ladies of Charity of Hotel Dieu in Paris, **1:152; 2:303**. See, *Charity (Ladies of)*. Missions in Bordeaux and Saintes, **2:32,51**.

1635. Ladies of Charity established at the royal court, **1:153**. Beginning of the seminary at Bons Enfants, **1:164; 2:249**. Establishment of the Congregation at Toul, **1:230**. Missions in the Cevennes, **2:35**.

1636. Mission at Auvergne, **1:167; 2:36 ff**. He sends Missionaries to the armies of Picardy. Guidelines that Vincent gave them, **1:174**. The Daughters of Charity are established in the village of La Chapelle near Paris, **1:136**.

1637. Services rendered to the Knights of Malta, **1:170**. Internal Seminary begins at Saint Lazare, **1:179**. His relations with Saint Cyran, **2:171,348**.

1638. Organization of the work of the foundlings, **1:161**. Establishment of the Congregation at Richelieu and at Lucon, **1:230**. At Troyes, **1:231**. Missions in Champagne, **2:47**. Missions in the Roman countryside, **2:55**. Mission at Saint Germain, **2:76**.

1639. Charitable intervention of Vincent in the Lorraine, **1:185; 2:317**. Aid to Toul, Verdun, Bar le Duc, etc., **2:318**.

1640. Assembly of the Ladies of Charity to decide to continue the support of the work of the foundlings, **1:161**. The poor of Lorraine take refuge at Paris, **1:185-87; 2:317,327-28**. Help at Metz, etc., **1:185; 2:318**. Brother Mathieu Regnard, **1:186; 2:329-30**. Work of Vincent for peace, **1:189**. Missions in Normandy, **2:43**.

1641. Daughters of Charity are established in the faubourg Saint Laurent near Saint Lazare, **1:136.** Mission to the village of La Chapelle, **1:187; 2:327.** Establishment of the mission at Crecy. **1:231.** Seminary at Annecy; first major seminary, **Ibid.** The missions begin in Rome, **1:231; 2:55 ff.,204-05.** Mission in the faubourg Saint Germain, **2:222 ff.** Vision of the souls of Francis de Sales and Jane de Chantal together in paradise, **2:283 ff.** Benedictine nuns who are in exile from the provinces because of the war settle in the faubourg Saint Germain, **2:328.**

1642. Tuesday Conferences at the College des Bons Enfants for the theology students of Paris, **1:147.** Foundation of the hospital for prisoners at Marseille, **1:150,231.** First General Assembly of the Congregation, and the attempted resignation of Vincent as superior general. The resignation is not accepted, **3:192.**

1643. Ordination retreats held at Rome, **1:140; 2:204-05.** Missions to the galleys of Marseilles, **1:150; 2:39.** Gift of Louis XIII to support the work of the foundlings, **1:162.** He assists at the death of Louis XIII, **1:190.** He is appointed to the Council of Conscience. His rule of conduct there, **1:192 ff; 2:372-73.** Services that he gave to the Church, to the episcopate, etc., **1:193; 2:382,385,391.** Religious opposition to Mazarin, **1:193; 2:375.** Foundation of the Congregation at Marseilles, **1:231.** Foundation of the seminary at Cahors, **Ibid.** Assistance given to Lorraine, **2:328.**

1644. The superior general of the Mission is named as Chaplain General of the Galleys in perpetuity, **1:150.** Foundation of the Mission at Sedan, **1:191,232.** Foundation of the Mission at Montmirail, **1:232.** Mission in Burgundy, **2:48.**

1645. Services given to Monsieur Olier, **1:116 ff.** Seminary of Saint Meen, **1:232.** Establishment of the Mission at Le Mans, **Ibid.** Foundation of the Mission at Tunis. Mission at Barbary, **1:233.** Establishment of the Mission at Genoa, **1:233; 2:66.** Vincent has a serious illness and one of his Missionaries offers his life to God for his, **1:251.** Services rendered by the Daughters of Charity to the Hospital of the Petites Maisons of Paris, **2:296.**

1646. Vincent dreams of giving the rules to the Daughters of Charity. First approbation of their Institute by the archbishop of Paris, **1:136.** Establishment and organization of the hospital at Marseilles, **1:149-50,231.** Foundation of the Mission at Algiers, **1:233.** New Missionaries sent to Tunis, **2:86.** Conversions of heretics and renegades in Algeria, **2:86,112.** Jean Barreau, consul at Algiers, **2:88.** Vincent wants to establish a hospital at Algiers, **Ibid., 2:125.** See, *Algiers.* The Missionaries serve as the vicars general of the archbishop of Carthage, **2:90,103,107.** Missions given in Ireland, **2:126.** Vincent condemns the heresy of the Jansenist Martin Barcos, **2:351.**

1647. Jean Le Vacher, consul and vicar apostolic at Tunis, **2:87.** Assistance to the poor slaves of Bizerte, **2:97,105.** See, *Bizerte.*

1648. Memorable meeting of the Ladies of Charity deciding in favor of the continuation of the work in with the foundlings, **1:162.** Mission at Madagascar; Messieurs Nacquart and Gondree, **1:233; 2:134 ff.**

1649. Troubles of the Fronde. Vincent meets with the queen at Saint Germain and suggests the departure of Mazarin, **1:198-99.** Visitation of the houses of the Company, **1:201.** He becomes ill at Richelieu. Return to Paris, **1:202.** Death of Monsieur Gondree. Monsieur Nacquart remains alone in Madagascar, **2:144.**

1650. Services rendered to the Daughters of the Cross, **1:195 ff.** First charitable interventions in Picardy, **1:204; 2:331.** Missions at Genoa, **2:66.** Vincent supports the appeal to Rome against Jansenism, **2:353.**

1651. Establishment of the Congregation in Poland, **1:136,233; 2:163.** Death of the prior of Saint Lazare, Adrien Le Bon, **1:206.** Missions to the islands of the Hebrides, **1:234; 2:173 ff.** Death of Monsieur Nacquart. New Missionaries are sent to Madagascar, **2:149.** Help to Champagne and Picardy, **2:337.** Letter to the French bishops to unite them in a common appeal to the pope against Jansenism, **2:353 ff.**

1652. Assistance to Champagne and Picardy continues, **1:205; 2:331,341.** He aids the areas around Paris; Etampes **1:208.** He himself teaches catechism to the poor who are received at Saint Lazare during the famine of 1652, **1:211-12.** His political intervention in the troubles of Paris, **1:213 ff.,219.** His spirit of charity and penitence in the midst of the troubles, **1:213,220.** Manner of preaching. Little method, **2:20.** Missions of Corsica, **2:69 ff.** He encourages the theologians who go to Rome to bring about the condemnation of the five propositions, **2:361.** He helps in the reforms of the abbeys, **2:385.**

1653. His firm and charitable conduct against Jansenism, **1:222; 2:366.** His conduct relative to his Company; to externs, **1:222; 2:367 ff.** Hospital of the Name of Jesus, **1:224.** First plan for the general hospital, **1:226.** Continuation of the assistance to Champagne and Picardy. See, *Public Misery.* He takes part in a mission on the occasion of the Jubilee of 1653; at the age of seventy-three, **3:99.**

1654. Missions in Brittany, **2:45.** Martyrs of Algiers. Pierre Borguny, **2:99 ff.** Missions to Scotland, **2:178.** Help continued in Champagne and Picardy, **2:338.** He aids the Irish refugees at Troyes, **2:340.**

1655. Alexander VII confirms the vows of the Congregation of the Mission, **1:111.** Missions given around Paris, **2:31.** Missions given in Piedmont, **2:76 ff.** Constitutions of the Daughters of Charity. Distribution, and explanation of the rules, **2:291,301.**

1656. Death of the Missionaries at Madagascar, **2:150,158; 3:103.** New disasters and shipwrecks, **2:159-60.**

1657. Vincent assists Monsieur Olier at his death, and presides at the election of his successor, **1:169.** He receives the exclusive privilege of the name of the Mission, **1:111.** Opening of the general hospital. He refuses its direction, **1:229.** Death of Monsieur Bourdaise at Madagascar, **2:162.** Services given to the Daughters of Providence, **2:303.** Conference given to the Ladies of Charity, **2:292.** Account of the work of the foundlings, **2:307.**

1658. Mission in Metz, **1:234.** Vincent gives the rules and constitutions to his Company, **1:237.** Distribution of the rules, **1:240.** Explication of the rules, **1:242.** He takes a dangerous fall from his carriage, **1:252.** Daughters of Charity are sent to nurse wounded soldiers, **2:298.** Loss of the farm at Orsigny, **3:162,249.**

1659. Infirmities and sickness, **1:253.** Hospital of Sainte Reine, **2:303.**

1660. Deaths of Antoine Portail, of Louise de Marillac, of Abbe Tournus, **1:246 ff.** Last Missionaries in Madagascar, **2:162; 3:277.** Final illness of Vincent, **1:253 ff.** His death and funeral, **1:261.**

2. *Testimonies given to the memory of Vincent.*

Homages of veneration at his death on the part of illustrious persons, **1:261.** Of his confessor on the purity of his soul, **3:75.**

Testimonies given to the memory of Vincent: by Pope Alexander VII, **1:258.** By Cardinal Berulle, **1:64,69.** By Cardinals Durazzo, Ludovisi, Bagni, **1:258.** By the Jesuit Fleuriau, **3:56.** By Monsieur de Lestocq, doctor of the Sorbonne, **1:119,122-23.** By Alain de Solminihac, bishop of Cahors, **1:232.** By the queen, Anne of Austria, **1:22.** By the queen of Poland, **3:38.** By the president de Lamoignon, **Ibid.** By the

inhabitants of Chatillon and Montmirail, **1:70,81**. By the parishoners of Clichy, **1:54**.
His works, all of Book 2
His virtues, all of Book 3.

Vincent (Francois), priest of the Mission. His death from the plague at Genoa, **3:54,276**.

Virgil (classical author). Cited **1:73**.

Virgin, (The Blessed). See, *Mary.*

Virgins. Explanation of the parable of the prudent and foolish virgins, **1:114-15**.

Virtues, (of Vincent according to Abelly), **Book 3 and throughout**. His virtues concerned the most ordinary things, but he lived them in a manner that was not common, **3:13**. He excelled in a great number, and often in those which appeared to be the opposite of each other, **3:14**. He was insatiable in his acquisition of the perfection of the virtues, **Ibid**. He was the only one who was unaware that they were living in him, **Ibid**.
Virtue is found between two opposing vices which are the absence and the excess, **2:313**. The devil tempts virtuous persons to try to do too much in their good works in order that they will be overworked and succumb, **Ibid**. An excess of virtues is praiseworthy in comparison with the lack of virtue and must be supported, **3:297**.

Visitation (Order of the), Vincent is chosen by Saint Francis de Sales and Saint Jane de Chantal to be superior of the monasteries of the Visitation at Paris, **1:90; 2:266; 3:208**.
The first monastery established in Paris (1619). Construction of the church in the rue Saint Antoine. Mission given to the workers (1633), **1:90; 2:211,266**. Three other monasteries are founded. Vincent takes great care of them for thirty-eight years, **1:242; 2:267**. How he was charged by Saint Francis de Sales with the direction of the house in Paris, **2:266**. Confidence of Saint Jane de Chantal in Vincent for her personal direction and that of her Congregation. Letters to the saint, **2:267 ff**. Vincent visits the monasteries of Paris and of Saint Denis. His conduct in these circumstances, **2:269,280-82**. His rules of direction with religious women, **2:270**. His devotion for sick religious, or those afflicted with interior spiritual pains, **2:270,281-82**. The saint refuses permission for visits to the Monasteries of the Visitation by princesses and ladies of high social position. Reasons for this refusal, **2:273-275**. He watches attentively to preserve them from the opinions of Jansenism, **2:271,280**. Vincent advises them to accept the direction of the work of the Madeleine for repentant women, **2:278-79**. Miraculous healing of a religious witnessed by Vincent, and obtained through the intercession of Francis de Sales, **2:280**. The part that was attributed to Vincent in this miracle, **2:282**. Testimony given by Vincent to the virtues of Madame de Chantal, **2:282-83**. He recommends unity to the religious and indicates two means to accomplish this, **3:110**. Testimony of a religious as to the merciful charity of Vincent, **Ibid**. He unsuccessfully tries to resign the direction of the Visitations. He takes it back under obedience, **3:208**.

Visits. Example of Vincent on the manner of making and receiving them, **1:243**. They are to be made only out of necessity, **3:316**.

Visits (To the blessed sacrament). Vincent makes a visit before the blessed sacrament each day after rising, **3:75**. He spent his spare moments there, and always goes there before leaving and after returning from a trip. He promotes this practice, **3:79**. Vincent reads the important letters that he receives while kneeling before the blessed sacrament, **3:78**.

Viterbo (diocese in Italy). Missions held there, **2:59**.

Vocation. Prudent conduct of Vincent when he is consulted about vocations, **1:182.** How he would resolve these questions during the retreat exercises, **2:231.** Perseverance. None of the apostles walked away from their responsibilities except when finally called to receive their crowns in heaven, **3:132.** How he imparted and followed wise advice on vocations. Examples, **3:225.**

Vocation (of the Missionaries). The evangelization of the poor proves the presence and activity of the Holy Spirit in the Church, **1:83.** The devil alone could find something to complain of in such a life, **1:117.** Vincent holds as an inviolable law never to say anything to attract anyone to his Institute. His particular teaching and his recommendations on this subject, **1:180-82; 3:181.** We must pray that God will send good laborers for the harvest, and then live ourselves so that our good example will attract many others, if God so wills, **1:181.** Charity of Vincent for those whose conduct in community was culpable, in order to give them the necessary time to correct themselves, **3:172-73.** Only self-love and pride will be able to destroy the vocation of a Missionary, **3:204,302,319.** Vincent suffers whenever someone left the company, **3:150-51.** Infidelity of a young Missionary who left the Congregation and joined the army. He was not there long before he was condemned to death for desertion, **3:161.** His discretion and his charitable silence towards those who had left the Congregation, **3:169,227.** He readmits a Missionary who had left the community, **3:237.**

Vocation (to the ecclesiastical state). The loss of vocation is inevitable for those who dare to enter there without being called, **3:194.**

Vocation (to the religious life). It is necessary in discerning a vocation to follow the maxims of the Gospel and not those of mere human prudence. One must prefer the communities that are best ruled, **2:230-31.** Vincent deters a religious tempted to transfer to a less rigorous order, **2:388.** He deters another celebrated religious from seeking a bishopric, **2:389.** He gives a religious motives for persevering in his vocation, **3:146.** He dissuades a discontented religious from taking his complaints to Rome. God will see to it that the order in which he has placed you will bring you happily to port, **Ibid.** The cross is everywhere. Trying to avoid those that one has found in one state by changing to another, **3:146.**

Vows (of the Congregation of the Mission). Approved by Pope Alexander VII (Brief of September 22, 1655), **1:111; 3:158-59.**

Vows (of the Daughters of Charity), **1:136; 2:292.**

W

Wars (of the Fronde), **1:198 ff.** Second Fronde (1651), **1:208 ff.** In Guienne, **1:216.** In Paris, **1:219.** The war is the cause of the damnation of a large number of persons. God is also using these events to procure the glorification of many others, **3:121.** See, *Public Miseries.*

Warsaw (Poland). Establishment of the Missionaries (1651), **1:233.** Their arrival, and the arrival of the Daughters of Charity in this city, **2:163-64.** Devotion of the Missionaries in the midst of the double scourges of war and the plague, **Ibid; 3:119,138.** Warsaw falls to the Swedes. Messieurs Desdames and Duperroy remain there because of illness, **2:166,169.** Site of a hospital served by the Daughters of Charity, **2:296.**

White (Francis). See, *Le Blanc, (Francois).*

Will of God. See, *God, (Will of)*.
Will (Self). To renounce it is one of the principal acts of mortification, **3:254-55**.
Wine (sobriety in the usage of). Example of Vincent, **3:270**.
Wisdom "Those walk most securely who travel the same path as the wise," **1:101**.
Wisdom (book of the Old Testament). Cited in Abelly: 8:1-**3:165,299,** 9:10-**3:231**.
Work. Many are inclined to an easy and soft life rather than to a solid and laborious one, **1:107**. We must serve those whose labor feeds us, **1:214; 3:240**. How Vincent was devoted to his work until the last moments of his life, **1:254-55**.
Their dedication to work is a virtue noted in the first Daughters of Charity, **1:136**. The Daughters of Charity are often overwhelmed with work. Letter of one of them to Vincent, **2:297**. See, *Idleness, Time, Zeal*.
Workers. Vincent arranges for missions given by the ecclesiastics of the conference of Saint Lazare to many of the workshops of Paris, **2:218-19**. He makes it possible for the workers to come to make their retreat at Saint Lazare by indemnifying their employers, **2:232**.
Works (of Vincent). Extent and diversity of those that he realized, **1:127 ff,242**. He knew that in order to accomplish them the hand of God had to be with him, **1:244**. He once said that he was only the "vile and contemptible mud that God formed into the mortar used in cementing the stones of his structure," **1:244**. *The works of Vincent*, They are almost miraculous which testifies that God approved the works of his servant, **3:325**.

X

Xavier (Francis), saint. Veneration of Vincent for this saint, **2:84**. He proposes that the Missionaries imitate the example of his zeal, **2:135;137; 3:100**. His words of apostolic zeal, **2:148**.

Z

Zacchaeus (New Testament figure), **2:61**.
Zeal.

   1. *Zeal in general.*

   The lack of zeal of priests for the country poor is one of the objections raised by a heretic before his conversion. The response of Vincent, **1:81**. The Church is compared to a great harvest that needs workers, but workers who will actually labor, **1:107**. Good example given by the first Missionaries, **1:117**. Only those who reflect on the pains of hell or on the price of the blood of Jesus Christ for even one soul can appreciate the value of conversions, **1:177**. "If you had but a spark of that sacred fire which consumed the heart of Jesus Christ, could you spend your life with folded arms, and abandon those who call for your help?" **3:107**.
   Monsieur Nacquart, a Missionary to Madagascar, writes to Vincent in the words of Saint Francis Xavier, "Where and who are the doctors and learned persons who waste their time in the academies and universities while so many poor unbelievers cry for food, but there is no one to give it to them," **2:148**. Monsieur Bourdaise, another Missionary in Madagascar, expresses the wish that the many capable ecclesiastics who were idle in France would reflect on the account they will have to render for all

the souls lost for lack of their help, **2:158**. Words of zeal of Jean Jacques Olier while giving a mission: "O Paris! You distract many who could with the grace of God convert a multitude of souls," **2:37**.

2. *Discretion of Zeal.*

In Vincent zeal is moderated by prudence. Example, **1:57**. Zeal is not effective if it is not also discrete. Vincent tells a Missionary in Algiers not to try to effect the conversion of Moslems and renegades because of the great dangers involved, **2:106**. It is a tactic of the devil to urge good souls to do more than they are capable of so that in the end they accomplish nothing, **2:313**. God only asks for our good will and a true and sincere readiness to seize every opportunity to serve him, **3:98**. Vincent was more anxious to do good than to receive any favors, **3:109**. Look upon your body as an instrument of God for the salvation of many, and care for it for this reason, **3:154**. A virtue is accompanied side by side by its vices; but the excess of a virtues is more acceptable than the lack of the virtue, **3:298**.

3. *Zeal of Vincent de Paul.*

Once when returning from the missions he dreamt that the gates of the city would fall down upon him because of the souls that still remained to be evangelized in the countryside, **1:116-17**. Vincent is consumed by that heavenly fire which Jesus Christ came to bring upon the earth; to respond to everything having to do with the glory of God, and the salvation of souls, **1:224**. Vincent expresses the desire to go to evangelize in the mountains of Cevennes even if it meant dying in this effort, **2:36**. He also wants to serve God in the foreign missions, **2:85**. He wants to accompany his confreres to the missions of Madagascar, **2:138**. His zeal for evangelization, **3:16**. His most ardent desire is that God would become better and better known, adored, served, obeyed, and glorified in all places and by all creatures, **3:37**. It is one of the characteristics of the conduct of Vincent, **3:293**. His examples and his teaching, **3:97 ff.** 1. Ardent Zeal, **3:97** Vincent, infirm and eighty years old still has the desire to go to the Indies even if he would die on the voyage, **3:98**. Merchants travel fearlessly by sea and soldiers fight fearlessly in war, "Should we then fail in our duty as helpers and saviors of souls because of the troubles and persecutions we may encounter?" **3:101**. 2. Disinterested zeal. He desires that everyone should imitate the zeal of the apostles, **Ibid**. 3. Constant and persevering zeal. Example of the missions in Madagascar and in Barbary, **3:102-03**.

4. *Zeal of the Missionaries.*

Vincent asks God two or three times each day to destroy the community if it is not being useful to his glory, **1:117; 3:89**. Vincent desires that all those who enter the company come there with the thought of martyrdom, **1:183**. "How happy is the Missionary who has no limit in this world on where he can go to preach the Gospel. Why then do we hesitate and set limits, since God has given us the whole world to satisfy our zeal," **2:84**. He cites the example of the sick Missionaries at Warsaw during the war in order to aid the plague-stricken, **2:166**. Ardent exhortation of the saint for the spirit of zeal, **2:170-71; 3:98-99**. A Missionary without zeal would only be the corpse of a Missionary, and a carcass from Saint Lazare, **2:236-37**. If our zeal is true we must desire that the whole world be evangelized, **3:27**. Whoever is called to be a Missionary is called by God to save souls. Explanations, **3:90**. It is impossible that a Missionary who lives in a cowardly way will succeed in his work and achieve his salvation, **3:104**. Resist any temptation to abandon the works of the company, **Ibid**. Regard as anti-christs the cowardly who will speak of abandoning the works that God has confided to the Congregation, **3:104-05.** If some Missionaries were obliged to beg for their bread or to sleep on hay and someone asked them: "Poor priest of the Mission! What has brought you to such an extremity?" What happiness if you could respond: "Charity," **3:107-08.** See, *Foreign Missions.*

Zelazewski (Stanislaus), priest of the Mission. Sent to Poland, **2:164.**